MW01556232

STRATEGIC MANAGEMENT
AND
BUSINESS POLICY

Second Edition

■ ■ ■

STRATEGIC MANAGEMENT
AND
BUSINESS POLICY

Donald F. Harvey

Eastern Washington University

MERRILL PUBLISHING COMPANY
A Bell & Howell Information Company
Columbus   Toronto   London   Melbourne

Cover Photo: Joseph A. DiChello, Jr.

Photo credits: Tom Brunk, pp. 25, 279; Jack Hamilton, p. 193; Honda of America Mfg., Inc., p. 243

Published by Merrill Publishing Company
A Bell & Howell Information Company
Columbus, Ohio 43216

This book was set in Serifa.

Administrative Editor: Paul Lee
Art Coordinator: James H. Hubbard
Cover Designer: Cathy Watterson
Text Designer: Cynthia Brunk

Library of Congress Catalog Card Number: 87-63488
International Standard Book Number: 0-675-20448-8
Printed in the United States of America
1 2 3 4 5 6 7 8 9 — 92 91 90 89 88

PREFACE

This is a book about strategic management—the management process aimed at improving organizational effectiveness by means of a systematic set of strategic goals, plans, and actions. In the changing business environment of the 1980s, top management's emphasis has shifted from more routine managerial functions to the development of both the organization's culture and managerial styles capable of functioning in varying situations. These new strategies focus upon the manager's style of thought and upon the development of new patterns of relationships among operating executives, to provide an anticipative mode of strategic management.

Strategic management has changed during the recent past because of two emerging forces. First, the manager of today is managing in a dynamic environment. The manager faces an accelerating rate of change in technical, social, political, and economic forces, through all of which he or she must steer the organization as it meets unprecedented challenges.

A second factor involves the changes in organization forms, which have expanded in scope and complexity. Organizations in the past were often relatively small and focused on one major product. Today, however, we see tremendous changes in the size and complexity of operations, as firms have diversified into multiple product lines and even multinational markets.

As a result of these changing forces, the management process has also become more difficult, requiring greater skills of analysis, planning, and controlling. These skills aim at controlling the future course of the firm in a changing and uncertain world.

The Purpose

This book has been developed for business policy courses in undergraduate degree programs. All such "capstone" courses study the job of the general manager or chief executive of an organization.

In recent years business policy has emerged as a distinct field of study focusing upon the formulation and implementation of strategy. Although these concepts and studies may not yet provide a conclusive theory of how to manage a firm, they do provide the manager with a framework for analyzing strategic problems.

Several new trends in this discipline are reflected in this text, including:

1 A focus on the role of the line manager as a strategist.
2 A view of the organization as an open, sociotechnical system of related subelements.
3 An emphasis on the strategic management process.
4 The separation of strategic management and operational functions.
5 A focus on the external systems, including social responsibility, business ethics, and multinational issues and problems.

The objective of this book is to examine in detail the current state of the art in the field of organization strategy and policy. The book is designed to bring present and potential managers into direct contact with the knowledge currently available in the field.

This edition develops in detail a model for the formulation and implementation of strategy. Text as well as case material considers in depth the formulation and implementation phases of strategy for both business and non-business organizations.

The text focuses on key areas of interest on at least three dimensions:

1 *Concern with practical "real world" applications.* The material emphasizes techniques and theory in actual organizational situations. Each chapter contains specific examples of the triumphs and failures of strategic management—the experiences of practicing chief executive officers bring the theories to life.
2 *Research orientation.* Studies utilizing experimental or field designs are included to develop the student's understanding of research in the field.
3 *Conceptual perspectives.* The book's focus throughout is on strategic management—

the process of defining business purpose, setting objectives, formulating and implementing a strategic plan, and finally monitoring performance and results.

New Material

As with the previous edition, the text continues to stress the basic elements of strategic management. A comprehensive model of the strategic management process provides a framework for the entire course. This edition, however, offers many noteworthy improvements in coverage.

First, the model presents a visual, graphic display of the major stages of the entire process, and shows the relationship between elements.

Second, many new models and diagrams have been included to supplement and focus discussion and to enhance the visual explanation of basic strategic concepts.

Third, the chapter on competitive analysis has been strengthened to include the pioneering work of Harvard's Michael Porter. This chapter thoroughly explores the concepts underlying competitive analysis.

Fourth, continuing emphasis is placed on strategy implementation and the fit between strategy and the "corporate culture." Several current diagnostic models are presented to emphasize the importance of strategy execution.

Fifth, there are numerous new strategy application capsules, integrating "real world" applications of strategic concepts and highlighting the importance of the topics.

Sixth, additional supplements are offered including computer software and video cases.

It is our position that strategic management is more than just a collection of experiences from successful practitioners. Rather, strategic management is an organized body of knowledge, with its own concepts, techniques, and necessary skills. In this text, we have attempted to present a complete picture of management's role and responsibilities in steering the course of a business and to demonstrate why these factors are essential in shaping an organization's future success. Moreover, because the practice of management by its very nature concerns people in organizations, emphasis also falls upon developing improved interpersonal skills.

Every successful strategy is the result of a concerted group effort, and each management failure is a failure for all the organization members. Therefore managers, not forces or structures, determine whether any strategy will be implemented effectively or ineffectively. Whether you will manage effectively will be determined not only by the concepts you learn, but also by your managerial style. Consequently, our emphasis is upon the experiential approach to learning about strategic management.

As you progress in the book, the cases will allow you to continually use your growing knowledge and experience to build a foundation of management experience to carry forward into your managerial career. By analyzing and critiquing your successes and failures in case analysis, you will begin to develop your ability to learn from your own experiences and develop insights into organizational functioning that would normally take years to acquire.

The book is designed so that you may assess your own managerial style and begin setting some personal development goals. Also, many opportunities are created whereby you may gain feedback on the effectiveness of your managerial style.

The text also contains a discussion of the case method and suggestions for case analysis, which provides a framework for analyzing and evaluating a company's situation. A checklist of areas to examine in sizing up a company's strategic position, what to look for in identifying company strengths and weaknesses, how to prepare a case for class discussion, and guidelines for written case analyses are included.

We have successfully utilized the material in this text with undergraduate management majors and MBAs as well as with graduate administration majors from many fields including public administration, health care administration, and planning. The material has also been used many times for management-training and executive-development programs in a variety of fields with bankers, engineers, teachers, public administrators, military officers, production managers, and marketing managers, at a variety of levels from first-line supervisors to top management teams.

Many topical features have been incorporated:

1 The nature of open systems and contingencies are thoroughly covered.
2 The cases are based on topics directly related to the text material.
3 Objectives have been provided at the beginning and review questions at the end of each chapter.
4 A full set of teaching aids can be provided.

The text includes twenty-nine cases, most of them newly published, written by experienced case writers from across the country who have generously contributed to this volume. All of the cases have been class-tested, and they provide an exceptionally well balanced mix of strategic problems and organizational situations. The comprehensive *Instructor's Manual* contains a suggested sequencing of cases, course outlines, transparency masters, and comprehensive teaching aids.

We are grateful to the many people who have contributed to making this book a reality. For assistance and encouragement offered throughout the development of the text, I would like to extend a special note of appreciation to Management Chairman Dr. Hugh Mills of Eastern Washington University. My sincere appreciation is also extended to Merrill Publishing for timely support and assistance.

In the preparation of this second edition we have been greatly assisted by the replies of Professors Warren Brown of the University of Oregon, Raghavan Parthasarthy of William Peterson College of New Jersey, Dennis Patzig of James Madison University, John H. Reed of Clarion University of Pennsylvania, and Benjamin Weeks of Governors State University to a survey by Merrill. We would also like to thank the reviewers of this edition, Professors Charles Stubbart of the University of Massachusetts at Amherst, D. Ray Bagby of the University of Baltimore, and, in particular, Dennis Patzig of James Madison University and Lew Taylor of the University of Miami.

Many colleagues in the School of Business at Eastern Washington University have been helpful, but special thanks go to Professor Hugh Hunter, who directed and coordinated the case materials. I would also like to thank Professors Rick Castaldi and Alec DeNoble of San Diego State University for support and review suggestions. Many students and managers have been involved in the development of the simulations and cases.

Beverly Mahrt (of Bev's Secretarial) did an outstanding job of typing the final manuscript. We thank the companies for providing the photos used in this book.

Finally, my wife, Becky, and sons Mike, Scott, and Dave have contributed in more ways than I can count—not just in allowing the time for writing, but in a form of involvement that can never be fully appreciated or repaid. As usual the author must accept the responsibility for any problems, in spite of the efforts of all contributors.

CONTENTS

PART FOUR
CASES IN STRATEGIC MANAGEMENT

order to meet new strategic challenges. This moderately complex case includes financial data and focuses on managerial style.   800

Case 27, *Wang Laboratories, Inc., 1986,* examines a strong computer company having problems adapting to changing market conditions and then adjusting its strategy under new leadership. This moderately complex case includes financial data.   813

Case 28, *Avon Products, 1986,* presents a leading company trying to plan for growth with limited opportunities and increasing competition. The case is moderately

complex.   826

Case 29, *Hewlett-Packard, 1986,* looks at strategy formulation and change in a competitive, high-tech environment. This relatively complex case examines corporate and business strategy and includes structural and financial data.   848

CHAPTER ONE

■ ■ ■

Strategic Management: An Overview

OBJECTIVES

After completing this chapter, you will be able to

■ Define strategy, policy, and strategic management

■ Describe the basic stages in the strategic management process

■ Discuss the importance of strategic management in achieving the organizational mission

■ Compare the characteristics of well-managed firms with those of firms managed strategically

■ Identify the levels of strategy

Hewlett-Packard's decentralized approach to managing information reflects its management philosophy. Managing people does not mean doing it all yourself. A good manager is one who makes it possible for employees to succeed. That means creating consensus and enthusiasm about a group's goals, as well as an environment where people can pursue those goals effectively.

John A. Young, CEO, Hewlett-Packard, Davos, Switzerland, 1984

Strategy at Hewlett-Packard

In the boardroom of the futuristic corporate headquarters of Hewlett-Packard (not far from the campus of Stanford University in Palo Alto), the executive committee, led by chief executive John Young, examines future strategic plans for this corporation. The strategic plan sets forth a map of targets and timetables projected five years into the future. These meetings provide a constant interplay between Hewlett-Packard's corporate goals and the ever-changing competitive conditions in which they exist. The meetings emphasize consensual-style decision making, with Young asking probing questions leading to agreement on future strategy.

John Young has been termed one of America's most admired chief executive officers (CEOs). He is perceived as strong at building morale and holding together a work force, yet tough at running things by numbers. Young builds consensus decisions by asking penetrating questions and listening closely to the answers; he is committed to "hands off" management and to coaching others in solving problems.

Entrepreneurship is a dominant value at Hewlett-Packard. John Young has been reorganizing the company to remain competitive in the rapidly changing computer business while seeking to maintain the risk-taking spirit that has made it an exceptional company.

There is a lot of risk-taking and continual innovation in product line. In any given year, over half of Hewlett-Packard's revenues come from products introduced in the preceding three years.

For example, 70 percent of Hewlett-Packard's total revenues result from products developed in the past five years. Consequently, the focus of strategic management is to identify key product amd market trends and to develop future competitive position. This low-key, informal style is known at Hewlett-Packard as "management by wandering around" (MBWA), and it has kept this firm a leader in the competitive high-tech electronics field.

A vital organization, Hewlett-Packard is constantly taking stock and changing to meet the needs of its corporate customers. John Young is reorganizing Hewlett-Packard into a company capable of designing and selling the integrated systems and networks currently in demand.[1]

INTRODUCTION

In meetings like those at Hewlett-Packard, organizations around the world hammer out strategic goals and plans. In this arena strategic management takes place, and strategic decisions are made.

John Young was one of the key leaders who developed the strategic management system, enabling Hewlett-Packard to program and plan its competitive position into the future. At monthly meetings like those described, managers examine financial reports of sales, profits, return on investment, and the status of their competitors. These managers try to analyze and anticipate virtually every existing or potential problem Hewlett-Packard is likely to face. The emphasis of these meetings is on problem solving for potential new products and markets in an uncertain economic environment. The purpose of strategic management is to develop an anticipative plan for future management actions.

The focus of this book will be on one of the most important aspects of managing in all types of organizations: strategic management. It should provide you with an understanding of the critical importance of policy and strategy in organizations.

The need for strategic management has increasingly become a fact of organizational life. The strategic plan, or lack of one, is often the starting point for the evaluation of the actions of management personnel and their organizations. Strategic management provides the basic direction and framework within which all organization activities take place. An understanding of strategic management, potentially the most advanced and sophisticated type, makes it easier for managers to develop a vision of the future for their organization.

This chapter should help you gain an increased awareness of the process used by managers in major corporations and government to determine organizational direction and strategy. An overview of the strategic management process will be presented in order to help clarify what strategic management is, why it is used, and what the basic stages of the strategic management process are. If you gain a thorough understanding of this process you are more likely to become an effective manager.

EXCELLENCE IN MANAGEMENT

What makes one organization a winner, while another fails to make use of the same opportunities? Why do some smaller companies move forward and seize new market and product opportunities, while other larger companies fail to take advantage of size and situation? How did CEO Jim Treybig lead Tandem Computers from virtual obscurity to the *Fortune* top 500, while at the same time Gulf Oil, once the ninth largest U. S. corporation, was taken over by another company?

In a recent survey, Hewlett-Packard was rated better than any other company at attracting and keeping talented people and among the top five in quality of management.[2] Good management does not mean trying harder by using out-of-date methods. Effective management involves developing techniques to come up with new products, making sure the products are what the customer wants, and getting the products to market in time to gain a competitive advantage.

Accelerating changes in technology, shorter product life cycles, and unexpected competition contribute to make succeeding in business harder than ever. The evidence indicates that managers play a major role in determining whether an organization performs or not. Managers make strategy, and strategy determines business success or failure.[3]

Management consultants Thomas J. Peters and Robert H. Waterman examined the qualities of forty-three "excellently managed" U. S. companies, including Hewlett-Packard, IBM, 3M, Boeing, Bechtel, Procter & Gamble, and McDonald's. These firms were not only consistently profitable over a twenty-year period, they were all unusually successful in responding to customer needs, providing a challenging working environment for their employees, and being good corporate citizens. Peters and Waterman concluded that these companies were successful because of emphasis on the basic elements of management.[4]

Although many company presidents agree with these findings (even encouraging and requiring managers to read the book), the book is not without its critics. Daniel T. Carroll, Peter Drucker, and others have criticized the methodological and conceptual problems in Peters and Waterman's work, including use of a small, nonrepresentative sample and a lack of a group of unsuccessful companies for comparison. There is also a lack of a detailed description of how the key characteristics were derived.[5]

From their research Peters and Waterman derived eight attributes, characteristics representing the management style of these excellent companies. The attributes emphasize the critical role of management in stressing the values and practices that lead to excellence. These excellent companies exhibit four core characteristics which suggest how these best-run organizations are managed (see figure 1.1).

1 *Managing into the future*   The first characteristic is the necessity to think constantly about new products and then to allocate resources and get them to the marketplace fast. Well-managed companies provide a clear sense of direction and strategic vision of the future. There is a bias toward action, rapid problem solving, and innovation.

2 *A strategic action plan*   The managers of best-run companies tend to develop a strategic game plan for achieving competitive advantage. Successful companies do their marketing homework. Staying close to the customer is a characteristic of successful firms: They seek what the customer wants. A related factor is staying close to what the competition is doing.

3 *The corporate culture*   In well-run organizations, people make things happen. There is a commitment to corporate values and objectives and a willingness to take risks. There is a sense of autonomy in entrepreneurship and a belief in the importance of value and service. The key factor in today's competitive world seems to lie in developing strategic entrepreneurship within the large corpora-

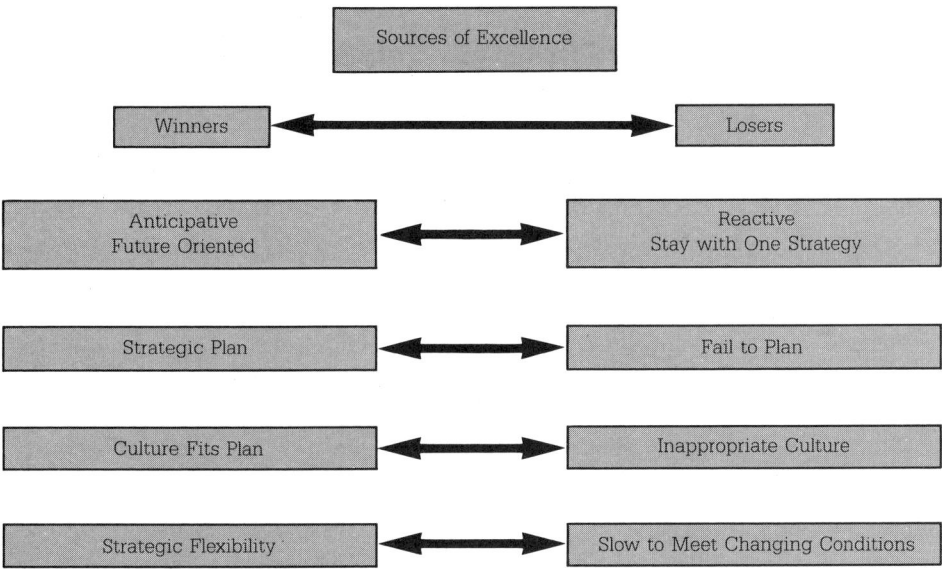

FIGURE 1.1
Strategic Characteristics of Best Run Companies

tion and managing creativity. IBM, for example, has developed new business groups that operate as autonomous units with complete responsibility for new product development.

4 *Strategic flexibility*   The companies that cope best with the rapidly changing environment try to anticipate changes, even if this means reformulating strategy or altering the corporate culture. These companies are results-oriented and market-driven. There is a belief in productivity through people that encourages change and supports risk-taking in order to gain success in both current and new product markets.

The answer, then, to the excellent firm lies in the strategic decisions made by top management of these organizations. Successful companies are effective in developing a strategic plan for achieving future objectives. Although many firms simply let their organizations drift toward uncertain goals, effective managers are able to design results-oriented systems for coordinating a diverse set of product and market endeavors. Some executives are unable to focus the resources of their organization, and the result is ineffective performance.

In a dynamic, competitive environment, an organization must either move forward with purpose and direction or fall back. There is no standing still. The difference between success and failure depends on how well a manager is able to perform the strategic management function: developing an effective, winning organization.

STRATEGIC MANAGEMENT

During the 1990s, traditionally managed business will be caught between advancing technology and changing markets. As a result, many firms will be squeezed out of existence. In order to survive in this changing environment of international competition, executives are finding that new strategic management approaches are necessary. Strategy becomes an important concept for the organization because it determines future success and survival.

Every organization has a strategy. For some, it is never explicitly formulated and involves merely responding to changes after the fact. But, for others, there is a well-defined plan of action termed strategic management—the planning and execution of a carefully targeted portfolio of industry-specific strategies.[6] The next sections examine strategic management, strategy, and policy.

Strategic management is defined as the process of formulating, implementing, and evaluating business strategies to achieve future objectives. Strategic management includes all of the activities leading to the definition of the organization's objectives and to the development of plans, actions, and strategies to accomplish these objectives. The focus of strategic management is on the external environment and on future operations, including three key elements:

1 *Strategic management deals with the future impact of current decisions.* Managers use competitive analysis to identify a set of cause and effect relationships associated with specific strategic decisions. This identification allows top managers to examine possible future results and to develop alternative strategies and plans.
2 *Strategic management determines the long-range direction of the organization.* Management is concerned with relating the resources and short-run objectives of the organization to broader opportunities that exist in the larger environment.
3 *Strategic decisions are made by operating managers.* At Hewlett-Packard, for instance, the executive committee meetings focus on the strategic management of the organization: developing a course of action and reviewing progress toward Hewlett-Packard's target objectives. Strategic management at Hewlett-Packard involves planning and implementing a carefully targeted system of business strategies at all levels to achieve future goals.

At General Motors, the change in strategic management is even more striking. Chairman Roger B. Smith is known throughout GM as the man who introduced strategic planning to the company. But he is also known as the man who, after three unsuccessful tries at establishing a strategic planning system at headquarters, decentralized the process and decreed that operating-division managers, not planners, should plan new strategies.[7]

These strategies involve a series of plans, each differing in terms of time frame, focus, and level of management involved. *Strategic planning* is perhaps more accurately viewed as the integrated structure of goals, strategies, and actions of the firm.

Strategic management is a formalized process with the following generally accepted characteristics:

1 *Strategic systems approach* provides a framework and process for integrating the various business, products, and units of the firm into a coordinated strategic system. The systems approach to strategic management views the organization as a system composed of interrelated parts. Rather than focusing on the separate parts of the organization, the systems approach gives managers a way of looking at the organization as a whole and as an interacting part of the larger industry environment (see chapter 3).
2 *Long-range planning* involves a longer time frame than traditional planning, usually extending from five to ten years into the future and tying together short-, medium-, and long-range plans.
3 *Competitive analysis* deals with the basic, gut issues of the organization: "What business are we in?" "Who are the customers?" and "Who are the competitors?"
4 *A comprehensive vision of the future* provides a sense of purpose and momentum for an organization's decisions and actions over time and a vision of what the firm will become in the future.
5 *A corporate culture* identifies and develops a sense of identity, motivation, and shared values to accomplish these future goals.

Strategic management involves both strategy and policy, which will be examined in the following sections.

Organizational Strategy

An organizational strategy is a course of action used to achieve major objectives. The term *strategy* is derived from the Greek *strategos*, meaning general. In a military sense, strategy involves the planning and directing of battles or campaigns. In the business world, this term refers to actions by a manager to offset actual or potential moves of competitors. Strategic decisions involve the determination of broad directions and the development of comprehensive plans to attain those objectives.

Richard Vancil of Harvard University defines the concept of strategy as follows: "The strategy of an organization, or the subunit of a larger organization, is a conceptualization expressed or implied by the organization's leader, of (1) the long-term objectives or purposes of the organization, (2) the broad constraints and policies, either self-imposed by the leader or accepted by him from his superiors, that currently restrict the scope of the organization's activities, and (3) the current set of plans and near-term goals that have been adopted in the expectation of contributing to the achievement of the organization's objectives."[8]

The strategy, then, is an action plan for achieving future objectives and competitive advantage relative to rival firms. In fact, by its very nature, a strategy has an impact on current competitive relationships.

One outcome of strategy is *organizational policy*. The term policy is generally used to refer to general guides for actions and decisions within the organization. A policy is often referred to as a standing decision made in advance to cover a pre-scribed set of conditions, thus setting the limitations or guidelines for making de-cisions or taking actions. Policies provide organization members with a framework for making decisions so that actions will be consistent throughout the system. At many companies, there is a policy of not acquiring or investing in product lines with a return below a certain level, say 20 percent. Firms may also have to deal with recurring situations. For example, most organizations have personnel policies that cover the basic situations of hiring, promoting, or terminating employees. Manda-tory retirement at age seventy is a typical policy of many organizations. Weyer-haeuser, for example, has a policy of promotion from within, whereas its competi-tion, International Paper, has relied upon hiring from other companies, such as Xerox and Du Pont, to inject new ideas and values.

At Hewlett-Packard organization policies facilitate communication and con-sistency through all levels of the organization. Policy evolves from strategy and includes the procedures, rules, and methods used in the implementation of strategic decisions (see figure 1.2).

Objectives are the overall strategic mission expressed in terms of five-year market share, return on investment (ROI), et cetera. The *strategy* and *plans* are designed as directions for achieving attainment of goals and missions, the steps that lead to the attainment of objectives. From strategy and plans, *policies* are then developed to provide guidance for operational decisions and actions. *Procedures* provide direction in handling specific sections but allow for a certain amount of judgmental discretion. *Rules*, which are quite rigid and very specific, deal with certain categories or situations in which little if any discretion is allowed.

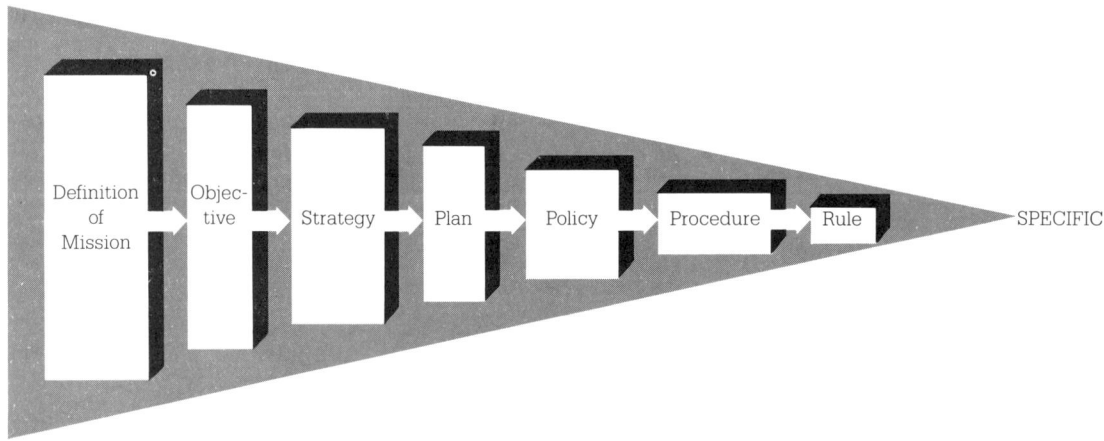

FIGURE 1.2
From Broad Mission/Strategy to Specific Rules/Job

WHY USE STRATEGIC MANAGEMENT?

Strategic management encompasses all the decisions and actions leading to the attainment of long-range objectives. The total organization is considered as an open system in determining the allocation of resources, the direction of organizational forces, and the plan of strategic actions. The open-system perspective emphasizes that an organization has a number of interacting elements and can be considered only in relation to its external environment. Without this system perspective, managers tend to see problems in isolation, often failing to recognize the dynamic interrelationship among subsystems of the organization and with other value systems.

The strategic manager's job, then, is one of managing systems. The strategist identifies system and subsystem relationships; develops goals, objectives, and plans; and integrates these activities into a broad course of action. The systems view recognizes the independent forces, both internal and external, which directly influence the organization. These influences include (1) external constraints; (2) opportunities for growth and survival; (3) internal processes, such as structure and climate; and (4) the degree of freedom that exists in strategic choice. The external environment includes those economic, political, and cultural systems that affect the firm. Because this external environment is becoming more unpredictable and complex, it is essential for the strategist to develop skills in coping with these changing forces.

What enables some managers and organizations to manage technical and market innovations with a true entrepreneurial style? They are able to execute well-planned business strategies with flexibility and speed and, as a result, have been winning market share away from bigger, slower competitors. The four main reasons for the use of strategic management include

1 Providing long-term direction
2 Adapting to an increasing rate of change
3 Gaining competitive advantage in a high-risk environment
4 Achieving a more effective organization

The strategic management process provides the organization members with clear direction and objectives. This understanding enables both short- and long-term goals to fit into the strategic plan.

Organizations are never completely static. They are in continuous interaction with external forces (see figure 1.3). Changes in consumer attitudes, new legislation, and technological breakthroughs all act on the organization to cause it to change.

The degree of change may vary from one organization to another, but all face the need for adaptation to external forces. Many of these changes are forced upon the organization, but others are generated internally.

Changing life-styles cause changing laws and changing strategies. In the liquor industry, for example, there is a powerful temperance coalition that is changing alcohol's role in American society. Anheuser-Busch has been marketing a low

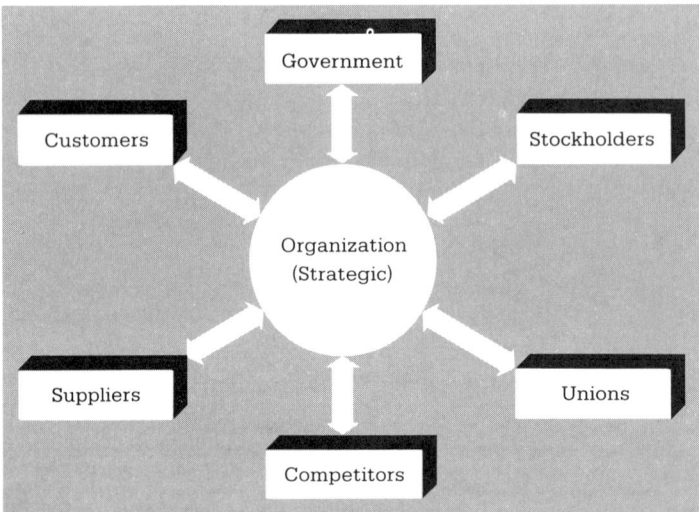

FIGURE 1.3
The Organizational Environment of Strategic Management

alcohol beer, and the industry in general has changed its advertising approach, because liquor sales have been decreasing.[9]

Because changes are occurring so rapidly, even more pressure is being placed on top management. The increased use of strategic planning and management provides one way to aid managers in dealing with this uncertain future.

Economic conditions change so fast that strategic management is the only way to anticipate future opportunities and problems. Given this increasingly complex environment, it becomes even more critical for management to identify and respond to forces of social and technical change.

Another reason for using strategic management is to allow the firm to identify and evaluate ways to gain competitive advantage. There is rarely only one strategy to pursue. There are usually many possible ways to allocate the resources of the organization, and many possible strategies. The analysis of the firm and the environment may generate aggressive-offensive strategies aimed at attacking the market or specific market segments; or they may generate alternatives for defensive purposes, for reducing spending, cutting costs, limiting growth, and even possibly selling off business units. The generation of many possible alternatives can be used in developing a new strategic approach and gaining competitive advantage.

In many decisions, the management team is placing the entire organization's assets on the line in selecting a certain course of action. This might be termed ''you bet your company!'' The decisions of IBM, in developing its new computer line, and Boeing, in developing its new 767 and 757 series of planes, are typical of the bold and daring strategic decisions organizations are making.

Not only are decisions harder to make, but the stakes keep getting higher. As a result, several studies have presented data to support the contention that strategic management tends to provide better sources of data and more reasoned decisions than more intuitive kinds of decision making do. A number of research studies on the impact of strategic planning indicate that companies using strategic management significantly outperform firms that do not.[10]

There are also several recent studies questioning the emphasis on strategic planning.[11] The issue is how best to use strategic management. Too often in the past, companies have tended to overload managers with meaningless "number-crunching" exercises that add little to an understanding of real competitive positioning. The current trend is toward simple but accurate competitive analysis leading to future strategy. At Hewlett-Packard, for example, the long-range plan is summarized in six to ten pages of narrative, with only a few key numbers but focusing on competitive product and market changes.

Strategic Management and the Personal Computer

One new technology affecting strategic management is the use of the personal computer (PC). Personal computers are becoming the primary method that managers use to analyze and manipulate competitive information. For example, a sales planning manager for a major division of General Foods uses a PC to transmit information on competitors' prices to a mainframe computer at General Foods' headquarters. She also uses the PC for tracking overhead costs and sales expenses against budget. It is estimated that 17 percent of the nation's managers and 13 percent of its top executives now have access to PCs, and the number will increase tenfold by 1990. By 1990, there will be more digital devices (i.e., PCs) than telephones in the business world.[12]

Managers who compute for themselves can build a small but useful database on a PC in a few days. After that, planning calculations take only minutes. Managers can quickly ask "what-if" questions on price, margin, ratios, and so forth by using spreadsheet programs like Lotus 1-2-3 or decision-support programs like LightYear to quickly calculate the effect of dozens of decisions. Should we allocate marketing resources to product A? Should we use a certain pricing strategy against competitor X? The computer will show how each alternative affects all the numbers in the equation.

The most far-reaching effect of PCs will probably be the flattening of the organizational hierarchy and the decentralization of strategic decision making. Managers will use PC technology increasingly to plan for and conceptualize the future. Travelers Insurance Corporation, for example, plans to put a PC on the desktop of every one of the company's thirty thousand employees by 1990.

The concepts that you will be learning in strategic management are being used more extensively at all levels by large and medium-sized businesses, and even by more sophisticated smaller businesses.

The CEOs of the generation now coming to power feel they are strategic thinkers—and believe that their key operating lieutenants should be as well. ''Those who succeed in thinking strategically and executing strategically are the people who are going to move ahead at this company,'' according to Hicks B. Waldron, chairman of Avon Products, Inc.[13]

Strategic management allows top executives to adapt to changes, to innovate in time to take advantage of new opportunities, and to reduce the risk of anticipated threats. Thomas H. Naylor of Duke University suggested that nearly two thousand firms in the United States, Canada, and Mexico are using or developing some form of corporate planning model.[14]

THE TYPES OF STRATEGIC MANAGEMENT

Organizations differ in their approach to strategic management. Clearly, strategic management involves a process or system linking strategic planning and decision making with the day-to-day business of operational management. Every organization has a strategy. That strategy may be implicit and informal, or it may be an explicit, formal strategic planning system (see figure 1.4). There are at least three approaches that may be used.

1   *Opportunistic decision making* prefers to use habit, experience, or gut feeling to respond to the environment. Intuitive decision making, as it is called, is usually used by the entrepreneurial-style manager in a smaller firm, and its success depends upon the quality of judgment of the individual.
2   *Strategic thinking* allows for creative entrepreneurial insights into a company, its industry, and its environment. Such managers typically tend to use a less formal approach. They may communicate their strategic plans verbally instead of writing them down, and managers may meet informally to select objectives and methods without an elaborate, systematic review process.
3   *Strategic planning* is the systematic, comprehensive approach to developing strategy. In larger organizations, the strategic process is likely to be rather formalized and involves a systematic implementation and review process. Each of these strategic approaches can be effective, but most large enterprises are, of course, too complex to be managed with only an implicit strategy. Consequently, in larger organizations, there is a tendency to develop more sophisticated strategic management systems.[15]

The strategy is a broad, long-range set of goals and plans for corporate success and survival. This strategic game plan must then be communicated and implemented by all units and levels of the organization, including corporate, business, and functional levels.

The typical large business firm applies three levels of strategy. The emphasis of strategic management, then, may be distinguished from other levels, as shown in

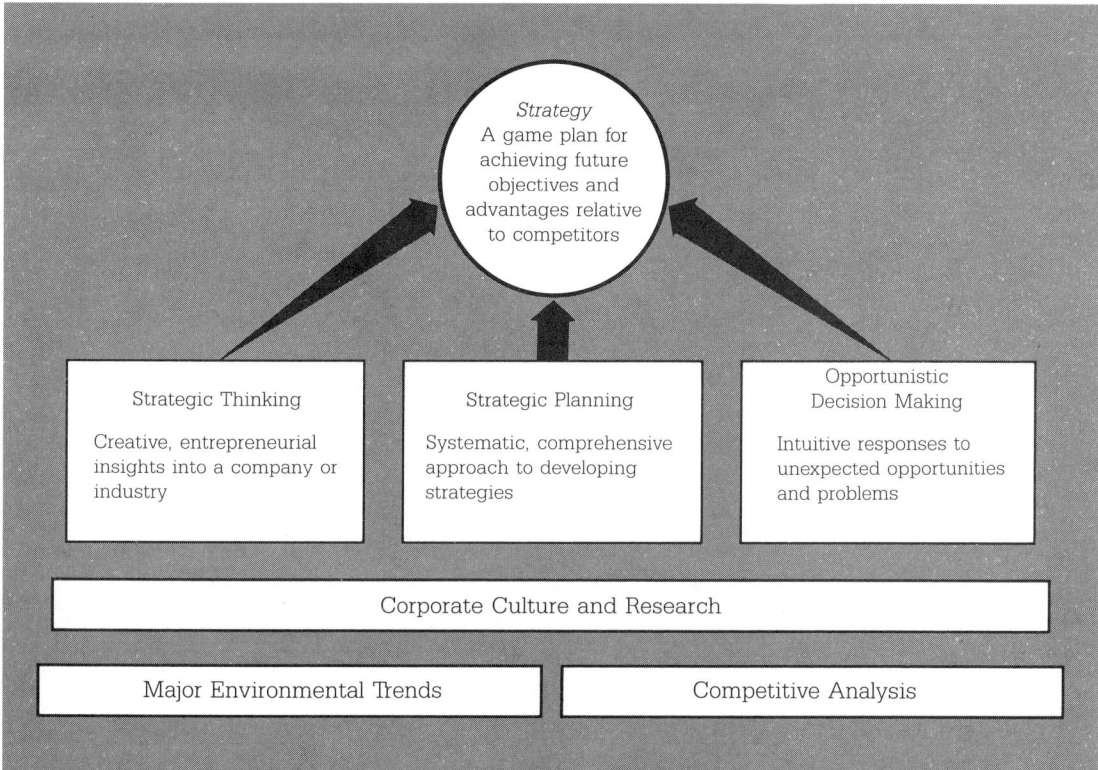

FIGURE 1.4
Three Strategic Approaches

Adapted from Frederick Gluck et al., "The Four Phases of Strategic Management," *Journal of Business Strategy* 2, no. 3 (Winter 1982):9. Reprinted with permission from *Journal of Business Strategy*. Copyright 1982, Warren, Gorham & Lamont, Inc., 210 South St., Boston, MA 02111. All rights reserved.

figure 1.5. The corporate level is concerned with the relation of the organization to its environment and with a comprehensive strategy. The business level is chiefly concerned with the divisional level strategy and stresses improving the competitive position of specific businesses or products in a limited industry or market segment. The functional level is concerned with maximizing the use of resources and productivity at a more detailed level.

The *corporate level* of strategy develops a long-range plan for the whole organization. It is concerned with the management of resources to achieve corporate-level performance objectives and with the integration of different businesses into a comprehensive organization strategy. Hewlett-Packard, for example, manages four different businesses or product sectors, which its strategic plan pulls into a single corporate strategy.

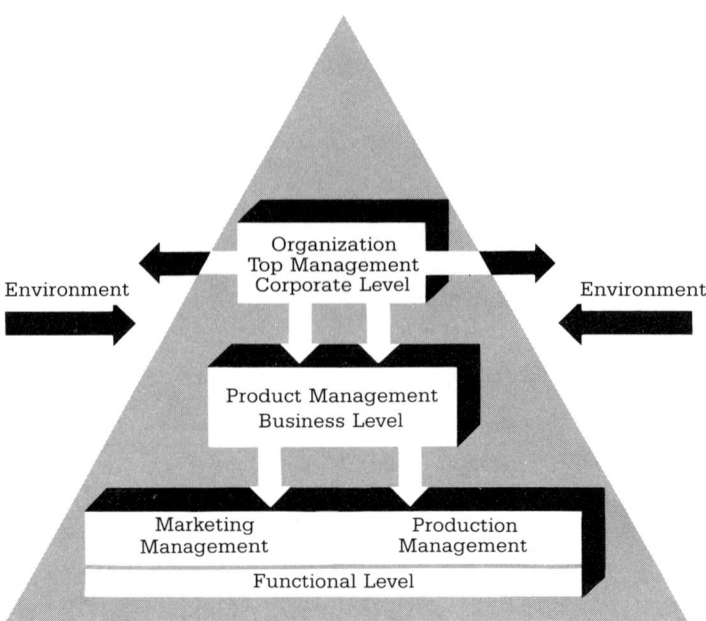

FIGURE 1.5
Three Levels of Strategy

Although the emphasis of the other levels is on smaller, internal problems, the strategic level is concerned with broad, externally oriented decisions. The strategic manager provides objectives and controls for lower-level internal units but not for detailed matters. The strategic level is concerned with long-range planning and makes decisions on the long-range direction of the organization and its interaction with the larger environment, including competitive, governmental, and social concerns.

The *business level* makes strategic decisions involving competitive position in a specific product, business, or market segment within that division. These divisions are often termed *strategic business units* (SBUs). A strategic business unit is an operating division of a firm that serves a distinct product/market segment, a well-defined set of customers, or a geographic area. The business unit makes its own strategic decisions within corporate guidelines to meet its own business objectives. The president of IBM's personal computer division, for example, develops a business strategy for the business to compete against Apple, Hewlett-Packard, AT&T, and others in the PC marketplace. This strategy includes allocating resources, developing marketing, pricing strategies, and so forth.

The *functional level* is concerned with managing product, geographic, or functional areas and the actual production and marketing of goods and services. The principal focus of functional strategy is on maximizing target objectives as an element of a business strategy, such as becoming the lowest-cost producer of a product. There is a functional strategy for each major segment of the business, including marketing, manufacturing, finance, human resources, research and development (R&D), and indeed for each functional unit that makes up a total business strategy.

An Integrated Strategic Plan

It is not enough to have a strategy for each of the business levels and segments. It is impossible for a company like Hewlett-Packard to be strategically managed without involving all levels of the organization. All members must understand and share the functional business and corporate strategy in order to implement it. At Hewlett-Packard, each individual's management-by-objectives (MBO) plan is integrated into the functional area's quarterly goals and plans.

The functional plans are integrated into the product group's quarterly and annual operating plans. And finally, the product group's plans are integrated into a corporate quarterly, annual, and five-year strategic plan. Of course, there is a continual updating and finetuning of the corporation's strategic plans to meet changing business conditions and competitive moves.

THE STRATEGIC MANAGEMENT PROCESS

Because of the success of strategic planning in such organizations as Hewlett-Packard, IBM, and General Electric, the emphasis has been shifting from policy or operational planning toward strategic management. This emphasis on strategic management reflects the growing impact of the outside world on the organization. The fast-changing and uncertain world situation is forcing organizations to do more strategic planning.

At Hewlett-Packard, for example, the strategic planning and review meetings are part of the system of management. Each year, Hewlett-Packard businesses develop a complete five-year business plan. The business plans are reviewed monthly, and the strategic plan is continually updated to meet possible changes and correct potential problems. In a rapidly changing environment, strategic decisions based on past conditions may become obsolete almost as quickly as they can be put into operation. Organizations are finding that strategic planning is necessary if they are to anticipate and adapt to changing conditions.

Strategic management appears to evolve over time through four distinct stages or phases: budgeting, forecasting, externally oriented planning, and, finally, strategic management. This conclusion is based on a study of a number of large companies around the world by McKinsey and Company, the consulting firm. The evidence suggests that as organizations grow and managers see the benefits of planning techniques, the planning activities tend to evolve into more complex strategic management systems.[16]

The McKinsey study found that the evolution of formal planning can be segmented into the four fairly distinct sequential stages shown in figure 1.6. Surprisingly, many companies (even firms with sales of several million dollars per year) did

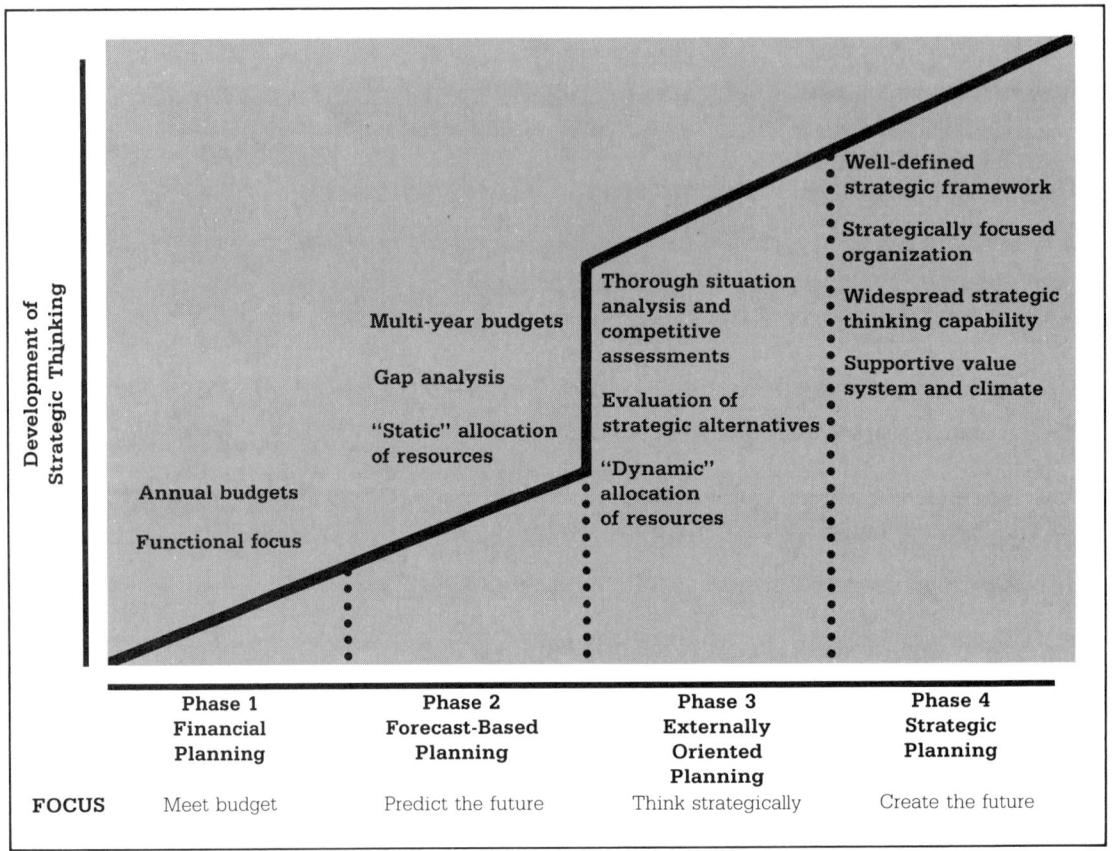

FIGURE 1.6
The Evolution of Strategic Planning

Adapted from F. Gluck, S. Kaufman, and A. S. Walleck, "The Four Phases of Strategic Management," *Journal of Business Strategy* (Winter 1982):11. Reprinted with permission from *Journal of Business Strategy*. Copyright 1982, Warren, Gorham & Lamont, Inc., 210 South St., Boston MA 02111. All rights reserved.

not use even a basic budgeting system. They are figuratively "flying by the seat of their pants."

Phase 1

Basic financial planning is the rudimentary form of planning practiced by most organizations. In this earliest phase of development, planning is viewed as a financial problem, and procedures are developed to forecast revenues, costs, and capital needs for one year in advance. In well over half of the business enterprises surveyed, including a number of highly successful companies, formal planning had never evolved beyond annual budgeting. In general, organizations in this phase have a short-term focus with little planning for the future.

Phase 2

Forecast-based planning emerges when the complexities of management increase—with, for example, an increased number of products, more markets, increasing sophistication of technology, or dynamic and turbulent economic swings. The second phase usually begins with the establishment of formal planning staffs. Their responsibility is to extend the budget beyond one year into a multiyear budgeting cycle. At first, forecast-based planning differs little from annual budgeting except that it covers a longer period of time. However, it is soon charaterized by the use of relatively sophisticated forecasting tools such as trend analysis, regression models, and simulation programs.

Phase 3

Externally oriented planning represents a quantum leap forward in planning capability. There are several distinguishing characteristics of phase 3 planning. First, planning begins with a thorough analysis of the environment that includes the competitive situation and strategy. Second, resource allocation is dynamic rather than static. The phase 3 planner looks for an opportunity to "shift the dot" of a business on a portfolio matrix into a more attractive sector (see chapter 6). Finally, the key characteristic of phase 3 plans is to present several alternative courses of action which force managers to think through all their options and the advantages and disadvantages of each.

Phase 4

Strategic management incorporates many of the planning advantages noted in earlier phases but attempts to overcome their limitations. The characteristics of phase 4 include

1 *A strategic framework and the development of strategic business units (SBUs).* A strategic planning framework involves lower-level managers in the planning process.
2 *A strategically focused organization.* Strategic planning becomes a part of management actions, plans, and decisions.
3 *A widespread strategic thinking capability.* Strategic decision making involves creative versus deterministic decision making among all levels of management.
4 *An integration of performance into the organization's reward system.* Managers are rated based upon planning performance against the firm's target objectives.

Strategic management appears to be a distinct, new phase in the evolution of the management planning process. Perhaps its most visible characteristic is the integration of strategic planning into decision-making aspects of management. Strategic management appears to improve a company's long-term business success. Top executives in strategically managed companies develop hard-hitting, effective business strategies supported by coherent, functional plans.

The Strategic Management Process Model

The evolving strategic management model is based upon the concepts of strategy and upon a process for managing strategy. An essential part of this process is the developing of a master strategy for the firm to provide positive, future-oriented direction to its business activities. A strategic management model of eight interrelated stages is shown in figure 1.7. The elements of the strategic process will be examined separately, although in fact they often happen simultaneously. Strategic management is a continuing process, and the stages are interacting parts of a whole system.

Stage 1: Define Strategic Mission/Vision

Organizations exist to accomplish a mission. The first step in the strategic formulation process is the definition of organizational purpose or mission. The mission of an organization presents a long-term idea of what that organization is striving to become in the future.

The strategic vision of what the firm will be in the future provides the broad initiation for mission, goals, and objectives. The strategic vision involves the general, abstract ideas that guide strategy formulation and give the organization purpose.

Stage 2: Determine Strategic Objectives

Strategic objectives for achieving the strategic vision in a complex environment must be identified. Organizational objectives refer to the results an organization seeks to achieve. An organization usually pursues many objectives, including primary (or strategic) objectives and secondary (or subunit) objectives.

Stage 3: Identify Strategic Opportunities and Threats

In determining a strategy, other factors are the opportunities and threats that exist in the environment. What economic and demographic factors have been and will continue to be important? Almost all organizations use economic forecasting and indicators to predict future conditions. The airlines, for example, must base future strategic moves on such factors as growth trends in air travel, overall economic conditions, and the future price of fuel. The strategic decision maker evaluates options based on the information about probable future situations influencing the attainment of strategic objectives. This evaluation includes an analysis of economic and market conditions. The strategy must take into account both the opportunities for the future and possible impediments to future actions.

The analysis of strengths, weaknesses, opportunities, and threats is termed a SWOT analysis (see chapter 3). Here the strategist tries to identify key competitive advantages and disadvantages, seeking a fit between the organization's distinctive competencies (what it can do) and its strategy (what it wants to do).

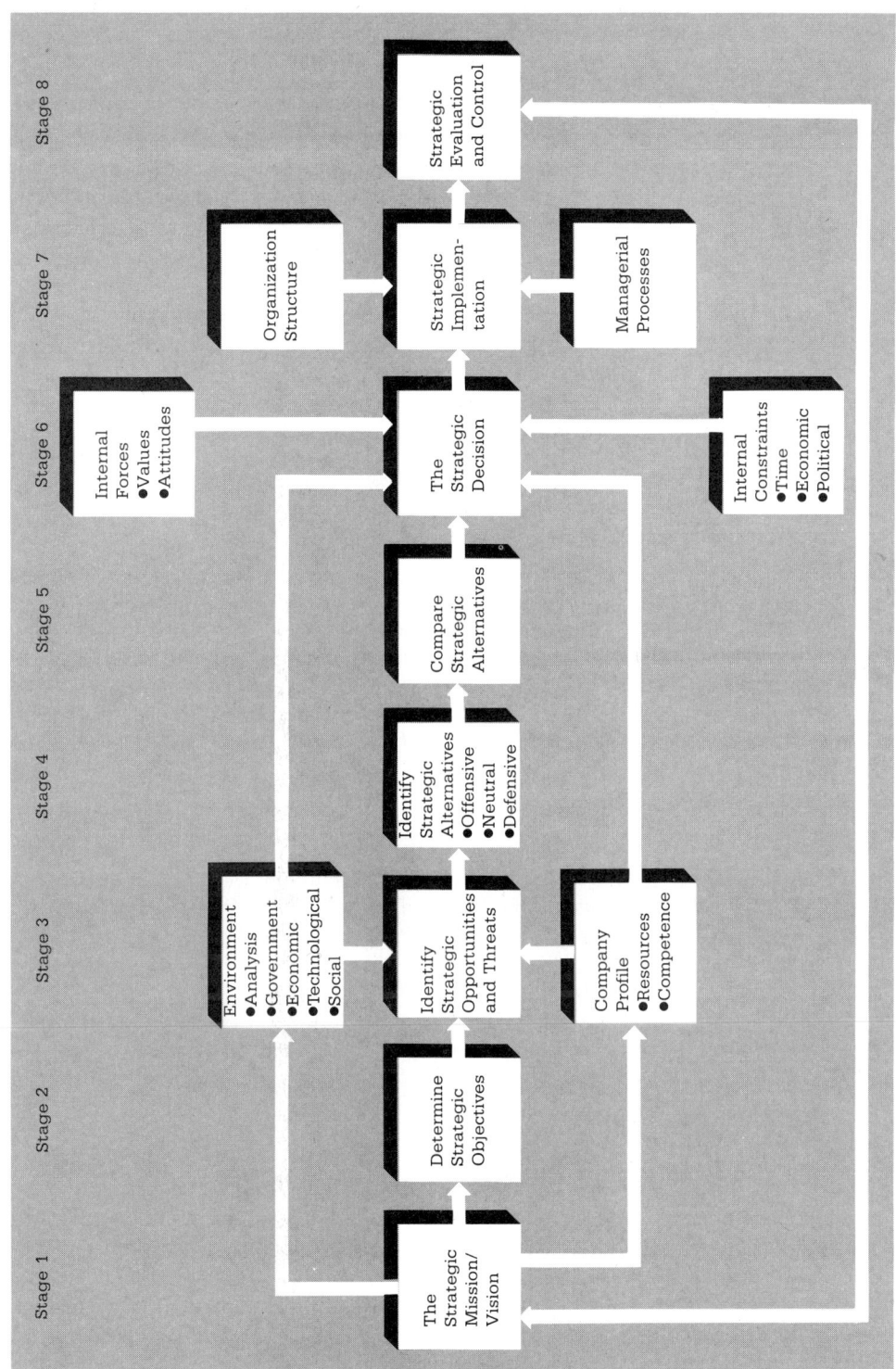

FIGURE 1.7
A Model of Strategic Management

19

Stage 4: Identify Strategic Alternatives

The next step is to identify and evaluate alternative strategies or options. There is rarely only one strategy to pursue. There are usually many possible ways to allocate the resources of the organization and many possible strategies. Depending upon the analysis of the firm and the environment, they may generate aggressive-offensive strategies aimed at attacking the market or specific market segments or they may generate alternatives for defensive purposes, for reducing spending, cutting costs, limiting growth, or even possibly selling off business units. The key here is the generation of many possible options or courses of action. What are the possible alternatives that could be used in developing a new strategic approach?

Stage 5: Compare Strategic Alternatives

Once strategic alternatives and possible actions have been identified, the relative advantages or disadvantages of each can be compared against some set of criteria. The alternatives can be examined to determine which strategy best matches the firm's resources and capabilities and which offers the best competitive advantage, in terms of potential opportunities or threats. Each strategic alternative will have advantages and disadvantages. Often they are in conflict: Should IBM concentrate on growth or on earnings? Should one subsidiary get a larger share of resources, or should another? At this point in the decision process, management must analyze the alternatives and compare them on the basis of certain criteria in order to separate the more promising options from the less likely alternatives.

Stage 6: Make the Strategic Decision

After the process of strategic evaluation, the next step is the most critical factor in the strategic management process: making the strategic decision. A decision is a choice from among possible alternative strategies. As the old saying goes, ''The buck stops here!'' The purpose of decision making is to direct resources toward objectives, and a decision to pursue one strategy usually means other possible actions are not being taken. The decisions may be good decisions or they may be terrible, but they must be made. At Boeing, Chairman T. A. Wilson's decision to invest $3 billion in designing two new airliner series (757, 767) has given Boeing a commanding lead among aircraft companies. At Rolls-Royce, however, a decision to design a new jet engine led that company into bankruptcy.

Stage 7: Implement the Strategy

The strategic plan alone is valueless until it is implemented to achieve the future objectives. Translating strategies into action is the function of strategy implementation. The strategic decision is implemented by developing specific and detailed policies, plans, and action programs aimed at the attainment of objectives. Once the strategic decision is made, the next step is the implementation of the action plan: the actual performance and activities that commit the organization's resources toward the desired goals. Implementation includes both the fit between strategy and structure and the fit with the corporate culture. Many strategists feel the implementation stage may be even more critical than the decision itself. Regardless of the merit of the decision, unless it is properly executed, it may end up being ineffective.

Stage 8: Evaluate the Strategy

Monitoring organization performance and results so that actual performance can be compared with planned objectives is the function of strategy evaluation. The purpose of strategic evaluation is critical to any plan. If actual results do not track with planned results, then changes must be made. Managers should be continually reviewing the process of strategic moves so that they can take corrective action or make countermoves if the original plan is not working or if conditions have changed. This final step involves the strategic review and evaluation of the game plan.

This eight-step strategic management process will determine future performance. How effectively managers are able to deal with these complex, ever-changing factors of market, competition, and economic conditions is what strategic management is all about.

THE PLAN OF THE BOOK

Strategic management is a fundamental process for solving complex organizational problems. The purpose of this book is to show how strategic management is important to you and to bring this field to life as you learn about it.

It is possible to use these same approaches in managing your own career or personal resources. You will very likely be making a series of strategic decisions about your life, career, and personal finances. What kind of job do you want, and in what career field? Will you want to pursue a graduate degree? If so, what is the return on investment of an MBA? Questions like these are not unlike the strategic choices a firm must make.

Most of you deal regularly with a large number of organizations: schools, businesses, churches, hospitals, and governmental departments. All of them need to be well managed in order to be effective. Thus, strategic management is an important, exciting, and challenging field and one that offers applications and rewards in numerous areas of activity and responsibility.

Included in the text are real-life situations that managers face on a day-to-day basis. The cases will allow you to become involved in and experience real managerial situations, using firms like Hewlett-Packard, Apple Computer, and Federal Express.

The organization of the text follows the flow of the strategic management model presented in figure 1.7, with each segment building on the earlier foundations.

The goal of the book is to help you as a manager to develop an improved way of thinking about problems and to form a broader point of view. Throughout the book the emphasis is on strategic practices, analysis, and theory, rather than on description and lists of advantages and disadvantages. The aim of the policy course is the stimulation of thought processes rather than the memorization of answers. Throughout the text there is an emphasis on new techniques and ideas that hold promise for the future development of strategic management rather than on the inadequate and unsystematic methods often used in the past.

MANAGERIAL SUMMARY

This chapter has developed the basic concepts of strategic management. At Hewlett-Packard, for example, the overall strategic planning of the company has caused it to change directions as economic conditions have changed. Hewlett-Packard, under CEO John Young, has become a leader in its field because of good strategic management systems.

Strategic management includes the decision-making process. These decisions formulate strategic goals and plans, implement these plans, and use control systems to ensure that these goals are achieved.

Strategic management is the keystone of the critical management function. All other organizational activities and functions are derived from strategic management. Strategic planning activities are becoming increasingly important because of the rapidly changing environment that managers must face. The strategic management model provides a means for anticipating the future and defining new strategic directions.

The strategic model identifies an eight-stage process. It translates the basic mission into objectives, strategy, plans, and policies, which are then implemented to achieve stated goals. There is evidence of a relationship between strategic management and the effectiveness of the organization. These concepts can be useful in all organizations, including large firms, smaller businesses, nonprofit organizations, and entrepreneurial startups.

Today executives manage in a changing and dynamic environment. This fact has important implications for organizations and strategic managers. Preparing managers to cope with today's accelerating rate of change is the central concern of this book. The modern manager must be not only flexible and adaptive in a changing environment but also must be able to diagnose problems, make strategic decisions, and implement strategic plans.

Because change is occurring so rapidly, there is increasing pressure on top management. The strategic decisions are harder than ever to make, and the stakes keep getting higher. Strategic management provides one way for organizations to become more effective in adapting to change.

Today's managers exist in shifting organizational structures and can be the central force in initiating strategic direction and establishing the means for adaptation. Most organizations strive to be creative, efficient, and competitive, maintaining a leading edge in their respective fields rather than following trends set by others. Effective strategic planning is vital to the continuing self-renewal and ultimate survival of the organization. The manager must recognize when changes are occurring in the external environment and possess the necessary competence to bring about changes in strategy when they are needed.

Review Questions

1   Read the Corporation section in a recent issue of *Business Week, Forbes,* or *The Wall Street Journal.* Find a company in your area of interest that is developing a new strategy.
2   As discussed in the chapter, Boeing risked $3 billion in developing its new series of planes (757, 767). Use the strategic management model to consider some of the important factors Boeing should have analyzed before making this decision.
3   What is competitive advantage? How would you measure competitive performance?
4   Is it necessary to have all levels of management involved in strategy? If so, why?
5   Does every organization have a strategy? Why or why not? See if you can identify the strategic process being used in a current movie or TV show.

Personal Objectives

Outside of class, list some of the specific objectives and expectations you have for this class. These objectives should describe what you will be able to do or demonstrate at the end of this course.

1   _____
    _____
2   _____
    _____
3   _____
    _____
4   _____
    _____

Notes

1   Based on personal interviews with Hewlett-Packard managers; see also John A. Young, "The Quality Focus at Hewlett-Packard," *Journal of Business Strategy* 5, no. 3 (Winter 1985):6–9; Kathleen K. Wiegner, "John Young's New Jogging Shoes," *Forbes*, Nov. 4, 1985, 44.
2   Patricia Sellers, "America's Most Admired Corporations," *Fortune*, January 7, 1985, 21.
3   See Andrew D. Szilagyi, Jr., and David M. Schweiger, "Matching Managers to Strategy," *Academy of Management Review* 9, no. 4 (1984):626–627; and LaRue T. Hosmer, "The Importance of Strategic Leadership," *Journal of Business Strategy* 3, no. 2 (Fall 1982):58.
4   Thomas J. Peters and Robert H. Waterman, Jr., *In Search of Excellence: Lessons from America's Best-Run Companies* (New York: Harper & Row, 1982), 285.

5 Daniel T. Carroll, "A Disappointing Search for Excellence," *Harvard Business Review* (November–December 1983), 78–88. See also *Wall Street Journal*, June 6, 1985; *Business Week*, June 3, 1985.

6 See John D. C. Roach and Thomas A. Schultz, "Strategic Planning in the 1980s," *Outlook* (Spring 1981):3.

7 "The New Breed of Strategic Planner," *Business Week*, September 17, 1984, 62.

8 Richard F. Vancil, "Strategy Formulation in Complex Organizations," *Sloan Management Review* (Winter 1976):1–18.

9 See "Liquor Makers Try the Hard Sell," *Business Week*, May 13, 1985, 56; "America's New Abstinence," *Fortune*, May 18, 1985, 20–23; and "The Sobering of America," *Business Week*, February 25, 1985, 112.

10 See the following:

   T. Scott Armstrong, "The Value of Formal Planning for Strategic Decisions," *Strategic Management Journal* 3 (July–September 1982):197–211.

   Joseph Eastlack, Jr., and Phillip McDonald, "CEO's Role in Corporate Growth," *Harvard Business Review*, May–June 1970, 150–163.

   David Herold, "Long Range Planning and Organizational Performance: A Cross Validation Study," *Academy of Management Review*, March 1972, 91–102.

   Delmar Karger and Zaraf Malik, "Long Range Planning and Organizational Performance," *Long Range Planning*, December 1975.

   Sidney Schoeffler et al., "Impact of Strategic Planning on Profit Performance," *Harvard Business Review*, March–April 1974, 137–145.

   Stanford Research Institute, as reported in "Why Companies Grow," *Nation's Business,* November 1957, 80–82, 84–86.

   Stanley Thune and Robert House, "Where Long Range Planning Pays Off," *Business Horizons*, August 1970, 81–87.

   D. Robley Wood, Jr., and R. Lawrence LaForge, "The Impact of Comprehensive Planning on Financial Performance," *Academy of Management Journal* 22, no. 3 (1979):516–526.

11 See Richard T. Pascale, "Our Curious Addition to Corporate Grand Strategy," *Fortune*, January 25, 1982, 115–116.

12 See "A PC per Desktop Remains Objective of Travelers Group," *PC Week*, December 1, 1986, 69; and John Deinden, "Will the Computer Change the Jobs of Top Management?" *Management Review* 25, no. 1 (Fall 1983/4):57–60.

13 "The New Breed," *Business Week*, September 17, 1984, 62.

14 Thomas Naylor and Daniel Gattis, "Corporate Planning Models," *California Management Review* 18, no. 4 (Summer 1976): 69–78.

15 Frederick Gluck, Stephen Kaufman, and A. Steven Walleck, "The Four Phases of Strategic Management," *Journal of Business Strategy* 2, no. 3 (Winter 1982):8.

16 Ibid., 9.

PART ONE

■ ■ ■

STRATEGY FORMULATION

CHAPTER TWO

■ ■ ■

Strategic Vision

OBJECTIVES

After completing this chapter, you will be
able to:

- Define and use the contingency
  approach to strategic planning

- Describe the strategic forces that
  influence objectives

- Discuss the factors contributing to the
  development of strategic vision and
  mission

- Compare the basic ways an
  organization can adapt to change

- Identify the key factors in strategic
  planning

The corporate objectives provide the basic framework for the management by objectives system, which gives the individual managers a lot of freedom to be entrepreneurial and innovative.

John A. Young, CEO, Hewlett-Packard

Management's job is to see the company not as it is . . . but as it can become.

John W. Teets, Chairman, Greyhound Corporation

Strategic Vision at Apple Computer

Sculley

John Sculley, Apple's chief executive, is changing management discipline by controlling costs, reducing overhead, and realigning the product lines in an organization that grew too fast. He moved quickly to develop tight cost controls and management reporting systems for Apple's chaotic operations.

One of the first things Sculley did on joining Apple was to put the highest priority on clarifying an erratic product grouping system, so that Apple had competitive products for low, medium, and top-of-the-line segments. Sculley, the pin-striped marketing genius, moved rapidly: He reorganized Apple's entire operation, fired several top managers, launched two successful new products, and showed the ability to work with the "laid back" corporate culture.

Sculley and his management team have indicated that Apple will renew its efforts to penetrate the office market, despite an unsuccessful attempt earlier.

John Sculley targets certain strategic goals and objectives for Apple in order to realize a strategic vision for the company. Apple is recognized for a culture and an environment in which each individual's achievement is given a high priority. There have been two results of this strategy: some incredibly great products and several products that were not compatible with each other, let alone with the rest of the world. John Sculley is working hard to retain this basic culture as the company grows, feeling that a company changes its culture not by any big decision, but by slowly making small compromises along the way.

John Sculley's strategic vision for Apple is to make it the second largest computer company by the 1990s. John Sculley wants Apple to become a clear alternative to IBM and to remain a leader in the computer industry. Apple is currently using what are described as "guerrilla tactics" to break into the corporate market.

Sculley wants to keep Apple "lean and mean," with a flat management hierarchy, while the company grows into a multibillion dollar corporation. Apple's sales per employee has been $300,000 for each of its 5,800 employees, which suggests a high level of productivity.[1] Sculley sees the recently reorganized Apple as a company that has grown from "visions tied to making technology exciting often for its own sake" to "market-driven visions focused on customer needs."[2]

INTRODUCTION

The strategic vision of what the firm will be in the future provides the broad initiation for mission, goals, and objectives. The strategic vision involves the general, abstract ideas that guide strategy formulation and give the organization purpose.[3] The goals and objectives translate this vision of the future into well-defined, measurable targets to be achieved within a specified time frame.

Strategic managers develop an entrepreneurial vision of the future. Managers make things happen, and it is their selection of goals, objectives, plans, and strategy that will eventually determine business success or failure.

This chapter examines the important role of mission, objectives, and plans in the strategy formulation process. We will approach the concept of strategic vision in three major parts: strategic leadership, goal and objective formulation, and adapting objectives to a changing environment.

The job of the CEO of a major organization is not an easy one. There have been many success stories of managers who have rescued seriously troubled companies and led them to a program of consistent growth. However, for every manager who becomes a winner, there are probably just as many who fail to turn their company around or even guide it from a leading position to a losing one. When we talk about organizational strategy we are really talking about the managers who develop the strategic vision: the mission, objectives, and plans for the future.

From a survey of companies, Thomas J. Peters, the author and management consultant, has found that successful corporate leaders tend to choose a single theme and never miss an opportunity to hammer it home. He suggested that the similarities that mark effective leadership styles may be a lot more important than the differences.[4]

Another study by Shaffir and Lobe reports that the impact of strategic leadership has been to

1 Help the companies sort their businesses into winners and losers
2 Focus attention on critical issues and choices
3 Develop a strategic vision among top and upper-level managers

The study suggests that strategic management results in improved competitive position, increased profits, and growth in earnings per share.[5]

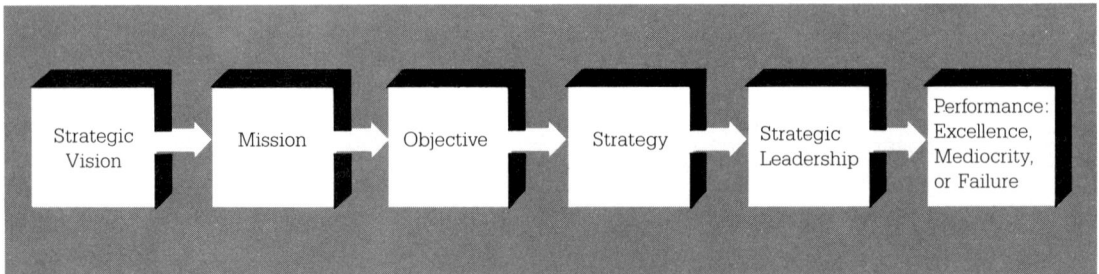

FIGURE 2.1
The Strategic Vision

Research on the best-run companies suggests that three key functions must be accomplished in the entrepreneurial process to providing strategic leadership for the organization (see figure 2.1). The basic steps in strategy leadership include

1   Defining the mission/vision for the firm
2   Developing strategic objectives
3   Formulating a winning strategy in a changing environment

DEFINING MISSION

The chief executive has responsibility for giving direction to the organization, that is, for creating the strategic vision of what the organization is to become in the future. The manager must be a strategic thinker, focusing on competitive position and building a solid set of values within the corporate culture. Somehow, despite the size of their organizations, the chief executives of high-performing companies have managed, through persistence and attention to detail, to keep autonomy, innovation, and entrepreneurial spirit alive all the way down to the shop floor, the sales branch, or the service desk. This sense of purpose flows from the corporate mission statement.

The first step in the strategic formulation process is the definition of organizational purpose or mission. The mission of an organization presents a long-term idea of what that organization is striving to become in the future. The mission statement defines the firm's business arena and serves as a guide to future executive action. It identifies the firm's basic image, philosophy, and thrust, including products, businesses, and markets. The identification of the mission is an awareness of a sense of purpose, the competitive environment, and the degree to which the firm's mission fits its capabilities and environmental opportunities.

The mission provides a starting point for dealing with technological innovation, product quality, customer service, employee satisfaction, and socially responsible conduct. The answers to these issues of mission have a significant impact on future strategy. As an example, when William Hewlett and Dave Packard founded Hewlett-Packard in 1939, they evolved a basic mission of (1) technological leadership, (2) high-quality products, and (3) good employee relations. Because of these basic premises, Hewlett-Packard does not use time clocks and bases its marketing approach on innovative design and product quality. In fact, it prefers not to use price as a strategy at the expense of quality.[6]

Corporate objectives then guide the organization in the direction set by the mission statement.

Hewlett-Packard's Strategic Objectives

1   Profit: To achieve sufficient profit to finance company growth and to provide resources we need to achieve our other corporate objectives.

2   Customer: To provide products and services of the highest quality and the greatest possible value to our customers, thereby gaining and holding their respect and loyalty.

3   Fields of Interest: To build on our strengths in the company's traditional fields of interest and to enter new fields only when it is consistent with the basic purpose of our business and when we can assure ourselves of making a needed and profitable contribution to the field.

4   Growth: To let growth be limited only by our profits and our ability to develop and produce technical products that satisfy real customer needs.

5   People: To help Hewlett-Packard people share in the company's success, which they make possible; to provide job security based on their performance; to help HP people share in the company's success, which they make possible; to provide job security based on their performance; to ensure them a safe and pleasant work environment; to recognize their individual achievements; and to help them gain a sense of satisfaction and accomplishment from their work.

6   Management: To foster initiative and creativity by allowing the individual great freedom of action in attaining well-defined objectives.

7   Citizenship: To honor our obligations to society by being an economic, intellectual, and social asset to each nation and each community in which we operate.[7]

Formulating the Mission

For a strategy to be implemented, it must become an integral part of the organization. The process of defining the mission evolves from the entrepreneurial vision of the top managers. In their study of well-managed firms, Peters and Waterman found several dominant beliefs that provide a sense of mission:

1   A belief in being the best
2   A belief in the importance of the details of the job, "the nuts and bolts"
3   A belief in the importance of people as individuals
4   A belief in superior quality and service
5   A belief that most members should be innovators, and the willingness to support failure
6   A belief in the importance of informality to enhance communication
7   A belief in the importance of economic growth and profits[8]

As the firm grows and changes its strategy, it may be necessary to redefine the mission statement.

Strategic Management at Chrysler Motors (Corporate Level) Strategy Formulation

Iacocca

The mission of strategic management at Chrysler is broad: to keep Chrysler on the leading edge of innovative design, production, and marketing, with the best quality in the industry.

The objectives at Chrysler include the following:

1   Achieve a return on investment (ROI) of 15 to 20 percent for the period 1988 through 1993
2   Achieve a market share of the *global* automotive market equal to that of the major competition by 1990
3   Increase domestic car and truck market share by 5 percent by 1989
4   Reduce unit costs by 6 percent per year

To achieve these objectives, the company has determined the following strategies:

1   Grow by concentrating all resources in the car and truck industry. Focus on developing fuel-efficient, stylish, high-quality cars and trucks to challenge competition
2   Vertically integrate and automate manufacturing facilities to reduce costs and to control raw materials
3   Engage in joint ventures with foreign auto manufacturers to build and sell cars and trucks[9]

DETERMINING ORGANIZATIONAL GOALS AND OBJECTIVES

All organizations need a sense of direction, mission, and objectives as guides to strategic action. Strategic management is based on goals and objectives because they give identity, purpose, and mission to the strategy. Strategic objectives give meaning to the general direction and allow the strategy to be converted into specific actions, programs, and targets. The objectives usually include expected targets for internal performance, such as profitability, sales, and cash flow, as well as anticipated impact on external factors, including rate of growth, innovation, market penetration, and market share.

Boeing, for example, under chairman T. A. Wilson, set as a strategic goal the development of a new generation of fuel-efficient aircraft — the 757 and 767 — while McDonnell-Douglas developed no new generation of planes to introduce in the 80s and 90s. Delta Airlines placed an order for sixty of Boeing's new 757, worth about $3 billion. Delta's order is just the beginning in the race to replace aging aircraft with new fuel-efficient planes like the 757, which burns about 40 percent less fuel per seat than the planes it will succeed.

Since the arrival of Lee Iacocca, Chrysler has moved from a "reactive" management style to an "anticipative" management style. The corporate organization has been streamlined for rapid decision making. Iacocca has recruited executive-level management talent primarily from Ford Motor Company, his former employer. The corporate culture can now be classified as innovative and adaptable to changes in the external environment and changes in corporate strategy, policies, and implementation.

Chrysler has returned to financial health following several years of a defensive-turnaround strategy. In 1984, revenues increased 47 percent, net income-to-sales ratio increased from about 3 percent to 12 percent, cost of goods sold decreased from about 85 percent to 80 percent, and return on total assets increased from about 10 percent to 16.5 percent. Chrysler has strong financial health and is positioned for implementation of growth strategies.[10]

What Are Goals and Objectives?

Organizational goals and objectives refer to the results which an organization seeks to achieve. An organization usually pursues many objectives, including primary or strategic objectives and secondary or subunit objectives.

Organizational goals are desired future states which the organization seeks to achieve. The goals are broad, general guidelines to thinking which provide levels of attainment that are relatively timeless. Goals are aimed at the broad purpose and mission of the organization and include survival, efficiency, and profitability. Most authors use the terms goal and objective interchangeably; however, many suggest that goals are broader and less specific than objectives.

Organizational objectives are the statements that help guide the activities of groups and members toward the overall goals. Objectives, which are more specific and timebound than goals, are (1) time-limited, (2) measurable, and (3) quantifiable. Plans and controls flow from the mission and objectives. Strategic objectives are selected by the strategist and are influenced by environmental forces.

The objectives are the end results or the end state toward which an organization is striving; for example, a 20 percent rate of growth or a 12 percent rate of return. The strategy is the plan or program for accomplishing the objectives; for example, an acquisition strategy or a cost-cutting strategy.

There are approaches to goal setting that research has found to be highly beneficial in obtaining desired results.[11] Difficult-to-reach goals led to higher performance than easy goals, "do your best" goals, or no goals. Goals should be specific, and feedback should be provided to show progress. In an organization setting, managers and supervisors should provide support. Goal setting should not only stress organizational goals but also provide opportunities for personal and career goals. It is imperative that individuals be committed to their goals. Goal setting has been shown to be effective at all levels in an organization without regard to education, position, or tenure of the employee. One example of goal setting is the lofty ambition of Xavier Roberts, creator of the Cabbage Patch Kids.

Out of the Cabbage Patch

Xavier Roberts is an entrepreneur who started his own company in 1978 and the creator of the Cabbage Patch kids. After developing his product, he sold the license to Coleco in 1983 and received revenues of $2 million. Today, total revenues reach about $1.5 billion. Roberts, who is single, owns four houses in Georgia and collects high-powered cars (including three Mercedes, two Jaguars, a Rolls-Royce, a Corvette, a BMW, and a Jeep); but he presents a good-ol'-boy image and wears a cowboy hat and well-worn jeans to the office. Instead of being satisfied with past performance, Roberts is looking to the future with even bigger and better dreams. His mission for the future: to become the next Walt Disney. Xavier Roberts has defined the following objectives as those which will enable him to achieve this goal:

1   Introduce Furskins, a new teddy bear with a personality
2   Create a cartoon series depicting his products
3   Build a hotel complex near his production facilities
4   Develop an amusement park
5   Introduce a new doll, "Bunny Bee"
6   Produce a Cabbage Patch movie

The final element in Roberts's strategy is to develop his toy-licensing business. He has now started work on a $25 million Cabbage Patch movie, a project he plans to finance himself. Still, for Roberts to attain the status of his idol, Walt Disney, he needs to prove that his creativity matches his ambition.[12]

The Importance of Organizational Objectives

Objectives play an important role in the strategic management process for at least four reasons.

1 *Objectives provide direction for organization efforts.* They give purpose to the organization's members. For example, both Mercedes Benz and Fiat produce automobiles. Mercedes Benz has stressed the production of high-quality and expensive cars, but at a low level of production. Fiat, on the other hand, specializes in high-volume, lower-priced models. The varying goals lead to different ways of manufacturing and marketing autos. Managers in each firm initiate strategy designed to focus organizational resources toward these goals.
2 *Strategic objectives perform an integrating function.* They provide a means for setting priorities and resolving conflicts between organizational elements. Marketing units may seek one set of objectives, research and development departments another, and financial groups yet another. The strategic objectives provide a means of integrating and coordinating these diverse activities and functions.
3 *Objectives provide a motivating force.* A clear sense of direction provides a unifying and motivating force for analytical members. At Tandem Computer, for example, employees see the big picture and are aware of strategic secrets; as a result, they feel a part of the team, see their own direction, and know what's happening on all sides of them. Tandem's productivity figures are among the five highest in the industry.[13]
4 *Objectives provide measures of organizational performance.* Objectives set out a target to be achieved and also provide a measure of how well these goals have been accomplished. Objectives, plans, and motivated workers all work toward the achievement of some end result. At Tandem, Jim Treybig and his associates are working toward building a successful company where everyone enjoys working.

Organizations have multiple sets of goals and objectives of varying importance. H. Igor Ansoff of the European Institute for Advanced Studies in Management has suggested that the firm formulates goals which are distinct and different from those of individual participants in the firm. He further noted that ''in our main area of interest, the strategic problem, objectives are used as yardsticks for decisions on changes, deletions, and additions to the firm's product/market posture.''[14] According to Ansoff, these objectives can take the form of a *threshold objective* (the minimum acceptable level of achievement) or a *goal* (the desired outcome or level of aspiration), and they are ranked in order of priority to form a goal hierarchy.

Charles A. Perrow has also noted the difference between official goals and operative goals.[15] The *operative goals* are the end results which managers seek to achieve and which annually guide the activities of the organization. The *official goals*, on the other hand, are those which are publicly announced by the firm. These are often termed ''motherhood and apple pie'' goals, statements with which no one can really take issue but which are of little practical use in actual operations.

How are these strategic goals and objectives formulated? Earlier economic theorists proposed a single owner-entrepreneur with a single goal: profit maximization. Others, such as Richard M. Cyert and James G. March, described the organization as a set of forces and interests, each seeking to influence goals.[16] Cyert and March contended that goals emerge from a *coalition of interests* and individuals who bargain with each other over objectives, using money, status, and power to press their views. Henry Mintzberg's power configuration model described a situation in which individual players seek to exert power within the rules of the game to attain goals acceptable to them as individuals.[17]

Frank Heller proposed another explanation: that goals evolve as a response to the values of top managers, in terms of what group or type of person is dominant and therefore influences the choice of goals.[18] Finally, James D. Thompson and William J. McEwen have argued that goals are dynamic variables evolved from review and adjustment and as such are formed as responses to external pressure.[19]

The Dimensions of Objectives and Plans

There are many performance criteria and results which organizations seek to achieve. The three basic dimensions most frequently discussed are level, priority, and time frame, as shown in figure 2.2.

Level

The strategic objectives and plans must be coordinated to involve all levels of the organization. Ari Ginsberg and John H. Grant suggested three levels of strategy domain:

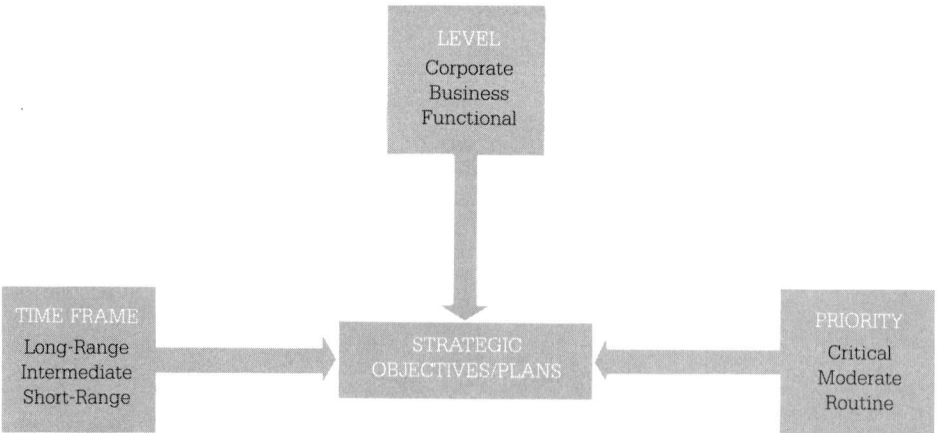

FIGURE 2.2
Strategic Objectives and Planning Dimensions

1 *Long-range corporate goals and strategic planning* are the plans and objectives that affect the entire organization. They are usually developed by the operating managers, and are usually long-term in nature.
2 *Strategic business unit objectives and plans* focus on the particular product line or service for which the business unit has responsibility. The business plan follows the lead of corporate objectives and must fit into the total organization plan.
3 *Functional or operating unit plans* are oriented toward short-term objectives, but must fit into longer-range business and corporate goals and plans as well.[20]

Finally, there is a detailed assessment of individual objectives and their fit with strategic objectives and plans.

Priority

Every organization and every manager has several objectives that they seek to achieve, often simultaneously. Multiple objectives may even be at cross-purposes, such as seeking growth and minimizing costs. Peter Drucker, a leading management consultant, suggested the importance of managing by objectives and indicated a number of areas in which objectives should be set:

1 Profitability
2 Market share
3 Efficiency or productivity
4 Increasing physical and financial resources
5 Innovation
6 Member satisfaction and development
7 Responsibility to shareholders and individuals
8 Public and social responsibility[21]

Some objectives are short-run targets and others are based on a longer time horizon. Many retail firms stress short-run objectives, while others, like Hewlett-Packard, aim at long-term results. The strategist must set priorities among conflicting goals and objectives.

Edson W. Spencer, chairman and CEO of Honeywell, feels that too much emphasis is placed upon short-term results. As he has commented:

> Unfortunately, shareholder value is almost entirely equated with short-term stock prices. By this yardstick, the higher the stock price, the better management has done its job. This forces management to put short-term earnings-growth before such interests as market development, and customer and employee satisfaction. These are interests that help ensure the long-term success of a company.[22]

Most management theorists and practitioners agree that too much emphasis is being placed upon short-term performance. Consequently, many organizations are developing reward systems related to long-term growth in shareholder value. If short-term profitability is the sole measure of performance, then investment in long-range projects will be diminished. The result of such a strategy would be a threat to long-run survival.

Make Your Numbers

One example of emphasizing short-term results is given by Richard Beeson, former president of Canada Dry, on the decision making of David Mahoney, then CEO of Norton Simon, Inc.

> "I had been on the job only a couple of weeks," Beeson says, "when we had a Canada Dry board meeting. I said to Mahoney, 'Dave, we're a little bit below budget now, and I think we can hold that for the rest of the year.'
>
> "Dave looked at me, smiled, and said, 'Be on budget by the six-month mark; be on by the year.'
>
> " 'But Dave,' I said, 'there isn't enough time to get on by the *half*. I inherited this situation, after all.'
>
> "Still smiling, Dave looked at me and said, 'Do I pay you a lot of money? Do I argue with you over what you want to spend? Do I bother you? Then don't tell me what the goals should be. Be on by the half; be on by the end of the year.'
>
> "What if I can't, Dave?" I asked.
>
> "Then clean out your desk and go home."
>
> Beeson . . . says he began running through the reasons why he could not meet the goals, but Mahoney said, "Not interested. My board and my stockholders want me to make my numbers. The way I make my numbers is for you guys to make your numbers. Make your numbers!"[23]

The pressure to show fast, short-term results "to make your numbers" can also have an unfavorable effect on long-range strategy. Research by Bruce and Judith Kirchhoff of the University of Nebraska at Omaha indicated that short-run optimization is not best for long-term results.[24]

In fact, long-term success may involve reduced return in the short-run. The Boston Consulting Group has suggested that sacrificing short-run profits to gain market share will yield the highest long-term gain.[25]

With this multiplicity of objectives existing throughout the organization, management must set priorities. Critical objectives are those of primary importance to the organization. For example, Teledyne corporation management has set profit margins as their critical objective. All other objectives, then, must be integrated into the strategic plan according to their priorities.

Time Frame

A third dimension of objectives is based on the time period over which results are to be achieved. Long-term objectives and plans refer to those which cover a five-year time period or longer. Short-term objectives usually cover one year or less. Intermediate range objectives, then, cover time periods of one year but less than five.

Hewlett-Packard, for example, has quarterly plans, an annual plan, and a five-year plan. The quarterly and annual plans are very detailed and complex. The long-range plans are concerned with long-range trends in markets, products, and competition. The only numbers on the plan are total revenues, costs, and profits. They also project long-term manpower needs (for example, how many electrical engineers will be needed by the 1990s) and facilities requirements.[26]

Typically, the short-term objectives and plans fit into the long-term projections. For example, a 20 percent market share in PC industry may be the long-term objective, with a 5 percent target in the first year, increasing to 10 percent share in the second year.

Every CEO has a unique managerial style which is most effective for accomplishing organizational goals and strategy. At Apple Computer CEO John Sculley has a critical role in shaping the direction and strategic decisions that will determine his firm's future position. Milton Leontiades of Rutgers University has suggested that managers make strategy and that this selection of key managers is what determines business success or failure.[27]

THE STRATEGY MAKERS

Who provides the strategic leadership for an organization? Three groups are generally involved in the strategic decision making of most organizations: the top manager (CEO) and the top management team, the board of directors, and the corporate planning group.

Although the board of directors has ultimate authority, as indicated in figure 2.3, the CEO (and top management team, who are often members of the board) plays a central role; and the corporate planning group is usually responsible for the strategic plan itself. Consequently, each of these groups has some influence on corporate decision making. Top management gives final approval to the strategic plans, and then the complete program is usually placed in broad outline before the board of directors. A financial plan is submitted to the board stating what management intends to accomplish and what the probable outcome will be. The CEO, such as John Sculley at Apple Computer, points out that the plan is based on certain economic forecasts regarding the future. The presentation of the strategic program to the board is something of a formality, but the board members must understand and approve its major aspects.

The trend among firms like General Electric, General Motors, and Hewlett-Packard is to decentralize strategic planning and involve operating managers at all levels. John Sculley has commented:

> Very few if any other $1.5 billion sales revenue *Fortune* 500 companies have the fifty or sixty key middle managers who run the business reporting only one level from the CEO. Vision and strategy are the fundamental principles we run our business on, yet we have no strategic planning staff nor want

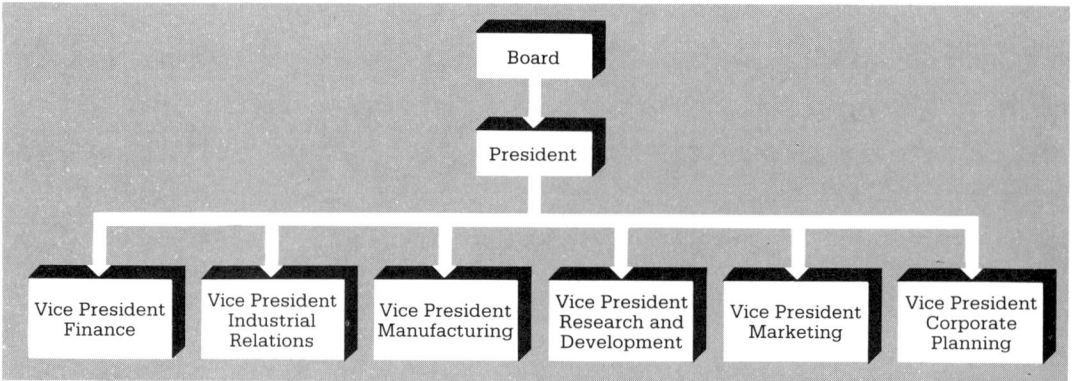

FIGURE 2.3
The Organization Chart

one. We continually test our management actions against our vision and strive to simplify our process. "Apple Values" is the function of our culture and we consider outstanding people to be our most important resource.[28]

The Team at the Top

The top management team of a firm includes the corporate managers, who are responsible for the success of the organization. The chief executive (who may also be chairman of the board) is responsible for the performance of the organization. It is the CEO (like John Sculley of Apple or John Young of Hewlett-Packard) who makes the strategic decision in most organizations. This is what CEOs get paid for (usually, very handsomely). Strategic management would not be effective without the involvement and leadership of the CEO. The job also involves tremendous pressures. Almost every strategic decision involves conflicting courses of action and options. Each of the options has some relative degree of risk and some potential rate of return. The selection of strategy is the job of the top management team, as is illustrated at Exxon Corporation.

Invariably the top management team and the CEO are the executives at the highest level who are responsible for the survival and success of the organization. They significantly influence the major strategic direction of the firm. The chief executive must create a strategic planning system such as the management review that John Young implemented so successfully at Hewlett-Packard. The CEO must also assess the degree of risk which is acceptable. Allied Corporation, under Chairman Edward L. Hennessy, undertook an overly ambitious program of acquisition, which resulted in a large debt position. Now, Hennessy is spinning off about thirty low-return businesses.[31] A similar program in 1979 led to large losses for the Singer Company and to the replacement of Donald Kircher as CEO.[32] On the other hand, a too cautious strategy may allow competitiors to take over market share.

Strategic Decisions at Exxon

At Exxon Corporation (number one in the *Fortune* 500), chairman and CEO Lawrence G. Rawl and the seven members of the executive committee meet monthly to make the major strategic decisions.

> The room is half the size of a tennis court, lined in uninterrupted walnut and carpeted in quiet luxury. The table is long and tapered, pieced from six massive sections of Indian laurel. The eight men who sit in the swivel chairs around it are a blur of blue, gray, and tan suits. They are here to make what for them is a routine decision involving the expenditure of several hundred million dollars. They run the Exxon Corp., the biggest industrial concern in the world.[29]

In the meetings, key managers make strategy presentations to the executive committee. These presentations, not unlike the case presentations in the business policy classroom, use slides, charts, graphs, and overheads to show ratios, models, diagrams, and information to support their conclusions.

In theory, the ultimate power of an organization resides with the board of directors, but in the case of most major corporations, the decisions are made by the executive committee. The committee reviews and evaluates performance to see that the firm is profitable and selects the new strategic approaches for allocating the firm's resources. At Exxon they also put a great deal of emphasis on developing future managerial talent—the Exxon person—a manager who has demonstrated the ability to solve problems, handle crises, and manage effectively. At the top in 1986 is a classic Exxon-type manager, Larry Rawl. A petroleum engineer from the University of Oklahoma, Rawl has spent his entire professional career with the company. He has run a refinery and managed the U.S. marketing operations and the company's European subsidiary before being appointed to the board. An analytical but personable manager, Rawl has a pragmatic understanding of the broader issues facing Exxon. But with the weakened petroleum market, Exxon may need a new strategic vision. A diversification strategy may be necessary, even though the results of earlier diversifications have been unsuccessful.[30]

The top manager must first be able to identify a gap between the current situation and some desired condition. Strategies are then aimed at improving effectiveness, efficiency, and participant well-being. Too often short-run, expedient programs, aimed solely at cost savings, are introduced. Such programs often have unintended, dysfunctional effects on participant satisfaction and the long-term goals of the organization. The manager, then, has an impact on organization strategy by identifying differences between "where it is" and "where it would like to be" and in designing and implementing appropriate strategic plans.

The Board of Directors

The board of directors in business and other institutions is responsible to the stock-holders or constituencies of the organization. It hires the CEO, rewards effective strategy, and fires the CEO if the strategy doesn't work. However, there have been many studies, including the work of Myles L. Mace, a professor emeritus at Harvard Business School, that have questioned the true authority of the board, suggesting that it often rubber-stamps management's decisions.[33]

Harold Geneen, former ITT chairman, has suggested that board members are often less independent than they should be to fully protect the interest of the share-holders. Geneen suggests that "in most corporations . . . the board of directors has little choice but to follow meekly where the chief executive leads."[34]

The degree of involvement of the board in strategic management can be placed on a continuum from very passive to very active (see figure 2.4). At one extreme, the board simply rubber-stamps management's proposals, but at the other, the board actually takes a leading role in strategic decisions.

The board of directors of a corporation is appointed or elected by the stock-holders to

1 *Hire, reward, and replace the CEO.* The major responsibility of the board is to ensure that the stockholders' interests are being protected. The actual strategic operation of the organization is in the hands of the CEO.
2 *Approve major strategic and financial decisions.*
3 *Protect financial integrity* and guard against actions that may place the company in jeopardy. One of the criticisms of the board of directors is that it often fails to do so.
4 *Guard against unethical actions by the CEO.* The board of directors must exert control over the ethics of the company. In one example, Lockheed's payment of over $9 million in bribes in connection with overseas sales resulted in the res-ignation of the key corporate executives.[35]

Whereas in the past the board of directors may not have been actively involved in strategic management, William R. Boulton of the University of Georgia suggested that current problems are leading to a more active role for board members, including increasing involvement in business strategy issues.[36]

As *Business Week* noted, "increasingly, outside directors are faced with a dilemma. They can be activists—strongly independent overseers who ask tough questions . . . or operate in a traditional mode: act as a rubber stamp for manage-ment . . . Either way, the job is a hot seat, as directors have a one-in-five chance of being privy to a stockholder suit." Gerald Ford, for example, reportedly serves on ten public boards, including American Express and Santa Fe International, earning $170,000 per year.[37]

There is evidence that a change is taking place, especially in corporations where stock is widely held. The forces underlying this change are both legal chal-lenges by stockholders and social reform movements relating to such issues as civil

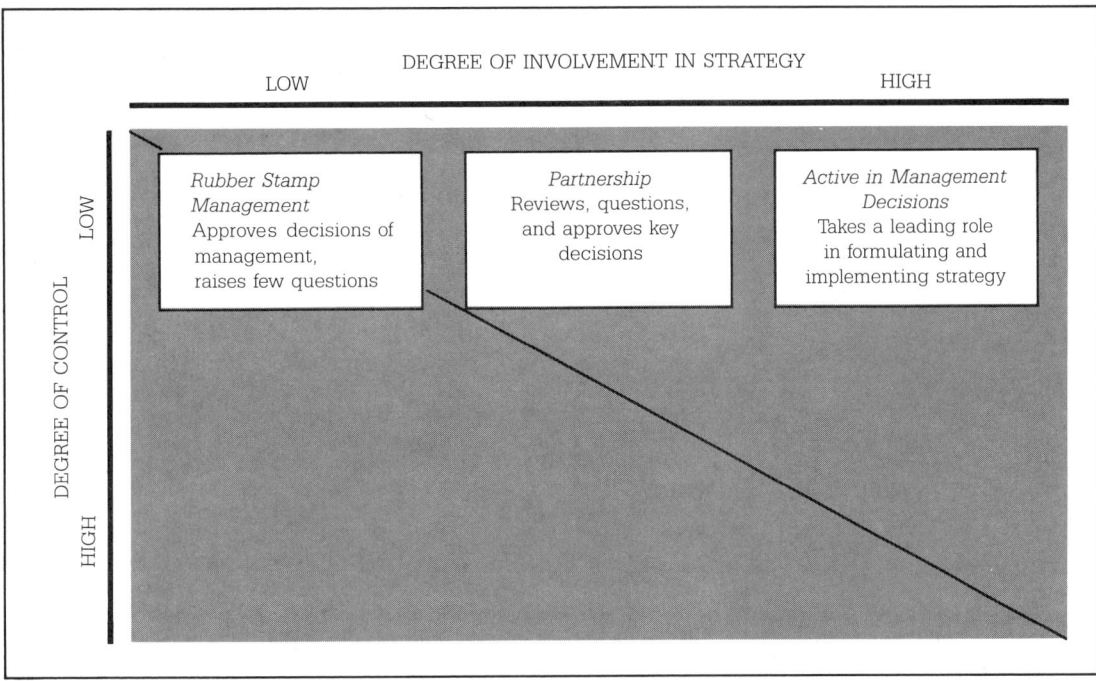

FIGURE 2.4
The Role of the Board of Directors

rights, women's rights, ecology, nuclear power, and questionable payments—all of which have added pressure on the duties of the board members.

The Corporate Planners

Most large organizations now use corporate planning staffs to coordinate the strategic function. George A. Steiner, a UCLA Business School professor, reported an increasing use of corporate planners as professionals who are responsible for the development and integration of companywide strategic plans.[38] Corporate planning may be handled by an individual, a small group, or, as in the case of General Electric, there may be as many as a hundred planners. These staff specialists are trained in planning techniques; they include economists, statisticians, computer modeling experts, and futurists who provide direction and support for overall planning efforts. The planners are most active in assessing the firm's capabilities, analyzing environmental forces, and generating strategic alternatives. However, evidence indicates that planners seldom take an active role in the actual strategic decision.[39]

Thomas H. Naylor of Social Systems, Inc., conducted a survey of 1,800 companies to determine the use of corporate planning models. Out of the 346 corporations that responded, 73 percent reported using some form of strategic planning model, and another 15 percent indicated the intention to develop such a model.[40]

One study reported that in companies with sales under $100 million, only one in five has a separate, formal planning department. Nearly all corporations with sales of at least $2 billion have such a department.[41]

One major development in current strategy is the emphasis on contingency planning. Whereas in the past a company would have one master strategic plan, now companies often have five or more separate tracks plotted to meet a variety of possible future economic environments.

There has been a recent shift away from the dependence on strategic planning groups. Few of their brilliant plans have been successfully implemented. As General Motors Chairman Roger Smith commented, "We got these great plans together, put them on the shelf, and marched off to do what we were going to do anyway."[42] Consequently, operating managers have become involved in strategic planning and there has been a focus on implementation. Corporate planners have important functions to perform, including

1 *Developing a framework for strategic planning and providing the data base.* The corporate planning group usually designs the strategic information system. This activity provides the information and forecasts, creates planning procedures, and integrates the multiplicity of plans into a single plan.

2 *Identifying and evaluating new product and market opportunities.* The life cycle of a product is much shorter, yet the time frame for new product research and development is growing. Consequently, the planning staff must keep tabs on new market trends.

3 *Monitoring, reviewing, and revising the strategic plan.* Companies now have to revise plans more frequently because of unpredictable and changing conditions. Many companies have a dynamic five-year plan, which is "rolled over" each month.

4 *Forecasting new economic conditions and trends.* Many of the large companies subscribe to national economic forecasting services, or run their own econometric models including pricing, cost, supply, and demand factors.

5 *Developing contingency plans and alternative scenarios.* Rather than developing only a single strategic plan, many firms now set up multiple contingency plans.

In summary, then, three groups are involved in setting strategic objectives: the corporate planner, in an advising and coordinating role; the board of directors, in overseeing and approving major decisions; and the top management team, in making most of the key strategic decisions. At General Electric, for example, the final decisions are made by the corporate policy committee, made up of the chairman, three vice chairmen, five senior vice presidents, and the vice president for finance.

STRATEGIC OBJECTIVES AND CHANGE

Objectives such as profitability, market share, and cost efficiency are influenced by the external and internal environment. These objectives, then, represent responses by the organization to competitive forces. Michael Porter of Harvard University has suggested that every firm competing in an industry has a competitive strategy, whether implicit or explicit. As he further pointed out, the essence of formulating strategy is relating a company to its competitive environment.[43] Strategic objectives define the long-term competitive position of the organization and also the performance levels that top managers seek to achieve in the future. As a result, strategic objectives are influenced by a number of internal and external forces, as shown in figure 2.5. Managers attempt to develop strategic directions that are acceptable to these external and internal power groups.

Strategic objectives are also derived from past activities and performance. Strategies that pay off are continued; for those that show a lack of results, new objectives and strategies need to be identified and implemented.

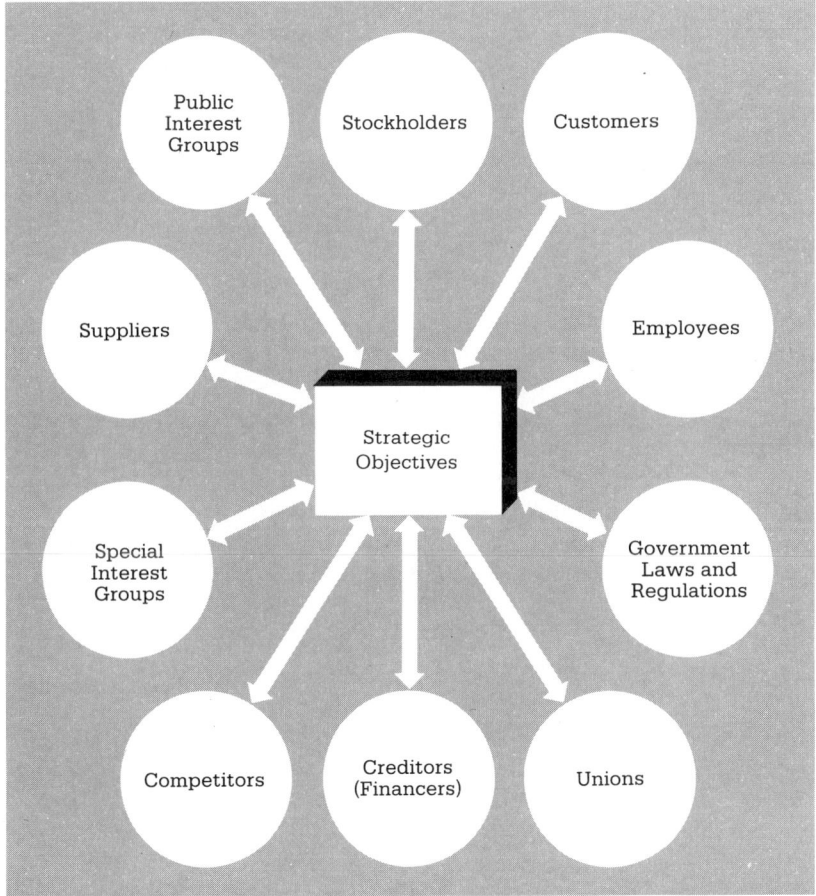

FIGURE 2.5
The Socio-political Influences on Strategic Objectives

Adapting to a Changing Environment

Change is inevitable. Executives are adapting to changing market conditions and, at the same time, facing the need for creating an anticipative rather than a reactive managerial system. They are searching for ways to manage an increasingly complex technology and a more sophisticated work force. To accomplish these diverse goals, managers need more than piecemeal, ad hoc decisions dealing only with current crises. They need some form of long-term strategic planning to prepare for future organization requirements.

There is a need for a continual examining and updating of the plan and objectives in order to adapt strategy to a changing environment. Adapting to change involves both the management orientation and the use of contingency approaches, as discussed in the following sections.

One danger in labeling any company as "excellently managed" is that both internal and external conditions may change. A company that demonstrates excellence in one year may stumble the next. Peters and Waterman's choices have been no exception; several of their "excellent" companies have since not performed as well.[44]

These problems are symptoms of an increasing rate of change and its impact upon strategic management. As a result, managers now face risk situations unlike those faced before. In an era of accelerating change, management's degree of excellence is judged by its ability to cope with these changes. Organizations become either more adaptive, flexible, and anticipative or they become rigid and stagnant, reacting to change after the fact, often when it is too late. Today's strategic management decisions cannot be based solely upon the extrapolation of historical experience. Many decisions are unique, innovative, and risky, involving new products and new areas of opportunity. Putting a new product or a new process into production is a major strategic decision.

Because an organization exists in a changing environment, it must have the capacity to adapt. As one consultant pointed out, "Nobody is moving faster on the experience curve than the high technology electronic companies, and the consequences of being late are most severe in that business."[45]

What makes for excellence in the management of a company? A study by the consulting firm of McKinsey & Co. found that, in the best-managed companies, one key factor is the "strategic fit" between the organization's goals, its strategy, and its competitive environment.[46] The company must constantly adjust to change while stressing key business values.

Why is change so difficult? Possibly because the culture of the organization becomes a part of the people who perform the work. At Alcoa, for example, change comes slowly because the organization structure and culture continue to reinforce prior patterns of behavior and to resist new ones. As a result, chairman Charles Parry said, "You can't transform the company overnight. When you have a $7 billion gorilla, you don't go into the cage and quickly change him."[47]

At Apple Computer, the organization structure, procedures, and relationships continued to reinforce prior patterns of behavior and to resist the new ones. As a result, strategic change sometimes results in upheaval and dissatisfaction, and possibly even resignations, dismissals, or transfers. An organization must develop an adaptive orientation and management strategy that is geared to its environment.

Dynamic Equilibrium

Every organization must have enough stability to continue to function satisfactorily without becoming too static or stagnant to adapt to changing conditions. This condition of both stability and adaptation, essential to continued survival and growth, is termed *dynamic equilibrium.*

An organization that operates in a mature field with a stable product and relatively few competitors needs a different adaptive orientation than a firm operating in a high-growth market, with numerous competitors, and with a high degree of innovation. The former operates in a relatively stable environment, while the latter is facing a more dynamic and turbulent set of conditions. A stable environment is characterized by unchanging basic products and services, a static level of competition, a low level of technological innovation, a formalized and centralized structure, and a steady, slow rate of growth. Such an environment remains relatively stable over long periods of time.

A dynamic environment, on the other hand, is characterized by rapidly changing product lines, an increasing and changing set of competitors, rapid and continual technological innovation, and a rapid market growth. For today's organization, change is necessary. A static organization can no longer survive. Yesterday's accomplishments amount to little in an environment of rapidly advancing markets, products, and life-styles.

In order to survive, organizations must devise methods of continuous self-appraisal. Managers must recognize when it is necessary to make strategic changes, and they must develop the systems capable of implementing these changes. To meet these conditions, many companies have created specialized strategic planning units whose primary purpose is planning for organizational changes. These units are developing new programs to help the organization improve its level of adaptation to the environment. They must also develop policies to maintain a stable identity, so that change is not overwhelming. To achieve successful change, both goals must be satisfied.

The effect of the environment on the strategy of the firm has attracted the attention of researchers for over two decades.[48] This research suggests that the way managers deal with environmental uncertainty is related to performance. In fact, a central tenet in strategic management is that a match between environmental conditions and organizational resources is critical to performance.[49] In essence, effective performance derives from developing a planning system that is appropriate to the organization's environment. Environment determines organization, which then determines effective performance. The researchers proposed that organizations develop flexible, organic styles to fit a turbulent environment, but that bureaucratic, mechanistic style may suit a firm in a stable environment.

A CONTINGENCY MODEL OF ENVIRONMENTAL-PLANNING ORIENTATION

Jeanne Liedtka has proposed a contingency model linking the planning process to other variables in a firm's environment, including four relevant characterizations of the environment and the corresponding planning processes.[50] The environment is based on two dimensions, as shown in figure 2.6. The first dimension is *uncertainty,* which refers to the frequency, extent, and predictability of change. The second, *complexity,* relates to the number of factors that are relevant to a firm's operations. Organizations can vary greatly on these dimensions, and the various combinations of these orientations can lead to differing adaptive styles.

The model proposes that key dimensions of the planning process vary systematically with the level of complexity and uncertainty of the organization's environment. Increased levels of complexity necessitate not only more extensive planning processes but also decentralization, significant staff support, increased comprehen-

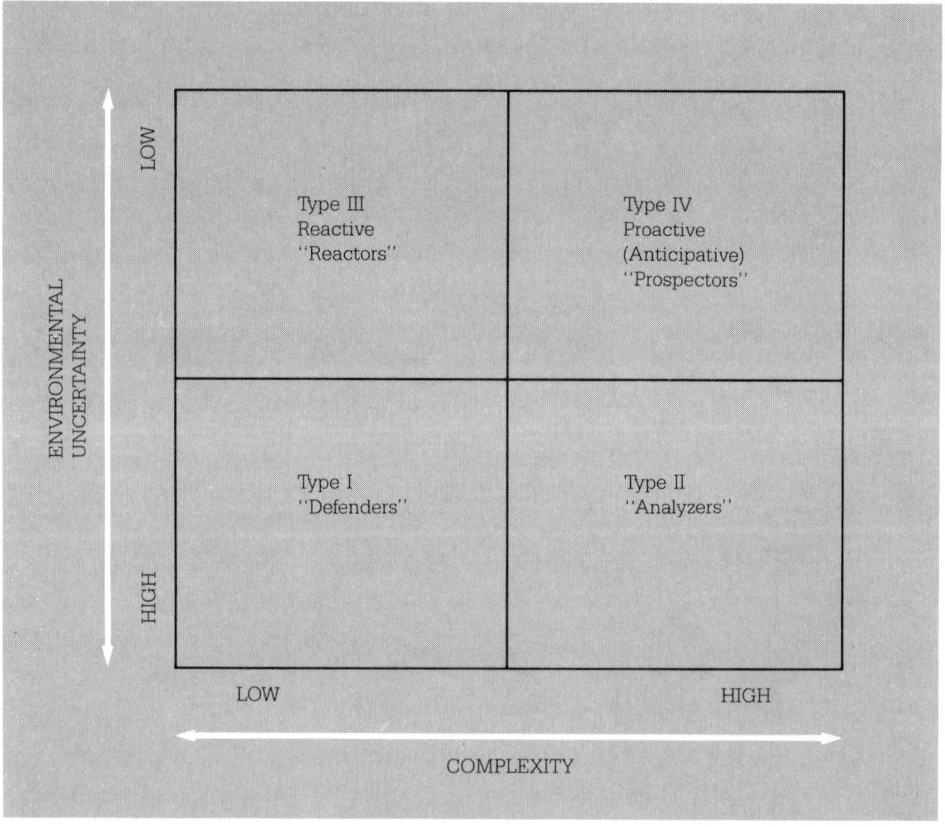

FIGURE 2.6
A Contingency Model of Environmental Planning Orientation

siveness, and an external, proactive (anticipative) management orientation. Similarly, increased levels of uncertainty render extensive planning processes less useful. Uncertainty fosters centralization, elimination of planning specialists, decreased comprehensiveness, and a mixed strategic orientation. Four planning orientations are possible.

Type I Organizations

Defenders tend to have minimal planning processes. They are characterized by centralization, lack of both comprehensiveness and staff roles, and an internal/reactive focus. These organizations are typically hierarchies whose goal is maintaining the status quo. These organizations fit into the "defender" strategic orientation, according to Raymond E. Miles and Charles C. Snow of Harvard University, who presented this continuum of strategic positions.[51] Defenders are firms that operate in a narrow product/market domain and guard it. They plan intensively, have centralized control, use limited environmental scanning, and are cost-efficient. This is one element of the strategic continuum. Type I organizations have a management style based on low risk, formalized procedures, stable goals, and a high degree of centralized structure and control. They also tend to have more managerial levels, a higher ratio of superiors to subordinates, and an emphasis upon formal control systems. They may tend to value tradition, to keep on doing things as they have always been done, to value seniority more than performance, and to be averse to new ideas. Alcoa has failed to keep pace with a changing environment and fits into the type I company.

Type II Organizations

Analyzers tend to have extensive planning systems. These systems are decentralized and comprehensive, aided by staff planners, and external/proactive (anticipative) in orientation. These firms are consummate planners and fit the analyzers category of Miles and Snow, one of two mid-positions falling between the two extremes of prospectors and defenders. Analyzers have some characteristics of both prospectors and defenders; in other words, this is a mixed strategic approach.

Type II managing emphasizes a decentralized decision-making structure that refers problems to the top. Because of the stable environment, there tend to be more levels of management, and coordination is usually done by formal committees. Planning and decision making are usually concentrated at the top, and procedures and roles are clear. Change occurs at a rate that is good enough to keep up with the industry but certainly well below the state of the art. Such organizations often accept strategies that are "good enough," because there is little pressure for change coming from the environment.

Type III Organizations

Reactors tend to have minimal planning, have a mixed strategic orientation, and include technical experts rather than staff planners. This mid-position category is characterized by firms that realize the environment is changing but are unable to effect the necessary change of strategy to meet the competition. Reactors either move into one of the other three positions or fail. It is an unstable strategic posture.

Type III organizations have a low level of adaptation in a rapidly changing environment and tend to deal with problems on a short-run, crisis basis. Reactive management represents a style in which one reacts to a stimulus after conditions in the environment have changed. Such adaptation often involves replacement of key people, hasty reorganization, and drastic curtailment of people and product lines.

A major food corporation, for example, was feeling the pressures of changing business conditions; it was losing momentum, experiencing product failures, and reporting decreased earnings. The new chief executive instituted massive changes, including a major management reorganization, a companywide efficiency drive, a 10 percent cut in salaried personnel, and a close scrutiny of all marketing programs. The reactive approach to change implies waiting until serious marketing problems that can no longer be ignored emerge and then taking drastic corrective measures.

Type IV Organizations

Prospectors tend to develop hybrid planning processes forged out of the inconsistent demands of highly complex, uncertain environments. They are characterized by decentralization, low comprehensiveness, an external/proactive (anticipative) orientation, and reliance on technical experts. With their broad planning approaches, decentralized controls and broad environmental scanning, and underutilized resources, *prospectors* aggressively seek new product/market segments.

Type IV organizations, with a high level of adaptation existing in a rapidly changing environment, tend to utilize the anticipative management style, planning for changes to deal with future conditions before they actually come about. The McKinsey study identified several examples of anticipative management, including corporations like IBM, Hewlett-Packard, McDonald's, and 3M, which have actively initiated programs of improvement before conditions became critical.

Modern organizations are increasingly finding the need for an anticipative orientation. In follow-up studies, McKinsey and *Business Week* found that many of the twelve firms who decreased in performance were inept in adapting to market changes.[52]

Contingency Theories and Strategic Managing

The increasing rate of environmental change and the increasing size and complexity of organizations have led to change in strategic management practices. One of the newer practices is termed the *contingency approach. Contingency planning* involves taking unexpected events into account as part of the planning process.

The contingency approach to strategy suggests that for a given set of organizational and environmental conditions, an optimal strategy exists. Contingency approaches are based upon the idea of contingent relationships between an independent variable—environment conditions—and a dependent variable—the organization's strategic response. This approach is in its formative stages, but it offers some interesting insights into future developments.[53]

Contingency planning involves planning events whose occurrence is uncertain but must be anticipated in the strategic plan. The probability of occurrence and the severe impact, should the events come about, call for anticipative planning. Alternative actions must be specified and strategic regrouping to meet possible contingencies must be considered.

A contingency plan forms a part of a company's strategic planning process. Its basic purpose is to achieve a state of anticipation in order to counteract possible problems and reduce risks. Contingency planning forces management to identify critical assumptions, to review the implementation of strategy, and to respond rapidly to contingencies. One of the basic factors affecting the use of contingency planning is the environment of an organization. The organization facing new problems and frequent changes needs flexible strategies that are highly adaptive, responsive, and open to innovation.

The development of contingency planning requires new procedures. The first step in arriving at them is to identify the critical environmental factors over which the company has little control. A possible downturn of the economy, a shortage of critical parts, a competitor's movement into the market, or labor problems are such contingency factors. The next step involves estimating the impact and scope of possible problems. A slowdown in the economy may affect all business areas of a company, but with differing impact on each segment. Contingency planning, then, provides alternatives, changes objectives, alters options for strategic adjustment, and, if necessary, revises the basic strategy.

Consequently, the very nature of strategic planning has undergone a dramatic change. Instead of relying on a narrow strategic plan, managers now develop a whole range of contingency plans and alternative scenarios. A wood products company such as Boise Cascade might develop a whole series of strategies based upon varying levels of housing demands. For example, at 2 million housing starts per year a growth strategy might be pursued, but at 1.5 million starts a retrenchment plan might be selected.

Many organizations also develop alternate plans for drastic changes, so-called *worst case scenarios*: if things go completely wrong, what can we do to maximize our objectives? Added to this, the economic and political uncertainty in the international situation causes many organizations to try to forecast possible economic or political hotspots or upheavals, such as the Iranian overthrow of 1979.

The contingency view suggests that managers in differing organizations face situations that may differ greatly on a number of dimensions. There may be varying degrees of structure, differing motivation levels, and a diverse potential for conflict. The manager, then, must recognize that there is no one best way for all organizations. The contingency approach suggests that the effectiveness of various strategies will vary according to the circumstances. The contingency variables that need to be considered and the relative emphasis depend on the type of problem being considered.

The development of strategic planning is becoming increasingly complex. Successful organizations in the future will be those that can adapt quickly to new techniques of planning. The contingency planning method offers multiple options based upon a given set of conditions. A series of possible plans—plan A, plan B, plan C, and so forth—are formulated on the basis of a relative economic outlook. Plan A may be based upon a high-growth economy, the most optimistic view, with each alternative plan keyed to a different level of economic activity. At the lowest level are the worst case scenarios, contingency plans that are based on possible economic or political upheavals and develop plans of action in the event that everything goes wrong.

Dow Chemical Company uses an economic simulation model to provide possible strategic scenarios. The effect of potential new chemical plants in various economic situations can be analyzed in terms of capacity, demand, and so forth to provide an estimated return on investment. Dow also has a product management team that analyzes social and political pressures around the world and forecasts the possible impact on its business of such things as overthrows of governments.[54]

For corporate planners and top managers, the environment has never seemed as turbulent as it does today. Uncertain economic outlooks make accurate planning for the future increasingly difficult. In such a rapidly changing environment, corporate plans may become outdated within less than a year and new strategic plans and goals must be devised to meet these changing conditions.

Key Factors in Strategic Objectives and Plans

One of the major reasons for the rapid adoption of strategic planning models is the fact that the absence of corporate planning efforts may result in organizational performance that is lower than potential. The experiences of managers and consultants in many industries and firms suggest that following factors are the keys to a successful planning system.[55]

1   *Invent the future*   Comprehensive long-range planning is not solely an attempt to blueprint the future by extrapolating from the present. If an organization plans by a statistical projection of current activities, it tends to make it difficult to adapt to changing conditions. Instead the firm must test assumptions and invent its future position.

2   *Stay flexible*   Any organizational plan that is more than one year old is probably obsolete, given the rapidly changing environment of most organizations. To achieve maximum value, strategic planning needs accurate information and timely updating.

3   *Avoid getting into a numbers game*   There is currently an increasing reliance on sophisticated quantitative tools at corporate levels. Often these systems translate broad organizational goals into specific financial targets. Unfortunately, these elements of financial performance are invariably related to time, and many of the key intervening variables (interest rates, technical innovation, and the like) are not controlled by a rigid time horizon. Consequently, the plan should not attempt to overemphasize forced numerical targets at the expense of broad goals.

4   *Involve top managers*   Corporate planning must be a way of life and a part of the corporate culture, not merely an annual exercise in number-crunching. The top managers of the organization need to develop a climate of effective corporate planning by active support and involvement.

5   *Have a flexible approach to contingency planning*   Strategic planning is based on predicting future conditions most likely to occur. Many other possible conditions and events also may pose serious threats or provide access to great opportunities. The planner must ask some "what-if" questions regarding the future and then derive likely responses from each possible scenario. For example, "what if there is a shortage of a critical raw material?" or "what if a new competitor enters the field?" Contingency planning should identify events that can occur during the planning time frame, their effect on strategy, and what actions the organization may take in the event that they occur.

6   *Don't make planning an end in itself*   Although the strategic planning process may produce periodically a written document, the process should be a continuous activity of top management. It is rare that the plan assesses future changes with complete accuracy. Therefore, the plan provides a framework and guideline for managerial action, but managers must be able to deal with changes if they are to maintain the needed flexibility of operation.

7   *Anticipate future problems*   Strategic planning deals with the future effect of current decisions. It involves the examination of cause-and-effect relationships among variables over time of an actual or proposed strategic decision. Consequently, an early warning of danger signals must be part of the planning process. Most companies can handle problems if they are alerted soon enough.

8   *Make planning flow from long-range goals*   Strategy precedes planning. Therefore, strategic goals should be established before the planning takes place. Strategy deals with the directions the firm desires to follow; planning focuses on how these goals will be attained. Otherwise, short-term, crisis management takes over.

In the past, strategists could be reasonably confident about long-term economic projections and plan accordingly. Today this is not true. The degree of risk is higher than ever. The strategic decision maker must deal with changing variables and must anticipate future conditions; thus, strategic planning and management are even more critical.

MANAGERIAL SUMMARY

This chapter has focused on the importance of mission, goals, objectives, and plans in strategy formulation. The process starts with the basic strategic visions of managers and leaders. The mission is used to develop well-defined, long-range objectives for the organization.

Corporate objectives are specific targets within the master strategy. There are different levels of objectives, including corporate, business, and functional, short and long term, which must be integrated into the master strategy. Organizations seek to achieve multiple objectives; therefore, there must be a set of goal priorities within the firm.

The increasing rate of change results in increasing complexity in the manager's job. How the manager adapts to these changes becomes a key element in strategic management.

The organization strategists formulate a strategy to accomplish goals on the basis of their estimates of organizational strengths and environmental opportunities and threats. The strategy makers include the top management team, the board of directors, and corporate planners. Research suggests that in most firms the strategic decision process is dominated by the CEO or a coalition of high-ranking corporate officers.

The strategic manager of today must manage within constraints. Organizations do not exist in isolation. Many external systems exert influence on strategy: governments, society, customers, special interest groups, and so forth. Strategy must be examined from an open system perspective, based on the assumption that the firm exists in a complex and dynamic environment.

Contingency planning approaches provide a way for managers to adapt strategic plans to changing market conditions.

Goals and objectives are a central element in a strategic process. They determine the direction in which the organization will move and position itself in a rapidly changing environment. The strategic goals come about from a series of negotiations and trade-offs among both internal and external forces.

Finally, the strategic manager must realize that there are no clear, unified solutions that apply to all situations. Instead, there are contingent strategies which may work best under a given set of circumstances. Certainly contingency approaches can provide guidelines for identifying strategies which are preferable in a specific situation over others.

Review Questions

1 Review current business publications or annual reports and compare the mission and objectives statements. How do they differ?

2 What is an organizational objective?

3 Find some examples of the use of contingency approaches in planning.

4 Compare and contrast the four types of management orientations used in relating to the environment. Can you find some firms or industries which fit these four types?

5 Select an organization and interview members at several levels to determine how the perception of objectives differs between levels.

Notes

1   Adapted from Ann M. Morrison "Apple Bites Back," *Fortune*, February 20, 1984, 86–100; "Apple's New Crusade," *Business Week*, November 26, 1984, 146–156; and "Apple Expects Increase," *Wall Street Journal*, November 5, 1985, 3.

2   "Apple CEO Lays Out Future plans," *PC Week*, February 18, 1987, 4.

3   Kenichi Ohmae, "The Secret of Strategic Vision," *Management Review*, April 1982, 10.

4   Thomas J. Peters, "A Style for All Seasons," *The Executive Summer*, 1980; and "Executive Style," *Wall Street Journal*, September 13, 1984, 1.

5   W. B. Schaffir and T. J. Lobe, "Strategic Planning: The Impact at Five Companies," *Planning Review*, March 1984, 40–41.

6   "Hewlett-Packard, "Where Slower Growth Is Smarter Management," *Business Week*, June 9, 1975, 50–54, 56, 59.

7   Hewlett-Packard Annual Report, 1985: 7–22.

8   Thomas J. Peters and Robert H. Waterman, Jr., *In Search of Excellence: Lessons from America's Best Run Companies* (New York: Harper & Row, 1982).

9   Adapted from Chrysler Annual Report, 1985-1986.

10 See Lee A. Iacocca, "Turnaround Strategies," *Journal of Business Strategy*, 4, no. 2 (Summer 1983): 67–69.

11 E. A. Locke, L. M. Saari, K. N. Shaw, and G. P. Latham, "Goal Setting and Task Performance: 1969-1980, "*Psychological Bulletin* 90, no. 1 (1981): 126.

12 Based upon Xavier Roberts, "Up from the Cabbage Patch," *Business Week*, March 3, 1986, 87; and "A Good Ol' Boy," *The San Diego Union*, March 7, 1985, E-4.

13 Myron Magnet, "Managing by Mystique at Tandem Computers," *Fortune*, June 29, 1982, 87.

14 H. Igor Ansoff, *Corporate Strategy* (New York: McGraw-Hill, 1965): 73.

15 C. Perrow, "The Analysis of Goals in Complex Organizations," *American Sociological Review* (December 1961): 854–866.

16 Richard Cyert and James March, *A Behavioral Theory of the Firm* (Englewood Cliffs, NJ: Prentice-Hall, Inc., 1963).

17 Henry Mintzberg, "Organizational Power and Goals: A Skeletal Theory," in Charles Hofer and Dan Schendel, *Strategic Management: A New View of Business Policy and Planning* (Boston: Little, Brown, 1979) 64–80.

18 Frank Heller, *Managerial Decision-Making: A Study of Leadership Styles and Power Sharing among Senior Managers* (London: Tavistock Publications, 1971).

19 James Thompson and William McEwen, "Organizational Goals and Environment: Goal-Setting as an Interaction Process," *American Sociological Review* (February 1985): 23–30.

20 Ari Ginsberg and John H. Grant, "Research on Strategic Change," *Academy of Management Proceedings* (1985): 11–15.

21 Peter Drucker, *The Practice of Management* (New York: Harper Brothers, 1954), 63.

22 Edson W. Spender, "The U.S. Should Stop Playing Poker with Its Future," *Business Week,* November 17, 1986, 20.

23 "The Way I Make My Numbers," *Forbes,* February 15, 1972, 26.

24 Bruce and Judith Kirchoff, "Empirical Assessment of the Strategy/Tactics Dilemma," *Academy of Management Proceedings*, (1980): 7.

25 Boston Consulting Group, *Perspectives on Experience* (Boston: Boston Consulting Group, 1968).

26 Personal interviews with Hewlett-Packard managers.

27 See Milton Leontiades, "Choosing the Right Manager to Fit the Strategy," *The Journal of Business Strategy* 3, no. 2 (Fall 1982); and Avil K. Gupta, "Contingency Linkages between Strategy and General Manager Characteristics," *Academy of Management Journal* 9, no. 3 (1984): 399–412. See also, Richard Castaldi, "Analysis of Work Roles and Strategic Orientation of Chief Executive Officers," paper presented at Academy of Management, August 1984.

28 Personal communication from John Sculley, June 1984.

29 See "Inside Exxon," by Anthony J. Parisi for *The New York Times Magazine*, August 3, 1980.

30 "Can Exxon Keep on Flying?" *Business Week*, August 19, 1985, 62–66.

31 "Hennessey Split Allied-Signal," *Fortune*, December 23, 1985, 9.

32 "Behind the Snafu at Singer," *Fortune*, November 5, 1979, 7.

33 See Mace's study, based on extensive research and interviews in *Directors: Myth and Reality* (Cambridge, MA: Harvard University Press, 1971), 4.

34 Harold Geneen, "Why Directors Can't Protect the Shareholders," *Fortune*, September 17, 1984, 32.

35 For discussion of overseas payoffs, see Peter Nehemkis, "Business Payoffs Abroad: Rhetoric and Reality," *California Management Review* (Winter 1975).

36 See Ahmed Taghakoni and William Boulton, "A Look at the Board's Role in Planning," *Journal of Business Strategy* 3, no. 3 (Winter 1983): 64; and William Boulton, "The Evolving Board: A Look at the Board's Changing Roles and Information Needs," *Academy of Management Review* (October 1978): 827–836.

37 "The Job Nobody Wants," *Business Week*, September 8, 1986, 56–61.

38 George A. Steiner, "Rise of the Corporate Planner," *Harvard Business Review* (September-October 1970): 133.

39 See, for example, M. Leontiades, "What Kind of Corporate Planner Do You Need?" *Long Range Planning* (April 1977); and P. Lorange, "The Planner's Dual Role," *Long Range Planning* (March 1973).

40 Thomas H. Naylor and Horst Schavland, *A Survey of Users of Corporate Simulation Models* (Durham, NC: Social Systems, Inc., 1975).

41 C. D. Burnett, D. B. Yeskey, and D. Richardson, "New Roles for Corporate Planners in the 1980s,"*Journal of Business Strategy* (Spring 1984): 67.

42 "The New Breed of Strategic Planner," *Business Week*, September 17, 1984, 62.

43 Michael Porter, *Competitive Strategy* (New York: Free Press, 1980).

44 Thomas J. Peters and Robert H. Waterman, Jr., *In Search of Excellence: Lessons from America's Best-Run Companies* (New York: Harper & Row, 1982).

45 "Hewlett-Packard: "Where Slow Growth Is Smarter Management," *Business Week*, June 9, 1975.

46 Personal communication. Robert H. Waterman, Jr., "The Seven Elements of Strategic Fit," *Journal of Business Strategy* 2, no. 3 (Winter 1982): 69.

47 "Too Big to Quit, Too Rich to Fail," *Forbes,* February 25, 1985, 115.

48 See, for example: H. I. Ansoff, "The Changing Shape of the Strategic Problem," in D. E. Schendel and C. W. Hofer (eds.), *Strategic Management: A New View of Policy and Planning* (Boston: Little, Brown, 1979); and J. S. Armstrong, "The Value of Formal Planning for Strategic Decisions: Review of Empirical Research," *Strategic Management Journal* 3 (1982): 197–211.

49 L. J. Bourgeois and D. R. Brodwin, "Strategic Implementation: Five Approaches to an Elusive Phenomenon," *Strategic Management Journal* 5 (1984).

50 Jeanne Liedtka, "Linking Strategic Management Processes to Organizational Environments: A Theory," *Academy of Management Proceedings* (1985): 21–24.

51 R. E. Miles and C. C. Snow, *Organizational Strategy, Structure and Process* (New York: McGraw-Hill, 1978).

52 See "Who's Excellent Now?" *Business Week,* November 5, 1984, 76.

53 C. W. Hofer, "Toward a Contingency Theory of Business Strategy," *Academy of Management Journal* (December 1975): 785–810.

54 From "Piercing the Future Gov in the Executive Suite," *Business Week,* April 28, 1975, 50.

55 Ibid., 46–52.

CHAPTER THREE

■ ■ ■

Strategic Issues: Opportunities and Threats

OBJECTIVES

After completing this chapter, you will be able to:

■ Define strategic issues analysis as an important determinant of strategy

■ Describe the role of management in optimizing the fit between the environment and the organization

■ Discuss the SWOT analysis and the major areas of opportunity for developing a strategy

■ Compare the major techniques used to monitor strategic issues and environmental forces

■ Identify the major reasons for using strategic issues analysis and environmental forecasting

I think the starting point is to assume that tomorrow will be different, may be radically different. That may sound obvious, but there are many executives who really believe that the future will be pretty much like today. They feel that if they continue doing what was successful until now, it will work tomorrow.

Alvin Toffler

"When It Absolutely, Positively Has to Be There Overnight"

Smith

Fred Smith is chairman and chief executive officer of Memphis-based Federal Express Corporation, an air cargo firm that specializes in overnight delivery door-to-door, using its own planes. Some feel that the significance of the company is that it created a $3 billion industry where none existed before, changing the way America does business and adding a new cliché—"when it absolutely, positively has to be there overnight"—to the language. Others say the significance is in showing how one man, Frederick W. Smith, could see trends in the world, conceptualize a product that would capitalize on those trends, and motivate an untested work force to build a $1.2 billion empire.

In his undergraduate days at Yale, Smith wrote a paper proposing the idea of an airline system to deliver small packages from city to city. This blueprint for his firm received a C grade from his unimpressed professor. Technological change had opened a radically new transportation market, he decided. To cut cost and time, packages from all over the country would be flown to a central point, there to be distributed and flown out again to their destinations—a hub-and-spokes pattern his company calls it today. Smith then spelled it all out in the overdue economic paper. Fred Smith had a revolutionary idea and converted it into a company that, starting from scratch and with heavy early losses, passed the $500 million revenue mark and had a 10 percent net profit margin within a few years. Although he was not able to convince his professor of his revolutionary idea, he was able to convince the financial world.

Except for his persistence and willingness to bet the ranch, Frederick Smith is not an easy fit into the image of the entrepreneur. Starting an air-freight business carries with it the cash-gobbling entry barrier of having to operate a fleet of planes, hundreds of vehicles, scores of offices, and a vast sorting and distribution system—costs that can digest an inheritance in a hurry. At one point, Smith met a payroll in part with $27,000 he won in blackjack. Apart from personal funds, his company would also require $70 million in venture capital before it went into the black in late 1975—four years after starting out. Fred Smith took a revolutionary idea, a market opportunity, and built it into a *Fortune* 500 company.[1]

INTRODUCTION

Strategic planning is based on an accurate forecast of future conditions. As Robert M. Price, the president and chief operating officer at Control Data, has noted, ''The gut issues for strategic planning in the face of uncertainty are adapting to future societal needs, creativity, and technological cooperation.''[2] As a result, managers must constantly be aware of changing forces in the environment. The organization's environment is the source of both potential opportunity and possible threats. Skillful strategic leaders are able to identify those market niches that offer the potential for increased growth and profitability.

The central focus of strategic management is that a match between environmental conditions and organizational capabilities is critical to performance. The strategist's job is to find or create this match.[3] In this chapter, the relationship between the organization's environment and strategy formulation will be examined. First, there is a detailed discussion of the major sectors of an organization's external environment: the strategic issues. Second, an examination of why environmental analysis is so important to the firm. And finally, a description of the various forecasting techniques used by organizations in the planning process.

STRATEGIC ISSUES

Strategic issues are important determinants of future business strategy and competitive positioning. A *strategic issue* may be defined as a major opportunity or threat which could critically affect the long-term future of the business.[4]

As Harold Koontz once commented, ''Long-range planning is not planning for the future, but planning for the future impact of present decisions.''[5] The assumption underlying strategic issues analysis is to avoid strategic surprise—a sudden and unfamiliar change in perspective in the form of the strategic threat or opportunity.[6]

In the McKinsey & Co. study of well-managed companies, one problem area for companies that had stumbled from the ranks was an inability to adapt to fundamental changes in their markets.[7] These firms became victims of strategic surprise. The competitive environment changed before they could adjust their strategy. The primary purposes of strategic planning are to optimize the fit between the business and its current and future environment and to anticipate future problems.

Effective management requires strategic issues analysis and planning, but strategic planning suffers from the instability and unpredictability of environmental forces. In a fast-changing world, the system must be designed to deal with alternative futures, with a constant monitoring and updating of plans. In an uncertain environment, the future can never be exactly predicted, but issues analysis can help the managers clarify their assumptions about the future and make rational choices.

The analysis of current and future trends is a starting point for the strategy formulation process. First, environmental forces are analyzed to determine current and future trends and how these trends shape alternative futures. This analysis then provides the issues and assumptions for the development of strategic plans.

Nathaniel H. Leff of Columbia University has identified four key issues which add to uncertainty in planning.[8]

1 *Predicted medium-term market growth rates, both in the United States and in global markets,* affect a company's strategic investment and marketing plans.
2 *Characteristics and identity of future competitors* must be anticipated. In a world of global investment and marketing, new competitors enter unexpectedly as major players in many industries. Similarly, with aggressive asset redeployment, many firms have exited past markets.
3 *Significant international currency fluctuations* also affect strategic decisions concerning new plant investment and product innovations. Unstable international market conditions decrease the accuracy of exchange rate forecasts.
4 *New technological developments* have always occurred rapidly for American managers, but new product innovations come increasingly from lateral fields and unexpected sources.

5) *Environmental Factors*

To illustrate the importance of strategic issues analysis, IBM reassigned chief financial officer Alan J. Krowe, who had been the main architect of IBM's ambitious growth plan. Industry analysts suggested that Krowe was demoted primarily because he failed to anticipate the slow growth in the computer market and IBM's lackluster financial performance. As head of planning, Mr. Krowe was the person most closely identified with IBM's projections that the industry would continue to grow at 15 percent a year.[9]

With instability and uncertainty likely to continue at high levels, strategic issues management becomes more critical than ever. What you don't know can hurt you!

In this rapidly changing environment a static organization can no longer be effective. Managers must recognize when changes are needed and be able to implement them. Organizations adapt to a dynamic environment by introducing internal changes that will allow the organization to develop more effective and competitive product lines or strategies.

One method for adapting to change is termed the *issues priority matrix*. The matrix allows managers to compare and rate possible opportunities or issues that

Megatrends

John Naisbitt, in his best-selling book *Megatrends*, suggested that America's present environment is in a state of turbulent change because we are moving into a new era. Naisbitt proposed that our society is being restructured by ten major forces or megatrends. The U.S. is moving from

1 an industrial to an information society
2 a forced technology to a high-tech/high-touch technology
3 a national to a global economy
4 a short-term to a long-term perspective with an emphasis on strategic planning
5 a centralized to a decentralized approach
6 a reliance on institutional control toward self-reliance
7 a representative democracy toward participative democracy
8 traditional hierarchical structures toward informal networks — "networking"
9 the north to the sunbelt regions of the south and west
10 a society with limited choices to one with multiple options[10]

These changing trends will have a significant impact on organizations. Strategic managers will need to be aware of issues that will affect their industry or organization.

---

may have an impact on their organizations on two dimensions: the potential impact on the firm and the probability of occurrence (see figure 3.1).

The manager can then compare a number of potential market trends in terms of their impact and probability. Levi Strauss, for example, might have been able to anticipate changing consumer tastes by using such a technique. Firms typically take action on those issues that fall in the three high-priority cells.

Issues management is a process for controlling changes that affect an organization. It is very important to involve key managers so that high-priority issues receive broad exposure.

The organization must adapt itself to the systems outside its immediate influence by introducing internal changes. To be successful, an organization has to develop a management strategy that will adequately handle the challenges and opportunities which it faces. The strategy adequate at one time under one set of conditions may become progressively less effective under changing circumstances.

Strategists try to target four areas of potential opportunity:

1 Technological or product innovation opening new markets
2 New product or market opportunity due to growth in underlying demand

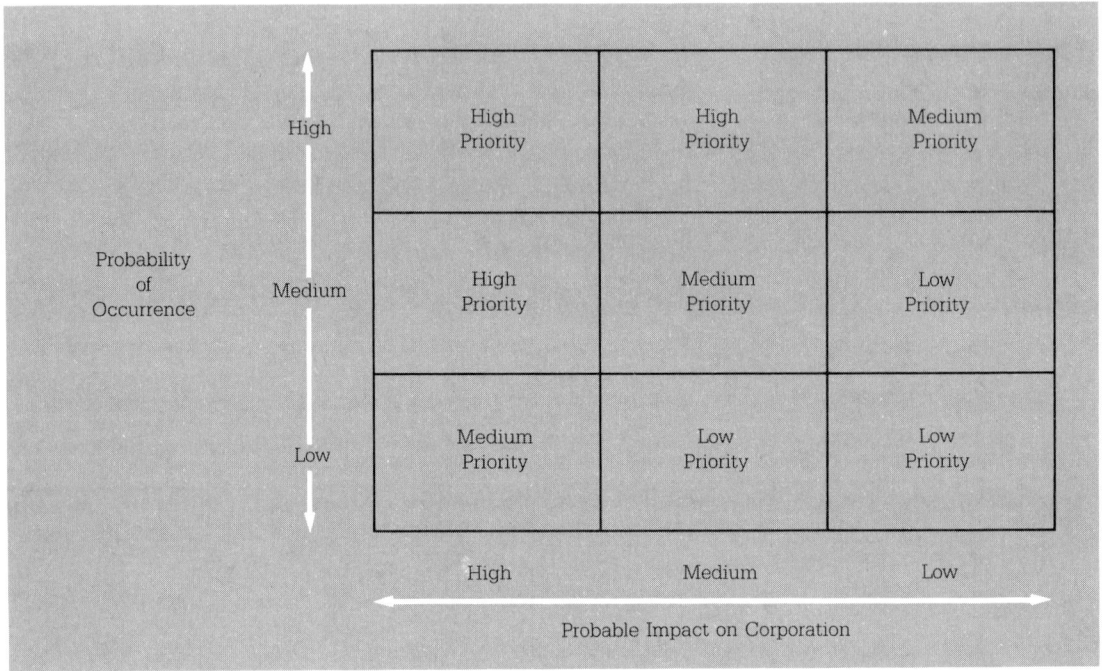

FIGURE 3.1
The Issues Priority Matrix

Adapted from William C. Ashley, "Issues Management—New Tool for New Times," *Bank Marketing*, August 1983, 12.

> 3 New opportunities in existing product or market segments in which the firm has a competitive advantage
> 4 New opportunities in expanding into additional market segments or geographic areas

At Federal Express, for example, Fred Smith and his management team constantly scan the environment for new market opportunities. After building a strong market share in overnight delivery of packages and documents, Federal Express then introduced Zap Mail, an electronic transmission service that moved copies door-to-door in two hours or less. Federal Express saw that America is becoming an information-based society and constantly seeks new opportunities to speed up in formation delivery. (Note: Unfortunately, Zap Mail was ahead of its time and has itself been zapped.)

STRATEGIC ISSUES ANALYSIS

Strategic issues analysis is the process of seeking "information about events and relationships in a company's outside environment, the knowledge of which would

Changing Market Trends for Levi Strauss

Levi Strauss, a successful family-run firm, built its business around three basic factors: product quality, a happy family corporate culture, and concentration on the jeans market. However, Levi's was ill-equipped to deal with a slowdown in sales growth and a market shift toward designer fashions. In the early 1980s, Levi's had problems with strategic issues, including diversification, fashion trends, and marketing: basically a failure by management to recognize changing trends. Levi's ran into problems for three reasons:

1 It lost touch with customers—the people who see changes coming.
2 It failed to anticipate customer shifts to new products. In retailing, fashions change rapidly, and Levi's could not react fast enough.
3 It failed to develop competing products to broaden its product base. Levi's brought out a line of designer clothing, but could not convince customers.

The challenge to Levi's management, then, is to anticipate and respond more quickly to changing market trends. Can Levi's pursue both the basic jeans and designer-fashion markets? Some have suggested that to do this, Levi's must become more market-oriented and less product-oriented. Certainly, the company needs to do more market analysis in order to foresee important strategic issues before they affect the firm.

Levi's hopes that "corporate culture shock" will overcome the complacency that stymied its past efforts to break into fast-changing fashion-merchandise markets. "The company is guilty of being too rigid and too deliberative in an industry made up of entrepreneurs who hustle," said Robert D. Haas, Levi's CEO, "and we're going to change."

The market for jeans—which accounted for about 75 percent of Levi's total sales—will be flat for the foreseeable future. Consequently, the company is seeking a new strategic vision and is moving into other types of apparel (such as men's and women's sportswear) for growth. Whether these new strategies will pay off remains to be seen.[11]

---

assist top management in its task of charting the company's future course of action."[12] According to Philip S. Thomas, effective environmental analysis is crucial to corporate planning. Factors needing analysis include the global context of governmental, economic, technological, and social conditions as they affect strategic planning.[13] Two factors that make environment analysis a critical stage in the management process must be considered.

First, the organization does not exist in isolation, but is interrelated with other elements in its environment. That environment itself is constantly changing as new products, technologies, and economic conditions emerge. In the past twenty-five years there have been many changes in the firms on the *Fortune* 500. The big companies do not just keep growing, and smaller companies, seizing new opportunities, have managed to take over spots in the top group. *Fortune* reported that only 262 (52.4 percent) of the original top 500 firms appeared in the 1980 ranking. Most of the missing companies were taken over by merger or acquisition, but several went out of business. Of the new additions to the top 500 in 1980, 147 (30 percent) were too small to even make the list in 1955.[14]

In many cases, this failure to survive stems from an inability to analyze and adapt to changing environmental conditions. Some research evidence suggests firms that do strategic issues analysis are more successful than those that do not.[15]

Second, environmental influence is complex and can affect many different parts of the organization. There is an increasing demand for energy by consumers, leading to the construction of new power plants. Yet environmental groups often delay the construction by demonstrations or legal delaying tactics. As a result, the lead time and cost for new plant construction are now almost double what they were previously. For example, Dow Chemical planned for several years to develop a new chemical complex in northern California but decided to cancel the plan because of environmentalist protests and delays, which kept stretching its lead time and increasing end costs. Environmental analysis is the process by which strategists analyze factors outside the firm to determine possible opportunities and threats.

SWOT Analysis

The first step for the strategist is to examine the determinants of strategy: to analyze the internal and external factors that exert a primary influence on the current and future position of the firm. This strategy, termed the *SWOT analysis*, identifies strengths, weaknesses, opportunities, and threats.

The strategist today is concerned with events external to the firm because they have an important impact on future results. For most organizations, the ability to control these external forces is considerably less than the ability to control operations inside the firm. The formulation of a formal, strategic plan involves elements which clearly interact, but which can be separately described and examined. These elements, as shown in figure 3.2, include

1   External environmental analysis: identifying and evaluating the organization's external market opportunities and threats
2   Internal advantage appraisal (see chapter 4): identifying and evaluating the organization's internal market strengths and weaknesses

This analysis of strengths, weaknesses, opportunities, and threats allows the strategist to identify key competitive advantages and disadvantages. They can then seek a fit between the organization's distinctive competencies and its goals. The

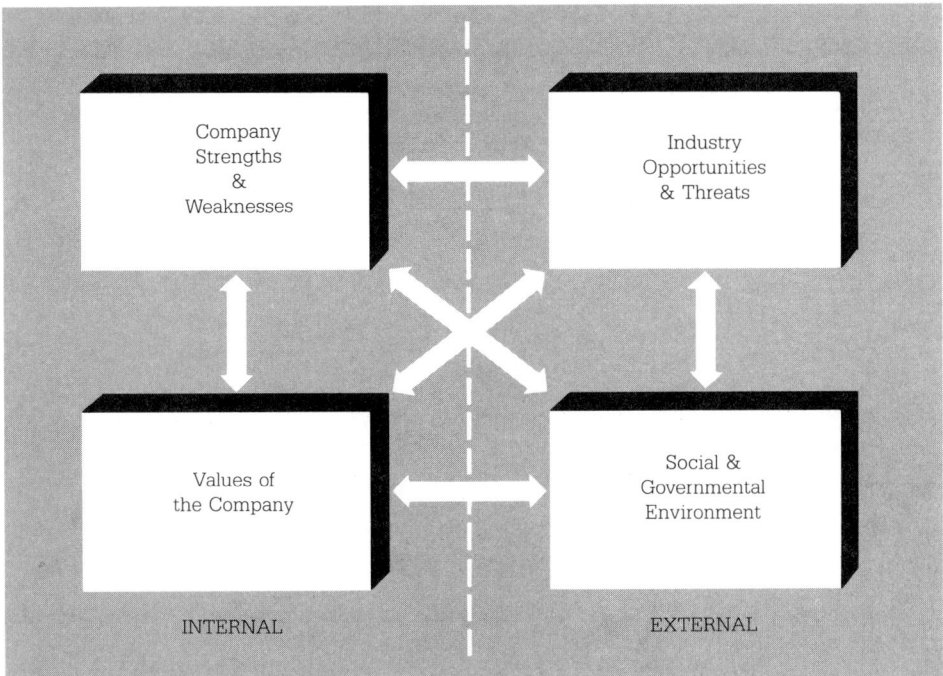

FIGURE 3.2
Components of Business Strategy (SWOT)

stronger the fit, the more likely the organization is to select a successful strategy. In the best-run companies, there is a close match between the organization's strategy and its place in the competitive market. The strategic decision maker must position his or her firm in relation to an uncertain future environment by analyzing the two basic determinants of strategy: the external environment and the firm's internal capabilities.

External environment analysis examines those factors that may influence the future success of the firm but are external and thus not under organizational control. In a study of large industrial firms, Harold Klein and Robert Linneman of Temple University found that a growing number of firms use formalized environmental analysis. They found that 92 percent of *Fortune*'s top 1,000 industrial firms have a corporate planning unit and 45 percent reported using a formal environmental analysis process.[16] In the environmental analysis process the firm identifies both its potential opportunities and threats.

The recognition of potential product or market opportunity is always an important factor. As one manager noted, "If you see an opportunity, put the plan on ice and seize the opportunity."[17] There will always be new product and market opportunities as long as consumers have unsatisfied needs. Managers must recognize the shifting trends in order to identify markets where demand is rapidly growing. For instance, certain demographic trends emerged from the baby boom of the 1950s, and as this age group moves into the home- and car-buying age segments in the next few years, one can predict increased demand in these markets.

The United States is going through some fundamental demographic changes that forecasters and policymakers must take into account. The economy is already feeling the impact of these shifts, and there is more—much more—to come in the future. "Demographic statistics make dull reading," said economist Michael J. Wachter of the University of Pennsylvania's Wharton School, "but they helped lay the ground-work for our current economic problems."[18]

The most obvious change in the U.S. population is simply that it is growing older. In 1970 the median age was just under twenty-eight. By 1982 it reached thirty, and by the turn of the century, it will hit thirty-five. Such a change means a shift in patterns of consumption and incomes and, inevitably, changes in social attitudes as well. Recent television ads for soft drinks have begun to focus on senior citizens drinking soft drinks and having good times, attempting to increase soft drink usage in these emerging market segments.

The strategic decision maker must first be aware of the potential growth areas and then identify those segments where the firm can exert some form of competitive advantage. Procter & Gamble, for example, saw an opportunity in the disposable diaper market because of favorable demographics and changing values among U.S. homemakers: the result was the dominant share of the market with its Pampers and Luv brands.

The strategic decision maker must also search the environment to identify factors that may pose potential threats to the organization's strategy. The more dynamic the environment, the greater the threat to strategy. As noted in chapter 2, many organizations react to environmental changes, rather than adopting a more proactive, anticipative approach. Among the many forces in the environment which can affect future strategy are technological developments. In the airline industry, for example, a competitor's use of newer, more fuel-efficient planes is a significant threat to airlines that are still flying older, less efficient planes. Airlines flying the new planes have a 50 to 60 percent cost advantage.

"Maybe 95 percent of all companies really don't pay much attention to the future," said Dale H. Marco, head of the industrial management group at Peat, Marwick, Mitchell and Co., one of the big eight auditing firms, which makes available management consulting services as well as accounting. "They react to history—history that is anywhere from one day to a few centuries old."[19]

Many companies are afflicted with what may be termed the "Jeanne Dixon syndrome." They see planning as an effort to predict the future. In reality, planning is a complex, sophisticated process of isolating developments that may affect the future. It involves monitoring the growth—or death—of these developments and-making adjustments as new facts are made available and placed alongside assumptions.

The economic conditions may be adversely affected during recession when customer spending decreases and during inflation when operating costs may rise drastically. The strategist must also be aware of changing consumer values and buying patterns. A few years ago, for instance, hardly anyone owned a hand-held calculator, but now almost everyone has one.

Finally, one must be aware of governmental and international influences upon future strategic moves. Factors such as the steadily rising price of energy and the impact of OPEC must be considered in all strategic planning. The airlines must base their planning on several possible supply and pricing situations, because the cost of jet fuel is such an important element in predicting their future financial position. Strategic managers must not only be aware of these potential threats, they must also develop strategic contingency plans for a number of possible conditions.

Strategists must determine how best to allocate scarce resources in order to minimize possible threats and take advantage of new opportunities. In the past, executives could be relatively confident about the long-term outlook and plan accordingly. However, today's strategist is confronted with unanticipated changes. The environment has never seemed so turbulent and unpredictable. These uncertainties make strategic analysis a critical stage in the planning process, for three important reasons:

1   *The accelerating rate of change* means that the strategist can no longer afford to ignore or guess at future trends. For example, demographic changes caught many universities unprepared for the declining enrollments of the 1980s. The reduced size of the 18-year-old group has created financial problems at many schools and even forced some to close, even though environmental analysis predicted this trend. AT&T has suffered huge losses because of the changing competitive environment in the computer industry, as shown in the accompanying box.

2   *Level of opportunity and threat* varies in a changing environment of new technological, cultural, and economic forces. In the watch industry, for example, the emergence of the solid state digital watch provided an opportunity for U.S. and Japanese watch companies to move into a market long dominated by the Swiss watch industry. The Swiss, on the other hand, using a reactive management style, failed to recognize this change and as a result their once dominant market share has eroded away.

3   *Use of environmental analysis* results in more effective companies. Danny Miller and Peter Friesen of McGill University, in a study of eight firms, found that in most cases the firm's level of effectiveness was related to the amount of environmental analysis.[21] In their study of twenty-one United Kingdom companies, Peter H. Grinyer and David Noerburn of the London Graduate Business School concluded that the more that environmental information was analyzed in strategic decisions, the more effective was the firm's financial performance.[22]

Technology and Strategy at AT&T

It has been speculated that AT&T lost some $800 million in its entry into the computer market. AT&T has been a recognized leader in technology, but also has a tradition of promoting from within and being run by managers who have spent their whole careers at the company. This stability has resulted in a culture with an unquestioning faith in its technical superiority. Unfortunately, these executives thought that AT&T's move into the computer market would succeed simply because of its past reputation.

Bell Labs, however, didn't make its mistakes in a vacuum. Many observers believe that the company failed to develop necessary marketing skills and that incompetence was tolerated far too often in AT&T's old-line management.

Although individual products have sold well (AT&T is the No. 1 PBX vendor in this country), overall, Information Systems has lost money—over $1 billion by some estimates. An AT&T executive revealed recently that the only AT&T computer product that was selling above expectations was the PC 6300, and most were selling very far below.

Although Information Systems' losses are not trivial, they won't bankrupt a company as big as AT&T. They do, however, hurt in a more subtle way: by contributing to the general lack of investor confidence that results in AT&T stock selling at depressed prices. AT&T's inability to carve out a position in the market for a high-tech product may discourage potential buyers of other AT&T products. To many analysts the losses affirm the charge that AT&T lacks marketing skills and is slow to adapt to the changing marketplace.[20]

Models for Environmental Analysis

The single most important factor in the strategic process is the analysis of the environment. The more dynamic the environment, the greater its impact on strategy. There are a number of significant relationships which need to be examined in formulating a plan of strategic action. A model of these interrelationships between the strategist and the key external and internal factors is shown in figure 3.3. First, the strategist must examine the fit between the firm's current strategy and the environment, and then predict probable future conditions.

The purpose of environmental analysis is to describe, analyze, and understand the impact which changing factors will have on the firm, its products, the market, and the industry during some future time frame. Operating managers use these vital data during the planning process.

In each broad strategic area, several topics or issues need to be considered. In performing the analysis four basic questions should be considered for each area:

1   What is the historical and present status of this strategic area?
   a   What is the sale potential of existing products?

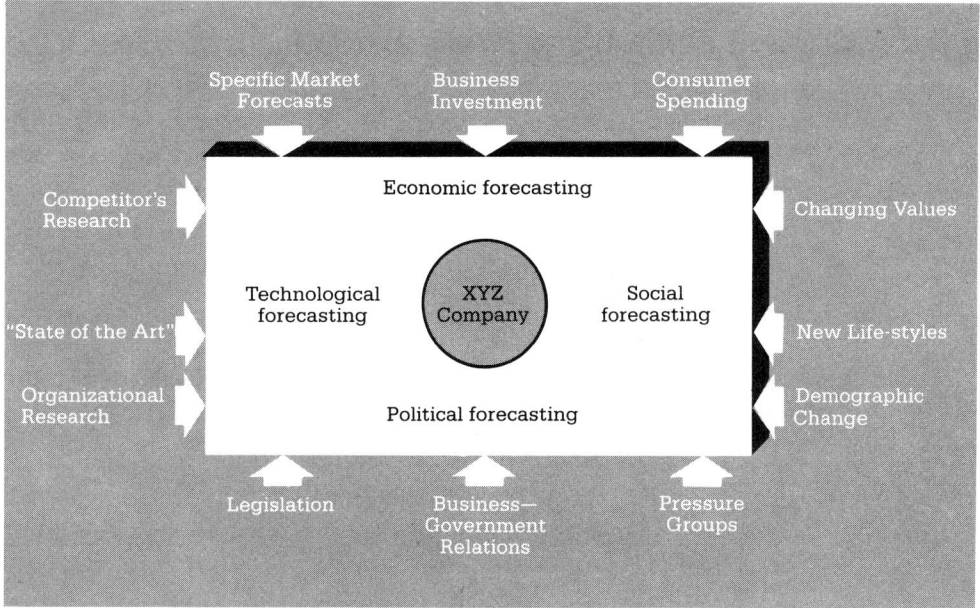

FIGURE 3.3
A Model for Environmental Analysis

Adapted from Ian H. Wilson, "Socio-Political Forecasting: A New Dimension to Strategic Planning," *Michigan Business Review*, July 1974, 19–20. Reprinted by permission from the July 1974 issue of the *University of Michigan Business Review*, published by the Graduate School of Business Administration, The University of Michigan.

  b   Is there an opportunity to introduce new products to fill an unserved or changing customer need?
2   What will the future competitive arena be like? The planning assumptions should represent the best approximation available at the time.
3   What are the implications of the future trends for the firm or product line? These answers are expressed as opportunities or threats.
4   What must the firm do to capitalize or take advantage of each strategic opportunity? What should the firm do to diminish (or eliminate) the impact of potential threats? These are referred to as *strategic issues*.

In the complex endeavor of strategic issues analysis, the organization may be viewed as an open system interacting with its environment. Governmental forces may exert one influence, while social forces may exert another. For example, the government exerted pressure on automobile manufacturers to incorporate air bags as a safety feature or option in new autos. The consumer, on the other hand, resisted this safety feature because of higher cost or lack of understanding.

The GETS Model

There are many ways to structure the external environment, but one easily usable method is to separate the outside influences into those dealing with government,

TABLE 3.1
The GETS Model: Important Factors in the Environment

G = Government	E = Economic	T = Technological	S = Socio-cultural
Government spending	GNP trends	Total federal spending for R&D	Life-style changes.
Antitrust regulations	Economic trends	Total industry spending for R&D	Career expectations
Environmental protection	Interest rates	Focus of technological efforts	Consumer activism
Tax regulations	Money supply	Patent protection	Family size
Special incentives	Inflation rates	New products	Working women
Foreign trade regulations	Employment levels	New developments in technology	Growth rate of population
Laws on employment and safety	Wage/price controls	Productivity improvements through automation	Age distribution changes in population
Attitude toward business	Energy costs/ availability		Regional changes in population
Industry deregulation			Life expectancies
Attitudes toward foreign companies			Birth rates
			Consumer/employee attitudes

economy, technology, and sociology—termed GETS for short.[23] The organization is also influenced by the constituent demands which are placed upon it from the outside, including customers, competitors, suppliers, employees, regulatory agencies, and special interest groups. The interaction of these elements is shown in figure 3.3 and table 3.1.

Government   As government gets bigger and bigger, federal, state, and local governments have an increasing effect on how business operates. Governmental forces influence a range of factors, including wage and price controls, equal employment opportunity, safety and health at work, consumer credit, environmental constraints, plant location, and other similar factors. These laws and regulations all influence a company's strategic operations.

In 1985 the government's budget of $850 billion made up almost a quarter of our total gross national product (GNP), and over one-third of the U.S. labor force is now employed in the public sector. As a result government affects strategy planning in several ways.

Economic Forces   Economic forecasts are often the most difficult for strategic planners. The condition of the economy has a direct bearing on what strategies are likely to be selected and upon the outcomes. A strategy that is successful in economic prosperity may well be a failure in a recession. As a result, managers typically forecast conditions under both optimistic and pessimistic scenarios. Economic factors include

1 The gross national product (GNP)
2 The state of economic cycle (i.e., recession or prosperity)
3 Income of consumers
4 Monetary policy—money supply, interest rates, and so forth

Each of these basic economic factors must be examined and evaluated in terms of potential impact upon the firm and upon future strategic moves. Strategic analysis and forecasting begins with the general economic situation, then moves to the industry as a whole, and finally to the economic situation for the specific firm.

Technological Forces The strategist must also be aware of changing technology which may affect the firm's future raw materials, production processes, and products and services. Changing technology can open up vast opportunities or threaten a firm's position in an industry.[24] Technological change can threaten even the survival of a firm that fails to keep up. The rapid rate of technological innovation not only is likely to continue, but may even accelerate. Technological advances can suddenly cause a firm's products or services to become obsolete, as competitors found when Fred Smith started Federal Express.

Technology can also change the life-style and behavior patterns of the consumer. AT&T risked a large-scale investment in the field of personal computers because it predicted that the computer would take its place with the telephone and television in every home. Whether or not this is true remains to be seen. Do you think you will have your own home computer, or do you already?

Social-Cultural Forces The social-cultural factor focuses on the values and attitudes of people, both customers and employees. Ian H. Wilson, in charge of General Electric's Business Environment Research and Forecasting unit, said

> It really began in 1967. A business environment studies unit was established as part of the personnel and industrial relations section of the company. There is no real logic to its emerging in that part of the company, except that the type of policy analysis, trend analysis, and forecasting that we were set up to do was essentially people–oriented rather than economics-oriented ortechnology-oriented. The charter that evolved for this work was the identification and analysis of the long-term social, political and in a broad sense, economic trends influencing the corporation, with particular emphasis on their impact on personnel relations, management style, organization of work union relations—the subfunctions of the major component to which we were attached.[25]

In this section, we have discussed the major factors to be considered in the analysis of the environment. By analyzing these factors, the strategist can recognize the potential opportunities and threats which must be faced. In addition, the strategist can compare the current strategy of the firm with the environment and identify those factors which remain important and those which may have changed.

Biotech's First Superstar

In 1976 in a San Francisco tavern, venture capitalist Robert A. Swanson and scientist Herbert W. Boyer agreed to form the first company to commercialize biotech products. Since then, Swanson (an MBA from the Sloan School of Management) has set forth a strategic goal of developing a billion dollar company by 1990. Genentech has come to symbolize the tremendous business potential of biotechnology. Swanson also has hired some of the best sales people in the business, relying on a small sales staff who have expertise in selling to the health care market.

In contrast, Herb Boyer is more laid-back and soft-spoken. He drinks coffee from a mug labeled, ''great minds have messy desks.'' His relaxed style and his impressive academic credentials have attracted a nucleus of bright young scientists to Genentech. Boyer spends most of his time in his cramped, cluttered laboratory at the University of California at San Francisco, conducting his research, even though he sits on the board of directors.

The atmosphere at Genentech is more like a college lab than a corporate research and development center. The employees' average age is only thirty-two, and cartoons and Three Stooges posters are pasted on the lab cabinets. The famous Friday afternoon keggers at Genentech, known as ''ho-ho's,'' date back to earlier times when the scientists, Swanson, and some secretaries would sit around with a couple of six-packs and cold cuts to discuss the week's progress. After a particularly tough week, the story goes that someone from the group sighed: ''Well, isn't this a ho-ho?''[26]

Because Genentech employees hold one-quarter of its stock, the idea that the company might become an acquisition target is doubted by its top executives. ''I've always said I wanted to build a fully integrated, major pharmaceutical company,'' said Swanson. ''The mission hasn't changed, but recently we've had to add 'independent' to that.''[27]

Swanson also hired an outstanding marketing department. Genentech, with some of the best sales people in the business, plans to rely on a small number of salesmen who are skilled at selling to hospitals and medical specialists.

Genentech and other biotechnology companies must face a number of issues clouding the industry's future. How well the early biotechnology patents will stand up to challenges is unknown at this point; however, Bob Swanson's goal doesn't seem too unrealistic. If Genentech keeps growing at the same rate as it has for the past ten years, it may become the first major biotech company.[28]

The success of these new biotech companies illustrates the far-reaching impact of new technology on the external environment of many types of firms and industries. The genetic engineering industry, for example, began with the first spliced gene just over a decade ago. By the mid-1980s, over $2.5 billion had been invested in the industry and more than 100 genetic engineering companies were pioneering many new products. It has been suggested that biotechnology will have more impact than any other technology in the history of man.[29]

According to Alan L. Frohman, the firm that integrates technology into its strategy significantly improves its chance of reaping benefits from changing technology.[30] The choice to become a technological leader should be based on the sustainability of the technological lead and the advantages and disadvantages of being the first to adopt a new technology. Regardless of the firm's decision, the results of integrating technology into strategy can improve a company's ability to set priorities, identify the resources necessary to achieve business goals, and speed up the movement of ideas into marketable places.

Technological change can either create or destroy profits, markets, or industries. The examples of significant technological impact on industry are numerous, from the invention of the steam engine to genetic engineering. The key to maintaining competitive position is knowing when to shift resources into a new technology.

THE TECHNIQUES OF STRATEGIC ISSUES ANALYSIS

The strategist must be able to predict probable future conditions before selecting strategic actions. Changes may emerge from unanticipated sources and disrupt a particular strategy. The introduction of new technology, a new pricing strategy by competitors, or decreased supplies of energy or materials will accentuate the advantages or disadvantages of possible strategic alternatives. As Don Lebell and O. J. Krasner have commented:

> Environmental forecasting in a dynamic and competitive business arena is challenging in concept and implementation. It is essential to remember the fundamental limitations of confronting the unknowable future. (1) We cannot always be certain of future purposes, objectives, and strategies. (2) We may not even know what questions to ask. (3) We may not know crucial cause-and-effect relationships, coefficients of those relationships, or impact coefficients which relate concerns to model outputs. Given such formidable obstacles, one might ask: "Why bother to forecast?" Of course, that question is pointless, because forecasts are an inescapable part of rational decision making.[31]

The external environment of the firm is one of the major determinants of strategy. Yet the tools and techniques used to monitor this important determinate are still relatively undeveloped in most firms. Basil W. Denning suggested that environmental forecasts are used primarily to provide assumptions on which strategic planning can take place and presented a summary of techniques which may be used (see table 3.2). What, then, are some of the techniques and methods strategists may use to anticipate the impact of environmental forces upon the firm?

Scanning and information gathering includes all sources of information gathering outside the firm, both informal and formal, and structured and unstructured methods. These sources include external contacts with customers, suppliers, competitors, bankers, consultants, and others. Information may also be gained by means of surveys, questionnaires, or interviews. Finally, there is a great deal of information available in published material such as trade journals, newspapers, and general publications.

Expert opinion/delphi is a source of information gained by contacting experts in various fields. These contacts may be with economists, university professors, consultants, or others with specialized expertise. The *delphi* method, originally developed by the RAND Corporation, involves using a group of knowledgeable people who make anonymous predictions. These predictions are summarized by computer and fed back to the panel until a consensus is achieved.

Forecasting-trend analysis is a technique used to analyze the environment by predicting, projecting, or extrapolating future events or conditions. There are several types of forecasts.

1 *Economic forecasts* involve general surveillance of the economy, including gross national product, consumer expenditures, income, sales, cash flow, and manpower forecasts for short- to long-range terms.
2 *Market/competitive forecasts* are based on surveys, market research, and industry analysis.
3 *Technological/supplier forecasts* are based on specific product market areas and are often made by futurists.
4 *Social forecasts* are performed by futurists or social scientists looking at the long-term social and political trends. They use nonquantitative techniques to forecast demographic changes, life-style shifts, political attitudes, and other socio-political developments.

Social forecasting, intended to supplement traditional forecasting, provides a view of the complete socio-economic-political-technological environment, so that strategic plans can be based on a more comprehensive set of premises. According to Kenneth E. Newgren of Indiana State University in a survey of *Fortune* 500 firms, sixty-three, or 34.4 percent, were classified as fully engaging in social forecasting, and these were the firms involved in very long-range forecasting. Newgren found that companies in the electronic, computing, and food preparation industries were least likely to use this technique.[32]

Competitive intelligence involves active intelligence or "spying" to gather information on competitors. Generally such information is gathered from suppliers, customers, or employees of the competitor. Often a firm will hire someone from a

TABLE 3.2
Environmental Forecasting for Planning Assumptions

	Sources of Information	Techniques
Economic Forecasts (a) National Economy (b) Sector Forecasts	(i) Government and private forecasts	(a) Critical appreciation of published forecasts (b) Development of models or relationships for sector forecasts
	(ii) Industry association, government, private forecasts (iii) Market research	(c) Input-output analysis (d) Large number of quantitative techniques
Technological Forecasts	(i) Technical intelligence service reports (ii) Technical market research (iii) Research into competitors' developments	(a) Demand and conditional demand analyses (b) Opportunity identification techniques. (c) Theoretical limits testing (d) Parameter analysis (e) Various systems analysis methods (f) Discipline reviews (g) Expert opinion
Sociological Forecasts	Wide variety of sources of data, including government reports, educational forecasts, population forecasts, regional forecasts, skilled labor forecasts, institutional changes, etc.	(a) National models such as built by Battelle (unlikely to be done in any one corporation) (b) Expert opinion
Political Forecasts	Political intelligence services and government reports	Expert opinion
Forecasting Competitors' Actions	Any intelligence about competitors	Any relevant technique to give information from intelligence

SOURCE: Printed with permission from *Long Range Planning*, vol. 11, March 1973, Basil W. Denning, "Strategic Environmental Appraisal." Copyright © 1973, Pergamon Press, Ltd.

competitor to gain more information about its activities. According to Robert Hershey, some of the activities a company of any size can normally afford to do include

- Buying a competitor's product, tearing it down, and evaluating it. (This is termed *reverse engineering* and is entirely legal and ethical.)
- Implementing a report system that requires field sales personnel to provide feedback on the activities of customers, suppliers, distributors, and competitors.
- Calling in all sales personnel once every quarter for a two-way debriefing with key officers in a face-to-face reporting and planning conference on competitive matters.
- Studying internal security to ensure that competitors cannot gain access to the company's secrets.
- Keeping aware of the inroads of overseas companies. (Frequently, foreign competitors have the full support of their governments.)
- Appreciating that giants are often clumsy. A smaller company's response time to user needs can frequently offset a larger competitor's advantage in advertising power, distributive competence, or cash flow.
- Questioning the vice-president of marketing about the kind of marketing data needed to enhance this function when drawing up the annual sales plan.[33]

Econometric models predict the effects of decisions by management or changes in the environment. Robert H. Turner saw the focus of such models as "the identification of relatively consistent economic relationships over a past period of time. Quantification (reduction to equations) of these relationships is the principal advantage of econometric models. To the extent that the equations remain valid, the computerized model can solve mathmatical problems beyond the capabilities of the human brain. But such quantification is often the biggest liability of the econometric models."[34]

Such models are designed to allow management to forecast the effects of various strategies, without actually trying them. The models allow managers to ask "what if" questions. If we raise our prices on product x by 10 percent, what would be the impact on profitability or on market share? At Ralston Purina, for example, a 1 percent change in the price of a prime commodity triggers a change in the company's cost models, and the whole corporate plan may change as a result. The econometric methods, then, are computerized models which aid managers in strategic decision making.

Scenarios are written descriptions of events that could occur in the future. Each scenario is usually based on a number of quantitative or qualitative factors used to develop a hypothetical sequence of events constructed to focus attention on causal factors and decision points.[35] Scenarios describe "what would happen if . . . " situations, are intended to broaden the outlook of managers, and help prevent strategic surprises.

What, then, are the relationships between environmental analysis techniques and other factors? Two proposed set of relationships have been set forth. First,

Environmental Change	Environmental Complexity	Type of Strategy	Forecasting Methods
Static	Simple	Cost-minimizing	No methods, or expert opinion
Static	Complex	Mixed and sales-maximizing	Expert opinion, monitoring, and trend extrapolation
Dynamic	Simple	Mixed and sales-maximizing	Expert opinion, monitoring, and trend extrapolation
Dynamic	Complex	Performance-maximizing	Above and simulation, quantitative and probabilistic models

FIGURE 3.4

Types of Environment Related to Forecasting Methods

James Utterback, "Environmental Analysis and Forecasting," in Charles Hofer and Dan Schendel (eds.), *Strategic Management: A New View of Business Policy and Planning* (Boston: Little, Brown, 1979). Reprinted by permission.

James Utterback of the Massachusetts Institute of Technology has suggested that a firm's environment largely determines its strategic planning process (figure 3.4).[36] Utterback identified four possible relationships.

1   *Simple-static* firms in a simple-static environment usually do not use formal forecasting techniques, but may use simpler informal and expert opinion methods.
2   *Complex-static* firms facing a complex-static environment use information scanning, monitoring, and expert opinion methods.
3   *Simple-dynamic* firms in a simple-dynamic environment use such techniques as economic forecasting, trend analysis, delphi, and other means suited to a limited data base.
4   *Complex-dynamic* firms facing a more complex and dynamic environment use more sophisticated forecasting methods, including simulation models.

In summary, Utterback suggested that a firm's environment conditions its strategy and its choice of forecasting methods.

Don LeBell and O. J. Krasner have proposed a similar relationship between the developmental stage of the firm and its choice of forecasting techniques.[37] As the firm moves into a more advanced state of development, a wider range of forecasting techniques becomes appropriate, and more sophisticated forecasting methods are used.

THE USE OF STRATEGIC ISSUES ANALYSIS

We have discussed a number of techniques used to gather environmental data for analysis and prediction. Informal planning in strategy formulation is still widely used. This approach may be satisfactory under stable conditions, but in a dynamic environment it is not sufficient for good management.

Trend forecasting and strategic issues analysis should be the cornerstone of strategic planning. The Klein and Linneman study of top industrial corporations examined the frequency of the use of major forecasting techniques.[38] They found that larger firms tend to use more sophisticated techniques and that trend extrapolation and scenarios are the most widely used methods. Other forecasting techniques, such as cross-impact analysis, were seen to be too time-consuming and complicated.

Despite uncertainty about the future and problems in accurate forecasting, it is still necessary to take environmental forces into account in making strategic decisions. As James B. Quinn of Dartmouth College has noted, "To be useful, technological forecasts do not necessarily need to predict the precise form technology will take in a given application at some specific future date. Like any other forecasts, their purpose is simply to help evaluate the probability and significance of various possible future developments so that managers can make better decisions."[39]

One thing is certain: strategic planners must expect the unexpected. They must be able to apply the most current techniques for forecasting and analysis or risk falling behind competitors.

Fred Smith says Federal Express has gone from its entrepreneurial phase into a transitional phase in which it will take new directions—he talks of getting into electronic transmission of information—before it matures. He spends a lot of time looking at the broad picture, searching for new "conceptual leaps." Arthur C. Bass, who had been president of the company, became vice-chairman and, with five other executive veterans of the entrepreneurial phase, moved into offices ten miles from Federal Express headquarters. There, this Advanced Projects and Research Group concentrates on such matters as developing a device that will enable pilots to "see" through fog and such possibilities as use of dirigibles and buying Concordes for an entry into the overseas market.[40]

The results of research by L. J. Bourgeois imply that firms should reduce uncertainty only under stable environmental conditions. In fact, uncertainty may even be functional in volatile environments, at least when it is experienced at the strategy-making level of the organization.[41] We have much yet to learn, but some of the findings at present indicate that most firms are not doing as well in environmental forecasting as they could or should do. A number of firms, such as General Electric and Xerox, are beginning to experiment with models of the external environment, and we can expect to see this type of forecasting becoming much more important and widely used during the next decade.

According to one survey of 358 large corporations, the most important factors mentioned were[42]

1	Changes in economy or economic policy	45%
2	New product innovation (internal)	32%
3	New product innovation (competition)	28%

4   Major new government regulations   19%
5   Major shifts in consumer preferences   18%

Environmental analysis is a critical stage in the strategic decision process and interacts with the next stage: the analysis of internal competitive advantages, which will be considered in chapter 4.

MANAGERIAL SUMMARY

Strategic issues analysis is an important determinant of strategy and "strategic fit" with the environment. The analysis of the organization's external and internal environments is one of the most important activities performed by the strategic manager. It is important not only because this analysis provides an evaluation of the current state of the firm, but also because the resulting strategic decisions will have long-term impact on the future of the organization.

Before strategy can be formulated, firms must scan the external environment for possible opportunities and threats. They must identify which strategic issues to monitor and assess those likely to affect the corporation in the future. They must analyze the resulting information and use it in strategic planning and decision making. Environmental scanning provides an understanding of future trends in the environment that are crucial for strategic management. A SWOT analysis of an organization's strengths, weaknesses, opportunities, and threats is the beginning of the strategic planning process.

Environmental analysis is important because resulting decisions to exploit opportunities or threats will have a long-term impact on the organization's performance. Most large organizations use some form of environmental analysis and forecasting to predict future events. Businesses and other organizations as well can survive only if they are able to manage in an environment of change and constraint. As the rate of change in the external environment increases, the manager must find new and more sophisticated ways to analyze, forecast, and plan for an unpredictable future.

Although environmental analysis is an important element in strategic formulation, it must be related to an internal competitive advantage analysis in determining what can be done with a given and limited set of resources. The advantages which are revealed will provide the chance to exploit opportunities in the environment. Weaknesses, whether technical, financial, or others, will prevent the strategist from moving in other directions.

There is an increasing emphasis on strategic issues analysis and forecasting and on the development of contingency plans to meet an uncertain future. Although larger organizations generally use more sophisticated techniques, there are indications that all firms are placing more and more emphasis on this aspect of strategic planning.

Although a variety of forecasting techniques, including scanning, time series analysis, technological forecasting, and econometric models, are available to the manager, it is important to remember that it is still a question of judgment. Managerial skills and judgment are important elements in identifying strategic issues. As Fred Smith found at Federal Express, there is still the managerial process, requiring creativity, flexibility, and entrepreneurial spirit in setting future directions for the firm.

Review Questions

1 What are some of the major consumer trends that you see emerging (for example, new eating, drinking habits)? What effect will they have on related industries? What strategies might these companies use?
2 What environmental analysis techniques do you feel would be most useful to you if you were a manager in a strategic position?
3 What are some of the major published sources of information in which you might find environmental analysis information?
4 Assume that your local real estate dealers ask you to forecast the future for your city or area. What key factors should be used to anticipate growth or decline?

Notes

1   Adapted from a speech given by Frederick W. Smith at the Apple Leadership Forum in 1984; "Lessons of Leadership," *Nation's Business*, November 1984; and "Frederick W. Smith of Federal Express," *Inc.*, April 1984, 89.
2   Robert M. Price, "Uncertainty and Strategic Opportunity," *Journal of Business Strategy* 2, no. 3 (Winter 1982): 3.
3   L. J. Bourgeois, III, "Strategic Goals, Perceived Uncertainty, and Economic Performance in Volatile Environments," *Academy of Management Journal* 28 (September 1985): 548–573.
4   William Ashley, "Issues Management," *Bank Marketing*, August 1983, 10; see also William R. King, "The Importance of Strategic Issues," *Journal of Business Strategy* 1, no. 3 (Winter 1981): 74; and Ian H. Wilson, "Environmental Scanning," *Business Environment Public Policy,* 1979 conference paper, 159–163.
5   Harold Koontz, "Making Strategic Planning Work," *Business Horizons* 19 (April 1976): 39.
6   See Igor Ansoff, "Managing Strategic Surprise," *California Management Review* 18, no. 2 (Winter 1975): 21.
7   Peters and Waterman, "In Search of Excellence," *California Management Review;* and "Who's Excellent Now?" *Business Week,* November 5, 1984, 76.
8   Nathaniel H. Leff, "Strategic Planning in an Uncertain World," *Journal of Business Strategy* 4, no. 7 (Spring 1984): 78.
9   See Lee A. Iacocca, "Turnaround Strategies," *Journal of Business Strategy* 14, no. 2 (Summer 1984): 67–69.
10 John Naisbitt, *Megatrends* (New York: Warner Books, 1982).
11 Based upon "Who's Excellent Now?" *Business Week,* November 5, 1984, 80; and "Levi is Promoting New Fashions," *Wall Street Journal,* January 31, 1985, 4.

12 Harold E. Klein and Robert E. Linneman, "Environmental Assessment: An Internal Study of Corporate Practice," *Journal of Business Strategy,* November 1984, 66.

13 See Francis Aguilar, *Scanning the Business Environment* (New York: MacMillan, 1967); and Philip S. Thomas, "Environmental Analysis for Corporate Planning," *Business Horizons,* October 1974, 27.

14 Linda Hayes, "Twenty-Five Years of Change," *Fortune,* May 5, 1980, 88.

15 See Danny Miller and Peter Friesen, "Strategy Making in Context: Ten Empirical Archetypes," *Journal of Management Studies,* October 1977, 253–280.

16 Klein and Linneman, "Environmental Assessment."

17 See Danny Miller and Peter Friesen, "Strategy Making in Context: Ten Empirical Archetypes," *Journal of Management Studies,* October 1977, 253–280.

18 "Americans Change," *Business Week,* February 20, 1978, 64.

19 Arthur Roalmn, "Why Corporations Hate the Future," *MBA,* November 1975.

20 Pat Bellaush, "AT&T Dials Wrong Number, Pays Price," *PC Week,* November 11, 1986, 65–71.

21 Miller and Friesen, "Strategy Making in Context."

22 Peter H. Grinyer and David Noerburn, "Strategic Planning in 21 U.K. Companies," *Long Range Planning,* August 1974, 80.

23 Louis E. DeNoya, "How to Evaluate Long-Range Plans" *Long Range Planning,* June 1978, 36.

24 P. Pascarella, "Are You Investing in the Wrong Technology?" *Industry Week,* July 25, 1983, 38. Copyright *Industry Week,* 1983. Reprinted by permission.

25 "Does GE Really Plan Better?" *MBA,* November 1975, 42–46.

26 "Biotech's First Superstar," *Business Week,* April 14, 1986, 71.

27 Ibid., 69

28 "Biotech's First Superstar," *Business Week,* April 14, 1986, 68–71.

29 "The Gene Doctors," *Business Week,* November 17, 1985; and "Bio Tech Comes of Age," *Business Week,* January 23, 1984, 84.

30 Alan Frohman, "Putting Technology into Strategic Planning," *California Management Review* 27, no. 2 (Winter 1985): 48–59.

31 Don LeBell and O. J. Krasner, "Selecting Environmental Forecasting Techniques from Business Planning Requirements," *Academy of Management Review,* July 1977.

32 Kenneth Newgren and Archie Carroll, "Social Forecasting," in *Proceedings, Academy of Management,* 1978.

33 Robert Hershey, "Competitive Intelligence for the Smaller Company," *Management Review,* 66, no. 1 (January 1977): 18–22.

34 Robert H. Turner, "Should You Take Business Forecasting Seriously?" *Business Horizons,* April 1978, 68.

35 H. Kahn and A. Weiner, *The Year 2000* (New York: Macmillan, 1967), 6.

36 James Utterback, "Environmental Analysis and Forecasting," in Charles Hofer and Dan Schendel (eds.), *Strategic Management: A New View of Business Policy and Planning* (Boston: Little, Brown, 1979).

37 LeBell and Krasner, "Selecting Environmental Forecasting," 373–383.

38 Klein and Linneman, "Environmental Assessment."

39 James Brian Quinn, "Selecting Environmental Forecasting," 373–383.

40 "Lessons of Leadership," *Nation's Business.*

41 Bourgeois, "Strategic Goals," 548–573.

42 William Glueck, *Business Policy,* 290; "Lessons of Leadership," *Nation's Business.*

CHAPTER FOUR

■ ■ ■

Competitive Advantage Analysis

OBJECTIVES

After completing this chapter, you will be able to:

■ define competitive advantage analysis and internal analysis profile

■ describe how the key success requirements for an organization are developed

■ discuss each of the major forms in the internal analysis profile

■ compare the technique and models which may be used to analyze competitive positioning

■ identify the five major factors which form the industry structure

I can beat these guys [IBM] at their own game.

Ken Olsen, CEO of
Digital Equipment Company,
October 27, 1986

Tandem Computers

It's 4:30 on Friday afternoon, and the weekly beer bust is in full swing at Tandem Computers' Cupertino, California, headquarters. Sun shines on the basketball court beyond the corporate patio and sparkles on the company swimming pool. . . .

Every week 60 percent of the company drops in to unwind at the beer bust for an hour as a reward for their hard work.

Jim Treybig is a lean Texan with a bachelor's degree in electrical engineering from Rice and an MBA degree from Stanford. He spent five years as marketing manager at Hewlett-Packard. He left that position in 1973 to join Kleiner, Perkins, Caufield, and Byers, a San Francisco venture capital firm, with the understanding that he would eventually leave to start his own firm. Treybig spent a year as a limited partner working on his business strategy and his plan for a fail-safe computer system.

It was while he was at Hewlett-Packard in the early 1970s that he first encountered customers looking for a computer that would not break down. He saw that people were spending large amounts of money to modify computers to get a computer system that would not fail.

That was when Jim Treybig decided to start Tandem. He added up the potential sales to all the companies that he knew of who wanted a nonstop computer system. He estimated a market of over $250 million, with no competitors and products that would be sold, not leased. Because of this competitive assessment, Tandem's revenues and profits have been doubling every year since 1976. In the past two years, the company has virtually replaced its entire product line to keep ahead of the competition.[1]

INTRODUCTION

Strategic management cannot be successfully developed in a vacuum. It requires an in-depth understanding of the competitive factors within both the company and the industry. Like Jim Treybig of Tandem, the strategist must take into account both emerging opportunities and potential threats to future operations.

The strategist must assess both the environment and the internal capabilities of the organization. What can the firm do with the available resources? An opportunity, no matter how attractive, is simply wishful thinking unless the organization has the resources to take advantage of it. Consequently, there must be an analysis which compares the strengths and weaknesses of the organization with those of its competitors.

The strategist must determine the fit between organizational resources and potential opportunities. An organization's strategic advantages allow it to seize new opportunities. Similarly, weaknesses such as a lack of financial resources may limit the possible avenues of opportunity. The next step in strategy formulation involves competitive advantage analysis: the determination of relative market position and the identification of internal areas of strength and weakness,[2] as shown in figure 4.1.

Every organization can analyze its strengths and weaknesses relative to those of its competitors. Some firms may excel in marketing and distribution channels,

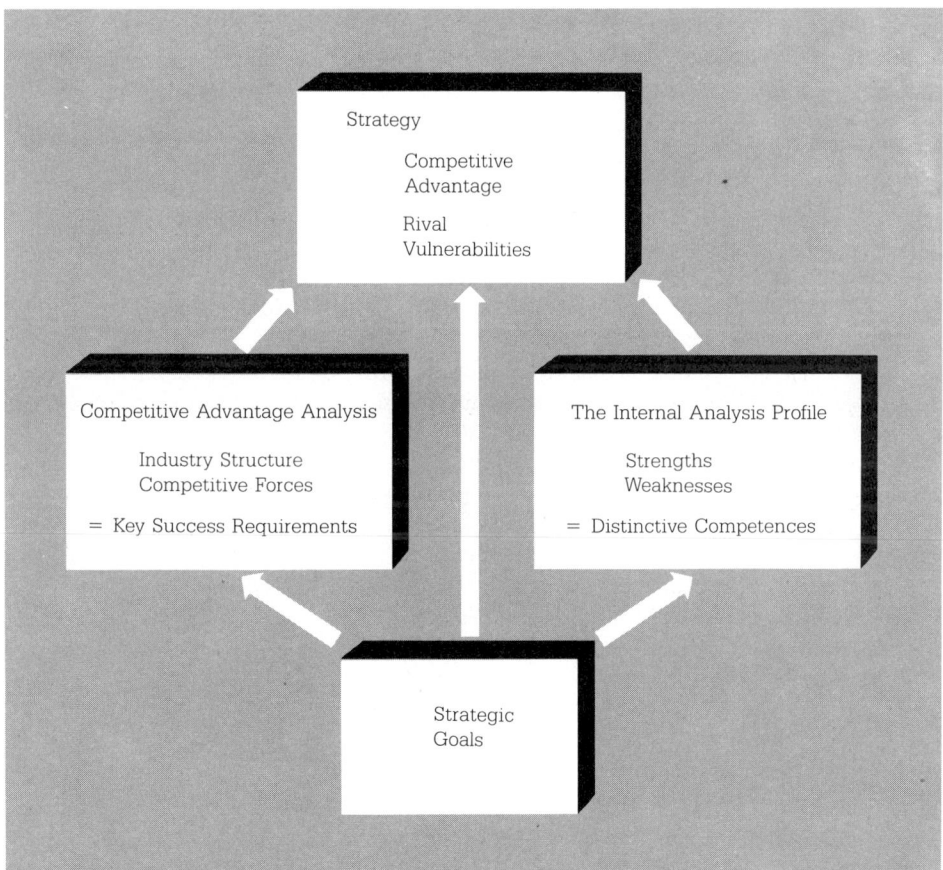

FIGURE 4.1
Framework for Analyzing Competitive Forces

while others may possess unique R&D or technical competence or some other special attribute. The strategist must determine how to utilize these strengths in taking advantage of existing opportunities. What sets this firm apart and provides a possible strategic advantage? In this chapter, we will discuss two critical factors affecting a firm's competitive strategy: competitive advantage analysis and the internal analysis profile.

COMPETITIVE ADVANTAGE ANALYSIS

As Michael Porter suggested, competition is at the core of the success or failure of firms. Competition determines if a firm's innovations, cohesive culture, or implementations can contribute to its performance. Competitive strategy focuses on developing a profitable and sustainable position against the forces that determine industry competition.[3]

The choice of competitive strategy is determined first by the long-term profitability of the industry, an essential ingredient in predicting the profitability of a firm. The second determinant of competitive strategy is the relative competitive position within an industry. Charles Hofer and Dan Schendel offered four steps for analyzing these forces.[4]

1   Develop an internal analysis profile of the organization's principal resources and skills in several broad areas such as financial, marketing, organizational, production, human resource, and technological.
2   Determine the *key success requirements* of the product/market segments in which the organization competes.
3   Compare the internal profile to the key success requirements to determine the major strengths on which an effective strategy can be based and the major weaknesses to be overcome.
4   Compare the organization's strengths and weaknesses with those of its major competitors to identify which key policies are sufficient to yield a competitive advantage in the marketplace.

The idea of competitive advantage is not new. The concept originated in the late 1970s, pioneered by McKinsey and Company and based upon the success of the Japanese in penetrating world markets.[5] *A competitive advantage is a position which offers the opportunity for higher profits relative to competitors* by

1   Differentiating products from the competition
2   Concentrating on specific market segments
3   Focusing on production or distribution channels
4   Using selective price/cost structures

Whatever method is used, the objective is to establish a distinct, favorable differentiation from rival firms.[6]

INDUSTRY STRUCTURE ANALYSIS

The industry structure analysis attempts to gain an understanding of the competitive relationships among a group of firms who compete for a specific market. First we begin with a broad analysis of the industry environment, as shown in figure 4.2. These factors include:

1 *Market size/age*   Is the market relatively large or small, and can it be broadly characterized in a stage of development (start-up, emerging, growth, mature, declining)?

2 *Number of competitors*   What is the level of competition for the market? Are there many smaller rivals or a few large, dominant firms? Also, how easy is it for new players to enter the game? Some industries are relatively easy to enter, others are difficult.

3 *The rules of the game*   How do firms compete in this market? Do they compete on price, quality, technology, service, etc? What is the average level of profitability? Is this a profitable market or is it a high-volume, low-margin field? As an industry matures there is usually a movement toward the cost advantage of

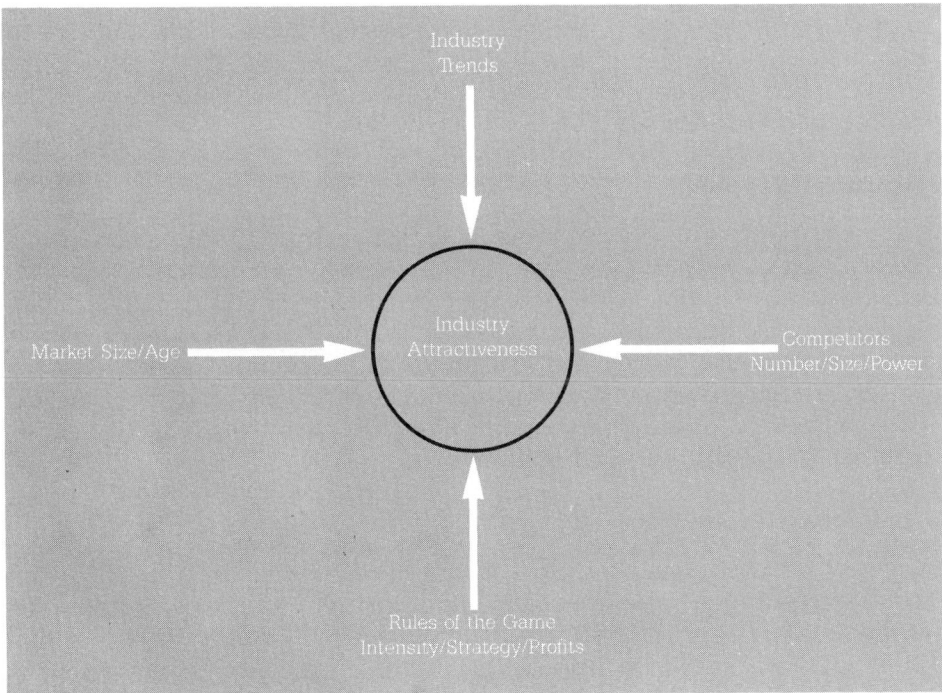

FIGURE 4.2
Industry Structure

economies of scale. When there is a major change in cost or profit structure, competition will tend to intensify, as for example, if price cutting strategies are used.

4   *Industry trends/driving forces*   What are the industry trends and how rapidly do they change? Is the industry growing and innovative or stable and slow to change? The rate of market growth is a critical factor because it influences the equilibrium between supply and demand forces. In a slow-growth industry, competition tends to increase because any growth must be taken from a rival's share.

5   *Industry attractiveness*   The overall attractiveness of an industry is determined by the interaction of these key structural forces. The higher the rate of growth and the weaker the competition, the more attractive the industry.

Techniques for Industry Structure Analysis

The initial analysis of industry structure provides a map of the competitive environment. The strategist also needs to anticipate future trends—new developments that may change the existing structure.

In young, emerging industries, there is often a wider spectrum of strategic approaches. Often firms survive simply because they got into the market early. Late entry to the market, on the other hand, may greatly reduce the available share of market.

There are several techniques which may be used to identify the underlying competitive alignments and the major players.

Structural Mapping

One method which may be used to examine industry structure developed is termed *structural group mapping*.[7] The map is developed by plotting competing firms on two industry dimensions; for example, product quality versus distribution channels, as shown in figure 4.3. Here the alignment of the appliance industry is plotted (with the size of the circles indicating relative market share) into three major competitive groups. The map shows both competitive structure and differing strategies: Maytag, for example, is known as the low-cost producer and builds its strategy around the high-volume, low-margin, low-end market segment.

Competitive Arena Mapping

A second industry analysis technique is termed *competitive arena mapping*.[8] The total market segment is diagrammed around customer needs and product offerings, as shown in figure 4.4. This map of the information-communication arena allows the strategist to examine all the likely moves by key players and to anticipate possible changes in competitive forces. By highlighting the biggest markets, one can visually portray the strategy and direction of key competitors. In the example, competitors

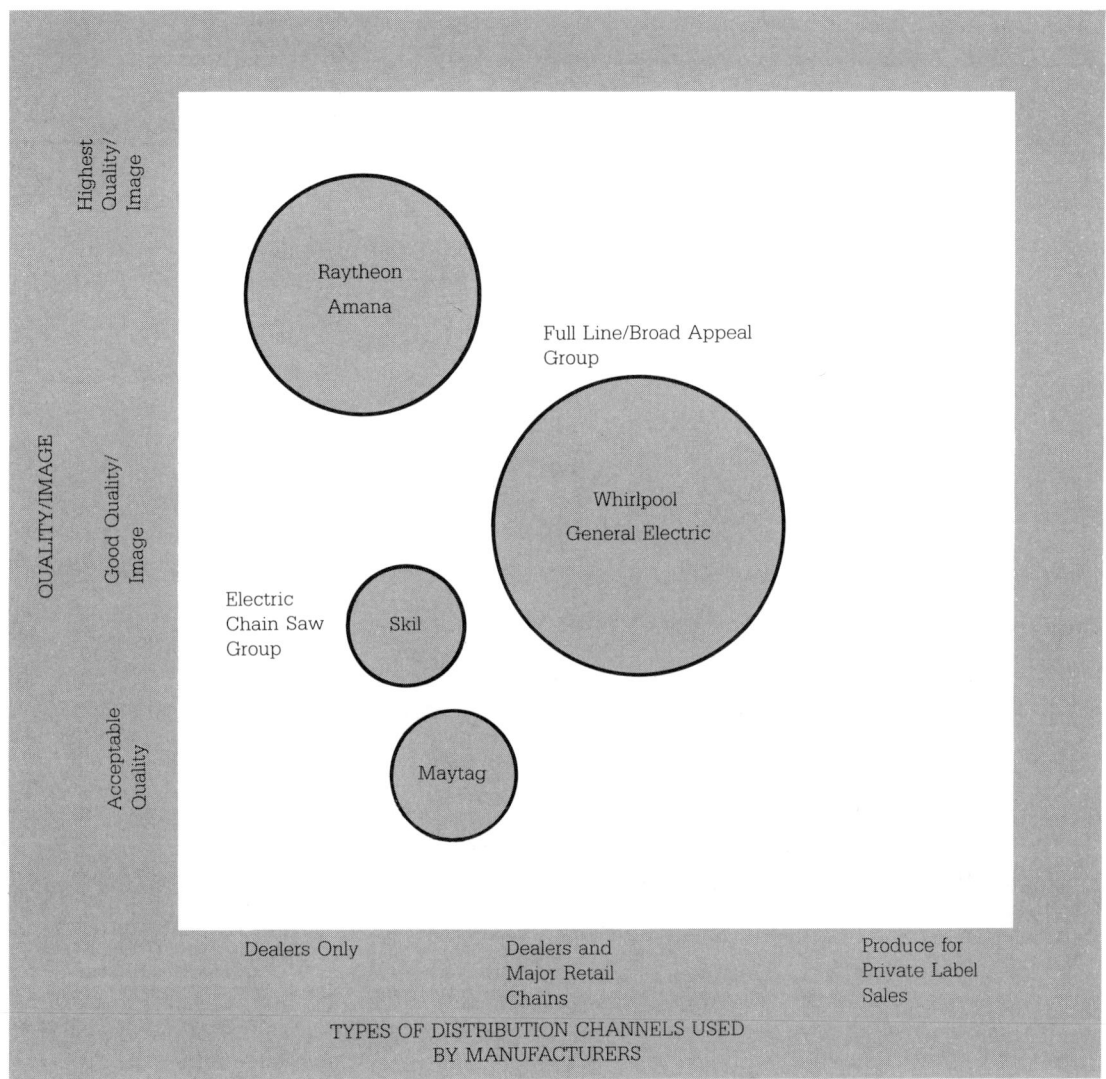

FIGURE 4.3
Strategic Group Map, Appliance Industry

from all directions are converging into the growing microcomputer and office automation markets.

This kind of evaluation can be extremely valuable for firms in these segments.
Firms such as Apple Computer, DEC, and Wang must be prepared for increased
competition from giants in other industries like AT&T and ITT. In the changing

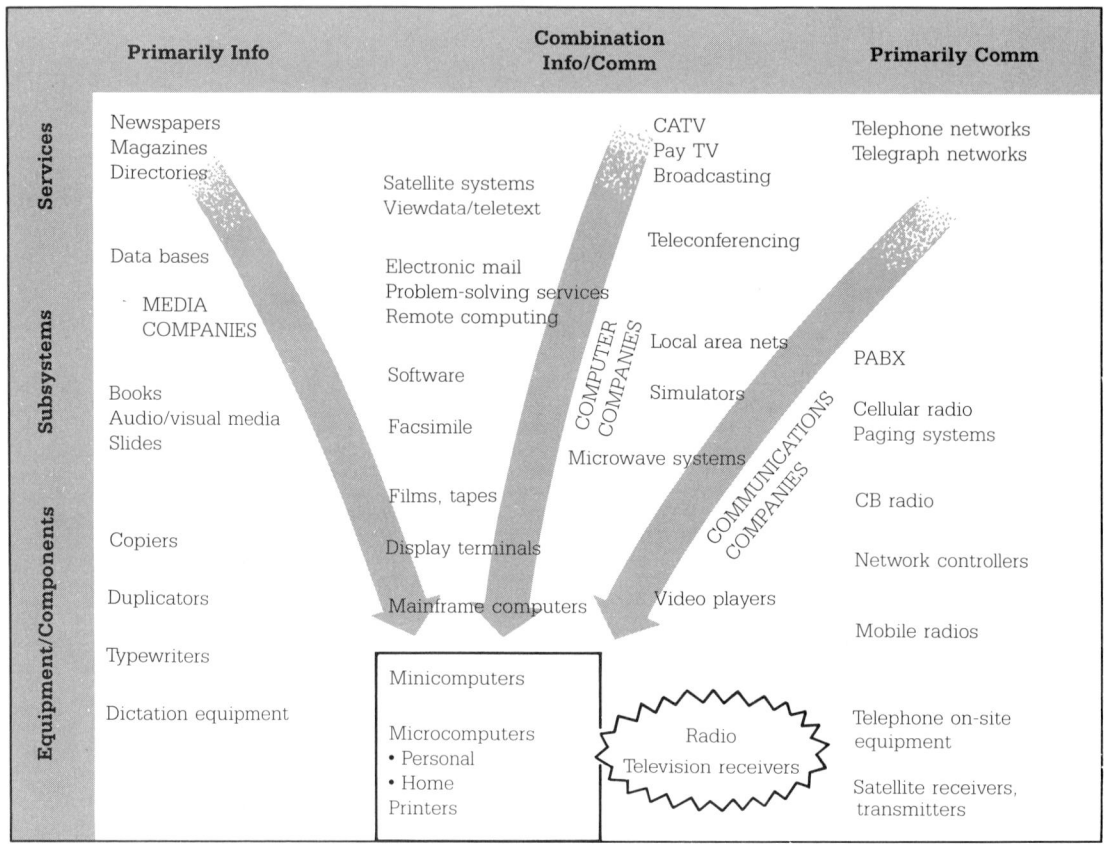

FIGURE 4.4
Competitive Arena Map

marketplace of today, managers must begin to think in terms of strategic arenas if they are to gain competitive advantage.

COMPETITIVE ADVANTAGE ISSUES

General Electric, a company known for its sophisticated strategic planning, identifies strategy as a statement of how resources are going to be used to take advantage of which opportunities and to minimize which threats to produce a desired result. This points to a critical element of strategy: How can we strengthen our competitive position relative to other competitors? Bruce Henderson, former chairman of the Boston Consulting Group, has suggested four basic managerial issues:

1 *The ability to understand competitive interaction as a complete dynamic system* including competitors, customers, money, people, and resources. In other words, how does the firm compete in each of its basic businesses or product groups?

2 *The ability to use this understanding to predict the consequences of a given intervention in that system.* In effect, how does the firm respond to changing conditions; how will it take advantage of new opportunities, reduce competitive threats, and strengthen the firm's own competitiveness?

3 *The availability of uncommitted resources* that can be dedicated to different uses and purposes in the present. How does the firm allocate its resources among various divisions and products? Which will it increase, and which will it choose to diminish?

4 *The willingness to deliberately act to make the commitment.* In effect, how can the firm integrate the activities of various divisions, products, and functions into a committed corporate culture and strategy?[9]

The purpose of strategy is to maintain or gain a position of advantage in relation to competitors. An advantage is gained by seizing opportunities in the environment so that the organization can capitalize upon its areas of strength. For example, IBM became aware of emerging competition and a decline in overall world market share. The IBM top management team then evolved new strategic goals and courses of action to meet potential threats and take advantage of new opportunities leading to the accomplishment of IBM's own objective for this world market (see box, p. 96).

The ability of firms to identify and capitalize on underlying industry structure varies tremendously. Many industries are characterized by one or more profitable leaders, a group of smaller, more focused competitors, and a large number of firms holding in the mid-ranges with lower performance. This pattern, termed the *V-curve effect,* compares sales volume with profitability, as shown in figure 4.5. Large firms tend to dominate the industry by achieving economies of scale, with resulting cost advantages. The smaller firms maintain a high profit level with lower volume by focusing on a specialized market segment.

The medium-sized firms remain at the bottom of the V-curve, unable to realize any competitive advantage. A firm that uses a basic strategy but fails to achieve its goals is "stuck in the middle." It possesses no competitive advantage and usually ends up with below-average performance. Such firms compete at a disadvantage because the cost leader will be better positioned to compete in any segment. In most industries, quite a few competitors are stuck in the middle.

Sometimes new players will enter the industry and change the equilibrium among established competitors. For example, Phillip Morris acquired Miller Brewing and dramatically restructured the beer industry. The industry structure analysis provides an overview of the competitive situation. In the next section, the specific competitive forces are examined.

COMPETITIVE FORCES ANALYSIS

The industry structure analysis provides a broad view of industry attractiveness, but the strategist also needs to identify key competitive forces and their impact on strategy. Michael Porter proposed a comprehensive methodology for analyzing in-

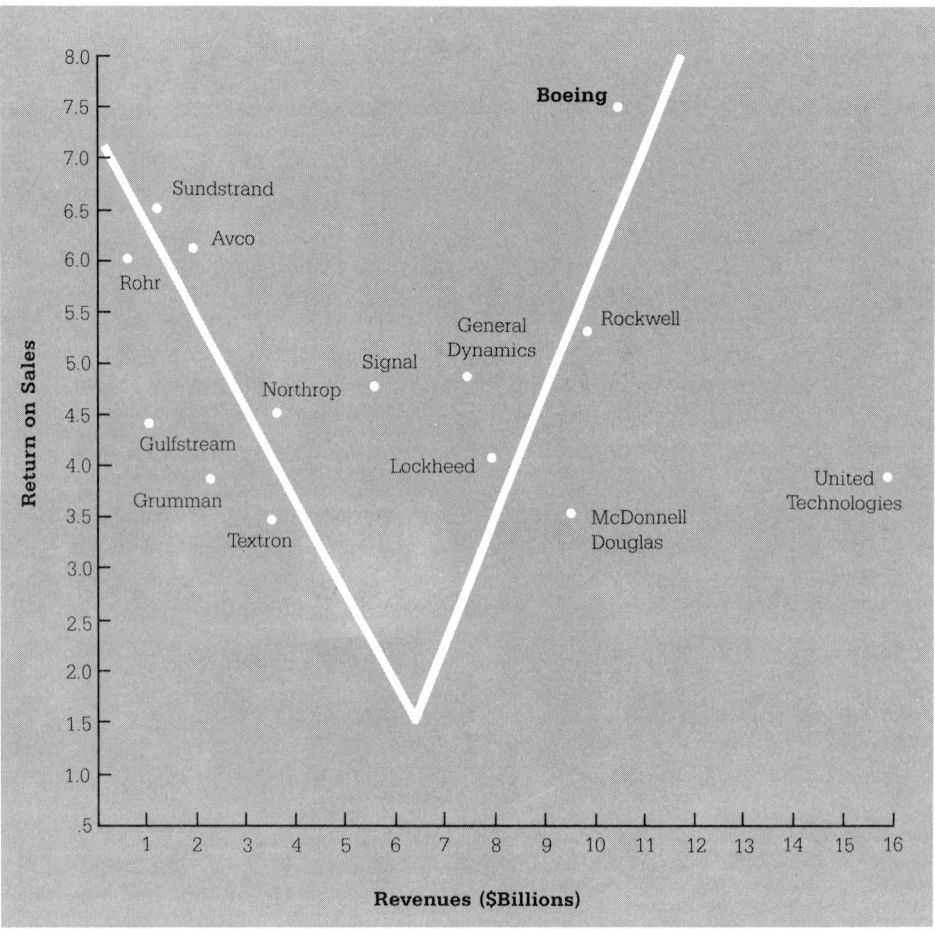

FIGURE 4.5
The V-Curve Model

dustry forces. "The collective strength of these forces," Porter said, "determines the ultimate profit potential in the industry, where profit potential is measured in terms of long-run return on invested capital."[11] The firm must understand its competitive situation, "the rules of the game," if it is to achieve competitive advantage.

The Five Forces Model

The critical factor in strategy formulation is coping with the competition. Porter has identified five basic forces as determinants of industry profitability, as indicated in figure 4.6. The impact of these forces is shown in table 4.1. The relative strength of

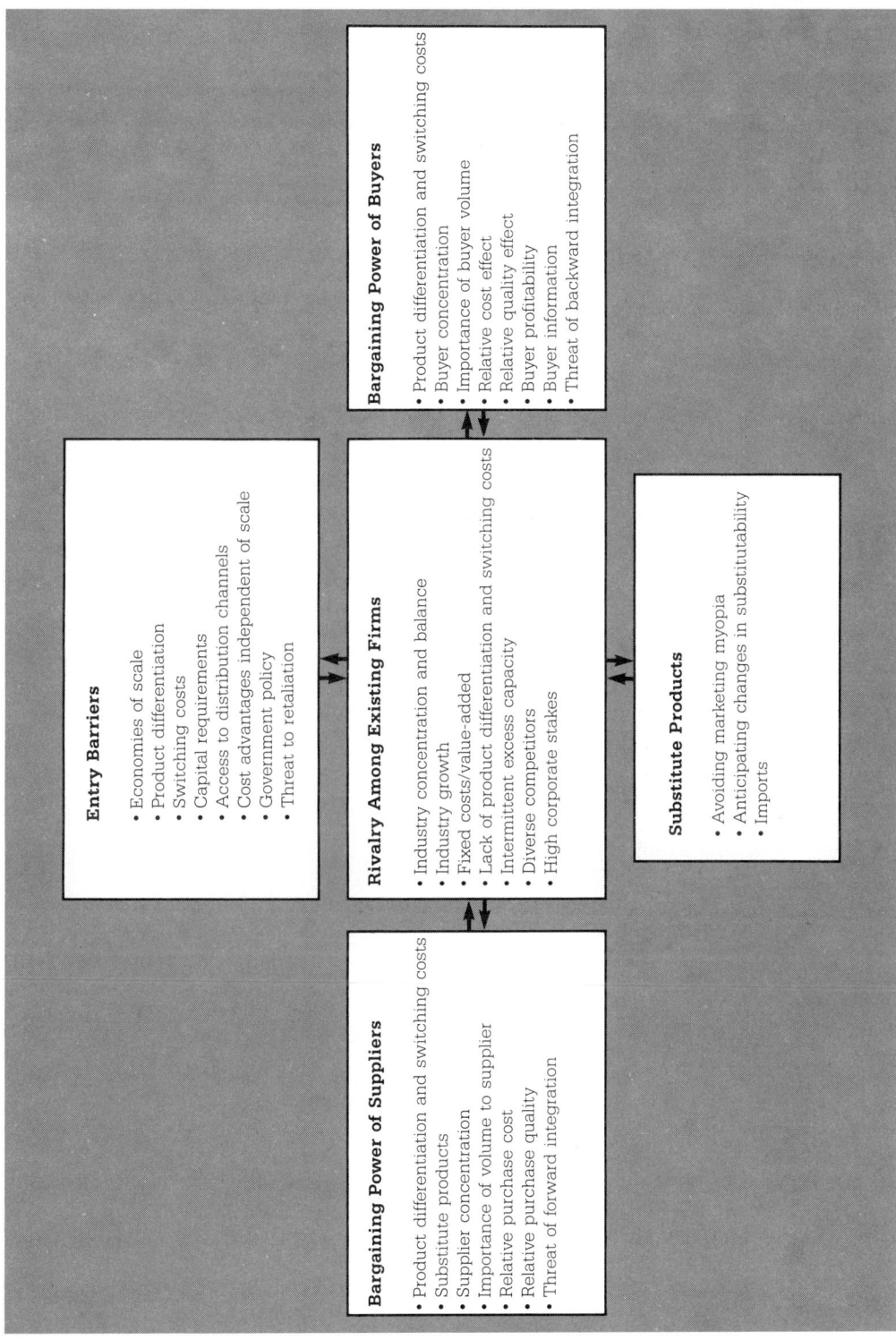

FIGURE 4.6
Industry Structure Forces

SOURCE: Michael Porter. *Competitive Advantage*, 5. Copyright 1985, Free Press. Adapted by permission.

Strategy at IBM

During the 1970s IBM fell behind in the explosively expanding computer industry as its share of the world market slipped from 60 percent in 1967 to roughly 40 percent in 1980. Under the leadership of Chairman John Opel and CEO John Akers, IBM has revolutionized the way it does business from its master strategy to lower-level tactical details and has emerged as a tougher opponent than ever before. IBM now speeds products to market faster than in the past, batters rivals with unprecedented price cuts, and outraces competitors to emerging new businesses.[10]

The new IBM strategy includes four key managerial elements:

1 *Competitive advantage*   IBM poured $10 billion into plant and equipment in an effort to become the industry's lowest-cost producer. This strategy gained a future competitive advantage for IBM relative to its competitors by providing the economies of scale that come with volume production so that it could cut prices to maintain demand and fend off new entries into its business.

2 *Response to changing conditions*   The IBM PC represented a major change in strategy. IBM's past performance in small computers gave it little reason for optimism as it developed a product for the personal computer market. In fact, John Opel himself admitted that the personal computer was an overlooked market. Two factors were involved: the decision to sell small computers directly to small users and the low selling price. The decision to build the PC, which sells for an average price of $3,500, a fraction of the price of IBM's regular computers, was difficult. Some board members questioned the idea of selling through independent retailers where IBM could not tightly control customer service. Other board directors were worried about whether the product could be profitable. The gross margin anticipated for the personal computer was 55 percent versus IBM's usual 65 percent or more, but the business of selling computers for this large market was too important to pass up, so IBM moved ahead.

3 *The allocation of resources*   To explore new markets, IBM spawned entrepreneurial business units that can cut through the corporate red tape. Since 1981, IBM has chartered fourteen independent business units (IBUs) and special business units (SBUs) to explore opportunities beyond the company's main business. For IBM, this has proved to be a low-risk way to enter emerging markets.

4 *Competitive analysis*   CEO John Akers and IBM's executive committee test IBM's results against the performance of more than 100 competitors worldwide grouped into fourteen business areas in what he calls a complicated and very thoughtful matrix. Each year, IBM's board reviews how IBM's growth stacks up against its competition.

John Akers is gambling that he can keep IBM's profitability and market share rising in tandem by strategically managing IBM's resources. As competition sharpens and IBM sells more and more small computers, the company's margins are likely to shrink. Akers plans to offset that trend by turning the company's assets faster so that return on investment stays high.

By changing its strategy rather than staying with its old plans, IBM increased its command over the future. The strategic game plan at IBM is aimed at increasing relative competitive position in a changing world marketplace.

---

each of these interacting forces determines the intensity of competition in an industry.

Entry barriers faced by potential entrants to an industry must be considered.

1   *The economies of scale necessary to compete* force the competitor to buy in on a large scale or to enter at a cost disadvantage. The more capital-intensive the industry (e.g., steel), the greater the necessary economies of scale. As world

TABLE 4.1
The Impact of the Five Forces

	Increase Profit		Decrease Profit	
	1	Weak, fragmented	1	Concentrated
	2	Threat of forward integration	2	No integration threat
	3	Supply a significant percentage to buyer	3	Buyer purchases big percentage
Buyers	4	High switching costs	4	No switching cost
	1	Weak, many	1	Strong, few
	2	Commodity product	2	Differentiated
	3	Backward integration threat	3	Forward integration threat
Suppliers	4	Concentrated buyers	4	Suppliers are weak
	1	Difficult to substitute	1	Easy to substitute
	2	High switching cost	2	Low switching cost
Substitutes	3	Passive substitutions	3	Aggressive substitution
	1	Difficult	1	Easy
	2	High cost	2	Lost cost
	3	High brand	3	Low brand
	4	Proprietary technology	4	Common technology
Entry	5	Restrained distribution	5	Open distribution

competition increases, the entry of foreign competitors into existing markets also increases.

2   *Product differentiation* to attract new consumers may be costly. For example, many firms spend $30 to $50 million to differentiate their product brand from others.

3   *Capital requirements* to enter limit the number of potential entrants.

4   *Access to distribution channels* may be limited, and sometimes a new player must create its own channels.

Substitute products as well as new players can enter the game. A strategy for many stable industries is to move into other markets by finding substitute uses for the product (aluminum, plastics, and so forth). Pressure from possible substitutes places limits on the industry's profit potential and theoretically forces a ceiling on the price firms are able to charge.

The key factors in assessing substitutes include:

1   Recognizing changing positions in the price-performance trade-off between products

2   Anticipating possible changes in designs and substitutability of products

3   Identifying new import products that may substitute existing products (i.e., cars, steel, etc.)

Buyer bargaining power can affect the industry as customers demand lower prices, higher quality, or better service and play competitors off against each other. The factors increasing buyer power include:

1   Product differentiation/low switching costs

2   Buyer concentration, few customers for product

3   Buyer volume

4   Alternative product sources

5   Backward integration

As an example, General Motors purchases a large volume of tires for its new models, making many demands regarding price, quality, delivery, and so forth. As a result, the tire suppliers are forced to operate on a low margin, and many firms have dropped out of this market.

Supplier bargaining power can raise prices or reduce the quality of products or services. The factors increasing supplier power include:

1   Product differentiation/high switching costs

2   Supplier concentration

3   The importance of supplier volume

4   Few alternate suppliers/substitutes

5   The threat of forward integration

As an example, certain integrated circuit microprocessor chips are used by many computer manufacturers. Consequently, the supplier has greater bargaining power unless there are other suppliers or substitute products. Hewlett-Packard decided to develop its own chip manufacturing facilities to reduce its dependence upon uncertain sources of supply.

Rivalry among existing firms can be expected to cause competitive countermoves. If one firm in an industry, for example, Pepsi Cola in the soft drink industry, tries a price-cutting or advertising promotion aimed at increasing share, then competitors can be expected to retaliate with counterstrategies. Coca-Cola, for example, countered the Pepsi challenge with its Bill Cosby ad campaign, featuring "It's the real thing." The key factors in rivalry include:

1 Industry concentration, balance
2 Industry growth
3 Fixed costs/capital-intensive
4 Lack of product differentiation/brand impact
5 Intermittent excess capacity
6 Diverse competition
7 High corporate stakes

The intensity of the competition is examined as changes in strategy cause immediate responses or relative complacency. It helps to understand the competitors' goals and past strategies, because the more committed they are to the market, the greater the probability that they will resist a loss of market share.

The purpose of competitive forces analysis is to gain an edge over competing firms. Therefore, the best strategy may depend on what others are doing. Porter suggested four basic questions in competitor analysis:

1 Is the competitor satisfied with current position?
2 If not, then what strategy shifts will that competitor make? What directions might this competitor's strategy take?
3 Where is the competitor vulnerable?
4 What moves are likely to provoke the most damaging retaliation by the competitor?

One example of the importance of competitive position is suggested by Profit Impact of Marketing Strategies (PIMS) data indicating that profitability is related to market share.

Competitive analysis provides a framework for diagnosing the competitive forces in the environment. The analysis can help prioritize strengths and weaknesses and locate possible vulnerabilities of rivals—a "strategic window" of opportunity that the strategist may be able to exploit. Competitive analysis should be an ongoing process if strategy formulation is to be effective. The strategy maker must identify the key success requirements for each industry situation.

The strategic window concept refers to the timing of market opportunities. It is easier to enter when the window opens and it is difficult to enter after it closes. For example, at one time the market for laptop PCs was opening (that is, pending) principally because the Internal Revenue Service was placing a large order. All of the players were waiting for IBM to come out with its entry, "The PC Convertible," but IBM missed this strategic window, and the million dollar order went to Zenith's Z-181. Since then competing products have entered the market, taking the limelight off the convertible, which has failed to fulfill IBM's initial expectation of becoming the market's leading laptop PC.

Strategic Window for Video Vending Machines?

If it's a risk you like, then Brandon Chase will fit right in; he loves a good bet. The former television newscaster, who became a Hollywood producer, wagered $3.6 million on a little-known film in 1982 and was rewarded when *The Sword and the Sorcerer* grossed more than $50 million. Chase currently plans to invest as much as $100 million on computer-operated vending machines. Chase is betting the machines will take a major share of the growing videocassette market. Chase believes that the strategic window for vending machines that dispense cassettes like soda pop has been opened, and his Group 1 Entertainment has ordered 2,000 Movie Machines from Diebold Inc., the nation's largest maker of automated teller machines (ATMs).

If all goes as planned, Group 1 will soon have 5,400 of the machines installed in groceries, office buildings, and hotels—and several other companies are close behind. Chase feels that vending machines have become a way of life and that people will also buy videocassettes from them.

Group 1's 7-foot-tall, 1,250-pound machine is a combination ATM and jukebox. To rent or buy a cassette, customers will insert a credit card into the machine.

One big question is whether or not customers will use the machines. Video rental stores often stock thousands of titles, and most cassettes are bought by young customers with cash, not credit cards. Other questions also remain. First, will the machines work? The video-vending machines currently in use have not been reliable, and the critical robotic arm of Diebold's new machine remains unproved. Even though Chase is confident that Diebold can make good on its guarantee of 98 percent reliability, it is still a major risk.

However, even 10 percent of the market could be profitable if the estimates of a $10 billion market a decade from now are right. Group 1's own projections call for its 5,400 machines to gross $400 million per year by 1988. Chase feels that Group 1's early entry makes his strategy a sure thing.[12]

INTERNAL ANALYSIS PROFILE

The second major determinant of strategy is the internal analysis of the firm's resources and capabilities.[13] The firm's internal analysis profile includes all resources, functions, and systems that exist within the organization. The internal competencies of the firm are examined to determine the driving forces which can lead to new strategic positioning. The key factors in the profile include the functional areas of marketing, engineering, and production. The internal analysis profile pinpoints the organization's strengths and weaknesses. The success of the firm depends on its ability to capitalize upon competitive opportunities.

According to Bruce Henderson of the Boston Consulting Group, taking advantage of this distinctive competence may include:

1   Following a course of action different from those of rival firms
2   Developing a strategy which will provide different and better outcomes than those of its competitors
3   Making it difficult for other firms to duplicate the strategy or enter the area of opportunity, if the strategy works[14]

The Value Chain

Another tool for analysis is the value chain, developed by Michael Porter. Every firm is a collection of activities that are performed to design, produce, market, deliver, and support its product. All these activities can be represented using a value chain. A firm's value chain is a reflection of its history, strategy, approach to implementing its strategy, and the underlying economics of the activities themselves.

The relevant level for constructing a value chain is a firm's activities in a particular industry (the business unit). An industry or sectorwide value chain is too broad because it may obscure important sources of competitive advantage. Though firms in the same industry may have similar chains, the value chains of competitors often differ. People Express and United Airlines both compete in the airline industry, for example, but they have very different value chains embodying significant differences in boarding gate operations, crew policies, and aircraft operations. Differences among competitor value chains are a key source of competitive advantage.[15]

This procedure is essentially the same as the one used by Kenneth H. Olsen, president and CEO of Digital Equipment Corp. (DEC), in launching a massive corporate overhaul. Olsen assembled and analyzed all available information on the company, including company, division, and product reports; interviews with operating managers, customers, and industry analysts; and his own observations. From this information, Olsen prepared an internal analysis profile of the organization pinpointing DEC's strengths and weaknesses. Using this internal analysis, Olsen is attempting to change DEC into a "tough, market-driven competitor" by

1   Developing a new product strategy with a broad range of products that can be networked, building on current product strengths

2 "Adopting aggressive new marketing tactics" for its users and more innovative promotions
3 "Streamlining an overgrown corporate bureaucracy." The purpose of the internal analysis, then, is to position the firm to become more competitive in the future.[16]

This analysis enabled CEO Ken Olson to determine what DEC was capable of accomplishing with its available resources. It provided a basis for future strategic determination by matching DEC's resources with potential market opportunities. Ken Olson felt that DEC's product line represented a real strength, one that he wanted to build upon by developing advanced technology products which could be marketed through the existing distribution system.

Every organization has distinct strategic advantages and disadvantages. One firm may excel at technical expertise but lack money. Another may have a cash surplus, but lack innovation. Unless the strategist is aware of these factors, the firm may be unable to exploit possible opportunities.

The strategist must investigate the opportunities and threats to the environment, but also must assess the firm's ability to meet these challenges and threats. This process of internal analysis may be termed the internal analysis profile, competitive advantage analysis, or strategic advantage analysis; but all refer to the same thing—an assessment of the firm's resources.

An Organizational System

The organization may be viewed as a system of interrelated parts. One may examine each of the subunits separately, then analyze the way the parts are incorporated into a functioning unit. In the analysis of the organization it is customary to review each of the key functional areas—marketing, finance, and production—as well as the managerial system that ties them together.

"People Express Airline," commented Harvard Professor D. Quinn Mills, "is the most comprehensive and self-conscious effort to fit business to the capabilities and attitudes of today's work force."[17] Chairman Donald C. Burr sought out young, aggressive, free spirits, using a decentralized style with only three layers of management, a system called "cross utilization" (where employees perform widely different tasks), and rewarding employees with a "piece of the action." Burr's low-fare, no-frills concepts, based on an analysis of strengths and weaknesses, led People Express to become a billion dollar sales firm in about five years. (Note: People Express has since run into financial troubles and has been acquired by another airline.)

Marketing is perhaps the most crucial of the functional areas because marketing brings in revenues—the life blood of the organization. The marketing function also provides a vital communication link between the organization and the external environment. Information gained through the marketing activity includes:

1 Competitive position and market share. Does the firm have a strong market share in the total market or its segments?

2   Product life cycle. Does the firm have new product leadership? In what phase of the life cycle are the main products?
3   Product mix. What are the range and quality of products and services?
4   Effective pricing strategy. Does the strategy include both products and services?
5   Effective sales force. Is there a dependence on a few customers?
6   Effective channels of distribution. Is there a broad geographic coverage, including multinational?
7   Advertising. Has the company's product and brand image been established?
8   Effective market research system. Is the firm a leader or follower?

Financial information determines the availability of cash resources to implement strategic actions. The firm's financial situation is important because it directly relates to the amount of resources it will be able to commit and to the degree of cost control over existing programs.

The primary purpose of financial analysis is to determine the strength of the firm's relationship to its needs and to competition. Questions addressed in financial analysis include:

1   Is the availability of capital relative to the industry and competitors?
2   Does the capital structure allow the effective use of financial leverage?
3   Is there a solid base of financial reserves and cash flow?
4   Is the firm using tax forms advantageously?
5   Is there access to new opportunities because of available resources?
6   How efficient are financial planning and budgeting procedures?
7   Are there effective accounting systems for cost, budget and profit planning, and auditing procedures?

Production, the nuts-and-bolts aspect of the organization, represents the firm's ability to produce goods and services. The production area contributes greatly to the firm's profitability through efficiency in the use of capital and human resources. The primary production factors include:

1   An efficient cost control of operations in comparison with those of its competitors
2   An adequate capacity and modern facilities
3   The relative level of raw materials cost and availability
4   Effective inventory control and purchasing systems
5   A strategic location of plant facilities
6   Efficient operations procedures for production control, design, scheduling, testing, tooling, and quality control
7   Effective management information and production control systems

Research and development (R&D) is an important function because it often determines the degree of innovation which a firm is able to apply in its strategic decisions. American companies spend large amounts of money on R&D, depending of course on the nature of the industry. Annual expenditures on R&D amounted to over $108.8 billion in 1985. R&D usually includes scientific research, both basic and applied, and the firm's engineering capabilities. The primary strategic questions about R&D include:

1   Does R&D reach the critical mass? Is R&D spending as a percent of sales, versus industry average?
2   What is the level of technical expertise relative to that of key competitors?
3   How modern and efficient are R&D facilities, laboratories, and equipment?
4   How well are the R&D efforts organized and managed?
5   What is the mix of R&D projects between basic, long-term projects and applied, short-term projects?

Human Resources

The organization is no more effective than its human resource capabilities. These capabilities all consider the factors that go into recruitment, training, selection, development, promotion, and compensation of the members of the organization, including:

1   How healthy is the organizational climate?
2   Is the company competitive with regard to salary and benefits?

Management Problems at Texas Instruments

Texas Instruments (TI) was one of the early entries in the home computer market. In theory, TI should have dominated the market; instead in 1983 TI folded its home computer business, taking a $660 million operating loss. This failure indicated some internal weaknesses:

1   *R&D*   TI's engineers lacked expertise in consumer markets. TI cut prices to create demand for its home computer, but was unable to provide a competitive product.
2   *Marketing*   The firm was product- rather than market-driven and failed to respond to customer needs.
3   *Management*   An overly complex management system, including matrix management and a domineering management style, lacked the flexibility to respond to changing high-tech markets.

TI is now attempting to develop an entrepreneurial culture that is more tuned to the market and to apply a strategy that builds on technological strength.[18]

3   How effective are the channels of communication and direction?
4   What managerial style is used and to what degree is delegation used?
5   Are there management development programs to gain involvement?

When all the internal factors have been analyzed, the strategist has an awareness of the firm's capabilities: what the organization can do. Then the manager can realistically determine how these resources can best be applied to take advantage of environmental opportunities.

MANAGERIAL SUMMARY

Competitive advantage analysis is a basic step in the formulation of corporate strategy. It is the process of examining the organization's marketing, financial, production, research, and human resource factors. Then, to enable it to meet possible threats or to dominate potential areas of opportunity, the organization can determine where the firm has critical strengths (advantages) or weaknesses. Primarily, the competitive advantage analysis determines what the firm is capable of doing and what it has the resources to accomplish.

Competitive advantage is at the core of success or failure of firms. Before strategy formulation begins, top management needs to assess the internal corporate environment for strengths and weaknesses. It must also develop an in-depth understanding of the industry strategic factors, including industry attractiveness and competitive forces. The outcome of competitive analysis is the identification of key areas of advantage and vulnerability.

The competitive analysis is one of the most important activities managers perform. The industry analysis provides a broad view of the dynamic relationship among the forces which determine competitive advantage.

The internal analysis profile focuses on the resources of the organization— technical, financial, marketing, and so forth—which establish constraints on the future strategy of the firm.

Strategy is determined by industry attractiveness and competitive position. In a dynamic environment, the flexibility to change direction as the industry changes or as new forces emerge will be critical elements in the firm's future success or failure.

Review Questions

1   Select a local company (or select an article about a firm from a business publication) and identify its competitive forces and industry analysis functions.
2   What are the key success requirements for a firm and how are they identified?
3   Why is competitive advantage always so important?
4   Can you find examples of companies that have used competitive advantage to develop a strong position in their industry?

Notes

1   Based upon "Managing by the Mystique of Tandem Computers," *Fortune,* June 28, 1982, 84–91; and "How Jim Treybig Whipped Tandem Back in Shape," *Business Week,* February 23, 1987, 124.

2   See Michael Porter, *Competitive Advantage* (New York: Free Press, 1985).

3   Ibid., 1.

4   Charles W. Hofer and Dan Schendel, *Strategy Formulation: Issues and Concepts,* 2nd ed. (St. Paul, MN: West Publishing, 1986). Strengths and weaknesses may also be related to the structure of organizations. See Ian C. MacMillan and Patricia E. Jones, "Designing Organizations to Compete," *Journal of Business Strategy* 4, no. 4 (Spring 1984): 11–26.

5   Stephen E. South, "Competitive Advantage: The Cornerstone of Strategic Thinking," *Journal of Business Strategy* 1, no. 4 (Spring 1981): 16.

6   See Porter, *Competitive Advantage,* 1–3.

7   Ibid., 152–154.

8   William E. Rothschild, "Surprise and Competitive Advantage," *Journal of Business Strategy* 4, no. 3 (Winter 1984): 10.

9   Bruce Henderson, "Understanding the Forces of Strategic and Natural Competition," *Journal of Business Strategy* 1, no. 3 (Winter 1982): 11.

10 Based upon "IBM: More Worlds to Conquer," *Business Week,* February 18, 1985, 84–98.

11 This summary of the forces driving competitive strategy is taken from M. E. Porter, *Competitive Advantage* (New York: Free Press, 1985), 4.

12 Based upon "In Goes Your Credit Card, Out Comes Amadeus," *Business Week,* November 10, 1986, 127.

13 For two excellent articles, see Robert B. Buchele, "How to Evaluate a Firm," *California Management Review* (Fall 1962): 5–76; and Howard H. Stevenson, "Defining Corporate Strengths and Weaknesses," *Sloan Management Review* (Spring 1976): 51–68.

14 Bruce D. Henderson, "Construction of a Business Strategy," in *Business Policy and Strategy: Concepts and Readings* (Homewood, IL: Irwin, 1975), 290.

15 Porter, *Competitive Advantage,* 36.

16 "A New Strategy for No. 2 in Computers," *Business Week,* May 2, 1983, 66–75.

17 "Up, Up, and Away?" *Business Week,* November 25, 1985, 80.

18 "TI: Shot Full of Holes and Trying to Recover," *Business Week,* November 5, 1984, 82.

CHAPTER FIVE

Strategic Alternatives

OUTLINE

OBJECTIVES

After completing this chapter, you will be able to:

- define the four different types of strategic alternatives available to the organization

- describe each of the basic alternatives and why they are used

- discuss how managers can develop an effective business and corporate strategy

- compare the corporate business and multinational approaches to strategy

- identify the three generic business level strategies

I'm particularly glad to see that reputation can be maintained and improved at a time when the banking industry and we ourselves are in a transition from what you might call the old days to the new days. Opportunistic is a word that could be used to describe our strategy. We're trying to spot the opportunities and run with them—conservatively, carefully.

Robert V. Lindsay
President of J. P. Morgan,
January 6, 1986

Managing a High-Growth Firm: Brae Corporation

Texido

When William J. Texido, former chairman and chief executive of Brae Corporation, sat down with 40 Brae executives recently in a Palm Springs meeting, he counted fourteen million-aires facing him around the table. The unique feature was that he had helped make them millionaires. They were all executives of San Francisco-based Brae Corp., one of the fastest growing smaller companies in the U.S.

Bill Texido was developing a fast-growth strategy for one of the nation's leading rail car leasing firms. His strategic game plan had evolved with fundamental changes to both operating strategy and corporate philosophy. One strategy he initiated was the acquisition and reorganization of American Sign and Indicator to move Brae into new high-tech fields. His impact on strategy changed the corporate culture of a firm that had been slow to adapt to changing markets. Texido was attempting to bring excellence to an old-line organization. He passed out copies of *In Search of Excellence* to each member of his management team in an attempt to develop new approaches.

The Brae CEO was known as a hard-driving executive who worked long hours and got involved in management operations when problems arose. He is also an active and competitive tennis player. "Some people say they play for the exercise," said Texido, "But I play for the 'iron' (trophies)."[1] "Playing to win" has led Brae to the number one position on *Inc.* magazine's 100 fastest-growing firms.

"Bill is a very warm person," says one Brae manager. "He likes to talk and listen to people."[2] But despite the collegial atmosphere he creates, Texido is a forceful and decisive strategist.

The strategies used by Texido included acting upon new market opportunities by using a diversification strategy, and he attempted an acquisition and turnaround strategy at American Sign and Indicator.

The changing strategy at Brae exemplifies an entrepreneurial, risk-taking entry into new high-growth markets. AS&I, for example, had a lease portfolio valued at approximately $100 million. The company was not very aggressive in R&D and maintaining market share, but Texido was committed to improving AS&I's product line, production cost-curve, and market penetration.

On the difficulty of reorganizing and revitalizing a turnaround, Bill Texido commented, ''The turnaround at AS&I was tougher than I expected. It takes a lot longer than you anticipate and involves a lot more problems than you originally are aware of.''[3]

INTRODUCTION

There is no perfect strategy. There are only strategies that work at a certain time and those that don't. No organization can continue to apply the same strategy or game plan indefinitely because conditions constantly change. AS&I was but one example of a successful company that became complacent, failing to change to meet new economic conditions and competition. In order to continue meeting these new and changing conditions, the manager needs to be developing an awareness of the various options which are open to the firm. In the strategic management process, the identification of strategic alternatives is an important element.

Sooner or later every strategy becomes ineffective; therefore, organizations must constantly reappraise their strategic plans and make necessary revisions and changes. There are times when only minor revisions will have to be made; a fine tuning of an existing strategy. At other times, the strategic plan may need a wholesale overhauling to revitalize and redirect organizational fortunes.

Because strategic management involves the selection of a corporate game plan, the strategic decision process begins with an analysis of possible moves and countermoves. One strategist, Henry E. Singleton of Teledyne, has been described in these terms, ''Everything he does has lots of deliberate thought behind it. He doesn't know what his opponent is going to do, but whatever the opponent does Henry has three possible moves.''[4]

One critical step involves a continuing appraisal of both corporate and business-level strategy. Competitive relationships do not remain stable over time. New opportunities emerge, new competitors or products enter the field, or other forces change. The key questions, then, involve which strategy within a given competitive situation will produce what level of operating results.

. In this chapter, we will examine stage four in the strategic management process: how decision makers develop alternative strategies. They seek to identify which courses of action are most likely to result in an increased level of performance for their firms. The focus of this chapter is on the major alternative strategies: corporate, business-level, and multinational strategies.

These strategic alternatives and decisions are the most critical facing the strategic decision maker. The answers to these questions will determine how well the firm will compare with its competitors in the future. The search for strategic alternatives involves three elements:

1   Corporate strategy   The strategist examines what businesses the firm should be in to achieve its basic goals of growth, profitability, and market leadership by managing the portfolio of businesses. At Exxon, for example, the executives manage a portfolio of thirteen autonomous strategic business units.

2   Business-level strategy   The strategist decides how to compete within a particular strategic business unit (or SBU).

3   Multinational strategy   The strategist considers using global expansion strategies in order to expand potential markets and increase the possible options open to the firm.

DEVELOPING CORPORATE STRATEGY

The development of strategic alternatives emerges from the analysis of the firm's competitive position and merges with strategic choice. Yet for our purposes we will discuss it as if it were a separate stage in the strategic formulation process. The development of strategic options involves several factors. One critical factor is, of course, the strategic fit between the alternative and the firm. The analysis of sources of competitive advantage is the starting point in seeking long-run profitability. The next phase is a process of creating a fit between the strategy and the corporate competence, because the closer the fit, the more likely the strategy can be implemented effectively.[5]

A strategic change is necessary whenever potential actions by competitors threaten to affect the firm's future goals. Although decision theorists suggest that the decision maker should consider all possible alternatives, strategists rarely do because the pressures of time and money limit the search. In most situations several alternatives should be considered to provide a superior comparison of trade-offs, advantages, and weaknesses for strategic selection.

The consideration of strategic alternatives involves several factors. First, the alternatives which will be considered are a function of the firm's resources and capabilities. If, for example, the firm is in a tight cash situation and has a shortage of capital, then major expenditure alternatives are unrealistic.

A second consideration is the firm's past strategy: What strategy has the firm used and with what results? Generally, strategists start with the past strategy and continue until conditions change and they are forced to adapt. James B. Quinn of Dartmouth College suggested that strategy is formed as an incremental process. He found successful strategists constantly reassess the future, find new directions as events unfurl, and direct the organization's skills and resources into new balances of dominance and risk aversion by incrementally modifying previous strategies.[6]

One useful construct in visualizing possible strategic options is the *product-market matrix*.[7] This matrix enables the strategist to identify a basic classification of strategies based upon product positioning, as shown in figure 5.1. This matrix is based upon two elements: market and product.

A *market penetration* strategy involves an attempt to increase market share in an existing market niche, one in which the firm already offers a product or service.

Market development introduces an existing product or service into new market areas, often by expansion into new market segments or geographic areas. For example, a new popcorn company has been successful in introducing its product in the midwest. Now it is attempting to expand into other areas, where it must compete against Orville Redenbacher, the market leader, and others.

Product development is a technology-based strategy that involves developing new or advanced products for existing markets. Hewlett-Packard is successful because it is continually developing new products for its markets. In fact, a high percentage of its revenues comes from products developed in the last few years.

Diversification involves the development of new products and services and entry into new markets. The degree of change often makes this a high-risk strategy, and many experts caution against going into a completely new market with a new product.

From the basic strategic question "What business are we in?" follow other questions such as "Should we stay in this business or should we get out?" These strategic issues involve a number of fundamental strategic alternatives as shown in table 5.1.

The *Strategic Alternative Matrix* is designed as a framework for the identification and comparison of strategic actions. It also indicates the relative frequency of use and the basic goals associated with each of these strategic alternatives. Each

		Customer	
		Existing	New
Product	Existing	Market penetration	Market development
	New	Product development	Diversification

FIGURE 5.1
The Product/Mission Matrix

SOURCE: Adapted from H. Igor Ansoff, *Corporate Strategy.* New York: McGraw-Hill, 1965, p. 109. Copyright 1965 by McGraw-Hill. Adapted by permission.

TABLE 5.1
The Strategic Alternative Matrix

	Strategy	Frequency (of use)	Goals	Uses	Examples
1	Growth Concentration Concentric Diversification Conglomerate Diversification Vertical Integration	54.4%	To increase sales/earnings	High market growth Economic prosperity	John Welch (General Electric)
2	Neutral Holding Harvest	9.2%	To increase profitability	In mature industry Stable environment	Charles Parry (Alcoa)
3	Defensive Turnaround/Retrenchment Divestment Liquidation	7.5%	Survival To cut costs To eliminate losses	In crisis Severe losses, etc.	Lee Iacocca (Chrysler)
4	Mixed Combination	28.7%	To increase earnings To cut costs	In economic transition Multidivision companies	Rand Araskog (ITT)

strategy can be effective depending upon the competitive position of the firm, its resources, the type of market, the competition, and so forth. In general, large multiproduct firms tend to take a more aggressive strategic approach than firms in weaker, less dominant positions.

One of the critical steps in the strategic process is the development of strategic alternatives. It is an important step because it allows a systematic comparison of the various trade-offs, risks, and rewards associated with each possible strategy. Therefore, the final strategic choice, such as the strategy of ITT, is likely to be more effective in terms of long-run performance.

The Growth Strategy

One of the most popular and frequently used strategic options is the *growth strategy*. In a study of 358 *Fortune* 500 companies, William Glueck found that over 50 percent chose growth as a primary strategy.[8] The growth strategy seeks to attack the market and dominate its product/market segment. This strategy involves attempting to increase the level of sales and market share at a higher rate than in the past and usually at a higher rate than that of competitors. In highly competitive industries with high rates of technological change (e.g., electronics), firms that do not use aggressive strategies will likely be left far behind. Not surprisingly, many firms feel that growth is a highly desirable, necessary objective and use dynamic growth strategies.

At ITT, for example, Harold Geneen was acclaimed for his aggressive program of acquisition and growth. The next CEO, Rand V. Araskog, was faced with sluggish profits and needs for internal growth as well as acquisition. The risk is that following both growth plans may be impossible.

A Change in Strategy at ITT

ITT, the giant conglomerate, has been restructured around what CEO Rand Araskog considers its core business: telecommunications—at a cost of some $1.5 to $2 billion. ITT has been in a desperate cash-crunch situation, resulting in the divestment of several past acquisitions to the tune of $1.7 billion. These acquisitions were part of former CEO Harold Geneen's strategy that built the giant conglomerate.

The sell-offs represent a major shift in strategy to meet a changing market place. As Rand Araskog has commented, "I really don't think much has changed here at ITT, except the nature of the world"[9]

But will this new strategy fit with the ITT's corporate culture and competence? The strategy represents a redeployment of assets into high-tech, high-growth markets. The question arises, can the company's management be effective in the volatile high-tech, telecommunications market? Although Araskog has restructured ITT, it still, reportedly, has a very top-heavy, highly centralized, and cumbersome top management structure. The past strategy at ITT under Geneen still affects new strategic moves.[10]

The first question to be asked, often termed the *key strategic variable*, is "What business are we in?" Peter Drucker, a leading management consultant, has suggested that this question can be answered only "by looking at the business from the outside, from the point of view of customer and market."[11] As Jacques Maisonrouge, a senior IBM executive, has stated: "We want to be in the problem-solving business—this is our mission. Our business is not to make computers. It is to help solve administrative, scientific, and even human problems. If your mission is broad enough, you do not find one day that a competitor's new product has outmoded all your equipment."[12]

Donald C. Burr, founder and chairman of People Express, built his firm into a $1 billion company in less than ten years. In 1980, the firm went public at $8.50 per share, and Burr bought seventeen used Boeing 737s to start the airline. By 1983 the firm had sales of \$287 million and the stock hit \$50 per share and split two-for-one. Burr used an aggressive-growth, market penetration strategy to exploit this market opportunity.[13]

One of the primary advocates of the growth strategy approach is Bruce Henderson of the Boston Consulting Group (BCG). The BCG supports getting the biggest market share as early as possible and then holding costs and prices down to reduce the attractiveness of the market to other possible entrants.[14]

There are many reasons why a growth strategy may be selected. First, many studies indicate that growth is associated with effectiveness (as measured by profitability and other standard measures).[15]

Second, there is much support for experience curve theories, which suggest that as the firm grows in size and experience there is an increase in effectiveness, including economies of scale (see chapter 6).[16]

Third, growth often hides other underlying problems. These problems, such as those at ITT, may not come to light until the growth rate stops or declines. At Litton, for example, several management problems developed during periods of rapid growth and affected later profitability. Fred Wittenbert has found that as the rate of growth accelerates, there tends to be a corresponding decline in profitability.[17] However, more recent data suggest that this is not always true.

Finally, there is the ego involvement of the manager. Most managers have "paid their dues," that is, they have worked their way up through years of hard work. They want to be remembered as the individuals who led their companies to new successes, not as persons who only occupied the office for five years.

In support of the popularity of the aggressive-growth strategy, there are a number of research findings which reinforce the effectiveness which strategic managers intuitively strive to grasp. In a study of fifty-three leading growth companies, Peter Gutman of City College of New York found that growth rates ranged up to 76.7 percent annually.[18] Gutman's findings conclude that the firms with the highest growth rates

1 Chose industries where sales increased more rapidly than the economy as a whole
2 Concentrated on the market segments within the industries which grew more rapidly than the industry
3 Entered the market earlier than competing firms
4 Operated in multinational markets

Michael Chevalier and Bernard Catry studied three U.S. industries and found that some growth strategies were more effective than others, namely:

1 Focus on products whose markets are growing. Never focus on slow-growth products unless there is technical or market know-how that can be applied to more promising markets.
2 Be a big fish in a small pond if the pond (market segment) is growing. Get out of small nongrowth markets. Don't be a follower.

3   Select specific market segments in which to compete. Don't try to compete against larger firms.[19]

These studies suggest that a growth strategy, when properly selected and implemented, can be very effective. In the following sections, each of the major growth strategy options will be described.

Concentration Strategy

One widely used growth strategy is to increase the sales and market share of the concentrated product line or market at an increasing rate. This strategy, like that of Kentucky Fried Chicken, involved doing only one thing but doing it very well.

1   *Market penetration:* increase market share in a high-growth field and attempt to dominate it. McDonald's strategy is an example of a high-growth strategy based on specializing in one product and doing it well in order to lead the growth in the fast-food field, at that time a high-growth area.
2   *Market development:* increase sales into additional geographic areas if the market stops growing. Coors, for example, was a highly growing regional brewing corporation, with a strong market share in the west. However, it decided to shift into a national geographic market in order to expand its total market.
3   *Market development:* increase sales by focusing on different market segments or distinctive product quality. Polaroid, for example, started in a high-growth field, and has since expanded from the low end (the One-Step camera) up to the high end (the SX-70) in instant photography. McDonald's sought to expand its market by moving into the breakfast segment, a move which other competitors have tried to follow as the basic market growth rate slowed. When Philip Morris, Inc., asked John A. Murphy to head its newly acquired Miller Brewing Company, it marked the beginning of a classic example of how sophisticated marketing can work miracles for a consumer product going nowhere. Murphy introduced new products such as Lite beer, upgraded Miller's distribution network, and spent advertising dollars freely. His strategy increased Miller's sales more than ninefold to $1.8 billion and challenged the nation's king of beers, Anheuser-Busch, Inc. Under Murphy, Miller jumped from seventh place, with 4 percent of the beer market, to second place, with 19 percent.[20]
4   *Market penetration:* increase sales by new pricing strategies. This strategy is not widely used, because the competition will rarely allow one firm to take market share on pricing moves: If you can do it, they will do it. However, it can be used if one firm has a pricing advantage. One example was Texas Instruments (TI), which used a learning curve pricing strategy to move into the watch market. It was able to assemble solid-state watches at an extremely low cost. With high-volume sales, TI was able to gain a significant share in a market dominated by others by offering a $10 digital watch. TI also attempted to apply a similar strategy to the computer market, but it failed to understand the market and has since withdrawn from both markets.

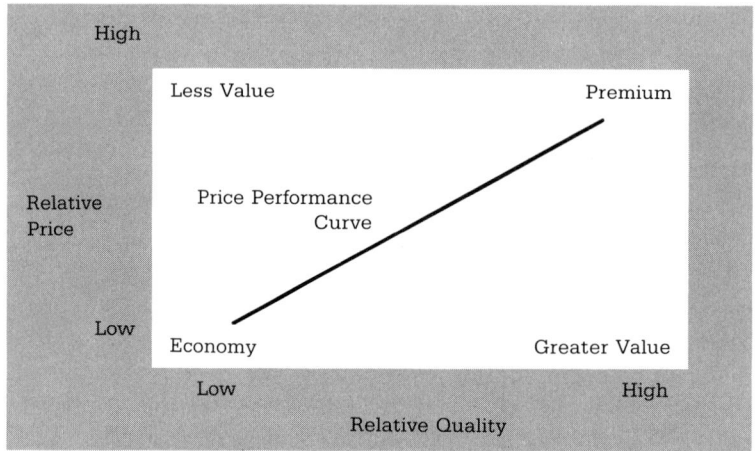

FIGURE 5.2
The Price/Performance Curve

5 *Product development:* increase price/performance. A final strategy is to improve product quality or performance. In a dynamic market, competitors may introduce products with a higher or lower price, changing its position on the price/performance curve as shown in figure 5.2.[21]

Concentric Diversification

When a firm can no longer grow through market penetration, it must add new products or markets. If a firm grows by adding related products, it is termed a *concentric diversification strategy.*[22]

Conglomerate Diversification

Conglomerate diversification is a growth strategy in which a firm seeks to diversify into products completely unrelated to its current product line. ITT is one example of a firm that used a conglomerate strategy to grow, as it manages some 265 different companies in a range of industries. Conglomerate diversification takes place for the same reasons as concentric diversification. Last year alone some 2,543 acquisitions took place for a staggering $122 billion.[24]

Norman Berg of Harvard University has identified some of the differences between diversified firms and conglomerates. His definition of a *conglomerate* is a firm which has at least five or six divisions which sell different products principally to external markets rather than to each other. Berg pointed out that conglomerates have diversified rapidly, primarily through mergers and acquisitions, into products unrelated to their prior business. In terms of growth in sales and earnings over the past ten years, Berg suggested that many conglomerates have far outpaced their

Strategic Changes for Kodak

For over a decade, Eastman Kodak Chairman Colby H. Chandler had been hearing arguments for breaking up Kodak's monolithic, bureaucratic management structure into smaller groups better able to adapt to fast-paced markets. He began a broad analysis of the company's management structure and practices.

Kodak polled its managers and called in outside consultants. McKinsey & Co. invited managers to test out scenarios that might cause problems. Finally, Chandler reshuffled Kodak's core photo business into seventeen entrepreneurial units—much as he had expected to do all along.

Such a measured approach to change has been the very essence of Kodak. In the last decade, Kodak dragged its feet while competitors ran away with new markets such as instant photography, 35-mm cameras, and video recorders. As growth in Kodak's photographic products slowed and as earnings suffered, Chandler recognized the need to expand into new business. "It's essential that we take more risks," he says. "We didn't need to take risks in the past."[23]

Chandler and his consultants identified "performance gaps" in several key areas and the need for a more entrepreneurial approach. In the past, Kodak favored caution over risk. Now, young managers have authority over new products, and decisions can now be made in a matter of days. By opting for a decentralized management, Kodak abandoned its traditional structure in which each executive reported through a separate chain of command. Decisions would have to filter up the management ladder, often taking months or years.

One of Kodak's greatest challenges will be managing its many new ventures, something it has muffed in the past. Still, Kodak's diversifications are minimal so far. Industry experts believe the company needs to make even larger acquisitions to build market share in fields such as electronics and biotechnology.

Indeed, the company is moving away from consumer electronics, such as its 8-mm video camera market, to focus its attention on nonconsumer applications of electronics. So far, the impact of such new technologies on the bottom line has been negligible. But in fifteen years, electronics could make up fully half of Kodak's business.

Will Kodak's diagnosis bring about the desired changes, and will Kodak's managers, trained in the company's staid old ways, be able to break out of its ineffective patterns?

---

more mature counterparts.[25] But the overall record of companies merged in recent years is not encouraging. In fact, one out of three mergers later fails.

Berg also suggested that conglomerate management style has three distinctive characteristics.

1 Conglomerates have much smaller central offices than diversified firms.
2 Conglomerates tend to place most major operating decisions at decentralized divisional levels.
3 Conglomerates' division managers are autonomous as long as the division delivers (i.e., is profitable).

By placing responsibility where it belongs—at the divisional level—conglomerate managers can evaluate performance better and do not become involved in operating decisions at lower levels of the organization.

The conglomerate strategy allows rapid growth primarily by purchasing (acquiring) other companies for stock when the conglomerate's stock is at a much higher price/earning ratio than that of the target company's stock. A merger occurs when two organizations literally merge all resources (human included). Acquisition occurs with outright purchase or through a stock-swap takeover.

There are many possible objectives underlying the selection of a conglomerate diversification strategy. The company may feel too dependent on one industry, such as the case of TWA, or may wish to move into higher-growth areas. Large-scale acquisition for the purpose of planned entry into a new industry is often a major strategy for corporate growth. Through forcing structural changes of business and management, it creates a synergistic condition—the addition of the parts is greater than the whole. The major objectives of conglomerate strategy include

Increasing the rate of growth   An exceptional company can grow internally at a 20 percent annual rate, yet the LTV Corporation averaged a 51 percent rate of growth over a ten-year period by using a conglomerate strategy. Teledyne (another conglomerate) averaged a 52 percent growth rate while acquiring 150 companies.[26]

Increasing the value of the company's stock   An effective acquisition can often result in an improved price/earnings ratio and a higher stock price. Litton's stock, during Tex Thornton's acquisition period, increased from about $15 per share to about $150 per share, including several stock splits.

Using excess cash to buy into high-growth or high-technology markets   Harry Gray's acquisition of Mostek, a small but highly innovative semiconductor company, is an example of buying into a new technology. He believed that a semiconductor company would give United's product designers a winning edge on the competition. "In the long run, every piece of equipment we manufacture is going to be controlled by microprocessors," said Gray. "The main reason we bought Mostek is to let the designers know what is possible to do now and what it will be possible to do, at what cost, in the next three, five, or ten years."[27] Some simply use excess cash to acquire other companies. Mobil Corp., for example, acquired Montgomery Ward, but has since tried to sell it off after losing millions.

Increasing financial synergy   Sometimes a highly leveraged company can merge with a low-debt company to the benefit of both. Also, experts on takeovers often seek companies with high cash positions.

Decreasing risk or increasing stability   A company in the defense industry may diversify into consumer products to spread the risk of economic downturn or diversify into countercyclical fields, thus reducing essential or cyclical fluctuation and stabilizing earnings. TWA's diversification program was aimed at smoothing out the wild, cyclical fluctuations of the airline industry.

Improving product line by expanding into new products or markets   Philip Morris's diversification into foods and beverages allowed it to expand its product line and yet build on its existing marketing skills and techniques, thus reducing its dependency on tobacco-related products.

Mergers and Acquisitions

The major method of conglomerate diversification is by merger or acquisition, although these methods may also be used in a concentric growth strategy. In this sense, merger or acquisition is a technique for accomplishing an accelerated level of growth by acquiring other firms. A *merger* refers to combining two firms into one. In an *acquisition,* one company purchases the assets of another and absorbs it into its own operations.

Mergers and acquisition can be accomplished in a number of ways and by several different techniques. The biggest single distinction is probably between cooperative (friendly) and hostile (takeover) mergers or acquisitions. The *friendly merger* is between two companies who agree upon the benefits of the acquisition and work together to achieve it. The *hostile merger*, often called a *takeover*, involves one firm forcefully acquiring a firm that is resisting the attempt. In this case, the "raider" gains control of the majority of the stock, displaces the current management, and puts its own plans into effect.

There are several methods of acquisition:

1   Purchase of stock on the open market at somewhat over the current trading price
2   Purchase of assets for cash
3   Purchase of assets for stock
4   An exchange of stock.   Frequently the relative values of the two firm's stock prices are considered or an equitable exchange worked out. For each two shares of company Y, one will receive three shares of company Z. The result is a share of ownership in the combined company of equal or greater value than that held in the former corporate entities.

According to one study, stock was used in 35 percent of all acquisitions, cash in 32 percent, and a combination of cash, stock, and debt in 33 percent.[29]

In using external expansion, however, a clear-cut business purpose is only part of a successful acquisition strategy. The takeover.climate has become so competitive that every corporation interested in acquisitions is finding it necessary to arm itself with the best advice and personnel available and to proceed in a careful and systematic manner.

The Corporate Raiders

Corporate raiders is a term used to describe the new wave of corporate takeover experts who are building huge personal fortunes by taking control of undervalued corporations. T. Boone Pickens (chairman of Mesa Petroleum and king of the corporate raiders) and other raiders have built large personal fortunes by taking over these undervalued companies. The raiders, heroes and modern-day Robin Hoods to some, sharks and predators to others, are the street-smart financiers who are currently shaking up the business world. They are power-hungry game players who are creating a shake-up in management and a redistribution of assets in large firms.

The fear of takeover is even changing corporate strategy. Managers are sacrificing long-term earnings for short-term gains, restructuring their companies, and even paying ''greenmail'' (paying a premium price for the company stock) to defend themselves from unfriendly investors. The raiders look for undervalued firms, mainly poorly managed companies that have failed to adjust to an upheaval in their business, and then purchase stock to gain a controlling interest.

How do the raiders accomplish all this? Well, it isn't easy although at times they make it look easy. Basically, this approach to acquisition involves maximizing the use of leverage; that is, borrowing money and then getting a higher return than the interest cost. The raider's method involves the following:

1 Borrowing under favorable terms
2 Analyzing and selecting an undervalued target
3 Acquiring a controlling interest in the target company
4 Splitting the acquired company into several autonomous parts
5 Keeping any desired (profitable) segments, then spinning off or divesting the remaining parts
6 Using the acquired cash to pay back the loan, plus making a sizable profit

To defend against raiders, corporate managers ask shareholders to approve anti-takeover measures, termed *shark repellant* or *poison pill* maneuvers. These include:

1 Requiring 70 percent to 80 percent, or super majority, stockholder votes to approve a takeover
2 Forcing the acquirer to sell stock in the merged entity at half price to existing shareholders
3 Issuing a new debt to equity holders as soon as a minority stockholder acquires a substantial portion of the firm's stock
4 Finding a friendly acquirer (a white knight) to purchase a controlling interest on friendly terms

5   Setting forth high payments (golden parachutes) to existing executives in
    case of a takeover

Despite these defenses, the merger-takeover strategy continues because the cost
of acquisition is less than starting a business from scratch.[28]

There are also certain pitfalls in the merger integration process. Alex De Noble
of San Diego State University has suggested several potential problems, including
low executive involvement, a breakdown in the reporting controlling relationship,
changes in the level of responsibility, and the attitude of members of the acquired
firm.[30] The seven basic problems of mergers are

1   Paying too much for the acquired company
2   Assuming market growth will continue
3   Leaping before looking, inadequate merger planning
4   Straying too far afield into businesses not well understood
5   Acquiring something too big to be successfully managed
6   Merging conflicting corporate cultures
7   Losing key managers. It is estimated that over half of top management leaves
    within three years of an acquisition.

A study by McKinsey & Co. of 58 major acquisitions between 1972 and 1983 examined two factors:

1   Did the return on the amount invested exceed the cost of capital?
2   Did they outperform the competition in the stock market?

The findings indicated that twenty-eight of the fifty-eight (48 percent) failed both
factors. They reported that mergers into unrelated businesses were most likely to
fail.[31]

Acquisition is becoming an increasing popular and complex strategy. Despite
the popularity, research indicates that almost half of all acquisitions fall short of
expectations. Several factors can significantly increase chances for success:[32]

1   Developing a comprehensive diversification plan as part of an overall corporate
    development strategy
2   Acquiring a firm that meets sound strategic and economic criteria—not what is
    available
3   Understanding the business being purchased strategically, its industry position,
    the competitive advantages, possible competitive reactions to the acquisition,
    and any changes in strategy
4   Understanding opportunity and having the resources to develop it and the man-
    agement commitment to take advantage of it

5 Evaluating the management of the acquisition candidate for competence, style, energy, and motivation. Experienced management is important, but the fit with your own corporate culture and values is equally important.

6 Determining the price beyond which the deal ceases to be attractive. Almost any company can be bought at some price. The key is to purchase at a price that allows for an attractive return.

A recent study by Galbraith and Stiles suggests a statistically significant relationship between merger strategy and relative market power.[33]

Vertical integration, another strategic alternative, is a growth strategy that involves the expansion of the business by moving backward or forward from the present product level. *Backward integration* refers to moving lower on the production process scale, so that the firm is able to supply its own raw materials or basic components. If McDonald's decided to buy cattle ranches and supply its own beef, this would represent backward integration. Another example of a primarily retail firm integrating down the scale is the move by Revco (a retail drug company) into manufacturing its own pharmaceuticals.

Forward integration is the other side of the coin and refers to moving higher up on the production/distribution process, toward the end consumer. If a cattle rancher were to open his own meat market or fast food restaurant and sell directly to the consumer, then this would be forward integration. For example, Xerox Corporation launched a nationwide chain of plushly appointed office equipment retail stores. The stores, which sell small copying machines, word-processing equipment, small computers, and telephone-answering devices, are aimed at the huge market of small businesses and move Xerox closer to the end consumer.

There are a number of reasons why firms might use the vertical integration strategy, including

1 *Economies of scale*   Firms may feel that by increasing scope they may reduce overall costs.

2 *Supplier dependability*   This lessens the influence of uncertain supplies and of price variation in raw materials.

3 *Better cost and quality control*   Cost efficiencies of stable operating level and quality level improve.

4 *Less dependence on uncertain suppliers*   Preventing possible shortages or loss of supply sources. For example, some firms who buy solid-state electronic components from Texas Instruments often find orders are delayed because TI cannot fill all orders and meet internal requirements.

5 *Increase in overall profit margins*

Joseph Vesey of Harvard University found that certain characteristics were associated with companies making successful use of vertical integration. These firms had

1 Sales of $1 to $2 billion which were highly diversified

2 Relatively few new products

3   Low investment per employee
4   Relatively concentrated customers (forty or more customers represented 50 per-
    cent of the business)
5   Low product value—the products produced are "unimportant" financially to the
    customers.[34]

Vesey also found that backward integration led to higher profit perfomance than
forward integration.

The Neutral Strategy

A neutral or satisfying strategy involves a continuation of past strategy or an incremental improvement in performance. In essence, companies using this strategy are
satisfied with the way things are going and hesitate to make drastic changes. Such
companies are usually dominant in their fields or in a relatively stable external
environment. These strategies may be termed "don't rock the boat" or "steer a
steady course" approaches to strategic decisions.

      This strategy is often used by companies like Coca-Cola or Anheuser Busch,
who hold a commanding lead in their industries and want to keep on doing what
they have been doing. However, such firms are also often what might be termed
counterpunchers. They are satisfied with the way things are going, but if a corporation starts to cut into their market share they will react aggressively.

      Often a neutral strategy is adopted after a company has been through a period
of rapid growth. For example, John B. Fery, CEO of Boise Cascade, and Doug
Danforth of Westinghouse attempted to solidify their firms' positions following high-
growth eras. Their emphasis has shifted to profitability rather than growth.

      The neutral or satisfying strategy is used when a firm is satisfied with its past
performance (sometimes unwisely so) and decides to continue with objectives in
line with prior achievements. The reasons for this relatively low-risk approach include:

1   The firm is already doing well. Why change or tamper with success?
2   The management may not wish to take the risk of greatly modifying its strategy
    but just keeps on doing what it has been doing. Some researchers have noted
    that too much growth too fast can lead to ineffectiveness.[35]
3   The firm is in the satisfying mode, and the current level of change is good
    enough. If the level of change for the industry is low, then a high-growth strategy
    may not be necessary. Arnold Cooper of Purdue University found that in many
    industries, firms with steady growth are more effective.[36]
4   The firm is unaware of changes in its environment. Sometimes a firm is simply
    unaware that it is not keeping up with the competition and so continues on the
    neutral course.

      There are two variations of the neutral strategy, termed holding and harvest-
ing. A *holding*, or sustainable growth, strategy may be defined as a steady rate of

growth but at a slower rate than that of the external environment. This strategy is usually followed by large, dominant firms, in a mature industry, where the goal is maintenance of position rather than rapid growth.

Often, a firm pursuing this strategy concentrates on one product but does this well. The firm grows slowly and incrementally by means of greater market penetration and slow addition of new products.

Some firms that use a holding strategy do so to pursue a low market share in their industry as a whole. Richard Hammermesh of Harvard University found that firms like Union Camp achieve excellent return-on-invested-capital objectives by effective market segmentation and operating efficiency and by lowering production and distribution costs.[37] A low-market-share firm is defined as one with less than half the industry leader's share. A characteristic of successful low-market-share companies is that they are content to remain small and emphasize profits rather than growth.

No product or market can grow indefinitely. A *harvesting* strategy is followed when the main objective of the firm is to generate cash for the corporation or stockholders. Harvesting is a decision to reduce investment in a business in the hopes of cutting costs and/or improving cash flow. Often market share is sacrificed to generate cash for other purposes. Firms like Carnation use a harvesting strategy to limit the amount of investment provided and to maintain market share.

Nothing much changes at Carnation Company. On the top floor dining room, Carnation's top managers still gather for their midday meal and drink milk. Earnings have risen annually for thirty-one years, the firm's 18 percent return on equity is among the food industry's highest, and the firm has some $250 million in cash. Now changes may be on the way as president and CEO Timm F. Crull, an outgoing and aggressive marketing expert, takes over, stepping up the company's growth and diversification. Otherwise, a takeover could be expected.[38]

Philip Kotler of Northwestern University suggested that a harvesting strategy will work if:

1   The business entity is in a stable or declining market
2   The business unit doesn't provide sales stability or prestige to the firm
3   The business entity's market share is small and it would be too costly to increase
4   The business does not contribute a large percentage to total sales
5   Sales will decline less rapidly than the reduction in corporate support[39]

The strategist must be aware that the market does not remain static. The nature of the market and competitors can change rapidly. Products mature or are surpassed by innovations. The firm may achieve a dominant position in one segment but still may be forced to look elsewhere.

Kathryn Harrigan and Michael Porter of Harvard University have described the harvesting strategy as an endgame strategy. They indicated that some firms have successfully profited from careful management of products which most firms felt were obsolete.[40] The functional strategies used by the successful endgame players include the ability to:

1   Dominate market share
2   Hold market share (relative to competitors)
3   Shrink selectively (get out of unprofitable segments)
4   Milk the investment (harvest strategy)
5   Divest now (sell before asset value shrinks too much)

The Defensive Strategy

The *defensive* strategy is the least used strategy, selected by only 7.5 percent of the firms studied. The use of defensive strategies, also termed *retrenchment,* is generally a reaction to operating problems stemming from either internal mismanagement or unanticipated actions by competitors. These strategies are used when the market is saturated or declining, the company is in trouble, and during economic recession or financial crisis. Survival is often the goal of a defensive strategy. In general, it is a short-run strategy used to weather the storm during periods of recession, financial strain, or inadequate performance.

Defensive strategies are generally used because of necessity, not by choice. There are reasons for using defensive strategies.

1   *The firm is doing poorly*   When A&P, the giant retailer, suffered lower earnings and profits, it closed down unprofitable stores and operations. In this way the company closed over one-third of its stores to halt the decline.
2   *The firm suffers major losses on one product*   General Electric, doing very well as a company, was losing heavily, about $10 million per year, in its computer business. Consequently, it got out of this business.
3   *The firm's survival is threatened*   At times a firm may find its very survival is in doubt, and some very drastic actions must be taken. Two recent examples of such firms include Lockheed and Chrysler, both of whom obtained government-backed loans to stay in business. When James H. Maloon became CEO of Itel, his top priority was "survival, period."

There are a number of possible alternatives within the defensive strategy mode. The *turnaround* or *retrenchment* strategy, as the name implies, is aimed at halting a firm's decline and improving its long-term efficiency. The short-term strategy is focused on cost reduction, while long-run strategy may be aimed at growth or holding strategies. The turnaround strategy usually emphasizes cost-cutting, personnel reductions, closing inefficient plants, or even closing out unprofitable products.

Dan Schendel of Purdue University found in a study of some fifty-eight firms that only about 20 percent of them actually changed prior strategy, while the majority (about 80 percent) applied some form of cost-cutting techniques.[41]

Since Lee Iacocca took charge at Chrysler, he has taken some basic steps to turn the company around. He has:

1   Reduced salary expense dramatically
2   Reduced fixed costs by closing old or obsolete plants
3   Simplified operations in its manufacturing system, cutting inventory cost by $1
    billion
4   Launched an all-out program to improve product quality
5   Restructured its balance sheet, converting debt to preferred stock
6   Embarked on a $6 billion product development program

Iacocca got Chrysler's financial house in order, got costs in line, cut break-even costs, and developed an exciting array of new products: a classic turnaround.[42]

If cost reduction methods don't solve the problems, the next strategic move may be necessary: the strategy of *divestment*, or selling, of part of the business in order to increase overall profitability. The divestment strategy is often the outgrowth of previous expansion or acquisition strategies which have resulted in a serious decrease in profits or cash flow for the firm.

General Electric, for example, entered the computer industry because it was a high-growth field. However, General Electric found that it could no longer afford the heavy drain on its financial resources and so decided to exit from that industry. As might be expected, divestment, like the turnaround strategy, is aimed at improving long-term efficiency by selling off unprofitable segments of the business.

There are many reasons for selecting this strategy. Profits may be lower than in alternative sources of investment, the market share may be too low, the market growth potential may be too low, the cash investment required to stay in the game may be too high, or the product may not fit with the total product line.

As the trend toward mergers increases, the number of divestitures also increases. A growing number of companies are slimming down and narrowing their focus by chopping out divisions and product lines that don't fit into a comprehensive corporate strategy.[43]

Divestment is often a difficult decision to make because (as was the case at GE) there has usually been much effort, investment, and commitment put into making the project succeed. GE had several plants with thousands of loyal employees and was reputed to have some of the strongest technical expertise in the field. Michael Porter of Harvard University has pointed out several of the factors that inhibit a decision to divest, including that it is often taken as a sign of failure or as a setback or a loss, and no one likes that.[44]

Divestment is often selected after there is a change in the management. The new manager does not have a proprietary interest in earlier decisions or in defending past errors in judgment. A study of three divestment case histories found that in all three cases a change in top management was required before the companies would divest unprofitable businesses. There is also evidence to suggest that divestment strategy is a way of increasing the value of the firm.[45]

At International Harvester Donald D. Lennox has been striving to save his firm from bankrupty. The outcome of his strategy is not yet certain, but at least International Harvester stands a chance of turnaround. In 1983, when Lennox took control, the plants were outdated, markets and sales were declining, and a heavy debt load of $4 billion placed the firm in jeopardy. However, since then, Lennox has sold off seventeen businesses, slashed headcount and payroll by more than 32 percent, and closed down inefficient operations, cutting costs by $1 billion per year.[46]

The most drastic defensive strategy is *liquidation*: the selling off of the entire company or liquidation of its assets. Although there are rare situations in which a company is "worth more dead than alive" and management chooses to sell out, this strategy is generally a last resort. There simply is no other way out. This strategy is obviously unpopular and is used only when there are no other feasible alternatives. For example, W. T. Grant, once a successful discount store with over 1,100 stores, was forced to liquidate.

In the ten months following his acquisition of Diamond International, corporate raider Jimmy Goldsmith sold off or negotiated sales of virtually all of its operations for total proceeds of $1.326 billion. After deducting the acquisition costs, Goldsmith stood to gain over $500 million in profits.[47] This undervalued company is an example of one whose assets were worth more in liquidation than in market value.

The defensive strategies which have been described are among a range of possible alternatives. In general, they are the hardest strategies to follow because their use suggests that earlier strategies have failed. However, often firms that are reluctant to use such strategies are taken over by other companies whose first move is to apply these approaches as a means of turning a so-called loser into a winner.

The Mixed Strategy

The *mixed* or *combination* strategy involves using elements of two or more basic strategies at the same time in different segments of the organization. If a firm is operating in several markets that are changing at different rates or if its products are in varying stages of the product life cycle, then a mixed strategy may be necessary.

The mixed strategy was the second most popular strategy among *Fortune* 500 firms (28.7 percent), according to a study by the late William Glueck.[48] It is most frequently used in large, multidivision companies and is typically selected to optimize the firm's profitable elements and minimize the effect of its losses. Such a strategy usually involves a growth strategy in certain divisions or product lines and harvesting or defensive strategies in others.

Westinghouse, for example, has adapted to changes in its environment after a period of growth, which emphasized increasing volume without regard to risk. CEO Doug Danforth tightened up operations by improving service, product quality, and worker productivity.

An example of a mixed or combination strategy is the approach of Doug Danforth of Westinghouse. First, he laid out several ambitious targets: yearly sales growth of 4 percent above GNP, operating margins of 8 percent to 9 percent, and record income in the next years. Danforth wanted to position his firm in what he terms the "winner's circle" of American corporations with superior financial performance and managerial excellence. He planned to shrink the traditonal, low-margin businesses and grow in higher-growth areas such as defense electronics. To improve the performance of any large business is a formidable challenge, but Danforth has accomplished much with a new strategy at an old-line firm.[49]

Time is the enemy of all strategic plans. From the time a strategic decision is made and implemented, it begins to become outdated. Therefore, for some firms, the mixed strategy provides a suitable approach for adapting to changing market conditions.

Mixed strategy is more appropriate in large multiproduct firms because a single strategy may not fit all products or markets. The times for using mixed strategies might include:

1   *When the firm has many different products and they are in different stages of the life cycle.* The strategy for an innovative, high-growth product should be different from that of a mature or declining product.
2   *During times of economic recession* there is often a need to tighten the belt in marginal or losing areas and concentrate on growth areas.
3   *When a firm reaches a certain size* there are often more opportunities than there are available resources. It is not possible to attack all markets with aggressive or growth strategies.

The mixed strategy, then, is usually used when a company has several businesses or products in differing stages of maturity. The purpose is to allocate resources to the high-growth and the high-potential areas of business, while reducing investment or selling off less profitable endeavors.

A Comparison of Strategic Alternatives

In the strategic decision process, the manager must consider a range of possible alternatives. These alternatives range from extremely aggressive and dynamic growth strategies to very defensive positions, including getting out of the business. Generally speaking, the appropriate strategy depends on the firm's position relative to external market and competitive positions and, of course, the firm's financial resources. A firm that has low cash resources will find it difficult to implement certain strategies, even though it might like to. In figure 5.3 a comparison of strategic alternatives is shown based upon two key variables: the potential market growth and the firm's competitive position.

Firms fitting the characteristics of quadrant 1, with weak competitive position and low-growth potential, would most likely select a *defensive* strategy. Because of the low probability for future growth, firms might look toward retrenchment or divestiture strategies and invest excess cash in areas where profit potential is greatest.

Those firms falling into quadrant 2, with a high market potential but with a weak competitive position, would most likely select some form of *mixed* strategy. In a high-growth field, there is an opportunity for the application of aggressive strat-

Characteristics	Possess Relative Corporate Strengths	Have Relative Corporate Weaknesses
Favorable Industry Traits for Endgame	"Dominate market" or "hold market share."	"Shrink selectively" or "milk."
Unfavorable Industry Traits for Endgame	"Shrink selectively" or "milk."	"Get out now!"

FIGURE 5.3
Matching Strategy and External Factors

egies, such as market penetration, or even diversification if the firm has the necessary resources. However, if the firm is not able to exploit such an opportunity, then it must consider the possibility of moving into other fields. In other words, in this situation, a firm must either aggressively seize the opportunity presented by the growth market and carve out a market segment or it should consider getting out of the field altogether.

Firms in quadrant 3, with strong competitive positions and low market growth, are most likely to select some form of *neutral* strategy, either a holding or harvesting approach, and use excess cash to invest in areas offering higher growth and return. In general, the firm tries to maintain its position and market share, with a minimum of investment, thereby generating cash for other strategic maneuvers.

Those firms in quadrant 4, high-growth and strong competitive position, generally should be using *growth* strategies, seeking to maximize market share and make it unattractive for competing firms to gain a foothold.

There are many factors to consider in the development of strategic alternatives, and each firm must consider the trade-offs, risks, and rewards associated with each possible option. Strategists consider the opportunities that are presented by the various markets, the firm's competitive strength, its financial resources, and possible moves and countermoves of its main competitors in shaping a master strategy.

BUSINESS-LEVEL STRATEGY

The business strategy focuses on how to compete in one particular business or market segment. Competitive advantage is the name of the game. This approach involves relating the analysis of competitive position and the underlying economics of the industry into a specific strategy. The basic strategies are similar to those at the corporate level and are based upon business and investment requirements.

1   *Offensive*   increasing share strategies and requiring large investments
2   *Neutral*   maintaining share or harvesting strategies requiring moderate investment levels
3   *Defensive*   decreasing or giving up share, or even exiting the market. This strategy involves minimum or no investment and may even generate new cash resources.

Michael Porter of Harvard University has identified three generic business level strategies:[50]

1   *Cost leadership* includes high-volume, large-scale facilities, cost control and reduction, and minimizing R&D and advertising. The basic strategy is to become the low cost producer in the industry.
2   *Differentiation* involves creating some special, unique product or service that provides a distinct separation from competing products. The name recognition of Mr. Coffee, for example, builds brand loyalty among customers. Differentiation seeks to gain advantage by offering distinct value to the consumer.
3   *Focus* strategies attack limited or specific target market segments and are similar to vertical marketing. The narrow-market focus is the means of gaining competitive advantage.

Mr. Coffee's New Product

Mr. Coffee is often associated with Joe DiMaggio, who did the TV commercials, but it is actually the brainchild of Vincent G. Marotta. Marotta developed the first coffee maker in 1972 and now holds some 40 percent of the drip coffee-maker market. Marotta recognized a market opportunity and used a market penetration strategy to build market share.

Marotta has introduced a new product to his existing market—a line of three special-blend ground roast coffees with the Mr. Coffee brand name. Marotta predicts his coffee will be a "blockbuster" product and he anticipates a 7 to 10 percent share of the $2.4 billion market within three years. His confidence comes from two factors: (1) name recognition and (2) a solid distribution system which is already in place. Vincent Marotta is betting some large advertising outlays that he can come up with another winner in a competitor's marketplace.[51]

Currently, Procter & Gamble, General Foods, and Nestlé control 60 percent of the market and many experts estimate that it takes $50 million in advertising to win an additional one percent of market share. Vincent Marotta is trying a differentiation strategy in an attempt to broaden his potential market.

The BCG Competitive Analysis Model

A technique similar to Porter's for analyzing business strategy is the matrix developed by the Boston Consulting Group as shown in figure 5.4. The assumptions underlying the BCG model are that (1) competitive advantage is necessary if the business is to be profitable, and (2) the ways to gain advantage vary by industry. The vertical axis identifies potential sources of advantage, and the horizontal axis presents the magnitude of the advantage. Each quadrant has certain strategy implications.[52]

In the *fragmented* sector, such as restaurants, there are literally thousands of kinds of advantages, but the size of the advantage is trivial. The suggested strategies are to minimize investment, improve profitability, and try to differentiate the product.

In the *specialization* quadrant, firms have large sources of advantage and many ways to achieve them. McDonald's is an example of a firm that moved from fragmented to specialized by concentrating on hamburgers and using large-scale advertising and low-cost production techniques. The strategy here is to maintain position and keep competitors out.

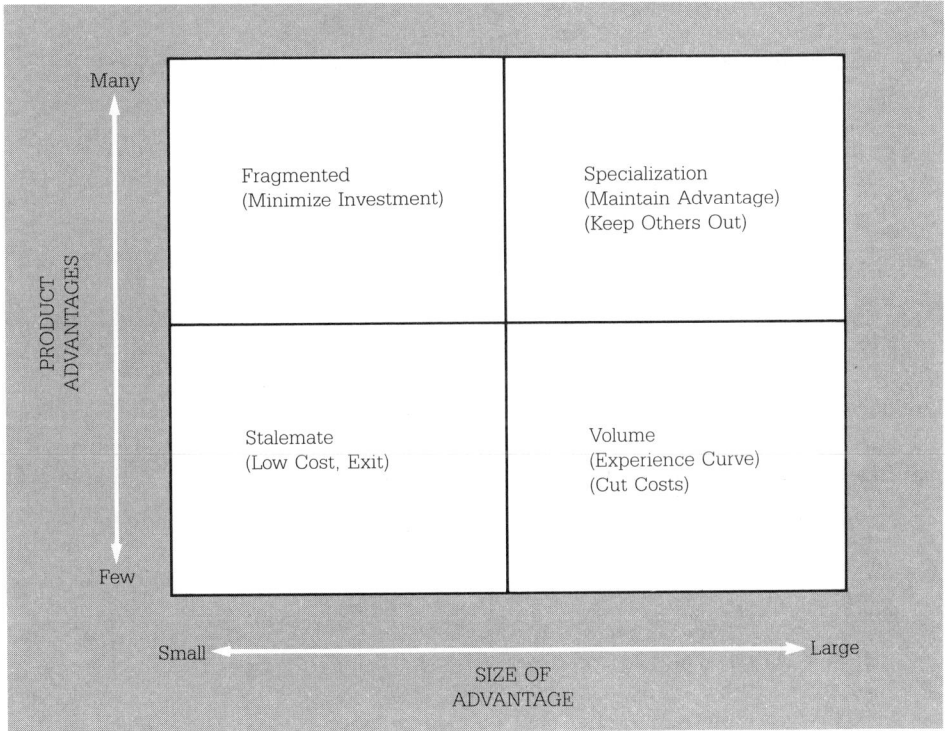

FIGURE 5.4
BCG 2 Model

SOURCE: Based on information presented by Alan Zakon to the Academy of Management, 1984.

Firms in *volume* industries have large advantages but few sources of advantage. In general these are commodity products so the advantage will be found in cost, as in steel and aluminum. The suggested strategy is to increase volume, use the experience curve, and cut costs.

Firms in the *stalemate* quadrant possess small advantages and few ways to achieve them. No one has advantage, so no one will be particularly profitable. The strategy here is to use intense cost control and reduction and look for the chance to exit—or to bail out.

This model allows the analysis of business strategy on the basis of the industry characteristics and finding a way to gain competitive advantage. Profit is the result of competitive differential.

MULTINATIONAL STRATEGY

In an era of rapid technological change and increasing international competition, the multinational firm occupies a unique position. Because of the diversity of national environments, the variety of products and markets, and the greater geographic dispersion, the multinational company faces a more complex array of strategic decisions.

The *multinational* company may be defined as a number of affiliated business establishments that function as productive enterprises in different countries simultaneously. To have such capacity the firm must possess host-country-based production units such as factories, mines, retail stores, insurance offices, banking houses, or whatever operating facilities are characteristic of its business.

Dow Chemical, one example of a multinational company with almost half of its revenues coming from outside the United States, demonstrates the increasing importance of the world environment in corporate strategy. To grasp the growing importance of multinationalism, the extent of the direct investment of the United States abroad increased more than two and one-half times from 1970 to 1980, while foreign trade doubled.

Organizations become multinational in order to expand potential markets and increase the alternatives which are open to them. They may apply a multinational strategy to benefit from cheaper labor costs, to gain access to scarce resources, or to compete more effectively with other companies. Multinational operations require new managerial strategies and more complex decision making than single-country businesses.

The expansion of multinational operations has significantly changed the strategic planning of many companies. There is a difference between a domestic company, which conducts business in a single country, an international export operation, which is based in one country but sells to others, and a multinational company, which is headquartered in one country but has subsidiary operations in many countries.[53] IBM, for example, markets multiple product lines in over 100 countries and claims a market share of 60 percent of the overseas data processing market.

The percentage of income from overseas generations is a significant factor. Profit potential more than national boundaries dictates the multinational manager's strategies. The rationale for such a multinational conglomeration is profit. This form of multinational interdependence literally explodes with strategic opportunities and threats.[54]

The integration of these diverse operations is an overriding problem. The distance and separation of units are barriers to effective communication and the volume of complex information that must be exchanged makes the nature of their interdependence even more complex. The high degree of differentiation caused by different cultures, languages, and currencies, in addition to the diversity of products and markets, causes integration to be difficult to accomplish. As a result, the multinational organization must find ways of organizing and managing to overcome these constraints.

Despite the inherent difficulties, nearly all large companies are involved in international or multinational business operations. There are many reasons why multinational operations have expanded. Donald A. Ball and Wendell H. McCulloch, Jr., categorized these as aggressive or defensive strategies.[55] *Aggressive* strategies support an attempt by the firm to:

1 Open new markets
2 Obtain higher profits
3 Acquire products for the domestic market (or *other* foreign markets)
4 Satisfy management's desire for expansion

Defensive strategies for expanding into international markets propose to:

1 Protect domestic markets
2 Protect foreign markets
3 Guarantee a supply of raw materials
4 Acquire new technology
5 Achieve geographic diversification
6 Seek politically stable bases for new operations

As these factors suggest, most companies move into multinational operations to increase the strategic alternatives available to them and to compete more effectively. For example, by moving into new markets, introducing new products, and adding capacity to produce old ones, Dow Chemical figures to add some 60 percent to its sales by 1990.

There are several types of international involvement, depending upon the circumstances which exist, ranging from export sales to full-scale subsidiary operations as indicated in figure 5.5. Each country and region of the world has unique characteristics, the observance of which is critical to operations. Managers must develop, devise, and implement structures, policy, and processes that best balance organizational goals with the local situation. The organizational form that is used is important in both an economic and cultural sense.

There is research evidence to support the evolution of the multinational organization. According to Daniels, Pitts, and Tretter, in a study of *Fortune* 500 firms,

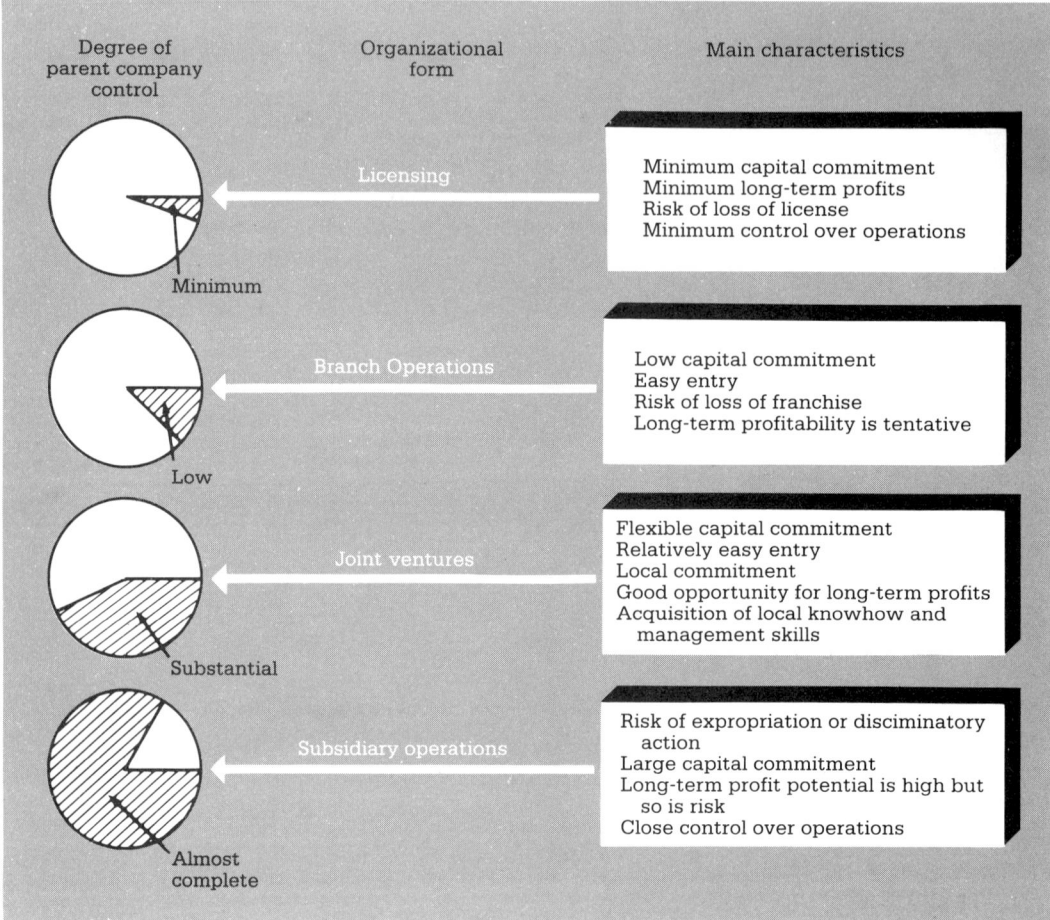

FIGURE 5.5
Basic Organizational Forms for Multinational Operations

SOURCE: G. John Hutchinson, *Management Strategy and Tactics* (New York: Holt, Rinehart and Winston, 1971), 508.

increasing dependence on foreign sales seems to be the major impetus for change from functional to worldwide product or to a matrix structure.[56]

Strategy for the multinational includes business-level strategy (the selection of markets, products, and segments), corporate-level strategy (managing a portfolio of businesses within national boundaries), and global strategy (matching worldwide business strategies against similar multinational corporations). The global strategy may suboptimize individual country markets to support thrusts in other geographic areas.[57]

William H. Davidson has identified two sets of factors as guides to selecting global strategies, as shown in figure 5.6. In the matrix, economic disadvantages,

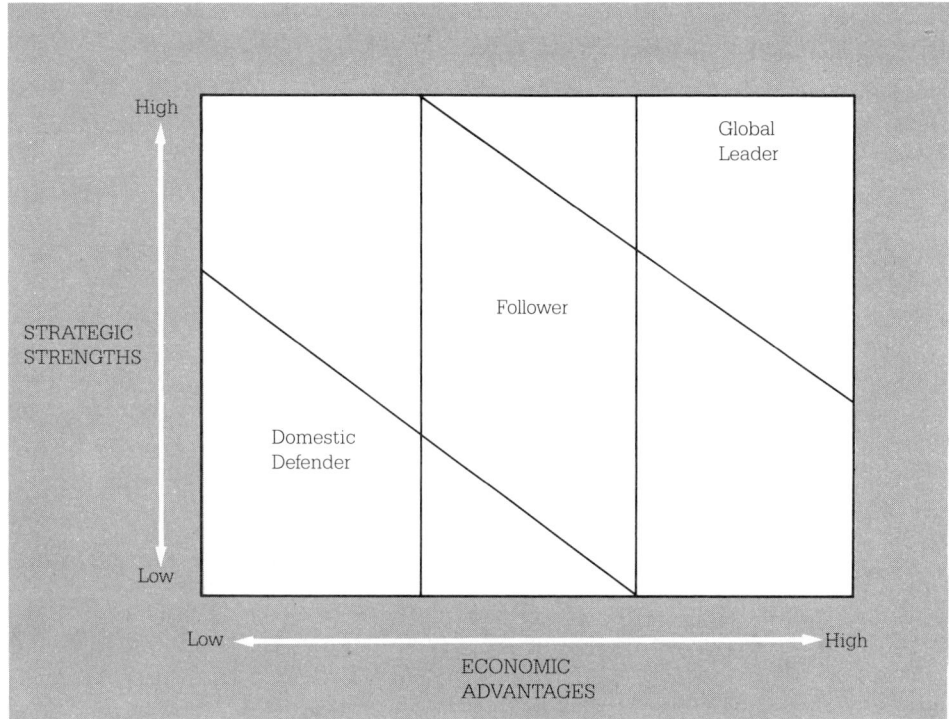

FIGURE 5.6
Global Strategic Factors

SOURCE: Adapted from D. Shanks, "Strategic Planning for Global Competition," *Journal of Business Strategy* 5 (Winter 1985): 84.

including labor, material, transportation, and energy costs, are plotted on the horizontal axis. On the vertical axis, strategic strengths are plotted, including skills in marketing technology, management, manufacturing, and information processing.[58] He suggested three possible global strategies:

1 *Domestic defender*   In the low sector in commodity markets, the prospect for global competition is low, so a strategy of defending the domestic market is used.

2 *Follower*   In the intermediate area, the challenge is to recognize how fast markets are developing so as to follow into emerging markets and preempt the competition. Being in too early may result in cash flow problems, while being too late may result in missing an opportunity.

3 *Global leader*   For firms in the high sector, an aggressive-growth strategy to gain product leadership is selected. Global competition is increasing and the expensive cost of strategic moves in the multinational arena has caused many firms to become more cautious in selecting a global strategy.

MANAGERIAL SUMMARY

During strategy formulation, management examines a variety of possible strategic alternatives. In this chapter, the major strategic alternatives for multinational business and corporate strategy have been presented. Strategy precedes planning. It deals with the options and directions that the organization will follow in the future. If more than one alternative is selected, then this strategy must be integrated into the cohesive framework. Once the strategist is able to compare the possible courses of action, it is possible to assess the likely outcomes and select the strategy that provides the best fit for that particular organization.

The identification of strategic alternatives emerges from the analysis done in preceding stages. From the environmental analysis, areas of growth and threat have been identified, and these are matched with the firm's competitive advantage profile. Out of this analysis evolves an assessment of the firm's current positition and an evaluation of the past strategy. The strategist must then decide whether to continue with a similar strategy or to change the game plan. Because the competitive environment is constantly changing and new areas of opportunity are emerging, new strategic alternatives need to be identified and evaluated.

If a change is necessary, there are a number of possible strategic approaches. Four different types of strategic alternatives have been presented: aggressive-growth, neutral, defensive, and mixed. Each strategy provides the firm with differing choices of action to meet differing situations and goals. These major strategic alternatives have been presented to enhance the reader's knowledge of possible strategic directions which organizations may pursue; however, there are many differing approaches, and those suggested should not be considered as all-inclusive.

The strategist makes many decisions about goals, decisions about markets and products, and decisions about strategies. The major strategic decisions, however, are important and far reaching and are often made under conditions of uncertainty. The strategic decision is a good one only if it is successful in achieving company goals. Better decisions are likely to be made when a range of possible strategic alternatives is examined to select the most appropriate strategy.

Often pressures toward short-term results create a tendency to concentrate only on current problems and crises at the expense of long-term perfomance. One of the advantages of strategic alternative evaluation is a consideration of these and other trade-offs and the possible consequences of each option.

Contingency approaches have grown in popularity because many strategic plans fail to take into account the changing environment. The crucial ''what if'' questions have caused strategic managers to include contingency approaches as a major factor in strategy selection.

The selection of a strategy is essentially a contingency decision. The best strategy will vary from industry to industry, from company to company, and from situation to situation. There is no simple set of strategic rules from which the manager can choose. Instead, the effect of many complex variables must be considered. There is an increasing emphasis on the development of contingency plans or scenarios for many possible future conditions, with varying strategic alternatives, depending upon the competitive situation.

This range of strategic alternatives highlights the variety of strategic options available and provides a framework for identifying and generating alternatives in a changing environment.

Multinational operations have been increasing in size and complexity for the past two decades, with emerging problems and opportunities. Organizations seek multinational expansion in order to broaden the scope of the options which are open to them, to obtain additional resources or labor, and to operate on a more effective competitive level.

Review Questions

1 Identify the basic strategic alternatives and their relative frequency of use.
2 Select a firm from an article in *Business Week*. Identify the strategy it is using.
3 Compare the use of mixed strategy with the use of a defensive or turnaround strategy.
4 Given the rate of potential market growth and relative competitive position for a local firm, suggest likely strategic moves for it.
5 Many analysts have pointed out that the fast food industry is in a slow-growth stage. What strategy might McDonald's, Burger King, or Wendy's use to meet these changing conditions?

Notes

1 Personal conversations with Bill Texido, 1984.
2 Based on "A Man Making Millionaires," *San Francisco Chronicle,* June 25, 1984; "A Plan for All Seasons," *Inc.,* 1983.
3 Ibid.
4 A. F. Ehrbar, "Henry Singleton's Mystifying $400 Million Flyer," *Fortune,* January 16, 1978, 66–67.
5 Joseph L. Bower, "Solving the Problems of Business Planning," *Journal of Business Strategy* 2, no. 3 (Winter 1982): 32.
6 James B. Quinn, "Formulating Strategy One Step at a Time," *Journal of Business Strategy* 1, no. 3 (Winter 1981): 42.
7 See H. Igor Ansoff, *Implementing Strategic Management* (Englewood Cliffs, NJ: Prentice Hall, 1986), 56–57.
8 William Glueck, *Business Policy and Strategic Management* (New York: McGraw-Hill, 1980), 290.
9 Adapted from "Caught in a Cash Crunch," *Fortune,* February 18, 1985, 70.
10 Ibid., 62–73.
11 Peter F. Drucker, *Management: Tasks, Responsibilities, Practices* (New York: Harper and Row, 1974), 77.

12 Jacques Maisonrouge, then president of IBM World Trade Corporation, quoted in *Harvard Business Review,* January-February 1972, 45.

13 "Up, Up and Away," *Business Week,* November 25, 1985, 80–83.

14 Bruce Henderson, *Henderson on Corporate Strategy,* (Cambridge, MA: Abt Books, 1979).

15 Robert Buzzell et al., "Market Share: A Key to Profitability," *Harvard Business Review,* January-February 1975, 97–106; see also William Hall, "Strategic Planning, Product Innovation and the Theory of the Firm," *Harvard Business Review,* Spring 1973.

16 Patrick Conley, "Experience Curves as a Planning Tool," in Robert Rothenberg, ed., *Corporate Strategy and Product Innovation* (New York: Free Press, 1977).

17 Fred Wittenbert, "Bigness vs. Profitability," *Harvard Business Review,* January-February 1970.

18 Peter Gutman, "Strategies for Growth," *California Management Review* 6, no. 4 (Summer 1964).

19 Michel Chevalier and Bernard Catry, "Don't Misuse Your Market Share Goal," *European Business,* Winter-Spring 1974, 43–50.

20 "Philip Morris: Turning 7-Up into the Miller of Soft Drinks," *Business Week,* April 2, 1979, 66.

21 Bradley T. Gale and Richard Klavans, "Formulating a Product Improvement Strategy," *Journal of Business Strategy* 5, no. 3 (Winter 1985): 21.

22 Ralph Biggadike, "Entry Strategy and Performance," *Proceedings, Academy of Management,* 1977; Charles Berry, *Corporate Growth and Diversification* (Princeton, NJ: Princeton University Press, 1975).

23 Quotation is from "Kodak Is Trying to Break Out of Its Shell," *Business Week,* June 10, 1985, 92; see also Clare Ansberry, "Analysts Speculate Kodak Is Considering Leaving 8-mm Video Camera Market," *The Wall Street Journal,* January 29, 1987, 8.

24 There is a large collection of literature on the subject. See David F. Linoes, *Managing Growth Through Acquisition* (New York: American Management Association, 1968), 105; Myles L. Mace and George G. Montgomery, Jr., *Management Problems of Corporate Acquisition* (Cambridge, MA: Harvard University Press, 1962).

25 Norman A. Berg, "What's Different about Conglomerate Management," *Harvard Business Review,* November-December 1969, 112–120.

26 See Rush Loving, Jr., "LTV's Flight from Bankruptcy," *Fortune,* June 1973, 134–145; "The Conglomerate Commotion," *Fortune,* May 15, 1969.

27 A. F. Ehrbar, "United Technologies' Master Plan," *Fortune,* September 22, 1980, 96.

28 See "The Raiders," *Business Week,* March 4, 1985, 80–90; and "Carl Icahn: Raider or Manager," *Business Week,* October 27, 1986, 89.

29 J. B. Young, "A Conclusive Investigation into the Causative Elements of Failure in Acquisitions and Mergers," *Handbook of Mergers, Acquisitions, and Buyouts* (1981), 605.

30 Alex F. De Noble, "An Analysis of the Association between an Acquiring Firm's Corporate and Business Level Strategies and Its Resulting Postmerger Managerial Decisions," Paper presented at Academy of Management, August 1984.

31 See "Do Mergers Really Work?" *Business Week,* June 3, 1985, 88.

32 Lionel L. Fray, David H. Gaylin, and James W. Down, "Successful Acquisition Planning," *Journal of Business Strategy,* 5, no. 2 (Summer 1984): 46.

33 Craig S. Galbraith and Curt H. Stiles, "Merger Strategies as a Response to Relevant Market Power," *Academy of Management Journal* 27, no. 3, 1984: 511–524.

34 Joseph Vesey, "Vertical Integration: Its Effect on Business Performance," *Managerial Planning,* May-June 1978, 11–15.

35 David Gerwin and Douglas Tuggle, "Modeling Organizational Decisions Using the Human Problem Solving Paradigm," *Academy of Management Review,* October 1978, 762–773.

36 Arnold Cooper et al., "Strategic Response to Technological Threats," *Proceedings, Academy of Management,* 1973.

37 R. G. Hammermesh et al., "Strategies for Low Market Share Businesses," *Harvard Business Review,* May-June 1978, 95–102.

38 "Carnation: Will a Corporate Recluse Come Out of Its Stall?" *Business Week,* August 6, 1984, 86.

39 Philip Kotler, "Harvesting Strategies for Weak Products," *Business Horizons,* August 1978, 17–18.

40 Kathryn Harrigan and Michael Porter, "A Framework for Looking at End-Game Strategies," *Proceedings, Academy of Management,* 1976; Kathryn Harrigan, "Structural Factors on the Exit Decision," *Proceedings, Academy of Management,* 1980.

41 Dan Schendel et al., "Corporate Turnaround Strategies: A Study of Profit Decline and Recovery," *Journal of General Management,* Spring 1976, 3–11.

42 See Lee A. Iacocca, "Turnaround Strategies," *Journal of Business Strategy* 4, no. 1 (Summer 1984): 67.

43 See "Splitting Up," *Business Week,* July 1, 1985, 50.

44 Michael Porter, "Please Note Location of Nearest Exit," *California Management Review,* Winter 1976, 21–33.

45 Surenda S. Singhvi, "Divestment as Corporate Strategy," *Journal of Business Strategy* 4, no. 4 (Spring 1984): 85.

46 "Harvester's Tough Boss," *Business Week,* July 1, 1985, 50.

47 Kinkead, G. "Jimmy Goldsmith's V.S. Bonanza" *Fortune,* vol. 108, October 17, 1983: 125–128.

48 Glueck, *Business Policy,* 290.

49 Based on "Operation Turn Around," *Business Week,* December 5, 1983, 124.

50 Michael Porter, *Competitive Strategy* (New York: Free Press, 1980), 34.

51 Based upon "Can Mr. Coffee's Own Brew Jolt the Giants?" *Business Week,* March 4, 1985, 76.

52 From a presentation by Alan J. Zakon, August 1983.

53 See Frederick Glueck, "Global Competition in the 1980's," *Journal of Business Strategy* 3, no. 4 (Spring 1983): 22.

54 James Leontiades, "Market Share and Corporate Strategy in International Industries," *Journal of Business Strategy* 5, no. 1 (Summer 1984): 30.

55 Donald A. Ball and Wendell H. McCulloch, Jr., *International Business: Introduction and Essentials,* 2nd ed. (Plano, TX: Business Publications, 1985) 39–48.

56 John D. Daniels, Robert A. Pitts, and Marietta J. Tretter, "Strategy and Structure of U.S. Multinationals: An Exploratory Study," *Academy of Management Journal* 27, no. 2 (1984): 247–270.

57 David C. Shanks, "Strategic Planning for Global Competition, *Journal of Business Strategy* 5, no. 3 (Winter 1985): 80.

58 William H. Davidson, *Global Strategic Management* (New York: John Wiley, 1982), 16.

CHAPTER SIX

Analyzing Corporate Strategy

OUTLINE

OBJECTIVES

After you have completed this chapter, you will be able to:

- define strategic gap, portfolio management, and experience curve concepts

- describe a framework for determining which alternative strategies are best for varying conditions

- discuss the proposed aims of differing alternative strategies

- compare the major strategic models and the differences in how these techniques are used

- identify the limitations associated with portfolio planning models

The growth strategy . . . being on the leading edge of every growth market . . . the driving force behind management selections of people . . . who can marry the products and services with changing markets, who understand the coupling of market niche with inherent GE strengths . . . and who possess the will and drive to make it work.

John Welch, Jr.,
Chairman and CEO of
General Electric

A New Strategy at General Electric

Jack Welch, Jr., chairman and CEO of General Electric, wants to transform his company into what he terms "world class competitors." Accelerating the development of growth businesses with innovation linked to markets will be the key to a new surge of growth.

Welch hopes to develop a new risk-taking culture at GE, with entrepreneurial style managers for each of the 250 businesses (SBUs), which are grouped into six product sectors. Because the pace of change is accelerating, GE is striving to move faster than the pack in each of its businesses to be sure they are on the leading edge of every market. Although GE is a big company (number nine on the *Fortune* top 500), it is made up of many small businesses, each of which possesses the same opportunities for entrepreneurship that exist in smaller, high-growth companies.

The new strategy places a greater emphasis on market share. Welch feels that market share is a critical measure of management because it represents the customers' evaluation of GE and is a function of competitive edge. He wants GE to be number one or two in all of its 250 businesses. Those that don't measure up will be candidates for divestiture in order to protect GE's reputation. GE has made a commitment for product quality and technological leadership.

Jack Welch put it this way: "We want to be a company that is constantly renewing itself, shedding the past, adapting to change."[1] In his book, that means concentrating on services and high-technology businesses. It also means keeping only those traditional businesses where GE can turn a respectable profit by dominating the market.

INTRODUCTION

In a turbulent and changing environment, managers like Jack Welch of GE are concerned not only with managing organizations as they exist currently, but also with developing new strategies to meet future conditions. New strategies do not happen accidentally. Instead, strategic alternatives are considered as options for allocating resources to best achieve overall corporate goals. These strategic decisions, such as the product leader strategy at General Electric, often represent a major alteration in organization directions and programs. Therefore, in stage five of the management process, strategic alternatives must be compared and analyzed prior to selecting an optimal strategy.

No organization can continue to apply the same strategy indefinitely. In an environment of change, any strategy will become ineffective or dysfunctional in accomplishing organizational goals. As a result, the organization, be it profit or nonprofit, must constantly reassess the environment for opportunities and reappraise its current strategic options.

Corporate strategy, as opposed to business unit strategy, is aimed at a higher level and is broader in scope. Top management is concerned with developing a total system of businesses that will all contribute to strategic position. Corporate strategy requires a careful allocation of resources. Some products will be increased, others harvested or liquidated, and new products will be added. Because this allocation process is similar to management of a financial portfolio, the term *portfolio management* is widely used to identify this form of managing.

In large corporations, such as IBM, ITT, or General Electric, the strategist must deal with several hundred distinct businesses and perhaps hundreds of differing countries and markets. Even in a smaller business, there are alternatives among products, customers, marketing methods, advertising techniques, pricing strategies, and so forth that must be decided. From these numerous possible strategies, a course of action must be selected and implemented.

In this chapter, a framework for comparing the various strategic alternatives will be discussed. This examination includes the major models for analyzing corporate strategy: the portfolio management models.

A FRAMEWORK FOR ANALYZING STRATEGIC OPTIONS

When Bill Texido, former CEO of Brae, assumed the leadership at American Sign and Indicator Company, his first move was to analyze the profitability of each product. He discovered that, in the past, no one had known precisely which products were profitable. Based on this assessment, Texido began a strategy aimed at phasing out older product lines and strengthening AS&I's position in new technologies. Similarly, when Jack Welch, Jr., took over as president of General Electric, he initiated a study to determine which products could gain larger market share and which could not. From this analysis, three major issues emerge:

1 Assessing the firm's current business portfolio positioning
2 Identifying the relative attractiveness and strength of each business
3 Determining how total corporate performance can be improved

These examples suggest that the evaluation of strategy in a complex organization is usually a multiple series of decisions, rather than one single decision. Strategic decision making involves examining various trade-offs and comparing alternatives in order to determine the best allocation of resources for maximum return.

At GE, Jack Welch, Jr., is known for his analytical decision making, his aggressive tactics, and his tough management style. Over a five-year span Welch has changed GE's strategy to focus on product quality, marketing, and innovation and has led GE into the top ten U. S. firms, with six product sectors and 250 SBUs. Like every strategist, Welch must consider how to allocate resources among these basic businesses to attain overall objectives.

There are many products, many competitors, and many possible actions. How does the manager select from all the possible strategic alternatives? The following sections present a framework for analyzing strategic alternatives.

Strategic Gap Analysis

Strategic gap analysis provides a mechanism for integrating the various products and businesses in multi-industry firms. The evaluative comparison of alternatives and options is a major determinant of long-term economic performance because these choices play a major role in allocating the firm's resources. Because of the impact on existing and potential strategies, it is essential that the evaluation of alternatives be accurate and complete in order to ensure that the proper course of action is selected.

The past decade has seen a widespread use of strategy analysis models; however, the models are not a substitute for strategic thinking. When properly used, the models can enhance the strategic planning process by helping to structure complex situations and to focus on important areas.[2]

The first step is to determine future results, assuming the current strategy (i.e., strategic mix of businesses) is continued relative to corporate goals. If there is a difference between the actual results and desired goals, then a *strategic gap* exists, as shown in figure 6.1. If such a gap exists, if current business strategies are not contributing sufficiently toward corporate objectives, then there are several possible actions which can be taken to reduce the differences.

1 *Change the business strategy of one or more SBUs* by gaining some type of competitive advantage (as discussed in chapter 4).
2 *Change the resource allocation among SBUs* by recognizing high performing businesses and allocating increased proportionate investment to these units.
3 *Add new businesses to the portfolio* to strengthen the mix of businesses.
4 *Delete some existing SBUs* if current businesses are in a weak competitive position or located in unattractive market segments.
5 *Change corporate performance goal levels.*

One other way to close the gap is to simply modify corporate goals to the levels projected with existing businesses. However, this solution is rarely satisfactory.

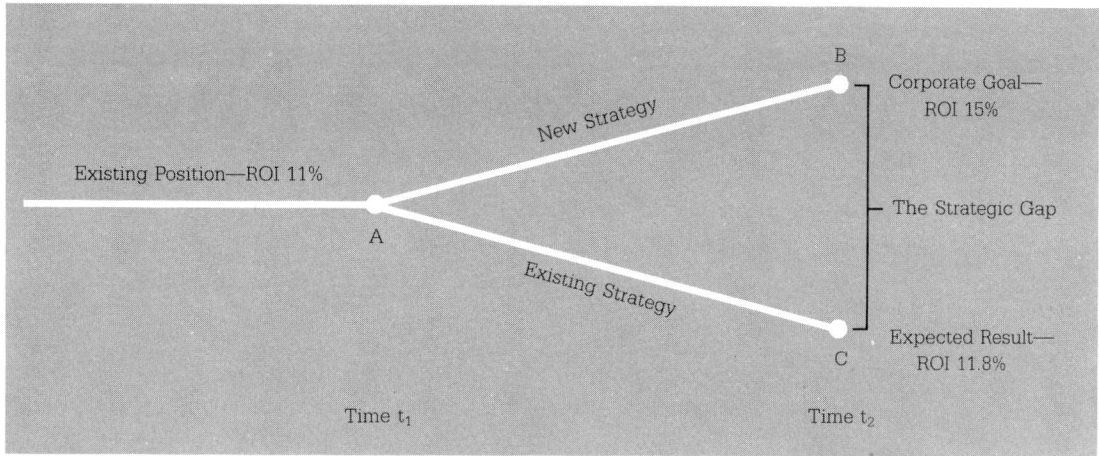

FIGURE 6.1
The Strategy Gap

The process of strategic gap analysis deals with two basic issues. Given the analysis of the emerging environmental conditions, how effective is the firm's existing strategy likely to be, and which of the possible strategic alternatives will be more effective in achieving desired goals? The outcome of the strategic evaluation process, then, is a strategy that will be most effective in positioning the firm in an uncertain future.

A solid strategy is evaluated by its probability of producing the desired short- and long-range results. A strategy that fails to consider changes is one that lacks future credibility. A strategy that is not supported by organizational activities at the coordinating and operational level is only partially effective and likely to suffer from weak implementation. As a result, an effective strategy must meet one basic test— is it workable?

How, then, do managers select certain strategies from an array of possible options? The purpose of critically comparing strategic alternatives is to ensure accuracy, feasibility, and compatibility between strategy and goals and to seek advantages that may be gained or synergies that may result from the way the firm deploys its resources. The managers of companies having a variety of products with differing life cycles, growth rates, and market shares often use *portfolio management* to find strategies that will optimize the company's long-run profits.

The Exxon Corporation doesn't really sell oil, chemicals, electronic typewriters, and motors; rather, it owns an array of companies that sell those things. It is, in effect, a fabulously wealthy investment club with a limited portfolio. Each year, it makes investments in thirteen affiliated companies that are expected to return that money plus a suitable profit. Those who can show they can make more with more, get more. Those who cannot, do not. It is just that simple, and just that complicated.[3]

The portfolio management strategy for a diversified corporation, such as Exxon, integrates several diverse considerations. The long-run strength and direction of combined businesses are the dominant criteria. Each of the various businesses is assigned a role derived from overall corporate goals. In the strategic plan, some businesses are aimed at rapid growth, while others are used to support this goal. Some businesses will be taking high risks, because the potential gains are high.

There are several portfolio models that can be used to evaluate strategic alternatives.

The Boston Consulting Group Model

The first of the analytical conceptual models which may be used to assist managers in making decisions about the overall deployment of resources is termed the *growth-share matrix*, or the *Boston Consulting Group (BCG) Model*.

The underlying concept of portfolio planning involves the allocation of resources according to a corporate strategic perspective of each of the businesses within the total portfolio. This model and others like it represent the first major advances in systematically identifying the main, underlying strategic characteristics of specific business segments. Each product and market segment is carefully analyzed as a separate business to determine its potential for sales growth and profitability. Each business may then be assigned to a specific substrategy; for example, growth, harvesting, or divestment within a comprehensive corporate plan (such as the Exxon example cited earlier). The resulting corporate portfolio of businesses should then be managed to optimize the allocation of resources within the firm.

At the center of a firm's business strategy is the issue of product and market segmentation. The analysis of a firm's scope of business interests provides a set of guidelines for developing present and future increases through the development and realignment of business segments. The BCG model is not confined to large corporations. The concept applies to small firms as well. In large firms, the portfolio can consist of businesses and products in several industries and markets. In a small firm, the portfolio revolves around products and markets.

Almost every company can find its businesses falling into one of the four basic types. Each type represents a firm's business interests. The specific form of a portfolio mix, however, affects the choice of strategic planning. These four types are summarized as follows:

1 *Single business*   Companies that are committed to a single business.
2 *Dominant business*   Companies that have diversified, but still focus the bulk of their resources into a single business.
3 *Related business*   Concentrically integrated firms in which diversification has been primarily accomplished by relating new lines to the major business.
4 *Unrelated business*   Companies that have diversified without regard to relationship between the new business and present activities. Conglomerate companies fall into this category.[4]

The Boston Consulting Group, under founder Bruce D. Henderson and Chairman Alan J. Zacon, uses the model to focus clients' strategy toward gaining the cost advantages of high market share. According to Henderson, "The BCG growth/share matrix cannot be applied to a company, administrative unit, or even a product line. To be of any value, it must be applied to the specific segments of a business. The segments must be defined as that combination of products, services, customers, and geography with respect to which that specific competitor has an absolute advantage compared to all other competitors. Even small businesses are composed of multiple segments with quite different characteristics."[5]

Henderson, a Tennessee native, believes that each market segment can support only about three competitors profitably. Thus BCG advises its clients to concentrate their businesses only in product areas where they are—or have a chance of becoming—number one or number two (or perhaps number three). If a product does not have this potential, it should be abandoned. Although Henderson and BCG have been arguing this case since 1966, it has become increasingly popular recently. Says one marketing professor at a Midwestern university, "Market dominance is the magic word in every management seminar today."[6]

There are three major advantages to be gained from using portfolio models. The models provide

1   A graphic display of relative business strengths and problems—a snapshot look at an entire business
2   An identification of cash flow generation and requirements
3   A tool to suggest strategic directions for each business

The essence of using portfolio models is to plan the movement of cash from one SBU to another.

The BCG model examines the structure of a firm's businesses in a continuous progression and is dynamic in nature. An optimal strategy enables a firm to position its resources to fully exploit business opportunities available as a function of competitive position in a given industry, market, or product. The BCG framework also provides a powerful tactical model. The strategist can estimate cash flows under a variety of pricing, cost, and growth conditions. In its design, the BCG model provides for a balanced strategic approach so that products have the synergistic force to resist business slowdowns and sustain long-term growth. In its management, the BCG model necessitates constant environmental scanning by the management of the changing characteristics and trends of industry and market needs so the strategist is able to redesign and realign business strategy as necessary. The BCG model is based on the application of two interrelated concepts, the experience curve and growth-share matrix.

The Experience Curve

The primary element underlying the model is the *experience curve theory*. This theory is based on the relationship between total cost per unit and the number of units produced (experience). The theory depicts that the unit costs of production, marketing, and distribution will decrease by 20 to 30 percent each time total output doubles. This decrease in cost with experience comes from economies of scale, improvements in labor, technology, and so forth. The BCG also found a relationship between cost and market share. The company that is able to produce more units than its competitors is bound to become the market share leader. Because of the greater volume of production, the market leader is farther down on the production curve than its competitors and therefore can turn out its product at the lowest cost. According to the BCG,

> Strategy is based upon competitive differences. If the experience curve permits you to confidently predict that one competitor can and should have a lower cost than another one, then the experience curve also permits you to predict that the low-cost competitor can and should displace the higher cost competitor if he provides identical products to identical customers with identical margins. That is the implication of the relationship between market share and the experience curve.
>
> It is an observable fact that companies make most of their profit from a very limited portion of their business. It is less obvious but equally certain that most of the profit is earned where the competitive advantage is the greatest.[7]

The experience curve is a rule of thumb. Its characteristic pattern is observable. *Value added* net unit production costs will characteristically decline 25 to 30 percent each time the total accumulated experience has been doubled. (This curve typically is plotted as a straight line on logarithmic coordinates.) The experience curve is based on the concept that people repetitively performing a task get better at it. In more technical terms, labor costs per unit decrease in a predictable manner with an increased volume of production.[8]

In the mid-1960s, Bruce Henderson and his colleagues at the Boston Consulting Group expanded this experience curve concept. They concentrated on total cost so that the vertical axis can be used as an index of total cost per unit. The horizontal axis, then, is used to plot the number of units produced or cumulative experience. The resulting slope, labeled the experience curve, can then be used to evaluate relative costs at various levels of production.

In order to establish market share, the product should be priced according to learning curve costs based on estimated volume. (Texas Instruments uses this pricing strategy.) This factor is *most* important for gaining large market share early.

The factors in this experience curve model include costs, volume, and market share. The greater the volume, the lower the unit cost; and the larger the market share, the larger the production volume. This model suggests a relationship between unit cost and the dynamics of market share. The company that has the greatest volume of production is operating farther down on the experience curve than its competitors. Consequently, the market share leader should be able to steadily increase its share at the expense of its competitors, whose unit cost should theoretically be higher. As an example, the relative production levels at B. F. Goodrich (4.5 percent), Sears (9.5 percent), and Goodyear (15.0 percent) are plotted on an experience curve in figure 6.2. Actually, of course, each firm is on its own experience curve, but Goodyear's profits have been higher than those of Goodrich, for example.

The BCG claims that the cost of most value-added items declines quite significantly each time accumulated experience doubles. Gerald Allan of Harvard University has suggested a number of factors that influence experience curves:

1   Labor efficiency
2   New processes and improved methods
3   Product redesign
4   Product standardization
5   Scale effect
6   Substitution in the product

The experience curve effect may be derived by dividing the accumulated costs by the accumulated product output. The economies of scale, the learning curve, critical masses of knowledge, and specializations all contribute to the result. The more experience a company has in producing a product, the lower its unit costs.[9] All

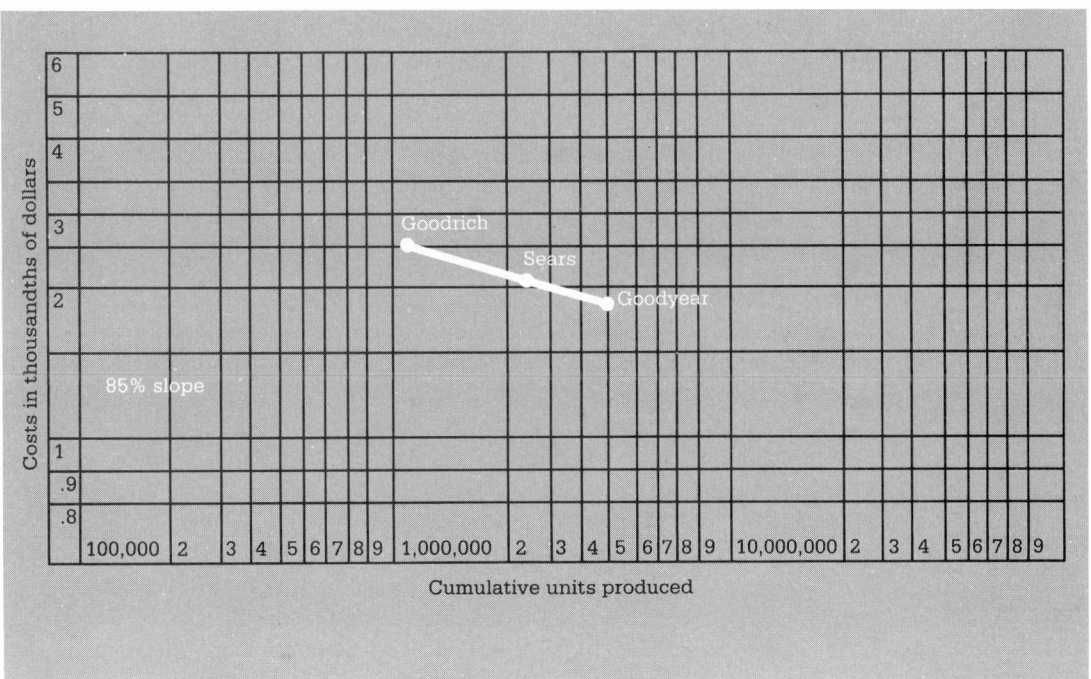

FIGURE 6.2
The Experience Curve Effect—An Illustration of Tire Companies

of the competitors in an industry come down the experience curve. The critical question is, who will become the low-cost producer in the fastest time?

The experience curve may be used as a basis for developing several strategic alternatives.

1 *Growth*   Expand market share as fast as possible to attain dominant position in the market.
2 *Divestment*   If the market share cannot be expanded and the firm is operating from a weaker cost position, then get out.
3 *Pricing down the curve*   By using the experience curve, a company can estimate probable costs at any given level of cumulative production. This information leads to a strategy of accepting lower profit margins in the short run in order to expand market share and perhaps the total market as well. The eventual outcome is an anticipated long-term increase in profitability.

Texas Instruments employed a pricing strategy based on high sales volume and relied on the concept of the experience curve. One example of pricing along the learning curve by Texas Instruments was its entry into the low-price digital watch market. The watch had to be simple in design and easy to assemble because millions had to be made annually to make a reasonable profit. This strategy of pricing down on the learning curve was an attempt to gain market penetration and maximize market share in a market long dominated by others.

As Richard Rumelt of UCLA has noted, although the underlying factors of experience curve theory are well established, the application is not so straight-forward.[10] The electronics industry appears to be an environment where the reality fits this model, but it is not so clear in other areas characterized by highly segmented markets with heavy brand advertising and promotion.

The Growth Share Matrix

The second element in the BCG model is termed the *growth-share matrix*. The growth-share matrix is a framework designed to provide a comparative analysis of businesses according to expected growth rates and relative market dominance.[11] In most instances, it is not possible for any one firm to gain full market dominance in all of its businesses. It is possible, however, to divide the market into a series of market segments and apply competitive advantages by concentrating on strategic market segments. A balanced strategy should include two basic features: (1) the identification and strengthening of the major market segments and (2) a common strategic pattern that relates the varied businesses into a total portfolio.

A firm's strengths lie in the main market segments from which it obtains its major revenues and in which it dominates the competition. This simple fact suggests that a firm should develop the main business segments for revenue, stability, and growth. No firm should allow these major markets to be neglected or unprotected, or it will find its position vulnerable and its growth and stability threatened. As Bruce Henderson has noted,

All misperceptions by competitors are strategy opportunities. The major un-known variable in strategy is the probable behavior and perceptions of com-petitors. If this were not true, all strategy would be merely an exercise in mathematical analysis. The ultimate creation of strategy depends upon the commitment of resources and reserves as investments in the future. The in-teraction of "competitive segmentation" and "experience curves" can provide a powerful insight into the most critical strategy factor of all: competitors' behavior.[12]

The main strength of the BCG approach is the assignment of a specific role or function for each product or segment and its integration into a total company strat-egy. Each product is evaluated in terms of its cash flow and growth potential, and the differences determine which products represent cash investment opportunities and which represent source of funds. The underlying strategy for relating varied businesses is the exploitation of competitive advantage. A company's advantages may consist of its production capability, its dominance of a specific market, its technological excellence, its financial strength, or its management excellence.

One dimension of the BCG approach involves balancing cash flows, or putting your money on the faster racehorse. The model seeks to shift cash from mature cash-generating units to high-growth products that use more cash than they gen-erate in the early product development stage. A second dimension is to balance the degree of risk and acceptable profit fluctuation. For example, companies in mature markets try to shift investment into new growth fields.

The growth-share matrix is based upon the idea that high market share in rapidly growing market segments leads to higher profitability and a strong compet-itive situation. If, on the other hand, the firm has markets in slow-growth areas, then increasing its market share requires large investments, often with diminishing re-turns. Therefore, the BCG approach recommends removing cash flow from these slow-growth areas and placing it in higher-growth market segments, even at the expense of market share.

There has been little empirical research to support the model. However, a study by Donald C. Hambrick, Ian C. MacMillan, and Diana L. Day strongly supports the primary assumptions of the BCG model.[13] The results (see table 6.1) are sum-marized in the following:

1   Return on investment was higher for high-share businesses than for low-share businesses.
2   The four types of businesses have significantly different cash flow outputs.
3   When ROI is adjusted for risk (four-year ROI variability), differences reflect high market share.
4   As expected, there were indications of greater share increases in growth mar-kets than in mature markets.

Overall, there is a clear indication that businesses differ in their performance ac-cording to life cycle stage and market share.

TABLE 6.1
Performance Levels of Businesses in the Four Cells of the BCG Matrix (Means Reported, with
Standard Deviations in Parentheses)

Performance Measure	Wildcats ($N = 181$)	Stars ($N = 114$)	Cash Cows ($N = 315$)	Dogs ($N = 418$)	2-Way Anova (Main Effects)	
					Life Cycle Stage	Market Share
Return on investment	20.55	29.58	30.00	18.48		**
(24.53)	(22.59)	(22.67)	(21.68)			
Cash flow on investment	−2.67	.74	10.01	3.41	**	**
	(18.79)	(18.26)	(17.03)	(16.17)		
ROI/ROI variability	2.37	3.96	4.57	2.80	**	**
(return per risk)	(3.53)	(5.20)	(4.15)	(4.68)		
Market share change	.39	.72	.38	.14	*	*
	(1.76)	(2.97)	(2.30)	(1.55)		

*p < .05
**p < .001

SOURCE: Hambrick, MacMillan, and Day, "Strategic Attributes," *Academy of Management Journal* 25, no. 3 (September 1982): 518.

The *growth-share matrix* is a model for analyzing how market share, market growth, and cash flow are related. The BCG model proposes that the organization should be managed as a portfolio of businesses, giving each a clearly defined strategy. The growth share matrix is used to evaluate business strategy in multi-industry firms, where a large array of businesses demand advanced techniques in selection and management. The BCG's use of growth-share analysis is based upon the well-known relationship between market share and profitability. The central thrust of matrix analysis is its emphasis on achieving balanced long-term growth in volume, revenue, cash flow, and resource allocation.

The basic element of the technique is the construction of a matrix that relates market growth or its attractiveness to a firm's relative competitive position. When a series of such matrices or charts is constructed, a company's product positions are diagrammed to show the changing relationships of these product segments at any critical time. To use growth-share analysis, a series of studies must be made to assess market attractiveness and competitive position and to plot the overall portfolio balance on charts. Once the plotting of the product portfolio chart is completed, growth-share management is perhaps the most challenging part of the whole scheme. Managing the portfolio of markets requires both economic considerations and a concern for people and the resources of the organization.

Each of the various businesses or products develops a strategy which best meets its competitive position and objectives. Because high market share and higher profitability are correlated, the competitive objective is market dominance in high-growth areas. In low-growth markets, where it is difficult and expensive to increase share, the strategy should be one of holding or harvesting and maximizing cash flow to other areas, even if this strategy results in loss of existing market share. Therefore, the strategic alternative that is selected depends upon the assessment of competitive strength, the costs of gaining market leadership in various segments, and the amount of capital that is available for investment.

The total organization is then managed to allocate resources in such a way as to maximize total profitability and to achieve the overall corporate goals. There are four steps in the application of the growth-share matrix.

Step One—Identification of Market Segments

The first step in using the growth-share matrix is to identify the distinct businesses, market segments, or product lines which make up the organization. The concept of what constitutes a market or business is often not easily defined in working terms. In fact, a product/segment can be defined in a variety of ways. These units should identify the natural businesses or markets of the organization, usually by product- or profit-center units. For example, General Electric has 250 business units, while Union Carbide has 150 strategic units. In general, a natural business should have primary responsibility for managing such basic functions as marketing, production, and research and development.

One problem in the identification phase involves the number of separate units which can be effectively managed. Research by Richard Bettis of Southern Methodist University and William Hall of the University of Michigan suggests that managers tend to group businesses (SBUs) into a manageable number of units, so that instead of several hundred product groups, these units range from six to forty-three major business units.[14] The key in each situation is to identify the economically distinct product/market segments of the firm's total operation as strategic business units. A second concern is that this number of businesses be manageable at the strategic level.

Step Two—Analysis of Competitive Position

Each basic business unit identified in the first step is then distributed into a matrix position based upon two criteria: (1) market potential and (2) relative market share as shown in figure 6.3. As a result there are four possible categories based on the SBU's position in the product portfolio chart.

1   *Build—high growth/low market share*   Businesses in this category are typically termed *question marks* or *wildcats* because they are in potentially lucrative market segments but are operating at a competitive disadvantage. These businesses must either expand to increase market share and to take advantage of the growth or suffer competitive disadvantage. If it is impossible to improve com-

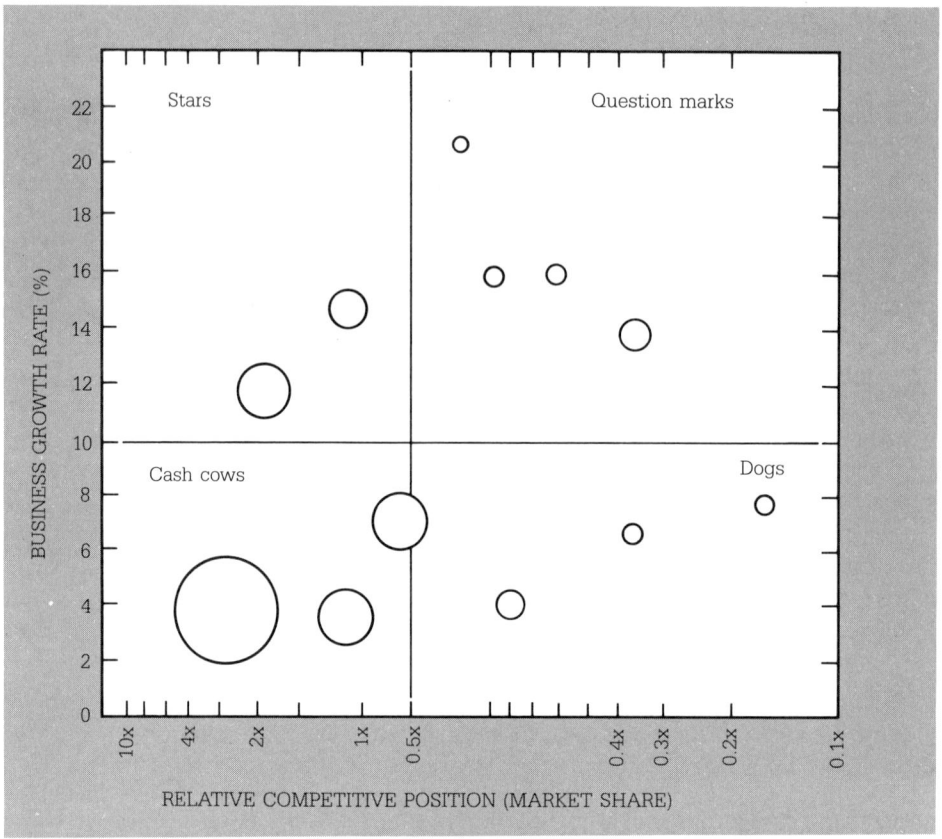

FIGURE 6.3
The Boston Consulting Group (BCG) Model

petitive position, then it may be strategically advantageous to withdraw from this business because cash demand is high, but cash generation is low.

2 *Withdraw—low growth potential/low market share*   A business in this category is typically termed a *dog* or *cash trap* because the low market share places it at a competitive disadvantage. A low-growth rate suggests a low probability for improvement. This business must maximize short-term cash flow by cost cutting, divestiture, or liquidation.

According to Donald Hambrick et al., empirical evidence shows that the average dog has a positive cash flow adequate to meet the cash requirements of the average question mark. Their research suggests that the positive cash flow of a dog may actually fund two or more promising new ventures.[15]

3 *Harvest—low growth/high market share*   These businesses with a strong competitive position in a stabilized market are termed *cash cows*. Because these businesses are already in a strong competitive position, the strategy is to invest

only enough to maintain the present market share while using the competitive advantage to build cash flow for use in higher-growth areas.

4   *Hold—high-growth/high-market share*   Businesses in this capacity are called *stars* and are the business segments where the firm's resources should be located. These businesses are attempting to use strong competitive position to grow at a rate faster than that of competitors in sales and profits.

The use of the growth-share matrix as a management tool permits management to array all of its businesses on one graph, called a *product portfolio chart*. BCG's use of product portfolio charts is based upon the relationships between market share and profitability, so that market dominance is the major strategic objective in high-growth markets.[16]

Step Three—Identify the Strategy

At Apple Computer, CEO John Sculley must decide which of his products are cash cows to be managed to maintain current share and which are rated as stars and should be allocated the majority of resources. At one company, it is reported that 80 percent of its resources are allocated to products in the star category.

Mead Corporation has twenty-four strategic business units and has moved managers into new slots so that their expertise matches the strategy of the unit they run. Richard Bettis and William Hall have suggested that managerial style should be matched to the business unit.[17] For example, they reported that one company associates a star mission with an analytical-type of manager, a cash cow with an engineer-type, a problem child with a salesman-type, and a dog with a cost accountant-type. The important point is that there must be a fit between the managerial style and the strategic mission of the business.[18]

William W. Wommack, vice-chairman of Mead, has also allocated money differently. Instead of funding projects with "fair share" allocation, he has funded strategies. This method lets the company weed out dog products, milk its mature cash producers, and concentrate investment on potential growth lines. "If you have a business you want a lot of cash out of instead of growth, you don't put a high-powered marketing man in charge, and if you want growth, don't put a conservative accountant in charge," explained Wommack.[19]

Step Four—Strategic Review

Each month, top managers, like Jack Welch, CEO of General Electric, must review the status of the strategic plan in light of economic conditions and competitors' countermoves and determine how well the portfolio plan is working. If there is a gap between plan and actual situation, then some corrective action must be put into effect. For example, at General Electric the market share declined in several product lines, resulting in short-term profit pressures and requiring a review of strategic decisions. According to *Business Week,* Welch used confrontation and constructive conflict to work out strategic approach. "Every day is a tryout for the new GE team," said one veteran.[20]

Although the BCG model has had wide application in industry, there are problems associated with the identification of market segments, the number of units which can be managed, and the idea that growth rate is always associated with profitability. There is no doubt, however, that such models do offer a useful tool for strategic evaluation and decisions.

The GE Business Screen Strategy for Planning

A second strategic planning model is the *business screen matrix,* or *stoplight strategy* approach, developed by General Electric and McKinsey & Co. The business planning matrix relates the multiple factors forming the firm's competitive advantage profile to its environmental opportunities and risks.[21]

General Electric uses stop-light strategy (a strategic business planning grid, as shown in figure 6.4) to evaluate critical factors in strategic planning for its forty-three SBUs, or strategic business units.

The GE grid is a nine-cell business planning matrix that provides a means of monitoring industry characteristics and has served to protect developing business units during business downturns. In the planning review each business is rated on a multiple set of strategic factors. Size, growth rate, market share, position, profitability, technology position, image, and people are GE business strength factors. Factors enhancing industry attractiveness are size, market growth, planning, market chemistry, technical role, competitive structure, and social, environmental, legal, and human factors.

The outcome of these ratings is high, medium, or low in both industry attractiveness and GE's position in the field, as shown in figure 6.4. If the product falls into the green section, then it has a green light and a go, the strategic decision to invest and grow. Products in the yellow light or caution section are question marks, borderline situations that might go either way. If the product falls in the red zone, a red light or stop strategy such as a retrenchment, consolidation, or divestment strategic decision is indicated.

"We don't give definitive weight to the nonnumerical factors," said Reuben Gutoff, corporate planner, "but they do have weights. At the end of our discussion there is a consensus on what's green, red, or yellow."[22] GE is currently attempting to get an unbeatable competitive advantage in each of its businesses and to become number one or two in each market. Another priority is to continue taking businesses that don't make significant ROI contributions (i.e., red zone businesses) and redefining their strategy, fitting them into new market niches, or divesting them.[23] The elaboration of the stoplight model specifies the functional areas and management styles for each major strategic alternative, thus providing a set of contingent actions for use in directing the strategic actions for each business unit.

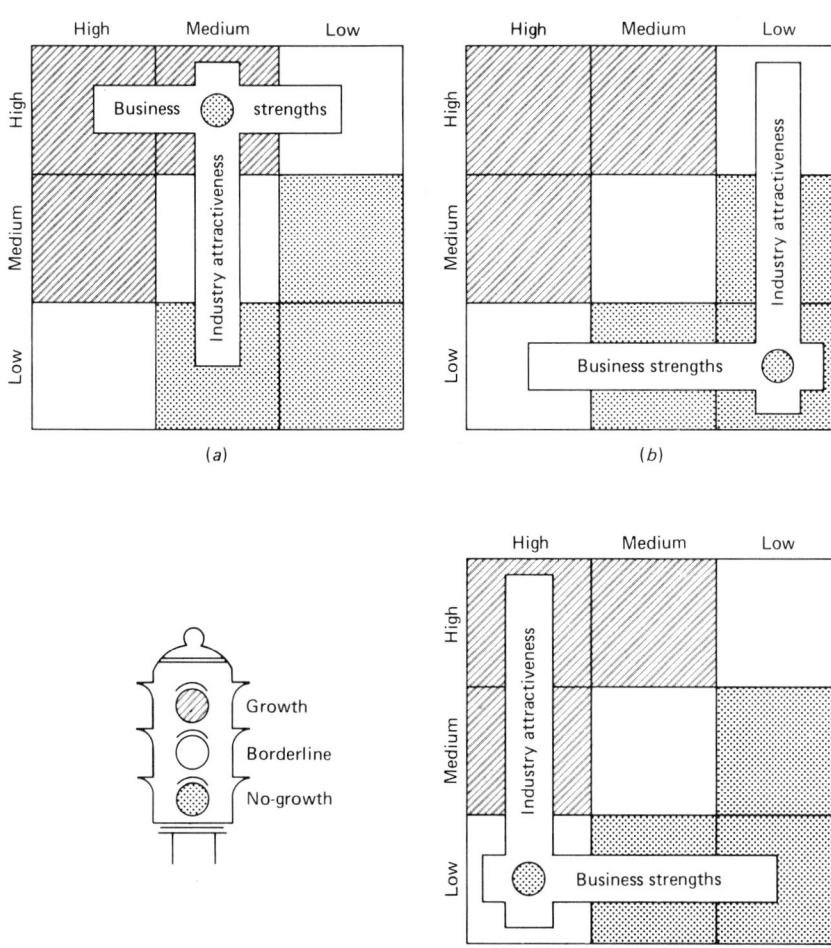

FIGURE 6.4
General Electric's Planning Grid

SOURCE: Reprinted from information in the March 15, 1975, issue of FORBES Magazine.

The Directional Policy Matrix

A third strategic planning model, the Directional Policy Matrix (DPM), has been developed by Royal Dutch Shell. This model, like the GE model, uses a weighted multivariate analysis to position a business on a three-by-three matrix and allows for greater complexity than the BCG model (see figure 6.5).

The major purpose of the DPM is to identify (1) the main criteria by which the prospects for a business sector may be judged to be favorable or unfavorable and (2) the criteria by which a company's position in a sector may be judged to be strong

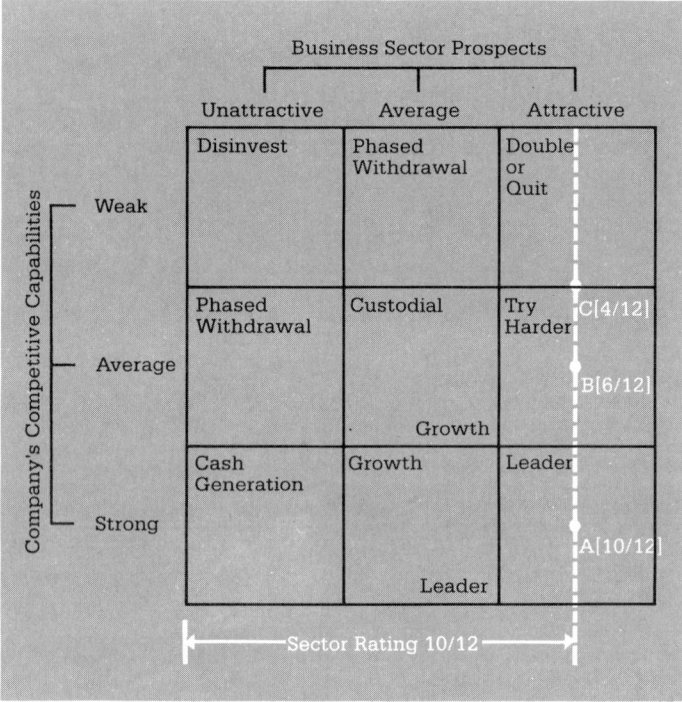

FIGURE 6.5
Comparison of Competitive Capabilities—Product X

SOURCE: Reprinted with permission from Long Range Planning, vol. 11, S. Robinson and others, ''The Directional Policy Matrix,'' Copyright 1978, Pergamon Press, Ltd.

or weak. These criteria are then used to construct separate ratings of *sector prospects* and of the company's *competitive capabilities,* and the ratings are plotted on a matrix. The matrix can be used to display all the competitors in one particular business sector, because the method evaluates competitors' ratings as well as those of one's own company.[24]

The DPM model, as indicated in figure 6.5, is developed by positioning each product/market unit within a nine-cell matrix. The basic technique analyzes each product on two primary factors and the results are plotted on the matrix. Because the various zones of the matrix are associated with different combinations of sector prospects and company strength or weakness, different product strategies are appropriate to them. These strategies are indicated by the various key words that suggest the type of strategy or resource allocation to be followed for products falling in these zones.

Leader   The largest producer with the lowest costs and a commanding technical situation, competitor A, is in the highly desirable position of leader in a business sector with attractive prospects. The indicated strategy is to give absolute priority to the product with all the resources necessary to hold its market position.

Try harder   The products located in this zone, exemplified by competitor B, can be moved toward an equality position by the right allocation of resources.

Double or quit   Products destined to become the future high fliers should be selected from this zone of the matrix. A company, competitor C, should not normally seek to diversify into any new sector unless the prospects for it are judged to be attractive. The firm must double its competitive market position or get out.

Growth   Products will tend to fall in this zone for a company that is one of two to four major competitors (four-star market position) backed up by commensurate production capacity and product R&D.

Custodial   A product will fall in the custodial zone of the matrix when the company concerned has a position of distinct weakness in either market position (below three star), process economics, hardware, feedstock, or two or more of these in combination.

Cash generation   A company with a strong position in such a sector can still earn satisfactory profits, and for that company the sector can be regarded as a cash generator.

Phased withdrawal   A company with an average-to-weak position in a low-growth sector is unlikely to earn any significant amount of cash. The key strategy in this sector is phased withdrawal. Efforts should be made to realize the value of the assets and put the money to more profitable use.

Disinvest   Products falling within this zone are likely to be losing money already. Even if they generate some positive cash flows when business is good, they will lose money when business is bad. It is best to dispose of the assets as rapidly as possible and redeploy more profitably the released resources of cash, feedstock, and skilled manpower.

This overall comparison of business units allows the development of a strategic plan within each SBU. At the corporate level, hard decisions about the relative future prospects are used as a basis for allocating scarce resources among the business units. In general, the DPM may represent a useful tool in strategic planning in narrowing the set of possible alternatives from which to choose.

Portfolio Planning Matrix

Another approach to the portfolio matrix is based on the life-cycle concept. The horizontal dimension represents industry maturity (the stages of the life-cycle) and the vertical dimension represents competitive position, as shown in figure 6.6.

The matrix is used to segment the businesses of the firm into SBUs to provide a systematic process for analyzing the stage of the product and to identify the

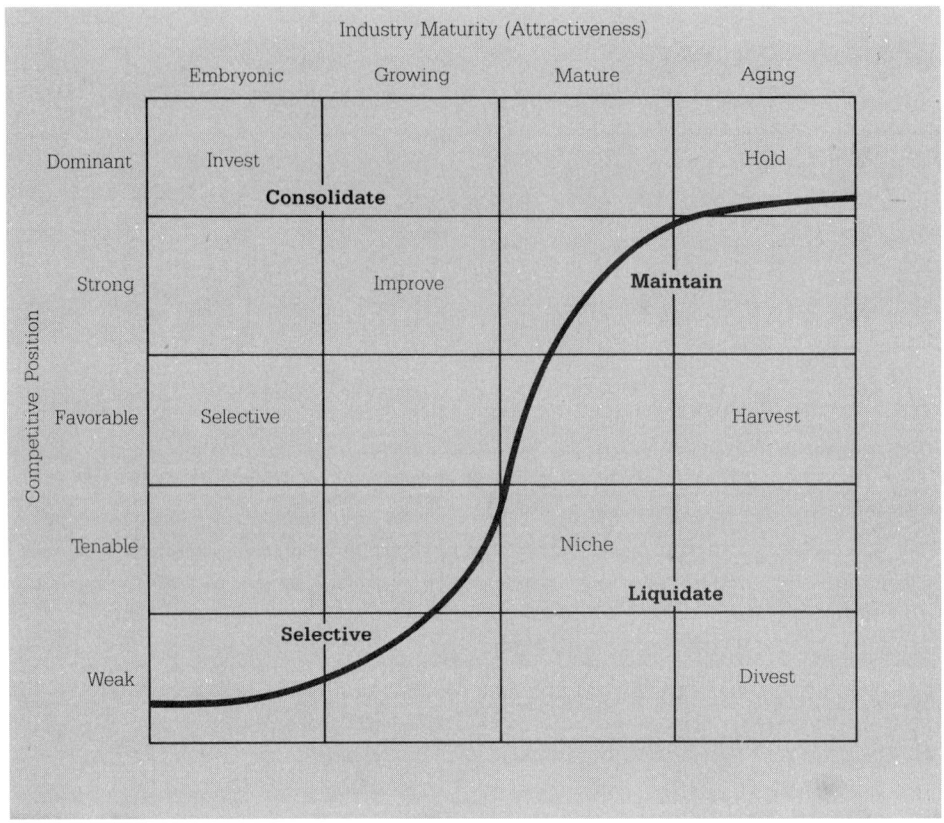

FIGURE 6.6
Portfolio Planning Matrix/Product Life Cycle

competitive position of each product. The advantage of this type of matrix is that it enables the manager to identify potential stars early and distribute businesses across the stages of the product life cycle.

This portfolio representation is used to determine the role of each SBU according to its classification in the product life-cycle. The firm is better off with a balanced portfolio. If too many SBUs are in the aging sector, then the firm may enjoy short-term profits but be neglecting future position. Similarly, if too many businesses are in the embryonic stages, the firm may have cash flow problems in the short term, but a bright future outlook.

THE LIMITATIONS OF STRATEGIC ANALYSIS MODELS

During the past decade there has been a widespread adoption of strategic analysis models in which resources are being allocated according to a strategic perspective of each business segment within the total portfolio of the firm.

The BCG model is one widely used technique for analyzing a company's stategic alternatives. One source estimates that over 40 percent of the *Fortune* top 500 firms are using the portfolio planning concept, while other research suggests that about 40 percent of firms studied use this technique.[25] Others have estimated that as many as 80 percent of the top 500, and a sizable portion of the second 500, are using some element of the BCG techniques. It has also been reported that at least seven major forest product companies are BCG clients, including Hammermill Paper, International Paper, Mead, Crown-Zellerbach, Boise Cascade, Great Northern Nekoosa, and Potlatch.

In the late 1970s and 1980s a new generation of strategic planning approaches emerged. Their application, however, has been limited. These strategic problems may apply with varying degrees to different models or within differing firms, but they should be recognized by the strategist. In fact, as experience has been gained in using these models, four serious limitations have been recognized.

Time Frame: Long- Versus Short-Run Trends

The BCG growth-share model for strategic analysis is based on the relationship between cash generation and market share and is derived from the effect of the experience curve. In other words, the firm with the greatest experience (market share) also has the lowest cost and the greatest cash generation. It is important to recognize, however, that the BCG approach is based on long-term relationships and is not a short-term adjustment technique.

The strategist must be able to identify future trends in the firm's relative market share. Tandy, for example, once held a dominant share in the growing PC market, but was unable to act on the longer-term trends. Tandy has consistently lost share and now holds a marginal position.

Market-Share Definition/Profitability

A second limitation of strategic analysis is the definition of market share. It is difficult to precisely determine the exact boundaries of any specific market, ander-rors here can make the analysis invalid. Similarly, there is often a serious problem of accurate product/market segmentation and relation of market share to strategy.

The relationship between large share and profitability does not always hold true, even though there is some evidence that a direct relationship does exist.[26] A study by Prescott, Kohli, and Venkatramen found that the relationships between market share and business profitability is context-specific. Although the relationship was found to be direct in three environments, it was spurious in four other environments. Even in environments with a strong direct effect, a sizeable spurious relationship was present. Therefore, the pursuit of market share as a goal must be done cautiously.[27]

In another study, Gale Buzzell and Ralph Sultan found that "on an average, a difference of ten percentage points in market share is accompanied by a difference of about five points in pretax ROI." The explanation was due to three factors: (1)

economies of scale—the ability to to capitalize on size; (2) marketing power—the capacity to apply power for competitive advantages; and (3) quality of management—the underlying strength for performance.[28]

The *quality* of the share is also important because the firm's position is not as vulnerable to competitive countermoves. When a firm has quality of share, a low-market-share business can be as attractive as a high-market-share business. High market share provides power and implies financial strength. However, within a corporation, it is often necessary to seek high market share for certain businesses, while accepting low market share for other businesses. In either situation market share significantly affects profitability. A study by Richard Hammermesh and others of Harvard University showed that low-market-share firms can outperform high-share competitors.[29]

To be successful, a low-market-share company must compete in the segments where its own strengths will be most highly valued and where its large competitors will be most unlikely to compete. But it is often possible to compete with large competitors. Procter & Gamble under CEO John G. Smale, for example, entered the disposable diaper market with Pampers, even though the market was controlled by Scott. This costly and risky action paid off: Pampers became the market leader despite the slow start. Johnson & Johnson, who had held 20 percent of the market, decided to pull out altogether as their share dropped to a meager 8 percent.

New Business Development/Identifying Growth Rate

A third problem area is that portfolio analysis does not address the issue of new business development. Firms that allocate resources among existing businesses may be underinvesting in potential new business development opportunities. Burroughs Corporation, for example, was slow to recognize the development of the PC market and as a result was forced to purchase its late entry, the B20, from another firm.

A related problem lies in the identification of the actual underlying growth rate of the market segment, a problem compounded by the impact of inflation. In the first place, there are no exact ways to determine the growth rates of new innovations, and forecasting methods often miss the mark. For example, how was one to determine the market for hand-held calculators or digital watches? Today we recognize the scope of these markets, but at one time the Swiss watch industry felt that the digital watch was only a small, insignificant segment of the entrenched mechanical watch industry. How quickly things can change! Similarly, what is the market potential for personal computers in the home? IBM, Apple, and others are betting that PCs will be a tremendous growth market, but it has yet to emerge fully.

This problem is especially important for strategic models where growth rate is a primary variable in developing strategy for various business elements. An inaccurate estimate makes strategic evaluation unreliable.

Managerial Motivation

Finally, there is the problem of management and employee satisfaction that emerges when a business is labeled as a dog or a cash cow. How motivated could you get if you were working on or managing a product identified as a target for divestment or for no growth? This labeling poses a special problem in applying the portfolio concepts as a strategic management tool.

There have also been examples of dogs or money-losing businesses in one company that were bought and turned into winners. For example, a group bought and successfully marketed Helena Rubenstein, a cosmetics company, even though Colgate-Palmolive had lost $50 million there in 1979. Another businessman, Victor Kiam, bought Remington shavers from Sperry, despite losses of $30 million in five years, and turned it into a market leader.

One recent study suggests that firms should avoid colorful labels such as star or dog and instead designate a strategy for each unit, such as build, hold, harvest, or withdraw, in the strategic planning activity.[30] Despite these limitations, portfolio models can be very useful in strategy analysis to clarify broad strategic objectives.

MANAGERIAL SUMMARY

An important stage in the strategic management process is the comparison and evaluation of strategic alternatives. There are always a number of possible strategic moves for allocating available resources to achieve organizational goals. These possible strategies must be evaluated to determine whether they are consistent with environmental opportunities and competitive advantages. The final choice must optimize the total return of the firm, subject to market and competitive constraints. Therefore, the evaluation of strategy in a complex organization is usually a multiple series of decisions rather than a single choice. Strategic decision making, then, involves the comparison of various trade-offs in order to select the most appropriate strategy.

In this chapter, several conceptual models were used to analyze strategic alternatives. The use of these models has grown rapidly over the past decade, and many of these techniques are being used as integral components of the strategic evaluation and decision process in large companies. These models represent the first major advances in systematically identifying the critical factors in strategic planning.

The use of these models provides one of the most detailed and important techniques in strategy selection. One of the keys to the successful application of these tools is accurate market segmentation. In this way, different strategies can be examined in terms of cash-flow generation and corporate resource allocation. The portfolio models (such as BCG, GE, and so forth) provide a mechanism for relating two key variables—business strength and industry attractiveness—to determine corporate strategy.

The analytical models are used to examine the current state of the organization and to analyze important trends that may be emerging. The manager's diagnostic skills, then, are particularly important in making these determinations.

Strategic evaluation involves developing and selecting a course of action for the future. At the higher levels of the organization, this evaluation tends to be broad in scope, but managers at all levels must be involved in determining how best to allocate the firm's resources. The use of strategic models reduces the extent of intuitive planning and "management by crisis" and provides a tool for the optimal use of various product/market business units within the firm.

There is no doubt that these models have not yet been perfected. They do not provide a simple mathematical solution to strategic questions but rather a framework for a rational comparison of complex factors. However, there are still a number of problems associated with their use, including the time frame, definition of market, identification of growth markets, and motivation of managers.

One problem is that financial performance is invariably related to time. However, many of the key factors in the model are not controlled by a rigid time horizon. Innovation does not usually occur on a planned, orderly basis. In other words, the strategist should not force-fit the strategy to meet a set of numbers, but rather must temper the analysis with common sense and business judgment.

In spite of these problems and shortcomings, strategic analysis models are a useful and growing element in evaluating strategies in large, diversified firms. The fundamental idea of a flexible strategic analysis system is one of regular review and evaluation. For maximum value, the strategist must not overlook the requirement for timely and accurate information and the element of managerial skill. The analytical models provide a means of managing future ventures with reduced risks and uncertainties.

Review Questions

1 Texas Instruments moved into the digital watch market a few years ago and took about 50 percent of the market. How was this done? What were the long-term outcomes? That is, was it successful? Describe experience curve theory and how it affects strategy.
2 General Electric is a diversified corporation. Find a recent article on GE. In view of changing demographics and life-styles, how would you manage a portfolio of businesses in this field? Explain the growth-share matrix and its role in strategic analysis.
3 Why do managers need to do strategic analysis? What is the difference between portfolio strategy and SBU strategy?
4 Describe GE's business screen strategy and its use.
5 What are some of the limitations of strategic analysis models?
6 At Tandy Corporation, managers are pondering what to do in the PC market. Using the BCG model, what would you do? Look up Tandy's annual report or *Value Line* report and see which strategic move might be most effective.

Notes

1   Quotation is from "GE: Giant Entrepreneur," *Planning Review*, 13, no. 1 (January 1985): 18. Based on "Electric Switch," *The Wall Street Journal*, July 12, 1982, 1; and "Can Jack Welch Reinvent GE?" *Business Week*, June 30, 1986, 62–67.

2   George Day, "Gaining Insights through Strategy Analysis," *Journal of Business Strategy* 4, no. 1 (Summer 1983): 51.

3   See Anthony J. Parisi, "Exxon: An Empire," *New York Times*, August 3, 1980; and "Can Exxon Keep Flying," *Business Week*, August 10, 1985, 62.

4   For more information, see Richard P. Rumelt, *Strategy, Structure, and Economic Performance* (Cambridge, MA: Graduate School of Business Administration, Harvard University, 1974), 11–32.

5   Personal correspondence from Bruce Henderson, November 25, 1980.

6   "Markets: It's Better to Be Big," *Forbes*, October 15, 1977, 132.

7   Boston Consulting Group, "The Experience Curve Revisited," *Perspectives*, Boston Consulting Group, 1980, n.p.

8   See Marvin B. Lieberman, "The Learning Curve, Diffusion and Competitive Strategy," paper presented at Academy of Management, August 1985.

9   See Gerald Allan, "A Note on the Use of Experience Curves in Decision Making," *ICCH #9-175-174*, June 1976; and Bruce Henderson, "The Application and Misapplication of the Experience Curve," *Journal of Business Strategy* 4, no. 3 (Winter 1984): 3.

10 Rumelt, "Evaluation of Strategy."

11 Based on Gerald Allan, "A Note on the Boston Consulting Group Concept of Competitive Analysis and Corporate Strategy," *ICCH #9-175-175*, June 1976.

12 Bruce Henderson, "Understanding the Forces of Strategic and Natural Competition," *Journal of Business Strategy* 1, no. 3 (Winter 1981): 12. See also *Perspectives*, Boston Consulting Group, 1980.

13 Donald C. Hambrick, Ian C. MacMillan, and Diana L. Day, "Strategic Attributes and Performance in the BCG Matrix," *Academy of Management Journal* 25, no. 3 (1982): 510–531.

14 See Richard Bettis and William Hall, "Implementing the Portfolio Concept," paper presented at the Academy of Management, Detroit, MI, 1980.

15 Hambrick et al., "BCG," 529.

16 Robert D. Buzzell, T. Gale Bradley, and Ralph G. M. Sultan, "Market Share—A Key to Profitability," *Harvard Business Review* (January-February 1975) 97–106.

17 Bettis and Hall, "Implementing the Portfolio Concept."

18 See Jeffrey Kerr, "Assigning Managers on the Basis of Life Cycle," *Journal of Business Strategy* 2, no. 4 (Spring 1982): 58.

19 "Olin's Shift to Strategy Planning," *Business Week*, March 27, 1978, 102.

20 "Can Jack Welch Reinvent GE?" *Business Week*.

21 For a comparison of GE to BCG, see Neil E. Swanson, "Measures of Strategic Attributes and Performance Using the GE Business Screen vs. the BCG Matrix," paper presented at Academy of Management, 1984.

22 "Piercing the Future Fog," *Business Week*, April 28, 1975, 49.

23 "GE, Giant Entrepreneur," *Planning Review*, January 1985, 18.

24 S. J. Q. Robinson et al., "The Directional Policy Matrix—Tool for Strategic Planning," *Long Range Planning*, June 1978, 8.

25 Philippe Haspeslagh "Portfolio Planning: Uses and Limits," *Harvard Business Review* (January-February 1982): 58–73.

26 See Carolyn Wood, "Does It Always Pay Off?" *Proceedings, Academy of Management* (1981): 7–11.

27 See John E. Prescott, Ajay K. Kohli, and B. Venkatramen, "What Is the Relationship between Market Share and Business Profit?" *Proceedings, Academy of Management* (1984): 32–36.

28 Gale Buzzell and Ralph Sultan, "Market Share," 97–106.

29 R. G. Hammermesh, M. J. Anderson, Jr., and J. E. Harris, "Strategies for Low Market Share Businesses," *Harvard Business Review* (May-June 1978): 95–102. "Make Way for Miller," *Forbes*, May 15, 1976, 45–47.

30 Anil K. Gupta and V. Govindarajan, "Build, Hold, Harvest: Converting Strategic Intentions into Reality," *Journal of Business Strategy* 4, no. 3 (Winter 1984): 34.

CHAPTER SEVEN

The Strategic Decision

OUTLINE

OBJECTIVES

After completing this chapter you will be able to:

- define the concepts of strategic decision and risk

- describe the strategic decision process

- discuss the major factors influencing the strategic decision-making context

- compare methods for assessing strategic risk

- identify the power and political tactics used to influence strategic decisions

The company has developed a strong culture that emphasizes hard work and clear thinking. Employees are encouraged to face all problems and differences of opinion openly and to pursue their point of view aggressively until a decision is made. Once a decision is made, we expect everyone to commit to its implementation, if he agreed with the original decision or not. We like decisions to be made at the lowest level in the organization where the required information is available. Very few decisions are made at the level of the Executive Office.

Gordon Moore, Chairman, Intel Corporation, July 1985

Strategic Decisions at Intel

Moore

In the rapidly growing semiconductor industry, Intel is regarded as a technological leader. Intel designed the first microprocessor, the computer on a chip, in 1971 and has continued to lead in the development of more powerful chips. "It's a Demolition Derby," says Intel president Andy Grove, about decision making in the hard-pressed semiconductor industry.

Behind Intel's success are the three engineers who founded the company, chairman Gordon Moore, vice-chairman Robert Noyce, and president Andrew Grove. At Intel, there is no staff or top management other than the partners themselves. Major decisions are made at weekly meetings of people from all parts of the operation, and problems are worked out right there in the room. Noyce wanted them all to keep internalizing the company's goals and to provide their own motivation, just as they had during the start-up phase. If they did that, they would have the capacity to make their own decisions.

At Intel, Noyce decided to eliminate the notion of levels of management altogether. He and Moore ran the show; that much was clear. But below them were only the strategic business segments, as they called them. They were comparable to the major departments in an orthodox corporation, but they had far more autonomy. Each was run like a separate corporation. Middle managers at Intel had more responsibility than most vice-presidents back east. They were also much younger and got lower-back pain and migraines earlier.

At Intel, if the marketing division had to make a major decision that would affect the engineering division, the problem was not routed up a hierarchy to a layer of executives who oversaw both departments. Instead, "councils," made up of people already working on the line in the divisions-that were affected, would meet and work it out themselves. The councils moved horizontally, from problem to problem. They had no vested power. They were not governing bodies but coordinating councils.[1]

Intel plans to spend $75 million over three years to transform itself from a producer of high volume (commodity) chips into a leading manufacturer of custom (specialized) microchips. "It is a very goal-oriented, output-oriented culture," says President Andy Grove. "We are a very paranoid company. We are in a very competitive industry, so we constantly look over our shoulder to see who is going to damage us."[2]

INTRODUCTION

The strategic manager is a decision maker. Gordon Moore, Robert Noyce, and Andy Grove of Intel have made a series of strategic choices that have resulted in the success of their firm to date. There are always a number of possible strategies and courses of action that might be taken, but the executive must make the strategic choice.

The purpose of this chapter is to explore the nature of the strategic decision process. The first section examines decision making and outlines the stages of the decision process and context. The next section is a discussion of the risk factors which influence decision making. Finally, some behavioral implications of the power-political process will be discussed.

THE STRATEGIC DECISION

After the alternative strategy evaluation, the next step (stage 6) is one of the most critical in the strategic management process: the strategic decision. A decision may be defined as a choice from among possible alternative strategies. As the old saying goes, "The buck stops here." The purpose of decision making is to direct resources toward objectives, and a decision to pursue one strategy usually means there are other possible actions that are not being taken. The strategic decisions may be good or bad, but they must be made. Boeing's decision to design a new generation of airliners, the 757 and 767, has placed it in a commanding lead among aircraft companies. But a decision by Rolls-Royce to design a new jet engine, the RB-211, led that company into bankruptcy.

After all the analysis of alternatives, there comes a point when the strategic decision must be made. The strategic decision is a process of systematically comparing how each possible strategy will affect the market and the firm. There are always several possible alternatives, and there are always trade-offs to be considered between differing courses of action.

The strategic decision narrows down to the business judgment of one person or group: the chief executive officer and the executive committee of the firm. The CEO finally makes the decision of how the firm's resources will be committed. At Intel, for example, the committee decided a major reorganization was necessary.

The goal of the reorganization is to let Intel exploit its technical strengths. According to Leslie Vadasz, an Intel veteran and vice-president for strategic planning,

> The best way to lose your shirt in this business is to go after the most visible commodity item. Our strategy is to look at our capabilities and see where we add most value to the piece of silicon. That means that Intel's core operation will continue to be in microprocessors and peripherals. These products are more than mere components, they are central to the whole development of computer technology, from microcomputers up to supercomputers. There will be a lot of systems business from which we can get leverage.[3]

Intel is solidly positioned in the microprocessor market because of its strategic decisions, and chips based on the 8086 family will account for about 83 percent of the microprocessor market.

These decisions to focus on specialized products will have a significant impact on Intel's competitive position for the next few years and will be a contributing factor to its anticipated high earnings.

A *strategic decision* is the choice by the decision maker of a course of action from among the alternatives available. Strategic management involves making the decisions which will ultimately determine the organization's survival. As Herbert Simon has noted, "If *all* behavior results from decision making and if management is a particular kind of behavior, then managing is decision making."[4]

The purpose of the strategic decision is the accomplishment of organizational goals and objectives. Consequently, the decision process is a fundamental part of strategic management. Many of these decisions require consideration of an uncertain and unpredictable set of future conditions. Therefore, the strategist must make a calculated judgment of what the future will be and then select a strategy that will enhance the firm's competitive position. Because of the uncertainty of the future, there is always an element of risk in such decisions. As an example, consumer goods companies often spend between $50 and $100 million on the introduction of new brands, many of which fail. Gillette spent over $100 million on the introduction of a new dry antiperspirant, and Coleco spent millions trying to promote its video game system.

At A&P stores, former CEO Jonathan Scott needed to make a strategic decision. One choice was to close down the company's worst operating units, store by store, warehouse by warehouse, plant by plant. A second more radical course of action was to shut down entire operating divisions. Scott opted for the first alternative. "We made a conscious decision to close down on a store-by-store basis," he recalled. "We decided to weed out the very worst and try to turn around the rest. We wanted to save as much as we could."[5]

Decision Factors

There is a range of strategic decisions which must be made. Sometimes these decisions involve relatively low levels of risk, but other times, the risk is substantial. One way to clarify decision elements is to examine the following factors:[6]

1   *What is the impact of the decision on the goals and objectives of the organization?* Effective decisions lead to a successful organization. The decisions by John Young, CEO at Hewlett-Packard, and Fred Smith, CEO at Federal Express, for example, led to growth and profitability for their companies. At International Harvester, W. T. Grant, and Rolls-Royce, on the other hand, strategic decisions led to disaster and failure.
2   *What is the scope of the decision?* A decision affecting one product or department in a small business will have a greater effect that one involving the same number of elements in a large organization.
3   *What level of financial outlay is involved?* The financial impact of a decision is, of course, relative to the size of the firm. A $100,000 purchase by a small business may be very important, yet the same amount for General Motors may be routine.
4   *What is the relative frequency of this type of decision?* Decisions which need to be made frequently tend to be routine. The decision to buy materials or hire workers is made routinely in most organizations. However, a decision to build a new research laboratory or chemical complex is made less frequently and is not a routine decision.
5   *What is the time frame?* Important decisions must often be made under conditions of urgency and the time given to make the decision may be short. Frequently, deadlines may be determined by the situation or by buyers, suppliers, or others outside the firm. A sudden breakdown of the supply of raw material may force a quick decision and action. In other decisions there may be enough time to study the situation in detail and determine alternative ways to solve the problems.

In order to make effective decisions, management must overcome the barriers to a rational, anticipative decision process. Irving L. Janis and Leon Mann have presented the reasons for several ineffective problem-solving approaches.[7] After a problem emerges, a manager may react to problems in four ineffective ways:

1   *Avoidance*   No decision is made because the consequences of inaction do not appear to be substantial.
2   *Easy alternative*   Rather than do a detailed decision analysis, the manager takes the first acceptable, low-risk alternative.
3   *Defensive avoidance*   Rather than seek alternatives, the manager avoids risks by avoiding a decision or ignoring possible risks.
4   *Panic*   When the manager is under time pressures, a rational alternative may not be searched out. Rather, any available solution is selected (such as shutting down stores at A&P).

Inadequate decisions are frequently the results of (1) not analyzing carefully enough the impact of the decision on the organization's objectives, (2) the tendency to ignore problems in the hope they may disappear, (3) insufficient evaluation of alternatives, and (4) the avoidance of risk.

The strategic decision is both an end and a beginning. It marks the end of the strategy formulation phase and the beginning of the implementation phase. The role of the executive in strategic choice is analyzing all information on the firm and the environment and using a rational process to translate the organization's mission and goals into action. The strategic decision signals the commitment of resources toward a specific goal: a new product, increased market share, or even acquiring or selling off a business. Roberto C. Goizueta, CEO at Coca-Cola, analyzed resources and the opportunities available. There were many possible choices, but he made a decision to invest $100 million into promoting the new Coca-Cola: a commitment to action.

The decision to market the "new Coke" was made on the basis of careful market research and on a declining market share, but rivals credited Goizueta with one of the biggest marketing blunders of the decade. Finally, four months later, he reversed the decision and brought back Coca-Cola Classic, the old Coke. Coke executives were staggered by the unexpected public response to scrapping the original cola. However, the company believes its three brands will increase total market share. "Time will tell," said Goizueta, "but I'm willing to take bets on this one."[8]

The Strategic Decision Process

The strategic decision is a deliberate attempt to modify the functioning of the organization to increase future effectiveness. Managers sometimes assume that a decision is an isolated phenomenon. However, a systems viewpoint shows that a number of interrelated factors affect strategic decisions. Decision making may be described as a sequential process of stages that enable the decision maker to structure the problem in a meaningful way, as shown in figure 7.1. CEO John Akers used this process at IBM.

IBM, one of the largest computer companies in the world, has long been known for its strategic planning excellence, timely decision making, and the seemingly endless stream of competent managers. An example is CEO John F. Akers. Like many managers, he has spent virtually his entire professional life inside the company, growing and learning new skills along the way to become a branch manager in Boston. Fellow salesmen from Boston say he lacked the polish he exhibits today. "He was an intuitive problem-solver and could build good esprit de corps," said one colleague, "but he had lots of enemies because he was so blunt." Akers was perhaps a "driving-driver" style manager, but he has managed to polish the rough edges, become a team player, and develop a deceptively laid-back style and a willingness to delegate decision making.[9]

An organization is a dynamic system, and major decisions often involve multiple forces. Decisions (like the one at Coca-Cola) are also likely to have both intended and unintended consequences that must be anticipated. The decision made

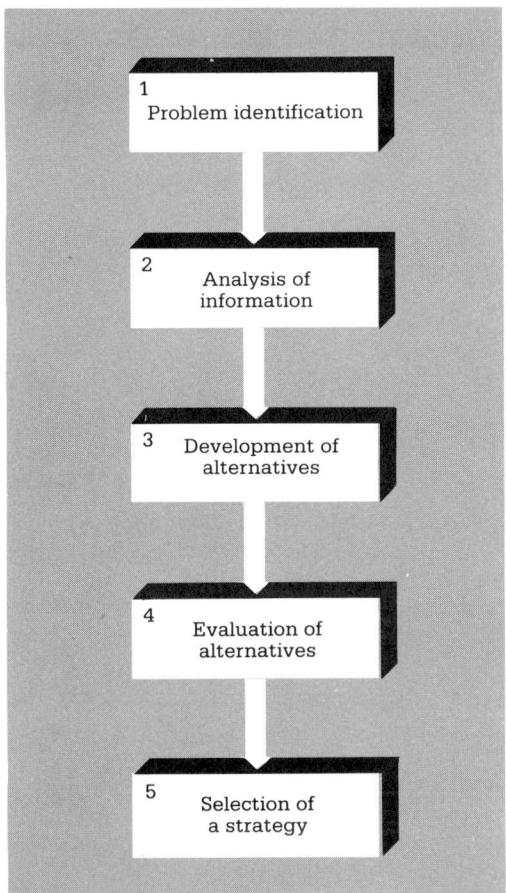

FIGURE 7.1
The Decision Process—The Rational Model

by the strategist today may have major ramifications on the future survival of the firm. John Akers made the major decision of moving IBM into communication systems and is aiming at long-range market trends and the improvement of IBM's competitive position to become a leader in each of its major markets.

Eberhard Witte of West Germany has researched the application of a five-stage model as follows (see figure 7.2):

1 *Problem identification* A necessary condition for a decision is a problem, or a gap between the desired level of achievement and the existing level.
2 *Analysis of information* A search process is undertaken for relevant internal and external information.

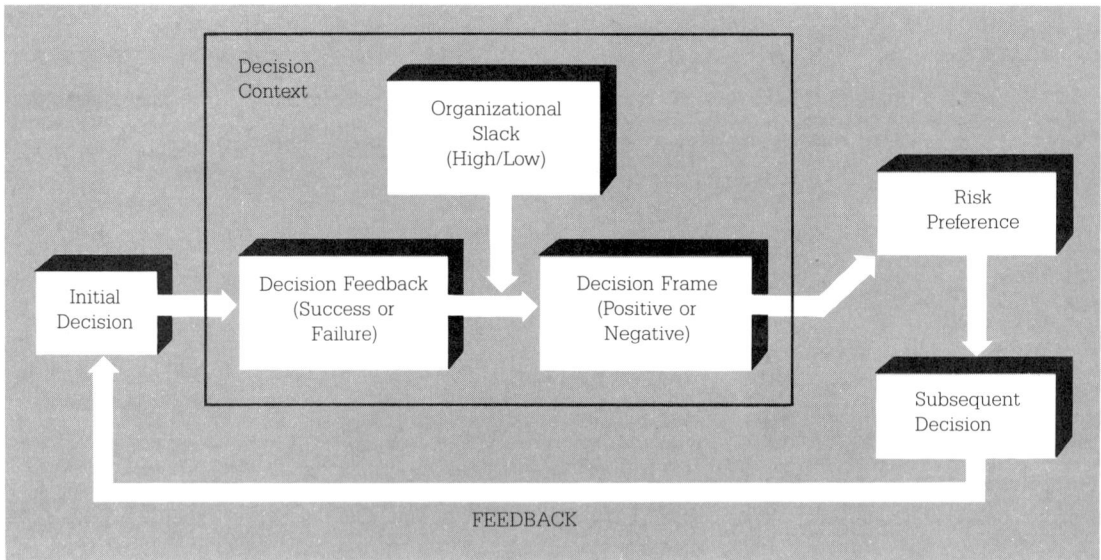

FIGURE 7.2
The Strategic Decision Context

SOURCE: Adapted from Bateman and Zeithaml, "The Context of Strategic Decisions" *Academy of Management Proceedings,* 1985:2.

3 *Development of alternatives*   Several possible alternative solutions are identified. These alternative strategies are the possible courses of action from which choices can be made. Obviously, the broader the range of alternatives to be considered, the more likely it is that an effective strategy will emerge.

4 *Evaluation of alternatives*   The relative worth of the various alternatives is examined and rated against some criterion or standard.

5 *Selection of a strategy*   The strategy that best meets the decision criterion is selected. The decision is not an end in itself, but rather the means to an end. The strategic choice also depends on the comparison of objectives and alternatives by the decision maker.[10]

Forces that influence the decision include the values of the decision maker, the risk-taking attitudes, and the internal policies of the situation.[11]

The rational model of decision making assumes that the decision maker has a full range of alternatives and a criterion for making the decision. However, in actual situations, the manager often has limited information and may not have the time to systematically search out all possible alternatives. Eberhard Witte has investigated the actual decision process in some 230 cases in three large international corporations, including IBM and Univac. His research, not surprisingly, showed that firms did not use the five-phase decision process, and he reported the following conclusions:

1 A complex innovative decision is a multi-operational process.
2 A complex decision process consists not of one final decision, but rather of a
   series of subdecisions.
3 The rational process can be found in actual decisions; however, they do not form
   distinct phases in time, but rather are distributed over the total duration of the
   process.[12]

In the broadest sense, managers do follow a decision process. However they
tend to rely more on action than diagnosis and frequently shortcut the decision
process by combining the steps. As James B. Quinn of Dartmouth College has
commented, "Any organization's ultimate direction is the result of many trade-
offs. . . . The attempt to find an acceptable and motivating compromise among
multiple competing goals is what forces much of the coalition behavior observed in
large organizations, including major businesses."[13]

There is research evidence to suggest that the rational decision process may
not be applicable to all industries. James W. Fredrickson found a consistently negative relationship between the rational process and performance in an unstable
industry, while finding a positive relationship in a stable industry.[14] This perspective
suggests that in a more dynamic, turbulent environment, it is less likely that the
rational process will be effective.

The Strategic Decision Context

In a world of changing technology and increasing shortages of energy and other
resources, the manager has to manage within constraints. The firm's strategic decision is dependent upon a multitude of constraining elements, including competitors, customers, suppliers, and so forth.

Thomas S. Bateman and Carl P. Zeithaml have described the sequential decision model shown in figure 7.2.[15] Strategic decisions are not impersonal, discrete,
or isolated events. They are made by individuals or groups that confront an array of
situational influences on the decision process. Strategic decision makers have experienced success or failure with previous decisions. They must consider the current issues facing the firm and weigh both the objective goals of the organization
and their subjective evaluation of the future. Each strategic decision is typically a
single episode in a series of decisions. It is affected by events in the past and the
present and by those anticipated in the future. Bateman and Zeithaml suggested
that strategic decisions are influenced by an array of situational factors. The model
contains three major components:

1 *Decision feedback (escalation of commitment)* emphasizes the sequential nature
   of decisions and the effects of success and failure feedback upon subsequent
   decisions. Barry Staw of Northwestern University found that as decision makers
   committed larger and larger amounts of time and resources to strategic deci-

sions, they tended to become personally involved with the decision, thus influencing later strategic choice.[16] When decision makers feel personally responsible, they tend to increase the amount of investment to a prior course of action, even though the current results are negative (see figure 7.3). Staw found that once the strategists become committed to a certain strategy, they tend to follow that strategy. In organizational situations, this finding may explain the tendency to replace top executives when a change in strategy is needed. At A&P, for example, even though the strategy of Jonathan Scott to cut unprofitable stores failed to reverse losses, it was continued until a new manager replaced Scott.

2 *Organizational slack (resources)* is defined as that cushion of actual or potential resources that allows an organization to adapt successfully to internal pressures

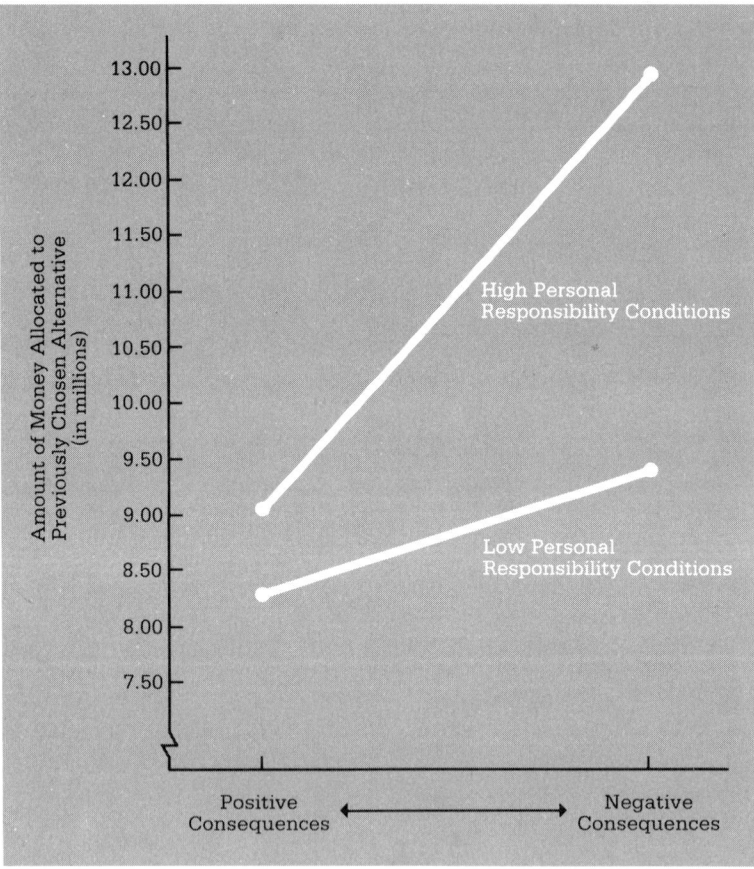

FIGURE 7.3
The Amount of Money Allocated to Previously Chosen Alternative by Personal
Responsibility and Decision Consequences

SOURCE: Adapted from Barry M. Staw, ''Knee-Deep in the Big Muddy: A Study of Escalating Commitment to a
Chosen Course of Action,'' *Organizational Behavior and Human Performance 16* (June 1976):27–44.

for adjustment or to external pressures for change in policy, as well as to initiate changes in strategy with respect to external environment.

3 *Decision frame (future prospects)* is the way in which decisions are presented. Positive or negative presentation influences the behavior and risk preference of the decision maker. Specifically, when decisions are phrased emphasizing the prospect of gain, decision makers tend to be risk-averse. When decisions are phrased negatively (emphasizing the possible loss) decision makers tend to be risk-seeking. In the Bateman study, it was found that future orientation had a greater impact on the reinvestment decision in a negative current context (losses) than in a positive current context. This tendency supports Staw's finding that decision makers will continue to invest in losing strategies. However, they also found that reinvestment was greater when a positive decision-frame future orientation was present. The managers at Exxon, for example, made a decision to enter the office automation market and continued that strategy for years even though suffering huge losses, until they finally sold off this unit and got out of this business.

RISK AND DECISIONS

T. Boone Pickens, chairman of Mesa Petroleum (see chapter 5), was asked if taking billion dollar risks was hard on his nerves. Pickens replied that because he had done his homework and analyzed the numbers and factors, making decisions was easy.

The strategist must make decisions to accomplish future objectives. These objectives may be immediate and short-term, such as the signing of a union contract by a certain date, or they may be long-term, such as the decision by AT&T to enter the PC market. Unfortunately, the future is rarely safe and predictable, but the strategist must make decisions based on the available information.

For any major decision a manager will probably have enormous quantities of information available. There are usually many possible alternatives and it would be extremely time consuming and costly to calculate them all. The amount of information available to the decision maker may vary as shown in figure 7.4. At one extreme is the condition of complete certainty and information, a condition rarely found in

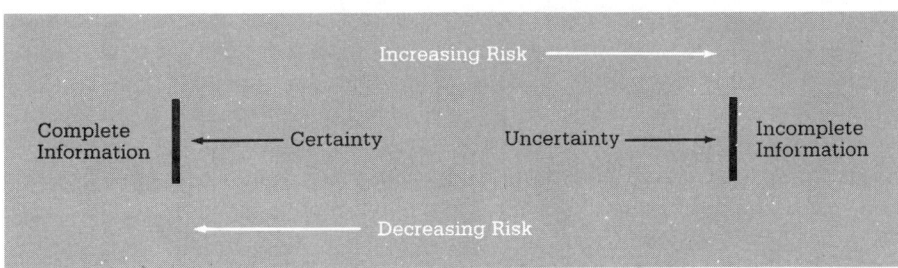

FIGURE 7.4
The Certainty-Uncertainty Continuum

strategic decisions. At the opposite end is a condition of complete uncertainty, where there is little or no information on which to base a decision.

This continuum between certainty and uncertainty, or more realistically between possible states of information, is called *risk*. The amount of information that the decision maker has becomes a critical factor. Theoretically, if all of the variables and their outcomes are known, then there is no risk. When you decide to invest your money in the bank at a fixed rate of interest, you are making a decision under certainty. The greater the amount of information available to the decision maker, the lower the level of uncertainty and risk. Conversely, the less information, the greater the risk.

Because managers tend to avoid risk, or more accurately to take calculated risks, information becomes an important element in effective strategic choice. Unfortunately, it isn't always that easy. Getting more information usually takes more time and money. Even then it is usually impossible to eliminate all risk. All the manager can do is try to minimize risk as much as possible.

Risk Analysis

The concept of risk is attracting increasing interest in strategic decision making. All strategic decision makers have one thing in common—they all require an estimate of both the expected result and the risk that the expected result will not be achieved. Risk may be defined as the uncertainty of achieving an expected result. Richard Bettis has noted that the term risk is taken in modern financial theory to be a precise, technical term defining the probabilistic distribution of future market returns. However, in strategic management it often is taken as a manager's subjective judgment of the organizational consequences that may result in a specific decision or action.[17]

In financial theory, two types of risk are specified: *unsystematic risk*, the proportion of total risk that can be eliminated by diversification; and *systematic risk*, the proportion of total risk that cannot be avoided, regardless of diversification.

In calculating risk, one useful concept is *beta*, a relative measure of price volatility. The average beta of all stocks is equal to 1.0; that is, the stock price will move up and down with the broad market average. A stock with a beta of less than 1.0 is less risky, and a stock with a higher beta is more risky. For example, a stock with a beta of 2.0 is twice as risky (or volatile) as the average stock. (See table 7.1 for a list of common beta coefficients.) The required rate of return increases in line with the beta of the project, as shown in figure 7.5. The expected return on an efficient portfolio is equal to a risk-free return plus a risk premium (a market premium based on the standard deviation of the portfolio returns). A higher return is associated with a higher risk, as shown in table 7.2.

Paul Samuelson stated, "Many economists think that businessmen on the whole act as if they dislike mere riskiness and hence they must on the average be paid a positive premium or profit for shouldering risks."[18]

TABLE 7.1
Illustrative List of Beta Coefficients

Stock	1983 Beta	1986 Beta
Diasonics	—	1.90
Apple Computer	2.74	1.70
Mesa Petroleum	1.86	1.20
Polaroid	1.15	1.05
Caterpillar Tractor	1.11	1.00
General Electric	0.92	1.00
Eastman Kodak	0.73	.80
General Motors	0.68	1.15
Anheuser-Busch	0.61	.75
Safeway Stores	0.58	.80
Campbell Soup Company	0.33	.70

SOURCE: *Value Line,* January 1986; Merrill Lynch, April 1983.

These betas are called "historic," or "ex post," betas because they are based strictly on historic, or past, data.

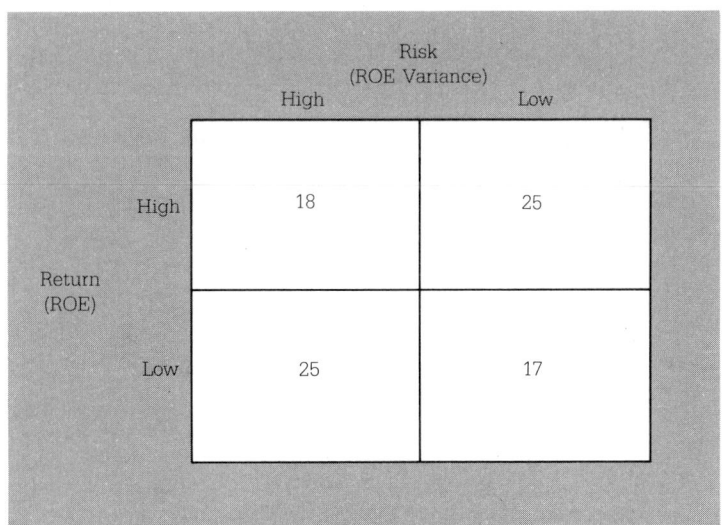

FIGURE 7.5
Risk-Return Relationship

TABLE 7.2
Investment Alternatives

| | | Investment Alternatives | | | |
Line	Expected Rate of Return or Risk Measure	T-Bill	Corporate Bond	Project #1	Project #2
1	k	8.00%	9.20%	10.30%	12.00%
2	Var (σ^2)	0.00	0.71	19.31	23.20
3	SD (σ)	0.00%	0.84%	4.39%	4.82%
4	CV	0.00	0.09	0.43	0.40

The Risk-Return Paradox

There should be a positive correlation between degree of risk and rate of return. However, Edward H. Bowman of MIT has noted the existence of a risk-return paradox: a negative correlation between business risk and return.[19] The essence of his finding is that in the majority of industries studied, higher-average-profit companies tended to have lower risk (i.e., variance) over time. The empirical results are shown in figure 7.6. The number of companies shown in each quadrant of the two-by-two contingency tables is based on each company's average profit over the five-year period, 1972 to 1976.

Bowman offered two possible explanations:

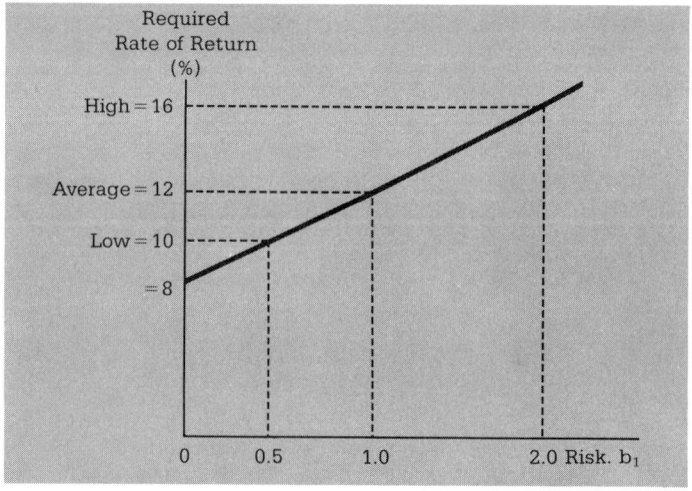

FIGURE 7.6
The Risk/Return Paradox

1   Strategic management and planning factors can increase returns and lower their variances.
2   The selection of high-risk strategies may be forced by financial problems.

Another explanation of the risk-return paradox may be the difference in markets. Risk measured by return on equity (ROE) includes total corporate risk and relates operating to financial risk, interest rate to exchange rate risk, and so forth. The financial models of risk return hold primarily for well-functioning and efficient markets. Financial markets are efficient, but most product markets are not. Richard Bettis and William Hall found that a negative relationship between risk and return is more likely to exist in related diversification firms.[20]

The outcome of these studies argues for risk measures that reflect the behavioral importance of total risk to strategic managers. The problem is that risk is taken before the resource commitment (an "ex ante" concept), but the return is typically measured over time, after the commitment ("ex post"). Strategic decision makers must focus on risk-return relationships.

Managerial Attitude Toward Risk

Research has indicated that individuals vary considerably in their propensity for accepting risk. Managerial attitudes toward risk vary from comfort with high risk to very strong risk aversion. A manager less inclined toward risk taking will set different goals, evaluate alternatives differently, and make different decisions than another manager who prefers risk. These risk attitudes vary by industry and firm, so that some managers need to be capable of withstanding higher levels of risk than others.

In industries where decisions need to be made quickly, as in the electronics industry where price levels must be shifted rapidly to meet competitors, risk takers can be expected to outperform low-risk managers because delays are usually associated with higher costs. Strategic decision making usually involves some level of risk. A major decision often involves the commitment of large resources, and a wrong choice may mean an executive's career. The strategic choice is the commitment of organizational resources to a specific course of action: to build a new plant or not to build, to invest R&D money in a new technology or not to invest, to invest in a large marketing campaign or not. These are the fundamental strategic questions, and making big decisions requires the courage to take a stand. There are many managers who prefer to take the low-risk option of no decision.

Studies show that individuals tend to reduce risk by collecting information on aspects of each alternative. However, once they have made the decision, they require considerably more information to adopt another alternative (as noted by Staw).[21] These studies reveal a good deal about the propensity of an individual decision maker for accepting or avoiding risk, as illustrated in figure 7.7.

The first decision maker has a high propensity for risk acceptance. This decision maker prefers a choice where the desirability of the outcome is highest and

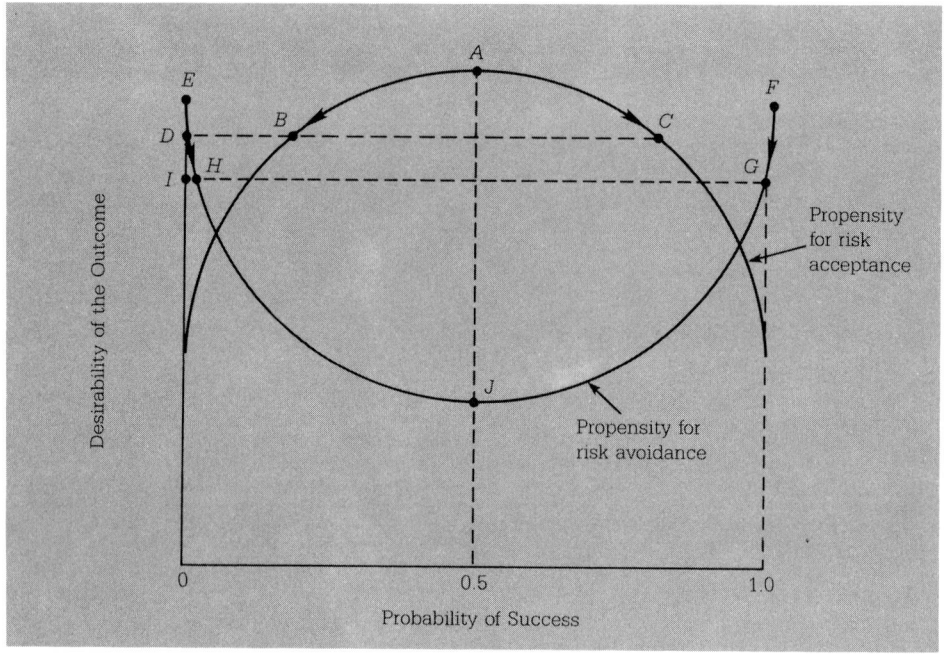

FIGURE 7.7
The Propensity of Risk Acceptance/Avoidance

uncertainty is greatest, at point A in the figure, with movement toward points B or C based upon success feedback. In a decision situation, the risk taker would prefer a higher risk to a certain lower return, because it offers a higher potential return.

These managers, like Charles "Tex" Thornton of Litton or T. Boone Pickens of MESA, could be classified as "Mississippi River Boat Gamblers." These managers look for high returns in high-growth, less stable markets. They are comfortable with highly leveraged positions and probably would not accept a no-debt position. They prefer to be the pioneers or innovators, seeking early entry into new high-growth markets.

There are some managers, like bankers, who are very uncomfortable in risk situations. They tend to be very low-risk takers in strategic decisions, preferring safer options, even though the payoff may not be as great. Similarly, such managers are more comfortable with very low-debt situations, and they prefer to be followers rather than innovators in newer, untried fields. The second type of decision maker is risk-aversive, therefore makes choices where the uncertainty or risk is lowest, at point F in the figure. In reality, there is a risk continuum between the propensity for risk acceptance and risk avoidance. In a decision situation the risk-averse manager would probably select a low-return strategy because it has a lower possibility of variation in return. Managers who pick the least risky investments are risk averse. Most managers recognize their investor's level of risk aversion and select strategy accordingly.

The Risk-Reward Trade-Off

The major factor in any strategic decision involves the level of risk associated with a given rate of return. The higher the rate of return offered by a strategy, the more attractive that alternative is likely to be perceived. Each manager has developed a set of criteria about which decisions are acceptable or unacceptable for his firm or industry and certain levels of risk which can be taken.

McDonnell Douglas Corporation called a special meeting of its directors to consider whether to risk manufacturing the MD-11 jumbo jet. However, the St. Louis-based McDonnell Douglas still hasn't met one other condition it laid down as a requirement for building the plane: obtaining an order from at least one major U.S. carrier. Building the plane without fulfilling that requirement would be taking a chance: McDonnell Douglas would never be able to recover the huge investment required to manufacture the big jet unless the plane caught on in the U.S. market, most analysts believe. A decision to go ahead would represent a high-risk decision, but for very high stakes.[22]

Each organization also has certain minimum rates of return which are attractive. Returns below these levels will be rejected. At Westinghouse, for example, a standard rate of return is 20 percent, although at many companies 25 percent or more must be achieved to make it worth going into. Fringe businesses with returns of less than 15 percent are candidates for divestment, and businesses below 7 percent are targets for oblivion.

Sometimes a firm is more concerned with other factors such as growth rate and market share. A cash-rich company, such as Exxon, may decide to get into a high-growth field like word processing even though it may sacrifice short-term rate of return for the longer-term potential. A firm may also place emphasis on gaining market share in a given product, with relatively less concern for profits. At Coors, for example, the company decided to switch its strategy from a relatively low rate of advertising to a head-to-head confrontation with the big guys because they wanted to gain market share.

At General Electric, managers are required to use more than just a single number, such as rate of return on investment or assets, to justify proposed programs. " 'In the past five years we have come to realize that a single number criterion doesn't work,' says Charles E. Reed, senior vice-president. 'People can make that number come out any way they want.' Instead, planning now consists of an analysis of the company's basic strengths in attacking the new business. These include relative competitive strength, competitors, economic, social, political and technological trends, and financial documentation."[23]

GE Bets on the Factory of the Future

Jack Welch, dynamic CEO of General Electric, made a strategic decision to bet heavily on the so-called factory of the future, where automated systems would improve quality and productivity even in older plants.

The vision has not materialized, and the project has cost GE over $120 million in losses since 1984. GE bought Calma, a fast-growing Silicon Valley maker of computer-aided design (CAD) equipment, eager to possess and successfully manage a high-tech generation company. However, political struggles broke out between Calma employees and GE managers. GE veterans were named to head up the company, causing defections of key engineers and marketing executives. The factory of the future was the most dramatic and visible element in Welch's decision to create a high-tech image for GE. The project also exemplified the chairman's wish to create "entrepreneurship" within the firm and to take more risks.[25]

A related factor is the degree of risk with which managers feel that they can live. Although management decision making always involves some element of risk, managers, as a rule, try to minimize risk. As a result, the strategic decision process involves taking calculated risks. The difference, of course, is how different managers calculate the degree of risk and how they perceive risk taking as a strategic factor.

Birger Wernerfelt and Aneel Karnani suggested that competitive strategy involves a trade-off between acting early and waiting and between focus and flexibility (see figure 7.8). They argued that in the typical situation, more competition makes earlier commitment more desirable. Smaller firms must take more chances and make focused bets; however, bigger firms can afford to wait and be flexible.[24] Their findings support Bowman's theory that firms are forced into riskier strategies.

Strategists can never know precisely what is going to happen tomorrow. They rarely have complete information about the past, present, or future. Each judgment about the outcome of a potential alternative must be conjectural and will contain an element of uncertainty. Strategic choice fundamentally involves judgment.

An example is the style of C. Peter McColough, chairman and CEO of Xerox Corporation. "If something bothers me," he said, "I don't rely on the reports or what other top executives may want to tell me. I'll go down very deep into the organization, into certain issues and certain levels of people, so I have a feel for what they think." McColough gets deeply involved in the "important decisions that are really critical to the business," such as the decision by Xerox to purchase Scientific Data Systems.[26]

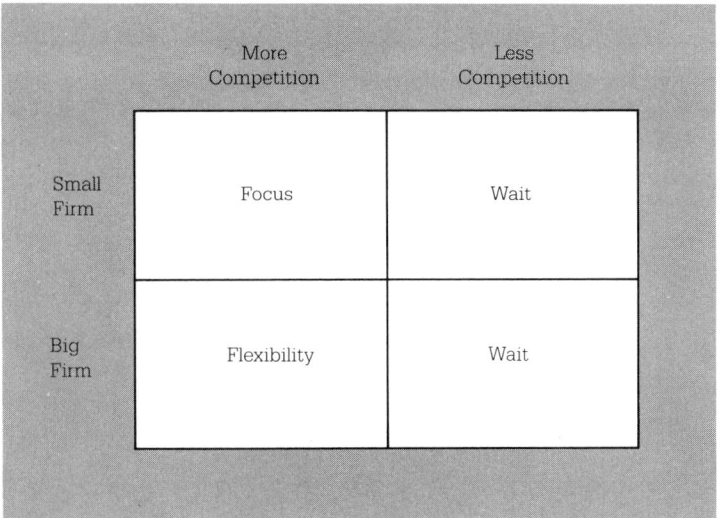

FIGURE 7.8
Typical Strategy Situations

SOURCE: Adapted from Wernerfelt and Karnani, "Competitive Strategy under Uncertainty," *Academy of Management Proceedings,* 1984, 45.

POWER AND POLITICAL FACTORS

Among the most critical but least discussed factors in decisions are the power relationships and political influences within the corporation. *Power* may be termed the "ability of a person or group, for whatever reason, to affect other persons' or groups' ability to achieve their goals."[27] For our purposes, political behavior in organizations refers to those activities that are not required as part of one's formal role in the organization but that influence, or attempt to influence, the distribution of advantages and disadvantages within the organization.[28]

Although both of these terms are often given a negative connotation, they are simply realities of organizational life, and the strategic decision maker needs to be aware of these forces. William D. Guth of New York University studied strategic decisions in a major corporation. He concluded that decisions were significantly influenced by interpersonal relations and the power relationships of top managers.[29]

Similarly, Peter Grinyer and David Norburn found that "those involved in the real process of strategic decision making recognized that it is ultimately a political process in which power and influence of individuals change with the nature of the challenges to the company."[30]

Why are there political or power struggles? Essentially, they are derived from the complex problems and multiple goals of the organization that result in differing views and vested interests. To cite only a few examples, marketing has different goals than manufacturing, doctors and administrators differ as to how hospitals should operate, and professors in the behavioral disciplines and those in the quantitative disciplines often differ over curriculum in the business schools. Each of these groups has some special interest it wishes to see advanced and opposing interests it sees as being of lesser value to the total organization. In one sense such conflicting interests are of value, for they bring different ideas and values to bear on problems. However, in another sense, this diversity can create conflict and the politicization of strategic decisions.

A number of studies have been conducted to explore political behavior and perceptions in organizations.[31] They found several basic political tactics, including

1 *Rule evasion*   Evading the formal rules and procedures in the organization
2 *Personal-political*   Using friendships to facilitate or inhibit the accomplishing of goals
3 *Educational*   Attempting to persuade others to think in terms of your departmental goals
4 *Organizational*   Attempting to change the formal or informal interaction patterns between organizational units

In another study conducted by Warren Bennis and Burt Manus, no common influence styles or traits were found. Instead, the researchers found that leaders share four common influence competencies:

1 The leaders had a sense of vision that compelled them to apply their energies and attracted others to this vision. Lee Iacocca, for example, was successful in attracting others to share his vision at Chrysler.
2 Successful leaders have the ability to communicate their visions so that others in the organization can understand and agree. Fred Smith at Federal Express, for example, was successful in communicating his innovative ideas to his team.
3 Leaders gain political influence when they are credible. Trust is an essential element in organizational functioning and is earned by developing credibility.
4 Successful leaders learn how to manage themselves. They learn how to fit their own strengths and limitations to the political realities of the organization. They have a positive self-image and tend to overcome minor setbacks without sacrificing long-term goals.[32]

The manager who hopes to change a strategy must be aware of the political nature of such a move. The past strategy may have been successful during an earlier time, and the managers who influenced these choices are probably still in positions where their support will be important in gaining acceptance of a new strategy. In order to gain support for a new strategy, the manager needs to win the support of key people and co-opt or neutralize the major opposing forces. The manager must be keenly aware of political forces, perceptive of strengths and weaknesses, and persuasive.

The result of such political tactics is often bargaining, compromise, and co-alition. *Bargaining* is simply the negotiation of agreement between two or more parties and is often necessary in organizations where power is not concentrated. Many strategic decisions are the result of bargaining among power groups. Another likely outcome is *compromise*. It has been said that politics is the art of the possible. Therefore, decisions are often the result of compromise between two groups. Finally, *coalitions* may be formed among two or more groups or persons to oppose or support a particular decision. Ian C. MacMillan of Columbia University has observed,

> Coalition members do not join the coalition without bringing with them their demands, and the support of these members could easily be given to alterna-tive coalitions. . . . Each member will, therefore, make a set of demands on-the coalition to commit itself to certain goals. . . . However, it is often impos-sible for the coalition to satisfy all the demands of all its members. A potential member will join only if he feels that the policy commitments of the coalition will promote his own goals, and he will stay only as long as he ex-pects the coalition to be successful.[33]

There are many examples of the importance of power struggles and politics, but one concerned the forced resignation of Richard Goodwin as CEO of Johns-Manville. There was a difference in strategic choice between Goodwin and the board, and nine of the twelve board members formed a coalition to achieve a ma-jority and force Goodwin out, even though he had done an outstanding job of managing the turnaround of the company.

Decisions are not always made on the facts of the situation. Generally, the more important the decision, the greater the probability that power and politics will be involved. Managerial decisions are often influenced by the political realities of the situation and these cannot be ignored. In a study of twenty-four strategic decisions, Henry Mintzberg found that in one-third of the cases, power and politics were significant factors and were important factors in all of the decisions.[34] The idea that politics is a factor, however, does not mean that managerial decisions are dishon-est — it simply implies that there are multiple forces involved in strategic decisions.

Decision Acceptance

Strategic decisions are never easy. That's why top managers are well paid. Their choices are based on complex sets of variables and unknown factors in imprecise relationships. If a certain set of economic conditions prevails, and if the competition takes one set of actions, then a given strategy may be very effective. If, however, conditions change or competitors take unanticipated actions, then the same strat-egy may prove to be disastrous.

Although the CEO is responsible for the strategic choice, a majority of impor-tant decisions take place in management review meetings. The strategic decisions are typically made in the boardroom as a result of group interaction after a careful consideration of all available information. When President John F. Kennedy made his famous Bay of Pigs decision, he first listened to a range of opinions, facts, view-points, and analyses from important members of government. There was not a "silver bullet solution." Instead there were a number of proposed plausible arguments from both hawks and doves, including many brilliant minds such as Robert McNamara, MacGeorge Bundy, Maxwell Taylor, and others. After all the meetings, discussion of alternatives, airing of opinions, and sifting of the pros and cons of each proposal, Kennedy made the decision. Unfortunately, the Bay of Pigs decision is generally regarded as a fiasco.

It is often said that a decision is no better than its implementation, that is, its acceptance by those who must carry it out. Because the strategic decision is influenced by external and internal coalitions, the decision maker needs persuasive and influential skills to gain that acceptance. No matter how brilliant the analysis, unless it can be sold to important forces (for example, the board of directors) the decision will not be carried out.

An example of a strategist with these skills would be Charles B. "Tex" Thornton, former chairman of Litton Industries. "Tex was one of the great managers of the fifties and sixties. He was a tremendous salesman. He turned on that Texas charm, deliberately using folksy colloquialisms. He had the gift of making everyone feel that they were valuable and important and worth listening to."[35]

Strategic problems are complex and controversial. There are facts, data, and arguments supporting several possible courses of action. No one person has all the expertise or all the information. Therefore, the decision maker must have the ability to function effectively in a group decision-making situation. The decision is usually based on the fluctuating and often vague realities expressed by experts in other fields and often based on uncertain information and differing analyses.

MANAGERIAL SUMMARY

The final stage in the strategic formulation process involves making the strategic decision. The strategic manager is a decision maker. Right or wrong, the decision must be made. Decision making is the most important activity of the strategic manager. In fact, some theorists suggest the term *decision maker* instead of manager. Decision making is involved in the entire strategic process, from goal setting and planning to controlling.

Decision making is an integral part of strategic management. More than any other factor, competence in this skill differentiates the effective manager from the ineffective. The manager's success as a strategic decision maker depends upon a combination of analysis, personal values, experience, and intuitive judgment.

Decision making is a dynamic process rather than a fixed, set procedure. Making a strategic decision is a process of systematically comparing strategic options and choosing between alternative courses of action. The actual choice is usually preceded by data gathering and the development of alternatives. Although the rational decision process is sequential in nature, this process is not always followed. Instead, managers take shortcuts, using bargaining or other power political techniques to deal with the complex forces involved in strategic decisions.

Decision making does not take place in a vacuum. Important elements in decision making are the external and constraining factors which influence decisions. The amount of information available, the time frame, and other forces place constraints on the decision outcomes. The three basic intervening variables are external constraints, internal values and attitudes, and political-power relationships. Managerial value systems influence the decision, and often strategic decisions are the result of compromises or coalitions between various power groups.

The strategic decision is the critical point in the strategic process because the choice sets the direction for the firm's future. The manager must analyze the various alternatives, sort out which important considerations are involved, and make a judgment regarding what to do.

The strategic decision process involves many managerial styles, skills, and roles. Because the strategic decisions are critical and involve risks, this stage is particularly crucial in the strategic management process.

In many situations, strategic decisions must be made quickly to be effective. However, there are many examples of decisions made under time pressures which result in ineffective choices—such as the Bay of Pigs fiasco.

Decision making is essentially a rational process, but there are limits to how orderly the strategic process actually is. Managers often approach decisions in intuitive, erratic ways rather than as a mechanical procedure. Because the stakes are high, there are usually differing power groups, inside and outside the organization, who have varying degrees of influence on the final choice.

Therefore, strategic decisions are more of an art than a science and are often the result of bargaining, compromise, and other political factors as much as pure rational analysis. In any event, decision making is an integral part of strategic management. In the final result, the quality of the decision sets apart the successful strategist from the unsuccessful.

Review Questions

1   Examine a major decision which you have made recently. Describe the process you used in making the decision.
2   Find examples of decisions made under certainty, risk, and uncertainty.
3   Find examples of managers who use high-risk and low-risk decision making. Where do you place yourself in terms of propensity for risk?
4   In what ways are intuition and political factors important to the rational decision process?
5   Many consultants advocate cost cutting and sacrificing short-term profit to build market share. (For example, TI's tactics in the digital watch field.) Do you agree with TI's decision? Why or why not?
6   Current research indicates that quantitative methods are not used as much in strategic decision making as was anticipated. Why?

7   In the text, it stated that the higher in the organization and the more important the decision, the less likely it is that quantitative methods will be used in the decision. Do you agree?

Notes

1   Wolfe, ''The Tinkering of Robert Noyce,'' *Esquire,* December 1983, 367. Based on personal communication from Gordon Moore, June 28, 1985 and ''Inside the Magic World of the Semi Conductor,'' *U.S. News & World Report,* December 24, 1984.
2   ''Inside the Magic World,'' p. 53.
3   ''How Intel Intends to Regain Momentum,'' *Electronics,* October 21, 1985, 48.
4   Herbert A. Simon, *The New Science of Management Decisions* (Englewood Cliffs, NJ: Prentice-Hall, 1977), 1.
5   Peter W. Bernstein, ''Jonathan Scott's Surprising Failure at A&P,'' *Fortune,* November 6, 1978, 36.
6   See F. Shull, A. Delbeque, and L. Cummings, *Organizational Decision Making* (New York: McGraw-Hill, 1970); D. Miller and M. Starr, *Executive Decision and Operations Research* (Englewood Cliffs, NJ: Prentice-Hall, 1960); S. Beer, *Brain of the Firm* (London: Penguin Books, 1973).
7   Irving L. Janis and Leon Mann, *Decision Making: A Psychological Analysis of Conflict, Choice, and Commitment* (New York: Free Press, 1977).
8   ''Coke's Man on the Spot,'' *Business Week,* July 29, 1985, 56.
9   Based upon ''In His Image,'' *Business Week,* February 18, 1985, 86.
10 Eberhard Witte, ''Field Research on Complex Decision-Making Processes,'' *International Studies of Management and Organization* 2 (1972): 156–182.
11 John Dewey, *How We Think* (Boston: Heath, 1933), 120.
12 Witte, ''Field Research.''
13 James Quinn, *Strategies for Change* (Homewood, IL: Irwin, 1980).
14 James W. Fredrickson, ''Rationalizing in Strategic Decision Processes,'' *Academy of Management Proceedings* (1983): 17.
15 Based upon Thomas S. Bateman and Carl P. Zweithaml, ''The Context of Strategic Decisions,'' *Academy of Management Proceedings* (1985): 2.
16 Barry M. Staw, ''Knee-Deep in the Big Muddy: A Study of Escalating Commitment to a Chosen Course of Action,'' *Organizational Behavior and Human Performance* (June 1976): 27–44.
17 See Richard Bettis, ''Modern Financial Theory, Corporate Strategy, and Public Policy: Three Conundrums,'' *Academy of Management Review* 8, no. 3 (1983): 406–415.
18 See Richard H. Bowman, ''A Risk/Return Paradox for Strategic Management,'' *Sloan Management Review* (Spring 1980).
19 Ibid.
20 Richard Bettis and William Hall, ''Diversification Strategy, Accounting Determined Risk, and Accounting Determined Return,'' *Academy of Management Journal* 25, no. 2 (1982): 254–264.
21 Staw, ''Knee-Deep in the Big Muddy.''
22 ''McDonnell Board to Weigh Risks,'' *The Wall Street Journal,* December 18, 1986, 16.

23 "The Opposites," *Business Week,* January 31, 1977, 64.

24 Birger Wernerfelt and Aneel Karnani, "Competitive Strategy under Uncertainty," *Academy of Management Proceedings* (1984): 42–45.

25 Based upon "What Welch Has Wrought at GE," *Fortune,* July 7, 1986, 3; and "GE Bets on the Factory of the Future," *Fortune,* November 11, 1985, 62.

26 "Where Management's Style Sets the Strategy," *Business Week,* October 23, 1978, 88–92, 94, 99.

27 D. Farrell and J. C. Petersen, "Patterns of Political Behavior in Organizations," *Academy of Management Review* (July 1982): 405.

28 Ibid.

29 William Guth, "Toward a Social System Theory of Corporate Strategy," *Journal of Business Strategy* (July 1976): 374–388.

30 Peter Grinyer and David Norburn, "Strategic Planning in 21 UK Companies," *Long Range Planning* (August 1974).

31 See Dan L. Madison, Robert W. Allen, Lyman W. Porter, Patricia A. Renwick, and Bronston T. Mayes, "Organizational Politics: An Exploration of Managers' Perceptions," *Human Relations* (February 1980): 79–100; Jeffrey Gantz and Victor V. Murray, "The Experience of Workplace Politics," *Academy of Management Journal* (June 1980): 237–251; and Robert W. Allen, Dan L. Madison, Lyman W. Porter, Patricia A. Renwick, and Bronston T. Mayes, "Organizational Politics: Tactics and Characteristics of Its Actors," *California Management Review* (1979): 77–83.

32 Warren Bennis and Burt Manus, *Leaders: The Strategies for Taking Charge* (New York: Harper & Row, 1985); Warren Bennis, "The Four Competencies of Leadership," *Training and Development Journal* (August 1984): 15–19.

33 Ian C. MacMillan, *Strategy Formulation: Analytical Concepts* (St. Paul: West Publishing Co., 1978).

34 Henry Mintzberg et al., "The Structure of Unstructured Decision Process," *Administrative Science Quarterly* (June 1976): 246–275.

35 "A Rejuvenated Litton," *Fortune,* October 8, 1979, 150.

PART TWO

■ ■ ■

STRATEGIC IMPLEMENTATION

CHAPTER EIGHT

Strategy Implementation

OUTLINE

OBJECTIVES

After you have completed this chapter, you will be able to:

- define the concepts of strategic implementation and structure

- describe the various ways an organization can be structured to fit the strategy

- discuss the key variables in the 7-S approach to strategy implementation

- compare the organizational structures which might be used in a national or multinational firm

- identify the key variables in the contingency approach to organizational design and explain how each can affect organizational structure

I'm trying to lead this company out of those areas that generate a constrained return, and into those areas that offer an increased return . . . [but] when you have a $7 billion gorilla, you don't go into the cage and quickly change him.

Charles Parry,
Chairman, Alcoa

A New Strategy At DEC—Overhauling the System

Kenneth H. Olsen, founder, president, and CEO of Digital Equipment Corporation (DEC), rode the data processing trend to become the second largest computer maker in the world, with annual revenues of $7.6 billion. In 1986, *Fortune* proclaimed him as America's most successful entrepreneur.

However, Olsen found that drastic changes in total system performance were necessary to retain competitive vitality as personal computers and office automation systems are putting computer power directly onto the desks of managers and executives. Instead of leading the trend, Olsen found himself having to play catch-up. DEC seemed to lose strategic direction—which markets it would go after and what its goals were.

To get the company back on track, Olsen moved into the company's day-to-day operations and launched a massive—and risky—corporate overhaul to transform his engineering-oriented company into a tough, market-driven competitor. The issues that led to this overhaul had to do with products and marketing.

Three key pieces of this restructuring are falling into place.

1 *Products* Olsen's new product strategy calls for a broad range of computers, from small desk-top machines to large office minicomputers, that can communicate easily with one another. Owing to a strategy Olsen adopted fifteen years ago, DEC now enjoys a wide technical lead in linking computers into networks.

2 *Marketing* DEC is adopting aggressive new marketing tactics for office automation, personal computers, and small-business users. It is working hard to develop closer ties with customers, organize new distribution channels, and launch more innovative promotions. In an effort to impress upon his managers the importance of the customer, Olsen ordered twenty-four senior executives to a warehouse where they spent a day uncrating and hooking up computers and learned just what customers had to contend with.

3 *Management* Olsen is streamlining an overgrown corporate bureaucracy and decentralizing decision making. Olsen has long been an advocate of delegat-

ing responsibility and he makes extensive use of committees. Olsen generally leaves the decisions up to the participants.

In the late 1970s and early 1980s, critics of Olsen questioned his ability to move DEC from a growth company to a mature, large corporation. There were some who thought he suffered from "founder's disease." In order to ensure DEC's future, Olsen led the company to a new computer line, a VAX superminicomputer. But the plan required DEC to perform new functions, such as engineering and manufacturing its own microprocessors and writing software to run networks.

In order to accommodate the new product line, DEC underwent a major reorganization and created a unified marketing organization. The corporate overhaul, which took five years, amounted to a major strategic and cultural redirection.

The change has paid off for DEC though not all of Olsen's lieutenants, including his brother, survived the changes. Olsen thinks that although he avoided founder's disease, many of his vice presidents fell victim to it by becoming complacent and ignoring changes in the marketplace. The new computers and networks have taken their competition by surprise and DEC is considered to be IBM's most serious competition in 20 years. Net profits were up 38 percent, sales up 14 percent, and stock prices rose 97 percent in 1986.[1]

INTRODUCTION

The next stage (stage 7) in the strategic process is the implementation of the stategic plan. The strategic plan is only that, a plan, until it is put into action. The strategic decisions, such as those at Digital Equipment Company, must be put into effect in order to achieve strategic objectives. At DEC, Kenneth Olsen implemented the strategy by developing specific plans and action programs aimed at shifting the firm's competitive position and decentralizing operations. After CEO Olsen and his top management team made the decision, the actual performance and activities aimed at achieving this plan, including developing new products, adopting new marketing plans, and reorganizing the structure, were put into effect.

Far too often, managers formulate a brilliant strategy, but they neglect the implementation: carrying out the plan of action.[2] Coleco, for example, developed a strategy to become a leader in the low-end home computer market with its Adam computer. Unfortunately, the firm was unable to implement this strategy. After losing some $500 million, Coleco called it quits, returned to its successful Cabbage Patch Kids product line, and got out of electronics.

In this chapter, we examine implementation—the means by which a strategy is carried through into successful goal achievement. First, a model of strategy implementation will be presented, setting forth the key factors in making strategy happen. Second, strategy and structure will be discussed, followed by a discussion of multinational factors.

STRATEGIC IMPLEMENTATION:
FROM STRATEGY TO ACTION

Strategic implementation, which involves the development of functional processes, as well as the organization structure and climate, is an extremely important and complex process in all organizations. Formulating policy and strategy and developing a game plan without carrying out the execution of the plan is a wasted effort.[3]

Implementation involves the carrying out or accomplishing of certain plans or goals. George A. Steiner of UCLA and John B. Miner of Georgia State University suggested that "the implementation of policies and strategies is concerned with the design and management of systems to achieve the best integration of people, structures, processes, and resources, in reaching organizational purposes."[4]

Daniel J. McCarthy, Robert J. Minichiello, and Joseph R. Curran, all of Northeastern University, argued that strategy implementation "consists of securing resources, organizing these resources, and directing the use of these resources within and outside of the organization."[5] On the other hand, Larry Alexander suggested that "implementation generally begins after a strategic decision has been made and carries through all the intermediary steps until performance achieves what the strategic decision had intended." Alexander also found that strategy implementation problems were experienced by about 50 percent of the organizations studied.[6]

Implementation might be defined as actually executing the strategic plan to achieve objectives. This procedure includes allocating resources, designing the organizational structure objectives, and developing a corporate culture to enable the attainment of organizational objectives. One recent report suggests that 90 percent of American corporations have been unable to develop and execute successful strategies, with implementation as the critical issue.[7]

If the strategic decision signals the commitment of resources, then the implementation phase means accomplishing the goals the firm has set out to achieve. This process includes the engineers who design the new product; the manufacturing people who convert raw materials into finished products; and the marketing people who must advertise, sell, and distribute this product to the customer. Therefore, the implementation involves the coordination of many differing groups and diverse skills into carrying out the strategic game plan.

In a rapidly changing marketplace, strategic opportunities often last only a short time. This favorable opening for a strategic move is termed a *strategic window*. If a firm cannot implement its plan and successfully get its product to market, then the window may close. As an example, Xerox originally developed the "mouse" and "window" concepts in computers, but Apple Computer was the first to bring it to the PC market place. A strategy must be implemented in the actual product and marketplace if it is to succeed. Otherwise, a market leader becomes a market follower. IBM was slow to bring out its laptop PC, thus missing the strategic window and becoming a follower.

Research has suggested that effective policy implementation is a key factor in the success of the strategy of the firm.[8] The resources of the organization must be allocated to reinforce the strategic plan. Therefore, the implementation phase involves the coordination of many diverse elements, products, and functions into an integrated course of action. The manager must be able to translate the game plan into action on the field.

The implementation phase is accomplished through adjustments in three major systems: (1) the technical system, allocating resources and organization structure; (2) the managerial system, providing leadership and responsibility; and (3) the cultural system, determining the behavioral processes and member values, as shown in figure 8.1.

The McKinsey 7-S Framework

Strategy implementation is more likely to succeed when the organization's elements are in alignment. Successful managers must attain a fit between the strategy and the internal factors available to achieve strategic goals. The closer the alignment, or fit, among these variables, the more effective the strategy is likely to be.

According to Robert H. Waterman, Jr., the McKinsey 7-S framework provides the way of thinking more broadly about the problem of organizing effectively.[9] It also provides an excellent tool for the analysis of management strategy and cases.

The 7-S model proposes that culture is a function of seven variables, as indicated in figure 8.2 and table 8.1. The McKinsey diagram may be thought of as a set of seven compasses. When the needles are aligned, the company is ready to implement a strategy; when they are not, it is likely the implementation will not be successful.

The 7-S framework provides a way of understanding how interrelated elements fit together in trying to implement a strategy. It is the degree of difference between what a firm does well and the requirements of a new strategy that determine the degree of difficulty of implementation. These problems were perhaps illustrated with the implementation of the new strategy at DEC. The key to implementing strategy is to ensure that all elements are in alignment, or fit, with the strategy.

The implementation stage is vital to the success of the organization. Without effective implementation, the strategy may become a set of unobtainable desires rather than a reality. The task of implementation involves a broad range of activities and requires the commitment and cooperation of all units, levels, and members if it is to succeed.

Organizations today face major, unpredictable changes that make strategic implementation more difficult and complex than in the past. Noel Tichy suggested a matrix of strategic tasks to be considered in the implementation phase when managing strategic change (see figure 8.3).[10]

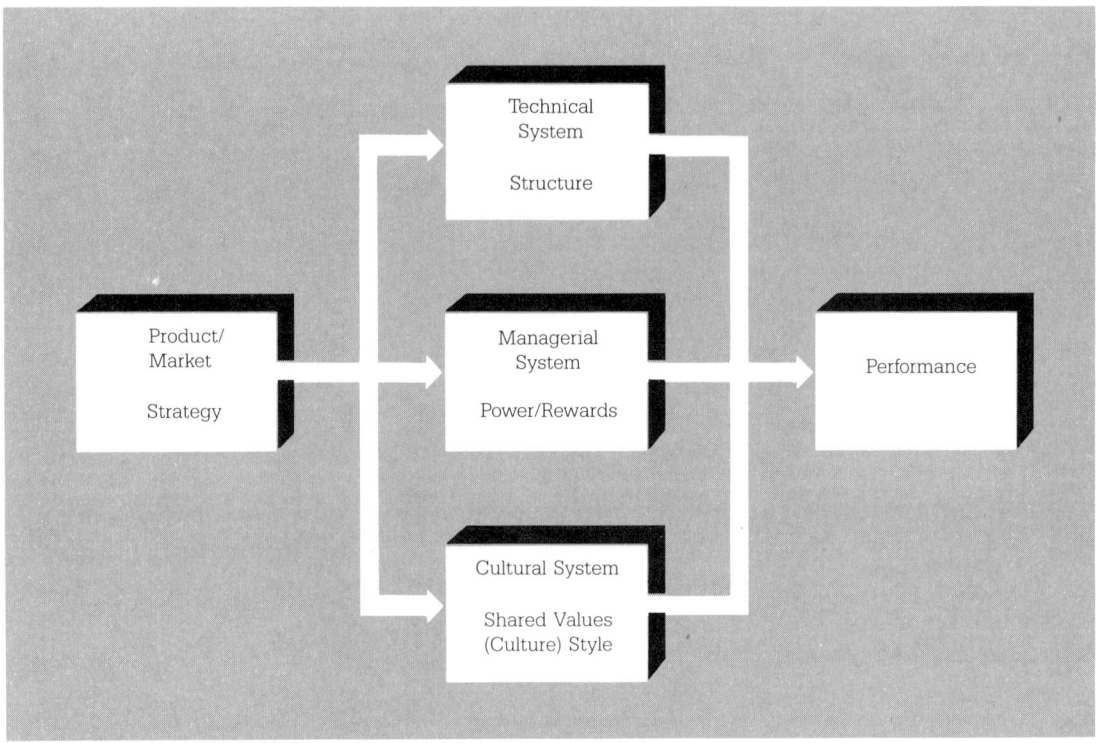

FIGURE 8.1
Strategy Implementation Model

Essentially, these basic functions may be incorporated in what may be termed the *strategic implementation model.* Peter Lorange of MIT, for example, has commented:

> It seems increasingly clear that the systems approach to strategy formulation and implementation, as signified by formal planning systems, is only one of the many aspects relating to effective strategy formulation and implementation. . . . Several other factors might contribute potentially equally as much or more to a corporation's strategic success. . . . Organizational structure and processes is another key area that impacts strategy implementation. . . . Finally, formal planning systems cannot function in a vacuum but need to be reinforced by other formal systems such as a management control system, a managerial accounting system, a management information system, and a management incentive/compensation system. . . . In total, formal planning systems is only one part of what seems to be an emerging *strategic administrative system.*[11]

The strategic implementation process is very complex because it involves several distinct but interrelated elements, as shown in figure 8.3: (1) the technical

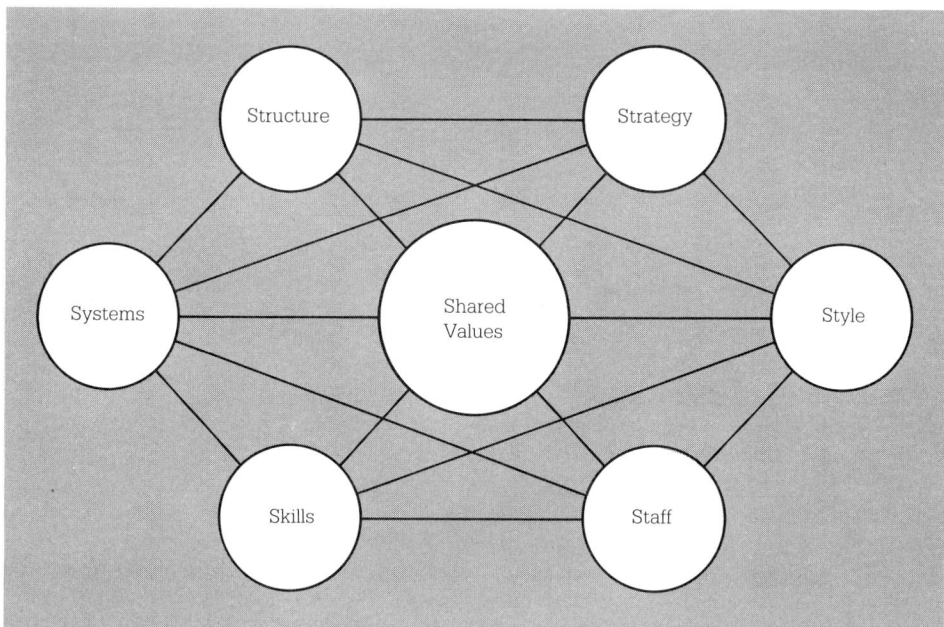

FIGURE 8.2
McKinsey 7-S Framework

SOURCE: R. H. Waterman, Jr., "The Seven Elements of Strategic Fit," 70. Reprinted by permission from *Journal of Business Strategy*, Winter 1982. Copyright © 1982. Warren, Gorham & Lamont Inc., 210 South Street, Boston, Mass. All Rights Reserved.

system, the alignment of structure to strategy; (2) the political managerial system, power, rewards, and leadership styles; and (3) the cultural system, the development and integration of a corporate culture to fit the strategy.

The strategist must integrate and coordinate these differing subsystems into a total, cohesive strategic system. In the following sections, we examine the technical and structural aspects of strategic implementation.

The Technical System

According to Tichy, all organizations face a production problem: arranging organizational resources to produce an output—structuring the organization.[12]

The first phase of the implementation process involves setting up systems to divide the strategic plan into its component parts (differentiation)—the subunit goals and plans. A subsystem plan is necessary because the overall master strategy is a comprehensive plan, but the carrying out involves all of the functions and areas of the firm. The purpose of the implementation process is to get members of the organization working toward accomplishing goals. Therefore, another problem facing the manager is how best to organize activities and people into functioning

TABLE 8.1
A Summary of the 7-S Elements

1 *Strategy.* A coherent set of actions aimed at gaining a sustainable advantage over competition, improving position vis-à-vis customers, or allocating resources.
2 *Structure.* The organization chart and accompanying baggage that show who reports to whom and how tasks are both divided up and integrated.
3 *Systems.* The processes and flows that show how an organization gets things done from day to day (information systems, capital budgeting systems, manufacturing processes, quality control systems, and performance measurement systems all would be good examples).
4 *Style.* Tangible evidence of what management considers important by the way it collectively spends time and attention and uses symbolic behavior. It is not what management says is important: it is the way management behaves.
5 *Staff.* The people in the organization. Here it is very useful to think not about individual personalities but about corporate demographics.
6 *Shared values (or superordinate goals).* The values that go beyond, but might well include, simple goal statements in determining corporate destiny. To fit the concept, these values must be shared by most people in an organization.
7 *Skills.* A derivative of the rest. Skills are those capabilities that are possessed by an organization as a whole as opposed to the people in it. (The concept of corporate skill as something different from the summation of the people in it seems difficult for many to grasp; however, some organizations that hire only the best and the brightest cannot get seemingly simple things done while others perform extraordinary feats with ordinary people.)

SOURCE: R. H. Waterman, Jr., ''The Seven Elements of Strategic Fit,'' 71, Reprinted by permission from the *Journal of Business Strategy,* Winter 1982. Copyright © 1982. Warren, Gorham & Lamont Inc., 210 South Street, Boston, Mass. All Rights Reserved.

systems—integration. This process includes resource allocation, information systems, and human resource systems.

Resource Allocation   One important aspect of the implementation phase is the allocation of resources to the operating units. The operating level must have the resources needed to carry out each part of the strategic plan.

Assigning responsibility is one of the first elements of implementation. At Boeing Co., for example, a new aircraft project may involve aerodynamic engineering, structural design, electronic and mechanical engineering design, and other special areas such as drafting, production, prototype development, tooling, testing, and marketing functions.

At advanced technology firms, like TRW Systems or Litton, the project system is used to organize the technical and staff specialties. In the project system, a project office is set up for each customer program. The project office reports to the appropriate company manager. At this point, the performing units, the responsible per-

Implementation Tasks

	Mission and Strategy	Organization Structure	Human Resource Management
Technical System	• Assessment of environment • Assessment of organization • Definition of mission and fit of resources	• Differentiation • Integration • Alignment of structure to strategy	• Fitting of people to roles • Specification of performance criteria • Measurement of performance • Staffing and development
Political System	• Determination of those who influence mission and strategy • Management of coalitional behavior around strategic decisions	• Distribution of power • Balance of power across groups of roles	• Management of succession politics • Design and administration of reward system • Management of appraisal politics
Cultural System	• Management of influence of values and philosophy on mission and strategy • Development of culture aligned with mission and strategy	• Development of a managerial style aligned with structure • Development of subcultures to support roles • Integration of subcultures to form company culture	• Selection of people to build or reinforce culture • Development to mold organization culture • Management of rewards to shape the culture

Implementation Systems

FIGURE 8.3
Strategic Management: Implementation Systems and Tasks

SOURCE: Adapted from Noel Tichy, "The Essentials of Strategic Change Management," *Journal of Business Strategy* (Spring 1983): 21.

sonnel, and individuals assigned to the program are determined. As Peter Drucker has been quoted as saying, "The test of a plan . . . is not how good the plan is itself. The test is whether management actually commits resources to action which will bring results in the future."[13]

The *budgeting* process is the second element of resource allocation. It provides the operating funds to actually design, produce, and market the product or service. The manager must decide what resources will be needed to get the necessary people, materials, and facilities. The program plan provides a detailed statement of activities necessary, while budgets lay out the cost of each activity specified in the plan.

Scheduling, the third aspect of resource allocation, involves the timing of interrelated activities leading toward the total goal accomplishment within a specific time frame. Typically, the planner begins with a start date and a completion date and must then calculate the estimated times for all interrelated activities, such as subassembly to assembly. The scheduling activity should involve several differentiation elements, including the following.

1   Clearly define all task activities and divide subtasks to the lowest operating level.
2   Sequentially lay out activities and identify responsible units for each segment of operations.
3   Specify the time of completion for every task and activity.

The manager must coordinate the departmental actions with those of other functional managers, thus making certain that companywide activities will fit together in the implementation phase.

Information Systems   Another primary task of the implementation process is to design and manage the information flow of the corporation in order to improve communication, productivity, and decision making. Efficient information systems are important because corporations are growing in size and complexity. As corporations become more decentralized, improved informational systems are needed to ensure that managers are operating to budgets and plans. Computers provide low-cost, dispersed information processing capabilities.

Human Resource Systems   In order to implement a strategy, the organization needs the proper quantity and quality of trained people. This requirement involves planning for human resource qualifications and appropriate recruiting, training, and reward systems. Companies like Hewlett-Packard include personnel planning in their long-range strategic plans, because they realize they must have the necessary human resources to accomplish these goals. They are already planning the need for engineers to meet their strategic plan in the 1990s, when a shortage of skilled personnel is predicted.[14]

Similarly, a capable management team must also be assembled as part of the implementation plan. Frequently, as an organization grows, it outgrows its management capability. Consequently, as part of the process, developing a solid management team is an essential function.

STRATEGY AND STRUCTURE

Organization structure might be defined as to the logical relationship of functions and authority arranged to accomplish objectives in an efficient manner. According to Peter Drucker, "Good organization structure does not by itself produce good performance—just as a good constitution does not guarantee great presidents, or good laws, or a moral society. But a poor organization structure makes good performance impossible, no matter how good the individual managers may be. To improve organizational structure . . . will therefore always improve performance."[15] The assumption underlying structural change is that task performance is improved by redefining the separation of tasks and the relationships between functions. As Ian C. McMillan and Patricia E. Jones have noted, "The challenge is not to design organizational structures that are perfect, but to design structures that are better than those of competitors."[16]

Structure involves the pattern of relationships among operating units of the organization. McKinsey & Co. studied one company where 223 separate operating committees had to approve an idea before it could be put into production. Imagine how long it would take to make decisions and how difficult it would be to use an innovative strategy in such an organization.

The strategist seeks to develop a structural arrangement that allows for the coordination and control of activities. At Westinghouse, for example, CEO Douglas Danforth decided upon a strategy of multinational growth. He found that a different structure was necessary to effectively carry out this strategy. Similarly, Dow Chemical, with over 2,300 different products, decided to become a global organization. In a sweeping move, Dow centralized its operations by using a matrix structure with autonomous geographic units in the expanding overseas markets. The strategist must identify the structural arrangement that allows for the effective coordination and control of activities.

An organization may be viewed as an interconnecting network of elements. Through this network or structure flow the resources, information, and materials that allow the major activities to be accomplished. A structural design change can improve organization efficiency by redefining the flow of authority (vertical) and responsibility (horizontal).

J. Thomas Cannon, a former consultant with McKinsey & Co., suggested that

> The experience of McKinsey supports the view that neither strategy nor structure can be determined independently of the other. . . . Strategy can rarely succeed without an appropriate structure. In almost every kind of large-scale enterprise, examples can be found where well-conceived strategic plans were thwarted by an organization structure that delayed the execution of the plans or gave priority to the wrong set of considerations. . . . Good structure is inseparably linked to strategy.[17]

There has been a great deal of research which demonstrates the relationship between strategy and structure. Eric Rhenman, for example, found that in Swedish firms strategic change without corresponding changes in structure led to problems.[18]

Westinghouse also found that a strategy of rapid growth without an appropriate organization structure caused problems. In place of an overall corporate design for growth and development, the company ran during most of the 1960s by the output of a computerized planning system that got most of its input from middle management sources. The corporation grew rapidly by entering promising fields and gaining volume without regard to risk. During the 1970s, poor management had let several businesses deteriorate. The new strategy and matrix structure implemented by CEO Doug Danforth provide a decentralized autonomy and a strong sense of accountability.[19]

The strategist is concerned with managing systems. The manager designs the organization, establishes objectives, and creates mechanisms to integrate the operational units. All organizations exist to maximize their effectiveness within the constraints of limited resources. Organizational design, then, is one factor of managerial choice. Given a certain strategy or game plan, the manager must then select the system design that best fits this strategic choice.

Alfred Chandler of the Harvard Business School first suggested that structure evolves from strategy in his study of seventy large firms. He found, for example, that when firms shifted to a diversification strategy, they tended to change their structure to a divisional form. Other studies have reported a similar relationship between strategy and structure.[20] Chandler noted that

> The comparison emphasizes that a company's strategy in time determined its structure and that the common denominator of structure and strategy has been the application of the enterprise's resources to market demand. Structure has been the design for integrating the enterprise's existing resources to current demand; strategy has been the plan for the allocation of resources to anticipated demands.[21]

As the organization's strategy changes from a single product to multiple-product diversification, the structure in effective organizations also tends to change. Several research studies have reported this shift as the firm diversifies. Leonard Wrigley of the University of Western Ontario found that almost 86 percent of the *Fortune* 500 companies used the divisional structure, and Richard Rumelt of UCLA found in a separate study of large companies that 75 percent used a divisional form.[22]

Organizational Growth Models

The concept of organizational stages of development has emerged as a result of Chandler's book *Strategy and Structure*. The organizational growth model suggests that as a firm evolves it tends to go through different stages of growth and development. Firms at different points in the cycle face different economic conditions and competitive situations and therefore require different structural designs to be effective.

There are several stages of development theories; for example, those of Cannon (1968), Thain (1969), and Scott (1973).[23] Although varying in the specific details, each of these models emphasizes that managerial style and organizational structure changes are associated with growth. These basic models propose that there is a continuum of organizational forms from a very basic extreme to a very complex one and that as the firm develops, there is movement toward more complex forms. Each stage represents an adaptation to changing conditions. In general, the development goes through a three-stage cycle from a small, single-product company (stage 1) to a specialized functional company (stage 2), and finally, to a multiproduct, diversified company (stage 3, see figure 8.4).

Stage 1—Entrepreneurial   A stage 1 firm is a small, single-product company that typically is operated as a one-man show. The top executive makes almost all strategic and operating decisions and works through an informal structure and communication network. All functions are handled by the entrepreneur, and most employees report directly to the boss. There is little formal strategic planning, and decisions are usually based on intuitive judgment.

As an example of a stage 1 firm, Hewlett-Packard was started by Bill Hewlett and Dave Packard in a Palo Alto garage in 1939 to build a piece of test equipment, an audio oscillator. The two engineer-managers did it all: they designed, built, tested, and marketed their product. They created the managerial style, set up an informal structure and made all the decisions.

Stage 2—Functional Development   A stage 2 organization is still a single-product company, but with an expanded size and scope of operation. Because of its increased size and complexity, it can no longer be managed by one individual with informal systems. As a result, the company is divided into specialized units, and operating decisions are delegated to managers in charge of marketing, production, and so forth. Group decision making is used in strategic decisions, and the planning and budgeting systems are now formalized. The organizational structure also is formalized, which means that it is based on areas of responsibility. The top manager makes the critical strategic decisions and spends more time on external concerns.

At Hewlett-Packard, as the firm grew out of the garage and began building greater volumes and types of test equipment, Hewlett and Packard's role became more of a top management job: making key strategic decisions. The functional managers were running the various segments of the company in a relatively autonomous manner, although still tying in closely with the owners. At this point, it was impossible for Hewlett and Packard to make the myriad of necessary operating decisions. They could no longer become as involved in detailed design decisions as they once had. Hewlett-Packard was now a functional organization.

Characteristics	Entrepre-neurial I	Functional Development II	Decentral-ization III	Staff Proliferation IV	Recentra-lization V
Strategic decisions	Made mostly by top person	Made more and more by other managers	May have "loss of control"	Corporate staff assists in decisions	Corporate management makes decisions
Organization structure	Informal operations	Specialization based on functions	To cope with problems of functionalization By industry or product divisions	Corporate staff assists chief executive	Similar to Stage II
Communication and climate	From leader down: informal communications	Internal communication is important, is difficult		Conservatism may result in slower communications	
Control system	Minimal need for coordination and control	Concerned with everyday situations	Problems with control	May be problems between line and staff	Tightening of control

FIGURE 8.4
Cannon's Stages of Development

SOURCE: Adapted from J. Thomas Cannon, *Business Strategy and Policy* (New York: Harcourt Brace Jovanovich, 1968), 525–28.

Stage 3—Divisional Diversified Firms   A stage 3 firm has outgrown its single-product line and became a multiple-product operation. The organization structure is more complex, divided into semiautonomous profit centers or product groups. The operating decisions are handled by the unit/division managers, and strategic planning and decisions are typically handled by corporate headquarters. There usually is a formal planning group for gathering information and communicating plans. In the divisionalized structure, the corporate headquarters usually is concerned with financial controls and allocating resources, but all other operations are delegated to the units, thus removing routine decision-making chores. In effect, the stage 3 firm is a collection of smaller businesses (see figure 8.5).

Hewlett-Packard's leadership position in instruments allowed it to diversify into computers, calculators, and components. For Bill Hewlett and Dave Packard the task became one of coordinating and controlling the activities of these semiautonomous units. The responsibility for operating decisions was delegated to plant,

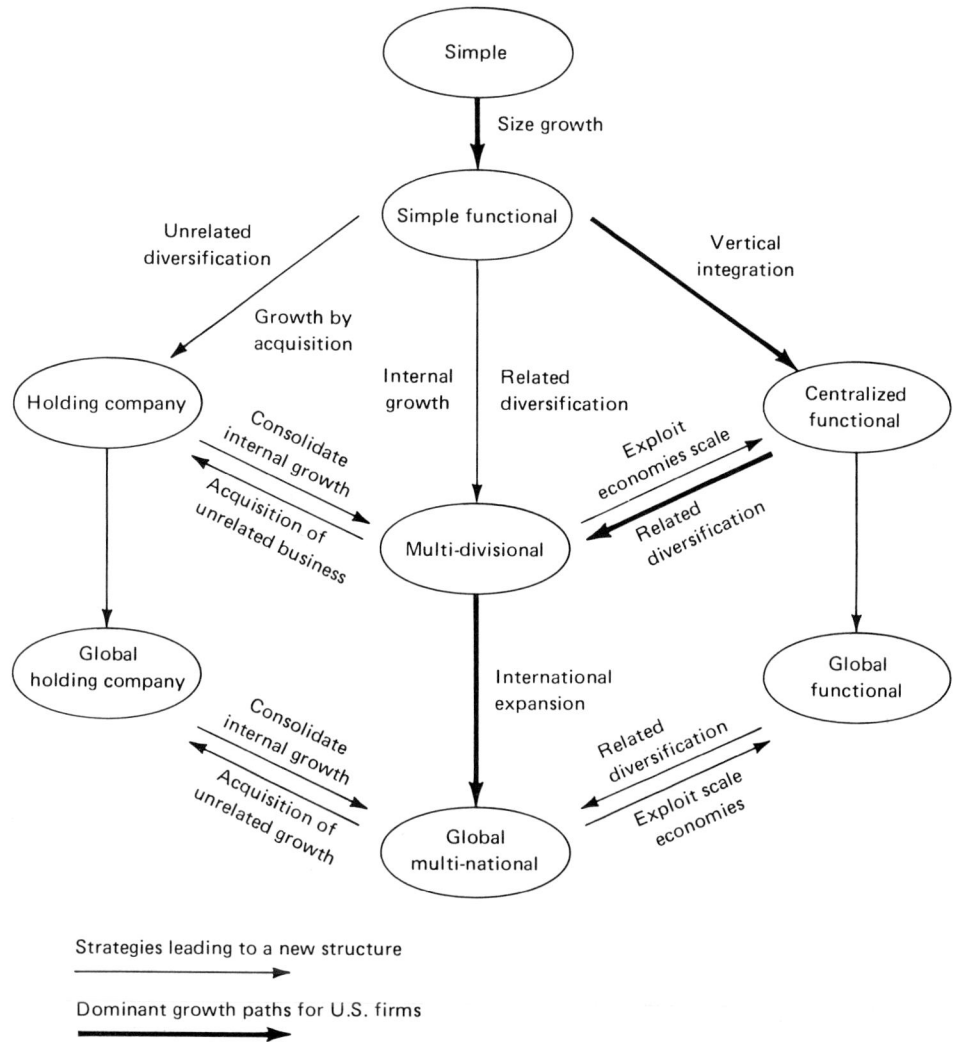

FIGURE 8.5
An Extended Stages-of-Growth Model

product, or division managers, while they retained the responsibility for tight fiscal controls and the strategic planning function.

None of Hewlett-Packard's forty-two divisions ever employs more than 1,200 people so that they maintain a manageable size. Hewlett-Packard is one of the top five companies or firms in the percentage of sales spent on R&D. Their famed decentralized management structure is a direct result of that emphasis on new products. As John Young commented, ''Nobody could plan that centrally, you'd be crazy to try. That's why we have forty-two divisions, because each of them has a general manager, they have all the marketing resources, they all have a product development team, they're really running a small business.''[24]

The move into stage 3 may be either by internal development of new products, as at Hewlett-Packard, or by acquisition. Donald H. Thain has suggested that ''the key skills necessary to be an outstanding general manager . . . shift from short-term operating ability in stage 1, to product and functional emphasis in stage 2, and to broader management abilities, including investment, trusteeship, diversification, and management supervision and development in stage 3.''[25]

Research by Bruce Scott indicates that firms moving into stage 3 are more profitable than those in stage 1 or stage 2. This finding is supported by the fact that almost 90 percent of the *Fortune* 500 firms are using the divisionalized structural form (stage 3). Perhaps the most important results obtained from this research related to the effectiveness of the firms. Scott compared firms whose strategies fit their structures—international divisions or area divisions under conditions of no diversification and worldwide product divisions when there was considerable diversification—with those whose did not. The results suggest that growth in sales is greatest when a diversified growth strategy is coupled with the appropriate structure.[26]

Stage 4—Staff Proliferation   As the organization grows, there is a tendency to add corporate staff to assist in top management planning and controlling. Often these staff units grow too large and create inefficiency; consequently, many firms today are reducing corporate staffs rather than increasing staff use.

Stage 5—Recentralization   Large organizations become very complex to manage, and as a result there is often a tendency to recentralize as a means of increasing management control over diverse activities. The computerization of planning and control systems often leads to the recentralizing of management operations.

It is apparent that all organizations move through stages of development, although the stages may be slightly different and unpredictable.

Structural Designs

There are a variety of structural designs, but certain basic types are found in modern, complex organizations. These designs include simple, functional, decentralized product/market, and matrix.

Simple   Smaller, emerging firms usually begin with a simple structure. Such a firm is usually manged by the owner or entrepreneur who performs most or all of the tasks that need to be done to provide a single product or service. This structure is useful for a small business in a relatively stable environment if the business is not growing.

Functional   The functional structure divides responsibility on the basis of basic business function, such as marketing, production, engineering, and so forth. The functional form enables the firm to take advantage of specialized expertise to deal with complex product problems. The functional form is appropriate as long as the firm remains basically a one-product business and operates in a stable environment.

Decentralized   When the firm grows and adds product lines, it may be organized along product or geographic divisions. The basic functions are then organized around producer, customer, or territory and typically formed into SBUs. These product segments are given primary responsibility for managing these autonomous areas.

A major emphasis of structural change is the concept of *decentralization,* which refers to moving decision making to lower levels of the organization, thus increasing the authority of lower managers. The real issue is not whether a company needs to decentralize but rather to what degree. In determining the actual amount of decentralization existing in an organization, the scope and level of decision making must be assessed. In a highly centralized structure, individual managers at lower levels in the organization have a rather narrow range of decisions or actions they can initiate. On the other hand, the scope of authority to make decisions and take actions is rather broad for lower-level managers in a decentralized organization. In a highly centralized organization structure, top management makes all major decisions.

Most large, multiproduct companies, such as General Electric, are organized using a product or market organization structure. As firms grow, sheer size and diversity of products make managing by functional departments too unwieldy. When the firm's departmentalization becomes too complex for the functional structure, top managers will generally create semiautonomous divisions, each of which designs, produces, and markets its own products.

A product or market organization typically follows one of three major patterns:

1 *Division by product*   Each department is responsible for a product or related family of products. For example, General Electric has a different sector for each of its major types of products. Product divisionalization is the logical pattern to follow when a product type calls for manufacturing technology and marketing methods that differ greatly from those used in the rest of the organization (see figure 8.6).

2 *Division by geographic area*   Each department is responsible for all activities performed in the region where the unit conducts its business. This arrangement follows logically when a plant must be located as close as possible to (a) its sources of raw materials, as with mining and oil-producing companies; or (b) its major markets, as with a division selling most of its output overseas that must locate abroad. Service, financial, and other nonmanufacturing firms are generally organized on a geographical basis.

3 *Division by customer*   Each department is responsible for a particular type of customer. An aerospace firm like Boeing, for example, might have separate

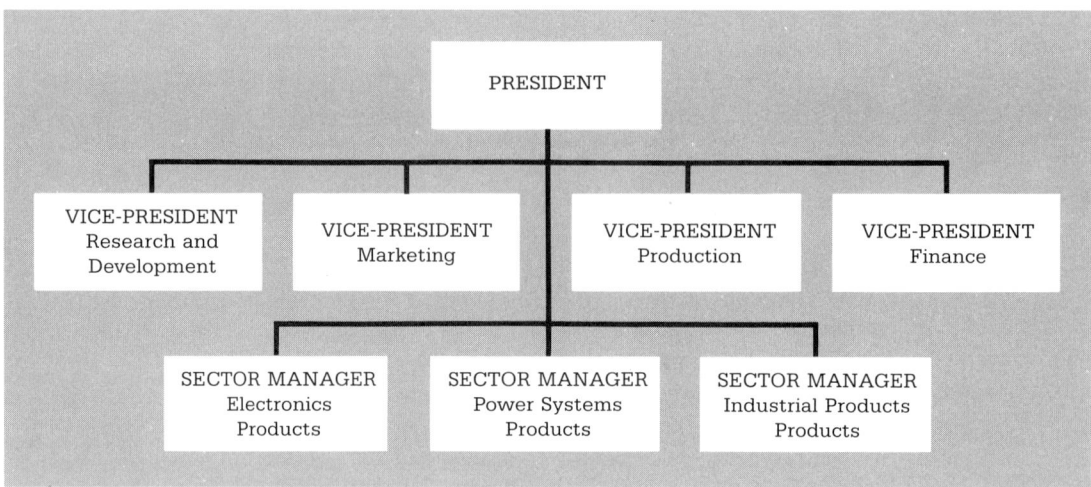

FIGURE 8.6
Product/Market Organization

divisions for military, industrial, and consumer customers. As a general rule, manufacturing firms with a highly diversified line of products tend to be organized by customer or by product.

In a decentralized structure, the decision-making responsibility is dispersed to business or product management. By opting for decentralization, Kodak abandoned a decades-old structure in which marketing and production executives reported through separate chains of command.[27]

A decentralized organization is possible whenever an organization's tasks are self-contained and centered on products or markets. In a decentralized organization, managers have only to worry about their own product or service. They have the resources to carry out these activities, and they don't have to compete for shared resources.

The strengths of the decentralized structure include:

1   The design is more flexible and suited for quick changes.
2   There is a high product, project, and program visibility.
3   There is a full-time task orientation (toward profits, for example).
4   The task responsibiltiy and contact points are clear to the customers.
5   The organization is able to process multiple tasks in parallel, and it is easy to cross functional lines.

The weaknesses of a decentralized structure include:

1   The restriction of innovation and growth to existing project areas.
2   The difficulty of allocating pooled resources.

3   The difficulty of coordinating shared functions.
4   The deterioration of in-depth competence.
5   The possibility of internal task and priority conflicts.
6   The high level of integration required in the organization.

In a study of decision makers' beliefs about the causes and effects of structure, Jeffrey D. Ford and W. Harvey Hagarty suggested that as size increases, delegation, formalization, and the division of work will also increase and that people-related variables tend to be most important in structural considerations.[28]

Matrix Organization

One new approach that has evolved out of contingency approaches is the matrix organization. This approach came into prominence during the late 1960s when the aerospace industry began using it. The matrix combines the functional and project types of structure and is often used to coordinate efforts on large, complex projects. The matrix organization may be defined as any organization that employs a *multiple command* system that includes not only a multiple command structure but also related support mechanisms and an associated organizational culture and behavioral patterns.[29]

The matrix organization is formed around specific products or projects (see figure 8.7) with individuals assigned to a project and a functional department.[30] The advantage of the matrix form is that it provides a horizontal group for a number of functions to accomplish project objectives under the direction of a project or product manager. It is most effective in large organizations with multiple products, innovative technology, and changing markets. TRW Systems is an example of a company using a matrix design where a team is formed for each special project, cutting across departmental lines. As a result, an employee may be a member of several project teams and report to a number of bosses.

In a matrix organization, employees have in effect two bosses—they operate under dual authority. One chain of command is functional or divisional, diagrammed vertically, while the second is shown horizontally in figure 8.7. This lateral flow forms a project team, led by a project or product manager who is expert in the team's assigned area of specialization. For this reason, the matrix structure is often termed a *multiple command system.*

Matrix organizations were first developed in the aerospace industry by firms such as TRW. The initial impetus was a government demand for a single contact manager for each program or project who would be responsible to the prime contractor for the project's progress and performance. To meet this need, a project leader was appointed, sharing authority with the existing technical or functional departments. Currently, matrix organization is used in the structure of many major companies, in management consulting firms, in advertising agencies, and in many other types of businesses. In some organizations, the matrix structure is found at all levels, while in others it is used only in certain departments.

TABLE 8.2
Characteristics of Matrix Structure

Advantages		
	1	Provides flexibility to organization
	2	Stimulates interdisciplinary cooperation
	3	Involves and challenges people
	4	Motivates people to identify with end product
	5	Allows experts to be moved to crucial areas as needed
Disadvantages		
	1	Risks creating a feeling of anarchy
	2	Encourages possible power struggles
	3	Requires high interpersonal skills
	4	Is costly to implement
	5	Risks duplication of effort by project teams

Not all employees function well in the matrix system. An effective matrix structure requires flexibility and cooperation from people throughout the organization. The complexity of the structure requires open and direct lines of communication at all levels. Special training in interpersonal relationships may be necessary for managers when a matrix structure is first introduced. The matrix structure is often an efficient means for bringing together the diverse specialized skills required to solve a complex problem (see table 8.2). Matrix structures are becoming more commonplace in today's environment. When used properly, they provide an excellent vehicle for managing and accomplishing complex projects.

In short, the matrix offers certain advantages and problems, but it can be an effective design under the right conditions. At Westinghouse, for example, top management needs greater flexibility and control in multinational operations and feels that the matrix is the answer. They recognize, however, that increased interaction skills, consensual decision making, and conflict management will be required if it is to work.

The Decision Tree Model

It appears that there is no one best way to organize to meet the demands of all situations. Management must analyze the relevant factors and develop a structure that best fits the situational demands. Robert Duncan of Northwestern University has developed a decision tree analysis technique to fit the demands of the environment.

FIGURE 8.7

Diagrammatic Representation: Matrix Organization

SOURCE: Adapted from J. Mee, ''Ideational Items: Matrix Organizations,'' *Business Horizons* 7 (Summer 1964): 70–72.

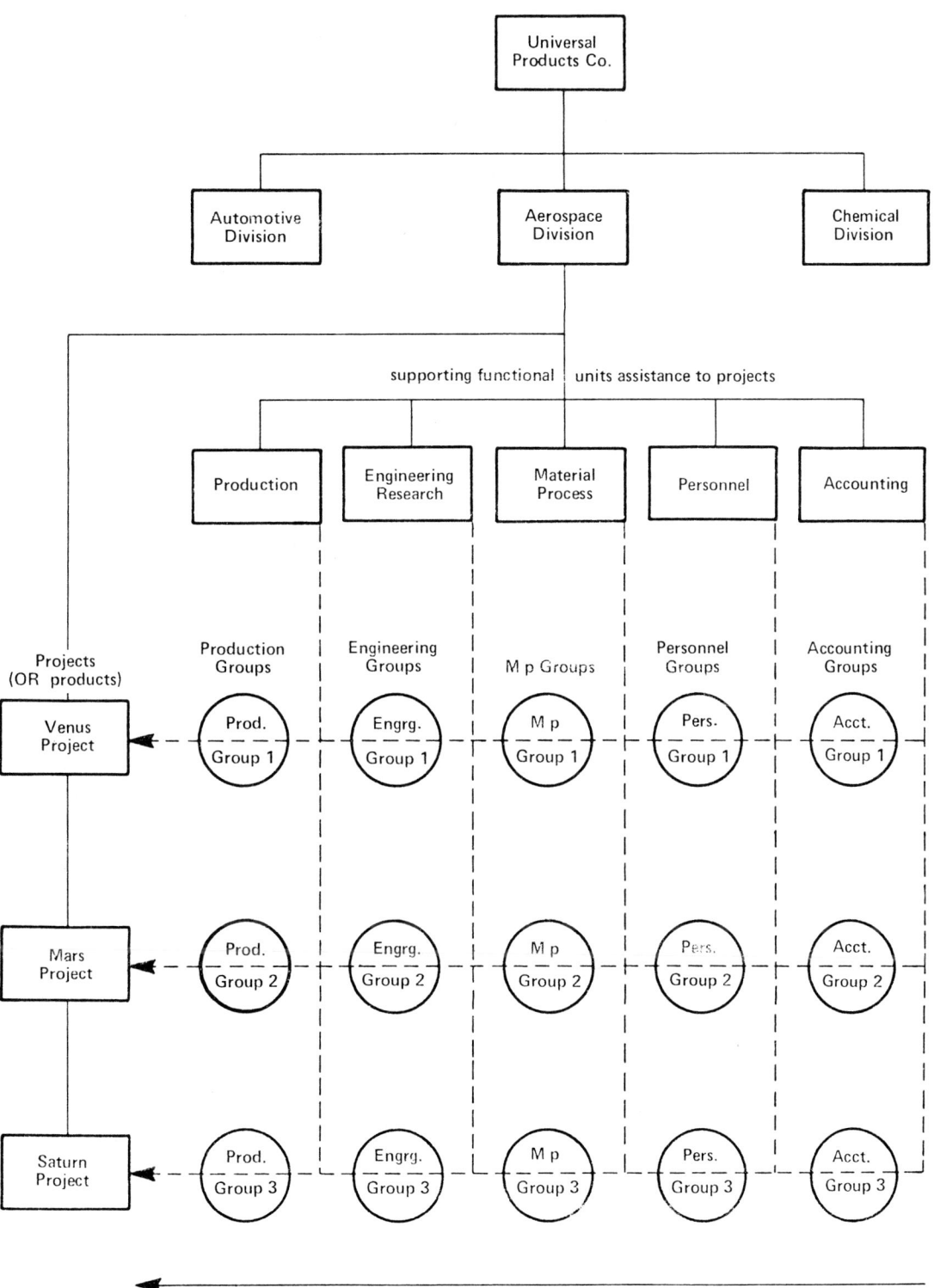

Matrix Structure at International Minerals and Chemicals

Tony Cascino, vice-chairman of International Minerals and Chemicals Corporation (IMC), faced a crisis that threatened to break down the company's problem-solving and decision-making processes. The company's structure had evolved from a simple, functional design to one that was a complex array of project management and decentralization. Cascino recognized, however, that internal complexities and external environmental turbulence can increase to such a degree that a more effective structure has to be devised. To IMC and Cascino, the answer was a matrix structure.

After six years with matrix management, Cascino learned a number of important lessons from which other managers may benefit. Some of the most important include the following.

1 In the early stages of implementation the structure should not only be put in place in manageable degrees, but minimal concern should be given to rules, titles, and authority. Experience is the best guide to establishing procedure.

2 Success rests more on the behavior of people than on structure. The internal operations, therefore must stress cooperation, not power plays.

3 Avoid the condition of two bosses. Refer to the peer group to minimize authority challenges.

4 Keep top management informed but uninvolved in day-to-day activities. Participation of superiors can cause otherwise good working sessions to deteriorate into a series of unproductive meetings and presentations.

5 The compensation package for managers must be structured to accommodate both vertical (functional) and horizontal (product) obligations.

6 Top management must, in spirit, philosophy, and practice, promote and support the matrix approach.

Matrix structure has helped IMC improve operations, productivity, profitability, and overall working relationsips. Its major contribution has been in the development of managers—with the matrix approach improving managerial skills and performance.[31]

As shown in figure 8.8, the decision analysis indicates when functional, decentralized, or lateral relations (matrix) should be selected. First, the manager must determine the state of the environment, simple or complex, and whether thesefactors are static or dynamic. Based upon these two factors, the manager can then identify the type of structure that best fits the environment. However, Duncan has cautioned that managers must be sensitive to the fact that environments are constantly changing, so contingency planning may be useful.[32]

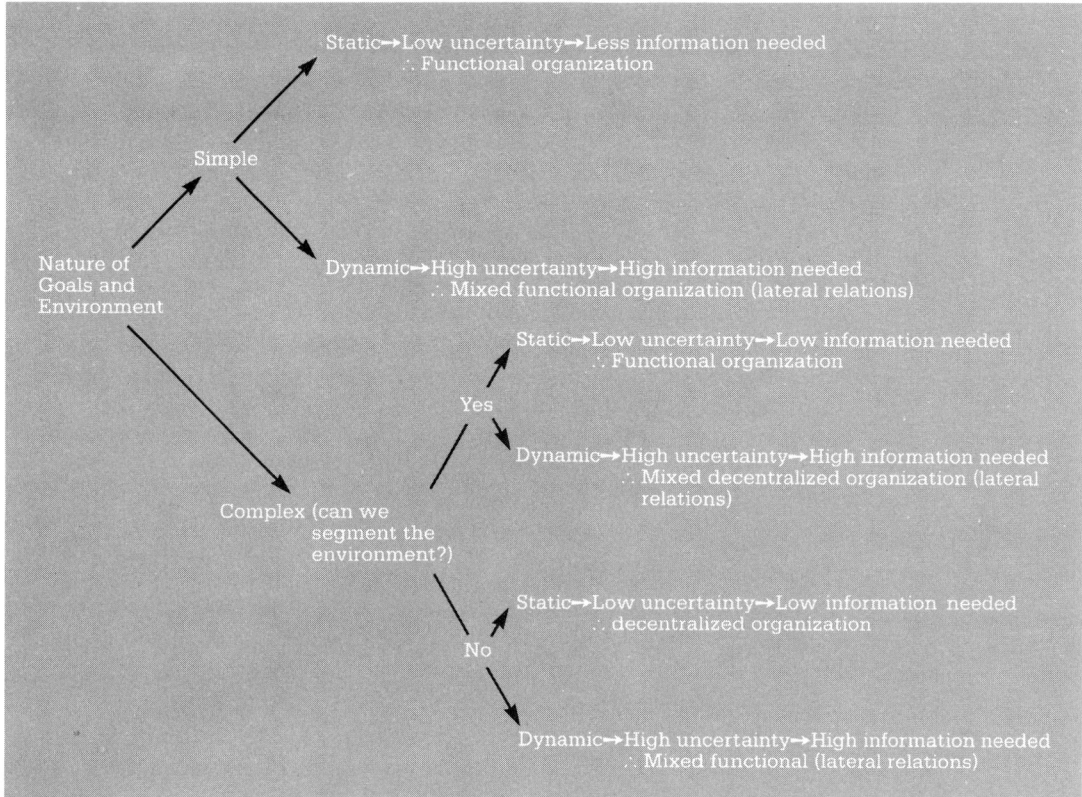

FIGURE 8.8
Organizational Design Decision Tree Model

SOURCE: Robert Duncan, "What Is the Right Organization Structure?" *Organization Dynamics,* Winter 1979. Copyright 1979 by *Organization Dynamics.* Reproduced by permission.

MULTINATIONAL STRATEGIC IMPLEMENTATION

Implementing strategy in the international environment is more difficult than deal-ing with problems in the domestic environment. Each overseas situation will be different from those for the home country and for other foreign countries, sometimes dramatically so. As the multinational corporation (MNC) becomes involved with more and more countries, the sheer number of situations strains the organization's ability to develop an effective strategy in each area. Another difficulty is that man-agers instinctively understand the home situation and the emerging trends of their environment. Often managers never achieve this understanding, as was exemplified in Iran, where the revolution took most American managers completely by surprise.

In an MNC, the managers must understand the current state of the interna-tional environment and monitor and predict changes. The primary focus is usually on the elements of the environment that involve change. Later, as managers gain experience in the host country, they can pay increasing attention to anticipating changes in the world environment.

The multinational manager faces some significant new challenges because of the more complex operational problems in overseas operations. Legal, economic, political, and cultural constraints can affect the formulation and implementation of strategy on a worldwide basis.

Legal Constraints   Multinational corporations have to be aware that each country has a unique set of laws and practices. There are also variations from country to country in the degree to which laws are enforced or overlooked. As an example, in the United States bribery is illegal, although in many countries around the world it is an unavoidable fact of life. In some countries, tax laws are expected to be avoided, but in others, exposed tax fraud brings legal action.

Economic Constraints   Because of the size and scope of multinational operations, the economic system must be taken into account. Countries exist in differing stages of development, and underdeveloped countries may offer lower levels of income but also provide lower labor costs. Also, the economy may be to a lesser or greater degree subject to governmental control and interference. Many countries are able to influence which companies are allowed access to certain markets.

Political Constraints   People who live in countries with established governments such as the United States or Canada take political stability for granted because the transfer of power from one political party to another occurs in an orderly manner without political upheaval. Unfortunately, in many countries, political instability is a constant way of life. MNCs doing business in politically unstable countries must be aware of these struggles for power, often a difficult task when several political parties are struggling for control of the government.

Political fortunes can shift quickly with dramatic impact in an unstable situation. The degree of political stability is an important factor because the large investments required to build a manufacturing complex are not factors to be taken lightly. The political aspects often overshadow all other elements of multinational management. An elected dictatorial, capitalist, socialist, or communist government also influences the way business is done. Generally, the more open the climate, the easier it is to operate; and the greater the restrictions, the more difficult it is to operate.

The top executives of multinational corporations often deal directly with top-level government officials and must consider the broader issues of public opinion and home government relations. However, the strategist faces greater turbulence abroad and operates from a position of less power than in the past. According to Louis Kraar, writing in *Fortune*,

Since U.S. corporations face ever fiercer competition abroad, and their own power has diminished, the leaders of these enterprises have only one choice—to get smarter about the world.

[Thus] . . . the top executives of major corporations are gradually acknowledging that they need both new skills and fresh insights to thrive overseas. The enjoyment of cordial personal relations with a head of state is no longer, if it ever was, a reliable way to appraise the prospects of their nation's market. Nor does the penchant of many CEOs for flying off to intriguing places, such as Islamabad or Peking, assure considered judgments back at their headquarters. Just as senior officers have long consulted their specialists on marketing and finance and law, they now sense the need for staff expertise to direct a more systematic approach to international affairs. Confronting the world these days cannot be a do-it-yourself job.

This new political-risk game requires anticipating the currents of change abroad, then plotting how to move with them. To do this demands going beyond economic forecasting to gauge other forces, from religious movements to nationalistic passions. It also requires U.S. executives, who have learned the hard way, to refrain from plunging into foreign ventures merely on the strength of Washington's judgments.

The potential for corporate disaster often lurks in seemingly stable places. A few years ago Aris Gloves, a division of Consolidated Foods, wanted to spread its risks beyond the Philippines, its only manufacturing base. In 1976, the company picked a spot that its vice president, James McCorry, says "everyone, including the U.S. embassy, described as a happy, sleepy country." This carelessly promised land was El Salvador. Within some two years, political turmoil hit the Aris plant, with leftist dissidents holding its president and about 120 local employees as hostages for nine days—until the company agreed to wage increases that it could not afford. In 1979, Aris fled from El Salvador.[33]

Political risk assessment has developed into a sophisticated activity.[34] Political risk may be defined as the probability that political forces will cause turbulent upheavals in a country's business environment, which may have an important impact on profit and other strategic goals of the enterprise.[35]

As *Business Week* reported, political risk assessment is rapidly becoming a fact of corporate life. Many firms are developing their own political assessment units to take a more accurate look at the risks inherent in operating overseas. Table 8.3 presents an assessment of the ten best and worst risk analyses by independent political risk consulting firms. Because MNCs are unable to dictate the political climate in a particular host country, they must learn to assess the risk of doing business under a given political climate. As Vernon Terpstra has commented: "Most host governments accept the need for foreign investment. Many realize that they need the resources, technology, management skills, capital, and foreign exchange that foreign investment can bring. But governments increasingly want foreign investment on terms that maximize the contribution to national goals and minimize

TABLE 8.3
Five Companies and Their Overseas Restaurants

Company	1981	1982	1983	1984	1985
McDonald's	1,185	1,341	1,527	1,709	1,831*
KFC	1,300	1,386	1,500	1,647	1,773
Pizza Hut	222	284	334	427	481
Burger King	205	256	289	321	364
Wendy's	109	125	153	177	201

SOURCE: *USA Today,* January 27, 1986, 46.

the threat to national sovereignty."[36] In other words, both parties seek a mutual exchange of benefits.

Cultural Constraints   Finally, the multinational firm must consider the cultural differences in multinational operations. Culture is the set of social norms and behaviors that are accepted, and cultural standards vary among nations. Thus, marketing a product may be very different in other cultures, and often TV advertisements when directly translated are insulting to foreign cultures. An example might be marketing Chevy Novas in South America. In Brazil, where Portuguese is spoken, "no va" means "It doesn't go." The name had to be changed.

Products that are prized in one culture may have little appeal in another. Similarly, there are traditions and practices among labor groups and status symbols that must be recognized if the firm is to operate effectively in that cultural setting.

> A Commerce Department study shows that U.S. companies operated 5,516 restaurant franchises in foreign countries in 1983 [see table 8.3], compared with 3,912 in 1979. Canada and Japan were the major markets for U.S. company franchises. "It's a much less competitive arena," says Michael Culp, an analyst with Prudential-Bache Securities Inc.
>
> McDonald's Corporation had about $665 million in capital expenditures in 1984. About $195 million went outside the USA. "That's a high proportion," says William Trainer, a Merrill Lynch and Co. analyst. "And as far as any other publicly held companies I cover, no one comes close to it."[37]

Because of the cultural and language differences, doing business abroad can be a sensitive venture. Wendy's International, Inc., occasionally runs into problems with certain words on its menu—hot stuffed baked potatoes, for example. " 'Hot stuffed' has a negative connotation in England," says Tom Lounds, director of international marketing. Wendy's dropped the adjectives. There's no good German translation for "stuffed," so Wendy's German restaurants sell "hot top" baked potatoes. Kentucky Fried Chicken cannot sell biscuits in England until it comes up with a new name. Biscuit means cookie to the British and, understandably, they are not turned on by the idea of a chicken-and-cookies dinner.[38]

In a cross-cultural study of similarities and differences among employees, Geert Hofstede compared employees from forty countries, looking for the main criteria by which the national cultures differed. Hofstede found four such criteria:

1 *Power distance* is the extent to which a society accepts that power of institutions and organizations is distributed unequally.
2 *Uncertainty avoidance* is the extent to which a society feels threatened by uncertain and ambiguous situations and tries to avoid these situations.
3 *Individualism* implies a loosely knit social framework in which people are supposed to take care of only themselves and their immediate families; its opposite is collectivism, which is characterized by a tight social framework in which people expect others in groups of which they are a part—family, organizations—to look after them.
4 *Masculinity* is the extent to which the dominant values in society are macho or masculine, that is, characterized by assertiveness, the acquisition of money and things, and the lack of concern for others or for the quality of life.

Based upon these four dimensions, Hofstede found certain distinct national cultural differences among employees.[39]

Multinational business is becoming increasingly important in a growing world economy. Yet because of the multiple challenges and constraints, the formulation and implementation of strategy is more complex and difficult.

MANAGERIAL SUMMARY

Strategic implementation is an important element of the strategic management process. Implementation does not occur automatically. The important organization factors must be managed to fit with the strategy, including technical systems (structure), managerial systems, and cultural systems.

Chandler's major contribution is the finding that structure follows strategy. Therefore, the structure is determined, in part, by the type of strategy which is chosen by the organization.

One means of finding a more effective way of allocating resources is the organizational structure. Structural change provides one technique for the strategist to implement strategy effectively. The successful use of this element requires that the structure be adapted to fit the environment, the technology, and the stage of growth of the firm.

The contingency approach to organizational design problems stresses an analysis of the environment, the internal culture, technology, and the strategy as key determining variables in the selection of the best form. As the environment becomes more complex and dynamic, a more decentralized structure becomes more appropriate.

The matrix design, which combines the functional and project structures, has become a popular form of organization structure. Although there are some problems with this design, it is often found to be effective for firms that operate in a dynamic and complex environment, as is the case for many multinational corporations.

Multinational implementation raises new legal, cultural, political, and economic problems as well. Because of these constraints, managerial strategies must vary from country to country, thus bringing increased problems of integration for the strategist. Effective managers must be aware of both the similarities and the difficulties offered by overseas operations, and they must remain sensitive to political and cultural norms and values associated with each locale. Strategic management in multinational corporations is a highly complex, risky process.

Coordinating the various departments and divisions of an organization is an extremely important and difficult management activity. Depending on the need for coordination, a number of structural mechanisms are available to the strategist. From the most basic policies to the most complex integrating departments, these structural techniques provide the desired level of managerial control, participant motivation, and organizational resources to the various operating units.

In the final analysis the selection of an organization structure is a strategic decision. Perhaps the most important lesson of this chapter is that the strategists should not accept the design as a given, without question. Instead the strategist must question the design, as strategy changes, to determine if the structure and culture fit the current strategy. If it does not, then the manager must consider changing to more innovative approaches to meet these new changing conditions.

Review Questions

1 Identify some of the key factors in designing an organization structure.
2 Explain the contingency theory of design.
3 How might one use a model (such as Duncan's) in determining an appropriate structure?
4 Under what conditions would you recommend the use of a matrix design? How might the matrix design be applied to the business school you attend?
5 Explain the sentence, "There is no one best way to design an organization."
6 How does organization strategy influence structure? For example, when a firm operates internationally, like Westinghouse, what are some of the considerations in selecting an appropriate design?
7 How should managers adjust management practices when planning for the international environment?
8 What special problems do the managers of the MNCs face when organizing international operations?

Notes

1   Based on "A New Strategy for No. 2 in Computers," *Business Week*, May 2, 1985, 66–75.
2   Walter Kiechel, III, "Playing by the Rules of the Strategy Game," *Fortune*, September 24, 1979.
3   Gordon C. Brunton, "Implementing Corporate Strategy," *Journal of Business Strategy* 5, no. 2 (Fall 1984): 6.
4   George A. Steiner and John B. Miner, *Management Policy and Strategy: Text Readings and Cases* (New York: Macmillan, 1977), 607.
5   Daniel J. McCarthy, Robert J. Minichiello, and Joseph R. Curran, *Business Policy and Strategy: Concepts and Readings* (Homewood, IL: Irwin, 1979).
6   Larry Alexander, "The Identification of Strategy Problems in Business and Government," paper presented at the Academy of Management, 1983.
7   See "The New Breed of Corporate Planner, *Business Week*, September 17, 1984, 62.
8   See Larry D. Alexander, "Strategy Implementation: The Neglected Element in the Strategic Process," paper presented at the Academy of Management, August 1980.
9   Robert H. Waterman, Jr., "The Seven Elements of Strategic Fit," *Journal of Business Strategy* (Winter 1982): 69.
10 Noel Tichy, "The Essentials of Strategic Change Management," *Journal of Business Strategy* (Spring 1983): 55.
11 Peter Lorange, "Formal Planning Systems: Their Role in Strategy Formulation and Implementation," paper presented at a conference on Business Policy and Planning Research: The State of the Art, University of Pittsburgh, May 1977.
12 Tichy, "Strategic Change Management."
13 David W. Ewing (ed.), *Long Range Planning for Management* (New York: Harper & Row, 1972), 5.
14 Peter Drucker, personal communication.
15 Peter Drucker, "New Templates for Today's Organization," *Harvard Business Review* 52, no. 1 (January–February 1974): 51.
16 Ian C. MacMillan and Patricia E. Jones, "Designing Organizations to Compete," *Journal of Business Strategy* (Spring 1984): 11.
17 J. Thomas Cannon, *Business Strategy and Policy* (New York: Harcourt, Brace, and World, 1968).
18 Eric Rhenman, *Organization Theory for Long-Range Planning* (New York: Wiley, 1973).
19 See "Operation Turnaround," *Business Week*, December 5, 1983, 124.
20 Alfred Chandler, Jr., *Strategy and Structure* (Cambridge, MA: MIT Press, 1967); and Richard Hill and James Hlavacek, "Learning From Failures," *California Management Review* (Summer 1977): 5–16.
21 Chandler, *Strategy and Structure.*
22 Leonard Wrigley, "Divisonal Automony and Diversification" (unpublished D.B.A. thesis, Harvard Business School, Boston, 1977); and Richard P. Rumelt, *Strategy, Structure, and Economic Performance* (Boston: Harvard University Press, 1974).
23 See Malcolm Salter, "Stages of Corporate Development," *Journal of Business Policy* 1, no. 1 (1970): 23–37.
24 *Spokesman Review* (Spokane), November 12, 1980.
25 Donald H. Thain, "Stages of Corporate Development," *Business Quarterly* (Winter 1969); and Luke Williams, "The American Sign Story," AS&I booklet, November 6, 1975.

26 Bruce Scott, ''The Industrial States: Old Methods and New Realities,'' *Harvard Business Review* (March–April 1973); and Derek F. Channon, *The Strategy and Structure of British Enterprise* (Boston, MA: Harvard University, Graduate School of Business Administration, 1973).

27 ''Kodak Is Trying to Break out of Its Shell,'' *Business Week*, June 10, 1985, 92–95; Robert Duncan, ''What Is the Right Organization Structure?'' *Organizational Dynamics* (Winter 1979).

28 See Jeffrey Ford and W. Harvey Hegarty, ''Decision Maker's Beliefs about the Causes and Effects of Structure: An Exploratory Study,'' *The Academy of Management Journal* 27, no. 2, 271–291; and Anant R. Negandhi and Bernard C. Reimann, ''Task Environment, Decentralization, and Organizational Effectiveness,'' *Human Relations* 26 (1973): 302–314.

29 Stanley M. Davis and Paul R. Lawrence, ''Problems of Matrix Organization,'' *Harvard Business Review* (May–June 1978): 131–142.

30 Donald Harvey, ''Organizational Adaptation and the Matrix Design,'' *Arizona Business* (Arizona State University) (August–September 1972): 19.

31 Adapted from A. E. Cascino, ''How One Company Adapted Matrix Management in a Crisis,'' *Management Review* (November 1979): 57–61.

32 Robert Duncan, ''What Is the Right Organization Structure?'' *Organizational Dynamics* (Winter 1977).

33 Louis Kraar, ''The Multinationals Get Smarter about Political Risks,'' *Fortune*, March 24, 1980, 87.

34 See, for example, Brian Leavy, ''Assessing Country Risk for Foreign Investment Decision,'' *Long Range Planning* 17, no. 3 (June 1984): 141–150; and Thomas W. Shreeve, ''Be Prepared for Political Risks Abroad,'' *Harvard Business Review* 62, no. 4 (July–August 1984): 111–118.

35 Robock and Simmonds, *International Business and Multinational Enterprises*, 342. See also Chris Lee, ''Cross-Cultural Training: Don't Leave Home Without It,'' *Training* 20, no. 7 (July 1983): 20 ff; and Philip S. Gutis, ''Bridging the Cultural Gap,'' *New York Times*, October 7, 1984, 15.

36 Vernon Terpstra, *The Cultural Environment of International Business* (Cincinnati, OH: South-Western, 1978), 240–241.

37 Haya el Nasser, ''USA Fast Food Speeds Abroad'' *USA Today*, January 27, 1986, 4B.

38 ''It May Not Play in Paris,'' *USA Today*, January 27, 1986, 4B.

39 G. Hofstede, ''Motivation, Leadership and Organization: Do American Theories Apply Abroad?'' *Organizational Dynamics* (Summer 1980): 42–63.

CHAPTER NINE

Changing the Corporate Culture

OUTLINE

OBJECTIVES

Upon completing chapter 9, you should be able to:

- define the concept of organizational culture
- describe the role of management style in the implementation of effective performance
- discuss how corporate cultures are formed, maintained, and changed
- compare approaches to implementing strategic change
- identify the possible effect of corporate culture on strategy implementation and performance

Innovation is crucial for 3M, which aims to continue generating at least 25% of sales each year from new products introduced in the previous five years. To do this, there has to be a culture; an environment for innovativeness. We try to say around here, "If you aren't making errors, you probably aren't doing anything."

Chairman Lewis W. Lehr, 3M,
January 6, 1986

Johnson & Johnson: Changing a Corporate Culture

Burke

Johnson & Johnson is a leading manufacturer of health-care products and has been rated as a well-managed company under chief executive officer James E Burke (a Harvard MBA). Burke is now attempting to change the strategy and move from a consumer goods firm into an advanced technology leader: from Band-Aids to high tech.

The company has been known for its unique decentralized operating structure, with each of its 170 businesses operated as autonomous profit-center units. However, the number of old, maturing products was slowing future growth. Therefore, Burke has focused more resources into high-growth, high-margin businesses (like pharmaceuticals) by consistently increasing research and development expenditures in these areas to well over the industry average. Burke has also used an acquisition strategy to move into new high-tech areas, including biotechnology, nuclear magnetic resonance (NMR), and surgical lasers.

However, J&J failed to adapt to these changes. The type of cooperation and communication between units needed by the new strategy has not been completely accepted by the old culture. In the old culture, managers operated as independent profit centers and were evaluated by their own results. Under the new plan, managers need to share marketing and R&D resources; this requires collaborative teamwork rather than the old independent operation.

This new strategy requires a change in the corporate culture. Where before each unit was autonomous, now they must cooperate; they need to work together, to break down the walls. The change poses big risks for a successful company. For years, the product managers have operated under a marketing-dominated, decentralized management structure. While most companies are struggling to eliminate corporate bureaucracies and give power back to operations, J&J is already there.

The managers of its 170 SBUs have a greater degree of autonomy than those in most corporations. Most divisions have their own boards. Corporate headquarters staff is a scant 750 people, and only one management layer separates division presidents from the fourteen-member executive committee to whom they report.

The kind of cooperation and communication that Burke deems essential for all J&J companies has been alien to its culture. Burke believes that sharing R&D and marketing resources is a key to speeding product development. This, he says, will enable J&J to regain share in such traditional markets as hospital supplies and to exploit new opportunities created by the movement toward preventive health care. For example, he says, combining J&J's expertise in magnetic resonance and biotechnology could revolutionize diagnostics. Even Burke has commented that persuading the divisions to work together as a team has required a change in attitude.

Many managers failed to adapt to these changes. Managing high-tech products required different managerial styles from those needed for the older consumer lines. The necessary communication and sharing of resources were in direct conflict with existing cultural values.

J&J is trying to gain share in its traditional markets and to exploit new strategies in biotechnology and magnetic resonance. The change in both strategy and culture has caused many problems and poses big risks for an old-line company. Will James Burke be able to implement this new strategy, and will he be able to change Johnson & Johnson old-line ways into a high-tech culture?[1]

INTRODUCTION

Strategic implementation must provide a fit between strategy and both managerial and cultural systems. Thomas J. Peters and Robert H. Waterman, Jr., suggested that management is the difference between successful and unsuccessful organizations. Their book *In Search of Excellence* presents their evidence and conclusions. The book, which topped the best-seller lists, drew a responsive reaction from management as well. The basis of the book is that managers have the power to reverse the trend of economic decay. Peters and Waterman identified the differences in managerial practice that affect organizational performance.

They first identified firms that had achieved uncommon success as measured by six criteria. The six criteria were (1) asset growth, (2) equity growth, (3) ratio of market price to book value, (4) return on total capital, (5) return on equity, and (6) return on sales. The firms that scored highest on these six criteria included IBM, Hewlett-Packard, and Procter & Gamble.[2]

What managerial practices were unique to these firms? Two of the key factors contributing to corporate excellence were a spirit of autonomy and entrepreneurship among employees and a corporate culture that gives meaning to the work of each employee.[3] In this chapter, the impact of managerial and cultural systems on strategic implementation efforts will be discussed.

MANAGEMENT STYLE

The managerial system is intended to solve the allocation problem—the distribution of managerial power and rewards within the organization.[4] One of the most critical factors in implementing organization strategy is the style of the top management team. This style sets the tone for the whole organization and influences the communication, decision-making, and leadership patterns of the entire system. Earlier, we have seen the impact that the style of CEO John Young had on Hewlett-Packard and John Sculley on Apple Computer.

In their study, Peters and Waterman found that one of the key factors in the best-managed companies was the quality of leadership. Abraham Zaleznik has also divided executives into leaders and managers. Leaders are entrepreneurial, often dramatic and unpredictable in style, and tend to be catalysts, creating a vision of change. They are often obsessed by their own ideas and, thus, stimulate others to higher performance. Managers, on the other hand, are hard working, analytical, and firm-minded, but are risk-averse and tend only to improve upon the status quo.[5]

At Apple Computer the managerial style emphasizes individual performance in a "laid-back, free-spirit culture," but John Sculley has instilled a sense of professionalism. Even as he is changing strategy, he is trying to preserve important connections to Apple's past.[6]

The CEO, by individual style, represents the managerial moral, ethical, and personal behavior that is valued in the organization. Thus, the managerial style of top management influences the organization's climate and interrelationships in all the interdependent activities that must be integrated into the organization's strategy.

The Wilson Model, developed by the Wilson Learning Corporation, focuses on changing interpersonal relationships into an effective managerial system.[7] The Wilson Change Model is shown in figure 9.1. Organizations go through three sequential stages of development involving a broad range of activities:

- *Stage 1 (entrepreneurial)* emphasizes innovation, creativity, and expanding markets and resources, with a focus on personal leadership and informal systems.
- *Stage 2 (transitional)* occurs as early growth causes problems. The organization becomes more formal and conservative with an emphasis upon stability and control.
- *Stage 3 (professional)* emphasizes adapting to the environment with decentralization of leadership and decision making.

Even successful companies will go through periods of transition. The conditions that allowed them to grow will evolve, and then the initially successful style and strategy must be changed. Some firms, such as Apple Computer, have tried to

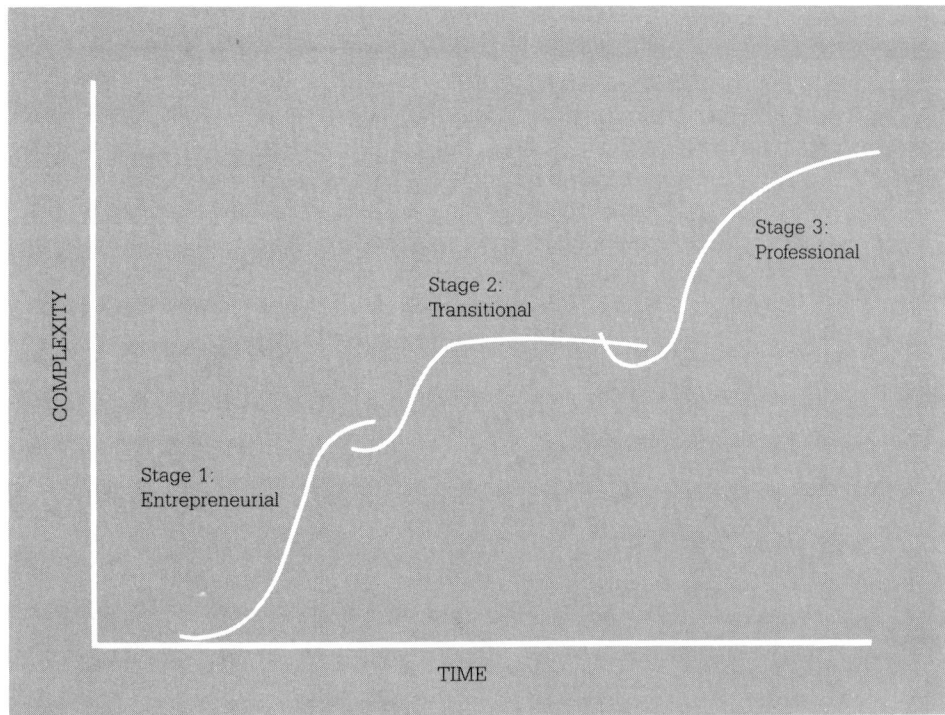

FIGURE 9.1
Wilson Change Model

go through the transitional phase and yet maintain the informal culture of the smaller firm. However, after a number of years of successful growth, Apple also reorganized to meet changing conditions.

As the time interval between new stimuli decreases, so does the time allotted to making appropriate responses—not only in the worlds of government and business, but for the person in the street as well. Everyone is under pressure to respond faster and more often to an ever more intense bombardment of changes.

The Wilson Model provides background for some of the questions Alvin Toffler, author of *Future Shock,* raised for the person of today. What *can* managers do, what *should* they do to enable themselves to better cope in a world of accelerating change? How should we as individuals best respond?

The Wilson Model offers insight into problems of implementing strategic change: the managerial style must fit the strategy. The model underscores the importance of strategy-style congruence and focuses on strategies as problems of power—who influences strategy in the organization?

Strategic Management Styles

What can we suggest about managerial styles of the strategist then? First, there seems to be a lack of consideration of the element of power. The job of a CEO, unless it is in a family-dominated business with an owner-manager, is subject to relationships with others, including the board of directors and subordinate managers. The managers may use their styles as a means of gaining strategic ends.

David McClelland and David Burnham of Harvard suggested that the power dimension is more important to the manager than affiliative or achievement motives and that a concern for power is essential to an effective managerial style. "Managers are primarily concerned with influencing others . . . [and have] a high need for power. . . . Thus, leadership and power appear as two closely related concepts, and if we want to understand effective leadership, we may begin by studying the power motive in thought and action."[8] Consequently, an effective strategic style may accurately reflect the needs for achievement and power dimensions, resulting in the managerial styles shown in figure 9.2.

The Administrator (Low Risk)

The manager with a low concern for achievement and for power tends to fit best in a slow-changing, conservative organization. The administrator style emphasizes low-risk, low-profile, low-threat approaches, with survival as the primary goal. Often companies that prefer no change and low-risk strategies will prefer this style of manager. As an example, when U.S. Steel was operating a low-percent growth rate

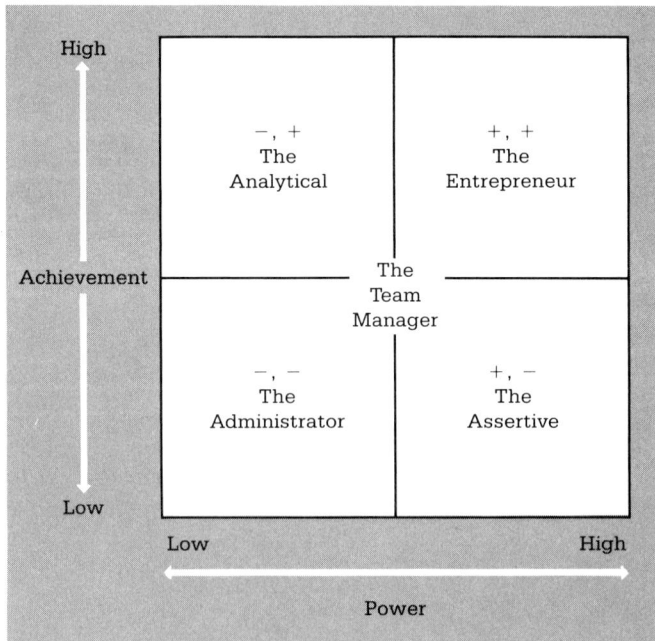

FIGURE 9.2
Strategic Managerial Styles

during a period of rapid economic expansion, its style would have been managerial. It might be called the Rodney Dangerfield style—"They get no respect."

The Analytical Manager

The manager with a high concern for achievement and a low concern for power fits into a more highly rational, low-key approach. Decision making is based on the analytical process and the logical analysis of information. This style might be termed the Orson Welles theory—"We will sell no wine before its time." This style is perhaps exemplified by the cool and intellectual style of John Sculley of Apple Computer. It is results-oriented, but with a low level of confrontation except around factual information. The emphasis is on the rational process and on detailed plans and programs.

The Assertive Manager

This managerial style is more aggressive and has a higher concern for personal control than the other styles. Although there is also concern with analysis, there is more open conflict and confrontation. Decision making emerges from the caldron of conflicting viewpoints argued through until the dominant strategy emerges. This style might be similar to that of Lee Iacocca of Chrysler, although there are many other managers who use this style. The style is results-oriented, uses a high level of confrontation, and exerts a high level of pressure. This style has three basic approaches:

1 *Problems must be highlighted.* For problems to be solved, there must be an early recognition of danger signals.
2 *Facts must be unshakable.* Analysis and research on problems must be painstakingly accurate.
3 *Face-to-face communication must be relied upon.* Many executives like to see the expression on the person's face as well as hear the information being presented.

This managerial style involves setting high, almost unattainable goals, having a demanding review and control process, and forcing people to make decisions and defend their positions.

The Team Manager

The team style is concerned with results, a winning team, and a balance between achievement and power. There is more reliance on confrontation or conflict in decision making than in the analytical style, but a less aggressive and competitive approach than in the more power-oriented manager.

The Entrepreneur

According to Michael Maccoby, the most successful executive seems to be the gamesman, the manager who sees business as a game like chess and whose motivation is to be a winner.[9] The entrepreneur is moderately high on both power and achievement motivation, but relatively low on affiliation needs or concern for people, who represent pawns on the field of play. The entrepreneur style has high standards tempered by the recognition of political realities. Interpersonal skills are used to persuade others and to negotiate positions of advantage; conceptual thinking emphasizes the long-run and total system aspects of the situation. Affiliation and emotional needs are underexpressed, a point of concern for Maccoby. This type of manager works toward long-range goals and is directed to climbing upward on a fast track.

In a study of managerial styles in different types of organizations, I have found that different styles are emphasized by differing organizational groups. For example, the mean scores for banking managers were higher in entrepreneurial and assertive styles, but low in the administrative style. University administrators, on the other hand, scored low in assertive style, but higher in the administrative style.[10]

REWARD SYSTEMS

In strategy implementation, a basic knowledge of motivation suggests that people perform to satisfy needs. Before they change, they will look for the payoff or reward. Because many of these rewards—salary increases, promotions, and preferred job assignments, to name a few—are organizationally controlled, the reward system becomes an important force in influencing strategic changes.

Performance involves results measurement. To reward members of the organization, therefore, requires agreed-upon criteria for defining performance. In implementing strategic change, effectiveness becomes difficult to measure, and the definition of performance becomes increasingly complex.

For senior managers in corporations, there is increased emphasis on linking rewards to performance. American Broadcasting, Security Pacific National Bank, Sears, and Dow Chemical are measuring the strategic plan and awarding rewards accordingly.[11]

There has been little research on the relationship between rewards and organizational commitment. Commitment to an organization strategy involves three basic attitudes: (1) identification with the organization's goals, (2) involvement in organizational tasks, and (3) loyalty toward the organization.

One study of managers in large organizations reported that certain organizational rewards significantly influenced the level of commitment:

1 *Personal importance*   The feeling of being considered a valuable member of an organization increased commitment.
2 *Realization of expectations*   Managers who were able to fulfill expectations reported higher commitment.

3 *Job challenge*   Challenging, interesting, and self-rewarding job assignments appeared to increase commitment.[12]

Consequently, managers must develop reward systems that focus on personal importance or self-esteem, integrate individual and organizational goals, and link challenging performance to strategy implementation. In the future, success will go to those managers who provide strategy-driven levels of reward which are related to performance.

THE CULTURAL SYSTEM

Each organization forms its own culture. An organization's culture includes the shared values, beliefs, and behaviors formed by the members of an organization over time. The leadership style of top management and the norms, values, and beliefs of the organization's members combine to form the *corporate culture.* Organization effectiveness can be increased by creating a culture that achieves organizational goals and at the same time satisfies members' needs. The CEO's words alone do not produce culture; rather, his actions and those of his managers do, as noted by *Business Week:*

"A corporation's culture can be its major strength when it is consistent with its strategies. Some of the most successful companies have clearly demonstrated that fact, including: International Business Machines Corp., where marketing drives a service philosophy that is almost unparalleled. The company keeps a hot line open twenty-four hours a day, seven days a week, to service IBM products."[13]

The corporate culture influences how managers approach problems, react to competition, and implement new strategies. The organization culture may also act to resist a strategy change. At Du Pont, for example, over the years a highly stratified, risk-averse organization developed which tended to stifle creativity and innovation. The company also failed to act on customer needs and market changes. But now Du Pont must change its mix of businesses and the way it does business. The company has had to change its corporate culture as well as shift its strategy.[14]

A number of studies have indicated that corporate strategy alone cannot produce winning results. Management consultants have suggested that only one company in ten can successfully carry out a complex change in strategy.[15] However, the need for devising and executing strategic changes has been rapidly increasing.

There is widespread agreement that organizational culture refers to a system of shared meaning held by members that distinguishes one organization from another. This system of shared meaning represents a set of key characteristics held by organization members. There appear to be five characteristics that describe an organization's culture.[16]

1 *Individual autonomy*   the degree of responsibility, independence, and opportunities for exercising initiative allowed members of the organization.

2 *Structure* the degree of rules and regulations and amount of direct supervision used to control member behavior.

3 *Support* the degree of assistance and warmth provided by managers.

4 *Performance-reward* the degree to which organization incentives (such as salary increases and promotions) are based on member performance.

5 *Risk behavior* the degree to which members are encouraged to be aggressive, innovative, and risk seeking.

By combining each of these characteristics, a composite picture of the organization's culture is formed. This culture becomes the basis for the shared understanding that members have about the organization, ''how things are done,'' and ''the way members are supposed to behave.''

The Strategy-Culture Fit

Culture provides a set of values for setting priorities on what is important and how things are accomplished. Culture is therefore a critical factor in the implementation of a new strategy. An organization's culture can be a major strength when there is a fit with the strategy and can be a driving force in successful change implementation.

To be successful, the strategy must be adaptable to the rapidly changing environment. When change occurs, the culture must be adjusted so that the firm can confront and deal with conditions that may contribute to it's failure, stagnation, or success. The culture influences each member in adjusting to these changes and in dealing effectively with fellow workers under a new set of conditions. Productive corporate changes increase the company's capacity to meet new challenges. To be effective, managers must motivate the company's employees and help them adapt to changing conditions. Success depends on management's skills and upon the level of acceptance by the organization's members: its corporate culture.

Every organization has a culture, but some are stronger than others. IBM, for instance, has a more tightly held culture than does a conglomerate of newly acquired companies or very young start-up firms. Harvard, perhaps, has a more cohesive culture than many state universities. AT&T has a more solid corporate identity than many of its newer competitors. In strong cultures, the behavior of members is constrained by mutual accord rather than by command or rule.

It has become increasingly popular to differentiate between strong and weak cultures. The evidence suggests that strong cultures have a greater impact on employee behavior and are more directly related to higher performances, reduced turnover, and so forth.[18]

A strong culture is characterized by the organization's basic values being both intensely held and widely shared, as figure 9.3 shows. Each dimension can be envisioned as existing along a continuum from low to high. The more members that share these basic values and the greater their commitment to those values, the stronger the culture. As John A. Young, CEO of Hewlett-Packard, has commented,

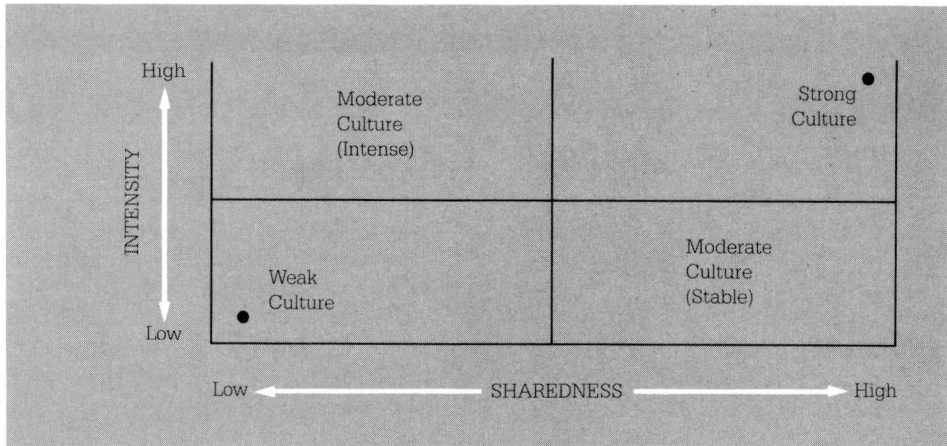

FIGURE 9.3
Strong vs. Weak Cultures

> Every company has kind of a culture to it, in the way it's grown up, it's got peculiar industrial relations things that are part of its history. By no means would I claim that the H-P style, the kind of people-oriented management system, is readily transportable. I think the fundamentals could apply to literally any business, but it takes a lot of work to change a company over to a different style. Any style change would be different because the culture of the company is deeply rooted.[19]

The Strategic Culture Matrix

Management Analysis Center, Inc., a consulting firm that deals extensively with corporate culture, has tried to simplify the cultural equation by linking culture to three broad factors: structure, systems, and people.

Howard Schwartz and Stanley Davis have proposed a two-dimensional matrix to examine cultural risk assessment, as shown in figure 9.4.[20] Any strategy change that rates on the matrix as being higher in strategic importance than in cultural compatibility is deemed an unacceptable risk. Every effort should be made to minimize the risk inherent in a proposed change. Schwartz and Davis suggested four basic alternatives to deal with cultural incompatibility: manage the change, reinforce the culture, manage around the culture, and change the strategy to fit the culture.

Manage the Change (Manageable Risk)

An organization in quadrant 1 is implementing a strategy change that is important to the firm and at the same time, potentially compatible with the existing corporate culture. It is possible to pursue a strategy requiring major changes but still manage

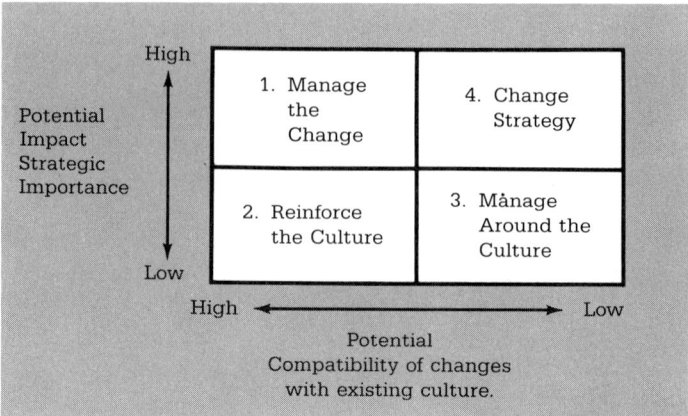

FIGURE 9.4
The Strategy-Culture Matrix

Cultural Clash at Pillsbury

The cultural clash within Pillsbury, a $5.85 billion packaged-food and restaurant giant, is intensifying as the restaurant sector (including Burger King) captures a growing role. Pillsbury's button-down executives seldom see eye to eye with the high-flying members of the company's Miami-based Burger King unit. Pillsbury's idea of a big splash is its biennial Bake-Off contest. Burger King executives favor brasher marketing battles—not to mention brighter clothes, darker tans, and flashier cars. Because of this cultural difference have come factional nicknames: "Miami Vice" and "Minneapolis Ice."

Pillsbury's internal tension reflects an industrywide war. Throughout the country, restaurant and packaged-food marketers, using radically different strategies and management cultures, are battling hard for the stagnating consumer-food dollar. More than any other big company, Pillsbury encompasses both arms of the industry, providing a close look at a struggle that is yielding more food and restaurant alternatives for consumers than ever. The war has Pillsbury competing within itself.

At Pillsbury's high-rise headquarters, dark business suits are the corporate uniform and conservative earth tones provide the decor. However, at Burger King's new $40 million tropical headquarters on Biscayne Bay in Miami, pink is the planned exterior color. With colorful and noisy surroundings, the headquarters has the Miami Vice look. Burger King also uses hard-hitting marketing tactics to attack McDonald's, the market leader.

Chairman and CEO John M. Stafford is trying to keep this conflict healthy. "My job is to make sure the competition is constructive, not destructive," he says. "It's a balancing act."[17]

the change by using the power of cultural acceptance and reinforcement. Those organizations should emphasize these basic elements:

1   The changes must be related to the overall goals and mission of the organization. This consistency builds on existing strengths and makes any changes legitimate to members.
2   Reshuffle power to raise key people to positions important in implementing the new strategy. Key people make visible the shared values and norms that lead to cultural compatibility.
3   Reinforce the new value system. If the new strategic direction requires changes in marketing, production, and so forth, the changes should be reinforced by the organization's reward structure.

People Express, for example, said Harvard Professor D. Quinn Mills, "is the most comprehensive and self-conscious effort to fit a business to the capabilities and attitudes of today's work force."[21] Chairman Donald C. Burr sought young aggressive, free spirits, using a decentralized style with only three layers of management and a system called "cross utilization" where employees perform widely different tasks, and rewarding employees with a "piece of the action." Burr's low-fare, no-frills concepts, based on managing a new strategy, led People Express to become a billion dollar sales firm in about five years.

Reinforce the Culture (Negligible Risk)

An organization in quadrant 2 needs relatively little strategic change, and the changes are highly compatible with the existing culture. Here the consultant should emphasize two factors:

1   Forge a vision of the new strategy and the shared value to make it work.
2   Reinforce and solidify the existing culture.

At Apple Computer, CEO John Sculley made changes to improve the firm's competitive position but also was determined to reinforce the existing culture in carrying out the new strategy.

Manage Around the Culture (Manageable Risk)

Organizations in quadrant 3 need to make some strategic changes, but these changes are potentially incompatible with the corporate culture. Here the critical question is whether these changes can be implemented with a reasonable probability of success. The key element is to manage around the culture, without confronting direct cultural resistance. These approaches include:

1   Reinforce the value system.
2   Reshuffle power to raise key people in critical position.
3   Use any available levers of change, such as the budgeting process or reorganization, to influence the changes.

At DEC, CEO Ken Olsen implemented new strategies even though some were not compatible with the existing culture.

Change the Strategy (Unacceptable Risk)

An organization in quadrant 4 faces a different challenge in strategic change because the change is important to the company, but incompatible with the entrenched corporate culture. First Chicago Bank, for example, illustrates the dilemma faced by an organization under these conditions. The company faced the challenge of attempting to change its culture from a risk-aversion to an aggressive, risk-taking style. The challenge of changing the culture is an expensive, long-term undertaking that is practically impossible to achieve.

When an organization is in this situation, facing large-scale change with a high probability of cultural resistance, the management must determine whether strategic change is really a viable alternative. The key question is: Can the strategic change be made with any possibility of success? If the answer is no, then the organization should modify its strategy to fit more closely with the existing culture.

Chairman Charles Parry is attempting to change Alcoa's strategy, but the old-line culture places limits on the extent of possible change. Parry must reshape a conservative, commodity-oriented set of corporate values into a new risk-taking culture. It remains to be seen if he can accomplish this task.[22]

Why Change the Culture?

Organization culture may also inhibit the implementation of a strategy and prevent a firm from meeting competitive threats or from adapting to changing economic conditions. This inflexibility can lead to the firm's decline, stagnation, or even ultimate demise unless the culture is changed. One company that has systematically changed its cultural emphasis is PepsiCo, Inc., under both former chairman Donald M. Kendell and current chairman D. Wayne Calloway.

Once the company was content in second position, offering Pepsi as a cheaper alternative to Coca-Cola. But today, a new employee at PepsiCo quickly learns that beating the competition, whether outside or inside the company, is the surest path to success. In its soft-drink operation, for example, Pepsi's marketers now take on Coke directly, asking consumers to compare the taste of the two colas. That direct confrontation is reflected inside the company as well. Managers are pitted against each other to grab more market share, to work harder, and to wring more profits out of their businesses. Because winning is the key value at Pepsi, losing has its penalties. Consistent runners-up find their jobs gone. Employees know they must win merely to stay in place—and must devastate the competition to get ahead.[23] Unfortunately, this level of pressure is not always acceptable and may result in the loss of key managers.

Allan Kennedy suggested that there are only five reasons to justify large-scale cultural changes:

1   The company has strong values that don't fit a changing environment.
2   The industry is very competitive and changes with lightning speed.
3   The company is mediocre or worse.
4   The firm is about to join the ranks of the very largest.
5   The firm is small but growing rapidly.[24]

For many businesses, changing the culture is not in the best long-term interests of the firm. For example, Apple Computer management recognized that its most important challenge is to retain its small-company culture even though it has grown into a top 500 firm.

A company's predominant culture may undergo changes from internal needs or be forced to change by competition. In the U.S. banking industry, pressures caused by deregulation have forced cultural change among established banks from what might be termed ''the old bureaucratic — make your books balance at the end of the day — culture'' to a culture that is more entrepreneurial, more oriented to sales, and aware of competition.[25] Peters and Waterman made the point that companies with strong cultures that are focused externally — that is, centered on service to the customer — may, in fact, be more sensitive to environmental changes and better able to adapt than companies without strong cultures.[26]

Changing an organization's culture is difficult. Vijay Sathe has shown that culture's durability and efficiency represent both an asset and a liability for an organization.[27] Therefore, the manager must learn when to discontinue a culture that is unresponsive to the needs of the environment. Often only top management has the power and influence to institute a strategic change in the organizational culture, a change of not merely structure and technology, but also shared behavior and values.[28]

MANAGERIAL SUMMARY

The key to success in implementation involves integrating the component elements into a total, organizational system. Successful implementation depends on the CEO's approach to planning, coordinating, and measuring performance toward strategic goals.

The managerial style of the strategic decision maker has an impact on the political system of the organization. The CEO's job is to make decisions and to gain effective performance from members. Harold Geneen, for example, had an impact on the way ITT was run and on the managers who worked there. He was reported to be a hard man to work for. ''I left because of hellish pressure I could not endure.'' ''He goes too far, he drives people up the wall.'' ''He sets almost unattainable standards that either stretch a person or breaks them. It stretched me!'' says one former manager.[29]

The key to all of these managerial styles is to bring the organization's managerial resources to focus on the biggest problems and biggest potential opportunities. The two biggest problems in most organizations are communication and planning. An effective style must have impact in these two areas. Each manager must examine his own decision-making style and critique it to become more effective.

Change is an inevitable consequence of operating in a dynamic environment. Strategic managers must recognize that organization development techniques can be used to change the corporate culture to fit the new strategy. Management style can also be a powerful determinant of performance when it is used to tie together the strategic goals, plans, and implementation.

Corporate culture includes the pattern of values, beliefs, and norms shared by organization members. It is usually taken for granted and tends to remain as a way of behaving. Corporate culture affects whether firms can implement new strategies and whether they can operate at high levels of excellence.

Many strategists feel that the implementation is perhaps more critical than the decision itself. As more and more chief executives recognize the importance of the implementation of longer-range strategies, they will have to consider the effect of the strategy upon the organization. It will be up to the CEO to decide whether to change the strategy to fit corporate culture or change the culture in order to ensure survival. At any rate, strategic implementation is an important and difficult process.

Strategic implementation involves integrating corporate strategy, structure, and human resource systems. It involves aligning the firm's technical, political, and cultural systems, using such tools and interventions as business strategy, organization structure, and human resource management.

Effective performance in the implementation phase is complex and requires more than recognition of effectiveness and efficiency. Multiple criteria are involved. There is no one best way to manage or to implement a strategy. There are no hard rules or equations. The key to implementation is the ability to analyze each situation, each organization, and each group of members. Managerial style is as important in this function as in the other stages of the strategic process. In the future, implementation will involve a greater concern over productivity, better ways of allocating resources, and more adaptive leadership styles.

Review Questions

1   What are some of the important factors in strategic implementation? If you were CEO of an old-line company like Alcoa, how would you implement a strategic change?
2   The development of a corporate culture calls for continuing action. What type of corporate culture would you like? How does this fit with your managerial style?
3   Compare two different organizational cultures (i.e., larger versus small, public versus private). What characteristics determine the differences?
4   What are the advantages or disadvantages of a strong culture?
5   Examine a recent merger or acquisition. What role did human factors play in it?
6   Compare and contrast managerial styles in two different organizations. How would your own style fit?

Notes

1   Based on "Changing A Corporate Culture," *Business Week,* May 14, 1984, 130; and Robert Bakken, "Picture of Health," *Barron's* (March 30, 1987): 15.

2   Thomas J. Peters and Robert H. Waterman, Jr., *In Search of Excellence* (New York: Harper & Row, 1982), 156–187.

3   Ibid.

4   Noel Tichy, *Managing Strategic Change* (New York: Wiley, 1983).

5   Abraham Zaleznik, "Managers and Leaders: Are They Different?" *Harvard Business Review* (May–June 1977), 67–70.

6   "Apple: Part 2," *Business Week,* January 27, 1986, 98.

7   Based on presentation of W. Matthew Juechter, *Managing Interpersonal Relationships,* Wilson Learning Corporation, 1980.

8   David McClelland and David Burnham, "Power Is the Fastest Motivator," *Harvard Business Review* (March–April 1976): 13.

9   Michael Maccoby, *The Gamesman* (New York: Simon & Schuster, 1976).

10 Donald Harvey, "Strategic Management Styles," Working Papers, November 1987.

11 "Executive Compensation: Looking to Long-Term Gains," *Business Week,* May 9, 1983, 80–83.

12 Bruce Buchanan, "To Walk an Extra Mile: The Whats, Whens, and Whys of Organizational Commitment," *Organizational Dynamics* (Spring 1975): 67–80.

13 "Corporate Culture: The Hard-to-Change Values That Spell Success or Failure," *Business Week,* October 27, 1980, 148.

14 Alan M. Freedman, "Giant Overhaul," *Wall Street Journal,* September 15, 1985, 1.

15 Bro Uttal, "The Corporate Culture Vultures," *Fortune,* October 17, 1983, 66.

16 Adapted from J. P. Campbell, M. D. Dunnett, E. E. Lawler, III, and K. E. Weick, *Managerial Behavior, Performance, and Effectiveness* (New York: McGraw-Hill, 1970), 393.

17 Based on "Cultural Clash at Pillsbury," *Wall Street Journal,* October 23, 1986, 1.

18 E. H. Schein, "The Role of the Founder in Creating Organizational Culture," *Organizational Dynamics* (Summer 1983): 13–28.

19 Quoted in *Spokesman-Review* (Spokane), November 12, 1980.

20 H. Schwartz and S. Davis, "Matching Corporate Culture and Business Strategy," *Organizational Dynamics* (Summer 1981): 30–48.

21 "Up, Up and Away," *Business Week,* November 25, 1986, 52.

22 "Alcoa: Recycling Itself," *Business Week,* February 19, 1987, 56.

23 "Pepsi's Marketing Magic," *Business Week,* February 20, 1986, 52.

24 See T. E. Deal and A. A. Kennedy, *Corporate Cultures: The Rites and Rituals of Corporate Life* (Reading, MA: Addison-Wesley, 1982), 65–66.

25 Raoul D. Edwards et al., "Marketing in a Deregulated Environment," *U.S. Banker* 95, no. 4 (April 1984): 34 ff.

26 Peters and Waterman, *In Search of Excellence,* 77–78.

27 Vijay Sathe, "Implications of Corporate Culture: A Manager's Guide to Action," *Organizational Dynamics* 12, no. 2 (Autumn 1983): 5–23.

28 Bro Uttal, "The Corporate Culture Vultures," *Fortune,* October 17, 1983, 66–72.

29 "They Call It 'Geneen II,' " *Forbes,* May 1, 1966.

PART THREE

■■■

STRATEGIC EVALUATION: THE REVIEW AND CONTROL PROCESS

CHAPTER TEN

■ ■ ■

Strategy Evaluation and Control

OBJECTIVES

After you have completed this chapter, you will be able to:

■ define the strategic control process and discuss the major elements

■ describe several strategic control system characteristics and problems

■ discuss the importance of key result areas and strategic control points

■ compare short- and long-term control systems

■ identify the relationship between strategic planning, decision making, and the control process

We sure as hell have taken a quick directional turn here, but my intent was not to shake things up. My intent was to create change and I think that the change is right on target.

Hicks Waldron, CEO, Avon, Inc.,
November 1984

The Sorcerer of Silicon Valley

Bushnell

Nolan Bushnell, a charismatic entrepreneur, founded an industry and developed his ideas into not one but two multimillion dollar companies. Termed the "Sorcerer of Silicon Valley" by *Inc.* magazine, Bushnell started Atari and then sold out to Warner Communications for $28 million. He then started Pizza Time Theatres, a restaurant chain that expanded so rapidly it twice made *Inc.*'s list of the 100 fastest growing public companies.

According to *Inc.*, his charisma was unmatched anywhere in the entrepreneurial wonderland of Silicon Valley. "Nolan walks in the front door with that smile on his face and puffin' on that pipe, and it's like a whirling dervish walked in," said the former president of a Bushnell company. "People's hair stands on end. Their eyes get like saucers, and they flock around him like J. C. the man just walked in."[1]

Bushnell, an electrical engineering graduate from the University of Utah, was the immensely popular leader of the high-tech wave of entrepreneurs in the Silicon Valley. When a group of engineers approached him about forming a company to produce robots, he agreed to form a company, find investors, and develop a marketing plan. "Androbot, Inc., as the company was called, was more than just a new plaything; it was part of Nolan Bushnell's evolving strategy for the 1980s, his attempt to create an entertainment and consumer product empire to rival Disney in size and scope."[2]

However Androbot was burning cash at the rate of several hundred thousand dollars per month. Pizza Time Theatres ran into cash-flow problems as well, and began losing money at the rate of nearly $20 million per month. At the beginning of 1984, Bushnell announced his resignation as Pizza Time CEO. Even entrepreneurial wizards like Nolan Bushnell cannot sustain their spells forever.

One of the major problems of managing high-growth companies is the need for accurate strategy evaluation and control systems.

INTRODUCTION

The world in which strategic managers operate is continually changing politically, socially, and technologically. The rate of change seems to have accelerated in recent years, making it impossible to develop strategic plans with complete certainty. There are too many forces in the external environment and too many unknowns to do so. If strategic management is to be effective in an ever-changing world, it must be able to review the results of strategic decisions and make changes if necessary.[3]

At a medium-sized electronic manufacturing firm, with over $35 million annual sales and over 500 employees, management began to find that although they were growing, they were losing money. As cash flow problems emerged, the CEO asked "What does it cost to produce one of our systems?" No one knew the answer! As in the situation described, control systems are often key factors in achieving organizational effectiveness.

Strategic control may be defined as "the process through which managers ensure that actual activities conform to planned activities," or making sure something happens the way it is supposed to happen.[4] The control process measures progress toward strategic goals and enables managers to detect deviations from the plan in time to take corrective action.[5]

In this chapter, we examine the final stage of the strategic management process (stage 8): strategy evaluation. This evaluation includes three basic elements: (1) the strategic control process, (2) the importance of controls, and (3) the characteristics and problems of control systems.

No Control System at A&P

The food giant, A&P, was in desperate straits when Jonathan Scott took over as CEO. Scott confronted a choice between two strategies: closing down the company's worst operating units or shutting down entire operating divisions. Scott opted for the first alternative. "We made a conscious decision to close down on a store-by-store basis," he recalls. "We decided to weed out the very worst and try to turn around the rest. We wanted to save as much as we could."[6]

At A&P, CEO Jonathan Scott implemented a retrenchment strategy by closing unprofitable stores. Unfortunately, the strategy did not work as planned. Apparently A&P failed to have a review system that would enable it to take corrective actions. Strategic evaluation is the process in which managers, like Scott, compare the actual outcomes of a strategy with planned objectives. The test of a strategy is not the formulation of the strategic plan. The true test is whether management's commitment of resources brings about results.

If results are not being accomplished, as was the case at A&P, then the strategy is ineffective. When properly formulated, strategic plans and controls are inseparable elements, because the first relates directly to the second. As Harold Koontz of UCLA has commented, "The two functions of planning and control are so closely interconnected as to be singularly inseparable . . . Certainly, no manager can control who has not planned, for the very concept of control incorporates the task of keeping the operation of subordinates on course by correcting deviations from plans."[7]

If actual results do not track with planned results then changes must be made. The top managers at A&P should have been continually reviewing the progress of strategic moves, so they could take corrective actions or countermoves if the original strategy had failed or if conditions had changed.

Richard Rumelt of UCLA has suggested that "strategy can neither be formulated nor adjusted to changing circumstances without a process of strategy evaluation. Whether performed by an individual or as part of an organizational review procedure, strategy evaluation forms an essential step in the process of guiding an enterprise."[8]

The development and formulation of strategies and plans is of little value if the strategy is not implemented or carried out to achieve company goals. Any strategy is only as effective as management's ability to put it into action: the plan is not the end result. If strategies are to be effective, the manager must also be able to measure performance, to determine where deviations from the plan are occurring (as was the case at A&P) and to make corrective moves where necessary.

The final stage (stage 8) in the strategic process, then, is the review and evaluation of the results of the strategic plans and decisions. This stage is critical for any plan or strategy because an ineffective or losing strategy should not be followed blindly or a company may end up like the W. T. Grant stores, going out of business because of uncontrolled expansion. Determining how effectively this strategy is being implemented is essential to accomplishing strategic objectives. Therefore, strategic evaluation and control is an important element in the strategic process. The strategic control process is designed to

1   Compare actual performance versus planned performance in key performance areas.
2   Surface issues and challenge the viability of critical points to a successful strategy.

THE STRATEGIC CONTROL PROCESS

The strategic control process involves the interlocking elements of strategic objectives, planning, decision making, and control. The focus of control is on results and ensuring that activities are producing the desired results. The strategic goals and plans remain only if they are well executed to achieve results. At A&P for example, Jonathan Scott set forth a strategic plan to improve its ailing financial position. His strategy was to close out losing operations, thus restoring a smaller but healthier company. However, A&P apparently lacked an adequate information and control system, and as a result the strategy failed to achieve the planned goals.

The Basic Stages

The basic stages of the strategic control process are presented in figure 10.1. To be effective, top management must be able to measure actual performance, compare it to the plan, recognize when deviations from the plan occur, and take corrective action.

The strategic objectives evolve into detailed plans during the implementation stage. The strategic control process begins with measuring performance to determine if it conforms to planned expectations. The review and control process generates information for decisions: decisions to continue a strategy, to increase or decrease the allocation of resources for specific elements, or to change strategic directions if something has gone wrong.

The basic purpose of control is to achieve strategic goals. The best type of control process is anticipative in nature, that is, it predicts possible deviations from plan by anticipating their potential occurrence.

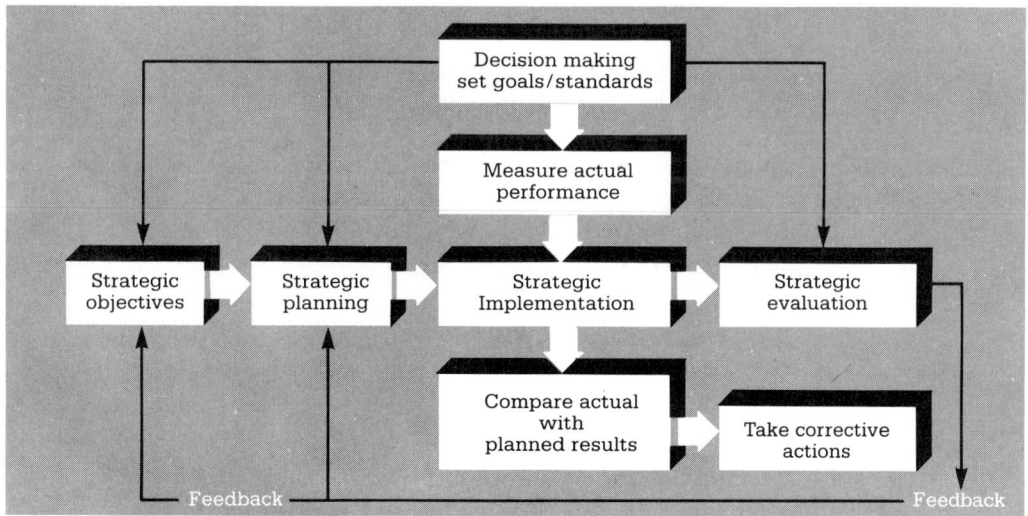

FIGURE 10.1
The Strategic Control Process

Strategic planning and evaluation work hand-in-hand in organizations. These elements, discussed in the following sections, are linked in the control process, which includes

1 Setting predetermined standards of performance.
2 Measuring actual performance results.
3 Comparing planned to actual performance.
4 Taking corrective action, if necessary.

Setting Standards

One of the most important aspects of the control process is to determine beforehand what results, or standards, are expected from a given strategic action. Standards are the units of measurement or criteria against which actual performance can be compared. Without comparative evaluation, control is impossible. Therefore, identifying the appropriate criteria is essential. Many retail stores, J. C. Penney for example, set objectives for store and department managers in terms of sales-per-square-foot of store space, or per labor hour. The stores use computerized cash registers to provide store and department managers with daily, detailed reports on such things as sales and volume so that managers can immediately determine how well they are doing.

Peter Drucker has suggested five criteria to evaluate performance.[9]

1 *Market standing*   The first real assessment of a company is its market standing relative to its competitors. (For one such ranking see *Forbes'* Yardsticks of Management in its annual reports.) Is market ranking going up or down?
2 *Innovative performance (R&D)*   How does the firm rank in R&D expenditures (as a percent of sales) in its industry? Is the company as successful or innovative (i.e., a market leader) as its market standing? Is the firm innovative in the market segment where future growth is likely?
3 *Productivity*   The third criterion relates the input to the "value added" output. Sales per employee is one measure of productivity.
4 *Liquidity and cash flow*   The fourth criterion measures liquidity by examining financial ratings and cash flow per share. A cash flow crunch is usually more damaging than a profit problem.
5 *Profitability*   Is the firm's profit margin increasing or decreasing?
6 ROI

These criteria present qualitative measures of how well the strategy is being implemented. The standards are often expressed in quantitative terms including such factors as:

Net profit

Stock price

Dividend rates

Earnings per share

Return on capital

Return on equity

Market share

Growth in sales

Production costs and efficiency

Employee turnover, absenteeism, and satisfaction indexes.

These quantitative criteria provide measures of how well the strategy is being implemented.

At Emerson Electric, the criteria of growth and profits have resulted in a relentless, almost heartless devotion to the true bottom line: return on investment. Former CEO Wallace R. "Buck" Persons has been compared to the late Green Bay Packers' coach, Vince Lombardi. Emerson's motto, to paraphrase Lombardi, might well be: Efficiency isn't everything; it is the only thing. Emerson does not hesitate to reduce sales growth in the interests of a higher return on capital. Control, discipline, tough-minded decision making are hallmarks of Emerson. The payoff has been a five-year average return on capital of 17.7 percent that placed Emerson well up in the ranks of large manufacturing companies in *Forbes'* Annual Report on American industry.

Emerson's planning sessions are among the most sophisticated in U.S. industry. The planning is done within a broad strategic framework that calls for doubling earnings every six years, which is an average of 12.5 percent earnings gain every year; no more than 10 percent of revenues from defense; no more than 20 percent to 25 percent from international; and $200 million worth of new products to be developed through corporate research and development by some target date.[10]

Many different criteria may be used, but they should provide a means to measure strategic performance.

Measuring Performance

Controls generate information for decisions. Former ITT chairman Harold Geneen had an impressive ability to ferret out the true "unshakable facts" about a company or a product, uncovering layers of false factors before he reached the truth. However, performance cannot be reviewed unless there is a means of determining what performance actually had been. Unless there is a reporting system and a basis for measurement, confusion can develop. Closing stores left A&P spread thin in certain regions, thereby sacrificing economies of scale that had been gained by geographic concentration. The reporting system did not provide adequate information.

The basic purpose of strategic evaluation is to assess the achievement of organizational goals. In this sense, evaluation is a positive process, because problems are anticipated before they emerge. The review meetings are aimed at predicting potential problems before they occur so that corrective actions can be taken. The process also, of course, points out problems after they occur. This identification of past mistakes results in the negative connotations often associated with the evaluation process: finding out where something has gone wrong.

The emphasis of strategic review is not so much on blaming someone for faults as it is on generating information. Consequently, an effective management information system that provides timely data on operating results for review by top management is necessary. There are several issues which arise around the design of strategic review systems in the evaluation of performance data.

Feedback is an integral part of the review process, because without feedback managers would be managing without information. Mike Miller, a young MBA, is a department manager for J. C. Penney. Each morning he receives a computer print-out on the previous day's sales activities. This information, or feedback, allows Miller to compare actual with intended results and use up-to-the-minute data to decide whether more fast-moving products should be ordered, slow-moving merchandise should be replaced, or personnel changes are needed.

There is considerable evidence that objective feedback about performance, or knowledge of results, can improve performance. A number of studies have focused on the way feedback affects performance. G. P. Latham and G. A. Yukl, for example, have indicated that feedback along with participation in goal setting was associated with improved performance.[11]

Often companies become bogged down in ritualistic annual review systems. To make more effective use of management time, different levels of strategy review may be used as indicated in figure 10.2.[12]

1 Maxi-reviews are for businesses that are clearly in trouble or face a major opportunity.
2 Mini-reviews are for businesses that are meeting targets but have one or more important issues ahead that may call for a modified strategy.
3 A simple strategy update is sufficient where no major problems or changes are foreseen.

Comparing Actual with Planned Performance

The next step in the control process involves the comparison of results against predetermined standards. The purpose of the comparison is to detect deviations— variances from the standard in time to make corrections. Because all performance has some degree of variation, it is important to determine the limits of regular performance variation. The manager must be able to distinguish the important variations, the potential problems or bottlenecks, from unimportant variances. One example is United Airlines' computerized system of reporting and controls.

> An intrinsic part of United's reporting system is what company executives like to call "the room with the 14,000 mile view." This is an information and

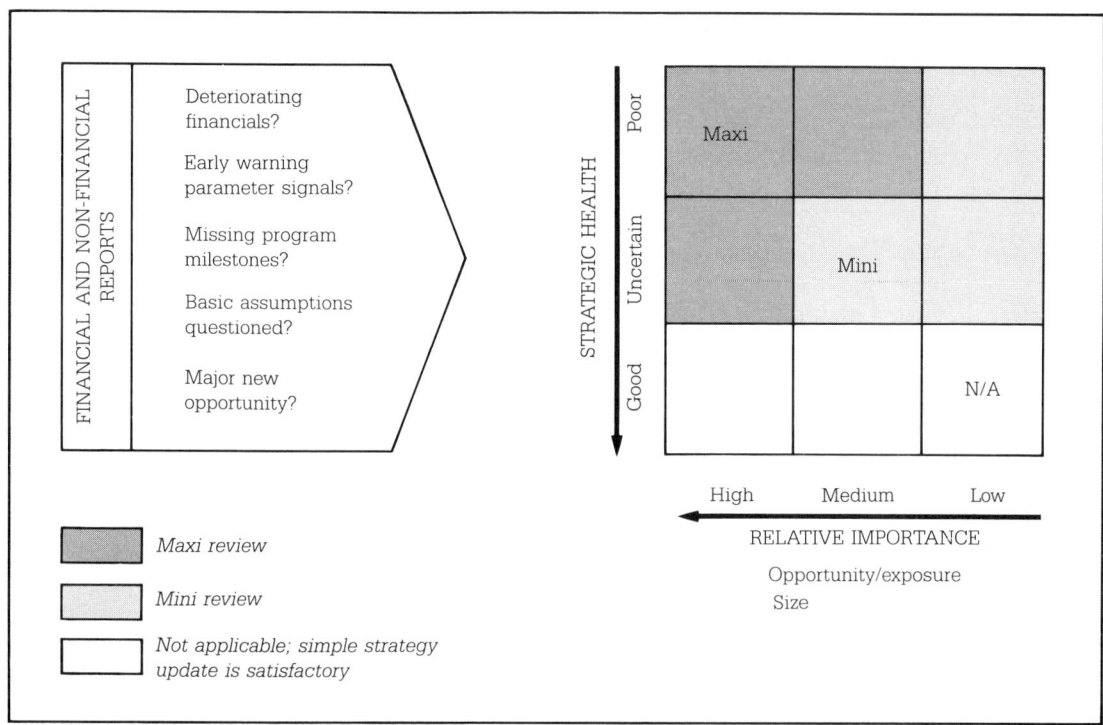

FIGURE 10.2
Levels of Strategy Review

SOURCE: Adapted from Arie J. Rijvnis and Graham J. Sharman, "New Life for Formal Planning Systems," *Journal of Business Strategy* 2, no. 4 (Spring 1982).

planning center at Denver which is the business world's equivalent of the military briefing room. Facts funneled daily into this center present a clear picture of operations throughout United's eighty-city system.

In keeping with the idea of expansive vision, the room has glass walls on one side. Modern white plastic chairs are grouped before a map of the United States, eight feet high and twenty feet wide, on which United's routes are outlined. Colored lights (red for weather, green for maintenance, and white for passengers) at major terminals show current operating conditions. If the red light glows steadily, for example, it means adverse weather; if it is flashing, the weather is marginal. Electric clocks above the map show the time in each zone through which United operates.

The room is designed to provide management with operational facts in the most convenient form. Data, such as mileage flown, delays at terminals by type of plane and total number of departures, are posted on lucite panels, flanking the map. Dozens of supplementary charts deal with payload volumes and load factors, weather, actual performance as compared with schedule and related information.

This reporting system helps to focus management attention on strategy areas which are most important.

The purpose of comparing performance with standards is not only to spot errors in strategy, but also to enable the manager to anticipate future problems. A good control system will allow top managers to make fast, accurate comparisons and identify future strategic problems—as Harold Geneen said, "No surprises." The graphing of actual versus planned performance over time will often reveal significant trends, suggesting possible danger signals before the problems have ever emerged.

As an example, Chrysler's chairman Lee A. Iacocca set strategic plans and control systems for a turnaround strategy.

Chrysler's Turnaround Strategy

Lee Iacocca came to Chrysler in 1979, when the Michigan State Fairgrounds were jammed with thousands of unsold, unwanted, rusting Chryslers, Dodges, and Plymouths. Foreign imports were draining profits out of the company. The Chrysler experience highlighted four painful realities.

- The quality of products had declined.
- Work practices had shortchanged productivity.
- The government had become an enemy instead of an ally.
- Foreign countries that the United States had defeated in war and rebuilt in peace were beating this country in its own markets.

Chrysler was faced with a choice. The company could go under—the suggestion of not a few—or efforts could be made to save the company.

In charting Chrysler's turnaround strategy, Iacocca identified six strategic success factors essential to a succesful turnaround. Chrysler executives used these six factors as the basis for their *strategic* control of the turnaround strategy. Careful, systematic attention was given to monitoring progress on each factor as an indicator of desired execution of the turnaround strategy.

1 Reduce wage and salary expenses by half the 1980 levels.
2 Reduce fixed cost by over $4 billion. Chrysler closed twenty plants and modernized the remaining forty with state-of-the-art robot and computer technology.
3 Reduce the number of different parts by one-third. Chrysler reduced the number of parts from 75,000 to 40,000, shaking $1 billion out of inventory in the process.
4 Improve its weak balance sheet. Chrysler retired its U.S. bank debt by converting $1.3 billion into preferred stock and some preferred into common stock.

5 Improve the quality of its components and finished products.
6 Implement a $6 billion product improvement program. Chrysler has a lead in front-wheel-drive technology; it has the best fuel economy in the industry; it offers a 70,000-mile warranty.[14]

For Chrysler Corp., the comparison of actual to planned results meant that drastic strategic action had to be taken if the firm was to survive.

Taking Corrective Action

The final step in the control process is correcting significant deviations from plan. The purpose of the control process is to allow the manager to identify problems and take needed corrective actions. The decisions made at this point are the culmination of the process. The manager must decide if corrective action is warranted and, if so, what actions should be taken.

The manager must assess the various possible actions. Managers must avoid taking corrective action where no action is needed; yet they must not fail to take action when a problem has emerged. If corrective action is called for, then they must also decide what type of action is best, given the specific situation.

As conditions change, plans and programs must also change. However, when there is a discrepancy between plan and results, the strategist will want to determine why. If the premises and assumptions underlying a given strategy are still sound, the strategist may wish to continue the strategy but with some modification. If, however, some major factors have changed, then a major realignment of strategy may be called for.

General Electric, for example, made a strategic decision to enter the computer industry in the 1960s in what was obviously a high-growth market. The strategic plan proposed early losses, then anticipated profits. However, as GE management reviewed the plan, it discovered losses of some $162.7 million. Consequently, it had to review this strategic move and determine what action to take. Its decision: to get out of the computer business. Another example of taking corrective action occurred at Wang Labs.

Strategic Controls at Wang

After years of extraordinarily rapid growth, Wang Labs, a leading producer of word processing equipment, is taking a beating. In the fiscal year ending in June of 1985, the firm's revenues were down by 93 percent. The price of its stock had also dropped sharply. At the beginning of the 1985 fiscal year, Wang had predicted a 30 percent increase in sales and hired some 4,500 new employees. However, business slowed, Wang was forced to make its first layoffs, and CEO An Wang began a cost-cutting program that included slashing executive salaries by

15 percent. The actual performance at Wang did not meet its strategic plans, thus corrective actions had to be taken.

CEO An Wang faced a formidable challenge. His company's greatest problem was also its greatest achievement—its tremendous rate of growth had outgrown many of its management systems. An Wang is a manager of great charisma who says, "When I look at these numbers, I can come out visualizing within 1 percent accuracy." A good manager uses these skills to anticipate potential problems. Most employees at Wang refer to him as simply "the doctor," and say that you can't find anyone who doesn't like and respect him. If An Wang is to have a great corporate legacy, he will have to write the final chapter himself in bringing his firm back.[15]

THE IMPORTANCE OF STRATEGIC CONTROL

Strategic control is necessary if the organization is to achieve its objectives.[16] There are several organization factors that make control so necessary in strategic management:

1 *Change* in market and economic conditions can cause rapid deterioration of strategic plans as at Wang Labs. Markets shift, competitors emerge, new technology is discovered. However, through the control process, managers detect changes which will affect their organization's performance.

2 *Complexity* in today's organizations requires a more formal and accurate approach to planning and control. IBM and General Electric, for example, are multiple product firms that market around the world, yet the performance of each business unit must be watched closely in order to appraise the effectiveness of corporate strategy.

3 *Decentralization* also increases the manager's need for effective controls. As managers delegate authority and planning, systems must be in place to determine if tasks are being accomplished as planned at the operating level. A control system allows managers to detect problems before they become critical. At Wang Labs, for example, financial deviations caused layoffs and severe cost cutting because it was late in detecting the problems.

In order for strategic managers to develop effective control systems, key result areas need to be identified. These are the critical elements of the organization's strategic plan that must function effectively if the strategy is to succeed. It is also important to identify strategic control elements in order to monitor actual performance relative to planned. Some typical strategic control elements include:

1 *Annual percentage of change analysis* compares the historic rate of change for key financial figures with the planned rate of change. These figures could include sales, cost of goods sold, profit margin, and so forth.

2 *Comparison of planned with actual performance data.* Pro forma or projected financial statements are constructed and used to evaluate the expected future financial position of the firm in such key financial areas as sales and profit margins.
3 *Annual business sales growth rate versus market growth rate* is analyzed to determine how actual growth rate of the product business unit compares with the rate of market growth.
4 *Percent of sales analysis* determines percentage of sales for key indicators relative to planned levels, based upon the assumption that all variables are related directly to sales. These indicators include cost of goods sold, selling costs, R&D, advertising, and profit margins.
5 *Sales per employee* analysis provides a rough measure of relative efficiency and is calculated by dividing sales dollars by number of employees (year-end).
6 *Relative market share* analysis assesses how effective the various product/business lines have been in achieving results in the environment in which each competes. Actual positioning on the BCG (or GE) matrix is compared to projected positions.

The most useful method of selecting strategic control points is to determine the critical indicators of measuring strategic change. Usually three consecutive months of declining indicators provide a warning of changing conditions.[17]

Characteristics of Strategic Control Systems

The development of effective strategic controls include certain characteristics. The relative importance of these characteristics varies, but can improve most control systems.[18]

1 *Accurate* Performance information must be accurate. Inaccurate reporting can cause the organization to take wrong actions to correct a problem or solve a problem that does not exist.
2 *Timely* Information must be evaluated on a timely basis if action is to be taken in time to correct deviations (as noted in the Wang example).
3 *Focus on strategic control points* The control system should be focused on those key result areas where deviations from the plan are most likely to take place or where deviations would lead to the greatest loss.
4 *Flexible* Organizations today operate in dynamic environments, and control systems must detect the possibility of changes. Controls must have flexibility built into them, so that managers can react quickly to overcome competitive changes or to take advantage of new opportunities.
5 *Acceptance* If the control system is to be accepted by organization members, the controls must be related to meaningful goals. The goals must reflect the knowledge and activities of the members to whom they pertain.

The control system also must be consistent with the organization's culture, or it will likely be ineffective. For example, the strategic control process at Wang indicated that either conditions were changing or the previous strategy was no longer working. As a result, Wang was developing new strategies to meet the changing conditions; these strategies had to be consistent with the culture regarding such things as layoffs.

Control Systems Problems

There are a number of problems associated with the measurement of performance in control systems. The fact that a control system is well designed and sophisticated, like the one used at ITT, may cause it to be opposed by lower levels of management. Even an efficient and reasonable system may be ineffective if members feel that irrelevant data are collected or that the standards are unfair or unreasonable. Often this opposition stems from "top down" planning where lower levels have not participated in the standard setting. No matter how technically sound the system may be, it will not work well unless it is accepted by organization members.

Similarly, there is a problem over what criteria of effectiveness are to be used. As Bruce Kirchoff has noted, "There is no ultimate criterion of effectiveness. Complex organizations pursue multiple goals. Real effectiveness can only be measured relative to a particular set of derived or prescribed goals."[19]

In a recent survey of 25 *Fortune* top 500 firms, Peter Lorange and Dedan Murphy found a number of barriers to implementing strategic controls, including invalid reporting, inadequate performance measures, excessive complexity, poor motivation and control systems, and inadequate rewards.[20]

Invalid Reporting   Many times the reporting data are invalid, or they include information not under the manager's control. There are also instances where managers are evaluated on a performance though they may not have total control of all factors. A manager may be measured as a profit center, for example, yet be forced to sell products to other divisions at unrealistic prices and thus be penalized.

Inadequate Performance Measures   The definition of adequate performance measurements for control also causes difficulties. The issue arises in the inability of the firms to agree upon a common unit of measure that permits a meaningful comparison of performance between businesses.

Often performance standards are set so that there are contradicting factors: as one element is maximized, another is minimized. As a result, whatever the manager does is wrong. For example, the manager may be expected to increase market share and profits yet lower expenditures. Or educators may be required to increase enrollments and maintain quality (such as class size) yet not add any new faculty members. Production people may be asked for increased production and fewer rejects yet be given no overtime nor allowed to hire new workers.

Excessive Complexity   Excessive complexity of the control system is another common problem repeatedly cited by the survey respondents. A control system that requires reams of paperwork may function too slowly to meet environmental changes.[21]

Poor Motivation and Control Systems   Strategy implementation and evaluation ultimately depend upon individual performance of organization members. Managers must consider the influence of control systems on human behavior. Given a good, fair system, employees may produce resistance in the form of "game playing" or "beating the system."

Cortlandt Cammann and David A. Nadler summarized the effects of control systems as shown in figure 10.3. The existence of measures has an effect on subordinate behavior but is not the only factor. These measures have to be perceived as being reasonably accurate, and they have to be used skillfully by the managers. Therefore, motivating and rewarding good performance is a key ingredient in effective strategy implementation.

Inadequate Rewards for Strategic Performance   Executive reward systems must be clearly linked to strategic performance. This relationship reflects recognition of the fact that the mission is to gain competitive advantage and achieve success, rather than to focus on short-term goals.[22]

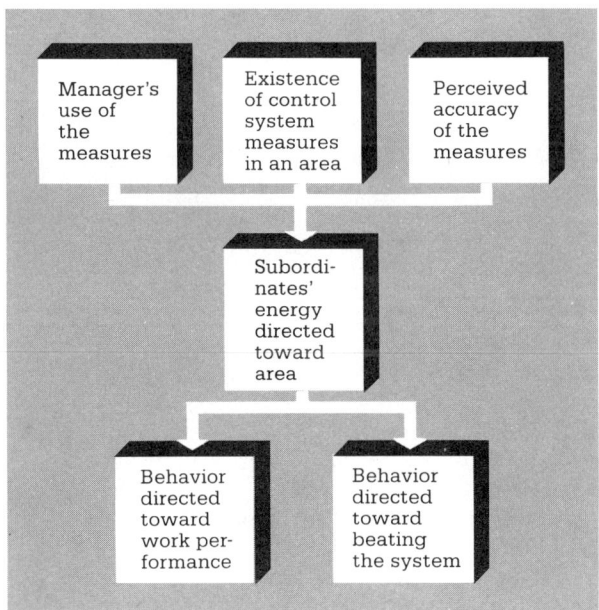

FIGURE 10.3
How Control Systems and Their Use Affect Behavior

As Cammann and Nadler suggested, control systems influence the way organization members direct their energies on the job. Managers are more likely to put time and effort into those areas covered by the control systems. Second, how members respond to control systems depends largely on the way managers use the systems. Third, different managers develop different strategies for using control systems. Finally, each control system has certain drawbacks and benefits.

It is necessary to integrate both short- and long-term concerns. An effective reward system should provide payoffs to enhance future performance.[23] For example, SBU managers might be measured against multiple criteria, such as growth or profitability targets, as shown in figure 10.4.

As Anil Gupta and V. Govindarajan have suggested, in firms that appear to have made maximum progress in matching incentive system to strategy, bonuses are based both on financial performance and accomplishments toward strategic milestones—long-range targets.[24]

Yardstick of Managerial Performance

One way to measure performance is by comparing the firm's results against those of other firms in the same or similar industries. There are two major published evaluations of large firms (by *Fortune* and *Forbes),* which provide objective comparisons

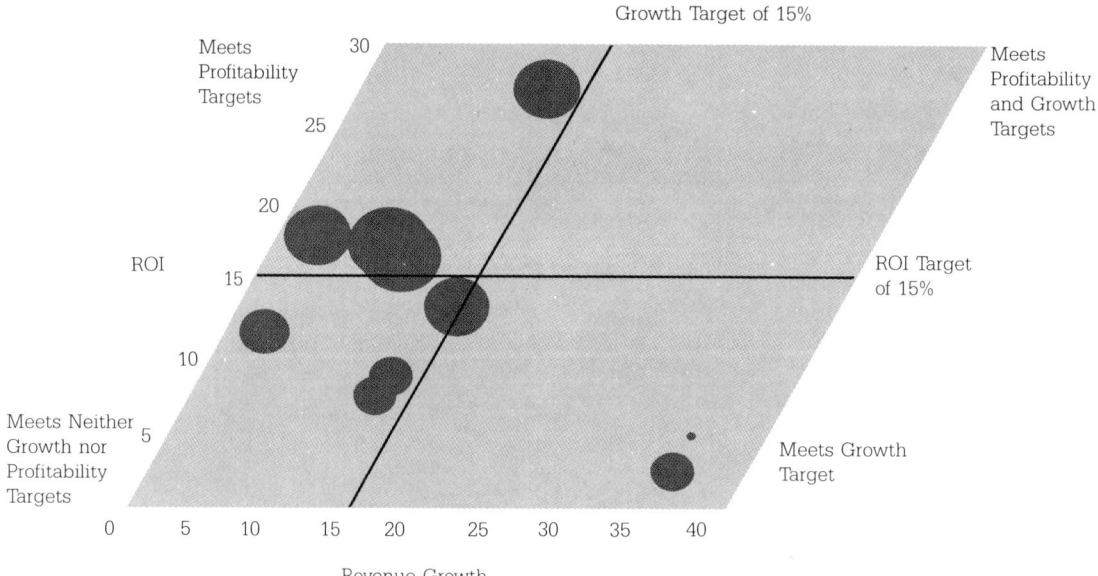

FIGURE 10.4

Measuring Performance: Growth and Profitability Target

SOURCE: Adapted from Louis Brindisi, Jr., "Paying for Strategic Performance," *Outlook* (Spring 1981): 21.

on a range of criteria. Fortune publishes its top 500 and second 500 largest manufacturing firms each year and ranks the best and worst performers on such financial criteria as sales, profits, growth, price/earnings, and return on investment. *Forbes* also presents an overall evaluation of the largest firms in its Annual Report on American Industry, ranking firms by industry on several key operating factors. *Forbes* also provides its "Yardsticks of Managerial Performance," in which rankings of the firms on their comparative performance are made against similar companies.

William Glueck noted, "It is easier to measure performance when a company shows consistent results on most of these measures in most years. In fact, research indicates that there is a high intercorrelation among organizational variables. If a firm is a 'winner' on three measures, chances are it is a winner on all measures. The most critical problem is the trade-off among measures."[25]

Both objective and subjective approaches to measurement become more difficult when using more than one criterion to rate success. For example, taking only two measures of success, efficiency and production effectiveness, four firms could be rated as shown in figure 10.5.

Value Line, another rating scale, uses a five-point scale to rate firms on two dimensions: (1) timeliness—short-term profitability and (2) safety—long-term growth and safety of investment. Both of these factors must be considered in the evaluation stage.

The evaluation of multiple factors is important. Several studies have found that it is possible for a company to make short-run results look better by firing or laying off employees (thus cutting direct labor costs). This strategy may achieve immediate

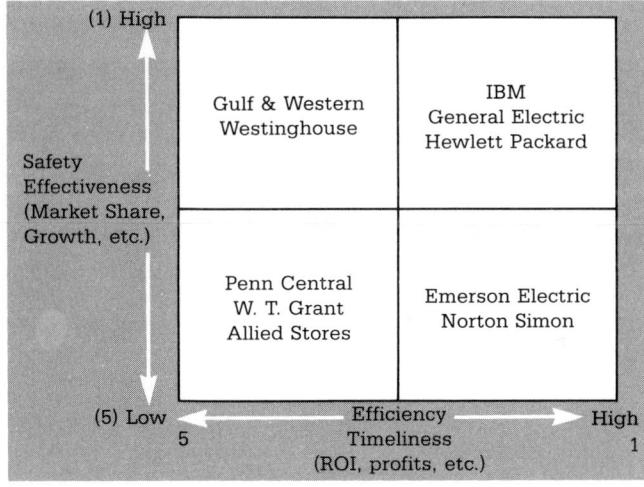

FIGURE 10.5
Company Efficiency to Effectiveness in Evaluation

SOURCE: Adapted from William Glueck, *Business Policy and Strategic Management* (New York: McGraw-Hill, 1980), p. 353.

financial improvement, but at the expense of deteriorating morale and performance in future periods.[26]

MANAGERIAL SUMMARY

The final stage of the strategic management process is the evaluation and review of performance. The strategic control system is intended to evaluate the results of the strategic decisions and plans. The control process is based on measuring and reporting actual performance and comparing it to the plan to see whether the plan is, in fact, being carried out.

Strategic control is the managerial function that ensures that actual organizational actions correspond to planned actions. Two aspects are important. First, control and review should take place at many stages of the implementation process. Second, control is closely related to other managerial functions such as goal setting, planning, and decision making. It is an interrelated function rather than a separate activity.

An effective strategist is aware that formulating stategies, implementing action, and controlling to evaluate results are essential elements of strategic management. The manager must be able to correct faulty moves and to adjust to meet changing conditions. The manager should understand the characteristics and use of an effective control and reporting system and must be constantly reviewing control systems and methods to be sure they are appropriate and realistic.

The changing environment of organizations, the increasing complexity of organizations, and the fact that managers must decentralize decision making are among the factors that make control necessary. The control function is one of the most important and detailed stages in the strategic process. One of the keys to successful control is developing a positive and participative feedback and control system. Therefore, not only do managers have a greater knowledge of the controlling operations, but because they are responsible for performance goals, they probably will be more highly motivated to work with the system.

The intent behind management controls is to generate information about performance. When something is going wrong, where there are deviations from plan, corrective actions must be taken. Perhaps if Nolan Bushnell had a better control and reporting system at Pizza Time, he would have been able to detect problems earlier, make strategic alterations, and possibly remain the CEO. For a control system to be effective, it must be accurate, timely, focused on strategic control points, feasible, and accepted by organization members.

Control systems must be flexible enough to adapt to changes in the external and internal environments. The best controls are anticipative in nature; that is, they allow the strategist to predict problems before they occur. Therefore, the control system is not only used to examine the current state of the organization but, more important, to predict any crucial, developing trends.

The control system analyzes the entire management process—from goals and plans to implementation—and helps to pinpoint potential advantages and problems. The managerial skills necessary for the control and evaluation stage are as important as those skills necessary for the earlier stages. Managerial skills are crucial for designing and analyzing control procedures, for the interpersonal exchanges involved in presenting data, for integrating control systems with the strategic plan, and for determining the future impact of strategic countermoves. The major key to success in the control process lies in integrating the controls into the local organization system and in adopting a broad-based, long-range approach to measuring performance.

Review Questions

1   What is the importance of the control function?
2   What are the relationships between objectives, planning, and controlling?
3   List the four basic steps in the control process. What are the key elements in each of these steps?
4   What organizational factors create the need for control?
5   What are key result areas?
6   What are strategic control areas? How may managers locate them?
7   What are the characteristics of effective control systems? Which of these characteristics is most important?

Notes

1   "When the Magic Goes," *Inc.,* October 1984, 83.
2   Ibid., 88.
3   Rajiv Tandon, "Strategic Planning in an Era of Uncertainty," *Journal of Business Strategy* 5, no. 3 (Winter 1985): 96.
4   Richard L. Daft and Norman B. Macintosh, "The Nature and Use of Formal Control Systems for Management Control and Strategic Implementation," *Journal of Management* 10, no. 1 (Fall 1984): 43–66.
5   Vijay Sathe, "The Controller's Role in Management," *Organizational Dynamics* 11, no. 3 (Winter 1983): 31–48.
6   Peter W. Bernstein, "Jonathan Scott's Surprising Failure at A&P," *Fortune,* November 6, 1978, 35–36.
7   Harold Koontz, "A Preliminary Statement of Principles of Planning and Control," *Journal of the Academy of Management* (April 1958): 48.
8   Richard Rumelt, "The Evaluation of Business Strategy," in William Glueck, *Business Policy and Strategic Management* (New York: McGraw-Hill, 1980), 359.
9   Peter Drucker, "If Earnings Aren't the Dial to Read," *Wall Street Journal,* October 30, 1986, 32.
10   "Emerson Electric: Efficiency Isn't a Goal; It's a Religion," *Forbes,* March 20, 1978, 41.

11 G. P. Latham and G. A. Yukl, "A Review of Research on the Application of Goal Setting in Organizations," *Academy of Management Journal* 23 (1970): 824–825.

12 Arie J. Rijvnis and Graham J. Sharman, "New Life for Formal Planning Systems," *Journal of Business Strategy* 2, no. 4 (Spring 1982): 102.

13 Philip Gustafson, "Business Reports: How to Get Facts You Need," *Nation's Business,* August 1956, 78–82.

14 Lee A. Iacocca, "The Rescue and Resuscitation of Chrysler," *Journal of Business Strategy* 4, no. 1 (Summer 1983): 67–69.

15 Based on Arthur M. Lane's "Doctor Wang's Toughest Case," *Fortune,* February 3, 1986, 106.

16 See Donald J. Cockburn, "Another Way of Looking at Internal Control," *CA Magazine* 117, no. 11 (November 1984): 74–77.

17 Dale W. Sommer, "Cycle Forecasting Spots Trends," *Industry Week,* April 25, 1977, 71.

18 Peter Lorange and Declan Murphy, "Considerations in Implementing Strategic Control," *Journal of Business Strategy* 4, no. 4 (Spring 1984): 27–35; and M. Lynne Marcus and Jeffrey Pfeffer, "Power and the Design and Implementation of Accounting and Control Systems," *Accounting, Organization and Society* 8, no. 2/3 (1983): 205–218.

19 Bruce A. Kirchoff, "Organization Effectiveness Measurement and Policy Research," *Academy of Management Review* (July 1977): 352.

20 Lorange, "Implementing Strategic Control," 21.

21 David B. Greenberger and Stephen Strasser, "Development and Application of a Model of Personal Control in Organizations," *Academy of Management Review* (January 1986): 164–177.

22 Cortlandt Camman and David A. Nadler, "Fit Control Systems to Your Managerial Style," *Harvard Business Review* (January–February 1976): 65–72.

23 Louis J. Brindisi, Jr., "Paying for Strategic Performance," *Outlook* (Spring 1981): 21.

24 Anil K. Gupta and V. Govindarajan, "Build, Hold, Harvest: Converting Strategic Intentions into Reality," *Journal of Business Strategy* (Winter 1984): 43.

25 William Glueck, *Business Policy and Strategic Management* (New York: McGraw-Hill, 1980), 290.

26 See Charles W. Hill, "Coxpomire Central Type, Strategy and Size and Financial Performance," paper presented at Academy of Management, New Orleans, August 1987.

CHAPTER ELEVEN

Epilogue: Summary and Emerging Trends

OUTLINE

INTRODUCTION

Keeping up with important trends, changes, emerging issues, and problems will be very important to organizations into the 1990s. Anticipating another energy crisis, a breakthrough in artificial intelligence, the entry of foreign companies into another industry, or changes in relevant laws may determine the very survival of many organizations. As noted in chapter 2, many organizations are giving formal recognition to this important predictive function by formally designating strategic issue managers. It is estimated that about thirty companies have such issue managers.[1]

In some firms a department of issue management has been created. Although ARCO probably uses the most comprehensive approach (the company is organized around the five areas of resources, environment, corporate planning, manufacturing, and trade associations), many other firms have experimented with issue managers. In this fast-paced, changing world, it is necessary for strategic managers to keep a step ahead of the competitive forces shaping the destinies of their organizations.

This final chapter brings the topic full circle. First, a brief summary of the major parts of the book is presented. This summary is followed by a discussion of some of the major trends that have emerged in recent years. These trends have affected and will continue to affect the field of strategic management. Finally, the chapter ends with a look into future challenges for the strategic manager.

STRATEGIC MANAGEMENT—A SUMMARY

In walnut-paneled boardrooms high above the major cities of the world, strategic decisions are being hammered out, strategic decisions that will lead to success or failure, to profitability or losses, and to survival or bankruptcy. Strategic management is the key concept underlying a new systematic approach to the management of the total enterprise. Strategic management is the key, critical management function, yet it is only recently that strategy has been recognized as the central element in business success.

The central aim of the strategy/policy course is to learn how to deal with all of the complexities and constraints involved in making strategic decisions. In this section, we will review some of the major points of strategic management.

The Strategic Management Process

This text has presented the stages of the strategic management process. Each stage has been examined separately to clarify the process. However, in reality the stages are not so distinct, but rather overlap and are interrelated in the real world of management. For our purposes, a strategy is that set of objectives, plans, and actions that taken together define the approach of the organization to its environment.

The strategic process begins with the basic purpose of the organization and is aimed at allocating the resources of the organization through a complex set of plans, procedures, and programs toward long-term goals. This process includes the formation of a strategy incorporating an analysis of all relevant factors, both internal and external forces, the development and evaluation of alternatives, a strategic choice, the implementation of the strategy, and finally, the evaluation and review of the strategy to determine how effectively the strategic plan has worked.

Effective strategic management requires a multidimensional thrust. Strategy is a general plan of action with an implied commitment of resources to achieve some basic goal. Broadly speaking, there are a number of dimensions to be considered. First, effective strategies determine the overall direction and action focus of the organization. Second, effective strategies are formed around a few key businesses or thrusts, so that resources are not scattered throughout ineffective endeavors.

Third, effective strategy deals with the future. Strategists must make decisions involving unpredictable and unknown variables without knowing precisely how all the complex forces will interact. They must base their strategy on a carefully calculated assessment of a probable future. Finally, an effective strategy aims at long-term goals, at developing a cohesive and comprehensive approach, and tying together in a systematic way many differing elements.

There is research evidence to suggest that firms that use the strategic process are more effective than those that do not and that the process itself is changing, becoming increasingly sophisticated and anticipative in nature.[2] The emphasis on strategic management reflects the growing complexity of the outside world and its impact upon the strategic manager.

Perhaps the most significant changes in the strategy field, however, concern the widespread adoption of advanced corporate planning and organization development techniques, so that the resource allocation and implementation processes are being increasingly emphasized. These recent techniques, including contingency theory and portfolio models, are the first major advances in systematically identifying the central, underlying strategic variables of large multibusiness firms.

There is one inescapable conclusion regarding strategic management. The real choice is not whether to use strategic management or not, but between management and nonmanagement. The degree to which a firm's strategy is effective will largely determine if the company will survive and be profitable, or decline and eventually fail.

The purpose of this book has been to clarify how and why strategic management can be used in making those crucial decisions that can mean the difference between winning or losing. The text has been aimed at easing the transition from the classroom to the real world of organizations by providing you an opportunity to practice your own managerial skills.

At some point in the future, you may well be in a boardroom making a presentation to the executive committee of a major firm. It is my hope that what you have learned here will help you get there and make the most of the opportunity when it arrives.

EMERGING TRENDS

The business climate of the 1990s will introduce dramatic changes. Strategic management is redefining the rules of the business strategy game and the game itself.

Major changes will be occurring in the environment, trends that will require an explicit identification and understanding of strategic concepts.

Computerized Management/Future Shock

The first of the changes involves a significant increase in the rate of change. This is the factor that Alvin Toffler termed *future shock*, the enormous, exponential changes in technological, political, economic and social forces. Because of these massive changes, managers will also be forced to implement strategic changes at an unprecedented rate.

The computer has been central to much of the focus on emerging trends, as well as to the topics covered in chapters 7 through 10, on strategic control. Computers have revolutionized the routine office functions through word processing, spreadsheet, and accounting packages and in factories through numerical control and robotics. Now the use of personal computers is revolutionizing both the way organizations are managed and the role of managers.

Contrary to common belief however, not all managers are using personal computers. In fact, there is some evidence suggesting that a majority of top-level executives do not use personal computers themselves and do not feel comfortable with the prospect of using them.[3] One might speculate that older senior managers might be in this category. However, the trends are in the direction of increasing use of personal computers, and the impact of this trend on strategic management is already being felt. Graduates now going into management should become fully familiar with all applications of the computer to strategic management, decison making, and problem solving.

"Yield management is the name of the game, and it requires sophisticated software and sophisticated humans to handle it," said James O'Donnell, vice-president of marketing at Continental Airlines. "We're using software that didn't exist five years ago."[4]

Consider, for instance the evolution of software and hardware requests made by Trans World Airlines. Xenophon Sanders, president of the airline's PARS computer-system subsidiary, recalled that executives used to confine their software needs to ticket-printing systems and other prosaic operations. Now, PARS has software that enables TWA not only to monitor the fares of competitors but also to create pricing scenarios on a flight-by-flight basis that predict the effect of fare adjustments on TWA's bottom line.

The Revolution in Management

The second significant change, one well documented by research, is the increasing size and complexity of organizations. These changes will undoubtedly continue and result in new challenges to the integrating role of the manager. How managers will coordinate and integrate complex and diverse structures is a continuing problem of strategic management, deemphasizing the importance of middle management. This new focus has been caused largely by the trends discussed previously (especially the impact of the computer) and by the more immediate competition problems faced by all organizations. The result has been a decreasing trend in the number of middle managers, especially corporate staff members, and restructuring and redefining of the management role. Some of these trends involve the flow of communications directly between upper- and lower-level management without being filtered through middle management.

Finally, managers of the 1990s will be managing in a world of change: making strategic decisions in an uncertain environment and with scarce resources. Although experts may argue over exactly how long it will take to exhaust our various nonrenewable resources, the fact remains that in the 1990s we will be faced with a growing world population and diminishing resources. We will be managing with constraints, new variables, more unknowns, and greater unpredictability than ever before. How can managers best use limited human, technical, financial, and material resources to accomplish objectives in a constantly changing environment?

FUTURE CHALLENGES

There are also several strategic challenges for the future. Strategic planning is being used less as a staff function and more directly focused on operating managers. At Hewlett-Packard, for example, where the line managers are responsible for developing strategic plans, the result has been more anticipative organization. Corporate planning staff probably will be substantially reduced or eliminated because it will be more effective to have line managers, who are closer to the business, develop strategy.

There is renewed emphasis on building an effective corporate culture based on excellence, a high level of performance, product quality, service, and innovation. Corporations believe that their culture will strongly influence future success or failure.

There is also an increased emphasis on developing entrepreneurial climates in large companies—entrepreneurship. Large firms like GE and IBM are attempting to create an entrepreneurial spirit to foster innovation and creativity in future strategy. These firms are finding a direct relationship between long-term success and the ability to discover their own entrepreneurs, before they leave and become competitors.

Emerging trends suggest what lies ahead for the field of strategic management. Strategic management has arrived as an identifiable and important field of academic study and has definite implications for the effective management of modern, complex organizations. This recognition of strategic management as a legitimate academic and management tool should become even greater in the future. More attention will be given to the field as it successfully addresses the problems stemming from declining productivity, foreign competition, the changing role of management, computerization, and the need for innovative strategic approaches.

Finally, the trend toward making strategic management more research oriented should continue. The successive editions of this text have evidenced the trend toward research and theory. The field is clearly aimed at developing more effective management of organizations. With increased research focusing on the relationship between strategic goal setting and performance appraisal, organizational structure, competitive strategies, leadership styles, organization development, and decision-making and control techniques; research applications should become clearer and lead to more effective strategic management in the years to come.

The future of the field of strategic management looks very challenging and exciting. Although there may be some shifting emphasis of conceptual frameworks and total coverage, the study and application of the topics covered in this book will help move toward better and more effective managers and toward increased excellence in organizations.

Notes

1   See Earl C. Gottschalk, Jr., ''Firms Hiring New Type of Manager to Study Issues,'' *The Wall Street Journal,* June 10, 1982, 21–28.
2   See R. B. Higgins and John Diffenbach, ''The Impact of Strategic Management on Stock Prices,'' *Journal of Business Strategy* (Fall 1985): 64–73.
3   Walter Kiechel, ''Why Executives Don't Compute,'' *Fortune,* November 14, 1983, 241.
4   ''Companies Permit Airlines to Cut Fares,'' *The Wall Street Journal,* February 2, 1987, 21.

APPENDIX: THE STRATEGIC MANAGEMENT STYLE MATRIX

Purpose   The purpose of this survey is to enable you to identify and to get feedback on your strategic managerial style. It will describe your behavior as a member of a team in order to examine your executive style. When you are a member of a team, what is your leadership behavior like? In what ways do you try to influence other team members toward accomplishing the team's goals?

There is no right or wrong way to manage; therefore, the best choice is the way you try to handle situations. Answer honestly, because the more accurate your response the more accurate the result.

Procedures   This survey presents eight situations with five alternative responses. Because you will rank order your responses to the situation, it is important that you read through all the responses before answering. Once you have read through all five responses, select the response that is most similar to the way you think you would actually behave or think in such a situation. Place the letter corresponding to that response (*a, b, c, d,* or *e*) somewhere on the "Most Similar" end of the ten-point scale (scoring form A) appropriate to the intensity of your feeling. Next select the response that is least similar to the way you would actually act or think. Again place the letter corresponding to that response somewhere on the "Least Similar" end of the scale. Complete the answers by placing the remaining three responses that reflect your actions or thoughts for those responses within the range of previously selected points.

Strategic Management Survey

In answering these questions, consider how you would act in the situation and how you perceive the nature of strategic management.

1 *Strategic Goals*   In determining strategic goals for the organization:
   a   Spell out clear-cut directions. "Push" people to higher performances.
   b   Specify the goals and values toward the direction by which success will be measured.
   c   Define the firm's strengths and weaknesses, then develop criteria and standards for future results.
   d   Set high standards for accomplishment, aiming for the best in the field.
   e   Stay with past practices and attainable goals.
2 *Strategic Management Style*   My style of management relies on:
   a   Rational emphasis and keeping options open until alternatives are analyzed.
   b   Developing a sense of urgency—"winning is everything."
   c   Using formal procedures and written reports and keeping a low profile.
   d   Frequent contact, participating and delegating duties.
   e   Pushing managers to set high standards by using competitive tactics.

3   *Strategic Planning*   The formal strategic planning system should:
   a   Emphasize strategic openings and improve short-term results against targets.
   b   Provide forceful leadership toward achieving major goals.
   c   Use qualitative and participative methods to coordinate goals.
   d   Develop plans at levels that have been successful in the past.
   e   Provide motivation toward future goals.

4   *Strategic Analysis*   The analysis of strategic factors should:
   a   Develop extensive econometric models by logical analysis.
   b   Identify the real issues of a situation by means of open discussion and confrontation.
   c   Analyze different ideas and approaches constructively.
   d   Use influence to create a winning strategy.
   e   Use formal procedures to compare each manager's performance with standards.

5   *Strategic Decision Making*   Strategic decisions are made by:
   a   Using quantitative methods to take calculated risks.
   b   Limiting your exposure to risk factors.
   c   Using assertive face-to-face communications and confrontation.
   d   Creating innovative new strategies that optimize return.
   e   Developing consensus on risk/reward trade-offs.

6   *Strategic Implementation*   In implementing the strategic decision:
   a   Emphasize group participation and commitment to new strategy.
   b   Gain the support of key power centers by persuasion or negotiation.
   c   Make things happen by pushing team members to perform well.
   d   Move slowly, maintaining company's past strengths.
   e   Follow the plan with detailed targets for each responsible manager.

7   *The Corporate Culture*   The corporate culture should:
   a   Focus on achievement with rewards related to goals.
   b   Focus on fun and action, using teamwork to accomplish goals.
   c   Focus on high risks with quick feedback and big rewards for winning performance.
   d   Focus on steady improvement, gradual change, and relatively low-risk activity.
   e   Focus on results with hard-driving, high-risk, big-stakes performance.

8   *Strategic Controls*   In controlling strategic action, the strategist will:
   a   Operate through questioning and fact finding.
   b   Have a rigorous review of company performance to stay on top of problems.
   c   Follow policy for improving problem areas.
   d   Use a shared responsibility approach with member participation.
   e   Use a high-risk approach to create winning performance.

SCORING FORM A

Question   **Rating**

1

| Most Similar | 10 | 9 | 8 | 7 | 6 | 5 | 4 | 3 | 2 | 1 | Least Similar |

2

| Most Similar | 10 | 9 | 8 | 7 | 6 | 5 | 4 | 3 | 2 | 1 | Least Similar |

3

| Most Similar | 10 | 9 | 8 | 7 | 6 | 5 | 4 | 3 | 2 | 1 | Least Similar |

4

| Most Similar | 10 | 9 | 8 | 7 | 6 | 5 | 4 | 3 | 2 | 1 | Least Similar |

5

| Most Similar | 10 | 9 | 8 | 7 | 6 | 5 | 4 | 3 | 2 | 1 | Least Similar |

6

| Most Similar | 10 | 9 | 8 | 7 | 6 | 5 | 4 | 3 | 2 | 1 | Least Similar |

7

| Most Similar | 10 | 9 | 8 | 7 | 6 | 5 | 4 | 3 | 2 | 1 | Least Similar |

8

| Most Similar | 10 | 9 | 8 | 7 | 6 | 5 | 4 | 3 | 2 | 1 | Least Similar |

Step 1: Scoring Instructions

On scoring form A you wrote your answers for each item. Transfer your values for each of the eight situations to scoring form B. Look at each score for all questions and complete filling in the scoring spaces. Once all values have been entered, total up the score for each column and determine your percentile score.

Step 2: To Enter the Scores on the Summary Form

1 Transfer the percentile scores from scoring form B to the summary form in *descending order* (enter in column 3).
2 In column 2 write the appropriate word description of strategic management style beside the score.
3 In column 4 place the numerical difference of your adjacent scores found in column 3. (The difference between the scores on the first and second lines of column 3 will be placed on the first line of column 4.)

Scoring Form B

	Entrepreneur	Team	Analytical	Assertive	Administrator
1	d _____	b _____	c _____	a _____	e _____
2	b _____	d _____	a _____	e _____	c _____
3	b _____	e _____	c _____	a _____	d _____
4	c _____	a _____	d _____	b _____	e _____
5	d _____	c _____	a _____	b _____	e _____
6	d _____	e _____	a _____	c _____	b _____
7	b _____	a _____	e _____	c _____	d _____
8	c _____	b _____	a _____	e _____	d _____
Totals	_____	_____	_____	_____	_____
PERCENTILES	_____	_____	_____	_____	_____

Executive Style Profile

You have just completed and scored the Executive Style profile. Following is a brief explanation of the five styles.

1   The *entrepreneur* sees life in terms of options and possibilities as if playing a game, likes to take calculated risks, and is fascinated by new technologies and methods. The main goal is to be known as a winner, and the deepest fear is to be labeled a loser. The entrepreneur is concerned with winning at all costs, seeks competition, sets a standard of excellence, and is results-oriented.

2   The *assertive* managerial style is more aggressive and has a higher concern for personal control. Although there is also concern with analysis, there is more open conflict and confrontation. Decision making emerges from the caldron of conflicting viewpoints argued through until the dominant strategy emerges. Thestyle is results-oriented, uses a high level of confrontation, and exerts a high level of pressure.

3   The *analytical* manager has a high concern for achievement, a low concern for power, and uses a low-key and highly rational approach. Decision making is based on the analytical process and the logical analysis of information. This style is cool and intellectual. It is results-oriented, but with low level of confrontation except around factual information. The emphasis is on the rational process and on detailed plans and programs. The analytical manager is concerned with achievement of long-term goals, applies rational, quantitative analysis to problems, assumes responsibility for results, and takes calculated risks.

4   The *administrator* bases his or her identity on being part of the organization, but lacks the daring to be innovative or competitive. The administrator is concerned with maintaining harmony and order, and with solid low-risk decisions. This style manager prefers group harmony, avoids conflict, and prefers slow, long-term goal attainment without drastic changes.

5   The *team* style manager is concerned with results and a winning team and a balance between achievement and power. There is more reliance on confrontation or conflict in decision making than in the analytical style, but a less aggressive and competitive approach than for the more power-oriented manager.

All of these styles can be effective. There is no one best style, but rather an adapting to the style that works best in each organization. A person does not operate using one type of executive style to the exclusion of the other styles. The purpose of the scoring is to indicate the relative importance you place on each of the five styles. The difference between your first and second styles indicates the strength of your performance and how quickly you will fall back on another style. Little difference between scores could indicate a tendency to vacillate between styles or vague thoughts about how you handle decisions. A large difference could indicate a strong reliance on the predominant style.

This survey should be used as a point of departure for further reflection and observation concerning the way you attempt to manage and influence others. To obtain a better understanding of your style, try to become aware of how you handle problems in your associations with friends, peers, and working associates. It may also be helpful to observe other people when they try to influence your behavior and become aware of how you react to their methods.

In plenary session, discuss the five managerial styles. Do your scores for your primary and backup managerial styles seem congruent with the way you think you

Executive Style Summary

Your Choice	Word Description of Style	Score	Difference between Scores of Adjacent Lines
1st	_____	_____	_____
2nd	_____	_____	_____
3rd	_____	_____	_____
4th	_____	_____	_____
5th	_____	_____	_____

operate in decision situations? Share your scores with class members with whom you have been working and get their feedback.

The Strategic Management Style index shows the norms for MBAs and banking, hospital, and university administrators. Percentile norms for undergraduates are shown on the index matrix as follows:

1 Entrepreneur = 17.3
2 Team   = 28.4
3 Analytical   = 20.7
4 Assertive   = 15.5
5 Administrator = 18.1

Plot your scores to see how they compare.

Strategic Management Style Index

Percentile	% Score	Entrepreneurial	% Score	Team	% Score	Analytical	% Score	Assertive	% Score	Administrative
100	23.8		38.5		28.4		26.0		28.2	
95	21.7		34.6		25.6		20.1		22.8	
90										
85										
80	20.5	Banking	32.1		24.3		19.0	Banking MBA	20.9	
75										
70	19.1	MBA	30.7		22.4	Hospital	17.0		19.8	
65										
60	18.5	University	29.9		21.6	University	16.7		18.9	University Hospital
55										
MEAN 50	17.4	Undergraduate	28.4	Undergraduate Hospital	20.7	Undergraduate MBA Banking	15.5	Hospital Undergraduate	18.1	Undergraduate
45										
40	16.4	Hospital	27.7		20.4		14.9	University	17.6	
35										
30	15.5		26.3	University Banking MBA	19.3		13.7		16.7	
25										
20	14.4		25.0		18.4		12.6		15.5	MBA
15										
10	12.8		23.9		16.7		11.4		14.1	Banking
5	12.2		20.7		14.7		10.0		12.5	
-1	11.0		18.2		11.9		7.9		11.1	

The percentile scores are based on the combined responses of 109 practicing managers and 212 Eastern Washington University undergraduate and 97 graduate students in management. (A raw score of 21 on Entrepreneurial means you scored higher on this dimension than 90 percent of the managers and students tested, and a score of 24 would indicate you scored higher than anyone in the population on which these norms are based.)

PART FOUR

■ ■ ■

CASES IN STRATEGIC MANAGEMENT

CASES FOR PART 1:
STRATEGY FORMULATION

CASES FOR PART 2:
STRATEGY IMPLEMENTATION

CASES FOR PART 3:
STRATEGIC EVALUATION: THE REVIEW AND CONTROL PROCESS

■ ■ ■

Cases in Strategic Management

TECHNIQUES FOR CASE ANALYSIS

The Business Policy/Strategic Management course may be approached in many different ways; however, in general, the classroom becomes the boardroom, and you become involved in making strategic decisions. At ITT and other major corporations, managers present plans, proposals, and projects to the executive committee. They usually use slides, charts, transparencies, and other visual aids to present complex problems and analyses. At ITT, Harold Geneen was famous for his probing questions and his search for "unshakable facts." In the classroom, your classmates and the instructor fill this role. In academic programs, you practice and develop your managerial skills in the case analysis sessions.

What Is a Case?

A case provides a written description of actual managerial problems, situations, and events. It includes factual information about an industry, an organization and its products, markets, competitive position, and whatever financial, structural, and economic data may be pertinent. In essence, the cases simulate the organizational problems managers face daily. Your role is to analyze, diagnose, and evaluate the problem situation, and present recommendations about what should be done. You have the responsibility of being prepared and of sharing your own ideas and solutions with the class.

Cases provide an opportunity to simulate actual experience by analyzing problems and making decisions. To learn strategic management, the student needs both knowledge of management techniques and experience at actually putting theory into practice. This method is known as *experiential learning,* or learning by doing. The experiential approach is different from traditional learning, because the major responsibility for learning is placed upon you.

Rather than looking for a right answer to memorize, you should be more concerned with identifying key problems, analyzing data, evaluating alternatives, examining the credibility of various strategies, and making and defending your own decisions.

In experiential learning a four-step process is involved, as shown in exhibit 1.

1 *Analysis*   Preclass preparation and analysis of the case, often including library research, determining financial ratios, and so forth.
2 *Case presentation and discussion*   Open debate and criticism of case presentations.
3 *Critique*   Comparison of analyses, approaches, decisions, and results of different strategies.
4 *Generalization*   Improvement of analytical and communication skills and the ability to find common elements and approaches to problem solving on a broader scale.

In experiential learning, the analysis and interchange that take place in the class discussion is more important than finding a right answer. There is an opportunity for you to sharpen your skills and develop your ability to apply your knowledge in real world situations. The purpose of the experiential approach is to become skilled in the process of thinking for yourself, making managerial assessments, and defending your plan of action.

How to Prepare a Case

There are a number of approaches to preparing a case, but it is helpful to develop a systematic procedure for case preparation. First, the case analysis requires time and effort for a conscientious preparation. Your main objective is not only to skim the case, but to comprehend its major points as efficiently as possible. Most cases need to be read through at least twice; therefore you should schedule a two- to four-hour block of time for case preparation.

Preparing cases involves two basic skills: analysis and presentation. Preparing cases requires sharpening your analytical skills. You will need to immerse yourself in the facts and behaviors presented in this segment of reality. Out of the confusing array of data, you must determine the critical issues and develop a plan of action. As you analyze the case, you should be asking questions:

What is the organization's current strategy?

What is the real problem facing this manager?

What factors have contributed most to past success or lack of success?

Second, you must organize your analysis in a form that will allow you to discuss it clearly in class. Your general approach to case preparation may proceed as follows:

A   Analysis
   1   Read the case through, underlining or making notes in the margin on im-
       portant facts. Try to get a feel for the overall content of the case, the industry,
       the management, and so forth.
   2   Examine all exhibits carefully. Exhibits typically include such information as
       operating statements, balance sheets, and organization charts. It is safe to
       assume that these items have been included for a purpose.
   3   Prepare any necessary financial analysis, ratios, or comparisons.
   4   Read the text again, this time forming your analysis into a logical outline,
       collecting common elements, and examining in detail goals, policies, symp-
       toms of problems, unresolved issues, and managerial roles.
   5   Do outside research to uncover economic and industrial information. These
       data should provide the necessary information for an in-depth analysis of the
       industry and of important competitors.
   6   Use the *SWOT* model to sum up the key strategic factors facing the corpo-
       ration: *S*trengths and *W*eaknesses of the company; *O*pportunities and
       *T*hreats in the environment.
B   Formulation
   1   Diagram the overall system and subsystems involved and specify the rela-
       tionships of their interaction. Try to define precisely the interactions and the
       roles of key characters.
   2   Identify problems and key issues.
   3   Analyze the causes by using strategy gap, portfolio models, and so forth.
   4   Develop a logical series of alternatives derived from the analysis to resolve
       the problem(s) or issue(s) in the case.
   5   Evaluate each major alternative in light of the company's environment (both
       external and internal), mission, objectives, strategies, and competition. For
       each alternative, consider both the possible barriers to its implementation
       and its financial implications.
   6   Make recommendations on the basis of the facts of the case. Don't say, "I
       don't have enough information." Managers often have the same or even less
       information than is in the case.
       a   Base your recommendations on a total analysis of the case and outside
           research.
       b   Provide the evidence to justify suggested changes.
       c   List the recommendations in order of priority—those to be done short-
           term and those to be done in the future.
       d   Show how your plan of action will solve each of the major problems.
       e   Explain how each strategy will be implemented. How will the strategy
           deal with possible resistance?
C   Written Presentation
   1   Use your outline to prepare the first draft of the case analysis.
       a   Don't rehash basic case material: instead supply the key evidence and
           data to support your strategy.

      b Develop exhibits on financial ratios and other data for inclusion in your report. The exhibits should provide meaningful information. Explain the key elements of an exhibit in the written analysis. If you include a ratio analysis as an exhibit, interpret the ratio in the text and cite only the critical ones in your analysis.

    2 Review your case analysis for content, spelling, and grammar. Make sure you've presented sufficient data or evidence to support your strategic analysis and recommendations. If the analysis requires rewriting, do so. Keep in mind that the written report is going to be graded not only on content but also on the format in which it is presented.

    Your plan of action should flow from your identification of problems. Regardless of the "rightness" or "wrongness" of your decision, you should have a solid, logical supporting analysis to defend your choice. Your ideas should be arranged in an organized form, so they will be clearly understood. If you present them in class, use visual aids such as graphs and diagrams on flip charts, overhead transparencies, or the blackboard. As the saying goes, "A picture is worth a thousand words." The visual aid gives you something to refer to as you talk. Try to sharpen your analyses to a few key points. Don't use overkill on your audience.

    In the following section, a review of important financial analysis techniques is presented. You should enjoy the case analyses and discussion sessions, if you are well prepared. Remember, the cases are used to help you learn about managing. One of the primary advantages of the case method is the opportunity to exchange views from a diversity of experiences. Only by taking positions and making your point can you test yourself against your fellow class members and your instructors. *Good luck!*

FINANCIAL STATEMENTS

    Accountants must collect data in great detail. Financial analysts must group data (accounts) for analysis. Below is a brief guide to the balance sheet and income statement.

    The balance sheet is a statement of financial position as of a specific date. With the usual caveat about the balance sheet's presenting historical rather than market values, here are the important account groupings:

Cash and securities	Current liabilities
Receivables	Long-term debt
Inventories	Preferred stock
Other current assets	
Current assets	Common equity
Fixed assets – net of depreciation	
Total assets	Total claims

The only detail, below the first level, is within the current assets because there is a vast difference in the liquidity (ease of conversion into cash) between the various current assets; and, current assets are held primarily for liquidity. (See the section on liquidity ratios.)

On the income statement, the expense accounts must be grouped into significant analytical categories. The result is as follows:

Net sales (revenues)

minus cost of goods sold

equals gross profit

minus selling and administrative operating expenses (net of depreciation)

minus depreciation

equals operating profit

minus interest charges

equals earnings before taxes

minus taxes

equals net income

Depreciation is separate from other operating expenses because it (and amortization, depletion, etc.) is not a cash expense. Therefore, the analyst may wish to separate this account, especially if liquidity is a matter of concern.

A particularly troublesome account which is appearing more commonly is lease expense. Leasing capital equipment is a popular alternative to borrowing and buying. With a lease, the firm incurs a fixed obligation, much like interest. Regardless of where it appears in the income statement, lease expense should be separated for analysis. (See the section on debt management ratios.)

Analyzing Financial Statements

In many of the cases, you are given financial data, sometimes in summary form, sometimes in greater detail. You should use the financial data in your case analysis, even if the primary theme appears to be nonfinancial. Financial data, properly analyzed, can often confirm tentative conclusions and may provide clues that lead to other discoveries about the firm. You may be provided with some or all of the following financial statements:

income

balance sheet

retained earnings

changes in financial position

Most commonly, you will have income statements and balance sheets, perhaps for the several most recent years. Financial ratios are used to analyze these two statements.

Financial data may well be the only quantitative data provided. Numbers connote precision; but, remember that you are looking at numbers condensed from many detailed accounting reports. These summaries may, in fact, be designed to convey a certain impression of the firm, and vast differences in procedure are allowed under the aegis of "generally accepted accounting principles." So, a word to the wise: Look for confirmation to your conclusions. Confirmation can be found in the data themselves—for instance, two or more financial ratios which support the conclusion. It is even better to find confirmation in the case text itself.

Using Ratios

A ratio is simply a means of converting two numbers into one. Interpretation depends on comparison. If you are provided with several years of data, you may analyze trends. Better yet, you may use industry average ratios. Two financial service organizations provide these ratios. Each has a unique set, however, so you may have to match your ratios to theirs. These services are Dun & Bradstreet, Inc., and Robert Morris Associates' *Annual Statement Studies*. In addition, the Federal Trade Commission's *Quarterly Financial Report* provides manufacturing ratios.

You may have access to computerized financial statements for major firms, such as Standard & Poor's *Compustat* or *Value Line*. They often provide statements for ten years, and sometimes calculated ratios and even industry averages, firm trends, and graphic displays. Securities brokerage firms are another source of (often voluminous) firm and industry data.

Keep in mind that "industries" are becoming increasingly difficult to identify. Diversification as a strategy, long practiced by such firms as General Electric, became popular in the 1960s. Using mergers, many firms were able to grow rapidly without arousing the ire of the U.S. Department of Justice. Throughout the 1970s and 1980s, diversification has remained popular as a means of protection against an increasingly volatile business cycle.

Financial Ratios

The ratios that follow can be calculated from the income statement and balance sheet. Ratios are commonly divided into five categories. Within each, several of the most useful ratios are presented. There is no one best set of ratios. Skilled analysts use those which they need and, on occasion, devise their own to fill a specific need. The five categories are liquidity, asset utilization, debt management, profitability, and common stock.

Liquidity is simply a measure of a firm's ability to generate sufficient cash to meet its current obligations. Because liquidity is essential for survival, it should take priority in the analysis. The two most common ratios are

$$\text{current ratio} = \frac{\text{current assets}}{\text{current liabilities}}$$

The higher the ratio, the greater the presumed ability of the firm to pay its current debt.

$$\text{quick (acid test) ratio} = \frac{\text{current assets} - \text{inventories}}{\text{current liabilities}}$$

Inventories are subtracted because they are the least liquid of current assets, and, in fact, in a forced sale, may be worth very little. Substantial deviation below 1:1 may indicate a cash crisis; a ratio of 3:1 or higher suggests a cash-rich firm.

Asset Utilization

These are sometimes called turnover ratios. All relate an asset to sales. Assets are acquired to produce sales. These ratios measure asset use efficiency. Holding any asset requires the use of increasingly high cost resources. The first two ratios deal with current assets—receivables and inventories—and, therefore, are also liquidity measures.

$$\text{average collection period} = \frac{\text{receivables}}{\text{average daily sales}}$$

Average daily sales are total yearly sales divided by 360 (or 365) days. The result is the average number of days for which receivables remain uncollected. If this number is high, it signifies either poor credit collection practices or a liberal credit policy.

$$\text{inventory turnover} = \frac{\text{sales}}{\text{inventories}}$$

This ratio measures the average number of times per year that inventory is turned over—purchased, processed, and sold. The higher the number, the greater the efficiency.

$$\text{fixed asset turnover} = \frac{\text{sales}}{\text{fixed assets}}$$

Fixed assets are the "productive" assets—plant and equipment. High numbers are generally desirable.

$$\text{total asset turnover} = \frac{\text{sales}}{\text{total assets}}$$

This ratio is a gross measure. A low turnover can mean an excess of either current or fixed assets.

Debt Management

Debt (and leasing) entails a fixed obligation. There is an opportunity to borrow at a low rate (interest is tax deductible), and invest this borrowed money at higher rates of return. This is called *positive leveraging*. It can greatly increase returns to the common stockholders and drive the firm's stock price up. The firm can also find itself in a negative leveraging position from a combination of high interest rates and declining return on investment. Nonetheless, U.S. firms have become increasingly (some say dangerously) leveraged in the past two decades. The use of debt implies both opportunity and risk.

There are two categories of debt management ratios. One proportions debt to assets or capital. The other examines the ability of the firm to meet its debt obligations. The ratios in the first category are:

$$\text{debt to total assets} = \frac{\text{current} + \text{long term debt}}{\text{total assets}}$$

The higher the ratio, the greater the leveraging.

$$\text{long-term debt to total capital} = \frac{\text{long-term debt}}{\text{long-term debt} + \text{preferred} + \text{common equity}}$$

This ratio differs from the debt to total assets ratio in that current liabilities are deleted from both numerator and denominator. It may be more meaningful because current liabilities are transitory and do not represent permanent financing sources.

The second category of debt management ratios includes:

$$\text{times interest earned} = \frac{\text{operating profit}}{\text{interest charges}}$$

This ratio is an important measure, because interest must be paid from operating profit. This ratio should be kept relatively high because operating profit can drop greatly under adversity, such as recession.

$$\text{fixed charge coverage} = \frac{\text{operating profit} + \text{lease payments}}{\text{interest} + \text{lease payments}}$$

This ratio is a modification of times interest earned to cover lease payments. Lease payments must be added to the numerator because they are usually included as an operating expense, and, therefore, have already been deducted in calculating operating profit.

Profitability

There are two categories of profit ratios. One consists of *margin* ratios, proportioning profit to sales. They are derived from the income statement and measure cost control performance. They are usually considered less important than the second category, called *return* ratios, which measure profit against resources committed to the firm. The primary margin ratio is

$$\text{profit margin} = \frac{\text{net profit}}{\text{sales}}$$

Other margin ratios, using gross, operating or before tax profit, can also be calculated.

Return ratios include:

$$\text{return on investment} = \frac{\text{net profit}}{\text{total assets}}$$

This ratio is the ultimate profit measure, because assets represent the total of the resources committed to the firm.

$$\text{return on equity} = \frac{\text{net profit}}{\text{common equity}}$$

This ratio is of primary interest to the firm's stockholders. This ratio will be most affected by positive or negative leveraging.

Common Stock

Three ratios of stock value that are useful to investors are

$$\text{dividend payout ratio} = \frac{\text{dividends}}{\text{net profit}}$$

Dividends paid for the year are found in the statement of retained earnings. It is important to know what proportion of earnings is paid and what is retained. First, dividends constitute a significant portion of the total yield on some stocks. Second, this ratio provides an indication of future prospects for the firm. A low payout, from a generally healthy firm, indicates that earnings are being reinvested for growth.

To calculate the next two ratios, the number of common stock shares outstanding must be given:

$$\text{dividend yield} = \frac{\text{dividends per share}}{\text{stock price}}$$

This ratio is the measure of current yield to the stockholders.

$$\text{price earnings ratio} = \frac{\text{stock price}}{\text{earnings per share}}$$

This ratio is a measure of the degree of acceptance of the firm's stock in the market. A high ratio connotes great acceptance. It may also mean that the stock is overvalued. Some securities analysts look for "low P/E" stocks, which may mean undervaluation in the market.

Another common and simple analytical technique is to "common size" the balance sheet and income statement. This technique allows for easy comparisons, because it provides percentages of all balance sheet items to total assets and all incomes to net sales.

Statement of Retained Earnings

This simple statement connects balance sheet common equity and net profit. Profit can be paid in dividends or added to common equity via retained earnings. The usual format follows:

retained earnings balance (previous year)

plus current year net income

minus dividends paid

equals retained earnings balance (current year)

Statement of Changes in Financial Position

This statement is also more descriptively called the source and application of funds statement. Funds are defined as net working capital—current assets minus current liabilities or the net liquidity position of the firm. This statement examines the change in net working capital (in dollars) from one year to the next and changes in those noncurrent accounts which contributed the change. Those noncurrent balance sheet accounts include fixed assets, long-term debt, and equity.

Sources of funds:	net profit
	depreciation
	sale of long-term debt
	sale of stock
	sale of fixed assets
Application of funds:	net loss
	purchase of fixed assets
	decrease in long-term debt
	stock repurchase
	dividends

EXHIBIT 1
Schematic Diagram of Experiential Learning Cycle

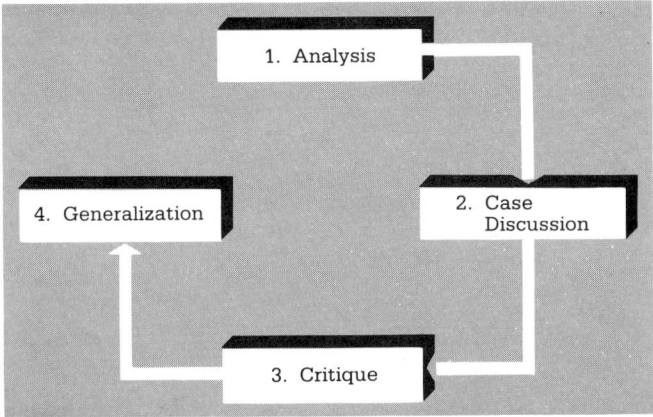

EXHIBIT 2
Financial Ratios

Ratio	Formula	How expressed
1. *Liquidity Ratios*		
Current	$\dfrac{\text{Current assets}}{\text{Current liabilities}}$	Decimal
Quick (acid test) ratio	$\dfrac{\text{Current assets} - \text{Inventory}}{\text{Current liabilities}}$	Decimal
2. *Profitability Ratios*		
Net profit margin	$\dfrac{\text{Net profit before taxes}}{\text{Net sales}}$	Percentage
Gross margin	$\dfrac{\text{Sales} - \text{Cost of sales}}{\text{Net sales}}$	Percentage
Return on investment (ROI)	$\dfrac{\text{Net profit before taxes}}{\text{Total assets}}$	Percentage
Return on equity (ROE)	$\dfrac{\text{Net profit after taxes}}{\text{Average equity}}$	Percentage
Earnings per share (EPS)	$\dfrac{\text{Net profit after taxes} - \text{Preferred burdens}}{\text{Average number of common shares}}$	Dollars per share
Productivity of assets	$\dfrac{\text{Gross income} - \text{Taxes}}{\text{Equity}}$	Percentage
3. *Activity Ratios*		
Inventory turnover	$\dfrac{\text{Net sales}}{\text{Inventory}}$	Decimal
Net working capital turnover	$\dfrac{\text{Net sales}}{\text{Net working capital}}$	Decimal
Asset turnover	$\dfrac{\text{Sales}}{\text{Total assets}}$	Decimal
Average collection period	$\dfrac{\text{Accounts receivable}}{\text{Sales for year} \div 365}$	Days
Accounts payable period	$\dfrac{\text{Accounts Payable}}{\text{Purchases for year} \div 365}$	Days
Cash turnover	$\dfrac{\text{Cash}}{\text{Net sales for year} \div 365}$	Days
Days of inventory	$\dfrac{\text{Inventory}}{\text{Cost of goods sold} \div 365}$	Days
Price earning ratio	$\dfrac{\text{Market price per share}}{\text{Earnings per share}}$	Ratio

EXHIBIT 2 (Cont.)
Financial Ratios

Ratio	Formula	How expressed
4. *Leverage Ratios*		
Debt ratio	$\dfrac{\text{Total debt}}{\text{Total assets}}$	Percentage
Times interest earned	$\dfrac{\text{Profit before taxes } + \text{ interest charges}}{\text{Interest charges}}$	Decimal
Coverage of fixed charges	$\dfrac{\text{Profit before taxes } + \text{ Interest charges } + \text{ Lease charges}}{\text{Interest charges } + \text{ Lease obligations}}$	Decimal
Current liabilities to equity	$\dfrac{\text{Current liabilities}}{\text{Equity}}$	Percentage

Note: In using ratios for analysis, calculate ratios for the corporation and compare them to the average ratios for the particular industry. Refer to Standard and Poors and Robert Morris Associates for average industry data. For an in-depth discussion of ratios and their use, refer to J. F. Weston and E. F. Brigham, *Essentials of Managerial Finance,* 7th ed. (Hinsdale, Ill.: Dryden Press, 1985), 59–93.

CASES FOR PART ONE

■ ■ ■

STRATEGY FORMULATION

■ ■ ■ CASE 1
KADC Radio

Douglas D. Baker and Mark Aucutt

BUILDING A MARKET

FM radio station KADC in Denver, Colorado, has just completed moving into a brand new broadcast facility. The new building was designed with the finest audio broadcast equipment, spacious offices, and high pile carpet. Yet, despite all the modern comforts, there is a noticeable difference in the working atmosphere. The station is now more formal than it had been at the old building, which it had occupied for the past five years.

As Program Director Keith Miller peered out of his second floor office at the vast lobby below, he thought back to how it was in the old days, when the station was housed in a much smaller building with fewer frills. The old building resembled an auto garage more than it did a radio station. There was not much space and most of the staff had to double up in the offices. It was a situation where everyone was forced to team up, which established a fraternal atmosphere. Sales people and disc jockeys (DJs) were grouped together, creating a novel sense of cohesion in the organization. It had been an unusually friendly and collegial place to work, a rare occurrence in the cutthroat radio business.

The old building was a place for everyone to get crazy and let out their aggressions. There were holes in the walls and coffee stains on the rug. The station manager's office doubled as an employee lounge, with DJs taking afternoon naps while Bob Easton, the station manager, was on the phone making important business decisions. The "shack," as it was most commonly referred to, did not even have a parking lot, so everyone was constantly on the lookout for the metermaid and her chalk stick. It was quite a sight, seeing virtually the entire staff roll out of the office at the same time to wipe the chalk off their tires. Those were the days.

With all the modern conveniences that the old building lacked, it made up for them in character. It was located in the "low-rent" district of town and it inspired the staff to be in a wild and raunchy mood, an attitude that seemed appropriate for playing rock and roll. Knowing that they could wreak havoc on the place, the DJs would do just about whatever they wanted, including drinking beer on the roof during the summer.

Despite all this "beautiful poverty" the station was growing in listenership and staff members, calling for more room in which to operate. Owner Victor Denton saw the need and decided to sell the AM sister station, KPC, to provide more capital for the improvement of KADC.

The new "home" located across town has every piece of equipment a DJ could ask for. There are three production studios, as compared to just one in the shack. Each sales person and director has an office or cubicle, and a parking lot and employee lounge is provided for the staff.

The new building is a beautiful sight, but the appearance seems almost too sterile for this group. It seems more like a dentist's office than the saloon everyone was used to. The receptionist can no longer sit at her desk with a beer and now has to adhere to a dress code. Keith thought of how a simple move had affected the atmosphere so dramatically and hoped that it would not disrupt the internal balance that had taken the station to number one in the market.

Description of the Industry

Climbing to the top of the market can be a very difficult task for a radio station. The competition is often intense, and listener preferences may vary from one period to the next. Age and gender demographics, geographical location, format trends, and new technology are all factors contributing to the strategy of a radio station. Adjustments to and possible abolishments of formats depend upon the hard-to-predict listener acceptance. There is a variety of formats that are predominant in the industry. They are characterized as follows.

1   News/Talk (NT)—NT features up-to-the-minute news, plus talk shows that range from current news to fashion trends. NT radio stations produce their own in-house newscasts along with having a network feed from one of the major radio networks (ABC, NBC, CBS, and Mutual). Stations located in towns with professional or college sports teams bid for the broadcast rights to the games. Sports programming usually increases listenership if the team appeals to the audience and has a good season. In general, NT stations appeal to both sexes ranging in age from eighteen up. However, the bulk of the listenership lies in the thirty-five to sixty-five age bracket.

2   Contemporary Hit Radio (CHR)—CHR is a fancy name for what is commonly referred to as Top 40 radio. CHR plays popular hits and features DJs who direct their dialogue to teenagers, who make up the greatest part of the audience. The CHR stations have traditionally been located exclusively on the AM band. Recently, there has been a movement of CHR to the FM band so that they can send out a higher-fidelity radio signal.

3   Album Oriented Rock (AOR)—AOR stations emerged on the FM band in the late 1960s, playing progressive music ranging from funk to acid rock for people who

liked "laid-back disc jockeys and no hype." Since that time, the formats have become narrower and the music is now primarily rock and roll. AOR stations that are successful reach that position because they have a focused direction and a loyal audience. The major market segments that AOR draws from are teens and males eighteen to thirty-four years old, with a few female rock and roll fans. With a distinct direction, AOR has become a major power in radio formatting and has given CHR a run for its money.

4   Adult Contemporary (AC)—In a nutshell, AC is a more middle-of-the-road version of CHR. The term *soft rock* applies here, as AC stations play the hits but add some country music and news to appeal to the middle demographics (women over twenty and both sexes over thirty-five).

5   Country Music (CM)—CM stations play "Top-40" country music with country specials and news. A popular promotional gimmick for them is the sponsorship of rodeos and roundups. CM appeals to both sexes between eighteen and twenty-five, but mostly to people twenty-five and up. It does especially well in country-oriented markets such as Nashville and Memphis.

6   Beautiful Music (BM)—Practically every dentist or doctor's office carries a BM station. The BM format plays orchestrated versions of the hits from years past and present. Along with commercial listeners, middle-age and older people constitute the major group dedicated to this format.

7   There are other smaller niches in the market that play jazz, black music, and religious programming.

This wide variety of formats represents the various listener interests. Although some people listen to a number of stations, most usually stick with one. Capturing the listener of this loyal audience is the station management's objective.

There is a concept in radio that is called the 20/80 theory, meaning that a station has die-hard listeners that represent 20 percent of their total audience, while the remaining 80 percent just follow the pack. What a station desires is to secure a loyal 20 percent and hope that the 80 percent casual listeners will become more committed to the station. It is not an easy task. In the large markets, there is usually more than one radio station with the same format, so there is often a battle between them to get the highest number of listeners. Naturally, ratings play a big role in the radio industry. Ratings help owners and management determine which way to program the station.

In the radio business, ratings are the bread and butter of existence. If the ratings are good, then advertisers will be inclined to buy time for their commercials. If the ratings sink, the advertisers will bail out and put their money where their potential customers can be reached.

The key to successful advertising in radio is repetition. The more someone hears an advertisement, the better the chance of remembering and identifying it with the product. Hence, if ratings are high, advertisers will buy a number of commercial spots, to insure audience recall. At some stations the repetition occurs at predetermined times of the hour or day. For instance, on NT stations, listeners tune in at the top of the hour to hear the news. Hence, repeated ads are run during this period. These high ratings also allow the station to charge up to three times the regular rate for advertisements run at peak ratings times.

The advertisers' choice of radio format to buy their commercial time on is critically important to the ad's success. Advertisements must be directed at the appropriate audience segment. For instance, a commercial on vitamins for geriatrics would not probably fare as well on a Top 40 station as it would on a beautiful music station. Similarly, a roller skating rink commercial would not be as effective on an adult contemporary station as it would be on a Top 40 station. Both advertisers and radio executives alike must be careful in choosing the proper products to sell on the air. An inappropriate advertisement can negatively affect listeners' attitudes about a station in a very short period of time.

The radio industry can be extremely volatile. A radio station can be one of the top stations in the market one rating period and then be struggling the next as listeners' preferences change. An example during the 1970s was the shift from rock and roll to disco music.

The choices of listeners also change as they get older. A Top 40 faithful today might be a News/Talk enthusiast ten years from now. A successful radio program director must be constantly looking ahead in order to keep ratings high. An example of the shifting preferences of large demographic groups is the case of AM-band CHR radio stations. In the 1960s, CHR was the king of contemporary music. There was an enormous audience which was boosted by the baby-boom-era listeners. The music was "poppy" and featured short songs, with fast-talking DJs who spoke after each song. As the 1960s wound down, there were new music movements which challenged the established Top 40 stations. Progressive music stations emerged throughout the country. Located primarily on the FM-stereo band, progressive stations played "underground" music cuts and long versions of CHR hits with laid-back DJs. Some of the selections ranged from funk to acid rock, with an open format. As the 1970s marched on, progressive music developed into a more sophisticated format. The end result was the emergence of AOR, which took a large market share from CHR and other formats.

The major attraction to AOR stations has been that they play uncut versions of popular music, not often heard on the CHR or AC stations, and the DJs communicate to the audience in a one-to-one manner. Another factor that has facilitated the growth of AOR stations is that they broadcast on the FM band. Being on FM is advantageous because the signal is clear, static-free, and in stereo. Virtually every radio household now has at least one FM receiver, enabling people to pick up the high fidelity music stations. Currently, some CHR stations are beginning to shift to the FM band, but the majority have stayed on AM. The advantage of AM is that its signal can reach a more physically distant audience, thus reaching more listeners. Some formats, such as NT, are not affected by the shift to FM because they are not concerned with reception fidelity.

Recent action by the Federal Communications Commission (FCC) has given AM stations some hope of increasing their fidelity. The FCC has approved that AM may be broadcast in stereo, instead of mono, and is considering the expansion of the AM dial to accommodate more stations. So far, FM stations have not been greatly affected by this decision, as it will take time for people to buy receivers that play AM stereo.

New technology can emerge in many forms to pose a threat to radio. Examples of recent technological advancements are tape cassettes, ''Walkman'' tape machines, video games and home computers. These advancements have had an effect on the music industry. For instance, listeners may tune out the radio stations and play a prerecorded tape or video game. Such new developments are in the minds of program directors who are trying to institute counterprogramming. Recently promotions have been attempted that tie in with video games and computers.

There are a number of market factors that affect the status of radio stations. The format must be directed toward the targeted audience, the advertisements must be appropriate and the technological changes must be considered. Management plays a major role in determining the success of a station by the manner in which they adapt to the changing internal and external environment.

Current Structure and Staff of KADC

KADC's management structure is shown on page 303. The structure of the station is fairly common in the industry. General manager Bob Easton oversees the entire operation. Easton has worked his way up the ranks and knows the many aspects of radio. He has sold for and programmed radio stations in his fifteen-year career. The employees respect him, as he is familiar with each department and knows how it should be run. Bob makes all the final decisions on internal and external station business. For instance, he is a liaison between the ownership and the business community and plays a variety of civic roles external to the organization.

Bob receives an allotted amount of company funds from the parent corporation and must prepare and adhere to a budget. He makes the money decisions and works very closely with program director Keith Miller in station format and hiring decisions. Bob also has a good working relationship with George Sampson, the sales manager, and his staff in deciding which products would be proper and effective when advertised on the station. Bob has an office staff, including a secretary who serves as his assistant. Easton also plays the role of traffic director and is responsible for scheduling commercials.

The sales manager position was created when KADC became the number one radio station in the market. With increased sales and demands by advertisers, the sales staff was growing and needed a department leader. Up to that point, the sales staff had reported to Bob. George Sampson was the logical choice for the job, as he had been with the station for five years and had sold well during that time. He showed leadership abilities and had a good rapport with the clients.

Upon assuming his new role, Sampson expanded the sales force from three to six, to ease the work load and allow for better customer service. The sales people

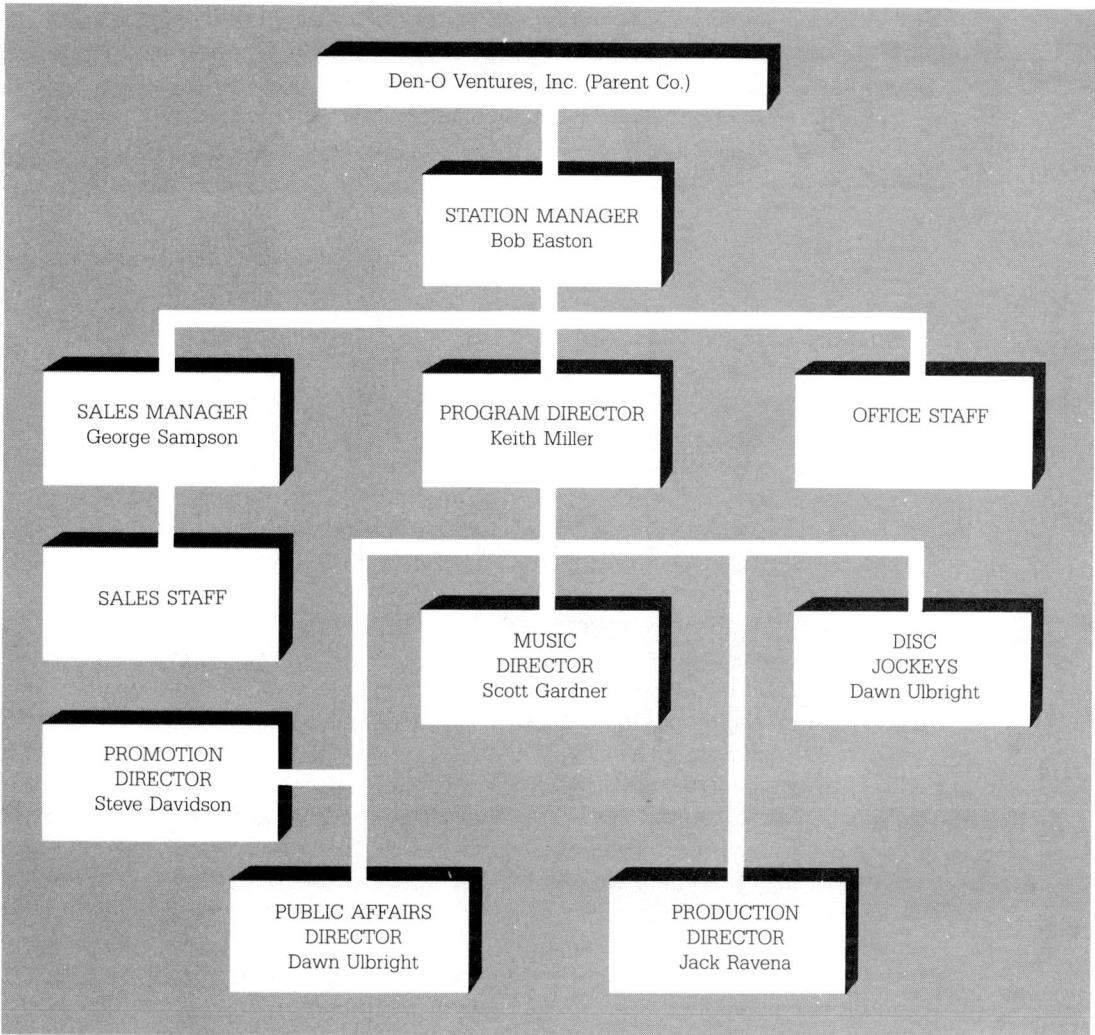

were each given an account list when they started at the station. It was up to the sales people to go out and make calls to acquire business. For stations that do not have high ratings, that can be a frustrating task. However, a good salesperson can often sell commercial time on stations with low ratings through determined effort.

The difficulty of sales at KADC is a different story. The station has had good ratings for two years, and clients are aware of the many listeners KADC reaches (for a description of market demographics see exhibits 1 and 2). The latest sales figures showed that the station allowed eight minutes an hour for advertisements, with rates varying depending upon the time of day. Currently, it has the next two and a half months of commercial time sold out. While the station has been at the top of the ratings, clients have come to KADC to advertise. Rather than the sales people having to pound the streets begging for business, they spend the bulk of their time servicing present accounts to update commercials and run promotions. The rest of the time is spent approaching prospective clients on the account lists to see if they are interested in future advertising.

Sampson has a sales secretary who handles the administrative chores in the department and works with the other office members. The station is represented regionally and nationally by the Carlson Guild, which acts as a consultant for the station in the sales department and spreads the station's name in the business community to attract clients.

Perhaps the most difficult job at the radio station belongs to Keith Miller, the program director. Miller must always be aware of the station format and feel the pulse of the future music trends that could surface. The program director is responsible for what goes on the air and has the final word on what will be broadcast. At KADC, Bob Easton oversees the entire operation, but the program director is directly in charge of the airstaff, music, promotions, production, and public affairs departments. He is, in a sense, the operations manager, and serves as the team captain, motivating the staff and DJs. Miller conducts meetings with DJs, evaluating each individual's performance and setting the format direction. He also works with Scott Gardner, the music director, in deciding whether a song will be aired. Over the years, they have developed a strong bond and can usually agree as to whether a group or song is appropriate for the format. In case of a disagreement, Keith has the final responsibility and authority.

Similar to baseball coaches, program directors can reap the harvest and get the credit when the organization performs well. However, they also get the blame if the station has poor ratings. The program director's job can be very expendable if the station's ratings fall. There are many out-of-work program directors who have failed to get a station out of the rating cellar or were unable to hold it in a high-market position. Miller has been at his job for four years, which is a long lifespan in this industry. Miller also works closely with the promotions director in conceptualizing new station promotion ideas and carrying them out. In addition, he establishes public affairs programs that fit the format and serve the public. The public affairs director, Dawn Ulbright, does on-the-street interviews and produces spots that are of interest to the listeners. The station features a Sunday morning talk show which addresses current issues. FCC license requirements require radio stations to air public affairs programming.

KADC also has a production department that produces commercials. National commercials usually involve dubbing from tape reel onto 4-track cartridges which enable the spots to be played on the air. KADC, which has a very talented airstaff, produces most of its own local spots that go on the air. Jack Ravena, the production director, along with the DJs, writes and records most of the spots. Miller supervises the production department and can pull a commercial off the air if he does not feel that it sounds right.

All in all, Miller has his hands full. He must be on the ball at all times to make important decisions and keep the morale up. Much of what goes on around the station revolves around the program director.

The music director must also have an ear for the appropriateness of songs. The music director usually doubles as a disc jockey, enabling him to get an instant response to a record or group from the listeners. Scott Gardner meets with the music representatives from the record companies on a weekly basis, as they attempt to sell their products. He listens to every new release to sort out the bad apples and then meets with Keith to make a decision on what to air. Scott is the only station employee to deal with the music representatives on a regular basis.

Most large-market stations have a promotions director who takes some of the burden off the program director by coming up with creative ideas to spread the station's name. Steve Davidson fills this role at KADC and has been with the station since he graduated from college with an advertising and graphics arts degree. His skills in graphic arts have saved money for the station that would normally have been spent on outside free-lance artists. Steve has been involved in the creation of many KADC trademarks, and the station has had a strong promotional department.

KADC is typified by having had a seemingly effective management staff. They have allowed their subordinates to be creative and experiment as much as they deem appropriate. The organizational climate has been very positive. Miller has kept the airstaff motivated so that they go on the air with aggressive, playful attitudes. It has been easy for listeners to pick up on this positive attitude. DJs project their attitudes, and KADC's jockeys are happy with their positions and the working atmosphere. It is a great improvement over what the station was like a few years earlier.

The History of KADC

KADC is an FM-Album Oriented Rock (AOR) radio station. It is owned by Den-O Ventures, Inc. Den-O consists of two owners: businessman Victor Denton and real estate developer Harold O'Connor. Den-O also owns two radio stations in each of the following cities: Salt Lake City, Utah; Sacramento, California; and Reno, Nevada. KADC and KSLT in Reno are the only AOR stations in the chain.

In addition to the seven radio stations, Den-O owns and operates Den-O recording studios in Colorado Springs. The Den-O studios have been used by major rock and roll recording artists, along with local groups who can foot the bill.

KADC first went on the air under different ownership in 1958, and operated as a classical music station for 15 years. In 1973, Den-O purchased the station to complement their highly rated AM band Top-40 station, KPC.

Upon acquisition, KADC was transformed into an open format rock and roll station, which would play anything from Stevie Wonder to Led Zeppelin in a twenty-minute music sweep. During this time, the station enjoyed a reasonable following. However, it lacked the consistent on-air talent and musical direction to pose a threat to the top rock station KMHC, which ranked as one of the top five stations in the local area during the mid- to late 1970s. As Miller put it: "KADC was just a station that didn't do anything really special, while KMHC was looked at as being 'The Rock Station' in the market."

In the latter part of 1978, KADC's then general manager, Craig Truax, was in search of a new program director. He wanted someone who would make changes and pull them out of the number sixteen position in the market. After an extensive interviewing process, Truax settled on a man who had worked in a major market (Minneapolis) as a disc jockey, but had no previous programming experience and had done limited work as a music director. Truax was ready for a change and took a chance on 27-year-old Keith Miller. Miller had suggested many musical and personnel improvements that set the station in a definite direction and increased their small 3 percent share of the market.

Shortly after Miller arrived, Truax left the station to become part-owner/manager of a Denver production studio. Den-O group manager Roger Peterson stepped into the position for an interim period, until a permanent replacement could be found. Peterson's stay lasted three months.

Victor Denton found a replacement for Peterson in Dan Waterfield, a veteran salesman who had been very successful at rival station KMHC for the previous seven years. The problems Waterfield faced at KADC were completely different from those he had previously encountered. He was not only in charge of the sales department, but was also Keith's boss. This meant he had to be familiar with programming, with which he had very limited experience.

Keith Miller recalls the period when Waterfield was KADC's station manager: "Dan was a great salesman at KMHC, very successful over there. But it was a different story for him at KADC. He ran the place like a dictator and didn't give us room to breathe or be creative. I was ready to quit if the situation didn't change. We were going nowhere and I couldn't do a thing about it. Then a change was made."

The change came in the form of Bob Easton. Easton, a veteran radio man, had served as station manager at KBLM in Boulder and program director at KRZR in Sacramento and KPC in Denver. Easton had a reputation for being a winner and brought a fresh attitude to KADC. Easton allowed Miller room to experiment and develop a format and station image that would lead KADC out of the mid-market blues to which it had become accustomed.

As Miller reflected, "Bob made all the difference in the world. He was the type of manager that could motivate people to want to work hard, while Dan was the type that created tension which in turn would alienate the staff from being productive." Easton gave Miller a broad span of authority from the start, allowing him to refine the format and make the airstaff realignments that would help the station gain listeners. Still, KADC lacked an image. They had been calling themselves "Denver's Choice Rocker," or "The Rocker," or "The Choice" for almost a year but had not really proven themselves worthy of that title.

The station hired the consulting firm of Sullivan/Bolinger/McConnell and Associates, Inc. of Chicago, to provide some suggestions that might help them become more identifiable. The consultants provided some general information that indicated that the station should make a commitment to rock and roll and go all out to become the number one AOR station in the market. Easton, Miller and Davidson had their work cut out for them.

The three sat down many times and discussed at length the approach they might take to establish KADC as "Denver's Choice Rocker." One thing they needed to do was create an image or logo that listeners could identify and feel secure with. The station had gone through three logo changes in two years, and none of them stood out as being anything special. Davidson spent almost two months at the drawing board trying to create a logo that would make KADC stand out in the minds of Denver's rock and roll listeners.

In the meantime, Miller worked on ways to improve the format. He was given permission by Easton to hire new and talented on-air personalities. Miller hired newsman Nick Martin to team up with John Pierce in the afternoons. He also hired DJ Paul McMahon to work the morning shift.

The new music that the station played set KADC in a unique niche. They "rocked" 24 hours a day, seven days a week. It was not uncommon to hear Ted Nugent or AC/DC blasting out of the radio at 7 A.M. No other station had adopted such a format. No others had dared, and the listeners started to take notice.

The timing of KADC's dedication to being the best rock and roll station in the market was perfect. When the change took place, the disco movement had reached its peak. The rock and roll lovers were ready to come out of the closet and bid farewell to John Travolta, the Bee Gees, and all-night discos. Rock and KADC were on the rise. "The Rock," as the station was commonly referred to, did its best to make sure that disco was pushed out of the public eye as quickly as possible. For instance, KADC began an antidisco attack known as "Disco Destruction." Veteran KADC disc jockey Scott Gardner became the self-appointed commander of the KADC "Rock and Roll Army," which had one goal in mind: "To destroy disco in your lifetime." On each show, Gardner set aside a segment for "Disco Destruction." During this time, he would take a disco record and destroy it on the air, using various sound effects. The concept was very effective and the listeners loved it.

In the meantime, Steve Davidson had created a logo that was far superior to anything the station had previously used. It incorporated "Denver's Choice Rocker" with a giant red and gold "Rocker" logo that was quite visible. It enhanced the station's image.

The rest of the radio stations had not taken KADC seriously. It just did not seem plausible to them that KADC could overtake the AOR powerhouse KMHC, which had been the top rock and roll station in the market for years.

The Climb

The climate at KADC in the fall of 1979 was upbeat. They had come from number eighteen to eleven in the market within a year (see exhibit 3) and wanted to continue the upward trend. If they made it to the top, it would be a dream come true.

Miller was happy with the airstaff, and the supporting management seemed to know their jobs. As the station began its quest up the ratings ladder, a strong collegial atmosphere developed. The air-sound at the station became distinctive, and KADC continued its rapid climb in the ratings. Ultimately, in 1981, KADC was the top-rated station in the entire market. For twenty-fours a day, they had consistent on-air talent and played ear-breaking rock and roll. Each disc jockey was unique and carried great audience appeal.

The morning team, Paul McMahon and newsman Jeff Whitson, combined to make one of the best morning shows in the country. They wrote original satirical material and became known as "The Mile-High Maniacs." They were followed in the morning by Miller. Miller was on the air for one year but quit DJing as his other station duties became too time consuming.

Rod "Midday" Moore was hired to fill Miller's time slot, and became a household name. He hosted an immensely popular "Noontime Snack" which played oldies rock from 12 to 1 P.M. Moore left to pursue other interests in late 1981 and was replaced by Shari Allen, who had been working the weekend shift.

The afternoon shift was held by former KMHC DJ John Pierce and newsman Nick Martin. Pierce and Martin were veterans of the business who also possessed a high degree of creativity. They called their 2 to 6 P.M. time slot the "Caribou Connection" and punctuated it with comedy skits. John Pierce was one of the first new DJs, coming to KADC in the summer of 1978. He had been a regular disc jockey in Portland, Oregon for six years, but was looking for a job change when he was hired at KADC. In Pierce's words: "I came to KADC because I was looking for a job that paid more. Also, I wanted to go to an organization that was run with better management. Victor Denton (the owner) was the person I wanted to work for." When John reached KADC he noticed a difference. "Coming to KADC was a shock, it was like going to work in a garage, they had speakers sitting on boxes and the equipment wasn't as new as KMHC's. It took about a year to get used to it." Pierce watched the managerial changes take place as Keith and Bob arrived and set the station on its course. "Keith put us in the right direction and allowed us to be creative. Bob Easton has been a big factor because he is such a people person, and everyone enjoys working for him."

This comment was echoed by Nick Martin, who was also a former KMHC staff member who came to KADC in 1979 for many of the same reasons as Pierce. "The station was beginning to climb back then, and no one believed that we could take the lead from KMHC, let alone be the number one station in the entire market." Nick added, "The atmosphere is so much better here, this is the kind of place you dream about, and Keith has given us so much room to be creative." Martin and the other DJs were very well rewarded financially. The station payed far above union scale and the staff felt equitably compensated during the climb of the station in the ratings.

Scott Gardner, the 6 to 10 P.M. DJ, has been with the station for seven years, making him the greybeard of the staff. He has been there through thick and thin and has seen the format change from free-form rock and roll, through various album rock formats, to the present concentrated format. According to Scott, "The station wasn't the force that it is today. It was a hole-in-the-wall station with five or six employees, and would play anything from Joni Mitchell to Deep Purple." He went on to say that, "the station has done well because of the commitment to rock and roll." The remaining DJs are experienced radio announcers and share the positive attitude about KADC.

In the two and a half years since the station set its course, it has consistently come up in the ratings (see exhibit 4). Promotions have been one of KADC's biggest weapons. They have had original promotions revolving around the theme "Denver's Choice Rocker." They operate on a modest budget and have had promotions success with selling T-shirts with the "Rock," window stickers, concert guides, concert ticket giveaways, record premieres, local talent searches, free drinking sprees at local bars, a rock and roll air force card with special discounts, and a racing car. These promotions, combined with the solid programming, added to the success of the station.

The results have been dramatic. KADC had five consecutive ratings increases and, by July of 1981, became Denver's first FM station to be number one, with 9.8 percent of the market share. They had quadrupled KMHC's ratings and stood on top of the heap. The nearest competition was KNTR-AM, a News/Talk station which had a 9.3 percent share. The dream had come true for KADC; they were at the top, and now the challenge was to stay there.

The Outlook

Miller rubbed his forehead and glanced back toward the plush lobby, thinking about the future. He knew that KMHC was planning to restructure their format back to rock and roll, and that it would take some listeners away from KADC. The big question that kept banging away in Keith's head was whether to stick with the same approach that took the station to the top, or switch to something different. Had the new building and the station's success changed the organizational climate for the worse? He had to act soon, the other stations were about to mount a charge . . . .

NEW PRESSURES

Three months after KADC reached the pinnacle of the Denver market, there was a celebration. The party was most impressive. Both owners, Victor Denton and Harold O'Connor, were in attendance and presented each employee with a bottle of champagne for a job well done. The staff thoroughly enjoyed themselves and breathed a sign of relief for amassing the number one position. KADC had done the impossible, not only becoming the top AOR station, but the most listened-to station in the entire market. Local newspapers and television stations even filed into the cozy confines to interview both Bob and Keith regarding their triumph. The feeling of euphoria was present throughout the following week and the airstaff never sounded better. But a number of threats to their top rating were on the horizon.

One threat came in the form of a mental let-down. The chase had been intense and exhausting. They had worked hard and taken many chances in the past three years. It was the perfect Cinderella story. However, it had taken its toll. The staff was tired and their enthusiasm began to wane. In the three months that followed, the internal climate at KADC began to take on a different light. After the initial let-down set in, the on-air and sales staffs started to take on an attitude of overconfidence. Despite a concentrated effort by management and staff to approach the high ratings modestly, KADC did show signs of self-righteousness. The airstaff were proud of their achievement and started to feel comfortable. Unfortunately, in radio, being comfortable can lead to complacency, and the program director, Keith Miller, felt cause for concern.

Another threat came from other stations. Seeing the success of KADC, they began to react. For instance, the owners of KFER were disappointed with the low ratings of their station and the management that produced those numbers. Consequently, both general manager Hank Stevens and program director Rich Elliott found themselves out of jobs. The parent company decided to restructure the format back to rock and roll and hired a new general manager, Joe Bowman, and program director, Mike King, to carry out the task. They began to attract KADC's listeners.

Miller knew that KMHC would be his most direct competitor, but what effect they would have remained to be seen. Counterprogramming was a factor to be considered to outfox the opponent. He felt a need to reiterate the importance of taking chances and being ''hungry'' for victory to the airstaff so as to avoid complacency. He was also compelled to not let the convenience and luxury of the new building create barriers to the internal atmosphere. Keith acted accordingly, sitting each disc jockey down within a week's time and discussing the importance of taking chances and striving for a repeat victory. The airstaff seemed to realize the importance of not being overly impressed with their accomplishments. Keith breathed a sigh of relief and felt confident that the aggressiveness would emerge again.

During the two rating months (April/May) that followed, KADC sounded very good, the airstaff was creative, and Keith and Scott's music programming was excellent. However, they were not the only station in the market to strive for an improvement.

KNTR had beefed up their programming and sounded very good on the air. KMHC had decided on a commercial-free rock and roll format and sounded stronger, although still not in the league of KADC. Meanwhile, KFER was establishing itself with its own commercial-free Top 40 sound and was gaining many women listeners. The activity in the market during the two rating months was very high-pitched. Everyone was trying hard, KADC to stay on top and the others to take their crown. When the ratings came out in June, KADC had dropped a notch.

With its overall appeal to a wider demographic group and carrying broadcasts of Denver's successful professional basketball team, KNTR emerged as the number one station with a solid 9.6 percent market share (see exhibit 5). KADC, while still showing a strong performance, came in second, dropping to a still respectable 8.9 percent market share. KMHC made a substantial gain, jumping from 3.1 percent to 4.8 percent, and started to take away KADC's teen listeners. Perhaps the biggest surprise in the new ratings was KFER, which had a paltry 1.6 percent share as a country station in December, but with its new Top 40 format had an impressive 3.7 percent share. Keith Miller was happy with KADC's performance despite its slipping to number two, and seemed unconcerned with the respectable showings of both

KMHC and KFER. He felt the commercial-free format some other stations were beginning to use was a fad and would burn out when people got tired of impersonal disc jockeys.

Continued Change in the Market

Despite its number-two ranking, KADC was still regarded as "Denver's Best Rock" in the minds of the listeners. But rock and roll was starting to go through some interesting changes. Many of the groups that had been trademarks for rock stations began to sound worn out or overplayed, and some of the new music being released was taking on a new sound. A change was taking place. For instance, the Who had announced that they were touring the United States for the last time. The relied-upon groups like Bob Seger, Styx, Pat Benatar, and Tom Petty had abandoned their cult rock images to become more commercial, and new groups like Men at Work and A Flock of Seagulls emerged with across-the-board popularity on Top 40, Album Oriented Rock, and Adult Contemporary formats. The influx of new music posed a serious problem. The movement had started to break away from album-oriented artists to pop artists, similar to what had happened in the early sixties.

While KADC's on-air talent sounded good, the music tended to come off as stale. Listener preferences were starting to go in two directions. Half of the diehard fans wanted to hear more heavy metal and classic rock and roll from groups such as Led Zeppelin, the Beatles, the Rolling Stones, and the Who. However, the other half of the listeners were yearning for new music and were tired of hearing the old standbys. The shift had started throughout AOR radio, and Miller was worried. These shifting listener preferences could cause serious problems. For instance, KADC had done a very successful job of promoting and marketing the station's image with the logo. There was a variety of apparel and stickers depicting the red "ROCKER," and the general public had come to associate rock and roll with KADC. With the recent change in music from hard rock to a pop sound, KADC was faced with a big decision. Should they maintain the rock image/logo and ride through this period, or switch to a new format, with a new image/logo, and stay ahead of the competition?

Pressure to Change

KADC was a relatively unique organization within the radio industry in that they took pride in providing a secure place to work. In other words, they did not believe in a revolving-door policy. Management opted to work with the employees and create a winning atmosphere. KADC had succeeded in building a secure, comfortable, working climate; but Keith wondered if it was too comfortable.

In the later part of 1982, the DJs were once again sounding overconfident and were not working on new material. Complacency was starting to show itself again. With such a secure relaxed atmosphere, the jocks did not feel like their jobs were in jeopardy and saw little reason not to let up a bit. Keith wanted to pull the station out of its slump and get the DJs motivated to perform better once again. He hated to threaten anyone with being fired, but he somehow needed to ignite a spark.

The Competition

A new round of ratings came out in mid-December and KADC slipped into third place with a 7.4 percent share (see exhibit 6). They followed adult contemporary station KLDF with 8.1 percent and KNTR with an outstanding 10.2 percent share. KADC's nearest rock and roll competitors, KMHC and KFER, had made substantial gains, grabbing 6.7 percent and 5.3 percent shares respectively. KADC had picked up more listeners in the twenty-five to thirty-four age bracket, but KMHC had closed in on the teen market.

The ratings indicated that KMHC and KFER were serious competitors in the Denver market. Keith came to grips with the fact that commercial-free radio was not a passing fad, and that it had made a bigger dent in the market than he had ever imagined it could. The situation was getting intense and he knew it was time to act.

The Outlook

With the combination of a new music movement and competition on his station's heels, Keith Miller was in a position to make crucial decisions that could determine the success of KADC. Three major dilemmas went through his mind. First was the issue of a format change. Miller knew that there were plenty of hard-rock fans in the audience to keep that format afloat, but not enough to allow the station to maintain the rating shares to which they had been accustomed. On the other hand, there were a lot of people growing out of the heavy metal rock age and who were shifting their tastes to new music. He did not want to be left with an out-of-date format if the new wave music took hold for an extended period of time.

Secondly, the promotional image of the station was of major concern. The ''Denver's Best Rock'' logo had served its purpose when the station played nothing but hard rock, but if they changed to a pop rock sound, the rock image/logo would be questioned by the public and would have to be modified or changed to create acceptance.

The third, and perhaps most difficult, problem that Miller faced was in regard to the DJs. The airstaff had virtually remained intact throughout the climb and during the year that followed, but was sounding complacent and uninspired. Keith had planned on working more intensely with each DJ on a one-to-one basis to motivate them.

He hated the idea of firing anyone, as it would break down the security and high morale that existed at the station, but he knew that if the ratings continued to fall, the morale would start to crumble anyway. It wasn't a pretty picture.

QUESTIONS

1   Describe the radio industry and its competitive nature.
2   What factors should be taken into account when planning format and programming for a radio station?
3   What do you think of KADC's current strategy? Why?
4   Describe the planning process at KADC.
5   What impact will reaching the top of the ratings have on KADC's competition? On the internal climate of the station?
6   Define KADC's market niche. How large is it? How large will it be in the future?
7   What impact will changing listener preferences and market demographics have on the station?
8   Describe the managerial style and climate of the organization. Will such a style persist if ratings fall?
9   What are the greatest dangers KADC faces?
10   What should KADC's strategy be in the future?

EXHIBIT 1
1980 Census Data

Years of School Completed (Number of Persons 25+)		Occupation (Percent Persons 16+)	
Elem./High	346,805	Managerial	25%
High Sch Grad	624,731	Technical	32%
College 1+ Yrs	710,731	Service Worker	13%
		Farm Worker	2%
		Precision Prod	14%
		Operator	14%

Value of Housing (Number of Units)			
Value in $	Number Units	Auto by Households	
Below 30,000	48,261	None	9%
30,000–49,999	113,074	1	33%
50K–79,999	232,377	2	35%
80K–99,999	78,067	3+	23%
100K–149,999	58,290		
150K+	26,475		
Median Value	$65,100		

Income by Households (Percent of Households)		Transportation to Work (Number of Persons 16+)	
Under $10,000	18%	Public	86,001
10K–14,999	9	Drive Alone	14,686
15K–19,999	10	Car Pool	238,848
20K–29,999	25	Other	127,831
30K–39,999	19		
40K–49,999	10		
50K+	9		
Median Income	24,883		

EXHIBIT 2
Population Estimates and Sample Distribution by Sex-Age Group, 1983

Total Survey Area		Estimated Population	Estimated Population As Percent of Total Persons 12+
MEN	18–24	204,800	8.2
MEN	25–34	289,000	11.6
MEN	35–44	200,800	8.1
MEN	45–49	69,500	2.8
MEN	50–54	65,900	2.7
MEN	55–64	133,800	5.4
MEN	65+	129,800	5.2
WOMEN	18–24	185,500	7.5
WOMEN	25–34	281,200	11.3
WOMEN	35–44	193,900	7.8
WOMEN	45–49	69,600	2.8
WOMEN	50–54	67,100	2.7
WOMEN	55–64	143,200	5.8
WOMEN	65+	188,200	7.6
TEENS	12–17	262,500	10.6
TOTAL PERSONS 12+		2,484,800	
MEN	18+	1,093,600	
WOMEN	18+	1,128,700	
ADULTS	18+	2,222,300	

EXHIBIT 3

Ranks of Area Radio Stations and Who Their Listeners Were for the Winter 1978 Period

1	KNTR-AM(NT): MEN 35–64(12.8), WOMEN 35–64(8.9)
2	KMHC-FM(AOR): TEENS(26.7), MEN 18–34(12.1), MEN 18–49(7.4), WOMEN 18–34(4.2)
3	KROV-AM(AC): WOMEN 35–64(10.7), MEN 35–64(6.3)
4	KPOA-FM(BM): WOMEN 35–64(12.1), MEN 35–64(7.7)
5	KUER-AM(CM): MEN 25–49(6.7), WOMEN 25–54(6.4)
6	KDKC-AM(NT): MEN 35–64(7.1), WOMEN 35–64(6.8)
7	KLBA-FM(CHR): TEENS(19.7), WOMEN 18–34(4.6), MEN 18–34(2.6)
8	KRXQ-FM(RELIGIOUS): MEN 35–64(8.7), WOMEN 25–64(8.1)
9	KBFR-AM(AC): MEN 35–64(7.7), WOMEN 35–64(6.2)
10	KSTS-AM(CHR): TEENS(16.5), MEN 18–34(7.8), WOMEN 18–34(5.1)
18	KADC-FM(AOR): TEENS(9.7), MEN 18–34(5.1), WOMEN 18–34(3.7)

EXHIBIT 4

Ranks of Area Radio Stations and Who Their Listeners Were for the Winter 1981 Period

1	KADC-FM(AOR): TEENS(34.1), MEN 18–34(17.1), WOMEN 18–34(7.6)
2	KNTR-AM(NT): MEN 35–64(14.1), WOMEN 35–64(9.1)
3	KPOA-FM(BM): WOMEN 35–64(13.2), MEN 35–64(9.7)
4	KPOV-AM(AC): WOMEN 35–64(10.4), MEN 35–64(7.8)
5	KLBA-FM(CHR): TEENS(11.1), MEN 18–34(9.7), WOMEN 18–34(9.6)
6	KUER-AM(CM): MEN 25–54(6.5), WOMEN 25–54(8.3)
7	KRXQ-FM(RELIGIOUS): MEN 35–64(8.3), WOMEN 35–64(7.8)
8	KSTS-AM(CHR): TEENS(9.1), WOMEN 18–34(6.2), MEN 18–34(5.7)
9	KTSR-FM(BM):WOMEN 35–64(9.1), MEN 35–64(7.7)
10	KITP-AM(BIG BAND): MEN 35–64(6.1), WOMEN 35–64(3.4)
13	KMHC-FM(AOR): TEENS(9.4), MEN 18–34(8.2), WOMEN 18–34(4.2)

EXHIBIT 5
Market Shares by Market Segments for 1981 & 1982*

12+ Monday–Sunday 6 A.M.–midnight		Spring 81	Fall 81	Winter 81	Spring 82	Fall 82
Popular (contemporary) AC:	5.0	4.7	4.2	7.8	8.2	12.5
KBLD(FM)	(2.7)	(2.5)	(2.3)	(2.8)	(2.4)	(2.5)
KETR(AM)	(1.5)	(1.5)	(1.1)	(1.2)	(1.0)	(1.2)
KMNR(AM)	(.8)	(.7)	(.8)	(1.3)	(.8)	(.7)
KLDF(FM)	MOR	MOR	MOR	(2.5)	(4.0)	(8.1)
Religious:	4.7	4.0	4.4	4.6	4.8	4.6
KRXQ(FM)	(4.7)	(4.0)	(4.4)	(4.6)	(4.8)	(4.6)
Beautiful Music:	8.1	9.6	11.1	13.5	12.3	12.5
KPOA(FM)	(4.3)	(5.4)	(7.1)	(7.9)	(8.1)	(6.4)
KTSR(FM)	(3.8)	(4.2)	(4.0)	(5.6)	(4.2)	(6.1)
Soft Rock:	9.7	7.8	7.7	8.7	9.1	9.7
KITP(FM)	(3.5)	(3.2)	(3.2)	(4.0)	(4.1)	(4.5)
KNBD(FM)	(3.3)	(2.9)	(3.0)	(2.7)	(2.8)	(2.5)
KPC(AM)	(2.9)	(1.7)	(1.5)	(2.0)	(2.2)	(2.7)
News and Information:	12.0	12.8	11.8	12.2	13.1	13.2
KNTR(AM)	(9.7)	(9.9)	(9.3)	(9.6)	(9.0)	(10.2)
KDKC(AM)	(2.3)	(2.9)	(2.5)	(2.6)	(4.1)	(2.9)
Classical:	3.2	3.7	4.2	4.0	3.8	3.6
KOBR(FM)	(3.2)	(3.7)	(4.2)	(4.0)	(3.8)	(3.6)
AOR:	15.1	15.5	16.1	14.9	14.8	15.5
KADC(FM)	(7.0)	(8.2)	(9.8)	(8.9)	(8.3)	(7.4)
KMHC(FM)	(4.4)	(4.1)	(3.1)	(4.8)	(5.5)	(6.7)
KHEO(FM)	(3.7)	(3.2)	(3.2)	(1.2)	(1.0)	(1.4)
Big Band:	4.6	4.2	3.7	4.1	4.3	4.2
KITP(AM)	(4.6)	(4.2)	(3.7)	(4.1)	(4.3)	(4.2)
Modern Rock/Wave:	2.1	2.5	2.8	2.4	2.1	2.7
KWAP(AM)	(2.1)	(2.5)	(2.8)	(2.4)	(2.1)	(2.7)
Country:	9.0	8.4	8.7	9.2	8.9	9.1
KUER(AM)	(4.3)	(4.4)	(4.6)	(5.6)	(5.3)	(5.7)
KWOB(FM)	(2.8)	(2.4)	(2.5)	(3.6)	(3.6)	(3.4)
KFER(FM)	(1.9)	(1.6)	(1.6)	CHR	CHR	CHR
Jazz:	1.1	.9	1.0	1.4	1.6	1.3
KPIG(AM)	(1.1)	(.9)	(1.0)	(1.4)	(1.6)	(1.3)
Top-40/CHR:	8.5	9.7	9.6	12.6	12.5	12.3
KLBA(FM)	(4.7)	(5.1)	(5.3)	(5.5)	(5.3)	(4.2)
KSTS(AM)	(3.8)	(4.6)	(4.3)	(3.4)	(2.8)	(3.0)
KFER(FM)	COUNTRY	COUNTRY	COUNTRY	(3.7)	(4.4)	(5.3)
Information(MOR):	10.7	10.8	10.1	9.7	9.6	9.3
KROV(AM)	(5.3)	(5.5)	(6.1)	(6.1)	(6.3)	(6.1)
KBFR(AM)	(3.0)	(3.2)	(2.8)	(3.6)	(3.3)	(3.2)
KLDF(FM)	(2.4)	(2.1)	(1.2)	AC	AC	AC

*The Denver market does not receive ratings during the summer.

317

EXHIBIT 6
Ranks of Area Radio Stations and Who Their Listeners Were for the Winter 1982
Period

 1   KNTR-AM(NEWS-TALK): MEN 35–64(16.2), WOMEN 35–64(10.1)

 2   KLDF-FM(AC): WOMEN 18–49(14.4), MEN 25–49(8.9)

 3   KADC-FM(AOR): MEN 18–34(23.7), TEENS(19.4), WOMEN 18–34(5.2)

 4   KMHC-FM(AOR): TEENS(27.3), MEN 18–34(14.2), WOMEN 18–34(4.7)

 5   KPOA-FM(BM): WOMEN 35–64(12.8), MEN 35–64(8.7)

 6   KROV-AM(MOR): WOMEN 35–64(11.7), MEN 35–64(8.4)

 7   KTSR-FM(BM): WOMEN 35–64(9.2), MEN 35–64(8.3)

 8   KUER-AM(COUNTRY): MEN 35–54(8.1), WOMEN 25–49(8.0)

 9   KFER-FM(CHR): WOMEN 18–34(11.1), TEENS(10.9), MEN 18–34(7.6)

10   KRXA-FM(RELIGIOUS): MEN 35–64(8.6), WOMEN 35–64(7.6).

The Neon Art Company
William M. Sukel

BACKGROUND AND HISTORY—COLLEGE FRIENDS START THE NEON ART COMPANY

In fall 1977 three college friends renewed acquaintance at a post-football game alumni reception and in the course of the evening conceived a new venture. The two Chicagoans were to supply capital and with the third as "primary worker" launch what they believed to be an innovative firm. The firm would design and manufacture neon art sculpture.

The Arrangement

Messrs. Toms and Bill contributed personal savings to the Neon operation. The original investment was $9,000, in exchange for three thousand (3,000) shares of stock each going to Messrs. Toms, Bill, and Richards. Mr. Bill loaned $3,000 to Mr. Richards to permit him to share as an equal. The loan repayment was to begin one year after the firm had been in operation and was an interest free arrangement. Upon repayment of the loan Mr. Richards would receive the stock certificate(s) based on the value of the loan. The Neon officials were similar to other entrepreneurs who rely on their own personal savings for start-up money.

Profile of the Principals of Neon Art Company

Mr. Toms, a Chicagoan, was a business school graduate and now employed with the largest insurance company in the midwest and was to be the firm's treasurer.

Mr. Bill, also a Chicagoan, was a writer and a business school graduate and was to serve as vice president.

This case was prepared by William Sukel, Associate Professor, DePaul University, as a basis for class discussion rather than to illustrate either effective or ineffective handling of an administrative situation. All company names, names of individuals, and facts and figures have been disguised to assure anonymity.

Mr. Richards, from Indianapolis, was a graduate of the Chicago Art Institute and had an MFA from Indiana University. At one time he was also an administrator at a midwestern museum. He was to serve as firm president and be the neon artist-technician.

Mr. Walters, who later joined the venture and contributed $3,000 capital, was a self-employed artist and managed his own properties. He had nothing to do with the conception or formation, until October of 1978 when he was also elected vice president.

The objective of the two Chicagoans was to make better use of their small accumulation of savings which resided in savings accounts. The objective of Mr. Richards was to transfer to a more cosmopolitan urban area, to improve the quality of life presently experienced in Indianapolis, Indiana, and improve his income by selling his neon art work in Chicago.

Preliminaries Before Operations:
Starting the New Neon Art Company

After the late 1977 meeting, Messrs. Bill, Toms, and Richards, the three entrepreneurs, agreed to conduct several telephone conversations clarifying their role, the capital contributions, dates for acquiring space, and pros and cons of incorporation, proprietorship or partnership, and printing business cards and stationery.

Prior to the Christmas holidays they agreed to consult with an attorney, Mr. Rogers, before formalizing any arrangement. Upon the recommendation of their attorney, all concerned agreed that the corporate form would best protect the personal assets of all involved.

In early January of 1978, they agreed to: (1) incorporate; (2) select officers; (3) open a bank account; and (4) secure appropriate state retailer tax forms.

A pre-organization subscription agreement was consummated on February 8, 1978. It provided for right of first refusal should any of the parties decide to withdraw from the enterprise.

On February 25, 1978, a corporate resolution was drafted and officers formally elected. Space for the neon studio was leased by the end of February for $335 per month.

The verbal arrangement with Mr. Richards was that he be considered an independent contractor, not an employee. He was to also receive living space and a stipend or salary of $600 per month with the understanding that he was to be the primary worker. Space was actually occupied March 15 and made livable for Mr. Richards. During March and April of 1978 actual work began on the technical aspects and making the facility operative.

OPERATIONS AND DECISIONS
BEGIN FOR THE CORPORATION

In late May 1978, the factory was operating and the first piece of neon art produced. May, June, and July were quiet months for this new business. Most of the money was already spent and little was coming in.

Without much consideration of a sales program, the men decided it was in the interest of minimizing cost and learning about the market to deal on a consignment basis with as many outlets as possible. This arrangement was well received by virtually all retailers they contacted. They became very aggressive in adding to the number of outlets.

Summer of 1978 overtures were made to secure a sales representative in the prestigious Chicago Merchandise Mart and this was consummated August of 1978 in time for the important August gift show which commenced late that month. The three men agreed to offer their most popular items to their "rep," the H-G Showroom.

The initial product line included:

Red neon apples

Green cloverleafs

Red and blue free form knots

Red neon hearts

Yellow and green tulips

As the technology became more familiar and as the design skills improved, the product line was extended. The offering included:

Lightning bolts

Pink swans

Free form geometrics

New York skyline

Neon cocktail tables

Chicago skyline

Hanging white neon triangles

Stars

Custom made initials

In addition to the products specifically offered and already designed, the firm undertook a number of ambitious custom orders for interior designers and special commissions such as a nine-foot sign for a special exhibit at an art gallery.

What to design and sell was a difficult area, for the impact of fad-fashion was unavoidable. It was never quite clear whether clients perceived neon for its "pop" appeal or whether clients could appreciate the real range and possibilities of neon in architectural and interior uses.

Frequently, customers would provide ideas about possible neon forms, but the principals in the firm were actually the more sophisticated.

The Chicago Merchandise Mart Arrangements

The welcome reception by the H-G representative in the Chicago Merchandise Mart eager to carry the Neon Art product was reinforcing to the entrepreneurs.

While the H-G representative accepted the product initially with a verbal arrangement, there was never an attempt to formalize a written contractual arrangement because it was not H-G's practice to do so. The Neon Art principals found this a comfortable arrangement because it also provided more flexibility to the new firm than a written contract.

However, the Neon Art Company was not exactly overwhelmed by orders from this Merchandise Mart representative, and the need for volume led the firm's investors (owners) to look elsewhere. Futurian and Associates agreed to carry the product line of Neon Art. Futurian and Associates showroom displayed a wide and diverse line of contemporary furniture and accessories, was larger in size than the other showroom, and seemed to offer a better "fit" for the Neon Art products.

Futurian and Associates required a formal contract, however, and insisted on an exclusivity clause which meant, of course, that the firm had to reconsider the friendly, informal, but less than impressive performance by the initial H-G representative.

The partners in Neon Art were stymied because the choice had to do with dispensing with their "rep" who gave them their first break, required no contract, and offered some fine suggestions. Sales, however, were just not being generated in sufficient volume.

The partners decided to postpone an immediate decision on which representative in the Chicago Mart would do most for the firm. They delayed in the hope that Futurian and Associates would waive the exclusivity clause, and it was thought that the delay would also permit the Neon Art firm an opportunity to assess the possibilities of the newer "rep."

The Gift Show

The August gift show was a revelation to the partners. The Neon sculpture received national visibility in a showroom which had a fine reputation for one-of-a-kind items. The results were encouraging but not overwhelming. People in the gift business remarked that the 1978 Summer Gift Show was slow in all quarters. Still the result was a few orders to other cities and this, it was felt, would generate interest.

At the time of the Gift Show an interesting shift in Neon Art officials' thinking occurred about the nature of the Neon product. Buyers at the Gift Show remarked that the Neon sculpture would be a perfect window display item.

The partners were required now to rethink the idea again. Was the neon to be sold as gifts by retailers or sold to stores as window display pieces. The idea of neon sculpture in windows had a certain appeal to the partners. For one thing, they would not need to concern themselves with price as much, for the retail stores have ample budgets for windows. Largely as a result of the gift show the partners began a program of contacting the display managers at the more prominent Chicago stores. Soon Neon was appearing at Bonwit Teller, Crate and Barrel, Tiffany's, and other fine stores on Chicago's Magnificent Mile. Still the business was erratic, and stores could not be depended upon to continue using Neon or imitating a neon sculpture already displayed in another retail window.

The partners were not sure about what direction the product should take— consignment in retail outlets, gift items for resale to the consumer, a window display item for sale to stores, custom, to order, or selling via the representatives in the Chicago Mart and completely "subcontracting" the sales part of the business to others. Some decision should be made, and the problem with the textbook solutions according to Mr. Toms is that this neon business needed to get sales wherever it could, and defining the product was a luxury the firm would rather leave to the professors.

Mr. Richards' Health

After the gift show in August, Mr. Richards, the Neon Art president and primary artist, became ill and was taken to one of the Chicago hospitals where he remained until late September 1978. Without the principal artisan, orders were not filled, the Neon studio was not staffed, call-in orders could not be taken, and the operations came to a halt. It became evident that without Mr. Richards, the enterprise could not produce. The person with no capital in the enterprise brought all the skill and expertise. What were Mr. Toms and Mr. Bill to do? Mr. Bill recalled an ad in the trade publication *Sign of the Times* placed by a neon firm in Kenosha, Wisconsin, and Mr. Bill subcontracted some of the work to the Kenosha firm. Although technically as good as Mr. Richards' work, artistically Mr. Richards was superior. Nevertheless, the firm at least had a source should Mr. Richards return to the hospital. When he was discharged from the hospital in late September, Mr. Richards and the other partners found the firm requiring funds to pay current debts. In addition Mr. Bill and Mr. Toms were not quite sure of the extent of Mr. Richards' dependence on cognac. The need for capital and Mr. Richards' health were both serious concerns.

Personalities and Interpersonal Differences

The two partners, Mr. Toms and Mr. Bill, were becoming impatient with Mr. Richards. Mr. Richards arrived in Chicago after the Christmas and New Year holidays and seemed to require constant direction. Not only was there a lack of initiative, there was a pattern to Mr. Richards' day of which the partners were not aware before entering the business arrangement. At about two o'clock P.M., Mr. Richards would begin sipping cognac and continue until the early morning. Messrs. Bill and Toms were in an awkward situation not knowing whether this was a temporary condition or regular practice. Since the start-up period for the corporation was slow for Mr. Richards, this may have had something to do with his routine.

Unfamiliar with the neon technology at the first, Mr. Toms and Mr. Bill began spending Saturdays and Sundays at the neon plant and learned how to bend glass, attach electrodes, and pump the glass with neon or argon or helium. It was gradually becoming clearer to Mr. Toms and Mr. Bill that Mr. Richards could be performing better and working harder. Since the corporation funds were the contribution of Messrs. Bill and Toms, and since Mr. Richards was the only partner to realize any financial return from the first days of operation by receiving a salary and a place to live in quarters immediately adjacent the Neon studio, expectations of Mr. Richards were considerably higher and his cognac ritual was a source of comment.

DESCRIPTION OF THE TECHNICAL ASPECTS

The neon technology has not changed since its early discovery in the 1930s. A length of glass which may be clear or coated with white powder comes in 36-inch lengths. The glass is first heated and then bent into shape by hand. In the truest sense, this is unit production. Pieces are custom made to order with the customer specifying size, color, and subject matter of the piece. Two electrodes are attached by hand torches to opposite ends of the piece of glass after the bending process. One of the pairs of electrodes has a small straw-like glass protrusion. The neon item is readied to receive the several most typical gasses—neon, freon, or argon. Before gas can be received, the glass must be purified or bombarded with a high-voltage electric charge. After bombarding and a short period of cooling, the glass tube can be pumped with one of the gasses which give neon lights their unique character. The straw-like glass protrusion is then capped or sealed by the simple application of heat which melts the glass.

The Production Process

Because of the technical aspects of the process the production process is a hand production and a craft-like process. Anything less than perfection in the accomplishment of any step in the technical process will result in waste. Wasted glass, wasted electrodes, wasted gas and electricity, and wasted time and effort can occur if anything goes wrong at any step in the process.

Since we are dealing with glass, even a perfectly completed piece involves substantial investment in time, effort, and cost, and breakage is a likely risk up until receipt by the customer.

While bending of glass might be suggested in a more mass production-like fashion, storage and risk of breakage discourage this.

Production scheduling poses somewhat of a problem, since customers for custom-made neon work were not predictable in the first year or probably later years of operation. Thus some days or weeks, there was no action whatsoever.

People have been and continue to be fascinated by neon. Commerce and business applications of signs for advertising were limited and unimaginative uses. This is not an inherent property of the medium itself. Neon can be subtle as to be completely unobservable except in absolute dark and even then might not be visible. The gaudy boisterous examples with which we are all familiar have nothing to do with the medium but with the businessman's need to have an eye-catching sign.

In the late seventies, an appreciation of the neon light medium as an art form was developing. There was potential for neon in the home, in restaurants, in architectural application. Almost any shape or form which could be linearly sketched could be made in glass. Animals, flowers, apples, geometrics, and initials could be executed in subtle green, blue, pink, lavender, yellow, and the more brilliant colors we are familiar with.

DECISIONS ON MARKETING AND SALE OF THE PRODUCT

How does one price art? How does one price a unique product? This decision faced the three college friends beginning their own first business.

Since it was unclear whether customers of neon art would be regular customers or retailers, it was difficult to solve many of the typical marketing "givens." Furthermore, it was difficult to anticipate demand for a product for which there was no real precedent. Neon signs were not the product; glass was not the product; so what was the product of this firm?

To recognize that Neon Art was confusing their role in the marketing channel is an understatement. The firm was selling directly to more customers (especially custom work), was acting as a wholesaler through their two representatives in the Chicago Merchandise Mart and the west coast representative in the Los Angeles Mart, as well as being the manufacturer of Neon Art.

Two partners in the venture, Mr. Toms and Mr. Bill, aware of the complexity, reasoned that the fledgling firm needed sales wherever they presented themselves and would not like to lose or turn down an order.

Most marketing textbooks assume a product and assume it is classifiable. How does one forecast demand for such a product? Neon signs were on a decline while neon art appeared to be emerging as an important area. Some museums began offering classes in neon in Minneapolis and Chicago.

A sales forecast in the traditional sense, suggesting past data or similar product data, would have been absurd for there was no past data, and it was unclear what product was similar, as for any small business.

The Advertising Situation

Unclear about the product and unclear who the customers were likely to be, a multiple approach was used. The consignment arrangements with some finer stores would provide visibility as well as referrals as income.

The manufacturer label on each piece could provide a potential customer access to the producer for custom-made work.

Selecting only better shops in the metropolitan area was essential (1) because of the cost and (2) to protect a quality and/or snob appeal of the product.

Raising Capital

How realistic would it be for the neon firm to consider a loan from the bank? Sales were only $8218.16 during the first year 1978. In September and October of 1978, capital was needed: (1) to pay some pressing creditors, (2) to order less costly transformers from Hong Kong, (3) to order a quantity of plastic containers and take the price quantity discount. The partners never pursued the possibilities of a bank loan. Lack of confidence, poor accounting and financial data, and lack of time by Mr. Toms and Mr. Bill prevented a trip to a bank for a loan.

One morning while at breakfast at the University Club in October, 1978, Mr. Bill encountered a former acquaintance, Mr. Walters, an artist and real estate developer. When breakfast ended Mr. Walters agreed to commit $3,000 for 3000 shares of stock. At the October 1978 meeting he was elected vice president. Not only was Mr. Walters considered to be a fine candidate as an investor, he was also quick to suggest his availability to do things which other partners could not schedule to help with the artistic elements, to be present at the studio as a motivator to Mr. Richards.

The quartet readied themselves for the 1978 Christmas season under the handicap of limited resources and no real idea about what to offer the public or the stores.

Mr. Richards and Mr. Walters collaborated on what actually was an innovation—using a red neon bow with a real evergreen wreath. Since neon burns cool, there was little threat of fire. The combination was very effective and several sales were made again to stores for use in window display. Trees, canes, and stars, all in red and green, were executed, and 1978 ended with mixed impressions about the financial conditions and future.

Sales were improving, the product was received enthusiastically, and two partners were optimistic. The other two partners did not think sales were sufficient to cover costs, knew that product reception did not always manifest itself in a sale, and in general were pessimistic.

Two of the original shareholders, Mr. Toms and Mr. Bill, realized now that although Mr. Walters brought capital, there was a problem of resolving conflict. Any two to two issue would result in a stalemate and the partners were sophisticated enough to know that conflict and conflict resolution is not a big business phenomenon exclusively.

Many such issues were to occur in fiscal 1979, and at one point it was suggested that Mr. Roger, the firm's attorney, would be the tie breaker but he declined the honor. Thus there was no mechanism, formal or informal, to resolve disagreements. The partners jokingly wondered what the professors would say but jokingly concluded that they would just suggest something upon which the vote would be two to two.

END YEAR ONE INFORMATION

The need to file 1979 federal taxes provided the first real information on revenues and costs. A certified public accountant prepared the financial statement and taxes for the Neon Art Company.

At this time there was considerable controversy about the merit of a strategy to reduce the price of the product and hope that volume would increase. Some explanations for the mild rather than enthusiastic interest in the product had been suggested as the high price. Lowering price with no guarantee of increased volume would be disastrous at bill-paying time. The dilemma of high price–low volume versus low price–high volume needed resolution.

Some members, Mr. Walters and Mr. Richards, of the firm were optimistic and pleased by the 1979 sales data. They argued that there was a consistent upward trend in sales and only the one isolated dip between February and March. The calls and interest in the product were certainly positive.

Other members of the firm, Messrs. Bill and Toms, were pessimistic and concerned with the fact that the costs were increasing and despite the fine sales performance the prospects for making a profit or realizing any return on investment in the next year or two was not likely.

The year was ending on a sour note. Two partners wanted to cease operation and the other two men wanted to proceed full speed ahead.

The future of the firm needed resolution. Would the firm survive or close? What changes in strategy were needed for success? Would the investors be well served with their interest and money elsewhere? Are the indicators favorable or unfavorable for this enterprise?

With friendships on the brink of dissolution, the principals of the firm held a meeting in early December. Two of the shareholders, Messrs. Bill and Toms, who held three-quarters of the stock, indicated they would look for a buyer for their shares.

EXHIBIT 1
The Neon Art Company

1978 Total Sales Month (1979)	May–December Monthly Sales	8281.16 Cum. Total
January	1792.50	1792.50
February	1206.00	2998.50
March	454.50	2453.00
April	800.36	4343.36
May	1945.00	6288.36
June	2285.64	8574.00
July	1261.50	9835.50
August	4404.00	14239.50
September	3999.00	17338.50
October	3749.00	20087.50
November	3258.90	23345.40

Average Monthly Sales   2123.30 (Breakeven 1259.11)

EXHIBIT 2
The Neon Art Company
Comparative Mart Representatives Sales Records

HOWEY-GRASHAM, INC.

August 1978	$1945.00
September 1978	2495.00 (includes $1865 custom order for Marchetti)
October 1978	885.26
November 1978	434.90
TOTAL	$5724.16

MAX FUTORIAN & ASSOCIATES

October 1978	$1319.00
November 1978	1175.00
TOTAL	$2494.00

EXHIBIT 3
Balance Sheet as of December 31, 1978 (Unaudited)

Assets			
Current Assets:			
Cash in bank		1,442.80	
Accounts receivable		1,028.79	
Inv.— Raw materials		615.00	
Inv.— Work in process		260.00	
Inv.— Finished goods		513.00	
Loans to shareholders		318.90	
Prepaid expenses		215.84	
Total Current Assets			4,394.33
	Cost	Net Book Value	
Property and Equipment:			
Leasehold improvements	2,520.00	2,520.00	
Machinery & equipment	3,232.22	3,232.22	
Furniture & fixtures	151.35	151.35	
Net Property and Equipment	5,903.57		5,903.57
Other Assets:			
Deposits		291.00	
Rent security deposit		335.00	
Organization expense		547.75	
Total Other Assets			1,173.75
Total Assets			11,471.65

Liabilities and Stockholders' Equity			
Current Liabilities:			
Accounts payable— trace		2,105.21	
Accounts payable— other		2,093.84	
Loans payable shareholders		400.00	
Total Current Liabilities			4,599.05
Stockholders' Equity:			
Common stock issued		12,000.00	
Net profit or (loss)		(5,127.40)	
Total Stockholders' Equity			6,872.60
Total Liabilities & Stockholders' Equity			11,471.65
Working Capital	(204.72)		
Current Ratio	.95 to 1		
Shares Outstanding	12,000		
Net Book Value per Share	.57		

EXHIBIT 4
Statement of Income and Expense (Unaudited)

	Nine months ended December 31, 1978	
Income:		
Sales	7,716.17	100.0
Cost of Sales:		
Purchases	5,352.11	69.4
Freight	22.24	.3
Ending inventory	(1,388.00)	(18.0)
Total Cost of Sales	3,986.38	51.7
Gross Profit	3,729.82	48.3
Operating Expenses:		
Advertising	92.00	1.2
Auto expense	116.70	1.5
Bank charge	17.49	.2
Casualty & theft	100.00	1.3
Commissions	3,447.95	44.7
Dues & subscriptions	34.04	.4
Entertainment	173.21	2.2
Insurance	173.16	2.2
Office expense	25.23	.3
Professional fees	200.00	2.6
Rent	3,182.50	41.2
Sales expense	75.00	1.0
Stationery and printing	182.00	2.4
Supplies	155.63	2.0
Telephone	449.33	5.8
Utilities	432.98	5.6
Total Operating Expense	8,857.22	114.8
Operating Profit (Loss)	(5,127.40)	(66.5)
Shares Outstanding	12,000	1.6
Earnings per Share	(.43)	

CASE 3 ■ ■ ■
The Mini-Storage Business: Entrepreneurial Decision Making

Marjorie G. Prentice

Dick and Judy LaVergne early in 1979 acknowledged that they have long wanted to expand their opportunities beyond full-time employment to include part-time management of a small business venture. The thrill of private entrepreneurship and the opportunity to make a substantial return on investment are key elements in their long term goals.

After much preliminary investigation into a variety of possible business ventures such as racquetball courts, fast food franchises and self-serve car washes, Dick and Judy have narrowed their consideration to an investment in the rapidly growing mini-storage industry. The decision to consider investing in this industry was made in response to their desire to find a business which (1) did not require a high level of technical expertise, (2) would have a high year-round customer demand, and (3) would be relatively easy to enter and operate.

At last they have reached the point of decision. Should they build in a mini-storage business? If they decide to build a mini-storage facility, where should it be located and what should be the mix of unit sizes? Can they handle the operations of a mini-storage business on a part-time basis? All of these questions, and many more, pass through Dick's mind as he and his wife review the information they have gathered over the past year.

GENERAL BACKGROUND

The LaVergnes live in Sacramento, the capital of California. Sacramento is surrounded by a number of "bedroom" communities, some relatively stable, and others growing rapidly. As the center of the state, county and city government, Sacramento has a large percentage of its labor force in service occupations. Within the extended metropolitan area there are two major Air Force Bases, Mather and McClellan, each with a relatively transient military population.

Beyond the immediate metropolitan area, there are still large expanses of undeveloped land which are of increasing interest to major industries wishing to expand or relocate in California. Such industries need space, not only for plant facilities, but for a major influx of production workers if a local labor supply is not already available. Hewlett-Packard is one such firm considering expansion in the Roseville area northeast of Sacramento. Should Hewlett-Packard exercise their land option, it is estimated that they will need 4,500 employees by 1985.

The mild climate of the Sacramento area is particularly appealing to the American public in the face of increasing energy costs for home heating. This asset to home owners, coupled with the property tax relief resulting from California's 1979 "Proposition 13" is encouraging increased migration to the area. Outdoor recreational opportunities are an important feature of California living. Within two hours, Sacramentoans can have their R.V.s in the campgrounds of the Sierra Nevada mountains. Within less than one hour, most Sacramento sailers, boaters and water skiers can be at the highly developed facilities of Lake Folsom, just northeast of the city. These combined factors make Sacramento a very desirable place for a family to locate.

INDUSTRY BACKGROUND

The mini-storage business, often referred to as private storage rooms, or by such terms as "rent-a-space" facilities or "U-lock-it" units, provides private and secure individual storage units for such varied items as household goods, business records, retail-wholesale inventory, sports and out-of-season equipment, and recreational vehicles. Most present firms operating mini-sized self storage units tend to use a similar design known as modified warehouse units. Typically, each location has eight or more cinderblock buildings subdivided by wooden partitions into 350 to 800 units. These individual storage units vary in size from $4' \times 6'$ closets to 10' by 30' indoor rooms. Many facilities also include outdoor parking areas for cars, campers, and boats. Each facility is surrounded by a chain link fence and has high intensity lighting and other extensive security precautions.

Customer Consideration

Customer access to most individual units is from the outside of the building through individually keyed roll-up doors; however, some of the smaller units have only interior hallway access. The facilities are usually open daily, with entrance controlled through a key card or with a sign-in-out sheet in the manager's office. Units are rented on a monthly basis, with charges in relation to both unit square footage and demand.

Demand

As both residential and business construction costs have risen, architects and owners have tended to decrease the internal storage space of living and working accommodations. With storage space at a premium, mini-storage units have become increasingly popular. In addition to business storage needs for records and inventories, and apartment and residential dwellers' needs for household and recreational storage, a currently expanding demand for storage exists for mobile home owners. The early 1980's recession appears not to have hurt the mobile home industry in California as it has conventional home construction.

According to managers of several operating mini-storage facilities, the demand for mini-storage units has resulted in a 90 to 92 percent average occupancy rate for all sizes of units during the late 1970s. They say the greatest demand is for the smaller units of 5′ × 10′ and under. Presently, mini-storage firms have larger numbers of these smaller units available, but there are still waiting lists for these small sized units. This is not to imply that the larger units are not needed, but only that the 10′ × 10′ and larger sizes are less popular than the smaller units.

Competition

At the present time there is such a high demand for self-storage units from conventional and mobile home owners, small business managers, and sports enthusiasts that competition does not seem to present a problem. Two examples support this view. Three mini-storage facilities operate adjacent to the Folsom Boulevard and Sunrise Boulevard freeway interchange in Rancho Cordova, just east of Sacramento. The two older original facilities have 95 to 100 percent occupancy and the newest firm is reported to be filling quickly without causing any decrease in demand for the others. The second example is a storage facility currently being constructed in Roseville adjacent to an older, established firm. The manager of the operating firm expects no decrease in her demand, and predicts sufficient demand for the new company to operate profitably. This apparently favorable climate may continue for the immediate future. However, in the long run, conditions may vary, depending upon the location selected.

Management Consideration

There are several major advantages for the owner of a mini-storage business. Three of these are (1) low maintenance, requiring little in addition to trash removal; (2) relatively low original land costs, as facilities can be built close to freeways, on odd-shaped parcels of commercially zoned land, or other less desirable locations; and (3) below average construction costs, due to limited requirements for plumbing, interior finishing work and other items requiring high-cost skilled labor.

Two of the primary problems in the mini-storage business are day-by-day management and security. Most owners hire one or more resident managers to maintain a residence at the mini-storage facility on a 24-hour basis. However, the storage facilities are usually open to the customer only from 7:00 A.M. to 11:00 P.M., seven days a week. The restrictive life-style coupled with the heavy paper-work flow required by high turnover customers, especially those with seasonal or inventory related needs, are undoubtedly reasons for the high turnover rate of resident managers within the industry.

An effective security system requires a perimeter chain link fence and high intensity lighting. Of the dozens of variations of security systems available, there seem to be three main types which are appropriate for this industry:

1 An alarm, deactivated by a key, installed in each door of each unit. The security key is issued to the customer at the time the unit key is issued.
2 Zoning surveillance and electronic monitoring, which relies on a centralized system. Each door is monitored to signal the central office whenever that door is entered.
3 Guard dogs, usually German shepherds or Doberman pinschers, can be either owned or rented. The dogs are usually used in pairs, and are in addition to the resident manager. The rental, per dog, per month, in the Sacramento area is $195, including transportation and required care. Dogs are used by most of the companies in the Sacramento area, often in combination with one or more other security devices.

FINANCIAL INFORMATION

From banks, credit unions, building contractors, real estate firms, and government agencies, the LaVergnes have carefully gathered a great deal of financial information. They feel they now are in a position to make a decision on entering the mini-storage business. They have learned that a typical facility would need about 2.5 acres of land (a lot approximately 210' × 520'). The entire area must be enclosed by a high quality chain link fence, and the entire surface within the fence must be asphalt covered, with the exception of the actual building footage.

Investigation has disclosed that, in this industry, the IRS expects the buildings to depreciate over a 30-year period, and fencing and asphalt to be depreciated over a 20-year period; accelerated depreciation is not permitted. A 65 percent occupancy rate is common for the first year, with a "conservative" 90 percent occupancy rate each year thereafter. Expenses and revenues should increase at the same rate over the foreseeable future.

Architectural considerations will influence the initial investment cost. For example, commercial building codes, maximizing fire and theft prevention while minimizing construction costs, and special code requirements for a live-in management unit must be considered in estimated cost projections.

Estimates of construction costs and actual operating expenses are shown in exhibits 1 and 2 respectively. Through the liquidation of several prior investments, Dick presently has the ability to raise $180,000 for the required 20 percent down payment on the $900,000 he will need for this new business. Thirty year loans are available at 14 percent interest through commercial outlets which will cover the remaining 80 percent needed for initial construction costs and first year working capital requirements.

SITE LOCATION INFORMATION

There seems to be a great deal of pricing consistency within the industry, at least in the Sacramento area. A comparison of unit sizes, numbers of units, and rental fees for three established firms are shown in exhibit 4.

In order to maintain a high unit occupancy rate, location is a primary consideration. Land availability, land costs, zoning laws, freeway/thoroughfare access, high density population and ease of travel from LaVergne's home are all important. His preferences for location are in the area north-northeast of the metropolitan area, in either Sacramento or Placer counties. From this general area, he chose four sites to investigate; Folsom, Citrus Heights, Carmichael, and Roseville. (See exhibit 3 for a map of the area and exhibit 5 for population figures of the area.)

Folsom would be a high demand area because of the excellent recreational developments around Folsom Lake and the resulting need for storage of boats and other recreational equipment. Folsom has many parcels of available commercial land for building. The drawbacks, however, are in the strict zoning limitations to protect the natural environment and the absence of good freeway access to the available land within the city.

Citrus Heights also seems to be a good site due to the fact that many new homes are being built in the area, most of which are smaller than in the past decade, and therefore, with limited built-in storage. There is also a present lack of competition from other storage firms in this area. The primary problems for a Citrus Heights location are (1) the limited availability of any easily accessible commercial land of sufficient size to handle this proposed development and (2) strict zoning regulations which would limit site and design options.

Carmichael is the nearest of the four cities to downtown Sacramento. It already has a high, relatively stable population. Many parts of the city are comprised primarily of older homes with an average larger amount of internal storage as well as basements and garages. Commercial land availability is limited due to the high residential population already established in the community.

Roseville's Chamber of Commerce reports that this city has a good growth potential, a wide variety of available commercial land near freeway access, and more new home construction under way than in the other three areas. In addition, a major firm has a land option for a proposed plant which will employ 4,500 persons within the next few years.

Recognition of site location is an important element in the mini-storage industry. Presently, the primary sources of advertising are: (1) multicolumn space in the yellow pages of the telephone directory and (2) on-building signs painted or mounted on the freeway-adjacent storage units. As other companies enter the market, there will undoubtedly be the need for other forms of advertising. A location away from major freeway visibility would make additional promotional strategies necessary.

OPERATIONAL INFORMATION

Once a facility is in operation, maintenance is usually at a minimum, with trash control often being the most complicated task. If customer turnover is high, office records can be a problem.

Operating considerations are directly related to the number of buildings containing the individual units to be managed. In addition, excessive turnover rates for live-in managers pose a critical problem which must be solved if the operation is to function effectively and profitably.

Based on a series of interviews with present managers, the LaVergnes have decided that if they build, the facility should have no more than five sizes of units: $5' \times 6'$, $5' \times 10'$, $10' \times 10'$, $10' \times 20'$, and $10' \times 30'$. The expected annual occupancy rate, after the first year, is 95 percent for the two smaller size units, 90 percent for the $10' \times 10'$ size, and 85 percent for the two larger size units. Dick wants to spend no more than $660,000 for construction costs and expects a payback of his total investment within seven years.

EXHIBIT 1
Estimated Start-Up Costs

1979 cost estimates for a "typical" self-storage facility in the Sacramento area:

Land acquisition	75,000
Architect fees	16,400
Construction costs for storage units	660,000[1]
Additional construction costs for live-in management	20,000
Asphalting costs	70,000
Fencing costs	6,300
Security system	20,000
Legal fees (incorporation)	2,300
Working capital (1st year)	30,000
	$900,000

[1]The greater the number of smaller units, the higher will be the total costs. For example, within a space of 10' × 20' you can build one storage unit at a cost of $2200, four 5' × 10' units at a cost of $2,400 or six 5' × 6' units at a cost of $2520. (Based on construction costs as follows:)

10 × 30 units at $11.50/sq. ft. *3,450   17,250*
10 × 20 units at $11.00/sq. ft. *2,200   11,000*
10 × 10 units at $10.75/sq. ft *1,075   5,375*
5 × 10 units at $12.00/sq. ft. *600   3,000*
5 × 6 units at $14.00/sq. ft. *420   2,100*
$38,725

EXHIBIT 2
Estimated Annual Operating Costs

Expenses for a "typical" medium-sized facility (575 units), include, but are not limited to, the following annual costs:

Insurance	$ 4,000
Security[1]	$ 5,000
Payroll—wages and fringes	$ 12,000
Advertising expenses	$ 5,000
Office supplies	$ 500
Property taxes	$ 14,000
Repairs and maintenance	$ 2,000
Depreciation[2]	$ 26,500
Utilities	$ 4,000
Loan repayment[3]	$102,800
Legal fees	$ 1,000
Accounting and auditing fees	$ 1,000
Corporate tax rate[4]	+

[1]Rental of two guard dogs for periods when the facility is not open.

[2]Actual Depreciation based on initial construction costs.

[3]Actual Loan payment based on size of loan; payment includes principal and interest (14%, 30 year loan on $720,000).

[4]Corporate form of structure is deemed advisable to minimize liability.

Corporate tax rates:		
	0–$ 25,000	17%
	$25,001–$ 50,000	20%
	$50,001–$ 75,000	30%
	$75,001–$100,000	40%
	over $100,000	46%

EXHIBIT 3
Map of the Area

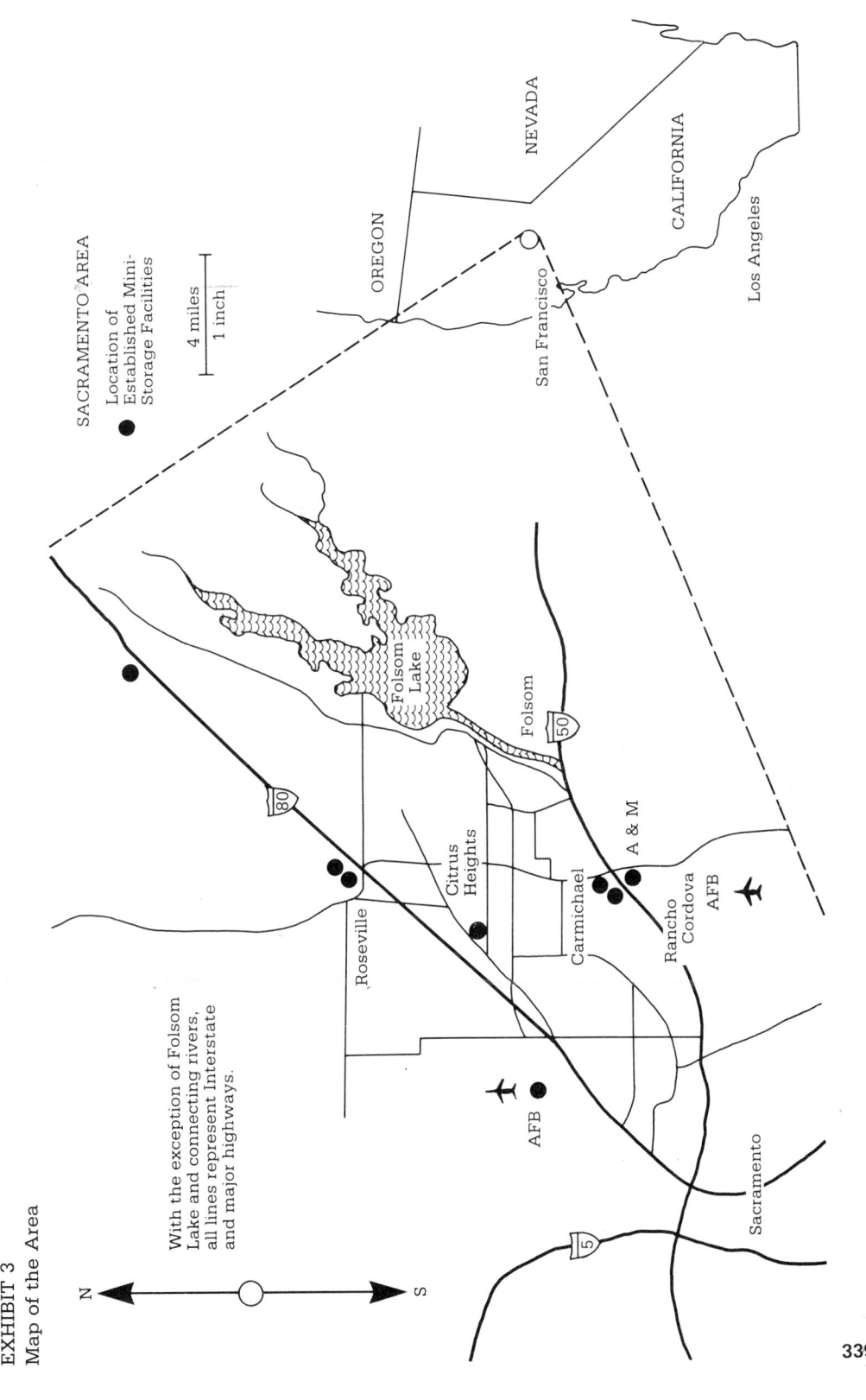

SACRAMENTO AREA

● Location of
Established Mini-
Storage Facilities

4 miles
1 inch

With the exception of Folsom
Lake and connecting rivers,
all lines represent Interstate
and major highways.

N

S

339

EXHIBIT 4
Pricing and Size of Typical Competition in Sacramento Area

	A & M Storage		Mini-Warehouse		Capital City Storage	
Unit Size	No. of Units	Monthly Rental per Unit	No. of Units	Rental per Unit	No. of Units	Rental per Unit
4 × 6	—	—	67	$15	—	—
5 × 6	15	$15	—	—	12	$15
5 × 10 (attic)	—	—	11	$10	—	—
5 × 10 (ground)	290	$22	299	$21	150	$21
6 × 10	76	$23	—	—	—	—
10 × 10	89	$36	69	$34	60	$34
10 × 12	—	—	28	$38	—	—
10 × 15	—	—	42	$42	50	$42
10 × 20	80	$54	85	$52	55	$52
10 × 25	—	—	34	$54	30	$64
10 × 30	36	$70	47	$74	25	$74
Parking Space for R.V. Units						
10 × 20	36	$15	60	$13	—	—
10 × 28	—	—	38	$18	—	—
10 × 30	24	$17	—	—	—	—

EXHIBIT 5
Population Figure for Target Area Locations

	Folsom	Citrus Heights	Carmichael	Roseville
1970	6,618	45,324	37,608	18,139
1971	6,312	45,328	38,391	18,600
1972	7,102	47,052	39,914	19,100
1973	7,073	51,459	40,199	19,800
1974	7,037	54,459	40,773	20,500
1975	6,858	55,520	41,489	20,850
1976	7,837	57,301	41,780	20,500
1977	7,900	62,492	42,125	21,050
1978				
1979				

Video Maker, Inc., 1986

Donald F. Harvey and Leon J. Munyan, Munyan and
Associates

INTRODUCTION

Video Maker, Inc., is a newly formed company established to capture a portion of the rapidly growing video camera rental market. The company's first location will be in Waikiki, Hawaii.

This location was chosen because recent surveys have shown that only 8 percent of the potential market is being serviced by the present rental outlets. Therefore, Video Maker, Inc., intends to service the remaining 92 percent of the market. This portion of the market represents potential sales of $36 million annually.

The only competition as of August 1986, included six camera rental businesses, five of which were not viable concerns. In addition, Video Maker, Inc., will employ an innovative marketing strategy designed to capture clients before they encounter the competition. This strategy will include utilizing contract accounts such as travel agencies, airlines, and major hotels. In addition to the market potential of tourists to Oahu, Video Maker, Inc., also intends to address the needs of residents, other commercial businesses, institutions, government agencies, and special events sponsored privately and publicly. Examples would be training tapes for employees, promotional tapes for other tourist-related businesses, taping of seminars and conventions, and so forth.

The business will be ably managed by two Salt Lake City, Utah, business people. The managers have proven experience in owning and managing small businesses. In addition, they will relocate to Waikiki, in order to devote full-time effort to the company.

Financial projections have been completed for the initial phase of the operation. This phase includes one distribution outlet and 100 rental cameras. Only 6 percent of the potential market will be addressed during this initial period. Future earnings will then be utilized to capture more of the video rental market.

Investment capital of $197,800 will be required for equipment and operating expenses. The projected profits during the first five-year period are $858,000, representing a return on investment of 34 percent (see exhibit 1).

DESCRIPTION OF BUSINESS

Video Maker, Inc., is a service business renting video camera equipment and accessories. Services will include delivery and instructions in camera use and editing.

Accessories will include tapes, tripods, battery packs, shoulder harnesses, and underwater covers.

The company intends to begin operations at a highly visible location in Waikiki, Hawaii. This location is ideally suited to meet the needs of the tourist market. The location was chosen because the greatest number of people arrive in Hawaii via air transportation and either pass through or stay in the Waikiki shopping center.

Video Maker, Inc., has a projected start date of early 1987. Sales operations will continue on a seven day-per-week schedule. Daily hours will be 7:00 A.M. to 7:00 P.M.

THE MARKET

Video Maker, Inc., has chosen the island of Oahu for the location of its first sales outlet. This outlet will address the needs of all visitors to the islands, whether their trip is for pleasure or business. The island of Oahu is the most visited island in Hawaii. In addition, the Waikiki shopping center is the location most frequented by shoppers.

The number of tourists present on an average day has been determined by the visitors bureau to be 67,370. Using the criteria shown below, a conservative estimate of the daily new visitors that would rent a video camera is 1,890. As shown in exhibit 2, this calculation is based on statistical data collected during recent surveys that consider:

1 That the percentage of visitors in Waikiki for pleasure only is high
2 That only one household head will rent a camera per group
3 That only 55 percent of these visitors would actually rent a camera

The potential market for all the islands and all the visitors, including business people and nonmainlanders, is much larger than the 1,890 used for calculating the Video Maker, Inc., potential market. However, using this conservative figure indicates that only 8 percent of the potential market is being serviced.

Video Maker, Inc., intends to aggressively pursue the entire potential market, which represents a total revenue of $3 million monthly. One strategy to assist sales is marketing packages through travel agencies. This method will be utilized to educate customers on the availability of video rentals in Hawaii. In addition, this method will capture potential clients before they are exposed to the competition. A similar method will be used to discount sales to major hotel accounts on Oahu.

THE COMPETITION

The video camera rental competition in Waikiki consists of six operations, with a total of 160 cameras. Five of the operations are not pursuing the market full time on a professional basis. The only viable competition is Video Vacation Camera Rentals, with 100 cameras. However, this company does not provide delivery service, have a yellow pages ad, promote corporate videos, or provide incentives to contract sales such as travel agencies or hotels.

Video Maker, Inc., intends to establish operations with 100 video cameras and expand as needed to meet the market demand.

MANAGEMENT

The two principals of the firm have proven track records in managing small businesses and in sales. Their past choices to be self-employed and to work on a commission basis have shown their drive and motivation to succeed.

Doralee Olsen, President of Video Maker, Inc., currently owns and operates a video production and editing company. This ten years of experience, in addition to expertise in advertising and marketing, makes Ms. Olsen an able manager for Video Maker, Inc.

Kristie Jensen is currently involved in managing and selling real estate. She has achieved several distinctions for exceptional sales ability, including membership in the million dollar club. Her recent experience also includes starting and managing her own small business. Ms. Jensen will oversee daily sales operations.

PROFITABILITY EXPECTED

Video Maker, Inc., will be profitable for the following reasons:

1   The service that Video Maker, Inc., will be offering lends itself greatly to the tourist and vacationer. In the 1984 census, the average number present on any given day during 1984 on Oahu and in the Waikiki area was 67,370 (see exhibit 3).
2   Because the greatest number of people arriving in Hawaii visit and stay in the Waikiki area for at least three to four days, the marketing of the service is more effective to reach the tourist.
3   Although the state does have its peak months for numbers of tourists, tourism is a year-round industry for the state, unlike other tourist locations in the states that are more seasonal (see exhibit 4).
4   The most important fact is based on the studies that the video camera rental business is an untapped market in Hawaii. Only 8 percent of the potential market for the services is being met.

MARKET GROWTH POTENTIAL

In exhibit 4, 23 percent of the visitors were not accounted for in the market potential. These visitors were from all other countries excluding the mainland and Canada. Because this percentage of the visitors is arriving from foreign countries, there may be possible marketing barriers due to culture and language differences.

However, this portion of the market is not going to be ignored. With thoughtful marketing planning targeted especially to this group, an additional 576 new visitors daily who will rent a camera while visiting Oahu can be expected.

The market's growth potential can also be expected due to the facts:

1   There is more demand than supply at this time in Waikiki.
2   The economics of home video making is swinging sharply away from film in favor of video tape. 75 percent of the visitors in Oahu own VCR recorders, creating more desire to videotape family vacations.
3   The total number of visitors to Oahu in the next twenty years is expected to increase 39 percent. The expectancy of a yearly increase of visitors is highly probable. Since 1964, there has only been one year that the number of visitors was less than the year before.

LOCATION OF BUSINESS

The initial location of Video Maker, Inc., will be in the Waikiki Shopping Center, at 2270 Kalakaua Avenue, the busiest street in the Waikiki area for foot traffic of tourists. The retail office space proposed for lease is approximately 400 square feet for $807 a month lease. A four month security deposit is required. Rent includes electricity, air conditioning, security, and fire protection. For an additional $100 per month, two parking stalls can be reserved (essential because parking in this area is very limited). A loading dock is accessible for quick deliveries. The office space will be divided into:

Sales/counter area

Equipment storage

Record and bookkeeping

The building hours are 6:00 A.M. to 2:00 A.M., with emergency access available after hours. The shopping center has five floors. The outlet space is located on the third floor. The center offers a variety of retail and merchandise stores. The center sponsors free to the tourist two nightly Hawaiian Hula shows called "Waikiki Calls," an advertising tool to bring tourists into the shopping center. Individual advertising spots from the merchants are available during the program.

The location advantages include:

1   High visibility to the target market
2   Reasonable walking distance from most hotels in the area
3   Cost- and time-effective foot or moped delivery
4   Cost-effective advertising. The shopping center advertises to promote the shopping center to the tourist, in addition to the free hula show. Also, the shopping center has a good mix of merchants attracting shoppers.

ADVERTISING

Customers will be attracted to Video Maker, Inc., by:

1   The location on a heavily traveled tourist route in Waikiki.
2   Advertising in the tourist magazines that are very effective for reaching the tourist market. Two other effective advertising media are in-room cable TV advertising in hotels, and in-room tourist magazines with free promotional give-aways.
3   Renting through contract accounts to businesses such as travel agencies, tour agencies, major hotels, and airlines.

PRODUCT SUPPLIERS

The two major types of suppliers necessary for the business will be a video camera supplier and blank cassette supplier. The video camera features that best met Video Makers criteria include:

1   A camera and recorder in one unit to eliminate the need to carry a separate recorder pack
2   Durability
3   Simplicity both in appearance and actual operation
4   Cost

It was decided that the Panasonic PCV 300 model would be best suited for present needs. The major supplier will be Panasonic Hawaii, Inc. A secondary supplier will be Tri-State Camera, New York.

The supplier for blank video cassettes will be 3M Scotch Tape Hawaii, Inc., which is a local Hawaiian distributor handling eight lines of tapes. A secondary supplier would be Tape One Hawaii.

CONCLUSION

After much preliminary investigation, Olsen and Jensen have reached the point of decision. What do you recommend? Should they go ahead with the Video Maker business? Why or why not?

EXHIBIT 1
Initial Capitalization Required

Rental Equipment	
Cameras (+ Tax)	$138,000
Battery Packs (50 × $30)	1,500
Tripods (5 × $40)	200
Lights (30 × $25)	750
Shoulder Harnesses (50 × $25)	1,250
Office Equipment	
Office Equipment	4,000
Office Supplies	500
Rent Deposit	3,332
Phone Deposit	200
Racks, Display Cases	5,000
Cash Register	2,000
Miscellaneous	
Travel	3,000
Tapes	4,960
Moped	675
Van Lease	1,000
Contingency (5%)	7,633
2 Months Working Capital	23,800
Total Start-Up	$197,800

Pro Forma Income Statement
For the Period Shown

	1st Qtr*	2nd Qtr	3rd Qtr	4th Qtr	Year 2
Total Sales	$ 72,637	$142,050	$159,803	$174,330	$697,320
Less: Cost of Sales	15,432	30,182	33,954	37,142	148,568
Gross Margin	$ 57,205	$111,868	$125,849	$137,188	$548,752
Less Operating Expenses:					
Office Expenses	$ 6,431	$ 6,681	$ 6,831	$ 6,931	$ 27,724
Auto Expenses	1,561	1,764	1,794	1,794	7,176
Payroll	28,575	35,212	35,212	35,212	140,848
Advertising	25,000	20,000	10,000	5,000	34,866
Depreciation	19,890	19,890	19,890	19,890	79,560
Total Operating Expense	$ 81,457	$ 83,547	$ 73,727	$ 68,827	$290,174
Net Income (Loss) Before Taxes	$(24,252)	$ 28,321	$ 52,122	$ 68,361	$258,578
Less: Income Tax	3,637	(4,248)	(7,818)	(16,748)	68,916
Net Income (Loss)	$(20,615)	$ 24,073	$ 44,304	$ 51,613	$189,662

*Detail months 1–3

	Month		
	1	2	3
Sales	$ 10,800	$24,100	$37,700
Less: Cost of Sales	2,200	5,100	8,100
Less: Operating Expenses	29,800	25,800	25,800
Less: Income Tax	3,200	1,000	600
Net Income (Loss)	$(24,400)	$ (7,800)	$ 3,200
Average Camera 1-day rentals per week	100	225	350

Sales Detail

	1st Qtr	2nd Qtr	3rd Qtr	4th Qtr
Cameras ($17.50/ea)	$51,187	$100,100	$112,612	$122,850
Tapes ($10/ea)	14,625	28,600	32,175	35,100
Battery ($2/ea)	1,755	3,432	3,861	4,212
Tripod ($3/ea)	195	385	430	468
Insurance ($5/ea)	4,875	9,533	10,725	11,700
Total Sales	$72,637	$142,050	$159,803	$174,330
Average camera 1-day rentals per week	225	440	495	540

Cost of Sales Detail

	1st Qtr	2nd Qtr	3rd Qtr	4th Qtr
Merchant Chgs. (Crdt. Cards)	$ 2,905	$ 5,682	$ 6,392	$ 6,973
Batteries	-0-	-0-	-0-	-0-
Tapes ($5.50/ea)	8,043	15,730	17,696	19,305
Rental Insurance	2,437	4,766	5,362	5,850
Commissions (20% of 20%)	2,047	4,004	4,504	4,914
Total Cost of Sales	$15,432	$30,182	$33,954	$37,042

Office Expenses Detail

	1st Qtr	2nd Qtr	3rd Qtr	4th Qtr
Rent	$2,427	$2,427	$2,427	$2,427
Telephone	900	900	900	900
Insurance	1,800	1,800	1,800	1,800
Licenses	63	63	63	63
Professional Fees	501	501	501	501
Bank Charges	60	60	60	60
Pagers	180	180	180	180
Supplies	500	750	900	1,000
Total Office Exp	$6,431	$6,681	$6,831	$6,931

Auto Expense Detail

	1st Qtr	2nd Qtr	3rd Qtr	4th Qtr
Lease Payment	$ 900	$ 900	$ 900	$ 900
Gas	346	519	519	519
Insurance	225	225	225	225
Maintenance	90	90	90	90
Total Auto Expense	$1,561	$1,734	$1,734	$1,734

Payroll Expense Detail

	1st Qtr	2nd Qtr	3rd Qtr	4th Qtr
Salaries	$22,500	$22,500	$22,500	$22,500
Wages (3.35/hr × 40 hr × 5 days)	-0-	5,226	5,226	5,226
Taxes (12%)	2,700	3,327	3,327	3,327
Benefits (15%)	3,375	4,159	4,159	4,159
Total Payroll Exp.	$28,575	$35,212	$35,212	$35,212

Equipment Replacement Detail (Depreciation Expense)

	1st Qtr	2nd Qtr	3rd Qtr	4th Qtr
Cameras $\frac{138,000}{1.5 \text{ Yrs}}$	$25,000	$23,000	$23,000	$23,000
Tripods $\frac{200}{3 \text{ Yrs}}$	15	15	16	16
Lights $\frac{750}{3 \text{ Yrs}}$	63	63	63	63
Shoulder Harnesses $\frac{1250}{3 \text{ Yrs}}$	104	104	104	104
Moped $\frac{675}{3 \text{ Yrs}}$	57	57	57	57
Total Depreciation	$25,239	$23,239	$23,240	$23,240

Revenue Potential (Camera Rentals Only)

Low	High
1,890—Daily rental potential (Mainland and Canada vistors to Oahu only)	2,466—Daily Rental potential (All visitors to Oahu)

Potential Weeky Income

	Low	High
Rent 1 day @ $17.50/day	$231,525	301,085
Rent 2 days @ $17.50/day	$463,050	604,170
Rent 3 days @ $17.50/day	$694,575	$906,255

Corporate Structure

Video Maker, Inc., Authorized Shares	200,000
Shareholders (November 15, 1986):	
DoraLee Olsen	40,800
Kristie Jensen	40,800
Infinite Images, Inc.	20,400
Unissued shares	98,000

Valuation of Shares

Value of Company based on five-year earning projections:	
Projected five-year profits	$858,000
(Valuation of Business)	
858,000 divided by 200,000 shares = $4.29 per share	
Total shares offered for sale	78,000
Times value per share	× $4.29
Total offering valuation	$334,600
Discount (41%)	136,800
Total investment	$197,800

EXHIBIT 2
Market Potential

(a) 2,901,310 .... Mainland yearly visitors (total)

(b) $\underline{\times\quad 79\%}$
     2,292,042 .... Total yearly visitors who came for pleasure only*

(c) $\underline{\times\quad 54\%}$
     1,237,702 .... Total yearly party heads who came to Hawaii for
                                                 pleasure only (average number per party 1.84)*

(d) $\underline{\times\quad 55\%}$
     608,736 .... Total yearly party heads who came to Hawaii for
                                               pleasure, who would actually rent a video camera
                                               (based on a random sampling from a
                                               questionnaire)

$$\frac{680,736}{360 \text{ (days)}} = \textit{1,890 NEW VISITORS DAILY WHO WILL RENT A CAMERA}$$

*Source: Hawaii Visitors Bureau, *Annual Research Report,* 1984. This market projection is supported by the (1984–1985) statistical census developed by the Hawaiian Department of Planning and Economic Development. The figures used are for those visitors from the mainland or Canada and visitors to Oahu only. This segment accounts for only 77 percent of the total visitors to Oahu, with another 23 percent from foreign countries.

EXHIBIT 3
Average Visitor Census, Daily

	State of Hawaii	Oahu	Island of Hawaii	Kauai	Maui
1980–	96,497	66,680	7,195	7,259	15,363
1981–	95,968	66,455	6,561	7,225	15,727
1982–	105,310	73,445	6,725	7,050	18,090
1983–	108,045	66,695	8,690	7,990	24,670
1984–	118,660	67,370	7,570	10,930	32,790

Source: Hawaii Visitors Bureau, release dated March 1985 and records. This table includes *all* visitors, westbound, eastbound, and northbound arrivals. Based on a 20 percent sample through 1983 and 10 percent sample for 1984.

EXHIBIT 4
1985 Monthly Breakdown of All Visitors Staying Overnight or
Longer*

January	421,800
February	415,000
March	464,680
April	405,140
May	351,440
June	372,970
July	454,460
August	344,320
September	344,320
October	364,990
November	376,340
December	444,840

Source: Hawaii Visitors Bureau, *Annual Research Report,* Tabular release dated March, 1985. All visitors include those visitors arriving westbound, eastbound, and northbound. Westbound visitors make up approximately 77 percent of all visitors. Eastbound and northbound combined to make up 23 percent of all visitors. Of the 23 percent of the eastbound and northbound visitors, approximately 72 percent are from Japan.

EXHIBIT 5
Top Three Competitors in Waikiki

BUSINESS NAME: Hawaii Holiday Video

ADDRESS: Waikiki Plaza Hotel, Kalakaua Avenue

LOCATION TYPE: Small counter-sized area. Approximately 4' × 8' on the outside of Waikiki Plaza Hotel. Excellent location for walk-by traffic.

OPERATING HOURS: 7 days a week—9:00 A.M. to 5:00 P.M.

RENTAL RATES: $ 5.00 per hour
$ 14.95 per 1/2 day (10 A.M.–4 P.M. or 4–10 P.M.)
$ 19.95 per day
$ 18.95 second day
$ 17.95 third day
$115.95 weekly rate

EQUIPMENT USED: Mostly VHS, Olympic cameras
2–3 Beta format

OTHER SERVICES: Sells a large supply of prerecorded Hawaiian videotapes.

NUMBER OF CAMERAS
IN USE: Approximately 10 to 12

NUMBER OF OUTLETS: 1 in Waikiki, 1 in Maui, 1 located by the Polynesian Culture Center

SOURCE OF ADVERTISING: 1¼″ × 3¼″ coupon ad in *Here In Hawaii* (Aug. 16–22, 1986) $18.95 with coupon.

MAJOR SOURCE OF MARKET: Tourists; walk-by traffic

AMOUNT OF BUSINESS: On a particular weekday, 9 cameras rented and 1 beta available. Most weekends all cameras rented.

STRENGTHS: Location, minimal overhead. Their location at the Polynesian Culture Center is one of the busiest tourist attractions.

WEAKNESSES: Minimal advertising, no delivery, lack of a professional posture. Their office was messy and a nonprofessional salesperson was in attendance.

BUSINESS NAME: Video Tropic

ADDRESS: 1750 Kalakaua Avenue

LOCATION TYPE: Located in high-rise condo, office. This portion of Kalakaua Ave. is not in the Waikiki area. It is not conducive to walk-in traffic. Approximately 400 to 500 square feet condo.

OPERATING HOURS: 24-hour answering machine

RENTAL RATES: $18.95 per day/camera
$11.95 / blank tape
If delivered, $27.00 for both ($3.90 discount for delivery)
$96.95 for weekly rate

EQUIPMENT TYPE: Panasonic AG 150 S
industrial grade TDK tapes

OTHER SERVICES: Delivery service, personalized instruction

NUMBER OF CAMERAS
IN USE: 25 full-size VHS

NUMBER OF OUTLETS: 1 in Oahu. They are planning to open outlet in Kuaii in September 1986.

SOURCE OF ADVERTISING: 1 ad in *Spotlight* (Aug 16–22, 1986)
2½″ × 3½″ ad in *Tropics.*

MAJOR SOURCE OF MARKET: Tourist

AMOUNT OF BUSINESS: On weekends all 25 cameras rented. Two internal sales staff. They have been in operation for 3 months.

STRENGTHS: Delivers to hotels to their customers
Two mopeds
Low rent ($500)
Uses a good rental contract, including much information pertaining to the tourists
Includes instruction booklet

WEAKNESSES: Location poor for walk-in. Does not advertise location, but encourages delivery through advertising. The quality of advertising is fair at best. Possible low capital for operating costs. Office was hard to find and had an unpleasant odor. Does not offer insurance to customer for possible theft or breakage.

BUSINESS NAME: Video Vacation Camera Rentals

ADDRESS: Waikiki Trade Center, Kuhio

LOCATION TYPE: Retail outlet located in shopping center, one block from Kalakaua Avenue. On ground floor. Approximately 500 to 600 square feet. High professional posture. Rent approximately $5 to $10 a square foot per month. Mauve and oak decor with three demo tables with cameras and thirteen JVC monitors with a 5-minute instruction tape. One camera pointed into the mall with live video of passerbys on monitor in front window.

OPERATING HOURS: 7 days a week; 9:00 A.M. to 9:00 P.M.

RENTAL RATES: $ 5.95 per hour
$19.95 per day
$99.94 per weekly rate
$ 4.50 for limited damage waiver/per day
$10.00 extended damage coverage/per day
$ 9.97 for high grade tape
$12.99 for camera high grade tape

EQUIPMENT TYPE: Magnavox cameras, VHS and Beta
3M Scotch brand tapes

OTHER SERVICES: Offers underwater diving cases for cameras; has 3 monitors to watch video for instructions in use of cameras; offers some additional accessories for rent, i.e., tripod, A/C light, D/C light, extra power pack.

NUMBER OF CAMERAS
IN USE: 100 total

NUMBER OF OUTLETS: One in Oahu. Will be opening additional outlet in Maui in late September, 1986. Currently in operation for 9 months. This is a pilot store for this company. Their headquarters are in Denver, Colorado. Plans to expand to other markets outside of Hawaii.

SOURCE OF ADVERTISING: Several. It is felt they spend a minimum of $60,000 a year on advertising in tourist magazines. Flyers in booths in hotel lobbies. Also for a period of time, advertised on the in-room cable television.

MAJOR SOURCE OF MARKET: Tourist. It has the largest share among the competitors.

AMOUNT OF BUSINESS: Most cameras are reserved and busy on weekends. Three internal sales staff.

STRENGTHS: Professional look and posture. Good location for walk-in traffic. Ads, flyers, and display tie in to give repetition of seeing ad. Professional looking ads. Apparent working capital available. Of all the competitors, it is by far the superior.

WEAKNESSES: No delivery services. Avoiding local market. No apparent direct sales or contract sales.

EXHIBIT 6
Tourist Publications and Readership

		(Refer to table below for column description)						
		(1)	(2)	(3)	(4)	(5)	(6)	(7)
1	*This Week on Oahu*	67	34	4.9	24	4.3	5.0	5.6
2	*Spotlight Hawaii*	52	29	4.2	27	4.1	4.8	5.3
3	*Guide to Oahu*	49	25	3.5	30	4.1	4.6	5.2
4	*Hawaii Island Guide*	49	29	4.2	29	3.9	4.4	5.3
5	*On the Go*	39	24	3.5	34	4.0	4.6	5.1
6	*Waikiki Beach Press*	30	10	1.8	49	3.7	4.1	4.5
7	*Here In Hawaii*	31	25	3.4	32	3.9	4.3	5.1

Table of Column Headings

(1) Readership of Tourist Publication (%)

(2) Minutes Read (mean)

(3) Number of Times Referred to Publication (mean)

(4) Read Once & Discarded (%)

(5) Shopping (mean)

(6) Dining (mean)

(7) Overall Usefulness (mean)

(Summary of the Loui/Singer/Ankersmit/Soom surveys Result Number 4 through 7 Tourist Publications Considered "Most Helpful: for Various Activities")

Ocean Shores Corporation

Donald F. Harvey
Research Assistant: Janet Nickerson

Gerald Diamond, Chairman of Ocean Shores, sat on the edge of his desk in his paneled office and spoke of his management team. "We're not doing badly with our current product line, but I feel we're in a growth market right now and we need to secure some new licensing agreements."

"I agree with that, Gerry," said president Tom Kirby, "but I also feel we need to develop and market our own product line as well."

The management team needed to examine these issues and determine a strategy for the future of Ocean Shores. What should Ocean Shores do? It has many options to consider.

BACKGROUND

Ocean Shores is a designer and manufacturer of active sportswear accessories that are marketed under separate brand names. In 1982, a ten-year license secured from Ocean Pacific (OP) granted Ocean Shores the exclusive right to manufacture and sell OP accessories as approved by OP. These accessors include wallets, bags, headwear, sunglasses, beachtowels, and backpacks.

In 1984, sales soared to $6 million and of the $6 million, OP accessories accounted for $5.9 million. In the midst of this large gain in sales (as shown in the financial statement analysis, exhibits 1 and 2), Ocean Shore's management structure has undergone numerous reorganizations. Ocean Shores is privately owned, and all four of its owners are active in the business.

Currently, Ocean Shores' concerns are

1 Answering the needs of the OP customer who is moving into an older age group.
2 Acquiring new licensing agreements for additional brands in the active sportswear industry. They plan to search out companies whose name brands are gaining popularity and who are not currently marketing an accessory line.
3 Increasing market share by manufacturing products that are geared towards the winter/fall season (current line is spring/summer).

This case was prepared as a basis for class discussion rather than to illustrate either effective or ineffective handling of an administrative situation. All company names, names of individuals, and facts and figures have been disguised to assure anonymity.

To achieve these objectives, Ocean Shores' designers work closely with upper management and designers from OP. This process keeps upper management informed of changing environmental conditions, such as styles, and achieves a clear line of communication.

Communication and reaction to changing conditions are important in the accessories market; if reactions to environmental conditions are slow, losses can occur. For example, in 1984 the market analysis was poor resulting in a $64,927 loss from operations.

PRESENT GOALS AND MISSIONS

Ocean Shore's mission revolves around acquiring new licensing agreements in the active sportswear industry. To achieve this mission Ocean Shores has set its strategy towards acquiring licenses whose products will even the product demand over the course of the year, for example, selling skiwear in addition to sunwear accessories. Ocean Shores' specific goal is to seek companies with an existing sales and distribution network that Ocean Shores can immediately tie into, as well as products that are easily adapted to Ocean Shores' current manufacturing process.

In the past, Ocean Shores' strategy was not clear. For example, Ocean Shores entered the accessory market by designing and manufacturing a jogger's key and money holder called the Trac Pac. At that time and in years to follow, there was not even a written business strategy or plan. However, by competing in the accessories industry and adding new products, Ocean Shores has gained an understanding of its direction. The key to this direction is gaining a larger market share in the accessories market.

Management and Corporate Style

Ocean Shores' management team offers solid leadership enhanced by the diversity of skills of its five members of the board. They appear to be suited to the responsibility of their position and to have a hands-on knowledge of their product. Because the corporation is small and privately owned, the managers at Ocean Shores appear to be team players who are open to input from other departments.

Product knowledge is important in this industry due to fast changing trends and styles. For example, Ocean Shores entered the market by anticipating the need for a jogger's key holder. Thus, it produced and successfully marketed the Trac Pac. However overall, Ocean Shores' corporate style is reactive. Trends and styles change and Ocean Shores tends to react to the wants and needs of the consumers.

INDUSTRY ANALYSIS

The garment industry is made up almost entirely of small privately owned (often family owned) businesses. The exceptions are the giants like Levi Strauss and a few others. Ocean Shores, being licensed under Ocean Pacific, is competing against many other small accessories manufacturers.

Ocean Shores is a manufacturer and wholesaler of garment accessories. It is difficult to classify accessories in a single industry classification. Ocean Shores produces a large variety of products, the majority of which fall into the standard industrial classification of small leather goods or other materials (SIC #3172).

The accessories market seems to be fairly insensitive to the economy. During recessionary periods, accessories sales have been more stable than other apparel sales. Consumers continue to update and accent their existing wardrobes. Market surveys reveal that the accessories market is expected to grow during 1986 to 1990.

Ocean Shores' primary customers are the active sportswear retailers. These include cloth, department, specialty sporting goods (such as surf and ski), running goods, fitness proshops, and chain clothing stores. They have retailers located all over the United States, primarily in the southwest and eastern seaboard, Hawaii, Alaska, and Puerto Rico. They also export to Canada, England, New Zealand, Australia, Panama, and Japan. The retail outlets tend to be located in shopping malls in large population areas.

Competition

Ocean Shores has different competitors for each product they produce. There is some overlap in these areas. In a survey of local retailers, the following list of competitors for the various products was identified:

Wallets	*Beach Towels*	*Hats*
Lightning Bolt	Hobie	Dorfman Pacific
Hang Ten	Offshore	Hobie
Hobie	Gotcha	Panama Jack
Offshore	Bolt	Sand Mfg.
Sunglasses	*Bags and Backpacks*	
Bausch & Lomb	Outdoor Products	
Buccie	Northface	
Carrera	Hobie	
Hobie	Nike	
Vuarnet	New Balance	
I Ski	Durango	
Bolle	Ciao	

Performance

Ocean Shores has a small share of the market, but that is the nature of the industry. Most of the competitors have an equally small market share. Due to the low costs and ease of entry and exit to the industry, the industry is made up of many small companies. In this sense, it is a purely competitive industry.

Government and Regulatory

The nature of the industry is such that there is little government intervention or industry regulation. The forces of competition eliminate the opportunity of cartels or monopolistic activities. The competitive nature of the industry keeps prices at reasonable levels. This market segment is basically price oriented.

INTERNAL ANALYSIS

Ocean Shores is a privately owned corporation managed by its four owners. The management team is made up of:

Gerald Diamond, Chairman of the Board
   Responsible for negotiations and new market opportunities
   Possesses strong entrepreneurial abilities

Thomas Kirby, President
   Manages and leads the company with a hands-on capability
   Possesses strong manufacturing and production expertise

Larry Baker, Chief Financial Officer and CPA
   Handles cash management and financial needs
   Effective manager of time, money, and people

Steve Carter, Vice President, Product Development
   Responsible for research, design, and adaptation to current market trends
   Received two patents on his designs

Organizational Structure

Due to the size of the company, there is no hierarchy or structure. The company is organized by department, each having a manager responsible for its function. The overall culture is very informal and decentralized, with considerable communication between departments. Because the corporation is small and privately owned, a sense of comradeship and team effort runs throughout the company. The company suffers little from intercompany conflict.

Production

Ocean Shores operates from two leased locations, the corporate office/warehouse and the 7000 square foot manufacturing plant. Production is very labor intensive, therefore plant and equipment costs are fairly low. There are three basic steps in the production process:

1   Raw materials are cut with die-cutting presses or electric knives.
2   Products are sewn on industrial sewing machines.
3   Products are silk-screened or embroidered, then dried on drying machines.

Production control is achieved through a system of work orders that control the flow of raw materials and labor. A perpetual inventory system is on-line with a computer system, and inventories are balanced daily. Raw materials are obtained exclusively through west coast suppliers who regularly offer the lowest prices, availability, and proximity. They have at least three suppliers for all raw materials.

Marketing

Marketing is a very important factor in the apparel industry in general. Products sell by the image they carry. Developing an image, therefore, is of utmost importance for a product to get off the ground and survive. Most of Ocean Shores' marketing is done by Ocean Pacific through their licensing agreement. Brand selling has proven to be the most economical and successful strategy for Ocean Shores. The licensor companies have large, well-established sales forces, and customer acceptance of the brand has been proven. Ocean Shores pays the licensor a fee (1 to 3 percent of sales) for these services. In addition, Ocean Shores offers retailers one-stop shopping by packaging related accessory items together on Ocean Shores' developed display stands. All merchandise is shipped directly by Ocean Shores.

Customers are willing to pay a higher price for name brand accessories because they relate the name to quality and value. Consequently, Ocean Shores' products are priced equal to or higher than the competition. Ocean Pacific has maintained its product image by not saturating the market thereby keeping a consistent market demand for the OP brand.

Ocean Shores describes its image as *active* accessories. Active separates these accessories from those in the *dress* or *high fashion* market segments. In addition, its image portrays the look and feel of a certain lifestyle (upbeat, mobile, healthy, and casual).

Research and Development

Ocean Shores' design team works together with designers from the licensor companies to create new and unique designs. Lifestyle trends and current fashions are monitored and are the basis for new design concepts. Fabric and material contents are constantly being analyzed for future use. New and more efficient production methods are always being developed.

Human Resources

Ocean Shores has followed the trend of small producers toward hiring buyers from large retailers. Retail-oriented people can use their expertise in dealing with the retailers. The production work force is made up of nonunion labor.

Financial

Ocean Shores is organized as a Sub S corporation. The stockholders assume federal tax liability for their proportionate share of the company's income. The company is very closely held and has issued only 1,500 of the 100,000 authorized shares. It is not a very capital-intensive business. In 1983, Ocean Shores' plant and equipment were valued at $241,169, with total assets of $1.83 million (see exhibit 1). It achieved $5.99 million in sales that year. The majority of its assets are current. The inventory at the end of 1984 was valued at $882,336, which is very high in relation to the industry. This high inventory was a result of poor planning and lack of market demand anticipation. Since then, Ocean Shores has reduced its average inventory (see exhibit 2).

In November 1983, the company entered into an agreement with a factor. The company sells most of its trade accounts receivable, without recourse, to the factor. This arrangement helps to steady the cash flow of the very seasonal business.

Ocean Shores has been experiencing a decrease in its gross margin. In 1983 this decrease was due to the introduction of towels and the increase in hat sales, which both have lower gross margins individually. In 1984 unrealistic sales forecasts led to large inventories which had to be sold at considerable discounts resulting in lower gross margins. Ocean Shores has developed its own sales forecasts and has reduced its reliance on its licensor's forecasts.

Ocean Shores has a deceptively high debt-to-equity ratio. Most of the debt is current, however, and is collateralized with inventory and nonfactored accounts receivable. The long-term debt is also collateralized by long-term assets. It is apparent that the owners of the company want to retain ownership of the company, but they could issue stock to raise capital if needed. Before issuing stock, however, they will have to improve the company's profitability.

CONCLUSION

Ocean Shores is currently limiting its future by depending solely on OP's marketing and established name. Such dependence could be detrimental to its survival in this competitive market. The OP name has passed its peak in the industry and is beginning to decline. This decline could greatly cut into Ocean Shores' sales if OP remains a main source of income.

Ocean Shores is reducing its future potential not only by depending on one source of income, but also by limiting the seasons toward which its accessories are geared. Presently, Ocean Shores' accessories are mainly spring and summer items. This emphasis completely ignores the fall and winter months and results in sporadic production cycles and lack of regular cash flow.

Ocean Shores carries its own product line but has not developed a positive sales record. It has not marketed under its own product name. Ocean Shores depends on OP's marketing expertise and has not developed an advertising and marketing team for its own product names.

EXHIBIT 1
Consolidated Balance Sheet—December 31, 1983

ASSETS

Current assets:

Cash	$ 4,678	
Receivable from factor, net of unapplied customer credits	212,526	
Accounts receivable, net of allowance for doubtful accounts of $52,000	403,219	
Inventory	881,366	
Loans receivable, officer-stockholders	49,150	
Prepaid expenses and other current assets	21,618	
Total current assets		$1,572,557
Property and equipment, net of accumulated depreciation		241,169
Other assets		19,382
		$1,833,108

LIABILITIES AND STOCKHOLDERS' EQUITY

Current liabilities:

Loan payable, factor	$602,680	
Accounts payable and accrued expenses	681,977	
Accrued officers' salaries	185,000	
Pension plan contribution payable	63,000	
Current maturities of long-term debt	48,360	
Total current liabilities		$1,581,037
Long-term debt, less current maturities		102,710
Stockholders' equity:		
Common stock; 100,000 shares authorized, 1,500 shares issued	1,500	
Retained earnings	147,861	
Total stockholders' equity		149,361
		$1,833,108

EXHIBIT 2
Financial Statement Analysis

	Year Ended 12/31/82 (UNAUDITED)		Year Ended 12/31/83 (AUDITED)		Year Ended 12/31/84 (UNAUDITED)	
NET SALES	$2,965,103	100.0%	$5,994,452	100.0%	$5,959,036	100.0%
COST OF SALES	1,325,530	44.7	2,932,220	48.9	3,342,589	56.1
GROSS PROFIT	1,639,573	55.3	3,062,232	51.1	2,616,447	43.9
OPERATING EXPENSES						
Selling	678,458	22.9	1,198,717	20.0	1,235,471	20.7
Shipping & Warehouse	121,769	4.1	291,896	4.9	137,377	2.3
Product Devel.	—	—	60,978	1.0	102,651	1.7
General and Administrative	813,632	27.4	1,420,642	23.7	1,205,875	20.2
TOTAL OPERATING EXPENSES	1,613,859	54.4	2,972,233	49.6	2,681,374	44.9
INCOME (LOSS) FROM OPERATIONS	$ 25,714	.9	$ 89,999	1.5	$ (64,927)	(1.0)
TOTAL ASSETS	879,584		1,833,108		1,317,043	
WORKING CAPITAL	29,777		(8,480)		(76,862)	
CURRENT RATIO	1.04		.99		.93	
INVENTORY TURNOVER	5.8		4.7		4.3	
DEBT TO EQUITY RATIO	13.1		11.3		5.2	

■ ■ ■ CASE 6
Alpha Electronics, Inc.

Donald F. Harvey
Research Assistant: Scott Union

In 1985, two young entrepreneurs, Bob Anders and Mitch Pepper, decided to start an electronics distribution firm in the San Diego area. The company is a start-up electronics distributor called Alpha Electronics, Inc. Anders, now president and chief operating officer, and Pepper, vice president, marketing, are former employees of Exile Electronics, Inc., a medium to large distributor. The venture is being financed by a large European distributorship.

The high-tech industry as a whole exists in the most dynamic and competitive environment of recent history. The technology is advancing at such an incredible rate that today's major breakthrough can become obsolete tomorrow. A well-publicized example is Adam Osborne's company (Osborne Computer), a $100 million corporation one year and a bankrupt corporation the next. Therefore, anticipative and innovative management is essential for a company to enter and compete effectively in the high-tech marketplace.

INDUSTRY STRUCTURE

Alpha is a distributor of semiconductors and subsystem products. The current industry consists primarily of two overlapping tiers of manufacturers and distributors. The first tier provides approximately 80 percent of total revenues for the major distributors. Exhibit 1 illustrates some of the key players broken down by tier in the San Diego market. Products in the second tier are necessary to the industry but not on a scale large enough to support a major distributorship. Therefore, although major distributors obtain and sell second tier products, it is more as a service to their main customers than as a principal selling objective. Alpha, focusing at the tier 2 level, operates using the following general philosophy: To offer a specialized leading edge, high technology, second tier product line (currently served by major/medium distributors as a second effort) to a broad range of clients (market penetration) through superior management (market acceptance).

This case was prepared as a basis for class discussion rather than to illustrate either effective or ineffective handling of an administrative situation. All company names, names of individuals, and facts and figures have been disguised.

Background

Distribution is a relatively low markup business compared with manufacturing or retail sales. The typical industry margins after markup are 25 percent. High sales generation and administration expense as a percentage of sales, interest, and taxes tends to cause a low operating profit. Also, high asset levels are required to maintain sufficient inventory levels. Thus, return on assets (ROA) is one of the most critical measures in evaluating well-managed companies. Alpha's financial goals are (1) high gross margins, (2) high asset turnover, (3) low operating costs, and (4) high profits.

Gross Margin Projections

Year	Sales (M)	Gross Margins (%)
1	$ 1.75	25
2	2.90	26
3	5.00	27
4	8.00	27
5	11.50	27

Alpha is projecting increased gross margin due to market acceptance, increased sales penetration, and account control.

Asset Turnover Projections

Year	Sales (M)	Inventory	Turns
1	1.75	$ 250,000	6
2	2.90	380,000	6
3	5.00	600,000	6
4	8.00	975,000	6
5	11.50	1,400,000	6

The industry average is four turns a year. Insight seeks to achieve high asset turnover by sales penetration, high gross margin, concentration on "A" (high demand, low supply) items, and high-tech products.

Market Share Projections

Year	Sales (M)	Market Share (%)
1	1.75	2.5
2	2.90	3.5
3	5.00	5.0
4	8.00	7.0
5	11.50	9.0

Projected Financial Statements (See Exhibits 2, 3, 4, and 5)

Projected balance sheet

Projected statement of income

Projected statement of sources and uses of cash

Notes to projected financial statements

Proposed Capitalization

$2,000,000 for proper personnel, solid financial status, viability, growth, and expansion.

Projected Start-up Costs

Legal	$ 5,000.00
Inventory	250,000.00
Building	6,000.00
Furniture	6,000.00
Phone System	12,000.00
Stationery	4,000.00
Warehouse	2,000.00
Contingency	10,000.00
TOTAL	$295,000.00

Management Strategy

Alpha: The ability to understand the integral workings of technology and people.

Mission Statement

To offer a specialized, high-technology, second tier product line to a broad range of clients through superior management.

Objectives

1   Specialize in leading edge products offering

- Limited competition
- High average selling price/gross margin
- High asset turnover

2   Provide a service level that is

- Superior
- Technical

3   Identify manufacturers that

- Manufacture high-technology products
- Require local/regional distribution
- Have proven capability to produce a good product
- Require technical coverage

4   Sell to an account base that

- Is mature and technically oriented
- Has ability to pay
- Has good growth potential

5   Provide long-term growth that is

- Consistent
- Conservative
- Profitable

Market

The high-tech industry is such a growing and expanding marketplace that many opportunities exist for small- to medium-sized companies that choose to specialize. The greatest area of growth and thus the greatest area for opportunity is in leading edge technology. The most effective way for a new distributorship to exist and compete with the larger established firms is to keep away from the highly volatile and competitive generic product markets. These markets, due to a softening of semiconductor orders, are currently experiencing a consolidation. Therefore, new firms should focus on the more sophisticated, specialized products that customers cannot get easily elsewhere. Advanced Micro Devices, Inc. (AMD), a specialized electronics manufacturer committed to ''out-innovating'' the competition, has grown from a start-up company in 1970 to a company expected to hit $1 billion in annual revenues in 1989 using this very strategy.

Market Definition

The major distributors handle both tier 1 and tier 2 product lines (exhibit 1); however, the bulk of their revenues is generated from the very high volume, low- to medium-technology product lines primarily in tier 1. The second tier products are necessary to the industry but not on a scale large enough to support a major distributorship. Therefore, the major distributors obtain and sell tier 2 product lines as a service or second effort to their main customers rather than as a specific selling objective. Exhibit 6 shows the current disposition of the key distributors at both the tier 1 and tier 2 levels in terms of a v-curve evaluating profit and revenues.

The San Diego area was selected because it has:

1   Quality personnel available
2   High-growth market
3   High-technology market
4   Limited competition in high-technology distribution

Market Profile

San Diego currently represents 2.3 percent of the U.S. semiconductor market. This percentage equated to approximately $140 million in 1984. Dataquest forecasts that real growth over the next three years will be 25 percent per annum, primarily due to the Sorrento Valley's emergence as the "Silicon Valley" of Southern California. Thus, San Diego will grow faster than most other markets and reach $225 million by 1988.

Distribution in San Diego historically has been 45 percent of the total market (Dataquest). The following calculations demonstrate probable distribution sales of semiconductors over the next five years:

Year	Growth (%)	Total Market (M)	Distribution (M)
1985	20	156	70
1986	20	185	83
1987	20	222	100
1988	12	250	115
1989	12	280	125

Trends

A national move to centralize inventory has met with some resistance from vendors who would prefer to have their lines carried at all locations. However, Charley Clough, president of Electronics Marketing, stated: "Centralized inventories will increase the business for their (vendors') product in total by having more product available to ship on short notice. There is no question this is the way to go in distribution."[1]

Distributors are increasing their overall market share of semiconductor sales. This increase is primarily because most new customers are small-to-medium-sized accounts which cannot be economically served by the manufacturers. These new companies typically possess much more favorable growth dynamics than the larger accounts handled by the manufacturers. Therefore, distributor sales should continue to grow more rapidly than overall semiconductor sales.[2]

Technological Developments

The distributor's role was once one of stocking and selling standardized products. However, the changing needs of the customer base and the new offerings of semiconductor suppliers have placed distributors in a potentially high-growth, but risky, business. These new application-specific or semicustom products are tailored to one specific user; thus the distributor is required to take a considerable amount of risk. Other issues in this area include valuation of the distributor's role in the design of the semicustom product and the question of who is responsible in the event of errors in the design or manufacturing process. These problems, in particular, are keeping many distributors from entering this very specialized market.[3]

Dataquest believes that the market for semicustom products will explode in the near future. This trend is supported by the large number (over 100) of new semicustom houses which have come into existence to help the manufacturer, distributor, and customer in the design of these specialized products.

The semicustom product area featuring gate arrays is particularly suited for the traditional client base of the distributor. Gate arrays allow a smaller manufacturer to enjoy the benefits of product customization. These benefits include size reduction of the total product package, proprietary design to guard against industry duplication, and increased cost efficiency through substitution of many products with one or a few. Presently, the following six major distributors are involved in gate arrays: Arrow, Diplomat, Hamilton/Avnet, Schweber, Western Microtechnology, and Wyle.

Government Regulatory Impact

The U.S. government on March 5, 1985, lifted the import quota restrictions on Japanese goods, primarily automobiles and semiconductors. Allowing a free flow of goods (semiconductors) into the U.S. places further pressure on U.S. manufacturers and suppliers. The impact of this regulatory change in terms of increased flow of Japanese goods is not immediately known. However, most U.S. electronics firms are quickly evaluating existing contingency plans and creating new ones to try and minimize the negative impact on their firms.

COMPETITION

Major Distributors—Tier 1[4]

Hamilton/Avnet   is the largest supplier of electronic components in the U.S. with 1983 sales of $1.164 billion. Highlights of the firm's income statement include:

Cost of goods sold	72.27%
Selling costs	19.85%
Pretax operating income	6.98%
Inventory turnover	4.1
Average collection period	69 days

Arrow is beginning to gain ground on Hamilton/Avnet in 1983 with total sales of $566 million. Income statement highlights appear below:

Cost of goods sold	75.98%
Selling costs	19.42%
Pretax operating income	3.91%
Inventory turnover	4.5
Average collection period	65 days

Schweber is very aggressive in the marketplace and believes in paying top dollar for personnel. Schweber is firmly committed to the tier 1 and risky semicustom markets. Recently, Schweber came into San Diego with its wallet wide open and hired a large number of key personnel from Hamilton/Avnet and Kierulff. However, Schweber poses little threat to Alpha because of its fierce commitment to dominating the tier 1 market. The firm's 1983 revenues were $342 million.

Kierulff boasts of the "broadest value-added connector program in the U.S." and is unquestionably committed to the tier 1 markets. 1983 revenues were $274 million.

Wyle reports 1983 sales of $294 million. Income statement highlights include the following:

Cost of goods sold	73.24%
Selling costs	19.95%
Pretax operating income	5.54%
Inventory turnover	5.2
Average collection period	66 days

Exile, the industry's most rapidly growing distributorship, more than doubled its 1982 revenues from $43 million to $95 million in 1983. Exile is a fairly new company and the smallest of the major distributors. However, superior sales and product management allow the firm to boast of the highest profit margins in the industry. Exile, primarily a west coast concern, with its topnotch management and aggressive, future-oriented outlook could prove to be a very serious competitive threat to Alpha. Currently, however, Exile and the rest of the tier 1 distributors service this market niche only as a second effort. Exile's income statement highlights include:

Cost of goods sold	74.20%
Selling costs	12.90%
Pretax operating income	11.90%
Inventory turnover	4.2
Average collection period	69 days

Major Distributors—Tier 2

Hallmark   is the fifth largest U.S. distributorship with 1983 revenues of $245 million. Hallmark offers ". . . the highest level of processing available for your engineering prototyping. From transistors, diodes, bi-polar ICs, memory, bi-polar and MOS memories, and micro processors . . ." as quoted from its brochure. However, management and sales expertise is currently insufficient to pose a major threat to a well-focused, talent-rich company in the leading edge of the San Diego market niche.

Marshall   is ranked seventh in total 1983 revenues of $171 million. Marshall, like the other large distributors, carries a full line of products such as capacitors, connectors, contacts and IC sockets, crystals, fans and blowers, filters, hardware, accessories, microprocessors, microcomputer boards, development systems, and so forth. This large spread of product lines, compiled from Marshall's brochure and line card keeps Marshall and most other large distributors from posing any real threat to Alpha. When a distributor gets this large, its management tends to ignore the relatively smaller, specialized, and highly technical market niches and focuses on generic, less technical markets more easily serviced. Marshall's income statement highlights include:

Cost of goods sold	74%
Selling costs	16%
Pretax operating income	9.8%
Inventory turnover	4.5
Average collection period	64 days

Bell   had 1983 revenues of $132 million. This firm concentrates more on the major markets such as Los Angeles and San Jose than on the relatively modest San Diego market.

Cetec,   according to its brochure, targets the "industry's state-of-the-art components." It also offers "a wide array of value-added services," including IDC mass termination assemblies; RF and other cylindrical connector assemblies; programmed PROMS, EPROMS, and EEPROMS. 1983 revenues totaled $72.8 million, up from $57 million in 1982. Cetec's strategy is to go after leading edge technology. Inventory turnover of over 6 times a year is excellent. However, the sales costs at 22 percent of sales is 6 to 9 percent too high. Overall, Cetec is a potential competitive threat and should be closely monitored by Alpha. Cetec's income statement highlights include:

Cost of goods sold	72%
Selling costs	22%
Pretax operating profit	4.6%
Inventory turnover	6.26
Average collection period	45 days

Diplomat is not a significant factor in the San Diego market. None of the customers we interviewed even knew of its existence.

Ryno is considered by Alpha to be its chief competitor in the San Diego market. However, poor capitalization coupled with an average sales and management talent pool prevents this concern from significantly affecting Alpha.

Time is a subsidiary of Hamilton/Avnet supplying "quality connectors" to the industry. Recently, it has begun carrying semiconductors and passive components. However, Time's new emphasis in semiconductors is focused mostly on the larger markets, not on the relatively small San Diego market.

Weatherford suffers from ineffective management, as illustrated by the decline in sales from $43.6 million in 1982 to $40 million in 1983. Sales costs of over 26 percent are also indicative of the firm's current weak position. Weatherford offers no consequential competitive threat to Alpha at this time or in the near future. Weatherford's income statement highlights are

Cost of goods sold	70.2%
Sales costs	26.3%
Pretax operating income	2.8%
Inventory turnover	3.9
Average collection period	70 days

Zeus focuses 100 percent on government and military markets.

The preceding presents a brief summary of each firm's key strengths and weaknesses. The following are 1983 industry averages of the income statement categories we have chosen to highlight:

Revenues	$4.64 billion
Cost of goods sold	72.1%
Sales costs	19.2%
Pretax operating income	7.6%
Inventory turnover	4.6
Average collection period	50 days

CUSTOMER PROFILE

The primary function of distributors is to sell high-technology products to small accounts that cannot be economically reached by the suppliers. Thus, any small- to medium-sized electronics firm is a potential customer. The key factors used by customers in evaluating distributors are

1 Supplies of printed technical information
2 Simplified purchasing
3 Local stock
4 Banking function
5 Fixed, fair prices
6 Service after sales

Alpha strives to deal with more than just purchasing and engineering. Its general customer profile is based on the following:

Products   Customer must be a viable manufacturer of technology products with a history of technological advancements and high R&D investment.

Markets   Customer must be committed to expanding markets, not the high-risk, fad markets.

Controls   Customer must exhibit proven materials and financial controls.

Risk   Customer must have the ability to pay, with limited bad debt exposure.

Relationship   Customer should have the potential to be sold at all levels.

ANALYSIS OF ALPHA ELECTRONICS, INC.

Alpha is a new electronics distributorship founded by the former general manager of Exile Electronics, Bob Anders, and one of the top sales representatives, Mitch Pepper. The firm began operating out of its new office located within La Jolla's coveted Golden Triangle in February 1985. Exile's former product manager and top salesman have since joined Alpha providing a strong initial talent base (see exhibit 7).

Alpha has chosen to pursue the smaller fringe markets, starting with San Diego and potentially expanding to Phoenix, Denver, Dallas/Houston/Austin, Seattle, Portland, and Salt Lake City. By concentrating on the fringe markets, Alpha hopes to avoid direct confrontation with the larger existing distributorships. This strategy should allow Alpha to serve its target markets with a minimum of competition.

Thus, with competition at a minimum, Alpha must still overcome the following three major obstacles or barriers to entry to be successful:

1 Developing credibility with manufacturers and customers
2 Obtaining qualified personnel
3 Obtaining adequate start-up money

People Resources

Alpha's number one strength rests with its founding partners. Bob Anders, president and COO, brings a proven and distinguished track record to Alpha. Anders was the driving force behind Exile's turnaround in the San Diego market from an insignificant distributorship to the area's fastest growing and most profitable firm, with 1984 revenues of over $7 million. Anders was offered the vice presidency of Exile's main and most-coveted San Jose office, along with a very generous pay increase, if he would reconsider his decision to leave. However, the excitement and thrill of his own company prevailed, and the future of Alpha lies heavily on his shoulders. Pepper brought money connections, sales expertise, and a strong existing customer base with him to Alpha. Alpha has hired Exile's former product manager to control and manage its inventory. Exile's top salesman in 1984 has also been acquired to assist Pepper in obtaining the firm's first year goal of $1.75 million in sales.

Financial Strength

A large European distributor has agreed to provide start-up funds and a $2 million line of credit for the new enterprise. The large European distributorship, with its assets of over $200 million and proven expertise in the electronics market, offers Alpha instant financial credibility.

Manufacturer Lines

The founders feel that ideally Alpha needs to acquire fifteen to twenty manufacturer lines to be a major force in the marketplace. The firm has acquired, to date, seven manufacturer lines. Two major tier 2 manufacturers, Fujitsu and Mitsubishi, both capable of producing $1 million in sales for Alpha the first year, create a strong product base. Data Delay, Integrated Device Technology, Thompson COF, Dallas Semiconductor, and IPS round out the list of seven. The firm is well on its way to acquiring the fifteen to twenty lines it desires. The signing of Fujitsu and Mitsubishi gives Alpha the base it needs to overcome the major barrier of manufacturer and customer credibility.

The major weakness is the fact that Alpha is a new company with no previous track record. In a market as competitive and dynamic as the electronics market, customers must be convinced of the future viability of a new company. Although both Anders and Pepper have been successful working within other companies, neither has previous experience with starting his own company.

Alpha's greatest opportunity is the potential to duplicate its San Diego operation in the areas previously listed that currently offer similar favorable conditions. Once this expansion is accomplished, Alpha may then be able to cost effectively enter the larger, more competitive major markets such as Los Angeles and San Francisco and become a major force in the overall distributorship picture.

The same dynamic marketplace which offers Alpha many opportunities also offers a corresponding amount of threats. These are

1 The entrance of one or more of the larger established firms into Alpha's previously ignored market niche. The possibility becomes greater as the current industry consolidation, due to declining semiconductor sales, continues.
2 Customer resistance to doing business with a new firm versus an older, established firm. Although Alpha has obtained some very good manufacturer lines, it has yet to book its first major order and break the often underestimated "first sale" barrier.
3 The underestimation of the strengths and resources of existing direct competitors such as Ryno.
4 Unforeseen negative economic, regulatory, or competitive issues detrimental to the firm.

CONCLUSION

To remain competitive, Alpha must manage its growth and profitability with care. It must keep its customers happy and develop new demand areas for its product lines. How can this company grow? Should Alpha compete against the giants, or should it expand into other geographic areas? What strategy would you recommend?

Notes

1 See *Electronic News* 30, no. 1506 (June 1984):62.
2 See Drexel, Burnham, and Lambert, *Research Abstract,* October 30, 1984.
3 See Dataquest, Inc., "Distribution Overview," October 30, 1984.
4 Revenue and income statement are figures from *Compustat,* "Wholesale Electronic Parts," 1983.

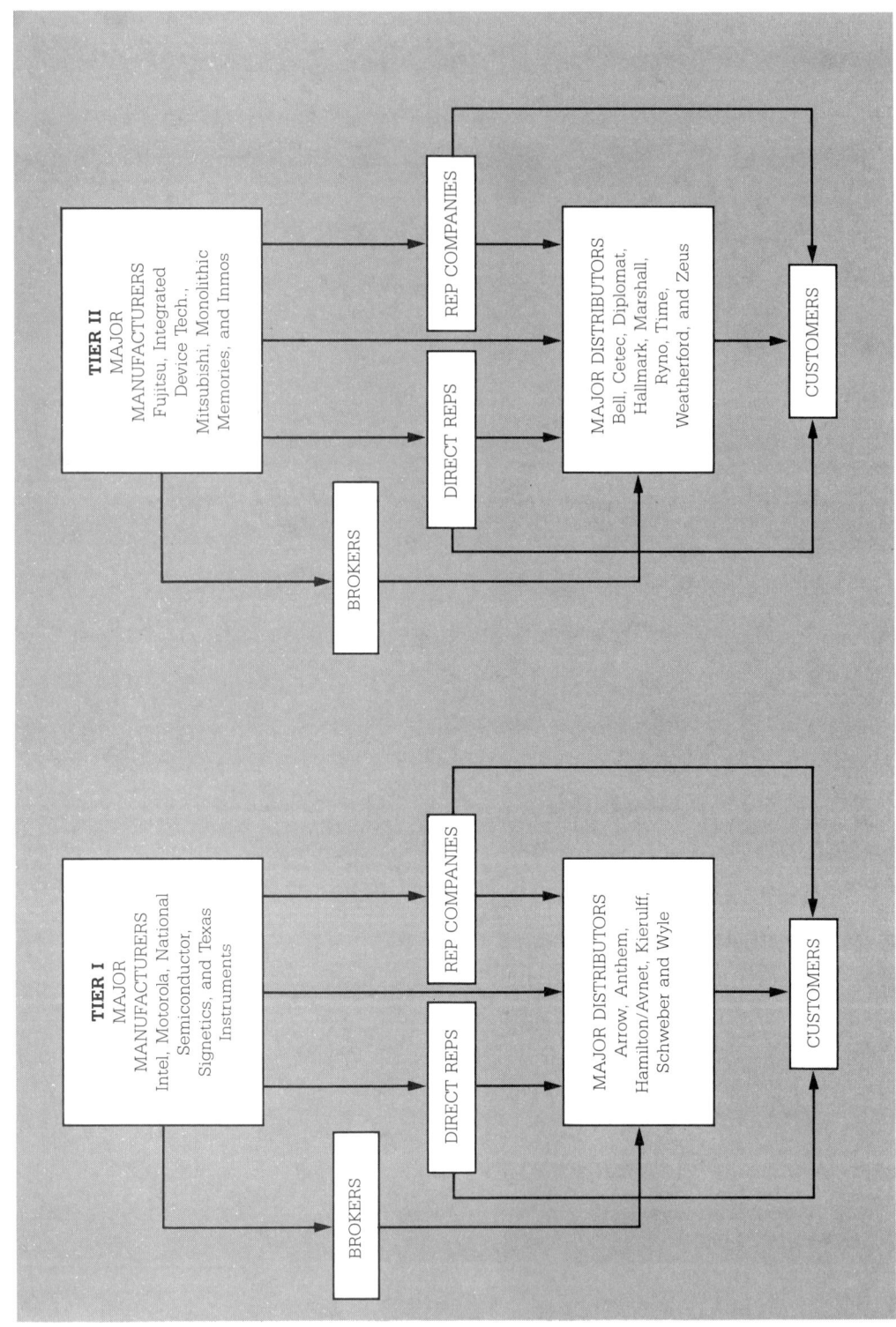

EXHIBIT 1
Tier 1 Major Manufacturers

EXHIBIT 2
Alpha Electronics, Inc. Projected Balance Sheet

			Year Ending		
	02/28/86	02/28/87	02/28/88	02/28/89	02/28/90
Assets					
Current Assets					
Cash	$429,616	$1,802,122	$2,027,671	$2,491,434	$3,334,519
Accounts Receivable	291,667	483,333	833,333	1,333,333	1,916,667
Inventory	218,750	357,667	608,333	973,333	1,399,167
	940,033	2,643,122	3,469,337	4,798,100	6,650,353
Property & Equipment					
Office Equipment	20,000	20,000	20,000	20,000	20,000
Less Accumulated Depreciation	4,000	8,000	12,000	16,000	20,000
	16,000	12,000	8,000	4,000	0
Other Assets					
Deposits	5,000	5,000	5,000	5,000	5,000
	$961,033	$2,660,122	$3,482,337	$4,807,100	$6,655,353
Liabilities & Shareholders' Equity					
Current Liabilities					
Accounts Payable	164,063	268,250	456,250	730,000	1,049,375
Shareholders' Equity					
Common Stock	700,000	2,000,000	2,000,000	2,000,000	2,000,000
Retained Earnings	96,970	391,872	1,026,087	2,077,100	3,605,978
	796,970	2,391,872	3,026,087	4,077,100	5,605,978
	$961,033	$2,660,122	$3,482,337	$4,807,100	$6,655,353

(See notes to projected financial statements on page 380)

EXHIBIT 3

Alpha Electronics, Inc. Projected Statement of Income

	Quarter Ending				Year Ending				
	05/31/85	08/31/85	11/30/85	02/28/86	02/28/86	02/28/87	02/28/88	02/28/89	02/28/90
Sales	$262,000	$350,000	$525,000	$613,000	$1,750,000	$2,900,000	$5,000,000	$8,000,000	11,500,000
Cost of Sales	196,500	262,500	393,750	459,750	1,312,500	2,146,000	3,650,000	5,840,000	8,395,000
Less: Purchase Discount	(1,965)	(2,625)	(3,938)	(4,598)	(13,125)	(21,460)	(36,500)	(58,400)	(83,950)
Gross Profit	67,465	90,125	135,188	157,848	450,625	775,460	1,386,500	2,218,400	3,188,950
Expenses									
Advertising	1,250	1,250	1,250	1,250	5,000	5,000	7,500	7,500	7,500
Automobile Expense	2,685	2,685	2,685	2,685	10,740	16,110	21,480	21,480	26,850
Bad Debts	2,188	2,188	2,188	2,188	8,750	14,500	25,000	40,000	57,500
Commissions	0	0	0	0	0	105,000	138,000	225,000	300,000
Depreciation	1,000	1,000	1,000	1,000	4,000	4,000	4,000	4,000	4,000
Dues & Subscriptions	250	250	250	250	1,000	1,000	2,000	2,000	3,000
Equipment Rental	500	500	500	500	2,000	2,000	3,000	3,500	5,000
Freight In	250	250	250	250	1,000	1,250	1,500	2,200	2,500
Freight Out	403	403	403	403	1,610	2,208	2,875	4,088	5,888
Insurance—Group	3,000	3,000	3,000	3,000	12,000	16,800	24,000	28,000	36,000
Insurance—Other	750	750	750	750	3,000	3,000	3,000	6,400	6,400
Insurance—Workmen's Compensaion	2,188	2,188	2,188	2,188	8,750	9,600	11,700	16,500	21,000

Legal & Accounting	1,250	1,250	1,250	1,250	5,000	6,000	7,000	8,000	9,000
Miscellaneous	575	575	575	575	2,300	2,500	2,500	3,700	4,500
Office Supplies	375	375	375	375	1,500	2,000	3,500	4,000	5,000
Payroll Taxes	4,375	4,375	4,375	4,375	17,500	19,200	23,400	33,000	42,000
Postage	375	375	375	375	1,500	1,500	2,000	3,200	5,000
Property Taxes	250	250	250	250	1,000	1,000	1,000	2,000	2,000
Rent	4,725	4,725	4,725	4,725	18,900	32,400	32,400	32,400	96,000
Repairs & Maintenance	1,020	1,020	1,020	1,020	4,080	4,080	4,080	6,480	6,480
Salaries and Wages	43,750	43,750	43,750	43,750	175,000	87,000	96,000	105,000	120,000
Shipping	500	500	500	500	2,000	3,000	4,000	5,000	7,000
Stock Plan	0	0	0	0	0	0	11,700	16,500	21,000
Telephone	2,325	2,325	2,325	2,325	9,300	11,500	14,000	18,000	20,000
Travel & Entertainment	1,250	1,250	1,250	1,250	5,000	5,000	8,500	13,000	15,000
Utilities	600	600	600	600	2,400	2,700	3,000	6,400	6,400
	75,833	75,833	75,833	75,833	303,330	358,348	457,135	617,348	835,018
Income (loss) From Operations	(8,368)	14,293	59,355	82,015	147,295	417,112	929,365	1,601,052	2,353,032
Other Income— Interest	3,580	3,580	3,580	3,580	14,321	74,391	127,660	150,637	194,098
Net Income Before Income Taxes	(4,788)	17,873	62,935	85,595	161,616	491,503	1,057,025	1,751,689	2,548,130
Provision for Income Taxes— Current	0	5,234	25,174	34,238	64,646	196,601	422,810	700,676	1,019,252
Net Income	($4,788)	$12,639	$37,761	$51,357	$96,970	$294,902	$634,215	$1,051,013	$1,528,878

(See Notes to Projected Financial Statements)

Notes to Projected Financial Statements
for the Periods Ending February 28, 1985—February 28, 1990

1   Summary of significant accounting policies:
Accounts receivable trade:
   Uncollectable accounts will be written off and expensed to bad debts when
   management determines them to be uncollectable.
Property, equipment and depreciation:
   Office equipment is stated at cost. Depreciation will be provided over the estimated
   useful lives of the assets using the straight-line method.
2   Interest income:
   Interest income is calculated using a 10 percent interest rate on average cash balances.
3   Rent expense:
   Rent expense for the period ending February 28, 1986, is net of rent subsidized by
   lessor.
4   Inventory:
   Inventory will consist of electronic components for resale.
5   Income taxes:
   An effective federal and California State combined income tax rate of 40 percent has
   been used. Income tax liabilities are assumed to be paid currently.

EXHIBIT 4
Alpha Electronics, Inc. Projected Statement of Sources and Uses of Cash

	02/28/86	02/28/87	Year Ending 02/28/88	02/28/89	02/28/90
Source of Funds					
Cash Flow From Operations:					
Net Income	$ 96,970	$ 294,902	$ 634,215	$1,051,013	$1,528,878
Depreciation	4,000	4,000	4,000	4,000	4,000
Decrease (increase) in Inventory	(218,750)	(138,917)	(250,666)	(365,000)	(425,834)
Decrease (increase) in Accounts Receivable	(291,667)	(191,667)	(350,000)	(500,000)	(583,334)
Increase (decrease) in Accounts Payable	164,063	104,188	188,000	273,750	319,375
	(245,384)	72,506	225,549	463,763	843,085
Other Sources					
Common Stock	700,000	1,300,000	0	0	0
	454,616	1,372,506	225,549	463,763	843,085
Applications of Cash					
Deposits	5,000	0	0	0	0
Equipment Purchase	20,000	0	0	0	0
	25,000	0	0	0	0
Net Increase in Cash	429,616	1,372,506	225,549	463,763	843,085
Cash Balance—Beginning	0	429,616	1,802,122	2,027,671	2,491,434
Cash Balance—Ending	$429,616	$1,802,122	$2,027,671	$2,491,434	$3,334,519

EXHIBIT 5

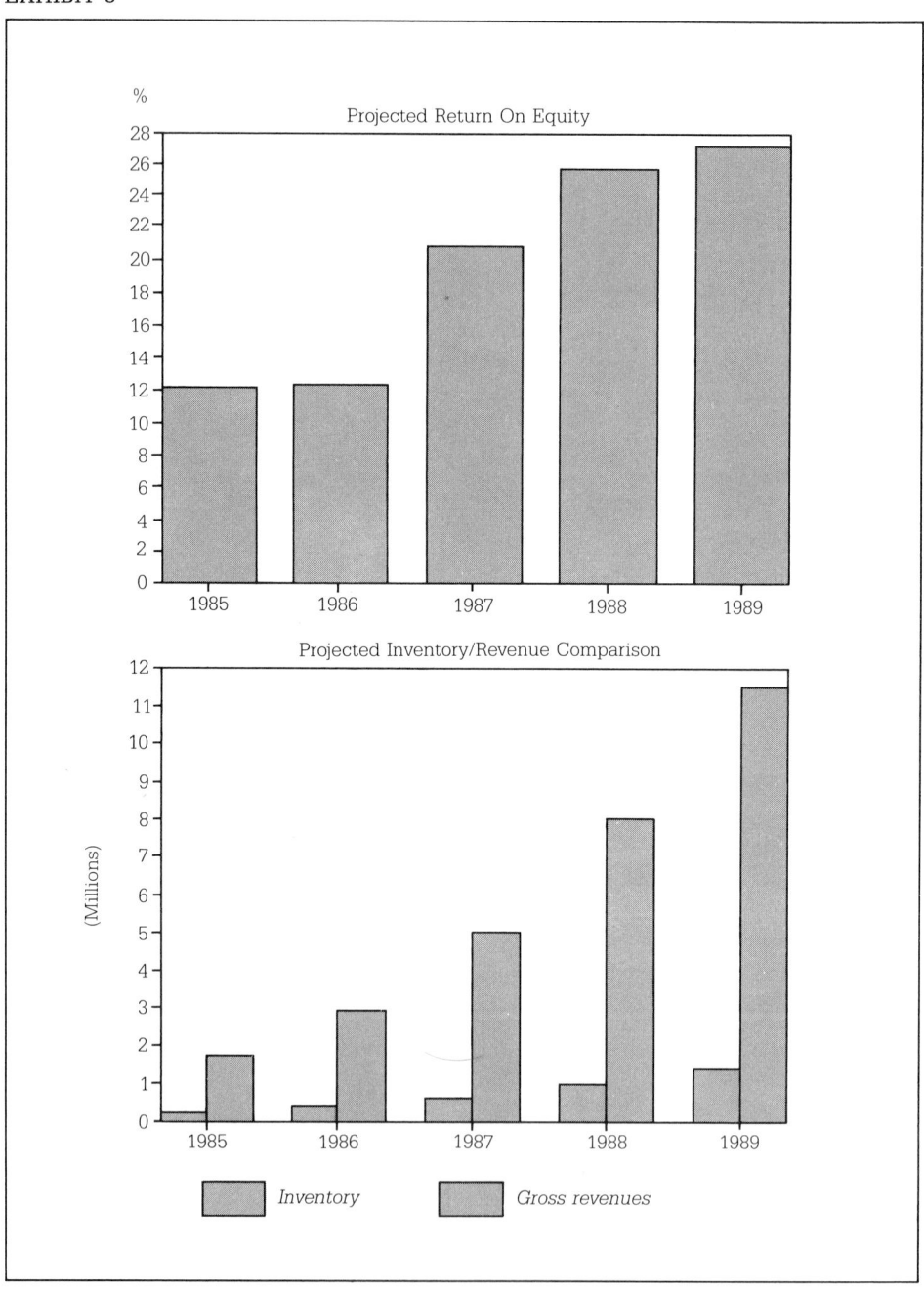

Alpha's Projected Financial Ratios

	1986	1987	1988	1989	1990	Industry Ave*
Current Ratio	5.73	9.85	7.60	6.57	6.34	3.00
Quick Ratio	4.40	8.52	6.27	5.24	5.00	1.50
Debt Ratio	.171	.101	.131	.152	.158	.46–.50
Debt/Equity	.215	.112	.151	.179	.187	.90–1.00
Inventory Turns	6	6	6	6	6	4.75
Total Asset Turn	1.82	1.09	1.44	1.66	1.73	1.75
Profit Margin	.055	.102	.127	.131	.133	.035
Ret. Total Asset	.101	.111	.182	.218	.230	.055–.075
Ret. Owner Equity	.122	.123	.209	.258	.273	.10–.155

*Source: Compustat: Wholesale Electronic Parts & Equipment, 1983.

EXHIBIT 6
Industry V-Curve Analysis

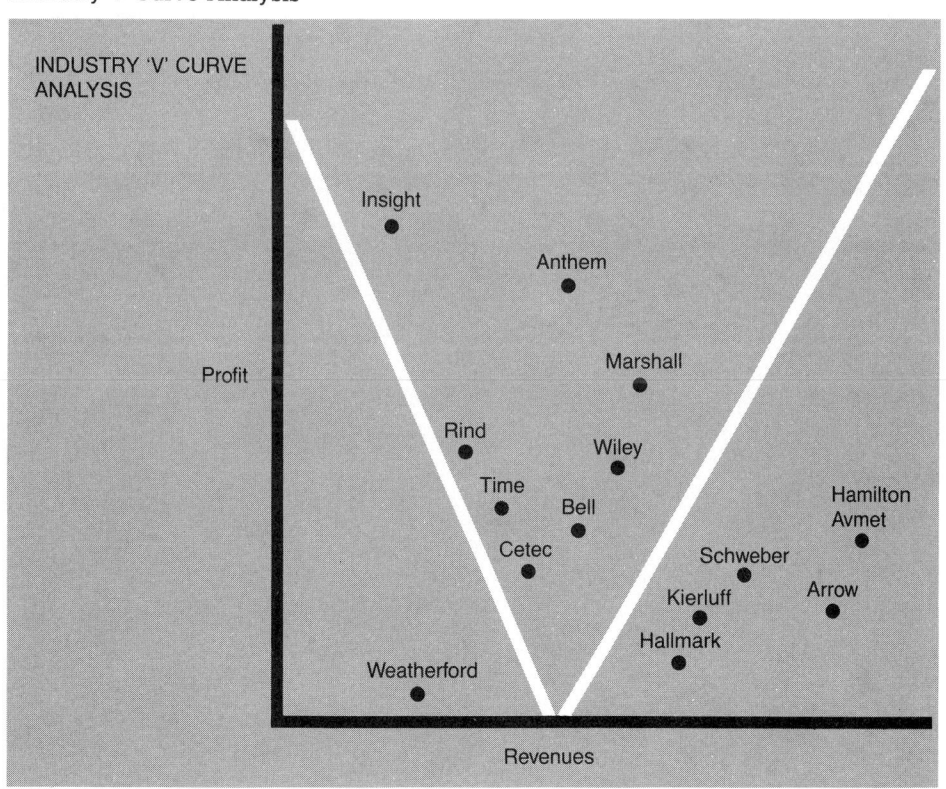

EXHIBIT 7
Organizational Structure

Board of Directors

President/COO, CFO

V.P. Sales Marketing

General Manager

Sales Manager   Operations Manager

Staff Projection

	Year				
	1	2	3	4	5
Management	1	1	1	1	1
Sales—Outside	1	2	3	3	4
Sales—Inside	1	1	2	2	3
Product Management	1	1	1	2	2
Support	1	2	3	4	5
Total	5	7	10	12	15

College Leasing, Inc.

Donald F. Harvey
Research Assistant: Robin Lensman

Robert Anderson, president of College Leasing, commented, "I have believed in this business from the very beginning." College Leasing, Inc., started out renting dorm refrigerators to West Coast University. The business was operated out of the family household. College Leasing now operates in four states and has over fifty employees. Its major emphasis in the past has been leasing dorm refrigerators to university students and operating rental shops located on military bases. College Leasing is, however, now moving into newer markets: leasing to the public, opening rent-to-own stores, and developing a wholesale business.

College Leasing may be divided into four strategic business units: (1) military; (2) college; (3) Pacific Sales; and (4) Pacific Rentals. Due to College Leasing's diversification and growth, it no longer can be viewed as a small family business. Consideration must now be given to restructuring the organization and implementing new strategic planning methods.

This case presents an overview of College Leasing's operations from a macro viewpoint. It deals with the management style of the organization, an analysis of the industries in which it is involved, and internal factors of the business.

PRODUCTS AND CUSTOMERS

The original mission of College Leasing, when it was formed in San Diego in 1970, was to provide appliance leases to college students and universities. Initially, mini-refrigerators were rented to students through individual contracts and major exclusive contracts through the universities. Later, College Leasing contracted with military bases; and equipment is now being rented to military bases in California, Hawaii, Georgia, and Alabama. These two areas are now taking a lesser role in College Leasing's overall plan, so that the company may pursue other markets with a higher growth potential.

Pacific Sales and Pacific Rental are College Leasing's new businesses, and both are trying to tap the high demand for consumer electronics such as televisions, video cassette recorders, and microwave ovens. Pacific Sales (appliance wholesaler)

This case was prepared as a basis for class discussion rather than to illustrate either effective or ineffective handling of an administrative situation. All company names, names of individuals, and facts and figures have been changed to assure anonymity.

is aimed at retail stores in southern California and in Mexico. Pacific Rentals is moving into the rent-to-own business stores aimed at the consumer. Pacific Rental's main customers are military personnel or low-income individuals who have not established credit or who have had trouble with their past credit record.

COMPETITION

Competition for College Leasing has, in the past, been minimal in San Diego. It has enjoyed strong market share position, and a lack of competition. In other areas north of San Diego and the three other operating regions (Georgia, Alabama, and Hawaii), College Leasing has not dominated the market. Polar Leasing, College Leasing's main competitor in college accounts, has maintained a strong 95 percent market share in these areas. Now, however, College Leasing is being threatened by the expansion of Polar Leasing into southern California.

Pacific Sales is moving into a market mainly dominated by a company called RTA. RTA currently holds 70 percent of the market share, while Pacific Sales holds a share of 20 percent, and other competitors retain about 10 percent. Pacific Sales is capitalizing on RTA's poor service and support and intends to acquire a larger market share by offering superior sales and service along with on-time delivery. Pacific Rentals is also moving into a market dominated by larger companies. In the rent-to-own market, there are many competitors. The main ones are RTO, Colortime, and Remco. Remco's recent acquisition of Curtis Mathis, another big competitor, now makes Remco a real threat.

CURRENT DEVELOPMENT STRATEGIES

Current plans do not extend very far into the future. Pacific Rentals plans to develop six new stores in San Diego within two years, then one store in Hawaii and one in the southern states. The company plans a slow phase-out policy in the military and college areas over the next few years. Pacific Sales plans to take over a larger portion of RTA's market share and will continue to develop an aggressive growth strategy.

In an effort to move away from the university leasing market, College Leasing is breaking into related new markets with high growth potential. College Leasing personnel supply and maintain the equipment in the military rental field with the exception of the U.S. Navy in San Diego which operates the business with its own personnel. College Leasing, however, prefers to manage the store with its own personnel.

College Leasing in the past year has expanded into serving the public as well as the military. This diversification strategy is twofold. First, College Leasing's contract with the Navy in San Diego expired in October of 1985. This arrangement had provided College Leasing with a monthly revenue of $37,000. Therefore, should College Leasing fail to renew this contract, it will already have a new facility off-base to utilize the existing customers of the on-base operations. Second, expanding into the rent-to-own stores provides additional growth revenue potential. Recently, College Leasing has penetrated the wholesale market under the name of Pacific Sales. This project involves purchasing the new equipment directly from the manufacturer and selling to retail stores in southern California and Mexico. This venture has proven to be highly profitable and expects to receive more attention in the future.

Corporate objectives at College Leasing are to:

1 Develop at a gradual, controlled pace.
2 Concentrate major growth in San Diego and current operation sites.
3 Seek additional products and services with a view toward diversification.

Management Style and Decision Making

Subtle power struggles among the family members exemplify the family-owned business atmosphere at College Leasing. The management decision making lies in the hands of the president, Robert Anderson, and his son, Vice President John Anderson. They also serve as two of the voting members of the company's board of directors. Because these two men serve as president and vice president and control half of the voting rights of the board, the company displays a highly centralized decision-making style. Although these two individuals carry much of the major decision-making power, they each display different management styles.

Robert Anderson, President or the "Colonel," as he is referred to by his family, exemplifies the characteristics of the classic gamesman. He assesses the degree of acceptable risk through market research and his own experience-based intuition. He is known for subscribing to as many as thirty magazines in order to broaden his knowledge of prospective business ventures. He is also fascinated by new fields and technologies. As a result of his awareness of new and changing markets, he has moved College Leasing into more profitable related areas. He has the power to influence the board members in his direction and accepts complete responsibility for the results of those decisions. Although he makes the major corporate decisions, the vice president has the authority to carry out necessary everyday decisions in response to the company's needs.

His son, John Anderson, possesses the qualities of an aggressive-competitive manager. His style is results-oriented, and he prefers face-to-face communications and control of all aspects of the organization from top management to delivery and maintenance personnel (see exhibit 1).

INDUSTRY ANALYSIS

Each of College Leasing's units competes in differing markets for the college and military segments. The market share is high in the San Diego regional market, but the industry growth is essentially zero. The income generated here could be used for expansion into other higher growth areas. Competition however, might easily erode College Leasing's high competitive advantage, shifting College Leasing's college and military units to a lower market share position.

Pacific Sales has low competitive position. This area is dominated by a company called RTA which has 70 percent of the market in Mexico and southern California. Pacific Sales' market share is 15 percent in Mexico and 5 percent in the United States. The industry growth is also slow. For this area, it should maximize short-term cash flow by cost-cutting or liquidation. Pacific Sales' short-term debt is financed by Borg-Warner. The Pacific Rentals' segment has a small market share in the rent-to-own business, but the industry growth is high.

The business strengths for College Leasing's military and college units are medium. Their market size is small and their growth rate is zero, but their market share in the San Diego market is high and their profitability is good. The industry attractiveness is also medium, because the market growth is zero and the competitive structure is high.

Pacific Sales' market share is low. However, its profitability is good and its growth rate is increasing, so the business strength factor is medium. The industry attractiveness is also medium, because the market growth is low and the competitive structure is high. The market size is large and there are few legal constraints.

Pacific Rentals has medium business strengths, but high industry attractiveness. Pacific Rentals has good financial backing, but little market share. The industry is growing quickly.

Environmental

College Leasing's military and college sectors are pursuing a conservative strategy. The environment stability is average; the growth is slow yet competition is increasing. College Leasing is taking a low adaptive position to keep its investment low in these areas. Pacific Rentals is in an environment with low stability and has a good adaptive orientation.

V-Curve Model

The V-curve model compares profits against revenues. It assumes that a V-type relationship exists as an organization starts out with low revenue and high profits. The company then moves into a middle stage with higher revenues and low profits before reaching a point of high revenues and high profits. The mature military and college segments are high in both revenues and profits. Pacific Sales is in the left end of the curve, with high profits in relation to low revenues. It is moving, with expansion, towards the middle of the V (see exhibit 2).

Government Policy and Regulation

In College Leasing's military and college segments, little or no government intervention exists. Contracts are fairly standard. Pacific Sales is also affected only slightly by government regulations. The future market share in Mexico is anticipated to be very positive. Sales revenues are increasing rapidly, and sales of $300 to $400 thousand can be expected by 1988. The environmental factors related to governmental actions should be monitored closely by Pacific Sales. The current import policy trends are for the most part favorable.

Pacific Rentals may be affected most by new laws concerning rent-to-own stores. Recently, a new law was passed requiring extensive disclosure of contract information. Another law in the works seeks to limit the total price charged for purchase of rental equipment.

INTERNAL ANALYSIS

Financial Analysis

College Leasing's sales revenue has achieved dynamic growth rates every year since the incorporation of the company, with the exception of the 1974 fiscal year. The highest growth rate was achieved from 1974 to 1975, with a sales growth rate of 93 percent. From 1980 to 1984, College Leasing obtained an average sales revenue growth rate of 36 percent. This impressive growth can be attributed to College Leasing's concentration on certain market segments that have grown faster than the industry. The service and equipment rental and leasing industry's sales revenue growth rate for the last five years has averaged only 4 percent. It is obvious that the industry in which College Leasing operates is a low-growth field. Yet College Leasing is generating revenue well above the industry median. This aggressive growth strategy is College Leasing's major financial strength (see exhibits 3, 4, and 5).

College Leasing has operated with a profit margin well above the industry median of 4.5 percent. Prior to 1984, the five-year profit margin average was 7.5 percent. The profit margin for 1984 dipped to less than 1 percent due to a sharp increase in the cost of sales. This increase was apparently caused by start-up expenses of the Pacific Sales' business segment. Previous to this start-up, College Leasing was not involved in selling products. They participated only in renting and leasing.

Debt Position   One of College Leasing's main objectives is to expand and diversify its products and markets. A prominent obstacle to this objective is the company's leverage position. The debt during the period from 1983 to 1984 equates to a long-term debt level of approximately 85 percent of total capital. The substantial increase of this ratio indicates that the company's dependence on debt financing has increased dramatically. This level of long-term debt represents almost four times the amount of the company's equity. Because creditors are understandably reluctant to lend additional investment capital, the company can't expect to receive additional debt financing from any institutional lenders. This lack of potential capital will hinder the expansion and diversification objectives that College Leasing has formulated. Highly leveraged firms are generally more vulnerable to business downturns than those with lower, more conservative debt positions.

Bank debt	$393,680
Borg-Warner loan	43,209
DeRocco/McLaughlin loan	130,287
Lyles loan	170,000
Credit union loans	53,982
Subtotal	$791,158
Notes payable—stockholder	274,625
Notes payable—student rentals	59,940
Total long-term debt	$1,125,723

Uncollectable Accounts

College Leasing has estimated that $40,000 to $60,000 of 1984's year-end accounts receivable will never be collected. Due to the nature of the rental and leasing business and College Leasing's dedication to service customers with little or no credit background, the estimated uncollectable accounts comprise approximately 24 percent of accounts receivable. Additionally, College Leasing has never acknowledged in their accounting system an allowance for doubtful accounts. In essence, accounts receivable has been overstated causing the quick and current ratios to yield inaccurate numbers.

Reporting of Financial Data   The current balance sheet and income statement for each operational division are currently being compiled for submission to corporate headquarters on a quarterly basis. Untimeliness of indications of cashflow advantages or deficiencies has caused delayed adjustments.

Organization Structure

The current organizational structure, presented in exhibit 1, is based on a regional and functional division of the organization. It is unclear in the middle to upper levels whether problems should be brought to the attention of the vice president or the comptroller. This uncertainty may lead to confusion among customers as well as employees.

Marketing

The marketing area is becoming a crucial one for College Leasing. Its move into the rent-to-own and wholesaling markets makes marketing more important than in its military and college segments. College Leasing's past marketing efforts have not needed to be well defined. With new, more competitive segments, its marketing skills need to be polished. The pricing, promotion, distribution, and product definition for each of College Leasing's strategic business units is examined in terms of marketing:

College Leasing (military) Pricing is set by contracts made with the military bases, and profit is based on a percentage of the sales made there. Distribution is determined by the position of the store on the bases. Very little is really done in the way of promotion, because the exclusive contracts guarantee customers from within the base.

College Leasing (College) Pricing is also set in the contracts made with the colleges, and profit is based on a percentage of sales. Promotion techniques, such as flyers and mailers at the beginning of semesters, as well as exclusive contracts are used.

Pacific Sales Pricing is a major factor in the wholesaling segment. Low prices are essential (10 percent to 14 percent) for the profit margin. Pacific Sales' strengths lie in its personal selling promotions that include good service and prompt delivery.

Pacific Rentals Promotion is critical. Stores must be located in low-income areas, and local papers must be used for advertising. Pacific Rentals currently offers a better selection of brands than its competitors, and its pricing policy is to price at or below the competition.

Human Resources

Employees are the lifeblood of any organization. The organization is no more effective than its employees. The ambiguities of College Leasing's current job titles and personnel evaluation system have led to a high turnover rate. College Leasing currently believes that it can easily replace employees without incurring excess training costs or reducing productivity. Its pay scale is low in comparison to comparable jobs in the industry.

CONCLUSION

College Leasing is a young and growing organization suffering from growing pains. It lacks organizational structure and centralized decision making. Its diversification strategies have resulted in problems with communications and monitoring growth. As President Robert Anderson and his management team plan for the future, they wonder what changes in strategy they should consider to maximize their strategic goals.

EXHIBIT 1
College Leasing Organizational Chart

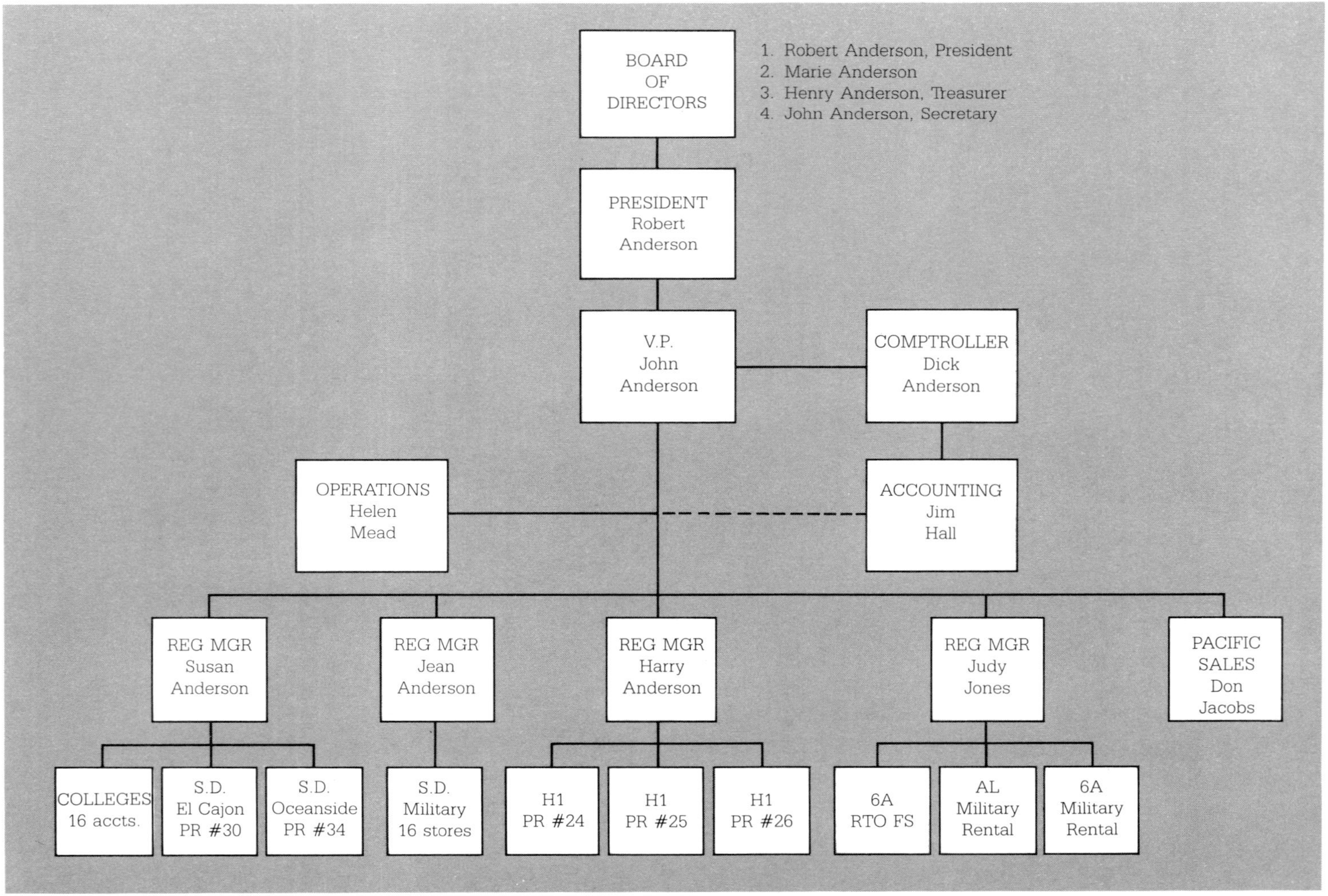

1. Robert Anderson, President
2. Marie Anderson
3. Henry Anderson, Treasurer
4. John Anderson, Secretary

BOARD OF DIRECTORS

PRESIDENT Robert Anderson

V.P. John Anderson

COMPTROLLER Dick Anderson

ACCOUNTING Jim Hall

OPERATIONS Helen Mead

REG MGR Susan Anderson

REG MGR Jean Anderson

REG MGR Harry Anderson

REG MGR Judy Jones

PACIFIC SALES Don Jacobs

COLLEGES 16 accts.

S.D. El Cajon PR #30

S.D. Oceanside PR #34

S.D. Military 16 stores

H1 PR #24

H1 PR #25

H1 PR #26

6A RTO FS

AL Military Rental

6A Military Rental

EXHIBIT 2
V-Curve

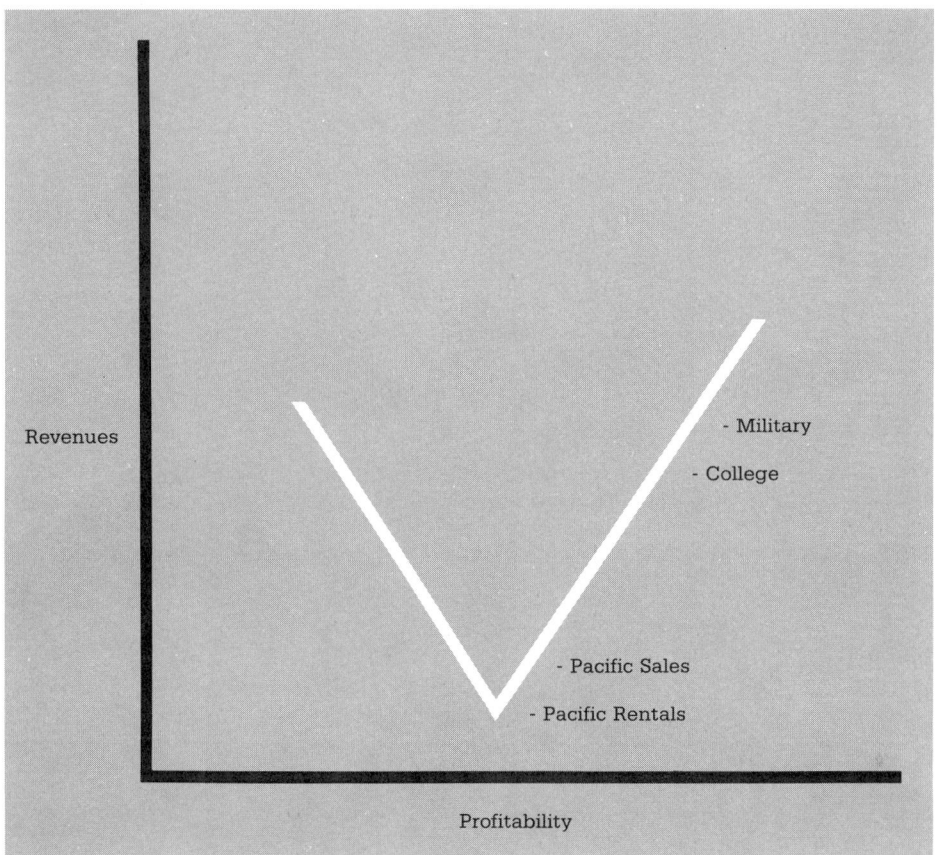

EXHIBIT 3
College Leasing Financial Reports and Pro Forma

	1982A	1983A	1984A	1985P	1986P	1987P	1988P	1989P	1990P
Assets									
Current Assets									
Cash in Bank	27569.00	28180.00	140788.00	172670.26	224471.34	291812.75	379356.57	493163.54	641112.60
Credit Union Share	76709.00	43074.00	2149.00	2158.38	2805.89	3647.66	4741.96	6164.54	8013.91
Petty Cash	.00	155.00	2650.00	3453.41	4489.43	5836.25	7587.13	9863.27	12822.25
Accts Receivable Trade	92944.00	81163.00	123097.00	151086.48	196412.43	255336.15	331937.00	431518.10	560973.53
Allow for Doubt Accts	.00	.00	.00	−15108.65	−19641.24	−25533.62	−33193.70	−4315181	−56097.35
Accts Receivable Shareholder	52633.00	4460.00	56000.00	64751.35	84176.75	109429.78	142258.71	184936.33	240417.23
Accts Receivable Employees	30679.00	44029.00	68281.00	86335.13	112235.67	145906.37	189678.29	246581.77	320556.30
Prepaid Taxes	.00	.00	3543.00	4316.76	5611.78	7295.32	9483.91	12329.09	16027.82
Inventory Watches	1187.00	553.00	553.00	647.51	841.77	1094.30	1422.59	1849.36	2404.17
Inventory Supplies	89.00	569.00	700.00	863.35	1122.36	1459.06	1896.78	2465.82	3205.56
Inventory	.00	.00	36662.00	43167.57	56117.84	72953.19	94839.14	123290.89	160278.15
Total Current Assets	281810.00	202183.00	434423.00	514341.55	668644.01	869237.22	1130008.4	1469010.9	1909714.2
Rental Equipment, at Cost									
Refrigerators	499140.00	510354.00	564472.00	733848.62	954003.21	1240204.2	1612265.4	2095945.0	2724728.6
Televisions	490755.00	590936.00	698247.00	906518.89	1178474.6	1532016.9	1991622.0	2589108.6	3365841.2

Others	47450.00	74465.00	240806.00	323756.75	420883.77	547148.90	711293.57	924681.64	1202086.1
Accum Deprecn	-414193.00	-553340.00	-700830.00	-906518.89	-1178474.6	-1532016.9	-1991622.0	-2589108.6	-3365841.2
Net Rental Equipment	623152.00	622415.00	802695.00	1057605.4	1374887.0	1787353.1	2323559.0	3020626.7	3926814.7
Property and Equipment, at Cost									
Furniture and Fixture	21356.00	43488.00	90642.00	107918.92	140294.59	182382.97	237097.86	308227.21	400695.38
Automobiles and Trucks	18915.00	33188.00	38112.00	43167.57	56117.84	72953.19	94839.14	123290.89	160278.15
Shop Equipment	3361.00	4193.00	4352.00	4316.76	5611.78	7295.32	9483.91	12329.09	16027.82
Building	.00	.00	663220.00	863351.32	1122356.7	1459063.7	1896782.9	2465817.7	3205563.0
Accm Depre	-19320.00	-26453.00	-52740.00	-64751.35	-84176.75	-109429.78	-142258.71	-184936.33	-240417.23
Net Property and Equip	24312.00	54416.00	743586.00	954003.21	1240204.2	1612265.4	2095945.0	2724728.6	3542147.1
Other Assets									
Security Deposits	1315.00	.00	.00	.00	.00	.00	.00	.00	.00
Escrows	2000.00	.00	.00	.00	.00	.00	.00	.00	.00
Deposits	.00	1715.00	12170.00	15108.65	19641.24	25533.62	33193.70	43151.81	56097.35
Cash Credit Union Rest	139706.00	473439.00	3541.00	4316.76	5611.78	7295.32	9483.91	12329.09	16027.82
Loan Fee	.00	.00	3865.00	4316.76	5611.78	7295.32	9483.91	12329.09	16027.82
Total Other Assets	143021.00	475154.00	19576.00	23742.16	30864.81	40124.25	52161.53	67809.99	88152.98
Total Assets	1072295.0	1354168.0	2000280.0	2549692.3	3314600.0	4308980.0	5601674.0	7282176.1	9466829.0

EXHIBIT 4
College Leasing Financial Reports

	1982A	1983A	1984A	1985P	1986P	1987P	1988P	1989P	1990P
Current Liabilities									
Notes Payable	258122.00	260388.00	454950.00	578780.15	752414.19	978138.45	1271580.0	1653054.0	2148970.2
Other Notes Payable	4786.00	4786.00	.00	.00	.00	.00	.00	.00	.00
Accounts Payable Trade	37860.00	46192.00	57007.00	71391.38	92808.80	120651.44	156846.87	203900.93	265071.21
Accrued Payroll Taxes	22613.00	11223.00	18922.00	22947.23	29831.40	38780.82	50415.07	65539.59	85201.46
Accrued Interest	7348.00	3916.00	16833.00	20397.54	26516.80	34471.84	44813.39	58257.41	75734.63
Sales Tax Payable	2239.00	1935.00	2980.00	3569.57	4640.44	6032.57	7842.34	10195.05	13253.56
Lease Deposits Payable	22000.00	37703.00	38357.00	48444.15	62977.40	81870.62	106431.81	138361.35	179869.75
Income Tax Payable	1995.00	1026.00	60.00	76.49	99.44	129.27	168.05	218.47	284.00
Total Current Liabilities	356963.00	367169.00	589109.00	745606.52	969288.47	1260075.0	1638097.5	2129526.8	2768384.8
Long-Term Debt									
Notes Payable LT	382169.00	527979.00	791158.00	1007128.5	1309267.0	1702047.1	2212661.2	2876459.6	3739397.4
Notes Payable Stockholder	123961.00	124047.00	274625.00	.00	.00	.00	.00	.00	.00
Notes Payable Student Rent	59940.00	59940.00	59940.0	73941.08	96123.40	124960.42	162448.54	211183.11	274538.04
Other Notes Payable LT	.00	.00	4786.00	5099.38	6629.20	8617.96	11203.35	14564.35	18933.66
Total Long-Term Debt	566070.00	711966.00	1130509.0	1086168.9	1412019.6	1835625.5	2386313.1	3102207.0	4032869.1
Total Liabilities	923033.00	1079135.0	1719618.0	1831775.4	2381308.1	3095700.5	4024410.6	5231733.8	6801253.9
Stockholder's Equity									
Capital Stock of No Par Value Authorized and Issued 1,000 Shares at Stated Value	100000.00	100000.00	100000.00	382762.00	563987.65	705364.17	889153.65	1128080.0	1438684.2
Retained Earnings	49267.00	175033.00	180662.00	262680.38	369304.26	507915.32	688109.69	922362.37	1226890.9
Total Stockholder Equity	149262.00	275033.00	280662.00	717916.86	933291.91	1213279.5	1577263.3	2050442.3	2665575.0
Total Liabilities and Equity	1072295.0	1354168.0	2000280.0	2549692.3	3314600.0	4308980.0	5601674.0	7282176.1	9466829.0
Financial Ratios									
Liquidity Ratios									
Current Ratio	.79	.55	.74	.69	.69	.69	.69	.69	.69

Industry Current Ratio	.90	.90	.90	.90	.90	.90	.90	.90	.90
Quick Ratio	.79	.55	.67	.63	.63	.63	.63	.63	.63
Industry Current Ratio	.60	.60	.60	.60	.60	.60	.60	.60	.60
Asset Utilization									
Average Collection Period	64.56	34.31	54.38	48.55	48.55	48.55	48.55	48.55	48.55
Industry Average Coll Period	43.00	43.00	43.00	43.00	43.00	43.00	43.00	43.00	43.00
Average Daily Sales	2730.25	3779.22	4548.74	5913.37	7687.37	9993.59	12991.66	16889.16	21955.91
Sales Per Employee	16073.23	22248.61	26778.89	34812.55	45256.32	58833.21	76483.18	99428.13	129256.57
Inventory Turnover	780.99	1229.42	43.79	48.31	48.31	48.31	48.31	48.31	48.31
Industry Inventory Turnover	45.00	45.00	45.00	45.00	45.00	45.00	45.00	45.00	45.00
Total Asset Turnover	.93	1.02	.83	.85	.85	.85	.85	.85	.85
Industry Total Asset Turnover	1.00	1.00	1.00	1.00	1.00	1.00	1.00	1.00	1.00
Debt Management									
Debt Total Asset	.86	.80	.86	.72	.72	.72	.72	.72	.72
Industry Debt Total Assets	.63	.63	.63	.63	.63	.63	.63	.63	.63
Debt to Equity	3.79	2.59	4.03	1.51	1.51	1.51	1.51	1.51	1.51
Industry Debt to Equity	2.30	2.30	2.30	2.30	2.30	2.30	2.30	2.30	2.30
Profitability									
Profit Margin	.08	.09	.00	.04	.04	.04	.04	.04	.04
Industry Profit Margin	.05	.05	.05	.05	.05	.05	.05	.05	.05
Return on Investment	.07	.09	.00	.03	.03	.03	.03	.03	.03
Industry Return on Investment	.05	.05	.05	.05	.05	.05	.05	.05	.05
Return on Equity	.53	.45	.02	.11	.11	.11	.11	.11	.11
Industry Return on Equity	.15	.15	.15	.15	.15	.15	.15	.15	.15
Number of Common Shares Outstanding	1000.00	1000.00	1000.00	1000.00	1000.00	1000.00	1000.00	1000.00	1000.00
Earnings Per Share	79.09	124.77	5.63	82.02	106.62	138.61	180.19	234.25	304.53

EXHIBIT 5
College Leasing Financial Reports and Pro Forma

	1982A	1983A	1984A	1985P	1986P	1987P	1988P	1989P	1990P
Statement of Income and Retained Earnings									
Revenue Sales	996540.00	1379414.0	1660291.0	2158378.3	2805891.8	3647659.3	4741957.1	6164544.3	8013907.5
Costs and Operating Expenses									
Cost of Sales	.00	2496.00	82481.00	43167.57	56117.84	72953.19	94839.14	123290.89	160278.15
Saleries and Wages	185616.00	239732.00	306324.00	388508.09	505060.52	656578.68	853552.28	1109618.0	1442503.4
Commission	199780.00	348438.00	397906.00	518010.79	673414.03	875438.24	1138069.7	1479490.6	1923337.8
Advertising	4703.00	3423.00	12831.00	15108.65	19641.24	25533.62	33193.70	43151.81	56097.35
Amortization	.00	.00	750.00	863.35	1122.36	1459.06	1896.78	2465.82	3205.56
Automobile	23527.00	25924.00	25288.00	32375.67	42088.38	54714.89	71129.36	92468.16	120208.61
Contributions	20.00	282.00	905.00	1079.19	1402.95	1823.83	2370.98	3082.27	4006.95
Bad Debt Expense	.00	73332.00	52090.00	66909.73	86982.65	113077.44	147000.67	191100.87	248431.13
Depreciation	124613.00	161665.00	189948.00	237421.61	308648.10	401242.53	521615.28	678099.87	881529.83
Equipment Rental	6862.00	8567.00	5688.00	6475.13	8417.68	10942.98	14225.87	18493.87	2404172
Employees Medical	.00	1715.00	451.00	431.68	561.18	729.53	948.39	1232.91	1602.78
Freight	14008.00	8247.00	20903.00	28058.92	36476.59	47419.57	61645.44	80139.08	104180.80
Insurance	25232.00	17190.00	31937.00	41009.19	53311.94	69305.53	90097.19	117126.34	152264.24
Interest	69598.00	117833.00	126220.00	155403.24	202024.21	262631.47	341420.91	443847.19	577001.34
Miscellaneous	19428.00	6596.00	3499.00	4316.76	5611.78	7295.32	9483.91	12329.09	16027.82

Office	32481.00	30478.00	48435.00	62592.97	81370.86	105782.12	137516.76	178771.78	232403.32
Penalties	2875.00	1211.00	2540.00	2158.38	2805.89	3647.66	4741.96	6164.54	8013.91
Professional Fees	46774.00	22421.00	32619.00	43167.57	56117.84	72953.19	94839.14	123290.89	160278.15
Rent	15075.00	18826.00	50276.00	64751.35	84176.75	109429.78	142258.71	184936.33	240417.23
Repair and Maintenance	49858.00	56675.00	64660.00	82018.38	106623.89	138611.05	180194.37	234252.68	304528.49
Storage	5780.00	6257.00	5407.00	6475.13	8417.68	10942.98	14225.87	18493.63	24041.72
Taxes and Payroll	25962.00	22040.00	29646.00	36692.43	47700.16	62010.21	80613.27	104797.25	136236.43
Taxes Other	829.00	1076.00	3129.00	2158.38	2805.89	3647.66	4741.96	6164.54	8013.91
Technicians	.00	.00	39114.00	49642.70	64535.51	83896.16	109065.01	141784.52	184319.87
Telephone	22158.00	18181.00	30034.00	43167.57	56117.84	72953.19	94839.14	123290.89	160278.15
Temporary Labor	49461.00	48621.00	44585.00	64751.35	84176.75	109429.78	142258.71	184936.33	240417.23
Travel and Entertainment	35951.00	42106.00	60126.00	86335.13	112235.67	145906.37	189678.29	246581.77	320556.30
Total Costs and Expenses	960591.00	1283332.0	1667792.0	2083050.9	2707966.2	3520356.0	4576462.8	5949401.7	7734222.2
Other Income									
Interest Earned	7151.00	25609.00	8911.00	8633.51	11223.57	14590.64	18967.83	24658.18	32055.63
Gain on Sales of Assets	39586.00	8138.00	4692.00	4316.76	5611.78	7295.32	9483.91	12329.09	16027.82
Miscellaneous	960.00	85.00	−213.00	215.84	280.59	364.77	474.20	616.45	801.39
Total Other Income	47697.00	33832.00	13390.00	13166.11	17115.94	22250.72	28925.94	37603.72	48884.84
Net Earning Before Income Taxes	83646.00	129914.00	5889.00	88493.51	115041.56	149554.03	194420.24	252746.31	328570.21
Income Taxes	4554.00	5146.00	260.00	6475.13	8417.68	10942.98	14225.87	18493.63	24041.72

EXHIBIT 6
College Leasing

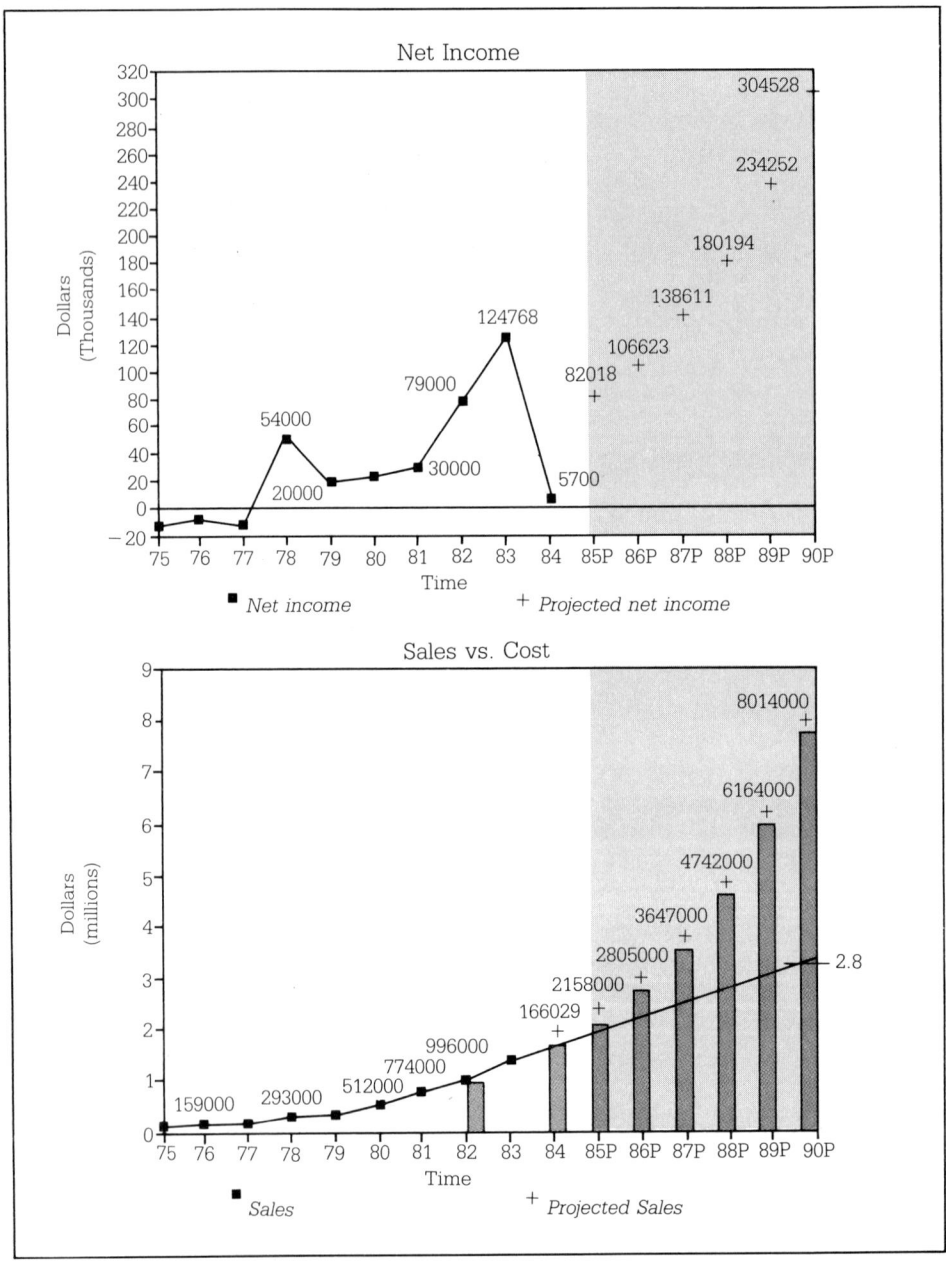

Net Income

320
300
280
260
240
220
200
180
160
140
120
100
80
60
40
20
0
−20

Dollars (Thousands)

304528 +
234252 +
180194 +
138611 +
124768
106623 +
82018 +
79000
54000
30000
20000
5700

75 76 77 78 79 80 81 82 83 84 85P 86P 87P 88P 89P 90P

Time

■ Net income   + Projected net income

Sales vs. Cost

9
8
7
6
5
4
3
2
1
0

Dollars (millions)

8014000 +
6164000 +
4742000 +
3647000 +
2805000 +
2158000 +
166029 +
996000
774000
512000
293000
159000
2.8

75 76 77 78 79 80 81 82 83 84 85P 86P 87P 88P 89P 90P

Time

■ Sales   + Projected Sales

CASE 8 ■ ■ ■
SeaFlite (Revised)

Jimmy D. Barnes
Viki Arbas
Revised by Hugh O. Hunter

INTRODUCTION

SeaFlite jetfoil ships were introduced to Hawaii in June 1975, marking the first water transport system since 1948. For two and one-half years Pacific Sea Transportation, Ltd., operated the jetfoil service amid mounting losses. The losses, caused by technical problems and disappointing passenger revenues, resulted in a cessation of operations by the end of 1977. In spite of a continuing interest in the state in a water transport system, additional financing for SeaFlite did not materialize, and the three ships were sold to a Hong Kong company.

In mid-1979, the owner of a Waikiki hotel bought one Boeing jetfoil ship. He announced that the new ship would transport passengers between the islands of Oahu and Maui by mid-1981. The jetship cost $10.8 million and an additional $3 million was to be spent on accessories. The total capital investment was estimated to be $18 million by 1981. (See exhibit 1.)

The dimensions of the new jetfoil were to remain the same as its predecessors', but the propulsion features and design would be improved. The new ship would hold 270 passengers, compared to 190 in the earlier ships. It was estimated that the new ship would have to run at 47 percent capacity for the two trips per day to be profitable. Fares were to remain in line with airline fares. A new jetfoil would be purchased one year from the beginning of operations, if demand proved high enough.

It was estimated that 60 employees would be hired, including a crew of 13 for the ship.

The Public Utilities Commission of Hawaii transferred the operating licenses to the new owner. The State Department of Transportation signed over the leases for the existing harbors on Honolulu and Maalaea in Maui. It was a promise for a new, more modest beginning of private industry implementing a waterway system between the Hawaiian Islands. The question was whether the company could achieve long-range survival where the prior company could not.

Following is an overview of the history of operation of Pacific Sea Transportation, Ltd., which had run the SeaFlite system and had failed.

HISTORY

The major industry of the state of Hawaii is tourism. Visitors who stayed overnight or longer in Hawaii numbered:

1975—2,830,000

1976—3,220,000

1977—3,434,000

During this period, the major interisland airlines reported 15,754,000 total revenue passengers. Visitors made up about half of those traveling between islands (see exhibit 2).

Oahu, home of the state capital of Honolulu and the famed resort of Waikiki, was the most heavily populated and traveled island. Traffic congestion was a problem in the higher density areas, particularly between the airport and Waikiki, as well as between the downtown business district and the residential suburb of Hawaii Kai.

Oahu's neighbor islands were basically agricultural, and population and per capita income were declining. The island of Maui had the fastest growing resort-destination traffic, and tourism contributed some revenues and jobs on the other islands.

Air traffic to and from Honolulu had increased dramatically over the years. Amid concern over congestion in the Honolulu area, there was also a strong desire by the state to encourage travel to and development of the neighboring islands. The results were creation of an Oahu General Aviation Master Plan to study air traffic dispersal, and creation of a state task force to study the feasibility of a marine highway.

Two types of marine service were studied. One was interisland passenger service; the other was a shuttle service between primary destination points on Oahu. The interisland service showed promise, but the shuttle concept seemed doomed for three reasons:

1 the harbor at Waikiki was dominated by pleasure yachts and boats which rendered it unusable.
2 no way was seen to provide fast and efficient baggage handling.
3 a large number of vessels required to provide peak period service would lie idle the rest of the time.

Interest in interisland service had begun in the 1950s. A number of studies had resulted, most centering on some sort of ferry service for passengers, autos and cargo. While these studies had generated questionable demand and cost forecasts, they did provide some consistent and useful findings. Among them were

1 The public indicated enthusiasm for water travel, but intentions to ride the ferry were more wishful thinking than a forecast of actual use.

2   There was some debate as to whether the ferry system could be handled by private enterprise without government subsidies.
3   Breakdowns could cancel the service altogether.
4   There was a strong preference among local residents for air travel.
5   Success hinged on low fares and fast, comfortable rides.
6   Although travel by air has the advantage of speed, high costs preclude it ever becoming the prime mover of people to the outer islands.
7   Demand for travel is price inelastic.
8   Patronage of a ferry system was dependent on sea conditions and was seasonal.
9   Passenger and cargo transport did not appear to be a good mix.
10 There was some opposition to the ferry by the public because of the long travel time involved.

In the mid-1970s two companies were providing marine transport service on Oahu. The most ambitious was the Sea Transit which operated a commuter run between Pearl Harbor, Hickam, and Iroquois Point. It charged 50¢ for the ride, and $1.00 each way for a trip between Kewalo Basin and Iroquois Point. Sea Transit also operated a Pearl Harbor cruise, but at $5.00 it was more expensive than some competing cruises. Sea Transit operated between 1972 and 1978.

The other company operated the Paradise Cruise which provided lavish and expensive excursions during the day. At night, it became a floating restaurant for a 2½ hour dinner cruise. On Saturdays, at 9 P.M., the boat would leave Kewalo Basin for a "disco rock boogie party." The business was sold in March 1978.

THE COMPANIES

SeaFlite resulted from a partnership between two giants in the aerospace industry— Boeing Company and LTV Corporation. Each had a great deal to gain from the partnership, LTV through its existing operating subsidiary in Hawaii, and Boeing through the sale of its hydrofoil ships.

Boeing

By the early 1970s, with the war in Vietnam coming to a close, Boeing was seeking commercial applications for some of its military hardware. Once in a while the application of military technology to commercial use can be phenomenally successful, as in the case of the 707 jetliner.

Some years earlier, Boeing had produced a 60-ton hydrofoil gunboat for the Navy called the Tucumcari. This was being converted into a 110-ton, 90 by 31 ft jetfoil capable of speeds of 48 to 52 miles per hour (42–45 knots).

Surface piercing hydrofoils were in use in Florida, travelling between the Keys and the Bahamas. These, however, had a tendency to roll over in waves six feet or more high. A submerged hydrofoil was then developed which could take waves up to ten feet high. Waters around the Hawaiian Islands exceed ten feet no more than 10 percent of the time year-round.

These ships were propelled by an inboard system of gas turbines which does to water what the jet plane does to air. Thus it was named the Jetfoil. The forward speed caused the vessel to lift several feet above the surface, minimizing water resistance. The ships were able to turn in short distances like banking aircraft. The Jetfoil could hold up to 250 passengers, but a model seating 190 was selected for SeaFlite operations.

LTV

LTV was a formerly highly successful Dallas-based conglomerate, engaged in aerospace, steel, and meat packing as its primary industries. As with many conglomerates, the end of the 1960s brought hard times, and in 1970, LTV nearly failed. As part of its survival strategy, the corporation began to expand into tourist-related activities, and by the mid 1970s, owned a Mexican hotel and a Colorado ski resort.

Kentron Hawaii, Ltd.

Kentron Hawaii was the catalyst bringing together these two corporate giants into the SeaFlite venture. Kentron is a subsidiary of LTV's Aerospace Division. It provides logistical and technical support to various government agencies on Hawaii, including the Department of Defense, NASA, and the Federal Aviation Agency. The company is also engaged in commercial tourist services in Hawaii.

Kentron had earlier participated in the Oahu General Aviation Master Plan. It had also produced a study for the state on an airport–Waikiki marine shuttle service. Kentron was hoping to be able to offer this service for an investment of $30 million. The planned fare was $4. The idea was shelved when no adequate harbor facility could be found on Waikiki.

With the shuttle service providing little promise, attention was shifted to interisland service. Kentron, through its participation in state marine transport studies, was aware that speed would be a primary factor in passenger acceptance. To provide the necessary speed, a high technology craft would have to be used. The British Hovercraft, which rides on a cushion of air, was considered, but it was deemed unsuited to the unpredictable Hawaiian currents, and it was excessively noisy.

Two U.S. companies, Grumman and Boeing, had been developing commercial models of hydrofoil ships which had originally been designed for military service. Versions of the hydrofoil models had been operating for some twenty years outside the English Channel between London and Ostend, France. Some were also operating on inland waterways in the Soviet Union.

Safety was a key factor in these models. Not a single fatality had occurred over some two billion passenger miles, and only very infrequent mishaps had occurred. However, Hawaii's rougher seas between islands, particularly through the Molokai channel, would prove to be a tougher test of the hydrofoil's technical capabilities.

Kentron's president became interested in Boeing's design of a passenger ship fashioned from a 60-ton hydrofoil gunboat, which had been used in Vietnam. Boeing had sold two of these to the Far East Hydrofoil Co. for the Hong Kong route, and was investigating further potential markets. Ultimately, Hawaii was to be a showcase for Boeing's jetfoils.

Pacific Sea Transportation, Ltd.

A decision by Boeing and Kentron to proceed with interisland jetfoil service resulted in the formation, in February 1973, of Pacific Sea Transportation, Ltd. (PSTL), owned 75 percent by Kentron and 25 percent by Boeing. The ships, purchased from Boeing at $4.8 million each, were named SeaFlite. The venture received the encouragement and support of the state administration and legislature.

From 1973 to June 1975, development of facilities was undertaken and SeaFlite was promoted. Because of the need to tailor the facilities on the ships themselves, PSTL elected to develop their own facilities. Terminals were built or upgraded on four islands: Pier 8 downtown Honolulu on Oahu, Nawiliwili on Kauai, Mallaea on Maui, and Kawaihae on Hawaii. The cost of facilities was $2.8 million.

Delivery of the new jetfoils to Hawaii was scheduled for November 1974, after testing in Puget Sound, Lake Washington, and the ocean. The delivery was first delayed until January 1975, and an accident at the Boeing plant caused further delay until May 1975.

On June 15, 1975, the first hydrofoil ship began service between islands, followed by the second in August and the third in October. By this time, an additional $6 million over the purchase price of the ships had been allocated to the program. (See exhibit 3 for Interisland Transportation Routes.)

SeaFlite was totally financed by private capital. The only indirect support was by the seventh legislature, which excluded use tax on the import of the three hydrofoils, and by the use of Title xi Maritime Administration Insurance on bonds which were sold by Pacific Sea Transportation. The company's goals, at that time, were to:

1 appeal to half the current interisland air travel market
2 develop greater demand for travel by promoting a mixed mode of travel: by surface and air, thus offsetting any passenger losses due to airlines
3 show a profit by 1977

4 service additional areas such as Molokai, Kahalui on Maui, Hilo on the Big Island
    of Hawaii, and Lanai, expanding the service to 18 ships by 1995
5 develop waterways connecting Oahu destination points

A plan developed in 1975 was to dredge near Hawaii Kai on Oahu to open a
channel for SeaFlite, connecting with downtown. Since nonpeak hours of interisland service were in the morning and late afternoon, a commuter service was
planned for these hours. This plan called for the state to purchase the ships, then
priced at $7 million each, and PSTL would lease them for operating the runs. Moon-
light rides could also be added for additional revenues. Some 80 percent of the
dredging costs could potentially have been financed by federal highway funds, in
conjunction with the Marine Highway proposal. This plan, however, was never
carried through.

Another plan developed to coordinate services with Young Brothers, a local
interisland marine cargo transportation company. The plan centered around jointly
transporting passengers and their autos. This idea also was dropped.

Other plans also died in their infancy, one for transporting sports fans to and
from Aloha Stadium, and another to have the state take over SeaFlite facilities.
SeaFlite contended that this latter transfer of facilities would simply put them on an
equal footing with other marine transport companies and the airlines, all of whom
used state facilities.

HYDROFOIL OPERATIONS IN HAWAII

Reliability

In the first year of operations, SeaFlite's vessels experienced 20 to 30 percent downtime, mostly due to mechanical failures. Only two weeks after the maiden voyage,
on a busy Fourth of July weekend, the two large turbines of the only ship then in
operation failed. As the ship skimmed over choppy water, it lifted six feet out of the
water, causing air to hit a water intake vent. The interruption of the flow of water
caused the engine to automatically shut down. The boat plopped in the water and
tossed about in the waves.

This automatic shutdown when air was ingested into the engine and chronic
gearbox problems caused SeaFlite's reliability to be below expectations. The gear-
boxes had an expected life of three years, but SeaFlite went through twenty in its
first year, at a cost of $200,000 each. There was also incidental damage from high
waves, and a fire aboard one of the ships. All of these meant that the third ship had
to be retained for what was essentially a two-ship schedule.

Boeing flew technicians to Hawaii to redesign some of its most troublesome
engine parts. Boeing honored all of its parts warranties, but some of the subcon-

tractors did not, claiming that usage had been harder than originally specified. SeaFlite ships in drydock became a common sight for passing motorists on the main highway between the airport and downtown Honolulu.

Costs

Total employment costs were higher than expected. In 1972, labor costs had been projected as:

On Oahu—69 full time, 12 part time, $750,000 per year

Other islands—2 full time, 3 part time $27,000 per year

By the second year of operations, actual employment figures were:

On Oahu—41 full time, 32 part time

Other islands—11 full time, 36 part time.

In 1978, after the close of operations, PSTL disclosed the following costs during its operating life:

$17,978,000 for materials, services, and labor
    252,918 paid to the state department of transportation for rent of state land and facilities.

In addition, the company had paid a public service tax of 4 percent of revenues. Diesel oil consumption had been projected at 420 gallons per hour at $200 per hour. Actual consumption was 560 gallons per hour.
    Operational losses were as follows:

1973	$209,000
1974	424,000
1975	1,990,000
1976	3,950,000
1977	4,494,000
Total	$11,077,000

Schedule Performance

Because of the continuing mechanical problems, on-time performance of SeaFlite was poor. (See exhibit 6: The Schedule of Departure and Arrival Times.) SeaFlite had planned ten trips daily. However, it seldom operated more than eight trips, and for a time, only six.

MARKETING AND COMPETITION

The Airlines

SeaFlite's primary competitors were the two major interisland airlines, Aloha and Hawaiian. The airlines had been in service for twenty-five years, and, in the mid-1970s were operating without federal subsidy. Hawaiian flew DC-9 jets, seating 138 passengers. Aloha flew 118-seat Boeing 737 jets. The airlines served all the major islands. Each had twenty-eight flights per day between Kauai and Honolulu, and forty flights between Maui and Honolulu.

Hawaiian and Aloha Airlines	1975	1976	1977
Total revenue passengers	4,787,000	5,263,000	5,724,000
Combined operating profits		$2,318,000	$2,193,000
Load factor	65.3%	64.3%	65.8%
Breakeven factor	65.1%	61.6%	65.6%

SeaFlite in the Interisland Passenger Market

The breakeven load factor for SeaFlite had been calculated at 54 percent for the ten scheduled trips per day. In 1977, the actual load factor was 38–40 percent. Passengers carried for the three years of operations were:

1975	69,000
1976	195,000
1977	260,000

SeaFlite served two publics, visitors to Hawaii and local residents. In its last year of operation, SeaFlite's passenger mix was 70 percent tourist and 30 percent resident. The two interisland airlines by contrast had approximately a fifty-fifty mix. (See a profile of Hawaii's visitors, appendix 1.)

In 1975, the *Honolulu Star-Bulletin* conducted a survey of local interisland travelers. It found that 96 percent had used an airline for their most recent business trip, as had 94 percent for their most recent nonbusiness trip. Only 6.2 percent had traveled on SeaFlite.

In 1976, the Hawaii Chamber of Commerce found that about one-third of the local travelers travel on business, while 80 percent travel for pleasure. (Some, obviously, do both.)

Terminal Location

Only in Honolulu did SeaFlite enjoy a locational advantage over the airlines. While the airport was 15–20 minutes driving time from downtown, SeaFlite was within walking distance. Advertising was directed to Honolulu business people, but this market never developed.

On the island of Hawaii, the SeaFlite terminal at Kawaihae was thirty miles from the popular destination area of Kona, while Ke-ahole Airport is only seven miles. The area surrounding the SeaFlite terminal maintained only 4 percent of the island's population. Another airport at Hilo directly served that popular community.

On Maui, the SeaFlite terminal was at Maalaea, which is close to the popular resort of Lahaina. The airport at Kahalui serves a region which contains 92 percent of the island's population.

Pricing

Both SeaFlite and the airlines operated as common carriers, with fares regulated by the State Public Utilities Commission. Fares were set to provide a fair rate of return on investment.

Fares for the major airlines were regulated by the Civil Aeronautics Board. These airlines offered a common fare for travel between the neighboring islands and Oahu with purchase of a round-trip ticket between Hawaii and the mainland. The Common Fare Plan applied only to interisland trips made by air. Under this plan, visitors could fly between islands for $13. SeaFlite's fare was $22. SeaFlite was not incorporated into the Common Fare Plan until early 1977.

During its brief life, SeaFlite experimented with a number of promotional fares. These included a $5 annual "membership" which entitled the passenger to a 15 percent discount. SeaFlite also offered military standby, youth, and group fares.

Between the two airlines, there was no price competition. Both charged the same fare. They also used promotional fares extensively. In 1976, they introduced Travel Clubs, which, for a membership fee of $5, allowed residents the same fares as those in the Common Fare Plan. The Travel Clubs also allowed fare reductions of 20 percent to 50 percent for off-hours trips.

Advertising and Promotion

Both SeaFlite and the airlines used mainland airline booking agents, tour operators, and travel agents to book visitors' travel.

SeaFlite's advertising budget was set at 3 percent of revenue after an initial promotional campaign. Advertising was directed, in more or less equal proportions, to the resident and visitors markets.

Advertising in the local print and broadcast media began in July 1975 and stressed novelty and scenic rides. Tourist advertising featured the navigational history of Hawaii, as well as repeated references to "flying" on SeaFlite. Departures were called "takeoffs" and journeys, "flights." Special flights were arranged for environmental groups, charities, and educational organizations. SeaFlite services were also provided to the *Hawaii 5-0* television series.

	1976	1977
Hawaiian Airlines		
Promotion and Sales Expense	$10,792,066	$12,185,998
Passenger Revenues	$57,243,393	$61,718,255
Aloha Airlines		
Promotion and Sales Expense	$ 8,388,827	$ 9,421,091
Passenger Revenues	$44,177,172	$47,851,442

PACIFIC SEA TRANSPORTATION, LTD. IN 1978

Late in 1977, in an effort to keep SeaFlite alive, the stockholders of PSTL sought a buyer for the company. When none materialized, SeaFlite operations were suspended and the three jetfoils sold to the Far East Hydrofoil Company for $5 million each. To date, these ships remain in service between Hong Kong and Macao.

The State Administration and the Governor's Advisor on Marine Affairs opposed the suspension of operations and sale of the ships, contending that such service was important to the state. The Public Utilities Commission, which granted permission for the suspension and sale, asked that PSTL continue to try to find a suitable operator. Through part of 1978, PSTL retained some key personnel, continued to search for a buyer, and made rental payments to the state for the terminal facilities.

Under terms of the facilities lease agreement with the state, PSTL was prohibited from subleasing the facilities. Finally, by August, 1978, PSTL's payments to the state were nearly half a million dollars in arrears, and the company proposed state takeover of the facilities.

In 1978, the state, along with the major airlines flying to Hawaii, began to extensively advertise travel to Oahu's neighboring islands. Advertisements appeared in *National Geographic, People, Smithsonian, Time, Newsweek,* and *Better Homes and Gardens.*

Thus, as the state continued to promote interisland travel, and encourage a sea transport system, a new operator came on the scene, and promised resumption of jetfoil service in 1981.

EXHIBIT 1

Projected Operating Expenses, 1980

Parking lot rent	$ 39,600
Rent	45,700
Maintenance	14,000
Utilities	13,120
Guard service	1,415
Property manager	18,000
Salary—President	25,000
Professional services	20,000
Insurance	8,000
Auto expense	1,200
Taxes	1,890
Estimated general excise tax	7,880
Total projected operating expenses	$195,805

EXHIBIT 2

Statewide Airport System
Interisland Passengers
(Arrivals, Departures, Thru)

Year	Passengers	Growth %
1967	4,235,114	
1968	4,695,898	10.8
1969	5,449,244	16.0
1970	5,985,554	9.8
1971	6,760,062	12.9
1972	8,186,676	21.1
1973	9,618,194	17.4
1974	10,349,828	7.6
1975	10,648,170	2.8
1976	11,746,276	10.3
1977	12,827,694	9.2

Interisland by Airport
1977

	IN	OUT
Total	6,413,847	6,413,847
Honolulu	2,568,533	2,601,860
Hilo	585,382	540,260
Upolu	1,512	1,297
Waimea	13,381	12,189
Ke-ahole	545,990	560,267
Kahalui	1,400,385	1,420,339
Hana	10,685	10,945
Kaanapali	46,935	47,708
Molokai	99,016	96,268
Kalaupapa	4,163	4,449
Lanai	23,814	23,324
Lihue	1,095,060	1,093,606
Other	991	1,335

SOURCE: Hawaii Department of Transportation, Air Transportation Facilities Division, *State of Hawaii Airport Statistics,* Myra Tamanaha, research statistician, 1978, p. 3 and 47.

EXHIBIT 3
The Principal Hawaiian Islands

Inter-island Transportation
period from 1974–1977

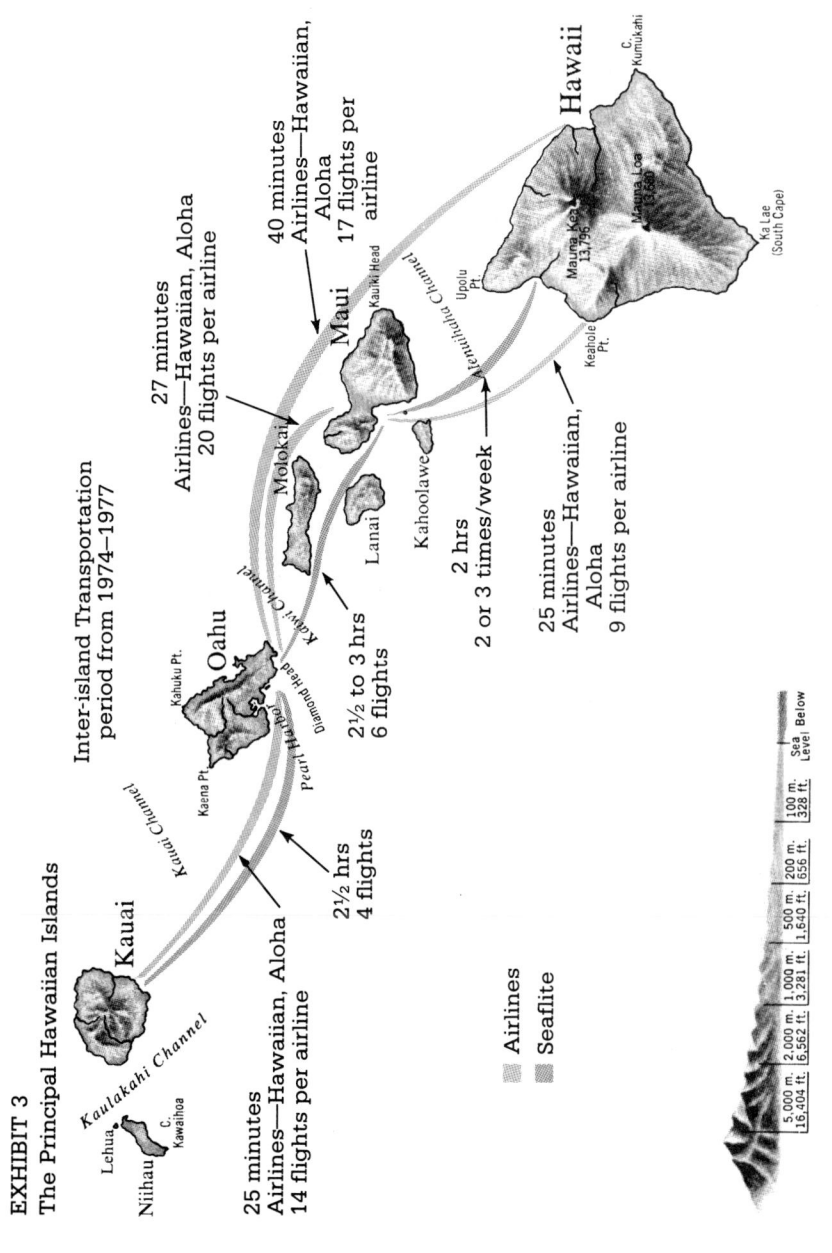

25 minutes
Airlines—Hawaiian, Aloha
14 flights per airline

27 minutes
Airlines—Hawaiian, Aloha
20 flights per airline

40 minutes
Airlines—Hawaiian,
Aloha
17 flights per airline

2½ hrs
4 flights

2½ to 3 hrs
6 flights

2 hrs
2 or 3 times/week

25 minutes
Airlines—Hawaiian, Aloha
9 flights per airline

Airlines
Seaflite

Kauai

Oahu

Molokai

Lanai

Maui

Kahoolawe

Hawaii

Niihau
Lehua
C. Kawaihoa

Kaena Pt.
Kahuku Pt.
Pearl Harbor
Diamond Head

Kauiki Head

Mauna Kea
13,796
Mauna Loa
13,680
Ka Lae
(South Cape)
Keahole Pt.
Upolu Pt.
C. Kumukahi

Kaulakahi Channel
Kauai Channel
Kaiwi Channel
Alenuihaha Channel

5,000 m.
16,404 ft.
2,000 m.
6,562 ft.
1,000 m.
3,281 ft.
500 m.
1,640 ft.
200 m.
656 ft.
100 m.
328 ft.
Sea Level
Below

413

EXHIBIT 4
Map Showing Principal Islands of State of Hawaii and the Statewide System of Airports

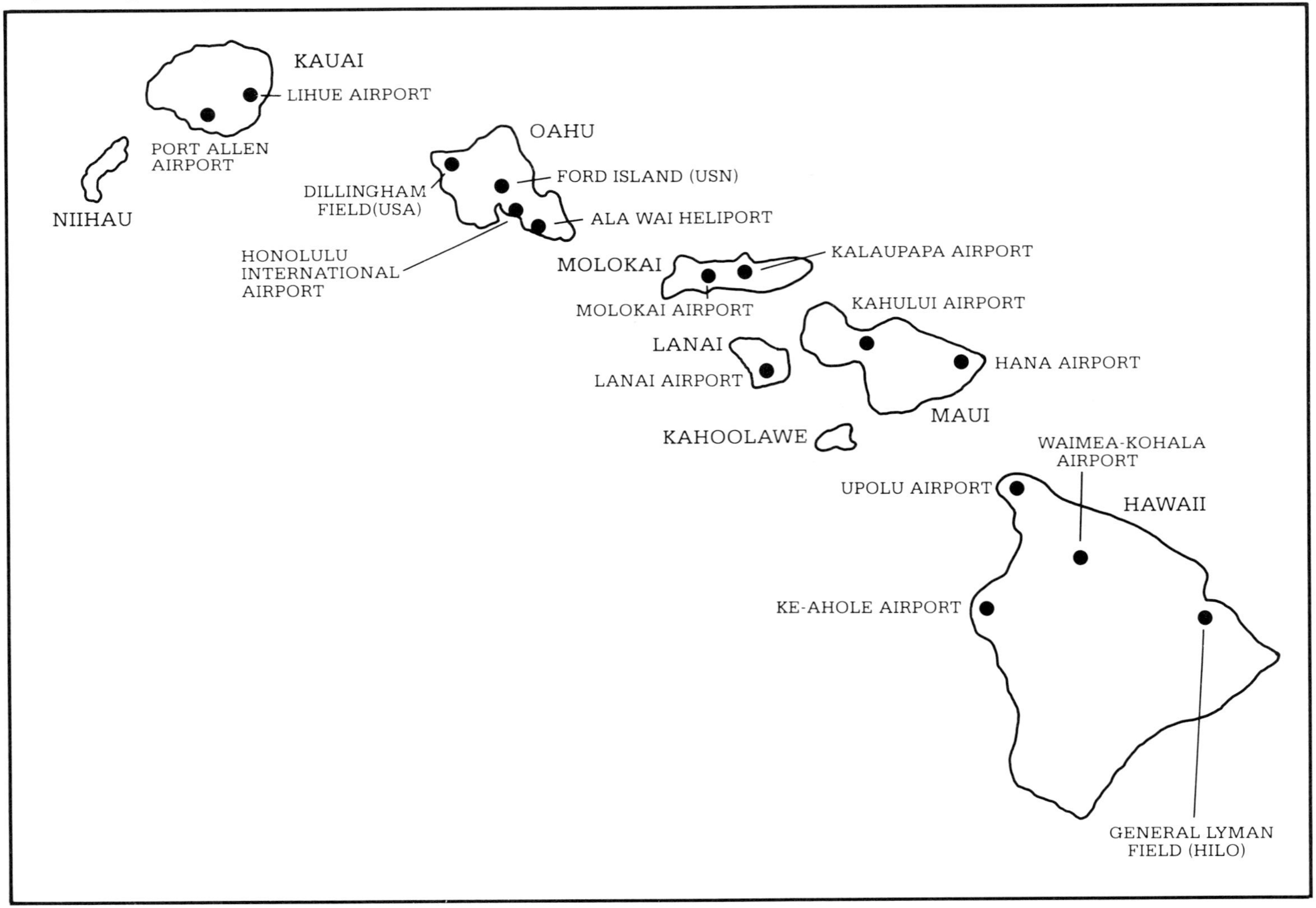

NIIHAU

KAUAI
LIHUE AIRPORT
PORT ALLEN
AIRPORT

OAHU
FORD ISLAND (USN)
DILLINGHAM
FIELD(USA)
ALA WAI HELIPORT
HONOLULU
INTERNATIONAL
AIRPORT

MOLOKAI
KALAUPAPA AIRPORT
MOLOKAI AIRPORT

LANAI
KAHULUI AIRPORT
LANAI AIRPORT
HANA AIRPORT

MAUI

KAHOOLAWE

UPOLU AIRPORT

WAIMEA-KOHALA
AIRPORT

HAWAII

GENERAL LYMAN
FIELD (HILO)

KE-AHOLE AIRPORT

EXHIBIT 5
SeaFlite Organization Chart

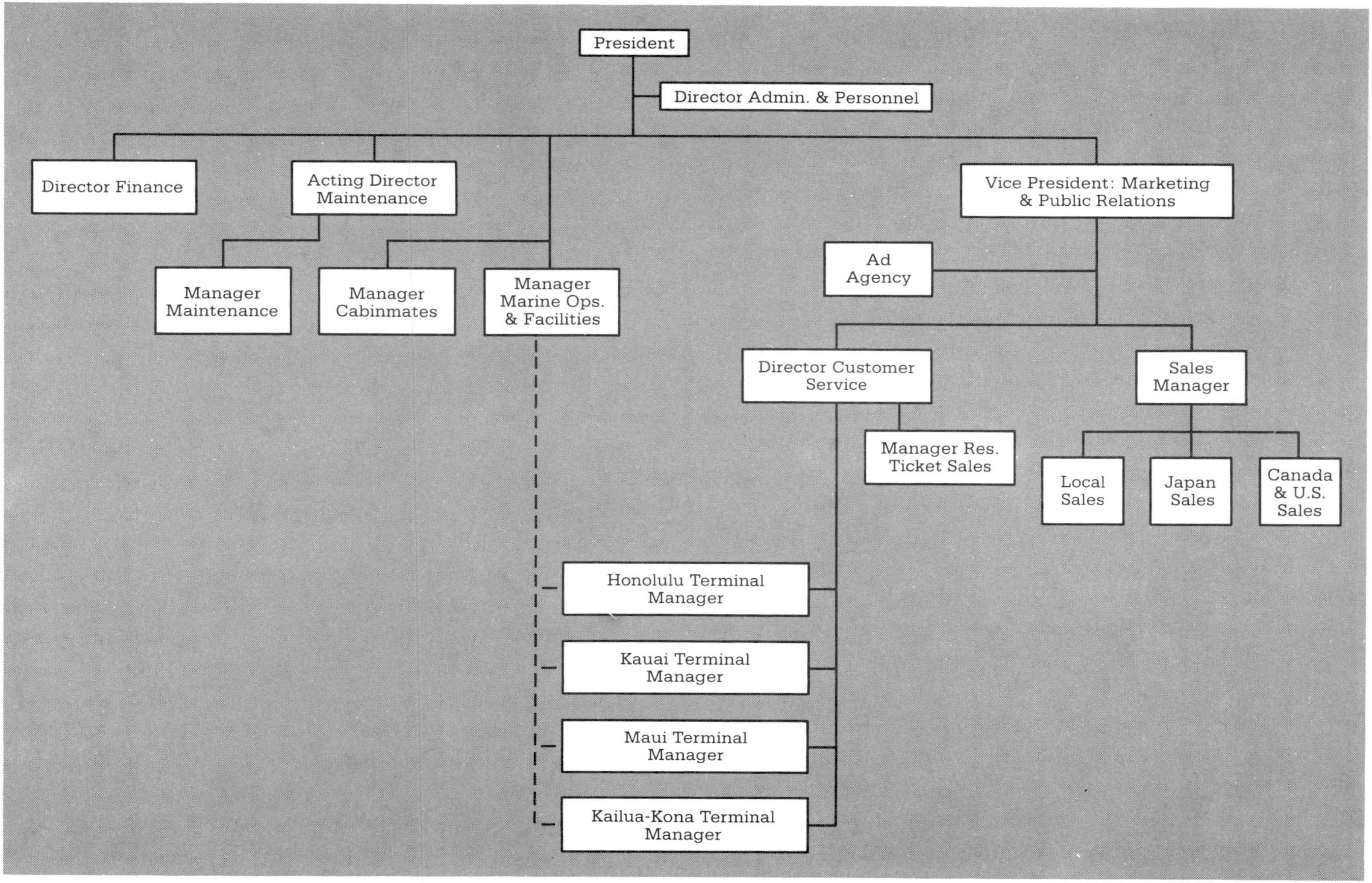

EXHIBIT 6
SeaFlite Schedules

Schedule of One Way Fares

		Nawiliwili Kauai	Maalaea Maui	Kailua-Kona Hawaii
Honolulu Oahu	FF	22.00	22.00	28.00
	MF	19.00	19.00	25.00
	YGF	11.00	11.00	14.00
Maalaea Maui	FF			22.00
	MF			19.00
	YGF			11.00

Children two through eleven years old pay ½ adult fare

Roundtrip fare twice one way full fare

FF = Full fare adult

MF = Military standby fare (active duty)

YGF = Youth group fare (passengers under 20 yrs. of age traveling as group of 10 or more accompanied by an adult fare passenger over 20 yrs. of age).

Ask about our hourly charter rates for special cruises, either local or interisland.

Baggage

3 Normal Size Bags per Passenger	FREE
Additional Bags	$3.00
Surfboards	$4.00
Bicycles	$4.00

SeaFlite Schedule Commencing 5/28/76

Eastbound		Daily 215	Daily 225	Daily Ex. Sunday 245	Daily 142	Sunday Only 226
Nawiliwili, Kauai	LV				4:10 pm	
Honolulu	AR				6:50 pm	
Honolulu	LV	7:30 am	8:00 am	1:50 pm		
Maalaea, Maui	AR	10:00 am	10:30 am	4:20 pm		
Maalaea, Maui	LV					11:00 am
Kailua-Kona	AR					1:00 pm

Westbound		Daily 502	Daily Ex. Sunday 512	Daily 522	Daily 241	Sunday Only 622
Kailua-Kona	LV					2:00 pm
Maalaea, Maui	AR					4:00 pm
Maalaea, Maui	LV	10:20 am	10:55 am	4:40 pm		
Honolulu	AR	12:45 pm	1:20 pm	7:05 pm		
Honolulu	LV				1:10 pm	
Nawiliwili, Kauai	AR				3:50 pm	

APPENDIX

Hawaii's Visitors: Type of Westbound Travelers to the State

Year	Westbound Travelers	Visitors	Intended Residents	Returning Residents
1967	893,103	754,910	44,117	130,995
1968	1,015,844	869,116	42,236	140,592
1969	1,181,029	1,008,802	41,162	152,404
1970	1,326,135	1,127,950	40,073	173,252
1971	1,430,325	1,207,898	41,562	162,967
1972	1,782,737	1,540,268	44,288	171,772
1973	2,067,861	1,815,443	36,886	194,974
1974	2,184,620	1,899,632	37,007	154,154
1975	2,207,417	1,935,396	39,233	178,040
1976	2,551,601	2,245,252	40,690	186,684
1977	2,763,312	2,453,541	43,617	179,298

Type of Travel—Percentage Distribution

	1977	1976	1975	1974
Organized tour group/ incentive trip	42.1	46.2	45.1	47.2
Individual basis	57.5	53.4	54.6	52.3
Government-military	.4	.4	.3	.5

Westbound Visitor Profile by Percentage

Family income	1973	1974	1975	1976
Under $5,000	2.5	1.7	1.5	1.5
$5,000–$7,499	5.4	4.2	3.6	2.8
$7,500–$9,999	8.5	6.9	6.1	4.6
$10,000–$14,999	21.8	19.5	18.1	16.8
$15,000–$25,999	33.3	35.0	33.3	35.5
$25,000 and over	28.5	32.8	37.4	38.8
Median income (dollars)	($18,600)	($20,100)	($21,200)	($21,800)
College graduates	47.3	48.6	47.9	47.9
Using travel agent	73.0	76.8	77.9	82.9
Arrangements for Outer Island travel				
made before arrival	79.7	81.4	82.3	81.7
made after arrival	20.3	18.6	17.7	18.3

21% of all westbound visitors remained on the island of Oahu exclusively.

Number of Trips to Hawaii by Westbound Visitor Party Heads by Percentage

	1977	1976	1975	1974
First trip	58.9	61.3	60.3	62.7
Second trip	17.5	16.9	17.1	16.2
Third trip	7.4	7.0	7.2	6.7
Fourth trip & over	16.2	14.8	15.4	14.4

Eastbound Visitor Profile

Year	Numbers		
1967	231,715	Intended length of stay:	
1968	298,727	1 to 6 days	90.7%
1969	345,988	7 to 12 days	7.2%
1970	420,835	13 days and over	2.0%
1971	388,619	Median stay: 5 days, 4 nights	
1972	461,640	Type of travel:	
1973	563,091	organized tour group	87.9%
1974	601,869	other	12.1%
1975	621,688		
1976	688,550	Neighbor islands are usually visited in one day.	
1977	670,355	Few visitors remain overnight.	

Westbound Visitors to the Neighbor Islands

Year	Maui	% of State Total	Hawaii	% of State Total	Kauai	% of State Total
1967	304,437	34.1	286,590	32.1	275,461	30.8
1968	364,364	35.9	369,509	36.4	327,813	32.3
1969	396,145	33.5	410,967	34.8	363,759	30.8
1970	447,985	33.8	445,401	33.6	410,075	30.9
1971	554,799	38.8	522,166	36.5	472,663	33.0
1972	710,050	39.8	637,562	35.8	565,386	31.7
1973	766,791	37.1	694,170	33.6	590,575	28.6
1974	852,204	39.0	742,839	34.0	601,703	27.5
1975	931,863	42.2	769,779	34.9	632,821	28.7
1976	1,110,726	43.5	816,514	32.0	699,275	27.4
1977	1,257,142	45.5	839,008	30.4	740,501	26.8

Percentage of Westbound Visitors by Their Intended Length of Stay in the State Who Traveled to the Respective Islands

1977			
Length of Stay	Maui	Hawaii	Kauai
1 to 6 days	3.6	4.2	2.8
7 to 12 days	56.1	51.8	51.4
13 to 18 days	33.9	38.3	39.6
19 to 24 days	4.3	3.8	4.3
25 to 30 days	1.2	1.1	1.1
31 to 60 days	0.7	0.6	0.6
60 days and over	0.1	**	**
Median (days)	(11.5)	(11.8)	(12.0)

** = less than .05%

Percentage of Westbound Visitors by Type of Travel Arrangements to the State

1977			
Travel Status	Maui	Hawaii	Kauai
Organized tour group	42.2	49.6	46.5
Individually arranged	57.7	50.3	53.4
Military	0.1	0.1	0.1

Residence of Westbound Visitors by Percentage

Area of Residency	State	Maui	Hawaii	Kauai
Pacific Coast	37.6	38.2	33.9	39.4
Mountain	5.9	6.5	7.3	7.7
West North Central	6.6	6.5	6.7	6.5
West South Central	5.7	5.8	7.1	6.0
East North Central	15.7	17.3	18.1	17.1
East South Central	2.1	1.7	2.2	1.6
New England	3.3	2.9	2.9	2.7
Mid Atlantic	10.4	9.6	10.2	8.7
South Atlantic	6.6	5.7	7.4	6.2
Canada**	4.9	4.9	3.1	3.1
Other foreign	1.3	0.9	1.0	1.0

**Only Canadians included in this survey are those arriving from American ports or on American carriers. Percentages can be assumed a good approximation.

■ ■ ■ CASE 9
Wavetek Corporation

Donald F. Harvey
Research Assistant: James Walsh

INTRODUCTION

Wavetek, Inc., operates solely in the electronic test and measurement equipment industry segment. Wavetek enjoyed strong financial operating results in this high-growth industry through 1983.

CEO John M. Thornton, the former boy wonder of the firm who took over as president at age 32 in 1965, led the company from a small $1 million dollar a year instrumentation firm to an $84 million high-tech company. Plans for 1984 were high, but management experienced unanticipated difficulties and profits were down to $1.4 million. Thornton acknowledged that the downturn in the instrumentation field in general and strong competition from formidable foes such as Hewlett-Packard were "a part of the problems we had," but he added quickly, "A lot of it was our own doing."[1] He said Wavetek "needed to make changes in marketing and selling, which we now have done, and we needed to drive a little more efficiently in new products. In the end, when you have problems, it always is your own doing."[2] Thornton also said that, despite high hopes, the instrumentation slump had an impact on Wavetek's sales. "What went wrong with our business strategy?" he wondered.

Company Profile

Wavetek designs, develops, manufactures, and markets worldwide general and special purpose electronic test and measurement (T&M) instruments and related products. These products are used in a variety of industrial, laboratory, and defense applications, and in specialized commercial applications that involve the design, evaluation, and manufacture of electronic circuits, devices, and equipment.

Wavetek was founded in 1962 to produce a unique function generator—its initial entry into the general purpose test and measurement market. Through a combination of internal product development and acquisitions, Wavetek has entered the following product areas: sweep generators, RF and microwave signal generators and frequency synthesizers, pulse generators, cable television (CATV), land-mobile

---

This case was prepared using published accounts and public documents for the purpose of the class discussion rather than to illustrate effective or ineffective handling of an administrative situation.

communications test instruments, filters, RF and microwave components, spectrum analyzers, microwave network analyzers, and power meters. Wavetek has facilities in California, Indiana, New Jersey, Pennsylvania, Washington, England, and West Germany.

Wavetek has been profitable each year since its incorporation in 1963 and has achieved a compound growth rate of 18.3 percent over the past five years. This growth has been financed through retained earnings and public offerings in 1981 and 1983.

Wavetek's main emphasis in business is the electronic T&M market. Recently, Wavetek has placed more emphasis on a divesting strategy of its data communications business and acquiring companies which offer products related to its T&M business. Wavetek is a major supplier of test equipment to the cable TV industry.

Corporate Strategy

Wavetek has established itself in niches in the T&M market, dominating the number one or two position. Wavetek first entered the T&M market using an intensive growth strategy to increase market share in a high-growth field, in an attempt to dominate it. As the market matured, the growth strategy shifted toward concentric diversification by adding related products to complement its existing product lines. With its desired portfolio, the company is now looking to increase profit margins by using a vertical integration strategy.

Mission

Wavetek's mission is to offer products in specific targeted markets and to become the leading competitor in those particular segments.

Goals

A Concentrate on marketing in electronic test equipment and selected application-oriented markets
   1 Increase market share in existing markets served
   2 Expand into higher frequency ranges
   3 Increase penetration into the ATE market
   4 Increase application-oriented market
   5 Link marketing with product development at the division level
   6 Integrate new products vertically
B Achieve sales and profit growth higher than industry averages
   1 Devise a worldwide distribution method dictated by product and market
   2 Utilize independent sales representatives and distributors for general purpose instruments
   3 Give direct factory support to representatives
   4 Have company direct salesmen in selected markets
   5 Establish advertising and promotion programs

    C Design products offering a superior price/performance ratio
        1 Maintain significant price/performance ratio
        2 Identify customer preferences
        3 Ensure that customers buy only what they need
    D Provide solution to customer problems
        1 Develop unified advertising and promotion programs
    E Increase market share through innovation
        1 Put more money into research and development[3]

INDUSTRY ANALYSIS

The electronic test and measurement industry is broad, diverse, and comprised of companies with products involving the use of electronic technology. T&M equipment is used mainly in research and development, manufacturing, and field service and maintenance in fields such as semiconductors, computers, communications, and other electronic areas. The overall growth of the T&M industry is related to the expansion of electronic technology. Contributing to the expansion is the rapid growth in the use of microprocessors in a wide variety of electronic equipment. The use of T&M equipment in manufacturing and field services is also adding to the growth of the industry. The highly competitive nature of the industry is caused by the rapid advances in technology. Wavetek's main competitor in the industry is Hewlett-Packard, which has much greater resources and does not restrict itself to the T&M industry.

Competition

The highly competitive electronic test and measurement instrument market is characterized by rapid advances in both integrated circuit and component technology. The market is divisible into many unique products that do not compete with each other. Thus, Wavetek has concentrated upon specific niches with innovative product designs and creative marketing techniques that enable it to capture and dominate market segments untouched by such industry giants as Hewlett-Packard and Tektronix.

Wavetek's ability to compete is dependent on several factors, including innovative design, price, quality, reliability, service capabilities, and the satisfaction of customers' delivery requirements. Many of Wavetek's competitors, the most significant being Hewlett-Packard, have substantially greater resources than does Wavetek. According to John Thornton, president and CEO of Wavetek, addressing the New York Society of Security Analysts, "We have seen Hewlett-Packard use price as a competing feature very effectively."[4]

The industry structure can be considered almost an oligopoly. Two companies, Hewlett-Packard and Tektronix, Inc., comprise approximately 55 percent of the worldwide market. Thus, the remaining 45 percent encompass Wavetek and a host of other small to medium-sized companies.

Technological and Product Development

Wavetek's initial T&M products were in the function generator area. Subsequently, through a combination of internal product development and acquisitions, Wavetek has entered the sweep generator, RF and microwave signal generator, pulse generator, CATV, land mobile communications test instrument, filter, spectrum analyzer, microwave network analyzer, microwave powermeter, and frequency synthesizer product areas.

Divestitures

    May 1980, sold Wavetek Computer Division

    August 1980, sold Wavetek Data Communications

Acquisitions

    May 1980, acquired Rockland System Corp.

    September 1980, acquired Mid-State Communications, Inc., into Wavetek Indiana, Inc.

    September 1981, acquired Spectrum Specialties, Inc.

    May 1983, acquired and merged Pacific Measurements, Inc.

Manufacturing operations

    San Diego and Sunnyvale, California

    Beech Grove, Indiana

    Rockleigh and Northvale, New Jersey

    Dorfen, West Germany

      Wavetek operations require the procurement, fabrication, assembly, and testing of a large number of electronic components and mechanical assemblies. Raw materials and components essential to Wavetek's operations are purchased through a number of established suppliers. Wavetek is not fully utilizing product capacity and can increase production 50 percent without having to make capital expenditures.

      Wavetek is predominantly known for *signal generation* products, including functional, signal, and sweep generators. These generators range from manually operated benchtop units to complex programmable units. Programmable generators are sold primarily to manufacturers and end users of automatic test equipment. The *broadband communications testing* area is growing rapidly for Wavetek. This area includes:

- sweep recovery systems
- system analyzers
- signal level meters
- communications test sets
- microwave meters

Equipment in this area includes special purpose test instruments used primarily in manufacturing, maintenance, and field service operations in television, CATV, land mobile and microwave communications, and local area networks.

Display and analysis products are used in patient monitoring equipment in medical centers. These products include:

■ Spectrum analyzers
■ Network analyzers
■ Display oscilloscopes

A fourth area is *filter products* used in radio frequency and microwave communications equipment. These products include:

■ RF and microwave ultra-miniature filters
■ Tubular filters
■ Adjustable filters

Although Wavetek is subject to some small restrictions on trading in foreign markets, government regulations do not have a significant impact on Wavetek or its industry.

INTERNAL ANALYSIS

Plans for fiscal 1984 were optimistic. Wavetek had just completed two consecutive years with record bookings and generally strong performance. The U.S. economy showed signs of improvement. The first quarter was plagued with abnormally low bookings principally due to a lack of general purpose product orders from the U.S. government. The CATV test equipment market softened considerably. Second quarter bookings improved about 15 percent over the first quarter, with CATV appearing stronger and increases in most other product lines. Third quarter orders deteriorated to below first quarter levels, again in the government and CATV areas and in most other product markets. Fourth quarter orders strengthened, in the normal seasonal pattern, but Wavetek was below the operating plan for the fiscal year.

Management's aggressive action substantially lowered the company's break-even point. Significant expenses and inventory write-downs were recorded, resulting in a loss for the fourth quarter and reduced earnings for the year. Net income was $1.4 million, or 15 cents per share, on sales of $81.5 million for the fiscal year ended September 30, 1984. For the 1983 fiscal year net income was $4.7 million, or 60 cents per share, on sales of $84 million. (See exhibit 1 for selected financial data.)

Results of Operations

Sales

Wavetek experienced a decline in sales during 1984 after substantial sales increases the prior two years. The factors contributing to this decline were a lack of general purpose product orders from the U.S. government, a strong dollar overseas, and a slowdown in the CATV industry that caused flat sales. Spectrum analyzers were up only slightly despite the inclusion of the results of a full year's operations of Nicolet Scientific Corporation for fiscal 1984 versus two quarters in fiscal 1983. Microwave products were relatively unchanged. Offsetting these factors were sales increases in the automatic test and component products areas.

Cost of Goods Sold

The percentage of cost of goods sold to sales was lower in fiscal 1983 than in fiscal 1982 because of improved efficiency, higher volume, methods improvements, and a favorable products mix. The percentage of cost of goods sold to sales was higher in fiscal 1984 than in fiscal 1983. The percentage in 1984 was affected by obsolete and excess inventory write-offs, inefficiencies, and excess plant capacity caused by a significant reduction in the workforce.

Inventories increased during fiscal 1984 in anticipation of significantly higher shipments. As a result of the low order levels, principally at the Indiana and Scientific divisions, staff reductions and spending controls were instituted over the course of the year to balance inventories to the ongoing level of business.

Selling, General, and Administrative

Selling, general, and administrative expenses in fiscal 1983 increased over those in fiscal 1982 mainly due to the addition of middle management staff, increased foreign sales support, increased product promotional efforts including trade shows and seminars, and the additional costs incurred in acquisition of Pacific Measurements Incorporated. Expenses in fiscal 1984 increased over those in fiscal 1983 because Wavetek anticipated higher sales than it achieved. The company also increased its foreign sales support to counteract the effects of the strong dollar. Several times during the year, staff reductions were made to adjust to a lower volume of business. However, significant termination costs were incurred, particularly in the fourth quarter. Also, many new products introduced in fiscal 1984 required a continued high level of sales promotional expenses to be brought to market.

Marketing

Both domestic and foreign sales are made through independent sales representatives and distributors. Wavetek's sales representatives act as sales trainers for their independent representatives worldwide. Foreign exports accounted for 24 percent of sales and are decreasing as domestic opportunities in CATV products drain corporate resources.

Wavetek's customer line is diverse and not dependent on any single customer except for the U.S. government. Even the percentage of dependency on the government for one product line is relatively small. In 1982, net government sales amounted to 15.6 percent. No other single customer or group of customers represents 10 percent or more of consolidated sales.

Management

Wavetek is composed of three U.S. divisions and two overseas subsidiaries. The three U.S. divisions report to John Thornton, chief executive officer. The two subsidiaries in England and Germany report to Robert S. Croshaw, vice president of international sales, because their primary thrust is in the marketing area. The domestic divisions are further segmented in SBUs. The differences between the SBUs are defined by the design technology required for the product line and the particular market segment served. Nine SBUs have been created to cover Wavetek's worldwide market. Each SBU is responsible for planning and implementing its own marketing, manufacturing, and R&D and generating its own profit.

Research and Development

Research and development expenditures were higher as a percentage (14.2 percent) and in the aggregate in fiscal 1984 than in fiscal 1983 due to both lower than anticipated volume and Wavetek's emphasis on an aggressive R&D program. Total aggregate expenditures came in at budgeted levels. As a result, many new products were introduced during fiscal 1984. R&D expenditures were reduced in the fourth quarter in order to improve efficiency and to provide a higher return on investment. From 1976 to 1983, Wavetek invested an average of 10.18 percent of sales in R&D. The industry average for 1983 was 8.0 percent.

Human Resources

Wavetek pays above-average wages to secure quality personnel for employment. The employee turnover rate is very low in all middle and upper level positions, but turnover is approximately 30 percent in the manufacturing positions in the Silicon Valley. Since 1983, Wavetek has laid off more than 22 percent of its employees, primarily from its Indiana facility because of a government contract cancellation.

CONCLUSION

The profitability ratios reflect the extent of Wavetek's poor 1984 performance. Reduced government orders coupled with Wavetek's poor product demand forecasts forced the company to absorb excessive inventory write-offs in 1984. Wavetek has limited foreign production facilities; therefore, the strengthening of the U.S. dollar deteriorates the company's price competitiveness throughout the product line in foreign markets.

Wavetek's high-cash position, in conjunction with its low long-term debt position, presents a two-fold problem. First, this environment makes it a primary target for a takeover. Second, its available $25 million line of credit is not being utilized to develop foreign manufacturing facilities similar to those of its industry competitors.

In April 1985, Thornton stepped down as CEO, naming John W. Battin as the new president. Thornton came to Wavetek in 1963 with a background in business and marketing, not engineering. Battin, however, is an engineer, and Thornton said that Battin's "background is more typical of people who run high-technology companies than mine is. Most guys are engineers, and actually he is well suited to marketing the rapidly changing world of high technology."[5]

What strategy should Battin use to get Wavetek back on the growth track?

Notes

1   "Thornton Steps Down," *San Diego Union*, April 3, 1985, E-1.
2   Ibid.
3   "Wavetek Corporation Presentation by John Thornton to the New York Society of Security Analysts," *The Wall Street Transcript*, April 25, 1983, 65, 570.
4   "Wavetek Corporation Presentation by John Thornton to the New York Society of Security Analysts," 65, 573.
5   Interview with John Thornton by Jim Walsh, February 20, 1985.

EXHIBIT 1
Selected Financial Data

SEPTEMBER 30	1984	1983	1982
STATEMENT OF INCOME DATA			
Total Sales[1]	**81,478**	84,004	64,634
Domestic Sales[1]	**58,969**	63,902	49,107
Export Sales[1]	**22,509**	20,102	15,527
Research and Development[1]	**11,527**	9,567	6,873
% of Sales	**14.1%**	11.4%	10.6%
Continuing Operations			
Income Before Taxes[1]	**212**	7,431	5,883
Income After Taxes[1]	**1,394**	4,687	3,401
% of Sales	**1.7%**	5.6%	5.3%
Discontinued Operations			
Income (Loss)[1]			
Net Income[1]	**1,394**	4,687	3,401
Per Share Data:			
Income from Continuing Operations	**$.15**	$.60	$.48
Net Income	**$.15**	$.60	$.48
BALANCE SHEET DATA			
Accounts Receivable[1]	**18,606**	19,774	16,647
Inventories[1]	**33,094**	26,164	21,497
Total Current Assets[1]	**57,516**	63,803	39,014
Property and Equipment – Net[1]	**28,455**	25,040	15,953
Total Assets[1]	**91,000**	94,670	56,602
Total Current Liabilities[1,2]	**10,240**	16,721	11,877
Long-Term Obligations[1]	**2,980**	3,085	3,762
Working Capital[1,2]	**47,276**	47,082	27,137
Retained Earnings[1]	**24,037**	22,643	17,773
Total Stockholders' Equity[1,2]	**75,006**	73,358	39,902
Equity per Average Share[2]	**$8.26**	$9.39	$5.58
Average Shares Outstanding[3]	**9,078**	7,814	7,148
STATISTICS			
Backlog[1]	**14,153**	11,187	16,150
Total Employees	**1,232**	1,581	1,603
Square Feet of Floor Space (thousands)	**459**	464	288
Sales per Average Number of Employees[1]	**57.9**	52.8	47.1
Sales per Square Foot (dollars)	**178**	181	224
Current Ratio[2]	**5.6**	3.8	3.3
Long-Term Obligations % of Equity	**4.0%**	4.2%	9.4%
Return on Average Stockholders' Equity	**1.9%**	8.3%	8.9%

[1] In thousands of dollars
[2] Restated in 1983 to reflect reclassification of cumulative foreign currency translation adjustment
[3] In thousands of common and common equivalent shares

1981	1980	1979	1978	1977	1976	1975
49,685	44,385	35,231	29,294	22,090	16,531	11,190
36,104	31,234	24,083	20,080	15,605	11,089	7,523
13,581	13,151	11,148	9,214	6,485	5,442	3,667
5,576	5,012	3,566	2,565	1,895	1,406	1,241
11.2%	11.3%	10.1%	8.8%	8.6%	8.5%	11.1%
3,749	4,890	5,174	3,424	2,440	1,863	641
2,175	2,666	3,044	2,065	1,499	1,153	443
4.4%	6.0%	8.6%	7.0%	6.8%	7.0%	4.0%
	(222)	(256)	125	(93)	51	176
2,175	2,444	2,788	2,190	1,406	1,204	619
$.38	$.53	$.61	$.43	$.32	$.25	$.10
$.38	$.49	$.55	$.46	$.30	$.26	$.14
11,680	10,755	11,510	9,015	6,921	5,750	3,883
13,939	11,230	8,513	5,644	5,284	4,084	2,672
32,417	22,964	20,838	15,429	12,797	10,461	6,873
12,969	9,401	5,349	3,571	2,857	2,541	2,186
46,877	33,485	26,315	19,099	15,820	13,171	9,423
6,601	11,617	10,778	6,732	5,217	4,817	2,335
3,407	4,276	1,509	1,478	2,064	1,403	1,430
25,816	11,348	10,060	8,697	7,580	5,644	4,538
14,372	12,346	10,059	7,271	5,097	3,691	2,487
36,149	17,156	13,836	10,772	8,470	6,944	5,619
$6.32	$3.41	$2.75	$2.25	$1.83	$1.53	$1.27
5,720	5,030	5,026	4,791	4,618	4,545	4,425
9,668	10,643	8,364	4,337	4,747	2,159	1,540
1,139	1,118	969	768	780	619	466
262	200	176	141	138	138	138
44.0	42.5	40.6	37.8	31.6	30.5	24.7
189	221	200	208	160	120	81
4.9	2.0	1.9	2.3	2.5	2.2	2.9
9.4%	25.0%	10.9%	13.7%	24.4%	20.2%	25.4%
8.2%	15.8%	22.7%	22.8%	18.2%	19.2%	11.7%

CASES FOR PART TWO

■ ■ ■

Strategy Implementation

■ ■ ■ CASE 10
Tandem Computers

Donald F. Harvey
Research Assistant: Monte J. Windsor

INTRODUCTION

Jim Treybig is a lean Texan with a bachelor's degree in electrical engineering from Rice and an MBA from Stanford. In 1973, after five years as marketing manager at Hewlett-Packard, he joined Kleiner, Perkins, Caufield, and Byers, a San Francisco venture capital firm, with the understanding that he would eventually leave to start his own firm. Treybig spent a year as a limited partner working on his business strategy and his plan for a fail-safe computer system.

Tandem Computers, with $1 million in start-up capital from the Kleiner, Perkins, Caulfield, and Byers firm, was incorporated in November 1974 by four founders: Jim Treybig, John Loustaunou (now retired) and two technical experts, James Katzman and Michael Green. All of the founders were employed at Hewlett-Packard prior to forming the company.

Jim Treybig knew that he wanted to start a company when he left his job at Hewlett-Packard in 1973. Because his background included employment with Hewlett-Packard and Texas Instruments, computers were a natural choice. While he was at Hewlett-Packard in the early 1970s, he first encountered customers looking for a computer that would not break down. He saw that people were spending large amounts of money to modify computers to get a computer system that would not fail, and he decided to start Tandem. He added up all the companies that wanted a nonstop computer system. "It came to $250 million. And the market was right," Treybig said, "no competitors and the products would be sold, not rented."[1]

> According to Treybig, the challenge was never market, but technology. The goal was to design and . . . produce a price competitive computer system that didn't fail, that didn't destroy data, that could be expanded from the power of a minicomputer to that of the largest mainframe, and also networked with as many as 225 systems in other locations, without changing software or hardware. The challenge was to do it technically, and to grow fast enough to be able to fend off competitors and provide opportunities for the talented and aggressive people they expected the venture to attract.[2]

"Jimmy T," as he is called by associates, is predicting a $1 billion market by 1990, but will Tandem be able to maintain its amazing rate of growth?

This case was prepared using published accounts and public documents for the purpose of class discussion rather than to illustrate either effective or ineffective handling of an administrative situation.

THE ENVIRONMENT

The Silicon Valley

The Silicon Valley, a peninsula between San Francisco and San Jose, is not simply a symbol of high technology. High technology exists elsewhere, but the Silicon Valley leads the world, and the corporations that have been the leaders are start-ups. The major corporations have for the most part been passed by newer ones in the swift-moving technologies. Fairchild Semiconductor was the progenitor and, in conjunction with Stanford University, attracted many scientists to the area. Soon Fairchild had trouble hanging on to its people as they began peeling off group by group to found literally scores of companies.

"There is nowhere else that we could have started this company," says Treybig. "The Silicon Valley is an attitude. We found risk capital, we found suppliers and vendors that wanted us to succeed, and we found people with an attitude that made us succeed."[3]

The Product

When an organization commits its vital functions to on-line processing (as opposed to batch processing), the business becomes truly computer-dependent. Tandem's products have been developed to provide simple, cost-effective solutions to the emerging on-line processing market.

Tandem designs, develops, manufactures, markets, and supports a unique computer system for the on-line transaction processing marketplace. Called the NonStop system, its innovative architecture virtually eliminates the risk of system failures and protects the customers' data bases from damage caused by electronic malfunctions. Tandem systems can be expanded modularly from a mid-sized to a large-scale system, or extended into a distributed data processing network of up to 255 geographically dispersed systems without hardware replacement or software conversion.

Tandem's NonStop systems are designed to run continuously during component failure and even during maintenance while parts are being removed or replaced. Each system protects the user's data base from damage or destruction. Tandem's systems have the capability to expand from the power of a mid-sized system through a large-scale mainframe. NonStop systems are capable of interconnecting up to 255 regionally dispersed systems at a fraction of the cost of networks based on conventional computers. Both system expansion and computer network connections can be accomplished without reprogramming or computer downtime. To facilitate the economic movement of large volumes of information over a corporate network, Tandem will offer a fully integrated computer/satellite communication system.

The Competition

Important considerations for potential purchases of computer systems include systems performance, software capability, systems reliability and maintainability, capability of a manufacturer to develop new products and enhance existing products, and price, including the relationship of price to one or more of these other factors.

The market for computer systems is highly competitive. Many companies have established reputations in the computer industry and have far greater financial, technical, and operating resources than Tandem. Present competitors are companies that offer redundant computer systems, including Burroughs Corporation, Data General Corporation, Digital Equipment Corporation, Hewlett-Packard Company, Honeywell Information Systems, Inc., and IBM Corporation.

Management believes that sales of dual processor systems constitute only a small proportion of such competitors' total computer sales, and that none of these companies presently offers a system with the same capabilities as NonStop systems. However, management also believes that these or other data processing companies could develop and market systems similar to or competitive with NonStop systems, and that one or more companies are likely to enter the market in the future.

The computer industry is also characterized by rapid technological advances. The company could be adversely affected if its competitors introduced technological advances. Accordingly, Tandem expects to continue to incur substantial engineering and software development expenses. Tandem is committed to the development and refinement of existing products.

Despite Treybig's tributes to the strength of his technology, some analysts suggest that Tandem's success may have as much to do with its applications of software. "More customers buy Tandem's machines for the nice software than anything else," said David Gold, a computer industry analyst. "Fail-safe is just a great marketing and advertising ploy."[4]

His words were echoed by Ted Costello, vice president of technology research at Sutro and Company: "The street doesn't seem to recognize yet that Tandem's strength is not in hard but in software. And Treybig is driving the company to keep improving the software like he's got the devil behind him."[5]

The question remains, however, whether Tandem's NonStop can continue to be a "nonstop" success. While Tandem still has no direct competition, Digital Equipment Corp., IBM, and several other companies are developing competitive systems. Tandem should be able to stay very competitive as industry observers predict that Tandem's rivals will have a difficult time duplicating the company's software developments in less than three years. "You can't have a baby in a month by making nine women pregnant," commented analyst Costello.[6]

The Customers

Tandem systems are sold to a wide variety of customers. Typical applications include electronic funds transfer, inventory control, manufacturing control, travel reservations, bank credit verification, and message switching. Sales have been made to approximately twenty-five different industries, including manufacturing, banking and other financial services, wholesale and retail distribution, health care, computer services, transportation, printing and publishing, legal services, and utilities. Systems have also been installed with government agencies in Australia, Mexico, the Netherlands, the United Kingdom, the United States, Venezuela, and West Germany.

By the end of fiscal 1981, 460 organizations were using over 2,500 Tandem processors to make their businesses better for themselves and for their customers (see exhibit 1).

The Economy

The company believes its advanced hardware/software solutions are favored by the market trends, and also that it is in a better position than any other company to evolve as the major force in the new wave of data processing in this decade. A turnaround for this industry appeared possible by 1984. For the most part, orders and earnings of computer and peripheral vendors continue at the mercy of worldwide economic sluggishness and the strength of the dollar overseas.

The growth sector of the industry is distributed data processing (DDP), which will require increasing computer power at remote work sites. This trend toward DDP should position Tandem to capture a healthy share of the future market.

THE INTERNAL SYSTEM

Financial

Tandem ranked at number 500 in the *Fortune* top 500 list, with sales of $418 million in 1984. Tandem Computer's fiscal 1981 operating results compared to those of 1980 showed consistently high growth: revenues increased 91 percent to $208,397,000; pretax operating margins were 19.3 percent compared to the 17.7 percent in fiscal 1980; and earnings per share increased 106 percent to $7.2. These financial results attest to the validity of the strategic market posture Tandem established in 1974, and in 1981 reflected both the company's technical leadership position in the market for on-line transaction processing systems and the productivity, creativity, and dedication of Tandem's employees.

Results of Operations

Exhibit 2 summarizes the changes in important operating indicators for the fiscal years presented. The numbers on the left account for the revenue dollar by showing various income and expense items as a percentage of revenue. The numbers on the right measure the yearly percentage increase in the same items.

Tandem has emerged as one of those enviable new companies that double their numbers year after year. Sales were $24 million for the year ended September 30, 1978, $56 million for 1979, $109 million the next year, and $208 million in 1981 to $26.5 million in 1982, pushing profit margins to 12.7 percent from 8.9 percent (see exhibit 3 for financial highlights).

Tandem continued to grow in 1982, although the recession has slowed this phenomenal growth rate. Revenues grew 60 percent over those for 1981, and net income increased 40 percent. Profit margins fell due to an increase in long-term debt that increased interest expense. Tandem's product mix is working in its favor. Fourth quarter earnings and sales increased in spite of the fact that Tandem delivered fewer processors than in the previous period (see exhibits 3 through 10).

This set-back in Tandem's growth rate should be only temporary. Tandem is poised for fast growth as it continues its efforts in R&D and marketing.

Geographic Segment Information

Exhibit 11 sets forth information about the company's operations in different geographic regions for the three years ended September 30, 1981.

CEO James Treybig has a good grip on financing Tandem's explosive growth. The company has almost no long-term debt, has a price to earnings ratio of 31, and uses its cash reserves to earn interest income. When he needs capital to finance the next phase of Tandem's expansion, Treybig can go again to the equity market, as he has done three times since going public. He avoids debt because "when you're selling against larger companies like IBM or Data General you have to look safe financially to your customer."[7]

Fiscal Performance

Making other businesses more efficient has been good business for Tandem. In fact, Tandem is one of the fastest growing publicly held companies in the world. Consistently, for eighteen consecutive quarters through Tandem's fiscal 1981 year-end, every period has been record-setting. Revenues have grown from under $8 million in fiscal 1977 to over $208 million in 1981. Operating margins during those four years were between 17.3 percent and 19.4 percent. This consistent performance is in accordance with the company's long-term plans, as is the manner in which Tandem has financed its growth through retained earnings and equity offerings instead of borrowings. Stockholders' equity has increased nearly 75 times since fiscal 1975.

Patents

Tandem has been awarded a patent on its system architecture claims by the U.S. Patent Office and by the Patent Office of Great Britain. Patent applications are pending with the U.S. Patent Office concerning numerous claims regarding other aspects of Tandem's products. Foreign patent applications are also in process in a limited number of countries. There can be no assurance that any of these applications will result in the award of a patent or that the company would be successful in defending its right to the patent should there be subsequent patent infringement actions.

Because of the rapid technological development in the computer industry with concurrent extensive patent coverage, and the rapid rate of issuance of new patents, certain components of the company's products may involve infringement of existing patents. If any such infringements do exist, the company believes that, based upon industry practice, any necessary licenses or rights under patent may be obtained on conditions that would not have a materially adverse financial effect on the company.

Manufacturing

Tandem has manufacturing operations in five locations in the United States and one in Germany. The company supports customers' NonStop systems throughout North America, Europe, and Asia from seventy-seven offices. By the end of fiscal 1981, Tandem had shipped over 2,500 processors to 460 customers. Fiscal 1981 earnings per share rose 106 percent on a 91 percent increase in revenues over the preceding year, while stockholders' equity grew 191 percent.

Manufacture of NonStop systems requires assembly and test of circuit boards, power supplies, and memory systems and the final assembly and testing of completed computer systems. In general, the company manufactures its systems from components and prefabricated parts such as integrated circuits, printed circuit boards, and metal parts fabricated by others. Tandem also purchases major assemblies such as disk drives, tape drives, and other peripheral equipment. Certain of the items manufactured by others, such as printed circuit boards and mechanical parts, are made to the company's specifications.

Approximately 40 percent of the production labor for the assembly of printed circuit boards, power supplies, and cables incorporated into the company's processors, main memories, and controllers takes place at the company's manufacturing facilities. The remaining 60 percent of the production labor for these items is provided by subcontractors. All purchasing, inspection, functional testing, final assembly, and systems integration and testing are performed within the company's manufacturing facilities.

The company purchases substantially all of the components and all the peripheral devices for its systems from other manufacturers. Most of the components and peripherals used in the company's systems are available from a number of different suppliers. Virtually all components are purchased from multiple sources and are standard, commercially available parts. Major items such as peripherals are generally purchased from single sources of supply. The company believes that alternative sources could be developed if necessary. Although the company has not experienced any significant problem in obtaining required supplies, future shortages of components or peripherals could result in production delays that would adversely affect its business.

Marketing

Tandem markets its computer systems primarily through its own sales organization, comprised of marketing, training, field service, and software support personnel. The marketing organization is divided into four divisions with a total of seventy-seven sales and service offices throughout the world. In addition to sales subsidiaries in Canada, Denmark, England, France, Germany, Hong Kong, Italy, Japan, the Netherlands, Singapore, Sweden, and Switzerland, the company has distributors in Australia, Finland, Greece (also serving the Middle East), Korea, Mexico, the Philippines, Taiwan, and Venezuela. In the foreseeable future, the company intends to continue to expand its direct marketing operations in the United States and abroad and to increase selectively international distributor representation.

In keeping with Tandem's end-user orientation, it tries to minimize the time that elapses from receipt of purchase orders to shipment of systems. Typically, the company ships its systems to customers within ninety days after receipt of orders. For this reason, and because of the possibility that customers will change delivery schedules or cancel orders, the backlog on any particular date may not be representative of the company's actual sales for any succeeding fiscal period.

The company has not generally financed, rented, or leased any of its systems, nor is such a program contemplated. Customers are free to obtain third party financing on their own.

Tandem Computers has achieved impressive business growth with an outstanding set of well-differentiated products. The company should be a major participant in the convergence of communications and data processing in the mid-1980s.

The future looks bright for Tandem and its marketplace. No other company has invested the time, energy, and resources to meet the onrush of demand for systems capable of efficiently and reliably driving an array of users' innovative on-line applications. Nor is any other company better prepared, or better positioned, to emerge as a major force in the changing marketplace during this decade.

THE PEOPLE

Every Friday afternoon Tandem stages its weekly "beer bust." This event is an opportunity for all employees to gather and socialize with their bosses and subordinates. The hierarchy of work is relaxed in this setting, and people have the opportunity to interact. Managers and subordinates are able to better know each other as equals thus promoting the corporate culture of Tandem and strengthening its team-building efforts.

Management Philosophy

Treybig's management philosophy consists of three major points: hire outstanding people, create an environment where they will be motivated to work, and perhaps most important, take an interest in every individual the company employs. Treybig has no qualms about hiring the best people for the job even if they are clearly overqualified. With such rapid growth, they don't stay overqualified for long. "If your people are only capable of filling the job they have right now, what do you do with them when the company grows," he asks, "change them all? The key is to look for highly motivated, intelligent people and pay them what they are worth."[8]

Tandem is continually striving to hire the best people, people with high internal motivations and high growth satisfaction who will deliver high quality performance. By hiring only high growth-need employees, Tandem avoids the possibility of "overstretching" a low growth-need employee. In this way Tandem avoids the moderating effects that a mixture of low and high growth-need employees causes.

Recent research has identified five core characteristics of jobs that elicit the above states.[9] They are the key to designing jobs with a high potential for motivating people. Three of the core job dimensions contribute toward meaningful work. They are skill variety, task identity, and task significance. The fourth dimension, autonomy, deals with developing personal responsibility. The final core dimension is feedback. Tandem applies these core dimensions.

In a survey late in fiscal 1981, 83 percent of employees said they believed advancement opportunities at Tandem are greater than at any other place they have worked. Tandem believes that promotions from within will perpetuate consistency and produce the management quality essential to the company's continued growth and prosperity.

Tandem's philosophy and environment also enable the company to keep its good people. In an industry that nationwide experiences a 26 percent annual turnover of employees (almost 29 percent in California's Silicon Valley, where Tandem is headquartered), only 6.7 percent left Tandem during fiscal 1981. Some of those 6.7 percent, of course, are asked to leave; 98 percent of Tandem employees, according to the survey, believe Tandem is the best place they've ever worked.[10]

Tandem employees are very productive. In 1981 when the electronic industry's median revenues per employee was under $50,000, Tandem employees averaged over $100,000 (see exhibit 12). Exceptional employees are recognized and rewarded through the company's TOPs (Tandem Outstanding Performers) program. According to Jim Treybig:

> A basic decision any manager has to make is whether to err on the side of goodness or to protect against badness. Ninety-nine percent of your people want to work and be responsible. But one percent will try to take advantage of you. . . . Now you can set up your system to protect against that one percent or to reward the other 99 percent. We chose to reward the majority. The other people may take advantage of us for a week or a month, but then they are gone. I contend that the net gain of treating the 99 percent right is far greater than the loss of the ones taking advantage of you.[11]

Work at Tandem is high in the core job dimensions. What manufacturing Tandem does itself is done in quiet, airy rooms more like labs than factories. Tandem's high-level assembly and massive testing require highly skilled workers. Most component and routing assembly jobs are farmed out. Combining high motivation potential jobs with systematically hiring high growth-need employees has enabled Tandem to keep its good people. Industry turnover is more than 25 percent, whereas Tandem's is less than 7 percent. "Because Tandem's growth demands high productivity, there simply is no room here for people who cannot be depended upon," said its director of research and development, Jerry Held. "Tandem is a society in which everyone is important; our people must consider work to be an important and desirable good rather than a necessary evil."[12]

Hewlett-Packard as a Model of Theory Z

Hewlett-Packard had to invent a model to prevent its scientists from defecting to its eastern competitors. This model, Theory Z, reflects attitudes that we think of as Japanese: paternalistic, flexible in work schedules, and caring. "H-P set the style," said Treybig, "it was informal, laid-back, and people-oriented."[13] Tandem and H-P both have corporate cultures based on Theory Z concepts. This similarity is not surprising because James Treybig, along with the other three founders—Michael D. Green, John C. Loustaunou, and James A. Katzman—all worked at Hewlett-Packard before forming the company. According to Treybig,

> This is a *culture*. It is oriented to *risk*. First of all, it is not a problem to fail here. If you live in Detroit, you want to be a vice president of General Motors. Here, if you start a company, that's as good as being president of General Motors, and the risk of a start-up is always failure. We have a pool of people willing to take risks, and we have thousands of risk-oriented decisions everyday. Which chip do you go with? The safe one or the one that might be superior? We know we have good people, and we do a lot of preaching. We depend on peer pressure.[14]

The goal is not utopia; it is profits. "Beneath all the camaraderie and teamwork are very tough, sophisticated management tools," said Richard Pascale, a professor at Stanford Business School.[15] Meeting the goals involves twelve-hour days and six-day weeks. Computer technicians talk about "burn-out" at thirty.

Theory Z takes the concept of the basic good in every employee and each employee's ability to work independently and combines it with management's trust in employees' ability to use their discretion in a manner consistent with the goals of the organization. The difference between a hierarchy and a type Z organization is the high state of consistency in the latter's internal culture. Z organizations can best be described as intimate associations of individuals who are working together towards the fulfillment of common goals.[16]

"Unions exist only because the management mistreated the workers," Treybig said, "people want to feel they're citizens of the company. This is a culture."[17]

Tandem has in place the mechanisms to perpetuate this corporate culture. Every employee is a stockholder and therefore has a stake in the success in the company. Treybig has developed a chart to show each employee how his or her performance can affect corporate profits. New employees go through up to twenty hours of interviews. A manager will never hire a candidate his or her people don't think is good. All employees go through a two-day indoctrination course. Tandem has eliminated time clocks, and managers often don't know how long employees work. Michael Green, a company founder, said, "We don't want to pay people for attendance but for output."[18] Through hiring the best people, providing a creative atmosphere, and taking an interest in each individual, Tandem has achieved productivity figures that are among the highest in the industry.

STRUCTURAL SYSTEM

The management policy at Tandem was largely established by its founders and its executive committee. The nine members of Tandem's board of directors are

- Thomas J. Perkins (1): Chairman of the Board; Partner Kleiner, Perkins, Caufield & Byers
- Morton Collins (2): Partner, DSV Associates
- Thomas J. Davis, Jr. (1)(2): Partner, Mayfield II
- Franklin P. Johnson, Jr.: Chairman, Asset Management Capital Company
- Eugene Kleiner (2): Partner, Kleiner, Perkins, Caufield & Byers
- Robert C. Marshall: Senior Vice President and Chief Operating Officer, Tandem Computers Incorporated
- Alvin C. Rice: President and Chairman, Imperial Bank
- Robert G. Stone, Jr.: Chairman of the Board, West India Shipping Company
- James G. Treybig (1): President and Chief Executive Officer, Tandem Computers Incorporated

The number (1) denotes member of the executive committee and the number (2) denotes member of the audit committee.

The Organization

Tandem uses a loose, flat organization structure with thirteen vice presidents reporting to CEO Jim Treybig and COO Robert Marshall (see exhibit 14 for organization chart).

Tandem's structure might be termed an adaptive-organic style. This style works well for high-growth companies. It adapts to environmental changes, has loosely defined roles, and has decentralized control. Authority is shared throughout the organization. Tandem's adaptive structure has enabled it to grow rapidly and still maintain organizational control.

"The most creative computer people are the semi-freakies, . . . and—especially in the case of the software designers who breathe the soul into Tandem's machines—they need freedom and solitude to perform their occult art. It's semi-channeled chaos."[19] Tandem's loose, flexible style reflects this industry reality.

GOALS AND VALUES

At Tandem, corporate goals and values are formed in consensus fashion. Treybig says that he has "100 percent disposable time" with which to work on people projects such as his new chart of 100 management concepts that he uses to guide the company. The chart emphasizes such notions as pushing responsibility down the employee ranks to develop managers faster, hiring the best person rather than the cheapest, and promoting from within.

At Tandem, employees have neither the time clocks nor the name badges usually found at other high-technology companies in Silicon Valley. Its workers have flexible hours, a swimming pool that is open before 6 A.M. and after 8 P.M., a volleyball court complete with locker room and showers, and an open-door policy that invites employees to drop in for a talk with their managers anytime.

Treybig's past experience with Hewlett-Packard helped him create a corporation with similar values. His perception of the task environment as one with a shortage of skilled labor led him to develop means to keep his people employed at Tandem.

Among his methods of upsetting the status quo has been to grant stock options to all employees at the same time the company makes a public offering. Perhaps as a result, employees as a group are now the largest single holder of Tandem's 10 million shares.

Treybig's own motivation, he said, has nothing to do with money. Some of it has to do with working with computers. But for the most part, he's out to prove that the kind of management style that works for Tandem now will still work five and ten years in the future when the company is five and ten times larger.

"There's a feeling here that we can create a big company where everybody enjoys working. Maybe that's a crusade. But we all want it, not just me. When people ask me how long this kind of organization can last, I tell them it will last just as long as each person here wants it to. We only lose it when people no longer care."[20]

MANAGERIAL SYSTEM

No one can truly manage 100 percent growth in the classical sense. There's less emphasis on management and more on information, on systems of providing information so people can work independently. But that does not mean that Tandem lacks control of company operations. The company has rigid procedures for implementing production controls, cost standards, quality control, and management reporting systems. To handle these jobs, Tandem has eight separate in-house computer systems.

Tandem uses this management information-decision system to monitor its operations and its growth. One of the ways Treybig has tried to promote creativity among Tandem's top management is to free them from the routine responsibilities of running a company. He encourages managers to delegate downward, both to give them more time to think creatively and to develop lower level managers.

Tandem tries to make sure the top people have no day-to-day responsibilities except to be interested in strategy, people, and creativity. The normal state of equilibrium is that there's no real place in a company for these types of things. So management's role must be to encourage people, to get them to think strategically, to reward creativity. Information on inventory, orders, costs, hiring, and payroll is entered and can be monitored by management the same day. Management knows immediately if there's a problem. As Jim Treybig commented, "You can make a lot of mistakes if you don't know about problems immediately."[21]

This basic control system, coupled with over 100 Tandem computer systems at more than forty locations all tied together into one large network, gives management on-line control of many aspects of their business. Its unique product features have directly assisted in the management of Tandem's growth.

Decisions are made informally, and executives get together in spontaneous meetings as problems arise. Admitted Chief Financial Officer Loustaunou: "We have no scheduled reviews of things like progress reports."[22] So far, the company has managed quite well without formal meetings. Outsiders often note that communications among the top executives flow as freely as the beer that is served every Friday afternoon. "If you ask the same question of several managers, you always get the same answer," said Alvin C. Rice, a Tandem director.[23]

A managerial grid, developed by Robert Blake and Jane Mouton as a means of categorizing management styles, shows that Tandem uses a team management style. Work is accomplished through committed people. Tandem spends a lot of time in hiring the right people and making sure that they are committed to the company. Tandem creates a common stake in organization purpose by making all employees stockholders. They develop relationships of trust through a comprehensive organization philosophy of individual respect.

Tandem uses a subordinate-centered leadership style. This style frees management to do the jobs of planning and control. This style works well at Tandem because employees can be monitored by their computer information system, and employees are extremely self-motivated.

Planning

The senior and middle managers of Tandem Computers participated in a training course in anticipation of the time when Tandem would become a $1 billion company. In two-day seminars they ran through courses on hiring, delegating responsibility, developing new markets and new products, and examining Tandem's basic corporate philosophy. When the time arrives, the problems and differences that come with bigness should seem old hat. "We use $1 billion not as a sales forecast, but to anticipate all the problems that come when you get that big," said Jim Treybig, "we need to recognize the problems that come with growth."[24]

A $100 million company doesn't need thirteen vice presidents, but a billion dollar company does. By the time Tandem reaches a billion, these people will be too busy to get to know each other. They are working together now, building an organization for the future.

Managerial Strategy

When Jim Treybig was asked about the factors that caused Tandem's success he replied:

> Having the right product and market, the right direction, and the right business strategy. If you have the right business strategy, you can make a lot more mistakes than if you have the wrong one. Another thing that makes a company good is having fantastic people. If you have the right business plan you can attract better people. The other thing you need is money. Without money, eventually you lose good people. Those three things were right at Tandem. We had the right business product/market concept. We started with outstanding people, which allowed us to hire more. Then we were able to do what we said we'd do, and that let us get more money and better people and keep growing in the right direction.[25]

CONCLUSIONS

Tandem Computers was founded in 1974 by Jim Treybig. It has grown rapidly, virtually doubling its revenues every year. Its location in Silicon Valley gives it ready access to a skilled labor force, vendors, and venture capital. This environment enabled Tandem to use the management techniques that it has used.

Rapid growth has caused Tandem to adopt a participative management style that emphasizes a broad area of control for management and a large amount of authority for subordinates. Tandem's high productivity has been accomplished by hiring the best people (both highly qualified and possessing a high growth-need) and providing an atmosphere that will motivate them. The integration of these concepts forms the basis of Theory Z.

William Ouchi, author of *Theory Z*, identified some problems that are inherent in running a Z-type corporation. Tandem may not be feeling the effects of these problems yet but should be aware of them. Xenophobia, a fear of outsiders, tends to develop in type Z firms, especially at the higher levels. Tandem deals with this problem by aggressively promoting from within, but care should be taken in maintaining a top-notch management team.

Type Z firms tend to resist deviance. Often new ideas are not developed in these firms because they do not conform. Tandem is young enough to still be creative, but it must carefully monitor research and development facilities to ensure continued creativity and diverse ideas.

When presented with changes in technology, type Z firms are unusually adaptive. However, if a change in corporate values is necessary for continued competitiveness, the organization is highly unadaptive. For example, Tandem might have trouble adapting if it were necessary to change to an assembly-line type manufacturing style in order to remain competitive.

Type Z corporations are highly productive and are especially well-suited to the high-growth industries. The problems that these corporations tend to have are not insurmountable. These problems may be dealt with if management is aware of them.

Tandem believes that its success emanates from a clear sense of direction throughout the company and from a sharing of responsibilities and rewards with all employees. The work environment is stimulating and challenging. Advancement opportunities abound for capable people who can take the initiative in accepting responsibility. Individual performance is nurtured by the company's belief that self-management and peer pressure in a high-technology environment is more productive than a strict structure.

The Tandem philosophy encourages teamwork by sharing corporate goals and objectives with all employees. The company impresses upon everyone that each area of the company and each individual contribute to Tandem's success.

Tandem's explosive corporate growth creates not only big profits and lavish benefits but also an acute need for new managers, rapid promotion, and employees able to manage themselves. With nearly half the employees at the company for less than six months, hierarchies are not fully defined, roles are relatively unfixed, and potential power and opportunity exist for all.

James R. Berdell of Montgomery Securities in San Francisco points out that Tandem's price-earnings ratio of thirty-six is the highest of all of the technology stocks that he follows and almost double the computer industry average. For Treybig, such success is merely part of his long-term plan. "I never started Tandem thinking only of a $100 million company," the brash executive exclaimed. "To build a $10 billion company where people loved to work would be a start."[26]

Notes

1   Myron Magnet, "Managing by Mystique at Tandem Computers," *Fortune,* June 28, 1982, 84.
2   Susan Benner, "Tandem Has a Fail-Safe Plan for Growth," *Inc.,* June 1981, 64–68.
3   Ibid., 65.
4   Ibid.
5   Magnet, "Mystique at Tandem," 85.
6   Ibid.
7   Ibid.
8   "What Makes Tandem Run?" *Business Week,* July 14, 1980, 73.
9   "Working in Tandem," *Mgr.,* 19.

10 See Donald F. Harvey and Donald R. Brown, *Organization Development,* 3rd ed. (Engle-
    wood Cliffs, NJ: Prentice-Hall, 1988), chapter 15.

11 Michael S. Malone, "Tandem Computers: No Recession Here," *The New York Times,*
    April 25, 1982, F9.

12 Magnet, "Mystique at Tandem," 90.

13 Ibid.

14 Thomas J. Murray, "The Hot New Computer Companies," *Dun's Review,* January 1979,
    52.

15 Magnet, "Mystique at Tandem," 91.

16 William G. Ouchi, *Theory Z* (New York: Avon Books, 1981), 68–79.

17 Kathleen K. Wiegner, "Beyond the Better Mousetrap," *Forbes,* June 22, 1981, 58.

18 Ibid.

19 Adam Smith, "Silicon Valley Spirit," *Esquire,* November 1981, 13.

20 Magnet, "Mystique at Tandem," 91.

21 Ibid.

22 Ibid.

23 Ibid.

24 Ibid.

25 Ibid.

26 Ibid.

EXHIBIT 1

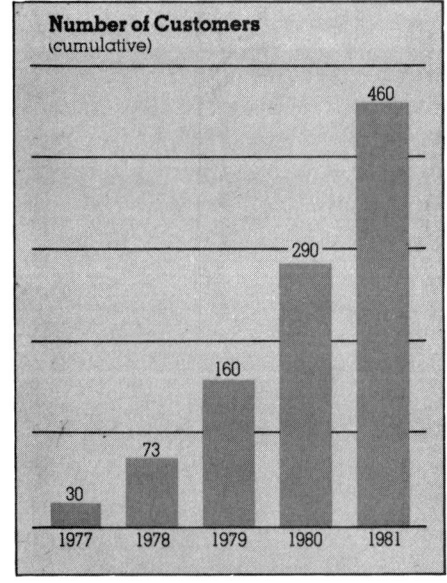

EXHIBIT 2

% of Revenue				% Increase		
1981	1980	1979		1981	1980	1979
100.0	100.0	100.0	Revenue	91	95	130
36.3	37.5	37.1	Cost of Revenue	85	96	129
8.6	8.1	8.3	Product Development	103	89	115
35.8	36.7	37.2	Marketing, General, and Administrative	86	92	136
19.4	17.7	17.3	Operating Income	109	99	129
5.1	1.6	.7	Interest (net)	509	342	54
			Earnings Per Share	106	76	100

EXHIBIT 3
Highlights

Fiscal year Ended September 30	1981	1980	% Change
Revenue	$208,397,000	$108,989,000	91
Operating Income	$ 40,391,000	$ 19,323,000	109
Operating Margin	19.4%	17.7%	
Net Income	$ 26,549,000	$ 10,687,000	148
Earnings Per Share	$.72	$.35	106
Working Capital	$179,102,000	$ 61,232,000	192
Total Assets	$255,971,000	$ 95,701,000	167
Equity	$204,810,000	$ 70,294,000	191
Number of Employees	2,730	1,387	97

EXHIBIT 4

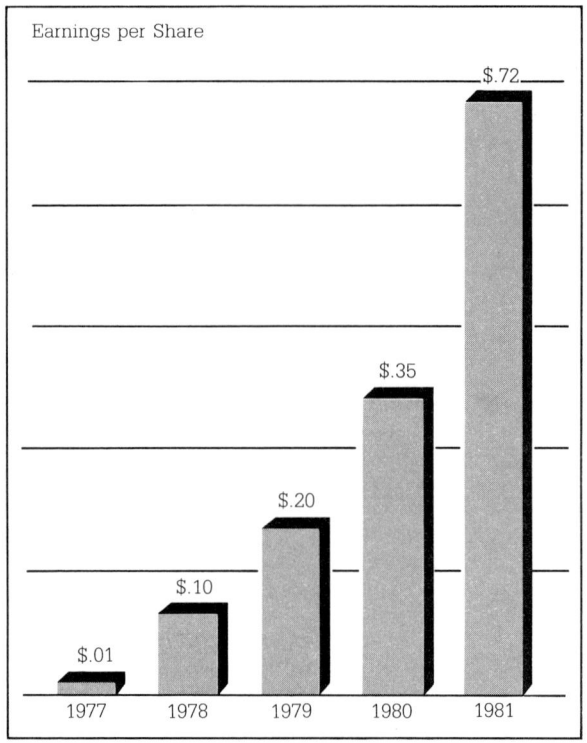

EXHIBIT 5

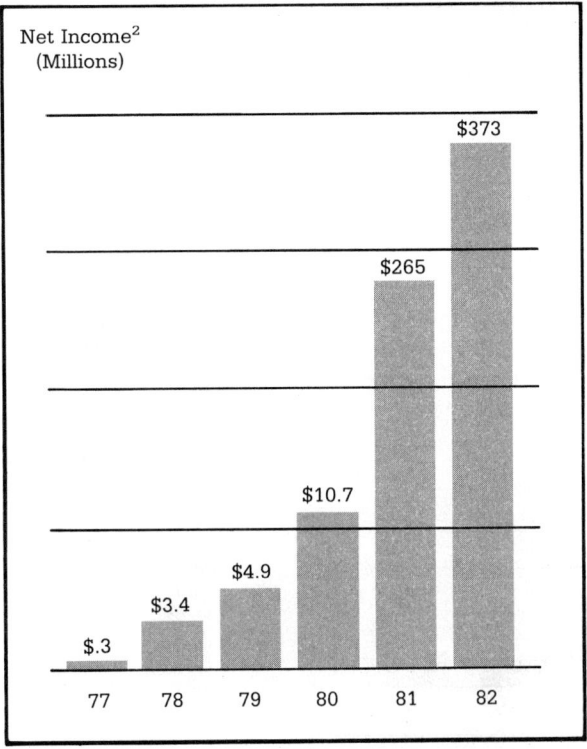

EXHIBIT 6

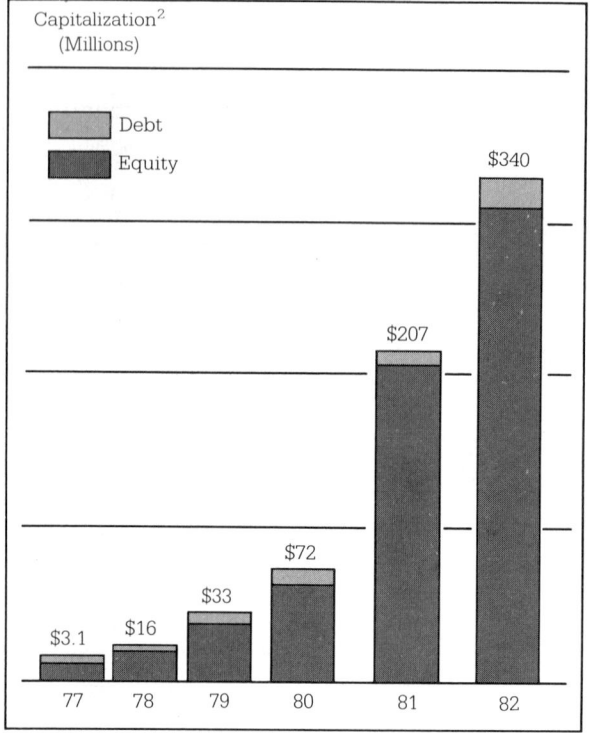

EXHIBIT 7

Selected Financial Data for the Five Years Ended September 30, 1981

TANDEM COMPUTERS INCORPORATED AND SUBSIDIARIES

SELECTED FINANCIAL DATA
For the Five Years Ended September 30, 1981

(In thousands except per share amounts)	1981	1980	1979	1978	1977
Revenue	$208,397	$108,989	$55,974	$24,305	$7,692
Cost of revenue	75,547	40,831	20,786	9,096	3,514
Product development	17,833	8,786	4,654	2,169	1,094
Marketing, general, and administrative	74,626	40,049	20,828	8,808	2,719
Operating Income	40,391	19,323	9,706	4,232	365
Interest income, net	10,707	1,759	398	258	(36)
Provision for income taxes	(24,549)	(10,395)	(5,184)	(2,337)	(171)
Income Before Extraordinary Credit	26,549	10,687	4,920	2,153	158
Net income	26,549	10,687	4,920	3,371	325
Earnings Per Share Before Extraordinary Credit	$ .72	$ .35	$ .20	$ .10	$ .01
Earnings per share	.72	.35	.20	.16	.02
Total Assets	$255,971	$ 95,701	$45,947	$22,051	$5,370
Long Term Capitalized Lease Obligations	2,054	1,651	1,144	715	316
Stockholders' Investment	204,810	70,294	31,530	15,538	2,735

Per share amounts have been adjusted here and throughout financial statements for three-for-one stock split effective June 30, 1981.

EXHIBIT 8

Consolidated Balance Sheet as of September 30, 1981 and 1980

TANDEM COMPUTERS INCORPORATED AND SUBSIDIARIES

CONSOLIDATED BALANCE SHEET
As of September 30, 1981 and 1980

(In thousands)	1981	1980
Assets		
Current Assets		
Cash	$ 9,377	$ 9,265
Cash investments	80,429	6,980
Accounts receivable, net of allowance for		
doubtful accounts of $1,000,000 in 1981 and $1,016,000 in 1980	70,671	42,552
Inventories	54,543	20,901
Prepaid expenses and other	5,046	1,965
Total current assets	220,066	81,663
Property and Equipment, at cost		
Production and test equipment	11,395	4,135
Computer equipment	11,122	4,702
Office furniture and equipment	2,466	1,083
Systems spares	8,610	4,391
Leasehold improvements	10,746	4,054
	44,339	18,365
Accumulated depreciation and amortization	(8,434)	(4,327)
Net property and equipment	35,905	14,038
Total Assets	$255,971	$95,701
Liabilities and Stockholders' Investment		
Current Liabilities		
Current portion of capitalized lease obligations	$ 682	$ 476
Accounts payable	23,634	11,063
Accrued liabilities	6,373	3,216
Accrued income taxes	10,275	5,676
Total current liabilities	40,964	20,431
Capitalized Lease Obligations	2,054	1,651
Deferred Income Taxes	8,143	3,325
Commitments		
Stockholders' Investment		
Common stock $.025 par value, authorized 60,000,000 shares,		
outstanding 36,409,631 in 1981 and 30,074,754 in 1980	910	251
Additional paid-in capital	161,468	53,555
Retained earnings	42,432	16,488
Total stockholders' investment	204,810	70,294
Total Liabilities and Stockholders' Investment	$255,971	$95,701

The accompanying notes are an integral part of this balance sheet.

EXHIBIT 9

Consolidated Statement of Changes in Financial Position for the Three Years
Ended September 30, 1981

TANDEM COMPUTERS INCORPORATED AND SUBSIDIARIES

CONSOLIDATED STATEMENT OF CHANGES IN FINANCIAL POSITION
For the Three Years Ended September 30, 1981

(In thousands)	1981	1980	1979
Working Capital Provided From (Used For):			
Net income	$ 26,549	$10,687	$ 4,920
Add back items not currently using working capital			
Depreciation and amortization	4,107	2,547	1,365
Deferred income taxes	4,818	2,284	1,041
Working capital provided from operations	35,474	15,518	7,326
Acquisition of property and equipment, net	(25,974)	(9,966)	(5,433)
Increase in capitalized lease obligations	403	507	429
Sale of common stock, net	105,702	27,271	10,837
Tax benefit from employee transactions in common stock	2,265	806	235
Net increase in working capital	$117,870	$34,136	$13,394
Working Capital Increase Represented By:			
Increase in current assets			
Cash and cash investments	$ 73,561	$ 9,487	$ 2,311
Accounts receivable	28,119	22,671	11,766
Inventories	33,642	9,597	4,985
Prepaid expenses and other	3,081	580	766
Increase in current liabilities			
Current portion of capitalized lease obligations	(206)	(101)	(172)
Accounts payable	(12,571)	(5,388)	(1,909)
Accrued liabilities	(3,157)	(1,947)	(316)
Accrued income taxes	(4,599)	(763)	(4,037)
Net increase in working capital	$117,870	$34,136	$13,394

The accompanying notes are an integral part of this statement.

EXHIBIT 10

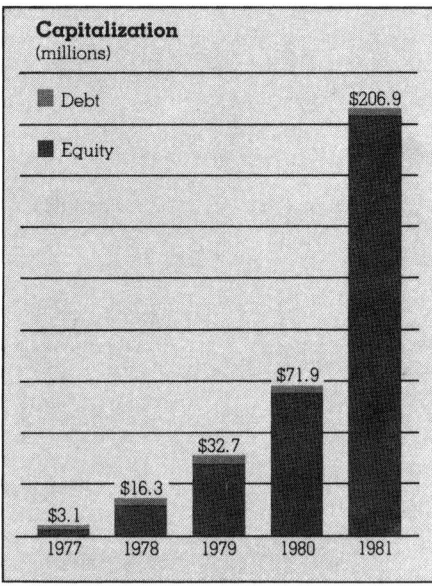

EXHIBIT 11

(In thousands)	Geographic Area			Adjustments and Eliminations	Consol- idated
	United States	Europe	Other		
1981					
Revenue-Customer	$144,392	$47,294	$16,711	$ —	$208,397
Revenue-Intracompany	37,580	—	—	(37,580)	—
Revenue-Total	181,972	47,294	16,711	(37,580)	208,397
Pre-Tax Income	50,297	4,145	2,139	(5,483)	51,098
Identifiable Assets	213,693	34,592	12,471	(4,785)	255,971
1980					
Revenue-Customer	$78,758	$25,760	$4,471	$ —	$108,989
Revenue-Intracompany	17,452	1,868	56	(19,376)	—
Revenue-Total	96,210	27,628	4,527	(19,376)	108,989
Pre-Tax Income	21,469	801	140	(1,328)	21,082
Indentifiable Assets	76,181	19,889	2,109	(2,478)	95,701
1979					
Revenue-Customer	$41,292	$13,501	$1,181	$ —	$ 55,974
Revenue-Intracompany	8,846	102	—	(8,948)	
Revenue-Total	50,138	13,603	1,181	(8,948)	55,974
Pre-Tax Income (Loss)	11,127	230	(173)	(1,080)	10,104
Identifiable Assets	35,667	10,113	1,319	(1,152)	45.947

Intracompany transfers are made at approximately arm's length prices, which include manufacturing profits attributable to United States operations. Identifiable assets are those assets of the Company that are identified with the operations of the corresponding geographic area. United States customer revenue included export sales of $7,397,000 in 1981, $3,973,000 in 1980, and $1,663,000 in 1979.

EXHIBIT 12
Employee Productivity (sales per employee; thousands)

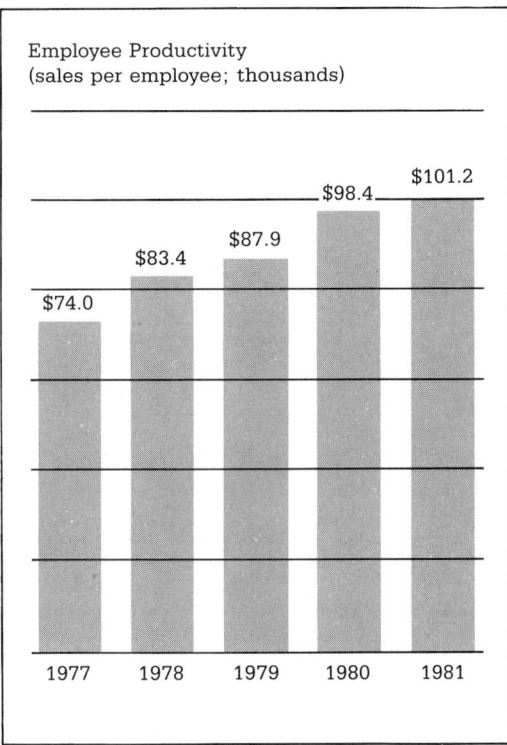

Employee Productivity
(sales per employee; thousands)

$74.0 $83.4 $87.9 $98.4 $101.2

1977   1978   1979   1980   1981

EXHIBIT 13
Organization Chart

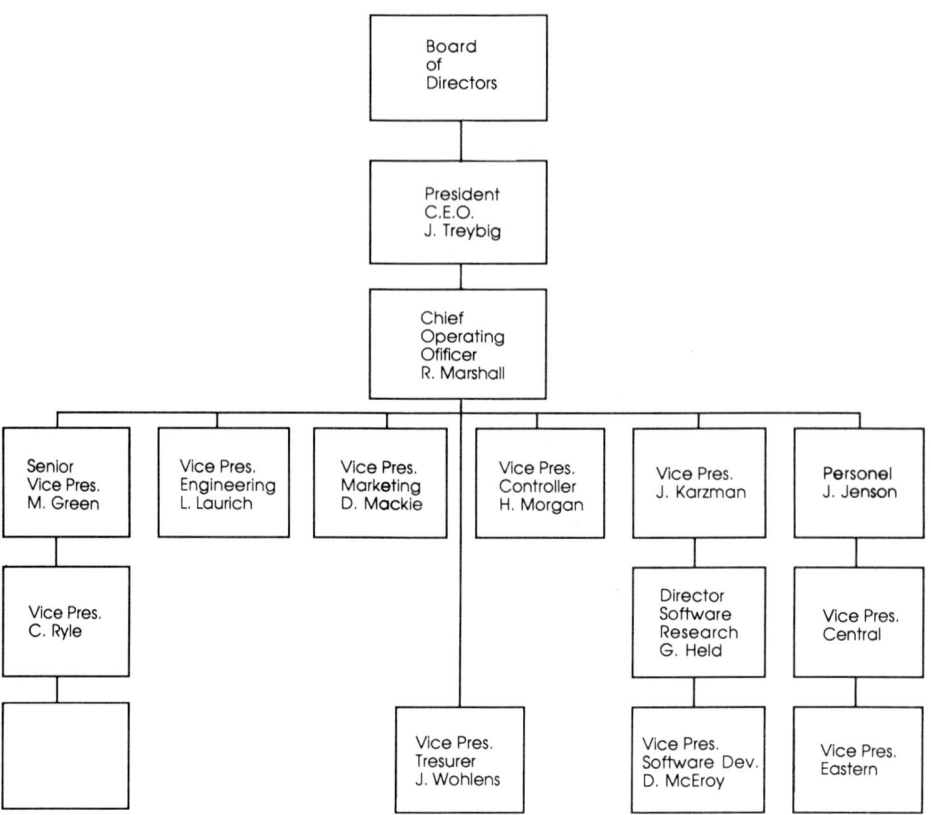

ISC Systems Corporation, 1986

Donald F. Harvey
Research Associate: Peter J. Carroll

INTRODUCTION

The year 1986 was very good for ISC. Its financial performance in fiscal year 1986 was the best in the nine-year history of the company, and ISC further improved its leadership position in the marketplace.

As Ted DeMerritt looked out of his office overlooking the Spokane River, he reflected on his new strategy for ISC. Successfully implementing systems is a much bigger challenge in today's complex data processing environment than simply building system components. ISC's turnkey approach satisfies a genuine and growing customer need and is an approach not fully embraced by its competitors. Although ISC's mission is demanding, DeMerritt believes he has the necessary people, knowledge, and management to succeed.

Background

ISC was founded by an entrepreneur who saw a need and then sought to satisfy that need for a profit. In 1977, Gary Norton, a self-taught programmer and former financial consultant, recognized that most financial institutions purchased their computer systems from larger computer companies with a vested interest in selling hardware. These large companies provide little if any software support or customization. Thus, the customers often had to adapt their operations to the limitations of the hardware. In response to this problem, Gary Norton developed a system using microcomputers and flexible software that addressed the need for software support and customization. The original system was the "4-window teller terminal system" developed for the savings and loan industry.

During the first few years of ISC's operation, the firm marketed its product exclusively to the thrift industry on the west coast. In 1979 the 8-window teller system was developed. The new system with its increased capacity, speed, and computing ability was well received by the thrift industry and allowed ISC to expand its market. On September 16, 1980, ISC went public with an offering of 658,992 shares at $19.50 each (not adjusted for four-for-one split). In 1981 ISC's geographic

This case was prepared using published accounts and public documents for the purpose of class discussion rather than to illustrate either effective or ineffective handling of an administrative situation.

market expanded to include the entire United States, but the company continued to focus on the thrift industry.

In June 1982, ISC formally introduced the "Pinnacle," a product designed to allow penetration into the commercial banking market. The unique Pinnacle system provided greatly expanded teller terminal capacity and applications in the platform area where new accounts are opened and where commercial and consumer loans are written. With the introduction of the Pinnacle system, ISC successfully penetrated the commercial bank market and continues in its bid to gain market share.

ISC's corporate headquarters and manufacturing facilities are located in Spokane, Washington. Until 1983 the focus of its business operations was on the needs of financial institutions within the domestic market. Since 1983 ISC has expanded into the international market by creating subsidiaries in the United Kingdom and in Canada. It has also developed relations with distributors in other areas of the world who market and support ISC products to their customers.

ISC has successfully established itself as the number one supplier of retail branch automation services in the domestic thrift market. It has also been successful in capturing 4 percent of the domestic commercial bank market and in expanding into the international market. Since the company began operations in 1977, it has installed 72,140 customer work stations; has 1,849 thrift institution customers, 167 commercial bank customers, two consumer finance customers; and, it has increased its net worth from $.2 to $67.7 million. Additional financial history information is contained in the financial section of this case and in exhibit 1. ISC fared well in its first eight years of existence, but it must continue to evaluate its environment and develop appropriate strategies if it wishes to survive through the twentieth century and beyond.[1]

CORPORATE MISSION

ISC, in a recent corporate publication, states that its mission is to

- Achieve leadership in the development, sales, and support of distributed processing systems to the financial industry.
- Provide solutions-oriented, turnkey system products responsive to the financial industry's needs.
- Deliver the highest level of comprehensive customer support available.[2]

There are four key components to ISC's basic statement of purpose: market position, areas of participation or business operations, type of products offered, and the market in which ISC wishes to participate. Because ISC states that it desires to achieve leadership in development sales and support, it is reasonable to assume that it wishes to dominate those areas—not necessarily a modest goal. Indeed, to obtain leadership in even one of the areas mentioned would be a substantial feat for a young company such as ISC. Yet, ISC's domination of the thrift industry makes it more than an idle threat to industry giants such as IBM and Burroughs Corp.

The areas of business participation were identified as development, sales, and support. In other words, ISC wishes to develop the very best systems available, have the largest volume of sales in the financial market, and provide unsurpassed service for the systems it sells. To attain a leadership position, ISC must invest heavily in research and development, expand its marketing capabilities, increase its advertising outlays, and increase its servicing capabilities by increasing the number of service centers and service personnel. Realizing ISC's mission will entail a great deal of capital outlay and well-organized plans and strategies.

The Product

The central product of ISC is distributed processing systems for the financial industry. Specifically, it produces solutions-oriented turnkey systems. ISC feels the turnkey approach is the best way to address customers' needs and therefore develops, markets, and sells *only* turnkey systems. The wisdom of such an approach is debatable, because most other market participants do not provide turnkey systems and yet still seem to make their required profit. Presently, IBM dominates the larger commercial bank market but does not provide a turnkey system. There are two limitations to using the turnkey-only approach. From a management and technical viewpoint, turnkey systems require additional time to produce, assemble, develop software for, and install. The added cost of combining these elements through project management tends to make cost containment and pricing difficult. From the customers' point of view, turnkey systems are limited both in the products they may wish to buy, such as a number of station terminals, and in the resulting amount of money they would be required to spend. Therefore, ISC's basic mission plan tends to exclude a number of potential customers because of its narrow focus.

Most companies develop their short- and long-term goals in support of the corporate mission, and it is advantageous to have a mission statement that allows the firm to take advantage of potential opportunities. ISC's mission statement restricts the potential opportunities the company may pursue to turnkey processing systems for the financial industry. There may be other opportunities that are consequently overlooked.

Management

In any organization there are a number of key decision makers whose knowledge, background, experience, and leadership style and skill aid the corporation in pursuit of fulfilling its mission. This section looks at ISC's key decision makers, their background, experience, and leadership style and provides a brief analysis of their effectiveness.

The man whose driving force brought ISC from its infancy to its present position is Gary A. Norton. Norton was formerly chairman of the board of directors and formerly president and chief executive officer of the company. For three years prior to founding the company, Norton was self-employed and engaged in the development and sale of telecommunications and front-end processing systems to financial institutions. He also served as a data processing consultant to financial institutions and others. He served in various capacities related to on-line terminal systems for Olivetti Corporation (the Italian systems firm) and Dade County Federal Savings and Loan Association.[3]

Several mid-level ISC managers indicated that Gary Norton tends to be moderately high in his need for both power and achievement. He tends to be results-oriented and uses his position power more often than he uses his personal persuasiveness. Two of the managers felt that Norton's executive style was that of an analytical gamesman because of his skill and experience in handling complex data and his creativity in obtaining results. The other two managers felt his style was that of an amiable gamesman because he got along well with most everyone.

Gerry Reeve (an ISC manager of investor relations) indicated in an interview that Norton does not engage in the day-to-day activities of managing ISC, but does at times drop in to work on some pet projects under development. This type of activity, related to his role of chairman of the board, often causes problems within the areas he delves into and is not considered appropriate. However, who is going to argue with the chairman? Because of conflicting lines of authority, such actions are counterproductive in most cases.

Most of the people who were approached regarding Norton held him in very high regard. He was described as having a mix of participative and directive management styles. Working with and around him was often intense, and he is said to be demanding.

The chairman of the company is Ted C. DeMerrit. DeMerritt has been with ISC since 1980. Since March 1981, he has also been a director of the Sacramento Savings and Loan Association. Outside of ISC, DeMerritt worked for seventeen years as the senior vice president and controller of the Sacramento Savings and Loan Association.

The four middle managers who were asked about DeMerritt's leadership style unanimously placed him in the middle of the Strategic Management Style Matrix. They each felt that DeMerritt's style was moderate in terms of both power and achievement. DeMerritt has a participative management style that is highly supportive of his subordinates, but he tends to provide only moderate levels of direction. He is characterized as a nice guy to work with and for; however, words like *dynamic, intense, inspiring,* or *aggressive* were absent from the descriptions given by the middle managers.

John Lindeblad is presently the president and chief operating officer of the company. Lindeblad has an accounting background and graduate degree, and he has served in various capacities with ISC since June 1978. Prior to coming to ISC he worked for eight years in the audit division of Arthur Anderson and Company. Lindeblad, who works closely with DeMerritt, is described as the man who holds the organization together. He is highly visible throughout the organization and is said to be assertive, providing equal amounts of direction and support. Of the senior executives, Lindeblad has been with the company for the longest time and many feel that he is the likely succesor to Ted DeMerritt.

Three of the top senior executives, Gary Norton, Ted DeMerritt, and David Stoner (vice president of marketing), came from the savings and loans industry. This fact may explain why the company did so well in the area of thrifts. Of the seven senior executives, not including Norton, only DeMerritt and Lindeblad were with the company prior to 1982. Apparently the company has had trouble holding on to its top people. This instability can cause real problems with continuity and morale, causing repercussions throughout the organization. Two of the senior executives, Hal Covert (vice president, finance) and Charles Furniss (vice president, human resources), were hired in 1984 and 1985, respectively.

Prior to 1984, most of ISC's executives were promoted from within the organization. Since that time, the company has pursued a strategy of bringing in seasoned professionals including: Glen Cavanaugh, vice president, product management; Ron Mason, vice president, eastern region; Brady Rackley, vice president, southern region; and, Anthony J. Nevison, managing director, ISC Systems Limited.

ISC's growth to its present size has required that outsiders with experience in dealing with and in a large corporation be brought on board. Their experience should be instrumental in leading the company into the future. However, it may also be necessary to bring in a new CEO to lead those executives.

Recent Top Organizational Changes

During the week of May 11, 1986, an important change to the top position of ISC took place. Gary Norton stepped down as chairman of the board of directors and was replaced by Ted DeMerritt. The vacated position of chief executive officer of the company was filled by John Lindeblad, whose position as vice president of operations was filled by Hal Covert, former vice president, finance. Covert's former position has been filled by Ken Olsen (formerly controller, Southwest Forest Industries).

The change has left the company in a state of flux until the dust settles. John Lindeblad should have no problem taking the reins of power with the full backing of DeMerritt, and Gary Norton's imprint on the company will continue to fade.

ORGANIZATIONAL STRUCTURE AND MANAGEMENT

After looking at the corporate mission and the key decision makers who oversee that mission, it is appropriate now to identify the way that those key decision makers have organized the resources of ISC to support its mission. This section describes the organizational structure of ISC, identifies some of the techniques ISC employs to ensure goals are being addressed, and examines the appropriateness of its present structure.

ISC has established a regional structure with decentralized management. ISC's organizational structure (see exhibit 2) consists of six administrative support groups, five domestic profit centers, and three international profit centers. The support groups assist the operating units of the corporation and administer and oversee those policies deemed necessary to keep the company on track toward realizing its short- and long-term goals. The six support groups are marketing, product development, operations, human resources, legal, and finance. (See exhibit 3 for a list of officers and directors.)

There are five domestic profit centers operating as semi-autonomous units of the organization: central, eastern, southern, and western regions, and manufacturing. Each profit center is responsible for developing and meeting its own goals in support of the corporate goals and mission. The majority of the decisions that affect the profit center's customers are left to its discretion. The manufacturing division operates as a for-profit company, selling its finished units to the regional centers. The regional centers act as distributors of those units with value added in the form of service, installation, customization, and support, somewhat like a franchise. The three international profit centers: ISC Computer Systems of Canada, ISC Systems, Ltd., United Kingdom, and ISC, Latin America, all operate similarly to the domestic profit centers.

When ISC moved from a centralized to a decentralized structure it also developed a number of management techniques and processes to ensure that corporate goals would continue to be addressed. The company initiated operation reviews, in which top management periodically visits each region for a general business review. These operation reviews allow management to appraise the progress of the region in relation to its objectives. Equally important, they ensure open communication between regional and corporate offices. Also to ensure open communication throughout the organization, formal and informal group meetings take place regularly and a formal grievance system is in place.

To remain on track toward goal fulfillment, the company recently implemented a quarterly forecast process with a twelve-month rolling horizon. This system attempts to predict revenue generation based on past, current, and forecasted sales and expenses. In the past, lack of emphasis on cost containment resulted in higher than needed inventories and greater than anticipated expenses. The new system has helped to reduce inventories and slow the upward spiral of expenses.

The question at this point is whether or not ISC's organizational structure is appropriate for its present stage of development.

THE EXTERNAL ENVIRONMENT

Government

Because the government regulates the banking system, ISC's primary customer base, it will continue to affect the way financial institutions conduct business and therefore the companies that supply financial processing systems.

Potential Threats

With the Depository Institution Deregulation and Monetary Control Act of 1980, the government set the stage for a major transformation of the financial industries. Since the passage of that act, the products and services offered by both banks and savings and loans have been deregulated to the point where the differences in the two types of institutions are difficult to identify. This deregulation has spurred fierce competition, which in turn has caused a number of financial institutions to file for bankruptcy. Should this trend continue, there may well be a push for a return to stricter regulation and a reduction in the product offerings of the various institutions. Stricter regulations may result in a lower demand for financial systems used in the platform area to cross-sell products.

The government controls the money supply of the country through its required reserve rate, the sale and purchase of bonds and T-bills, and the rate it charges member banks to borrow money. The Federal Reserve then has a direct impact on the amounts of money that individuals and businesses desire to spend, borrow, or save. Should interest rates rise from their present low levels, financial institutions will no doubt see a slowdown in the rate of borrowing, with a resulting reduction in revenues and fewer dollars to invest in new processing systems.

The Gramm-Rudman deficit reduction bill has effectively cut government spending across the board, which in turn reduces the money that banks (that is, those banks that hold the accounts of organizations receiving government funds) would have on deposit. Consequently, the amount of money such banks may loan to other customers is reduced, resulting in a reduction in revenues and a decline in the dollars available to purchase new systems.

Potential Opportunities

If the Federal Reserve continues its present monetary policy of low interest rates, the banks and savings and loans should continue to see an expansion in their loan portfolios. Revenues should continue to increase, and the money to purchase new and updated systems to handle the increased loan demand will be available. At present, with mortgage and car loan rates so low, many of the loan departments are swamped with business that could be expedited with improved systems. For example, most bank-originated car loans (e.g., Seafirst) take anywhere from one to three days to process. With ISC's Pinnacle system, loans can be processed in less than thirty minutes.

If the financial system continues toward deregulation, and the type and variety of financial products are allowed to expand, there will be a continued need for sophisticated systems to automate transactions, improve cost position, and cross-sell those products.

Economic Forces

The U.S. economy has been expanding moderately for the past four years. Whether it will continue to expand is difficult to predict, but regardless of which direction it takes, the economy will have a definite impact on ISC's customers, its competitors, and its general business condition.

Potential Threats

In the event the economy slows down or goes into a recession, it will reduce the desire of individuals and businesses to borrow and save. The demand for financial products and services would decline and result in a slackening of demand for new processing systems. Smaller companies such as ISC would be financially weakened with a probable reduction in sales revenue and profit. There would be a shortage of money for R&D, sales, and marketing expenses and also a possible erosion of market share.

Potential Opportunities

If the economy continues to expand, ISC's customers should continue to see ample demand for its financial products. The availability of money directly affects the type and volume of financial services made available by banks and savings and loans. As demand for services continues to increase, the need for processing systems with greater speed and capacity will also expand and create new business for companies in the financial systems field.

A survey of executives, conducted by *Fortune* magazine, showed that 79 percent of the executives polled felt that the economy will continue to expand steadily. GNP growth in 1987 is expected to be 3.5 percent, according to those surveyed. *Fortune's* estimate is slightly more conservative at 2 percent.[4]

With the value of the dollar down against most major foreign currencies, the products of ISC should be more affordable to its overseas customers. *Fortune* believes that many countries will also have more discretionary income because of lower oil prices and expects to see U.S. export earnings increasing 9 percent annually.[5] This increase may provide a prime opportunity to move more aggressively into the overseas markets.

Market Forces

The financial services industry is an extremely dynamic market. With only minor differences between various institutions, the banks and savings and loans compete for customer deposits with new and varied financial services. The way individuals access, borrow, and invest their money is changing and consequently presenting both threats and opportunities to companies such as ISC whose systems support those markets.

Potential Threats

A recent bank operations report by Warren, Gorham, and Lamont, Inc., addressed the topic of *electronic funds transfer* (EFTS). It predicted that banks, savings and loans, the federal government, and the retail businesses will continue to move away from paper transactions and toward EFTS, motivated by the demonstrated cost reductions. Consumers will also come to accept and eventually demand EFTS services as a more convenient way to manage their finances.[6]

As EFTS gains acceptance within the population, businesses will begin to use automated clearinghouses to handle labor-intensive paper transactions. A move away from the customer paper transactions toward a greater use of EFTS should reduce the need for tellers and therefore for teller stations. The teller stations make up a large portion of ISC's annual sales.

This phenomenon is already evident in the banking system. Many employees at a branch that installed a cash machine were forced to reduce work hours due to a noticeable reduction in lobby traffic. Branches have been closed and replaced by smaller drive-up branches with only one to three tellers and a cash machine. Should this trend continue, ISC must make appropriate adjustments in its product offerings.

Potential Opportunities

According to a recent report, banks currently provide at least 155 separate and distinct services to consumers.[7] As the type and variety of these services continue to change, there will be a continuous need for information processing systems to handle and cross-sell those services. Also, with EFTS gaining in acceptance, the equipment and software to handle it will continue to increase in demand. As consumers repeatedly use automated teller machines (ATMs), their popularity will grow and create new demand. It is predicted that ATM sales will grow by 33 percent per year through the 1990s. We are already seeing ATMs popping up in supermarkets and shopping malls across the country. There may be a big market for replacement, upgraded machines, and integrated software in the future.

Insurance companies and brokerage firms are entering financial markets with an assortment of financial products and services. Also, as companies like Sears and GM expand into traditional financial markets, they may create a demand for the types of financial processing systems offered by ISC.

Competitive Factors

ISC operates in a fiercely competitive market. There are a number of market participants, all of whom should be considered as potential threats.

Potential Threats

ISC's major competitors are IBM, NCR, Olivetti, Bunker Ramo, and Burroughs. IBM is by far the largest player in the financial systems market. According to Jim Stafford, marketing manager of ISC, IBM holds about 35 percent of the commercial bank market and 25 percent of the thrift institution market. IBM's 3600 system has been replaced by the new FCS4700, a basic controller terminal system that will be continually enhanced with both hardware and software throughout its product life.

IBM has a large direct-sales force (the number devoted to financial systems was not available) and has the best name in the business for service after the sale. Its equipment, although rating high in reliability and ease of operations, rated lower than ISC's in a survey of 631 branches using ISC's systems and 616 using IBM's systems.[8]

IBM is by far the low cost producer of financial systems and consequently offers its equipment at lower prices than ISC. Although IBM's after-sale service is similar to that of ISC, it does not offer nearly as much customized software. IBM will continue to be a dominant force in the industry for the foreseeable future, and consequently a constant threat.

Burroughs Corporation has lost some market share due to the influx of several new vendors. In the commercial bank market, Burroughs has approximately a 25 percent market share, while in the thrift market its share is 7–9 percent. The company's BMT series, its primary on-line system, is being replaced by Burroughs's new EF7000. The EF7000 Financial Workstation is Burroughs's main product for on-line teller transactions. Each unit contains its own microprocessor similar to ISC's Pinnacle. Burroughs also has a large direct-sales force. It is a higher cost producer than IBM, and its equipment price is lower than ISC's. Overall, a Datapro survey rated Burroughs lower than both IBM and ISC. It also received lower ratings in terms of software customization and vendor support.[9]

Burroughs added to its strength as a producer of information processing equipment by acquiring Sperry Corporation, making it the second largest computer firm. The merger enhances its production and R&D capabilities and may prove to be an increasing threat in the future.

NCR has approximately 10 percent of the commercial bank market and less than 5 percent of the thrift market.[10] NCR recently introduced the Branch Automation System 5000, a modular system that includes a powerful branch processor and a variety of workstation components from which a user can establish an appropriate configuration. NCR also offered an integrated passbook posting terminal for thrift institutions (model 2270) and the 2262 Financial Teller Terminal for commercial banks. NCR's system is like IBM's in that intelligence is not resident in the individual teller terminals. The branch processors are the main processing units of the system. Should the branch processor go down, all transactions would have to be done by hand. ISC's teller stations can continue to process a number of transactions without the branch processor. NCR, which makes the ranks of the *Fortune* 500 along with IBM and Burroughs, is a lower cost producer than ISC. Its hardware is very competitively priced, at a lower price than ISC, but it does not offer nearly as much software customization and after-sale service.

Olivetti has less than a 5 percent market share in both the commercial bank and thrift markets.[11] Its Line 1 Distributed Data Processing System incorporates many of the features of its older product, but with several significant enhancements. The vendor plans expansion of its marketing efforts in the United States and aims to find a greater proportion of commercial banks among its users. Olivetti's system resembles ISC's Pinnacle more closely than it does any other market participant.

Olivetti works with Docutel Corporation (a pioneer ATM vendor) in the United States and markets its financial systems as a subsidiary. Olivetti has extensive software customization and does provide after-sale service. Its pricing is also similar to that of ISC.

Olivetti's competitive position may also be further enhanced by the presence of David M. Stoner, who left ISC without notice in November of 1985. Stoner was formerly ISC's executive vice president of marketing.

Bunker Ramo Corporation has less than 5 percent of both the commercial bank and thrift markets,[12] but also offers a product line similar to ISC's Pinnacle system. Bunker Ramo provides two distinct hardware systems, the Bank Control System 90/Thrift and System 90. The basic hardware elements are identical in the two versions, with appropriate applications software defining the necessary differences. Bunker Ramo's newest offering is the Aladdin 30 system, a distributed multiprocessing system that provides traditional teller and administrative functions in addition to personal computing, word processing, and electronic spreadsheet capabilities. All of those features are also available with the Pinnacle system. Bunker Ramo has high ratings for reliability, but does not offer as much service and support as does ISC. Information on pricing was not available.

Other smaller operators within the financial systems market are Lundy Electronics and Systems, Inc., SCI systems, Systeme Corporation, Ericsson, and Fujitsu Systems of America. These are recent entries into the financial systems on-line teller market, with each having only a fraction of the total market share in both commercial bank and thrift markets. Like all competitors, they bear watching.

Supplier Factors

Because ISC is in the business of manufacturing, it must be concerned with the availability of material and labor to meet its customers' needs.

Potential Threats

ISC has moved away from its participation in the manufacturing of many of the subassemblies and most of the peripheral hardware units used in its systems. Although the company has not experienced any production delays caused by limited supplies in the past, the potential is there. Most of its subassemblies and hardware are purchased from outside suppliers. ISC usually has more than one source of supply; however, some parts and subassemblies currently have only one. If problems arise because of defective material or workmanship, there could be considerable delays in production, delivery, and installation. ISC must identify those key parts and subassemblies that are critical to production flow and seek additional potential suppliers.

Potential Opportunities

As more and more companies enter the high-tech electronic industry, the availability of quality suppliers should continue to make pricing competitive. ISC should continually survey the market and seek low-cost, high-quality vendors of parts and subassemblies. Also, it should seek vendors who can work closely with ISC production schedules and thereby reduce inventories and carrying costs.

Technology Factors

Potential Threats

The basic threat facing any high-tech company is the development of new technology or lower cost delivery of the product. Both major and start-up firms could develop customized software to compete in this market. Also, there is always the danger of being underpriced in either hardware or software from some competitor seeking to take away market share.

ISC exists in an industry characterized by extremely high technological opportunity. As new technology becomes available, it provides greater market opportunities. Those who make it to market first usually reap the greatest rewards. However, if a competitor beats them there, they may lose sales and market shares.

Potential Opportunity

Since 1970 the processing power of computers per dollar spent on them has risen a remarkable 30 percent a year, on average. However, computers cannot run without software, and software developers have been able to increase useful software at only an estimated 4 percent to 7 percent per year. The result: a software gap that is a barrier to computer progress but a possible boon to a company that can close that gap.[13] ISC's systems are unique because they are designed to accommodate the software, unlike most systems in which the software is designed to accommodate the system. Over 250 software people in ISC have developed proprietary software that helps to generate new software. ISC has many of the necessary assets to pursue the opportunity.

A possible opportunity lies ahead with the development of Intel's new 32-bit chip. It is said to have the potential for making personal computers twice as powerful and twice as fast. It was designed to be compatible with IBM's 16-bit chip for ease of upgrading and replacement on systems that use IBM-compatible software. Most of ISC's equipment is IBM-compatible, and it should seek to upgrade its product line to include that chip as soon as possible.[14]

Social Factors

There are no apparent social threats or potential opportunities that would have serious impact on ISC, at least none in the domestic market. It may have to keep close tabs on its international marketing areas, where the laws and social climate differ greatly from our own, especially if it expects to expand overseas markets.

Techniques for Environmental Analysis

ISC's environmental analysis maintains an awareness of customers' needs through a product advisory council and continued communication with present and potential customers. The company has no formal analysis methods to assess the impact of changes due to government, technology, or social factors. The marketing department keeps track of competitive market factors merely by monitoring new product offerings and advertisements.

THE INTERNAL SYSTEM

Marketing

According to Paine Webber, ISC's share of the thrift market was 43 percent, while in the commercial bank market its share was a mere 1 percent as of June 1984. ISC's lack of experience in the commercial bank market resulted in greater than expected time and expense involved in obtaining orders. This problem appears to have been overcome, as evidenced by the increased commercial bank orders. In 1985 net orders from the commercial banking market were $68.7 million, a 124 percent increase over fiscal 1984.[15]

Product

The marketing strategy ISC currently pursues positions its product to address the needs of various market segments. The basic teller and platform system applications contain 80 to 85 percent of the functions that most customers ultimately decide they want. It is the customization that completes the total systems package that differentiates the end product sold to various market segments. The software, service, and support are tailored to the specific needs of the customer.

ISC's products are used at the customer interface level. The company has intelligence resident at each work station and at the branch level. IBM's and NCR's systems do not have that feature. All of ISC's major applications are designed to improve and speed customer transactions. In addition, it has developed a great deal of expertise to support its customers and thereby to implement its product strategy of targeting the front office of financial institutions.

ISC's hardware is designed for a specific vertical market which permits it to be very exacting in its specifications. As a result, ISC has a number of visible advantages. System response time is much more rapid than that of its competitors. With intelligence located at the workstation, requirements for host support are much less than for systems without distributed intelligence. The trade-off here is in price: ISC's systems cost more. ISC, as mentioned earlier, offers only turnkey systems, providing the purchaser with a fully customized and operational system. ISC works closely with the purchasing organization to assess its processing needs, designs the appropriate system configuration, handles the details of installation and software customization, trains the new operators, and provides continuous after-sale service. No other competitor offers such a comprehensive product package. There are, however, limitations to so comprehensive an offering: namely, it costs a lot more and not everyone needs or wants a comprehensive package.

Distributed processing systems are still in the growth phase of the product life cycle, but are nearing maturity. Projected growth in the thrift industry is expected to be 2–4 percent through the eighties, and in the commercial bank market there is a larger expected growth rate of 16 to 18 percent.[16] ISC does not have new product leadership, but its products have an excellent reputation for quality, capability, and dependability.

Promotion

ISC promotes the sale of its systems principally through the use of a regional direct-sales force. Each region is divided into sales territories in which individual salespersons sell directly to the large banks and thrifts. The company concentrates its sales force on the 300 largest commercial banks and the 200 largest thrifts. ISC sells to smaller institutions through distributors and service bureaus including Electronic Data Systems and Citicorp Associates (an affiliate of Citicorp).

ISC also promotes its products by direct mailings, displays at conventions, advertisements in journals and magazines that cater to financial institutions, and word of mouth. The company periodically sends product brochures to potential and present customers announcing new or upgraded product offerings. Full-page color ads are purchased in publications geared to bankers and financiers, such as *Bankers World.* ISC normally purchases space for displays at conventions where information processing equipment is featured.

The sales and marketing expense in 1985 was fifteen times greater than when the company went public in 1980. In 1985 sales and marketing expense was $17.64 million, a 53 percent increase over 1984. That 53 percent increase resulted in a mere 8 percent increase in net sales. There was, however, a 66 percent increase in service and other revenues. The number of newly installed workstations (21,000) in 1985 compared to the number installed in 1984 (20,940), shows an increase of only 0.3 percent. ISC is spending a lot more money with little change in the amount of hardware it sells, an indication that the market may be closer to maturation than presently thought. Regardless, ISC needs to take a hard look at where its sales and marketing dollars are going. If it has to spend 53 percent more to maintain the same sales volume (in terms of units sold), it is in for trouble in the long run.

Distribution

ISC utilizes a direct sales organization to market its products primarily throughout the United States, Canada, and the United Kingdom. Additionally, independent distributors and service bureaus assist ISC in marketing to small- and medium-sized financial institutions. ISC sells its systems to independent distributors at a discounted price, whereas the company's sales personnel and independent service bureau representatives are compensated on a commission basis.

Internationally, relationships have been established with independent distributors to market the company's products in countries throughout South America, Australia, Asia, and Africa. Since 1983 ISC has greatly expanded into the international markets, but it is difficult to say how well these areas are doing because they are not broken out on the annual financial reports. In 1985, however, the number of workstations installed annually increased only minimally, indicating that the expanded market isn't generating too many new sales. If that is indeed the case, ISC needs to assess what must be done to improve this condition. There is a problem somewhere in the system.

Pricing

According to Jim Stafford, ISC's pricing strategy is competitive with that of other market participants. He also said that price was dependent on a number of variables such as the number of workstations to be purchased, the host system of the purchaser, the number of functions required in each workstation, and the geographic location of the purchaser.[17] There are apparently price differences in quantity orders and with systems that will be hooked up to host systems. Also, the price varies with the complexity of the system. There is an apparent improvement in the pricing effort because ISC realized an 8 percent increase in revenues with only a 0.3 percent increase in units sold.

There is some evidence that the company is pricing its equipment at the margin and making up the difference in service contracts. This compensation is probably a "penetrating strategy" to increase market share in the commercial bank market. This strategy would also help to explain a 66 percent increase in service revenues and the fact that service revenue now accounts for 23 percent of total revenue, up from 16 percent in 1984 and 14 percent in 1983. The increase was the largest percentage of total revenue jump since the company went public in 1980. No other information on pricing was available.

Production

The new ISC facility uses a fairly modern assembly line process, but it falls far short of a continuous flow system. Such a system would have greatly enhanced the company's production capacity, reduced unit labor cost, and throughput time. Consequently, ISC's production capabilities for producing low-cost units is not as competitive as most of the other market participants. Fortunately, the new facility is highly integrated with the major functional areas of the firm through the use of ISC's Interact System. Interact is a corporate management information system that ties together forecast demand, production planning, master production scheduling, bills of material, material requirements planning, capacity planning, inventory control, purchasing, shipping and receiving, and production control. Interact enables all departments to work together to "meet the plan."[18]

When ISC moved its production to the new facility, its capacity increased by 57 percent with only an 8 percent increase in required labor. With the new facility, ISC now has plenty of unused capacity. If we assume a one-shift operation, ISC is using only 60 percent of available capacity. It has the capability of three shifts, which would put it at a capacity utilization of 30 percent.[19] With such a low utilization rate, it is no wonder ISC's return on assets is only 10.6 percent. A comparison of ISC's net sales to net fixed asset ratio of 2.21 to the Robert Morris industry average of 5.4 for electronic computing equipment companies demonstrates that ISC is not using its productive assets effectively.

Currently, ISC purchases a number of subassemblies and hardware components from external sources. Given its present capacity utilization, ISC should consider producing some of those units in-house where doing so can be cost-justified? Also, ISC should continue to modernize its facility and move toward a continuous flow system. Currently, ISC outsources many components (e.g., keyboards) it considers commodity products.

Considering that most of the larger financial institutions are located in the east and southwest, one has to wonder about the wisdom of constructing a new production facility so far from most of its customers, cheap transportation, and possibly cheaper and more available labor.

Research and Development

In the financial markets there is increasing emphasis on the use of technology to improve productivity and profitability. The pace of technological change is increasing due to technology spillover from other, often unrelated, industries and intense competition, even from foreign competitors like Olivetti. In addition, future markets are more uncertain, capital requirements are large, and the cost of capital is uncertain. This section examines ISC's technological effort in the area of research and development and assesses a strategy for the future based on opportunities already identified and ISC's capabilities, competitors, and potential customers.

To assess ISC's technological effort, Hambrick and MacMillan's model for R&D efficiency will be used. ISC's performance will be compared to results of companies they evaluated in the Profit Impact of Market Strategies (PIMS) data base[20] (see exhibit 4).

In all cases, ISC scored considerably higher than the mean scores of the PIMS companies. This performance may be due to the fact that the PIMS companies are considerably larger than ISC. Also, in applying the model to ISC, it was assumed that all R&D expenses were applied to the Pinnacle system, but they more than likely were not. That fact would not reduce the scores below the PIMS means, but would in fact raise its scores.

Three factors that lead to ISC's high innovative efficiency and follow the factors addressed by Hambrick and MacMillan are (1) the technological opportunity in the field in which ISC operates, (2) ISC's use of market input through its product advisory board, and (3) the relatively new equipment in its new production facility.

In 1985 ISC spent $17.07 million (11 percent of its sales revenue) on R&D. That figure is lower than its 1984 R&D expenses of $19.52 million (15% of sales revenue) because the company stopped including project/customer-specific related R&D in the figure. Those amounts are now included in cost of sales and service. This accounting change has the effect of passing the project-specific development costs on to the customer. The experience that ISC gains in developing software customization for various host systems will allow it to use the learning curve to be more competitive in pricing future systems. ISC is presently working on a system to be introduced in 1990 that incorporates many of the recent advances in technology.

Human Resources

People are important to the success of any organization, and ISC is no exception. This section looks at ISC's human resource capabilities, the health of the organizational climate, salary and benefits, communication channels, and the managerial style employed.

Presently, the organizational climate is under the pressure and strain of restructuring. Internal changes have resulted in what one ISC employee described as a general atmosphere of chaos. Although the company is on target for its five year objectives, there is some concern for ISC's long-term future.

ISC claims to have competitive salaries and benefits. However, interviews with ISC personnel indicate that the salaries for professional positions within the firm may be low in comparison to companies like Hewlett-Packard and Keytronics. Although the company has a reputation of paying higher than market to attract high-tech people, ISC personnel who were interviewed said only that their salary was "OK for Spokane." However, they feel the company does have excellent medical, tuition reimbursement, and profit sharing benefits.

ISC has an open and healthy communication system. The company has an open door policy, is experimenting with formal groups such as quality circles, and has a formal grievance and suggestion system. Most of the people interviewed felt that there was a real commitment to open and honest communication and that the steps taken thus far to encourage healthy communication have been positive.

The managerial style in ISC appears to be reactive in most areas of operations. In many instances, problems must emerge or something must go wrong before any form of action takes place. However, once a problem or concern has surfaced, managers react fairly quickly to make the appropriate changes. There is a considerable amount of participative management, with decisions made collectively or at least with the requested input of those affected by the decision. This participation helps to promote a greater degree of commitment and to develop employee decision-making capabilities.

FINANCIAL ANALYSIS

ISC must have the required resources available to bring potential opportunities from the drawing board to the market place. This section examines the financial stability of ISC by looking at such factors as availability of capital, capital structure, cash flow measures, and the accounting system.

ISC's revenues and earnings grew explosively from its inception in 1977 through fiscal 1982 as the company quickly established itself as the major supplier of microprocessor-based, on-line, modular teller, and administrative terminal systems for the savings and loan industry. However, from 1984 to 1986 as the company has broadened its marketing thrust to go after the much larger commercial bank market, earnings declined. Despite this decline, revenue growth has continued to improve. Fiscal 1985 revenues were a record $149,998,000, a 17 percent increase over 1984's revenues. Earnings, on the other hand, have been hurt because it has proved to be more complex, more expensive, and more time-consuming to develop, sell, and install systems for commercial banks than for thrifts. In 1984 the net income increased 152% over 1983 results.[21] In 1985, net income fell 18 percent from 1984's record $9,987,000.

The disappointing earnings figure for 1985 ($8,190,000) was due to a number of increases in costs and expenses and interest expense (see exhibit 5). From fiscal 1984 to 1985, the cost of sales and services increased by 24 percent, whereas the production rate remained relatively the same at 21,000 workstations per year. Sales and marketing expense increased by 53 percent, and general and administrative expense increased by 25 percent. The largest increase was the 439 percent increase in interest expense, caused primarily by the capitalized interest on the long-term debt associated with the new production facility, which became due when the company occupied the building. This one-time payment explains the large decrease in ISC's times interest earned ratio from 27.84 to 5.104. 1986 should be brighter if sales volume and cost of goods sold remain the same. That's double its net income for 1985.

A comparison of ISC's results with those of some of the industry averages reported by Robert Morris and Associates (RMs) shows that ISC is not doing too badly. ISC's cost of sales as a percentage of revenue was 56 percent compared to an industry average of 59 percent. Income before taxes as a percentage of sales was 9 percent compared to a slightly higher industry average of 10.6 percent. Operating expenses were 10 percent as compared to the average of 29.3 percent.

ISC is more or less maintaining its present position, but what about its ability to continue to expand and take advantage of opportunities? ISC's balance sheet indicates that the company has been steadily improving its position over the years (see exhibit 6).

The figures in exhibit 7 shows that ISC is capable of meeting its short-term obligation with some reserve left over for other ventures should it wish to pursue them. The company's current and quick ratios of 3.26 and 2.15, respectively, for 1985 compare favorably with the RMs industry averages of 3.3 current and 2.0 quick.[22]

Looking at cash and equivalents, receivables, and inventories provides a clear picture of the liquidity and cash flow of the firm (see exhibit 7).

Exhibit 8 shows a major improvement in cash and receivable accounts and also a reduction in inventory that may indicate a trend toward greater cost control. Of the three accounts, cash compares least favorably with the industry average. As a percent of sales revenue the average for the industry was 24 percent, compared to ISC's meager 4 percent. The company did marginally better in the other accounts. The industry average for receivables as a percentage of sales was 21 percent and for inventory 24 percent, whereas ISC had 24 percent and 16 percent respectively. These percentages indicate that ISC has more money tied up in receivables than the average company, but less money tied up in the not-so-liquid inventories. The total working capital of the firm is 44 percent of sales revenue, compared to a 69 percent industry average. Those figures show that ISC has less capacity to take on additional capital requirements than the average firm in the industry. However, it is difficult to base a concrete conclusion on averages because they include the highs and the lows. Nonetheless, $6.660 million in cash is not all that much money in the computer business.

The company could not expect to accommodate any large increase in working capital demand with a cash reserve of only $6.660 million. They would have to look to other, long-term sources of capital such as stock offerings and taking on more debt. In 1986 ISC stock sold for $11.25.[23] That price is below the original issue value of $19.50, and it has been as low as $8.75 in 1986. For the most part, stock fluctuated between $11 and $16 from 1984 to 1986. Without introducing a new product in four years, and a return on average assets of 10.6 percent compared to RMs industry average of 10 percent, ISC would no doubt have a difficult time obtaining the necessary funds for a major new venture. (See exhibits 8 and 9 for ISC financial statements.)

ISC's ability to take on additional debt in comparison to industry averages brightens its financial picture. The industry average of debt to equity is 50 percent according to RMs; ISC's is only 30.7 percent. If we use the average as a guide and let the creditors assume equal risk with the shareholders, then the company could conceivably borrow as much as $22 million. That's about the best it can muster at this point, having just taken on an additional $20 million in long-term debt in 1985. There is trouble ahead without some type of new product offering to keep unit sales from flattening out altogether.

On the bright side, ISC has taken some steps to even out the cash flow by going to a percentage-of-completion accounting system. Previously, during the installation of a system in an institution, it did not transfer any amount of money to accounts receivable until the project was complete; but all the while it was incurring the cost of production and installation. Now, with project management, the turnkey system is priced by stages of completion and billed to the receiving firm as each stage of the project is completed. Also, ISC has stopped bundling the prices of systems packages, and instead has broken out and assessed a price to each specific identifiable portion of a project. This technique helps regional managers to better measure performance during the course of a large project and aids in ensuring accountability. These new accounting techniques will not push ISC into the ranks of the *Fortune* 500, but they will help to stabilize ISC's cost of goods sold and have a positive impact on the bottom line.

Most of the analysts feel that ISC is positioned for a turnaround. Donaldson, Lufkin, and Jenrette predict revenue to increase by 25 percent and net income to increase by 83 percent in 1986.[24] For 1986, *Value Line* estimates revenue will increase by 20 percent and net income by 65 percent.[25] Operating margins are predicted to recover to the 13.4 percent level. These short-term estimates may be fairly accurate; in fact, third quarter returns show that projected earnings for the company for 1986 were 100 percent of target. (See exhibit 10 for ISC's five-year forecast.)

CONCLUSION

Managing a rapid-growth company with an extremely dynamic environment is difficult. ISC appears to be doing well. Its goals are being pursued, and employees seem happy and productive. The company is financially sound and ready to continue growing. The structure is changing to meet and more effectively plan for and control that growth. The ISC products are needed in financial institutions, and state-of-the-art technology is being used to produce and develop new products to meet future needs.

The future looks good for ISC, but it cannot relax its efforts for continued customer support and systems improvement. The banking industry is rapidly changing and so are its needs, and ISC must know what those needs will be and meet them.

As Chairman Ted DeMerritt and his executive committee plan for growth, DeMerritt wondered what strategy ISC should follow in the future. His strategic decisions had focused on the banking industry, but he felt changing strategy might be a big gamble. As DeMerritt said, "Even though we are proud of our record, we cannot relax our efforts for continued improvement of our system and support of customers. The fast-changing environment in which our banking customers operate today—and will operate for the foreseeable future—challenges us not to let them down. We accept that challenge with confidence."[26]

As a people-based company, ISC has no corner on technology, no secret formula. Its strength is the talent and dedication of the employees. ISC must continue to emphasize attracting, developing, and rewarding top quality professionals. ISC's strategy of industry focus and turnkey products dictates this direction.

Notes

1 "Corporate Overview," ISC Systems Corporation, Spokane, WA, 1985.
2 Ibid., 3.
3 ISC Systems Corporation, Prospectus, September 1980.
4 Todd May, "Business Foresees Solid Growth Ahead," *Fortune,* May 26, 1986, 28–30.
5 Ibid.
6 Bank Operations Report, Warren, Gorham, and Lamont, May 1985.
7 Ibid.
8 "A Guide to On-line Teller Terminals," Datapro Research Corporation, October 1985.
9 Ibid.

10   Ibid.
11   Ibid.
12   Ibid.
13   John P. Newport, "A Growing Gap in Software," *Fortune,* April 1986, 132–142.
14   "Intel's Hot Superchip," *Fortune,* June 9, 1986.
15   ISC Systems, Annual Report, 1985, 1986.
16   "On-Line Teller Sales," Frost and Sullivan, 1984.
17   Interview with James Stafford, ISC, November 1985.
18   ISC plant tour, May 1985.
19   Interview with Gerry Reeve, ISC, October 1985.
20   Donald Hambrick, "Strategic Attributes and Performance," *Academy of Management Journal,* vol. 25, no. 3, 1982, 501–531.
21   ISC Systems, Paine Webber Bulletin, April 24, 1985.
22   "Manufacturers of Electronic Computing Equipment," Robert Morris, 111.
23   "ISC Systems," *Value Line,* 1985.
24   Ibid.
25   ISC Systems Corporation, "Financial Presentation," 1985.
26   Ibid.

EXHIBIT 1
Performance Highlights for Year Ending in June

	1985	1984	1983	1982	1981	1980	1979	1978
Financial ($Millions)								
Revenues	150.0	127.7	79.9	63.8	32.9	14.4	3.8	.7
Earnings	8.2	10.0	4.0	8.1	4.4	1.7	.4	(.1)
Net Worth	67.7	58.5	48.1	42.4	16.0	2.6	.8	.2
Order Backlog	130.5	91.9	73.4	32.3	30.4	9.2	6.9	.3
Customers								
U.S.								
Thrifts	1844	1450	916	486	243	114	22	4
Commercial Banks	163	110	65	20	4	2	—	—
Consumer Finance	2							
International								
Thrifts	14	4	2	1	0	—	—	—
Commercial Banks	9	5	2	1	1	—	—	—
Totals	2032	1569	985	508	248	116	22	4
Workstations (000s)								
Installed	72.1	51.1	30.2	18.7	8.8	3.4	.99	.1
In Backlog	21.4							
Employees	1696	1671	1392	1135	586	243	67	23

Source: From ISC's Corporate Overview, 1985

EXHIBIT 2
International Operations prior to May, 1986 reorganization

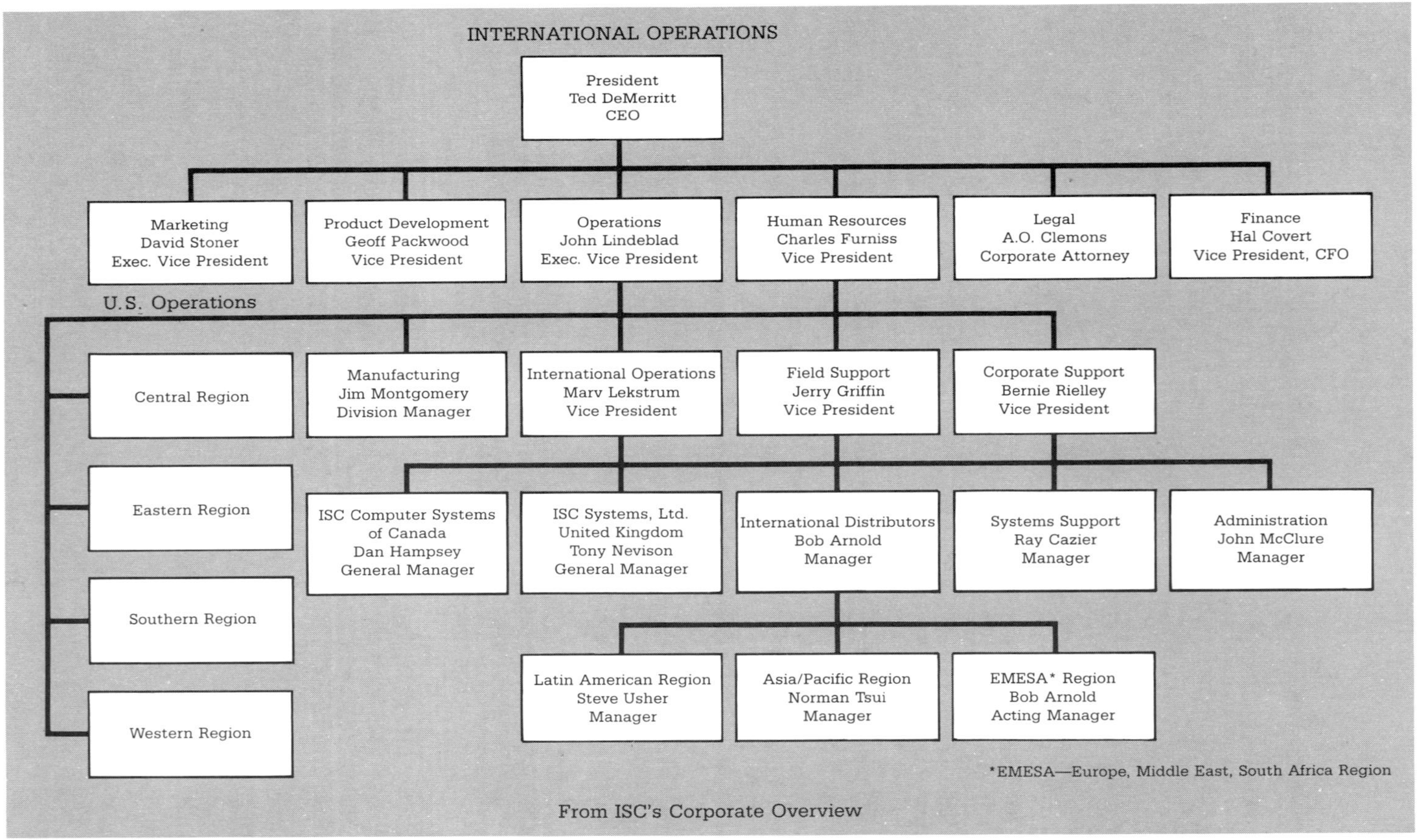

INTERNATIONAL OPERATIONS

U.S. Operations

President
Ted DeMerritt
CEO

Marketing
David Stoner
Exec. Vice President

Product Development
Geoff Packwood
Vice President

Operations
John Lindeblad
Exec. Vice President

Human Resources
Charles Furniss
Vice President

Legal
A.O. Clemons
Corporate Attorney

Finance
Hal Covert
Vice President, CFO

Manufacturing
Jim Montgomery
Division Manager

International Operations
Marv Lekstrum
Vice President

Field Support
Jerry Griffin
Vice President

Corporate Support
Bernie Rielley
Vice President

ISC Computer Systems
of Canada
Dan Hampsey
General Manager

ISC Systems, Ltd.
United Kingdom
Tony Nevison
General Manager

International Distributors
Bob Arnold
Manager

Systems Support
Ray Cazier
Manager

Administration
John McClure
Manager

Central Region

Eastern Region

Southern Region

Western Region

Latin American Region
Steve Usher
Manager

Asia/Pacific Region
Norman Tsui
Manager

EMESA* Region
Bob Arnold
Acting Manager

*EMESA—Europe, Middle East, South Africa Region

From ISC's Corporate Overview

Source: From ISC's Corporate Overview, 1985

EXHIBIT 3
Officers and Directors

ISC Systems Corporation

Ted C. DeMerritt
Chairman and Chief Executive Officer

John Lindeblad
President and Chief Operating Officer

Harold L. Covert
Executive Vice President—Operations

Bruce C. McGilaway
Senior Vice President—Corporate Sales

Glen Cavanaugh
Vice President—Marketing Operations

A.O. Clemons, Jr.
Vice President—Corporate Administration

Charles Furniss
Vice President—Human Resources

Jerry Griffin
Regional Vice President and
General Manager—Western Region

Allen P. Hardin
Regional Vice President and
General Manager—Central Region

J. Marvin Lekstrum
Vice President—International

Ron Mason
Regional Vice President and
General Manager—Eastern Region

Jim W. Montgomery
Vice President—Field Support and Manufacturing

Kenneth M. Olsen
Vice President—Finance and Chief Financial Officer

Geoffrey W. Packwood
Vice President—Development

Bernard D. Rielley
Vice President—Product Management

Frank Wypychowski
Vice President—Operations Programs

Stanley Yagerman
Regional Vice President and
General Manager—Southern Region

ISC Computer Systems of Canada Inc.

Wayne D. Gillies
General Manager

ISC Systems Ltd.

Anthony J. Nevison
Managing Director

Ted C. DeMerritt
Chairman and Chief Executive Officer

John Lindeblad
President and Chief Operating Officer

John D. Mangels
President—Rainier Bancorporation

Gary A. Norton
Director

Kenneth C. Schmitt
Investor

Andrew V. Smith
President—Pacific Northwest Bell

Max J. Steinmann
President—VIMAC Corporation

EXHIBIT 4

	ISC	PIMS Mean
R&D Inputs	12.50	1.99
New Product Outputs	60.00	7.88
Innovative Efficiency	32.50	.39
Innovative Efficiency %	1.18	.32

Source: Hambrick, 1985, 537

EXHIBIT 5
Consolidated Statements of Income

| | For the three years ended June 27, 1986 | | |
(In thousands, except share data)	1986	1985	1984
REVENUES			
Net sales	**$122,536**	$115,685	$107,032
Service	**43,550**	34,313	20,638
	166,086	149,998	127,670
COSTS AND EXPENSES			
Cost of sales and service	**87,792**	87,209	75,780
Systems development and engineering	**14,884**	13,120	11,138
Selling, general and administrative	**38,031**	32,728	23,598
	140,707	133,057	110,516
OPERATING INCOME	**25,379**	16,941	17,154
INTEREST			
Expense	**2,858**	3,319	616
Income	**1,234**	20	55
	1,624	3,299	561
INCOME BEFORE INCOME TAXES	**23,755**	13,642	16,593
Provision for income taxes	**9,900**	5,452	6,606
NET INCOME	**$ 13,855**	$ 8,190	$ 9,987
NET INCOME PER SHARE	**$.90**	$.55	$.67

The accompanying notes are an integral part of these financial statements.

EXHIBIT 6
ISC Liquidity Analysis (in thousands)

Year	Current Assets	Current Liabilities	Working Capital	Current Ratio	Quick Ratio
1980	$ 6,497	$ 4,397	$ 2,100	1.47	.64
1981	17,699	5,157	12,542	3.43	2.1
1982	39,751	8,931	30,820	4.45	2.5
1983	43,765	11,880	31,885	3.68	1.8
1984	60,295	21,834	38,461	3.34	1.47
1985	72,769	22,305	50,464	3.26	2.15

EXHIBIT 7
ISC Selected Current Asset Accounts (in thousands)

Year	Cash & Equivalents	Receivables	Inventories
1980	$ 184	$ 2,626	$ 3,674
1981	1,865	8,051	6,997
1982	6,608	14,521	17,654
1983	2,433	19,689	21,401
1984	2,259	29,245	28,101
1985	6,660	36,073	24,686

EXHIBIT 8
Consolidated Balance Sheets

(In thousands, except share data)	June 27, 1986	June 28, 1985
ASSETS		
CURRENT ASSETS		
Cash and short-term investments	$ 46,966	$ 6,660
Accounts receivable	40,640	36,073
Inventories	24,237	24,686
Other current assets	718	5,350
Total current assets	112,561	72,769
PROPERTY AND EQUIPMENT		
Land	3,328	3,221
Buildings and improvements	22,359	21,866
Equipment	18,360	16,826
Furniture and fixtures	13,479	10,264
Property and equipment, at cost	57,526	52,177
Less accumulated depreciation	16,461	11,387
Property and equipment, net	41,065	40,790
OTHER ASSETS	897	681
TOTAL ASSETS	$154,523	$114,240
LIABILITIES AND SHAREHOLDERS' EQUITY		
CURRENT LIABILITIES		
Current portion of long-term debt	$ 225	$ 187
Accounts payable	7,339	6,032
Compensation and benefits	8,724	3,603
Income taxes payable	12,759	9,046
Other accrued liabilities	6,195	3,437
Total current liabilities	35,242	22,305
DEFERRED INCOME TAXES	4,206	3,458
LONG-TERM DEBT	20,590	20,797
SHAREHOLDERS' EQUITY		
Common stock, no par value		
authorized—25,000,000 shares		
outstanding—15,991,567 shares and		
14,874,467 shares, respectively	699	688
Additional paid-in capital	43,506	30,509
Retained earnings	50,488	36,633
Foreign translation adjustments	(208)	(150)
Total shareholders' equity	94,485	67,680
TOTAL LIABILITIES AND SHAREHOLDERS' EQUITY	$154,523	$114,240

The accompanying notes are an integral part of these financial statements.

EXHIBIT 8 (Continued)
Consolidated Statements of Shareholders' Equity

For the three years ended June 27, 1986

(In thousands, except share data)	Common Stock Shares	Amount	Additional Paid-In Capital	Retained Earnings	Foreign Translation Adjustments
BALANCE AT JUNE 30, 1983	14,682,846	$686	$28,931	$18,456	$ —
Common stock issued under stock option plans, and related tax benefits	95,275	1	173	—	—
Common stock issued under profit sharing plan	16,322	—	248	—	—
Foreign translation adjustments	—	—	—	—	(62)
Net income	—	—	—	9,987	—
BALANCE AT JUNE 28, 1984	14,794,443	687	29,352	28,443	(62)
Common stock issued under stock option plans, and related tax benefits	7,428	—	99	—	—
Common stock issued under profit sharing plan	72,596	1	1,058	—	—
Foreign translation adjustments	—	—	—	—	(88)
Net income	—	—	—	8,190	—
BALANCE AT JUNE 28, 1985	14,874,467	688	30,509	36,633	(150)
Common stock issued under public offering	1,000,000	10	11,913	—	—
Common stock issued under stock option plans, and related tax benefits	60,245	1	367	—	—
Common stock issued under profit sharing plan	56,855	—	717	—	—
Foreign translation adjustments	—	—	—	—	(58)
Net income	—	—	—	13,855	—
BALANCE AT JUNE 27, 1986	15,991,567	$699	$43,506	$50,488	$(208)

The accompanying notes are an integral part of these financial statements.

EXHIBIT 9

Consolidated Statements of Changes in Financial Position

(In thousands)	For the three years ended June 27, 1986		
	1986	1985	1984
OPERATIONS			
Net income	**$13,855**	$ 8,190	$ 9,987
Non-cash charges to income:			
Depreciation and amortization	**5,619**	5,433	3,370
Deferred income taxes	**748**	1,367	2,091
Working capital changes:			
Accounts receivable	**(4,567)**	(6,828)	(9,556)
Inventories	**449**	3,415	(6,700)
Accounts payable	**1,307**	(818)	793
Compensation and benefits	**5,121**	(1,925)	2,005
Income taxes payable	**3,713**	8,160	—
Other current assets	**4,632**	(4,660)	(449)
Other current liabilities	**2,796**	1,054	1,156
Funds provided by operations	**33,673**	13,388	2,697
INVESTMENT ACTIVITIES			
Acquisition of property and equipment	**(6,780)**	(9,948)	(22,290)
Net book value of property and equipment retired or sold	**1,069**	3,290	543
Other, net	**(457)**	(280)	4
Funds invested in the business	**(6,168)**	(6,938)	(21,743)
FINANCING ACTIVITIES			
Issuance of common stock:			
Public offering	**11,923**	—	—
Employee plans	**1,085**	1,158	422
Increase in long-term debt	**28**	20,072	12,977
Repayment of long-term debt	**(235)**	(17,279)	(528)
Increase (decrease) in short-term borrowings	**—**	(6,000)	6,000
Funds provided by financing activities	**12,801**	(2,049)	18,871
INCREASE (DECREASE) IN CASH AND SHORT-TERM INVESTMENTS	**$40,306**	$ 4,401	$ (175)

The accompanying notes are an integral part of these financial statements.

EXHIBIT 9 (Continued)
Notes to Consolidated Financial Statements

Note 1
Significant
Accounting Policies

Fiscal Year—The Company operates on a fifty-two, fifty-three week fiscal year ending on the Friday nearest June 30. Fiscal years ended June 27, 1986, and June 28, 1985 and 1984 each were comprised of fifty-two weeks.

Principles of Consolidation—The consolidated financial statements include the accounts of ISC Systems Corporation and its wholly-owned subsidiaries after eliminating intercompany accounts and transactions.

Revenue Recognition—For all contracts except major turnkey projects, revenue is recognized at the customer's acceptance of the software and shipment of the hardware. For major turnkey projects, revenue is recognized using the percentage-of-completion method of accounting based on the ratio of costs incurred to total estimated cost. Unbilled revenue related to turnkey projects, included in accounts receivable, was $6,228,000 at June 27, 1986, and $5,671,000 at June 28, 1985. Service and other support revenues are recognized ratably over the contractual period or as the services are provided.

Foreign Currency Translation—The accounts of foreign subsidiaries are maintained in the currencies of the countries in which they operate and are translated to U.S. dollars in conformity with Financial Accounting Standards Board Statement No. 52. Translation adjustments are accumulated in a separate component of shareholders' equity.

Accounts Receivable—Management reviews accounts receivable to determine an appropriate allowance for doubtful accounts and, accordingly, receivables were net of an allowance of $400,000 at June 27, 1986. No allowance for doubtful accounts had been established in prior years.

Property and Equipment—Property and equipment is valued at cost less accumulated depreciation. Expenditures for maintenance, repairs and minor renewals are charged to expense as incurred. Additions, improvements and major renewals are capitalized. Depreciation is computed principally using the straight-line method over estimated useful lives of 3-40 years for buildings and improvements, and 3-5 years for equipment, furniture and fixtures.

Software Costs—All software costs are charged to expense as incurred until technological feasibility has been established for the product. Beginning in fiscal 1986, in accordance with Financial Accounting Standards Board Statement No. 86, costs incurred after technological feasibility has been established are capitalized. For each product, these costs are amortized either using the straight-line method over estimated economic lives, or based on current and estimated future revenues. At June 27, 1986, $370,000 of unamortized computer software costs were included in other assets, and $20,000 of amortized costs were charged to expense during the year.

Net Income Per Share—Net income per share is computed using the weighted average number of common shares outstanding, including the dilutive effect of stock options. The number of shares used in the computation was 15,388,000 in 1986, 14,948,000 in 1985 and 14,887,000 in 1984. Fully diluted earnings per share have not been presented separately since they would not be materially different.

Reclassifications—Prior period amounts associated with cost of sales and service and systems development and engineering have been reclassified in order to conform to the current period presentation.

EXHIBIT 10
Long-Range Financial Plan for 1986–1990

	1986	1987	1988	1989	1990
Financial ($Millions)					
Net Orders	179.0	218.0	241.5	289.3	329.4
Backlog	165.7	189.2	205.3	225.3	230.8
Net Revenue	184.0	217.8	263.1	318.8	379.4
Net Income	14.2	17.1	19.3	25.1	29.8
Earnings Per Share	$.95	1.14	1.29	1.67	1.99
Total Assets	129.2	164.3	185.1	218.5	256.4
Shareholder's Equity	83.2	101.6	122.9	150.3	183.2
Key Ratio Targets					
Current	2.5				
Long-Term Debt/ Total Capitalization	20%				
Return on Equity	18%				

Source: Projected from ISC Annual Report, 1986

Integrated Software Systems Corporation

Donald F. Harvey

INTRODUCTION

Peter Preuss looked around the table at the executive committee of Integrated Software Systems Corporation (ISSCO). He had started the company in his own San Diego home in 1970. By 1985 it was a $30 million company with nearly 300 employees and was the world's leading independent supplier of visual information system software. According to Preuss,

> While past accomplishments deserve review, it is the future that commands your management's attention. We are committed to remaining the leading independent supplier of visual information system software and continuing to grow in revenue and income. The corporate formula for growth focuses on four integrated product strategies, and leverage strengths we have built over fifteen years. ISSCO today is very sound financially. We enjoy a broad-based reputation for product quality and customer support. We believe our expanding product line is well-suited to today's market needs. And we have a seasoned management team, talented technical experts and a professional sales force.[1]

ISSCO develops, markets, and supports a broad line of visual information system software used on mainframe and microcomputers to access and manipulate data and convert information into high-quality graphics.

Corporate Mission, Goals, Strategies, and Plans

Mission

To solve business problems

Goals

1　To increase the company's potential markets
2　To provide users with flexibility in choosing graphics output devices

This case was prepared using published accounts and public documents for the purpose of class discussion rather than to illustrate either effective or ineffective handling of an administrative situation.

3   To permit users the continued use of ISSCO software in a rapidly changing computer hardware environment

4   To be the largest independent software house

5   To keep developing improved, lower cost, and faster products that will result in more efficient ways of communicating data

6   To remain a leader in the development and marketing of graphics software and related software packages

Strategies

1   To provide innovative products of high quality

2   To provide custom-tailored presentation graphics that serve the communication needs of executives and managers

3   To expand in the following directions: system integration, applications software, graphics technology

4   To stay close to the graphics and related software industry

5   To take advantage of market expansion

6   To increase internal expansion and acquisitions of other software development companies

Plans

1   To design software so that the company need modify only a few sections of computer code for the software to operate on different computers and graphics output devices

2   To design individual graphics products as a form of ''tool kit'' for constructing graphics tailored to a user's specific data, analytical, aesthetic, and communications requirements[2]

THE COMPANY

ISSCO develops, markets, and supports a family of integrated software products consisting of graphics software to produce high-quality graphics, system integration software to integrate the company's products with other software and hardware, and applications software for applications that can be significantly enhanced by graphics. The company's products increase the ability of users to understand, analyze, and present information, while saving time, money, and effort. ISSCO's products operate on mainframe computers, minicomputers, and certain large microcomputers to convert data of various sources and character into a wide variety of easy-to-understand graphics representations in forms such as bar, line and pie charts, tables, maps, and planning charts. The company's graphics software allows a wide range of users such as business executives, scientists, and secretaries to use and produce graphs. The company's customers include manufacturing and service businesses, financial institutions, government agencies, research organizations, and educational institutions. ISSCO markets its products in the United States, Canada, Germany, the United Kingdom, and France through its direct sales force and in other parts of the world through a direct sales force or independent sales representatives.

The company believes that it is the leading independent supplier of data representation and business graphics software. It presently has more than 2,500 installations throughout the world of TELL-A-GRAF® and DISSPLA® software, its primary software products. These installations typically have multiple users, ranging from a few to several hundred individuals. ISSCO markets its products through a sales organization of 91 persons located in 20 United States cities, a Canadian city, and 6 European cities. Its software is also marketed by independent representatives located in Austria, Greece, Israel, Italy, Japan, the Netherlands, Singapore, South Africa, Sweden, and Switzerland.

TELL-A-GRAF and DISSPLA software allow a user to produce high-quality graphs and charts meeting specific data representation requirements with a flexibility not permitted by standard formats. TELL-A-GRAF software is designed for use by persons without programming skills. DISSPLA software is designed to meet the more complex requirements of programmers.[3]

The company's family of software presently consists of the following nine software products:

Graphics Software	System Integration Software	Applications Software
TELL-A-GRAF	IVISS MANAGER$_{TM}$*	TELLAPLAN®*
DISSPLA	THE DATA CONNECTION®*	MegaCalc$_{TM}$*†
CUECHART®*	DEVICE DRIVERS	
TABLES$_{TM}$*		

*First installation by ISSCO after 1984.

†A trademark of The Mega Group, Inc.

EXTERNAL FORCES

In the past, graphics were drawn manually by trained artists and generally for only a few specialized purposes. However, in recent years the use of computers to generate charts and graphs has grown substantially as a result of major reductions in the cost of computers and graphics output devices, the increased use of computers for data handling, and the greater availability of high-capability graphics software. ISSCO's graphics software products produce data representation graphics, by which information such as financial data, research results, performance statistics and market data is graphically displayed. These graphics produced by ISSCO's software meet high aesthetic standards, which in the past could be achieved only by graphic artists. Data representation graphics include what is commonly known as business graphics.

The business graphics market arose from the growing number and acceptance of computers in the business community. As the volume of data became increasingly unmanageable, the need for data representation graphics developed. A simple chart or graph can summarize conditions, reveal trends, and communicate a message in a more direct and easy-to-understand manner than a computer printout.

The production of data representation graphics requires a computer, a terminal or other data input device, graphics software, and a graphics output device. A typical user produces graphs on two or more graphics output devices of different manufacturers. In addition to creating graphs, ISSCO's software products provide the interfaces that enable these components to communicate with each other. These interfaces allow the user to sit at a keyboard and to display a graph on a terminal screen, a mechanical plotter, or other graphics output device, or to produce 35mm slides, overhead transparencies, or report illustrations. Because ISSCO software serves as the interface which allows a user to produce graphics output, the software's availability and usefulness depends, in part, upon the number and variety of computers and graphics output devices with which such software will operate.

ISSCO's products are designed to operate with many computers and graphics output devices. This strategy is intended to increase the company's potential markets, provide users with flexibility in choosing graphics output devices, and permit them the continued use of ISSCO software in a rapidly changing computer hardware environment. ISSCO software products operate with more than 225 graphics output devices. DISSPLA software operates in 40 different types of computer operating environments.

To implement this strategy economically, ISSCO designs its software so that the company need only modify a few sections of computer code for the software to operate on different computers and graphics output devices. This design, combined with ISSCO's considerable experience in adapting its software to different kinds of equipment, generally allows the company to execute such modifications in a systematic, predictable, and timely manner. For these reasons, ISSCO believes that its modification process is more like a production process than typical software development. Although ISSCO's products operate on many mainframe computers and mini-computers, the majority of its installed products are presently operating on computers of IBM and Digital Equipment Corporation. In 1983 and 1984, ISSCO's products were adapted to operate on certain 32-bit microcomputers, and modified to facilitate transfer to additional 32-bit machines.[4]

Products

Graphics Software

The company's line of graphics software products is designed around a central graphics software technology that has been continuously developed and refined by ISSCO since its founding in 1970. ISSCO's products are intended primarily for business, scientific, and research applications in numerous markets and to meet the individual requirements of many different users. ISSCO's individual graphics products are a form of "tool kit" for constructing graphs tailored to a user's specific data, analytic, aesthetic, and communication requirements. The tool kit approach is designed for ease of use and flexibility in representing data and in designing and modifying charts and graphs without the limitations inherent in standard chart formats (see exhibit 1).

ISSCO's graphics software technology can generate many types of charts and graphs, including:

- bar charts
- pie charts
- line charts
- numerical tables

- diagrams
- contour plots
- calendar charts
- planning charts

- word charts
- 3-D charts
- maps
- symbol tables

ISSCO has developed a broad range of design features which give users numerous choices as to exactly how their data can be represented, including:

- unlimited color choices
- wide variety of line widths, line textures and symbols
- area fill with wide pattern variety
- flexible annotation
- multiple type fonts

- multiple geographical databases
- curve interpolations
- layout control for multiple graphs
- windowing and outlining capabilities
- varied axes and scalings

ISSCO has incorporated in many of its products, in an automated form, the artistic judgment and experience of graphic artists. This function, termed "Layout Intelligence," helps the users of the company's products, who are not trained in graphic design, to make the complex decisions required to produce aesthetically pleasing and effective graphics. The user may specify the intended use of the graphics (e.g., slides, viewgraphs, report illustrations), the desired color theme (e.g., fall, spring, summer, winter, black-and-white), and the quality level desired. The graph is then designed according to these wishes and the characteristics and limitations of the graphics output device. A more skilled user may choose to use the automated design process selectively or to control every aspect of the graphic design (see exhibit 2).

- TELL-A-GRAF software was designed for what the company believes is one of the largest markets for data representation and business graphics users: those who want a great number of choices in designing charts and graphs but have no experience in computer programming. TELL-A-GRAF software's capabilities include many chart and graph types and design features, including all of those that the company believes to be most frequently used. A user can also license options with TELL-A-GRAF software which include additional types of charts and graphs and design features. To construct charts, a user instructs TELL-A-GRAF software through simple commands. A typical user of TELL-A-GRAF software, with no programming or computer knowledge, can develop professional quality graphics after only a day of training.

- DISSPLA software has all of the presentation capabilities and design features available from the company's graphics software technology. As a result, DISSPLA software offers extensive flexibility for data representation and addresses a very broad range of user needs for high-quality graphics. This product was designed for use by persons with some familiarity with computer programming, who instruct DISSPLA software using FORTRAN or compatible languages to develop the desired charts. DISSPLA software, introduced in 1970, was the company's initial product and has been continuously revised and enhanced since that date. Approximately 33 percent of the company's customers have licensed both DISSPLA and TELL-A-GRAF software. As with TELL-A-GRAF software, various options are available with DISSPLA software.

- CUECHART software enables users with no computer programming skills and no training on the company's products to create charts and graphs. This product is designed for use with TELL-A-GRAF software to permit the easy input of data and creation of charts for users who frequently use the same chart formats. CUECHART software contains a built-in library of the most commonly used chart formats and ''reads'' each format to construct a series of questions to prompt a user who wishes to generate a chart with specific data. For example, when creating a chart which graphs monthly sales by individual salespersons, CUECHART software might prompt the user by asking, in turn, for the month, the salespersons' names, and the sales volumes in terms familiar to the user rather than in computer terminology. Users trained in TELL-A-GRAF software can add formats of their own design to the CUECHART software library. CUECHART software was first delivered in August 1982, and approximately 76 percent of TELL-A-GRAF software licensees have licensed this product.

- TABLES software, first delivered in December 1984, is an option to TELL-A-GRAF software that produces tables of numbers, words, and symbols. Like TELL-A-GRAF software's other graphic formats, these tables may be produced with full color and high-quality typestyles suitable for presentation or publication. TABLES software may be used for certain kinds of data that are not suitable for graphical representation. A table can also complement graphical representation; by displaying the information side-by-side in graphics and tabular form, the precision and detail of a table may be combined with the visibility and impact of graphics. TABLES software draws upon TELL-A-GRAF software data files to convert charted information into tabular form. It also works with THE DATA CONNECTION software so users can access data files and manipulate the data to be tabulated. TABLES software has been licensed and installed by approximately 13 percent of TELL-A-GRAF software licensees.[5]

System Integration Software

- IVISS MANAGER software, first delivered in February 1985, is a system integration software product that supervises the operations of ISSCO graphics software in an IBM environment, providing a user interface that follows standard IBM protocol. IVISS MANAGER software gives each user a library of charts, auto-matically updated on a customer's chosen schedule. End-users may ask IVISS MANAGER software to display or print selected charts, or they may browse through its libraries at their leisure. It also provides a user full-screen panels for chart access, chart modification and new chart creation, and on-line "help" functions wherever needed, requiring neither understanding of graphics design nor computer expertise. Charts in IVISS MANAGER software may be produced on TELL-A-GRAF or DISSPLA software or by any other graphics software that works with IBM's standard graphics utilities. Because this product makes access to comprehensible information very convenient and gives executives a complete visual information system, ISSCO believes that it will change the way managers in large corporations use data. As of February 11, 1985, 11 percent of the TELL-A-GRAF software customers on IBM and IBM-compatible computers have li-censed IVISS MANAGER software.

- THE DATA CONNECTION software, first delivered in October 1982, is a group of four software products which enter data into TELL-A-GRAF software by ac-cessing data stored in standard computer files and data base management systems, or generated by applications programs created in-house or licensed from software vendors. THE DATA CONNECTION software operates as a stan-dardized data interface that eliminates the need for data entry by keyboard or through customized data interfaces or the need of the user to know specific data formats. The product also allows the user to accumulate and summarize data and perform mathematical calculations. The calculation capabilities available are those the company believes to be most frequently used in transforming data for graphic presentation in business and scientific environments. To date, THE DATA CONNECTION software has been licensed by approximately 62 percent of TELL-A-GRAF software licensees.

- DEVICE DRIVERS are the software which a computer graphics system employs to produce a graph on a graphics output device. Device drivers operate as an interface between graphics output devices and ISSCO's products by expressing their graphic commands in a form that the device can understand. Device driv-ers are sold in combination with ISSCO's graphics software products and indi-vidually.

ISSCO's customers require a variety of graphics output devices. Therefore, ISSCO offers "off the shelf" device drivers which interface with more than 225 different graphics output devices, including graphics terminals; pen plotters or im-pact, electrostatic, ink jet or laser printers; microfilm recorders; 35mm slide-making machines; and machines to make overhead transparencies. As new graphics output devices are introduced, ISSCO evaluates them and develops device drivers for those it believes to be important in the market place. See exhibit 3 for typical customers.

As part of this ongoing program, the company developed in 1983 a device driver which enables a leading microcomputer, the IBM personal computer, to func-tion as a graphics terminal for the company's software products. Using this device driver, customers are able to input commands or data through an IBM personal computer, access a mainframe computer's data base and processing power to produce graphs, and view the resulting graph on the screen of the microcomputer. These graphs, after being previewed on the IBM personal computer, may be reproduced on a high-quality graphics output device. In 1984, ISSCO developed device drivers for two new graphics-oriented IBM personal computers.[5]

Applications Software

- TELLAPLAN software, first delivered in November 1983, is an applications software product directed to managers and engineers as a tool to plan and control the scheduling of a project. It has easy-to-learn English commands, runs with TELL-A-GRAF software, offers the ability to make Gantt-type planning charts, and has the capacity to update the plan during its progress. It provides the capabilities to prepare plans and monitor schedules and collect a large set of statistics like reporting of staff requirements by skill type and actual-versus-budget costing by department during the process of generating the plan. Although project planning and scheduling are considered essentially nongraphic in nature, TELLAPLAN software extensively employs graphics in the solution of project planning and schedule monitoring. As of February 11, 1985, TELLAPLAN software has been licensed by approximately 26 percent of TELL-A-GRAF software licensees.

- MEGACALC software is a full-function financial spreadsheet for IBM mainframe computers that can also accept microcomputer spreadsheet data uploaded and downloaded from leading microcomputer spreadsheet products. In October 1984, the company entered into a nonexclusive license agreement with the Mega Group, Inc. to market, distribute and sublicense MegaCalc software. Development is currently underway to link MegaCalc software directly to TELL-A-GRAF and IVISS MANAGER software to enable users to develop simple to very large and complex spreadsheets, and then generate related charts with supporting data and retrieve them with the push of a single terminal key. Compared to having numerous spreadsheet programs on personal computers, MegaCalc software lowers the cost per user, reduces difficulties with compatibility, cooperation and control, and links all users to common mainframe data bases and graphic production facilities. MegaCalc software was developed by and is the property of The Mega Group, Inc. of Irvine, California.[6]

Competition and Performance Levels

The markets for ISSCO's products are highly competitive with the continuing entry of new competitors and broadening of the product range from very low price, limited capacity software products for small home computers to high capability software products.

The company has identified various categories of competitors. They consist of independent software vendors, including certain mainframe applications software suppliers, and various hardware manufacturers, such as IBM and others that are far larger than the company, which offer competitive software packages. In addition, certain turnkey system vendors, including Hewlett-Packard, offer competitive products as part of their applications. With the expanding power and presence of microcomputers, many microcomputer hardware and software suppliers have also developed competitive products.

ISSCO believes that the graphics software products offered by these competitors are, at present, generally more limited in graphics capability and quality and can operate on fewer graphics output devices and computers than its products, but they are often less expensive. The company's other products compete with numerous software packages that vary widely in capability and price. There are many competitors or potential competitors which have substantially greater financial, technical and marketing resources than the company and have the ability to develop and market software products competitive with those of ISSCO.[7]

Computer graphics software continues to exhibit exciting growth and future potential. More than $700 million of graphics software and services were forecasted to be sold worldwide in 1985. Of this amount ISSCO should at least maintain its current market share of 6.5 percent or $46 million. Expectations are that these sales will grow to $1.5 billion by the end of the decade with an overall growth rate averaging between 25 percent and 30 percent a year. With this potential, the graphics market has become highly competitive, with a continuing entry of new competitors and a broadening of the product range from very low-price and limited-capacity software products for small home computers to high-capability products on the more sophisticated devices.

ISSCO has identified various categories of competitors producing these products. They consist of independent software vendors, such as Precision Visuals and ASAS Institute; various hardware manufacturers, such as IBM; and turnkey system vendors including Hewlett-Packard. According to ISSCO users, the products offered by these competitors are, at present, generally more limited in graphics capability and quality and can operate on fewer computers and graphic output devices. Though these products are often less expensive, ISSCO has found its target market willing to pay for the quality and flexibility it offers (see exhibit 4).

Overall, ISSCO does not consider independent software vendors threatening. Most of these companies use the classic niche formula of tailoring software to a specific need; but lacking experience and a reputation in the graphics market these companies find it dicult to branch out from that niche. There is obviously always the threat that a major corporation with more resources will decide to compete head-to-head with ISSCO products. For example, if IBM were to suddenly decide to offer a comparable product, there is not much ISSCO could do to counteract this move. However, there are no signs of a large corporation willing to invest the time and money it would take to develop the high quality standards of ISSCO products.

Technology and Government Influences

ISSCO and its users—which include forty-one of the fifty *Fortune* 500 companies—believe the company leads the industry in software graphics technology and is constantly updating its products. However, there is always the possibility that someone could produce a new technology rendering the company's product obsolete. For instance, the company programs its product for Vector use, but a new technology using Raster may be forthcoming. If this is the case, the company will have to convert its programs to Raster.

With the exception of computer program piracy becoming an issue in the future, there is little, if any, government regulation in the computer graphics industry.

INTERNAL ANALYSIS

Financial

Total revenues of the company increased 45 percent and 39 percent in 1983 and 1984, respectively. (See exhibit 5 for selected financial data.) This growth resulted principally from the licensing of more software products and options and to a lesser extent, from the introduction of new products and options and price increases. Although some growth is attributed to expansion into new geographic market areas, much of the growth reflects the expansion of the market for graphics software which was approximately 40 percent in 1984 and 1985 (see exhibits 6 and 7).

Product license fees from TELL-A-GRAF and DISSPLA software increased 15 percent in 1983 and 37 percent in 1984, accounting for a total of $10,596,000, $12,164,000, and $16,685,000 in revenues in 1982, 1983, and 1984, respectively. Product license fees from CUECHART and THE DATA CONNECTION software, first delivered in 1982, accounted for $1,435,000, $3,987,000, and $4,913,000 in license revenues in 1982, 1983, and 1984, respectively. Product license fees from TELLA-PLAN software, first delivered in November 1983, accounted for $662,000 in 1983 and $1,290,000 in 1984. Product license fees from TABLES software and MEGA-CALC software, first licensed in December 1984, accounted for $796,000.

Customer support and renewal fees increased 53 percent in 1983 and 30 percent in 1984, primarily from maintenance and enhancement fees being purchased by a greater number of customers, more customers utilizing the company's training programs and larger purchases of product publications.

Total foreign revenues (including both direct from foreign customers and through foreign subsidiaries) increased from $2,433,000 in 1982 to $3,662,000 in 1983 and to $4,565,000 in 1984, despite a strengthening of the U.S. dollar during that period. These revenues represented 15 percent, 15 percent, and 14 percent of total revenues in each of 1982, 1983, and 1984.

Total revenues from various agencies and departments of, and certain contractors to, the United States government were $2,618,000, $5,139,000, and $7,286,000 in 1982, 1983, and 1984, respectively. These represented 16 percent, 21 percent, and 22 percent of total revenues, respectively. Overall, the company is in a good financial position. It has virtually no long-term debt, a substantial balance of cash and equivalents, and is able to internally generate most funds for normal operating needs. However, major nonrecurring expenditures for capital equipment and facilities and acquisitions of companies or product lines may require external debt and equity funds. On Thursday, March 7, 1985, ISSCO sold 300,000 shares of new stock in just a few hours for $22.75 a share for a total just over $6.5 million. These funds are targeted for possible acquisitions of software companies and products, but as yet no prospective firms have been named.

Management

ISSCO is a public corporation with a five-man board of directors. Two are internal board members: Peter Preuss, president and CEO of ISSCO; and Allen T. Paller, president of AUI Data Graphics, Inc., an ISSCO subsidiary. The rest are external board members: Howard E. Cox, Jr., general partner of Greylock Partners and Company, a venture capital limited partnership; John J. Thornton, chairman of the board and CEO of Wavetek Corporation and chairman of the board of Micom Systems, Inc.; and G. Larry Willson, president and CEO of Policy Management Systems Corporation, a supplier of insurance processing software systems (see exhibit 9).

ISSCO management is essentially structured on three levels. At the top is Peter Preuss, founder, president, and chief executive officer. Mr. Preuss is the leader, spokesperson, and ultimate decision maker. He has, however, delegated the responsibility for planning and strategy formulation to the senior vice presidents who work in coordination with the vice presidents of sales, contracts, and European operations. The day-to-day running of the company is entrusted to the various operations directors.

Although the company currently has a functional type structure, management feels the company's growth will force it into a division structure. In anticipation of this growth, the company plans to organize its markets into strategic business units based on user needs.

Marketing

The company markets its products in the United States, Canada, Germany, France, and the United Kingdom. The U.S. marketing operations are organized into four regions with regional offices located in Chicago (midwest region), Dallas (southeast region), New York (northeast region), and San Francisco (western region).

The company identifies prospective customers primarily through advertising in magazines, direct mailing, executive level seminars, promotions at trade shows, and referrals from current customers. A typical customer is a large *Fortune* 1000 business, university, or government agency.

The sales force is staffed with experienced sales-oriented people who are backed up by technical personnel. ISSCO believes it takes this kind of marketing professional to communicate with corporate officers who are the ultimate purchase decision makers.

Collectively, sales and marketing has a budget consisting of approximately 50 percent of projected revenues. This expenditure reflects management opinion that marketing is essential to future sales.

Customers

More than 2,500 installations of DISSPLA and TELL-A-GRAF software had been completed by 1985. Each installation usually has multiple users, ranging from a few to several hundred individuals. A typical customer is a large business, university, or government agency which has mainframe computers or minicomputers and whose needs for data analysis and presentation allow it to benefit from the speed and cost savings of using a computer to represent its data graphically. Approximately 33 percent of the company's customers have licensed both TELL-A-GRAF and DISSPLA software. In 1982, 1983, and 1984, licenses to various agencies and departments of, and certain contractors to, the United States government represented 16 percent, 21 percent, and 22 percent, respectively, of ISSCO's revenues. No other single customer accounted for 10 percent or more of revenues in each of the years 1982, 1983, and 1984.

Of the top fifty *Fortune* 500 industrial companies, forty-one have at least one installation of ISSCO software and collectively have 542 installations of DISSPLA or TELL-A-GRAF software. Included among ISSCO's customers are AT&T, Exxon, Gulf Oil, Schlumberger, Dow Chemical, Du Pont, Boeing, Lockheed, McDonnell Douglas, Ford, BMW, Pepsico, 3M, Time Inc., Citicorp, Chase Manhattan Bank, Federal Reserve Bank of New York, the World Bank, Harvard, Yale, Princeton, Los Alamos National Laboratory, and the U.S. Bureau of the Census.

ISSCO has generally benefitted from the rapid acceptance of its new products. Within eighteen months after initial delivery, TELLAPLAN, THE DATA CONNECTION and CUECHART software had been licensed by approximately 26 percent, 49 percent and 67 percent, respectively, of the TELL-A-GRAF software installed base. One month after its first shipment in December 1984, TABLES software had been licensed by approximately 13 percent of the TELL-A-GRAF software installed base. Since its first shipment on February 1, 1985, IVISS MANAGER software has been licensed by approximately 11 percent of the TELL-A-GRAF software installed bases that operate on IBM and IBM-compatible computers.[8]

Research, Development, and Production

Because the computer software industry is characterized by rapid changes in user needs, frequent introduction of new hardware technology and relatively easy entry of new competitors, the company maintains a continuing program of product development. During 1982, 1983, and 1984, product research and development expenses were $2,917,000, $4,207,000, and $6,451,000, respectively. These costs are expensed as incurred.

Because the computer software industry is characterized by rapid changes in user needs and frequent introduction of new hardware technology, the company maintains a continuing program of product development. The R&D department is also the production department. This department's activities consist of developing new products, enhancing the graphics capabilities of its existing products, and modifying its semi-standardized products to meet different user needs. The importance of R&D is reflected in the company's decision to invest 19 percent of revenues ($6.5 million) in the department during 1984, a favorable comparison to the industry average of 12 percent, according to Value Line and Standard and Poors.[9]

Human Resources

ISSCO currently has 284 employees, sixty of whom are engaged in product research and development, forty-two in technical support, 155 in sales and marketing, and twenty-seven in general administration. The company feels it has the best collection of graphics software employees in the country. It also recognizes that in order to recruit and retain skilled personnel in an industry where competition for these skills is intense, it must somehow distinguish itself from other firms. One avenue ISSCO has chosen is to maintain a competitive salary base, along with periodic bonuses, profit sharing, employee discount stock purchases, and stock options. However, ISSCO is very selective in the employees it hires. No matter how qualified an individual is for the position, it is imperative that his or her attitude and personality fit the corporate culture. Currently morale seems to be high among employees. They think ISSCO is the greatest and are working hard to make it stay that way.

CONCLUSION

Managing a rapid growth company, with an extremely dynamic environment is difficult. ISSCO appears to be doing well. It is pursuing its goals and employees seem happy and productive. The company is financially sound and ready to continue growing. The structure is changing to meet and more effectively plan for and control that growth. Its products are needed, and state-of-the-art technology is being used to produce and develop new products to meet future needs. The future looks good for ISSCO, but it cannot relax its efforts for continued customer support and systems improvement. The industry is rapidly changing and so are its customers' needs. ISSCO must know what those needs will be and meet them.

As President Peter Preuss and his executive committee plan for growth, he wondered what strategy ISSCO should follow in the future. "Even though we are proud of our record, we cannot relax our efforts for continued improvement of our system and support of customers. The fast changing environment in which our customers operate today—and will operate for the foreseeable future—challenges us not to let them down. We accept that challenge with confidence."[10]

Notes

1   ISSCO Annual Report, 1984.
2   Ibid.
3   "ISSCO Common Stock," Preliminary Prospectus, 1985.
4   Ibid., 11.
5   Ibid., 14.
6   Ibid., 15.
7   Ibid., 14.
8   Ibid., 19.
9   *Value Line,* 1985.
10 Peter Preuss, "Computer Graphics: Visual Information Systems of the '80's," *Computer Pictures,* November 1984, 34–38.

EXHIBIT 1

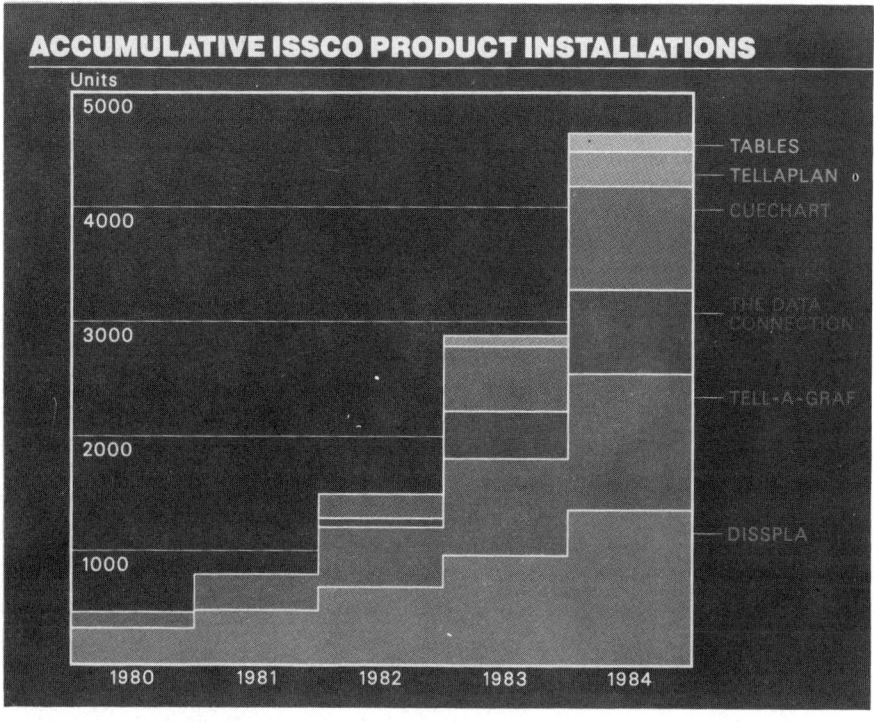

EXHIBIT 2

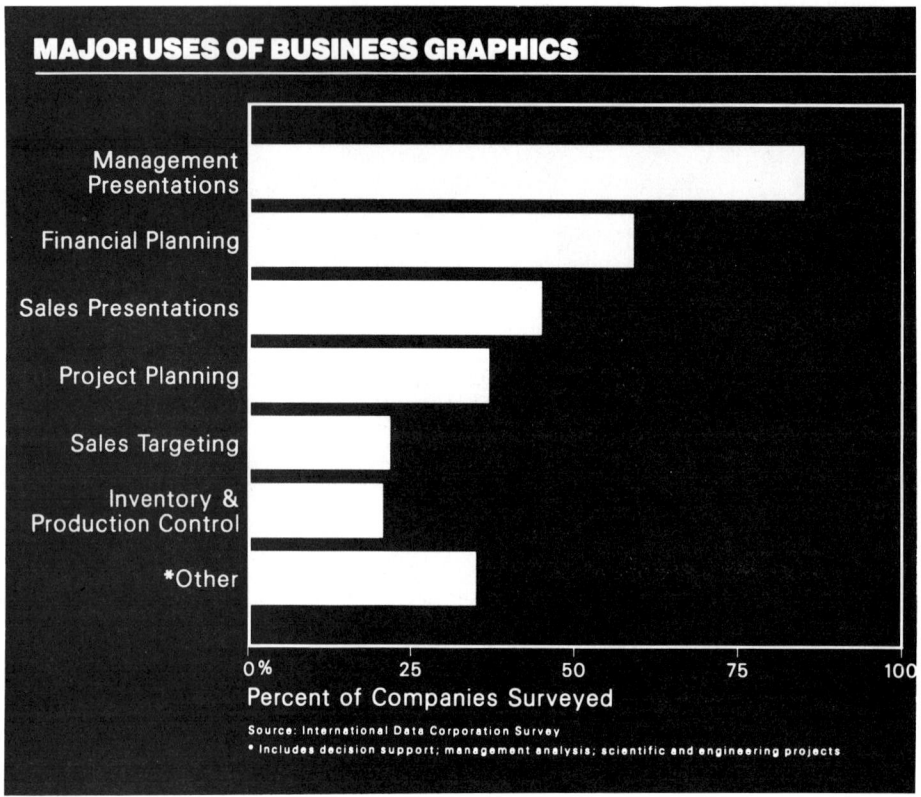

Source: International Data Corporation Survey

EXHIBIT 3

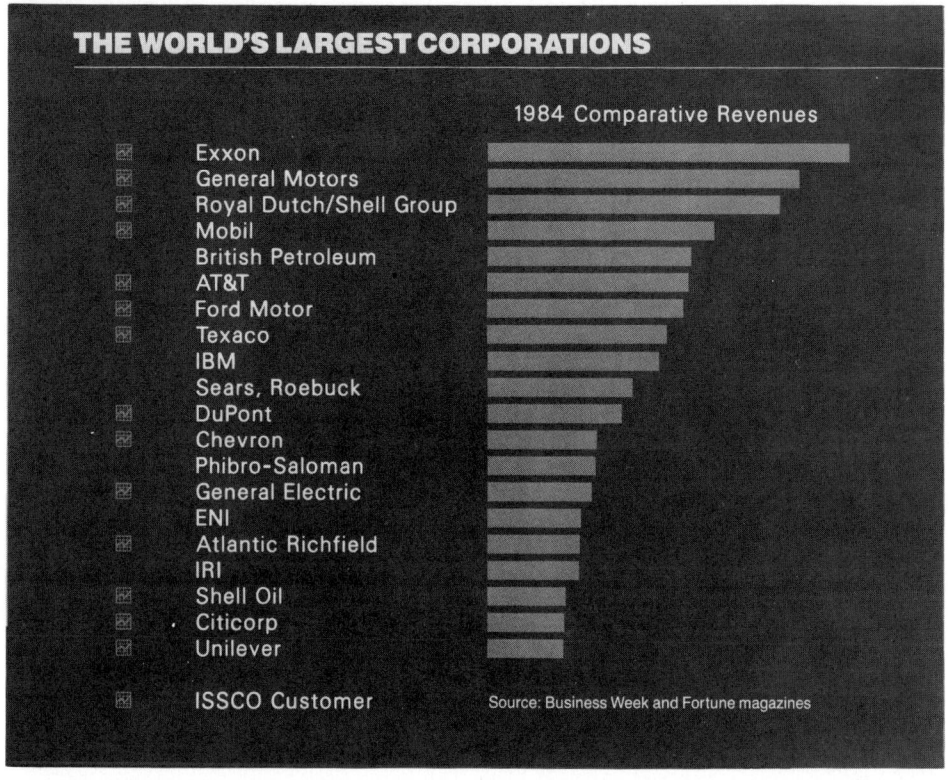

EXHIBIT 4

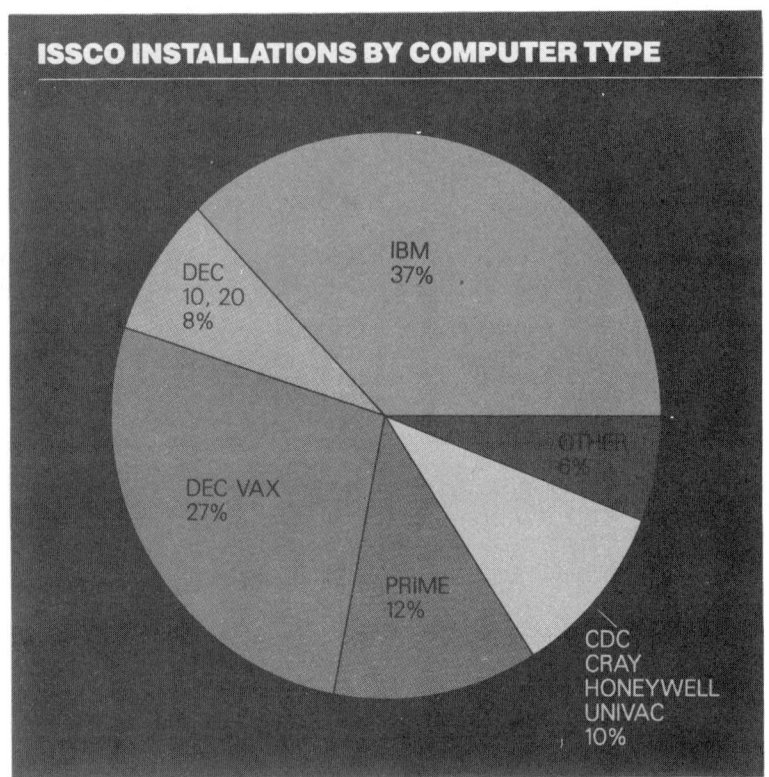

ISSCO INSTALLATIONS BY COMPUTER TYPE

IBM
37%

DEC
10, 20
8%

DEC VAX
27%

OTHER
6%

PRIME
12%

CDC
CRAY
HONEYWELL
UNIVAC
10%

EXHIBIT 5

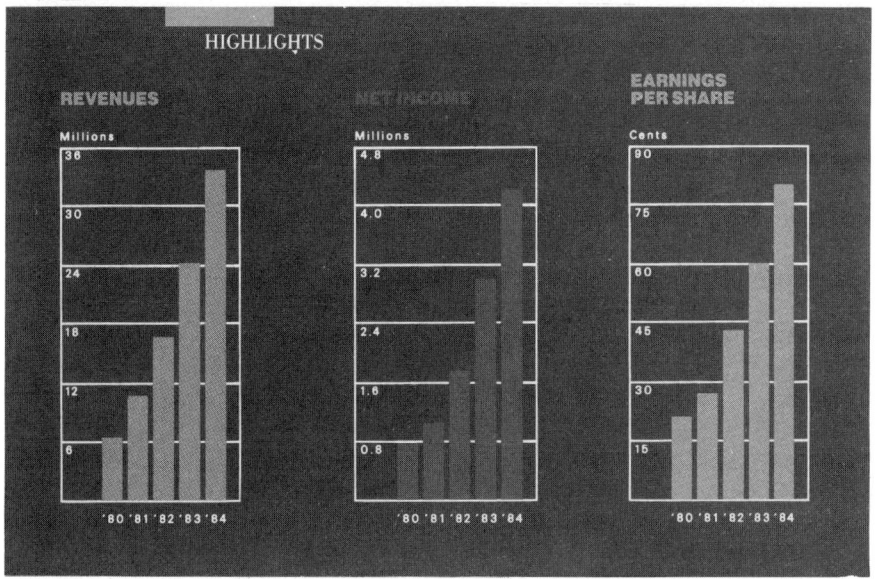

FINANCIAL HIGHLIGHTS	1983	1984	Percent Increase
(In thousands, except per share amounts)			
Revenues	$24,177	$33,632	39
Net income	3,001	4,228	41
Earnings per share	.60	.80	33
Weighted average shares outstanding	5,023	5,293	5
Assets	31,821	40,618	28
Stockholders' equity	23,638	28,493	21

OPERATING HIGHLIGHTS			
(December 31)			
Employees	217	280	29
Sales offices	24	27	13
Basic software installations to date (more than)	1,800	2,500	39

EXHIBIT 6

(In thousands, except per share amounts)	1984	1983	1982
Revenues			
Product license fees	**$24,492**	$17,138	$12,031
Customer support and renewal fees	**9,140**	7,039	4,592
Total revenues	**33,632**	24,177	16,623
Operating Expenses			
Product research and development	**6,451**	4,207	2,917
Sales and marketing	**17,202**	12,911	7,825
General and administrative	**3,619**	2,636	2,714
Total operating expenses	**27,272**	19,754	13,456
Operating Income	**6,360**	4,423	3,167
Non-Operating Income, principally interest	**1,808**	1,128	162
Income Before Income Taxes	**8,168**	5,551	3,329
Income Taxes	**3,940**	2,550	1,580
Net Income	**$ 4,228**	$ 3,001	$ 1,749
Earnings per share	**$ .80**	$ .60	$ .43
Weighted average shares outstanding	**5,293**	5,023	4,084

See notes to consolidated financial statements.

EXHIBIT 7

ASSETS (Dollars in thousands)	1984	1983
Current Assets		
Cash and equivalents	$18,247	$16,697
Receivables – net, principally trade	13,744	10,337
Other	1,415	779
Total current assets	33,406	27,813
Property		
Equipment	7,280	4,128
Leasehold improvements	422	223
Total	7,702	4,351
Less accumulated depreciation	1,958	1,094
Property, net	5,744	3,257
Other Assets	1,468	751
TOTAL	$40,618	$31,821

LIABILITIES AND STOCKHOLDERS' EQUITY (Dollars in thousands)	1984	1983
Current Liabilities		
Accounts payable	$ 1,335	$ 666
Accrued liabilities	1,745	1,069
Deferred revenue	3,772	2,572
Income taxes payable	328	49
Deferred income taxes	4,309	3,395
Total current liabilities	11,489	7,751
Long-Term Liabilities	636	432
Stockholders' Equity		
Common stock, without par value: Authorized – 12,000,000 shares;		
Outstanding – 1984, 5,180,027 shares; 1983, 5,116,107 shares	17,385	16,758
Retained earnings	11,108	6,880
Total stockholders' equity	28,493	23,638
TOTAL	$40,618	$31,821

See notes to consolidated financial statements.

EXHIBIT 8
Management

Directors and Officers

The directors and officers of the Company are as follows:

Name	Age	Position
Peter Preuss	41	Chairman of the Board, President, Chief Executive Officer and Director
Meldon K. Gafner	36	Senior Vice President
Anders Vinberg	35	Senior Vice President
Carl E. Zeiger	42	Senior Vice President—Finance and Administration and Chief Financial Officer
Alan T. Paller	39	President of AUI Data Graphics, Inc.(1) and Director
Richard E. Brown	41	Vice President—Sales
Louise B. Courtier	49	Vice President—Contracts
Friederich Schaaf	63	Vice President—European Operations
Stephen A. Hurwitz	41	Secretary
Howard E. Cox, Jr.(2)	41	Director
John M. Thornton(2)	52	Director
G. Larry Wilson(2)	38	Director

(1) Wholly-owned subsidiary of the Company.
(2) Member of Audit, Compensation, and Stock Option Committees.

Mr. Preuss, a founder of the Company, has been a director of the Company since its incorporation in 1970, President since 1978 and Chairman of the Board and Chief Executive Officer since 1984.

Mr. Gafner joined the Company in August 1980 as Director of Marketing. He was Vice President—Sales and Marketing of the Company from December 1981 to February 1985, when he was elected a Senior Vice President. From September 1973 to August 1980, he was with the Information Display Division of Tektronix, Inc., a company engaged in the computer graphics hardware business. Mr. Gafner's last position at Tektronix, Inc. was that of marketing manager, after having been a sales manager for the western half of the U.S.

Mr. Vinberg joined the Company in January 1977 in a combined technical, sales and product research role. He was a Vice President of the Company from January 1979 to December 1981 and Vice President—Research and Development from December 1981 to February 1985, when he was elected a Senior Vice President.

Mr. Zeiger joined the Company in August 1981 and has been its Chief Financial Officer since December 1981. He was Vice President—Finance and Administration of the Company from September 1982 to February 1985, when he was elected Senior Vice President—Finance and Administration. From 1979 to 1981, he was Vice President—Finance of Arden Group, Inc., a company operating a chain of grocery stores, as well as a Vice President of Arden's subsidiary, Telautograph Corporation, a company engaged in the manufacture and sale of facsimile telecopier equipment. From 1975 to 1979, he was President of a division of Republic Corporation.

Mr. Paller has been a director of the Company since November 1980 and President of AUI Data Graphics, Inc., a wholly-owned subsidiary of the Company, since March 1982. For more than five years prior to joining the Company in December 1981, he had been President and Chairman of the Board of Directors of Applied Urbanetics, Inc., a software company. Until December 30, 1981, Applied Urbanetics, Inc. was marketing agent for the Company for a portion of the East Coast of the United States.

Mr. Brown joined the Company in November 1984 in the appointed position of Vice President of Sales, and his position was made an officer position by the Board of Directors in February 1985. From 1981 until November 1984, he was Vice President, General Manager and director of Computer Sciences Canada, Ltd., a computer services and consulting firm. He was National Sales Director of Computer Sciences Canada, Ltd. from 1980 until 1981.

Ms. Courtier joined the Company in November 1977. She has held various staff and management positions and served as director of contracts from 1980 to February 1985, when she was elected Vice President—Contracts.

Mr. Schaaf was elected Vice President—European Operations in February 1985. Since October 1979, he has been the Managing Director of ISSCO Deutschland GmbH, a West German subsidiary of the Company. Since July 1981, Mr. Schaaf has been a director of ISSCO U.K. Limited, an English subsidiary of the Company, and since May 1984, he has been a director of ISSCO France S.A.R.L., a French subsidiary of the Company.

Mr. Hurwitz, Secretary of the Company since December 1981, has been a partner since 1973 in the Boston law firm of Testa, Hurwitz & Thibeault, general counsel to the Company.

Mr. Cox became a director of the Company in November 1980. He has been a Vice President of Greylock Management Corporation, an investment service organization, since January 1977, and a general partner of Greylock Investors & Co. and Greylock Partners & Co., venture capital limited partnerships, since January 1976 and January 1979, respectively. He has been a director of Stryker Corporation since April 1984.

Mr. Thornton has been a director of the Company since September 1981. Since October 1976, he has been Chairman of the Board of Directors of Micom Systems, Inc., a company in the electronic data communications business. He has been a director since 1963 of Wavetek Corporation, a company in the electronics industry, and has served as President or Chairman of the Board of Directors of Wavetek Corporation since 1965 and as its Chief Executive Officer since February 1978.

Mr. Wilson became a director of the Company in January 1984. Since October 1981, he has been President, chief executive officer, and a director of Policy Management Systems Corporation, which is a supplier of insurance processing software systems and related services to companies in the property and liability insurance industry. From 1974 to 1981, he was President of the PMS Division of Seibels, Bruce & Company and a senior vice president and a director of Seibels, Bruce & Company, a wholly-owned subsidiary of The Seibels Bruce Group, Inc., which is a holding company for several insurance companies in the property and liability insurance industry. Since 1980 he has been a vice president and a director of The Seibels Bruce Group, Inc.

Mr. Paller serves as President of AUI Data Graphics, Inc., pursuant to an employment agreement that continues from year to year unless terminated by either party. Mr. Paller is the only officer who has an employment agreement with the Company. See "Executive Compensation" and "Certain Transactions."

All directors are elected at the annual meeting of stockholders to serve for one year or until their successors are elected and have qualified. The officers are elected annually and serve at the pleasure of the Board of Directors.

EXHIBIT 9
Corporate Structure

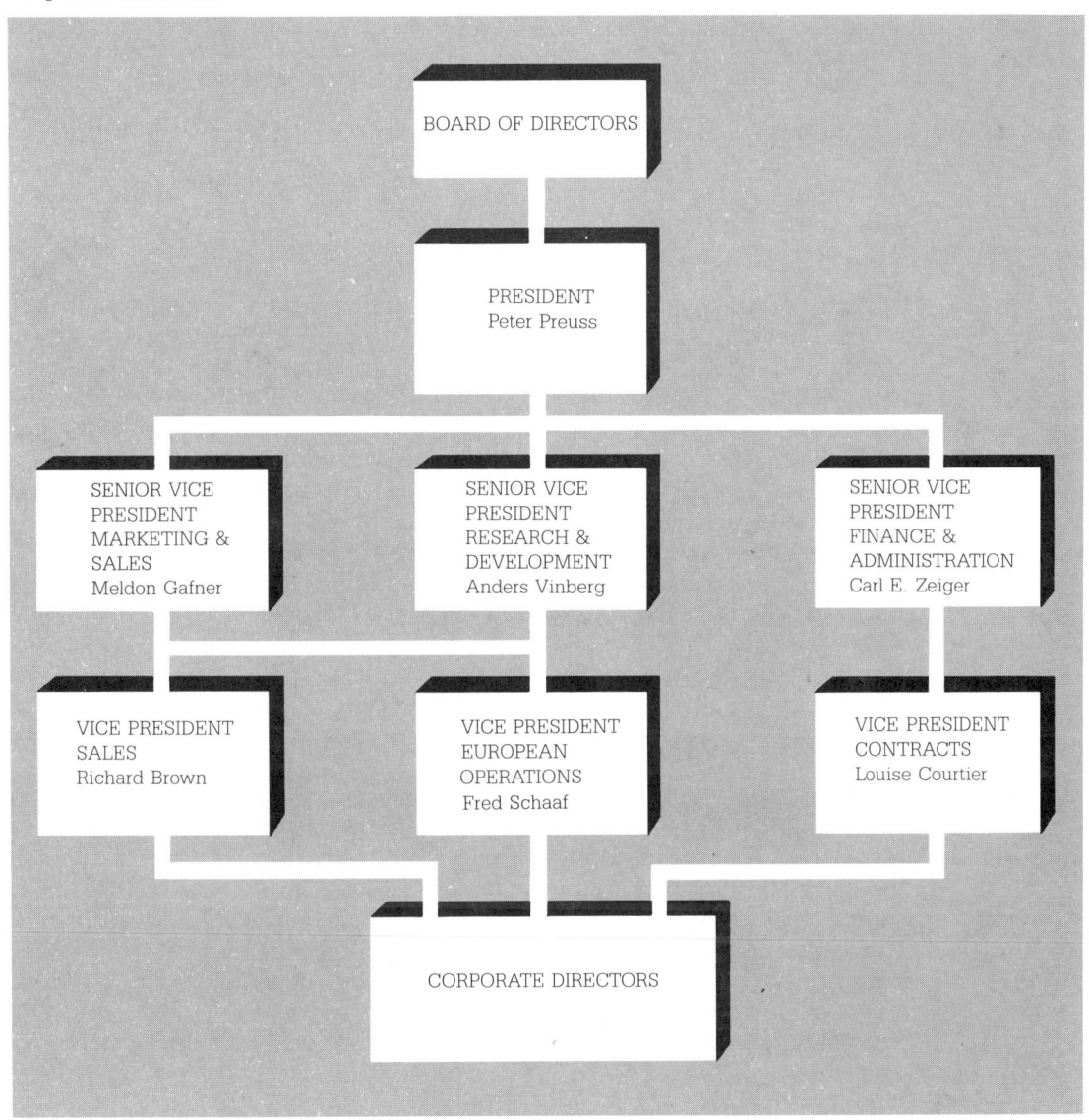

■ ■ ■ CASE 13
Federal Express

Donald F. Harvey
Research Assistant: Mike Crow

INTRODUCTION

The history of Federal Express Corporation has become a parable of sorts. Some feel that the significance of the company is that it created a $7 billion industry where none existed before, changing the way America does business and adding a new cliché—"when it absolutely, positively has to be there overnight"—to the language. Others say the significance is in showing how one man, Frederick W. Smith, could see trends in the world, conceptualize a product that would capitalize on those trends, and motivate an untested work force to build a $3.2 billion empire.

Ours is an information-based society. American in its genesis, this phenomenon has become international. The United States has exported not only the technology but, with it, an entirely new economic paradigm. Time is no longer of the essence, it *is* the essence. Business has become increasingly more urgent. Logistic networks to support this fast-paced economy have become integral parts of it. High-priority goods and documents continue to proliferate, reflecting the changed work environment. Over half of all working Americans, for example, earn their living by processing information.

Federal Express is near the heart of this phenomenon. It was the first to apply the idea of a central national distribution system for the movement of express shipments. Federal Express continues to be the leader in its field, enjoying impressive growth.[1] In December 1982, a single-night record of 208,000 pieces passed through the new Superhub. A year-and-a-half later, traffic soared to 351,000 pieces.

Smith anticipated the explosion of small-package commercial activity in the 1970s and recognized the shift of airline service from smaller hubs to larger cities. He realized that a growing service/computer industry that relied on a faster and faster pace of information flow would support a small-package express business. The company has grown from a handful of deliveries to an average of 850,000 packages per day. This volume represented an annual sales figure of approximately $3.2 billion in 1987.

This case was prepared using published accounts and public documents for the purpose of class discussion rather than to illustrate either effective or ineffective handling of an administrative situation. The author expresses appreciation for the cooperation of Anne Manning and Fred Smith of Federal Express in supplying information.

Business

Federal Express Corporation was incorporated in 1971 and commenced operations in 1972. The company provides an overnight, door-to-door express delivery service for high-priority packages and documents Monday through Saturday between 145 airports in the United States, certain points in Canada and Puerto Rico, and on a limited basis to Europe and the Far East. Local offices are maintained in approximately 300 cities. This service, which serves approximately 98 percent of the United States' population, is provided through an integrated air-ground transportation system utilizing company personnel and equipment. In addition to the overnight services, a one-to-two hour electronic document transmission service was introduced in July, 1984.[2]

The acceleration of technology in this century necessitates a faster information flow, which provides the competitive edge in the information processing world of today. If a computer part is needed, or software, or special materials, or even the original copy of a pending contract, it is almost always needed yesterday; and companies will pay whatever is necessary to be on-line and on time. Thus, the need for express service. The pre-Federal Express era was serviced by Emery, U.S. Postal Service, UPS, and the Hub-to-Hub airline delivery service, but these companies were large-package and two- to three-day delivery service segmented.

Company Profile

Frederick W. Smith graduated from Yale and served two distinguished tours of duty in Vietnam, first as a platoon leader and then as a reconnaissance pilot. Although Smith could not convince his economics teacher of his plan's viability, he managed to convince venture capitalists six years after his graduation. Unlike many entrepreneurs, Smith was already wealthy when he began Federal Express. The son of a Memphis millionaire who died when Fred was four, he put $4 million of his own money into the idea of Federal Express and went to New York City in search of more. Smith was able to persuade a half-dozen institutional investors with his intellect, directness, and research reports predicting that Federal Express would work. He returned to Memphis with $72 million in venture capital from organizations such as Chase Manhattan and Citibank.

The greatest challenge that Smith faced was that of creating a complete delivery system and having it in place before Federal Express had so much as accepted its first package. This accomplishment was possible due to the ability of Smith to motivate people as well as his planning capabilities and financial backing.

Losses were high at first, $29 million in the first twenty-six months because fuel prices jumped after the 1974 Arab fuel embargo; however, after that the revenues and fortunes of Federal Express rose sharply. By the mid-1970s, revenues were running at 50 percent above projections and Smith has the flexibility to expand the service base.[3]

EXTERNAL SYSTEMS

What external factors must Federal Express deal with in its increasingly competitive marketplace? Determining strategic direction in a world of shifting market competition and economic forces is difficult.

Market

Federal Express is the leader in the small-package delivery service industry, with Purolator, UPS, Express Mail, Emery, and Airborne following. Armed with the knowledge of the success of this market segment, the competition is becoming fierce. Advertising strategies to grab and steal market share are increasing along with ad budgets.

Federal's share of total small-package industry advertising approximates $150 million annually. Federal's growth in standard air packages per day indicates the level of aggressive promotion which Federal used to capture market share:

March 82	June 82	July 82	Dec 82	Mar 83	June 83	July 83	Aug 83
8,635	8,971	9,350	19,199	23,971	27,103	29,087	32,300

Federal has more than 345,000 customers including most of the *Fortune* 500 firms.

Staying Ahead in the Information Age

Market research clearly indicates the need to move documents instantaneously from one desk to another regardless of distance. ZapMail is a major step in that direction. This new service delivers reproductions of documents door-to-door almost anywhere in the country within one or two hours from customer contact. The quality of reproduction is extremly faithful to the original—achieved by combining state-of-the-art digital scanning and electronic transmission technology. These technologies are then used in concert with Federal's nationwide ground courier force. They pick up the document (or the customer may take it to a Federal Express facility), transmit it from one ZapMail machine to another, and deliver it. ZapMail puts Federal far ahead in an industry that is under increasing pressure to move documents even faster and with total reliability. The introduction of ZapMail has given Federal Express an advantage in this new field, but as use increases and demand grows, many companies in telecommunications and package/mail express will follow.

Federal's aggressive use of computer technology for tracing a package (COSMOS) from origin to destination to the DADs, which enable messages to be left for the courier even when the vehicle is not occupied, coupled with the constant research and development applied to customer and consumer reports, enables Federal Express to be a forerunner in service development.

COSMOS, a computerized system for tracking shipments from pickup through delivery, is being improved and expanded. Using a satellite and telephone network, COSMOS will soon be able to locate a customer's shipment at any time as it passes through six electronic gates during transit. Automated sorting systems, based on computers and optical character recognition, are under development as well. Improved productivity and customer service will result from this application of technology.

Several regional sorting centers are being built to expedite service and reduce costs. Its air and ground fleet is unmatched, and international growth is planned. Local efforts to improve value of services provided are

- Expanding of air/ground transportation system and sorting capacity
- Extending its network of services both domestically and internationally
- Increasing the convenience of its services by opening "store-front facilities"
- Utilizing the state-of-the-art technology more fully to enhance its package tracing capabilities, billing, and communications systems

Sort Systems Development

The sharp increase in volume makes it more efficient for Federal Express to move a portion of its volume point-to-point rather than through the Memphis Superhub. At regional sorting centers, it selectively segregates volumes that justify direct transport between cities. Where feasible, packages and documents move by truck between points close enough to permit Federal Express to meet service commitments. Construction of the first of several such regional sorting centers began in 1987 in Newark, New Jersey.

Corporate Highlights

Federal Express operates a network of full-service stations and business service centers in 300 major markets and 40,000 communities. It specializes in electronic image transmission of documents and the transportation of documents and packages up to 150 pounds. Federal Express completely controls its transmissions and shipments from pickup to delivery because it uses only company-owned or leased equipment.

Federal Express owns and operates seventy-five aircraft. The fleet is comprised of eight DC 10s, eleven 10-30s, thirty-six 727-100s, and twenty-one 727-200 Boeing aircraft. The company has agreed to purchase five DC 10-30s from McDonnell-Douglas. In 1984 it agreed to purchase two Boeing 727-233ADV from Air Canada and eighty-six Cessna 1 aircraft from Cessna. The company also operates more than 17,000 computer- and radio-dispatched vans, which pick up and deliver shipments (see exhibit 1).

Federal Express became a publicly held company on April 12, 1978, when its first stock issued went on sale over-the-counter. The stock split two for one in September, and on December 29, 1978, was listed on the New York Stock Exchange.

Competition

The rapid growth in package volume of Federal Express (over 45 percent) is attributed to economic recovery, new programs for service, and price discounts. Factors which affected Federal's sales success are (1) the largest express sales force, which is trained in personal selling (5,000 couriers); (2) couriers and sales personnel who have shared revenue goals; and (3) the emphasis on teamwork between couriers and sales staff.

Company	Percentage of Market Share		
	July 1981	July 1982	July 1983
Express Mail	14	13	14
Emery	3	3	3
Airborne	3	3	3
UPS	22	19	16
Federal	19	19	21
Purolator	19	20	20

The market for the company's overnight package service is highly competitive. Federal Express's principal competitors are air freight forwarders, passenger airlines, other all-cargo airlines, United Parcel, and the Express Mail service offered by the U.S. Postal Service. The company's most direct competitor is United Parcel Service. Several air freight forwarders have chartered purchased aircraft and established a hub system in order to compete more effectively in this market.

The principal competitors for the electronic services are digital data transmission systems, such as MCI Mail and Western Union Easy Link, and facsimile equipment manufacturers/marketers, such as Xerox and Panafax. None of these offer a pickup and delivery service of electronic facsimile reproductions; however, all could do so in the future and are believed to be considering such a service. See exhibit 2 for financial highlights.

Governmental Regulation of Air Transport

Under the Federal Aviation Act of 1958, the Federal Aviation Administration (FAA) exercises regulatory authority over Federal Express. The FAA's regulatory authority relates primarily to the safety aspects of air transportation, including aircraft standards and maintenance. The operating certificate is for unlimited duration and remains in effect as long as operational standards are kept within the guidelines of parts 121 and 135.2 of the Federal Aviation Regulations.

The company holds a nationwide motor carrier certificate issued by the Interstate Commerce Commission (ICC), authorizing the express carriage of general commodities between points in the forty-eight contiguous states. The ICC falls within the scope of the Department of Transportation, which regulates safety aspects of motor vehicle operation. Because of extensive use of radio and other communication facilities in the aircraft and ground operations, the company is subject to the Federal Communications Act of 1934, as amended.

SERVICES[4]

Overnight Services   Federal Express provides three overnight delivery services —Priority 1^{SM}; Courier-Pak Overnight Envelope^{TM}, Box^{TM}, and Tube^{TM}; and Overnight Letter^{SM}. Packages and documents are either picked up at the shipper's place of business or are dropped off by the customer at a Federal Express Business Service Center or Overnight Delivery Counter strategically located throughout the country. They are scheduled for delivery not later than 10:30 A.M. local time, in most communities, the following business day.

Priority 1 Service is designed for large packages weighing up to 150 pounds, with a maximum combined length and girth of 120 inches. Rates for Priority 1 Service are based on package weights.

Courier-Pak service is designed for time-sensitive documents, reports, machine parts, and instruments. This service utilizes three specially designed, company-provided containers: a 12″ × 15½″ overnight envelope, a 16″ × 12½″ × 3″ overnight box, and a 38″ × 3″ × 3″ overnight tube. Rates for Courier-Paks are the same as for Priority 1 packages for deliveries in the continental United States.

Overnight Letter^{SM} Service is a fixed-rate service designed for important business correspondence utilizing a company-provided 9″ × 12″ envelope that will hold up to 20 pages.

Standard Air Service   The company provides Standard Air^{SM} Service for less time-sensitive shipments. Packages up to 150 pounds and 120 inches in combined length and girth shipped by Standard Air Service are scheduled for delivery to the consignee by the close of business no later than the second business day following pick up. Standard Air rates are based on the weight of the package.

ZapMail Service   On July 2, 1984, Federal Express began offering ZapMail^{SM} Service, which allows same-day delivery of documents and graphics. Couriers are dispatched to pick up original documents on receipt of a customer request through the customer service center network. The documents are taken to a Federal Express transmission location, where specially designed terminals scan the input and convert it into electronic signals which are sent, utilizing land data lines and a satellite-based network, to a companion terminal at the destination. The reproduction of the original document is then delivered to the designated recipient. This process occurs, in most cases, within two hours of initial customer contact but may vary, based on the number of pages and the destination.

Weekend Service In October 1983, the company initiated Saturday package pick-up service for delivery the following Monday. This service expanded upon the existing service for packages delivered before noon on Saturdays.

Special Services Federal Express provides special handling services for which a surcharge is added to the rate otherwise applicable. Restricted Articles service is available either on an overnight or second-day basis for the shipment of items such as radioactive materials, flammables, and chemicals. Items such as these are classified as hazardous by the Department of Transportation and require special handling. Signature Security service is available on an overnight basis and provides a record for the shipper of the persons responsible for custody of the package from origin to destination. Government agencies and their contractors are the principal users of Signature Security service. Out of Area service is available for packages addressed to a consignee outside the company's delivery areas. During fiscal 1984, less than 1 percent of the company's average daily package volume involved such services.

PartsBank Service Federal Express operates an inventory management service called PartsBank^{SM}. PartsBanks customers deposit inventory in the company's warehouse located in Memphis, Tennessee. As needed, customers request shipments of designated items from their segregated inventory, either by Federal Express or other carriers. Revenues of the PartsBank operation did not exceed 1 percent of total revenues during any one of the three years ended May 31, 1984.

Cargo Charter Service The company also offers a cargo charter service utilizing its aircraft when such aircraft are not required for package delivery operations. Customers can charter aircraft on a one-time or contractual basis. Revenues from the company's charter operations did not exceed 1 percent of total revenues during any one of the three years ended May 31, 1984.

International Service

Federal Express provides small-package and letter delivery service, including customs clearance, from any point in the company's domestic system to 243 Canadian cities under an agreement with Cansica, Inc., an unaffiliated Canadian licensee. Revenues from Canadian service did not exceed 2 percent of total revenues during any one of the three years ended May 31, 1984. The company is further developing a system to expand its foreign services. As an entry into this market, in January 1984, the company purchased Gelco Express International, a small courier service company, which provides service mainly to Europe and the far east. Although plans are being developed for extensive overseas operations beginning in 1985, revenues and expenses associated with international operations in 1984 were less than 1 percent of the company's total revenues and operating expenses.

Exhibit 3 shows the dollar amount in thousands of revenue generated for each class of service offered for fiscal years 1982 through 1984.

The company's customer base is diversified, and at the end of fiscal year 1984, included over 745,000 customers. No single customer accounted for as much as 1 percent of the company's total revenues.

INTERNAL SYSTEMS

Operations

General   Services are provided through the operation of the company's integrated air-ground transportation system. The company's aircraft are operated over a hub-and-spokes pattern with Memphis as the hub. Each weekday evening, aircraft carry packages consigned for overnight delivery from cities throughout the United States to Memphis, where they are sorted, generally between midnight and 2:00 A.M., reloaded onto the aircraft, flown to their destination cities by early morning, and delivered to the consignees by the company's couriers. As a result of sharply increased volumes, in 1984 Federal Express began trucking a small percentage of packages point-to-point, utilizing several regional sorting centers, thereby bypassing the Superhub in Memphis. Also, some city stations are now segregating packages consigned to high-volume destinations. At the Superhub, these segregated packages are simply transferred to the destination aircraft. In addition, the company provides package and letter delivery service between the United States and Canada through an agreement with an unaffiliated Canadian licensee.

Service Locations   Federal Express operates local offices near each of the airports it serves and in most of the cities served by truck. Each city station employs customer service agents, handlers, loaders, and a staff of couriers who pick up and deliver packages in the station's service area. In some cities, the company operates business service centers which are staffed, store-front facilities located in high-traffic, high-density areas. These centers offer package delivery services, as well as other business services, such as high-quality copying. Overnight delivery counters primarily serve Courier-Pak and Overnight Letter customers.

Customer Service

The company has an advanced package tracking and billing system, COSMOS, that utilizes electronic scanning equipment and computer terminals. This system provides proof of delivery information and a facsimile airbill to the customer and information regarding the location of a package within the company's delivery system.

The company also maintains computerized telephone customer service centers in fourteen U.S. cities.

Fuel Supplies and Cost

A large portion of the company's jet fuel supplies is purchased under agreements with Exxon Corporation and other suppliers. Those suppliers have at times reduced allocations of jet fuel to amounts less than Federal Express has requested. However, it has been able to accommodate these reduced allocations and operate its schedule without interruption. The company believes that the effect of reduced fuel allocations or fuel shortages may be mitigated by its ability to reroute aircraft through cities with adequate fuel supplies. Exhibit 4 sets forth certain aircraft fuel cost information for fiscal years 1980 through 1984. Federal Express has agreements with fuel suppliers to provide the bulk of the fuel required by its vehicle fleet, but also relies on retail purchases at some city station locations.

Financial

The annual growth of revenue is directly attributable to increases in package volume, which totaled 67 million in 1984, compared to 43 million in 1983 and 32 million in 1982. Expansion of services has increased operational expenses from $684.4 million dollars in 1982 to $857.4 million in 1983, and $1,271.1 million in 1984. Increased services and geographical expansion have continually pushed up capital expenditures as well. 1984 expenditures were $649 million compared to $230 million in 1983 and $155 million in 1982.

In the fiscal year ending in May 1983, Federal Express was grossing $800 million, and its $15.5 million in interest payments was no problem. The company was earning $78 million after taxes compared to the $4 million in 1978. Capital expenditures for 1985 were estimated at $450 million. As of May 31, 1984, the value of future minimum lease payments for capital lease obligations was $168,538,000.

The effective tax rates of 24 percent in 1984, 40.8 percent in 1983, and 40.2 percent in 1982 differ from statutory federal income tax rates primarily due to utilization of investment tax credits related to the disposition of certain aircraft and related equipment and accelerated depreciation. The 1985, 1986, and 1987 aircraft purchase agreements were expected to approximate $147.7 million, $186.5 million, and $120.2 million respectively. In May 31, 1984, the cost of property and equipment, net of accumulated depreciation, was $1,127,119,000.

Operating results for 1984 reveal another year of impressive growth as Federal Express continued its commitment to provide a superior service that satisfies the increasing demand for the rapid movement of high-priority goods and documents. Express service revenues reached $1.4 billion, a 42 percent increase over 1983; and net income was $115 million, up 30 percent for the year. Earnings per share rose 24 percent in 1984 to $2.52, compared to $2.03 in 1983. Although revenue for 1984 was substantial, margins declined as the company intensified its efforts to improve the value of its existing services and to offer new services by:

- Significantly expanding its air-ground transportation system and sorting capacity
- Extending its network of services both domestically and internationally
- Increasing the convenience of its services by opening store-front facilities (business service centers) in high-density areas, offering additional weekend services, raising the maximum weight-limit for Priority I and Standard Air packages, and introducing a "hundredweight" shipment program
- More fully utilizing state-of-the-art technology to enhance its package tracking, billing, and communications system

In addition, significant expense associated with the development of the two-hour ZapMail service contributed heavily to the lower margins for 1984. The introduction of this service in July 1984, along with the company's commitment to invest in the development of new and improved services, will continue to exert pressure on margins in the short run, but should position Federal Express to better meet the needs of customers and challenges of the future.

The annual growth in revenues is directly attributable to higher package volumes which totalled 67 million packages in 1984, compared to 43 million in 1983, and 32 million in 1982. Although package volumes have risen significantly, package yield has gradually declined, reflecting a much higher growth in the lower-priced Standard Air and Overnight Letter services and a more attractive customer discount program. Together, these programs comprised 44 percent of total package volume in 1984, compared to 31 percent in 1983, and 23 percent in 1982. Additionally, competition in the air express market has heightened and has resulted in the company's implementing certain pricing actions aimed at increasing market share with minimal increases in the prices of services. Federal Express continues to evaluate various pricing strategies and marketing programs that will assume superior service to customers at the best price.

Operating expenses rose 48 percent in 1984, compared to 25 percent in 1983, and 40 percent in 1982, and are, in general, indicative of the company's growth in operations, as evidenced by higher package volumes, geographic expansion, increased capacity, and the development of new services. Greater employment levels, general wage and salary increases, and higher fringe benefit costs were the major factors behind the increases in salaries and employee benefits. Employment levels were up 47 percent in 1984, compared to 24 percent in 1982. The higher level in 1984 is attributable to the introduction of weekend services, an accelerated effort to expand geographically, and preparation for the introduction of ZapMail Service.

Delivery capacity has increased each year in response to higher volumes and expanded service areas. Aircraft capacity has expanded considerably as twelve 727-200s and four DC 10-30s were added to the fleet in 1984; seven 727-100s and two DC 10-10s were added in 1983, and six 727-100s were added in 1982. The vehicle delivery fleet has increased significantly, with approximately 10,000 vehicles in operation at the end of 1983, almost double the number at the end of 1983. Consequently, this growth in the aircraft and vehicle fleet and other additions, primarily data processing and telecommunications equipment, were the main factors leading to increases in depreciation and maintenance and repair expenses. Fuel costs have continued to rise, reflecting higher consumption related to the expanded fleets which has been partially offset by a declining price for aircraft fuel since 1982.

Federal Express's use of leased facilities increased significantly through geographic expansion into new market areas and the opening of business service centers in 1984. As a result, rental expense increased 52 percent in 1984, 28 percent in 1983, and 31 percent in 1982. Also affecting the 1984 increase was the short-term lease of a McDonnell Douglas DC 10-30 aircraft. Vehicle rental costs increased only 22 percent in 1984, as the company began purchasing delivery vehicles during the year. As a percentage of revenue, equipment and facility rentals remained at a relatively constant level from 1982 through 1984.

Other expenses constituted 20 percent of total operating expenses in 1984 and 19 percent in 1983 and 1982. Higher package volumes, improvements to services, and the development of ZapMail Service resulted in higher supply and communications costs which comprise a significant portion of other expenses. In addition, freight charges, previously billed to the customer, were absorbed by the company beginning in March 1983.

To finance major capital expenditures necessary for operating capacity expansion, long-term borrowings increased which, in turn, caused higher interest expense each year. Capitalized interest increased significantly in 1984, primarily associated with the purchase of Boeing 727-200 aircraft, the construction of corporate facilities, and the expansion of the Superhub. Interest income increased in 1984 and 1982 as a result of a higher level of invested funds, but decreased in 1983, reflecting the decline in interest rates. Gains from aircraft dispositions consisted of the sale of ten Falcon aircraft in 1984, the sale of two aircraft purchase positions in 1983, and the sale of one Boeing 737 aircraft and two aircraft purchase positions in 1982 (see exhibits 5, 6, 7 and 8).

Management

Federal Express' management philosophy is summed up in these excerpts from Frederick W. Smith's address to the Apple Computer Leadership Forum:[5]

> Now I think it's important to spend just a moment with you to talk about the people side of our business. Obviously in the conversations that I have had with Steven and Mark and Sue, I've learned a few things about Federal Express. I will say this, we are obviously much more labor intensive organization than Apple. And we are probably more blue collar if you will, if you'll pardon that sort of frayed terminology, than Apple is. However, there are many parallels. We have an average age in our work force of about thirty-two

and a half years of age. Yours is somewhat less than that. We have had a tremendous record of esprit de corps, motivation, innovation, and a sense of humor which I also attribute to Apple. So our trick has been how to maintain, again, the type of motivation and interest on the part, not of a few thousand employees, but tens of thousands of employees. And what we've done is to recognize that almost every human being fits in one category or another in terms of a value system hierarchy.

We consciously set out to address those things which we could identify as key human needs. For instance, job security. The company has been right up front with no ambiguity, the fact that it will never lay off an employee unless the company's future is at stake. And more importantly, that any employee who's displaced because of technological advance or changed business circumstances, will be retrained to another worthwhile position within the company. It's in the handbook and permeates the organization.

I think the number one criterion, bar none, is do we think that person has the interpersonal skills and the leadership skills to be able to manage our people? And among those traits I'm speaking of, do they have the commitment to put people first? We have a corporate philosophy. It's on everything. People-service-profit. People-service-profit.

Smith has earned the undying loyalty of those who work for him. "He was a fantastic motivator of people," said Charles Tucker Morse, the company's first general counsel. "I have not worked since in a situation so intense and so free of politics."[6] (See exhibit 9 for organizational chart.)

CONCLUSION

Federal Express has been successful to date and prospects for the future are favorable. However, managing a high-growth company in a dynamic environment is difficult.

As CEO Fred Smith, COO James Barksdale, and the management team plan for growth, they wonder what strategic changes will be needed to meet this uncertain future. As Fred Smith stated in the 1984 *Annual Report,* "Events have dictated our moving quickly and decisively to stay at the forefront of this market of our own making. We have done so in a number of ways. At least two are completely new, but all are of sweeping importance to the future of Federal Express."[7]

Notes

1 Based upon information supplied by Federal Express Corporation.
2 Federal Express Corporation Annual Report and Form 10-K, 1984.
3 See "Sagas of Five Who Made it," *Time,* February 15, 1982, 42.
4 Annual Report, Form 10-K.
5 Excerpts from Frederick W. Smith's address to the Apple Computer Forum.

6 Henry Altman, "A Business Visionary Who Really Delivered," *Nation's Business* (November 1981), 57.

7 Annual Report, 1984, 5.

EXHIBIT 1
Overview of Federal Express

	Fiscal Year				
	1980	1981	1982	1983	1984
Aircraft Operated					
DC 10-10	2	4	4	6	6
DC 10-30	—	—	—	—	4
Boeing 727-100	17	25	31	38	35
Boeing 727-200	—	—	—	—	12
Dassault Falcons	32	32	32	32	—
Courier Vehicles	2,156	2,500	4,000	4,825	8,358
Full-Service Stations	139	166	180	225	403
Business Service Centers	33	50	69	87	182
Overnight Delivery Counters	114	1,500	3,750	3,693	4,300
Theoretical Maximum Lift Capacity (000#)[1]	1,262	1,612	1,852	2,342	3,318
Max. Sorting Capacity[2] (packages per sort)	90,000	135,000	205,000	260,000	339,000
MSA Served[3]	224	241	275	302	328
Customer Base	240,500	320,300	467,300	550,000	745,000

[1]Individual cargo capacities in pounds: DC 10-30: 148,000; DC 10-10: 105,000; Boeing 727-200: 58,000; Boeing 727-100: 40,000; Dassault Falcon: 6,000

[2]Assumes a sorting time of approximately two hours

[3]Metropolitan Statistical Areas

EXHIBIT 2
Selected Consolidated Financial Information

| | Years Ended May 31 | | | | |
	1984	1983	1982	1981	1980
Income Statement (in thousands except per share data)					
Revenues	$1,436,305	1,008,087	803,915	589,493	415,379
Net Income	$115,430	88,933	78,385	58,136	37,729
Earnings per share	$2.52	2.03	1.85	1.42	1.00
Shares Outstanding	45,448	43,316	41,788	40,222	36,564
Balance Sheet Data					
Current Assets	$328,136	265,171	194,265	166,952	85,454
Current Liabilities	$255,910	175,293	114,596	113,846	64,351

EXHIBIT 3

| | Years Ended May 31 | | |
	1984	1983	1982
Priority 1	$625,501	$469,422	$427,940
Courier-Pak	445,917	355,952	263,030
Overnight Letter	193,093	94,978	55,993
Standard Air	153,614	77,376	48,868
Other	18,180	10,359	8,084
Total	$1,436,305	$1,008,087	$803,915

EXHIBIT 4
Fuel Cost

Fiscal Year	Gallons of Fuel Consumed*	Total*	Average Price per Gallon	Percent of Operating Expense
1984	80,488	$73,444	$ .92	5.8%
1983	58,226	58,473	1.00	6.8
1982	54,681	59,095	1.09	8.6
1981	47,447	49,560	1.05	10.1
1980	43,094	37,346	.85	10.7

*In thousands

EXHIBIT 5
Consolidated Statements of Income for Years Ended May 31

	1984	1983	1982
	In thousands, except per share amounts		
Express Service Revenues	**$1,436,305**	$1,008,087	$803,915
Operating Expenses (Notes 4 and 8):			
Salaries and employee benefits	**622,675**	419,644	320,345
Depreciation and amortization	**111,956**	77,421	56,353
Fuel and oil	**93,520**	71,262	69,282
Equipment and facility rentals	**89,775**	59,115	46,116
Maintenance and repairs	**59,482**	44,083	38,795
Advertising	**39,345**	34,558	25,302
Other	**254,344**	151,267	128,256
	1,271,097	857,350	684,449
Operating Income	**165,208**	150,737	119,466
Other Income (Expense):			
Interest expense	**(36,350)**	(23,451)	(15,933)
Interest capitalized	**11,851**	5,831	2,852
Interest income	**13,166**	9,679	11,994
Gain on disposition of aircraft and related			
equipment	**2,463**	4,224	7,318
Other, net	**(4,078)**	3,196	5,383
	(12,948)	(521)	11,614
Income before Income Taxes	**152,260**	150,216	131,080
Provision for Income Taxes (Note 7)	**36,830**	61,283	52,695
Net Income	**$ 115,430**	$ 88,933	$ 78,385
Earnings Per Share (Note 6)	**$ 2.52**	$ 2.03	$ 1.85
Average Shares Outstanding (Note 6)	**45,448**	43,316	41,788

The accompanying Notes to Consolidated Financial Statements are an integral part of these statements.

EXHIBIT 6
Consolidated Balance Sheets for Years Ended May 31

		1984	1983
		In thousands	
Assets	**Current Assets:**		
	Cash, including short-term investments of		
	$35,500,000 and $105,233,000	$ 37,690	$105,437
	Receivables, less allowance for doubtful accounts		
	of $7,821,000 and $5,284,000	207,256	124,841
	Spare parts, supplies and fuel	39,725	16,203
	Refundable Federal income taxes (Note 7)	27,282	5,058
	Prepaid expenses and other	16,183	13,632
	Total current assets	328,136	265,171
	Property and Equipment, at cost (Notes 3, 4 and 9):		
	Flight equipment	742,444	416,283
	Package handling and ground support equipment	206,372	124,954
	Other property and equipment	478,465	276,413
		1,427,281	817,650
	Less accumulated depreciation and amortization	314,642	221,258
	Net property and equipment	1,112,639	596,392
	Construction Funds in Escrow (Note 3)	32,168	47,839
	Equipment Deposits and Other Assets (Note 9)	52,862	82,315
		$1,525,805	$991,717

The accompanying Notes to Consolidated Financial Statements are an integral part of these balance sheets.

EXHIBIT 6 (Continued)

		1984	1983
		In thousands	
Liabilities and Stockholders' Investment	**Current Liabilities:**		
	Current portion of long-term debt and redeemable		
	preferred stock (Notes 3 and 5)	**$ 22,001**	$ 12,171
	Note payable	**—**	15,912
	Accounts payable	**129,960**	59,047
	Accrued expenses (Note 2)	**103,949**	88,163
	Total current liabilities	**255,910**	175,293
	Long-Term Debt, less current portion (Note 3)	**435,158**	247,424
	Deferred Income Taxes (Note 7)	**112,439**	59,094
	Commitments and Contingencies (Notes 3, 4, 5, 8 and 9)		
	$9.50 Cumulative Preferred Stock, $1.00 par value; stated at $100		
	mandatory redemption value, less $1,534,500 for shares		
	currently redeemable; 61,120 and 76,465 shares authorized and		
	issued (Note 5)	**4,577**	6,112
	Common Stockholders' Investment (Notes 3 and 6):		
	Common Stock, $.10 par value; 100,000,000 shares authorized,		
	46,386,287 and 21,970,049 shares issued	**4,639**	2,197
	Additional paid-in capital	**321,768**	222,782
	Retained earnings	**391,314**	278,815
	Total common stockholders' investment	**717,721**	503,794
		$1,525,805	$991,717

EXHIBIT 7

Consolidated Statements of Changes in Financial Position for Years Ended May 31

	1984	1983	1982
	In thousands		
Funds Provided By:			
Net income	$115,430	$ 88,933	$ 78,385
Charges to income not requiring working capital:			
Depreciation and amortization	111,956	77,421	56,353
Deferred income taxes and other	54,206	26,141	21,336
Working capital provided from operations	281,592	192,495	156,074
Increase in long-term debt	258,791	37,745	65,479
Proceeds from issuance of common stock	99,224	65,414	2,077
Disposition of property and equipment	20,536	13,947	14,512
Decrease in construction funds in escrow	15,671	4,746	—
Decrease in equipment deposits and other assets	28,589	—	—
Total funds provided	704,403	314,347	238,142
Funds Used For:			
Acquisition of property and equipment	648,736	230,188	155,187
Reduction of long-term debt	71,057	14,177	4,328
Mandatory redemption of preferred stock	1,535	1,534	1,535
Payment of dividends on preferred stock	727	872	1,018
Increase in construction funds in escrow	—	—	32,855
Increase in equipment deposits and other assets	—	57,367	16,656
Total funds used	722,055	304,138	211,579
Increase (Decrease) in Working Capital	$ (17,652)	$ 10,209	$ 26,563
Increase (Decrease) in Working Capital by Component:			
Cash and short-term investments	$ (67,747)	$ 44,545	$ (5,216)
Receivables	82,415	27,470	34,021
Spare parts, supplies and fuel	23,522	1,041	(2,205)
Refundable Federal income taxes	22,224	5,058	—
Prepaid expenses and other	2,551	(7,208)	713
Current portion of long-term debt and redeemable preferred stock	(9,830)	(6,778)	(885)
Note payable	15,912	(15,912)	—
Accounts payable	(70,913)	(26,302)	(1,993)
Accrued expenses	(15,786)	(11,705)	2,128
Increase (Decrease) in Working Capital	$ (17,652)	$ 10,209	$ 26,563

The accompanying Notes to Consolidated Financial Statements are an integral part of these statements.

EXHIBIT 8

Federal Express Corporation Product Line Statistics and Product Growth for Fiscal
Years 1980–1984

	1980	1981	1982	1983	1984
Packages (thousands)					
Priority 1 and Courier-Pak	15,244	20,117	24,800	29,221	38,080
Standard Air	1,966	2,029	2,207	4,555	11,136
Overnight Letter	—	—	5,093	8,830	18,211
TOTAL	17,210	22,146	32,100	42,606	67,427
Yields					
Priority 1 and Courier-Pak	$24.40	$26.88	$27.86	$28.25	$28.14
Standard Air	18.55	21.18	22.15	16.99	13.80
Overnight Letter	—	—	10.99	10.76	10.60
Composite	23.73	26.29	24.79	23.42	21.03
Percentage of Revenues					
Priority 1 and Courier-Pak	89.5%	91.5%	85.9%	81.9%	74.6%
Standard Air	8.8	7.3	6.1	7.7	10.7
Overnight Letter	—	—	7.0	9.4	13.4
Other	1.7	1.2	1.0	1.0	1.3
TOTAL	100.0%	100.0%	100.0%	100.0%	100.0%
Pounds/Package	9.8	8.4	6.5	5.8	5.5
Revenue/Pound	$2.43	$3.15	$3.81	$4.02	$3.80

	1980	1981	1982	1983	1984	Five-Year Compound
Product Growth Rate						
Priority 1 and Courier-Pak	51.0%	32.0%	23.3%	17.8%	30.3%	30.4%
Standard Air	23.6	3.2	8.8	106.4	144.5	47.6
Overnight Letter	—	—	—	73.4	106.2	—
TOTAL	47.3	28.7	44.9	32.7	58.3	42.0

EXHIBIT 9
Organizational Chart

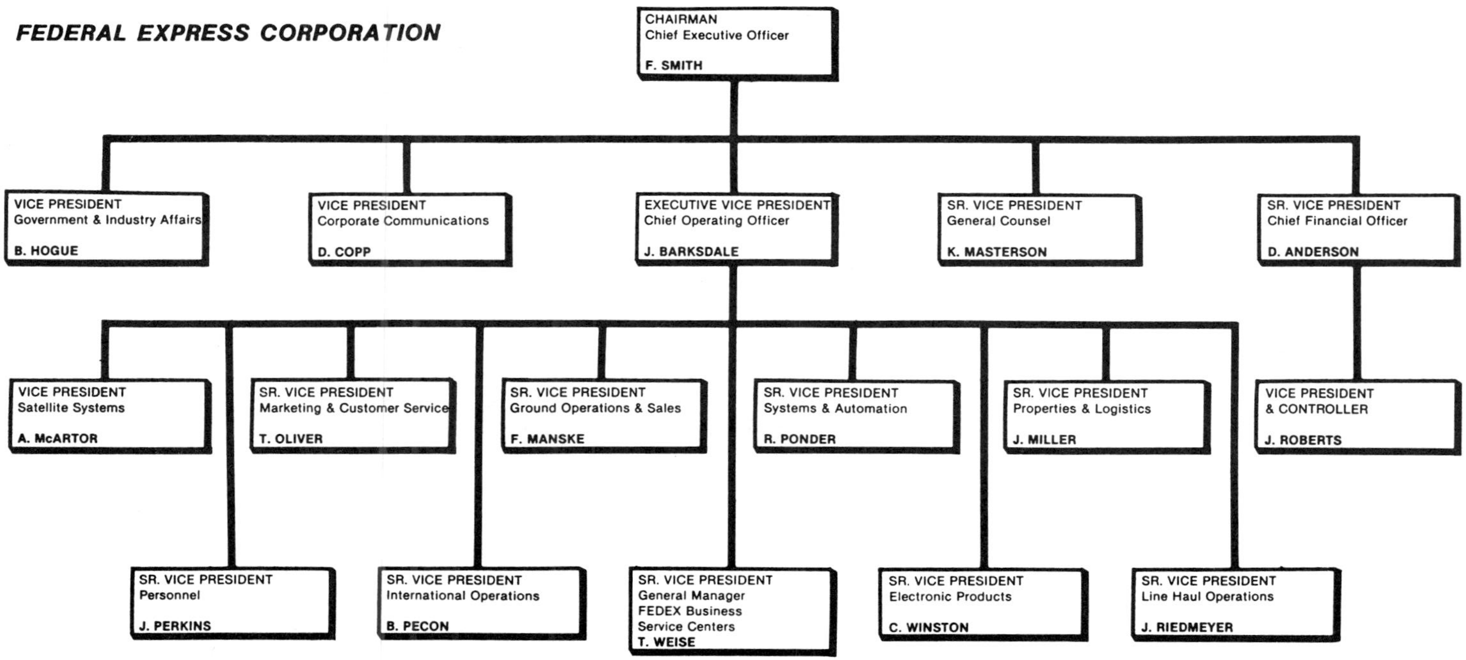

FEDERAL EXPRESS CORPORATION

CHAIRMAN
Chief Executive Officer
F. SMITH

VICE PRESIDENT
Government & Industry Affairs
B. HOGUE

VICE PRESIDENT
Corporate Communications
D. COPP

EXECUTIVE VICE PRESIDENT
Chief Operating Officer
J. BARKSDALE

SR. VICE PRESIDENT
General Counsel
K. MASTERSON

SR. VICE PRESIDENT
Chief Financial Officer
D. ANDERSON

VICE PRESIDENT
& CONTROLLER
J. ROBERTS

VICE PRESIDENT
Satellite Systems
A. McARTOR

SR. VICE PRESIDENT
Marketing & Customer Service
T. OLIVER

SR. VICE PRESIDENT
Personnel
J. PERKINS

SR. VICE PRESIDENT
Ground Operations & Sales
F. MANSKE

SR. VICE PRESIDENT
International Operations
B. PECON

SR. VICE PRESIDENT
Systems & Automation
R. PONDER

SR. VICE PRESIDENT
General Manager
FEDEX Business
Service Centers
T. WEISE

SR. VICE PRESIDENT
Electronic Products
C. WINSTON

SR. VICE PRESIDENT
Properties & Logistics
J. MILLER

SR. VICE PRESIDENT
Line Haul Operations
J. RIEDMEYER

■ ■ ■ CASE 14
Cubic Corporation

Donald F. Harvey
Research Assistant: Dave Todd

Cubic Corporation, a major supplier of electronic systems to the military, has followed a pattern of consistent growth. Walter J. Zable, chairman and chief executive officer, reflected on his firm's thirty-five years of operation,

> As our company begins its thirty-fifth year of operations, it does so with a record high backlog. We are well positioned in new and exciting growth markets, with a strong financial position to capitalize on our opportunities. In addition, we have established a team of highly skilled and trained managers and employees.
>
> Management philosophy, over the past three decades has been one of conservative, steady growth. Our business policies are aimed at three major areas: First, providing our customers with good products and services at a fair price. Second, utilizing the resources of our investors in the most prudent and productive manner with a minimum amount of risk. Third, providing a work environment for our people that will produce the ultimate in efficiency and creativity to best benefit every person in the Cubic family, as well as the corporation.[1]

Company Profile

Formed in 1951 in San Diego, California, Cubic has, through a conservative but decisive plan of achievement, developed into a high-technology, growth company. (See exhibit 1 for financial highlights.) The corporation has set out to achieve the following corporate goals:

- Conservative, steady growth
- Good products at fair prices
- Prudent and productive use of resources
- Minimizing risk
- Work environments that facilitate efficiency and creativity
- Expansion through judicious acquisition
- Growth in new directions

This case was prepared using published accounts and public documents for the purpose of class discussion rather than to illustrate either effective or ineffective handling of an administrative situation.

All of these goals reflect current and expected market trends in electronic warfare systems which are estimated to receive funding increases, at least through 1990, at rates greater than the defense budget as a whole. Financially strong with 1.3 million square feet of modern facilities, Cubic feels it will remain a viable competitor in its chosen business fields well into the future.

Cubic's divisions' and subsidiaries' product lines hold important positions within their respective markets. Cubic's division and subsidiary operations are best grouped into three main product segments: electronic defense systems, electronic elevator operations, and industrial operations.

- *Electronic defense systems*   work under U.S. and foreign government contracts relating to electronic defense systems and equipment, advanced flight training aids, navigational aids, simulators, antennas, and transceivers.
- *Electronic elevator operations*   involve the design, construction, installation, and servicing of passenger and freight elevators.
- *Industrial operations*   include design, production, and servicing of fare collection systems; manufacture of surveying systems, radio communication equipment, and paper products: distribution of safety and medical products; and operation of a computer service bureau.

Business segment financial data for the three years in the period ended September 30, 1984, are presented in exhibit 2. Certain prior year amounts have been reclassified to conform to current year classifications.

COMPANY SYNOPSIS AND RELEVANT TECHNOLOGICAL DEVELOPMENTS BY DIVISION

Defense Systems

In fiscal 1984, over 90 percent of the revenue from the division came from the training and simulation systems business segments. The company expects that training will receive greater emphasis as the cost and complexity of weapons systems continue to increase. As a result, the market for systems of this type will continue to grow.[2]

Many new features and developments are under way that will enhance simulation systems product lines. These features, many of which are truly scientific achievements, will add technical advances to present product lines, allowing them to become systems of the future. All will play important parts in providing key training tools to the military through the 1990s. These advances to the company's simulation and training systems are not blue sky or engineering pipe dreams, but are actual funded and applied research projects that are vital to the success of military training and free world defenses.[3]

Competition

The leaders in the defense electronics industry are E-Systems, Loral, Sanders Associates, Watkins-Johnson, and Westinghouse Electric. In comparison to these companies, Cubic ranks fifth on sales and market share (see exhibit 3).

In the early seventies, the Navy chose Cubic over General Dynamics, McDonnell Douglas, Grumman, and Singer for the air combat training system that was called ACMR. Since then, Cubic has remained at the leading edge of training and simulation systems technology.[4]

Despite government attempts to channel contracts to minority firms, big companies are increasing rapidly. As these big companies get bigger, they make it more and more difficult for small businesses to compete.

Tactical Aircrew Combat Training System, and Air Combat Maneuvering Instrumentation (TACTS/ACMI)

TACTS/ACMI is the most "advanced and realistic" training and tactical warfare simulator available. The first fully operational TACTS/ACMI system was accepted by the Navy in 1973. Since then, Cubic has continued to develop, build, and enhance its capabilities. TACTS/ACMI is a computer-based data communication and tracking network that provides information to a range training office and observers on flight dynamics, weapons system status, and weapons firing of each aircraft engaged in a training mission, and does it in real time.[5]

For more than ten years, this division has been an international leader in tactical training systems. New and advanced military requirements will dramatically change the mission of this already dynamic product line. New systems being developed for the U.S. Navy and Air Force will be able to simultaneously track and monitor thirty-six high-performance aircraft. The current state-of-the-art permits only eight. Advanced applicants will encompass training within a complete battle scenario, including:

- Air-to-air combat
- Air-to-ground combat
- Ground-to-air combat
- Fighting helicopters
- Tactical vertical takeoff and landing aircraft
- Ground troops

Military commanders will be able to view the performance of all combat as the training mission is taking place. Views of any segment of the exercise can be seen with the push of a button. A replay capability of each mission offers a closer study of every facet of the training exercise. All information is stored and can be replayed from any angle, cockpit view, or in stop-action in order to study each facet of the training exercise. In 1984, TACTS/ACMI provided over 90 percent of the defense division's revenue. The market will continue to grow as the emphasis on cost considerations and the complexity of weapons systems increases. Additional applications are being built into the TACTS/ACMI systems in the form of GPS, or Global Positioning System, which uses satellite capabilities to improve the overall system.

Cubic Western Data

Recognized as a world leader in the technology of revenue collection systems, Cubic Western Data during the 1984 calendar year added new customers to its already prestigious client roster. These include:

- Singapore Mass Rapid Transit System
- Southern California Rapid Transit District (Los Angeles)
- Long Beach Transit District (California)
- Massachusetts Turnpike Authority

With more than a decade of direct fare collection experience, this subsidiary is a known and respected prime contractor. Earning this position world-wide required a good deal of on-the-job learning as the needs of various transit authorities are often diverse. Since 1971 a great deal of applied research has resulted in the perfection of fare collection technology, which will contribute even more to the customer's future.

Every day, more than three million people board buses, high-speed commuter trains, and subway cars or drive over toll roads and have their fares collected by Cubic equipment. Since entering the market in 1971, the company has recorded sales of more than $300 million. The customers are among the world's most prominent transit bus and turnpike authorities. Not a single client has ever wanted for technical or management assistance in the operation of their fare collection systems. Cubic has committed its resources to this business.

Cubic has applied research into the development of its fare collection system and feels it has the most technologically advanced equipment on the market. During that period when Cubic lacked competition, however, its equipment was "plagued with problems" and gained a bad reputation for performing below specifications.[6]

The backlog of unfilled orders at Cubic Western Data is up 100 percent over fiscal 1983 levels to nearly $45 million. The market prospects in fiscal years 1985, 1986, and 1987 looked just as promising.

Until fiscal 1983, Cubic confined its markets to rail transit systems. In fiscal 1984, the business was expanded to include toll roads, buses, and automated parking lots.

The computerized farebox Cubic developed in 1984 will be installed in Los Angeles Rapid Transit District buses in early 1985. This new product is what the industry calls *intermodel* because it allows riders to travel on commuter trains, city buses, and subways with one ticket. The new farebox also accepts dollar bills and any denomination of U.S. coins, as well as magnetically coded multirider passes. Transit systems such as those in New York, Los Angeles, Washington, D.C., and Miami, as well as every other major city's bus system, have requirements for this new farebox. The established product line of computerized fare collection equipment is a proven entity in the world marketplace. The addition of this new product adds still another dimension to serve Cubic's customer base. The entire fare collection business has limited competition, both domestically and overseas. "I would call this segment of the company explosive, and I feel we have all the financial resources, management, engineering maturity, and product ingenuity to achieve outstanding success," says CEO Walter J. Zable.[7]

U.S. Elevator

U.S. Elevator, the nation's fifth largest producer of passenger and freight elevators, has been a wholly owned subsidiary since 1969. A national company, it operates from a 240,000 square-foot administrative, engineering, and manufacturing complex in San Diego County. Fifty-seven branch offices comprise the marketing, service and installation facets of the company. Calling on the strong technical and financial resources of the parent company, U.S. Elevator has made significant strides within the industry. Recognized as a technology trend-setter, many of the engineering innovations developed by the company have become standard products in the market place. Among these are microprocessor-controlled systems.

U.S. Elevator's major sales lever is the development of high-tech products, as well as innovative related systems, which afford the company market penetration. Continued expansion to broaden market penetration is a matter of corporate priority. The fast-growing regions of Austin and San Antonio, Texas, were added to U.S. Elevator's operation region in 1984.

U.S. Elevator has relied on high-tech development and innovation to gain market penetration. The company is recognized as a technology trend setter and many of its innovations have become industry standards. U.S. Elevator offers the more than 100-year-old elevator market something the industry cannot refuse: technology. As pioneers in the use of solid state circuitry and microcomputer controls, Cubic has been in the forefront of scientific achievement since acquiring this subsidiary in 1969.

Labor relations within the industry are more stable than ever as the result of five-year union contracts. Nonresidential construction indicators show increased building in the national market regions served by Cubic.

Cubic's business policy in this market is not short-term. Fifteen years in the elevator industry is a relatively brief period. From initial acquisition of approximately $2 million in sales volume to $100 million, Cubic is building a business on firm profits with a keen eye to the future. It's difficult for Cubic to lose in the elevator industry. Its initial investment has paid off, and it has laid the vital foundation for future success.[8]

Otis Elevator is dominant in the industry. Significant segments of total business available are taken up by mainly five other competitors, the most significant of which is Dover Elevator. U.S. Elevator Corporation believes that it now ranks fifth in sales in the industry.[9] Competition is keen because of price tightening within the market. However, U.S. Elevator has had success in penetrating the market by using state-of-the-art electronics in its products and systems. An example is the use of microprocessor-controlled elevators, now a standard production item sold by the company.

Although the elevator business is not seasonal, it does tend to be cyclical, as do all construction industries. Incident to the sale of its elevator products, U.S. Elevator is subject to possible liability by reason of warranties against defects in design, material, and workmanship.

Cubic Precision

The newest member of the Cubic family of companies, this subsidiary, located in Tullahoma, Tennessee, is the headquarters for the corporation's line of surveying and positioning systems. The positioning systems, called Argo and Autotape, have been marketed successfully worldwide for many years. These established products continue as the industry standard for accuracy and reliability.

Used in conjunction with offshore oil exploration, hydrographic research, and dredging, these systems also have a variety of uses where long-range, high-accuracy positioning is required. New, low-cost products for land surveying that are fully automatic, simple to operate, and highly portable are in the final stages of development.

Aside from producing surveying instruments, this complex provides the corporation with additional high-volume, precision production capability. Another new area of business opportunity for this subsidiary is subcontracting to support other firms' manufacturing needs.[10]

The Argo and Autotape positioning systems lead the industry in accuracy and reliability. They are used for:

- Oil exploration
- Hydrographic research
- Dredging
- Long-range situations requiring highly accurate positioning

New surveying products are in the final stages of development. These products will be economical, fully automatic, simple to operate, and highly portable.

Cubic Communications

An increasingly important part of Cubic's future, this family member has made impressive progress in recent years. These corporate contributions include development of new state-of-the-art communications equipment that has expanded this unit's customer base. Significant technical advances have been made in systems for electronic surveillance and two-way radio communication. The powerful, portable systems are small and lightweight. They are used by such agencies as the Department of Energy, drug enforcement, U.S. Coast Guard, undercover authorities, U.S. Navy, U.S. Air Force, and allied powers. These new microprocessor-powered, modular design systems are in the frequency ranges suited for varied applications and have enhanced this company's position in the marketplace.[11]

Cubic Data Systems

Created through acquisition in 1968 to support the data processing needs of the expanding parent company and its then new subsidiaries, this unit is also a profit center. Aside from computer services, the subsidiary performs direct marketing functions to clientele in a variety of businesses, including fundraising organizations, advertisers, and publishing companies.[12]

Because of its strong computer hardware, software, and systems marketing experience, Wang Laboratories, Inc., accepted the unit as an authorized national distributor in 1983. As a profit center, it performs computer services and direct marketing functions.

G. S. Parsons Companies

This member of the Cubic family of companies is a distributor of welding equipment, industrial, medical and cryogenic gases, safety supplies, fire protection systems/ equipment, carbonics, and medical apparatus. Since becoming a wholly owned subsidiary in 1969, this unit has generated $156 million in revenues. The company has grown into a major business operation with modern stores and warehouse facilities in six locations throughout San Diego and neighboring Imperial County.[13]

Consolidated Cover Company

Developing from a one-product company when acquired by Cubic in 1969, this converter of sanitary paper products today has many diverse lines within the paper industry. Among the major new products are corrugated containers used for packaging and shipping, plus the special "Hot Box" pizza carton employed by fast food chains. The company is highly automated, with computerized machines that print, cut, fold, and glue corrugated paperboard to customer specifications.

With financial support from Cubic and knowledgeable internal management, Consolidated Cover Company has grown a remarkable 10-fold since its acquisition.[14]

Goverment and Social Influences

Cubic, because it is involved in government defense contracts, must deal with the following:

1   Government regulation and performance requirements
2   Pentagon funding which relies on congressional approval

3 Pentagon demands regarding workmanship, materials, and performance; increased sophistication; simplified operations; and rapid updating of current systems
4 Federal limits on profit margins
5 State Department export limitations
6 Increased scrutiny of defense budgets to reduce unreasonable costs
7 Legislation to facilitate competition by small business
8 National security and sentiment towards budget expenditures for defense versus social programs
9 Maintenance of employment, economic, and environmental stability
10 Community involvement
11 Prudent use of natural resources

FINANCIAL

Cubic's financial position continues strong in virtually all areas of measurement. Net working capital, including cash and securities of $39.5 million, has increased to $94.4 million from an already strong $80.2 million at the beginning of 1984. Long-term debt as a percentage of total capitalization at 21.2 percent reflects a decrease from 1983, further strengthening the company's financial position. Because of this strong liquidity, Cubic had not utilized all of its available short-term credit lines nor did it anticipate that such bank credit would be needed in fiscal 1985.[15]

Although sales for 1984 were slightly higher than those for 1983, the combination of a number of circumstances adversely affected net income. As was reported in the third quarter, management decided to set aside approximately $3 million, the equivalent of 19 cents per share, for possible disallowance of costs relating to a disputed government contract. Also affecting the company's performance in 1984 compared to 1983 was the return to more traditional overall profit margins on defense systems contracts as a result of a lower ratio of foreign versus domestic government contracts. Accordingly, costs of sales as a percent of sales was 73 percent in 1984 compared to 71 percent in 1983.[16]

Research and development expense increased by 9 percent in 1984 over that for 1983, reflecting Cubic's continuing efforts to improve market and competitive positions. This effort is especially evident in the expansion of the company's mass transit product lines into buses and tollroads. Interest, dividends, and other income at over $5 million in 1984 represented an increase of $2 million over 1983, reflecting the higher levels of invested funds provided from operations.

In 1983, management determined that the decline in the market value of certain noncurrent marketable securities required a write-down of $2.5 million. In 1984, these securities were sold for an amount approximating the adjusted carrying value at September 30, 1983.

A substantial portion of Cubic's business consists of long-term contracts. Many of these contracts are with agencies of the United States government and are cost reimbursable, which permits recovery of inflation costs. Other contracts with the government or other customers are fixed-price and include estimated costs for inflation in the contract price. Generally, Cubic has been able to increase prices to offset its increased costs (see exhibits 4, 5, and 6).

Research and development expenses increased over 9 percent in 1983 and are expected to increase at an even higher rate in the future as Cubic continues to improve its market and competitive positions in its volatile environment. The estimated dollar amounts spent for customer-sponsored research activities relating to the development of new products or services was $50 million in 1984 and $53 million in 1983. The dollar amounts of company-sponsored research activity were $4,066,000 for the fiscal year ending September 30, 1984, and $3,742,000 for the fiscal year ending September 30, 1983.[17]

ORGANIZATION STRUCTURE

Cubic is run with an informal organizational structure. Employees report both formally and informally to various, limited levels of management. Due to the lack of a formal organizational structure, the occurrence of duplicate efforts, poor communication, and inefficiencies among departments may be significantly increased. Cubic does not have an overall strategic plan that encompasses the corporation as a whole. Instead, each strategic business unit engages in its own planning that best fits its goals and objectives.

Human resources have been one of the key factors in Cubic's success since its beginnings. The goals of finding and developing qualified people sometimes call for special efforts, and Cubic is willing to use its resources to find qualified individuals in all areas of the community. Cubic recognizes that people are its most critical resource and plans to keep this resource on a top priority in the years to come. There were 3,700 persons employed by the firm as of 1984.[18]

CONCLUSION

As CEO Walter Zable reflected on thirty-five years of success, he also wondered about the future. Cubic is a high-tech firm with a consistent record of strong profit growth. On this Mr. Zable commented:

> From my personal experience, I sincerely believe that when one combines all the many parts of our company into a whole, our optimism is justified.
>
> When we mesh good products with very strong growth markets, add a viable financial position with a motivated, stable work force, I cannot help but feel our future is strong for both the long- and short-terms.
>
> One must understand that this company is not in business on a day-to-day or year-to-year basis. We are, by the very nature of the business, in operation for the long pull. The parts of the company have been carefully organized over the past three decades to accommodate the present and prepare for the future.

As president, with a heavy investment in Cubic, I am committed to do everything possible to protect the interests of all stockholders. To that end, strong emphasis is placed on conservative growth.[19]

As Chairman Walt Zable and his executive committee plan for the future, he wondered what strategy Cubic should follow to best maintain its position.

Notes

1   Cubic Corporation, Annual Report, 1984, 3.
2   Ibid.
3   See *Business Week,* September 20, 1982, 80.
4   Cubic Corporation, Defense Systems literature, 1985.
5   Ibid., 14.
6   See *Forbes,* September 26, 1983, 68.
7   Cubic Corporation, Prospectus, 1985.
8   Ibid., 19.
9   *Value Line* Investment Survey, February 8, 1985, 1051.
10 Cubic Prospectus, 10.
11 Ibid., 14.
12 Ibid., 21.
13 Cubic Annual Report, 6.
14 Ibid., 7.
15 Ibid., 8.
16 Cubic Prospectus, 22.
17 Ibid., 24.
18 Ibid., 25.
19 Cubic Annual Report, 4.

EXHIBIT 1
Financial Highlights (in thousands, except per share data)

	1984	1983
Sales	$275,097	$273,244
Net Income		
(after provision of $1.5 million for a disputed contract in 1984)	$ 14.018	$ 17.341
Earnings per Share	$ 1.77	$ 2.19
Backlog	$213,000	$200,000
Average Number of Shares Outstanding	7,926	7,926
New Order Bookings	$302,000	$284,000

EXHIBIT 2
Business Segment Financial Data

Business segment financial data for the three years in the period ended September 30, 1984, is presented below. Certain prior year amounts have been reclassified to conform to current year classifications:

	1984	1983	1982
		(in millions)	
Revenue:			
Electronic defense systems	**$126.0**	$122.2	$116.8
Electronic elevator operations	**86.7**	91.1	108.0
Industrial operations	**62.9**	60.1	69.3
	275.6	273.4	294.1
General corporate revenue	**4.8**	3.0	2.0
CONSOLIDATED TOTALS	**$280.4**	$276.4	$296.1
Operating profit:			
Electronic defense systems	**$ 18.2**	$ 23.0	$ 17.2
Electronic elevator operations	**5.9**	6.1	9.5
Industrial operations	**5.9**	8.6	9.7
	30.0	37.7	36.4
General corporate expense	**(1.0)**	(4.0)	(2.5)
Interest expense	**(2.9)**	(2.7)	(2.5)
CONSOLIDATED TOTALS	**$ 26.1**	$ 31.0	$31.4
Identifiable assets:			
Electronic defense systems	**$ 76.0**	$ 64.5	$ 70.4
Electronic elevator operations	**27.1**	29.0	30.4
Industrial operations	**40.2**	35.1	31.0
	143.3	128.6	131.8
Corporate	**56.5**	48.4	24.0
CONSOLIDATED TOTALS	**$199.8**	$177.0	$155.8
Depreciation and amortization:			
Electronic defense systems	**$ 2.5**	$ 2.5	$ 1.8
Electronic elevator operations	**1.2**	1.1	1.0
Industrial operations	**1.9**	2.0	1.9
	5.6	5.6	4.7
Corporate	**.6**	.3	.2
CONSOLIDATED TOTALS	**$ 6.2**	$ 5.9	$ 4.9
Gross capital expenditures:			
Electronic defense systems	**$ 1.8**	$ 4.6	$ 5.4
Electronic elevator operations	**1.5**	.9	1.4
Industrial operations	**4.4**	2.3	2.3
	7.7	7.8	9.1
Corporate	**1.7**	.1	1.0
CONSOLIDATED TOTALS	**$ 9.4**	$ 7.9	$ 10.1

Intersegment sales of $2,388,000, $3,714,000 and $3,391,000 in 1984, 1983 and 1982, respectively, have been netted above and are recorded at approximate cost. Sales of $115,241,000, $116,548,000 and $104,101,000 in 1984, 1983 and 1982, respectively, were made to United States Government agencies, primarily from the electronic defense systems segment. No other single customer accounts for 10 percent or more of the Corporation's revenue. Domestic revenue includes $30,330,000, $23,519,000 and $44,422,000 in 1984, 1983 and 1982, respectively, for export. The Corporation's foreign revenue comprises less than 10 percent of consolidated revenue.

EXHIBIT 3

Company	Company Sales	Market Share
Westinghouse Electric	$10,264,500,000	29.4%
E-Systems	819,353,000	2.4
Sanders Associates	746,100,000	2.1
Loral	478,300,000	1.4
Cubic	275,097,000	0.8
Watkins-Johnson	210,510,000	0.6

(1984 Defense Electronics Sales: Approximately $34.9 billion)

EXHIBIT 4
Statement of Consolidated Financial Position

	September 30, **1984**	1983
	(in thousands)	
ASSETS		
Current Assets		
Cash and short-term investments	**$ 36,285**	$ 26,391
Marketable securities—Note B	**3,188**	4,177
Accounts receivable:		
Trade and other receivables	**14,724**	11,932
Long-term contracts—Note C	**64,380**	65,170
	79,104	77,102
Less allowance for doubtful accounts	**698**	1,399
	78,406	75,703
Inventories and costs relating to long-term contracts in process—Note D	**18,657**	17,237
Refundable income taxes	**6,402**	
Prepaid expenses and other current assets—Note I	**11,188**	6,381
TOTAL CURRENT ASSETS	**154,126**	129,889
Property, Plant and Equipment		
Land and land improvements	**6,178**	6,104
Buildings and improvements	**14,617**	13,717
Machinery and other equipment	**41,560**	35,166
Leasehold improvements	**2,076**	1,916
Construction-in-progress	**135**	69
Allowance for depreciation and amortization	**(29,935)**	(24,937)
	34,631	32,035
Other Assets		
Marketable securities—Note B	**548**	12,059
Other assets	**10,465**	3,064
	11,013	15,123
	$199,770	$177,047

EXHIBIT 4 (Continued)

	September 30, 1984	1983
	(in thousands)	

LIABILITIES AND SHAREHOLDERS' EQUITY

Current Liabilities

Trade accounts payable	$ 14,152	$ 12,259
Customer advances and other current liabilities—Note F	16,084	9,396
Salaries and wages, and amounts withheld from employees' compensation	7,599	7,227
Income taxes payable		2,198
Deferred income taxes—Note I	18,643	16,056
Current portion of long-term debt	3,212	2,509
TOTAL CURRENT LIABILITIES	59,690	49,645

Long-Term Debt, less current portion—Note E 27,432 25,452

Other Liabilities

Deferred income taxes—Note I	9,270	9,833
Deferred compensation	1,648	1,256
	10,918	11,089

Shareholders' Equity—Note G

Common Stock, no par value:
Authorized 20,000,000 shares

Issued and outstanding—7,925,614 shares	234	234
Additional paid-in capital	12,123	12,123
Retained earnings—Notes B and E	89,373	78,504
	101,730	90,861

Leases—Note H

	$199,770	$177,047

See notes to consolidated financial statements

EXHIBIT 5

Statement of Consolidated Income

Year Ended September 30,	**1984**	1983	1982
	(in thousands, except per share data)		
Revenue:			
Net sales	**$275,097**	$273,244	$293,610
Interest and dividends	**4,966**	2,963	2,106
Other income	**291**	229	422
	280,354	276,436	296,138
Cost and expenses:			
Cost of sales	**201,424**	194,825	218,544
Selling, administrative and general expenses	**45,727**	41,510	41,048
Research and development	**4,066**	3,742	2,532
Interest	**2,988**	2,841	2,612
Write-down of noncurrent marketable securities—Note B		2,489	
	254,205	245,407	264,736
INCOME BEFORE INCOME TAXES	**26,149**	31,029	31,402
Income taxes—Note I	**12,131**	13,688	15,180
NET INCOME	**$ 14,018**	$ 17,341	$ 16,222
Earnings per share	**$ 1.77**	$ 2.19	$ 2.05
Average number of shares outstanding	**7,926**	7,926	7,926

See notes to consolidated financial statements

	Common Stock		Additional Paid-in Capital	Retained Earnings
	Shares	Amount		
	(in thousands)			
Balance at October 1, 1981	7,928	$234	$12,157	$49,819
Cash dividends paid ($.33 per share)				(2,615)
Net unrealized gain on marketable securities				90
Fractional shares purchased in connection with stock split	(2)		(34)	
Net income for the year				16,222
Balance at September 30, 1982	7,926	234	12,123	63,516
Cash dividends paid ($.36 per share)				(2,853)
Recognition of previously unrealized loss on marketable securities				500
Net income for the year				17,341
Balance at September 30, 1983	7,926	234	12,123	78,504
Cash dividends paid ($.39 per share)				(3,091)
Net unrealized loss on marketable securities—Note B				(58)
Net income for the year				14,018
BALANCE AT SEPTEMBER 30, 1984	**7,926**	**$234**	**$12,123**	**$89,373**

See notes to consolidated financial statements

EXHIBIT 6
Statement of Consolidated Funds Flow

	Year Ended September 30, 1984	1983	1982
		(in thousands)	
Provided from (used for) operations:			
Net income	**$14,018**	$17,341	$16,222
Items not requiring outlay of funds:			
Depreciation and amortization	**6,244**	5,856	4,885
Deferred income taxes	**2,484**	1,865	1,632
Deferred compensation	**392**	323	449
Write-down of noncurrent marketable securities—Note B		2,489	
	23,138	27,874	23,188
Working capital changes:			
Accounts receivable	**(2,703)**	3,587	(18,338)
Inventories	**(1,420)**	3,293	2,285
Prepaid expenses	**(3,810)**	(5,414)	(408)
Accounts payable	**1,893**	(6,589)	2,806
Customer advances and other current liabilities	**6,688**	2,452	4,183
Salaries and wages	**372**	(1,404)	2,215
Income taxes payable or refundable	**(5,139)**	(352)	(4,179)
	(4,119)	(4,427)	(11,436)
Capital expenditures, net of disposals	**(8,693)**	(7,709)	(9,851)
Sale of (investment in) noncurrent marketable securities—Note B	**11,453**	(13,500)	
Other	**(526)**	(57)	(672)
Net provided from operations	**21,253**	2,181	1,229
Provided from (used for) nonoperating items:			
Benefits from (investments in) tax leases—Note I	**(2,491)**	20,066	(9,565)
Investment in direct financing and leveraged leases—Note I	**(9,449)**		
Long-term borrowings—net of repayments	**2,683**	(186)	517
Dividends paid	**(3,091)**	(2,853)	(2,615)
Net provided from (used for) nonoperating items	**(12,348)**	17,027	(11,663)
Net funds (cash, short-term investments and current marketable securities) generated (expended) during the year	**8,905**	19,208	(10,434)
Funds at the beginning of the year	**30,568**	11,360	21,794
Funds at the end of the year	**$39,473**	$30,568	$11,360

See notes to consolidated financial statements

CASE 15
E&J Gallo Winery

Patricia J. Hall
Boise State University

The average American drinks 37 gallons of soft drinks a year, 24 gallons of beer, but only 2 gallons of wine. Even so, wine marketers are excited about the prospects for the 1980s. The decades since 1960 have seen significant changes in the American wine market, changes that experts believe place the American wine industry in an enviable growth position. Total U.S. wine consumption in 1990 is expected to be at least one billion gallons, double that of 1981.

The E&J Gallo Winery of Modesto, California has been the leading marketer of wines in the United States since the mid-1960s. The "E" and "J," of course, stand for Ernest and Julio, the two brothers who started the winery in 1933 and have ruled it, some would say with an iron hand, ever since. Gallo's market share in 1981 was a commanding 26 percent, while its closest competitor, United Vintners (UV), was able to get only a 10 percent share.[1] The wine industry has, in the words of industry analyst Marvin Shanken, become a "form of warfare," as old and new entrants battle for position and market share.[2] Gallo's greatest challenge comes from Wine Spectrum, Coca-Cola's entry in the wine business. It was the advertising campaign for Spectrum's new wine label, "Taylor California Cellars," that changed the nature of competition in the industry from "clubby" to a form of "capitalist hardball."[3] In 1983, Seagram, owner of Paul Masson winery, purchased Wine Spectrum from Coca-Cola, thus increasing its market share to 11 percent.

THE WINE INDUSTRY

Wines are now available to suit every occasion, taste, and budget. For impressing that special someone, the purchaser might choose an award-winning "Private Reserve Cabernet Sauvignon" from Beringer, a premium California winery. A six-pack of Taylor "California Cellars" rosé could be just the thing to pack along with a picnic lunch. The dieter might well substitute a glass of light chablis for his customary martini before dinner. For the working couple, a bottle of Gallo "Hearty Burgundy" might add a festive touch to a hurry-up dinner of steak and salad.

The current cascade of new products, new brands, and new packages was not the first source of confusion to the actual or potential wine purchaser. "All wine

Richard Faw of Stein Distributing, Boise, Idaho; Brooks Tish of the Wine Merchantile Company, Boise, Idaho; and John Movius, editor of *Wine Scene,* provided valuable assistance to the writer.

marketers agreed . . . that wine had to be demystified if it were to succeed in the popular market."[4] For example, almost everyone is familiar with the term *vintage year,* but which years are vintage years, and for which wines? There is a saying that for California wines, "every year is a vintage year;" for the purist that is not so, but for most people it is true enough to act as a guide to buying wine.

There is also the matter of which foods go with which wines. Some wine experts are willing to say that this is a matter of individual preference, but the experts have written several volumes explaining which foods go best with which wines and why, and the public is at least vaguely aware of this. The average consumer may also have overhead a friend or two talk about "balance" or "micro-climate" or "color" and concluded that there is simply too much to know about wine and too many ways to make a mistake.

Although Wine Spectrum's market research has shown that only 4 percent of the population accounts for 53 percent of the total U.S. wine consumption, evidence shows that the consumer base is beginning to "thaw."[5] It is a truism in the industry that consumer taste moves from sweet to dry, and one of the factors that has helped to change the American wine market in the last two decades was the introduction of new types of sweet, light wines.

During the late 1960s came the apple wines from Gallo. These wines joined Gallo's family of "special natural" or fruit-flavored wines that already included "Ripple" and "Thunderbird." Other vintners soon came out with their own versions such as "Annie Greensprings" from UV. The special naturals were a big success on college campuses. In the 1970s, came the Italian imports, sweet, slightly fizzy wines especially blended to be "chillable." These wines such as "Riunite" and "Cella" found favor among many who were not wine drinkers. Imported wines of all types now account for about 26 percent of U.S. wine consumption. The special naturals were a fad, but the Italian imports appear to have staying power.[6]

The House of Banfi, the U.S. importer of the "Riunite" brand of lambrusco wine, is planning on keeping those of its customers who are interested in trying a more traditional dry table wine. It will soon be introducing a line of red, white, and rosé wines not made from lambrusco-type grapes. American wine marketers do not expect to make any inroads into markets now held by importers of Italian lambrusco-type wines, but the success of these wines has encouraged Wine Spectrum to bring out a line of "Lake Country Soft" wines that have many of the same characteristics.

Special natural wines peaked at shipments of 58 million gallons in 1972 (17 percent of total wine market), held steady until 1975, and then began a decline which has since become precipitous. *Impact Review* for 1979 noted that "the one true disaster area in the wine business today continues to be special natural wine."[7] Although this is good news in many ways because it means that many consumers have switched to table wines, it is bad news in that the special naturals served a definite purpose in the wine market, that of introducing young people to wine. In a country like the United States where wine is not an ordinary accompaniment to meals, some sort of easy introduction to drinking wine is necessary.

It is possible that light wines may take over the function of special naturals, but these wines are simply lower in alcoholic content than ordinary table wines and are not sweet. Light wines were first introduced by Franzia in 1979, and have not done very well in the market possibly because ". . . of the extremely light taste—some would call it watery—that is characteristic of most."[8] Paul Masson and Taylor California Cellars have light wines on the market, but Gallo has not yet made up its mind about whether or not to market light wines.[9]

The real growth market since 1970 has been in table wines, both domestic and imported. Table wines finally reached 50 percent of total U.S. wine consumption in 1970; from 1970 to 1980, the table wine market grew at a compound annual rate of 10.4 percent, and *Impact* expects this market to sustain an annual growth rate of 11 percent between 1980 and 1990.[10] Table wines accounted for 75 percent of the national wine market in 1980, and that percentage is expected to increase. The market for dessert wines—high alcohol sweet wines such as port and sherry—is expected to decline at about 5 percent a year between 1980 and 1990. Sales of vermouth are expected to remain level, and special naturals may decline at a 6 percent annual rate. Champagne and sparkling wines are expected to be the only types of wine other than table wine to show a positive rate of growth over the 1980 to 1990 time period.[11]

Table wines are classified as either red, white, or rosé. The reds are the most complex wines and therefore the most interesting. The table wine boom in the United States has been largely fueled by the increases in the sales of white wine during the late 1970s. Americans like cold drinks, and white wine is usually served chilled; it is becoming increasingly popular as a cocktail beverage. In 1975, red wines accounted for 44 percent of the table wine market, whites for 32 percent, and rosés for 24 percent. White wines grew at an average annual rate of 24 percent from 1975 to 1980, and by 1980, they accounted for 54 percent of the table wine market.[12]

Domestic table wines are available in two basic types: generic (or proprietary) and varietal. Generic and proprietary wines may be blends of any type of grapes that the vintner wishes to use. Generic wines are named for the various famous wine-growing regions of Europe such as Burgundy and Chablis. Proprietary names are names made up by the winery such as Gallo's "Paisano" wine. Varietals are generally (but not always) better wines than the generics. California varietal wines must contain at least 51 percent of the grape variety named on the label, and if the wine has any pretensions, it usually contains at least 70 percent of the named grape because at least that much is needed for the purchaser to be able to taste the grape variety. By 1983, all varietals will have to contain at least 85 percent of the named grape variety by law.

California varietal names include whites such as Sauvignon Blanc and Riesling and reds such as Pinot Noir and Zinfandel. There is general agreement that the best California red wine is made from the Cabernet Sauvignon, and the best California white wine comes from the Chardonnay grape. The varietal wines are expected to be the real growth area for table wines in the 1980s as consumers move up the spectrum of wines. Varietal wines carry a higher price tag than most generics, and with the introduction of a $6 Cabernet Sauvignon from Gallo, these prices could go even higher. The so-called premium wineries such as Paul Masson and Taylor

California Cellars (TCC) cannot afford to offer lower prices on their top of the line varietals than Gallo. On the other hand, given the price-value relationship for which Gallo is noted, those wineries now pricing their varieties significantly above those from Gallo may be forced to reduce prices somewhat.

Fortunately for the large wineries, a preference for varietals does not mean that the consumer has stopped drinking the generics and proprietaries. Although consumers seldom go back to drinking special naturals after they have "graduated" to traditional table wines, this does not hold true for the step between generics and varietals. Those whose tastes have broadened to include varietals, however, are going to insist on high quality in their *vin ordinaire*. In the United States, they can be reasonably sure of getting it, and most writers do not hesitate to give much of the credit for this to the winery of Ernest and Julio Gallo.

A more expensive wine is a better wine—maybe. In the sometimes confusing world of wine, consumers often take price as a guide to quality. Wine marketers have not agreed on common terminology with regard to the prices of wines and the way in which brands fit into categories, and this makes it impossible to interpret most of the available data on purchases of wine by price category. Most wine from the larger wineries is sold in 1.5-liter or 3-liter jugs. Gallo "virtually owns the low-priced area with its Carlo Rossi jug wines . . ."[13] The trade generally considers "Carlo Rossi" to be in competition with "Colony" wines from UV and most of the "Franzia" wines from the Wine Group. In the majority of its markets, Gallo wines are priced above "Colony," but below the other premium producers such as Paul Masson and Almaden.

STRUCTURE AND COMPETITION

A patchwork quilt of state liquor laws governs the sale of wine. Wine can be purchased along with the week's groceries in twenty states. In some states, wine can be sold only in state-owned liquor stores; in others wine can be purchased in the supermarket if the wine department has a special entrance; in still other states only liquor stores can sell wine. In 1980, supermarkets accounted for 30 percent of all wine sales.[14] There is a real effort being made to change state laws to permit the sale of wine in supermarkets, particularly in some of the more highly populated northeastern states like New York, but this push is being led by distributors on a state-by-state basis, rather than by wine marketers at either the state or national level.[15] Because 60 percent to 70 percent of all wine purchases are made on impulse, a uniform law permitting the sale of wine in supermarkets in all states could cause wine sales to expand even more rapidly than already predicted.

The distributor plays a major role in the success of any winery. In larger cities, each major winery has its own distributor, but in smaller markets a distributor must often handle two or more of the major wineries. Good distributors can help the winery get space on retailer's shelves and in the store's "cold box" (refrigerator); they can also influence the "adjacencies" or the wines next to which the wines from their wineries are placed. Gallo, for example, would prefer to have its wine bearing the Gallo label in the same section as Paul Masson and Almaden rather than together with Colony or Franzia. Distributors also set the price of the wine in their markets. At least before the entry of Coca-Cola into the wine business, most of the competition in the wine industry was carried on at the distributor level rather than at the winery level. This, no doubt, was a major reason for the rather gentlemanly competition that characterized the industry before 1977.

The label on a bottle of wine may tell the consumer absolutely nothing about what kinds of grapes are in the wine, where they were grown, who made the wine, and who bottled it. Yet every bottle of wine must have the name of the business responsible for the wine printed on the label along with a business location. What that means is that the winery listed on the label is responsible for the taste of the wine and sometimes for very little else. This is the case, for example, with Taylor California Cellars, although it will soon have its own bottling and blending facility in Gonzales, California. Although there are supposed to be guidelines to let the purchaser know how much the winery named on the bottle had to do with making the wine that went into the bottle, these guidelines differ among wine writers; however, if the label says that the wine was "vinted, cellared, and bottled by," then the winery on the label did everything from crushing the grapes to putting the wine into the bottle.

None of the large wineries are publicly held, although Canandaigua, one of the smaller wineries, is traded in the over-the-counter market. The competitive structure of the wine market is undergoing significant change with some formerly strong companies (*e.g.*, United Vintners) slipping and others such as Wine Spectrum and Paul Masson gaining ground. Because "there is really no limit to be set on the possible future extent of wine sales expansion in the United States . . ." it is little wonder that many companies see it as a good industry to get into.[16]

The entry of Coca-Cola into the wine industry would have been enough to give other vintners pause even if Coke had not started out by directly challenging premium vintners such as Inglenook and Almaden. Coke is a superb mass marketer with experience in the beverage industry and annual profits of around $400 million a year. They have "deep pockets," and it has become clear that Wine Spectrum can tap these pockets to the extent necessary. In 1977, Coke purchased the Taylor Wine Company of New York and two highly regarded small California wineries, Sterling Vineyards and Monterey Vineyards. Because California supplies about 70 percent of all domestic wines, Coke believed that it needed a California wine in the same category as Paul Masson and Almaden, so it created the "Taylor California Cellars" label and did comparative tasting ads that got it into trouble with the Bureau of Alcohol, Tobacco, and Firearms and with other members of the wine industry.

The comparative ad campaign—or something—worked because TCC was the largest successful new brand in wine marketing history. The wine could not have succeeded unless it was good, and part of the reason it was good may have been Richard Peterson, the winemaster at Monterey Vineyards when Coke acquired it. Peterson had spent ten years at Gallo before leaving because he was unhappy with Ernest Gallo's management style.[17] Spectrum has also drawn heavily on Gallo's sales talent.[18] There is no doubt at all that Gallo and Wine Spectrum have their eyes firmly fixed on each other. Spectrum wants to become the number one U.S. vintner, and Gallo is determined to maintain its position. Most observers expect Gallo to remain number one in part at least because "the company's sole mission continues to be making and selling wine."[19]

The second largest winery, United Vintners, has seen its position erode almost steadily since it lost first place to Gallo during the mid-1960s. The decline started before the purchase of United Vintners (UV) by Heublein in 1969. The purchase was challenged by the Federal Trade Commission and was not settled until 1980 when Heublein was allowed to keep UV. Heublein decided against investing much in a subsidiary that it might not be able to keep, but it claims to be planning a comeback.[20] It recently introduced the "Colony" line, which competes on a price basis with Gallo in some markets; it still markets some types of wine under the "Italian Swiss Colony" label. "Inglenook," its premium brand, comes from the Inglenook winery, which has a long and honorable history. UV lost ground again in 1981, and nobody has suggested that it is even in the running in the battle between Gallo and Wine Spectrum.

The two U.S. vintners expected to compete for third place in the new lineup are Almaden, which is owned by National Distillers, and Paul Masson, which is owned by Seagram, the large Canadian distilling company. Almaden is currently the third largest vintner, and Paul Masson is number six. In 1981, Almaden experienced the first sales decline in its history. Paul Masson's sales were up slightly.[21] Wine shipments in 1980 outpaced liquor shipments for the first time, partly as a result of the recent popularity of white wine as a cocktail. Because of this, wine may look even more interesting to Seagram and National Distillers than it has in the past.

Dart and Kraft has recently announced that it intends to enter the wine industry in 1982. According to *Advertising Age*, Kraft executive personnel are not entirely happy with this decision, and it is the Kraft sales force that will have the job of selling the new wine.[22] Paul Solomon, formerly of Gallo, will head the marketing effort for the new wine.

In addition to the major vintners, there are several smaller California wineries with excellent reputations who distribute their wines on a national basis. Charles Krug, Robert Mondavi, Beringer, and Sebastiani are among the more important members of this group. Although *Impact* expects non-California vintners to remain unimportant in the U.S. market, vintners in the Pacific northwest are excited about the prospects for a major wine area in the states of Oregon, Washington, and Idaho.[23] They expect to be able to produce not only good wines, but great wines.

THE WINERY OF ERNEST AND JULIO GALLO

In 1970, William Massee wrote, "When the nation wants well-made wines of fine quality, and is willing to pay for them, Gallo will make them."[24] The time Massee wrote of has come, earlier perhaps than anyone expected, and Gallo is now producing fine wines. Its only real problem seems to be getting the public to accept the idea that the makers of "Pagan Pink Ripple" can also produce a fine quality Cabernet Sauvignon.

The founding of the E&J Gallo Winery in Modesto in 1933 was "it could be argued . . . the most decisive single event in the post-Prohibition history of California wine. . . ."[25] Julio made the wine, Ernest sold it; so it was then, and so it is now. Julio's early efforts were sold to distributors for bottling, the beginning of a strong distribution effort that continues to this day. The profits in the first full year of operation were $34,000, which was not a bad return on an initial investment of $5,900. The profits were reinvested in the business.[26]

Those figures are the earliest reliable financial data on the company. Sales for 1981 were estimated to be between $500 million and $1 billion, but the *Wine Investor* estimate of $750 million looks as good as any.[27] In the early 1970s, pretax profit margins were estimated at 8.5 percent.[28]

The Gallos did not put their name on a bottle of wine until 1940, but they were still dissatisfied with the quality. Their efforts to produce a quality wine have led them to innovate in production techniques and to be among the first to make use of the innovations of others, notably the world-famous group of research scientists at the University of California at Davis. "The Gallos claimed that screw caps protected their wines better; that corks don't breathe as is generally believed, but only leak."[29] In 1961, *Time* said, "His [Ernest's] stainless steel vats and presses are by far the most technologically advanced in the world ('You won't find a stick of wood in our winery.'). . . ."[30] The Gallos even developed a type of glass that they believe better protects the wine, and they make their own glass bottles right at the winery. They also own one of the largest trucking firms in the state of California, partly in order to haul sand to the bottle-making facility.

This innovativeness has worked against Gallo in some quarters because many wine buffs believe that one should not meddle with an art as old as human history, but art as well as science is still involved in making the wine at Gallo. The brothers taste every master blend, and none is released until it is considered acceptable by both.[31] The wineries (there are four) now have computerized blending, but they also have facilities for inserting corks into bottles, and beneath the main buildings at Modesto are caves containing hundreds of 4,000-gallon barrels of Yugoslav oak.

The main Gallo winery at Modesto is not the largest of the Gallo wineries. The world's largest winery is the 100 million-gallon Gallo winery at Livingston, California. There are two smaller wineries at Healdsburg and Fresno. Gallo has about 10,000 acres of its own grapes and has fifteen-year contracts with growers who own 100,000 acres.

Ernest and Julio together make all major decisions concerning the winery.[32] There are Gallo sons and sons-in-law in top management, but the Gallos also have some extremely capable managers who know about wine and wine marketing and are not relatives. Among the Gallo relatives is a sales executive named Charles Rossi, the Italian version of whose name is on jugs of wine throughout the country. Julio is considered to be the more amiable and open of the brothers, but it is difficult to find evidence of anyone who has spoken to him. Ernest, on the other hand, is the stuff of which management legends are made.

John Movius, internationally known authority on food and wine, spent a day with Ernest in 1969. He says that Ernest is willing to "seek out the facts" and "hear all the sides of the argument" before reaching a decision.[33] Ernest inspires fierce loyalty, but seems to generate other kinds of feelings among some who are now ex-employees.[34] The list of Gallo alumni now holding high positions elsewhere is long and getting longer.[35] Ernest is conceded to be a marketing genius. Although in his late seventies, he has if anything increased his ability to market the products Julio produces.

Marketing at Gallo is also a blend of art and science. Until the 1960s, Ernest visited every market nearly every year, sometimes calling on fifty stores in a day. He still visits stores whenever possible.[36] On the other hand, Gallo makes maximal use of all the science that the field of marketing has been able to come up with. During the late 1950s, Ernest simply went to some of the major consumer products companies (such as Procter & Gamble) and hired himself a marketing department, but the guts of the company's marketing efforts are its large sales force and its network of distributors.[37] Although *Wine Investor* was referring to distributors when it said "much of the credit for the current success must go to the guys in the trenches-—the offensive line, if you will, out there every day romancing retailers, checking the facings, and doing all the other stuff that so many wineries neglect (or can't afford)," they could equally well have been describing the activities of Gallo's own sales force.[38]

Gallo has been a national advertiser for decades. "Ripple—the wine with that ring-a-ding flavor . . . oh-oh, that ring-a-dinging taste" is an example of an ad campaign from the early 1960s. It is a long way from "ring-a-ding flavor" to the studied tastefulness of the 1980 campaign "the wine remembers" or the current romantic emotional "share the joy of Gallo wine." Gallo spends about $25 million a year on advertising; about 80 percent goes to television advertising and most is spent on wines bearing the Gallo label.[39]

STRATEGIES FOR THE 1990s

As late as 1960, Gallo was known mainly for its dessert wines, which found most of its market among the skid-row set. By 1980, everything had changed, including the market. In 1960, 53 percent of the wine sold in the United States was dessert wine; now 75 percent is table wine. The typical wine purchaser today is a woman between 30 and 39 with a family income of $25,000 or more, living in the west. She probably also has had at least some college and lives in or near a large city. Wine Spectrum research has shown that the average college-educated person, twenty-five years of age or older, with an income of $20,000 drinks an average of 220 glasses of wine a year.[40] Ten states, led by California and New York, account for 65 percent of all wine consumption.

"The elevation of taste and quality has been quietly but steadfastly led by E&J Gallo. . . ."[41] In 1961, Ernest apparently believed that the way to introduce the novice to wine drinking was through dessert wines.[42] There is no evidence that this progression ever took place in any great numbers, but the basic idea (sweet to dry) was sound, the product just wasn't right. With the introduction of the first special natural wine, "Thunderbird," in 1957, Gallo had found the secret. It was another ten years before the strategy really took off with the introduction of "Boone's Farm" apple wines.

Even before "Boone's Farm" came on the market, Gallo was already at work on the next phase of its strategy.[43] In 1965, it broke with industry precedent and gave growers fifteen-year contracts. Growers were told to plant large quantities of varietal grapes and given financial assistance if it was needed. In 1964, Gallo had released "Hearty Burgundy," which has won praise from some wine writers. "Hearty Burgundy" is made from 100 percent varietal grapes, as are the Gallo generics. In 1974, Gallo released a line of varietals, mainly whites, such as Chenin Blanc and Riesling. Gallo began for the first time to enter competitive tastings, and their line of cork-tipped varietals began to win prizes.[44]

The wines sold well, but Gallo was not satisfied. The Chardonnay and Cabernet that were to top the line were never released. In 1979, Gallo released a new line of varietals together with a new rosé. The varietal names were the same, but the wines were different and better. The oak-aged Chardonnay and Cabernet were due to be released in 1980. The Chardonnay from the 1977 grape crop did not satisfy Ernest and Julio, and the wine was dumped into the Chablis Blanc.[45] The Chardonnay was released in 1981 and the Cabernet in the early fall of 1982.

According to *Wine Investor,* these two wines finally broke the barrier to the acceptance of Gallo by wine snobs, but *Business Week* seems somewhat doubtful that Gallo will be able to successfully upgrade its image. They said that wine writers are often "embarrassed" to talk about Gallo.[46] Movius said that this is because many wine writers feared objections from their readers. Yet even before the release of the top of the line varietals, comments such as the following could easily be found:

> The brothers Ernest and Julio Gallo command American market, command respect of the industry, and, increasingly, command interest of critics.
>> Bob Thompson, *The Pocket Encyclopedia of California Wines* (1980), 52.
>> Preliminary blind tastings by your editor tend to support the conclusion that the new (1979) Gallo line of white varietals is the finest varietal line coming out of the great central valley of California with the exception of Papagni.
>> John Movius, "The Wine Scene," March–April, 1980, 52.
>> If Ernest and Julio say the wine's okay, the wine's okay. Gallo is to *ordinaire* what Rothchild is to Lafite. In each case there has been enormous investment in love and pride and treasure in building that name. . . .
>> Forrest Wallace and Gilbert Cross, *The Game of Wine* (1976), 148.

Movius rather subtly pointed to one of the reasons that Gallo is sometimes given short shrift by wine writers, "it has tended in the past to ignore the wine buff and the wine press. It has no tasting room, and Ernest and Julio have granted no press interviews for decades."[47] The Gallos' passion for secrecy extends to not even having their name on their headquarters in Modesto. Ernest did speak with a writer from the *New York Times* in 1974 and apparently with Leon Adams in the early 1970s, but his reputation for silence comes with good reason.[48] Although the Gallos' secrecy with regard to financial details is understandable, their unwelcoming attitude toward visitors and their inattention to the wine press are not characteristic of the California wine industry. Adams said that Ernest plans to build a wine tasting room and a wine museum in Modesto "someday."[49]

Gallo has had little success in the important restaurant market. Although only 11 percent of all wine is consumed in restaurants, the market is important because it gives consumers a chance to try new wines.[50] A survey by *Family Circle* showed that 59 percent of wine purchasers give as one of the reasons for selecting a particular brand "My own experience—had tried it in a restaurant or someone else's home."[51] Gallo has formed a special division to try to gain entrance into this market and has tried to put together a package deal with some of the smaller but highly regarded California "boutique" wineries.[52] *Wine Investor* believes that they may not need to do this once the Chardonnay and Cabernet have made their mark. There is also the possibility that wines may move into fast food restaurants. Customers of Skipper's Seafood 'n' Chowder House, a chain of fish and chips places in the west, can now have a glass of Paul Masson Chablis or rosé with their fish dinner.

Gallo first began producing champagne in 1968 and today has about 40 percent of the U.S. market for champagne and sparkling wines.[53] In 1982, its sales force was split into two divisions, one of which is now going to handle only champagne and sparkling and dessert wines. This may mean that new emphasis will be placed on these wine categories.

A line of imported wines may also be on the drawing boards. *Wine Investor* says Ernest and Julio have made a number of trips to Italy, and there is speculation that the purpose may have been to explore the possibility of producing Italian wines for sale in the United States.[54]

In 1983, the E&J Gallo Winery marked the fiftieth anniversary of its founding. In those fifty years, Gallo has managed to move America a few steps further along the road to a nation in which the "civilized custom" of drinking wine with meals has become a national habit.

Notes

1 *Impact,* March 15, 1982, 4.
2 *Newsweek,* September 1, 1980, 57.
3 *Newsweek,* September 1, 1980, 57.
4 C. Burck, "The Toyota of the Wine Trade," *Fortune,* November 30, 1981, 162.
5 *Business Week,* March 15, 1982, 109.

6   C. Burck, ''The Toyota of the Wine Trade,'' *Fortune,* November 30, 1981.

7   *Impact American Wine Market Review and Forecast,* 1979, 15.

8   C. Burck, ''The Toyota of the Wine Trade,'' *Fortune,* November 30, 1981, 162.

9   C. Burck. ''The Toyota of the Wine Trade,'' *Fortune,* November 30, 1981, 162.

10 *Impact American Wine Market Review and Forecast,* 1981, 52.

11 Ibid.

12 Ibid., 17.

13 *Business Week,* March 15, 1982, 108.

14 *Supermarket News,* November, 1981, 23.

15 *New York Times,* July 14, 1979, L25, L28.

16 *Wine Marketing Handbook,* 1980, 93.

17 *Business Week,* February 23, 1974, 67.

18 *Business Week,* March 15, 1982.

19 Ibid., 114.

20 Ibid., 118.

21 *Impact,* March 15, 1982, 1.

22 *Advertising Age,* November 11, 1981, 1.

23 *Impact American Wine Market Review and Forecast,* 1981, 53, 55.

24 W. Massee, *McCall's Guide to Wines of America* (New York: McCall Publishing Company, 1970), 131.

25 F. Wallace and G. Cross, *The Game of Wine* (New York: Harper & Row, 1976), 131.

26 *Business Week,* March 15, 1982.

27 *Wine Investor,* Feburary 1, 1982, 5.

28 *New York Times,* November 3, 1974, 5F.

29 L. Adams, *The Wines of America,* 2nd rev. ed. (New York: McGraw-Hill, 1978), 438.

30 *Time,* November 3, 1961, 52.

31 J. Movius, ''The Wine Scene,'' *Friends of Wine,* March–April, 1980, 51.

32 L. Adams, *The Wines of America,* 2nd rev. ed. (New York: McGraw-Hill, 1978), 439.

33 J. Movius, ''The Wine Scene,'' *Friends of Wine,* March–April, 1980, 50.

34 *Business Week,* February 23, 1974.

35 *Business Week,* March 15, 1982.

36 L. Adams, *The Wines of America,* 2nd rev. ed. (New York: McGraw-Hill, 1978), 439.

37 *Business Week,* February 23, 1974.

38 *Wine Investor,* February 1, 1982, 2.

39 *Impact American Wine Market Review and Forecast,* 1981, 42, 44.

40 Ibid., 49; *Marketing News,* November 11, 1980, 15.

41 *Time,* January 14, 1980, 66.

42 *Time,* November 3, 1961, 52–53.

43 The account of Gallo's strategy over the 1974–1980 period is taken from J. Movius, ''The Wine Scene,'' *Friends of Wine,* March–April, 1980, 50–52, unless otherwise indicated.

44 L. Adams, *The Wines of America,* 2nd rev. ed. (New York: McGraw-Hill, 1978), 439.

45 *Wine Investor,* February 2, 1982, 2.

46 *Wine Investor,* February 2, 1982, 2–5; *Business Week,* March 15, 1982.

47 J. Movius, ''The Wine Scene,'' *Friends of Wine,* March–April, 1980, 50.

48 L. Adams, *The Wines of America* (New York: Houghton Mifflin, 1973), 308–312.

49 L. Adams, *The Wines of America,* 2nd rev. ed. (New York: McGraw-Hill, 1978), 438.

50 *Impact American Wine Market Review and Forecast,* 1981, 48.

51 *Wine Marketing Handbook,* 1980, 91.

52 J. Movius, ''The Wine Scene,'' *Friends of Wine,* March–April, 1980, 51; *Wine Investor,* February 2, 1982, 4.

53 *Impact American Wine Market Review and Forecast,* 1981, 25.

54 *Wine Investor,* February 2, 1982, 4–5.

EXHIBIT 1

The Big Five: Top Wine Advertisers.* Total Advertising and Major Brand Changes for First Six Months of 1983 vs. 1982 (thousands of dollars)

Company**	1982	1983	Change Dollars	Change Percent
1. E. & J. Gallo	$11,888.0	$13,359.6	$ 1,471.6	12.4%
Carlo Rossi	334.4	1,215.8	881.4	263.6
Polo Brindisi	—	315.0	315.0	+
2. Jos. E. Seagram, USA	$ 9,649.3	$ 7,634.2	$−2,015.1	−20.9%
Paul Masson Light	3,453.2	1,126.3	−2,326.9	−67.4
Black Tower	1,684.9	1,153.9	−531.0	−31.5
3. Villa Banfi, USA	$ 5,787.6	$ 7,030.9	$ 1,243.3	21.5%
Riunite	5,058.4	7,030.9	1,972.5	39.0
Bell'Agio	729.2	—	−729.2	−100.0
4. Heublein (R. J. Reynolds)	$ 5,979.0	$ 6,316.3	$ 337.3	5.6%
Inglenook	2,772.9	3,147.8	374.9	13.5
Harveys Bristol Cream	1,108.9	1,368.9	260.0	23.5
Colony	1,241.8	720.0	−521.8	−42.0
5. National	$ 6,043.7	$ 3,317.3	$−2,726.4	−45.1%
Almaden	5,322.2	3,057.0	−2,265.2	−42.6
SELECTED OTHER				
Wine Spectrum	$ 8,810.7	$ 1,995.4	$−6,815.3	−77.4%
Taylor California Cellars	8,253.8	1,966.7	−6,287.1	−76.2
Taylor	551.7	24.3	−527.4	−95.6

*Includes LNA six media total (network radio, spot and network TV, magazines, outdoor and newspaper supplements), which does not contain data on spot radio or newspapers.

**Companies are ranked according to first six months 1983 advertising expenditures.

Sources: LNA and Impact Databank

EXHIBIT 2
U.S. Wineries Market Shares Are Changing

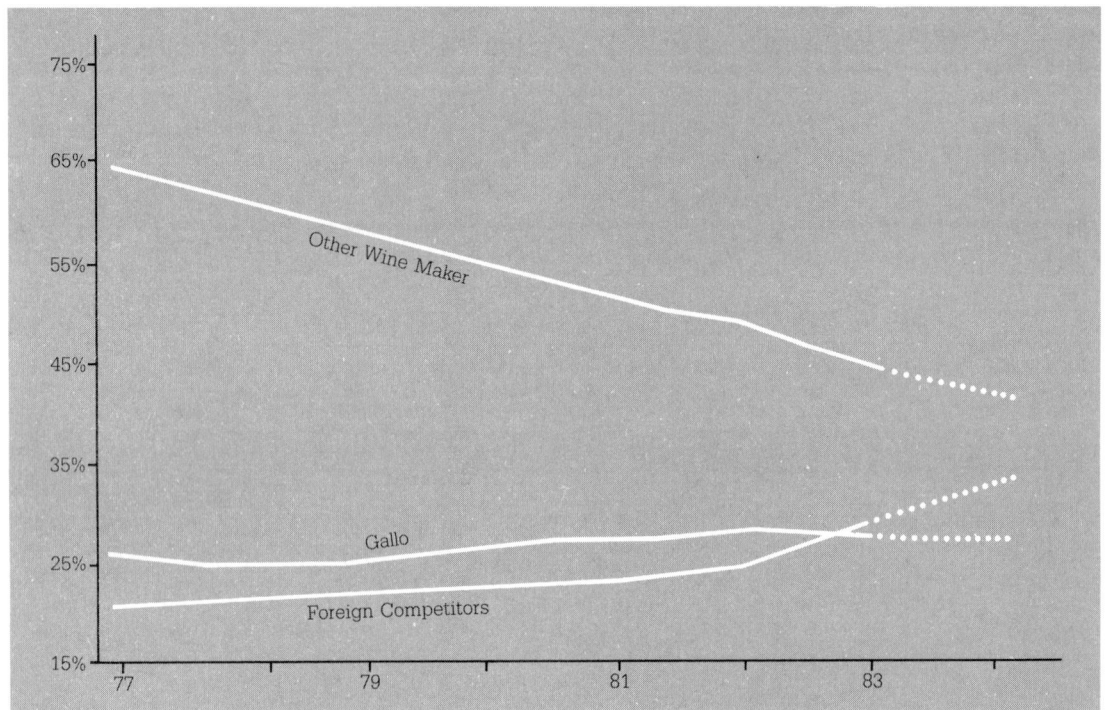

EXHIBIT 3
Ernest and Julio Gallo Winery Organization Chart

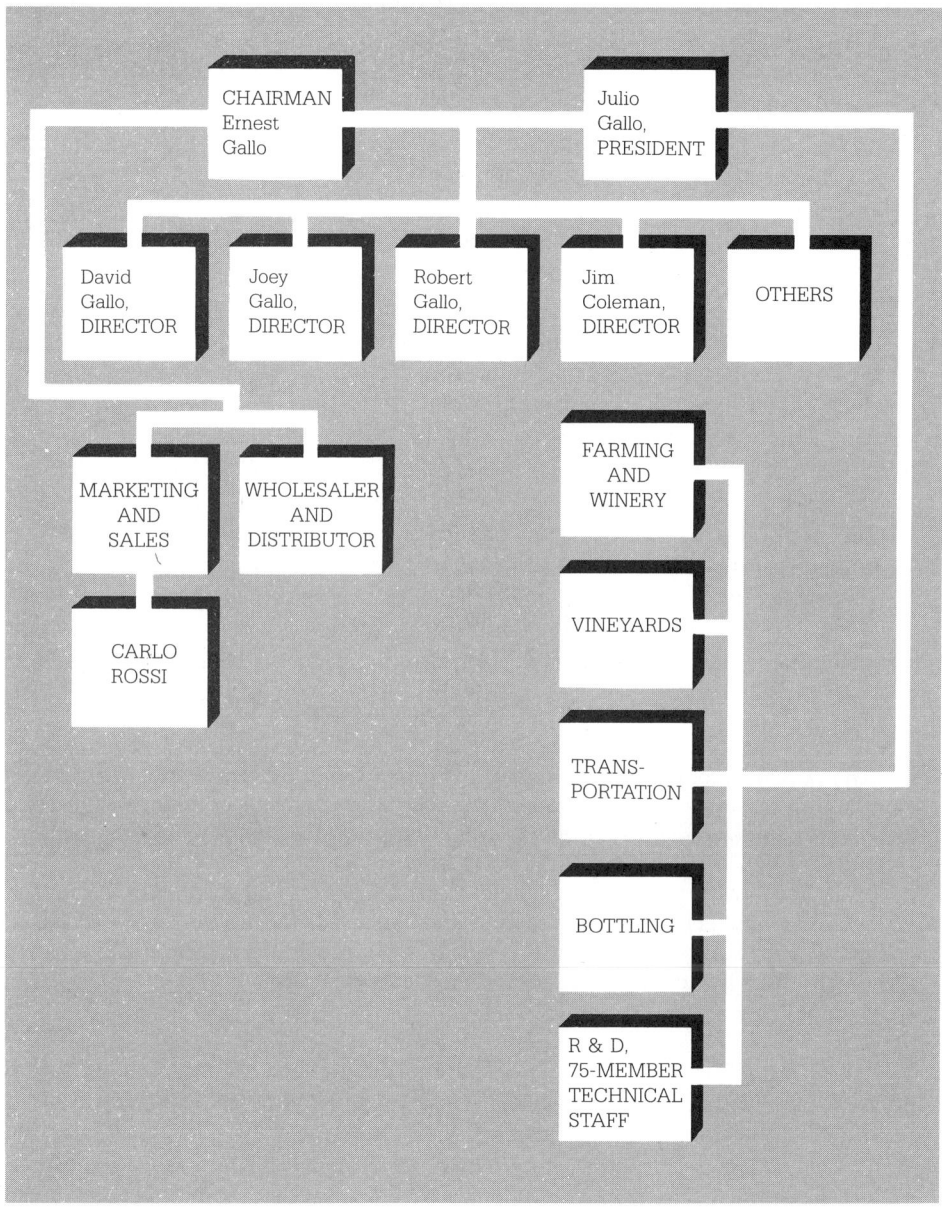

■ ■ ■ CASE 16
The Future Is Now: The Apple Computer Company, 1986

Donald F. Harvey
Patrick Clifford
Eastern Washington University

INTRODUCTION

In 1975, two young entrepreneurs, who would later found Apple Computer, designed and built the first personal computer—it spawned a new industry. Despite a legendary beginning, Apple Computer, Inc., has run into problems stemming from a breakneck growth rate and increasing competition from giant companies. After some problems with the introduction of its second major personal computer, the Apple III, President Mike Markkula and Vice-Chairman Steve Jobs were looking for ways to make a "quantum jump" in computer technology. A 1981 management shake-up, including the firing of forty employees, had brought out differing views on how to manage the explosive rate of growth.

Reflecting this increasingly competitive marketplace, Apple's top management, led by CEO John Sculley, began redirecting strategy toward steady, profitable growth. Managing rapid growth often places extreme stress on management systems, and Apple is working to deal with these forces. Apple's strategy is based on two basic elements:

> The personal computer is the heart of Apple. We do not view the world through the eyes of a mainframe. Since we don't have to protect other parts of our business, we do not have conflicting priorities that force product compromises.
>
> We have just one goal: to lead the industry in innovation. For those who use personal computers daily—and especially for the millions who have *never* used a personal computer—we want to provide the most flexible and technologically advanced computer solutions available.[1]

BACKGROUND

The personal computer is part of a continuum that illustrates the acceleration of technology in this century. A milestone year, 1986 marked the fortieth anniversary of the first electronic computer, the fifteenth anniversary of the integrated circuit, the fifteenth anniversary of the microprocessor, and the tenth anniversary of the personal computer.

This case was prepared using published accounts and public documents for the purpose of class discussion rather than to illustrate either effective or ineffective handling of an administrative situation.

There is probably no company more closely identified with the personal computer revolution than Apple Computer. Founded in 1977 by two college dropouts, Steven P. Jobs, then twenty-one, and Stephan G. Wozniak, twenty-six, their rags-to-riches success story has been well documented. They designed their first machine in Jobs's bedroom, built it in his parents' garage, and showed it to a local computer store owner, who promptly ordered twenty-five. Demand for the personal computer, mainly from hobbyists, soon outstripped the young men's ability to produce, so they began looking for help. They joined forces with A. C. Markkula, an experienced marketing manager, and the meteoric growth began.[2] In April 1977, when the two unveiled Apple II, the first fully programmable personal computer was priced from $1195 to $1395. Selling their entry level machine through computer stores, Jobs and Wozniak saw sales skyrocket from $773,977 in fiscal 1977 to $334.8 million in 1981 and to $1.9 billion in 1985.

The company currently designs, develops, produces, markets, and services microprocessor-based personal computer systems for individual use in solving computing programs commonly encountered in business, education, science, engineering, and the home. Products manufactured and distributed by Apple are sold in the United States and Canada through approximately 2,000 independent retail computer stores and internationally through twenty-one independent distributors that resell to approximately 2,000 retail dealers. Apple's products are primarily serviced in the United States and Canada by approximately 700 of the retail stores and in other countries by independent retail dealers.

Apple's Goal

The goal of Apple Computer, Inc., is to produce high-quality, low-cost, easy-to-use products that incorporate high technology for the individual. Apple wants to prove that high technology does not have to be intimidating for noncomputer experts.[3]

To accomplish this goal, Apple intends to keep its product lines simple, providing a few high-volume, high-quality products; encouraging the aftermarket to complete the customer's solution; and continuing to market products that are completely different from those of competitors.

Recent Trends and Current Situation

The period from 1977 to 1979 marked the beginning of Apple Computer's success story. The company posted a profit of only $41,575 in 1977. Through aggressive marketing and advertising strategies, the demand for the Apple computer grew in the next two years as sales increased from $774 thousand in 1977 to $47.8 million in 1979. Profit also soared to $5.1 million by 1979, over a 100 percent profit increase compared to 1977.

The period from 1979 through 1981 saw geometric growth in the computer industry. At this time, Apple had a 12.4 percent share of the business computer market and a 16 percent share of the home and educational market in the United

States. The company was able to cash in on its position as the industry leader and profits jumped from $5 million in 1979 to $11.6 million in 1981—a 132 percent increase in profit within two years.

Beginning in 1981 and continuing through 1983, there was an influx of competitive products from other computer companies and, consequently, the need for a new strategic plan to maintain or increase Apple's market share. In its attempts to increase sales and fight off competition, Apple reduced the price on the Apple II systems and also increased marketing and distribution expense to 23 percent of sales in 1983. This strategy was successful as sales revenue for 1983 rose to $983 million, a 69 percent increase over 1982. Profit for the period was $76.7 million, a 25 percent increase from 1982.[4]

In 1983 John Sculley was appointed to the position of chief executive officer (CEO). As president and CEO of Apple Computer, Mr. Sculley set about developing marketing, cost planning, and control systems (see exhibit 1). He also reduced the work force and restructured the corporation into one manageable organization. Recognizing that retail distributors account for about 80 percent of the industry's sales, Mr. Sculley scuttled Apple's network of outside representatives and marshaled a 350-person sales force to blunt IBM Corporation's mounting domination. He expanded Apple's retail network by 33 percent to 2,000 dealers; tripled Apple's advertising budget to $100 million, and promoted new products with aggressive and effective advertising (like the famous Macintosh-1984 TV commercial) and the sole sponsorship of *Newsweek's* Special Election Issue.[5] In an attempt to further broaden its product line and also capture some share of the fast-growing business computer market, Apple Computer, Inc., introduced its Macintosh business computer and the Apple IIc. Net sales for 1984 were $1.5 billion, an increase of $533 million, or 54 percent, over 1983. The primary reason for the increased sales was the introduction of the Macintosh, which accounted for 34 percent of the sales. Sales of Apple IIe and IIc were 58 percent of revenue, whereas maintenance and services generated 8 percent of revenue (see exhibit 2).

In 1985 Apple Computer recorded the first quarterly loss in its nine-year history. The year also saw a complete shake-up in the organization's management. Steve Jobs relinquished his position as the chairman of the board after having been removed as the manager of the Macintosh division and left with no operating role. In the same year, CEO John Sculley adopted a functional organizational structure, replacing the former divisionalized structure in which each product division had its own general management, product development, marketing, manufacturing, finance, and management information systems. In the new functional system, all product operations (development, manufacturing, and distribution) are handled by one group. Finance and management information systems are handled by another group. Restructuring the organization in this way allowed the elimination of redundancy in Apple's operation and improved the management process (see exhibit 3).

In 1985 three manufacturing facilities owned by Apple Computer, Inc., were closed to adjust for the general slump in the computer industry. As a result of these measures, the company eliminated 1,200 jobs and, more importantly, lowered its break-even point from quarterly sales of $430 million to $360 million.[6]

As of October 1985, the balance of Apple Computer, Inc., remained strong, and the company enjoyed a cash and temporary cash position of over $526 million. Furthermore, the company had no long-term debt. This strength in Apple's balance sheet was particularly impressive given the continuing slump and the increased competition in the computer industry. A look at the total asset turnover ratio from 1982 through 1985 reveals that the increased revenue derived from the development and introduction of the Macintosh and Apple IIc had come with a relatively small capital outlay.[7]

There were several notable developments in 1985 that reflected a new direction in Apple's product and marketing strategies for the years ahead. First, the company changed its distribution system from the use of independent manufacturer's representatives to the use of its own trained sales force. This change helped Apple to be more responsive to day-to-day store traffic and to work with its dealers as partners. Eventually, this partnership should help both Apple and the dealers improve the merchandising of products.

Another important change was Apple's marketing of its Macintosh to *Fortune* 500 companies. Apple's strategy was to generate and secure a minimum of fifty orders from major corporations so that those companies could be used as "showcase accounts" to generate purchases among small- and medium-sized businesses.[8]

Finally, and of critical importance, was Apple's announcement that it would start producing devices to let Macintosh communicate with IBM PCs. This strategy could be a step in the right direction, as many people have blamed the less-than-expected sales of the Macintosh on its noncompatiblity with IBM PCs. On the negative side, however, this strategy might also negate Apple's marketing strength as the only computer that is not IBM-compatible.

EXTERNAL SYSTEMS

What external factors must Apple deal with in its increasingly competitive market-place? Determining strategic direction in a world of shifting market competition and economic forces is difficult.

As a first step in the development of strategies to meet the goals of Apple Computer, the environment in which Apple operates must be analyzed, and those key areas must be factored into the planning and strategy of the company.

ECONOMIC ANALYSIS

Computer experts had predicted that 1986 would not be a spectacular year for the computer industry.[9] As a result, suppliers of computers, software, and services expected relatively sluggish growth, coupled with lower margins and profit. The industry was expected to grow 7 percent to 8 percent in 1986 by John F. Akers, chief executive officer of International Business Machines. This growth rate was about the same as in 1985, but half the rate of previous years. By most accounts, prices were expected to drop about 20 percent for mainframes and minis and about 30 percent for the micros.[10]

The strength of the U.S. dollar has hurt export of technology. And with stiff competition from the Japanese and European manufacturers, the stronger the dollar, the more expensive computers shipped out of the United States become. The weakness in the manufacturing sector of the national economy has also slowed computer purchases.[11]

The major problem, however, appears to be not lack of demand, but rather an oversupply of products and overcrowding of companies in the marketplace. Too many companies specializing in the same product line have been formed. IBM has its XT and AT PCs to compete with Apple's IIc, and other companies such as COMPAC have also come out with similar versions of such a computer, thereby overcrowding an already small market niche.

Market

The company's systems are used by persons both with and without prior computer experience in business, education, scientific, and engineering applications and, to a lesser extent, in the home.

Over a third of Apple's projected market through the mid-1990s falls into the business category. Historically, the business, professional, and managerial segment has accounted for over 40 percent of revenues; but ultimately, the greatest demand will come from a broader spectrum. An estimated 140 million people around the world could justify the purchase of a personal computer.

Apple's computer systems are used with a variety of peripheral products such as video monitors, disk drives, printers, and graphics tablets. Apple's computers incorporate standard interfaces permitting the use of peripherals designed and manufactured by others as well as those offered by Apple. These peripherals include medium-speed printers for home and business applications requiring letter quality output; modems that provide a data communications link using a telephone network to access time-sharing services, computerized bulletin boards or other computers; music synthesizers; and portable power units that allow Apple systems to be operated in automobiles and elsewhere.

Apple has aimed its sights at two markets: very small businesses with less than $2 million in revenues that could use its computer to automate accounting procedures and major corporations where a department could use the machine in a specialized area, such as sales forecasting, without tying up the central computer.

Originally, the company produced one type of computer—the Apple II. As the needs of the consumer changed over the years, Apple Computer expanded its product line to meet these needs. Presently products being marketed include Apple IIc, Apple IIe, Macintosh, and Macintosh-Plus. Both the Apple IIc and Apple IIe are targeted primarily toward the home and educational market, whereas the Macintosh and Macintosh-Plus are targeted toward the business market.

The Apple IIc is a compact computer with a base memory capacity of 128 kilobytes and is expandable to 512 kilobytes. The Apple IIe, more powerful than the IIc, comes with a base memory capacity of 128 kilobytes, which is expandable to 1 megabyte. The Macintosh is produced with a base memory capacity of 512 kilobytes, which is expandable to 1 megabyte. The Macintosh-Plus, an enhanced version of the Macintosh, comes with a base memory capacity of 1 megabyte.

Currently Apple Computer, Inc., has three manufacturing facilities. A highly automated plant in Fremont, California, builds the Macintosh, Macintosh-Plus, and the Apple IIc. The Apple IIe is currently built at an existing plant in Singapore, and the European Model IIs are built in Ireland.

Apple's products are sold in the United States and Canada through approximately 2,000 independent retail outlets. The twenty-one independent foreign distributors are located primarily in Europe and to a lesser extent, in the Far East, Middle East, Australia, Philippines, and South Africa. During 1985 foreign sales of Apple's products, including sales in Canada, were approximately 22 percent of net sales. (See exhibit 4 for financial highlights.)

Competition

In a full-page *Wall Street Journal* ad in 1981, Apple heralded the entry of International Business Machines Corporation into the personal computer field by stating "Welcome, IBM, Seriously." Apple itself maintains that IBM's presence confirms that personal computers as not just a fad but a major growth industry. After all, Apple's personal computers—compact, desktop machines designed to balance checkbooks, play games, and handle a variety of other tasks—kicked off an industry that now encompasses some 350 companies with sales expected to reach approximately $20 billion in 1990. Nevertheless, because of the new competition and the internal strain of managing its prodigious growth, Apple is facing a critical period that will see the development and introduction of new products.

The personal computer market is highly competitive and has been characterized by rapid technological advances in both hardware and software development that have substantially increased the capabilities and applications of personal computers. The principal competitive factors in the personal computer market are product quality and reliability, relative price versus performance, marketing and distribution capability, service and support, the availability of hardware and software accessories, corporate reputation, and ease of understanding and operation of the system.

The company believes it competes favorably with respect to all of these factors, but its reliance on independent retail dealers for product distribution may not provide the extent of market penetration of Radio Shack (a subsidiary of Tandy Corporation), which sells through a large number of company-owned retail stores and distribution outlets. In addition, Commodore International, Ltd., has broader international retail distribution than Apple. Apple may also be at a competitive disadvantage because it purchases integrated circuits and other component parts used in its computers from vendors, whereas a number of its competitors manufacture such parts. In addition, a substantial portion of the peripheral equipment used with Apple's systems is purchased from outside vendors, while certain competitors design and manufacture their own peripheral equipment.

Apple expects intense competition from several substantially larger firms that have entered or are expected to enter the personal computer market, including Hewlett-Packard Company, IBM, COMPAC, and various foreign manufacturers, all of which have considerably greater financial, marketing, and technological resources than Apple.

As many as a dozen large companies have joined the battle, offering personal computers costing less than $5,000. ITT, AT&T, and Digital Equipment are all marketing PCs. Meanwhile, at least eight Japanese companies, including Nipon Electric, Casio, and Sharp, have introduced personal computers and are preparing to come to the U.S. market.

Apple Computer, Inc., is the nation's leader in the home and educational computer market.[12] This segment is a low-margin business and only a fraction of the size of the home and business market. Recently, IBM, the number one computer maker in the world, discontinued the production of its PC Jr.—a strong competitor of the Apple IIc in the home market. Apple IIc is expected to pick up some of the market share left by PC Jr. and sales of Apple IIc should increase.

Market research by several companies indicates that Apple Computer, Inc., has been losing business market share to competitors such as IBM, ITT, Hewlett-Packard, Commodore, and various Japanese manufacturers. In particular, IBM may be considered to be dominant in the business market. Future Computing, Inc., a market research concern, put Apple's share of the business market at 12.6 percent in 1985 compared to 16.2 percent in 1984. In contrast, IBM's share increased from 4.4 percent in 1984 to 31 percent in 1985. The forecast for 1986 predicted further lower business market share of 10.8 percent for Apple Computer, Inc., and increased business market share for IBM at 37.5 percent (see exhibit 5). This trend is expected to continue into the 1990s.

Apple's declining share of the business market suggests the company has been making some strategic errors in the last few years. For example, Apple for a long time unofficially had limited its promotions aimed at selling Apple II computers to businesses, fearing those efforts might detract from its big push to establish its Macintosh personal computer as its flagship product for the business market. As a result, sales of Apple IIs to businesses fell, but Macintosh failed to pick up the slack.[13]

Another explanation for the declining market share is that unlike the Apple II and IBM PC, the Macintosh has no slots into which outside manufacturers could slide printed circuit boards for expanding the computer's memory or for adding a super-fast mathematical processor. Meanwhile, the great strength of the original Apple and the IBM PC is that they attracted swarms of outside suppliers whose specialized add-on hardware and software vastly expanded the market for those machines. One way to make the Macintosh more appealing to businesses is to open up the systems to third party hardware and software companies. Apple could also include in the Macintosh the equipment consumers want, such as larger disc drives, or produce more powerful versions of the machine itself.

Price is another reason for Apple's loss of market share. A look at the PC comparison chart reveals that the Macintosh and IBM PC XT, both of which are directed toward the business market, are priced equally (see exhibit 6). However, the IBM XT has more memory capacity (640K) than the Macintosh (512K). Also, while the IBM XT has seven slots into which outside manufacturers or programmers can slide printed circuit boards to expand the computer's memory or to add a super-fast mathematical processor, the Macintosh has absolutely no slots. Therefore, a consumer who is shopping for value (relative price/performance) would probably lean toward purchasing an IBM XT as opposed to a Macintosh. A price review and market incentive by Apple Computer, Inc., should reverse this situation.

The International Market

Apple Computer, Inc., a leader in microcomputer sales in Europe, intended to boost foreign sales from 22 percent of revenue to 35 percent in the 1986 fiscal year. Dataquest, Inc., forecasted an annual growth of up to 50 percent overseas, compared with growth of only 8 percent in the United States. Apple's goal is to get its share of that overseas market. Meeting the 35 percent target is critical to Apple's effort to halt a slide in its share of the world market, from nearly 19 percent in 1984 to less than 11 percent in 1986.[14]

A maturing European market, however, threatens Apple's goal and calls its strategies into question. Since 1984, IBM has overcome a late start in European microcomputers and has pulled ahead of Apple. Meanwhile, European manufacturers such as West Germany's Nixdord, France's Bull, and Italy's Olivetti have gained considerable market share by selling computers that are compatible with IBMs. By some estimates, IBM captured 33 percent of the European market in 1985.

The excess of both domestic and foreign competition also points to another change that will make it more difficult for computer companies to make tangible profit in the future. The impact of this overcrowding was especially felt at Apple Computer, Inc., as its worldwide market share dropped from 19 percent to less than 11 percent in two years (see exhibit 7).

INTERNAL SYSTEMS

Apple Computer must assess its strengths and weaknesses in product quality and reliability, relative price/performance, marketing and distribution capability, service and support, availability of hardware and software accessories, corporate reputation, and ease of understanding and operation of the system to determine how best to proceed toward its goals.

Advertising

Among the ten largest computer advertisers in the nation, Apple Computer is second only to IBM. While IBM spent an estimated $518 million (representing 2 percent of its sales revenue) on computer advertisement in 1984, Apple spent $180 million. This expenditure represents 11.8 percent of Apple's computer revenue, an amount significantly higher than the average of 4.0 percent of revenue spent on advertising by the ten largest computer advertisers. Expenditures of this size have become a requirement in the microcomputer market. As competition escalates, Apple has increasingly turned to advertising to differentiate itself and its products from those of competitors.

Although many advertisements for machines in direct competition with IBM products emphasize the benefits of those machines over IBM's and mention compatibility for software and perhaps peripherals, Apple's ads make no allusion to IBM. Instead, they challenge the reader or viewer to test Apple products, so that they would subsequently want to buy them. Many thought this marketing position would doom the company; but with the 1984 introduction of the successful Macintosh, Apple proved it can survive the industry shake-out by maintaining its uniqueness as "an alternative to IBM."[15]

The newness of the products and the high number of market participants in the computer industry require that Apple's advertising be designed to do double duty. It must first persuade consumers to make a purchase. Then, it must differentiate a specific product and firm from all others. Apple Computer had the highest name recognition rating (97 percent) of any computer firm.

In the long run, Apple might want to advertise its product directly against IBM. Because IBM is the present market leader in computers, Apple must prove to the consumers the superiority of its product relative to IBM.

Production

The corporation has an efficient arrangement for production because its manufacturing facility in the United States is located in one area—Fremont, California. Its manufacturing facilities in Singapore and Ireland are also concentrated, allowing for efficient management and ease of coordination of each of the facilities.

Because Apple is a high-cost producer compared to IBM, one of John Sculley's primary goals is more cost-efficient production. Recently, he adopted a functional structure in which all product operations are handled by one group. Functionalizing the organization in this way allowed the elimination of redundancy in the company's operation and should lead to lower production cost in future years.[16]

Raw materials essential to Apple's business are generally available from multiple sources. Certain components such as power supplies, integrated circuits, and plastic housings are obtained from single sources, although other sources for such parts are available. To date, Apple has not experienced significant production delays or problems due to shortages in material or components.[17]

Research and Development

The computer industry is subject to rapid technological changes. Apple's ability to develop new products and improve existing products is important to its future. To respond to industry needs as they arise, Apple maintains a continuing program of research and development.

Expenditures for research and development increased from $60 million in 1983 to $71 million in 1984. R&D as a percent of sales was 6.10 percent and 4.69 percent for those years, respectively. This amount is relatively small when compared with other leading computer manufacturers such as IBM and Hewlett-Packard. IBM spent $2.5 billion in 1983 and $4.2 billion in 1984 on R&D. This amount represents 6.2 percent and 9.1 percent of IBM's sales in 1983 and 1984. R&D as a percentage of revenue is a useful indicator of the degree of a firm's technological activity. The absolute level of R&D expenditure, however, can be misleading. For example, it would be wrong to conclude that Apple with the lower R&D expenditure is less technologically advanced than IBM. IBM manufactures mainframe computers which require more intensive R&D expense; Apple does not. Apple's present low R&D expenditure as a percent of sales (4.7 percent) compared to the industry average of 9 percent calls to question its ability to come up with innovative products necessary to remain competitive in the future.

Financial

Apple's revenues grew explosively, from about $177 million in 1980 to about $1.9 billion in fiscal 1985, as the company established itself as one of the leaders in the computer industry. Net income also increased from $11.6 million in 1980 to $76.7 million in 1983—a 56 percent revenue increase. Owing to increases in the marketing and advertisement costs and price reduction brought on by competition within the industry, net income declined by 10 percent and 4 percent in 1984 and 1985, respectively.

Liquidity

The company has no liquidity problems as it currently enjoys a current cash and temporary cash investment in excess of $441 million.[18] Apple should be able to continue its research and development programs with internally generated funds.

Apple has experienced significant increases in net sales and net income during each of its fiscal years, reflecting the growth in the personal computer market as well as continued market acceptance of Apple's products. The company made no significant changes in prices for its products during the period. In addition, economies of scale and certain product cost efficiencies have offset the effects of inflation (see exhibits 8, 9, and 10). In fiscal 1985, Apple posted record sales of $1.9 billion, a 27 percent gain, and a 10 percent earnings gain to $61.2 million.

In December 1980, the company went public with the sale of 4.6 million shares at $22 a share, raising $96.8 million. The sale placed the total market value of Apple at $1.2 billion. In calculating the price, the underwriters Morgan Stanley and Company compared Apple with nine somewhat similar companies. These companies were selling shares at an average eighteen times their anticipated 1981 earnings. The underwriters figured that Apple's spectacular growth rate—earnings went up 700 percent in 3 years—and a faddish enthusiasm for the stock made the company worth a lot more, perhaps thirty-five to forty-five times anticipated earnings. Investors are again infatuated with high-technology issues.

Apple has no long-term debt position. Its strong liquidity position would enable the company to use leverage, when and if necessary, to finance a new acquisition or product line. The company's profit outlook should be stronger in 1990 as cost-cutting measures (such as the recent reduction of its work force by 20 percent and the closing of three manufacturing facilities) should lower the overall cost of production. The result of this cost control measure is already evident as Apple's break-even point has been lowered from $400 million in revenues per quarter to $325 million. Cash on hand has also ballooned to $441 million, igniting speculation that Apple might acquire another company.

Technological Analysis

Apple's ability to operate successfully depends upon, among other things, its ability to adapt to the rapid technological changes of the computer industry. The company maintains a continuing program of research and development for which it spent approximately $72,526,000 in fiscal 1985.

A key reason for the rapid technological change is the frequent change in consumers' demand. The current taste of the home and education computer market is for easy to use and nonsophisticated computers. However, the computers available to meet this market segment have been criticized as being too sophisticated and difficult to use. There is a gap between consumers' demand and manufacturer's supply, and therefore a need to change the technology. The business computers presently on the market have been criticized for not being sophisticated, so they also do not meet the specialized needs of many consumers. Technological innovation is a crucial aspect of remaining competitive.

Another reason for the dynamic technological change in the industry is a law referred to as the "standing ten feet away and squinting test" (Apple *v.* Digital Research, Inc., 1985). This law requires computer companies to differentiate their product from that of a competitor so that it does not look the same from ten feet away.

Governmental Policies

FCC Regulation

In October 1979 and April 1980, the Federal Communications Commission adopted orders imposing radio frequency emanation standards on computing equipment.

The regulations distinguish between computing devices marketed for use primarily in a commercial, industrial, or business environment and computing devices marked for use primarily in a residential environment. Neither regulation poses a compliance problem for Apple.

Tariff and Export Control Policies

Since August 1980, sales to the foreign distributors have generally been made in local currencies and are subject to the risks of exchange rate fluctuations. Restrictive tariff and export control policies are potential risks of foreign sales, but the company has experienced no material problems to date.

Canada

To get a bite of Canada's minicomputer market, which Apple estimates to be 10 percent to 15 percent the size of the U.S. market, the company had to bargain with Canadian bureaucrats. Apple's products were being sold in Canada by retailers who imported them from the U.S., but it was "a very clumsy arrangement."[19] To sell large volumes, Apple would need a Canadian subsidiary and distribution system, but as a new business, such a subsidiary would have to be approved by Canada's Foreign Investment Review Agency. In return for approval to set up operations in Canada, the company promised to look for competitive Canadian-made parts that could be used in Apple's worldwide production. It also agreed to begin production in Canada after sales reached a specified volume.

Litigation

The company is a defendant in two separate lawsuits, primarily antitrust actions; the plaintiffs in both are former distributors of the company's products. These suits were filed in 1980 and occurred around the time Apple was revamping its marketing and distribution channels. Antitrust lawsuits are long, drawn-out affairs and can go on for years before settlement or a decision is reached.

> In February and March 1984, six class action complaints were filed against the company and fourteen of its officers and directors alleging violations of federal and state securities laws, including allegations of fraud and insider trading based on the company's alleged failure to make certain disclosures of material facts during the time period from November 12, 1982 to September 23, 1983. The company believes that the suits are without merit and intends to litigate vigorously the asserted claims in these actions. The company maintains a directors and officers insurance policy that it believes should defray a substantial portion of any liability and costs of defense.[20]

Marketing

In the personal computer industry, Apple is unique, offering a broad range of products to satisfy most market segments. To further penetrate the business market,

Apple Computer, Inc., is beginning to market its business computers to *Fortune* 500 companies. Apple's ultimate goal is to sell not only to the large companies, but also to the five million small and medium-sized businesses who (according to Dataquest, a California computer consulting firm) account for more than 80 percent of all personal computer sales. The success of this strategy is already evident as Apple was able to secure a $5 million order from Federal Express and commitments worth about $2.5 million each from General Motors, GTE, Honeywell, and Motorola.[21] The impact of these purchase orders on the total demand of Apple's business computers is, however, yet to be measured (see exhibits 11 and 12).

ORGANIZATION CLIMATE/MANAGERIAL STYLE

Apple has grown from a small, single-product, single-nation, private company to a medium-sized, multiproduct, multinational public company. Today, it is a healthy and focused organization with excellent technology, seasoned management, and a strong balance sheet.

Apple's management conducts a multilayered program of internal communications, employee-management meetings, training programs, and publications to help its people better understand and participate in their company. Apple encourages an environment in which employees can bring issues to the attention of decision makers. Apple also has a "loan to own" program whereby employees can get their own computer, and the company estimates that 40 percent of the company's employees now have their own Apple.

Much of Apple's growth is attributed to astute marketing, but the firm is also aggressive in its research. To handle the rapid growth, Apple works hard at internal communications. Michael Scott, who resigned from Apple's presidency in a management shuffle, believes the company is divisionalizing "too fast. . . . It's become like a cluster of little companies, and there's too little understanding of how manufacturing relates to inventory." Mr. Scott saw another problem, "Apple's still fat from its public offering so it's hard for them to run as lean and mean as they should." A future problem, some observers say, lies in the fact that Apple has made many personal fortunes. It may be hard to be motivated and strive for ingenuity when you've already made it big.[22]

In the management shake-up, John Sculley took over operation of the company from founder Steve Jobs. (See exhibit 13 for a full list of officers and directors.)

Employees like the fact that top executives operate with a "walk-around management" style, meaning that the president and the chairman mingle with workers on an assembly line or in the cafeteria. "It gives a whole different feeling from having to walk into the president's office."[23] There are also employee bonuses and stock option, stock purchase, and profit participation plans available.

Training Managers Dennis Mahoney and Beth Richardson put together a three-week crash course called Sell With Apple Training, or SWAT. These "boot camps" introduced new recruits to Apple's product lines and the corporate resources they'd be using in their new jobs. Every part of Apple sent people, each week for sixteen weeks, to teach the new salespeople about Apple's history and organization. Those Apple salespeople even practiced their new techniques in a mock retail store set up by Mahoney's team.[24]

Apple employees, whose average age is 29, want the freedom to get things done, not the constraints of a rule book.

To attract and keep great people, Apple holds management levels to a minimum so each person has more influence on the direction in which the company moves. At Apple the chief executive officer is just one reporting level away from the more than seventy middle managers who run the company day to day. We know of no other *Fortune* 500 company in which the chief executive is so close to middle management.

Even as a billion-dollar corporation, Apple still acts like an eight-man garage shop in some ways—most notably in the way employees get their jobs done. With a minimal hierarchy of management (typically only two or three levels between a general manager and an individual contributor) and Apple's breakneck do-it-now scheduling, people spend a lot of their time in action. The pace and the movement sometimes leave people little time to slow down and *learn*.

For short periods this might work. But when Apple introduces two major products within 100 days, then hires and builds an entire sales force in the next 100 days, there's a tendency to live from crisis to crisis, for management and individual contributors alike. But Apple can't afford to have reactive-mode managers; it needs leaders inspired with vision, not managers preoccupied with problems.[25]

Goals, Objectives, and Planning— Managerial Strategy

Apple wants to remain one of the top three or four companies in the personal computer market. Faced with a growing crowd of competitors, the company is polishing its image with a $100 million marketing and promotional budget. The aim is to retain or possibly increase the company's market share.

Because of the demand and Apple's high expectations for Macintosh, the company will also want to get the various peripherals and software package accessories designed for the capabilities of the machine on the market as fast as possible. The company says, "Apple will be able to run operating systems used by IBM's personal computers. That ability, which will require the Apple user to install an accessory microprocessor, is a strategic move aimed at IBM's customer base."[26]

Apple's objectives include gaining tighter inventory control ($109 million vs $261 million), enhancing direct training of dealers, and gaining better access to end-users. To reinforce its new strategy, Apple launched the Apple Means Business (AMB) program designed to help dealers go after targeted markets. AMB gives dealers a series of objectives and, equally important, the means for implementing them, including sales seminars, structured presentations, and a kit of 172 color slides illustrating the various applications.

CONCLUSION

Apple has suffered some growing pains and problems attendant on early success, such as how to assimilate growth and how to defend its market share in personal computers against a field that now includes formidable competition. The company has endeavored to stay on course after management shake-ups. The company has experienced wide inventory fluctuations, from nearly exhausted supplies in 1980 to overbuilt stocks in 1985. With a closer access developed over time to the end-users and better anticipation of future needs, this problem may subside.

The company believes it can compare favorably in factors affecting competition but notes that its reliance on independent retail dealers may not provide the market penetration of Radio Shack (Tandy Corporation). Apple's reliance on purchased parts also may place it at a competitive disadvantage. It may want to study and increase the use of a sales force in the near future in an effort to maintain or increase its market share.

Service on future products may require greater technical expertise than it does currently, and future products may require on-site service. In addition, the continued growth of Apple's distribution network will require the establishment of other company-owned service centers and inventory of spare parts in different geographic locations to provide prompt service and warranty repair.

To stay in command of the industry, Apple must manage its product entries, its growth, and its profitability with exquisite care. It seems to be fully aware of the challenges that lie ahead, and that is good in itself. Now that it is a dominant market force, it needs to straighten out its small problems to keep the customers and dealers happy and thus retain the demand for its product. "The need to be a contender in the office of the future is enticing every major data processing operator in the business. New product development and marketing muscle is the name of the game. If Apple falters, Tandy and others will be there to pick up any slack."[27]

In the past, the temperamental, but never dull, Steve Jobs encouraged a risk-taking spirit at Apple. Now CEO John Sculley and the young executive team must determine the strategic direction for this dynamic young company. Should Apple start its own distribution network? Should it develop its own software and move toward more vertical integration? Finally, how can it best compete with the giants such as IBM and Hewlett-Packard, who have entered this high-growth field?

Notes

1   See "Behind the Fall of Steve Jobs," *Fortune,* August 5, 1985, 20–24; and "How Apple Plans to Stop IBM from Taking an Even Bigger Bite," *Business Week,* October 3, 1983, 79.
2   "Apple Reaches out for a Marketing Pro," *Business Week,* April 25, 1983, 27–28.
3   Annual Report to Stockholders, and Form 10-K, 1984.

4   Ibid.
5   "Apple's Counterattack against IBM," *Business Week,* January 16, 1984, 78–81.
6   "Apple Has Loss of $17.2 Million," *The Wall Street Journal,* July 19, 1985, 4.
7   Annual Report, 1984.
8   "Apple's Pitch to the Fortune 500," *Fortune,* April 15, 1985, 53–56.
9   "The Long Awaited Rebound," *Business Week,* January 13, 1986, 86.
10 Ibid, 87.
11 "Computer Industry in Severe Slump," *The New York Times,* June 10, 1985, F-1.
12 *The Wall Street Journal,* July 19, 1985.
13 Ibid.
14 "Apple's Point Man in the Fight to Catch IBM," *Business Week,* February 10, 1986, 43–46.
15 "Marketing Methods Bring Apple Back," *Advertising Age,* December 31, 1984, 21–23.
16 "Current Market Outlook," Apple Computer, July 1985.
17 Annual Report.
18 Ibid.
19 "Apple's Foreign Touch," *Newsweek,* January 27, 1986, 42.
20 Annual Report.
21 "The No-Nonsense Era of John Sculley," *Business Week,* January 27, 1986, 96–98.
22 Ibid., 96.
23 Ibid., 97.
24 Annual Report, 1984.
25 Ibid.
26 Ibid.
27 Ibid.

EXHIBIT 1
Current Trends at Apple Computer, Inc.

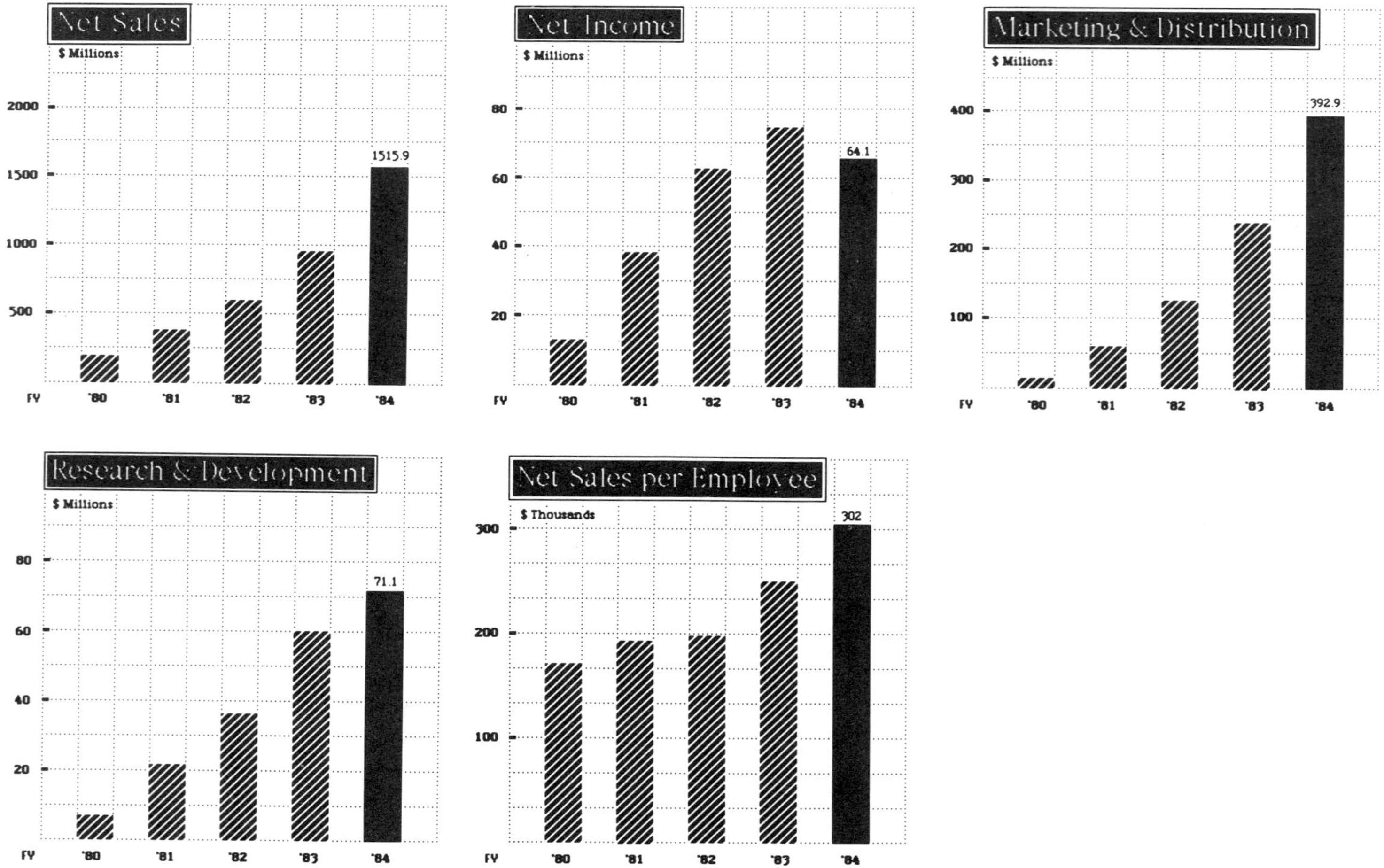
Net Sales
$ Millions
2000
1500
1000
500
1515.9
FY '80 '81 '82 '83 '84
Net Income
$ Millions
80
60
40
20
64.1
FY '80 '81 '82 '83 '84
Marketing & Distribution
$ Millions
400
300
200
100
392.9
FY '80 '81 '82 '83 '84
Research & Development
$ Millions
80
60
40
20
71.1
FY '80 '81 '82 '83 '84
Net Sales per Employee
$ Thousands
300
200
100
302
FY '80 '81 '82 '83 '84

EXHIBIT 2
Revenue by Product Segment (%) from 1983–1984 for Apple Computer, Inc.

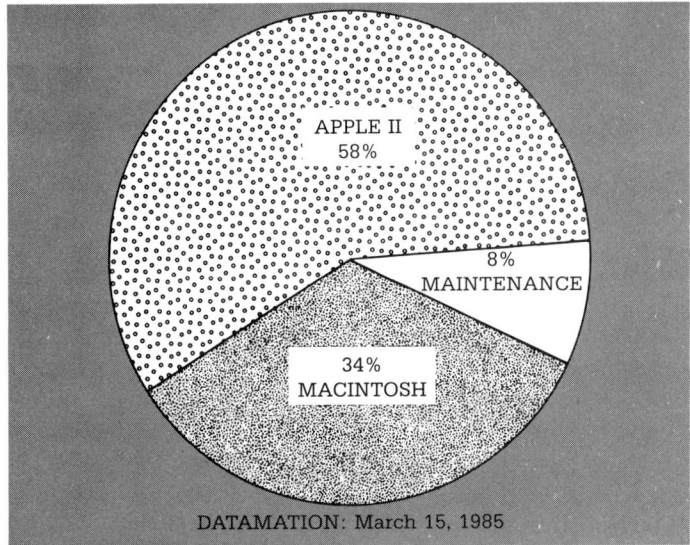

Source: *Datamation,* March 15, 1985

EXHIBIT 3
Apple Computer Management Structure

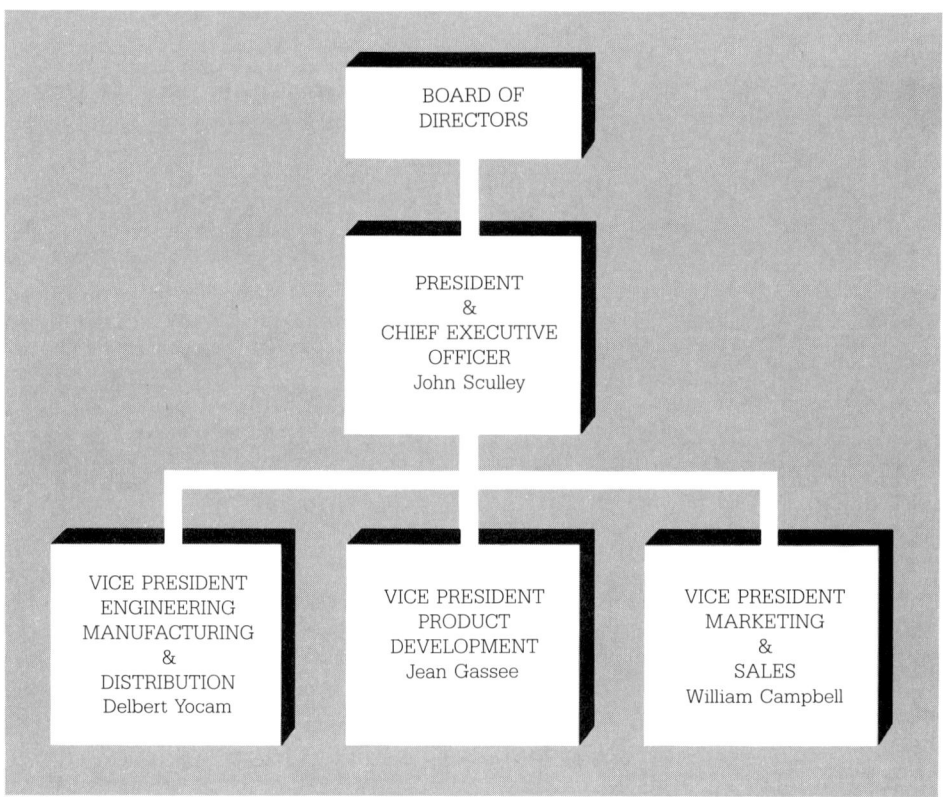

Source: *Fortune*, August 5, 1985

EXHIBIT 4
Selected Financial Information

Annual   (In thousands, except per share amounts)

Five years ended September 26, 1986

	1986	1985*	1984	1983	1982
Net sales	$1,901,898	$1,918,280	$1,515,876	$982,769	$583,061
Net income	$ 153,963	$ 61,223	$ 64,055	$ 76,714	$ 61,306
Earnings per common and common equivalent share	$ 2.39	$ .99	$ 1.05	$ 1.28	$ 1.06
Common and common equivalent shares used in the calculations of earnings per share	64,315	61,895	60,887	59,867	57,798
Cash and temporary cash investments	$ 576,215	$ 337,013	$ 114,888	$143,284	$153,056
Total assets	$1,160,128	$ 936,177	$ 788,786	$556,579	$357,787
Noncurrent obligations under capital leases	$ —	$ —	$ —	$ 1,308	$ 2,052

Apple has not paid any cash dividends on its common stock. The present policy is to reinvest earnings to finance future growth.

Quarterly (Unaudited)   (In thousands, except per share amounts)

1986	Fourth Quarter*	Third Quarter*	Second Quarter	First Quarter
Net sales	$ 510,786	$ 448,279	$ 408,943	$ 533,890
Gross margin	$ 272,463	$ 236,032	$ 231,360	$ 270,931
Net income	$ 32,893	$ 32,333	$ 31,812	$ 56,925
Earnings per common and common equivalent share	$ .51	$ .49	$ .50	$ .91
Price range per common share	$37¾–$30½	$38⅞–$26¾	$ 28¼–$22	$ 22⅜–$15

1985				
Net sales	$ 409,709	$ 374,930	$ 435,344	$ 698,297
Gross margin	$ 188,039	$ 154,467	$ 175,415	$ 282,495
Net income (loss)	$ 22,357	$ (17,210)	$ 9,977	$ 46,099
Earnings (loss) per common and common equivalent share	$ .36	$ (.28)	$ .16	$ .75
Price range per common share	$18⅛–$14½	$22⅞–$14¾	$ 30⅝–$21½	$ 28⅜–$21⅞

The price range per common share represents the highest and lowest closing prices for Apple's common stock in the NASDAQ National Market System during each quarter.

At September 26, 1986, there were approximately 35,000 shareholders of record.

*The third and fourth quarters of fiscal 1985 include $40 million and $(3 million), respectively, charged (credited) to income before income taxes related to the consolidation of the Company's operations, as discussed in the notes to the consolidated financial statements.

EXHIBIT 5
Reverse Fortunes. Apple Computer's share of the business market for personal computers has declined steadily while archrival IBM's share has risen.

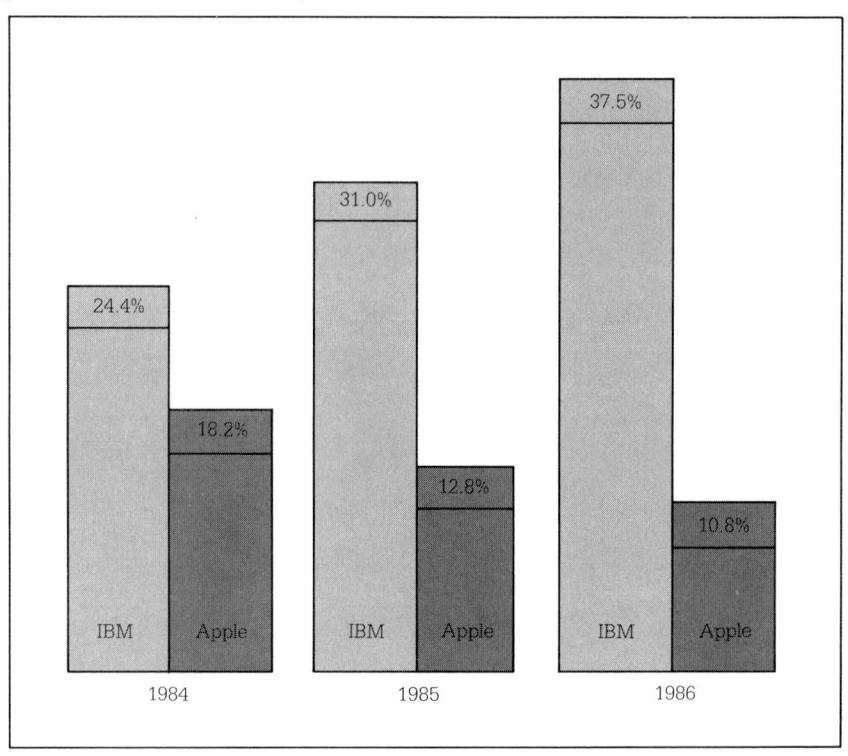

EXHIBIT 6
PC Comparison Chart

Feature	Macintosh	IBM PCXT	Mac Plus	IBM AT
RAM	512 K	640 K	512 K	640 K
Floppy Disk Drives	400 K	2 @ 360K = 720K	800 K	1.2 MEG
Board Expansion	0	Seven Expansion Slots	0	Seven Expansion Slots
Keyboard	Detachable	Detachable	Detachable	Detachable
Monitor	Built-in	Optional	Built-in	Optional
Word processing	√	√	√	√
RAM Maximum Memory	1 MEG	2.5 MEG	1 MEG	4 MEG
With Hard Disk	20 MEG	20 MEG	30 MEG	20 MEG
Price	$3,595	$3,595	$4,095	$3,995

Source: COMPUSHOP, West 510 Riverside, #101, Spokane, WA 99201

EXHIBIT 7
Market Share of Apple Computer, Inc.

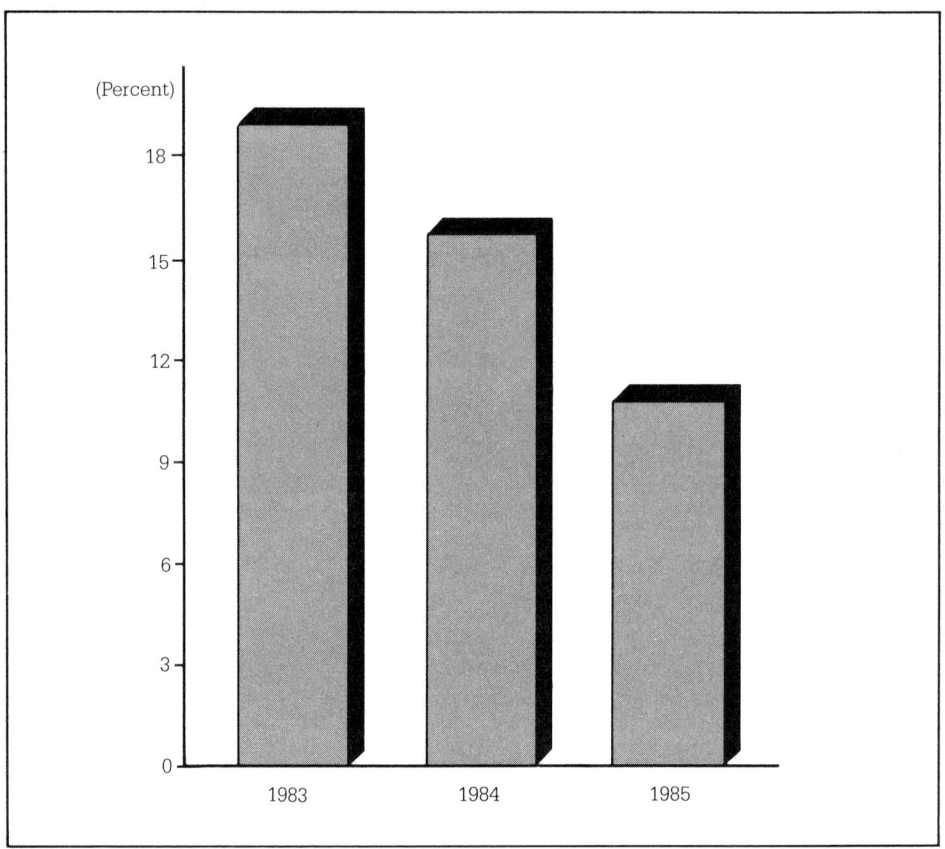

EXHIBIT 8
Consolidated Statements of Income

(In thousands, except per share amounts)

Three years ended September 26, 1986

	1986	1985	1984
Net sales	$1,901,898	$1,918,280	$1,515,876
Costs and expenses:			
Cost of sales	891,112	1,117,864	878,586
Research and development	127,758	72,526	71,136
Marketing and distribution	476,685	478,079	398,463
General and administrative	132,812	110,077	81,840
	1,628,367	1,778,546	1,430,025
Operating income before unusual item	273,531	139,734	85,851
Unusual item—provision for consolidation of operations	—	(36,966)	—
Interest and other income, net	36,187	17,277	23,334
Income before income taxes	309,718	120,045	109,185
Provision for income taxes	155,755	58,822	45,130
Net income	$ 153,963	$ 61,223	$ 64,055
Earnings per common and common equivalent share	$ 2.39	$ .99	$ 1.05
Common and common equivalent shares used in the calculations of earnings per share	64,315	61,895	60,887

See accompanying notes.

EXHIBIT 9
Consolidated Balance Sheets

(Dollars in thousands)

September 26, 1986 and September 27, 1985

Assets	1986	1985
Current assets:		
Cash and temporary cash investments	$ 576,215	$337,013
Accounts receivable, net of allowance for doubtful accounts of $21,792 ($16,209 in 1985)	263,126	220,157
Inventories	108,680	166,951
Prepaid income taxes	53,029	70,375
Other current assets	39,884	27,569
Total current assets	1,040,934	822,065
Property, plant, and equipment:		
Land and buildings	25,660	23,621
Machinery and equipment	103,963	78,725
Office furniture and equipment	44,237	38,551
Leasehold improvements	48,179	34,738
	222,039	175,635
Accumulated depreciation and amortization	(114,724)	(85,189)
Net property, plant, and equipment	107,315	90,446
Other assets	11,879	23,666
	$1,160,128	$936,177

Liabilities and Shareholders' Equity		
Current liabilities:		
Accounts payable	$ 118,053	$ 74,744
Accrued compensation and employee benefits	37,238	25,595
Income taxes payable	14,652	27,800
Accrued marketing and distribution	83,577	75,934
Accrued cost of consolidation of operations	3,735	20,173
Other current liabilities	71,280	71,179
Total current liabilities	328,535	295,425
Deferred income taxes	137,506	90,265
Commitments and contingencies		
Shareholders' equity:		
Common stock, no par value; 160,000,000 shares authorized; 62,627,613 shares issued and outstanding in 1986 (61,849,802 shares in 1985)	227,075	234,625
Retained earnings	474,287	320,324
Accumulated translation adjustment	(966)	414
	700,396	555,363
Notes receivable from shareholders	(6,309)	(4,876)
Total shareholders' equity	694,087	550,487
	$1,160,128	$936,177

See accompanying notes.

EXHIBIT 10
Foreign Subsidiaries

Geographic financial information is as follows:

	1986	1985	1984 (In thousands)
Net sales to unaffiliated customers in:			
United States	$1,411,812	$1,490,396	$1,187,839
Europe	298,843	247,609	192,187
Other	191,243	180,275	135,850
Total net sales	$1,901,898	$1,918,280	$1,515,876
Transfers between geographic areas (eliminated in consolidation):			
United States	$ 204,454	$ 220,653	$ 142,059
Europe	12,709	31,041	20,533
Other	187,834	269,265	210,885
Total transfers	$ 404,997	$ 520,959	$ 373,477
Operating income:			
United States	$ 161,192	$ 57,538	$ 43,503
Europe	47,814	2,712	14,559
Other	58,241	53,976	32,791
Eliminations	6,284	(11,458)	(5,002)
Unallocated	36,187	17,277	23,334
Income before income taxes	$ 309,718	$ 120,045	$ 109,185
Identifiable assets:			
United States	$ 427,746	$ 469,654	$ 534,251
Europe	108,232	85,098	104,081
Other	55,717	66,387	46,385
Eliminations	(7,782)	(21,975)	(10,819)
Corporate assets	576,215	337,013	114,888
Total assets	$1,160,128	$ 936,177	$ 788,786

Transfers between geographic areas are recorded at amounts generally above cost and in accordance with the rules and regulations of the respective governing tax authorities. Operating income is total revenue less operating expenses, and does not include either interest and other income, net, or income taxes. Identifiable assets of geographic areas are those assets used in Apple's operations in each area. Corporate assets are cash and temporary cash investments.

EXHIBIT 11

Desktop Computers in U.S., Units Installed (percentage distribution)

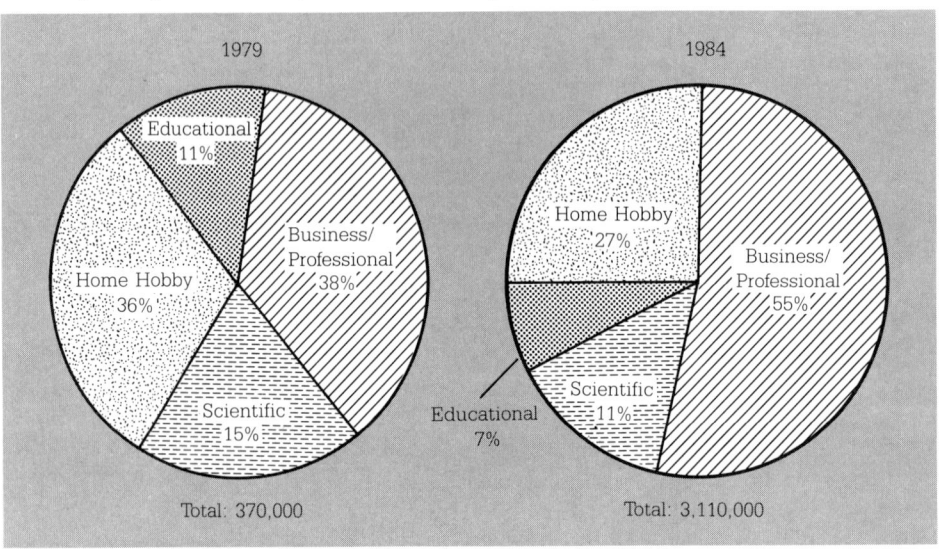

Source: International Data Corporation

EXHIBIT 12
Growth Record for Desktop Computers

	1980	1981	1982	1983	1984
Revenues (Adjusted for inflation: 1967 = 100) (in thousands)					
Apple		$ 698	$1,215	$2,048	$3,158
Compaq		—	—	100	—
Commodore		1,438	2,346	5,238	9,746
Tandy		474	569	693	767
Earnings Record (% change)					
	(5-yr.growth)				
Apple	65.0%	237.6	55.6	25.1	−16.4
Compaq	—	—	—	—	—
Commodore	90.0%	53.7	63.1	116.7	63.6
Tandy	27.0%	51.8	31.8	24.5	1.1
R.O.E. (%)					
Apple	65.7	38.1	27.8	23.8	15.1
Commodore	58.0	50.9	48.5	59.1	55.8
Tandy	46.9	37.6	32.2	28.7	28.4
R.O.A. (%)					
Apple	27.0	23.9	19.7	16.5	9.4
Commodore	22.3	21.1	21.4	20.6	22.2
Tandy	17.5	19.3	20.6	19.8	18.4
Operating Income (% of revenue)					
Apple	21.3	22.3	20.4	15.5	8.5
Commodore	19.9	21.1	21.3	19.9	20.9
Tandy	17.6	20.3	20.9	21.7	19.6
Net Income (% of revenue)					
Apple	10.0	11.8	10.5	7.8	4.2
Commodore	12.9	13.4	13.3	12.9	11.3
Tandy	8.1	9.1	8.4	11.6	15.6

No Dividend Payout

EXHIBIT 13

Board of Directors

Peter O. Crisp
General Partner
Venrock Associates
Venture capital investments

Albert A. Eisenstat
Senior Vice President, Secretary,
and General Counsel
Apple Computer, Inc.

A. C. Markkula, Jr.
Chairman, ACM Aviation, Inc.
Private flight service

Arthur Rock
Principal, Arthur Rock & Co.
Venture capital investments

Philip Schlein
Partner, U.S. Venture Partners
Venture capital investments

John Sculley
Chairman, President, and
Chief Executive Officer
Apple Computer, Inc.

Henry Singleton
Chairman, Teledyne, Inc.
Diversified manufacturing
company

Officers

John Sculley
Chairman, President, and
Chief Executive Officer

Delbert W. Yocam
Executive Vice President and
Chief Operating Officer

Albert A. Eisenstat
Senior Vice President, Secretary,
and General Counsel

William V. Campbell
Executive Vice President,
U.S. Sales and Marketing

Michael H. Spindler
Senior Vice President,
International Sales and Marketing

David J. Barram
Vice President, Finance
and Chief Financial Officer

Charles W. Berger
Vice President, Business Development

Deborah A. Coleman
Vice President, Operations

Jean-Louis Gassée
Vice President, Product Development

Lawrence G. Tesler
Vice President, Advanced Technology

Roy Weaver, Jr.
Vice President, Distribution

Robert W. Saltmarsh
Treasurer

Pizza Time Theatre

Donald F. Harvey
Research Associates: James A. Love and Mark G. Craze

INTRODUCTION

Nolan Bushnell, a charismatic entrepreneur, founded the video game industry and developed his ideas into not one, but two multimillion dollar companies. Termed the "Sorcerer of Silicon Valley" by *Inc.* magazine, Bushnell had started Atari and then sold out to Warner Communications for $28 million. He then started Pizza Time Theatres, a restaurant chain that expanded so rapidly it twice made *Inc.*'s list of the 100 fastest growing public companies.

Pizza Time Theatre, Inc., began in 1977 and for its first year was a division of Atari, a Warner Communications subsidiary. In June 1978, Nolan K. Bushnell, one of the developers of Pizza Time, purchased all assets and rights from Atari for $500,000 and formed a separate corporation.[1]

Incorporated in California on May 12, 1978, the company grew from one prototype restaurant to over 260 company and franchised centers by December 31, 1983. Total company employment reached 8,120 during this period.

Capitalization included $5.5 million in venture capital and two public stock offerings in 1981 of nearly 2.4 million shares. Outstanding shares totaled 6,108,165 on December 31, 1983. In addition, $50 million in convertible subordinated debentures were issued in May of 1983.[2] Cash flow problems led to ten store closings in the fourth quarter of 1983 and over twenty in the first quarter of 1984. The Kadabrascope division was discontinued, and over 900 employees lost their jobs.

Pizza Time Theatre

Pizza Time Theatre, Inc. (PTT), operates and franchises "Chuck E. Cheese's Pizza Time Theatre" family-oriented restaurant and entertainment centers. These centers focus on the concept of combining a restaurant with coin-operated electronic video games and musical entertainment by computer-controlled robot characters. The Pizza Time Theatre, Inc., concept expands the dining-out experience into a total package of family entertainment.

PTT has created and manufactured fifteen robot characters and the system of control, computers, and software that synchronizes their voices and body and facial

---

This case was prepared using published accounts and public documents for the purpose of class discussion rather than to illustrate either effective or ineffective handling of an administrative situation.

movements to the dialogue of original and popular songs in 283 separate two- to three-minute presentations.

The family-oriented restaurants and entertainment centers are generally located in attached, general purpose, one-story leased space in middle-class suburban shopping centers. Each center generally consists of the following restaurant and entertainment areas:

Order and Food Service Area   A multiple line, fast service-type order area features a uniform menu that includes a variety of pizza selections, sandwiches, salad bar, and a "make-your-own ice cream sundae" bar. A variety of beverages is offered, including beer and wine. Television-type monitors in each area indicate when orders are ready to be picked up at the adjoining food service area.

Theatre Dining Room   The main dining area, comprising approximately 50 percent of the informal bench-and-table seating, is the focal point of the center and contains a majority of the robot characters used in PTT's Cyberamics entertainment system. The characters are either mounted on the walls at a height designed to permit unobstructed viewing of the entire show, or appear on an elevated stage that allows viewing of the entire cast at once. Approximately every eight minutes the cast of robot characters performs an original two- to three-minute cabaret-like presentation of songs and dialogue drawn from a library of eleven musical skit tapes created by the company. In addition, special event presentations for birthdays and major holidays can be played as required.

Cabaret Lounge   The cabaret lounge, a secondary dining area with a seating capacity of approximately seventy-five, is quieter than the Theatre Dining Room and has a token-operated piano bar featuring a Cyberamics character. Most centers also contain an additional dining area with capacity for approximately sixty-five persons, which in some cases has additional Cyberamics characters, for special parties.

Fantasy Forest and Game Preserve   Approximately 2,500 square feet of a typical center is devoted to coin- or token-operated games of the following three basic types:

> Arcade games such as air hockey, skeeball, and other games which are not video or kiddie in nature represent between 20 percent and 30 percent of total center games.

> Video games utilizing a television monitor represent between 30 percent and 40 percent of total center games.

> Kiddie rides such as miniature helicopters, rocketships, carousels, and ferris wheels represent between 15 percent and 40 percent of total center games.

In order to encourage family-oriented activity, the centers do not contain pinball games, and children under eighteen years of age are required to be accompanied by an adult.

Merchandise Outlet   Approximately 200 square feet is devoted to a merchandise outlet which sells a line of toys, small gifts, T-shirts, and candy.

Company Center Network

Of the 266 company centers in operation as of 1983, 148 were company-owned and the balance were franchised (see exhibit 1). These centers vary from approximately 5,000 square feet to 22,000 square feet, with most centers averaging 10,000 to 15,000 square feet. Seating at most centers is in the range of 300 to 400 persons, and most centers have seventy-five or more games. Leases for centers generally have ten-year terms with renewal options.

Company-owned centers are generally open every day from 11:00 A.M. to 11:00 P.M. Approximately 57 percent of the revenues of a center is attributable to food, 17 percent to beverages, 25 percent to games, and 1 percent to merchandise purchases.

PTT developed a highly decentralized management style with an aggressive growth strategy in an attempt to capture market share before competitors could develop other versions of an entertainment restaurant. An overly aggressive growth strategy was selected because of management's limited perception of the product, as well as the ego involvement of Bushnell. Growth in revenues and market share were achieved by increasing the number of restaurants in operation. Exhibit 1 illustrates the growth from 1979 through 1983.

Company center personnel generally include a general manager, three center managers, a service and repair technician, and approximately eighty part-time food preparation and service employees. Operational standards of company centers are the responsibility of the company's executive vice president of operations, the director of company center operations, three regional directors, and nine district directors who regularly visit the centers.

In the company's experience, new company centers do not reach full operational levels of revenue and income until four to eight months after opening.[3]

Franchise Center Network

PTT offers franchises for centers on both a territorial and an individual unit basis, generally only in areas where there is no existing or planned concentration of company centers. PTT expects to franchise about half its stores.

Of the eighty-six franchised centers in operation as of 1982, nine were in California and the balance were located in twenty-eight other states, Canada and Australia. Franchised centers tend to be slightly smaller in size than company centers and have fewer games.

PTT's standard franchise agreement grants the franchisee the right to use the company's trade names, trademarks and service marks and the right to develop and operate a center in accordance with the company's system, which includes standards and specifications related to quality, preparation and service of food, maintenance of premises, and employee conduct. The franchisee is required to select the center site (though PTT retains the right of site approval), to provide necessary financing, and to bear all other costs in the development and opening of the center.

Under PTT's franchise agreement, the franchisee pays an initial fee of $20,000 and continuing fees based on the addition. Franchisees are required to spend at least 3 percent of monthly gross sales on advertising, and may be required to contribute an additional 1 percent of monthly gross sales to an association of franchises for regional and national advertising. The franchise agreement has an initial term of twenty years with two five-year renewal options, which may be exercised upon payment of an amount equal to 25 percent of the then-current initial franchise fee and compliance with certain other conditions.[4]

Cyberamics

PTT has created and developed Cyberamics as an entertainment system for use in company centers and for sale to franchisees. Cyberamics currently includes fifteen pneumatically operated robot characters and character sets driven by a computer-controlled tape system, and software programs designed and developed by the company to synchronize the characters' voices and body and facial movements to songs and dialogue in original presentations. The Cyberamics characters, not all of which appear at each center or in the same presentation, include the following, many of which are trademarks of Pizza Time Theatre, Inc.:

Chuck E. Cheese	Master of ceremonies
Pasqually	Italian chef
Helen Henney	Folk-singing chicken
Madame Oink	Parisian pig
Foxy Colleen	Irish fox
Sally Sachet	Disco skunk
Warblettes	Singing magpies
Dolli Dimples	Piano-playing hippopotamus
Artie Antlers	Flashy moose piano player
The King	Memphis rock singer
Jasper J. Jowls	Banjo-playing hound dog
Mister Munch	The purple pizza eater
Beagles	Rock and roll quartet
Harmony Howlette	Country and western coyote
The Four Little Shavers	Barbershop quartet

PTT has developed 283 separate original two- to three-minute presentations made available in eleven program tapes, rotated among the centers to permit changes of program about every six months. The company produces all program materials internally, occasionally utilizing outside consultants and writers.[5]

PTT designs, engineers, and assembles its robot characters and their computer-control system, including the creation of the software programs and the design of related tape encoding, programming, and reproduction systems. Its robot designs incorporate interchangeable parts and simplified production techniques. The company also designs, engineers, and assembles various other devices used in the centers, including television order/call-out systems and token dispensers. The company employs 120 persons in its engineering, design, and assembly departments, twenty of whom are also engaged in research and development efforts. The company's Cyberamics development and manufacturing facilities currently consist of approximately 20,000 square feet, including a test theatre in its principal offices in Sunnyvale, California, and a 4,000 square foot research and development facility in Victorville, California.[6]

Employees

As of December 27, 1981, PTT employed approximately 4,100 persons, of whom 3,566 were center employees and 534 were general office employees, corporate personnel, center management personnel, or center management trainees. Of the 534 corporate employees, twenty-seven were involved in corporate management, 100 in manufacturing, twenty in engineering and design, 110 were general office employees, 224 were center management personnel, and 53 were center management trainees.

MARKET

Target Market

Pizza Time's target market was children two to twelve years old. The emphasis was on maximizing the fun for children in this age group. Pizza recipes were tested on this target market, resulting in slightly sweet food that lacked spice. Parents, who were responsible for the purchase decision, disliked the taste, quickly tired of the surroundings, and often did not return.

Pizza Time Theatre, Inc., is expanding its market to include international development. It has signed franchise territorial agreements in England, France, Puerto Rico, Hong Kong, Canada, and Australia. The company's target is to have 1,000 of its family fun center restaurants in operation across the United States by 1990.

Pizza Time Theatre is more than just a pizza parlor; it is really selling entertainment. The marketing game now is to downsize the "Disney World" or "Magic Mountain" entertainment concept and get it closer to population centers. Pizza Time Theatre is the first legitimate effort to downsize the theme park, cross-positioning it with family dining and then putting it in high demographic areas at reasonable real estate costs. PTT sees the American market as becoming burger-bored, and will continue to emphasize the family entertainment concept in the U.S. and abroad.

Product

Bushnell's perception of the Pizza Time concept (which set the tone of management) was an arcade/entertainment center that sold pizza as well. In contrast, the market viewed PTT as a restaurant. Complaints about food quality were dismissed by Bushnell, and as a result, revenues suffered. By 1983 the central issue of food quality was first addressed when formulating turnaround strategies. However, the focus of the strategies remained a mixture of new robots, new animation, and new video games. According to Bushnell, "It turned out to be a little more of a restaurant than I intended."[7]

The restaurants had an exorbitant degree of operating leverage and depended on cash flow generated by video games for income. Games accounted for 25 percent of a restaurant's sales and provided around 50 percent of the pretax net income. The long-run viability of the Pizza Time concept was tied to the video game industry that Bushnell created.[8]

Price

Pizza Time's pizza was overpriced compared to competing pizza restaurants. PTT's food cost was a low 20 percent of sales compared to an industry average of 28-30 percent. Low food costs were achieved by a reduction of quality/quantity of ingredients on the pizza or overpricing, depending on the point of view. As Senior Vice President of Development Gene Landrum noted: " . . . our customers pass two or three pizza places for the opportunity to spend 15-20 percent more for pizza."[9]

However, several larger companies (Gizmo's: The Greatest Food and Game Invention, Bally's Tom Foolery, Sega Enterprises, and Warner Communications) have opened chains of entertainment centers similar to the Pizza Time Theatre's concept and competition will become increasingly intense.

Competition

PTT's definition of the product narrowed its perception of the competition. Bushnell felt PTT's only competitor was ShowBiz Pizza Place because of its similar format. However, the pizza segment of the fast food industry was experiencing numerous changes that PTT ignored. Industry pizza sales grew from $700 million in 1977 to $6 billion by 1984. Consumer demand shifted from thin crust pizza to "deep dish" or "pan style" pizza—a trend unnoticed by PTT. Pizza Hut, Godfather's, and Domino's grew aggressively during this period.

PTT competes principally with restaurants that offer pizza, although, to a certain extent, it also competes with restaurants offering other types of food. The pizza market is currently dominated by chain restaurants. The pattern of market share is generally regional with the exception of Pizza Hut, a subsidiary of Pepsico, Inc., Pizza Inn, and Shakey's.

Pizza Hut units represent more than 50 percent of the chain-affiliated pizza restaurant market with about 4,000 restaurants in its nationwide chain. Pizza Inn and Shakey's each represent about 10 percent.[10] The balance of the market is fragmented, with most chains operating on a regional basis. PTT also faces competition from local, individually owned pizza restaurants. Many of the company's food service competitors have been established longer and have greater financial and other resources than the company; however, competition in the food industry is generally based upon the quality and price of food products offered, location and attractiveness of facilities, advertising, and quality of service. Based upon these competitive criteria, PTT feels that it will be able to compete successfully in the food industry.

Many of PTT's competitors offer limited entertainment and amusement activities and have provided, and can be expected to continue to provide, entertainment and amusement activities similar to those offered by the company.

ENVIRONMENTAL OUTLOOK

Market Trends

Current trends in the restaurant market suggest an increased emphasis on health and nutrition as a weight-conscious attitude develops. Through the seventies, consumption of poultry and fish increased 38 percent and 21 percent on a per capita basis.[11] In response to changing tastes, menu diversification has been a key strategy. In many situations diversification can hurt profitability if it slows service or increases operating costs. Consumers are demanding increased service, ambience, and comfort for their dollar, suggesting that a high price/value relationship is the key to success.

Pizza Market

The pizza segment of the fast-food market has been growing at a rate of 20 percent annually. In 1980 there were sixty-six franchise pizza chains that amassed sales of nearly $2.4 billion.[12] Sales in 1985 were expected to top the $7 billion mark. The market is appealing because of market share potential. In 1980 Pizza Hut commanded a 22 percent market share as the industry leader. Domino's, in the number two position, had a 6 percent share; and, Godfather's had 5 percent in third place. The remaining market was divided among smaller regional chains (see exhibit 2).

Each of the market leaders has been successful due to its market niche. Pizza Hut is a full-service restaurant that attracts a family clientele. Domino's competes based on convenience in a delivery-only segment. Godfather's appeals primarily to a younger adult crowd.

Economy

The exceptionally strong performance in the restaurant sector should continue, predicts Roger Lipton of Ladenburg, Thalmann and Company. Food prices should be up only modestly, and chains should be able to increase prices in excess of the inflation rate. Further, he doesn't believe that the rate of growth of customer traffic, which has fallen rapidly since the onset of the recession, will deteriorate any more.[13]

Labor and food, the industry's two main expense items, should show only nominal growth. The federally mandated minimum hourly wage was not scheduled to increase in 1982 for the first time since 1973.

With both parents working in more and more families, a higher amount of dining out is ingrained in our life-styles. However, the economic conditions of the U.S. are not predicted to improve much until late second quarter of 1988.[14]

Governmental

PTT is subject to various federal, state, and local laws affecting its business. Federal and state environmental regulations have not materially affected the company's operations, but more stringent and varied requirements of local governmental bodies with respect to zoning, land use, and environment factors have increased, and can be expected to continue to increase, the cost and time of constructing new centers. The most significant of these laws are zoning regulations that restrict the location of facilities which include coin-operated games. In most instances, PTT must obtain zoning variances and use permits for its centers. Although the company has been able to obtain needed variances and permits in the past, changes in zoning laws or in their application could impair the company's ability to open centers in desired locations.

Social

Pizza Time Theatres, Inc., is committed to community service and the education of America's youth. As an example of the total commitment from the top down and throughout the Pizza Time family, Nolan Bushnell, chairman of Pizza Time Theatre, recently received a presidential appointment to serve on the National Advisory Council for Vocational Education. Bushnell will be helping create a national training strategy for America's technological needs over the next two decades. He says, "We need to direct our energies toward job training for industries of the future, and to provide leadership in looking toward our needs for the year 2000."[15]

Another example of social responsibility is Chuck E. Cheese's quest for national computer literacy. The program is offering schools the opportunity to earn a computer through their local Pizza Time Theatres. Pizza Time has a commitment from four leading computer manufacturers to make their computers available to the program at a discount of approximately 50 percent. Schools can earn the balance of the cost of a computer by participating in the Chuck E. Cheese Computer Program.[16]

Financial

Pizza Time Theatre, Inc., has a strong financial base from which to pursue its aggressive growth plans. Since PTT went public, it has raised $37 million with two public offerings. Those funds will be expended to develop new company centers and for working capital purposes. The stock of the company is commanding a price-earnings multiple of thirty-six, which would appear to allow the company to continue to go to the stock market to assist in its growth needs.[17]

PTT's objective is to open sixty to seventy new centers. PTT has never declared or paid a cash dividend and anticipates that, for the foreseeable future, its earnings will be retained for use in its business.

The cost of developing new centers depends on the size of the center and varies considerably among metropolitan areas, primarily due to differences in land prices, construction codes, and labor costs. Currently, PTT's cash investment to develop and open a typical 12,000 to 15,000 square foot center averages approximately $495,000, although actual costs range from approximately $450,000 to $750,000.[18]

Exhibit 3 sets forth certain information regarding the present estimated costs of developing a typical 12,000 to 15,000 square foot company center and the financing provided by the company, the lessor of the land and building, and the lessor of equipment. The sales breakdown for a family entertainment center is

57%:	Food
25%:	Games
17%:	Beverages
1%:	Merchandise

The arcade games usually generate 40 to 50 percent of a center's profits. Partly for this reason, a center typically spewed out three to four times the sales of regular chain pizzerias and up to nine times the profits.

PTT centers averaged $1.19 million in revenues in 1983 compared to ShowBiz's average of $1.45 million. No other competitor in the pizza business touches these results. Pepsico's Pizza Hut, the largest national chain with 20 percent of the $5 billion-a-year pizza market, mustered average sales of $320,000 at each of its 4,000 restaurants in 1983.

Profit margins also rank with the most appetizing among restaurant chains. In 1983, PTT company centers averaged $237,200 in pretax profits, a margin of 20 percent of sales, as compared to ShowBiz's $320,900 and 22.1 percent margin on sales. A 10 percent margin is about par for competing pizza chains. Part of the difference is size, PTT has four to five times the capacity of most chain pizzerias. However, the main reason is all those quarters that go into the games.

The company believes that its business is somewhat seasonal, each center having slightly lower revenues in the second quarter.

FINANCE

Each store opening required almost $500,000 in working capital. The public stock offerings in 1981 brought the company $37 million to fund expansion. The addition of sixty-five company restaurants in 1982 placed considerable demands on working capital, as shown in exhibit 4.

Although assets showed only a slight decline from 1981 to 1982, the company nearly exhausted its cash reserves. Exhibit 5 details the major accounts comprising the assets of PTT. Spending more than $18 million of its cash reserves in 1982, PTT faced 1983 short of the cash required to continue its growth strategy. Given the expansion rate in 1982 and 1983, PTT gambled on operating revenues from existing company centers to fund the growth.

Pizza Time restaurants were sensitive to changes in volume because of their operating leverage. In the second quarter of 1982, pretax margins dropped from 14.2 percent to 12.8 percent.[19] Third quarter pretax margins dropped further to 6 percent. Some stores experienced sales declines that suggested a lack of repeat business.

The $4 billion decline in the video game industry—coupled with poor locations, food, and management—devastated store volume by 1983. Customer counts in 1983 dropped by 18 percent over the previous year as product dissatisfaction grew.[20] Store sales dropped by 15 percent in the first quarter and 20 percent in the second quarter of 1983. An analysis of exhibit 6 illustrates the decline in profitability experienced in 1983.

Although sales revenue increased 53 percent in 1983 over the previous year, operating expenses increased nearly 100 percent. The sharp increase in operating expenses suggests per store sales volumes dropped below the break-even point in most company-owned restaurants. The sharp increase in operating expenses is graphically illustrated in exhibit 7. (See exhibits 8, 9, and 10 for financial statements.)

ShowBiz Pizza Place experienced sales declines in the second half of 1982 as well. Brock promptly discontinued plans for further expansion in 1983 and concentrated instead on improving customer counts. Although aware of the problems, Pizza Time continued to expand in 1983. Almost fifty company stores were built, indicating the inertia of PTT's fast-growth strategy.[21]

Research and Development and Production

Pizza Time Theatre, Inc., has expanded its research and development efforts in two major areas. The first relates to the quality and variety of food offered at Chuck E. Cheese's Family Entertainment Centers. The second relates to Cyberamics.

Pizza Time Theatre, Inc., is opening new family entertainment centers at the rate of one every five days, mainly in the sunbelt and midwest. This rapid growth has put a strain on the entire company. Due to the highly adaptive structure of the company, the materials department, which supplies everything from birthday fliers to children's rides, has reduced the average time an order takes to complete from fourteen days to only three. The distribution center has been reorganized for faster material withdrawal and fewer errors. The traffic manager has reduced outbound freight costs by 40 percent by negotiating a contract with North American Van Lines, by evaluating air forwarders for the lowest cost, and by using new packaging for shipment. Another change is that one person now has sole responsibility for seeing that promotional material gets to the centers.[22]

PTT emphasizes the ''nuts and bolts'' of store operations. In order to achieve this goal, it has improved its training programs, increased the tenure and professionalism of center managers, and provided greater incentives and recognition of store personnel.[23]

Marketing

PTT has one of the best-defined primary markets of any restaurant or entertainment operation that exists today—families with children aged fifteen and under. An important secondary market is group business. With an average restaurant size of 12,000 square feet, PTT encourages group sales. PTT entertainment package and large seating capacity allow it to market with equal success to a soccer team of twenty or a bowling league of 200. Nonprofit organizations are encouraged to use PTT's Community Involvement Nights as a means of fundraising.[24]

PTT relies heavily on local advertising and community promotional activities to develop local patronage. The company conducts a pre-opening marketing program about six weeks prior to the opening of a center, utilizing community relations, newspaper advertisements, direct mail, billboards, radio and television spots, and special promotions, generally involving discounts on food or free merchandise. Once a center is open, the company's marketing strategy is focused on community activities directed at families with children fifteen years old and younger. The company also attempts to ensure maximum customer exposure to its robot characters. Walk-around costumes for a number of the company's robot characters are used in the centers, and their images and names are employed on proprietary merchandise. Use of the walk-around characters in a visitation program to schools, hospitals, sports activities, and community events ensures maximum exposure and consumer recognition and allows creative marketing of the PTT concept outside the centers.

PTT believes its use of tokens is an important factor in its marketing strategy. Generally, games and amusement devices in the centers will accept both quarters and Chuck E. Cheese tokens. To encourage game play, a certain number of free tokens, depending on the size of the food order, accompany food purchases. Tokens are also offered for sale through bill-changer machines at the rate of five tokens per $1.00 and twenty-eight tokens per $5.00. Because the tokens are valid only for game play within a Pizza Time Theatre center, customers are encouraged to use all their tokens in the center.

The family-oriented marketing has added attraction both for parents and the community. PTT discourages the traditional game arcade clientele—males aged thirteen to seventeen—by posting signs outside each restaurant stating that anyone under the age of eighteen must be accompanied by a parent.

PTT capitalizes on the twenty-minute order cycle (a disadvantage for conventional pizza restaurants) by diverting waiting parents and young children with electronic animals singing and laughing at their own silly jokes. Those customers not thrilled by skits wile away the time in electronic game arcades, having been lured in by a few free tokens given away with food orders. The typical customer comes back once every two months, there to linger for one-and-a-half hours on average. A family of four spends $22 to $24 a visit. PTT hopes to increase those visits to once a month with additional advertising on children's television programs and direct mail promotional campaigns. A new sandwich program and a special lunch promotion program were introduced in 1983, aimed toward working adults and increased daytime sales.

Structure

PTT has a flexible organizational form. This form is appropriate because the environment is relatively uncertain and turbulent, the goals are diverse and changing, the technology is complex and dynamic, and there are many nonroutine activities in which creativity and innovation are important. Heuristic decision-making processes are utilized and coordination and control occur through reciprocal adjustments (see exhibit 11).

Managerial

Bushnell has served as chairman of the board and chief executive officer of PTT since its incorporation in May 1978. Bushnell and Keenan conceived the basic idea of the company in 1976 at Atari, Inc., a pioneer in the video game industry, and organized an operating group to implement the concept. Bushnell, a founder of Atari, served as one of its chief executive officers until he left to develop PTT in early 1979. He continues to serve in a consulting capacity to Atari. (Exhibit 12 lists the present executive officers of PTT.)

Keenan joined PTT in 1979. Mr. Keenan was the cofounder and president of Kee Games, Inc., and operated that company until its merger with Atari in 1974. Following the merger, Keenan became president of Atari and, in November 1978, became chairman of the board. In September 1979, Keenan resigned as chairman of Atari (where he continues to serve as a consultant) to become president and chief operating officer of PTT.

Koenig joined PTT in September 1980. From August 1979 to September 1980, he served as vice president of finance and administration for First International Service Corporation, a franchiser of beauty salons.

Scott joined PTT in 1981. Prior to joining the company, he had been employed for more than five years by Wendy's International, Inc., a hamburger restaurant chain, as director of franchise sales and development.

Landrum joined PTT in May 1978 and served as its president until September 1979. He was employed by Atari from May 1976 until May 1978 as assistant to the chairman of the board and chief operating officer of Atari's restaurant division.

CONCLUSION

Pizza Time Theatre, Inc., is a dynamic, growth-oriented, family entertainment company that believes its pizza restaurants are places for families to enjoy their leisure. The company has proven its adaptive organizational style by recognizing the need for change and continual refinement of its product. People are the key and will continue to be the key to success at PTT, and management has established an environment, a Pizza Family atmosphere, that motivates and appropriately rewards its employees.

Growth is both a blessing and a potential handicaap at PTT. Growth has helped create the exciting family atmosphere and synergy now enjoyed. However, if that growth is not able to be managed, and strategies designed to deal with it, PTT might become just another flash in the pan in the fast-food restaurant industry.

QUESTIONS

1 How many family entertainment centers will the market bear? The growth objective of PTT is to have 1,000 centers in the U.S. by 1985; however, ShowBiz (PTT's only serious competition) predicts it will also have 1,000 restaurants, and no one knows how much the market can consume.
2 Is the PTT concept just another flash in the pan for the fast-food restaurant industry?
3 What changes will be needed in the management team and the structure to allow everyone to perform their jobs adequately, given the high-growth stage PTT is currently encountering?
4 What is the future availability of prime sites for Chuck E. Cheese's Pizza Time Theatres? Obtaining prime sites is important in the competitive battle with ShowBiz, because they compete with relatively slender distinctions.
5 When is the best time to issue more stock to finance the growth objectives?

Notes

1 Pizza Time Theatre, Inc., Annual Report, 1981.
2 Pizza Time Theatre, Inc., Form 10-K, December 27, 1981.
3 Pizza Time Theatre, Inc., 3rd Quarter Interim Report, September 6, 1982.
4 Annual Report.

5 Form 10-K.

6 Ibid.

7 David Pauley, Richard Sanders, and Marilyn Achiron, "Hard Times for Pizza Time," *Newsweek*, January 23, 1984, 48.

8 Ibid.

9 Betsy R. Gullickson, "The Electronic Restaurants," *Restaurants and Institutions*, February 1, 1982, 48.

10 Form 10-K.

11 Standard and Poors, "Industry Surveys," January 26, 1984, 132.

12 Ibid.

13 "Making Dough at Pizza Time," *Dun's Business*, December 1981, 56.

14 Ibid.

15 Suzie Crocker, "Bushnell Appointed to National council," *The Pizza Times*, October 1982, 4.

16 Suzie Crocker, "Chuck E. Cheese Computer Program," *The Pizza Times*, October 1982, 6.

17 Form 10-K.

18 Ibid.

19 Stephen Taub, "A Noisy Decline," *Financial World*, November 30, 1983, 40.

20 "The Pitfalls in Mixing Pizza and Video Games," *Business Week*, March 12, 1984, 33.

21 Stephen Taub, 42.

22 John Scott, "Operations Outlook," *The Pizza Times*, October 1982, 3.

23 Ibid.

24 Ibid.

EXHIBIT 1
Pizza Time Theatre, Inc., Centers in Operation, December 31

Year	Company	Franchised	Revenues (in thousands)
1979	6	1	$ 3,066
1980	14	11	11,426
1981	44	44	36,219
1982	109	95	99,286
1983	148	118	151,843

EXHIBIT 2
Distribution of Market Share for the Pizza Industry

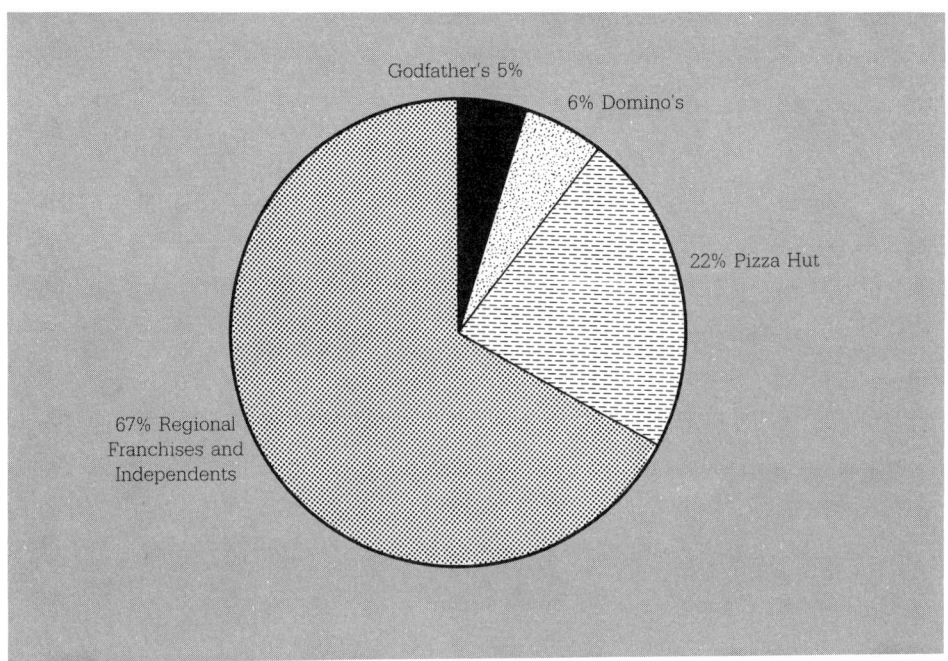

EXHIBIT 3
Estimated Cost of Developing a New Center

| | | Approximate Financing Provided | | |
Description	Approximate Cost	Company	Real Estate Lessor	Equipment Lessor
Land and building	$ 800,000	$ —	$800,000	$ —
Leasehold improvements	280,000	240,000	40,000	
Cyberamics	103,000			103,000
Games	175,000	145,000		30,000
Furniture, fixtures, and equipment	177,000	10,000		167,000
Pre-opening expenses and working capital	100,000	100,000		
TOTAL	$1,635,000	$495,000	$840,000	$300,000

EXHIBIT 4
Pizza Time Theatre, Inc., Liquidity Analysis (in thousands)

Year	Current Assets	Current Liabilities	Working Capital	Current Ratio
1979	$ 687	$ 1,085	$ (398)	.63
1980	2,665	2,075	590	1.28
1981	31,496	9,994	21,502	3.15
1982	26,060	21,818	4,242	1.19

EXHIBIT 5
Pizza Time Theatre, Inc., Selected Current Asset Accounts (in thousands)

	Cash & Equiv.	Receivables	Inventories
1979	$ 127	$ 59	$ 429
1980	194	661	1,666
1981	22,179	2,364	6,524
1982	3,736	5,131	12,647
1983	—	5,430	3,372

EXHIBIT 6
Pizza Time Theater, Inc., Consolidated Statement of Income and Expenses (not consolidated through 1981) (in thousands)

Years Ended 12/31	Sales, Revenues	Costs, Expenses	Depreciation Depletion	Income Tax	Net Income
1978	$ 348	$ 733	$ 140	$ —	$ (525)
1979	3,066	4,088	302	—	(1,324)
1980	11,426	10,548	786	—	92
1981	36,219	30,623	2,344	651	2,201
1982	99,286	81,546	8,922	1,310	7,508
1983	151,483	163,003*	21,060	(1,283)	(31,297)**

*Before asset writedown of $45,412

**Before asset writedown above and losses from discontinued operations $4,907

EXHIBIT 7
Pizza Time Theatre, Inc, Comparison of Sales Revenues to Operating Expenses

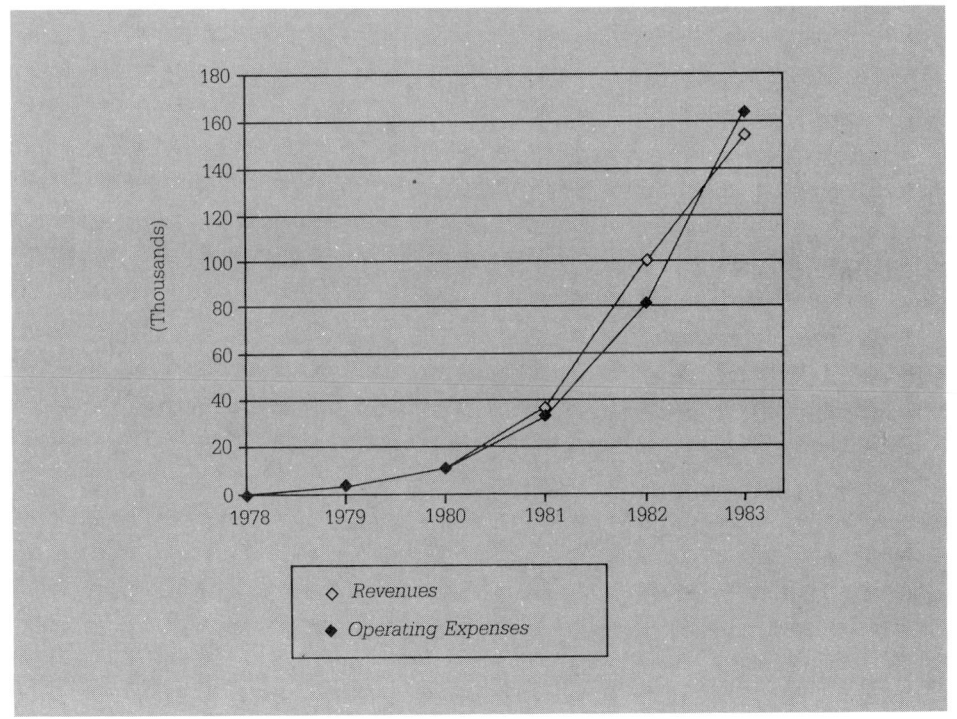

EXHIBIT 8
Pizza Time Theatre, Inc. (Debtor in Possession) Consolidated Statements of Operations

	Fiscal Year Ended		
	December 27, 1981	December 30, 1982	December 29, 1983
Revenues			
Company centers...	$29,547,007	$82,580,391	$132,180,101
Royalties and franchise fees	2,624,254	8,508,940	10,477,789
Other revenues	4,047,653	8,196,737	9,185,415
Total revenues	36,218,914	99,286,068	151,843,305
Costs and expenses			
Company centers:			
Cost of sales...	13,472,154	36,539,861	64,429,551
Operating expenses	9,592,524	29,712,603	66,022,015
Product costs...	2,834,582	6,101,313	9,360,078
Research and engineering	—	—	559,775
Selling, general and administrative expenses.....	7,503,188	17,155,941	35,818,202
Interest expense (income), net...........................	(435,590)	959,114	7,872,796
Provision for center closings/asset writedown....	—	—	45,412,353
Total costs and expenses.......................	32,966,858	90,468,832	229,474,770
Income (loss) from continuing operations before income taxes	3,252,056	8,817,236	(77,631,465)
Income taxes (benefit)	651,000	1,309,500	(1,282,597)
Income (loss) from continuing operations.......................................	2,601,056	7,507,736	(76,348,868)
Income (loss) from discontinued operations	—	—	(3,357,220)
Provision for loss on disposal of discontinued operations...	—	—	(1,550,000)
Net income (loss)	$ 2,601,056	$ 7,507,736	$ (81,256,088)
Earnings (loss) per common share and common share equivalent:			
Continuing operations	$0.58	$1.27	$(12.65)
Discontinued operations, including loss on disposal...	—	—	$ (0.81)
Net earnings (loss)	$0.58	$1.27	$(13.46)
Weighted average number of common and common equivalent shares outstanding	4,492,265	5,893,098	6,035,874

EXHIBIT 9
Pizza Time Theatre, Inc. (Debtor in Possession) Consolidated Statements of Shareholders' Equity (Deficit)

PIZZA TIME THEATRE, INC.
(DEBTOR IN POSSESSION)

CONSOLIDATED STATEMENTS OF SHAREHOLDERS' EQUITY (DEFICIT)

	Common Stock		Preferred Stock		Retained Earnings (Accumulated Deficit)	Total
	Number of Shares	Amount	Number of Shares	Amount		
Balance at December 28, 1980	2,925,746	$ 4,233,043	730,980	$3,323,907	$ (1,672,465)	$ 5,884,485
Sale of stock under stock option plans	102,519	394,467	—	—	—	394,467
Sale of stock to public	1,933,166	35,938,344	—	—	—	35,938,344
Conversion of preferred to common stock	730,980	3,323,907	(730,980)	(3,323,907)	—	—
Net income	—	—	—	—	2,601,056	2,601,056
Balance at December 27, 1981	5,692,411	43,889,761	—	—	928,591	44,818,352
Sale of stock under stock option plans	90,395	242,923	—	—	—	242,923
Issuance of stock in connection with acquisitions	44,435	1,191,466	—	—	—	1,191,466
Net income	—	—	—	—	7,507,736	7,507,736
Balance at December 30, 1982	5,827,241	45,324,150	—	—	8,436,327	53,760,477
Sale of stock under stock option plans	17,781	118,315	—	—	—	118,315
Issuance of stock in connection with acquisitions	263,143	2,067,859	—	—	—	2,067,859
Net loss	—	—	—	—	(81,256,088)	(81,256,088)
Balance at December 29, 1983	6,108,165	$47,510,324	—	$ —	$ (72,819,761)	$ (25,309,437)

See accompanying notes to consolidated financial statements.

EXHIBIT 10
Pizza Time Theatre, Inc. (Debtor in Possession) Consolidated Statements of
Changes in Financial Position

PIZZA TIME THEATRE, INC.
(DEBTOR IN POSSESSION)

CONSOLIDATED STATEMENTS OF CHANGES IN FINANCIAL POSITION

	Fiscal Year Ended		
	December 27, 1981	December 30, 1982	December 29, 1983
Sources of working capital:			
Net income (loss) from continuing operations	$ 2,601,056	$ 7,507,736	$ (76,348,868)
Items which do not use working capital:			
Depreciation and amortization	2,256,267	8,922,145	21,060,215
Deferred income taxes (benefit)	334,000	1,000,665	(1,334,665)
Reserve for center closings	—	—	34,453,437
Write-down of property, equipment and leasehold improvements	—	—	8,500,000
Working capital provided (used) by continuing operations	5,191,323	17,430,546	(13,669,881)
Net income (loss) from discontinued operations, including loss on disposal	—	—	(4,907,220)
Depreciation and amortization	—	—	409,175
Working capital provided (used) by operations .	5,191,323	17,430,546	(18,167,926)
Net book value of property and equipment dispositions	163,223	146,364	7,141,355
Decrease in long-term receivables	—	145,000	—
Decrease in other assets	—	—	74,377
Proceeds from long-term borrowings	11,407,433	41,212,325	41,173,732
Proceeds from subordinated debentures	—	—	50,000,000
Additions to deferred income	188,588	784,994	—
Sale of stock	36,332,811	242,923	118,315
Issuance of stock in acquisitions	—	1,191,466	2,067,859
Decrease in working capital	—	17,521,304	98,768,309
	$53,283,378	$ 78,674,922	$181,176,021
Uses of working capital:			
Additions to property and equipment	$23,508,754	$ 62,348,207	$ 57,473,375
Additions to other assets	228,577	2,733,912	—
Decrease in deferred income	—	—	973,582
Repayment of long-term debt	8,004,786	13,592,803	53,119,838
Reclassification of long-term debt to current.....	—	—	69,609,226
Increase in working capital	21,541,261	—	—
	$53,283,378	$ 78,674,922	$181,176,021
Changes in components of working capital:			
Increase (decrease) in current assets:			
Cash	$21,984,627	$ (18,443,291)	$ (3,735,505)
Receivables	1,703,041	2,766,911	298,794
Inventories	4,858,246	6,123,228	(9,275,093)
Prepaid expenses	284,800	870,629	(973,661)
Center pre-opening expenses	1,292,000	1,955,000	(3,247,000)
Net assets of discontinued operations	—	—	4,388,647
	30,122,714	(6,727,523)	(12,543,818)
Increase (decrease) in current liabilities:			
Bank overdraft	—	—	2,515,567
Accounts payable	5,813,162	2,092,813	(620,203)
Accrued liabilities	972,370	1,894,388	2,772,912
Income taxes payable	317,000	99,264	(416,264)
Current debt.............................	628,421	7,197,831	31,139,605
Subordinated debentures	—	—	50,000,000
Deferred income	850,500	(490,515)	832,874
	8,581,453	10,793,781	86,224,491
Increase (decrease) in working capital	$21,541,261	$ (17,521,304)	$ (98,768,309)

See accompanying notes to consolidated financial statements.

EXHIBIT 11
Pizza Time Theatre's Organizational Chart

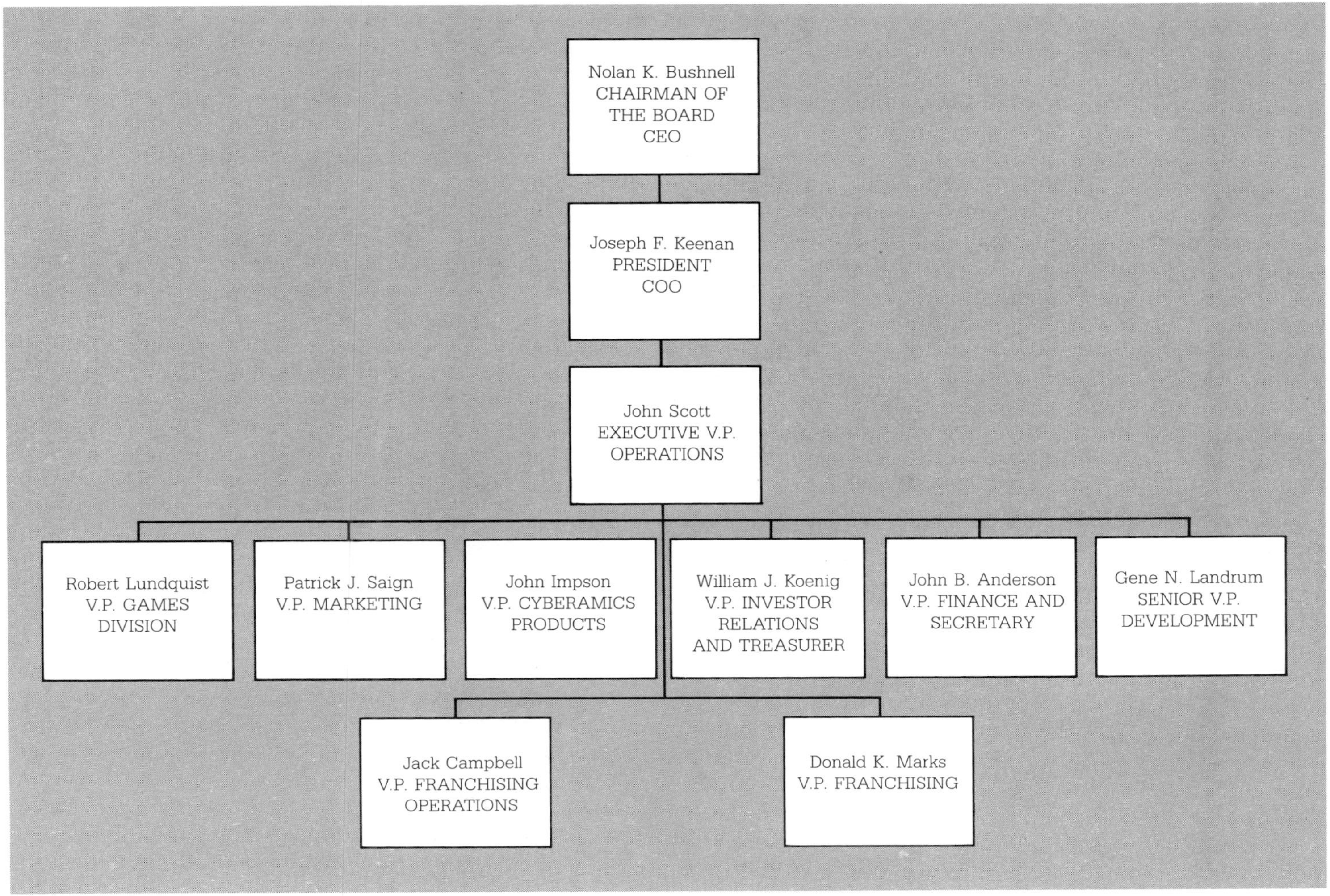

EXHIBIT 12
Executive Officers of Pizza Time Theatre

Name	Position with Company	Age in 1983
Nolan K. Bushnell	Chairman of the Board and Chief Executive Officer	39
Joseph F. Keenan	President, Chief Operating Officer and Director	40
William J. Koenig	Vice President, Investor Relations and Treasurer	51
John Scott	Executive Vice President, Operations	38
Gene N. Landrum	Senior Vice President, Development	45
Donald K. Marks	Vice President, Franchising	38
John Impson	Vice President, Cyberamics Products	38
Patrick J. Saign	Vice President, Marketing	34
John B. Anderson	Vice President, Finance and Secretary	38
Robert Lundquist	Vice President, Games Division	32
Jack Campbell	Vice President, Franchise Operations	38

The American Sign and Indicator Corporation

Donald F. Harvey

INTRODUCTION

At American Sign and Indicator, management was reflecting on twenty-five consecutive years of growth. This was a rewarding example of opportunity and fulfillment, working within the framework of the American free enterprise system—an achievement that could only happen in America. Looking ahead, it was clear that a continued high level of activity would be required to meet the challenge of successfully expanding their marketing thrust into the dynamic electronic information industry. Changes that had been made within the company over the past year would help assure that success.

As chief executive officer Luke G. Williams noted,

> June 25, 1977 marked the 25th anniversary of the American Sign and Indicator Corporation. During this period of time, our company has grown from an embryonic beginning with $600 capital to the largest on-premise sign company in the world.
>
> We are naturally proud of this accomplishment and feel it is a tribute to the American free enterprise system—living proof that in a free society the opportunity still exists to invent a product and develop an organization that will provide real and valuable services to users. With these elements identified, capital and creative people can be attracted to chart the course and provide the energy to build a new industry.
>
> However, even with the past growth record of our company, we stand today on the threshold of future opportunities that pale our past accomplishments. We anticipate these opportunities with great enthusiasm and confidence.

COMPANY BACKGROUND

The American Sign and Indicator story is one of American entrepreneurship. Luke Williams Jr. and his brother Chuck started the business in 1946 with $600 capital. They were inspired by their father, who was a commercial sign painter and a pictorial artist.

Over the years the company experienced many ups and downs, hovering near bankruptcy at times. It has expanded its production facilities, hired more employees, and diversified into different kinds of signs.

Today, American Sign and Indicator remains the largest specialized sign leasing company in America and the only sign company that operates nationally. It believes its customer base will be expanding shortly with the new unisplay technology. Unisplay technology, marketed under the trade name "Unex," provides total flexibility and versatility in many aspects of signs. Letter sizes, letter styles, languages, and graphics of many varieties will be available.

The company is engaged in the electronic visual communications business. It designs, engineers, and manufactures a broad range of electronic visual-communications display products and systems. It also provides for the installation of such products and continuing maintenance. Two basic technologies are used in its products: the lamp-matrix technology, which uses individual incandescent lamps and the dot-matrix display, which is basic to the Unex technology and utilizes computer-controlled electromagnets to open and close apertures to reveal light from a common light source. Its lamp-matrix products include alternating time and temperature displays, message centers, and indoor and outdoor sports scoreboards for university and professional stadiums. Its dot-matrix Unex display products are used for public service messages, advertising, internal corporate communications, flight information, and other applications. The company believes that it is the leading producer of lamp-matrix electronic display products and systems in the world and is the only manufacturer of Unex technology products in the world, excluding Japan. Although the company's customers consist primarily of banks and savings and loan associations, they also include an increasing number of industrial and commercial concerns. The company is presently serving over 7,200 customers on a worldwide basis.

As of October 31, 1980, the company employed 598 persons, of whom 187 were engaged in production activities (including supervisors, technicians, and assembly personnel), 167 in sales and marketing, 132 in service and installation, and 112 in executive, supervisory, clerical, administrative, and accounting positions. In October 1979, the company employed 691 persons.

FINANCIAL OPERATIONS

The consolidated statement of operation represents the consolidated operating results of American Sign and Indicator Corporation and subsidiaries for the five years ended April 30, 1980 (see exhibit 1).

MARKETING

The company designs, engineers, manufactures, and provides installation and maintenance services for a broad range of electronic visual communications systems and display products. These consist of alternating time and temperature displays, lamp-matrix message centers, indoor and outdoor sports scoreboards, and Unex display systems.

From the organization of the company in 1952 through approximately 1970, the company's principal source of revenues was derived from the sale and lease of alternating time and temperature displays to financial institutions. During the 1970s the company expanded the basic time and temperature display technology to include a variety of sequential message and sports information display systems and, in 1975, it purchased the rights to manufacture, sell, and exploit patented technology which is being marketed by the company under the name "Unex." Recognizing the appeal of certain of its products as an advertising medium, the company has begun to broaden its market to include commercial customers such as automobile dealerships and shopping centers. The company has also begun to market certain of its products to industrial customers seeking a medium through which to communicate with their employees.

Principal Products

Lamp-Matrix Displays

Time and Temperature Displays   Time and temperature displays consist of an incandescent lamp-matrix display that shows time and temperature alternately. The time and temperature display is typically installed outside a building and advertises the name, slogan, and/or logo of the customer combined with the alternating time and temperature display. The time and temperature display was invented by Charles Williams, senior vice president and co-founder of the company, and is marketed under the name "Double TT"™ primarily to banks and savings and loan associations throughout the country. The time and temperature display can be programmed to show both Fahrenheit and Celsius readings. The company has installed in excess of 5,200 time and temperature display systems, with over 80 percent owned by the company and leased to customers. Sales prices for time and temperature display systems currently range from approximately $10,000 to $20,000.

Message Centers   Electronic message-center displays ("Message Centers") consist of an incandescent lamp matrix that is capable of displaying sequential messages and a microprocessor data-base controller which is programmed to display such messages. The control system generally consists of a signaling and information storage device such as a computer. The signaling and storage device sends a message through data cable or telephone lines to a lamp-matrix controller in the vicinity of the display. The controller then sends an on–off signal to each lamp in the display resulting in a message. Message Centers can combine the features of a time and temperature service with a message; they are primarily used by financial and commercial customers to promote their services and products and to provide community service information. To date, the company has installed over 1,200 Message

Centers, with more than 80 percent owned by the company and leased to customers. Sales prices for Message Centers currently range from approximately $12,000 to $120,000.

Other   The company also manufactures several products which utilize Message Center components, including displays showing the Dow Jones stock averages and highway displays indicating traffic patterns and warnings. The company designed a display system known as "Spectacolor," a multicolor lamp matrix capable of providing continuous messages with animation features. The company was granted a limited license for the sale of its multicolor animation system. Spectacolor is typically used by a customer to produce revenue from the sale of advertising time on the display. The most well-known Spectacolor system is located in New York City's Times Square.

Sports Information Systems

A sports information system is a display which consists of a combination of animation panels, Message Centers, Unex displays, and scoring formats for the various events held in sports complexes. Sports information systems can include large computer-memory storage capacities, four-color display capability, and grayscale capability, which is an enlarged simulation of black and white television. The company manufactures these systems for university and professional sports complexes. Recent installations include systems in the Rose Bowl, Oklahoma University, University of Alabama, University of Notre Dame, Reunion Arena in Dallas, RFK Stadium in Washington, D.C., and Balboa Stadium in San Diego. Other sports information systems manufactured by the company include those in Madison Square Garden in New York City, Riverfront Stadium in Cincinnati, and Pontiac Stadium in Detroit. The company is currently designing a mobile system for the Tournament Players Association, Inc., for use at golf courses on the PGA tour.

Sports information systems are generally sold, as opposed to leased, and payments are sometimes made on an installment basis over a period of up to ten years. In connection with the sale of a sports information system, the company often arranges for advertisers to purchase and donate the scoreboard to a university or professional stadium. To date, the company has installed in excess of 250 sports information systems in the United States.

Unex

Unex displays consist of fluorescent lights in an enclosure, the design of which is a matrix of apertures that may be selectively opened or closed magnetically by a computer-controlled head which sweeps the face of the enclosure changing the message displayed in a matter of seconds. The company has developed several computer controllers for the Unex system, which provide versatility in the letter sizes, letter styles, languages, colors, and graphics used in the display of messages. In addition, computer memory sources make it possible for numerous messages consisting of both text and graphics to be programmed for sequential display. Messages are displayed in light with an extremely high resolution which provides greater clarity with lower energy requirements than conventional incandescent lamp-matrix displays. Unex displays lend themselves to both interior and exterior use and are being used for transportation information systems in airports and train stations, as advertising displays for stores, shopping centers, automobile dealerships, and broadcast stations, and for marquees at arenas and public entertainment facilities. Recent Unex installations include transportation information systems at Miami International Airport and Taiwan's International Airport. The company has also recently begun to market Unex display systems for internal communications in industrial plants.

The company obtained the right to manufacture, sell, and exploit the Unex technology pursuant to a license agreement entered into in April 1975 with Unisplay S.A., a Swiss corporation that is the owner of the patent related to Unex. The license agreement granted to the company the exclusive right to sell in North and South America, excluding Canada, the West Indies, and the Republic of Guyana. The license agreement was amended in February, 1979, to give the company the exclusive right to manufacture, sell, and exploit such technology in Canada, and on a nonexclusive basis, to do so elsewhere in the world, except Japan. The company is required under the license agreement to pay presently a minimum royalty of $33,000 per quarter, subject to adjustment, to Unisplay until the applicable U.S. patent expires in 1988. The company spent an aggregate of approximately $3,500,000 on the development and improvement of the Unex display.

Through 1980, the company has installed in excess of 585 Unex units. The sales price for a single Unex display system, including a controller, currently ranges from approximately $5,000 to $70,000, while the sales prices for multiple unit Unex installations, such as a transportation information system, range up to $1,000,000.

Marketing and Customers

The company markets its products from three regional offices located in Jacksonville, Florida; Dallas, Texas; and Spokane, Washington. The company has divided each region into a number of districts which are the exclusive territory of individual salespersons. Regional offices provide administrative, art, and other support services for marketing and sales personnel. The company obtains customer leads through advertising programs, industry trade shows, referrals from customers, and unsolicited direct calls by company sales personnel.

At the beginning of fiscal 1980, the company shifted its marketing emphasis toward the sale or lease of newly manufactured products and away from rewriting contracts for existing installations. The company also changed its sales force compensation arrangements to provide for the payment of a substantially larger commission on new product sales or leases than on renewals, as well as for the payment of a bonus based upon designated quotas.

The company's products are sold abroad in over ten foreign countries through company personnel and independent sales representatives, including, in Mexico, sales through a 49 percent company-owned corporation. To date, foreign sales have not been material to the company's operations.

Historically, the company has sold or leased its products principally to banks and savings and loan associations. However, the company has more recently attempted to broaden its customer base to include commercial and industrial concerns. During the five fiscal years ended April 30, 1980, and six months ended October 31, 1980, no single customer of the company accounted for as much as 10 percent of net sales of installed displays in any period.

Competition

Although there are no reliable statistics available, the company believes that it is the leading producer of lamp-matrix electronic display products and systems in the world. The company is one of the few manufacturers of electronic display systems which markets its products nationwide directly to end users. The company competes with numerous firms, most of whom operate regionally or locally. In certain instances, some of these competitors may realize cost advantages for particular displays. However, the company believes that its reputation for innovation, quality manufacture, and complete service, together with its ability to maintain leasing programs and to undertake large display commitments, can, in many cases, overcome competitor's price advantages.

The company competes, through the sales of its products, for customers' advertising dollars with numerous advertising media, including billboards, newspapers, radio, and television. The company believes that its products compete effectively for advertising expenditures on the basis of lower overall costs to reach the desired customer in a user's primary advertising market area.

Major U.S. competitors are

1 Everbrite Electric Signs, Inc., South Milwaukee, Wisconsin. 1978 sales $29 million. 430 employees.
2 Cummings Incorporated International Sign SV, Nashville, Tennessee. 1978 sales of $29 million. 666 employees.

Cummings makes, installs and maintains electrical signs which are sold or leased throughout the United States and Canada. Through a system of local sign firms (about 170 as of December 31, 1979) licensed by it, Cummings offers nationwide installation and maintenance service to its national customers. Financial ratios of Cummings Incorporated are shown in exhibit 3.

Research and Development

The company devotes a substantial portion of its operating budget to research and engineering of new products and improvements to its current product lines. During the fiscal year ended April 30, 1980, the company spent approximately $1,155,000 for redesign of the Unex display and engineering, an increase from approximately $673,000 during the preceding fiscal year. In October, 1980, forty-nine employees of the company, including approximately fifteen engineers, were engaged in research and engineering activities.

The company is currently concentrating its research and engineering efforts upon improving and expanding the capabilities of its existing products and upon applying its technology to reduce the energy costs associated with the use of its products. The company expects to market in fiscal 1981 a new product line known as the "Solar Matrix." As part of the Solar Matrix line, the company has recently introduced a low-energy "7-Segment Time and Temperature Display" which utilizes light-reflective modules.

MANAGEMENT

Exhibit 4 outlines principal management personnel and their relationships.

The organization chart of AS&I is as follows (as of October, 1980):

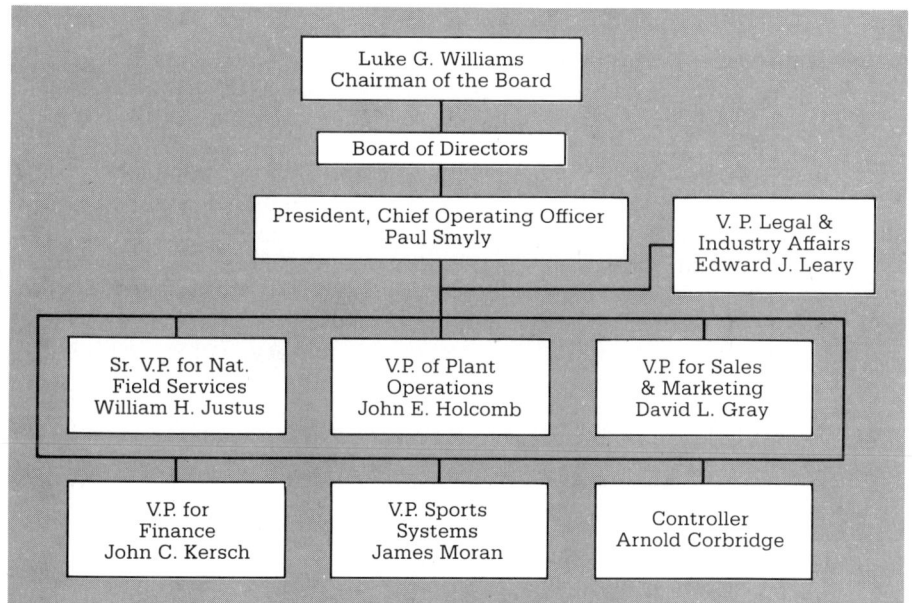

CONCLUSION

In 1980, Luke G. Williams was looking ahead to the 1980s:

> In the 79–80 fiscal year ending April 30, American Sign and Indicator Corporation generated gross sales of $46,008,000, a four percent increase over the

previous year, but short of our $51 million budgeted goal. The decline in our sales occurred during the first quarter of calendar year 1980 when interest rates soared creating a "wait and see" attitude by our market. Revenues from installations for the fiscal year were $42,900,000 as compared to our plan for the year of $42,539,000. Net earnings were $1,055,000 as compared to our fiscal year projections of $1,511,000. Earnings were materially impacted by higher than projected interest rates which, essentially, diluted our earnings from potentially record levels to the lowest in years.

The 79–80 fiscal year was a difficult and uncertain period; however, necessities of the times precipitated certain changes and alterations in our organization which assure our continued confidence in the company's future.

At the beginning of the 79–80 fiscal year, an overhead reduction plan was implemented. This plan was carried on through the year and resulted in more than $2 million in cost savings. The plan called for reduction of overhead in all areas in the company. One area dramatically affected by the overhead reduction plan was the sales and service organization, wherein we reduced our number of regional offices from six to three. The three former regional offices were converted into sales and service facilities. These changes, while significant in cost reduction, have not affected our ability to sell our products and service our customers.

Another notable accomplishment during the year was the completion of the Unex development project. The initially designed product lacked a reliability factor associated with our product lines. The greatly improved reliability factor as well as customer acceptance of this product during the past twelve months has indeed been gratifying. In each succeeding month sales have increased, proving the early optimism we had for this unique communications technology. We continue to find new applications and markets for the Unex technology and look to it as being a major product line in our future.

Our company is placing greater emphasis on professional management. Paul Smyly joined our company early last fiscal year as Executive Vice President and was elected President on May 1, 1980. We are planning other high-level additions in the future to support orderly management succession and to upgrade the leadership of our company.

As Luke Williams prepared to meet with his management committee, he wondered what direction American Sign and Indicator's future strategy for growth should take.

EXHIBIT 1

	Year Ended April 30,					Six Months Ended October 31,	
	1976 (Unaudited)(b)	1977	1978	1979	1980	1979 (Unaudited)	1980 (Unaudited)
Net lease sales (c)	$ 7,610,734	$11,252,169	$13,151,962	$15,056,771	$15,702,444	$ 5,693,355	$ 5,318,922
Direct sales	4,334,609	4,907,797	9,163,820	9,729,547	9,639,584	3,588,925	5,781,724
Net sales of installed displays ..	11,945,343	16,159,966	22,315,782	24,786,318	25,342,028	9,282,280	11,100,646
Cost to build, ship and install displays (Note 4)	5,196,188	8,178,341	9,088,844	11,441,891	12,272,176	4,304,783	5,611,862
Gross profit	6,749,155	7,981,625	13,226,938	13,344,427	13,069,852	4,977,497	5,488,784
Finance revenue earned	8,066,301	8,928,080	9,306,083	9,726,552	11,220,340	5,641,177	5,625,729
Maintenance revenue earned ..	2,744,484	3,191,640	3,648,740	4,201,399	4,973,764	2,321,326	2,492,771
Net revenue on installed displays	17,559,940	20,101,345	26,181,761	27,272,378	29,263,956	12,940,000	13,607,284
Gain on sale of contracts (Note 11)	—	—	—	126,483	1,190,095	—	2,523,770
	17,559,940	20,101,345	26,181,761	27,398,861	30,454,051	12,940,000	16,131,054
Operating expenses: Interest (Note 11)	3,033,477	3,036,486	3,932,942	6,278,749	10,523,173	4,408,216	4,965,520
Maintenance	2,467,381	3,132,167	3,530,107	3,594,579	4,116,771	2,050,688	2,227,763
Selling, general and administrative	8,906,051	11,581,968	15,072,810	17,501,992	15,625,841	7,274,133	6,956,430
Total operating expenses	14,406,909	17,750,621	22,535,859	27,375,320	30,265,785	13,733,037	14,149,713
Operating income (loss)	3,153,031	2,350,724	3,645,902	23,541	188,266	(793,037)	1,981,341
Other income (deductions): Interest (Note 11)	—	661,298	179,987	159,836	153,007	50,410	85,173
Other, net	(120,969)	162,121	479,144	54,434	145,131	279,186	117,803
	(120,969)	823,419	659,131	214,270	298,138	329,596	202,976
Earnings (loss) before income taxes	3,032,062	3,174,143	4,305,033	237,811	486,404	(463,441)	2,184,317
Income tax provision (benefit) (Note 9)	1,316,524	1,324,823	1,738,739	(214,474)	59,160	(340,625)	950,851
Net earnings (loss) (Note 14)	$ 1,715,538	$ 1,849,320	$2,566,294	$ 452,285	$ 427,244	$ (122,816)	$ 1,233,466
Earnings (loss) per share	$ .75	$ .81	$1.13	$ .20	$ .19	$(.05)	$ .54
Ratio of earnings to fixed charges(d): Actual	1.96	1.99	2.05	1.04	1.05	.90	1.43
Pro forma (unaudited) ..					1.05		1.38
Average shares outstanding ...	2,272,500	2,272,500	2,272,500	2,272,500	2,272,500	2,272,500	2,272,929
Dividends per share	$ .14	$ .20	$ .20	$ .10	$ .05	$ .05	$ –0–

Numerical note references are to Notes to Consolidated Financial Statements.

EXHIBIT 1 (continued)

NOTES TO CONSOLIDATED STATEMENTS OF OPERATIONS

(a) See Note 1 to Consolidated Financial Statements for a summary of significant accounting policies.

(b) Although the financial statements for the year ended April 30, 1976 were originally audited, they were not reaudited subsequent to being adjusted to conform with new lease accounting principles set forth in Statement of Financial Accounting Standards No. 13, "Accounting for Leases", which was issued in November 1976.

(c) The amount of net lease sales is derived as follows:

	Year Ended April 30,					Six Months Ended October 31,	
	1976 (Unaudited)	1977	1978	1979	1980	1979 (Unaudited)	1980 (Unaudited)
Gross lease sales..	$20,378,798	$28,122,539	$30,561,007	$35,333,282	$36,259,166	$15,199,856	$13,233,473
Less:							
Unearned finance revenue	10,034,169	12,997,420	12,676,925	15,406,420	19,191,260	8,507,367	6,710,047
Unearned maintenance revenue .	2,733,895	3,872,950	4,732,120	4,870,091	1,365,462	999,134	1,204,504
	12,768,064	16,870,370	17,409,045	20,276,511	20,556,722	9,506,501	7,914,551
Net lease sales	$ 7,610,734	$11,252,169	$13,151,962	$15,056,771	$15,702,444	$ 5,693,355	$ 5,318,922

(d) For the purpose of calculating the ratio of earnings to fixed charges: (1) earnings have been calculated by adding to net earnings (loss), interest expense, the amount of taxes on earnings and the interest component of rent expense, and (2) fixed charges comprise total interest and the interest component of rent expense. The pro forma ratios of earnings to fixed charges give effect to the issuance of the Debentures offered hereby, the elimination of interest expense on the bank borrowings to be repaid with the net proceeds of this offering and the reduction in the effective interest rate on bank borrowings resulting from the new term loan and revolving credit agreement. The Debentures will require initial annual interest payments of $3,750,000.

EXHIBIT 2

Management's Discussion and Analysis of Financial Condition and Results of Operations

MANAGEMENT'S DISCUSSION AND ANALYSIS OF FINANCIAL CONDITION AND RESULTS OF OPERATIONS

NET SALES OF INSTALLED DISPLAYS	Year Ended April 30,					Six Months Ended October 31,	
	1976	1977	1978	1979	1980	1979	1980
	(in thousands of dollars)						
Net sales of installed displays	$11,945	$16,160	$22,316	$24,786	$25,342	$ 9,282	$11,101
Cost to build, ship and install displays	$ 5,196	$ 8,178	$ 9,089	$11,442	$12,272	$ 4,305	$ 5,612

Net sales of installed displays increased at an annual compounded rate of 36.7% over the three fiscal years ended April 30, 1978. This increase was attributable to the growth of the Company's customer base, expansion of its product line and renewals of existing leases during this period. Since 1978, the Company's net sales of installed displays increased at a lower rate due primarily to its emphasis on developing a market for the Unex system. Net sales increased by approximately $1,819,000 (20%) during the six months ended October 31, 1980 from the prior comparable period due to substantially higher sales of Unex displays and sports information systems. The Company's cost to build, ship and install displays as a percentage of net sales during the first six months of fiscal 1981 increased from approximately 46% to 51% over the prior comparable period as a result of a change in product mix and promotional markdowns primarily associated with Unex sales. See "BUSINESS." The Company historically experiences greater sales during the second half of its fiscal year. See "Interim Results" for a discussion of the decrease in net sales of installed displays during the two months ended December 31, 1980 as compared with the two months ended December 31, 1979.

NET FINANCE INCOME	Year Ended April 30,					Six Months Ended October 31,	
	1976	1977	1978	1979	1980	1979	1980
	(in thousands of dollars)						
Finance revenue earned ...	$ 8,066	$ 8,928	$ 9,306	$ 9,727	$11,220	$ 5,641	$ 5,626
Interest expense	3,033	3,036	3,933	6,279	10,523	4,408	4,966
Net finance income	$ 5,033	$ 5,892	$ 5,373	$ 3,448	$ 697	$ 1,233	$ 660
Effective average interest rate paid*	9.4%	9.2%	8.9%	12.8%	17.7%	15.4%	16.0%

* The effective average interest rate paid was determined by using the interest expense for the fiscal year divided by the weighted average monthly outstanding debt during the period.

Most of the Company's borrowings have been made pursuant to the Credit Agreement under which interest payments have been based upon a formula tied to the prevailing prime lending rate. Recent high interest rates have resulted in substantially increased interest expense. During fiscal 1979 and 1980, interest expense increased approximately $2,346,000 (60%) and $4,244,000 (68%), respectively, over the prior comparable periods. Interest expense increased by approximately $557,000 (13%) during the six months ended October 31, 1980 over the prior comparable period. Implicit interest rates in the Company's lease contracts have been raised to reflect the Company's increased costs of borrowing, but the income recognized on such contracts will be realized over a period of years as compared with the immediate recognition of the increase in interest expense. Similarly, increased payments to the Company under its lease contracts as a result of the provision for cost of living increases have not entirely offset increased interest expense. The Company's lease contracts provide for a maximum annual 4% increase under such cost of living provision. Finance revenue earned in fiscal 1980 increased approximately $1,493,000 (15%) in comparison to fiscal 1979 primarily due to a lower estimated maintenance reserve requirement. Excess maintenance reserves were transferred to, and earned as, finance reserves. Finance revenue earned remained relatively constant during the first six months of fiscal 1981 compared with the prior comparable period due to the sale of certain lease receivables and the resultant loss of the related finance revenues. See Note 11 to Consolidated Financial Statements.

EXHIBIT 2 (continued)

NET MAINTENANCE INCOME	Year Ended April 30,					Six Months Ended October 31,	
	1976	1977	1978	1979	1980	1979	1980
	(in thousands of dollars)						
Maintenance revenue earned	$ 2,744	$ 3,192	$ 3,649	$ 4,201	$ 4,974	$ 2,321	$ 2,493
Maintenance expense	2,467	3,132	3,530	3,595	4,117	2,051	2,228
Net maintenance income ...	$ 277	$ 60	$ 119	$ 606	$ 857	$ 270	$ 265

Maintenance revenue earned increased during the past five fiscal years due to the Company's expanding customer base. Net maintenance income increased during the past three fiscal years as a result of the Company's control of its maintenance expenses. As a percentage of maintenance revenue earned, maintenance expense declined from a high of 98% in fiscal 1977 to 83% in fiscal 1980.

SELLING, GENERAL AND ADMINISTRATIVE EXPENSES	Year Ended April 30,					Six Months Ended October 31,	
	1976	1977	1978	1979	1980	1979	1980
	(in thousands of dollars)						
	$ 8,906	$11,582	$15,073	$17,502	$15,626	$ 7,274	$ 6,956

During fiscal 1980, the Company implemented an overhead reduction plan for its selling, general and administrative expenses ("SG&A") which had almost doubled from fiscal 1976 to fiscal 1979. Specific measures implemented included the closing of three regional sales offices, the reduction of the number of production and administrative personnel and the consolidation of certain departments at the Company's executive offices. During fiscal 1980, SG&A decreased by approximately $1,876,000 (11%) from the prior fiscal year. The Company's overhead reduction plan was implemented without significant adverse impact on sales or service. Additional budget reduction measures were taken during the six months ended October 31, 1980 which resulted in a decrease of approximately $318,000 (4%) in SG&A from the prior comparable period.

NET EARNINGS (LOSS)	Year Ended April 30,					Six Months Ended October 31,	
	1976	1977	1978	1979	1980	1979	1980
	(in thousands of dollars)						
Earnings (loss) before income taxes	$ 3,032	$ 3,174	$ 4,305	$ 238	$ 486	$ (463)	$ 2,184
Income tax provision (benefit)	1,317	1,325	1,739	(214)	59	(341)	951
Net earnings (loss)	$ 1,715	$ 1,849	$ 2,566	$ 452	$ 427	$ (122)	$ 1,233

Earnings (loss) before income taxes have been affected by the factors discussed above and, in addition, in fiscal 1980, benefited from a gain of approximately $1,190,000 recognized on the sale of certain lease receivables. Earnings (loss) before income taxes increased significantly during the six months ended October 31, 1980 from the prior comparable period as a result of a gain of approximately $2,524,000 on the sale of certain lease receivables and a $1,818,000 increase in net sales of installed displays. Net earnings (loss) in fiscal 1979 were benefited by a $214,000 net operating loss carryback for income tax purposes in 1979 and a significantly reduced effective tax rate in 1980.

LIQUIDITY	Year Ended April 30,					Six Months Ended October 31,	
	1976	1977	1978	1979	1980	1979	1980
	(in thousands of dollars)						
Total minimum lease payments to be received ..	$75,481	$81,627	$92,070	$103,128	$110,542	$107,425	$111,393
Net investment in sales type leases	$41,887	$46,805	$54,972	$ 62,865	$ 68,797	$ 69,176	$ 72,948
Debt	$36,663	$44,377	$44,278	$ 51,236	$ 60,907	$ 62,685	$ 63,587

EXHIBIT 2 (continued)

Leasing operations have required the Company to raise capital in order to finance the costs associated with products under lease. Such capital has been provided primarily by bank borrowings under the Credit Agreement, cash generated from operations and sales of certain lease and installment sale receivables. The Company also offers a prepayment program which permits substantially all of its customers to prepay annually their lease obligations at a discount, which discount is less than the effective interest rate in their respective lease contracts. During 1980, approximately 55% of the Company's customers participated in this program through the prepayment of approximately $11,442,000. See Note 2 to Consolidated Financial Statements.

The Company believes that its greatest potential source of liquidity is its lease portfolio. As of October 31, 1980, the total minimum lease payments to be received by the Company were approximately $111,393,000, of which approximately $81,206,000 was expected to be collected over the next five years. See Note 3 to Consolidated Financial Statements. In 1979, the Company initiated a policy of selling from time to time certain of its lease and installment contract receivables for cash. See Note 11 to Consolidated Financial Statements. As described under "USE OF PROCEEDS AND FINANCING REQUIREMENTS," the Company has available to it various methods of financing, including borrowings under the new term loan and revolving credit agreement.

The Company has budgeted $323,000 in capital improvements during its current fiscal year which will be financed internally. No other material commitments have been planned.

EXHIBIT 3

	1978	1979	1980
Current ratio	2.43	2.10	2.15
Quick ratio	2.60	1.52	1.72
Sales/total assets	1.86	2.02	1.86
Long-term debt to total assets	38.25%	31.06%	37.41%
Net sales (millions)	$28.863	$30.595	$31.065

EXHIBIT 4
Management

Directors and Executive Officers

The following table sets forth certain information regarding the directors and executive officers of the Company:

Name	Age	Position with the Company
Luke G. Williams*†	57	Chairman of the Board of Directors; Chief Executive Officer
Charles M. Williams*	59	Senior Vice President; Director
Paul Smyly†	45	President and Chief Operating Officer
Donald Sherwood*†	79	Treasurer; Chairman of the Finance Committee; Director
Cameron Sherwood	80	Director
Horton Herman*	69	Secretary; Director
Edward J. Leary	33	Vice President for Legal and Industry Affairs
William H. Justus	59	Senior Vice President for National Field Services
John E. Holcomb	56	Vice President of Plant Operations
David L. Gray	45	Vice President for Sales and Marketing
John C. Kersch	50	Vice President for Finance
Arnold Corbridge	41	Controller

* Member of Executive Committee.
† Member of Finance Committee.

Directors serve until the next annual meeting of stockholders and until their successors are elected and qualified. Under the by-laws of the Company, the date of the Annual Meeting of Stockholders is scheduled for the third Thursday in August of each year. Each executive officer of the Company is elected or appointed by the Board of Directors and holds office until his successor is elected and qualified. Paul Smyly has an employment contract with the Company which expires in August 1982. See "Other Transactions." The Chairman of the Board and Chief Executive Officer of the Company has the power to appoint additional officers to serve at his discretion in addition to those elected or appointed by the Board.

Luke G. Williams, a co-founder of the Company, has been Chairman of the Board and Chief Executive Officer since May 1980. Mr. Williams had previously served as President, Chief Executive Officer and a Director for more than the past five years. Mr. Williams also serves as a Director of Sea-First Corporation and the Seattle-First National Bank, one of the lenders to the Company under the Credit Agreement. Mr. Williams has been acting as Chief Financial Officer.

Charles M. Williams, a co-founder of the Company, has been Senior Vice President and a Director for more than the past five years. In addition, Mr. Williams is in charge of research and development for the Company. Luke G. Williams and Charles M. Williams are brothers.

EXHIBIT 4 (continued)

Paul Smyly has been President and Chief Operating Officer of the Company since May 1980. Mr. Smyly joined the Company as Executive Vice President and Chief Operating Officer in August 1979. From 1975 to 1979, Mr. Smyly was President of Key Electro Sonic, Inc., a subsidiary of Applied Magnetics Corporation, which at the time was principally engaged in the manufacture of food processing equipment.

Donald Sherwood has been Treasurer and a Director for more than the past five years. From 1976 to May 1980, Mr. Sherwood was also Chairman of the Board of Directors of the Company. Mr. Sherwood owns Pioneer Investment Company, a personal holding company engaged in investments. See "Other Transactions."

Cameron Sherwood has been a Director for more than the past five years. Prior to 1976, Mr. Sherwood served as Secretary to the Company and was a member of the law firm of Sherwood, Tugman, Gose & Reser. Mr. Sherwood continues to practice law in the State of Washington. Donald Sherwood and Cameron Sherwood are brothers.

Horton Herman has been a Director since 1975, and since 1976, Secretary. Since January 1974, Mr. Herman has been of counsel to the law firm of Paine, Lowe, Coffin, Hamblen & Brooke, formerly Paine, Lowe, Coffin, Herman & O'Kelly. See "Other Transactions." Mr. Herman also serves as a Director of Hecla Mining Company.

Edward Leary has been Vice President for Legal and Industry Affairs since September 1979. From October 1978 to September 1979, he served as Director of Legal Affairs for the Company. Prior to joining the Company in 1976, he was District Supervisor in the Office of Support Enforcement for all departmental programs in Eastern Washington.

William Justus joined the Company in 1952 and has been Senior Vice President for National Field Services since 1978. From 1975 to 1978, he was Vice President for Transportation Information Systems.

John Holcomb, who joined the Company in 1962, has been Vice President of Plant Operations since May 1980. From 1979 to 1980, Mr. Holcomb served as Vice President of Manufacturing and from 1976 to 1979, he was Vice President of Williams Brothers Manufacturing Company, a wholly owned subsidiary of the Company. In 1975 and 1976, Mr. Holcomb was Manufacturing Manager of the Company.

David Gray, who joined the Company in 1972, has been Vice President for Marketing and Sales since April 1979. From May 1976 to April 1979, Mr. Gray was a Regional Sales Manager. Prior to that time, Mr. Gray was a District Sales Manager.

John C. Kersch has been Vice President for Finance since January 1981. From 1979 to 1981, Mr. Kersch was Treasurer for Enterprises Incorporated in Olympia, Washington, a publicly owned holding company primarily engaged in the manufacturing of material handling systems for the pulp and paper industry. Prior to 1979, Mr. Kersch was Vice President for Finance of Pullman Torkelson, a subsidiary of Pullman Incorporated, which at the time was involved in engineering, construction and manufacturing.

Arnold Corbridge joined the Company as Assistant Controller in 1974 and became Controller in September 1976.

James Moran, who joined the Company in 1969, has been Vice President of Sports Systems since May 1976. Prior to that time he was Regional Manager for Sports Systems. Management considers Mr. Moran's contribution to the sales of Sports Information Systems to be significant. Mr. Moran is 38 years old.

The American Sign and Indicator Corporation, 1986

Donald F. Harvey
Research Associate: Deborah Russell

INTRODUCTION

As Michael Quinn, American Sign and Indicator's chief executive officer, worked in his large, well-appointed office with paneled walls, expensive oil paintings, and color-coordinated furnishings, he reflected on strategy for the sign company, head-quartered in Spokane, Washington. His strategic decisions had cut back many of AS&I's old-line businesses and moved aggressively to redeploy its assets into the new electronics area, but he felt that transforming the company might be a big gamble.

Quinn settled on his new strategy for a handful of what seem to be pragmatic reasons. "Of our basic businesses, electronic signs have consistently shown the highest return on investment," he declared. "Because we think electronic signs have by far the greatest growth opportunities in the 1990s, that's where we have decided to concentrate our investment."[1]

American Sign and Indicator (AS&I) is following a strategy of applying its technological and financial strength to the development of high-margin products for selected high-growth electronics markets.

BACKGROUND

American Sign and Indicator Corporation has undergone major changes since 1983. Founded in 1952 by Luke and Charles Williams, the company invented, manufactured, and sold time and temperature displays, the state-of-the-art in electronic sign technology at that time.

In 1983, the BRAE Corporation purchased AS&I and began to operate it as part of a larger organization. BRAE owns another company that manufactures component parts for electronic signs, such as those produced by AS&I. Together these two companies comprise the Electronic Visual Communications Systems (EVCS) segment of BRAE's business. The second company in this segment is Integrated Systems Engineering (ISE). This segment has been part of BRAE since fiscal 1983, with ISE joining the parent company in fiscal 1984.

This case was prepared using published accounts and public documents for the purpose of class discussion rather than to illustrate either effective or ineffective handling of an administrative situation.

As a segment, EVCS has not shown a profit resulting from operations since acquisition by BRAE. Through aggressive cost reductions (continuing a process begun in 1980), BRAE has been attempting to bring AS&I to the point of profitability once more.

Changes Within the BRAE Corporation

In order to develop a strategy for AS&I, it is necessary to understand the changes that have occurred in the parent corporation. BRAE has been involved with many acquisitions and divestitures since its formation in 1977 (see exhibit 1). BRAE has been primarily in the production and leasing of transportation business. Its diversification into the electronic sign industry has broadened its product base, however, some market analysts feel that this lack of focus has been a factor in the less than vigorous acceptance of BRAE stock by the stock market.[2]

Presently BRAE is concentrating its efforts on the development of its electronic segment through aggressive plans for acquisitions of local sign companies. BRAE has exited the "piggyback" industry with the sales or intents to sell of its subsidiaries in this segment. The remaining segment, the rail division, continues as part of BRAE Corporation.

BRAE sold three of its companies, National Piggyback Services, Inc., and Intermodal Brokerage Services, Inc., which provided services as licensed property brokers, and National Piggyback Specialized Commodities, which operated a fleet of refrigerated piggyback trailers, to American President Companies for $60 million during fiscal year 1985. These sales, along with the sale of AS&I's lease portfolio for $97.3 million, improved the cash position of the corporation.

During fiscal 1986, BRAE Intermodal (a separate company) and BRAE Partners were sold to Greenbrier Leasing Corporation. The corporation was also seeking to sell Cargo and BRAE Trailers, the two remaining components of its "piggyback" business. In addition, BRAE has agreed in principle to sell BRAE Marine.

An article in the August 12, 1985, *Business Week* stated that "although the deal left BRAE flush with cash, Texido was forced to sell two related rail operations below book because they were less valuable on their own. The subsequent write-off left a loss of $2.3 million in the quarter ended June 30 [1985], though revenues were up 40 percent, to $37.5 million. Texido says he'll make up the loss when he sells his two remaining piggyback operations."[3] The sale date of July 24, 1985, for BRAE Partners and Intermodal would appear to make these the two subsidiaries that former CEO Texido expected to sell at a profit, although figures are not available.

The event that will have major impact on the future for AS&I has been the purchase of 48 percent of BRAE's stock by a company called Leucadia National, headed by Chairman Ian Cumming and President Joseph Steinberg. This relative newcomer to the financial world has been making a name for itself by attempting hostile takeovers of companies, only to end up with a greenmail gain on the buy-up of the targeted companies' stock. An article in the November 11, 1985, *Barron's* recounts Leucadia's attempts at company buyouts, which finally resulted in Leucadia's forcing the targeted company to buy back its own stock or find another merger partner. In the instance of Avco Corporation, this technique was successful, netting Leucadia $61 million before taxes. During 1984, Leucadia began attempting to buy up control of National Intergroup, later attempting an unsuccessful proxy fight to take over the board of directors. This time Leucadia was forced to sell National Intergroup's shares back to the company at a loss.[4]

Leucadia's primary business, selling investment-oriented life insurance products, has not proven to be highly profitable but has not incurred significant losses. Its most recent acquisition was OPM, a computer leasing firm, just as it was coming out of bankruptcy.

Leucadia purchased 41.5 percent of its 48 percent of BRAE's stock from Edward L. Scarff. Scarff and Texido had entered into an agreement in July 1985 to sell Texido the 41.5 percent of stock on or before December 31, 1985, for $13 per share. Scarff had the right to sell his stock prior to receipt of the required ten days' notice for more than $13 per share to any third party.[5] Texido formed a general partnership, BRAE Associates, for the purpose of raising $23 million from investors to purchase the stock. On December 18, 1985, Leucadia purchased Scarff's stock for $12 per share, giving it control of BRAE Corporation.[6] Apparently Texido was not able to attract enough interested investors to raise the capital needed to purchase Scarff's share of BRAE's stock.

On April 7, 1986, when Texido resigned as chairman and chief executive officer of the BRAE Corporation, Leucadia principals Ian Cummings became chairman and Joseph Steinberg became president.

Goals of American Sign and Indicator

The goals of AS&I are inextricably entwined with the goals and mission of the BRAE Corporation. During fiscal 1985, BRAE began a program of divestiture and consolidation that effectively turned the focus of the corporation's growth toward expansion of its electronic sign segment.[7]

The stated goals of AS&I are to continue to expand its market share by acquiring local static sign companies. This acquisition will allow the company to penetrate a market that has not yet been touched by AS&I.[8] Static signs do not utilize the technology incorporated in the various electronic systems found in the time and temperature displays, sports systems, and message centers that have been the focus of AS&I since 1952. Purchasing local sign companies throughout the country is seen by the BRAE and AS&I leadership as a way to heighten the company's visibility as well as to expand market share through horizontal integration. Horizontal integration is defined as acquiring competitors to increase market share.[9] The purchase of smaller local sign companies to achieve these ends will have the further advantage of avoiding additional shipping and delivery costs that would be incurred if the static signs were manufactured in Spokane and shipped to customers.

ECONOMIC ANALYSIS

The sign industry as a whole is a $2.3 billion industry; $200 million of that represents electronic signs. According to the trade journal *Signs of the Times,* the industry is in a rather flat sales growth pattern. In a 1985 survey, the average sales declined by 6.7 percent from the previous year.[10]

During April 1986, AS&I and ISE were reorganized by BRAE into a single company. This vertical integration will allow AS&I to have more control over ISE and benefit from its strengths. The 1985 BRAE Annual Report stated that ISE is a research and development organization charged with developing state-of-the-art technologies for the sign industry.

Principal Products

Lamp-Matrix Displays

Time and temperature products consist of an incandescent lamp-matrix display that shows time and temperature alternately; such displays are typically installed outside a business for the purpose of advertising. Primary customers have been banks and savings and loans around the country. Prices for such displays begin at around $10,000.

Electronic Message Centers

These displays consist of an incandescent lamp-matrix that is capable of displaying sequential messages and a microprocessor data base controller programmed to display the messages. Primary customers are financial and commercial customers for product promotion and community services. Sale prices begin at around $12,000.

Sports Information Systems

These systems are made up of a combination of animation panels, message centers, Unex displays, and scoring formats for events held in sports complexes. These displays are currently used in many sports arenas around the country including the Rose Bowl, the University of Notre Dame, and the RFK Stadium in Washington, D.C.; there is even a mobile system for PGA golf tours. The company installed an impressive $9 million sports information system for the 1984 Summer Olympic Games in the Los Angeles Coliseum.

Unex

The Unex technology is an advancement over the original dot matrix design, in that the light source for the displays is fluorescent rather than incandescent. A computer-controlled head sweeps the face of the enclosure, changing the message displayed in seconds. This design has an extremely high resolution, which allows the signs to be used indoors as well as outdoors. The price range for these signs is from about $5,000 to $1 million for a multiple Unex installation.

Technology

The technology that American Sign pioneered in 1952 with the time and temperature displays, using a dot matrix format with incandescent bulbs, was the most advanced in the industry at that time. Its expansion into the Unex technology and the inclusion of computerized control for the message systems have kept the company abreast of technological advances in the industry. However, it was the ISE advancement called ISEglo that brought the company up to date in sign technology. ISE is considered by BRAE to be a research and development organization.

AS&I is currently negotiating with other sources for technology that can be incorporated in its sign production. Mike Quinn, AS&I's president, is negotiating a joint venture with Japan's Mitsubishi Electric Company to acquire new technology and has been seeking other technology from General Electric.[11] This awareness of the need to be competitive in the industry will be an important factor in the future growth of the company.

According to the 1985 BRAE Annual Report, AS&I has installed an automated manufacturing system:

> Recognizing the need to produce the highest quality product at the lowest possible price, AS&I has instituted a series of measures to further enhance its manufacturing operations. This year, the company will be installing a computer-aided design and manufacturing system anticipated to significantly improve productivity. Coupled with this "CAD/CAM" system, a new front-end automatic routing system is likely to boost productivity of some operations by as much as 80 percent. The manufacturing department is also restructuring the layout of its facility to better control and streamline the flow of the manufacturing process.[12]

Competitive Advantage Analysis

AS&I offers the only national sales and service organization in the sign industry to its national and international customers, who represent the financial, commercial, employee communications, sports, and transportation markets.[13] The sports systems are sold by a direct sales staff, and the remaining products—financial/commercial (time and temperature displays, primarily), and transportation/international—are sold by distributors located around the country. Presently, there are ninety-five service representatives located in all fifty states.[14]

AS&I has many competitors throughout the country; however, most of these are local or regional companies. Forty-five percent of the industry is comprised of companies with less than $500,000 in sales.[15] The company's national presence allows it to reach all parts of the country.

Quinn, who became the CEO in 1985, said that one motive for acquiring a national network of static sign companies, beyond expanding into new markets, is heightening visibility of its electronic signs to customers requiring a variety of signs for their business.[16]

The relative market share enjoyed by the EVCS segment of BRAE is based on the previously reported industry estimates of the electronic sign industry as a $200 million market and the total sign industry as a $2.3 billion market. The reported revenue figures for the EVCS segment of BRAE for 1984 and 1985 are as follows:

Year	% of Total Sign Market	% of Electronic Sign Market
1984	1.5% ($35,145,000)	17.5%
1985	1.0% ($23,598,000)	11.5%

The relative market share represented can be roughly determined for each of the product divisions of AS&I by dividing each division's percentage of total sales by the percentages of the EVCS percentage of each market. The results for 1985 are

Division	Total Sales (%)	Electronic Sign Market (%)	Total Market (%)
Sports System	73	8.4	0.7
Financial/Commercial	22	2.5	0.2
Transportation/International	5	0.6	0.05

FINANCIAL ANALYSIS

As can be seen in exhibit 2, revenues, net income, and cash categories were up sharply in 1985 from previous years, as were the operating profit and equity positions. Additionally, the debt to equity ratio, return on equity, and return on assets measures showed improvement. What this means is that BRAE was able to pay off some of its long-term debt ($34,700), increase its profit from $4,345 to $27,779, raise its stockholder's equity from $52,575 to $79,668, and greatly boost its cash position from $21,372 to $87,825 (figures in thousands). The quick ratio, which measures how quickly a company can become liquid (that is, produce cash for paying debts), nearly doubled.

This financial situation looks very favorable for BRAE, but upon closer examination it becomes apparent that much of the revenue generated during fiscal 1985 resulted from the sale of company assets. That in itself was not a problem, but these events are not repeatable in the future. This fact must be taken into consideration when projecting future operations.

The Operating Segments report (exhibit 3) shows that the Electronic Visual Communications Systems segment had an operating profit of $10,584,000. The 1985 BRAE annual report showed a $6.6 million loss in operations and a $17.2 million gain on the September 1984 sale of AS&I's lease portfolio. BRAE sold the portfolio of lease agreements for AS&I's products for $97.3 million. The purchase of AS&I in 1983 was for 85 percent of the company's stock at $14,794,000. The remaining 15 percent of the stock was purchased in September 1984 for $1,941,000, bringing the total purchase price of AS&I to $16,735,000. This sale translates into a payback to BRAE of nearly five times its purchase price in just eighteen months. This figure was computed by adding the costs to BRAE for purchasing AS&I, the operating losses to BRAE, the costs of unsuccessful attempts to sell the portfolio; that figure was divided into the $97.3 million selling price of the lease portfolio. According to CEO Mike Quinn, AS&I incurred a $2.5 million loss in 1985. Assuming that the proportion of the $98,000 loss incurred by the EVCS segment of BRAE that represents AS&I is the same as that in 1985 (38 percent), the loss in 1984 was $.037 million.

The other sale that enhanced BRAE's balance sheet in fiscal 1985 was the sale of three of its property brokerage companies for $60 million. The corporation realized a gain on this sale of $26,202,000.

According to Quinn, in the third quarter of fiscal 1986, which ended in December 1985, AS&I showed a $675,000 net profit. He had projected that AS&I would break even if sales reached $27 million. BRAE's available working capital for expansions or acquisitions, also improved by the sale of the property brokerage companies and the lease portfolio, is shown in exhibit 4. For a summary of AS&I's operations from 1978 through 1982, see exhibit 5.

In 1986 CEO Mike Quinn and his management team were using turnaround strategy at AS&I. A *turnaround* strategy is an attempt to halt a firm's decline and improve its long-term efficiency. The short-term strategy is focused on cost reduction, while longer-run strategy can be aimed at growth or holding strategies. Further, a turnaround strategy can emphasize cost-cutting, personnel reductions, closing inefficient plants, or closing out unprofitable products. AS&I has engaged in all of these activities, with the exception of elimination of products.

One long-term goal that has been publicized by AS&I is to expand into static signs. This move, seen by upper management as a way to broaden the market base, requires the acquisition of other sign companies around the country. The initial probings into this market, according to Mike Quinn, will be in the form of the acquisition of a "couple of companies in the sun belt."[17]

Capital for these acquisitions must come from BRAE because AS&I is not in a cash-rich position. The capital needed to purchase such a sign company would be in the range of $1 million for each company, based on the fact that 45 percent of the sign companies in America have $500,000 or less in sales yearly. In order to compete effectively, AS&I would need to purchase established companies with high visibility and good competitive position in their markets. AS&I can use the market share already gained by the company to its advantage.

Currently, AS&I has electronic signs using a variety of technologies in place in Sweden, Taiwan, Hong Kong, and Saudi Arabia. These have served as a good base for continued market penetration overseas. AS&I has a marketing and sales force of approximately thirty individuals, eight of whom are direct sales employees in the company's sports market. The remaining twenty-two salespeople are distributors for

AS&I, purchasing the products outright from the company and selling them to the end-users.[18] This distribution method can prove to be beneficial to AS&I because the overhead costs of maintaining an international sales force would prove to be prohibitive, particularly during these times of economic retrenching by the company.

The criteria to be considered in determining the markets to enter overseas include ranking each country's market size, market growth, cost of doing business, competitive advantage, and risk level. Armed with this marketing information, AS&I seeks to establish those distributors that best meet the company's standards of quality product representation and service to customers.

Research and Development

In order to enhance technological leadership in the electronic sign industry, the R&D conducted by the EVCS of BRAE Corporation must keep pace with industry standards. The available data for this particular type of electronic equipment were limited to the electronic industry as a whole, as reported in the 1985 United States Statistical Abstract. The industry standard for electronic research and development was 8.6 percent. The amounts spent by the BRAE EVCS for R&D were $899,000 (2.5%) in 1984 and $920,000 (3.8%) in 1985.

CEO Mike Quinn projected $30 million in sales for fiscal year 1987. If the static sign segment is penetrated through acquisition during this period, sales can be larger by as much as $1 million, depending on the size of the companies purchased. If the $30 million in sales is primarily from electronic signs, the R&D expenses incurred by AS&I should reach $2.58 million, better than double the figures of the previous two fiscal years.

Management Analysis

The corporate culture at AS&I appears to be changing. According to interviews with former and present employees of AS&I, the current management has increased morale among the Spokane staff.[19] The low morale prior to BRAE's takeover, according to these same sources, was frustrating for middle managers, who perceived a lack of specific long-range strategy and mission in the upper management, led by Luke Williams, co-founder of the company. The corporate culture was characterized as reactive, not proactive.

At the time of BRAE's takeover, the plan was to continue operations with the same management, with Heath Matthews as the president. However, Texido was not pleased with the results of operations, according to these former employees, and brought in Brent Brown from ISE as president. This period was marked by no long-range planning, with Brown preferring to use a stated work ethic as the guidance for the company goals. Operational results continued to be less than favorable, and morale to be low.

During this time, Vice-President Larry Hirschfield, a Stanford MBA, came to the Spokane operation from BRAE headquarters to prepare a proposal for potential buyers of AS&I's lease portfolio. According to a former employee (responsible for the data processing function that provided the information needed to draw up this proposal), Larry Hirschfield's attitude seemed to be that the employees of AS&I failed to understand the complexity of the problem facing BRAE in the attempt to sell the lease portfolio. Therefore, the data processing and accounting departments received only bits and pieces of the information needed to draw up the necessary documents. These mid-level managers had no idea of the larger picture.

BRAE CEO Bill Texido was commuting from San Francisco to Spokane four days a week during this time and attempting to bring the costs and revenues into line by cutting operating expenses. One of the two manufacturing locations at the Spokane Industrial Park was closed during fiscal year 1984. Spokane employees felt that the leaders from BRAE were totally task-oriented, with little concern for the employees. Exhibit 6 shows the management changes since BRAE's takeover of AS&I.

Mike Quinn, the current president of AS&I, began with the company in April 1985. He has continued to reduce operating costs at AS&I by cutting an additional seventy members from the staff. Interviews with the current employees of AS&I reveal that Quinn treats his staff as if they are competent to do their jobs. There is evidence among remaining employees that morale is improving with the long-range plans to expand the business into static signs. At the time of the layoffs in June 1985, after Mike Quinn's arrival, tension was elevated. However, the corporate culture is reported by the employees as team-oriented and pulling toward the same goal.[20]

The Wilson Model depicts the relative assertiveness and objectivity found in leaders of an organization. Mike Quinn is placed in the amiable section of the upper right quadrant, the "Drivers." This placement is based on the information received in interviews of the Spokane employees. Bill Texido is placed in the "Driver Driver" quadrant, based on the input from former employees of AS&I. They perceived Texido to be totally task-oriented, reducing costs to improve the financial performance of the company and pursuing the sale of the portfolio of AS&I's leases for a profit.

Ian Cummings and Joseph Steinberg, the principal leaders of Leucadia National, are placed also in the "Driving Driver" quadrant based on information received from Ralph Tozier, former vice president of finance at AS&I. He stated that both Cummings and Steinberg were highly assertive and highly objective individuals.[21] Leucadia is very aggressive in its pursuit of takeovers of companies' stock.[22] Although Leucadia has attracted attention because of its attempted takeovers of diverse companies, Cummings and Steinberg resolutely refuse to be interviewed. The message one gets in the media about Leucadia is that the company is in business to make money, not to maintain a high-profile, friendly image.

Management and Organization

CEO Mike Quinn has come into the company with the team of managers that was with him at American Hospital Supplies and had worked with him on two previous corporate turnarounds. The message here is that Mike Quinn wanted to work with individuals he knew and respected, in order to accomplish the turnaround of AS&I (see exhibit 7).

With the expansion into static signs and the emphasis on international and transportation markets, opportunities can arise for mid-level managers to take supervisory or managerial roles in these areas of the company.

CONCLUSION

American Sign and Indicator is at a crossroads in its corporate development. The company has survived a variety of management styles, cost reductions, plant closures, and personnel layoffs. With a staff of 300 people, reduced from approximately 550 when BRAE took over, and plans for expansion, AS&I can look to that future with its strategic goals firmly in mind. The development of the transportation and international divisions and the stabilizing of manager morale through programs designed to develop the individual can work to bring the entire organization to a point of success and goal achievement.

CEO Mike Quinn is excited about AS&I's redirection and believes in the capabilities, commitments, creativity, and loyalty of company employees. Most observers of AS&I credit Quinn with a well-conceived and bold positioning of his company in attractive high-technology markets. Many of them, however, contend that he faces a huge challenge in making the highly praised strategy work.

Despite AS&I's progress in developing such multidivision efforts, outsiders remain doubtful that the company can develop the kind of interaction between units needed to make it click as a force in the electronic sign business. So far, the company appears to be doing well, but it is much too early to predict how well it can all be tied together.[23]

Mike Quinn wondered what other strategy could be used to bring AS&I back to a profitable future.

NOTES

1 "AS&I Seeking Acquisitions," *Journal of Business (Spokane),* February 6, 1986, 1.
2 Merrill Lynch Opinion, BRAE Corporation, May 31, 1985.
3 "Boxcars to Billboards," *Business Week,* August 12, 1985, 53.
4 "Elusive Leucadia," *Barron's,* November 11, 1985, 6.
5 *BRAE News,* July 11, 1985.
6 *Standard and Poors,* "Company Report—BRAE Corporation," June 1985, 9528.
7 "Boxcars to Billboards," 53.
8 "Neon Sign Brought Big Business," *Spokane Week,* January 31, 1984, 3.
9 Philip Kotler, *Marketing Management: Analysis, Planning and Control* (Prentice-Hall, Englewood Cliffs, NJ, 1984), 59.

10 "The State of the Custom Sign Industry," *Signs of the Times,* Vol. 207, No. 7, July 1985, 80.

11 "AS&I Seeking Acquisitions," 1.

12 BRAE Corporation, Annual Report, 1985, 10.

13 Ibid.

14 Interview with Shelly Winkleman, AS&I, April 1986.

15 "AS&I Seeking Acquisitions," 1.

16 "The State of Sign Industry," 80.

17 "AS&I Seeking Acquisitions," 1.

18 BRAE Corporation, Annual Report, 1985.

19 Interview with Bill Donner, AS&I, April 1986.

20 Interview, S. Winkleman.

21 Interview with Ralph Tozier, Vice President, Finance, AS&I, February 1986.

22 "Elusive Leucadia," 7.

23 "AS&I Seeking Acquisitions," 1.

EXHIBIT 1
BRAE Corporation Acquisitions and Divestitures

1977	1979	1980	1981	1982	1983	1984	1985
Began Rail Division	Formed BRAE #Intermodal Corporation	Acquired *National Piggyback Services, Inc.	Acquired *Intermodal Brokerage Services, Inc.	Acquired °Cargo, Inc.	Acquired American Sign and Indicator Corporation	Acquired Integrated Systems Engineering	Formed BRAE Associates
		Began *National Piggyback Specialized Commodities	Began °BRAE Trailers	Began #BRAE Partners			
			†TRICO Offshore Services (Acquired)			Sold AS&I Lease Portfolio	

*Sold to American Presidents Companies

#Sold to Greenbrier Capital Corp.

†Agreed in Principle to Sell

°For Sale

EXHIBIT 2
Financial Analysis of BRAE (in thousands)

Year	Revenues	Net Income	Long-Term Debt	Operating Profit	Equity	Total Assets	Cash	Working Capital
1985	$146,397	$27,779	$140,770	$10,879	$79,668	$329,933	$87,825	$78,200
1984	117,546	4,345	174,989	(987)	52,575	349,169	21,372	21,700
1983	47,580	3,960	166,064	689	44,328	322,575	22,230	20,300
1982	34,789	3,899	122,317	3,619	41,482	229,796	63,069	17,300

Ratios

Year	Debt/ Equity	Industry Averages	Return on Equity	Industry Averages	Return on Assets	Quick Ratio
1985	1.83	2.94	.348	.07	.148	2.32
1984	3.15	2.94	.08	.07	.077	1.18
1983	3.12	2.94	.09	.07	.058	1.36
1982	2.26	2.94	.093	.07	.082	1.42

Industry averages were established by a weighted average of the industry averages for the electronic industry for the years 1980 through 1983. These industry figures were obtained from the 1985 *Statistical Abstract of the United States,* 105th ed., pp. 532 and 533.

EXHIBIT 3
Business Segments

	(In Thousands)		
	1985	**1984**	**1983**
OPERATING REVENUES:			
Electronic Visual Communications Systems	$ 55,445	$ 51,932	$ —
Surface Transportation	63,130	37,161	15,577
Rail	26,776	26,356	27,772
Total	145,351	115,449	43,349
Equity in Net Income from Domestic Joint Ventures and Partnerships	247	213	286
Corporate and Other	799	1,884	3,945
Total Operating Revenues	$146,397	$117,546	$ 47,580
OPERATING PROFIT:			
Electronic Visual Communications Systems	$ 10,584	$ (98)	$ —
Surface Transportation	4,564	2,515	2,730
Rail	(1,104)	(1,577)	(745)
Total	14,044	840	1,985
Corporate and Other	(3,165)	(1,827)	(1,296)
Total Operating Profit	$ 10,879	$ (987)	$ 689
IDENTIFIABLE ASSETS AT YEAR-END:			
Electronic Visual Communications Systems	$ 85,143	$108,105	$ 95,450
Surface Transportation	22,724	62,086	50,801
Rail	156,849	152,248	152,666
Total	264,716	322,439	298,917
Investment in Net Assets of Joint Ventures	3,645	4,242	4,034
Corporate and Other	61,572	22,488	19,624
Total Assets	$329,933	$349,169	$322,575
CAPITAL EXPENDITURES:			
Electronic Visual Communications Systems	$ 964	$ 411	$ —
Surface Transportation	28	107	5,114
Rail	1,595	1,064	779
Corporate and Other	27	1,957	92
DEPRECIATION AND AMORTIZATION:			
Electronic Visual Communications Systems	$ 2,039	$ 1,497	$ —
Surface Transportation	276	1,185	941
Rail	6,271	5,533	5,537
Corporate and Other	375	241	204

EXHIBIT 4
BRAE Corporation and Subsidiaries

CONSOLIDATED BALANCE SHEETS
(Dollar amounts in thousands, except par values)

Assets March 31	1985	1984
Current Assets:		
Cash and temporary investments of cash	$ 62,825	$ 21,372
Cash equivalents	25,000	—
Receivables	25,423	45,217
Inventories	11,703	9,727
Net Investment in sales-type and direct-financing leases	1,952	7,542
Prepaid and deferred expenses	1,761	5,861
Total current assets	128,664	89,719
Non-Current Receivables	12,981	7,680
Net Investment in Sales-Type and Direct-Financing Leases	18,195	57,754
Investment in Joint Ventures	3,645	4,242
Property and Equipment, at cost:		
Railcars		
Owned	158,937	158,097
Capitalized leases	8,692	8,733
Trailers	8,803	8,621
Equipment, furniture, and leasehold improvements	7,117	8,022
Land and buildings	4,973	6,359
	188,522	189,832
Less— Accumulated depreciation and amortization	(34,815)	(28,352)
	153,707	161,480
Other Assets:		
Excess of purchase price over related underlying assets in subsidiaries acquired, net of accumulated amortization of $822 and $871 at March 31, 1985 and 1984, respectively	8,245	22,579
Other Assets	4,496	5,715
	12,741	28,294
	$329,933	$349,169

EXHIBIT 4 (continued)

Liabilities and Stockholders' Equity March 31	1985	1984
Current Liabilities:		
Current maturities of long-term debt	11,907	14,422
Trade accounts payable	8,847	37,166
Other accounts payable and accrued expenses	19,924	6,387
Due to former shareholders of acquired subsidiaries	3,492	3,022
Accrued interest payable	3,373	3,507
Unearned revenue on maintenance contracts	2,676	3,279
Preferred dividends payable	205	231
Total current liabilities	50,424	68,014
Unearned Revenue on Maintenance Contracts	7,761	5,776
Notes Payable to Former Shareholders of a Subsidiary	5,857	7,231
Long-Term Debt and Capitalized Lease Obligations	140,770	174,989
Deferred Income Taxes	35,955	28,344
Total liabilities	240,767	284,354
Minority Interest	627	2,406
Commitments and Contingencies		
Redeemable Preferred Stock:		
9-1/4% Senior Cumulative Preferred Stock, $1 par value, 1,000,000 shares authorized—900 and 1,000 shares issued and outstanding at March 31, 1985 and 1984, respectively, with $1,000 aggregate par value (aggregate value in liquidation—$9,000 and $10,000 at March 31, 1985 and 1984, respectively)	8,871	9,834
Common Stockholders' Equity:		
Common Stock, $1 par value, 10,000,000 shares authorized—4,248,470 and 4,221,313 issued and outstanding at March 31, 1985 and 1984, respectively	4,248	4,221
Non-Voting Common Stock, $1 par value, 1,000,000 shares authorized—34,534 issued and outstanding	35	35
Capital in excess of par value	30,583	30,427
Retained earnings	44,792	17,892
Total common stockholders' equity	79,668	52,575
	$329,933	$349,169

EXHIBIT 5

American Sign and Indicator Corporation, Statements of Earnings for 1978–1982

	1978	1979	1980	1981	1982
Net sales of installed displays:					
Lease sales	$30,561,007	$35,333,282	$36,259,166	$26,333,365	$26,280,534
Less:					
Unearned finance revenue	12,938,222	15,706,420	19,191,260	14,816,642	14,799,057
Unearned maintenance revenue	4,894,852	4,870,091	1,365,462	2,206,102	2,658,780
	17,833,074	20,576,511	20,556,722	17,022,744	17,457,837
Net lease sales	12,727,933	14,756,771	15,702,444	9,310,621	8,822,697
Direct sales	9,163,820	9,729,547	9,639,584	16,066,609	16,286,448
Net sales of installed displays	21,891,753	24,486,318	25,342,028	25,377,230	25,109,145
Costs to build, ship, and install displays	9,581,844	11,542,891	12,272,176	13,319,681	13,474,972
Gross profit	12,309,909	12,943,427	13,069,852	12,057,549	11,634,173
Finance revenue earned	9,672,007	9,853,035	12,410,435	10,895,266	9,257,143
Maintenance revenue earned	3,648,740	4,201,399	4,973,764	5,130,223	5,331,415
Net revenue from installed displays	25,630,656	26,997,861	30,454,050	28,083,038	26,222,731
Gain on sales of contracts	—0—	—0—	—0—	5,343,118	7,254,638
				23,426,156	33,477,369
Operating expenses:					
Interest	3,932,942	6,278,749	10,523,173	11,186,236	11,206,943
Maintenance	3,530,107	3,594,579	4,116,771	4,963,757	5,132,850
Selling, general and administrative	14,843,699	17,782,218	15,453,126	15,499,048	15,556,257
Total operating expenses	22,306,748	27,655,546	30,093,070	31,649,041	31,896,050
Operating income	3,323,908	(657,685)	360,981	1,777,115	1,581,319
Other income:					
Interest	179,987	159,836	153,007	328,974	390,906
Other, net	(57,546)	476,315	127,584	183,295	445,784
Earnings before taxes	3,446,349	324,064	427,244	2,289,384	2,418,009
Income tax provision	1,356,390	2,517,154	433,577	983,953	905,009
Net earnings	$ 2,089,959	$ 2,841,218	$ 860,821	$ 1,305,431	$ 1,513,000

EXHIBIT 6
American Sign and Indicator Corporation (November 1986)

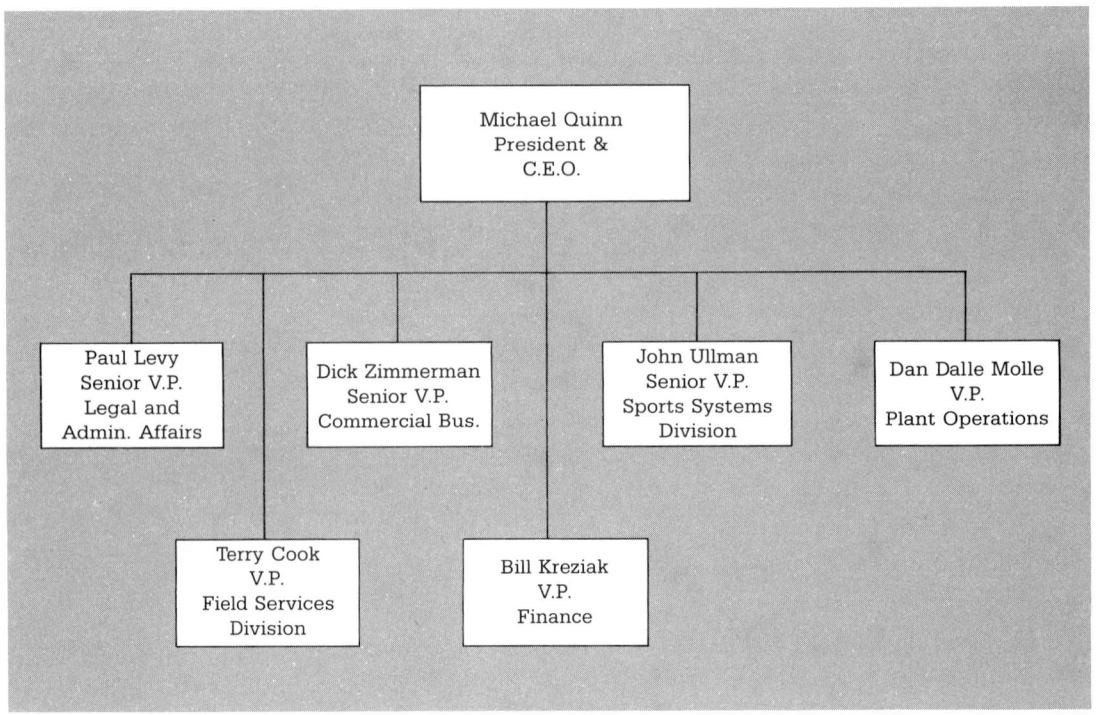

EXHIBIT 7
Upper Management of American Sign and Indicator

1986	1985	1984	1983
President and CEO: Michael Quinn	President and CEO: Michael Quinn	Chairman of the Board: Luke Williams	Chairman of the Board: Luke Williams
Vice President, Commercial Business: Dick Zimmerman	Vice President, Operations: Bill Collinsworth	President and CEO: Brent Brown	President and CEO: Heath Matthews
Vice President, Sports Business: John Ullman	Vice President, Sales and Marketing: D. Alexander Maxwell	Executive Vice President: Lawrence Hershfield	Senior Vice President, Legal and Industry Affairs, and Assistant Secretary: Edward Leary
Vice President, Operations; Dan Dalle Molle	Vice President, Finance: Ralph Tozier		Senior Vice President, Sports Systems: James Moran
Vice President, Finance: Bill Kreziak	Vice President, Commercial Sales: Lawrence Hershfield		Senior Vice President, Sales and Marketing: John Rutherford
Vice President, General Counsel: Paul Levy	Vice President, Sports Systems: Gregory Schmidt		Vice President, Finance, and Assistant Treasurer: Arnold Corbridge
Vice President, Service Business: Terry Cooke	Vice President, Manufacturing: Charles Wedge		Vice President, Corporate Development: Lawrence Hershfield
	General Counsel and Assistant Secretary: Paul Levy		Controller: Connie Munekiyo
	Controller: James Brown		

Source: BRAE Corporation Annual Reports 1985, 1984, 1983

CASES FOR PART THREE

■ ■ ■

STRATEGIC EVALUATION: THE REVIEW AND CONTROL PROCESS

■ ■ ■ CASE 19

The Washington Public Power Supply System: A Question of Managerial Control and Public Sector Accountability

Darryll Olsen
Robert J. DeFillippi

The Supply System's financial strength lies in its project participants who provide electrical service to the broad and diverse economic base of the Pacific Northwest. This helps make the Supply System's revenue bonds one of the most secure investments one can make.

Supply System Annual Report, 1980

Washington Public Power Supply System [WPPSS] projects nos. 4 and 5 bondholders are victims of the nation's largest municipal bond default and massive fraud. Many class actions have already been filed. Some parties to this WPPSS bilking are suing one another while others are trying to escape culpability by just blaming each other. Major underwriters and brokers are involved. Likewise, prominent law firms, engineering companies, and public utilities are among those who participated in the misrepresentations and omissions that wiped out our WPPSS investments . . . as U.S. Senator James McClure accurately charged: "This [WPPSS] is one huge mess and anyone who deals with it gets their hands dirty."

Supply System Bondholders Association, Inc., January 1984

As the year 1976 came to a close, the Washington Public Power Supply System, a state-authorized consortium of Pacific Northwest utilities, commenced construction activity on nuclear projects four and five (WNP-4/5). These two projects formed the capstone of an ambitious nuclear power program second in scale to only the nuclear program undertaken by the federal government in the Tennessee Valley. For Pacific Northwest electric utility officials, this decision reflected earnest concern

Darryll Olsen is a research associate with the Office of Applied Energy Studies, Washington State University. He specializes in energy and natural resources policy analysis. Robert J. DeFillippi is assistant professor, Department of Management and Systems, Washington State University. His current research focuses on information use and misuse within public and private organizations. The authors would like to thank Professor Robert E. Berney, member of the Executive Board of Directors of the Washington Public Power Supply System, for helpful comments on an earlier draft of this article. Please address reprint requests to Dr. Darryll Olsen, Office of Applied Energy Studies, Washington State University, Pullman, Washington, 99164-4430.

for providing the region with an adequate supply of energy to satisfy the burgeoning economic activity that electric power demand forecasters promised would come. But instead of the promising vision held by Supply System and electric utility officials, the future brought decreases in the rate of electric power consumption, colossal project cost overruns, and project schedule delays beyond the capacity of Supply System management to control. Following the aftermath of planning miscalculation and management disarray, Supply System officials were forced to terminate construction of WNP-4/5, and in July 1983 the WNP-4/5 participants defaulted on their bond payment obligations. In less than a decade, the Supply System descended from the status of nuclear power development leader to a utility group besieged in the courts and despised by ratepayers and bondholders alike.

The Supply System bond default took many of the WNP-4/5 bondholders by surprise; it proved to be the event that conventional thinking deemed impossible. Historically, the municipal bond market offered a relatively safe investment outlet, and in the case of WNP-4/5 bonds, additional security existed in the form of a ''hell or high water'' bond resolution that guaranteed bond payment regardless of whether the nuclear projects ever produced a single kilowatt-hour of electricity. Perhaps equally blind to the impending crisis, bond-rating firms continued to appraise WNP-4/5 securities as largely risk-free investments until the construction moratorium in June 1981. In effect, the investment community was largely baffled by an unpredictable and rapid succession of events.

The economic, legal, and political froth left in the wake of default promised to keep electric utility officials, government leaders, and federal judges searching for answers for several years. But in addition to the obvious questions surrounding investment in public securities and public power systems' ability to manage large--scale development projects, a more fundamental set of issues arises concerning public sector accountability in general. The Supply System enigma leaves serious questions unanswered as to how the public sector responds to planning crisis and protects the public interest.

THE STORY BEGINS

Throughout the mid- and late 1960s, the development of nuclear power was vigorously explored in the Pacific Northwest. Representing the state of Washington, the House and Senate Joint Committee on Nuclear Energy studied the questions surrounding nuclear power development and made the following recommendations to the state legislature in 1968:

> Nuclear power plants offer the most economical long-term solution to the state's power needs . . . we must now turn to nuclear power plants to supply our growing needs for industry, jos, and an increasing standard of living . . . state government should be structured to participate in the timely and successful siting of nuclear power plants to balance our growing energy demands . . . within state government a procedure must be established

wherein all state agencies having an interest in the siting of nuclear power plants may resolve their various interest into a single policy for the state of Washington and this enunciated formally as the policy of state government (Joint Committee, 1968:6–7).

The Joint Committee on Nuclear Energy was not the only governmental authority from the state of Washington encouraging nuclear power development, for Governor Daniel Evans also looked approvingly upon nuclear energy:

> . . . no market offers more promise than that of nuclear energy . . . [We] must be prepared to take the action necesary to assure maximum development of this great resource so that Washington becomes the nation's center of nuclear industry (Joint Committee, 1968:22).

State government gave its sanction to nuclear energy development and promoted Washington as the "nuclear progress state."

The state legislature and Governor Evans spurred nuclear power development in another important way. At the request of the Chairman of the Joint Committee on Nuclear Energy and the State Advisory Council on Nuclear Energy, Governor Evans, by executive order, created the Thermal Power Plant Site Evaluation Council on July 29, 1969. Enabling legislation for the council, at the request of Governor Evans, was drafted and passed into law in the spring of 1970; this legislation was later amended in 1976 creating the Energy Facility Site Evaluation Council (EFSEC). The key purpose of the site evaluation council was to reduce siting lead time, eliminate duplication of review, avoid overlapping regulatory requirements, improve representation of the public interest, institute a rational process to bring about a "reasonable compromise between conflicting values of energy development and the environment," and "to provide abundant energy at reasonable cost" (Rev. Code Wash. 80.50). These objectives were sought through a "one-stop siting concept," where a single administrative body would review all issues affecting the construction and operation of any major energy facility (Northwest Public Power, 1970; McCarthy, 1971; Granger and Wise, 1980; Ching, 1981).

The realization that new, large-scale hydroelectric power resources were becoming limited had existed within the Bonneville Power Administration, the region's federal wholesale power distributor, and the electric utility industry prior to the 1960s. This realization, coupled with increased electric power demands and even larger demands predicted for the future, made energy planners anxious to prevent any kind of future electric power shortage. According to the prevailing attitudes of the 1960s, the solution to meeting future electric power demand left no other option except building thermal electric generation plants. But financing their construction constituted a formidable challenge to public power systems. Most public power systems depended upon the federal hydroelectric system for power —power they could purchase and then resell—and as a result, these utilities, on an individual basis, possessed scant financial resources. BPA officials were not insensitive to this problem, and in 1968, BPA Administrator H. R. Richmond requested that the Joint Power Planning Council, an organization consisting of BPA and 108 public and private utilities, study the possibility of adding large thermal electric plants to the Pacific Northwest power grid (Bonneville Power Administration, 1980; Lee, 1980).

Brainstorming by the Joint Power Planning Council produced recommendations for a Hydro-Thermal Power Program, a far-reaching power plan that effectively linked BPA, the public utilities, and the investor-owned utilities in an energy-economic-planning triangle. The Hydro-Thermal Power Program, initially presented in 1968, circumvented the public utility's financing problem through a "net billing" agreement. Under net billing, BPA assumed the public power system's share of the cost for the new thermal plants and acquired the power generated. BPA would pay these costs by giving power credits to the public power system's account for their share of the thermal plant's costs, reducing their annual bills for power purchases and other services from BPA (Bonneville Power Administration, 1980). BPA planned to combine the cost of thermal power with the cost of hydropower once the thermal plants were "on line," internalizing the public power systems' cost of building thermal units. Simply stated, BPA was indirectly backing thermal power plant construction with the financial resources of the United States government, an action which would ultimately become visible to BPA's customers as rate increases to pay for the combined power costs (see exhibit 2).

In the estimation of the region's power planners, the need for new thermal electric power generation was beyond question. So much so in fact, the BPA and the region's electrical utilities originally projected the siting of twenty nuclear reactors for the Pacific Northwest power grid by 1990—should future load growth follow historical trends. Under the Hydro-Thermal Power Program's first proposed "package," regional investments for electric power generation transmission and distribution—within the period 1970 through 1990—were expected to cost approximately $17 to $18 billion, the federal portion expected to be approximately $5.5 billion. Nonfederal thermal generation was projected to cost approximately $4 billion (Bonneville Power Administration, 1969a; Bonneville Power Administration, 1969b; U.S. Comptroller General, 1974). By 1970, electric power planners scaled down the scope of the Hydro-Thermal Power Program, and seven thermal plants were scheduled to come on line between 1971 and 1981.

At this time, few utilities or utility groups in the Pacific Northwest were thought to be in a better technical or organizational position to sponsor new power plants than the Washington Public Power Supply System. As a joint operating agency of the state of Washington, the Supply System could build, buy, own, and operate electric power and transmission facilities and sell electric power. Over one hundred utilities participated under the consortium umbrella provided by the Supply System. The policy and management control of the Supply System rested in its twenty-three member board of directors along with a managing director who handled daily affairs (Rev. Code Wash. 45.32). The board of directors consisted of representatives from the full-member utilities, the majority being elected officials from rural public utility districts. Like the public power systems that comprised the

Supply System, the joint operating agency was authorized by law to protect the public interest and adhered to the standards of "prudent utility practice." The Supply System's obligation to prudent utility practice was expressed in clear terms by former Managing Director J. J. Stein:

> Prudent utility practice requires the Supply System to accomplish its task at the lowest reasonable cost consistent with the reliability, safety, and expedition. . . . The matter of prudent utility practice is a protective clause . . . to keep the Supply System from making decisions undertaking those things that might not be in the interest of all of the people concerned (Stein, 1975).

Because of the Supply System's perceived ability to sponsor satisfactorily thermal plants, the Public Power Council—a Northwest public utility planning organization working in cooperation with the Joint Power Planning Council—requested the Supply System to sponsor one of the planned nuclear plants (WNP-2); and again in 1972, the Public Power Council requested the Supply System to sponsor two more plants (WNP-1 and 3). The Supply System gave an affirmative reply to the Public Power Council's request, and by the end of 1972, BPA had prepared net-billing agreements for all three plants (Power Planning Committee, 1969, 1972; Olsen, 1983).

Support for the Hydro-Thermal Power Program and particularly nuclear energy was actively voiced by a variety of electric power planners and actors. Representatives from the Northwest Public Power Association contended that "nuclear power offers the brightest hope as an alternative to hydro. . . ." Frank M. Warren, president of the Portland General Electric Company, stated that "these arrangements [Hydro-Thermal Power Program] will be an adequate and reliable source of power at low cost for both investor-owned and public utilities." Owen W. Herd, Managing Director of the Supply System, noted that "the Bonneville Power Administration program is a realistic plan for meeting the low-cost supply objectives of Washington Public Power Supply System members and all the public agencies of the region . . . public power interest as well as those of private utilities are well protected" (Northwest Public Power, 1969). Likewise, the Bonneville Power Administration vigorously promoted the necessity of the Hydro-Thermal Power Program and gave thermal power development highest priority. With almost evangelistic zeal BPA officials proclaimed:

> Failure to meet regional power requirements as they develop will result in economic and social penalties. Increased use of electricity has contributed importantly to the emancipation of people from poverty and drudgery and to expansion in the human capacity to live the good life. Any further efforts to extend these benefits to a larger segment of our society will require more electricity . . . significant growth and power requirements cannot be stopped without compromising the future well-being of people . . . failure to meet future power requirements is an unacceptable alternative (Bonneville Power Administration, 1971:v−vi).

The confidence Bonneville Power Administration and others placed in the Hydro-Thermal Power Program proved to be short-lived. In less than five years, the program was in economic jeopardy, and BPA was forced to terminate "Phase One" of the program. Escalating project costs threatened the financial capabilities of net-billing, and changes to Internal Revenue Service regulations removed the Supply System bonds' tax exempt status. In 1973, BPA announced an end to net billing for new plants, and later in 1976, BPA issued "notices of insufficiency" to public power systems stating that BPA lacked sufficient power resources to meet their expected power demand beyond 1983. The only resource BPA could offer the region became known as the "Phase Two" proposal. Under Phase Two, BPA would continue to augment its own hydropower capacity and to expand the Pacific Northwest power grid to the advantage of public power systems and privately owned utilities, but the utilities would have to build their own generation facilities to meet future power demand (Power Planning Committee, 1980; Bonneville Power Administration, 1980).

Even though the Hydro-Thermal Power Program did not live up to the expectations of its designers, concern over expanding electric power loads prompted the Public Power Council to approach the Washington Public Power Supply System again in 1974 with a proposal to build two more nuclear plants (WNP-4/5). The Supply System accepted the Public Power Council's proposal and began the process of selling to utilities shares of the plant's power generation, because Washington state law required joint operating agencies to guarantee total plant capacity purchase prior to issuing revenue bonds. The financing of WNP-4/5, as provided under the Phase Two proposal, did not receive federal backing by Bonneville Power Administration, and this meant that the participating utilities would be directly financing the plants through their own borrowing capabilities (Olsen, 1983).

The lack of a regional financing mechanism made some participants mildly hesitant to join in the WNP-4/5 venture. However, some of the participants, through discussions with Bonneville Power Administration officials, mistakenly drew the conclusion that BPA would eventually assume financial responsibility for WNP-4/5. BPA officials, according to former BPA Deputy Administrator Ray Foleen, "certainly made a case for signing [agreements] . . . but there was nothing at the time that promised" that BPA would assume financial responsibility of the plants. Also, in letters to potential participants, BPA Administrator Donald Hodel made it clear that BPA did not have any existing plans to join in plant financing. Still, according to Snohomish County Public Utility District Commissioner Stan Olsen, BPA and the private utilities "pleaded with the eighty-eight participants to commit to build the projects" (Hodel, 1976; Gleckman, 1981; *Oregonian,* 1981; Personal Communication Foleen, 1981). In a special report prepared by the United States General Accounting Office, GAO investigators concluded that "BPA and utility officials as well as documents obtained from their files, agree that BPA endorsed the need for additional generating units to meet regional power needs." GAO noted further that, while it would be impossible to "quantify the impact" of BPA's notice of insufficiency on the utilities' decision to participate in WNP-4/5, the notice of insufficiency "was a strong factor in their decision to participate in the plants" (GAO, 1982). Regardless of what some BPA officials may have inferred, the participants agreed to join in the building of WNP-4/5, thus committing the Supply System to build five nuclear power plants at the same time—a construction plan of unprecedented size.

While the Supply System was responsible for the overall nuclear construction program, the actual design and construction of the five projects was performed by engineering firms and private contractors hired by the Supply System. Three different architect/engineers were employed to design the plants, and in varying degrees, these firms served as construction managers, participating in construction management and engineering, project scheduling, and contracts preparation. By 1978, the Supply System sought a stronger role in construction management and integrated its own staff with the architect/engineering management staff. The Supply System later reverted to the old system, with WNP-3 and 5, at the Satsop construction site. The Supply System hired, under competitive bidding, the contractors to perform the work specified by the architect/engineers, with contractors hiring their own laborers. The Supply System relied upon "fast-track" engineering scheduling, where construction contracts were awarded and construction began physically before engineering and design were completed, an engineering scheduling program commonly employed by the nuclear industry (Senate Energy and Utilities Committee, 1981). The benefit of a fast-track schedule was that the project construction time could be reduced by overlapping activities instead of scheduling construction activities in a sequential manner. Naturally, because of overlapping construction and management activities, management complexity became exacerbated, and since the design was not completed prior to construction and initiation, contracts had to be amended in many instances, as engineering design was completed.

Although the Bonneville Power Administration did not hold any financial or direct managerial obligations regarding the construction of WNP-4/5, the agency, under the net billing agreements, was ultimately responsible to pay the costs associated with WNP-1, 2, and 3. Because of BPA's enormous financial responsibilities and because of its legislative responsibility to the public, it was necessary for BPA to assume an oversight role over the construction of WNP-1, 2, and 3. BPA's oversight role included review of Supply System construction program analysis, engineering and construction contract modifications, construction budgets, and economic planning and schedule changes (Institute of Public Management, 1979; Personal Communication Holberg, 1981).

SOUNDING THE ALARM

The decisions made by Supply System participants to build five nuclear power plants were founded on the belief that the region's future electric power demand would continue a 4 to 5 percent average annual increase as it had in the past. The "Long-Range Projection of Power Loads and Resources" prepared by the Pacific Northwest Utilities Conference Committee (PNUCC) served as the Pacific Northwest utilities' primary electric power demand forecast; and based on the long-range projections, the utility planners determined that the "projects are needed in the area to assure an adequate power supply . . ." for the future (Stein, 1975; WPPSS, n.d.). While Supply System officials recognized that a forecasting error on the "high side" could lead to a surplus of generating capacity, it was assumed that forecast projections which turned out too low could have serious social and economic consequences:

> An industrialized economy depends on electricity. Two-thirds of all electric energy, both in the nation and the Pacific Northwest, is used in commerce and industry. An inadequate power supply for industry means reduced capital investment, fewer jobs, decreased payroll, less production, and lower living standards. To government it means the increased burden of welfare and unemployment benefits concurrent with the decrease of personal and corporate tax receipts. . . . In the Pacific Northwest, the thermal generating resources must be scheduled to allow the region to serve the firm load requirements . . . (WPPSS, n.d.).

In the following years, it became apparent to the region's energy planners that previous long-range projections—1969 through 1976—significantly overestimated actual load growth. For example, in 1976, the year the Supply System committed itself to build WNP-4/5, forecast projections indicated an average annual rate of growth of 4.4 percent between 1977–78 and 1987–88. By 1980 the Pacific Northwest Utilities Conference Committee substantially revised its past projection, reducing average annual load increases to a maximum of 3.1 percent over a twenty-year period, and four years later, the PNUCC projections dropped further still to 1.4 percent average annual rate of growth (Power Planning Committee, 1969, 1972, 1976, 1980; PNUCC, 1981; PNUCC, 1984). As the above change in long-range projection indicates, load forecasting was and continues to be a complex and imperfect science.

The reasons for forecasting errors during the late 1960s and early 1970s were numerous. One assessment has been provided by the Army Engineers in their review of regional power demand forecasts:

> Electricity demand from 1973 to 1977 was overestimated by an average of 7.85 percent. In 1973, a critical power shortage due to a lack of water and the Arab oil embargo led to a crisis-induced conservation program throughout the region. About the same time, Pacific Northwest Utilities began to increase their rates to pay for the higher cost of thermal power plants they were building. These events, followed by the 1974–75 regional economic recession, all led to lower electricity consumption than had been projected. In general, . . . forecast[s] tended to underestimate actual electricity demands until the mid-1960s, and overestimate them after that. . . . However, except for the 1973–74 rate increases, the magnitude, timing, and impact of the events which lead to these underestimates and overestimates [bad weather, water shortage, embargo, recession] probably could not have been accurately predicted by any forecasting technique (U.S. Army Engineers, 1978:23).

It has been suggested that one reason for the forecasting errors transcended all others: the region's utility officials felt compelled to honor stringent service standards. Electrical utility officials possessed a "moral obligation" to provide adequate service to their customers despite any unforeseeable circumstances (Ernst and Ernst, 1976). This obligation led utility officials to plan for a surplus of electric power generation beyond the bounds of necessity.

While forecasting demand proved difficult, surprises awaited on the supply side as well, and few energy analysts, economists, or engineers were aware of the dramatic costs surrounding nuclear power plant construction. Even so, not all seers foretold a bountiful future for nuclear power development in the Pacific Northwest. As the Hydro-Thermal Power Program began in 1970, BPA Administrator H. R. Richmond conveyed his own foreboding thoughts about thermal power economics before the BPA Advisory Council:

> The next more serious problem is financing. Twenty billion dollars to raise in the region is going to be very difficult. Whether you are going to the federal treasury, the private money markets, or the municipal bond markets. It may be more difficult than the environmental problem, I do not know. For the nation as a whole, the question I have is that the nation needs to invest in electric facilities in the next twenty years some $360 billion. The only other figure approximately that large is the national debt. The question is, 'Can the electric industry literally raise this kind of money?' They have a difficult job. The other problem we have is construction delays. We talk about how to figure deficits and supply, that is assuming that all these projects stay on schedule. Of course, the extent to which they slip for one reason or another, the regional generating capacity changes, and they change for the worse. The final problem, I think, in implementing this program is cost escalation. The cost of anything that anybody builds, including power plants and transmission lines, is escalating at a very alarming rate. That will present some real problems (Bonneville Power Administration, 1970:5).

History has since demonstrated that Administrator Richmond's early concerns over the successful implementation of the Hydro-Thermal Power Program were extremely farsighted for his day.

By the end of the 1970s, widespread anxiety over the large-scale cost overruns affecting the Washington Public Power Supply System became intense. The danger posed by cost overruns, though, became apparent in the early months of 1975, as the estimated cost for WNP-1, 2, and 3 increased by almost one billion dollars. Later in the year, Supply System Managing Director J. J. Stein issued the following warning in the Supply System's annual report:

> It now appears that completion of many of the thermal plants is running behind schedule. . . . These delays increase plant cost for an industry already encountering high financial charges and escalating labor and equipment costs. The rise in cost ultimately will be borne by the consumer in the form of higher electric rates (WPPSS, 1975).

In 1976, the Thermal Projects Division of the Bonneville Power Administration discussed internally the Supply System's cost overrun problem; and in 1977, BPA Acting Administrator Ray Foleen began to question formally Supply System cost overruns and management problems:

> There is some concern over the nineteen percent increase in owner's cost for the three net-billed projects during the past year. These costs approach or exceed the architect/engineers cost for each project. There appears to be a duplication of effort between the owner and architect/engineer in several management areas and we would like to continue working with your staff on this item (Foleen, 1977).

Later BPA Administrator Sterling Munro would write Supply System Managing Director Neil Strand and express apprehension over cost overruns in even stronger terms:

> As mentioned in our meeting, we are very concerned with the lack of progress [by WPPSS] over the past six months. . . . The current cost of the net-billed projects have a very substantial impact on our projected rate increase in 1979. Delays in the presently scheduled commercial operation dates and increased project costs will have a significant impact on BPA's resource planning and future rate studies . . . (Munro, 1978).

The Supply System's ability to finance its nuclear projects depended upon the issuance of revenue bonds, and as late as 1980, the eastern bond market did not question the economic credibility of the Supply System's far-reaching construction program. However, two factors began to work against the Supply System's financing program. First, the escalating capital costs surrounding nuclear plant construction forced the Supply System to make more and more frequent trips to the bond market. Investors, while not openly worried by the Supply System's ever-more-frequent borrowings, now began to watch Supply System actions with a more critical eye. Second, the bond market as a whole was becoming saturated, forcing the Supply System to raise interest rates to a record high level to make the bonds competitive within the market. In effect, rising capital costs, a saturated bond market, and high interest rates began to tumble the Supply System into a synergistic spiral with chances of recovery diminishing daily (see exhibit 3).

While the saturated bond market and escalating interest rates represented cost factors beyond the Supply System's control, the overall growth in the estimate of total nuclear plant costs caused Bonneville Power Administration and the Washington State legislature to scrutinize carefully the Supply System operation. BPA contracted with the counseling firm of Theodore Barry and Associates (TBA) to prepare a management study of the Supply System and to review the unique oversight role BPA held because of the net billing agreements on WNP-1, 2, and 3. Study results, published in 1979, criticized the Supply System for inefficient contract arrangements with project architect/engineers, weak accounting and internal auditing procedures, and most importantly, a management system unable to control project progress and quality (TBA, 1979). The Washington State Senate Energy and Utilities Committee conducted a special inquiry of Supply System operations in 1980 and reached similar conclusions to the TBA study regarding important issues like the Supply System's inefficient contractual relationships with project architects and engineers. Moreover, the Senate Inquiry Committee stressed other problems, such as the "apparent absence of any realistic discipline in budget and schedule processes," failure of the board of directors to address adequately policy considerations associated with Supply System project decisions, "duplicative efforts resulting from the poor management of the many contractors on the same site," and the failure to prepare cost estimates "at a sufficient level of detail to assure accuracy" (see exhibit 4). But above all, the Senate Inquiry Committee determined that "WPPSS management has been the most significant cause of cost overruns and schedule delays on the WPPSS projects" (Senate Energy and Utilities Committee, 1981).

In defense, Supply System officials stressed the aggravating problem of regulatory costs, claiming that 30 to 50 percent of the cost overruns were directly attributable to design and construction changes caused by ever-increasing regulatory requirements. Though the Senate Inquiry Committee concluded that an inadequate "change management system" accentuated the difficulty of adapting to regulatory requirements, the committee did bring to light a significant point: the Supply System did not have any acceptable method of accurately isolating regulatory costs. In fact, as later noted by Supply System manager of licensing programs, Gerald Sorenson, neither the Supply System nor any other utility building nuclear power plants had included or attempted to estimate with reasonable precision the effects of primary and secondary costs—such as increased work scope from new or revised regulations, design change delay, site certification delay and inflation costs associated with permit and construction delay—were not calculated into Supply System budgets, because satisfactory calculation methods did not exist (Personal Communication Sorenson, 1981).

The Supply System's failure to control costs was not atypical of the experience of other utilities throughout the nation—many nuclear power construction programs incurred project delays, escalating construction costs to satisfy regulatory changes, and the indirect costs associated with inflation and the utility industry's inability to take advantage of a "learning curve" due to the simultaneous timing of most nuclear power plant construction programs. But to a larger degree than most utilities, the Supply System issued bonds to pay not only for construction costs, but also for interest costs coming due on money borrowed during project construction—the capitalizing of interest charges. As a result, the Supply System faced high debt-service charges during the period of construction, adding to the total debt-service charges that would have to be paid when the plants were completed.

Perhaps the most significant common denominator between the Supply System and the national electric power industry was how utility managers reacted to the supply and demand situation during the 1965–1980 period. In previous years, 1945–1965, utility managers witnessed sustained rates of high economic growth, with corresponding growth rates for electric power demand: demand met by larger power plants capable of providing more efficiency and economy of scale. After 1965, costs of production increased rapidly, but utility officials did not immediately alter rate policies to reflect higher product costs, and customers continued demand patterns that bore little relationship to the changing cost structure of new power supply (Hyman, 1983). Even when utility managers began to adjust upward electric power rates in the mid-1970s, conventional industry thinking held that rates of demand would remain relatively constant; utility economists believed that society's firm reliance on electric power made demand for this commodity inelastic. However, when prices did shift upward, consumers defied the ''myth of inelasticity,'' lowering their rate of demand, and leaving utilities with high fixed costs and a declining rate of new revenues to pay for power units coming on line (see exhibit 5). Consequently, by 1982, over seventy-five nuclear power plants were cancelled throughout the nation due to cost overruns coupled with low demand growth (Rosa and Freudenburg, 1984). The impact of the economic forces described above was especially pronounced in the Pacific Northwest, because most utility customers had been nurtured on extremely low-cost, federal hydropower, and even modest increases of about 1¢ to 1.5¢ per kWh were regarded as intolerable. The only alternative, in the minds of utility customers, was to use less electricity.

Confronting the reality of insurmountable economic obstacles, the Supply System's Board of Directors ordered a construction moratorium on WNP-4/5 in June 1980. As the future of the two nuclear projects took an obvious turn for the worse, Washington Governor John Spellman and Oregon Governor Victor Atiyeh asked business and financial leaders John Elorriage, U.S. Bankcorp Chairman; George H. Weyerhauser, Weyerhauser Company president; and Edward E. Carlson, UAL, Inc., Chairman, to ''investigate the economic consequences to the region of the future construction or disposition'' of WNP-4/5. This ''blue-ribbon panel'' concluded that the projects should be mothballed for two to two and one-half years, preventing the project participants from paying immediately the interest and principal due on the revenue bonds, as stated in the bond resolutions (Governors' Panel, 1981). The Supply System Board of Directors accepted this advice. But despite a serious attempt to secure mothballing, participating utilities owning 30 percent of project shares forced the Supply System's board of directors to terminate WNP-4/5 on January 22, 1982. The bond resolutions required participants to begin paying interest and principal due on the bonds twelve months later.

Reflecting the concerns of a bewildered constituency, the Washington State legislature commissioned the Office of Applied Energy Studies at Washington State University and the Energy Research Center at University of Washington to conduct an ''independent study'' of WNP-4/5. University researchers concluded that:

> The total cost at completion, including financing costs, ranges from $12.5 billion for completion in 1987 upward to a projected $23.6 billion for completion in 1997–98 after a ten-year deferral. However, when costs for completion at the later dates are adjusted for general inflation, they are roughly equal in value. Total costs at termination are approximately one-half the cost of com-

pletion when both are expressed in inflation-corrected values (Office of Applied Energy Studies, 1982:2, 17–19).

Given the above conclusions, university researchers recommended that "every effort to avoid irrevocable termination" should be made, and that "regional power plans continue to include WNP-4/5 ahead of more expensive new-start projects in the region's thermal power plant construction schedule . . . ."

WOMEN AND CHILDREN LAST

When economic analysis ends and payment for past miscalculation begins, lawsuits usually follow, and the case of WNP-4/5 did not prove otherwise. Shortly after formal termination, the Supply System faced multiple lawsuits for breach of contract on WNP-4/5, where utilities sought to extract themselves from their bond debt. Oregon utilities received tentative legal relief from their WNP-4/5 debt when Lane County Circuit Judge George Woolrich ruled that the WNP-4/5 contracts violated the utilities' state enabling legislation; however, the state Supreme Court disagreed and overturned the original ruling. Utilities in Idaho and Wyoming also received at least temporary legal relief, with the Idaho Supreme Court prohibiting municipal utilities from raising rates to pay their WNP-4/5 obligations, and the Wyoming Public Service Commission denied the inclusion of the WNP-4/5 debt into utility rates, because state enabling legislation, in the Commission's view, did not allow utilities to pay for "dry holes." The Wyoming Public Service Commission held that the cost of WNP-4/5, once terminated, "falls upon the investor, not the consumers" of the participating utilities (see Olsen, 1983).

In Washington State, the courts followed an erratic path. Chemical Bank of New York, a trustee for the $2.25 billion in revenue bonds issued on WNP-4/5, sought a declaratory judgment action to force the utilities to make payments according to their participant agreement schedule. In a summary judgment, King County Superior Court Judge H. Joseph Coleman ruled that Washington State utilities did have authority to enter the Supply System contracts, though Coleman reserved judgment on contract validity. Coleman planned to make a final ruling in mid-January 1983, but the state Supreme Court granted the utility's motion for discretionary review, setting the court date to late spring. In an earlier review of the Chemical Bank case, the State Supreme Court supported Coleman's summary judgment regarding the utility's authority to enter into Supply System contracts (see Olsen, 1983). Nevertheless, most Washington utilities gave no indication they intended to pay their WNP-4/5 debt unless forced to do so by the courts. In the words of former Clark County Public Utility District Commissioner Frank Lambert, "I don't think we'll be paying unless the guy in the black robe tells us to" (*Seattle Post-Intelligencer,* 1982).

In the flurry of lawsuits and the utilities' attempts to circumvent their WNP-4/5 debt, Bonneville Power Administration did not escape unscathed, and two "seduction" lawsuits were filed against BPA in the U.S. Claims Court by eleven Washington public power systems. According to the Washington utilities, BPA's role in promoting WNP-4/5 created a breach of existing power sales contracts and violated statutory preference customer status by issuing a formal "notice of insufficiency." Because of this action, the utilities claimed "BPA knew or should have known at all times relevant therein that the attempt by the public utilities to meet load growth through participation in WNP-4/5 would expose the public utilities to costs which they would not have incurred had BPA discharged its obligations under its contracts with the public utilities . . . ." Because of BPA's alleged contract violations, the public power systems demanded that BPA share the utilities "financial obligation and liabilities, if any, arising out of their involvement in WNP-4/5." The seduction suit gathered further momentum when Snohomish County and Clallam County public utility districts filed a separate lawsuit against BPA in the U.S. Claims Court. These utilities not only stressed the above violation, but they also asserted that BPA failed to exercise adequately its oversight responsibilities on WNP-1, 2, and 3. This oversight failure, as noted in the claim, caused cost overruns and time delays which forced the Supply System to make additional demands on the bond market, creating a saturated market that further jeopardized the completion of WNP-4/5. And, the utilities claimed BPA promised to seek congressional legislation "to acquire the output WNP-4/5 thereby removing the financial risk from the participating preference customer sponsors" (see Olsen, 1983). The utilities' desired outcome was to force BPA, through the courts, to "regionalize" the WNP-4/5 debt.

By January 1983, the story of WNP-4/5 resembled a classic Greek tragedy, with the specter of default lurking in the wings and, from time to time, moving boldly to center stage. Many of the utilities, in the view expressed by Washington Governor John Spellman, still clung to the desperate belief that the "tooth fairy [was] going to come along and pay the cost of those projects" (*Seattle Post-Intelligencer*, 1982). Bonneville Power Administration executives drew the conclusion that "investors believe 4/5 participants (utilities) are able to pay but won't" and took a serious look at the implications of default on WNP-4/5 bonds. Under default, BPA officials speculated that all municipal institutions would be "penalized by limited market access and higher interest rates," and the price of WNP-1, 2, and 3 bonds could "rise dramatically," or WNP-1, 2, and 3 bonds would be denied market access. The region's utilities would probably be denied market access for many years, and investors would likely try to seize the total assets of the Supply System, including WNP-1, 2, and 3, in order to wrestle forth payment for the WNP-4/5 bonds. BPA officials further concluded that "bondholders will not be passive, Chemical Bank will have new alternative to pursuing vigorous and drastic steps to ensure payment" (Bonneville Power Administration, 1982).

The financial community's anxiety surrounding default came to a head when, on June 15, 1983, the Washington Supreme Court ruled that the state's public power systems lacked authority to enter the 1976 participants' agreements for WNP-4/5 (Clearinghouse Service/Information Resources, 1983). The Court's ruling, which reversed the summary judgment of the King County Superior Court, was labeled as "putting risk where it belongs" by supporters and as "an avowedly political decision" by opponents. Shortly thereafter, Superior Court Judge Coleman ruled that the non-Washington participants could not be held liable given the state Supreme Court ruling. No longer receiving payments from the participating utilities, Supply System officials admitted that they lacked sufficient funds to cover WNP-4/5 bond interest accounts, and the Supply System entered technical default. The proverbial line had been crossed, and Chemical Bank and a bondholders' association filed two separate lawsuits against the Supply System, the eighty-eight participants, and others—the lawsuits alleged securities fraud. Perhaps ironically, Chemical Bank and the bond-holders intended to use the state Supreme Court decision as proof that the Supply System participants had knowingly misled bond buyers when the bonds were ini-tially issued. And again in October 1984, the bondholders filed a liability claim against the state of Washington, because the WNP-4/5 bond sales had been certified by the state auditor.

The default raised the question of whether Pacific Northwest utilities and other municipal entities would be barred from the municipal bond market or forced to pay high interest-rate penalties for future borrowings. Foreseeing economic disaster ahead, Washington and Oregon governors John Spellman and Victor Atiyeh formed a special Governors' Commission to reconcile bondholder and ratepayer interests and to avoid the financial wrath of Wall Street (Governors' Advisory Panel, 1983). Chaired by former BPA Administrator Charles Luce, the Commission reached three major conclusions concerning the WNP-4/5 situation: (1) federal legislation should be passed that would create a federal corporation with legal power to assume the assets and liabilities of the Supply System; (2) WNP-4/5 bondholders should be reimbursed partial payment, amounting to approximately thirty-six cents on the dollar; and (3) to secure the funds for partial bondholder repayment, Bonneville Power Administration should impose a surcharge on all Northwest power sales to collect funds. Needless to say, the Commission's findings represented a rational compromise to a complex problem, but each of the Commission's major points faced formidable institutional and political obstacles.

OF LIGHT IN DARK TUNNELS

The immediate aftermath of the Supply System default portrays an incomplete story. As a result of the Hydro-Thermal Power Program debacle, the state legislature refashioned the structure of the Supply System's Board of Directors, creating an eleven-member executive board composed of five representatives from the twenty-three member full board, three representatives selected by the full board from out-side the Supply System community, and three representatives selected by the state governor. Rate payers likewise desired to institute direct changes to the Supply System's governing body and, through local elections, several utility and Supply System commissioners were removed from office. The Supply System management composition was drastically changed as well, with experienced managers in the nuclear power industry brought in from outside. Lawsuits involving the Supply System continue, and whether the Luce Commission report will ever see the light of day may require several years to determine. Despite the worse fears of utility managers and government officials, the bond market did not punish either electric utilities (for individually owned projects) or the state in subsequent borrowings—an action of seemingly inexplicable logic. Even so, the Supply System was barred from the bond market to continue financing for WNP-1, 2, and 3, forcing the region to seek other funding sources for these units (see exhibit 6).

But the greatest single change to regional power planning involves the decision-making process itself, a change that has been brought about through political and economic forces ironically exclusive from the WNP-4/5 default. On December 5, 1980, Congress passed the Pacific Northwest Electric Power Planning and Conservation Act (PNEPPCA, 1980). Under the act, regional power planning has been spearheaded by the Northwest Power Planning Council, which consists of two representatives from each of the Pacific Northwest states (Washington, Oregon, Idaho, and Montana). The Council has based its power plan on the technical information and comments gathered from not only the electric utilities and Bonneville Power Administration, but also from the recommendations of its planning staff, special interest groups, and the general public. In effect, the Regional Power Act has considerably "opened" the decision-making process.

The Northwest Power Planning Council has adopted a "planning for uncertainty" strategy as the lynchpin for the new regional power plan. The Council recognized that the development of new resources necessitates sound thinking about how new power projects can be acquired by Bonneville Power Administration and how the risks of scheduling new products can be minimized. The major components of the planning for uncertainty strategy consist of a multiple scenario power demand forecast, a resource "portfolio" to match with varying power demand scenarios, a list of "resource options" to fill the portfolio, and a systematic power plan monitoring program (Northwest Power Planning Council, 1983). Following the Council's planning for uncertainty strategy, the development of resource options to meet a range of forecasts, instead of building new resources to meet a specific forecast, is expected to promote planning flexibility, to avoid irreversible decisions, and to provide a degree of control over the problem of under- or overbuilding new power generation units.

The Northwest Power Planning Council's proposed use of policy monitoring relates directly to the policy "systems perspective" illustrated by the Conceptual Model of electric power policy in exhibit 7. Because regional power planning activities will be based on a two-year planning cycle, the Council's monitoring program will be part of a periodic "action plan." Monitoring will involve a comparison of "forecast or desired system behavior with actual behavior." The Council's monitoring process will incorporate an information feedback loop, whereby the evaluation and analysis done during one planning cycle will lead to improved methods and data during the next planning cycle. By electing to redraft the regional power plan every few years, based on knowledge gained from a policy-monitoring program, the Council has institutionalized the feedback loop of the policy formulation system.

As this new power planning venture moves forward, policy analysts will be able to comprehend more fully the regional power plan's strengths and weaknesses.

But regardless of what the future may bring, the call for change is here, for the Pacific Northwest and the United States are entering a new era of economic and energy planning. The unanticipated results from past energy development plans and the panoramic nature of societal expectations places new challenges before the managers of energy resources.

References

Bonneville Power Administration. (1969a). *A Ten-Year Hydro-Thermal Power Program for the Pacific Northwest.* Portland, Oregon: BPA.

Bonneville Power Administration. (1969b). *The Hydro-Thermal Power Program: An Analysis of Investment Cost.* Portland, Oregon: BPA.

Bonneville Power Administration. (1970). *Conference Proceedings of the Bonneville Regional Advisory Council.* Portland, Oregon: BPA.

Bonneville Power Administration. (1971). *The Hydro-Thermal Power Program: Status Report.* Portland, Oregon: BPA.

Bonneville Power Administration. (1980). *Final Environmental Impact Statement, The Role of the Bonneville Power Administration in the Pacific Northwest Power Supply System, Including Its Participation in a Hydro-Thermal Power Program.* Portland, Oregon: BPA.

Bonneville Power Administration. (1982). "Background Papers for WNP-4/5 Discussion." Portland, Oregon.

Ching, C. R. (1981). "Energy Facility Siting: Recent Models of Reform." *Washington Law Review,* 56, 467–486.

Clearinghouse, Service/Information Resources. (1983). "Supreme Court Opinion, No. 49186-1." *Clearing Up.* No. 57.

Ernst and Ernst. (1976). *Incentives for Electric Utilities to Overforecast.* Portland, Oregon: Bonneville Power Administration.

Personal Communication with Ray Foleen, Special Consultant to the WNP-4/5 Participants' Committee, November 24, 1981.

Letter to Neil Strand, Managing Director, Washington Public Power Supply System, from Ray Foleen, Acting Administrator, Bonneville Power Administration, December 9, 1977.

Gleckman, Howard. (1981). "Fate of WPPSS 4, 5 Hangs on Planned Halt to Bonding, Building." *The Weekly Bond Buyer,* 225, No. 4615.

Granger, J. A. and Wise, K. R. (1980). "A Critique of One-stop Siting in Washington: Streamlining Review Without Compromising Effectiveness." *Environmental Law,* 10, 457–482.

Governors' Panel. (1981). *A Report on the Economic Impacts of the Alternatives Facing the Region on Washington Public Power Supply System Units 4 and 5.* Olympia, Washington: Office of the Governor.

Governors' Advisory Panel. (1983). *Recommendations for Solutions to the Major Problems Involving, or Arising from the Washington Public Power Supply System.* Olympia, Washington: Office of the Governor.

Letter to the City of Albion, Idaho, from BPA Administrator Donald Hodel, April 16, 1976 (example of Hodel's letters to WNP-4/5 participants).

Personal Communication with William Holberg, Thermal Projects Manager, Bonneville Power Administration, November 18, 1981.

Hyman, Leonard S. (1983). *America's Electric Utilities: Past, Present, and Future.* Arlington, Virginia: Public Utilities Reports, Inc.

Institute of Public Management. (1979). *Federal, State, and Regional Oversight: With Particular Reference to Supply System-BPA Relationships.* Richland, Washington: Report to WPPSS Board of Directors, Committee on Management Consultant.

Joint Committee on Nuclear Energy. (1968). *Report to the Legislature.* Olympia, Washington: Washington State Legislature.

Lee, K. N. and Klemka, D. L. with Marts, M. E. (1981). *Electric Power and the Future of the Pacific Northwest.* Seattle, University of Washington Press.

McCarthy, J. L. (1971). "The Evolution of Washington Siting Legislation." *Washington Law Review,* 47, 1–8.

Letter to Neil Strand, Managing Director, Washington Public Power Supply System, from Sterling Munro, Administrator, Bonneville Power Administration, March 23, 1978.

Northwest Power Planning Council. (1983) *Northwest Conservation and Electric Power Plan* Vol. I. Portland, Oregon: NPPC.

"Northwest Utility Leaders Praise Thermal Plan." (1969). *Northwest Public Power Bulletin,* 23, No. 5.

Office of Applied Energy Studies. (1982). *Independent Review of Washington Public Power Supply System Nuclear Plants 4 and 5.* Pullman, Washington: OAES.

Olsen, Darryll. (1983). Ph.D. dissertation, Washington State University.

The Oregonian, 13–20 September 1981, "WPPSS: The Power Struggle," special reprint.

Pacific Northwest Electric Power Planning and Conservation Act. 16 U.S.C. 837–839 (1980) [P.L. 96-501].

Pacific Northwest Utilities Conference Committee. (1981). *Long-Range Projection of Power Loads and Resources for Resource Planning.* Bellevue, Washington: PNUCC.

Pacific Northwest Utilities Conference Committee. (1984). *Northwest Regional Forecast.* Portland, Oregon: PNUCC.

Power Planning Committee. (1969, 1972, 1976, 1980). *Review of Power Planning in the Pacific Northwest.* Vancouver, Washington: Pacific Northwest River Basin Commission.

Revised Code of Washington. Chp. 43.52.

Revised Code of Washington. Chp. 80.50.

Rosa, Eugene A. and Freudenburg, W. R. (1984). "Nuclear Power at the Crossroads." in William R. Freudenburg and Eugene A. Rosa. *Public Reactions to Nuclear Power: Are There Critical Masses?* Boulder, Colorado: Westview Press.

Seattle Post-Intelligencer, 30 November 1982.

Seattle Post-Intelligencer. 30 December 1982.

Personal Communication with Gerald C. Sorenson, Manager of Licensing Programs, Washington Public Power Supply System, November 11, 1981.

Stein, J. J. (1975). Managing Director, Washington Public Power Supply System. Testimony before the State of Washington Thermal Power Plant Site Evaluation Council. October 8. Application No. 73-2, Vol. 24, 4457–4519.

Theodore Barry and Associates. (1979). *Management Study of the Roles and Relationships of Bonneville Power Administration and Washington Public Power Supply System.* Portland, Oregon: BPA.

U.S. Army Corps of Engineers. (1978). *Electrical Energy in the Pacific Northwest.* Seattle: Seattle District.

U.S. Comptroller General. (1974). *Pacific Northwest Hydro-Thermal Power Program—A Regional Approach to Meeting Electric Power Requirements*. Washington, D.C.: GAO.

U.S. General Accounting Office. (1982). *Bonneville Power Administration and Rural Electrification Administration Action and Activities Affecting Utility Participants in Washington Public Power Supply System Plants 4 and 5*. Washington, D.C.: GAO.

Washington Public Power Supply System. (1975). *1975 Annual Report*. Richland, Washington: WPPSS.

Washington Public Power Supply System. n.d. Application for Site Certification before the State of Washington, Thermal Power Plant Site Evaluation Council Application No. 73-2, Report Statement, Section 100(4), Amendment No. 2.

Washington State Senate Energy and Utilities Committee. (1981). *Causes of Cost Overruns and Schedule Delays on Five Nuclear Power Plants*. Olympia, Washington: WSSEUC.

"Washington State Thermal Plant Act Proposed." (1970). *Northwest Public Power Bulletin*, 24, No. 2.

EXHIBIT 1
Major Actors Concerning Nuclear Power Development in the Pacific Northwest

Washington Public Power Supply System: Joint Operating Agency of the State of Washington (Municipal Corporation); "Construction Arm" of the Public Power Systems Responsible for Building WNP-4/5.

Public Power Systems: Consumer-Owned Utilities, Public Utility Districts, Municipals, Cooperatives. Board of Directors or Council Leaders are Elected by the Customers of Each Utility.

Investor-Owned Utilities: Privately Owned Utilities, Accountable to Stockholders.

Bonneville Power Administration: Federal, Wholesale Power Distribution Agency; Provides Financial Support for WNP-1, 2, and 3 Through Net-Billing Agreements and Sells Electric Power from the Federal Columbia River Power System to Public Power Systems and Investor-Owned Utilities.

Pacific Northwest Utilities Conference Committee: Planning Organization Consisting of Pacific Northwest Public Power Systems, Investor-Owned Utilities, and Direct Service Industries (BPA's Large Industrial Customers); Responsible for Electric Power Demand Forecasts.

Thermal Power Plant Site Evaluation Council: Washington State's Siting Authority, Later Changed to Energy Facility Site Evaluation Council in 1976; Agency Reviews Utility Plans to Construct Large-Scale Power Facilities.

EXHIBIT 2

Estimated Public Power Systems' Operating Expenses and Revenue Obligations in Washington, 1982

Source of Expenses and Obligations	Cost	Percentage
Debt Service WNP-1, 2, and 3	$158,532,000	16.3
BPA Transmission Costs	56,147,000	6.7
Federal Hydro Amortization	52,844,000	5.4
BPA Administration and Operation	29,725,000	3.1
Debt Service Trojan Nuclear and Hanford N-Reactor	13,211,000	1.3
Public-Private Power Exchange	13,211,000	1.3
Conservation Programs	22,197,000	2.3
Nongenerating Utilities: Operation, Purchased Power Other than BPA	214,131,000	22.1
Generating Utilities: Operation, Power Production, and Debt Service	410,752,000	41.5
TOTAL	$970,750,000	100.0

Source: Washington State Energy Office, *Washington State Energy Use Profile*. Olympia, WA: WSEO, 1984.

Does not include operating expenses and revenue obligations of investor-owned utilities.

EXHIBIT 3
Washington Public Power Supply System Project Status, 1982 Estimate

| Project | Estimate Date of Commercial Operation | | Slippage (months) | Estimated Cost in Millions | | Estimated Cost Overrun (in millions) |
	Original	1982 Estimated		Original	1982 Estimated	
WNP 1	9/80	6/86	69	$1,204	$ 4,268	$ 3,064
WNP 2	9/77	2/84	77	504	3,216	2,612
WNP 3	9/81	12/86	63	1,402	4,532	3,130
WNP 4*	3/82	6/87	63	1,610	5,510	3,900
WNP 5*	3/83	12/87	57	1,951	6,261	4,410
			329	$6,671	$23,787	$17,116

Source: Senate Committee on Energy and Utilities, *Energy Transition to the 80s* (Olympia, Washington, 1980).
WPPSS, "Construction Budget Summary: 1982 Estimate at Completion," 1981.
Personal Communication with Thermal Projects Division, Bonneville Power Administration, December, 1981.
*Commercial operation dates and cost estimates given do not take into account mothballing.

EXHIBIT 4
Major Causes of Overruns and Schedule Delays Identified by the Senate WPPSS Inquiry

- Failure to manage effectively construction contractors
- Selection of inappropriate contract formats, methods, and contractual terms
- Failure to hold the architect-engineers and construction contractors accountable to the terms of their contract
- Decision to integrate construction management between WPPSS and the architect-engineers
- Failure to delegate adequate authority and responsibility for project management
- Failure to develop a project management system which interrelates costs and schedules
- Failure to develop schedules which integrate construction, engineering, and procurement
- Failure to develop an effective change management system

Source: Washington State Senate Energy and Utilities Committee, "Causes of Cost Overruns and Schedule Delays on the Five WPPSS Nuclear Power Plants," Olympia, WA, January 12, 1981.

EXHIBIT 5
Electric Utility Industry Characteristics, 1945–1980

Year	Percent of Change in kWh Sales	Price of Electricity for All Sectors (¢/kWh)	Electricity Use per Customer for All Sectors (kWh)	Cost of Incremental General Plant ($/kWh)
1945	−2.3	1.73	5,762	—
1950	12.9	1.81	6,377	173
1955	17.1	1.67	9,265	165
1960	9.0	1.69	11,704	149
1965	7.0	1.59	14,694	101
1970	6.4	1.59	19,380	147
1972	7.5	1.77	20,964	192
1974	−0.1	2.30	21,488	247
1976	6.6	2.89	22,361	309
1978	3.4	3.46	23,315	678
1980	2.0	4.49	23,167	553

Source: Leonard S. Hyman, *America's Electric Utilities: Past, Present, and Future* (Arlington, VA: Public Utilities Reports, Inc., 1983), chapters 13 and 14.

[1]U.S. investor-owned utilities.

EXHIBIT 6
Supply System Bond Ratings: Historical Summary

Date	WNP-1, 2, 3		WNP-4/5	
	Moody's	S & P	Moody's	S & P
June 1973*	A-1	AA		
Nov. 1974	Aa	AA		
March 1975	Aaa	AAA		
July 1975**	Aaa	AAA	A-1	A
Feb. 1977	Aaa	AAA	A-1	A+
June 1981	Aaa	AAA	Baa-1	A
Jan. 1982	Aaa	AAA	Suspend	BBB+
March 1982	Aa	AAA	Suspend	BBB+
May 1982	A-1	AAA	Suspend	BBB+
Nov. 1982	A-1	AAA	Suspend	B
March 1983	A-1	AA	Suspend	CC
May 1983	Baa	AA	Suspend	CC
June 1983***	Suspend	Suspend	Withdrew	CC
Oct. 1983	Suspend	Suspend	Withdrew	D

Source: *Background Information*, Washington Public Power Supply System, October 1984.

Notes: Moody's is Moody's Investor Services, Inc. S & P is Standard and Poors

*Project 2 initial long-term bond sale

**Projects 4/5 initial long-term bond sale

***Washington Supreme Court ruling on authority

EXHIBIT 7

Conceptual Model of Pacific Northwest Electric Power Policy Formulation under
the Regional Power Act

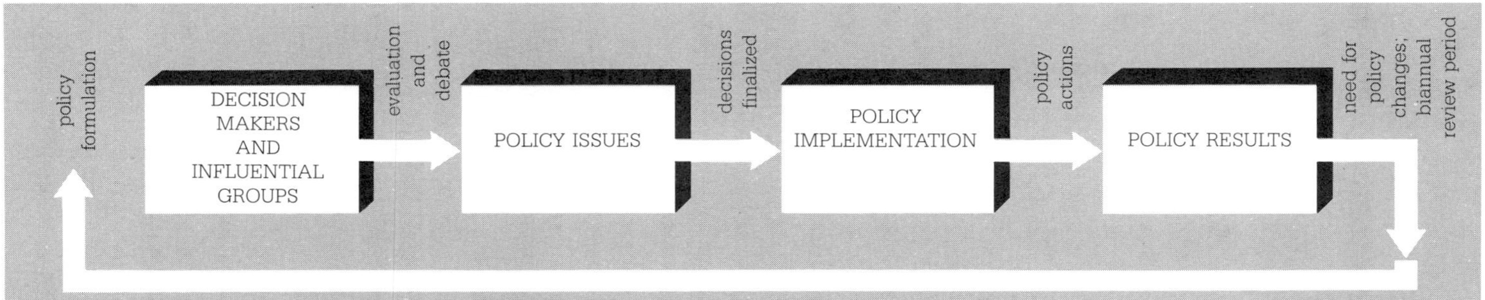

POLICY RESULTS

Policy benefits changing through time
Policy detriments changing through time
Changes to social, economic,
or environmental order

POLICY
IMPLEMENTATION

Institutional constraints
Decision makers' accountability
to public
Acknowledgeable social purpose
Policy monitoring
Unexpected technical, institutional,
and economic factors

POLICY ISSUES

Defining loads and resources
Economic structure
Public values and attitudes
Environmental constraints
Impact on industrial customers

DECISION MAKERS
AND
INFLUENTIAL GROUPS

Regional Power Council
Bonneville Power Administration
Public power systems
Investor-owned utilities
Federal, state, and local governments
General public
Direct service industries
Special interest groups

■ ■ ■ CASE 20
Johnson & Johnson, 1986:
From Band-Aids to High Tech

Donald F. Harvey
Research Assistant: Deborah Schauls

Johnson & Johnson's sleek, modernistic aluminum and glass headquarters building's structure symbolizes the changes taking place in one of the most successful firms in the United States. Chairman James E. Burke is trying to change the management style and corporate culture "from Band-Aids to High Tech."[1] Johnson & Johnson's decentralized management structure has successfully marketed its consumer products but also, through its franchises, hospital supplies and prescription drugs. A vital company, Johnson & Johnson continues to invest heavily in biotechnology and has important programs under way in nuclear magnetic resonance, ultrasound, surgical lasers, monoclonal antibodies, and intraocular and contact lenses.

As Burke has commented, "The events of the last eighteen months have put great pressure on our worldwide Family of Companies. Our people have responded magnificently. As a result of their efforts, we believe our organizations are stronger than ever before as they pursue the significant opportunities before us."[2]

BACKGROUND

Johnson & Johnson, known as the world's most diversified healthcare company, manufactures and distributes products worldwide from Band-Aids to hospital supplies and equipment. The mid-1880s marked not only the birth of this company but also the beginning of what we know today as asepsis. In 1886, J&J entered the antiseptic surgical dressing business in New Brunswick, New Jersey, utilizing fourteen employees in an antiquated wallpaper factory. By 1910 the company had firmly established itself as a leader in the healthcare field, barely keeping abreast of demand. International growth, beginning first with Canada and extending to Europe, began in the 1920s.[3]

Basic Mission

Today, Johnson & Johnson's decentralized family of 170 companies markets products in more than 150 countries and employs over 70,000. It abides by a credo

This case was prepared using published accounts and public documents for the purpose of class discussion rather than to illustrate either effective or ineffective handling of an administrative situation.

emphasizing strong commitment to consumers first and stockholders last. Charitable contributions, community service, and a dedication to equal opportunity for all are stressed as important factors for J&J, as indicated in *Fortune*'s 1984 survey of America's most admired corporations. Over 8,000 executive peers and financial analysts rated J&J as number two within the community and environmental responsibility category.[4] Johnson & Johnson's commitment to healthcare is total.[5] Its core businesses remain solidly profitable, and the scope of its product lines has become increasingly diverse. Three segments represented J&J's family of companies in 1985. J&J has positioned itself in a high-technology arena in order to stay abreast of the scientific healthcare revolution.

Strategic Action

J&J is on the threshold of either growing within the healthcare industry or becoming stagnant. In April of 1986, J&J divested itself of Technicare, its medical equipment subsidiary, because it was not competing profitably within the medical equipment market. This subsidiary was an unfamiliar, high-technology product line for J&J. A concentric, aggressive-growth strategy in familiar biotechnology pharmaceuticals is planned for the next five years. Acquisitions, internal ventures, and joint ventures are the recommended methods of entry.

The company plans to continue aggressive marketing strategies to retain its present market share leadership and to expand new product lines. Increased investment spending in research and development is imperative for J&J to gain technological advancement through all corporate segments.

Although the J&J organizational structure is quite decentralized, top management needs to incorporate some form of lateral relations via venture teams for increased success in high-tech research endeavors.

Before 1980 the healthcare industry was a stable economic environment. Since 1980 the government, in an effort to decrease healthcare costs, has imposed strict budget cuts that have contributed to a loss in sales and earnings for some J&J product lines. Products such as biotechnological pharmaceuticals, that are not directly affected by these budget cuts, need to be developed and marketed for increased profits.

DESCRIPTION OF JOHNSON & JOHNSON

Internal Structure

Exhibit 1 shows the organizational structure of one of the three main segments within the J&J corporation. Exhibit 2 lists the corporate officers and directors.

When corporations become as large and diverse as J&J, this tall organizational structure can adapt to change and facilitate the coordination of activities within each product line. However, the narrow span of control for each subsidiary manager created by this structure can cause job dissatisfaction. Johnson & Johnson has started rotating its general managers through different subsidiaries to increase managerial training,[6] to help lateral relations, and to reduce job dissatisfaction.

As exhibit 1 shows, a general manager has direct responsibility for each individual subsidiary and reports directly to a group chairman. The group chairman reports to a member of the executive committee. In 1985, J&J created three individual segments, each headed by a vice-chairman of the executive committee, to speed up the decision-making process. This decentralized organizational structure has worked well for J&J's mature product lines. Subsidiary managers in this multinational corporation are knowledgeable about the culture and the political and monetary systems of their environments. This knowledge enables the decentralized subsidiary's products to be quite adaptable to change because of each general manager's external focus and able to react quickly to competition or new consumer needs.

The major disadvantages of J&J's decentralized structure, which need to be changed by using venture teams within the organization, are (1) the difficulty of maintaining economies of scale when duplication of functions such as marketing/research and development occur across all subsidiaries, and (2) lack of cooperation and communication between product segment managers, two essentials for successful technological advancement.

Subsidiaries Extracorporeal (kidney dialysis equipment) and Technicare (medical equipment) have suffered from this strict decentralized structure. They were unable to adapt to the environment to make their products marketable.

Top management has had difficulty in progressing toward more centralized, lateral communications between general managers. Managers have been reluctant to work together because of firmly embedded decentralized procedures of the past. Also, top management has not always been consistent in supporting the newly devised centralized plan. For example, general managers in the professional segment implemented a proposal to save costs by jointly packaging medical supplies across three subsidiaries. It took top management approximately three months to finally accept this cost-saving proposal.[7] Centralized marketing and research and development procedures would enhance cost savings and product innovation for J&J's product lines.

James Burke has been lauded by *Forbes* for his strategic management decision-making style in both Tylenol poisoning crises. After working at Procter & Gamble, Burke joined J&J in 1953. His background, as well as that of the members of this corporation's executive committee, lies mainly within consumer and pharmaceutical marketing.[8]

Broad Organizational Objectives

Johnson & Johnson has consistently shown continuous growth and introduction of new products within each company segment. Chairman Burke's vision for his corporation involves advancement within high-technology endeavors. Burke strongly believes that some of J&J's maturing product segments limit long-term growth. Since 1980, he has acquired twenty-five companies for high-technology diversification.[9]

Burke has been quoted as saying, "J&J has been a high-technology company for decades."[10] His incorporation of the acquired high-tech companies within J&J's conservative culture often inhibited their ability to remain competitive within the fast-paced technological environment. Consequently, many of them have been liquidated or sold. Burke needed to keep these high-tech subsidiaries separate from J&J's present corporate culture and management principles until a communication system to help them understand the new high-tech business was developed. This communication system should have been incorporating venture teams for increased centralization between parent and subsidiary.

ENVIRONMENTAL ANALYSIS

Economic Analysis

Although J&J had been segmented into four distinct product areas in the past, steps were made in 1985 to consolidate the relatively small industrial product area into the other remaining three product areas.

The overall external environment has not been favorable toward multinationals in general. On a broad scope, J&J has shown decreased sales internationally because of the strong U.S. dollar and productivity competition from other international companies. For example, Japan's wage costs are only about 60 percent of the U.S. manufacturing average.[11] Competition is especially strong in J&J's professional segment, which carries medical devices.

Governmental Analysis

Newly imposed domestic governmental regulations regarding the healthcare industry have ricocheted, affecting all three of J&J's product lines. The Gramm-Rudman deficit reduction amendment threatens to close many less than well-managed hospitals.[12] Medicare reimbursement for hospitals, which had previously been based on fees for service, looks dismal. Congress has not yet completed the cuts in reimbursement fees that were phased in over the last three-year period as an attempt to curb the rising healthcare industry's costs. All of these legislative cost-cutting amendments affect every J&J product division because reduced hospital admissions and implicit cost-containment measures impede growth in supplying hospitals, which accounts for 40 percent of the healthcare industry's market share.[13]

Social Analysis

The healthcare cost-containment wave has given rise to a multitude of alternative-care providers, such as health maintenance organizations. Their main goal is prevention oriented: to keep their insured clients out of the hospital. Third-party insurers, such as Blue Cross, also are showing signs of collaborating with Medicare reimbursement schedules, which usually reimburse hospitals at least 30 to 40 percent less than previous fee-for-service charges.

Because much patient care is now done on an out-patient basis through ancillary services, J&J will have to focus its product lines to supply this newly created demand. Consumers will be involved in caring for their ill family members. Johnson & Johnson needs to redesign healthcare products that were once utilized only by professionals for easy consumer use.

Healthcare has become more technologically advanced within the last few years, and the emphasis is on less invasive treatment procedures. Johnson & Johnson must anticipate every opportunity to capture new ideas through research and development for new treatment modalities. Now that consumers are performing more medical tests (e.g., tests for cancer, diabetes, pregnancy) at home, and with the shift toward home healthcare, J&J will need to concentrate on this growing area.

JOHNSON & JOHNSON SEGMENT DESCRIPTIONS

Consumer Segment

Shown in exhibit 3, the consumer segment is J&J's largest business sector, representing 43.2 percent of total sales in 1985. Sales by J&J's domestic companies accounted for 59.7 percent of the total; international subsidiaries accounted for 40.3 percent. These figures were almost identical to 1984 sales. The consumer segment consists mainly of toiletries, hygiene products, first-aid products, and nonprescription drugs. These product lines are marketed through wholesale distributors and J&J's direct sales force.

Exhibit 4 shows consumer segment sales, operating profits, and profit margins.

As shown in exhibit 4, domestic sales of consumer products have risen steadily, with a modest overall increase in 1985 of 0.9 percent since 1984. International sales have been disappointing since 1983, showing slight declines, a reflection of the continuing decline in international exchange rates.[14] Even though sales of personal care products have remained sluggish, the economic outlook for industry profits is for a modest improvement. Demand for these types of products, which are for the most part discretionary, was hurt by consumers cutting back on impulse buying which accounts for roughly two-thirds of all personal care purchases.[15]

Because J&J has significant competition in all lines of its consumer products, heavy advertising and promotion costs reduced both operating profit and profit margins substantially. As shown in exhibit 4, operating profit decreased 23 percent from 1983 but showed a 26 percent increase in 1985. Profit margins have been unsteady, reflecting an overall slowing in consumer demand for personal products. Johnson & Johnson has been implementing stringent cost reduction programs through production and diversifying into more rapidly expanding businesses within its other two product-line segments.

Following robust sales in the 1960s and 1970s, the personal products industry began to slow in the 1980s as the overall economy slowed. As can be seen in exhibit 5, producers such as J&J experienced a price leveling after an upward climb since the 1970s. High operating profits have been extremely difficult to achieve since the recent Tylenol crises, primarily because of the public relations expenses necessary to regain market share.

The product life cycle demonstrates that J&J's consumer segment is in the most expensive stages of its life cycle. Sales of J&J's individual products do not necessarily follow a general pattern through the product life cycle; however, J&J can consider the life cycle for its "whole product categories," including current and potential competitors, when planning market strategies. An example would be J&J's analgesic product line vis-à-vis any competitor's analgesic product line.

Many of J&J's strong consumer products such as Band-Aids, baby shampoo, and Tylenol have been in existence for years. Two of its outstanding products within this consumer segment are feminine hygiene products and Tylenol. J&J's feminine hygiene products are progressing toward the end of their growth stage. To earn its much-acclaimed number one worldwide franchise accomplishment, J&J has had to build strong product familiarity and launch a number of innovative product features to this existing line. Successful leadership from increased promotion and advertising along with personal selling will decrease operating profits in this growth stage.

Tylenol has been in existence for twenty years and achieved market leadership by consumers through full acceptance by the medical profession. This analgesic line is now in the first phase of maturity, the growth maturity stage. Because of two recent re-entries into the marketing product life cycle, this line of products has had to fight to regain market share. Even so, Tylenol is still viewed as being in the maturity stage because its product concept has not been changed. If Tylenol had changed in chemical composition or if the use of the product had changed, then it could be viewed as entering the introduction stage in terms of gaining market share in the product life cycle.

Proprietary, or over-the-counter (OTC) drugs, account for approximately one-fifth of all drug industry shipments and have shown modest growth in recent years. OTC analgesics account for about 25 percent of the total OTC volume, and projections for OTC internal medicines are expected to expand by about 45 percent over the next five years.[16] Although this growth sounds promising for J&J's Tylenol line, a new nonaspirin analgesic compound, Ibuprofen, received approval by the FDA for marketing in 1984. Known more commonly as the OTC analgesics Advil and Nuprin, they had 3 percent of the total market share of analgesics in 1984. Ibuprofen is in the growth stage of the product life cycle. This analgesic did not have to enter the maturity stage because it is a different chemical compound than Tylenol analgesics and has different features, such as anti-inflammatory properties, on which to capitalize. The real shake-up may yet to be seen, because Ibuprofen's patent expired in mid-1985, making it possible for any drug company to copy this analgesic with its own brand.

Tylenol's past success in regaining the number one market share after two separate incidents of accidental poisonings has been attributed to J&J's sound business practices and responsible corporate philosophy. Chief executive Burke took full responsibility for winning back market share leadership after Tylenol was pulled from the shelves during each episode of poisonings. His latest marketing strategy for Tylenol involves ending capsule use altogether. There has been evidence some major producers of analgesics are following suit (see exhibit 6).

Overall, the consumer products segment is operating in an oligopolistic demand market making the fight for market share extremely difficult. Because of J&J's kinked demand curve, competition in price usually will be its least favored mode of competing for increased market leadership. The fight for market share is the heart of its marketing efforts, although Tylenol is one example where price lowering proved beneficial. Mainly, J&J strives for product differentiation. For example, its Band-Aid line has been in existence for many years, but it has consistently added new and improved products within this line. Its latest improvement to differentiate the Band-Aid line is marketing a medicated adhesive strip. If J&J resorted only to price-cuts to attempt market leadership with its high market share position in most product lines, competitors would probably feel compelled to do the same. Market shares for everyone would remain more or less unchanged, and essentially everyone would be worse off because of the lower price charged for the same quantity sold. J&J looks average in comparison with similar consumer products producers (see exhibits 7, 8, and 9). Because of the difficulty of earning high profits in this segment, most consumer products producers have diversified significantly. Although J&J is steady with respect to sales, earnings per share, and return on equity, it must be remembered that it is J&J's, as well as all corporations shown, total diversified sales that are being compared in this survey.

The consumer segment ranks number one in comparison with all J&J segments in advertising. Advertising expenditures for this segment were $210.7 million out of a total $300 million in 1985. This advertising expense is necessary to retain leading market share in the following consumer products:[17]

1	Feminine hygiene products	42%
2	Baby toiletries Sunscreens First-aid products Adhesive bandages	64%
3	Tylenol product line	33% (With 98% of dollar share it had preceding 1982 Tylenol poisonings)

Johnson & Johnson must increase market penetration in lower market share products. Promotion appeals aimed at persuading present markets to use present products will be necessary. Increasing sales of products through multinational expansion will be mandatory to penetrate new markets. Expenditures are heavily weighted in this segment toward advertising product modifications for constant consumer appeal. Such advertising will be a continuing necessity. New product introductions from the pharmaceutical segment will continue to be important because of the trend toward home testing and OTC remedies. Innovation in biotechnology is imperative for these new product introductions. The consumer segment now actively markets a new pregnancy test called Advance, which gives accurate results within 24 hours. This biotechnology product was first marketed by J&J.

PHARMACEUTICAL SEGMENT

Johnson & Johnson's pharmaceutical segment consists mainly of prescription drugs and includes contraceptives, therapeutics, antifungals, and veterinary products. These products are distributed through wholesalers and direct selling staff (see exhibit 10).

Even though pharmaceutical sales and operating profits increased 9.1 percent and 4.7 percent over 1984 respectively, the profit margin decreased slightly to 32 percent in 1985 from 33.4 percent in 1984. Significant research activities account for much of this decline.[18]

During 1983 through 1986 the pharmaceutical industry encountered slow sales and earnings growth as it struggled to adjust to medical cost containment in major world markets.[19] Domestic companies doing business in the pharmaceutical segment accounted for 54.2 percent of sales, whereas international subsidiaries held 45.8 percent of total sales in 1985.

The drug industry ranks as one of the nation's most profitable in terms of return on sales and return on investment, reflecting a relatively high and inelastic pricing structure for prescription drugs. Johnson & Johnson's research and development costs are paying off significantly, with many prescription and nonprescription drugs being approved by the FDA for marketing. New pharmaceuticals have traditionally carried high operating profit margins and are expected to continue to do so well into the 1990s.[20] The number of persons sixty-five years of age and older, who average eleven prescriptions per year (as opposed to about seven for the general population), is expected to increase by 26 percent by the end of the century. This increase is twice that projected for the overall population. Also, the projected 30 percent increase in the number of physicians by 1990 should help the prescription business.[21]

Demand for pharmaceuticals, especially for drugs with special chemical properties, is highly inelastic. Inelastic demand for a particular drug would allow J&J to price at a higher level for a substantial gain in revenue. Because the drug is a necessity for the person who buys it and lacks a good available substitute, higher price is usually not a factor in the purchase decision.

Although inelastic demand sounds very good for all pharmaceutical corporations, recent legislative action may affect this demand curve. Although President Reagan signed into law legislation that extends the patent life of prescription drugs, which would lengthen inelasticity, he also signed legislation that speeds approval of less expensive generic versions of brand name drugs whose patents have expired. By 1990, seventy-nine of the top 100 U.S. prescription drugs will no longer have patent protection and will be open for generic copying. As substitutes become available the demand curve becomes elastic, making higher prices less profitable.

The pharmaceutical industry has gone through some major governmentally induced changes within the last few years. Medicare reimbursement, previously mentioned, has affected drug sales in this population group. Sales were down to 10.7 percent in 1983 from 11.9 percent in 1982. Continued governmental control can be expected in the next few years to curb the 35 percent rise in drug prices since 1983. This percentage should be compared to the 13 percent in the overall producer price index for the same time period.[22]

In mid-1985, the Department of Health and Human Services initiated a plan that would cut as much as six months from the two years or more it normally takes to get a new drug approved for marketing in the United States. Although this should help J&J in realizing potential earnings on its newly developed products, generic sales on expired patents are expected to double from $3.6 billion to $8.2 billion by 1989.

Johnson & Johnson will need to concentrate heavily in new product development through increased research and development. Concentration in biotechnology (genetic engineering) is essential, for it is predicted that these genetically engineered pharmaceuticals could expand to $15 billion by the end of this century from essentially zero in 1980[23] (see exhibit 11).

J&J has approximately 18 percent of the leading competitor's market share. Judged by only pharmaceutical sales for each competing corporation, American Home Products (AHP) is the clear leader, with nearly twice the market share in pharmaceuticals of J&J. Pfizer is almost even with AHP, and Bristol-Myers has a slightly larger market share than J&J.

Although Johnson & Johnson is relatively strong within the drug industry as a whole, it must be constantly aware of its leading competitor's strengths and weaknesses in various drug research capabilities. To capitalize on this growing market, J&J must develop new products in such areas as cardiovasculars, antidepressants, monoclonals, and antipsychotics, to name an important few.

Exhibits 12, 13, and 14 show how J&J ranks among the pharmaceutical companies as compared by *Forbes*. The industry medians for the healthcare industry include more than just pharmaceuticals.

Exhibit 15 shows how J&J ranks on a scale from 1 to 500 within the pharmaceutical industry in various comparisons from sales to sales per employee, as determined by *Fortune* magazine. Number 1 is the highest and number 500 is the lowest within this categorical range. J&J looks very strong in sales, assets, and net income within this table; however *Fortune* included total sales of each diversified company, not just pharmaceutical sales. Johnson & Johnson's diversification compares favorably with that of some pharmaceutical companies that have greater drug sales. The information contained in exhibit 15 shows that within the pharmaceutical industry J&J:

1   Has higher diversified sales
2   Has the lead in assets
3   Has higher diversified net income
4   Has not shown a dramatic sales change from 1983–1985. (Most pharmaceutical companies rely heavily on international drug sales, and the U.S. strong dollar has limited sales growth and therefore, limited sales change.)
5   Has experienced a static profit change compared with some pharmaceutical companies. J&J is average.
6   Has the highest number of employees through its three segments
7   Has the top one-fourth of net income as a percentage of diversified sales
8   Is ranked in the upper third with respect to net income as a percentage of stockholder's equity
9   Is ranked in the middle for ten-year earnings per share growth
10 Is ranked second from the bottom on total return to investors (ten-year average)
11 Is ranked in the lower one-third on total return to investors in 1984
12 Is ranked highest for assets per employee
13 Is ranked in the middle one-third for sales per employee

It is not surprising J&J ranks highest in assets per employee because it manufactures heavily within all three segments. The most disturbing aspect of this comparison is its low return to investors as compared with other pharmaceutical companies. The low return to investors is a problem of assets growing at a faster rate than sales. This discrepancy represents ineffective asset utilization.

PROFESSIONAL SEGMENT

The last J&J segment of products is the very important professional segment. It is comprised of ligatures and sutures, mechanical wound closure products, diagnostic products, dental products, surgical dressings, surgical apparel, instruments, and accessories. These products are distributed to markets both directly and through surgical supply dealers.

Professional sales increased 7.4 percent from 1984 to 1985. Of the total professional segment sales in 1985, domestic companies accounted for 70.4 percent and international subsidiaries 29.6 percent. As shown in exhibit 6, the operating profit margin increased to 6.8 percent in 1985 from 5.8 percent in 1984. The lower profit margins of this J&J segment are a direct reflection of the previously mentioned government imposed cost containment measures as well as heavy investment spending.

Some of the more exciting breakthroughs in this professional segment in the past few years have been the introduction of surgical lasers and magnetic resonance imaging scanners. Both of these introductions are important in the fast-paced, emerging technical healthcare market today. Laser surgery has been shown to reduce postoperative infections as well as pain and bleeding. They can be used for surgical procedures in the physician's office. New uses for lasers are expected to substantially increase into a multibillion dollar market by the end of this decade. The medical laser market escalated to $330 million in 1984, up from $181 million in 1983.[24] Johnson & Johnson has introduced through its Xanar subsidiary a new portable surgical laser system that eliminates the need for bulky gas tanks. The emerging markets in dentistry, veterinary medicine, as well as neurosurgery show substantial promise for this subsidiary.

Magnetic resonance is used for both diagnosis and research purposes. J&J announced closure of Technicare, the producer of these medical scanners, in April 1986.

General Electric, a leader in all forms of medical electronic equipment, was one of J&J's main competitors. J&J incurred substantial losses since acquisition of Technicare in 1979 (see exhibit 17). Technicare was essentially a near-bankrupt biomedical equipment company which Chairman Burke hoped to turn around into a profitable imaging subsidiary. J&J was never able to match GE's efficiency in servicing medical imagers. It also failed to do market research to determine how to make its medical equipment easy for technical personnel to use. Therefore, it did not gain the needed physician loyalty and trust for increased purchases of their imaging product line. With heavy investment spending as well as marketing costs necessary to become accepted into this high-tech field, J&J found it difficult to compete with the ever-changing technological advancements being made by such competitors as General Electric.

Although J&J's market share looks very good as compared to other manufacturers (see exhibit 18), marketing efforts included two-for-one sales of its scanners, so its machines would be placed within many research and development centers. The costs incurred with this marketing strategy along with the significant product line development prompted J&J to divest with an accumulated $260 million in losses since acquisition. Johnson & Johnson, very protective of its reputation, has left this business without abandoning clients who have Technicare units. General Electric will take over the servicing of these units as well as installation of the backordered Technicare units already sold to customers.

J&J showed strong market share within the magnetic resonance division, but unfortunately was not particularly strong within any other medical equipment division (see exhibit 19). Its strength in CAT scanners looks favorable, but this form of medical diagnostics is giving way to new technology such as magnetic resonance and positron-emission tomography.

Johnson & Johnson should not have acquired Technicare with the expectation of having its medical equipment on the market within a five-year period. Technicare was not performing well within the industry, and medical equipment was an unfamiliar product for J&J. Internal product development with this described combination usually demands at least an eight-year time span for strong competitive ability.[25] Johnson & Johnson expected to gain experience, trust and loyalty of physicians, and profits on this medical equipment line in too short a time span.

Medical supplies are one of the major product lines of the professional segment. Over the last two years, J&J has developed an inventory information system for its hospital accounts. This system allows each J&J salesperson to monitor and maintain inventory levels of J&J products, keeping each hospital's inventory level as low as possible for hospital cost savings. With hospital in-patient utilization decreasing from government budget cuts, J&J has found it necessary to offer this added service to maintain market leadership of 32 percent in this product line.

J&J ranked number one within this product line for market share in 1984 (see exhibit 20). With decreased hospital in-patient utilization, medical suppliers have experienced a decline in sales within this target market. Johnson & Johnson must now target ancillary services that are benefiting from hospital patient losses such as home health agencies, minor emergency clinics, hospice facilities, and nursing homes. Although J&J market share looks favorable, it must strive to serve its customers through increased cost containment measures. Eliminating excess distributors as well as increased sales staff education will be necessary.

FINANCIAL PERFORMANCE

The healthcare industry was relatively stable until 1980. Government healthcare budget cuts and the internationally strong U.S. dollar have decreased J&J sales growth since 1980. The 1980–1985 total sales show only a 30 percent increase. J&J showed decreased working capital in 1984, and assets did not increase enough to offset liabilities in 1985. This lowered liquidity was a result of a stagnant growth in sales in the years 1983 and 1984. The increase in dividend payout ratios to 42 percent in 1984 means J&J has incrementally increased its dividends to shareholders. This payout ratio declined to 38 percent in 1985 even though the dividend increased from 1.17 (1984) to 1.27 (1985). A substantial net income increase of 19 percent from 1984 to 1985 caused this ratio to decrease even though an increased dividend was paid to common shareholders.

Exhibit 21 indicates that research and development expense has increased steadily since 1975. This increase is a good indication J&J is interested in a consistent research and development program.

Cost containment measures have been important for J&J since 1984. Total sales for J&J in the years 1983 and 1984 were low due to the strong U.S. dollar and the government healthcare budget cuts. J&J has realized the necessity of consolidating distribution facilities for cost-effective warehousing. J&J's expense-to-sales ratio declined in 1985, a direct result of warehouse consolidation across all three segments (see exhibits 22, 23, and 24).

As shown in exhibit 22, J&J's overall combined segment sales indicate steady growth with earnings also climbing. Profit margins held tight at eight percent with an increase shown for 1985 due to expense reductions as well as increased sales shown from international subsidiaries.

The "ultimate" profit measure of J&J's ability to use its assets to generate profits is return on investment. Johnson & Johnson's ratio indicates that management is, on the average, effectively using the capital entrusted to them by both their creditors and stockholders over the ten-year period. All of these industry ratios do not exactly fit J&J because of its wide product diversification. They must be used only as guidelines for measurement purposes.

The final profitability measure to be addressed measures the profits attributable to the shareholders as a percentage of their equity in the corporation. Because the measure focuses specifically on stockholders' profits and investment in relation to financial leveraging it shows that J&J's stockholders are receiving a return higher than the return on assets. This return indicates positive leveraging. Healthcare industry return on equity ratios have shown a decline in the last two years because of increased governmental cost containment measures. Johnson & Johnson ratios also reflect this volatility.

Comparing J&J's long-term debt with that of the pharmaceutical industry as a whole is most important, as the majority of new product developments come from this particular segment. The drug industry incurs less debt because of the risky nature of its research projects. With the fast technological advancements that are occurring in this industry, J&J must continually introduce innovative products for increased sales and earnings. It takes two years to legally introduce many of J&J's new product lines because of strict FDA approval requirements. Revenue increases are sometimes not realized until at least three years after initial product development. Therefore, the pharmaceutical industry can increase shareholder wealth more effectively through less long-term debt during these periods of continual product development and introduction. More of the cash flow is available to the shareholder wealth if minimal debt is incurred. This cash flow is especially important in the years of low sales and earnings because of no successful product introductions. When the expected net income stream associated with or following a divestiture is greater than the income stream of continued operation, it is in the best interests of the shareholders to sell the business unit. Because J&J announced publicly that selling Technicare was necessary for profitability the market viewed this action favorably. Johnson & Johnson will set a reserve of $230 million before taxes. These charges are in addition to the $85 million J&J incurred for withdrawing Tylenol in capsule form from manufacturing. Capsules will now be caplets for increased consumer safety. Efforts to cut out unprofitable areas will result in an increased share profit in 1986.

CONCLUSION

Future strategic decisions concern growth in a highly technical and dynamic environment. Can J&J continue to grow and diversify while maintaining strategic control? The multinational business environment may become too complex and too dynamic to allow an efficient operation of such diversification, size, and technical complexity. Johnson & Johnson ranks seventy-fourth in size among the 500 largest industrials. Can managers be developed who can keep up with this expanding diversification, complexity, and dynamic environment? CEO James Burke must remain an adaptive decision maker. The future does hold vast opportunities especially in healthcare technology. Burke must continue to lead future technological trends or see his corporation become obsolete. He must also consider the ill effects of too much diversification in an unstable and complex environment.

Burke is a great "P.R." representative. His statements concerning Tylenol seem optimistic. Behind the scenes, he invested great energy and resources in salvaging Tylenol's market share. So far he has moved faster than the competition in developing market strategy and the tamper-resistant bottle. Burke must continue this proactive behavior, not only to recover Tylenol's market share, but also to stay ahead in J&J's dynamic environment.

Managing a rapid growth company with an extremely dynamic environment is difficult; J&J appears to be doing well. Its goals are being pursued, and its employees seem happy and productive. The company is financially sound and ready to continue growing. The structure is changing to meet and more effectively plan for and control that growth. The J&J products are needed, and state-of-the-art technology is being used to produce and develop new products to meet future needs.

The future looks good for J&J, but it cannot relax its efforts for continued customer support and systems improvement. The health care industry is rapidly changing, and so are its needs. J&J must know what those needs will be and meet them.

As CEO James Burke and his executive committee planned for growth, he wondered what strategy J&J should follow in the future. "Even though we are proud of our record, we cannot relax our efforts for continued improvement of our system and support of customers. The fast-changing environment in which our customers operate today—and will operate for the foreseeable future—challenges us not to let them down. We accept that challenge with confidence."[26]

But, there are uncertainties clouding the medical technology markets. General Electric's CEO John F. Welch cautioned that the wisest strategy is simply to have "the best. There's no room for the third-best machine." In hardware, Welch scoffed that J&J is no match for GE. His advice to Burke: "People who go afar from what they know run into some ground holes."[27] Burke's challenge is to prove J&J can climb out of them.

Notes

1 *Brief History of Johnson & Johnson* (New Brunswick, New Jersey: 1986), p. 2.
2 Ibid.
3 Ibid.
4 Patricia Sellers, "1984 Survey of America's Most Admired Corporations," *Fortune*, January 7, 1985, p. 20.
5 *Johnson & Johnson 1984 Annual Report* (New Brunswick, New Jersey: 1985), p. 3.

6   Ibid., p. 5.

7   "Changing A Corporate Culture," *Business Week*, May 14, 1984, p. 133.

8   "Corporate Strategy," *Forbes*, March 24, 1986, p. 72.

9   "Changing A Corporate Culture," *Business Week*, May 14, 1984, p. 131.

10 Yvan Allaire, "How to Implement Radical Strategies in Large Organizations," *Sloan Management Review* (Spring 1985), p. 19.

11 General Electric Company 1985 Annual Report (New York: 1985), p. 3.

12 Dean C. Coddington, "Strategies for Survival in the Hospital Industry," *Harvard Business Review*, May–June 1985, p. 129.

13 "Healthcare-Hospitals, Drugs, Cosmetics," *Standard and Poors Industry Surveys*, September 12, 1985, p. H27.

14 *Johnson & Johnson 1985 Annual Report* (New Brunswick, New Jersey: 1985) p. 36.

15 "Healthcare-Hospitals, Drugs, Cosmetics," *Standard and Poors Industry Surveys*, September 12, 1985, p. H30.

16 "Healthcare-Hospitals, Drugs, Cosmetics," *Standard and Poors Industry Surveys*, September 12, 1985, p. H21.

17 "Johnson & Johnson Ranks 25," *Advertising Age*, September 26, 1985, p. 98.

18 *Johnson & Johnson 1985 Annual Report* (New Brunswick, New Jersey: 1985), p. 37.

19 "Healthcare-Hospitals, Drugs, Cosmetics," *Standard and Poors Industry Surveys*, September 12, 1985, p. H19.

20 Ibid.

21 "Healthcare-Hospitals, Drugs, Cosmetics," *Standard and Poors Industry Surveys*, September 12, 1985, p. H20.

22 "Healthcare-Hospitals, Drugs, Cosmetics," *Standard and Poors Industry Surveys*, September 12, 1985, p. H16.

23 "Healthcare-Hospitals, Drugs, Cosmetics," *Standard and Poors Industry Surveys*, September 12, 1985, p. H17.

24 "Healthcare-Hospitals, Drugs, Cosmetics," *Standard and Poors Industry Surveys*, September 12, 1985, p. H29.

25 Edward B. Roberts, "Entering New Businesses: Selecting New Strategies For Success," *Sloan Management Review*, Spring 1985, p. 28.

26 *Johnson & Johnson 1984 Annual Report*.

27 "Changing a Corporate Culture."

Bibliography

"A Medical Inventor Beats a Goliath in Court," *Business Week*, 16 December 1986, p. 32.

"Advances in Technology to Affect Planning Hospitals," *Hospitals*, 20 January 1986, p. 128.

"American Home Sues Johnson & Johnson Over Tylenol Ads," *The Wall Street Journal*, 26 June 1985, p. 16.

"America's Most Admired Corporations," *Fortune*, 7 January 1985, pp. 18–21.

Allaire, Yvan and Firsiroth, Michaela, "How to Implement Radical Strategies in Large Organizations," *Sloan Management Review*, Spring 1985, p. 19.

"Baxter Travenol Bid Is Rejected by Board of American Hospital," *The Wall Street Journal,* 30 September 1984, p. 3.

"Brief History," *Johnson & Johnson,* 1986

"Burke-Johnson & Johnson," *Computer Decisions,* 15 September 1983, pp. 12–15.

Buzzil, Robert, and Chussil, Mark, "Money for Tomorrow," *Sloan Management Review,* Summer 1985, pp. 13–16.

Chapin, Christopher K., and Jermain, David O., "Increasing the Success of Your Diversification Program," *Sloan Management Review,* Summer 1985, pp. 51–55.

"Convict in Tylenol Case Sentenced for Tax Fraud," *Wall Street Journal,* June 1984, p. 16.

"Corporate Autophagy," *The Economist,* 7 September 1985, p. 18.

"Corporate Image," *Sloan Management Review,* Summer 1985, pp. 73–81.

"Cutting The Guesswork Out of Surgery," *Business Week,* 8 April 1985, p. 80–81.

"Diamonds in the Rough?" *Business Week,* 18 April 1986, p. 251.

"Diasonics Agree to Buy Partner's Stakes in Venture," *The Wall Street Journal,* 8 March 1985, p. 27.

"Diasonics, Inc., Says Award Against It Is Overturned by Court," *Wall Street Journal,* 1 January 1984, p. 56.

Drug Industry Statistics, *Value Line* (New York, N.Y.) February–May 1986, pp. 12, 818, 981, 1250–51, 1258–59.

"Drug Tampering Warnings Come In A Calm Voice," *The Spokesman Review and Spokane Chronicle,* 23 March 1986, p. 14.

Drugs-Medicines, *RMA Annual Statement Studies,* 30 June 1983, 31 March 1984, p. 92–93.

Fisher, Ann B., "In Health Care", *Fortune,* 17 February 1986, p. 105–115.

"Generic Drugs Will Double In Sales From 1984 To 1989: Study", *Hospitals,* 20 February 1986, p. 92.

"G.E.'s Len Vickers", *Sales and Marketing Management,* 3 June 1985, p. 66.

Gobeli, David H. and Rudelius, William, "Managing Innovation: Lessons From The Cardiac Pacemaker Industry," *Sloan Management Review,* Summer 1985, p. 29–35.

Gorden Judith R., *A Diagnostic Approach To Organizational Behavior,* (Allyn and Bacon, Inc., 1983).

"Gramm-Rudman: Hospitals Budget Nightmare", *Hospitals,* 20 January 1986, p. 32–35.

Hambrick, Donald C. and MacMillan, Ian C., "Efficiency Of Product Research And Development In Business Units: The Role Of Strategic Context", *Academy of Management Review,* 1985, Vol. 28, No. 3, p. 527–547.

Harvey, Donald F., *Business Policy and Strategic Management,* (Charles E. Merrill Publishing Company, 1982).

Health and Allied Services, *Industry Norms and Key Business Ratios,* (Dun & Bradstreet Credit Services) 1984–1985, p. 194.

Heilbroner, Robert L. and Thurow, Lester C., *Understanding Microeconomics,* (Prentice-Hall, Inc., 1981).

Heins, John, "Take Two Of These and Call Tokyo in the Morning," *Forbes,* 24 March 1985, p. 178–179.

"In Today's Market The Concept Is The Thing", *Business Week,* 30 December 1985, p. 106.

International 150, *Business Week,* 18 April 1986, p. 292.

Johnson & Johnson Annual Report—1984, James E. Burke, Chairman; Chief Executive Officer, New Brunswick, N.J.

Johnson & Johnson Annual Report—1985, James E. Burke, Chairman: Chief Executive Officer, New Brunswick, N.J.

EXHIBIT 1
Organizational Structure

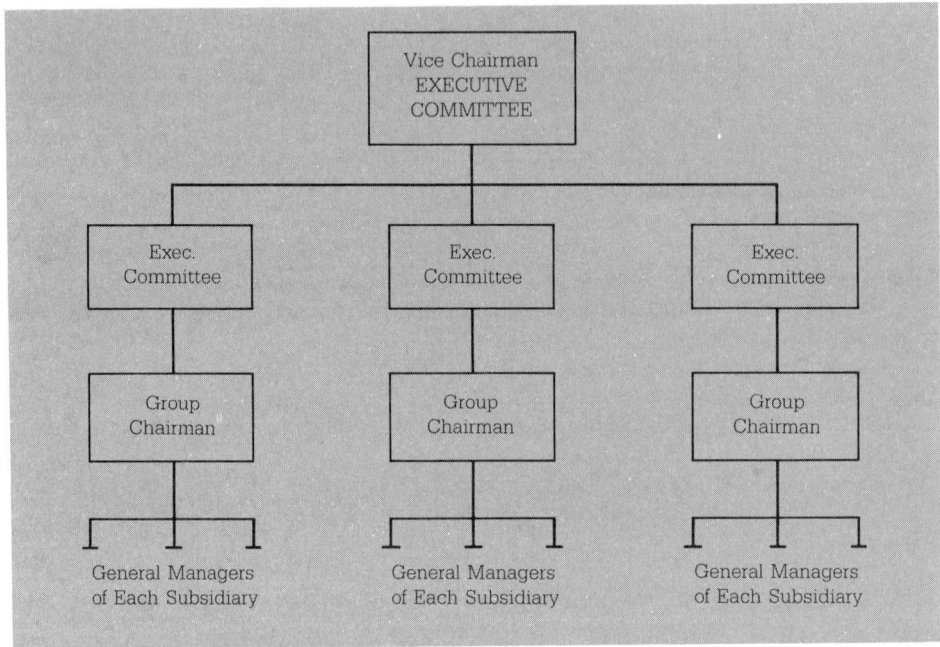

Source: Johnson & Johnson Annual Report (1985)

EXHIBIT 2
J & J Corporate Officers

Corporate Officers

Board of Directors

James E. Burke
Chairman, Board of Directors and
Chief Executive Officer

David R. Clare
President
Chairman, Executive Committee

Ronald J. Brenner, Ph.D.
Vice President
Corporate External Research

Robert E. Campbell
Executive Committee

David E. Collins
Executive Committee

Victor J. Dankis
Executive Committee

Frank De Angeli
Executive Committee

Lawrence G. Foster
Vice President, Public Relations

George S. Frazza
General Counsel

Robert A. Fuller, Ph.D.
Vice President, Science and
Technology

John J. Heldrich
Vice President, Administration
Executive Committee

Donald D. Johnston
Executive Committee

Andrew J. Markey
Treasurer

Wayne K. Nelson
Executive Committee

Joseph S. Orban
Secretary

Arthur M. Quilty
Executive Committee

Herbert G. Stolzer
Executive Committee

John C. Walcott
Vice President, Finance
Executive Committee

Verne M. Willaman
Executive Committee

Robert N. Wilson
Executive Committee

The Executive Committee of Johnson & Johnson is the principal management group responsible for the operations of the Company. Its members typically have responsibility for a group of domestic and international companies. Operating management of each company is headed by a President, General Manager or Managing Director who reports directly or through a Company Group Chairman to a member of the Executive Committee.

Company Group Chairmen

John E. Avery, Jr.

Frank H. Barker

Stuart A. Christie

Edward J. Hartnett

Paul A. J. Janssen, M.D.

Thomas M. Lane

Ronald R. Morris

Giorgio Petronio

Raymond P. Regimbal

William O. Baker, Ph.D.
Chairman of the Board, Bell
Telephone Laboratories,
Incorporated, retired

James E. Burke

Robert E. Campbell

David R. Clare

Ann D. Cook
Director of the Social Services
Department, Chicago Lying-In
Hospital

Joan G. Cooney
President, Children's Television
Workshop

Victor J. Dankis

Frank De Angeli

Robert S. Hatfield
President, Board of Governors,
The Society of the
New York Hospital

John J. Heldrich

Donald D. Johnston

Irving M. London, M.D.
Director, Harvard-M.I.T. Division of
Health Sciences and Technology

Donald S. MacNaughton
Chairman of the Board,
Hospital Corporation of America

Robert Q. Marston, M.D.
President and Professor of
Medicine, University of Florida,
Gainesville

Thomas S. Murphy
Chairman of the Board and Chief
Executive Officer, Capital Cities
Communications, Inc.

Arthur M. Quilty

Paul J. Rizzo
Vice Chairman,
International Business Machines
Corporation

Herbert G. Stolzer

John C. Walcott

Verne M. Willaman

EXHIBIT 3
Sales by Segment of Business

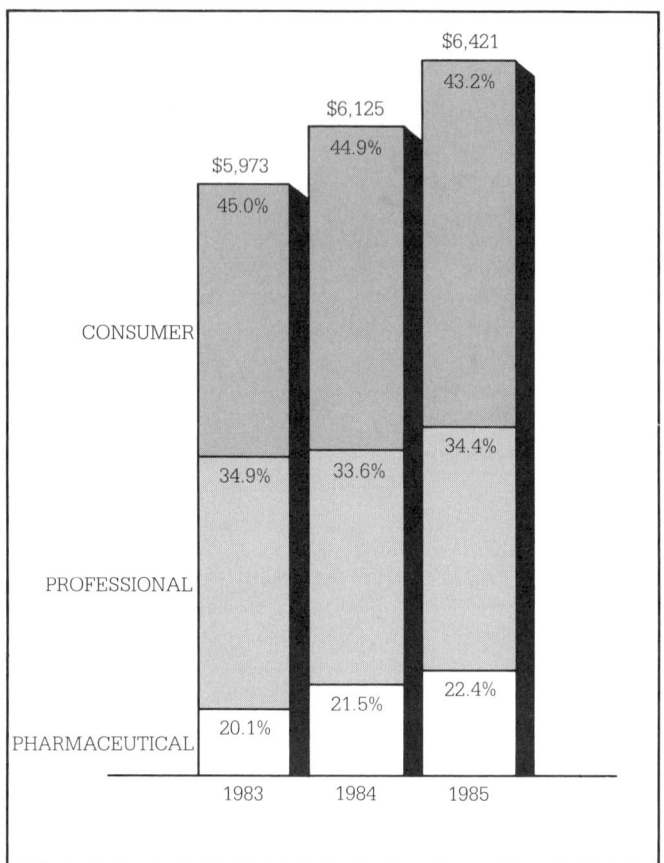

Source: Johnson & Johnson Annual Report (1985)

EXHIBIT 4

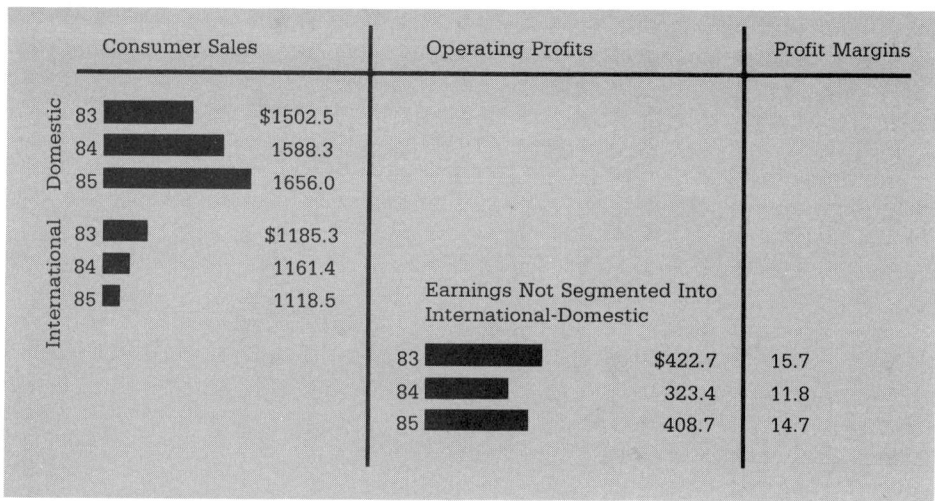

Source: Johnson & Johnson Annual Report (1985)

EXHIBIT 5
Producer Commodity Prices (1967 = 100)

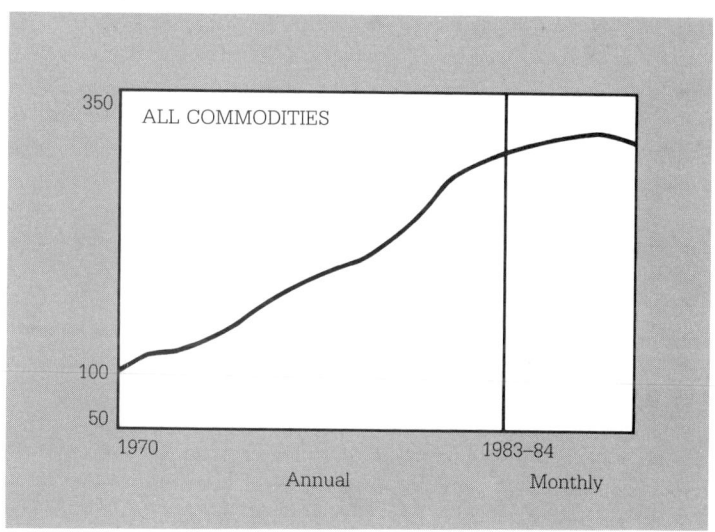

Source: Bureau of Labor Statistics; Standard and Poors; *Health Industry Report,* January 1985, p. H30

EXHIBIT 6
Estimate of the Over-the-Counter Market Share of Analgesics

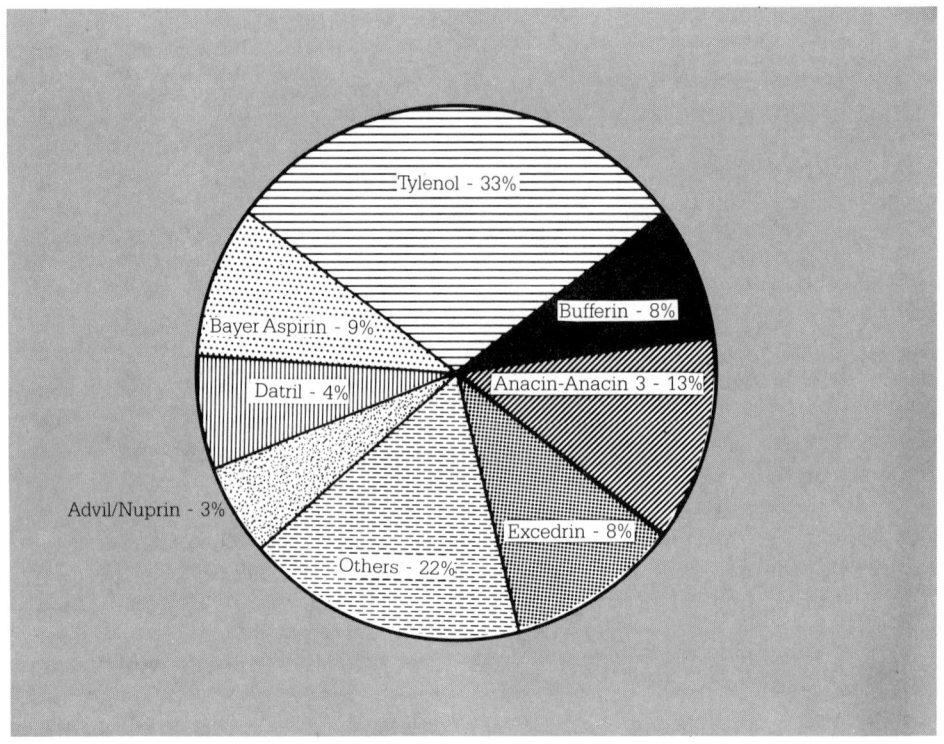

Source: Standard and Poors; *Current Analysis/Health Care,* January 17, 1985, p. H21

EXHIBIT 7

Comparative Consumer Segments Within the Personal Products Industry*

Company	Rank	5-Year Average	Latest 12 Months	Earnings Stability
Bristol-Myers	1	14.3	12.5	Very High
Chesebrough/Ponds	6	5.5	−3.2	Average
Shaklee	7	1.3	−2.0	Very Low
Procter/Gamble	3	9.4	−21.8	Very High
Avon Products	13	−14.2	−10.7	Very High
Gillette	5	6.7	−0.6	Very High
Johnson & Johnson	**4**	**7.1**	**30.0**	**High**
Hillenbrand Ind.	2	9.6	−3.2	Very High
Schering/Plough	9	−4.0	6.4	Average
Kimberly Clark	10	−4.3	25.4	Low
Colgate Palmolive	11	−5.7	−73.8	Very Low
Revlon	12	−11.6	0.3	High
Scott Paper	8	−3.2	20.2	Very Low
Medians		1.3	−0.6	
Industry Medians		**1.5**	**−2.6**	**(Earnings Per Share)**

*Calculated from 1985 company figures

Source: *Forbes,* January 13, 1986, p. 129

EXHIBIT 8
Comparative Consumer Segment Profitability*

Company	Rank	5-Year Average	Latest 12 Months	Debt % of Equity	Net Profit Margin
Bristol Myers	1	23.3	24.2	4.8	11.9
Chesebrough-Ponds	2	21.0	16.8	39.0	4.3
Shaklee	3	20.6	8.3	17.2	3.2
Procter/Gamble	4	19.7	12.8	16.6	4.8
Avon Products	5	19.3	13.9	38.1	5.5
Gillette	6	19.2	20.0	56.0	6.8
Johnson & Johnson	**7**	**19.2**	**20.3**	**7.7**	**9.4**
Hillenbrand Ind.	8	18.8	15.2	28.1	7.2
Schering/Plough	9	16.0	14.2	9.6	9.9
Kimberly Clark	10	14.7	16.9	34.4	6.8
Colgate Palmolive	11	13.4	4.2	22.9	1.1
Revlon	12	13.0	11.8	48.1	5.0
Scott Paper	13	10.1	13.0	40.7	6.8
Medians		19.2	14.2	28.1	6.8
Industry Medians		**13.1**	**14.1**	**28.5**	**4.8 (Return on Equity)**

*Calculated from 1985 company figures

Source: *Forbes,* January 13, 1986, p. 129

EXHIBIT 9
Comparative Consumer Segment Growth*

Company	Rank	5-Year Average	Latest 12 Months
Bristol-Myers	4	8.3	5.1
Chesebrough/Ponds	3	8.8	38.6
Shaklee	5	8.0	−11.6
Procter/Gamble	8	6.2	3.9
Avon Products	9	5.8	−5.5
Gillette	12	1.4	2.8
Johnson & Johnson	**6**	**7.6**	**4.5**
Hillenbrand Ind.	1	10.1	6.2
Schering/Plough	11	4.3	1.4
Kimberly-Clark	2	9.4	11.5
Colgate/Palmolive	13	0.6	−6.8
Revlon	10	5.6	0.4
Scott Paper	7	7.4	16.4
Medians		7.4	3.9
Industry Medians		**5.6**	**3.4 (Sales)**

*Calculated from 1985 company figures
Source: *Forbes,* January 13, 1986, p. 129

EXHIBIT 10
Pharmaceutical Segment Sales, Earnings, and Profit Margins

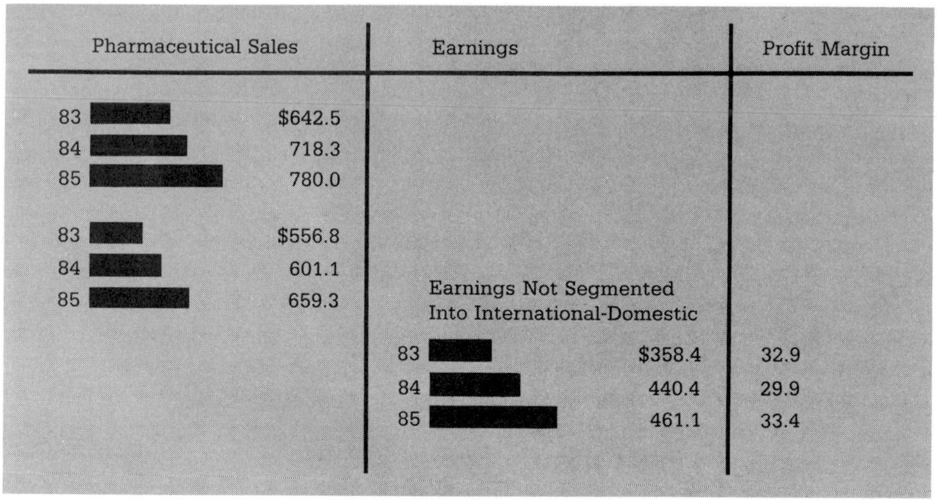

Pharmaceutical Sales	Earnings	Profit Margin
83 $642.5		
84 718.3		
85 780.0		
83 $556.8		
84 601.1		
85 659.3	Earnings Not Segmented Into International-Domestic	
	83 $358.4	32.9
	84 440.4	29.9
	85 461.1	33.4

Source: Johnson & Johnson Annual Report (1985)

EXHIBIT 11
Leading Market Shares of the Drug Industry

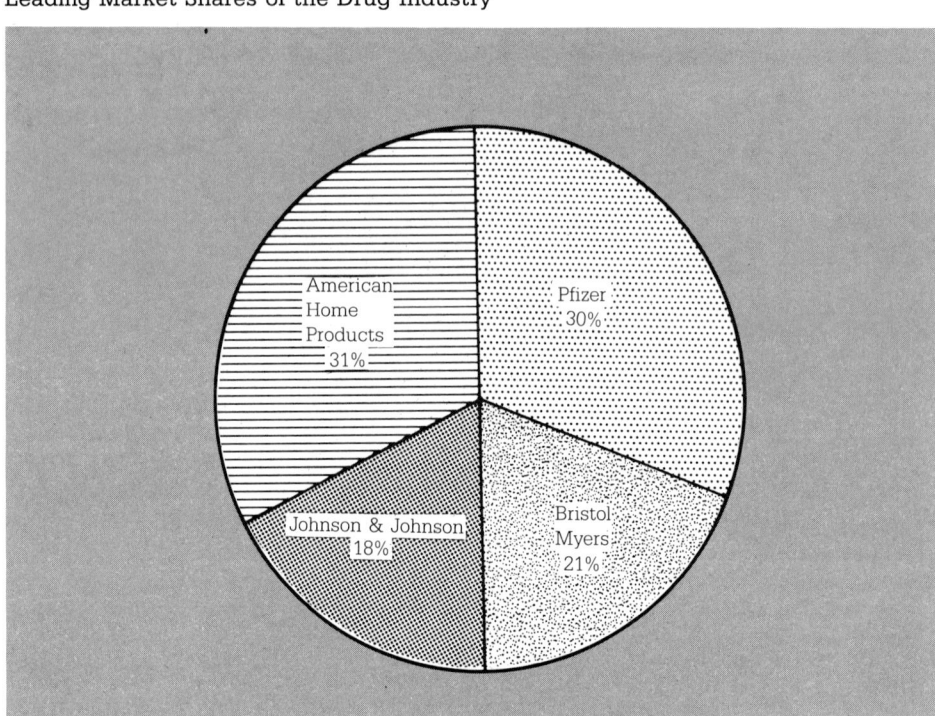

Source: *Value Line,* May 1986 (using only drug sales information)

EXHIBIT 12
Comparative Pharmaceutical Segment Profitability

Company	5-Year Average	Latest 12 Months	Debt % of Equity	Net Profit Margin
Upjohn	17.9%	16.4%	33.7%	9.2%
Schering/Plough	16.0	14.2	9.6	9.9
McKesson	14.0	12.5	33.4	1.3
Squibb	14.0	16.2	15.1	11.0
Warner-Lambert	12.6	16.7	35.6	7.4
Bristol-Myers	23.3	24.2	4.8	11.9
Johnson & Johnson	**19.2**	**20.3**	**7.7**	**9.4**
Industry Medians for Health Care Industry	18.9	16.7	29.0	7.7 (Return on Equity)

EXHIBIT 13
Comparative Pharmaceutical Segment Growth

Company	5-Year Average	Latest 12 Months
Upjohn	6.4%	−6.5%
Schering/Plough	4.3	1.4
McKesson	4.2	20.5
Squibb	4.6	7.3
Warner-Lambert	−1.3	2.2
Bristol-Myers	8.3	5.1
Johnson & Johnson	**7.6**	**4.5**
Industry Medians for Health Care Industry	8.3	6.2 (Sales)

Source: *Forbes*, January 13, 1986, p. 157

EXHIBIT 14
Comparative Pharmaceutical Segment Earnings Per Share

Company	5-Year Average	Latest 12 Months	Earnings Stability
Upjohn	0.0%	6.9%	Very Low
Schering/Plough	−4.0	6.4	Very High
McKesson	−4.9	0.5	Average
Squibb	7.4	12.9	Average
Warner-Lambert	18.7	9.8	Low
Bristol-Myers	14.3	12.5	Very High
Johnson & Johnson	**7.1**	**30.0**	**High**
Industry Medians for Health Care Industry	9.3	9.2	

Source: *Forbes*, January 13, 1986, p. 157

EXHIBIT 15
The Pharmaceutical Industry Ranked by Fortune

Company	Sales	Assets	Net Income	Sales Change from '83	Profit Change from '83	Stockholder's Equity	Number of Employees	Net Income % of Sales	Net Income Stockholders' Equity	10-Year Earnings per Share Growth	Total Return to Investors 10-Year Average	Total Return to Investors 1984	Assets per Employee	Sales per Employee
Abbott Laboratories	131	97	48	334	230	85	115	15	27	39	152	274	171	280
American Home Products	78	102	22	437	286	64	73	9	11	139	372	166	302	244
Baxter Travenol Laboratories	207	154	357	449	408	128	124	413	433	345	407	449	299	464
Bristol-Myers	92	93	41	316	231	63	107	28	39	100	217	37	185	191
Johnson & Johnson	**57**	**63**	**33**	**393**	**302**	**41**	**40**	**63**	**120**	**152**	**408**	**309**	**321**	**326**
Lilly	130	81	39	394	294	60	137	5	38	177	423	83	104	211
Merck	110	62	38	250	279	51	111	11	79	201	398	165	97	238
Miles Laboratories	281	264	363	380	365	251	256	377	405	—	—	—	218	279
Pfizer	101	73	34	386	248	54	96	13	61	130	320	66	147	250
Rorer Group	450	387	283	242	308	370	393	57	93	310	333	349	225	303
Richardson-Vicks	261	270	205	155	119	257	272	172	203	283	311	157	199	185
Robins	404	—	484	193	—	—	—	—	—	—	389	293	—	—
Schering/Plough	193	127	106	377	341	103	159	45	249	279	440	213	143	347
Searle	266	184	113	68	295	168	288	14	92	212	204	10	63	169
Smith-Kline Beckman	136	95	35	469	313	66	128	3	29	43	202	254	144	258
Squibb	191	146	93	325	246	101	162	36	205	238	364	70	172	329
Sterling Drug	196	201	117	448	303	157	166	93	182	251	399	137	294	322
Upjohn	166	140	107	245	290	125	163	85	191	199	395	61	159	268
Warner-Lambert	126	104	83	405	263	93	90	111	178	287	385	64	260	352

Source: *Fortune*, April 29, 1985, p. 310

EXHIBIT 16

Professional Segment Sales, Earnings, and Profit Margins

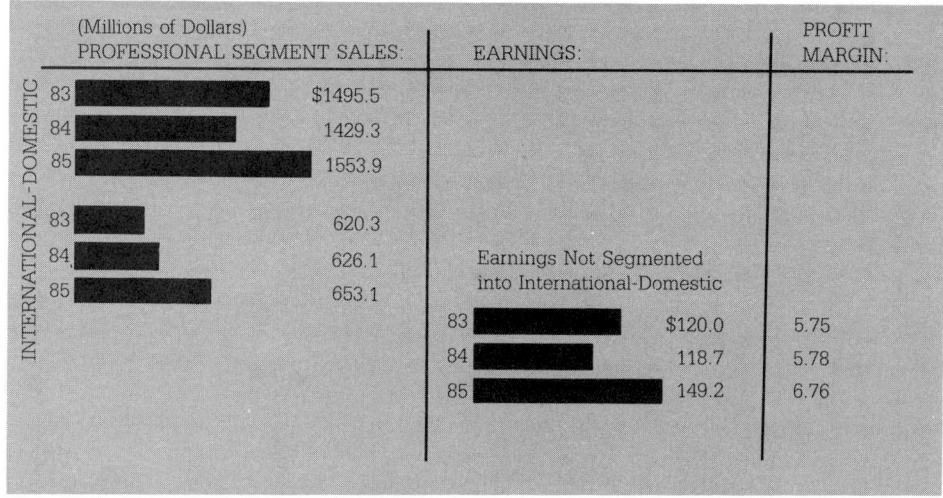

Source: Johnson & Johnson Annual Report (1985)

EXHIBIT 17

Comparison of General Electric and J&J Imaging

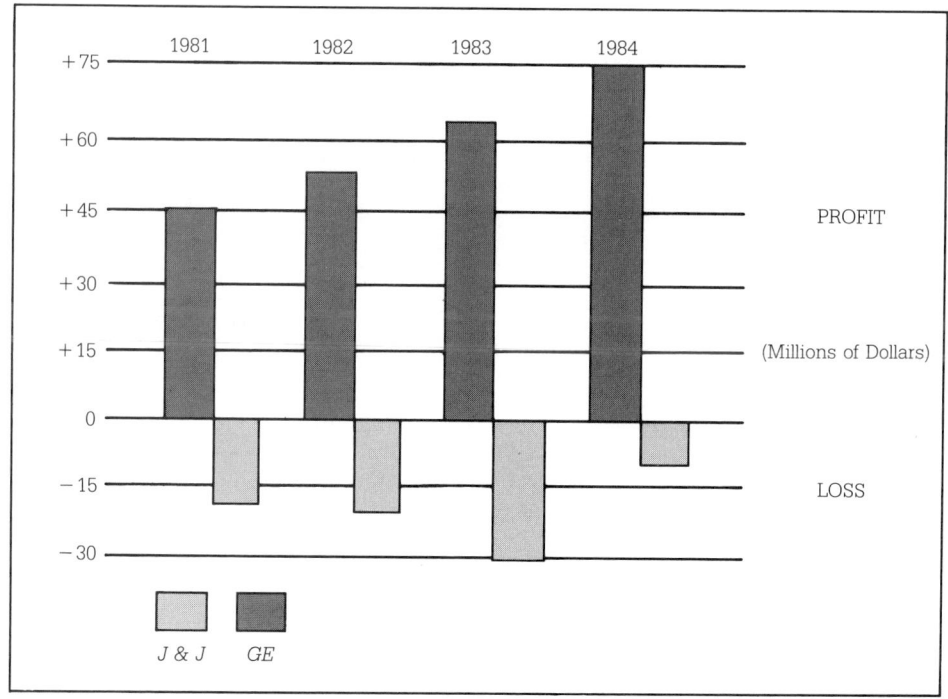

Source: *Business Week*, May 14, 1984, p. 138

EXHIBIT 18
Magnetic Resonance Scanner Market Share as of January, 1985

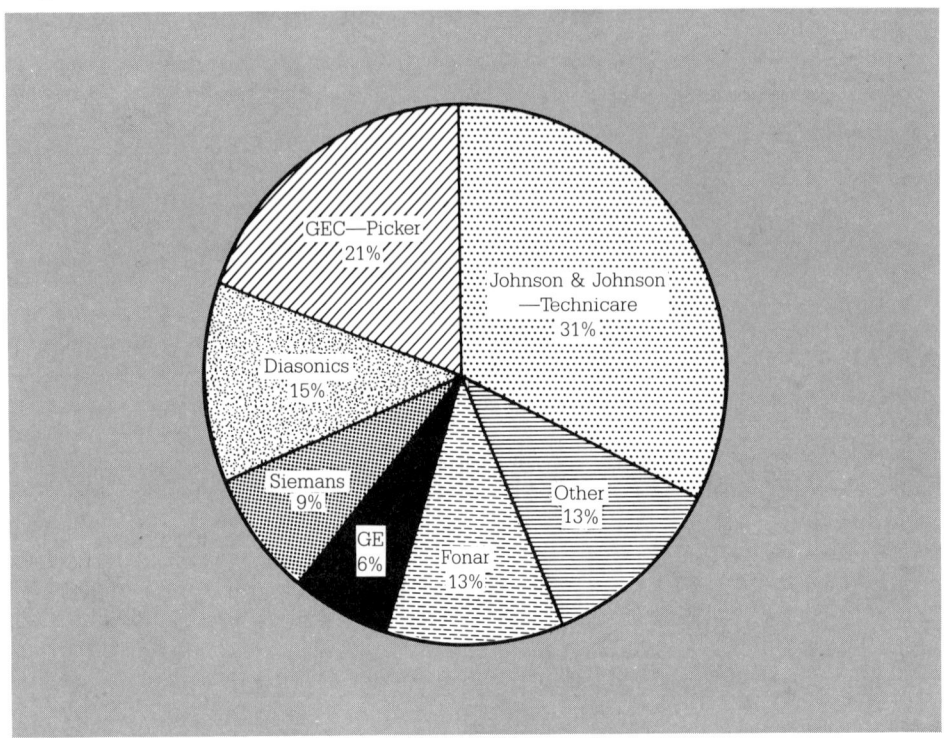

Source: *The Economist*, January, 1985, p. 70

EXHIBIT 19

Sales Units of the Top Ten Diagnostic Imaging Firms

Company	X-Ray	CAT Scanners	Nuclear	Ultra-Sound	Magnetic Resonance	Worldwide Sales
General Electric	380	210	35	20	25	670
Siemans	340	210	50	25	20	645
Philips	300	50	—	65	20	435
Picker International	160	80	25	20	45	330
Toshiba	180	60	10	55	12	317
Technicare (J&J)	**35**	**110**	**30**	**45**	**70**	**290**
CGR	200	40	—	10	6	256
Hitachi	80	40	—	20	8	148
Elscint	10	80	25	10	20	145
Diasonics	15	—	—	75	30	120
All Others	450	30	65	200	15	760
Total:	2,150	910	240	545	271	4,116

Source: Standard and Poors, Survey Biomedical Equipment, January 1985, p. H28

EXHIBIT 20
Medical Supplies Market Share as of January 1, 1985

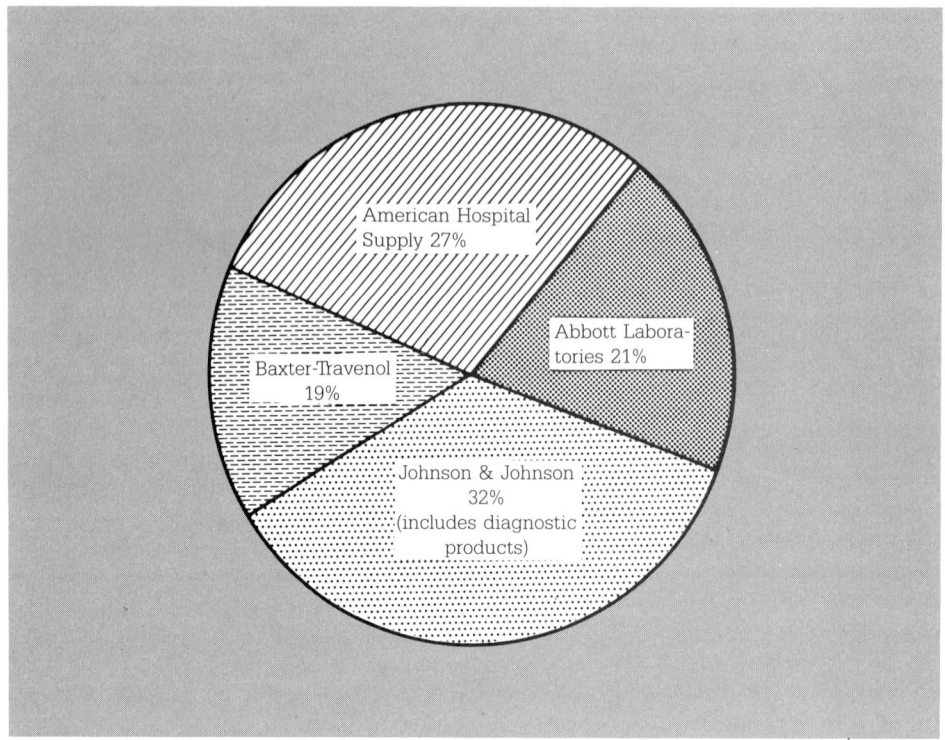

Source: Standard and Poors, Healthcare Industry Survey, September 12, 1985, p. H34

EXHIBIT 21
Research and Development

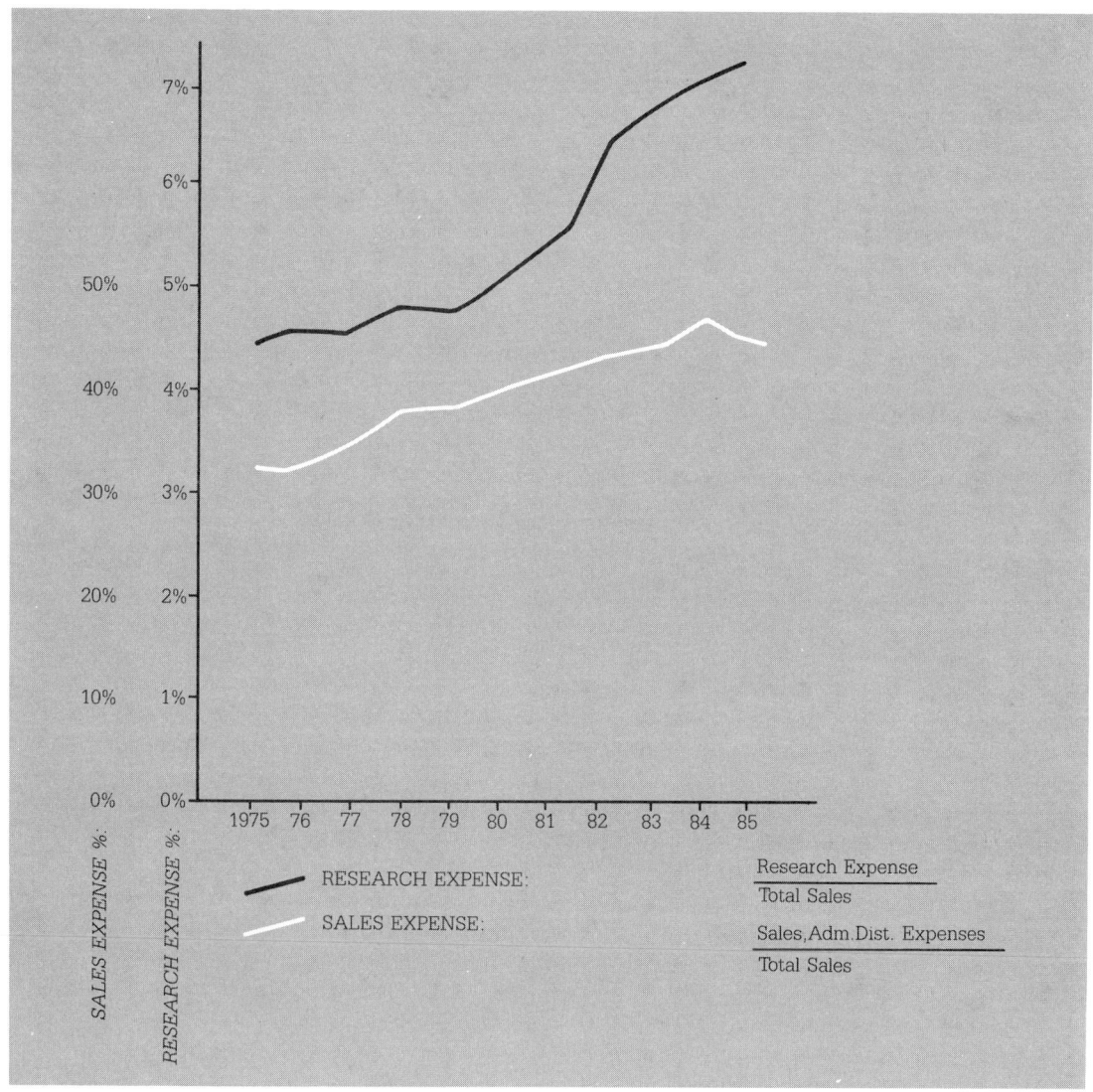

Source: Johnson & Johnson Annual Report (1985)

EXHIBIT 22
Total Sales, Net Profits, and Profit Margins for J&J (1975–1985)

Year	Sales (millions of dollars)	Net Profit	Profit Margin
1975	$2224.7	$183.8	8.3%
1976	2522.2	205.4	8.1
1977	2914.1	247.3	8.5
1978	3497.3	299.1	8.6
1979	4211.6	352.1	8.4
1980	4837.4	400.7	8.3
1981	5399.0	467.6	8.7
1982	5760.9	473.4	8.2
1983	5972.9	489.0	8.2
1984	6124.5	514.5	8.4
1985	6421.3	613.7	9.5

Health Industry Median 1985 = 7.7% (Profit Margin)
Drug Industry Median 1985 = 9.6% (Profit Margin)

Source: Johnson & Johnson Annual Report (1985)

EXHIBIT 23
J&J 1985 Balance Sheet

Johnson & Johnson and Subsidiaries   Consolidated Balance Sheet

At December 28, 1986 and December 29, 1985, Dollars in Millions (Note 1)	1986	1985
Assets		
Current assets		
Cash and cash items	$ 166.7	129.2
Marketable securities, at cost, which approximates market value	785.8	606.4
Accounts receivable, trade, less allowances $40.5 (1985, $39.7)	856.6	959.4
Inventories (Notes 1 and 5)	1,010.5	955.1
Prepaid expenses and other receivables (Notes 2 and 9)	382.0	246.4
Total current assets	3,201.6	2,896.5
Marketable securities, non-current, at cost, which approximates market value	156.4	148.7
Property, plant and equipment, net (Notes 1 and 6)	1,916.3	1,839.9
Deferred taxes on income (Note 9)	43.2	—
Intangible assets, net (Notes 1 and 7)	393.1	76.9
Other assets	166.1	133.1
Total assets	$5,876.7	5,095.1
Liabilities and Stockholders' Equity		
Current liabilities		
Loans and notes payable (Note 8)	$1,010.3	229.3
Accounts payable	512.3	401.4
Accrued liabilities (Note 2)	502.2	328.7
Taxes on income	94.2	65.3
Salaries, wages and commissions	116.7	95.1
Miscellaneous taxes	57.0	52.5
Total current liabilities	2,292.7	1,172.3
Long-term debt (Note 8)	241.9	185.3
Deferred taxes on income (Note 9)	—	121.3
Certificates of extra compensation (Note 14)	58.5	58.0
Deferred investment tax credits (Note 1)	30.3	40.2
Other liabilities	429.1	167.1
Stockholders' equity		
Preferred stock—without par value (authorized and unissued 2,000,000 shares)	—	—
Common stock—par value $1.00 per share (authorized 270,000,000 shares;		
issued 191,834,000 and 191,832,000 shares)	191.8	191.8
Additional capital	186.2	247.6
Cumulative currency translation adjustments (Note 10)	(171.9)	(291.9)
Retained earnings	3,584.4	3,499.6
	3,790.5	3,647.1
Less common stock held in treasury, at cost (18,984,000 and 8,980,000 shares)	966.3	296.2
Total stockholders' equity	2,824.2	3,350.9
Total liabilities and stockholders' equity	$5,876.7	5,095.1

See Notes to Consolidated Financial Statements

EXHIBIT 24
J&J 1985 Consolidated Income Statement

| Johnson & Johnson and Subsidiaries | | Consolidated Statement of Earnings and Retained Earnings | |

Dollars in Millions Except Per Share Figures (Note 1)	1986	1985	1984
Revenues			
Sales to customers (Note 3)	**$7,002.9**	6,421.3	6,124.5
Other revenues			
Interest income	**99.9**	107.3	84.5
Royalties and miscellaneous	**65.0**	48.1	38.0
Total revenues	7,167.8	6,576.7	6,247.0
Costs and expenses			
Cost of products sold	**2,630.1**	2,594.2	2,469.4
Selling, distribution and administrative expenses	**2,867.9**	2,516.0	2,488.4
Research expense	**521.3**	471.1	421.2
Interest expense	**87.4**	74.8	86.1
Interest expense capitalized	**(21.8)**	(28.9)	(35.0)
Redirection charges (Note 2)	**540.0**	—	—
Other expenses (Note 3)	**152.1**	50.3	61.8
Total costs and expenses	**6,777.0**	5,677.5	5,491.9
Earnings before provision for taxes on income	**390.8**	899.2	755.1
Provision for taxes on income (Note 9)	**61.3**	285.5	240.6
Net earnings (Notes 2 and 3)	**329.5**	613.7	514.5
Retained earnings at beginning of period	**3,499.6**	3,119.1	2,824.5
Cash dividends paid (per share: 1986, $1.375; 1985, $1.275; 1984, $1.175)	**(244.7)**	(233.2)	(219.9)
Retained earnings at end of period	**$3,584.4**	3,499.6	3,119.1
Net earnings per share (Notes 1, 2 and 3)	**$ 1.85**	3.36	2.75

Consolidated Statement of Common Stock, Additional Capital and Treasury Stock

	Common Stock Issued		Additional Capital	Treasury Stock	
Dollars in Millions, Shares in Thousands (Note 1)	Shares	Amount	Amount	Shares	Amount
Balance, January 1, 1984	191,562	$191.6	$272.1	234	$ 1.0
Employee compensation and stock option plans	291	.2	6.5	(1,248)	(38.7)
Repurchase of common stock	—	—	—	10,000	328.8
Other	(22)	—	—	—	—
Balance, December 30, 1984	191,831	191.8	278.6	8,986	291.1
Employee compensation and stock option plans	—	—	(31.0)	(2,666)	(117.4)
Repurchase of common stock	—	—	—	2,660	122.5
Other	1	—	—	—	—
Balance, December 29, 1985	191,832	191.8	247.6	8,980	296.2
Employee compensation and stock option plans	—	—	(61.4)	(2,470)	(152.2)
Repurchase of common stock	—	—	—	12,474	822.3
Other	2	—	—	—	—
Balance, December 28, 1986	191,834	$191.8	$186.2	18,984	$966.3

See Notes to Consolidated Financial Statements

EXHIBIT 25

Ten-Year Summary of Operations and Statistical Data

Summary of Operations and Statistical Data 1976–1986

(Dollars in Millions Except Per Share Figures)	1986	1985	1984
Earnings data			
Sales to customers			
Domestic	$3,972.0	3,989.9	3,735.9
International	3,030.9	2,431.4	2,388.6
Total sales	7,002.9	6,421.3	6,124.5
Interest income	99.9	107.3	84.5
Royalties and miscellaneous	65.0	48.1	38.0
Total revenues	7,167.8	6,576.7	6,247.0
Cost of products sold	2,630.1	2,594.2	2,469.4
Selling, distribution and administrative expenses	2,867.9	2,516.0	2,488.4
Research expense	521.3	471.1	421.2
Interest expense	87.4	74.8	86.1
Interest expense capitalized	(21.8)	(28.9)	(35.0)
Redirection charges	540.0	—	—
Other expenses	152.1	50.3	61.8
Total costs and expenses	6,777.0	5,677.5	5,491.9
Earnings before provision for taxes on income	390.8	899.2	755.1
Provision for taxes on income	61.3	285.5	240.6
Earnings before extraordinary charge	329.5	613.7	514.5
Extraordinary charge (net of $50.0 taxes)	—	—	—
Net earnings	$ 329.5	613.7	514.5
Percent of sales to customers	4.7[1]	9.6	8.4
Domestic net earnings	$ 32.4	376.6	305.6
International net earnings	$ 297.1	237.1	208.9
Per share of common stock	$ 1.85	3.36	2.75
Percent return on average stockholders' equity	10.7[1]	19.5	17.3
Percent increase (decrease) over previous year			
Sales to customers	9.1	4.8	2.5
Net earnings per share	(44.9)[1]	22.2	7.0
Supplementary expense data (2)			
Cost of materials and services	$3,823.3	3,441.0	3,285.8
Total employment costs	2,091.4	1,941.1	1,935.8
Depreciation and amortization	275.2	250.5	226.3
Maintenance and repairs (3)	170.4	132.7	124.0
Total tax expense (4)	284.4	466.2	418.6
Total tax expense per share (4)	1.59	2.55	2.23
Supplementary balance sheet data			
Property, plant and equipment-net investment	$1,916.3	1,839.9	1,720.6
Additions to property, plant and equipment	445.7	366.3	366.0
Total assets	5,876.7	5,095.1	4,541.4
Long-term debt	241.9	185.3	224.8
Common stock information			
Dividends paid per share	$ 1.38	1.28	1.18
Stockholders' equity per share	$ 16.34	18.33	16.04
Average shares outstanding (millions)	178.4	182.9	187.4
Stockholders of record (thousands)	52.1	53.5	53.8
Employees (thousands)	77.1	74.9	74.2

(1) After one-time charges of $380 million. —1986 net earnings percent of sales to customers before one-time charges is 10.1%.
  —1986 percent return on average stockholders' equity before one-time charges is 21.6%.
  —1986 net earnings per share percent increase over prior year before one-time charges is 18.5%.

EXHIBIT 25 (continued)

1983	1982	1981	1980	1979	1978	1977	1976
3,610.5	3,304.0	3,025.9	2,633.6	2,372.1	1,991.3	1,713.6	1,493.2
2,362.4	2,456.9	2,373.1	2,203.8	1,839.5	1,506.0	1,200.5	1,029.3
5,972.9	5,760.9	5,399.0	4,837.4	4,211.6	3,497.3	2,914.1	2,522.5
82.9	88.9	78.8	50.0	43.3	28.7	18.9	19.3
49.4	49.3	28.6	26.4	23.1	17.2	16.8	16.7
6,105.2	5,899.1	5,506.4	4,913.8	4,278.0	3,543.2	2,949.8	2,558.5
2,471.8	2,450.9	2,368.4	2,194.3	1,950.2	1,580.3	1,368.0	1,222.9
2,352.9	2,248.8	2,030.6	1,794.2	1,505.3	1,258.9	1,002.3	847.9
405.1	363.2	282.9	232.8	192.7	163.6	131.8	112.5
88.3	74.4	60.7	37.0	21.9	13.5	8.5	6.3
(36.9)	(46.3)	(43.5)	(32.7)	—	—	—	—
—	—	—	—	—	—	—	—
99.9	20.9	23.4	12.9	16.2	12.7	7.0	7.4
5,381.1	5,111.9	4,722.5	4,238.5	3,686.3	3,029.0	2,517.6	2,197.0
724.1	787.2	783.9	675.3	591.7	514.2	432.2	361.5
235.1	263.8	316.3	274.6	239.6	215.1	184.9	156.1
489.0	523.4	467.6	400.7	352.1	299.1	247.3	205.4
—	(50.0)	—	—	—	—	—	—
489.0	473.4	467.6	400.7	352.1	299.1	247.3	205.4
8.2	8.2	8.7	8.3	8.4	8.6	8.5	8.1
281.8	235.8	262.2	184.6	172.4	144.4	129.3	107.5
207.2	237.6	205.4	216.1	179.7	154.7	118.0	97.9
2.57	2.52	2.51	2.17	1.92	1.67	1.41	1.18
16.8	17.8	19.5	18.8	19.1	18.8	17.8	16.7
3.7	6.7	11.6	14.9	20.4	20.0	15.5	13.4
2.0	.4	15.7	12.8	15.2	18.2	19.8	11.0
3,205.9	3,078.1	2,843.4	2,532.4	2,200.1	1,803.0	1,494.5	1,294.4
1,920.8	1,821.7	1,693.6	1,535.2	1,337.4	1,101.6	892.0	785.1
209.8	176.2	152.4	138.7	121.2	103.1	86.5	77.5
119.6	123.6	126.2	116.1	118.2	102.0	89.1	74.8
415.2	436.3	477.0	425.3	373.2	323.0	274.9	231.1
2.18	2.32	2.56	2.30	2.04	1.80	1.57	1.32
1,668.2	1,577.9	1,335.6	1,161.9	947.8	788.2	652.4	568.5
401.3	470.2	388.5	364.0	273.3	228.5	171.7	119.2
4,461.5	4,209.6	3,820.4	3,342.5	2,874.0	2,382.4	2,019.8	1,730.7
195.6	142.2	91.7	70.1	69.5	52.1	37.1	26.7
1.08	.97	.85	.74	.67	.57	.47	.35
15.82	14.80	13.51	12.24	10.82	9.47	8.43	7.45
190.5	188.0	186.4	184.8	183.3	179.4	175.2	174.6
49.3	43.0	38.2	35.6	35.6	31.9	31.2	31.1
77.4	79.7	77.1	74.3	71.8	67.0	60.5	57.9

(2) Excludes in 1982 an extraordinary charge of $100 million ($50 million after taxes or $.27 per share) associated with the withdrawal of TYLENOL capsules.
(3) Also included in cost of materials and services category.
(4) Includes taxes on income, payroll, property and other business taxes.

The Boeing Company, 1985 — "The Sporty Game"

Donald F. Harvey
Captain R. S. Eresman
United States Air Force
1985 information supplied by
James Clanton and Steve Kane

INTRODUCTION

In 1984, Boeing ranked number twenty-nine in sales, thirty-three in assets, and nineteen in after-tax profits on *Fortune's* top 500 industrial corporations. Boeing is clearly a giant company with sales of some $10.3 billion and relatively high profitability and growth rate. The firm's return on stockholder equity was 12.3 percent, its growth rate in earnings per share from 1974 to 1984 was 6.1 percent, and the company's total return to investors (dividends plus capital gains) was 17.8 percent during the same period, a ranking of 232 out of 500: an impressive scorecard.[1]

John Newhouse, writing in the *New Yorker,* said,

> The business of making and selling jet airliners, whether profitably or, as is more often the case, unprofitably, is oppressively difficult and, by anyone's standards, intensely competitive. There are a few industries—automobile manufacturing, for one—that consume as much capital; certain others rely as heavily on highly skilled manpower. Probably no other is involved with as many advanced technologies. But two things really set the commercial airplane business apart: the size of the risks and the costs that must be accepted.

Because of this risk, Newhouse calls it "the sporty game."[2]

As Chairman T. A. Wilson and President Frank Shrontz examined Boeing's strategic direction, they felt the company was well positioned to meet the market opportunities of the 1990s. Even so, the company faces some potentially serious problems. Both the energy situation and the general economy, if they should become substantially worse, would seriously affect the profitability of the airlines. Their ability to order the next-generation aircraft, which they need to improve fuel efficiency, could be sharply limited by such lack of profitability.

BACKGROUND

Boeing Company, the world's leading commercial airplane maker, is facing better times. Cash was being drained further by the decline of airplane deliveries, the loss of progress payments from airline customers canceling or postponing orders, and heavy financing costs on undelivered planes. (Boeing has fourteen unsold 747s, worth about $1 billion, sitting at its military airplane complex in Wichita.)

E. H. "Tex" Boullioun, Boeing's senior vice-president for commercial airplanes, is sanguine. He thinks the company's commercial prospects will pick up. "We can hang on for that long," he said. "We're in ten times better shape than we were in 1970," when the company's three basic businesses—airliners, defense, and space—were all down at once and the company slashed its workforce in only 2 years from 101,000 to 38,000.[3]

Today there are approximately 6050 commercial jet airplanes in service in the western world. Approximately 3400 of these aircraft have been built by Boeing.

As of January 1, 1985, Boeing had sold a total of 3401 of the most modern of its airplanes now in service—the 727s, 737s, and 747s. Of these, carriers outside the United States bought one-third of the 727s, two-thirds of the 737s, and well over two-thirds of the 747s. With its domestic competition fading, Boeing is of course doing even better than before at home, but it worries about the trend in the overseas market.

Since it produced the first 707, this remarkable company has come to corner 60 percent of the world market for jet airplanes and 70 percent of the U.S. market. Though most famous for its family of commercial jet aircraft, Boeing is also a producer of airplanes, helicopters, missiles, and hydrofoils for the U.S. military. The company is also involved in such diversified areas as computer services, wastewater treatment, portable asphalt plants, and advanced energy systems using wind turbines and solar power. In business, Boeing's name has become synonymous with quality. The largest division of Boeing, the Boeing Commercial Airplane Company, accounts for almost 80 percent of Boeing's revenues; however, Boeing has been losing some of its overseas market to the A-300 Airbus.

The Boeing Company is presently emerging from a three year slump in the market for commercial aircraft. In 1983 it delivered 204 aircraft for a total revenue of $6.998 billion, up from $5.135 billion in 1982. This increased sales revenue reflects the first year of substantial 757 and 767 aircraft deliveries. Thirty-nine percent of the 1983 total delivery figure is attributed to these planes.

In 1984, only 138 aircraft were delivered, a decrease from 296 in the peak year of 1980. However, in 1985, the company delivered 191 airplanes worth approximately $6 billion, and in 1986 estimates indicated an increase to 226.[4]

The company's military-oriented business is expanding in importance. Sales grew 10 percent in 1983 following a 41 percent increase in 1982. Thanks to Saudi Arabia and the U.S. Air Force, demand for the AWACS is quite strong. In 1985, for example, Boeing was awarded a $1.2 billion Air Defense System contract for Saudi Arabia. The B-1B bomber program and other military aircraft and helicopter orders added to the strength of this segment in 1985.[5]

FINANCIAL

In 1985 Boeing recorded revenues of over $14 billion, a 32 percent increase over 1984 sales. When revenues are broken down among Boeing's various divisions, commercial aircraft and related services accounted for 62 percent of total sales, military aircraft and services accounted for 23 percent, missiles and space accounted for 10 percent, and Boeing's other divisions accounted for the remaining 5 percent. After taxes, Boeing's net income was over $600 million, or an increase of 28 percent over the 1984 income. Although the increase in revenues was consistent with aerospace industry norms, the increase in profit was far above the average 6.5 percent increase for related companies. Earnings per share also increased over the 1984 figure (see exhibit 1).

According to Chairman T. A. Wilson, Boeing today is the only manufacturer in the United States and perhaps in the world that makes a profit on commercial jets. This success stems from several factors. First is the popularity of the company's airplanes. One of the major problems facing airplane manufacturers is being able to recover the costs associated with the research and development of new aircraft. Two of Boeing's airplanes, the 737 and the 747, have sold well enough to become what analysts call *cash cows* or profit makers for the company. The popularity of the 737 saved Boeing from financial disaster in 1980, and the 747 provides the capital needed to support the company until the 757 and 767 aircraft series become profitable. The profits generated by the 737 and the 747 allow Boeing to charge research, development, and planning costs directly against earnings instead of borrowing money to cover the costs through sufficient sales until the debt is amortized.

Boeing maintains tight controls on costs. Each manager follows an annual operating plan, and control is maintained through a formal computerized system requiring managers to send data to headquarters on how well they are meeting their targets—including progress in production and research and development and use of resources such as working capital, labor, and materials. In addition, each manager meets with the president to discuss new developments or to iron out any deviations from the operating plan.

A final method by which Boeing has protected its financial position is by sharing the risk in its new projects. By including subcontractors in sharing the profits and risks of research and development, Boeing generates a new source of capital. By developing subcontractors overseas who will participate in this type of venture, Boeing attempts to acquire insurance against an outbreak of economic nationalism that could hurt sales overseas. The only requirement is that the subcontractor produce the part or system for less than what it would cost Boeing to produce it internally.

As Boeing heads toward the 1990s, it finds itself on pretty solid financial ground. At present, there is a backlog of over $20 billion dollars for Boeing products. The cash generated from these early sales will also allow Boeing to finance its 757/767 costs without incurring too much additional debt. See exhibit 2 for industry segment information.

T. A. Wilson, Boeing's chairman, and Frank Shrontz, chief executive officer, expect future airline growth and see a need for more airplanes in the 1990s. They predict a $140 billion new aircraft market in the 1990s (which would mean eventual orders of 1,000 each for the 757 and 767) as airlines strive to remain competitive, reduce fuel consumption, and comply with noise regulations.

Boeing's balance sheet is one of the strongest in the aerospace industry. As of December 31, 1985, the company had cash assets of $1,595 billion—a substantial sum in anyone's back hangar. Also, long-term debt was $299 million, with total current assets of $6,170 billion.[6] Other financial data of importance are itemized in exhibit 3.

Although the company experienced profitability problems because of the weaknesses in the commercial airplane business in 1982 (operating and net profit margins were down 12.33 percent and 33.33 percent, respectively from 1981), the company performed well in 1983 and is in excellent financial condition. Its operating margin of 6.5 percent of sales is sufficient to service the current portion of the company's debt as well as allow some cash to be socked away for future use. Although sales declined in 1982, they had been on a six year general upward trend. Sales decline in 1982 over 1981 is equal to 7.7 percent. Sales rebounded in 1983 to $11.129 billion as the commercial aircraft industry picked up greatly in the last six months of 1983. Sales in 1983 increased 23.18 percent over those in 1982. Revenues (63 percent of total) also helped to restore sales and profitability to former levels. Because of these two factors, it was estimated that the company would have a 3 to 5 percent increase in earnings in 1986. A significant sign of health in the balance sheet is the company's working capital line of almost $1.9 billion.[7]

Exhibit 4 provides a summary of operating profit margins by business segment and a clear look into the devastating effects of the downturn of the commercial airline industry in two and one-half years. (See exhibit 5 for the industry breakdown of sales in the military segment. Exhibit 6 shows Boeing's sales of aircraft by type from 1983 through 1985; and exhibit 7, its projected sales through 1998.)

RESEARCH AND DEVELOPMENT

Boeing has developed a reputation for innovation, reliability, and plain downright engineering excellence that is unmatched in the industry. Boeing's research and development has been a major contributor to this fine reputation. The typical Boeing development course is to plan several years in advance and then take calculated risks (see exhibit 8).

> Boeing hasn't built a fighter plane in four decades. But since 1976 it has put about $125 million into fighter technology, and it currently has about fifty contracts for such related projects as ejection seats and wing design. In its huge black Boeing Developmental Center, just down the road from corporate headquarters, 200 Boeing Military Airplane Company employees are testing wind-tunnel models and working on computer designs to offer the Air Force.[8]

The secret of success in engineering is to go the extra mile. Consequently, the company stands as proof that over the long haul the only lasting standard or profit is quality. Boeing engineers take full advantage of existing technology and in many areas advance it. In the new fuel-efficient 757 and 767 series, Boeing engineers used computers to aid in the design of the aircraft. The 757 and 767 flight decks have more space than any current two-crew airplane, the best visual outlook, and the most sophisticated electronic equipment available for commercial airplanes. The digital flight management computer can coordinate the autopilot and autothrottle so that climb, cruise, and descent will be done at maximum fuel efficiency. The automatic navigation system allows the 757 and 767 to conserve fuel by guiding itself over the most direct route at the optimum air speed. This control enables a gain of almost 40 percent in fuel efficiency, thus providing lower operating cost per flight, a greater utilization factor, and higher operating profitability. Other features of these aircraft include the use of composite materials, advanced aerodynamics, and commonality of design. Though it can also be considered a management triumph, the first 767 aircraft was completed to design weight (unusual for new designs) and to the exact schedule date set when the program was launched in 1978.[9]

Research and development expenses for the last eight years and their percentage of sales are detailed below:

Year	Expenditure (MM)	% of Sales
1985	$700,000 (est.)	4.9
1984	500,000 (est.)	4.9
1983	429,000	3.9
1982	691,000	7.5
1981	844,100	8.4
1980	767,500	7.8
1979	525,200	6.2
1978	276,100	4.9

Boeing's R&D expenditures rose dramatically over five years and dropped off sharply in 1983. Much of the high R&D expenditure levels can be attributed to the cost of developing the 757 and 767, which is estimated at $3 billion. What does not surface here, however, are the millions in transferable R&D dollars that the U.S. government pumps into the company through its numerous defense contracts. R&D expenditures in 1986 were expected to reach the $700 million level as R&D increases to previous levels. The company would not survive in its selected markets if it did not possess a high-caliber R&D department staffed with competent engineers.

PRODUCTION

Approximately once a day, or at the rate of twenty-eight a month, a Boeing aircraft rolls off the assembly line. At the present time Boeing is building the 737, 747, 757 and 767. This rate of production is the maximum capacity for Boeing, and is three times the level for McDonnell Douglas Corporation. Backorders for new airplanes will keep Boeing at this level of production well into the mid-1990s. The basic philosophy of management in controlling Boeing's production rate has been to avoid the boom or bust cycle of the late 1960s. By maintaining stability of production, Boeing hopes to achieve stability and security for itself and its customers. Boeing production managers feel that maintaining a constant backlog of orders by not cyclically changing production rates will allow greater efficiency and better quality on the product line.

Boeing airplanes are not built from scratch in Boeing's Washington plants. Major parts are constructed in different states and by different companies. Northrop, for example, builds the fuselage for the 747, and Boeing Military Aircraft Company in Wichita, Kansas builds the cockpit for the 747 and the fuselage for the 737. Having a vast array of suppliers and subcontractors can become a management headache; however, managers carefully monitor the construction process by the use of computers to control shop loading, scheduling, and inventory. The result is an aircraft built in the minimum time possible through the efficient use of labor and materials.

> When Boeing sells planes, it benefits from an extremely low cost structure, built on a high degree of automation and, particularly in its 747 and 737 lines, high production rates. Manufacturing efficiencies, in fact, enabled the Boeing Commercial Airplane Company unit to build 203 planes last year with 37,200 employees—20 percent fewer than it took to make as many airliners in 1970.
>
> Aircraft parts normally are produced only after a design group creates a drawing and then manufacturing people analyze it and choose the needed tools and machinery. But with advanced design methods that Boeing's military side developed, "the engineering department generates a tape and the computer does all the rest, even to putting out the orders for parts," says H. K. Hebeler, the president of Boeing Electronics Company. That unit services both military and commercial programs.[10]

MARKETING

A major reason for Boeing's strength in the marketplace has been its policy of developing whole families of airplanes to meet the total needs of the commercial market. Since the 707 first rolled off the line, Boeing has offered a new aircraft model or a new derivation of the basic model at an average of once every ten months. In keeping with this tradition, Boeing has begun producing the 767 and 757. This production has been costly to the company and represents a high risk. However in a fuel conscious age, Boeing has reaped huge profits because of this ability to meet customer's demand for aircraft of diverse range, size, and configuration.

The second reason for Boeing's success in marketing has been its sales force and the loyalty of the company's customers. Each salesman is expected to keep close continuous contact with customers and to keep track of traffic patterns and airlines' current requirements. Computers at company headquarters store data from seventy air carriers about the number of people who fly between each city each day and the frequency of service. With such information, salespeople can predict the proper combination of different sized airplanes and airline needs to make the best return on investment.

By taking the long view in its dealing with customers, Boeing has received their confidence and trust. Not only does Boeing's sales force represent Boeing's interests to the customers, it also represents the customers' interests to Boeing. The salespeople, most of whom are engineers, routinely confer with company design engineers on aircraft modifications that will meet the specific needs of a particular airline; the so-called Omni combined passenger and cargo carrier was developed for Sabena Airlines on the recommendation of a salesperson.

A final factor that has helped Boeing in the market place has been its service record. Concerned with competition as well as customer satisfaction and loyalty, Boeing has trained maintenance teams and has spare-parts pallets that can be dispatched quickly anywhere around the world to aid in the repair of Boeing aircraft.

STRUCTURE

Boeing's current corporate structure is considered one of the most streamlined in industry. Boeing's various businesses—commercial aircraft, military and space aircraft, missiles, computer services, engineering and construction, and hydrofoil ships—are divided into seven operating units or companies. Although each company has almost complete production and marketing authority, corporate headquarters closely monitors their financial, labor, and inventory management. The management structure is designed to provide as much involvement as possible in the company's total effort (see exhibit 9). For example, Kenneth F. Holtby not only heads new programs for the Boeing Commercial Airplane Company but also oversees engineering for the entire company. W. W. Buckley is vice-president for operations (all airplane programs) and overseas operations resources for the company. As Holtby explained, "We are set up in such a way that people can't back away and say 'That's his problem,' we've got everybody on the spot."[11]

The corporate structure follows what might be termed a *matrix* type of organization. When Boeing starts a project, a project manager is named to gather the required people from the traditional functional areas including marketing, engineering, and manufacturing. The size of the project force changes during the life of the project. Partly in an attempt to prevent boom or bust hiring, Boeing is careful in allocating and assigning its workforce among its many projects. An example is the way Boeing's engineers are allocated among the various programs so that new projects receive the required assistance without damaging other efforts. When a project manager requires engineering assistance, a request is submitted to a skill team composed of experienced people who will weigh the requirement and available talent before making a decision. From the top management to the lowest production level the most costly factor of production, labor, is used in the most efficient manner possible.

GOALS AND PLANNING

As with any typical American business, the basic goal of the Boeing Company is to profit from the sales of its various products. Through its offering of a family of jetliners and by developing its image of quality engineering, sales, and service for all its products, Boeing hopes to achieve this goal. Because the risks are so great, the industry has been inclined—though necessarily less so of late—to take them for granted. Joseph Sutter of Boeing, one of the world's pre-eminent designers of large airplanes, says, "In this business, you have to put the company on the line every three or four years."[12]

The general manager of the 767 program is Dean Thornton, a highly regarded Boeing vice-president, who said that "most of Boeing's net worth is riding on this ship." The 767 program's costs are widely estimated at $2 billion, but Thornton said that more money is involved. "It is more than two and less than ten," he commented circumspectly with regard to a figure of great interest to Boeing's customers and competitors.[13]

Exactly where between $2 billion and $10 billion Boeing's actual investment in this airplane will come to rest defies close calculation. "You may spend three hundred to four hundred million dollars on the facility, and even more on the tooling," Thornton said.[14] "And the certification is very expensive." M. T. Stamper, while president of Boeing, said,

> Just defining your nonrecurring costs is hard, because you may add a building or new tools and not know which program to charge them to. Or you may decide later on to improve the wing, or design a new and better one—a truly enormous additional cost—or make a freighter version of the airplane. A new customer may want something different; no two airplanes are alike, and the more versions you make, the higher the costs. Another customer may want variations in the airplanes already earmarked for him. Furthermore, by the time he has bought the third or fourth airplane—sometimes even the second—there are improvements, some of which may have to be folded into the planes already delivered.[15]

Perhaps the most unique aspect of Boeing in comparison to many other companies is its heavy emphasis on planning. After the near-disastrous consequences of poor planning in the late 1960s, Boeing's management is vitally concerned with making timely and accurate plans. The basis for company planning is a computerized long-range forecasting system. Computers are constantly being fed with information on passenger travel, and by adding in its own set of economic assumptions, Boeing has been able to analyze the future needs of the airlines fairly accurately.

The 767 program is an example of the methodical planning done by Boeing. In the mid-1970s, Boeing engineers knew that the next aircraft would be a medium-sized, medium-range vehicle. Knowing the general shape of the landing gear that would be needed, Boeing ordered the huge forgings that would be required. These forgings require a long lead time and were ordered heavier and longer than necessary, so that they could be machined later to precise dimensions when the final decision was reached. By doing this homework and ordering on time, Boeing delivered the first 767 off the line at the exact 1981 date set when the program was initiated in 1978.

Another achievement of Boeing planning has been its ability to integrate the vast number of subcontractor parts and services into its products without causing log jams in the production lines. Boeing's build-up in its commercial aircraft production has taxed the entire industry, ranging from raw material producers to manufacturers of galleys and engines. The result has been some out-of-sequence assembly while waiting for parts; however, early ordering and comprehensive planning have been able to keep Boeing production lines at full capacity.

A final aspect of Boeing's planning is the desire of the company to avoid the cyclical boom or bust cycles that often plague the aircraft industry. Maintaining a constant production rate while allowing huge backorders, Boeing management has given itself a preplanned full production and hence a sound financial structure well into the mid-1990s. By creating stability and hence security, Boeing expects more efficient operation and better prices on its products.

MANAGERIAL STYLE

The Boeing Company has been commended several times as being one of the best-managed companies in the United States. This distinction does not come lightly in a time when poorly managed and financially failing companies are the rule rather than the exception. Boeing's success is due to several factors that include the style of Boeing's chief executive office, upper level management, and Boeing management's tight system of controls (see exhibit 10 for a roster of officers).

Boeing's successful pre-eminence in the aerospace industry can be traced directly to 1968 when its present chairman Thornton A. Wilson assumed control. An engineer by profession, Wilson became chairman at a time when Boeing was beset by problems stemming mainly from the way the company was being run. One survey indicated that production workers spent only 26 percent of their time on the task because of associated activities such as obtaining approvals. Wilson is a powerful man and reserves for himself the final say on a broad range of Boeing decisions. His conservative business style and philosophy are felt at all levels of the organization. Some officers of the company complain that he considers himself to be the chief aerodynamicist of the company and gets involved in areas where he shouldn't. Ultimately, Wilson has the final say on all major decisions. Of his decision-making style, "I shoot from the hip," conceded Wilson, a native of rural Missouri. He contrasted himself with the more deliberative Frank Shrontz, a Harvard MBA who spends more time talking to people, and tends to use a more analytical approach.[16]

Ambitious projects such as the 747 and the SST were undertaken with little market or cost planning and no internal controls. By slashing the workforce, decentralizing the corporation, and installing planning and cost control systems, Wilson was able to return the company to its current strength. Although the head of a large company, Wilson dislikes the rigidity of a giant corporation and tries to promote a feeling of creativity among his managers. He stresses innovation and encourages managers to bend rules when necessary. Wilson believes that Boeing benefits from a small-company flexibility resulting from this type of managerial style.

Upper level management has also been effective in the success of the company. Top management has gone through a baptism of fire that has made them mature leaders without costing them their entrepreneurial spirit. Analysts are impressed with Boeing's top management team, particularly President Frank Shrontz, who is chief operating officer, and E. H. (Tex) Bouillioun, former head of the commercial aviation division. Boullioun was in charge of the computers that have helped Boeing forecast airline requirements and guided the company's development of the 767.

Boeing's management is successful at all levels because its key people tend to remain at Boeing throughout their careers. Corporate memory is exceptional and the errors of the past are prevented by the current system of controls.

Boeing's management strategy includes the efficient use of its own people and subcontractors. By the use of computers, Boeing's managers skillfully control planning and scheduling of the company's workforce. As one example of the effectiveness of this control, the labor required to build a 747 today is only one-fourth of that needed in the late 1960s. Boeing also uses borrowed engineers from its subcontractors and subcontractor services in order to keep its employee force stable. Consequently, Boeing's employees can expect fairly stable and secure employment, a factor management hopes will lead to even greater efficiency and productivity.

CONCLUSION

Boeing will enter the 1990s as the pre-eminent manufacturer in the aerospace industry. Even with an airline profit downturn, Boeing still expects to receive approximately 50 percent of the world market for new commercial jet aircraft. Its existing airplanes and new designs will allow Boeing to meet the needs of the airline industry for the foreseeable future. Boeing's military division also expects a bright future. As prime contractor for the Air Launched Cruise Missile and the MX Missile and a major subcontractor for the B-1 Bomber, Boeing is well entrenched in the major military programs of the 1980s. Thus, Boeing's chief executive officer Frank Shrontz can relax knowing that his company will not lack long-term business. Remembering that Boeing's success nearly destroyed it in the 1960s, he must maintain the controls that have made the company profitable and continue to encourage the research, development, production, and sales that have been a trademark of Boeing. As Chairman Wilson said,

> Our market projections indicate that a continuing demand for commercial jet transports will require that airlines purchase some $122 billion (in constant 1981 dollars) in new equipment during the next ten years. Boeing has a family of jet transports that meets virtually all airline requirements and we believe we can continue to maintain a substantial share of this market. . . .

Although political and economic uncertainties exist in both the national and international arenas, there are numerous opportunities that can enhance the long-term growth of the company. We are confident we can make strong contributions to several programs that will strengthen the country's military posture and retain our ability to respond to a resurgence of commercial jet transport markets.[17]

Will Boeing be able to bear the cost of both developing new models and helping domestic airlines to buy them—a practice that has included lending money to customers? (Boeing is reported to have lent Braniff nearly $100 million a few years ago and has not been repaid.) Boullioun—an acute and very direct man—said of these financing arrangements, "We will very soon be accumulating a large inventory," and added, in reference to the 767s and 757s, "and won't begin to get back any of our investment in the airplanes any time soon." He concluded, "If the airlines can't finance their purchases, we will have to slow down."[18]

CEO Frank Shrontz insists that "Our priorities will continue to be to put pressure on costs and to aggressively pursue opportunities on the commercial side of the business."[19] Yet he pondered on future strategy for Boeing—should the company continue its past traditions or should it now consider some major diversification, such as its unsuccessful $5 billion bid for Hughes Electronics?[20]

Notes

1   M. Magnet, "The 500," *Fortune,* April 29, 1985, 266.
2   J. Newhouse, "A Reporter at Large—The Aircraft Industry, Part 1," *The New Yorker,* June 14, 1982, 48–105.
3   "Boeing Tries to Maneuver Out of a Downdraft," *Business Week,* April 26, 1982, 97.
4   Boeing Annual Report, 1985.
5   Boeing Form 10-K, 1985.
6   Ibid.
7   Ibid.
8   *Current Industry Outlook,* Boeing, 1985.
9   *Value Line Investment Survey,* 1986, 555.
10 "Boeing Angles for More Military Business," *The Wall Street Journal,* May 13, 1986, 6.
11 "Boeing Tries," *Business Week,* 97.
12 J. Newhouse, "A Reporter at Large," 48.
13 Ibid., 51.
14 Ibid., 53.
15 Ibid., 103.
16 "Airwars, 1980's-Style," *Forbes,* July 29, 1985, 38.
17 "Clouds on Boeing's Horizon," *Forbes,* July 8, 1985, 80.
18 "Boeing Tries," *Business Week,* 98.
19 "Boeing Turns to Guns for More of Its Bread and Butter," *Business Week,* September 23, 1985, 101.
20 See "Boeing Angles for More Military Business," *The Wall Street Journal,* May 23, 1986, 6.

EXHIBIT 1

Five-Year Comparative Financial Data

Dollars in millions except per share data
Per share data restated for stock splits

	1983	1982	1981	1980	1979
For the year:					
Sales	**$11,129**	$ 9,035	$ 9,788	$ 9,426	$ 8,131
Net earnings	**$ 355**	$ 292	$ 473	$ 600	$ 505
Percent of sales	**3.2%**	3.2%	4.8%	6.4%	6.2%
Per share	**$ 3.67**	$ 3.02	$ 4.90	$ 6.23	$ 5.25
Average common shares outstanding (thousands)	**96,813**	96,535	96,455	96,341	96,214
Cash dividends paid	**$ 136**	$ 135	$ 135	$ 135	$ 135
Per share	**$ 1.40**	$ 1.40	$ 1.40	$ 1.40	$ 1.40
Salaries and wages	**$ 2,825**	$ 2,983	$ 3,020	$ 2,713	$ 2,241
Average number of employees	**84,600**	95,700	105,300	106,300	98,300
Additions to plant	**$ 223**	$ 331	$ 545	$ 668	$ 569
Depreciation of plant	**$ 337**	$ 324	$ 271	$ 194	$ 122
At end of year:					
Working capital	**$ 1,957**	$ 1,800	$ 1,471	$ 971	$ 873
Long-term customer financing	**539**	339	390	277	208
Facilities—at cost	**3,659**	3,485	3,204	2,723	2,083
Facilities—net	**1,671**	1,785	1,778	1,505	1,031
Investments and other assets	**99**	82	64	49	34
Total assets	**7,471**	7,593	6,954	5,931	4,897
Long-term debt	**301**	315	327	76	81
Deferred taxes	**743**	666	499	260	126
Deferred investment credit	**184**	212	222	151	92
Stockholders' equity	**3,038**	2,813	2,655	2,315	1,848
Per share	**$ 31.33**	$ 29.12	$ 27.52	$ 24.02	$ 19.19
Common shares outstanding (thousands)	**96,961**	96,590	96,494	96,363	96,277
Firm backlog	**$18,043**	$19,025	$19,389	$20,032	$18,011
Floor area (million square feet)					
Boeing owned	**38.7**	38.4	38.4	36.2	33.5
Leased	**6.1**	6.2	6.8	6.7	5.8
Government owned	**.1**	.1	.2	.2	.3

Source: The Boeing Company and Subsidiaries

EXHIBIT 2

Industry Segment Information

Dollars in millions

Year ended December 31,	1983	1982	1981
Revenues:			
Transportation equipment and related services:			
Commercial	$ 6,998	$5,135	$ 7,004
Military*	2.617	2,372	1,687
Total transportation equipment	9,615	7,507	8,691
Missiles and space*	1,047	938	667
Other industries	569	682	525
Operating revenues	11,231	9,127	9,883
Corporate income	77	79	190
Total revenues	$11,308	$9,206	$10,073
Operating profit:			
Transportation equipment and related services:			
Commercial	$ 98	$ 16	$ 308
Military*	289	269	223
Total transportation equipment	387	285	531
Missiles and space*	95	96	39
Other industries	8	3	10
Operating profit	490	384	580
Corporate income	77	79	190
Corporate expense	(92)	(99)	(79)
Earnings before taxes	$ 475	$ 364	$ 691
Identifiable assets at December 31:			
Transportation equipment and related services:			
Commercial	$ 4,782	$5,801	$ 4,704
Military	988	831	679
Missiles and space	225	196	246
Other industries	270	384	324
	6,265	7,212	5,953
Corporate assets	1,206	381	1,001
Consolidated	$ 7,471	$7,593	$ 6,954
Depreciation:			
Transportation equipment and related services:			
Commercial	$ 202	$ 205	$ 185
Military	71	62	42
Missiles and space	21	20	20
Capital expenditures, net:			
Transportation equipment and related services:			
Commercial	$ 104	$ 204	$ 329
Military	65	77	100
Missiles and space	21	17	51
Export sales by geographic area:			
Europe	$ 2,081	$1,454	$ 2,638
Asia	1,742	1,427	1,834
Western Hemisphere	456	430	772
Africa	354	299	271
Oceania	186	269	591
	$ 4,819	$3,879	$ 6,106

*Principally U.S. Government.

Source: The Boeing Company

The Company operates principally in two industries, (1) transportation equipment and related services, and (2) missiles and space. Operations in transportation equipment and related services primarily involve production and sale of such equipment and services to both commercial and military customers. Operations in missiles and space primarily involve production and sale of various offensive and defensive missiles, and space exploration products.

Financial information by industry segment for the three years ended December 31, 1983 is summarized at the left. Corporate income consists principally of interest income from corporate investments. Corporate expense consists of interest on debt and other general corporate expenses. Corporate assets consist principally of cash and short-term investments.

EXHIBIT 3

Item	1983	1982	1981	1980	1979	1978
Sales (MM)	$11,129	$9,035	$9,788.2	$9,426.2	$8,131	$5,463
Operating Margin	6.5%	6.4%	7.3%	9.3%	8.5%	9.2%
Net Profit (MM)	355	292	473	600.5	505.4	322.9
Net Profit Margin	3.2%	3.2%	4.8%	6.4%	6.2%	5.9%
Working Capital (MM)	1,957	1,800	1,471.3	971.7	874.2	920.9

EXHIBIT 4
Operating Margins by Year

Business Segment	1983	1982	1981	1980
Commercial Transportation	.2	.3	4.4	8.8
Military Transportation	15.0	11.3	13.2	8.5
Missiles and Space	10.0	10.2	5.9	5.1
Other	1.0	.4	1.8	3.8

EXHIBIT 5
Industry Breakdown Military Segments

Company	Market Share (% of military industry)
General Dynamics	22.9
Lockheed	22.4
McDonnell Douglas	21.6
Boeing	14.1
Northrop	10.0
Grumman	6.6
G-Systems	2.1
International Controls	.3

EXHIBIT 6

Sales of Aircraft by Type, 1983–1985

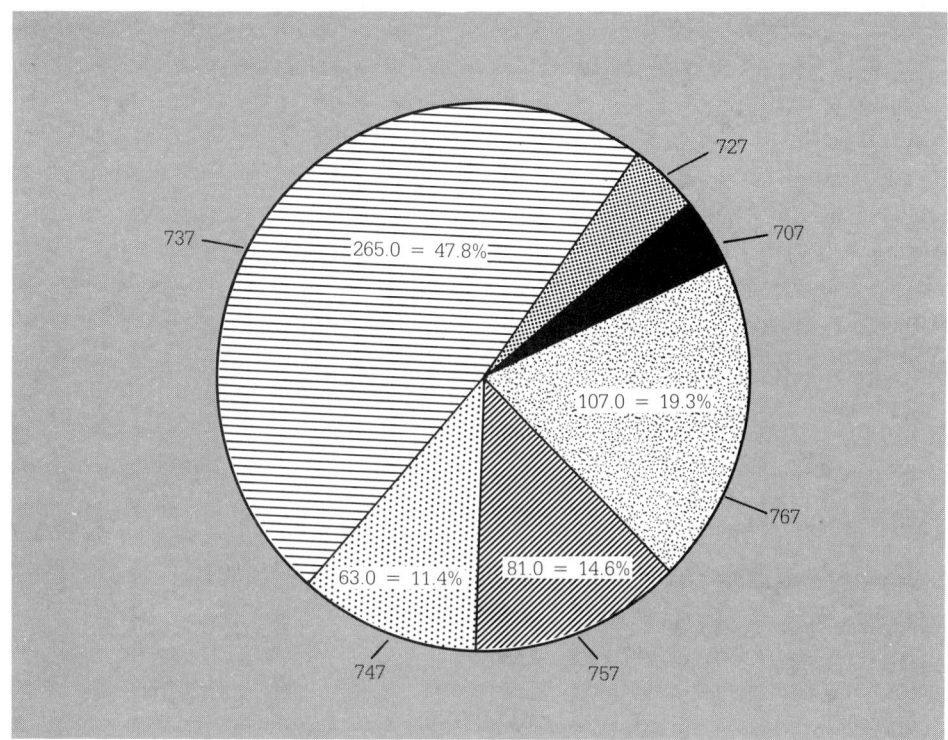

Source: Boeing Annual Reports (1982–1984)

EXHIBIT 7
Projected Aircraft Sales, 1985–1998

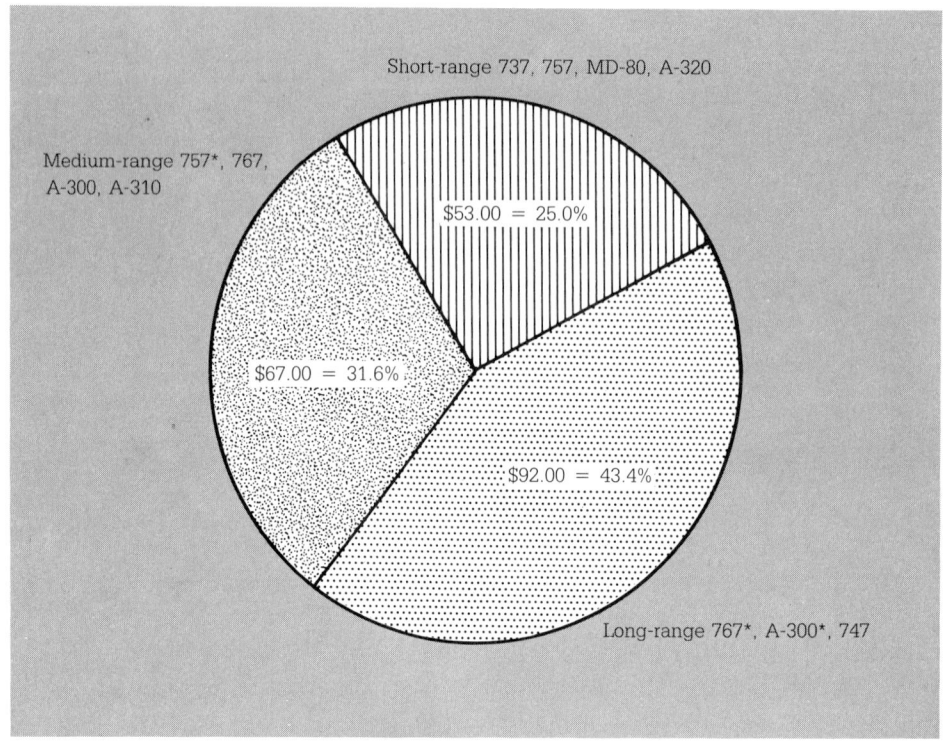

Source: U.S. Department of Commerce

EXHIBIT 8
The Prudent Step Up in Capacity

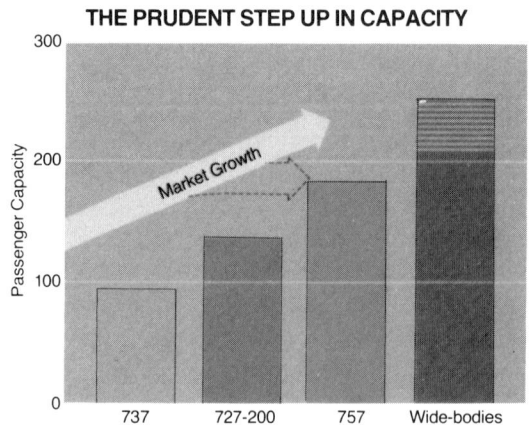

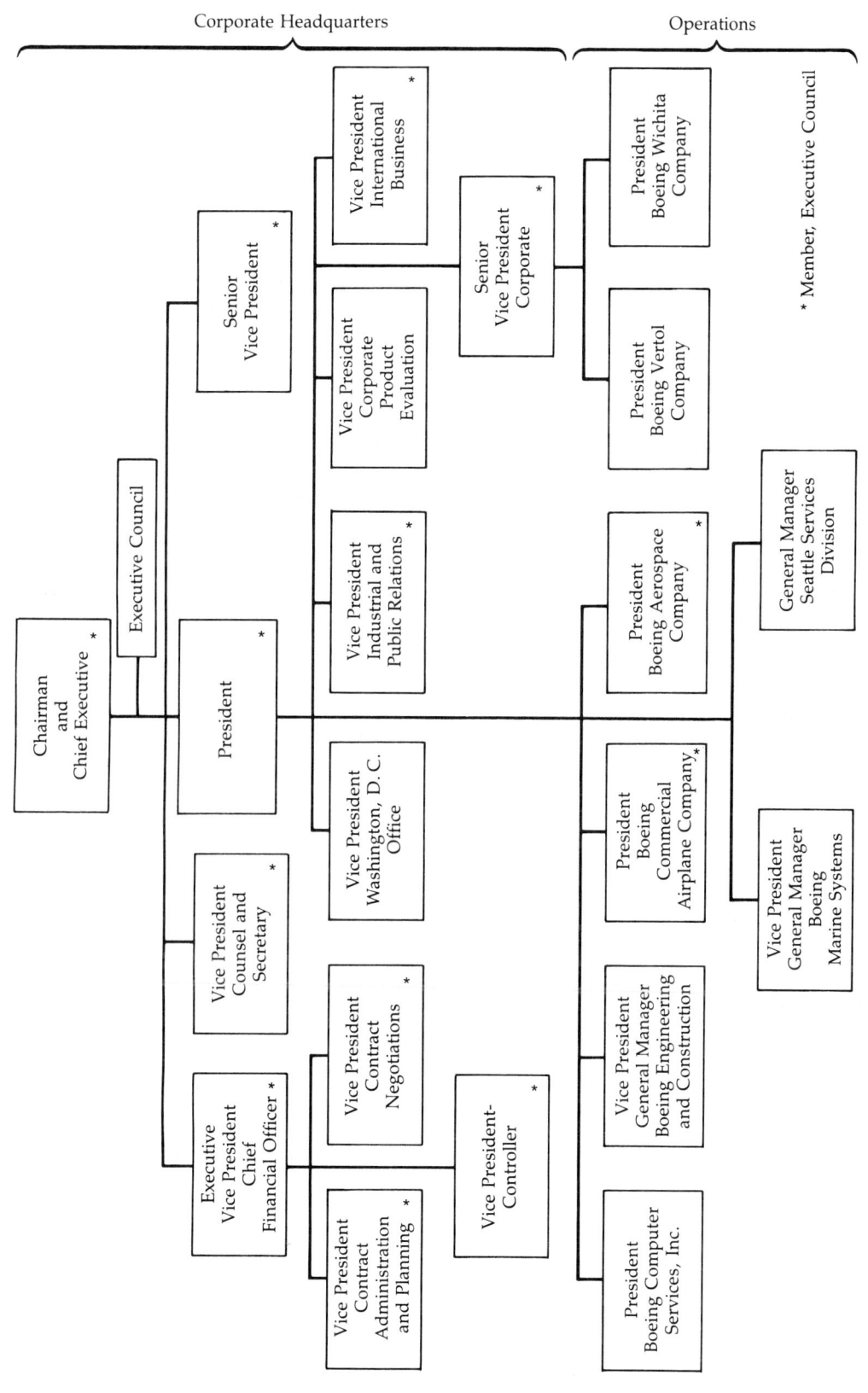

EXHIBIT 9
The Boeing Company: Corporate Organization

EXHIBIT 10
Executive Officers of the Registrant

Executive Officers of the Registrant

Executive officers are elected or designated as such annually on the date of the organization meeting of the Board of Directors. There are no family relationships between any of the executive officers listed below.

Name	Age	Positions and offices presently held and business experience
T. A. Wilson	64	Chairman of the Board and Chief Executive Officer since 1972. Director since 1966.
M. T. Stamper	59	Vice Chairman of the Board effective February 25, 1985. Prior thereto President from 1972. Director since 1972.
F. A. Shrontz	53	President and Director effective February 25, 1985. Prior thereto Vice President; President, Boeing Commercial Airplane Company from April 1984. Prior thereto Vice President-Sales and Marketing, Boeing Commercial Airplane Company from 1982. Prior thereto Vice President-General Manager-707/727/737 Division, Boeing Commercial Airplane Company from 1978.
H. W. Haynes	62	Executive Vice President-Chief Financial Officer since 1975. Director since 1966.
L. D. Alford	59	Senior Vice President since February 1984. Prior thereto President, Boeing Military Airplane Company from 1977.
R. E. Bateman	61	Vice President-General Manager, Boeing Marine Systems since 1975.
D. P. Beighle	52	Vice President-Contracts, General Counsel and Secretary since 1981. Prior thereto Vice President, Contracts from 1980. Prior thereto Partner in the law firm of Perkins, Coie, Stone, Olsen & Williams from 1967.
R. L. Dryden	51	President, Boeing Computer Services Company since 1981. Prior thereto Executive Vice President, Boeing Computer Services Company from 1980. Prior thereto program director, International Business Machines Corporation from 1971.
A. M. S. Goo	59	President, Boeing Military Airplane Company since February 1984. Prior thereto Executive Vice President, Boeing Military Airplane Company from 1979.
H. K. Hebeler	51	President, Boeing Aerospace Company since 1980. Prior thereto President, Boeing Engineering and Construction Company from 1975.

EXHIBIT 10 (continued)

Name	Age	Positions and offices presently held and business experience
K. F. Holtby	62	Senior Vice President since February 1982. Prior thereto Vice President-New Programs, Boeing Commercial Airplane Company from 1978.
A. H. Lowell	57	Vice President and Controller since April 1984. Prior thereto Controller from 1981. Prior thereto Controller, Boeing Commercial Airplane Company from 1977.
J. Mallen	58	President, Boeing Vertol Company since 1980. Prior thereto Vice President-Operations, Boeing Vertol Company from 1979.
W. M. Maulden	59	Senior Vice President since 1974.
J. B. L. Pierce	51	Treasurer since 1968.
C. E. Skeen	68	Senior Vice President since 1979.
R. W. Tharrington	65	Senior Vice President; President, Boeing Electronics Company since January 1985. Prior thereto Senior Vice President from 1981. Prior thereto Vice President; President, Boeing Computer Services Company from 1970.
D. D. Thornton	56	Senior Vice President; President, Boeing Commercial Airplane Company effective February 25, 1985. Prior thereto Senior Vice President from April 1984. Prior thereto Vice President-Customer Services, Marketing and Contracts, Boeing Commercial Airplane Company from June 1983. Prior thereto Vice President-General Manager-767 Division, Boeing Commercial Airplane Company from 1978.
R. W. Welch	64	Senior Vice President since April 1984. Prior thereto Vice President; President, Boeing Commercial Airplane Company from 1981. Prior thereto Executive Vice President, Boeing Commercial Airplane Company from 1975.

■ ■ ■ CASE 22
Gulf Resources/Bunker Hill Corporation

Donald F. Harvey
Robert Neilson
Eastern Washington University

INTRODUCTION

In 1981, Gulf Resources ranked number 459 in sales (down from 413 a year earlier), 396 in assets, and 481 in after tax profits, with a loss of $77 million in *Fortune's* top 500 U.S. industrial corporations. As he reflected on these rankings, Robert H. Allen, chairman and chief executive officer, looked out of his forty-seventh floor office window high above Houston, Texas, and pondered a difficult strategic question: what to do about the Bunker Hill subsidiary. Gulf Resources had initially invested $65 million in 1968 when it took over Bunker Hill. The figures through July 1981 showed a total of $122 million invested.

Allen needed to face the hard decision of the divestment of Bunker Hill. As reported in the *Wall Street Journal,*

> Gulf Resources and Chemical Corporation estimated that the cost of closing its Bunker Hill Company mining operation at Kellogg, Idaho, will result in an after-tax charge of $82.2 million against third quarter and nine months earnings. A Gulf Resources and Chemical spokesman said the closing is permanent. Although the Company is still seeking buyers for Bunker Hill, he said, "There's little hope, because after an exhaustive search there's been no offer." Gulf Resources stated that "further support of losses at Bunker Hill could only result in forcing capital and operating constraints upon the other subsidiaries to such an extent as to damage their competitive position and operating cost structure.[1]

Background

Ninety-six years ago, a little mining company started operating in a North Idaho valley town known today as Kellogg. It was to become Idaho's second largest employer and one of the nation's principal suppliers of strategic metals. The Bunker Hill Company, located in the famous Coeur d'Alene Mining District of north Idaho, was an important supplier of the nation's lead, zinc, silver, and cadmium. The company's Kellogg operations annually produced approximately 125,000 tons of refined lead, 100,000 tons of metallic zinc, 8 million troy ounces of silver, over 1 million pounds of refined cadmium, and a variety of by-products. A wholly owned subsidiary of Gulf Resources and Chemical Corporation, Bunker Hill employed 2,200 people in north Idaho and eastern Washington.

The company was founded following the discovery of the Bunker Hill Mine, which has become one of the world's largest underground lead–zinc–silver mines. The mine is composed of over 130 miles of tunnels, crosscuts, and drifts extending from approximately 3,600 feet above sea level to nearly 2,000 feet below sea level. Since the mine's discovery in 1885, over 35 million tons of ore have been extracted. Bunker Hill also operated the Pend Oreille Mine located in Metaline Falls, Washington, and has a 70 percent ownership in the Star-Morning Mine located at Burke, Idaho. In addition, the company also owns the Crescent Mine, a silver property located near Kellogg.

The daily production of the Bunker Hill Mine, together with lesser amounts of purchased ore, are processed through a 2,400-ton-per-day concentrator. This operation separates the metal values from the waste rock (tailings), producing a lead concentrate (approximately 64 percent lead with 40 ounces of silver per ton) and a zinc concentrate (approximately 55 percent zinc). The tailings are either pumped back underground to fill mined out areas or impounded in a 160-acre disposal area.[2]

GENERAL ENVIRONMENT

Cultural

The environmental system discussed in the following section is diagrammed in exhibit 1. Bunker Hill's beginning, the story goes, involved a jackass and a down-and-out grubstake miner, Noah Kellogg, who wandered into Murray in 1885 looking for work. Two mine speculators, O. O. Peck and Dr. J. T. Cooper, took pity on the old man and offered him a stake. They gave Kellogg an old burro and $18.75 worth of provisions and sent him to the South Fork of the Coeur d'Alene River to seek his fortune. Kellogg scoured the hills for two months and scraped together a few ore samples. He showed the minerals to a friend, Phil O'Rourke, who took one look and told Kellogg he had stumbled onto a fortune. The ore was galena, a lead ore often containing silver and similar to rich discoveries in Colorado. Kellogg dissolved his business obligations with Peck and Cooper, picked up some new partners, and headed back to the South Fork. The team of Kellogg, O'Rourke, "Dutch Jake" Goetz, and Harry Baer tramped through the valley with a string of pack mules and a promising future.

A jackass bolted one day and was later found standing on a huge exposed vein of galena. The men hurried to Murray and filed their claim as The Bunker Hill, in honor of America's first victory in the Revolutionary War. The men turned to James Wardner for financial backing. He found enough money to finance construction of the company's first mill in 1886, and in the following year the Bunker Hill and Sullivan Mining Company was in operation. Eventually, the mine's production superseded the mill's capabilities and a new mill was built across the valley. To move ore from the mine to the mill, an aerial tramway was built directly over the frontier town of Wardner. During its eleven years, the tram had its problems. Ore-laden buckets frequently dropped their load or fell from the cable onto the town's streets. Several people and horses were killed by falling ore.

The mill lasted until 1889, when it was blown up in the first of Bunker Hill's many labor disputes. It was so serious that Idaho Territory Governor Frank Steudnberg declared martial law and called in the army. Bunker Hill operated until 1980 with the only major change being the acquisition by Gulf Resources and Chemical Corporation; 1981 proved to be a bad year, however, as many factors caused Bunker Hill to show a heavy loss for Gulf Resources. In February of 1982, Bunker Hill closed for good.[3]

This case involves the critical period between 1980 and 1982. In 1980, the Bunker Hill Company produced approximately 25 percent of the nation's primary refined silver and 21 percent of its primary lead and zinc. By-products such as zinc oxide, refined gold, cadmium, antimonial lead, and phosphatic fertilizers were also important to its operations.

Bunker Hill's production was derived in part from its own ores and in part from purchased and tolled ores. Production from Bunker Hill-owned mines in 1980 and 1979, including Bunker Hill's 70 percent share of the Star Mine, was 2.2 and 2.3 million ounces of silver, respectively, 23 and 24 thousand tons of lead, respectively, and 26 thousand tons of zinc in both years.

Demographic

The majority of Bunker Hill and its mines were located in Kellogg, Idaho. Bunker Hill was Kellogg's major employer with 2,200 jobs directly involved in the company. A great number of indirect jobs, about 3,150, were also associated with Bunker Hill, meaning that a total of 5,350 jobs were directly and indirectly attributed to Bunker Hill. The 5,350 jobs were approximately 40 percent to 50 percent of the employment in Kellogg and Shoshone County. The majority of the workers for Bunker Hill were brought up in the town because their fathers and their fathers's fathers worked for the mining company at some time. The demographic makeup of Kellogg was basically skilled in the mining industry.

Natural Resources

A mining and smelting industry's most basic need—abundant natural resources—is the reason Bunker Hill was started in the Kellogg area. In 1980, the natural resource containing zinc concentrates began running out, resulting in lower outputs of both zinc and cadmium. The outlook for zinc concentrates had not improved through 1981. The quantity of other natural resources (including people) was good for Bunker Hill. In fact, there are still many untapped veins of galena in and around the hills of the Coeur d'Alene mining district.

Economic and Political

The year 1980 was extremely uncertain and difficult, not only for business but also for the general populace of the country. Interest rates and capital availability fluctuated tremendously throughout 1980 to 1982. Economic trends were downward. The important markets for Bunker Hill, the automobile and construction industries, suffered drastically.

Lead and zinc markets are largely dependent on conditions in the automobile and construction markets. These two sectors were more seriously affected by the recession than any other domestic industry. As a consequence, demand for lead and zinc and their pricing were at unsatisfying levels. Although the longer-term prospect for price improvement was excellent, the near term reflected the poor economic conditions.

The demand and price of silver also fluctuated widely. In 1980 silver sold for as high as $45.00 per ounce, but in late 1981, the price dropped to a low of $8.00 per ounce. The economic picture of Bunker Hill from 1978 to 1980 can best be shown by the financial, production, and reserves information provided in the Gulf Resources and Chemical Corporation 1980 Annual Report (see exhibit 2). Because of the sharp downturn in the economy in 1980 to 1982, the demand for lead and zinc also sharply decreased.

The major political occurrence affecting Bunker Hill was the sale forced by the Federal Reserve of a large amount of the Hunt brothers' silver. An overabundance of silver on the market in 1981 immediately drove down the price of the metal. The chain reaction caused a drastic drop in earnings for Gulf Resources and Bunker Hill. This glut was not a political ploy to injure Bunker Hill (or anyone) but was deemed necessary because of the market-cornering attempt by the Hunt brothers. The placing of silver on the market was not the only factor that caused the Bunker Hill demise, but it was one of the most important external factors affecting the company.

TASK ENVIRONMENT

Technological

Bunker Hill was basically an old mine, but capital expenditures on equipment and processes to improve efficiency and mining technologies were at industry level over the years. These improvements and the use of new technologies increased production capabilities at Bunker Hill.

Production of silver in all forms was a record 10.2 million ounces in 1980. Production of lead in all forms, at 129,000 tons, was 21 percent above 1979, the highest since 1973. The increase was partly due to the constant-volume air control system developed within Bunker Hill, for which patents are pending. It provides for a uniform flow of air through the total area of the furnace and is unique in that air control is applied separately to each pipe. The system made a significant contribution to blast furnace performance, and Bunker Hill was able to achieve a furnace availability of 95.5 percent during 1980, with the balance of the time almost entirely accounted for by routine preventive maintenance. In addition to reduced maintenance, lead concentrations in ambient air and coke consumption decreased while processing costs improved.

Refined silver production was aided by the expansion and modification of the silver refinery in early 1980, resulting in a significant reduction in the recycle load, lower processing losses of silver, and lower inventories of materials in process. Total cast zinc production in 1980 was approximately 77,000 tons despite the fact that zinc plant output was reduced from April through July due to shortfalls in concentrate receipts. The outlook for concentrate availability in 1981 was for continued tightness in supply.

Improvements were to have been made in the electrolytic zinc plant in 1981. Large anodes and cathodes, used in only a portion of the cells, were scheduled to be introduced throughout the electrolytic cell room. As a consequence, electrolytic current densities could have been reduced and more efficient electrolytic solutions employed. The results of this technological improvement should have increased operating performance and decreased labor costs. The larger anodes make possible a reduction in the amount of silver used in anodes. The changeover will be accomplished by lowering the cells involved below their present levels, and the capital cost needed is minor.

The domestic activities of GRC Exploration Company, Gulf Resources' mineral exploration subsidiary, were focused on molybdenum, lead, zinc, silver, gold, lithium, and coal during 1980. During that year, GRC Exploration continued its evaluation of the Cardiff coal property in eastern Tennessee. This work consisted of drilling to expand the proven reserves and obtaining cores for washability determinations. In addition, geotechnical analyses were made of the roof and floor characteristics of the coal seam. The findings increased confidence that the mining conditions were favorable, particularly with respect to tunnel support conditions and a dilution during mining. Geological and geochemical work was conducted at a large molybdenum prospect in southern Colorado; additional work was planned on the property during 1981. Foreign exploration projects included a promising lead–zinc–copper–gold project in Colombia and potash brines in the Atacama desert of Chile. The Bunker Hill material flow sheet and production process is shown in exhibit 3.

Competitors

Bunker Hill was very competitive, even though there were many producers of these metals. In 1980 the Bunker Hill Company produced approximately 25 percent of the nation's primary refined silver and 21 percent of its primary lead and zinc—a clear indication that competition was not a major factor in the downfall of Bunker Hill. The poor economic conditions of the early 1980s adversely affected all of the major metal producers. Zinc concentrates were difficult for everyone to obtain, and lead demand was low. The placement of silver on the market by the Federal Reserve affected everyone equally; however, the sharp decrease in silver prices especially hurt companies with large reserves.

Parent Company

Because Bunker Hill is a subsidiary of Gulf Resources, it is necessary to analyze the relationship between the two. A look at the events involving the Bunker Hill closure as they relate to Gulf Resources will also help in this analysis.

Gulf Resources and Chemical Corporation, a major domestic industrial company, is a leading producer of a broad range of natural resources and related products. The company's technical capabilities are in mineral extraction, metal and chemical processing, industrial explosives technology and research, oil and gas exploration and development, and process engineering for the oil and gas industry. The company's major products are coal, precious and base metals, lithium chemicals and metal, fertilizers, salt, industrial explosives, oil and gas, and specialty clays. Gulf Resources has many subsidiaries including the following:

C & K Coal Company

Cambria Coal Company

Charter Coal Corporation

GRC Coal Company

GRC Mining Company

Shannon Coal Company

W. P. Stahlman Coal Company, Inc.

The Bunker Hill Company

Lithium Corporation of America

IRECO Chemicals

Great Salt Lake Minerals and Chemical Corporation

Pend Oreille Oil and Gas Company

GRC Exploration Company

GS&B Engineering Company, Inc.

Industrial Mineral Ventures, Inc.

Gulf Resources Asia, Ltd.

This list shows the relative size of the company and the natural resources with which it is involved. The company's total assets are over $587 million, and in 1980 revenues were in excess of $671 million. The company is listed on the New York Stock Exchange and the Spokane Stock Exchange.

FINANCIAL

Chairman Robert Allen said,

> The accomplishments of 1980 were particularly pleasing because they were
> achieved in a year of extreme difficulty and uncertainty, not only for business
> but also for the general populace of the country. Efforts to curtail the rate of
> inflation were unsuccessful; interest rates and capital availability fluctuated
> tremendously throughout the year; economic trends were confusing and diffi-
> cult to analyze. In addition, the automobile and construction industries, im-
> portant markets for some of the company's products, suffered levels of stress
> that were inconceivable only a few years ago. Finally, precious metals' price
> fluctuations, influenced by fears of inflation and international turmoil on the
> one hand, and high interest rates, speculative excesses and disillusion on the
> other, exacerbated the year's uncertainties.[4]

Financial highlights are shown in exhibit 4, income statements are shown in
exhibit 5, balance sheet information in exhibit 6, information in exhibit 7, and a
ten-year review of financial information in exhibit 8.

Management

The company operated with each subsidiary as an operating entity or profit center.
The list of officers and directors is shown in exhibit 9. In 1981 a strategic decision
was made by Gulf Resources to close down Bunker Hill because of low profits due to
the declining silver market, lack of demand for lead and zinc, and high operating
costs. These high costs were the result of many factors including labor costs, high
energy costs, and an aging facility. Announcement of the closure caused a panic in
Kellogg, Idaho, because of the impact on the economy of the area. People banded
together to stop the closure, but the decision had been made.

The White Knights

In late 1981 a group of investors decided to try to save the mine by putting together
a package to purchase the mine from Gulf Resources. It would cost the investors $65
million in notes, cash, and future income, plus another $25 million in working cap-
ital. Gulf Resources would have accepted this offer; however, it wasn't that simple.
Before Bunker Hill could become a viable investment for the investor group, operating cost would have to be reduced or the banks would not loan the money required
for the takeover.

The six-member investor group was led by Harry Magnuson, a Wallace, Idaho,
millionaire, and Coeur d'Alene, Idaho, businessman Duane Hagadone. Other members included engineering consultant Bill Pfeiffer of Kellogg, Idaho, and Dallas,
Texas; and Boise-based potato millionaire J. R. Simplot and Co. The only way to cut
current operating costs was to reduce the labor costs at Bunker Hill. Union conces-

sions would have to be made by the United Steel Workers Union Local 7854 members in order for the mine to survive.

"If the numbers work out, we'll have the money," Magnuson said on January 6, 1982. Making the "numbers work out" was phase two of the process, which would ultimately end in the investor team deciding whether to exercise the option to buy Bunker. According to Duane Hagadone, consultants and principals spent the next two or three days studying the Bunker Hill books, cost and income projections, and the worth of the mines, the smelters, and the refinery. By Friday, January 9, he said, the group would know what concessions it would have to ask of the 1,800 union employees.[5]

Union

The proposal given to the union by the investors called for rehiring 1,500 workers and cutting wages by 25 percent in 1982. It then called for a 5 percent raise in 1983 and 15 percent raise annually in 1984, 1985, and 1986. Nonunion workers would be asked to take a 15 percent pay cut.

The union did not react favorably to the proposal, saying:

. . . it calls for "sweeping concessions in noneconomic areas which were not necessary for the rehabilitation and operation of the Bunker Hill facility."

"The purchasers demanded changes in virtually every provision of our agreements, including major reductions in wages, vacations and holidays, shift differentials, overtime pay, hazard pay, and elimination of all incentives," Flatt said. "In addition, they have demanded drastic cutbacks and changes in insurance and other benefit protections at a time when workers can least afford them."

. . . Union officials said they were ready to concede wage cuts of 10 to 20 percent. But they aren't willing to give up benefits or seniority or live with what they said would be the skeleton of a grievance system.

. . . Hagadone said all union rights were written into the new agreement and stressed that all safety rules were left intact.

. . . Union officials disagreed, saying the pact gives the company the bottom line of every issue.

. . . "In every area where there might be a dispute, the company retains the right to make the final decision," a union official said. The proposal "totally disrupts seniority," he said.[6]

The union officials were against the investors' proposal, but the rank and file voted for it. On Tuesday, January 19, 1982, the local union members elected new officers who supported the position of the rank and file and the investors group's proposal.

The crisis in the Silver Valley grew more complex the following Tuesday when a judge issued a temporary restraining order prohibiting the United Steelworkers from interfering with the mandate of Local 7854 union members. A hearing on the class action suit was then scheduled for the following Friday, January 22. The critical problem was the deadline faced by the investor group interested in purchasing Bunker Hill. The investors needed the national union's approval, or the labor agreement would have been tied up in court, and the investors would not be able to get the capital necessary to purchase the company.

On Thursday, January 21, 1982, Duane Hagadone announced that their (the investor group) lawyer recommended they terminate the purchase offer. That day the last nails were driven into the coffin of Bunker Hill. There would be no chance for the members of the United Steel Workers Local 7854 to return to work at Bunker Hill.

CONCLUSION

This case examines the environmental system and its subsystems and how they affected Bunker Hill and Gulf Resources and Chemical Corporation. The Bunker Hill management made decisions that influenced the lives of thousands of people in and around Kellogg, Idaho. Bunker Hill provides an example of what changing environmental factors can do to a large company.

Ninety-six years ago a little mining company started operating in a city later called Kellogg in a northern Idaho valley. It grew to become Idaho's second largest employer and one of the nation's principal suppliers of strategic metals. Now, Bunker Hill Company, a victim of a bad economy, poor metals prices, high operating costs, a shortage of concentrates, a breakdown in union negotiations, and an absentee owner, is about to be ravaged by scavenging scrap metal dealers and demolition companies.

Although Gulf Resources and Chemical Corporation says "our problems are behind us," a newly formed group disagrees. It insists that many shareholders aren't behind the company. The shareholder protective group, generally dissatisfied with management, specifically objects to the decision to close the Bunker Hill Company unit's mining and smelter operations in northern Idaho. Thus, Gulf's troubles may be just beginning.

The protective group claims support or financial commitment from holders of 25 percent of Gulf Resources' common stock outstanding. The group spokesman said, "they haven't any intent to seek control of the company," but Mark Yarry, a San Diego writer who is organizing the group, doesn't rule out a proxy fight for a change in management. He asserts that many holders also think the timing of the Bunker Hill closing is "deplorable."[7]

Robert Allen, chairman of Gulf Resources, said he hasn't any "reason to believe most shareholders are unhappy with the company's management."[8] He adds that many holders have expressed support for closure of Bunker Hill, which was expected to incur a $20 million loss in 1982 and perhaps a $40 million deficit in 1983. Many stockholders, Robert Allen said, "realize we hadn't any other alternative." Gulf Resources announced November 10, 1981 that it would take a $82.2 million write-off against third quarter earnings because of the cost of ending work at Kellogg, Idaho. Robert Allen also said the company will be able to focus attention on its growing operations in coal, lithium, oil, and natural gas. "Our problems are behind us,"[9] he asserted. But are they?

Notes

1   Annual Report, Gulf Resources and Chemical Corp., 1980, 1981, 1982.
2   *The Bunker Hill Company*, Lawton Printing, Spokane, 1966, 1–2.
3   Ibid.
4   Gulf Resources Annual Report, 1981.
5   R. Hibbard, "Bunker Hill Crisis," *The Spokesman-Review*, January 20, 1982, B-1.
6   B. Tabor, "Union: We'll Reject Investor's Pact," *The Spokesman-Review*, January 15, 1982, B-1.
7   "Bunker Hill's Demise Is Not Sudden," *The Seattle Times*, February 21, 1982, F-1.
8   Ibid.
9   Ibid.

EXHIBIT 1
Environmental System and Subsystems

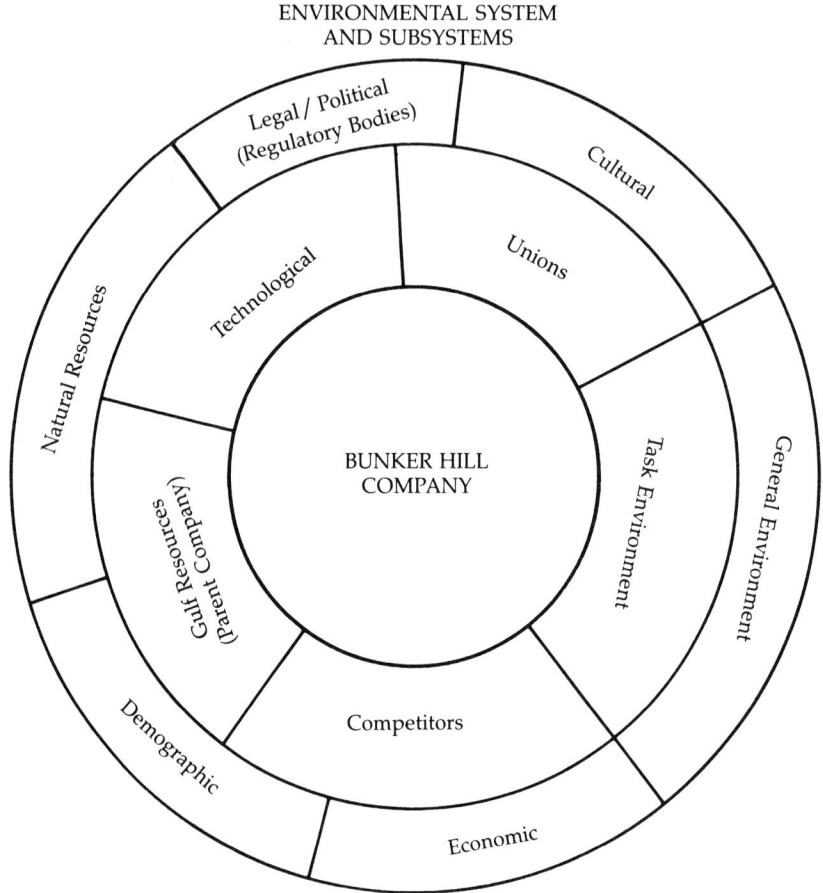

ENVIRONMENTAL SYSTEM
AND SUBSYSTEMS

EXHIBIT 2
Earnings Overview (in thousands)

	1980	1979	1978
Financial			
Silver, Lead, Zinc			
Revenues	$338,237	$228,913	$158,161
Earnings (losses)	31,499	13,976	(953)
Production			
Lead, all forms (tons)	129	107	110
Zinc, cast (tons)	77	81	84
Silver, all forms (ounces)	10,184	8,756	9,471
Reserves			
Silver, Lead, Zinc (proven and probable tons)	3,391	3,362	3,436
Metals Contained			
Silver (ounces)	11,884	11,776	11,189
Lead (tons)	115	110	106
Zinc (tons)	149	152	147

EXHIBIT 3
Bunker Hill Material Flowsheet

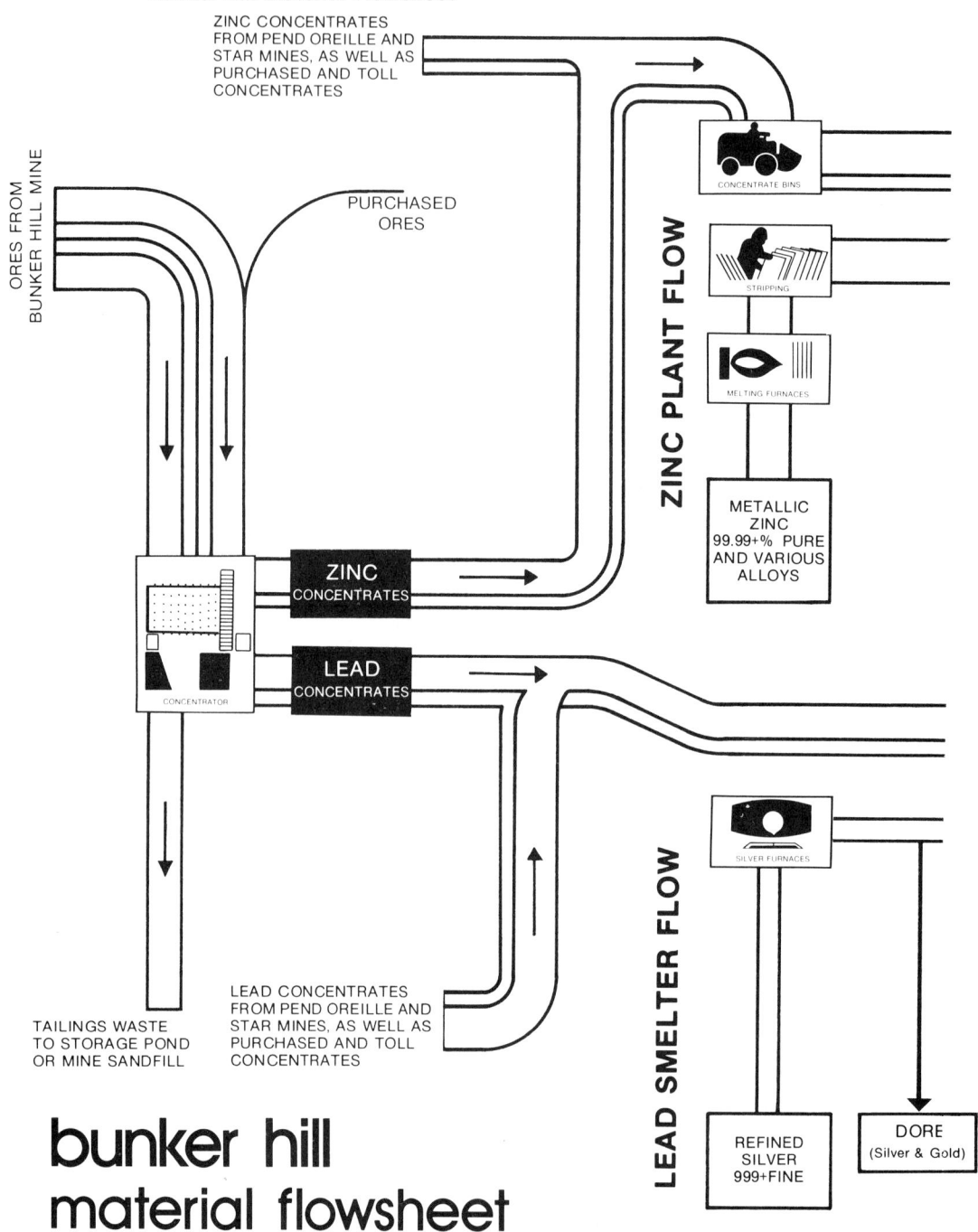

bunker hill
material flowsheet

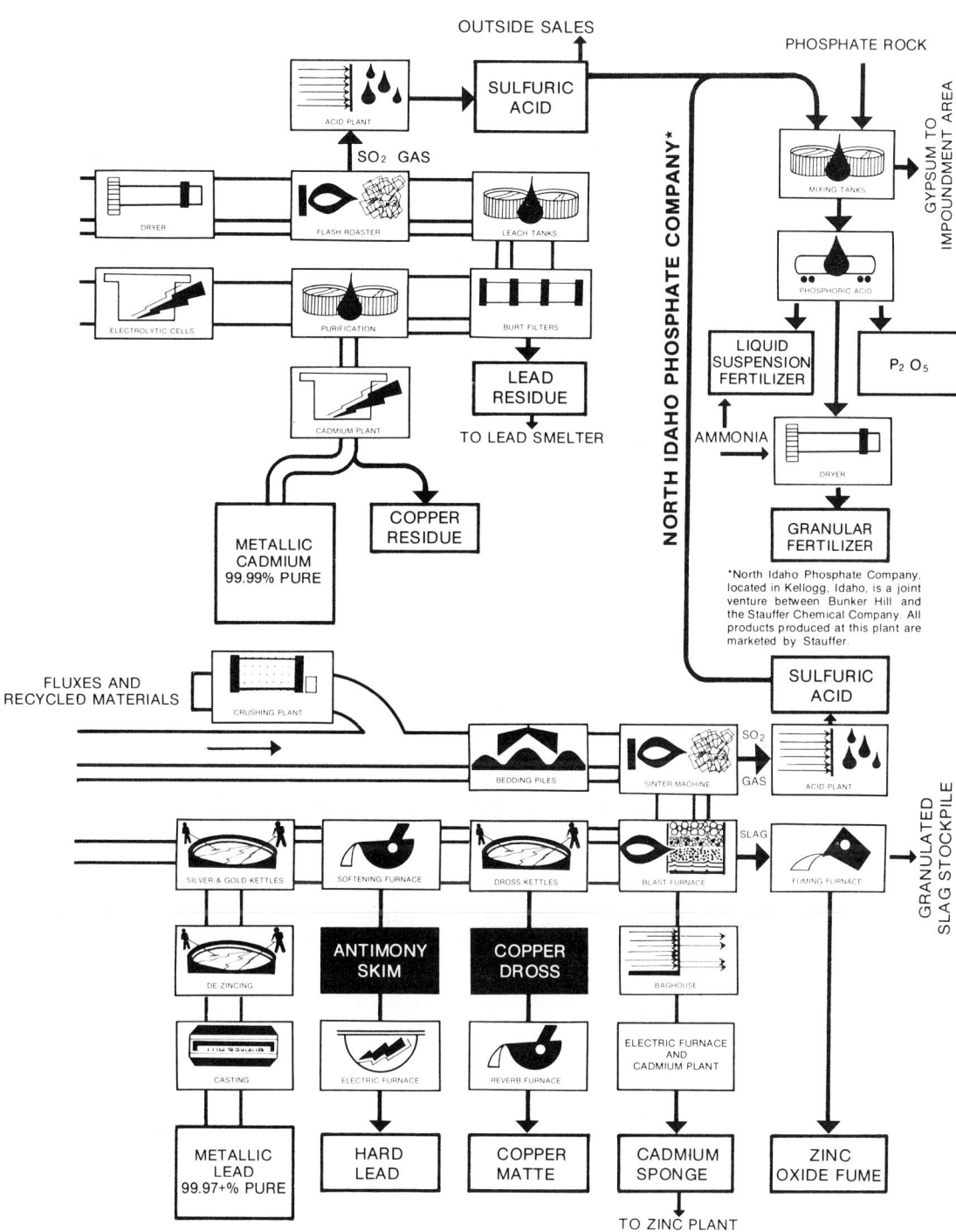

*North Idaho Phosphate Company, located in Kellogg, Idaho, is a joint venture between Bunker Hill and the Stauffer Chemical Company. All products produced at this plant are marketed by Stauffer.

EXHIBIT 4

Financial Highlights for Gulf Resources & Chemical Corporation

Financial Highlights

Gulf Resources & Chemical Corporation

Year Ended December 31,	1980	1979	1978
(In thousands except earnings per share)			
Revenues	$671,410	$510,015	$390,110
Income before extraordinary item and cumulative effect of changes in method of accounting	21,361	15,146	13,596
Net income	25,072	13,998	13,596
Earnings per share on common shares assuming full dilution— Income before extraordinary item and cumulative effect of changes in method of accounting	2.08	1.50	1.37
Net income	2.44	1.38	1.37
Working capital	195,545	120,039	107,859
Capital expenditures—net	46,608	50,182	31,353
Property, plant and equipment—net	203,089	188,116	159,496
Total assets	587,087	507,624	408,635
Long-term debt—net	225,723	195,822	148,227
Stockholders' investment	188,254	167,338	157,968
Contribution to revenues:*			
Coal	114,413	119,542	120,500
Silver, lead, zinc	338,237	228,913	158,161
Lithium	58,080	54,361	42,093
Industrial explosives	56,161	52,248	39,592
Fertilizer and salt	31,784	26,382	23,644
Oil and gas	10,581	7,946	4,166
Specialty clays	2,136	2,143	—
Engineering services	48,270	16,652	—
Contribution to earnings:*			
Coal	16,172	15,616	20,793
Silver, lead, zinc	31,499	13,976	(953)
Lithium	11,167	12,873	9,856
Industrial explosives	2,799	4,412	4,296
Fertilizer and salt	2,717	2,325	3,346
Oil and gas	2,936	1,694	952
Specialty clays	(9,760)	(2,098)	—
Engineering services	(9,863)	(2,559)	—

*Before taxes, interest expense, parent company overhead and elimination of intercompany transactions.

EXHIBIT 5
Statements of Income for Gulf Resources & Chemical Corporation

Statements of Income
Gulf Resources & Chemical Corporation

Year Ended December 31,	1980	1979	1978
Revenues:			
Sale of products and services	$638,311,508	$496,226,890	$379,502,060
Interest income.	9,254,141	3,600,615	3,522,224
Gain on sale of investment in Bethlehem Copper Corporation (Note 1). . .	18,739,438	—	—
Other	5,104,735	10,187,669	7,085,779
	$671,409,822	$510,015,174	$390,110,063
Costs and expenses:			
Cost of sales.	$530,736,872	$410,867,263	$310,963,213
Depreciation, depletion and amortization.	23,635,054	21,561,511	18,096,424
Selling, general and administrative.	39,911,213	33,277,074	19,764,753
Research, development and exploration.	5,972,849	4,568,083	3,833,466
Interest and debt expense.	26,494,623	19,544,170	17,063,322
Write-down of certain assets (Note 2)	13,232,708	—	—
Other	3,897,409	1,051,430	1,156,928
	$643,880,728	$490,869,531	$370,878,106
Income before taxes on income, extraordinary item and cumulative effect of changes in method of accounting	$ 27,529,094	$ 19,145,643	$ 19,231,957
Provision for taxes on income (Note 3)	6,167,820	4,000,000	5,636,000
Income before extraordinary item and cumulative effect of changes in method of accounting.	$ 21,361,274	$ 15,145,643	$ 13,595,957
Extraordinary item (Note 5).	—	(1,147,694)	—
Cumulative effect on prior years of changes in method of accounting (Note 1).	3,711,015	—	—
Net income	$ 25,072,289	$ 13,997,949	$ 13,595,957
Earnings per share (Note 4):			
On common and common equivalent shares—			
Income before extraordinary item and cumulative effect of changes in method of accounting	$ 2.24	$ 1.58	$ 1.41
Extraordinary item	—	(.14)	—
Cumulative effect on prior years of changes in method of accounting . .	.42	—	—
Net income.	$ 2.66	$ 1.44	$ 1.41
On common shares assuming full dilution—			
Income before extraordinary item and cumulative effect of changes in method of accounting	$ 2.08	$ 1.50	$ 1.37
Extraordinary item	—	(.12)	—
Cumulative effect on prior years of changes in method of accounting . .	.36	—	—
Net income.	$ 2.44	$ 1.38	$ 1.37

EXHIBIT 6
Balance Sheets for Gulf Resources & Chemical Corporation

Balance Sheets
Gulf Resources & Chemical Corporation

December 31,	1980	1979
Assets		
Current assets:		
Cash	$ 10,350,151	$ 12,315,449
Temporary cash investments	98,541,697	49,739,145
Accounts receivable—		
Trade	115,721,855	81,878,993
Unbilled receivables	10,412,577	4,742,847
Other	7,551,950	4,365,690
Inventories	83,571,889	64,939,023
Prepaid expenses and other	19,971,618	24,995,853
Total current assets	$346,121,737	$242,977,000
Investments:		
Bethlehem Copper Corporation	$ —	$ 32,711,211
Other	2,159,470	1,572,545
	$ 2,159,470	$ 34,283,756
Property, plant and equipment, at cost (Note 5):		
Land, mineral and oil and gas properties	$ 86,581,096	$ 76,502,784
Plants, facilities and equipment	278,886,740	259,357,875
Construction in progress	12,859,711	9,934,656
	$378,327,547	$345,795,315
Less—Allowance for depreciation, depletion and amortization	175,238,139	157,678,927
	$203,089,408	$188,116,388
Other assets:		
Cost of investment in The Bunker Hill Company in excess of underlying book value at date of acquisition	$ 14,854,417	$ 14,854,417
Patents and licenses (Note 2)	—	10,944,020
Deferred mine development costs	2,854,797	4,864,630
Other	18,007,076	11,584,041
	$ 35,716,290	$ 42,247,108
	$587,086,905	$507,624,252

EXHIBIT 6 (continued)

December 31,	1980	1979
Liabilities and Stockholders' Investment		
Current liabilities:		
Current installments on long-term debt, including mandatory prepayments of $12,736,000 (Note 5)	$ 16,685,601	$ 10,166,149
Notes payable to banks	5,032,151	3,782,552
Accounts payable	72,969,208	61,867,841
Accrued liabilities—		
Taxes on income	10,163,829	4,782,748
Payroll	9,098,971	9,379,350
Interest	9,045,957	6,180,620
Other	27,580,666	26,778,718
Total current liabilities	$150,576,383	$122,937,978
Long-term debt (Note 5)	$225,723,076	$195,822,155
Deferred income taxes (Note 3)	$ 22,533,615	$ 21,525,880
Commitments and contingent liabilities (Note 6)		
Stockholders' investment:		
Preferred Stock, $1 par; authorized 4,000,000 shares—aggregate involuntary liquidating preference of $11,541,617 at December 31, 1980 (Note 7)		
Series A	$ 72,589	$ 88,484
Series B	470,249	595,046
Series C	—	1,234,900
Common Stock, $.10 par; authorized 20,000,000 shares, outstanding 8,872,151 and 7,188,896 shares (Note 8)	887,215	718,890
Common stock purchase warrants (Note 8)	1,645,417	1,461,750
Capital in excess of par	73,659,704	71,151,098
Retained earnings (Note 5)	111,518,657	92,088,071
	$188,253,831	$167,338,239
	$587,086,905	$507,624,252

EXHIBIT 7
Segment Information for Gulf Resources & Chemical Corporation

Segment Information
Gulf Resources & Chemical Corporation

(In thousands)	1980	1979	1978	1977	1976
Financial[1]					
Coal					
Revenues..	$114,413	$119,542	$120,500	$ 98,162	$ 84,289
Earnings	16,172	15,616	20,793	14,741	16,127
Silver, Lead, Zinc					
Revenues..	338,237	228,913	158,161	130,200	140,402
Earnings (losses)	31,499	13,976	(953)	(6,677)	8,537
Lithium					
Revenues..	58,080	54,361	42,093	41,304	34,289
Earnings	11,167	12,873	9,856	9,953	8,637
Industrial Explosives					
Revenues..	56,161	52,248	39,592	35,660	34,735
Earnings	2,799	4,412	4,296	1,588	3,481
Fertilizer and Salt					
Revenues..	31,784	26,382	23,644	19,325	15,549
Earnings	2,717	2,325	3,346	2,798	2,653
Oil and Gas					
Revenues..	10,581	7,946	4,166	4,807	5,193
Earnings	2,936	1,694	952	1,806	2,572
Specialty Clays[2]					
Revenues..	2,136	2,143	—	—	—
Earnings (losses)	(9,760)	(2,098)	—	—	—
Engineering Services[2]					
Revenues..	48,270	16,652	—	—	—
Earnings (losses)	(9,863)	(2,559)	—	—	—
Production					
Coal—raw tons.......................................	5,254	5,915	5,871	5,453	5,031
Lead, all forms—tons	129	107	110	100	108
Zinc, cast—tons	77	81	84	52	100
Silver, all forms—ounces	10,184	8,756	9,471	7,483	7,791
Lithium—carbonate equivalent in pounds..................	26,742	30,045	26,493	27,563	25,641
Sulfate of Potash—tons	202	183	196	177	158
Common Salt, produced for sale—tons	533	603	391	312	185
Natural Gas—mcf	2,502	2,280	1,120	1,223	1,371
Condensate—bbls	110	112	92	140	171
Reserves					
Coal—recoverable tons................................	69,553	68,905	70,889	70,195	66,144
Silver, Lead, Zinc—proven and probable tons	3,391	3,362	3,436	3,681	4,222
Metals Contained—					
Silver—ounces.....................................	11,884	11,776	11,189	11,221	9,078
Lead—tons..	115	110	106	112	119
Zinc—tons..	149	152	147	150	179
Lithium—proven and probable tons (avg. 1.38% lithia)	25,700	26,300	27,000	27,600	29,600
Oil and Gas—proved					
Gas—mcf...	24,292	17,158[3]	7,565	7,170	8,456
Condensate—bbls	715	476[3]	324	367	498

Notes:
(1) Revenues and earnings (losses) are before taxes, interest expense, parent company overhead and elimination of intercompany transactions.
(2) Includes results of these operations since date of respective acquisition.
(3) Includes 5.1 billion cubic feet of gas and 105,000 barrels of condensate acquired by purchase in early 1979.

EXHIBIT 8

Selected Financial Information Ten-Year Review for Gulf Resources & Chemical Corporation

Selected Financial Information
Ten-Year Review

Gulf Resources & Chemical Corporation

Year Ended December 31,	1980	1979	1978	1977	1976	1975	1974	1973	1972	1971
(In thousands except per share amounts and employees)										
Revenues	$671,410	510,015	390,110	330,918	315,484	301,304	250,522	147,615	127,249	116,288
Income (loss) before extraordinary items and cumulative effect of changes in method of accounting	$ 21,361	15,146	13,596	8,910	16,188	27,937	33,022	6,032	2,478	(4,210)
Net income (loss)	$ 25,072	13,998	13,596	8,910	16,188	27,937	35,870	7,439	2,834	(21,992)
Earnings (loss) per share on common shares assuming full dilution—										
Income (loss) before extraordinary items and cumulative effect of changes in method of accounting	$ 2.08	1.50	1.37	.81	1.80	3.26	3.97	.87	.28	(1.00)
Net income (loss)	$ 2.44	1.38	1.37	.81	1.80	3.26	4.33	1.13	.35	(4.41)
Cash dividends declared per common share	$ .455	.32	.25	1.00	1.00	1.00	.25	—	—	—
Working capital	$195,545	120,039	107,859	116,474	119,918	72,814	64,427	39,156	20,558	19,751
Capital expenditures—net	$ 46,608	50,182	31,353	27,025	31,349	44,840	32,245	10,163	8,406	7,076
Property, plant and equipment—net	$203,089	188,116	159,496	146,240	134,158	117,611	84,732	59,937	46,948	43,634
Total assets	$587,087	507,624	408,635	396,122	331,193	277,331	218,408	144,258	112,066	105,184
Long-term debt—net	$225,723	195,822	148,227	157,989	110,786	80,948	89,126	73,575	53,087	48,610
Stockholders' investment	$188,254	167,338	157,968	148,708	149,216	117,340	75,799	41,689	34,096	31,730
Number of employees	5,000	5,000	4,400	4,400	4,400	4,300	3,700	3,300	2,900	2,700

The above table sets forth selected financial information regarding Gulf's financial position and operating results. This information should be read in conjunction with the Review of Operations, and the Financial Statements and Notes thereto, included herein.

EXHIBIT 9
Directors and Officers

Directors		Officers

Directors   **Officers**

Director Since

Robert H. Allen* 1960
Chairman of the Board and
Chief Executive Officer of
the Corporation

Raphael Bernstein‡ 1972
Partner
Bear, Stearns & Co.
(investment bankers
and brokers)

Robert E. Brown 1968
Partner (retired)
Brown, Peacock,
Keane & Boyd
(attorneys)

George A. Butler* 1961
Senior Partner (retired)
Butler, Binion, Rice,
Cook & Knapp (attorneys)

Donald P. deBrier 1976
Vice President and
General Counsel of the
Corporation

Jerry E. Finger*† 1977
Chairman of the Board
Republic National
Bancshares, Inc.

Dan M. Krausse 1981
President
The Krausse Company
(oil and gas consultants)

Robert G. Peters‡ 1978
President
Peters & Company
(stockbrokers)

Director Since

George Rieveschl, Jr.* 1967
Vice President, Emeritus
University of Cincinnati

Richard H. Skinner†‡ 1973
Vice Chairman of the Board
and Chairman of the
Executive Committee
First Mortgage Company
of Texas, Inc.
(real estate and mortgage
banking)

Jackson W. Smart, Jr.‡ 1972
Chairman of the Board
and President
Central National Chicago
Corporation
(commercial banking)

Thomas G. Stevens 1981
Vice President
Clayton W. Williams, Jr.
Companies
(oil and gas exploration and
production)

Jack T. Trotter*† 1956
Investments

Frank G. Woodruff 1970
President and
Chief Operating Officer of
the Corporation

Robert H. Allen
Chairman of the Board and
Chief Executive Officer

Frank G. Woodruff
President and Chief
Operating Officer

Donald P. deBrier
Vice President and
General Counsel

William M. Wolf
Senior Vice President

Gene M. Baker
Vice President,
Environmental Affairs

Robert E. Bowman
Vice President and
Executive Assistant to the
Chairman of the Board

Keith E. Dyas
Vice President,
Special Projects

Robert H. Gow
Vice President, Planning
and Corporate Development

Robert E. Holt
Vice President, Exploration

Donald M. Rose
Vice President, Controller

Arthur M. Urech
Vice President, Finance
and Treasurer

Jack M. Webb
Vice President,
Government Relations

Jose Diaz de Leon
Assistant Treasurer

Jerry T. Northcutt
Assistant
Controller-Accounting

Elsie D. Wilson
Secretary and
Assistant General Counsel

List of Directors as of May 12, 1981

*Members of Executive Committee
†Members of Audit Committee
‡Members of Compensation Committee

Tandy Corporation, 1985

Donald F. Harvey
Research Assistant: Charlotte Sullivan

INTRODUCTION

From his well-appointed office in Tandy Center overlooking Fort Worth, John V. Roach, chairman and chief executive officer of Tandy, reflected upon future strategy. Roach, a handsome, dapper man who speaks with a soft Texas drawl, is not one to blow his own horn. "It's been totally a team effort," he insists. "There is no question that our share of the computer market has decreased," Roach concedes. "But our computer centers will allow us to remain strong competitors."[1]

> The opportunity to start a new chain has been demonstrated dramatically by our Radio Shack Computer Centers, now numbering 400 in the United States plus at least 45 outside this country. We've been able to expand this chain rapidly and have proven that retail outlets for computers are very popular. IBM, Xerox, Digital Equipment, and Sears have indicated they also think computer stores are viable. Presently, our toughest competition in computer centers comes from the Computerland franchise group and hundreds of independents, but we won't be outdone. We will open more than 50 new Radio Shack Computer Centers in the next twelve months, a rate of growth second to none in the challenging computer field.
>
> The opportunity to push into new frontiers grows steadily. As we expand into business and educational electronics, we see the prospects of some day being as big in these areas as we are in consumer electronics. Our business product line will grow steadily. We currently spend substantial sums for product development in the educational area.[2]

Thus, future sales growth is based on present research and development and on the expansion of Radio Shack Computer Centers.

BACKGROUND

Tandy Corporation is a U.S. manufacturer and retailer of consumer electronic equipment. Founded in Fort Worth in 1918 by Norton Hinkley and Dave Tandy, Tandy Corporation began as a shoe leather and repair supplier. It prospered and expanded until 1955, when it was sold to financially troubled American Hide and Leather Company. Charles Tandy, son of Dave, resented American Hide and Leather and in

1958 used options and creative financing to purchase 50,000 shares of stock to regain control. By 1960, Tandy had sold off all of the unprofitable divisions.

Charles Tandy's initial strategy was to integrate Tandy vertically as a leather products firm, and he purchased Corral Sportwear, Cleveland Crafts, Tex Tan Division, Craftool Company (a leather tool manufacturer), Clarke and Clarke, Limited, Merribee, and Pier I (eventually sold because it required too much capital).

In 1963 Tandy bought financially troubled Radio Shack, which consisted of nine retail stores in the Boston area and a mail order house started in the 1920s to supply ham operators and other electronic hobbyists. Radio Shack's 1963 sales were $20 million; in 1986, Radio Shack's net sales were over $3 billion.[3] Charles Tandy reduced Radio Shack's inventory from 25,000 items to 2,500, eliminated the catalog business, established cost controls, and emphasized rapid inventory turnover. Today Radio Shack is widely known as the largest electronics retail chain in the United States.

Until his death, Tandy ran his firm using the following strategies:

1 Retain earnings for capital investment and pay no dividends.
2 Borrow money only to finance seasonal requirements.
3 Do not acquire companies unless a 25 percent return on assets before taxes can be achieved.
4 Carry only fast-moving items, that is, carry only high-turnover inventory.
5 Pay managers on a profit-sharing basis.

Since 1963 Tandy has spun off all its nonelectronic businesses to other corporations. It is now an electronics retailer and manufacturer.

Tandy is basically a consumer electronics retailing business, despite the fact that some 1,200 of the company's 2,800 products are manufactured in-house. Tandy's ability to develop and quickly market innovative products has enabled it to capitalize on trends in the consumer electronics marketplace. Management constantly reviews the product line in terms of sales trends and adds or discontinues products in response to changing consumer demands. Thus, the total number of products offered today is only 17 percent greater than the 2,400 items offered ten years ago. Exhibit 1 presents contribution to net sales, projected growth rate, and probable sales contributions in fiscal 1988 for each major product category. Newer product lines are expected to contribute the major share of sales growth in the future.

1 Tandy is a major player in the personal computer industry. Tandy competes in the personal computer industry on the basis of price, product quality, and service, with an estimated 24 percent compound growth rate over the next five years.
2 Tandy controls the retail stores that sell its products. All 8,100 plus stores sell the lower end line, and over 200 computer centers sell all computer products.
3 Tandy has implemented the separate computer store concept to serve first-time business and professional users.

4   Tandy has an extensive product line.

5   Tandy has a high-quality management team. The corporation is run as a profit center, with all employees compensated on the basis of their units' sales increases and profits.

6   The company's cash position is strong.

7   Tandy sells other fast-growth consumer electronic products.

Environment

Tandy Corporation operates in a highly dynamic environment. Due to rapid technological advances, its product line experiences dramatic changes in a highly competitive industry characterized by foreign and domestic competition.

One-third of Tandy's 1981 sales were made in product lines that five years earlier were either nonexistent or minor; therefore, short-range forecasts are made for all product lines and their development, and wrong forecasts, as in the CB market, can be disastrous.[4] The audio market generally seems to be declining, but audio manufacturers increased production 20 percent in a flat sales year with the result that products must now be discounted in order to reduce inventories.

Except for technological advances in digital recording technology, no major audio advances are occurring. According to Bernie Appel, executive vice-president for marketing, the audio market is still strong in audio accessories, rack systems (receivers, amps, and so forth sold in a rack or shelf system), miniature portable AM/FM radios equipped with lightweight headphones, and AM/FM cassette car players. Declining markets exist for open reel tape decks, 8-track tape players, ordinary car radios, and stereo consoles. CB radio sales are stable at about 1.5 million units—down from 10 to 12 million units sold during the CB craze days.[5]

Radio Shack predicts increased markets in electronic toys and calculators; however, other marketing experts believe that although electronic toys are a significant market, the electronic hand-held game device has peaked. Other growth markets include consumer-owned telephones and security systems. Long-term growth for the videocassette and video disk markets is possible, but Tandy has production problems in meeting the market. The market for personal computers has been exploding ($2.4 billion dollar sales worldwide—40 percent growth rate currently; 15 percent growth rate through 1991), especially in business and education. The growth in the home computer market is slowed, largely because of application software shortages.[6]

Tandy's market is characterized by an extensive and expanding distribution system. It is the largest retail electronics firm in the world, with 5,147 company-owned stores and more than 3000 dealer/franchise outlets.

The company-owned store dealer program—offering exclusive product line distribution in towns of less than 25,000—is expanding; while in towns of less than 8,000, local businesses carry Radio Shack products for a small franchise fee. Sales to these dealers are on a cash basis with dealers establishing their own prices. Company-owned stores, on the other hand, are managed by Radio Shack employees. In the United States, 150 company-owned stores and 100 computer stores were projected to open in 1982, while some older stores were to be remodeled or relocated. Tandy's marketing is done mainly through retail outlets with support from fifty-three service centers.

The environment, especially competition and the general market, has a decided impact on Tandy Corporation. Tandy's survival depends on its ability to predict and meet changes in the technological area, as well as to be competitive in pursuing aggressive marketing strategies (see exhibit 2).

Financial Data

As a retailer, Tandy has set increased sales and percent of market share as major corporate goals. John Roach, the chief executive officer, also wants to consolidate Tandy's lead in low-cost computers and generate a mass market of users. Currently, Tandy's TRS-80 has 200,000 users. Roach envisions a convenience system for users to include electronic mail, banking, and educational uses. His strategy is to develop a communications network that encourages users to start small and upgrade their systems with more costly and sophisticated equipment. This strategy was successfully used in Detroit by the Big Three auto companies for several decades. Thus, Radio Shack computer stores are pushing hardware, but not software. Of course, software sales will follow sales of the hardware base.

Tandy strives to be the "Biggest Name in Little Computers." One technique used to achieve this status is upgrading the Radio Shack image with new computer stores, a professional image, and classes for users that are also free to educators. Over the long run, Tandy plans to increase its gross profit margin by holding down costs through self-manufacturing more and more of its own computers. Tandy is a growth company, and as a retailer, its concern is increasing sales. For the past ten years, sales have increased 17 percent annually. A review of operations is shown in exhibit 3. Tandy regards gross profit as one of its key figures. Founder Tandy's statement, "If you don't have it [gross profit] going in, you won't have it [profit] coming out, and volume will not solve your problems," is widely quoted.[7]

Gross profit in Canada increased in spite of currency fluctuations, but it declined in Europe largely due to currency fluctuations. Currency fluctuations are a risk in international markets. As Tandy expands in the international market, this risk will increase. Exhibit 4 shows operating profit of Tandy Corporation by region.

The largest group of stockholders in Tandy Corporation includes its officers and employees. Tandy has a generous stock purchase plan where the firm matches employee contributions at rates of 40 percent and up, according to the length of employment. Tandy does not pay dividends; it prefers instead to plow the earnings back into new computer stores. Thus, for investors and employees, the increased return on equity is the critical factor because there are no dividends (see exhibit 5; exhibits 6 and 7 show comparison).

Research and Development

Tandy's early lead in the personal computer market resulted when the price of microprocessors fell during the mid-1970s. Perhaps luck more than planning figured into Radio Shack's lead in the micro market because the company did not expect the TRS-80 to be the winner it has become. The developer of the TRS-80 left Tandy because he said he liked being a department of one better than being one of 800. Today, the head of research and development at Tandy has less Tandy experience than any other corporate officer. Research and development is based in two design centers, one in Fort Worth and one in Tokyo, each a part of Tandy's research department. Two areas for new product development include semiconductor manufacturers and design centers. Both show forward looking trends. Tandy doesn't rely on customers or competitors for product design, which means Tandy is rarely behind in introducing new products to the highly dynamic consumer electronics market. In short, Tandy is a market leader in the area of research and development for new product development.

Tandy is attempting to move toward a more vertical company integration. Currently, 43 percent of Tandy products are manufactured by Tandy in twenty-eight factories—twenty-four in the United States and one each in Japan, Canada, Korea, and Taiwan. Tandy regards reliance on outsiders, such competitors or suppliers that sell to the competition, as a distinct liability. Whether Tandy has the technical expertise to become totally integrated without massive outside investments in non-retailing enterprises is doubtful. Thus, there appears to be a conflict between the sales and growth strategies and the preference of management for equity financing.

One reason for Tandy's success in the personal computer market is the distribution of its computers and the rest of its electronic products. Opening computer stores takes priority over regular stores. Tandy also emphasizes product-specific advertising. The 1000 and 2000 IBM-compatibles are doing well.

Tandy's strengths in marketing include an effective distribution system, low competitive prices, products that most consumers demand, and a sales force motivated by commissions and increased shares of stock in Tandy Corporation. Weaknesses include growing competition, a weak product development procedure, and a perceived poor image of the Radio Shack logo.

Structurally, Tandy Corporation is divided into Radio Shack, the retailer for the United States; Tandy International Electronics; and Tandy Electronics Manufacturing (see exhibit 8). A&A Trading Company purchases components overseas and sells them to Radio Shack and Tandy Electronics Manufacturing.

MANAGERIAL

Until Charles Tandy's death in 1978, Tandy Corporation was marked by his personal relationships. After Tandy's death, he was replaced by childhood friend Phil North, a Fort Worth newspaperman. When he became chief executive officer, North had no professional merchandising or management experience. John Roach, a former data processing manager, is president, currently chairman, and chief executive officer of Tandy. Until 1982, Lew Kornfeld was president of Radio Shack. Like other old Tandy executives, his title and expertise did not necessarily match. As a former college English teacher, his specialty was product development and advertising. He reportedly kept his TRS-80 computer shut up in the closet in his office! Bernard Appel, vice-president of marketing, runs most of Radio Shack's noncomputer business (85 percent). Jon Shirley, vice-president for computer merchandising runs the computer end of Radio Shack.[8] Tandy is characterized by a senior staff that has been with the company for a long time (see exhibits 9 and 10).

The most dynamic areas, research and development and manufacturing, are characterized by the most recent additions to the staff. As Exhibit 10 suggests, Tandy generally promotes from within.

PROBLEMS

One significant problem for Tandy is increasing competition from strong computer companies. Tandy has made a major commitment to the personal computer business but has been unable to meet customer demands for peripherals and software. In the past, it relied on users to produce software not found in Radio Shack stores. Tandy will not sell any software unless it can "back it up," but it has been unable to develop enough to meet demands. Because most users are not data processing experts, they need software as well as hardware. Failure to meet software demands may send potential customers to other producers.

Tandy was lucky with the TRS-80. Apparently, the success of the product was a surprise to most people. Whether Tandy will have available the next "hot" product depends on marketing research and product development.

The increase in interest rates has caused reduced inventory levels in retail outlets, and upsurges in demand could cause strain. In April 1980, when the TRS-80 Model III came on the market, delays of several weeks were common between order and delivery.

CONCLUSION

John Roach has many strategic moves to consider. Should Tandy use the opportunity to acquire other firms? In the coming battle for the personal computer market, many firms will go under. Tandy could be aided by acquiring companies with strong product development bases, manufacturing capabilities, and software development.

What should Tandy do about the software problems? It does not currently produce enough quality products to supply needs. Opening computer stores to software produced by outsiders and having trained persons to evaluate that software would be a real help to the masses of customers who are not computer experts. Developing an MS/DOS-compatible system would aid users if Tandy believes it must stay in software. Tandy has done this. In the short run, it may cut into software sales, but in the long run, it could only aid hardware sales.

Should Tandy consider ventures in offshore (labor-cheap) markets to produce peripherals in demand? It is currently working with Datapoint on disks. More cooperation may be considered. Should Tandy consider hiring more managers from outside to bring in fresh ideas? Only two of Tandy's thirty-seven top managers are women, and both of them have been with Tandy over twenty-five years. Should more women be moved into management?

John Roach felt that the next few years would be critical to Tandy. With increased competition and the pressure for product development, Tandy may gain or lose a large share of the market.

> Some observers, in fact, predict that if Tandy is to survive and prosper in tomorrow's information processing market, it may have to abandon the private-label strategy. Customers, these experts say, want retail stores to carry several brands of computers so that they can do one-stop comparison shopping.
>
> Despite the many changes being made at Tandy, Roach insists that he is not changing basic strategies and is not about to sacrifice profits to win market share. By controlling its own stores, Tandy can avoid any price-cutting going on at other retailers and maintain its own profit margins. Roach says the company is still taking between 10 percent and 20 percent of nearly every market it enters. "We are a distribution system for technology," Roach says. "The beauty of our business is that we always seem to have a good basic business plus good product innovations."[9]

Notes

1 Paul Bornstein, "Can Tandy Stay on Top?" *Forbes,* April 11, 1983, 43–44.
2 Tandy Corporation, Annual Report, 1981, 1.
3 Ibid.
4 Annual Report, 1981, 2.
5 K. Wiegner, "It's the Response That Counts," *Forbes,* November 23, 1981, 125.
6 Ibid., 126.
7 "Tandy Unttandied," *Financial World,* May 1, 1980, 61.
8 S. Slom, "Radio Shack's Retail Star Is Rising," *Chain Store Age Executive,* May 1980, 37.
9 Richard A. Shaffer, "Tandy May Have a Hot Seller," *The Wall Street Journal,* November 28, 1983, 1.

EXHIBIT 1
Estimated Five-Year Growth Rates by Product Category

	Fiscal 1983 % of Total	Five-Year Annual Compound Growth Rate	Percentage-Point Contribution to Five-Year Growth Rate	Fiscal 1988 % of Total
Radios, phonographs, and television sets	12%	10%	1	6%
CBs, walkie-talkies, scanners, and public address systems	7	(10)	(1)	1
Audio equipment, tape recorders, and related accessories	25	10	3	14
Electronic parts, batteries, test equipment, and related items	14	10	1	8
Toys, antennas, security devices, timers, and calculators	14	25	4	15
Telephones and intercoms	6	25	2	6
Microcomputers, software, and peripheral equipment	22	40	9	40
Other	—	NC	5	10
Total	100	—	24	100

EXHIBIT 2
Estimated U.S. Market for Personal Computers (units in thousands)

	Number of Units Installed		Compound Annual Growth Rate	Cumulative Number Installed by 1985	Estimated Market Size in 1980	Market Penetration by 1988
	1980	1985				
Business	130	1,000	50%	2,900	26,000[a]	11%
Home	90	700	50	1,950	24,000[b]	8
Education	70	350	35	1,100	58,000[c]	2
Scientific	30	150	35	450	3,500[d]	13
Total	320	2,200	45–50	6,400	111,500	6

[a]20 million executives and business professionals plus 6 million small businesses

[b]Number of households in the United States with annual income of $24,000 or more

[c]58 million students in the United States

[d]Approximate number of engineers in the United States

EXHIBIT 3
Review of Operations and Financial Information

Consolidated Statements of Income
Tandy Corporation and Subsidiaries

In thousands, except per share amounts.
Per share amounts restated for two-for-one stock splits in May 1981,
December 1980, June 1978 and December 1975.
Fiscal 1983 and 1982 amounts reflect the adoption of FAS No. 52,
Foreign Currency Translation.

	1983	1982	1981
Net sales	**$2,475,188**	$2,032,555	$1,691,373
Other income	**38,109**	28,657	15,697
	2,513,297	2,061,212	1,707,070
Costs and expenses:			
Cost of products sold	**1,008,187**	826,842	701,777
Selling, general and administrative, net of amounts allocated to spun-off operations in fiscal 1976 and prior	**930,244**	780,378	645,934
Depreciation and amortization	**38,679**	29,437	23,288
Interest expense, net of interest income and interest allocated to spun-off operations in fiscal 1976 and prior	**8,905**	1,168	15,454
	1,986,015	1,637,825	1,386,453
Income from continuing operations before income taxes	**527,282**	423,387	320,617
Provision for income taxes	**248,761**	199,302	151,015
Income from continuing operations	**278,521**	224,085	169,602
Loss from discontinued operations, net of income taxes	**—**	—	—
Net income before income from operations spun off	**278,521**	224,085	169,602
Income from operations spun off, net of income taxes	**—**	—	—
Net income	**$ 278,521**	$ 224,085	$ 169,602
Income (loss) per average common share and common share equivalent:			
Continuing operations	**$2.67**	$2.17	$1.65
Discontinued operations	**—**	—	—
Spun-off operations	**—**	—	—
Net income	**$2.67**	$2.17	$1.65
Average common shares and common share equivalents outstanding	**104,335**	103,395	102,578

The Review of Operations and Financial Information, pages 16 to 47, is an integral part of these statements.

			Year Ended June 30,			
1980	**1979**	**1978**	**1977**	**1976**	**1975**	**1974**
$1,384,637	$1,215,483	$1,059,324	$949,267	$741,722	$528,286	$411,241
11,360	11,403	5,629	3,763	2,649	3,963	2,153
1,395,997	1,226,886	1,064,953	953,030	744,371	532,249	413,394
594,841	535,549	491,509	434,031	331,400	249,006	198,067
546,325	484,249	403,173	350,878	270,308	204,107	158,792
19,110	17,121	13,879	11,140	8,034	7,392	5,461
25,063	28,466	30,260	15,192	7,282	14,044	8,544
1,185,339	1,065,385	938,821	811,241	617,024	474,549	370,864
210,658	161,501	126,132	141,789	127,347	57,700	42,530
98,423	78,272	59,986	69,970	63,066	29,078	20,669
112,235	83,229	66,146	71,819	64,281	28,622	21,861
—	—	—	(2,777)		(1,820)	(7,072)
112,235	83,229	66,146	69,042	64,281	26,802	14,789
—	—	—	—	3,243	7,794	5,657
$ 112,235	$ 83,229	$ 66,146	$ 69,042	$ 67,524	$ 34,596	$ 20,446
$1.12	$ .81	$ .69	$ .54	$ .44	$ .20	$ .13
—	—	—	(.02)	—	(.01)	(.04)
—	—	—	—	.02	.05	.03
$1.12	$ .81	$ .69	$ .52	$ .46	$ .24	$ .12
103,644	106,004	96,136	132,336	144,824	145,408	169,992

EXHIBIT 4

Operations by Geographic Area for Tandy Corporation and Subsidiaries (in thousands)

Operations by Geographic Area

Tandy Corporation and Subsidiaries In thousands.	United States	Canada	Europe	Pacific/ Asia	Elimina- tions	Consoli- dated
1983						
Sales to unaffiliated customers . . .	$2,088,851	$187,129	$130,856	$ 68,352	$ —	$2,475,188
Transfers between geographic areas	75,936	5	91	398,300	(474,332)	—
Total revenue	$2,164,787	$187,134	$130,947	$466,652	$(474,332)	$2,475,188
Operating profit	$ 498,340	$ 26,349	$ (8,212)	$ 26,624	$ (1,012)	$ 542,089
General corporate expenses						(5,902)
Interest expense, net						(8,905)
Income before taxes						$ 527,282
Identifiable assets at June 30,1983	$ 966,305	$ 79,671	$100,792	$ 96,098	$ (20,999)	$1,221,867
Corporate assets						360,041
Total assets at June 30,1983 . . .						$1,581,908
1982						
Sales to unaffiliated customers . . .	$1,684,540	$160,198	$117,816	$ 70,001	$ —	$2,032,555
Transfers between geographic areas	87,349	—	65	347,269	(434,683)	—
Total revenue	$1,771,889	$160,198	$117,881	$417,270	$(434,683)	$2,032,555
Operating profit	$ 398,917	$ 22,657	$ 2,313	$ 19,218	$ (11,100)	$ 432,005
General corporate expenses						(7,450)
Interest expense, net						(1,168)
Income before taxes						$ 423,387
Identifiable assets at June 30,1982	$ 764,119	$ 66,693	$ 88,631	$ 98,982	$ (19,987)	$ 998,438
Corporate assets						229,206
Total assets at June 30,1982 . . .						$1,227,644

Note: Operating income represents all revenues of the geographic segment less all operating expenses attributable to that segment. The operating profits of a geographic location exclude corporate expenses, net interest expense and income taxes. Transfers between geographic areas are generally recorded at market price.

Income Tax Expense

In thousands.

	Year Ended June 30,				
	1983	1982	1981	1980	1979
Current					
Federal	**$200,492**	$159,007	$122,678	$ 84,992	$64,858
State	**19,051**	15,981	10,568	6,552	5,147
Foreign	**25,007**	21,604	15,882	9,996	5,515
	244,550	196,592	149,128	101,540	75,520
Deferred					
Federal	**3,118**	3,879	2,318	(1,223)	1,649
Foreign	**1,093**	(1,169)	(431)	(1,894)	1,103
Total income tax expense	**$248,761**	$199,302	$151,015	$ 98,423	$78,272

Statutory vs. Effective Tax

In thousands.

	Year Ended June 30,				
	1983	1982	1981	1980	1979
Components of pretax income:					
United States	**$474,776**	$367,970	$285,089	$183,842	$146,827
Foreign	**52,506**	55,417	35,528	27,316	14,674
Income before income taxes	**527,282**	423,387	320,617	210,658	161,501
Statutory tax rate	**× 46%**	×46%	×46%	×46%	×47%
Federal income tax at statutory rate ...	**$242,550**	$194,758	$147,484	$ 96,903	$ 75,905
Investment tax credit	**(5,494)**	(5,310)	(2,992)	(1,499)	(695)
State and provincial income taxes, less federal income tax benefit	**12,075**	10,177	6,970	4,418	3,430
Other, net	**(370)**	(323)	(447)	(1,399)	(368)
Total income tax expense	**$248,761**	$199,302	$151,015	$ 98,423	$ 78,272
Effective tax rate	**47.2%**	47.1%	47.1%	46.7%	48.5%

EXHIBIT 5
Corporate and Financial Objectives

June 30	Asset Turnover — Sales / Avg. Assets	×	Return On Sales — Net Income / Sales	=	Return On Assets — Net Income / Avg. Assets	×	Financial Leverage — Avg. Assets / Avg. Equity	=	Return On Equity — Net Income / Avg. Equity
1974	1.47	×	3.6%	=	5.3%	×	2.41	=	12.8%
1975	1.71	×	5.1	=	8.7	×	2.53	=	22.0
1976	2.04	×	8.7	=	17.7	×	2.18	=	38.7
1977	2.16	×	7.3	=	15.7	×	2.37	=	37.2
1978	2.06	×	6.2	=	12.8	×	3.39	=	43.6
1979	2.09	×	6.9	=	14.3	×	3.35	=	47.9
1980	2.10	×	8.1	=	17.0	×	2.69	=	45.7
1981	2.06	×	10.0	=	20.6	×	1.93	=	39.7
1982	1.88	×	11.0	=	20.7	×	1.56	=	32.3
1983	**1.76**	**×**	**11.3**	**=**	**19.8**	**×**	**1.45**	**=**	**28.8**

Accumulated Depreciation In thousands.	**Balance at Beginning of Period**	**Depreciation Expense**	**Retirements and Sales**	**Other**	**Balance at End of Period**
Year Ended June 30, 1983					
Consumer electronics operations:					
Buildings	$ 3,985	$ 927	$ —	$ 20	$ 4,932
Furniture, fixtures and equipment . .	65,844	22,686	(3,593)	(178)	84,759
Leasehold improvements	33,171	11,369	(697)	(418)	43,425
	103,000	34,982	(4,290)	(576)	133,116
Tandy Center:					
Buildings and other	11,360	2,902	—	—	14,262
	$114,360	$37,884	$(4,290)	$ (576)	$147,378
Year Ended June 30, 1982					
Consumer electronics operations:					
Buildings	$ 3,183	$ 736	$ —	$ 66	$ 3,985
Furniture, fixtures and equipment . .	56,030	16,782	(5,622)	(1,346)	65,844
Leasehold improvements	26,390	8,634	(528)	(1,325)	33,171
	85,603	26,152	(6,150)	(2,605)	103,000
Tandy Center:					
Buildings and other	8,562	2,827	(29)	—	11,360
	$ 94,165	$28,979	$(6,179)	$(2,605)	$114,360
Year Ended June 30, 1981					
Consumer electronics operations:					
Buildings	$ 2,594	$ 630	$ (41)	$ —	$ 3,183
Furniture, fixtures and equipment . .	45,286	13,700	(2,956)	—	56,030
Leasehold improvements	20,926	6,170	(706)	—	26,390
	68,806	20,500	(3,703)	—	85,603
Tandy Center:					
Buildings and other	5,879	2,705	(22)	—	8,562
	$ 74,685	$23,205	$(3,725)	$ —	$ 94,165

Note: With the adoption of FAS No. 52, Foreign Currency Translation, the foreign fixed assets and related accumulated depreciation are translated into U.S. dollars at the rates in effect at the date of the balance sheet. The amounts shown in the "Other" column for fiscal 1983 and 1982 reflect the changes in currency values between the balance sheet dates.

EXHIBIT 6
Comparative Income Statement Data (dollars in millions)[a]

	Net Sales		Computer-Related Sales as % of Total	
	1978	1981	1978	1981
Tandy[b]	$1,059.3	$1,691.4	2.4%	21.8%
Apple[c]	7.9	334.8	100.0	100.0
Commodore[b]	50.2	186.5	24.3	71.0
	Gross Margin		SG & A as % of Sales	
Tandy	53.6%	58.5%	38.1%	38.2%
Apple	49.6	46.1	22.8	20.1
Commodore	30.5	44.4	13.7	21.3
	Operating Income		Operating Margin	
Tandy	$150.7	$320.4	14.2%	18.9%
Apple	1.5	66.1	19.4	19.9
Commodore	6.3	10.1	12.6	18.6
	Pretax Income		Pretax Margin	
Tandy	$126.1	$320.6	11.9%	19.0%
Apple	1.5	76.5	19.7	22.9
Commodore	5.2	30.8	10.4	16.5
	Taxes		Tax Rate	
Tandy	$70.0	$151.0	49.4%	47.1%
Apple	0.8	37.1	48.7	48.5
Commodore	1.8	5.9	35.0	19.1
	Net Income		Net Margin	
Tandy	$66.1	$169.6	6.2%	10.0%
Apple	0.8	39.4	10.1	11.8
Commodore	3.4	24.9	6.8	13.3
	Average Share and Equivalence Outstanding (millions)		Earnings per Share	
Tandy	$96.1	$103.0	$0.69	$1.65
Apple	31.5	56.2	0.03	0.70
Commodore	9.5	10.3	0.36	2.42

[a]Fiscal year ending June 30

[b]Data for Apple Computer calculated on balance sheet as of June 30, 1981, and trailing 12-month income statement

[c]Calculated on Consumer Electronics fixed assets only

EXHIBIT 7
Comparison of Selected Financial Ratios

	Tandy[a]	Apple[b]	Commodore[a]
Current ratio	3.48	4.03	2.23
Quick ratio	0.90	1.56	1.15
Cash and equivalents as % of current assets	20.0%	38.6%	8.5%
Accounts receivable as % of current assets	5.9%	17.8%	43.1%
Inventories as % of current assets	72.4%	38.8%	47.3%
Average inventory turnover (times)	1.48	2.75	2.33
Days to sell inventory	243.4	130.9	154.3
Average life of accounts receivable	7.2	33.1	70.8
As % of total capital			
Short-term debt	4.8%	3.8%	6.8%
Long-term debt	17.2	0.9	31.9
Equity	78.0	95.4	61.4
Return on average equity	39.7%	33.7%	51.3%
Return on average capital	26.3	30.8	30.4
Return on average total assets	20.6	22.2	21.3
Sales/average total assets	2.05	1.94	1.59

[a]Fiscal year ending June 30
[b]Data for Apple Computer calculated on balance sheet as of June 30, 1981, and trailing 12-month income statement
[c]Calculated on Consumer Electronics fixed assets only

EXHIBIT 8
Tandy Corporate Structure

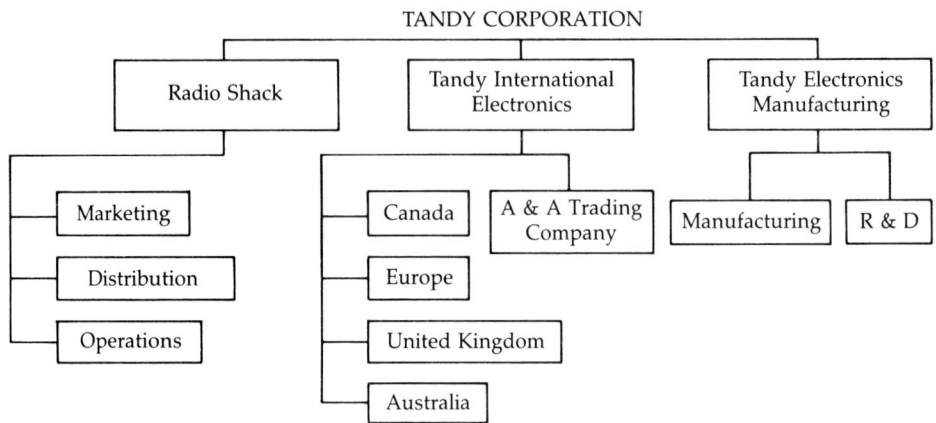

EXHIBIT 9
Tandy Corporation Officers and Board of Directors

TANDY CORPORATION OFFICERS

		Age	Years with Company*
John Roach	Chairman of the Board, Chief Executive Officer and President	44	16
John McDaniel	Senior Vice President and Controller	65	17
Charles Tindall	Senior Vice President and Treasurer	57	17
Herschel Winn	Senior Vice President and Secretary	51	14
Billy Roland	Vice President	57	29
Loyd Turner	Vice President	65	11
Donald Bock	Assistant Treasurer	41	15
Louis Neumann	Assistant Secretary	51	9

Radio Shack Officers

Bernard Appel	Executive Vice President—Marketing	51	24
Robert Keto	Executive Vice President—Operations	42	19
David Beckerman	Vice President—Advertising	55	27
George Berger	Vice President—Director of Personnel	44	20
Robert Bourland	Divisional Vice President	42	19
Jerry Colella	Vice President—Franchise International	54	25
Timothy Diachun	Vice President—Telephone Marketing	42	8
Ray Hicks	Vice President—Distribution	61	11
Dean Lawrence	Divisional Vice President	53	28
Carroll Leu	Vice President—Tandy Data Processing	46	17
Robert Miller	Vice President—Merchandising-Consumer Products	40	4
Caroline Nemser	Vice President—Merchandising Control	69	29
Jim Nichols	Divisional Vice President	40	15
Dick Richards	Divisional Vice President	47	18
E. W. Spieckerman	Vice President—Real Estate	50	15
Ron Stegall	Vice President—Computer Marketing	36	13
Paul Wofford	President—Tandy Transportation, Inc.	61	14
Chuck Wyse	Divisional Vice President	39	15

Tandy International Electronics Officers

David Christopher	Senior Vice President—TIE	41	16
Clifford Atfield	Vice President—Operations-TIE Europe	36	19
Marvin Cash	Vice President and Managing Director—Radio Shack Canada	50	27
Mike Murray	Vice President—Australia	34	15
Robert Owens	Vice President—Marketing and Support-TIE Europe	46	23
John Sayers	Managing Director—United Kingdom	44	9
Elaine Yamagata	President—A&A Trading Companies	61	28

Tandy Electronics Manufacturing Officers

Sy Bogitch	Senior Vice President—TEM	57	12
John Humphreys	Vice President and General Manager—Memtek Products Division	43	13
Robert McClure	Vice President—North American Manufacturing	47	11
Jim Mortensen	Vice President—Computer Manufacturing	49	16
John Patterson	Vice President—Research and Development	42	5

* Includes prior service with companies acquired by Tandy Corporation.
Radio Shack, Tandy International Electronics and Tandy Electronics Manufacturing are divisions of Tandy Corporation.

EXHIBIT 9 (continued)

TANDY CORPORATION BOARD OF DIRECTORS

John V. Roach[3,4]
Chairman of the Board,
Chief Executive Officer
and President
Fort Worth, Texas

Donald L. Bryant[2,4]
Business Consultant
Boynton Beach, Florida
Business Executive-in-Residence
Texas Christian University
Fort Worth, Texas
Retired Executive Vice President
The Equitable Life Assurance Society
New York, New York

William C. Conner[1,2]
Co-founder and Chairman Emeritus
Alcon Laboratories, Inc.
Pharmaceutical Manufacturer
Chairman
Hearing Health Group, Inc.
Chairman
Medcon, Inc.
Prepaid Health Care Plan
Fort Worth, Texas

Lawrence E. Dempsey[1,4]
President
Batavia Enterprises, Inc.
Industrial Leasing
Batavia, Illinois

Lewis F. Kornfeld, Jr.[1,3]
Former Vice Chairman of
the Board, Executive Vice
President of Tandy Corporation
and President of Radio Shack
Fort Worth, Texas

Robert R. Lowdon[3,4]
Chairman
Stafford-Lowdon
General Printing Company
Fort Worth, Texas

Phil R. North[2,3]
Chairman of the Board
First City National Bank of Fort Worth
Former Chairman of the Board,
Chief Executive Officer
and President of Tandy Corporation
Fort Worth, Texas

George R. Nugent[2,3]
Former Chairman of the Board
and Chief Executive Officer
Tandycrafts, Inc.
Hobby and Handicraft Company
Fort Worth, Texas

William T. Smith[1,4]
Chairman of the Board and
Chief Executive Officer
Champlin Petroleum Company
Fort Worth, Texas

Alfred J. Stein[1,2]
Chairman of the Board and
Chief Executive Officer
VLSI Technology, Inc.
Semiconductor Manufacturer
San Jose, California

Jesse L. Upchurch[2,3]
Chairman of the Board,
Chief Executive Officer and President
Upchurch Corporation
Private Diversified Holding Company
Fort Worth, Texas

John A. Wilson[1,4]
Chairman of the Board,
Chief Executive Officer and President
Color Tile, Inc.
Home Improvement Company
Fort Worth, Texas

[1]Member of Audit Committee
[2]Member of Organization and
  Compensation Committee
[3]Member of Executive Committee
[4]Member of Nominating Committee

EXHIBIT 10
Tandy Executive Statistics

Corporate Officers
8 offices Average age 51.8 years Average time with   Tandy–14 years

Radio Shack	Tandy International Electronics	Tandy Electronics Manufacturing

17 offices
Average age 48 yrs.
Average time with
    Tandy–17 yrs.
	7 offices
	Average age 43 yrs.
	Average time with
	    Tandy–16 yrs.
		5 offices
		Average age 60 yrs.
		Average time with
		    Tandy–9.6 yrs.

■ ■ ■ CASE 24
Executone Corporation: Managing on the Down Side

Daniel Harris
Research Assistants:
Steve Husband
Catherine Crawford
John Solberg
Lisa Solberg
Seattle Pacific University

COMPANY BACKGROUND

Executone Corporation, headquartered in the western United States, was founded in 1968 to develop innovative products to meet the needs of the telecommunications industry. The company employs approximately 450 people in three plants. Executone's products include specialized electronic components and software-based systems which receive, transmit, and convert voice, data, or simultaneous voice/data signals in public and private networks. The corporation has four major divisions and manufactures and markets a broad line of telecommunications products.

Historically, Executone has been a conservative, profitable, cash generating company with a strong commitment to its employees through competitive wages and benefits, strong options, profit sharing, and a general attitude of employee support. Through the years, the corporation has had a reputation for its commitment to quality, reliability and customer service. The corporation has been noted as a good community neighbor and in 1980 embarked on a formal contributions program for external organizations and a scholarship program for employees' children.

MANAGEMENT AND OPERATIONS

Donald Johnson is chairman and chief executive officer of Executone and was one of the company's founders in 1968. Johnson feels that an ongoing commitment to both product development *and* employee development are critical in maximizing the company's performance. In 1981 Davis Wentworth was hired to serve as president. In 1984 he resigned because of a disagreement over management philosophies and the firm's economic difficulties. Johnson remarked, "The company has been used to a participatory style of management. Mr. Wentworth's style just hasn't been that way." Currently no replacement has been found.

INDUSTRY AND PRODUCT DEVELOPMENT

With the advent of AT&T's breakup, all telecommunication equipment manufacturers were wide-eyed in anticipation of new markets, more sales, bigger profits. The

This case was prepared as the basis for class discussion rather than to illustrate either effective or ineffective handling of an administrative situation. All company names, names of individuals, and facts and figures have been disguised to assure anonymity.

sky was the limit. The breakup of AT&T created the need for systems to monitor local services charges, so in 1983 Executone embarked upon two major product developments. Management felt that the support of these projects was necessary for the future of the company. These products, Private Branch Exchange (PBX) and the CallData System (CDS), each took longer to develop and bring to market than expected and cost about $3 million per year each for continued research.

PBX Executone entered the digital PBX market via a license agreement with British Telecom. The Cascade 400, the Executone version of this switch, has been enhanced to comply with FCC rules to include several features required in the U.S. market such as least-cost routing and an expanded capacity of 400 ports. The Executone PBX will handle interactive data at 9,600 baud over existing telephone lines, and batch data up to 56,000 baud through the voice matrix.

Planned for shipment in fiscal 1984, Executone offered small to medium-sized applications a complete voice and data communications package in a variety of architectures to meet their specific requirements.

CDS In order to increase revenues and satisfy regulatory requirements for equal access to other common carriers (such as Sprint and MCI), the telephone operating companies are expected to install universal measured service equipment that will record billing information on every local call. Executone's CDS is a fully integrated system for the collection and management of billing data. Most telephone companies operate with a mix of electromechanical and digital switching systems in their central offices; the CDS electronically links any combination of these. The CDS consists of three basic computer components: central office sensors that collect call data, local storage modules that process and store the data, and host computers that poll the storage modules from a remote location and generate billing data on magnetic tapes. Each call record includes the calling and called numbers, date and time, billable call duration, class of call, and toll center information.

The Bell Operating Companies were the major market for the CDS. Because the operating companies were expected to implement measured service in phases, the CDS was designed as a modular and evolutionary system capable of linking central offices in a variety of stages. However, development of the CDS became significantly behind schedule. Bringing the CDS to market is dependent on the in-house completion of hardware, software, and systems integration aspects for this product. The cost of the system ranges from $10,000 to $300,000. Competition in the area flooded the market, as shown in exhibit 1. This increased competition has caused the market to fall (see exhibit 2). Since 1985 telecommunications manufacturers have come back to earth—Executone has crash landed.

Says Donald Johnson, chairman,

> When you have a change as dramatic as we had in telecommunications, an awful lot of people think they can jump in and make a killing. The tendency is for your eyes to be bigger than your stomach. That's what happened to us. It was a hard lesson. Two years ago we launched some ambitious programs

that have since given us severe indigestion. I told our employees that the problem with our company isn't that we don't do enough, it's that we try to do too much. We were an inch deep and a mile wide. Deregulation created an atmosphere where it was easy to bite off more than we could chew.

As a result, in 1985 Executone was forced to lay off about a hundred employees and the remaining staff suffered pay cuts ranging from 3 to 25 percent. Management also reduced the corporate contribution program by 50 percent.

STOCKHOLDERS

There is no established public trading market for Executone's common stock. Although the board of directors declared and paid dividends in past years, in fiscal 1983 it adopted a policy of retaining all earnings to fund business development and growth. Due to an aggressive stock option program, there are over 750 shareholders. Of the outstanding shares of stock, 21 percent are owned by employees; 42 percent of the employees own shares of stock in the company.

Executone has enjoyed steady growth in sales and its gross margin, but since 1982 profits have fallen dramatically. Sales grew from $34,124,000 in 1982 to $40,956,000 in 1984, but before-tax profits went from $5,750,000 to a loss of $1,216,000 in the same period. Earnings per share went from $.59 in 1982 to a $.28 loss per share in 1984. In 1982, Executone declared a $.04 per share dividend but no dividends were declared for 1983 or 1984 (see exhibit 3).

The price of Executone's stock also decreased from over $9.00 per share in 1983 to approximately $6.00 per share today. Some of the major reasons for these declines were Executone's commitment to develop its new product lines. Although productivity remains good, these additional product-line development costs affected the efficiency and profitability of the company as seen in exhibit 4.

Executone also expanded its plant and equipment. As shown in exhibit 5, total assets almost doubled since 1982.

The corporation is currently experiencing some growing pains. It has aggressively pursued new product lines and at the same time expanded its facilities to handle the production of these new products. The short-term profitability suffered from this strategy but on the other hand, long-term growth and profits may be much greater by choosing to take these risks. Executone is highly regarded for producing quality products and its reputation should help in marketing new developments.

OUTLOOK

Revised forecasts for Executone indicate that profitable operation is some time away. Management is struggling with the reality that continued losses would erode the financial strength of the company. Johnson would like to develop a plan representing a balance of interests among Executone's shareholders, employees, and corporate contribution program.

EXHIBIT 1
Executone's Competitors

Company	1984 Revenues (in millions)
Executone Corporation	$41
Commander Systems	15
Saturn Corporation	15
Automatic Products	10
Daylight Industries	10
Meco Labs, Inc.	10
Gamble & Associates	9
RCW, Inc.	5
Macon, Inc.	5
Supreme Air	3.5

EXHIBIT 2
Relative Strength (Ratio of Industry to Value Line Comp.)

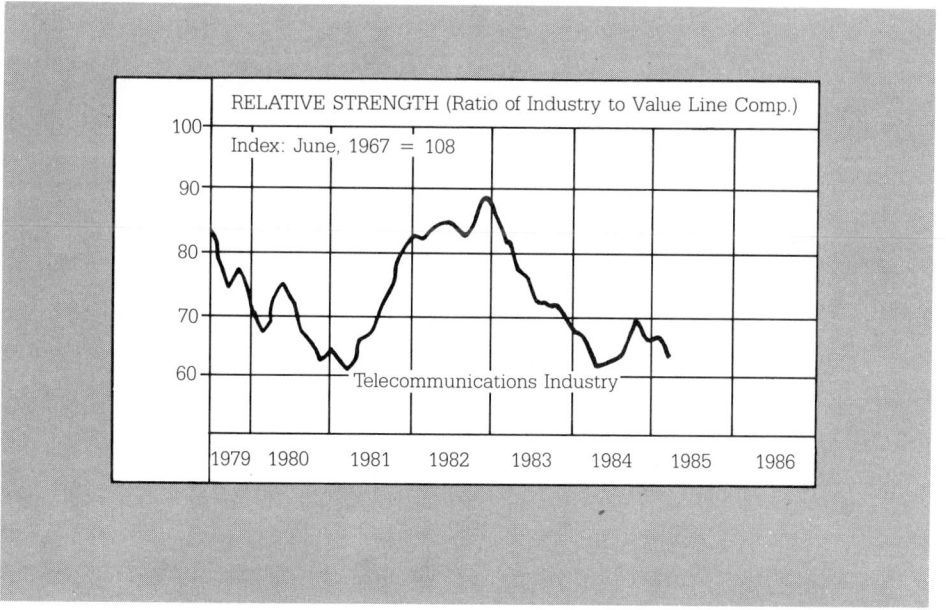

EXHIBIT 3
Income Statement

	1982	1983	1984
Net sales	$34,124,000	$36,227,000	$40,956,000
Gross margin	16,116,000	18,036,000	19,006,000
Income (loss) before tax	5,750,000	4,869,000	(1,216,000)
Net income per share	.59	.56	(.28)
Dividends per share	.04	.00	.00

EXHIBIT 4
Comparison of Selected Financial Ratios

	1982	1983	1984	Median Industry Average
Productivity (revenue/person)	N/A	N/A	$87,500	$90,000
Quick ratio (times)	1.5	1.4	.9	1.9
Current ratio (times)	2.8	2.9	2.5	2.5
Current liability to net worth (%)	41.2	36.5	43.5	49.8
Current liability to inventory (%)	75.6	79.6	75.3	111.7
Total liability to net worth (%)	61.0	57.5	77.6	78.5
Fixed assets to net worth (%)	39.8	41.0	N/A	35.7
Collection period (days)	44.4	49.7	67.5	69.3
Sales to inventory (times)	4.6	4.4	3.5	4.6
Assets to sales (%)	64.9	78.0	87.8	87.9
A/P to sales (%)	6.0	9.9	6.8	7.3
Return on sales (%)	9.2	8.6	3.9	5.6
Return on assets (%)	14.1	11.0	4.4	6.4
Return to net worth (%)	22.7	17.4	7.8	12.7

EXHIBIT 5
Assets and Liabilities

	1982	1983	1984
Working capital	10,431,000	12,485,000	13,436,000
Property/plant/equipment (net)	5,479,000	7,359,000	12,556,000
Total assets	22,143,000	28,256,000	35,975,000
Long-term obligations	2,726,000	3,774,000	6,899,000
Stockholders' equity	13,750,000	17,941,000	20,256,000

■ ■ ■ CASE 25
Westinghouse, 1986

Donald F. Harvey
Eastern Washington University
Research Assistant: Richard Helmer

INTRODUCTION

Westinghouse is not the company it was ten or even five years ago. The firm has undergone drastic change. In his office, twenty-three floors above the junction of Pittsburgh's three rivers, Chairman Douglas Danforth outlined his strategic goals for record revenues and profit margins. Westinghouse had not been performing poorly, but it wanted to do better. The great electrical equipment maker had gained a reputation abroad for being internally disorganized and at times arrogant. Danforth was worried about this image because demand was growing faster overseas than in the United States.

One decision that emerged was to reorganize into a matrix structure. The transformation promised to be turbulent. Most Westinghouse executives were raised in a management structure based on *product* lines—a structure that was accentuated, if anything, when the company was reorganized in 1980 into thirty-seven operating groups known as *business units*. These units, somewhat akin to those set up earlier by arch rival General Electric, were given a great deal of autonomy, including a free hand abroad. Now, however, the unit managers would have to mesh their foreign strategies and operations with those of a new international hierarchy headed by John Marous and organized along geographic lines.

They would be learning to live within the more complex matrix system, which has two chains of command instead of one. The manager of a circuit-breaker factory in Brazil would now report to a new Westinghouse manager who oversees the activities of all business units in that country, as well as to a stateside business unit that makes electrical transmission and distribution equipment. In effect, the Brazilian manager will be serving two masters. Many Westinghouse executives will have trouble adapting to this new arrangement, which requires considerable interaction and consensus decision making at all levels. Danforth told the company's top 220 managers, "some of you will adjust and survive, and some of you won't."[1]

The Westinghouse Electric Corporation is a multinational diversified manufacturer of electrical equipment with sales in 1986 of over $10.8 billion. The firm was ranked thirtieth in sales, thirtieth in assets, and thirty-second in net income on

---

This case was prepared using published accounts and public documents for the purpose of class discussion rather than to illustrate either effective or ineffective handling of an administrative situation.

Fortune magazine's list of the top 500 U.S. industrial corporations. Westinghouse is clearly a giant in the industry, the second largest manfuacturer of electrical equipment and a leader in nuclear power. The firm's return on stockholder equity of 14.3 percent ranked 218th, and its growth rate in earnings per share from 1974 to 1984 was 34.66 percent and ranked sixth among the 500. However, the total return to investors (dividends plus capital gains) was 24.14 percent and ranked Westinghouse 136 for the ten-year period.[2]

Westinghouse is included in the *Forbes* magazine ranking of the 500 largest companies in the United States. *Forbes* ranked the corporation number forty-sixth in sales, 122 in assets, fifty-eighth in market value, and fiftieth in profits. *Forbes* also ranked the companies based on jobs and productivity. Westinghouse's work force is the twentieth largest out of 785 ranked. In sales per employee, Westinghouse ranked 659 with $89,000, and in profits per employee it ranked 549 with $4,200.[3] (See exhibit 1 for financial highlights.)

Background

Westinghouse began business as the Westinghouse Electric Company, founded in 1886. In 1889 the name was changed to Westinghouse Electric and Manufacturing Company; in 1945 the name was changed to its present form. Over the last ninety-nine years, the firm has increased its assets to $9,150,000 and its work force to approximately 117,000. Westinghouse today is the second largest diversified electrical company in the country. It is heavily involved in electrical products, defense electronics, commercial nuclear power, broadcasting and cable television, and financial services.

In 1983 Westinghouse made a number of organizational changes. The restructuring provided specialized management for high-growth advanced technology businesses, for its traditional businesses, and for its diversified commercial businesses. The restructuring resulted in some former company and group staff organizations being reduced and some business unit responsibility increased. The firm is currently organized into four major operating groups: Energy and Advanced Technology, Industries and International, Commercial, and Broadcasting and Cable.[4]

Westinghouse applies a strategic business unit (SBU) concept for planning purposes. Business units consist of one or more divisions or subsidiaries that meet certain internal criteria for profit center decentralization. Internationally, some Westinghouse multiproduct in-country organizations are designated business units. Currently there are twenty-four business units within the four major operating groups plus the Westinghouse Credit Corporation, which is a wholly owned non-consolidated subsidiary of Westinghouse.[5]

Westinghouse has evolved from a basically mainline electrical equipment manufacturer to a highly diversified electrical and electronics corporation serving a worldwide range of markets and customers.

Business Segments

The company has organized the business into the four operating groups for corporate financial reporting purposes. Financial results of manufacturing entities outside the United States, export sales, and foreign license income are included in the financial information of the organizational group which has operating responsibility. (See exhibits 2 and 3 for segment information.)

Energy and Advanced Technology Group

The Energy and Advanced Technology Group consists of Defense, Nuclear Energy Systems, Power Generation, Advanced Production Technology, and Transportation business units.

The Defense business unit provides research, development, production, and support services for such advanced technology products as radar, electro-optical, and electronic control systems. The major products of this unit involve ground and airborne radar, space and information systems, missile launching and handling, and marine equipment. Additionally, this business unit manufactures selected products for commercial aircraft and instrumentation and controls used in nuclear reactor ship propulsion and in commercial power generation.

Westinghouse is a leader in defense electronics and, even if military spending is slowed, this unit should continue to do well because growth in military electronics will feed itself. As increasingly sophisticated electronics are used in weapon systems and communications equipment, increasingly sophisticated monitoring and service systems will be required. One area of strong growth could be the new command, control, and communications programs. The Defense Department is striving to build extremely expensive strategic and tactical communications networks that would be radiation-hardened to survive a nuclear war. This business unit encounters heavy competition, primarily from large companies, on the basis of technology, price, service, warranty, and product performance. This unit is also influenced by changes in the diplomatic and political posture as well as in the budgeting plans of the United States government.[6]

The Nuclear Energy System business units are responsible for commercial nuclear energy activities and engage in developing advanced energy technologies. They design, manufacture, and market commercial nuclear pressurized water reactor systems and reactor components. Their service businesses consist primarily of the maintenance and upgrading of existing equipment and systems, the sale of spare parts, technical advice, and the installation of power generation equipment. This unit also acts as agent for the Department of Energy in the management of several government laboratories involved in engineering, fuel reprocessing, nuclear waste disposal, and naval propulsion.[7]

The Power Generation business unit designs, manufactures, sells, and services steam turbine generators, combustion turbine generators, and combined cycle plants. Both Nuclear Energy Systems and the Power Generation units serve utilities and industrial organizations which generate or distribute their own electricity. However, due to excess capacity among utilities, no new domestic power plants have been ordered over the past several years and it appears unlikely that any will be started before 1992 in the United States.[8] The Nuclear Energy Systems unit has entered the business of construction and operation of waste-to-energy plants that utilize water-cooled rotary combustors manufactured by Nuclear Energy Systems. These two units are in competition with both domestic and foreign firms for the waste-to-energy market. Technology, service, and worldwide presence are considered pluses for Westinghouse. However, foreign competition is increasing.

The Advanced Production Technology System business unit offers broad industrial automation services, integrating Westinghouse resources in robotics, artificial intelligence, controls, and factory communications networks. Unimation Incorporated is a subsidiary making robots for material handling, spot-welding, and machine loading. The robotics market is growing; however, the rate of growth is slower than expected, as a result of several factors. For example, the market was overestimated as a result of exaggerated media coverage and a lack of sound statistics on this industry. The forecasters had "tunnel vision" and failed to anticipate that alternative forms of automation might do the jobs of robots. The actual production of units increased by only 8 percent during the 1983–1984 period. However, the U.S. Department of Commerce expects the robotics industry to grow at a 10 to 15 percent rate during the 1990s. Moreover, the peripheral equipment and service areas of the robotics industry are expected to grow very rapidly. Long-term growth will be the result of strong research and development efforts in the development of vision, sensory, and software applications.[9]

The Transportation business unit manufactures and installs propulsion and automatic control equipment for local and intracity mass transit systems and for airport and other automated people-moving systems. Its customer markets include foreign and domestic airport authorities, transit authorities, transit car manufacturers, and other public and private development authorities.

Industries and International Group

The Industries and International Group contains Marketing and Services, which includes Westinghouse Electric Supply Company (Wesco) and the Industry Services business unit. Additionally, Control Equipment (which includes the Distribution and Protection and the Electronics Measurement and Control business units), Transmission and Distribution, the Motor Divisions, and the International business units are all part of this group.

The Marketing and Services organization operates a nationwide distribution business through Wesco. This supply company distributes Westinghouse-made electrical products as well as non-Westinghouse products, such as conduit and cable. Its customers are in the construction, industrial, and electric utility markets. Products are also distributed through a network of approximately 700 independent distributors.

The Industry Service business unit provides project management, installation, start-up, and maintenance services, in addition to repair of electrical and mechanical apparatus. Its major customers are electric utilities, the metals industry, and petroleum and chemical plants.

The Distribution and Production business unit designs, manufactures, and sells electrical distribution and control products. A joint venture with the Toshiba Corporation was formed to produce high-resolution color display tubes for various types of computer terminals, office automation, professional graphic equipment, and television tubes. Westinghouse also joined Sanyo Electric Corporation in the production and sales of selected electronics products for the cable TV market.[10]

The Electronics Measurement and Control business unit designs, manufactures, and sells watt-hour meters and load survey equipment, automatic metering equipment, energy management systems, and computer-based process control systems.

The Industrial Control business unit is involved with electrified drive systems, inverters, converters, ARC heaters and related power equipment, motor control, high-power semi-conductors, high-power thermo-conductors, electro-optical devices, radiation detection devices, and various sensor and control products.

The Transmission and Distribution business unit sells electrical power transformers and other transmission and distribution equipment, primarily to electric utility customers. The market for these products has been depressed for the past several years and, because of excess capacity, will probably remain so for the remainder of the decade.[11]

The Motors business unit manufactures and markets electric motors, from fractional horsepower sizes to the largest sizes used in steel mills and mining excavation equipment. The weak demand for commercial products has driven prices down; demand is expected to remain weak, with little growth.[12]

The International unit integrates the international activities of the domestic business units with the in-country operations in key markets of the world, mainly Canada, Europe, the Far East, the Middle East, and Latin America. This unit provides a management structure tailored to adapt to the marketing and economic conditions of each trading area or country. It is responsible for the overseas activities of domestic Westinghouse businesses as well as the management of subsidiaries and manufacturing facilities in other countries.

In 1984 subsidiaries located outside of the United States produced approximately 8.3 percent of total corporate sales and operating revenues. Exports accounted for an additional 11.4 percent. In addition, patent license and technical assistance agreements produced approximately $105 million in revenues during 1984, which was 20 percent below 1982 levels.[13]

The Industries and International Group supplies a variety of products and services to a broad range of customers in the capital goods, industrial, electric utility, construction, and consumer markets. There is a high degree of competition for all products and services by both large and small competitors. General economic conditions, including the strong dollar, have had a negative impact on foreign business, as well as resulting in a marked increase in foreign competition in United States markets.

Commercial Group

The Commercial Group consists of the Westinghouse Elevator Company, the Thermo King Corporation, the Material business unit, the Westinghouse Beverage Group, Inc., the Westinghouse Furniture Systems business unit, Westinghouse Communities business group, and the Longines-Wittnauer Watch Company.

The Westinghouse Elevator Company is the second largest elevator and escalator operation in the country. The company also provides installation and maintenance service for its products throughout the United States, Canada, and Puerto Rico. Production facilities are currently being restructured due to weak demand.

Thermo King manufactures a complete line of transport temperature control equipment. It also produces warehouse refrigeration equipment and air conditiioning units for buses. Thermo King has dealerships worldwide, with more than eighty countries using its equipment.

The Materials business unit consists of the Insulating Materials, Micarta, and Wire Divisions, in addition to Fortin Industries. The products of this division include electrical insulation materials and copper-clad laminates for the expanding electronics markets along with decorative laminates and copper wire for industrial use. Multilayer copper-clad laminate materials for printed circuit boards are also produced by this unit.

The Westinghouse Beverage Group, Inc., is the world's largest bottler of 7-Up. The product line of this business unit includes Dole Whole Fruit Coolers, Schweppes, Like Cola, Perrier, A&W Root Beer, Sunkist, Welch's, Hawaiian Punch, and Country Time Lemonade. Management of this unit was recognized by *Beverage Industry* for outperforming a highly competitive industry in both profit and volume.[14]

Westinghouse Communities engages in land and community development and related activities, primarily in Florida. With its focus on the sun belt, this unit should remain profitable.

The Longines-Wittnauer Watch Company assembles and distributes watches and clocks. The company distributes direct to a national network of retail outlets in both the United States and Canada using its own sales force.

Broadcasting and Cable Group

Westinghouse Broadcasting and Cable, Inc., is a wholly owned subsidiary of Westinghouse and provides a variety of communications services, consisting primarily of commercial broadcasting, cable television systems, six AM and five FM radio stations, and sales of broadcast time to radio and television advertisers through national sales organizations. Westinghouse competes with its numerous competitors mainly on the basis of audience ratings, price, and service.

The cable television business provides service to over two million basic subscribers. However, the peak activity in franchising is over. Consequently, more resources are being targeted to marketing and to servicing its customers. The firm operates 140 cable systems covering 605 communities in thirty-four states. Although existing systems are being upgraded and rebuilt, the firm is actively trying to find a buyer for its cable business.

Westinghouse's commercial broadcast television business is experiencing competition from cable television, which offers improved reception along with program diversification. Both broadcast stations and cable television systems are also competing with other communication and entertainment media, including videocassette recorders and movie theaters. Additional, competing firms have announced plans to provide direct broadcast service from a satellite transmitter. Because of the rapid pace of technological advancement and regulatory changes in the communications field, broadcast television stations and cable systems can expect new forms of competition in the future.

The program production and distribution business supplies series and special shows through national syndication to television stations throughout the country. The company reported that this unit achieved record sales and operating profits during 1984.

Westinghouse Credit Corporation

The Credit Corporation is a large, diversified finance company. However, less than one percent of its total receivables outstanding results from financing Westinghouse products. The services provided by this business include inventory financing, bulk purchase of home equity mortgage loans, financing and leasing of industrial equipment, financing leverage buyouts, providing venture capital, financing investment in real estate syndicates, leverage leasing, and line-of-credit financing for manufacturers, wholesalers, and retailers. Westinghouse faces competition in the various markets it operates in from factoring companies, leasing companies, commercial finance companies, and commercial banks. In view of the market fragmentation resulting from the multitude of local and regional competitors, it is not possible to provide a meaningful description of its competitive position.

FINANCIAL PERFORMANCE

Sales and operating revenues reached $10.731 billion in 1986. This is only a slight increase over 1985, with sales of $10.7 billion. The expected sales figure for 1985 reflects a 4.4 percent compound growth rate since 1980. Although sales in the 1981 to 1983 period were relatively flat, during Danforth's first year as CEO they increased by 7.7 percent (see exhibits 4 and 5).

Net income, which leveled out in 1981 at $438 million and was only $449 million in 1983, increased 19 percent during 1984 and was projected to increase approximately 12.7 percent during 1987 to $670 million. Due to the reorganization that occurred after 1981, only group financial data recorded in 1982 and later were reviewed. Sales figures for 1987 were estimates based on actual nine-month results plus the estimated fourth quarter figures.

The Energy and Advanced Technology Group increased sales from 1983 to 1986 at a compound rate of 6.3 percent. The Industries and International Group has seen very little growth over the period—its rate was 2 percent. The Commercial Group has experienced a growth rate of 6.6 percent, and the Broadcasting and Cable Group sales have grown at a rate of 13.1 percent.

The following three-year compound growth rates of operating profits have been computed using best estimate of 1985 results:

	1985 (millions)	Rate (%)
Energy and Advanced Technology	$408.5	10.5
Industries and International	0	(7.1)
Commercial	189	18
Broadcasting and Cable	105	32.6

From 1982 to 1984, there was a positive change in the profits to asset ratio of all groups except the Industries and International.

	P/A (%) 1982	P/A (%) 1984
Energy and Advanced Technology	15.2	15.7
Industries and International	2.6	(.2)
Commercial	15.8	19.7
Broadcasting and Cable	3	4

This change in profitability is in keeping with the goals established by Mr. Danforth and further highlights the problems within the Industries and International Group.

Expenditures for facilities expansion, modernization, and operating efficiencies rose steadily from $317 million in 1979 to a record high of $724 million in 1982. The expenditures for 1983 dropped to $716 million and the decline continued into 1984, when expenditures were $662 million—a 14 percent decrease from 1982.

Research and development expenditures have been declining since 1982 also. For example, the 1982 expenditure on Westinghouse-sponsored R&D was $265 million. By 1984 it had dropped to $233 million. Additionally, expenditures on programs sponsored by customers increased from $537 million to $615 million. The Energy and Advanced Technology Group expended approximately 95 percent of the funds used on customer-sponsored programs.[15]

Sales and operating revenues from manufacturing subsidiaries outside the United States have been steadily decreasing since 1981, when they amounted to 13 percent of the total. In 1984 those subsidiaries contributed 8 percent to the total sales and operating revenues.

Operating profit from those manufacturing subsidiaries outside the United States held steady from 1979 to 1982 at around 16 percent of the total corporate operating profit. However, in 1983 they contributed only 11.6 percent of the total. This contribution declined further to an estimated 8.8 percent in 1985. Manufacturing assets outside the United States peaked in 1982 at $806.6 million and dropped to $622.6 in 1984. The operating profit to assets ratio has been declining steadily from 15 percent in 1979 to 8.6 percent in 1984.

Westinghouse is this country's fourteenth leading exporter. However, although there was an 18.72 percent decline from 1983 to 1984, exports totalled $1.1 billion in 1984. Total products sold outside the United States, including foreign manufactured goods, have been contributing less since 1982. The contribution was 26 percent of sales and operating revenues in 1982 to only 20 percent in 1984. The strong dollar and soft overseas markets are major reasons for this decline.

Westinghouse's prime source of capital has been from operations. The funds provided have decreased from the 1982 level of $918 million to 1984's $555 million. The decline can be attributed to the increase in customer receivables and to changes in programs' billing and related costs on uncompleted contracts. The corporation initiated the sale of commercial paper in 1981, and this source has become an important (88 percent) source of short-term funds. Westinghouse reduced its reliance on a revolving credit agreement from 14.6 percent in 1982 to 9.5 percent in 1984. The long-term debt of the corporation is currently 33 percent of the total combined short- and long-term debt. Stockholders' equity increased at a compound growth rate of 10.2 percent from $2.5 billion in 1980 to $3.7 billion in 1984.

Westinghouse's ability to generate cash to meet its current obligations is less than average compared to the industry average for a major diversified electrical equipment company. Its current ratio of .97 is well below the average of 1.34 that's maintained by General Electric. When a shorter time perspective is considered and inventories are disregarded, it is apparent that Westinghouse is in a very vulnerable cash position.[16] Its ability to cover current liabilities is reduced considerably when inventories are removed from the computation. Its acid test ratio is .75 as compared to the average of GE and RCA of 1.01. A more disturbing point is that at the end of June 1985 it was down to .715. A significant change in liquidity occurred during 1981, and there has been little improvement since that time. The liquidity problem was further confirmed when net working capital was compared to total assets. Westinghouse's percentage is .4 percent, whereas the average of its two competitors is 12.9 percent. The reservoir of cash is a little shallow at Westinghouse (see exhibit 6).

Westinghouse's debt to total assets ratio of .18 is not considered a problem. Its long-term debt to total capital ratio has held fairly constant since 1979 and was only 13 percent of the total capital at the end of 1984. Preliminary figures for 1985 indicated the percentage had decreased slightly to 11.9 percent during 1985. The long-term debt to total capital comparison did not indicate any debt problem. When Westinghouse's ability to cover interest charges with operating profit was evaluated, it was determined that operating profits were 3.45 times greater than 1984 interest expense. Based on the first six months of the year data, this figure has increased to 3.77. This measure is important because interest must be paid from operating profit.

Profit margins at Westinghouse were fairly flat, around 4.7 percent from 1978 through 1983. In 1984 they climbed to 5.2 percent, and the best estimates for 1985 were 5.8 percent. General Electric's margin was 8.2 in 1984, and it was anticipated to be 8.5 for 1985. RCA's profit margin was 2.6 percent in 1984. The third quarter industry average was 4.1 percent, which was down 26 percent from the same period in 1984.[17]

Westinghouse's return on investment at the end of 1984 was 5.8 percent. At the same time GE recorded 9.2 percent. At the end of 1986, Westinghouse's ROI was still only 6.3 percent. In fact, this corporation's ROI has changed very little since 1980.

MANAGEMENT/ORGANIZATION

Doug Danforth, chairman and CEO and by training a mechanical engineer, has been with Westinghouse for thirty years. Prior to replacing Kirby, he was the vice chairman and chief operating officer. Prior to that he ran the Industry Products business when it was Westinghouse's most profitable division.

Edwin V. Clarke, Jr., is the senior executive vice president of corporate resources. Prior to his present position, he was president of the Industry Products Company.

John C. Marous, Jr., is the president of the Industries and International Group; and prior to his current position, he was the president of the International organization. Westinghouse's most serious problems are still associated with the Industries and International Group. Marous, who has headed this group since February 1983, took dramatic action to meet his 1986 goals. He forced a major restructuring of his division during 1983 and increased sales from $3.4 billion to $3.6 billion while cutting the operating deficit from $19.3 million to $3.7 million in just one year. He is expected to increase sales this year to over $3.7 billion while eliminating the operating deficit. Marous has been with Westinghouse for more than thirty-six years.

Matthias J. McDonough has been president of the Commercial Group since February 1983. Prior to that time he was senior executive vice president of Corporate Resources.

Thomas J. Murrin is president of the Energy and Advanced Technology Group. Prior to that he was president of the Public Systems Company. Murrin has been solving problems within this group of businesses since the 1960s. Murrin's ability was recognized early, and he has risen steadily up the corporate ladder. In the major reorganization of February 1983, he and Mr. Marous came out as big winners.

David L. Ritchie has been the chairman and chief executive officer of Westinghouse Broadcasting and Cable, Inc., since November 1981. Prior to that time he was the vice president of Westinghouse Broadcasting Company. Ritchie increased the number of cable subscribers from 1.3 million in 1981 to 2.1 million in 1985.

Westinghouse had been criticized for an emphasis on growth, but Doug Danforth is now attempting to change. He has tightened operations and is concentrating on profits. Many customers complained that Westinghouse was difficult to do business with. For example, not long ago a company salesman called on a Saudi businessman. After the preliminaries, the Saudi reached into his desk drawer and drew out the business cards of twenty-four other Westinghouse sales representatives. Spreading them out on his desk, the Saudi inquired, "Who speaks for Westinghouse?"[18] Westinghouse had few vice presidents abroad, and they had little clout back in Pittsburgh. Indeed, the prevalent attitude at headquarters was that those in the overseas operations were second raters who could not cut it in the United States. By adopting a matrix organization, Danforth hopes to better coordinate overseas operations.

Westinghouse's Matrix Organization

Westinghouse uses a very effective matrix system to coordinate foreign strategies and operations of business unit managers with those of the Industries and International Group. This structural system requires considerable interaction and consensus decision making at all levels and allows for effective coordination and control of the activities involved in multinational growth. An unofficial chart is shown in exhibit 7.

Jay R. Galbraith and Daniel A. Nathanson suggest several tracks of growth are possible, with some firms moving on one track (from functional to divisional) and other firms following the holding company to a multidivisional track. Using a managed growth strategy, Westinghouse has moved from the multiproduct divisional form to a global multinational matrix organization.[19] The matrix organization allows the international manager to develop strategies based on the plans of in-country managers. These strategies are then coordinated with the product-oriented plans developed by business unit managers. Westinghouse's multiple products, innovative technology, and changing markets make the matrix style of organization most effective.

Westinghouse's activities in foreign countries involve licensing agreements, joint ventures, branch operations, and subsidiary operations. Currently it has manufacturing operations in seventeen foreign countries, with larger facilities in Canada, Australia, Brazil, West Germany, and Ireland.

The board and management committee are concerned with broad strategy issues, while the four product groups operate as profit centers with some twenty-four strategic business units (SBUs) within these products. The international managers will integrate the strategy and develop markets in specific areas of the world. In addition, the Corporate Resources Group, including finance, productivity, research and development, human resources, and so on also will have dotted-line responsibility for their activities worldwide.

In addition to developing strategies for foreign markets, the area managers will centralize staff functions to eliminate the duplication that existed in the past. The business unit managers will continue to have profit and loss responsibility for their units in any country, but the area manager will have responsibility for the foreign market as a whole.

The process of adjusting to the new matrix system will take time. D. J. Povejsil, corporate planner, said, "We've spent thirty years trying to convince the managers of our profit centers that they're really responsible for their own areas. We've nearly succeeded. And now we're asking them to change."[20] John Marous's staff will develop foreign strategies based on the plans of in-country managers. These strategies will then have to be meshed with the product-oriented plans drawn up by the business unit managers. "We'll have to make our strategic plan fit," explained Harry Weingarten, manager of the switch gear unit, "The country manager can't say, 'I'm going to expand switchgear in Brazil by forty times,' while I say, 'I'm going to expand by 50 percent.' "[21]

The business units retain control of technology, product pricing, and capital budgets. When the unit and country managers disagree, which is likely to happen frequently in the early years, the matter will move to a higher level. The country manager will be able to appeal his case all the way up through Marous to Westinghouse's management committee. Danforth anticipates situations in which the committee may decide to have the corporation finance a project that a country manager needs badly, but cannot persuade the units to participate in. The chairman foresees a few such apparently irreconcilable problems bubbling to the top in the early days of the new system. Then, he figures, managers will get tired of receiving Solomonic judgments from above and find ways to resolve their differences.

Ian K. MacGregor, chairman of Amax, Inc., the mining company that is also expanding rapidly, said in assessing the difference between GE and Westinghouse management, "GE is a highly decentralized business. They do a good job of training their people, they are very profit conscious, and they have good engineering and cost-out practices. They have also diversified intelligently within the framework of their skills . . . Westinghouse certainly has been a little less flexible and, as a result, hasn't been able to adapt to changing circumstances as rapidly."[22]

Danforth is adapting to change by tightening operations and concentrating on profits. Fringe businesses with returns of less than 15 percent are candidates for divestiture. Below a 8 percent return they are sure targets for oblivion.[23]

Managerial Style

Danforth set the tone for his reign as chairman in October 1983 when he spoke to the top 230 executives. At that time he said, "You can expect tough but realistic objectives. Failure to deliver will be considered a management failure."[15] One veteran executive reported that Danforth's speech was the toughest speech he had ever heard from a Westinghouse CEO. Although his predecessor, Robert Kirby, liked to determine policy, Danforth is considered to be more of a hands-on manager. An ideal leader for implementing strategy, he likes to get out and meet the people and see firsthand what's going on inside the firm. Observers say that he is a much warmer manager than Kirby. Danforth gets involved with his workers and is seen as being more decisive and less tolerant of excuses than Kirby. He has decentralized the organization and given his managers more authority. They share a strong sense of accountability because they know they must meet their agreed-upon targets.

Danforth drives himself and his subordinates hard. He wants managers who aren't afraid to make mistakes. He recognizes that risks must be taken to stay ahead of the pack.[24]

Corporate Culture

For many years General Electric was the standard by which Westinghouse's performance was judged. Many corporate officials reportedly felt that Westinghouse lacked a winning attitude and could therefore expect to remain behind GE. Whether or not Westinghouse has what it takes to be a winner will be determined as Danforth continues to emphasize superior financial performance and managerial excellence at all levels of the corporation.

Corporate Strategy and Goals

Westinghouse follows a strategy of managed growth in selected areas where its financial, technological, and marketing expertise provide the firm significant advantages. It has expanded its technology base and increased its investment in services business. Danforth stated at the recent annual shareholders meeting that Westinghouse will continue on a program of acquisitions and divestitures "designed to increase portfolio value, balance diversity and provide a foundation for future growth."[25]

In 1985 Westinghouse established and met the following goals:

- Operating margins of 8 percent to 9 percent
- Record revenues in 1986 (the former record, set in 1984, was $10.264 billion)
- Sales growth at least three or four percentage points higher than the real increase in gross national product

CONCLUSION

Will this new strategy work? Former Chairman Bob Kirby said of this approach,

> You know . . . we can buy growth in almost all our ongoing businesses. On the other hand, growth is worth buying only if it increases the *value* of a business. So let me give you a few more ground rules. We'll put new capital money into a business only if we get 'yes' answers to three key questions: First, will the investment increase the value of the business to Westinghouse shareholders? Second, is the nature of the business in tune with our growth strategy for the 90's? Third, is the business worth more to us than it might be to a potential purchaser outside Westinghouse? If the answer to any of

these questions is 'No,' chances are good our corporate resources will work harder doing something else.[26]

The Management Challenge of the 1990s

Westinghouse management has noted:

> Westinghouse accomplished a lot in 1985, despite some of the worst market conditions we've faced in many years. We can be proud of that . . . as long as we don't get lulled into a false sense of satisfaction. We're playing in a tough league. Our domestic and foreign competition is not going to get any easier. Our customers here and abroad are not going to become any less demanding. I'm confident that our corporate strategy for the '90s is a good strategy. But it's not worth a damn to us unless every Westinghouse manager conveys a sense of purpose and dedication to the people he or she supervises.
>
> Our future ultimately depends on prudent allocation of resources . . . innovative technology and marketing . . . and total dedication to customer service based on better product quality and improved productivity. These things are achieved by people, not plans. . . . From now on, Westinghouse will have to walk a tightrope, balancing its books to provide for probable uranium payouts and exploration and development of uranium mines, and to stay abreast of its competition in its core businesses at the same time.[27]

There will almost certainly be no room in its calculations for any extensive new products or lines. But perhaps the very problems it will have both from its competitors and from the necessity of getting its act together will do for the company what it has been unable to do for itself—make it more manageable and more responsive to the marketplace.

Notes

1 H. D. Menzies, "Westinghouse Takes Aim at the World", *Fortune,* January 14, 1980, 48–53.
2 Westinghouse Annual Report, 1984, 1986, 3.
3 "The *Forbes* 500," *Forbes,* April 29, 1985, 244–266.
4 Annual Report.
5 Ibid.
6 Ibid.
7 Ibid.
8 Ibid.
9 Ibid.
10 Annual Meeting Report, First Quarter Report, Westinghouse, 1985, 3.
11 Ibid.
12 Ibid.

13 Annual Report.
14 U.S. Department of Commerce *Industry Surveys,* 1985:E-4
15 Annual Report.
16 Westinghouse form 10-K Report.
17 Ibid.
18 Menzies, 52.
19 J. Galbraith and D. Nathanson, *Strategic Implementation* (St. Paul: West, 1978):96.
20 Menzies, 53.
21 Ibid, 49.
22 "The Opposites: GE Grows While Westinghouse Shrinks," *Business Week,* January 31, 1977, 60.
23 Ibid., 66.
24 Interviews with Westinghouse Managers.
25 "Operation Turnaround," *Business Week,* December 5, 1983, 124–127.
26 "Kirby Talks Strategy," Westinghouse Annual Report, 1981.
27 Annual Report, 1986.

EXHIBIT 1
Financial Highlights (in millions except common share data)

Financial Highlights

(in millions except common share data)

	1986	*1985*	*1984*
Sales and operating revenues..............	**$10,731.0**	$10,700.2	$10,264.5
Net income	**$ 670.8**	$ 605.3	$ 535.9
Common share data:			
Primary earnings per share................	**$ 4.42**	$ 3.52	$ 3.04
Dividends	**$ 1.35**	$ 1.15	$ .975
Book value at end of year................	**$ 21.13**	$ 21.03	$ 21.40
Market price at end of year	**$ 55¾**	$ 44½	$ 26⅛
Shares outstanding at end of year	**142,456,796**	153,788,933	174,770,376
Capital expenditures	**$ 440.0**	$ 568.0	$ 662.0
Depreciation and amortization	**$ 371.0**	$ 449.0	$ 426.0

Source: Westinghouse Annual Report (1986).

EXHIBIT 2
Financial Information by Segment (in millions)

Financial Information by Segment
(in millions)

	1986	1985	1984
Sales and operating revenues:			
Energy and Advanced Technology....	$ 4,807.7	$ 4,407.8	$ 4,077.3
Industrial....................	3,602.4	3,732.3	3,638.0
Commercial	1,699.7	1,750.8	1,843.7
Broadcasting and Cable	838.8	1,069.2	981.9
Other......................	110.7	119.9	114.1
	11,059.3	11,080.0	10,658.0
Intersegment sales	(328.3)	(379.8)	(393.5)
Total sales and operating revenues....	$10,731.0	$10,700.2	$10,264.5
Operating profit:			
Energy and Advanced Technology....	$ 434.8	$ 417.8	$ 375.0
Industrial....................	123.2	61.2	(3.7)
Commercial	178.2	134.7	194.0
Broadcasting and Cable	149.9	138.7	71.2
Other......................	(15.3)	(10.3)	(26.5)
Gain from sale of Group W Cable (note 17)	651.2	–	–
Provision for major business restructuring and other unusual items (note 17)	(790.0)	–	–
Operating profit after unusual items...	732.0	742.1	610.0
Equity in income of financial services subsidiary and other affiliates	111.1	120.8	105.2
Other income, net...............	103.8	118.0	123.6
Interest expense	(145.9)	(185.0)	(176.6)
Income before income taxes and minority interest	$ 801.0	$ 795.9	$ 662.2
Segment identifiable assets:			
Energy and Advanced Technology....	$ 2,878.0	$ 2,896.7	$ 2,392.9
Industrial....................	1,743.7	1,875.9	1,850.1
Commercial	1,053.2	1,005.1	980.8
Broadcasting and Cable	313.9	1,680.9	1,762.0
Other......................	367.1	318.5	298.6
Adjustments and eliminations	(92.2)	(120.2)	(118.1)
	6,263.7	7,656.9	7,166.3
Investments...................	893.6	762.3	694.8
Corporate assets	1,324.5	1,292.1	1,289.3
Total assets	$ 8,481.8	$ 9,711.3	$ 9,150.4

Source: Westinghouse Annual Report (1986)

EXHIBIT 3
Financial Information by Geographic Area (in millions)

Financial Information by Geographic Area
(in millions)

	1986	*1985*	*1984*
Sales and operating revenues:			
United States....................	**$ 9,799.2**	$ 9,795.9	$ 9,415.8
Subsidiaries outside United States	**931.8**	904.3	848.7
	$10,731.0	$10,700.2	$10,264.5
Operating profit before unusual items:			
United States....................	**$ 816.2**	$ 675.3	$ 555.9
Subsidiaries outside United States	**54.6**	66.8	54.1
	$ 870.8	$ 742.1	$ 610.0
Segment identifiable assets:			
United States....................	**$ 5,648.7**	$ 6,972.9	$ 6,543.7
Subsidiaries outside United States	**615.0**	684.0	622.6
	$ 6,263.7	$ 7,656.9	$ 7,166.3

Source: Westinghouse Annual Report (1986)

EXHIBIT 4
Consolidated Statements of Income and Retained Earnings (in millions)

Consolidated Statements of Income and Retained Earnings

(in millions)

Statement of Income

Year Ended December 31	1986	1985	1984
Sales and operating revenues.........................	**$10,731.0**	$10,700.2	$10,264.5
Cost of sales..	**(7,771.2)**	(7,737.9)	(7,579.8)
Marketing, administration and general expenses	**(1,718.0)**	(1,771.2)	(1,648.7)
Depreciation and amortization	**(371.0)**	(449.0)	(426.0)
Gain from sale of Group W Cable (note 17)..........	**651.2**	—	—
Provision for major business restructuring and other unusual items (note 17)	**(790.0)**	—	—
Equity in income of financial services subsidiary and other affiliates	**111.1**	120.8	105.2
Other income, net	**103.8**	118.0	123.6
Interest expense	**(145.9)**	(185.0)	(176.6)
Income before income taxes and minority interest....	**801.0**	795.9	662.2
Income taxes (note 3)...............................	**(129.0)**	(188.6)	(122.6)
Minority interest...................................	**(1.2)**	(2.0)	(3.7)
Net income	**$ 670.8**	$ 605.3	$ 535.9
Net income per common share (note 14)			
Primary	**$ 4.42**	$ 3.52	$ 3.04
Fully diluted.......................................	**$ 4.31**	$ 3.45	$ 3.01

Statement of Retained Earnings

Year Ended December 31	1986	1985	1984
Retained earnings at beginning of year...............	**$ 3,470.7**	$ 3,063.5	$ 2,698.3
Net income	**670.8**	605.3	535.9
Dividends	**(204.2)**	(198.1)	(170.7)
Retained earnings at end of year	**$ 3,937.3**	$ 3,470.7	$ 3,063.5

The information on pages 32 through 46 is an integral part of these financial statements.

Source: Westinghouse Annual Report (1986)

EXHIBIT 5
Five-Year Summary of Selected Financial and Statistical Data (dollars in millions except per share amounts)

Five-Year Summary
Selected Financial and Statistical Data

(dollars in millions except per share amounts)

	1986	1985	1984	1983	1982
Sales and operating revenues	$10,731.0	$10,700.2	$10,264.5	$9,532.6	$9,745.4
Equity earnings and other income	$ 214.9	$ 238.8	$ 228.8	$ 131.9	$ 212.4
Interest expense	$ 145.9	$ 185.0	$ 176.6	$ 151.1	$ 185.8
Income taxes	$ 129.0	$ 188.6	$ 122.6	$ 4.1	$ 94.6
Net income	$ 670.8	$ 605.3	$ 535.9	$ 449.0	$ 449.3
Net income as a percentage of sales	6.3%	5.7%	5.2%	4.7%	4.6%
Return on average equity	20.7%	16.0%	15.1%	13.8%	14.9%
Primary earnings per share	$ 4.42	$ 3.52	$ 3.04	$ 2.54	$ 2.58
Dividends per share	$ 1.35	$ 1.15	$ .975	$ .90	$ .90
Cash and marketable securities	$ 597.5	$ 702.1	$ 611.5	$ 548.3	$ 542.4
Plant and equipment, net	$ 2,188.7	$ 3,300.2	$ 3,295.4	$3,090.0	$2,935.8
Total assets	$ 8,481.8	$ 9,711.3	$ 9,150.4	$8,569.0	$8,349.8
Short-term debt	$ 596.9	$ 2,039.2	$ 1,115.1	$ 953.2	$ 650.1
Long-term debt	$ 518.2	$ 525.3	$ 567.3	$ 354.8	$ 493.0
Stockholders' equity	$ 3,009.6	$ 3,234.7	$ 3,740.8	$3,410.3	$3,175.0
Average shares for primary earnings per share	152,331,187	172,488,375	177,301,873	176,881,388	173,981,498
Market price range per share	$62½-42	$46¾-25⅜	$28⅜-19¾	$28¼-18⅝	$20¼-11
Common stockholders at year end	123,859	134,096	140,799	143,731	154,440
Average number of employes	117,267	124,935	126,849	132,927	145,251

Source: Westinghouse Annual Report (1986)

Quarterly Financial Information *(unaudited)*

(in millions except per share amounts)

Quarter Ended	Sales and Operating Revenues	Operating Profit After Unusual Items	Net Income	Primary Earnings Per Share	Dividends Per Share	Common Stock Prices High	Low
1986:							
March 31	**$ 2,553.7**	**$169.7**	**$135.2**	**$ .88**	**$ .30**	**55**	**42**
June 30	**2,733.7**	**63.9(a)**	**163.1**	**1.05**	**.35**	**57¾**	**49½**
September 30	**2,574.5**	**211.8**	**169.3**	**1.11**	**.35**	**60¼**	**48½**
December 31	**2,869.1**	**286.6**	**203.2**	**1.38**	**.35**	**62½**	**52½**
	$10,731.0	**$732.0**	**$670.8**	**$4.42**	**$1.35**	**62½**	**42**
1985:							
March 31	$ 2,314.1	$151.8	$129.7	$ .74	$ .25	32⅞	25⅜
June 30	2,557.5	173.1	143.9	.81	.30	35¼	28⅞
September 30	2,608.9	178.1	148.6	.85	.30	39⅞	32
December 31	3,219.7	239.1	183.1	1.12	.30	46¾	36⅝
	$10,700.2	$742.1	$605.3	$3.52	$1.15	46¾	25⅜

(a) Includes gain on the sale of Group W Cable of $651.2 and provision for major business restructuring and other unusual items of $790.0.

Consolidated Statement of Cash Flows

(in millions)

Year Ended December 31	1986	1985	1984
Cash flows from operating activities			
Net income..	$ 670.8	$ 605.3	$ 535.9
Adjustments for noncash items included in net income:			
Depreciation and amortization.............................	371.0	449.0	426.0
Equity in income of financial services subsidiary and other affiliates	(111.1)	(120.8)	(105.2)
Income taxes deferred	(64.6)	56.7	82.7
Gain from sale of Group W Cable	(651.2)	—	—
Writedown of assets under major business restructuring program..	251.3	—	—
Remaining liability for major business restructuring program..	484.3	—	—
Minority interest	1.2	2.0	3.7
(Increase) decrease in customer receivables, current and noncurrent	125.8	(212.0)	(259.6)
Increase in inventories and costs of uncompleted contracts net of progress billings	(147.2)	(163.0)	(171.4)
Increase in accounts payable...............................	45.6	25.3	50.9
Decrease in uranium settlement items......................	(23.2)	(63.2)	(44.0)
Other changes in working capital	14.4	63.8	(26.3)
Other noncurrent items, net................................	27.4	137.7	62.6
Net cash flow from operating activities	994.5	780.8	555.3
Cash flows from investing and financing activities			
Capital expenditures.......................................	(440.0)	(568.0)	(662.0)
Proceeds from sale of Group W Cable	1,710.4	—	—
Sale-leaseback of buildings................................	—	149.2	—
Net increase (decrease) in short-term debt	(1,440.7)	924.1	161.9
Proceeds of long-term debt	309.3	11.4	355.5
Repayment of long-term debt..............................	(316.4)	(53.4)	(143.0)
Common stock purchased for treasury	(806.6)	(975.1)	(47.6)
Common stock issued to employes	29.0	50.6	28.6
Dividends	(204.2)	(198.1)	(170.7)
Other, net	60.1	(30.9)	(14.8)
Net cash flow from investing and financing activities	(1,099.1)	(690.2)	(492.1)
Increase (decrease) in cash and marketable securities	$ (104.6)	$ 90.6	$ 63.2

Certain 1985 amounts have been reclassified for comparative purposes.
The information on pages 32 through 46 is an integral part of these financial statements.

Source: Westinghouse Annual Report (1986)

EXHIBIT 7
Matrix Organization of Westinghouse (unofficial)

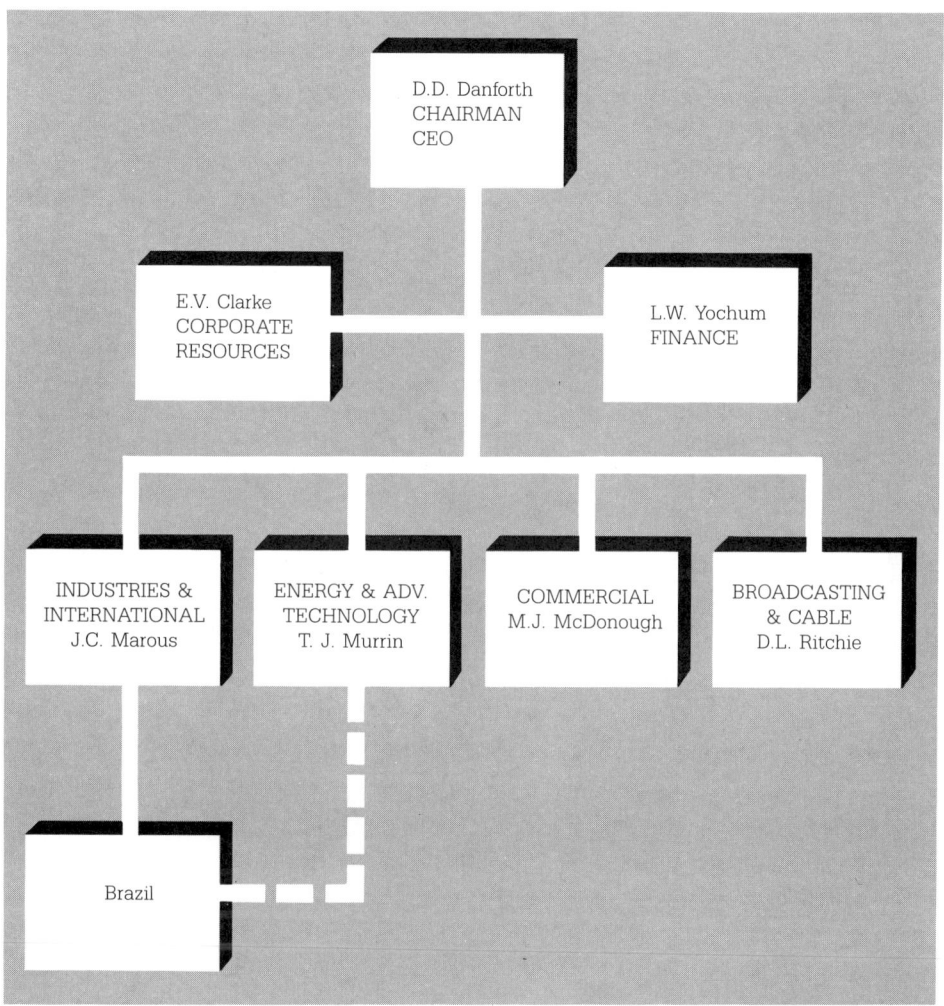

The Rise and Fall and Rise and Fall and . . . Rise? of Atari

Donald F. Harvey
Eastern Washington University
Research Associate: John D. Bowden

In the Oriental game of Go, two players compete for territory and power on a two-dimensional gameboard. With each new move, the advantage shifts from one player to the other. But as the game progresses, a time comes when one player takes control, when the outcome of the game becomes apparent. There is a word for this moment; a word that is less a signal of intent than it is an announcement of the inevitable. That word is . . . ATARI.

Though the electronics industry is full of rags-to-riches stories, few can compare with the tumultuous history of Atari. California's Silicon Valley, just south of San Francisco, has had little time to build traditions in its short history as the electronics capital of the world. If it has one, however, it would be Atari's rise from an engineer's backyard experiments to a hot public corporation.

Atari has experienced three distinct phases in its thirteen-year lifetime. It was born at the home of an engineer in Silicon Valley. After being near bankruptcy and undergoing a meteoric rise, Atari was sold to a large entertainment corporation. For the first six years Atari gave its parent company sizable profits, but then the public's infatuation with video games began to fade. The losses were staggering. In one year alone, the loss was over half a billion dollars.

In a desperation move to stop the hemorrhaging, Atari was partially given away. A "bulldog" of an entrepreneur now has Atari under his tight control, and though the company is privately held, the industry is watching closely to see if the new owner can raise Atari from its deathbed.[1]

HISTORY

In the beginning there was a young research engineer at Ampex who had some wild ideas about building video games people would want to play again and again. In 1969 Nolan Bushnell, a young research engineer for the Ampex recording-tape company, began working on a plan for the world's first commercial video game.

After two years of experimenting in his workshop, improvised out of the bedroom of one of his daughters, Bushnell completed Computer Space, the first commercial video game. Like today's top games, 1971's Computer Space pitted space-ships against flying saucers with the background of the Milky Way galaxy. Bushnell showed it to his friends, and they all loved it. He began selling it to tavern owners with the help of Nuting Associates, a marketing firm.

Computer Space flopped. No one would play it and less than 2,000 were made. Unlike Bushnell's friends, who themselves were all computer scientists, the average guy in the bar was simply bewildered by the game. The public had never seen anything like it. Computer Space was ahead of its time.[2]

Bushnell went back to the drawing board, realizing that his game would have to be simpler. The rules of the game would have to be immediately comprehensible to the average person, so he decided to draw on tennis as an analogue. "People don't read instructions," Bushnell reasoned, "so the key was creating a game that was analogous to a game people already knew."[3] Thus Pong was born. Instead of selling his design to other manufacturers as originally planned, Bushnell decided to found his own company, Atari. In its first year, Atari rang up sales of $3 million, and before the more sophisticated games came along, Pong sold over 100,000 units.

MANAGEMENT

Nolan Bushnell has been described as a big bear of a man with a child's passion for games. He was a fair chess player and quite good at go. He lived for fun and spent most of his time finding ways to amuse himself—the climate he created at Atari.

Atari became something like Bushnell's version of Disneyland, the perfect place for creative, fun-loving engineers to work. The management style was California casual. At Atari, business and pleasure not only mixed; they were inseparable. Bull sessions between top management and design engineers were reportedly often fueled with cannabis and Coors. Bushnell had the reputation of being combative with business adversaries but running Atari with a carefree hand.[4]

Under Bushnell

Nolan Bushnell had managed to pull the company out of near bankruptcy in 1974 with the development of the first home-game console of Pong and the financial backing of Sears. But in 1976, the home video market was so heated that Bushnell knew that new developments must be made in order to keep the public's interest. Once again Atari needed cash in a hurry. Bushnell had three options: assume huge loans; go public with its stock, which he felt was uncertain; or sell out to a cash-rich, established company.

Bushnell made his decision and put Atari up for sale. MCA, an entertainment conglomerate, and Disney both looked at it but declined. Finally, Warner Communications made an offer. Warner's other divisions—records and music publishing, film production, and a cable TV venture—were all performing poorly, and the quarters that poured down Atari's coin chutes were very enticing.

Video games had become the fastest-growing segment of the $4.3 billion-a-year toy business at a time when the market for hand-held electronic games, such as Mattel's Football II, had softened. Among all the companies in this fast-growing business, only Atari manufactured both coin-operated games for arcades and a video game player for the home.

The chaotic market conditions mirrored the situation inside Atari. A *bon vivant* and a conceptualist with a disdain for detail, Bushnell never intended to oversee Atari's operations after the sale to Warner, even though he had stayed on in a top post. "I'm not a very good chief operating officer," he conceded, "I like to develop the strategy, not to work it."[5] Soon after the company was sold, Bushnell began showing up only rarely for work.

Nolan Bushnell stayed for a year at Atari but spent less and less time managing the business. He felt he had little to contribute, and the day-to-day operations bored him. He was finally ousted in 1978. Overseeing the daily chores was left to then Atari president Joseph Keenan, who himself had become a millionaire from the Warner deal.

As Part of Warner Communications

The year 1978 was not only when Bushnell was forced out of Atari, but it was also the year that the VCS 2600 programmable computer game began to catch on. Prior to the VCS 2600, home games could play possibly four different games. Atari's VCS 2600 was the first home game console that allowed the owner to change games by plugging in a new read only memory (ROM) cartridge.

"Then in 1979, some hard-partying wizards from the coin-op department teamed up to create the Atari 400 and 800 computers."[6] The new home computers and the video game player suddenly made Atari a billion dollar a year company. Tensions between old Atari employees and Warner newcomers began to rise. Warner felt that more control was needed in the management of Atari to capture larger and larger market shares in the expanding industry.

Raymond Kassar was placed in charge of Atari. He changed the once open and free-floating atmosphere found at Atari to one found at many large corporations. Kassar instituted formal reporting systems and tried to implement sales and marketing goals. The sales at Atari were indeed growing, but fewer and fewer people at Atari knew what the products they were selling were all about. The biggest problem for Atari became its own bigness.[7]

Raymond Kassar began changing the corporate climate at Atari. He recruited experienced managers from other corporations, created formal reporting procedures, established financial controls, outlined detailed sales and marketing goals, and tightened security measures to protect confidential information. "I knew I had a consumer-marketing company and I had nobody who understood the consumer business," he said.[8] Kassar put his stamp on the corporate culture as well. "Things were kind of casual here," he recalled. "People didn't work very hard."[9] He made it clear that he expected people to be at work at 8:00 A.M. sharp, to answer the phones promptly, and to wear ties and jackets instead of T-shirts.

Design engineers felt Kassar's presence more than most other employees during this transition from entrepreneurial to the managerial style. Once-pampered engineers during the Bushnell era were described as over-emotional prima donnas by Kassar in a newspaper interview. Labs had locked doors that could be opened only with magnetic cards, and engineers' names were kept top secret to guard against competitors stealing them away.

Kassar divided the company into three divisions: coin-operated games, home computers, and consumer electronics, which produced the home video players. These divisions worked independently of one another. Most damaging to Atari was the split between home computers and the home games division. These products were meshing in the minds of consumers, but the two divisions were becoming rivals within the company. Their failure to work together probably cost Atari the high end of the games market, which went to Coleco, and the low end of the home computer market, which went to Commodore. But many of the problems were being hidden by Atari's explosive growth.

Atari was "videotripping" in 1981 and 1982. Its revenues were over a billion dollars in 1981, with more than a quarter of that in profits. "After Pac-Man became a national rage, Atari, which marketed the home version, reported 1982 sales of $2 billion and profits of $323 million, both records."[10] However, before 1982 had ended, the boom was fizzling. Many of the game cartridges that had been sold were being returned and by the year's end actual sales had fallen back to $1 billion.

As Atari changed, so did the staff. It was no longer a "fun" place to work. It takes a special sort of person to create a video game with appeal and then translate it into programming language and the electronics of a computer. The engineers felt that the new management ignored the fact that creativity could not be regulated by traditional nine-to-five work hours. Gradually Atari's best resource, its design engineers, left the company.

Events of 1983–1984

Atari has had its ups and downs over the last twelve years, and the story is not yet over. Though Warner Communications' massive loans and a structured management style helped Atari achieve record profits for several years, some in the industry and in the company feel Warner may also have hurt Atari, especially in the appointment of Raymond Kassar as CEO. Kassar and Warner are accused of being too cautious in an industry where risk-taking is a way of life. Kassar had top management experience but no experience in the high-tech electronics industry. In alienating key personnel within Atari, they lost much of their innovativeness and creativity. And in hesitating to enter the home computer market, they lost valuable market share.

The year 1983 proved to be a difficult one for Atari and Warner Communications. Once Atari had proven the potential in the video game business, many corporations quickly entered the market. At the same time demand fell from its 1982 peak, causing large inventories of unsold products. Also in 1983, the home computer industry faced severe price competition.

However, the market was not the only problem, and some believe not the primary problem. Negative publicity faced by Atari was impossible to overcome. As one Atari employee stated, "It wasn't so much the market that hurt Atari, it was all the bad press due to the layoffs, the move of manufacturing to Taiwan, and local anti-video game organizations banning the arcades in their towns."[11] Kassar was responsible for most of the bad press. He was close-mouthed and openly antagonistic towards the media. As a result, certain events were blown out of proportion or not reported accurately. For example:

1   The move of manufacturing to Taiwan was reported in the national news. What was not reported was that Atari was the last company in the Silicon Valley to move its manufacturing overseas. Also, only part of that division went overseas, two-thirds of the manufacturing division went to El Paso, Texas.
2   Massive layoffs by Atari were reported in 1983. What was not reported was that layoffs had been gradually happening since late 1972 and those in 1983 occurred over a nine-month period.
3   In the Bay area, it was reported that Atari was throwing away video cartridges. People were going to the dump, picking up game cartridges, and selling them for $10 to $15 each. Atari finally had to dispose secretly of cartridges, using security guards and unmarked trucks. At one point, a truck was mobbed when a security guard mistakenly wore a hat with an Atari logo. What was not reported was the fact that the cartridges were defective: cartridges that did not pass quality control or were returned by customers.

Warner made a last-ditch effort to save Atari in September 1983. It appointed James Morgan, a former Philip Morris executive, as chairman at Atari. Morgan slashed Atari's worldwide work force from 9,800 to 3,500 in an effort to cut costs, but the tactic was "too little, too late" for Warner. The decision to sell Atari came in April of 1984.[12]

Management's policy at Atari was largely established by the management team (see exhibit 2).

FINANCIAL

Atari started fast, contributing over $1 billion in revenues and over $285 million in operating profits by 1981. However, by 1983 there was a loss of over $500 million. Warner Communication ranked 114 in the *Fortune* top 500 list, with total revenues at the $3.4 billion level in 1984. Warner's revenues and earnings per share have increased steadily over the past ten years.

However, the year 1983 was the most difficult in Warner's 22-year history. The problems experienced by the Atari subsidiary caused the first earnings downturn in corporate history.

For Atari, 1983 was a year of both extraordinary problems and profound, positive changes. The Consumer Electronics Division reported revenues of $1.1 billion and an operating loss of $539 million (see exhibit 2).

Warner executives became frustrated at Morgan's inability to extract Atari from its decline and sent one of its senior executives to assist. Warner's effort proved futile. Finally, Warner chairman Steven Ross, without consulting Morgan, decided that attempts to salvage Atari should be abandoned. Warner turned its video game and computer divisions of Atari over to Jack Tramiel, founder and former CEO of Commodore International for $240 million in ten- and twelve-year notes. Warner's sale of Atari to Jack Tramiel in July of 1984 was ironic—it was Tramiel's "success at marketing rival electronic products from Commodore International [that] contributed so much to Atari's abrupt collapse."[13] Also with the sale came a new phase in the existence of Atari.

The sale of Atari to Jack Tramiel was not the end of Warner's financial association with the company. Warner Communications, Inc. (WCI) has had a very difficult time divorcing itself from Atari. "Until late 1982, it netted close to $700 million for WCI, which bought it for only $28 million. . . ."[14] However, the losses in 1983 and 1984 probably wiped out all of the previous profits, and the fact that Atari continues to drain resources away from Warner undoubtedly will leave it in the red when the eight-year enterprise is really divested.

"The sale-of-assets agreement was a 300-page monument to expediency, full of qualifications, loopholes, and doors left open to be closed later."[15] Tramiel paid no cash to acquire all but Atari's telephone and coin-operated games division. He did pledge to use $75 million of his own fortune to recapitalize Atari and he signed $240 million in ten- and twelve-year notes. Tramiel was able to get below-market interest rates on the notes (which Warner valued on its books at $160 million).[16]

Also as part of the deal both sides exchanged stock warrants. Tramiel got an option to buy one million Warner shares at $22 each. (Shortly after the sale was announced, Warner stock fell from 23-3/8 to just under 19. The stock traded for approximately 34-5/8 in 1985.) Warner was given the option of purchasing up to 14.3 million shares of Atari stock at $2 per share.[17] The chance to own 32 percent of the company was Warner's only real chance to profit on the deal. Many industry analysts observed that WCI had practically given Atari away, and as Fred Anschel of Dean Witter Reynolds said following the sale, "In effect, Warner is financing the whole thing."[18]

Though Tramiel agreed to inject $75 million into the company, he has yet to do so. Thus far he has put $30 million into Atari—$26 million of his cash and the rest from his sons and lieutenants. "The remaining $45 million is tucked away in investments such as municipal bonds."[19] To finance future advertising and product development, Atari will need to raise more capital, but Tramiel seems to have no intention of dipping into the $45 million reserve. Instead, he has been returning to Warner for more money. Tramiel demanded cash from WCI in August of 1984 when many of the receivables proved to be uncollectable. For the nine months ending September 30, 1986, Atari reported earnings of $21 million on sales of $164 million.

Jack Tramiel can best be described as a competitive jungle-fighter. He is reputed to be a man who must have complete power and control. Tramiel is reportedly bitter about the treatment he received from his old company, Commodore, and will use Atari to get even. Within a month of his purchase of Atari, he had cut the staff from 1,100 to approximately 300. All divisions were eliminated but marketing and some finance. Tramiel is viewing Atari as a start-up operation and hopes to beat Commodore at its own game of price slashing: a strategy that Tramiel knows so well.[20]

The obvious question about Atari's smashing success is: How long will it last? Video games might just be the latest toy industry fad. In the meantime, the profitability of video games is attracting plenty of new competitors. Since 1983 at least half a dozen companies have started making coin-operated video games. Japanese companies have invented some of the most successful games and have established manufacturing facilities in the United States.

MARKETING AND THE MARKET

Historically Atari has been very poor at marketing its products. In 1979 Atari introduced two of the most advanced and best-designed low-end machines in the industry: the 400 and 800 home computers. But Atari let the computers languish for four years and lost money on them every year. By the time Atari realized that the problem lay with its sales efforts and not the hardware, other firms had entered the market and Atari was bleeding. Atari built a reputation as only a game company; consumers did not perceive it as being a computer company. This image is a problem Tramiel will have to face.

In 1983 Pac-Man threatened to gobble up the world; however, by 1985 there were only two surviving independent manufacturers of low-priced home computers: Atari and Commodore. Martin Romm, an analyst with First Boston Corporation, a New York-based investment company, has put the market in perspective by stating that video games and home computers may be "the electronic hula-hoops of the 1980s."[21] These firms will probably have to move up-market if they wish to survive.

Tramiel announced that he will expand Atari's product line and has already brought the 520ST to market in record time. Tramiel hopes the ST (promptly dubbed the Jackintosh by those within the industry) will compete directly with the Apple Macintosh. Atari has run advertisements comparing the ST to the Macintosh and IBM's PC and touting its machine as being equal to, but selling at a lower price, than its competitors' machines.

Although Atari may have produced a machine that can compete with Apple and IBM in power and ability, it still faces some formidable obstacles in marketing the new computer. It must first convince software writers to write an adequate number of programs. Tramiel must reverse the image he had at Commodore of not caring about software. When he spoke to a group of software executives in January 1985 promising assistance and even financial aid to software developers, there was some snickering. So far, Atari has persuaded few software companies to write programs for the ST. Market researchers insist that the new breed of sophisticated consumer won't look at a machine without an abundance of programs. "The ball game is won or lost in software," said Egil Juliussen, Future Computing's Chairman.[22] But Tramiel thinks consumers will buy a computer with a small amount of rudimentary programs and as the machines find their way into the homes, software will follow.

To get the machines into the homes, Tramiel must first get them into the market. When the 520ST started appearing in stores in July 1985, there was no publicity. "People who are buying right now are well versed in technology," said Dan Williams, an owner of Home Computing Center in San Bruno. "Reaching the first-time buyer is a much harder sale."[23] Atari is trying to reach a confused market. Until 1984, cheap computers ruled the market. Tramiel's price wars had driven the cost of basic machines to well below $300, making them impulse items. During the Christmas season of 1984, the market did a flip-flop and consumers were drawn to the specialty shops. Demand for the mass-market home computers leveled off; the impulse buyer went after VCRs instead.

COMPETITION AND TECHNOLOGY

Sales of the 520ST are reported to be brisk (150,000 by September 1986). Atari is placing its ST against Apple's Macintosh at $2,795, Commodore's Amiga at $1,795, and IBM's PC-AT at $4,675 and declaring the competition to be "rip-offs." At $799 the 520ST seems to be making some gains.

If Atari can get software developers to write programs and retailers to sell its machines, its products could undercut both IBM and Apple on the low end of the personal computer market; but this feat would defy past odds. The home computer market is littered with casualties. In 1985 the two giants captured 30 percent of the $2.8 billion consumers spent on home computers. The latest victim was Coleco, which abandoned its Adam and had a final write-down of over $100 million. Other companies such as Mattel, Timex, and Texas Instruments left the market earlier with losses totaling more than half a billion dollars.

The collapse of the low end of the home computer market has effectively forestalled the planned invasion by Japanese consumer electronic companies. More than a dozen Japanese firms have built home computers around a common operating system known as MSX that allows all the computers to run the same software. These machines have had respectable sales in Europe and Japan since their introduction, but dealers in the United States have greeted them with little enthusiasm. Consumer giants such as Sony and Matsushita have, therefore, cancelled their plans to sell their computers in the United States.

Atari's ST (its main hope for the future) is based on the Motorola 68000 microprocessor—the same chip used in Apple's Macinitosh. The ST closely resembles the Macintosh, but it is able to use color, while the original Macintosh is only black and white. Also, unlike the Macintosh, which sells in one unit, the ST's components are designed to be bought in affordable increments. With the average credit card limit set at $500, this marketing ploy may prove to be positive.

Apple spent tens of millions of dollars on advertising in 1985 to familiarize the public with its Macintosh. Tramiel thinks he can capitalize on Apple's efforts and can use the ST to lure customers away from IBM's PCjr and the Apple IIc, which are based on less sophisticated technology.

Atari officials say the company will soon demonstrate a computer that can process thirty-two bits at once, likely to be called the TT. The TT will be aimed at the business markets and Atari claims the computer will have the power of a VAX superminicomputer (Digital Equipment Corporation, selling for more than $100,000). Atari says its computer will have a microprocessor from National Semiconductor and an operating system based on Bell Laboratories' Unix. Most astonishingly, Atari says the computer, nicknamed the "Vax-in-a-box," will sell for under $1,000. If Atari can, indeed, come to market with such a machine at that price, it will have a tremendous advantage over its competition.

Before Atari looks too far ahead, it must think about surviving month-to-month. Its best bet, the 520ST, is facing an uphill battle to move into the domain of IBM and Apple. Both larger companies have far greater resources than Atari and machines that have tons of software available for them.

ORGANIZATIONAL STRUCTURE

Because Atari is a privately held company, it does not publish an annual report listing the various officers. An analysis of the organizational structure is therefore extremely difficult. The organization chart (see exhibit 3) was drawn using information gleaned from numerous newspaper and magazine articles. Like a jigsaw puzzle with many missing pieces, the picture remains unclear. Because Atari is a small company with fewer than 200 employees in the United States, the structure becomes less important.

CONCLUSION

Three important questions arise in researching Atari. First of all, how large can a company grow before the management style must change to accommodate that growth? Second, what effect does the management style have on creativity and innovativeness? Can balance be achieved? And third, how much knowledge and experience must a CEO have, either in the company's technology or in management, to lead a company to success?

Although he continues to make all major decisions; Jack Tramiel says he is pulling away from Atari's day-to-day operations. In 1984 few analysts would have predicted that he could raise Atari from the near-dead. There are still those who believe the company will stumble. But Tramiel isn't listening. His next goal is nothing less than overtaking Apple. He said, "I've created one billion-dollar company and I intend to do better this time." [24] Jack Tramiel has both an electronics background and corporate management experience. The final question is: Under Tramiel, will Atari rise again?

Notes

1 John Anderson, "Atari," *Creative Computing*, March 1984, 51.
2 "When the Magic Goes," *Inc.*, October 1984, 82.
3 Ibid.
4 Ibid.
5 Ibid., 84.
6 Michael Miller, "Atari Sees Boost from Write-off of Debt to Warner," *The Wall Street Journal*, February 19, 1985, 114.
7 Michael Miller, "Atari, Commodore Target IBM, Apple in Market for Higher Cost Computers," *The Wall Street Journal*, January 7, 1985, 14.
8 "When the Magic Goes."
9 Ibid.
10 Gary Hector, "The Big Shrink Is On at Atari," *Fortune*, July 9, 1984, 23.
11 Interviews with Atari employees.
12 "Jim Morgan's Unhappy 10 Months at Atari," *Business Week*, July 23, 1984, 90.
13 "Electronic Disaster," *Financial World*, August 8, 1984, 6.
14 Ibid.
15 Peter Petre, "Jack Tramiel is Back on the Warpath," *Fortune*, March 4, 1985, 49.
16 Ibid.
17 "Electronic Disaster."
18 Peter Giffen, "A Canadian Buys Atari Using No Cash," *MacLeans*, July 16, 1984, 28.
19 Petre, 50.
20 Andrew Pollack, "Jack Tramiel Dreams Big," *The New York Times*, February 10, 1985, F33.
21 Giffen, 28.
22 Petre, 48.
23 Michael Miller, "Atari Turnaround Depends on $799 Machine," *The Wall Street Journal*, September 30, 1985, 6.
24 "Father Knows Best," *Business Week*, December 15, 1986, 108.

EXHIBIT 1
Organization Chart

EXHIBIT 1 Organization Chart

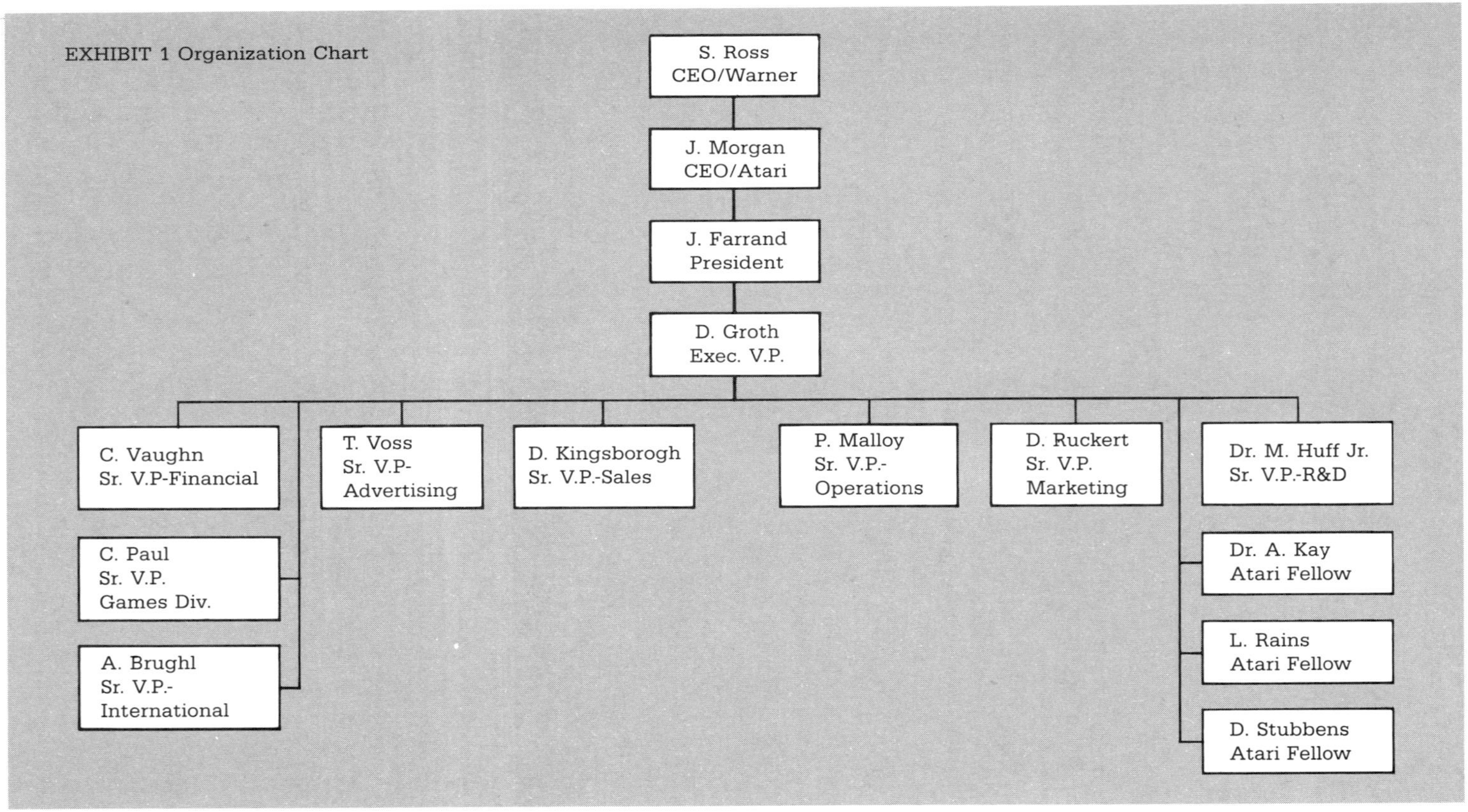

EXHIBIT 2
Segment Information

Information as to WCI's operations in different industry segments is as follows (Thousands):

Years ended December 31	1983	1982	1981
Revenues from unaffiliated customers:			
Consumer electronics	$1,121,346	$2,008,805	$1,227,135
Filmed entertainment	877,846	694,088	755,175
Recorded music and music publishing	765,933	752,317	811,257
Consumer products	660,147	635,441	500,181
Total revenues	$3,425,272	$4,090,651	$3,293,748
Operating income (loss):			
Consumer electronics	$ (538,578)	$ 323,288	$ 286,553
Filmed entertainment	109,404	101,796	24,748
Recorded music and music publishing	60,724	58,656	85,014
Consumer products	43,252	40,160	40,897
Operating income (loss)	(325,198)	523,900	437,212
Unallocated expenses, net	(205,905)	(144,000)	(72,019)
Income (loss) before income taxes	(531,103)	379,900	365,193
(Provision) benefit for income taxes	113,300	(122,089)	(138,700)
Net income (loss)	$ (417,803)	$ 257,811	$ 226,493
Total assets:			
Consumer electronics	$ 661,316	$ 752,778	$ 576,568
Filmed entertainment	858,494	939,988	781,578
Recorded music and music publishing	374,907	384,159	381,553
Consumer products	430,898	409,960	453,912
Corporate (a)	796,691	699,470	480,030
Total assets	$3,122,306	$3,186,355	$2,673,641
Net capital expenditures:			
Consumer electronics	$ 71,689	$ 74,063	$ 43,844
Filmed entertainment	8,122	8,484	18,195
Recorded music and music publishing	7,622	9,997	19,915
Consumer products	10,230	8,565	6,585
Corporate	20,790	23,924	12,971
Total net capital expenditures	$ 118,453	$ 125,033	$ 101,510

(a) Principally cash, marketable securities, other investments and deferred income taxes.

EXHIBIT 3
Atari Organizational Chart

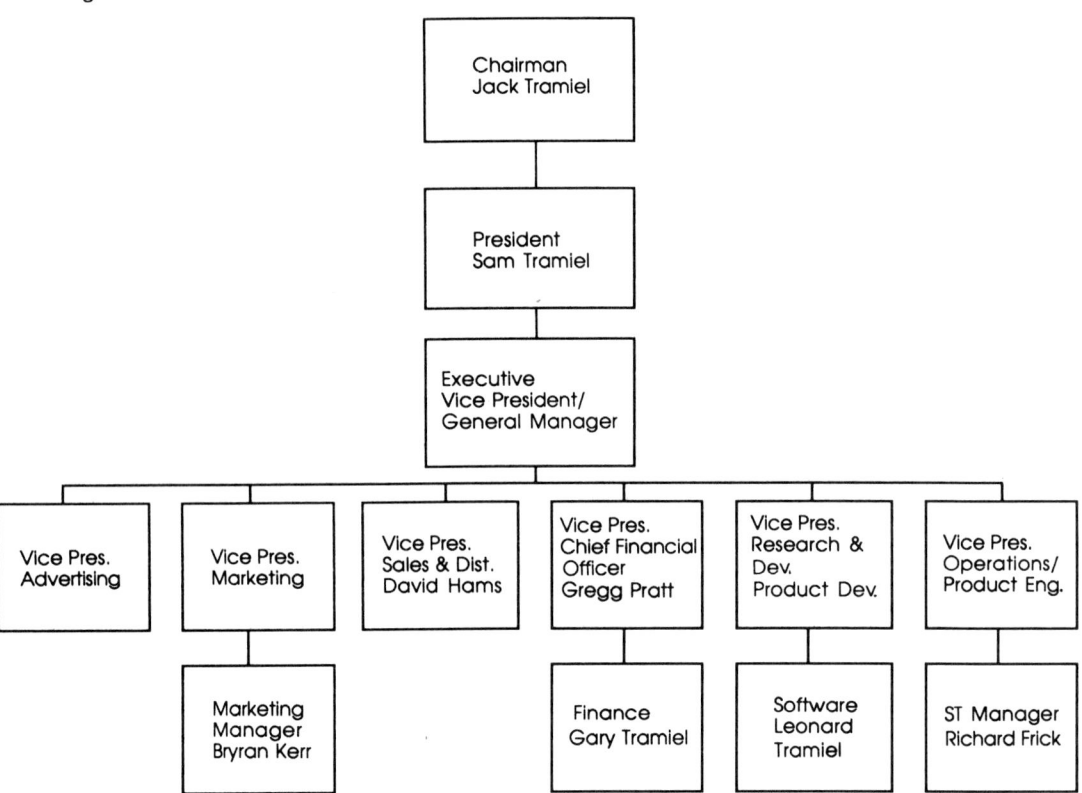

Wang Laboratories, Inc., 1986

Donald F. Harvey
Eastern Washington University

INTRODUCTION

Dr. An Wang has come a long way from his Shanghai birthplace to the Wang headquarters in Lowell, Massachusetts. With a personal worth of more than $1.5 billion, the man known to his employees as the "Doctor" is believed to be one of the ten richest men in America.

Strong leadership is essential at Wang Laboratories these days. Sales at the $2.6 billion, 30,000-employee company used to grow by more than 30 percent a year, but in 1985 sales rose only 8 percent. Earnings, which stood at $210 million in 1984, sagged to $16 million in 1985, including a $109 million fourth-quarter loss. Only recently has the company begun to climb back to modest profitability. Its stock languishes near its fifty-two-week low of $15.

Frederick A. Wang's first two months as president of Wang Laboratories, Inc., were anything but dull. As soon as he took over day-to-day operations from his father (founder An Wang) the new president announced a reshuffling of the company's sales and marketing organizations. Then, he unveiled yet another restructuring—with the layoff of 1,000 employees and a 6 percent pay cut for the 30,000 workers who remained. The reason: The $2.6 billion computer company was facing the most precipitous downturn in its thirty-six-year history. Says Fred Wang: "We've got to get back on track."[1]

> Wang Laboratories, Inc., designs, manufactures, and markets computer systems and provides related products and services for the worldwide operations automation marketplace. The company's products are used primarily for data and text processing, and offer image and voice processing functions as well. These products provide extensive communications capabilities, and can be incorporated into networks of interconnected systems. The company's products and services are designed to provide its customers with automation solutions that enable them to manage their operations and communicate information more effectively (see exhibit 1).[2]

Background

The company was founded in 1951 as a research laboratory for the development of scientific and engineering products produced to meet the demands of a variety of large customers. In the early 1960s, Wang took an entirely new course, which included developing its own direct sales organization. Landmark products at that time were the LOCI and 300 series programmable calculators, which were designed and sold to fill a market need not met by the large-scale digital computers of the day.

In the early 1970s Wang established its presence in the data processing market with its 2200 small business system, another fundamental corporate transition in response to changing technology and customer requirements. By 1986 the more than sixty-five thousand 2200 system customers were supported and serviced by Wang's field organization throughout the world. In the mid-1970s, Wang marketed its first CRT-based text processing systems. The success of these systems helped Wang pass the $100 million revenue threshold in 1977.

In the late 1970s and early 1980s, the company integrated previously distinct word, data, and communications technologies in its families of VS and integrated information systems. In 1980 Wang defined the Six Technologies of Office Automation: word processing, data processing, voice processing, image processing, networking, and human factors.

During each of these transitions, Wang Laboratories adapted its marketing focus through refinements in management and organizational structure, product offerings, and the expertise of its people. Recently Wang has expanded its integrated information architecture beyond the confines of the office or a single vendor environment to provide operations automation throughout the organization and across vendor boundaries. Under this systems integration framework, Wang delivers not only information processing capabilities but also information transport and a full range of information services.

Products

Wang has sales, service, and support operations in more than 360 cities in the United States and in more than 100 nations. Manufacturing facilities are located throughout Massachusetts and in Ireland, Scotland, Puerto Rico, Taiwan, Australia, Mexico, and Korea. Research and development centers have been established in Taiwan, Belgium, Mexico, and Hong Kong, with a new center currently being built in British Columbia. The majority of its business is presently generated from data processing and communications products and services, not word processing or office automation.

Large-scale systems integration brings together Wang technology with that of competitors through adherence to communications standards in a cohesive network of systems and services. Wang's upgradable and compatible systems meet the operational needs of departments and branches in large organizations, as well as the total operational needs of small- and medium-sized organizations. The foundation and infra-structure of large-scale systems integration and integratable products were developed under the framework of an integrated information architecture.

Wang extended its product family at both the low end and high end with VS 5, VS 6, and VS 300 and expanded its desktop offerings with the Advanced Professional Computer and a wide range of new workstations. Wang made significant strides in its ability to provide both strategic and application software, greatly enhancing Wang OFFICE, delivering new operating systems throughout the VS product family, and upgrading its PACE fourth generation relational base. The product strategies of large-scale systems integration and integratable products and the synergistic relationship between sales and development has helped Wang extend its integrated information architecture beyond the confines of the office.

Competition

There is a lot of tough competition for Wang Laboratories, Inc., from IBM, Digital Equipment, and Xerox. Each of these major competitors is attempting to enter the office systems market from one of its three technological bases—data processing, word processing, or communications. Wang's advantage is that it already has a product line featuring all three. Wang is the eleventh largest computer company following IBM, Digital Equipment, UNISYS, Apple, Xerox, Commodore International Ltd., Radio Shack, Hewlett-Packard, and Data General. However, Wang is the second largest office automation company, after IBM (see exhibit 2).

Wang expects intense competition from several large firms that have entered or will enter the office automation market, including Hewlett-Packard, IBM, and others. During 1987 as many as a dozen large companies were expected to join the battle, including several major Japanese firms who are preparing to enter the U.S. market.

Management and Organization

Wang has put into place a well-planned course of action to bring it closer to its customers and to make it more responsive to their needs. Management layers were reduced from eight to five distinct levels of management between the customer and the chairman's office. (See exhibit 3 for Wang's organizational chart.)

Until recently Wang had no system for tracking material usage during production. There was also little or no communication and coordination between functional groups in the company, and people often worked at cross-purposes. Wang engineers, for instance, never took into account how much it would cost to manufacture or service a product when they were designing it.

Ironically, it was An Wang's centralized and highly personal management style—so important to the company's success—that caused its growing pains. "The company took longer to go through adolescence because of the tight control at the top," admitted a member of Wang's board of directors.[3] An Wang managed largely on an ad hoc basis, reserving final decision-making power for himself. As a result, formal strategic planning and delegation of duties were given little emphasis. An executive operating committee had been established in 1985 to handle top management decision making during the doctor's increasingly frequent absences. However, the most significant transfer of responsibility came in 1986 when Wang

turned over corporate operations to his eldest son, Frederick A. Wang, and promoted
him to president.

"In the long term," said Fred Wang, "the committee will make general strategic decisions, and the functional arms will carry them out."[4] The group also was
formed to broaden top management's perspective. Managers continue to run their
own division on a day-to-day basis. The committee then provides a good forum to
air issues that cut across functional lines. Decisions once made during casual hallway conversations now are brought before the committee through formal presentations. "We are institutionalizing processes that were once informal," said one
manager.[5]

For the first time, too, decisions are being made by consensus rather than by
autocratic leadership. An Wang is largely silent unless the other members cannot
reach a decision or unless he feels that their judgment runs dramatically counter to
his. To counteract the belief among lower-level managers that "the doctor" still calls
all the shots, the committee has begun to issue orders on its own letterhead.

Wang Present and Future

By conservative estimates, sales by America's computer industry were expected to
grow 8 percent in 1986, to $95 billion—not bad in a sluggish economy. The business
is stuck in its worst slump in a decade. What began in 1985 with consolidation
among makers of low-priced home computers now has spread to manufacturers of
more expensive personal computers, minicomputers, mainframes, and the silicon
components that fuel them all.

Industry sales have slowed to a crawl. Profit margins, and in many cases profits
themselves, are evaporating. Layoffs, plant closings, and shortened workweeks
abound. Total employment in computers and semiconductors has fallen 30,000, or
2.5 percent, since January 1985. Sales changes from the previous year are

1981	15.0%
1982	15.5%
1983	14.2%
1984	16.5%
1985 (est.)	7.9%

Beginning in 1975, the company's earnings rose every quarter for ten years. However, in the quarter that ended in March 1985, they fell by two-thirds. In June 1986
Wang fired 1,600 employees—5 percent of its work force.

The computer slump has hit Wang hard. It must cope with a strategic shift that
brings it up against IBM. Unlike Apple Computer, which suffers in its competition
with IBM from lack of big company accounts, Wang is at home with *Fortune* 500
companies. Wang achieved this status by selling word processors—computers that

manipulate only text—to department heads and secretaries, not to information systems managers. The success of multipurpose personal computers has weakened Wang's word-processor market.

One of Wang's biggest weaknesses is its sales organization. A company's data processing managers, not just department heads, get involved in decisions about integrated office systems. These managers know and like IBM. Wang has not been making its case to them.[6]

Another problem is that, unlike IBM, Wang has been secretive about the specifications of its personal computers, thus putting off independent software writers and equipment producers. Until 1986, Wang had been reluctant to provide links from its computers to IBM's. All the problems Wang is facing now put a premium on management skills that were not in demand during the early years.

The problem Wang must remedy is its reputation for failing to help customers integrate their word processing systems with computers made by other companies. A hardware designer by training, An Wang tended to see "software as a necessary evil," said a former staffer. "Wang used to say: 'If you want to hook up with somebody else, that's your problem,'" said Dennis Barnes, a systems analyst at Thousand Trails, Inc., a private campsite organization that uses Wang equipment. "Now," he added, "that's starting to change."[7]

Although Wang failed to anticipate the need for different brands of computers to communicate with each other inside an office, it did foresee its customers' larger communications needs. Wang Labs bought a range of satellite frequencies long before their usefulness for data communications was fully understood, and it now sells satellite time to corporate customers.

The fallout from Wang's current troubles may be difficult to overcome. Vincent Flanders, who edits *Access 86,* an independent magazine for Wang customers, feels Wang has become a technological follower instead of a leader. "IBM used to be scared of Wang because they had the best and brightest people," he said. "That is no longer the case."[8]

CONCLUSION

Wang has been in business for over ten years but only recently is it being truly tested. Wang had never had a losing quarter until 1985. Wang will now have to do some strategic planning to turn the situation around. To stay in front in the industry, Wang must manage its product entries, growth, and profitability with care. Wang seems to be aware of the challenges that lie ahead. Now that it is a major market player, it needs to straighten out the problems addressed in this case to keep customers and dealers happy. The need to be a contender in the office of the future is enticing every major data processing operator in the business. New product development and marketing muscle is the name of the game. If Wang falters, IBM and others will be there to pick up any slack. For Fred Wang, this is a time of opportunity and risk: a time for a new strategy at Wang.

Notes

1   "Strong Medicine from the Son of Doctor Wang," *Business Week*, January 19, 1987, 33.
2   Wang Annual Report, 1986.
3   "Wang Labs' Run for a Second Billion," *Business Week*, May 17, 1982, 102.
4   Ibid.
5   Ibid.
6   "The Market Isn't to Blame for All Wang's Woes," *Business Week*, June 10, 1985, 48.
7   "Wang Labs Wrestles with the Question: What Happens After An Wang?" *Business Week*, June 30, 1986, 82.
8   Ibid., 23.

EXHIBIT 1
Financial Highlights (dollar amounts in millions except per share data)

	1986	1985	Change (%)
Revenues	$2,642.5	$2,351.7	+ 12
Net earnings	50.9	15.5	+228
Net earnings per share	.35	.11	+218
Total assets	2,649.3	2,375.9	+ 12
Stockholders' equity	1,447.6	1,248.3	+ 16
Average number of employees	31,000	31,700	− 2

EXHIBIT 2
The Top 10 in Minicomputers

DTM 100 Rank	Company	1984 Revenues (in millions)	1983 Revenues (in millions)	% Change
1	IBM	3,000.0	2,627.0	14.1
2	Digital Equipment Corp.	1,527.0	1,000.0	52.7
11	Wang Laboratories Inc.	970.0	892.9	8.6
8	Hewlett-Packard Co.	950.0	735.3	29.1
18	Data General Corp.	840.0	706.0	18.9
3	UNISYS	700.0	650.0	7.6
13	Ing. C. Olivetti & Co. S.P.A.	540.1	490.5	10.1*
40	Prime Computer Inc.	479.1	416.5	15.0
45	Tandem Computers Inc.	477.1	387.4	23.1
22	Toshiba Corp.	421.0	378.9	11.1*

*In actual accounting currencies, Olivetti mini revenues were up 27.4% to $949 billion; Toshiba mini revenues were u 11% to $100 billion.

Source: Pamela Archbold and John Verity "A Global Industry . . . The Datamation 100," *Datamation* 31 (June 1, 1985), 38.

EXHIBIT 3
Wang's Organizational Chart

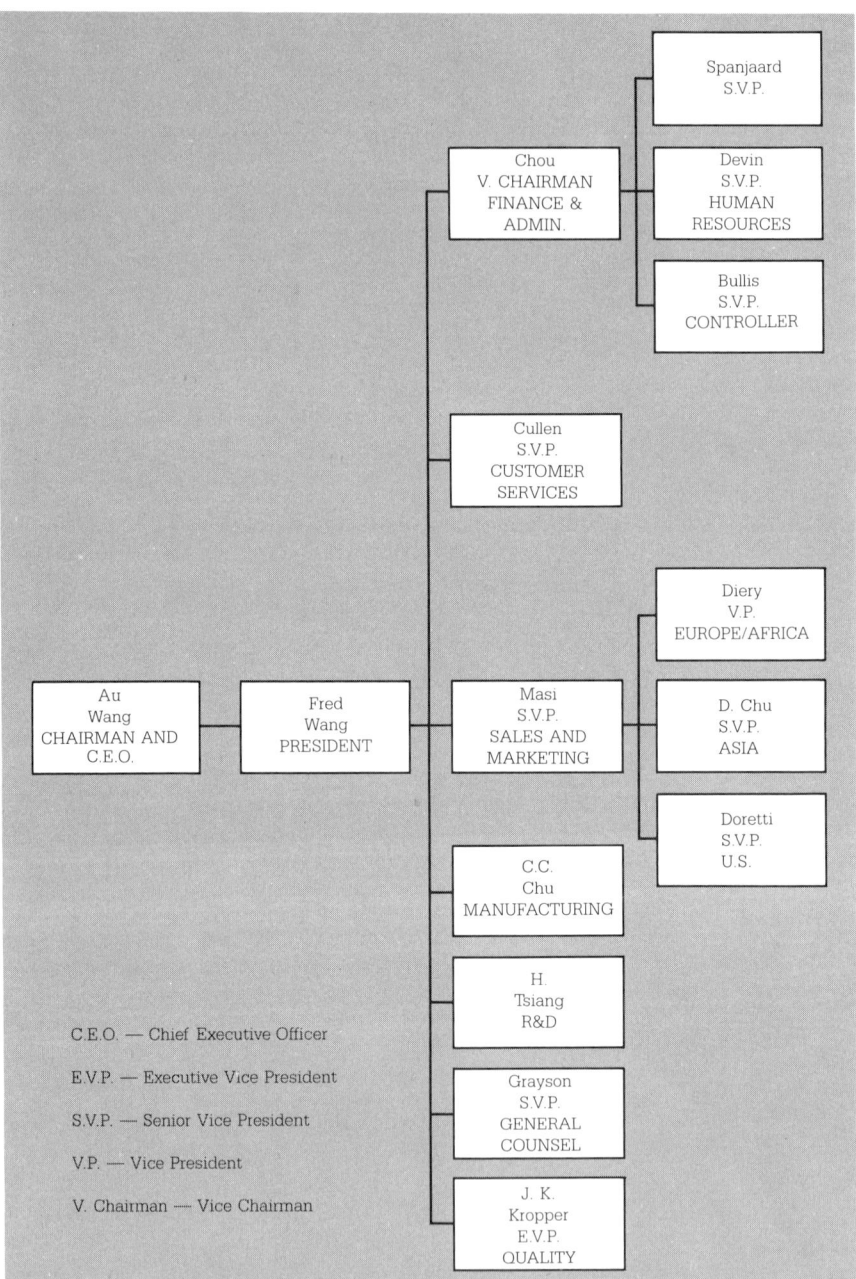

EXHIBIT 4
Revenues (See Exhibits 5–8 for operating statements)

Revenues
Revenue increases by major geographic areas were as follows:

	1986	1985	1984
United States	**4.7%**	5.9%	39.8%
International:			
Europe, Africa and Middle East .	33.3	6.4	42.1
Asia/Pacific	15.7	38.9	48.3
Americas	21.1	(10.9)	62.5
Total International	26.5	10.9	46.7
Consolidated	**12.4%**	7.6%	42.0%

( ) denotes decrease

International revenues were affected by fluctuating international currencies against the U.S. dollar. Had such currencies remained constant during each year against the U.S. dollar compared to the previous year, international revenues would have been approximately $96 million lower in 1986, $107 million higher in 1985 and $48 million higher in 1984.

Increases in product sales in 1986 and 1985 are attributable to international operations, as the prolonged weakness in the U.S. computer market has resulted in flat domestic product sales for both years.

Percentage increases in service and rental income exceeded corresponding increases in net product sales due to the effect of the increasing installed base of equipment and the attendant maintenance contract income.

Costs and Expenses
Product cost in Fiscal 1986 was 51.1% of product revenue, compared to 54.4% in 1985 and 43.7% in 1984. Improvements in product cost in 1986 compared to 1985 resulted principally from reduced spending for manufacturing labor

and overhead. Increases in product costs as a percentage of revenue in 1985 reflected increasingly competitive pricing practices in the industry for all products as well as the effect of an increasing proportion of revenues from the Professional Computer class of product, which has lower gross margins than the Company's other products. Gross margins in 1985 also reflected increased volume of indirect sales to software vendors, dealers and distributors, which have higher discounts and lower selling costs than direct sales to end-users. Increased product costs in Fiscal 1985 also reflected higher manufacturing fixed costs resulting from investments in additional production capacity and attendant overhead without commensurate increases in shipment volume. Gross profit margins have also been affected by the impact on revenues of fluctuating international currencies.

Gross margins from service and rental were 34.5% in 1986, 26.4% in 1985 and 22.9% in 1984, reflecting increasing productivity of service activities through improvements in customer service logistics as well as improved product quality and reliability.

Increases in research and development expense reflect continuing commitment to development of new hardware products and associated operating system software. During 1986, the Company adopted a change in accounting for costs of computer software, which reduced 1986 research and development expense by $21.1 million.

Increases in selling, general and administrative expenses reflect investments in additional sales and support personnel as well as investments in marketing and customer and employee training programs. The average number of sales and sales support employees increased approximately 6% in 1986 compared to 1985, and approximately 22% in 1985 compared to 1984.

During 1986, the Company made investments in new communications and services ventures, which reduced earnings before income taxes by approximately $23 million.

EXHIBIT 5

Consolidated Balance Sheets Wang Laboratories, Inc., and Subsidiaries

(Dollar amounts in millions) June 30	1986	1985
Assets		
Current Assets		
Cash	$ 38.0	$ 31.1
Temporary cash investments	119.7	17.2
Accounts receivable, less allowances ($27.8 in 1986 and $22.3 in 1985)	530.1	479.4
Inventories	448.4	469.4
Prepaid expenses and other current assets	68.0	52.2
Total Current Assets	1,204.2	1,049.3
Spare parts and rental equipment, less accumulated depreciation ($218.0 in 1986 and $164.4 in 1985)	347.4	311.2
Property, plant and equipment, less accumulated depreciation ($443.5 in 1986 and $319.9 in 1985)	737.7	715.1
Investments	240.2	220.9
Other assets	119.8	79.4
	$2,649.3	$2,375.9
Liabilities and Stockholders' Equity		
Current Liabilities		
Notes payable to banks	$ 10.1	$ 64.0
Commercial paper		2.7
Accounts payable, other payables and accruals	333.0	268.9
Unearned service revenue	122.1	90.7
Income taxes	12.1	9.4
Dividends payable to stockholders	6.0	5.5
Portion of long-term debt due within one year	54.6	13.8
Total Current Liabilities	537.9	455.0
Long-Term Debt, less current portion (including subordinated long-term debt of $426.1 in 1986 and $420.2 in 1985)	656.5	666.6
Deferred Income Taxes	7.3	6.0
Stockholders' Equity		
Class B Common Stock (144,937,333 shares outstanding in 1986 and 133,622,841 shares outstanding in 1985)	72.5	66.8
Class C Common Stock (6,028,945 shares outstanding in 1986 and 6,174,550 shares outstanding in 1985)	3.0	3.1
Capital in excess of par value	781.5	595.1
Unrealized foreign currency translation adjustments	(66.7)	(47.0)
Retained earnings	658.9	630.9
Less cost of treasury stock	(1.6)	(.6)
	1,447.6	1,248.3
	$2,649.3	$2,375.9

EXHIBIT 6
Geographic Information

Certain information on a geographic basis follows:

(Dollar amounts in millions)	1986	1985	1984
Revenue from unaffiliated customers:			
United States, including direct export sales ...	$1,689.3	$1,616.0	$1,555.2
Europe	602.4	431.6	385.8
Asia/Pacific	247.7	210.4	148.5
Americas	103.1	93.7	95.2
	$2,642.5	$2,351.7	$2,184.7
Interarea transfers:			
United States	$ 232.9	$ 265.7	$ 179.3
Europe	43.7	44.8	25.4
Asia/Pacific	65.9	145.7	74.5
Americas	6.3		
	$ 348.8	$ 456.2	$ 279.2
Earnings (loss) before income taxes:			
United States	$ (8.9)	$ (158.0)	$ 178.4
Europe	57.7	48.6	52.5
Asia/Pacific	.2	58.8	30.6
Americas	(5.0)	(.2)	4.9
Eliminations	11.9	(3.7)	(5.2)
	$ 55.9	$ (54.5)	$ 261.2
Identifiable assets (excluding intercompany):			
United States	$1,896.1	$1,816.5	$1,720.1
Europe	464.8	325.6	317.3
Asia/Pacific	232.4	189.9	175.7
Americas	75.8	68.6	66.7
Eliminations	(19.8)	(24.7)	(27.9)
	$2,649.3	$2,375.9	$2,251.9
United States direct export sales to:			
Europe, Africa and Middle East	$ 30.8	$ 43.5	$ 60.8
Asia/Pacific	29.6	29.3	24.1
Americas	34.7	20.1	32.5
	$ 95.1	$ 92.9	$ 117.4

Liabilities related to operations outside the United States amounted to (in millions): $200.6 in 1986, $156.8 in 1985 and $150.8 in 1984, excluding intercompany accounts.

Realized foreign currency exchange and translation gains (losses) amounted to (in millions): $(6.8) in 1986, $.7 in 1985 and $2.4 in 1984.

EXHIBIT 7

Statement of Consolidated Earnings Adjusted for Changing Prices for the Year Ended June 30, 1986 and Five-Year Comparison

Statement of Consolidated Earnings Adjusted for Changing Prices for the Year Ended June 30, 1986

(Dollar amounts in millions except per share data)	As Reported in Financial Statements (Historical Cost)	Adjusted for Changes in Specific Prices (Current Cost)
Revenues	$2,642.5	$2,642.5
Cost of products and services sold (a)	1,341.5	1,314.6
Depreciation and amortization	223.2	191.8
Other operating expenses (a)	961.6	961.6
Interest — net	60.3	60.3
Provision for income taxes	5.0	5.0
	2,591.6	2,533.3
Net earnings	$ 50.9	$ 109.2
Net earnings per share	$ .35	$ .75
Net assets at June 30, 1986 (b)		$1,529.5
Purchasing power (loss) resulting from holding of net monetary assets during the year		$ (6.6)
Increase in the specific prices (current cost) of inventories, rental equipment, spare parts and property, plant, and equipment		$ 29.2
Less increases in the general price level (constant dollars) of these items		10.3
Excess of increase in specific prices over increase in general price level		$ 18.9
Aggregate translation adjustment on a current cost basis		$ 20.8

(a) Excludes depreciation.
(b) At June 30, 1986 the current cost of inventory was $446.5 and the current cost of rental equipment, spare parts and property, plant, and equipment net of accumulated depreciation was $1,168.8.

Five-Year Comparison of Selected Financial Data Adjusted for Inflation

(Dollar amounts in millions except per share data) Year Ended June 30	1986	1985	1984	1983	1982
Revenues	$2,642.5	$2,419.2	$2,335.1	$1,704.3	$1,339.3
Net earnings, adjusted for specific price changes	109.2	46.8	236.1	158.3	118.3
Net earnings per share, adjusted for specific price changes	.75	.33	1.70	1.21	.97
Excess (deficiency) of increase in specific prices of inventories, rental equipment, spare parts and property, plant and equipment over increase in general price levels	18.9	(.7)	(.7)	40.9	11.8
Purchasing power gain (loss) resulting from holding of net monetary assets or liabilities during the year	(6.6)	(13.5)	(5.0)	(1.1)	6.7
Net assets at year-end, adjusted for specific price changes	1,529.5	1,367.3	1,354.2	1,021.4	706.6
Cash dividends declared per share adjusted for general inflation:					
Class B	.16	.16	.13	.10	.07
Class C	.11	.11	.07	.04	.01
Market price per share at year-end adjusted for general inflation:					
Class B	15.13	18.52	30.20	41.69	15.96
Class C	15.00	18.26	29.93	42.66	13.72
Average consumer price index (Calendar 1967 = 100)	325.9	316.8	304.9	294.1	282.1

EXHIBIT 8
Directors and Officers

Board of Directors	An Wang	Chairman of the Board, President and Chief Executive Officer
	*Leo L Beranek	Communications engineering consultant
	*Peter A Brooke	Managing Partner of TA Associates (venture capital management)
	Louis W Cabot	Chairman of the Board, Cabot Corporation (specialty metals, performance chemicals, and oil and gas products)
	Harry H S Chou	Vice Chairman and Chief Financial Officer
	Martin Kirkpatrick	Patent lawyer
	Richard A Smith	Chairman of the Board and Chief Executive Officer, General Cinema Corporation (soft drink bottler and film exhibitor)
	*Ernest F Stockwell, Jr	Senior Vice President, Bank of Boston
	Paul E Tsongas	Partner, Foley, Hoag & Eliot (law firm)
	Frederick A Wang	Executive Vice President and Treasurer
	Lorraine C Wang	Founding director of the Company, Stockholder

Members of Audit Committee

Corporate Officers	An Wang	Chairman of the Board, President and Chief Executive Officer
	Harry H S Chou	Vice Chairman and Chief Financial Officer
	Frederick A Wang	Executive Vice President and Treasurer
	Eugene M Bullis	Senior Vice President and Corporate Controller
	Dodge Chu	Senior Vice President
	Raymond C Cullen, Jr	Senior Vice President
	Edward J Devin	Senior Vice President
	Ian Diery	Senior Vice President
	Robert L Doretti	Senior Vice President
	Edward D Grayson	Senior Vice President, General Counsel, Clerk, and Secretary
	Paul Guzzi	Senior Vice President
	Johannes Spanjaard	Senior Vice President
	Horace Tsiang	Senior Vice President and Chief Development Officer

Other Officers	Harold P Ano ... Vice President	Thomas R Henninger ... Vice President	
	Robert E Aspell ... Vice President	Herbert S Holzman ... Vice President	
	Geoffroy de Belloy ... Vice President	Stephen P Jonas ... Vice President	
	Robert Bozeman, Sr. ... Vice President; President, Wang Information Services Corp.	A Laurence Jones ... Vice President; President, Wang Financial Information Services Corp.	
	Carleton A Brown ... Vice President	Joseph Klementovich ... Vice President	
	John J Bucsi ... Vice President	Robert S Kolk ... Vice President	
	Robert E Carr ... Vice President	Robert N Lesnick ... Vice President	
	John T Chambers ... Vice President	Martin A Miller ... Vice President, Assistant Treasurer	
	Leo C Chan ... Vice President	Paul L Mucci ... Vice President	
	Chauncey C Chu ... Vice President	Eoin O'Driscoll ... Vice President	
	Michael F Clarkin ... Vice President	Richard J Orlando ... Vice President	
	Peter J Conley ... Assistant Treasurer	Rosallie Papoutsy ... Vice President	
	Richard Connaughton ... Vice President	Gerald Paul ... Vice President	
	C Ernest Cornelssen ... Vice President	Rhea Pomerleau ... Vice President	
	Timothy C Cronin ... Vice President	Paul W Sandman ... Vice President, Assistant Clerk and Assistant Secretary	
	Ralph Crusius ... Vice President		
	Robert Curtis ... Vice President	Dennis J Shepard ... Vice President	
	Paul Demko ... Vice President	Donald R Shriner ... Vice President	
	Donald J Desrochers ... Vice President	Eugene L Shugoll ... Vice President	
	Michael P Downes ... Vice President	Ronald A Smith ... Vice President	
	Donald Dunning ... Vice President	John C Thibault ... Vice President; Designated Executive, InteCom Acquisition	
	Michael B Fox ... Vice President		
	Samuel F Gagliano ... Vice President	Han van de Ven ... Vice President	
	Edward V Garcia ... Vice President	Arend Vleggeert ... Vice President	
	Martin Goldman ... Vice President, Assistant Treasurer	Eli Wackstein ... Vice President	
	Louis B Green ... Vice President	Courtney S Wang ... Vice President; President, Wang Communications, Inc.	
	Noel E Greiner ... Vice President		
	David J Hennessey ... Vice President	Edward V Yang ... Vice President	
		Florence F S Yen ... Vice President	

Avon Products, 1986

William R. Wynd
Donald F. Harvey
Eastern Washington University

INTRODUCTION

Hicks Waldron has probably not even had the time yet to fully savor the spectacular view of Central Park his luxuriously appointed office affords. The chairman and CEO of Avon Products, Inc., has been putting the 100-year-old direct seller—the world's largest—through some pretty stiff paces. He is rethinking, replotting, and reorganizing Avon's basic business plan because the direct selling division, which still makes up 74 percent of the company's $3 billion sales, is in serious trouble.

"This company was built on the practice that all you had to do was get 10,000 representatives out in the field and sales went up, earnings went up, and the stock price went up," related Waldron. "But beginning in 1979 and 1980, you couldn't just add 10,000 or 20,000 salespersons. The old system that had worked for ninety-six years failed to work."[1]

In 1986, Hicks Waldron was faced with a dilemma. Since David H. McConnell founded the small California perfume company in 1886, Avon has relied on canvassing agents to sell its products. McConnell's experience as a door-to-door salesman was refined by P. F. E. Albee, America's first Avon lady. In a dozen years she had organized and trained a sales force of 5,000 representatives. Today Avon has 425,000 salespersons in the United States, and many executives still believe that direct selling is the primary reason for their success. However, Avon's earnings have been sagging in recent years, and many managers have begun to question direct selling as the best way to market Avon's products.[2] Hicks Waldron, chief executive officer, wanted to review the distribution strategy and find ways of strengthening the company's position. (See exhibit 1 for financial highlights.)

MARKET

Industry

The toiletries and cosmetics industry is mature. Analysts say it is capable of generating an annual unit volume growth of no more than 2 percent on a sustained basis. Too many vendors are aggressively competing for a larger share of a market that is not expanding rapidly enough to keep them all happy.

This case was prepared using published accounts and public documents for the purpose of class discussion rather than to illustrate either effective or ineffective handling of an administrative situation.

During the sixties and seventies, companies in the industry grew at above average rates as more and more women entered the labor force and purchased cosmetics in increasing amounts. Now that trend has about run its course, and future volume growth should return to no more than the expansion in population. Continuing competition for market share often means costly new product introductions, heavy advertising, and price restraints. Furthermore, the strength of the dollar will continue to adversely affect sales overseas, a market that accounts for a significant portion of sales and earnings for some firms in the industry.

One analyst believes cosmetic firms are finally realizing that the consumer is more sophisticated than they may have thought.[3] In 1980 when the unit volume in the industry was flat, manufacturers hit the panic button and boosted prices 15 to 20 percent. The next year they increased again by 12 to 15 percent. They hoped to preserve historical profit margins; however, it didn't work, and volume declined. In 1983 they dramatically increased advertising budgets, but still failed to see much of an increase in volume. Now firms are taking a serious look at their research and development labs to create differentiated products. Some are reviewing their distribution structure. Mary Kay Cosmetics, which also employs the direct selling approach, has strengthened its position by new incentives designed to reward top recruiters and sales representatives generously. In addition, they have fine-tuned various rules of the game to enhance the productivity of the reps. Mary Kay has also concentrated on the fastest growing segment of the cosmetic industry: skin care. Margins for skin care products are about twice as high as they are for makeup.[4]

Some analysts believe that direct distribution, not only in cosmetics but also in other industries, is becoming obsolete. With increased labor force participation by women, the number of available sales representatives has declined. Not as many women want to work part-time for low wages. Moreover, women are often not home when the Avon Lady calls or are not available for a Tupperware Party.

Products

Avon Products, Inc., is a diversified company which includes the Avon, Health Care, and Direct Response divisions. Avon's products division accounts for about three-quarters of the company's sales. In 1982 Avon began acquisitions in the rapidly growing health care industry. In that year it acquired Mallinkrodt, Inc., a maker of diagnostic products in addition to chemicals for cosmetics, flavors, and fragrances. In 1984 it strengthened its position by acquiring Foster Medical Corporation, a distributor of wheelchairs, hospital beds, and other items. Acquisition of these two companies has resulted in a decline of working capital and a significant increase in long-term debt (see exhibit 1). Some analysts believe that Avon paid too much for its latest acquisition.[5] In 1986 Avon divested Mallinckrodt for $675 million.

When Avon began selling woman's clothing by direct mail catalogue in 1974, sales were brisk. However, since then sales have fallen off dramatically. Avon has added children's and men's apparel to its catalogues in an effort to revive sales. They are encountering stiff competition from direct mail experts such as L. L. Bean, Inc., and Land's End.

Waldron is also trying to change Avon from a distribution-oriented company to a brand-marketing firm. Avon was also slow to recognize a growing trend toward skin-care products. Although Avon has carried an excellent line of skin-care products, it failed to capitalize on this segment, letting Oil of Olay and others take a significant share of the market.

Sales Representatives

Avon has found it increasingly difficult to recruit sales representatives for its door-to-door sales. In 1983 the number of sales people in the United States fell 3.4 percent to 425,000, its lowest level since 1980. In the first quarter of 1984 the count was down 5 percent from the same period in 1983. Beyond the fact that more women are working full time, those that are left want more from part-time employment. Avon doesn't offer such benefits as a medical plan, life insurance, or paid vacation. The average Avon representative with a territory of 100 homes earned $1,800 in 1982 on sales of $4,600. The average "beauty consultant" for Mary Kay Industries earns $1,450 on $2,900 in sales. That works out to an average sale of $40 per customer for Mary Kay and $8 per customer for the typical Avon representative.[6]

New Plan

Recognizing incentive compensation as a problem, Avon initiated a new, three-part plan which took effect in 1984. First, Avon offered representatives a 5 percent bonus on the sales of each new representative brought into the business for as long as both continue their association with the company. Second, Avon initiated an enriched group sales leader program that gives an additional 3 percent bonus on new recruits in that leader's group. Third, the company established a new compensation structure that enables representatives to earn higher percentages based on their sales volumes.

New Methods

Avon is also exploring new ways to reach its changing consumer. In some test markets Avon mails brochures with an order form to women who are not currently purchasing Avon products. In other markets, the company runs local television ads offering product samples and the Avon brochures through free phone calls to an 800 number. The caller's name is given to a direct sales manager who then asks a local representative to visit the prospect.

Avon has also changed its emphasis on brand name. The latest brochures stress the Avon brand name and the company's cosmetics, fragrances, and newly introduced skin-care products. Gifts and jewelry are deemphasized.

Advertising has also been given a boost. In 1983 the company began a serious effort to rebuild its media pressure. Media expenditures in that year were in excess of three times the 1982 level. Another 30 percent increase was programmed for 1984.

The company's advertising agency, Ogilvy and Mather, is augmenting the sales representative's most important sales tool by designing television spots to highlight specials in the brochures. These sixty-second spots appeared on the top-rated daytime soaps beginning in 1984. Coverage of both the Feraud and Fantastique high-priced cologne and the lesser priced Pave Elle fragrance (targeted towards a younger customer) will continue on daytime and prime time television.

Competition

Meanwhile, several competitors in the beauty sphere have gone after this customer with a vengeance. Most notably, Maybelline and Cover Girl have been highly successful in their product pitches, which promise clean, yet pretty, fashionable looks at prices which promise value. Their product lines are focused and their messages clear.

The major trouble spot for Avon Products will be in weathering the difficult transition period in the all-important direct selling arm. Avon showed only modest improvements in profits in 1984, 1985, and 1986; however, Waldron anticipated a 10 percent increase in both sales and profits by 1988.

Problems

The problems besetting Avon are complex ones. The company has been caught in sociological, psychological, and competitive changes. As more women leave their homes for work in offices, there are fewer potential buyers to open their doors to Avon representatives. Reaching these women in the evening is iffy. Neither buyer nor seller may be keen about venturing out in the evening or letting someone in after dark. And for women away from the homestead during the daytime, the evening hours are often reserved for tending to family and household chores.

Also, while this working woman, theoretically at least, may have more money to spend on cosmetics, fragrances, and personal items, her interest in Avon products seems to be on the wane. Avon's image has been seen as somewhat old-fashioned, sensible, and not too exciting. Avon's image has been further undermined by a product line so broad that it blurred the division's identity. Selling so many diverse items ranging from makeup to fragrances, to toothbrushes, to shaving cream, has made customers feel Avon has no real expertise in any one area.[7]

FINANCIAL

Avon will have to boost its cash flow if it wants to make any significant purchases. Although borrowing should be no problem for Avon, which has long-term debt of less than 24 percent of total capitalization, the company would go deeply into debt if it tried to buy anything that might affect its earnings significantly. The direct-selling business overshadows all else. Investor disenchantment may reflect a long-term problem; too many suppliers eager for a bigger slice of a pie that's not expanding rapidly enough to keep them all happy. Lack of industry growth is not conducive to healthy margins; and profit margins are expected to remain below those of the late 1970s throughout the 1980s.

The greenback's dramatic appreciation against all foreign currencies since 1980 has made life very difficult for the large, multinational companies. Avon, Cheesebrough-Pond's, Gillette, and Revlon all depend on overseas markets for a significant portion of their sales and earnings. (See exhibits 2, 3, 4 and 5 for 1985 financial statements.)

INDUSTRY SEGMENTS

Avon's business is primarily composed of four industry segments. These segments are the manufacture and sale of cosmetics, fragrances and toiletries; the manufacture and sale of fashion jewelry and accessories; the rental and sale of home health care equipment and the sale of medical supplies; and the sale of apparel (see exhibit 6). Operations are conducted in the United States, Europe, Latin America, the Pacific, and Canada.[8] The two principal industry segments are the manufacture and sale of cosmetics, fragrances, and toiletries and of fashion jewelry and accessories. These products are sold directly to customers by Avon representatives. Over 650 products are currently marketed in the United States. Although the products offered in Europe, Latin America, and other parts of the world are not as varied as those sold in the United States, most are substantially the same as those marketed domestically (see exhibit 7).

The Health Care segment was established as a result of the acquisition of Foster Medical Corporation in May 1984. Foster Medical is a leader in the home health care industry and distributes medical supplies. Since the merger was accounted for as a pooling of interests, all financial data and statements have been restated to include the results of Foster Medical.

MARKETING

Avon's newest CEO recognizes that the days of direct selling may be on the wane. He recently announced, "Our future is still in direct selling. That's the goose that laid the golden egg. But we cover only half of the U.S. with representatives. That's a marketing man's dream. We will attack those other thirty-five to forty-five million households. I want to make it possible, yes, even convenient, for every woman in the free world to buy Avon products. We can't do that with direct selling alone."[9]

On the other hand, Yvonne Daly, a direct sales manager in charge of the recruiting, supervising, and training of 200 Avon representatives, said: "The basics haven't changed. The big difference is that twenty-five years ago every order was taken one-on-one. We all knocked on doors. That time is no longer. We do business by dropping off brochures and calling people. Going house to house, that's pie-in-the-sky thinking."[10]

One outside analyst indicated that even if Avon solved its recruiting problem, he couldn't get excited because during the last ten years, every time the company tried something new it lasted for a year to eighteen months only to peter out. The analyst went on to say that there hasn't been much consistency or implementation in past programs.[11] Furthermore, Avon has concentrated on the negative by complaining that there are fewer women at home. On the other side of the coin, there are virtually hundreds more women in the office. Those women buy differently. For example, women are still buying upscale fragrances and cosmetics for sexual-social reasons, but they are buying a different type of fragrance, usually purchased from a mass merchandiser for functional office wear. So far Avon has been unable to penetrate that market.

ORGANIZATION AND MANAGEMENT

The problems at Avon forced Hicks Waldron to conclude that the firm could not go far without a major overhaul and to launch one of the most far-reaching attempts to reorganize a major U.S. corporation. Most analysts agree that what's impressive is how fast these changes are being implemented. "The company has been staid for so many years that any change is very dramatic," noted Allan Mottus, a beauty industry consultant. "Turning around Avon is like turning around an ocean liner."

"We sure as hell have taken a quick directional turn here," agreed Waldron. "But my intent was not to shake things up. My intent was to create change and I think that the change is right on target."[12]

Waldron initiated the overhaul by encouraging his managers to think like strategic planners: developing strategies and contingency plans through an arduous analysis of resources, competitors, economic environment, and opportunities and threats.

John S. Chamberlin was recruited to be the company's president and chief operating officer. He is providing the operational support needed by the chairman and chief executive officer. His appointment also provides for succession and continuity of top management in the longer term.

Stephen F. Nagy was promoted to executive vice president of the company and president of Foster Medical. He has directed Foster Medical's growth to a position of national leadership in home health care. The company also recruited Cam Hoak to be group vice president of human resources and William R. Henn to be group vice president of strategic planning and development. All four officers are members of the corporate management committee. General management, marketing, planning, and operations talent was added in all three divisions (see exhibits 12 and 13).

CONCLUSION

Hicks Waldron was excited about Avon's redirection and believes in the capabilities, commitments, creativity, and loyalty of the employees who will make it work. Most observers of Avon, as well as insiders, credit Waldron with a well-conceived and bold repositioning of his company in attractive markets. Many of them, however, contend that he faces a huge challenge in making the highly praised strategy work.

"We'll do that by selective investment," said Waldron. "If they have ten projects they want to work on, we'll only let them work on eight next year. Then we'll take those cost reductions and reinvest them into other parts of the business."[13]

While Waldron seems to have weighed carefully the risks involved in taking dramatic steps to bring about a new strategy, the plan is faced with potential problems. Avon must learn how to compete strongly in areas it has never before emphasized—such as health products—at a time when competitors are only getting stronger and the sales environment more competitive. Good luck, Avon.

Notes

1 "A Troubled Avon Knocks at Several New Doors," *Marketing and Media Decisions,* November 1984, 68.
2 Ibid., 69.
3 "Avon Tries a New Formula," *Business Week,* July 2, 1984, 46.
4 "Avon, You've Looked Better," *Sales and Marketing Management,* April 5, 1982, 54.
5 "Avon Outlook—Analysts Differ," *The New York Times,* August 29, 1984, F2.
6 "Avon Sets Campaign to Recruit Saleswomen," *The New York Times,* January 6, 1983, F4.
7 "A Troubled Avon," 69.
8 Avon Annual Report, 1986, 8.
9 Beyond Door-to-Door Sales," *The Wall Street Journal,* October 30, 1984, 1.
10 "A Troubled Avon," 70.
11 Ibid.
12 "Avon Tries a New Formula," 48.
13 Ibid., 126.

EXHIBIT 1

Avon Financial Highlights for Year ended December 31 (in millions, except per share amounts)

	1985	1984	1983
Net Sales	$2,470.1	$2,605.3	$2,607.6
Earnings From Continuing Operations			
Before Taxes	224.3	274.1	243.2
Taxes on Earnings	96.1	122.2	108.3
Net Earnings From Continuing Operations	128.2	151.9	134.9
Discontinued Operations:			
Earnings, Net of Taxes	34.9	29.8	38.0
Loss on Disposal, Including Taxes	(223.0)	—	—
Net (Loss) Earnings	(59.9)	181.7	172.9
Per Share of Common Stock:			
Continuing Operations	$ 1.61	$ 1.80	$ 1.61
Discontinued Operations:			
Earnings	.44	.36	.45
Loss on Disposal	(2.81)	—	—
Net (Loss) Earnings	$ (.76)	$ 2.16	$ 2.06
Cash Dividends	$ 2.00	$ 2.00	$ 2.00
Average Shares Outstanding	79.35	83.84	83.58
Cash and Short-Term Investments	$ 86.1	$ 118.5	$ 194.7
Inventories	374.5	356.1	349.5
Working Capital	352.3	284.9	365.9
Long-Term Debt	617.8	412.8	301.2

EXHIBIT 2
Financial Statement

In September 1985, the Company's Board of Directors authorized the purchase of up to 20 million shares of the Company's common stock. In October 1985, the Company signed an agreement with Merrill Lynch, Pierce, Fenner & Smith, Incorporated under which Merrill Lynch purchased 7.8 million shares of the Company's common stock during 1985. The Company had an option to purchase these shares, which it exercised on February 20, 1986. In addition, the Company purchased approximately 2.0 million shares of its common stock during January and February 1986. The cost of these shares was approximately $270 million.

On January 22, 1986, the Company and The Mediplex Group, Inc. ("Mediplex") signed merger agreements under which Mediplex will become a wholly owned subsidiary of the Company. Under the agreements, the Company will acquire all of the outstanding common stock of Mediplex for approximately $182 million in cash and $25 million in notes. Options to acquire approximately 650,000 shares of Mediplex common stock will be purchased for about $11 million. The merger agreements also provide for contingent payments of up to $61 million based on the annual earnings increases of Mediplex over the next three years.

On December 19, 1985, the Company signed an agreement with International Minerals & Chemical Corporation to sell Mallinckrodt, Inc. for $675 million in cash. The sale is expected to close in the first quarter of 1986, subject to completion of regulatory filings and other conditions. Proceeds from the sale of Mallinckrodt will be used to acquire The Mediplex Group, Inc., to make the scheduled purchase of 10 million shares of the Company's common stock and to reduce debt.

During the past three years, the Company has modernized major facilities in several countries. Capital expenditures during this three-year period totaled $305.7 million, a significant portion of which was financed by long-term borrowing. Construction programs in progress at December 31, 1985, carried an estimated cost to complete of $20 million. Capital expenditures in the next three years are expected to be at a higher rate than in the previous three years, primarily as a result of the acquisition of Retirement Inns of America and The Mediplex Group. Based on current projections, the Company will need to finance some of these projects with long-term borrowing.

The maximum amount of additional borrowing during 1986 for seasonal operating needs and facilities expansion projects, primarily in the United States, is estimated to be $85 million. The peak level of borrowings during 1986 for all purposes is not expected to exceed $760 million.

Short-term borrowing consists primarily of borrowings from banks by international subsidiaries. The peak level of such borrowings during 1986 is not expected to exceed that of 1985, which approximated $100 million. Unused lines of credit at December 31, 1985, were approximately $885 million. Of this amount, $630 million was revolving credit facilities used to support the commercial paper issued by the Company. The remaining $255 million was primarily related to international operations.

Discussion of 1985 and 1984

Consolidated net sales were $2.5 billion in 1985, a decrease of $135.2 million from 1984. U.S. net sales decreased 3% to $1.6 billion, and international net sales decreased 8% to $887.9 million. Net earnings from continuing operations decreased 16% to $128.2 million. Net earnings per share from continuing operations were $1.61, compared with $1.80 in 1984.

On December 19, 1985, the Company signed an agreement with International Minerals & Chemical Corporation to sell Mallinckrodt, Inc. for $675 million; accordingly, the financial results of 1985 and 1984 have been restated to reflect Mallinckrodt's results as a discontinued operation. Earnings from discontinued operations, net of taxes, were $34.9 million, compared with $29.8 million in 1984. The loss on disposal of discontinued operations, including taxes, was $223.0 million resulting primarily from capital gains and other taxes and the write-off of goodwill. As a result, the Company incurred a net loss of $59.9 million in 1985.

Financial results for 1984 have been restated to reflect the Company's acquisition of Foster Medical Corporation, which became effective in May 1984.

The decrease in net earnings from continuing operations of $23.7 million (19¢ per share) was caused principally by the following factors:
• Lower net sales, which decreased net earnings by $8.5 million (10¢ per share).
• An increase in marketing, distribution and administrative expenses as a percentage of net sales, which decreased net earnings by $14.4 million (17¢ per share).
• An increase in other deductions—net and interest expense, partially offset by an increase in interest income, which decreased net earnings by $3.9 million (5¢ per share).

The decrease in net earnings from continuing operations of $27.6 million (33¢ per share) was partially offset by the following factors:
• A decrease in the effective income tax rate, which increased net earnings by $3.9 million (5¢ per share).
• Fewer shares outstanding as a result of the purchase of treasury stock during 1984 and 1985, which increased earnings per share from continuing operations by 9¢.

Net sales of the Avon Division's domestic and international operations each decreased by 8%, primarily as a result of the decreased number of representatives. Sales of the Health Care and Direct Response Divisions increased compared with last year.

Cost of goods sold decreased by $51.0 million, but remained level as a percentage of net sales, at 38.8%. Increased cost ratios experienced in the Avon Division's domestic operations and the Direct Response Division were partially offset by a decreased cost ratio in the Health Care Division.

Marketing, distribution and administrative expenses decreased $41.4 million, but increased as a percentage of

EXHIBIT 2 (continued)

net sales, to 50.9% in 1985 from 49.8% in 1984.
Decreases in the Avon Division were partially offset by
increases in the Health Care and Direct Response
Divisions.

Interest income increased $12.1 million primarily as a
result of increased amounts of short-term investments
outside the United States. Interest expense increased
$13.5 million principally due to increased borrowing.
Other deductions—net increased $5.6 million primarily
as a result of higher foreign exchange losses in Mexico.

Taxes on earnings decreased by $26.1 million, and the
effective income tax rate declined to 42.9% in 1985 from
44.6% in 1984. Major factors were lower effective tax
rates on international earnings before nondeductible
foreign exchange losses and tax benefits derived from the
write-off of investments in certain foreign subsidiaries.

EXHIBIT 2 (continued)

The consolidated summary of earnings adjusted for changing prices for the year ended December 31, 1985, follows (in millions):

	As shown in the financial statements (historical cost)	Adjusted for changes in specific prices (current cost)
Net sales	$ 2,470.1	$ 2,470.1
Cost of goods sold	959.5	969.6
Marketing, distribution and administrative expenses	1,256.3	1,267.5
Interest income	46.5	46.5
Interest expense	(63.4)	(63.4)
Other income (deductions)—net	(13.1)	(13.1)
Taxes on earnings	96.1	96.1
Net earnings from continuing operations	$ 128.2	$ 106.9
Income tax rate	42.9%	47.3%
Depreciation included in:		
Cost of goods sold	$ 22.2	$ 29.8
Marketing, distribution and administrative expenses	33.1	44.3
	$ 55.3	$ 74.1
Purchasing power gain on net monetary items		$ 28.0
Decrease in current cost of inventory and property held during the year		$ (84.6)
Effect of increase in the general price level		54.0
Decrease in current cost over rate of increase in the general price level		$ (138.6)
Adjustment—foreign currency translation		$ 41.7
At December 31, 1985:		
Inventories		$ 412.7
Property—net of accumulated depreciation		1,047.2

Selected financial data adjusted for changing prices in average 1985 dollars (in millions, except per share amounts):

	Year ended December 31				
	1985	1984	1983	1982	1981
Net sales	$2,470.1	$2,698.2	$2,816.7	$3,021.2	$3,223.2
Net earnings from continuing operations	106.9	99.3	113.0	132.9	247.5
Earnings per share from continuing operations	1.35	1.18	1.35	1.73	3.91
Purchasing power gain on net monetary items	28.0	22.7	20.8	10.6	8.6
Increase (decrease) in current cost over (under) changes in the general price level	(138.6)	77.9	261.4	166.1	(.1)
Adjustment—foreign currency translation	41.7	(54.7)	(55.2)	(169.8)	(77.8)
Net assets, December 31	1,338.8	1,779.3	2,131.6	1,978.8	1,512.4
Dividends per share	2.00	2.07	2.16	2.79	3.54
Market price, December 31	27.19	22.34	26.68	29.55	34.34
Average consumer price index (1967 = 100)	322.2	311.1	298.4	289.1	272.4

EXHIBIT 3

Consolidated Statement of Financial Condition for Avon Products, Inc., and Subsidiaries (in millions of dollars)

	December 31	
	1985	1984
Assets		
Current assets		
Cash and short-term investments	$ 86.1	$ 118.5
Accounts receivable (less allowance for doubtful accounts of $38.6 and $28.6)	264.6	202.5
Inventories	374.5	356.1
Prepaid expenses	169.8	144.5
Total current assets	895.0	821.6
Property	989.4	855.1
Less accumulated depreciation	323.0	270.9
	666.4	584.2
Excess of cost over net assets acquired	106.1	73.1
Deferred charges	96.6	77.6
Net assets of discontinued operations	524.9	731.0
	$2,289.0	$2,287.5
Liabilities and Shareholders' Equity		
Current liabilities		
Notes payable	$ 58.8	$ 67.8
Accounts payable	134.2	130.9
Accrued expenses	137.3	131.5
Accrued compensation	41.9	33.6
Retail sales and other taxes	66.3	67.2
Taxes on earnings	104.2	105.7
Total current liabilities	542.7	536.7
Long-term debt	617.8	412.8
Other liabilities	50.4	48.9
Deferred income taxes	151.7	132.0
Shareholders' equity		
Common stock, par value $.50; authorized 200,000,000 shares		
Issued 85,582,904 and 85,421,032 shares	42.8	42.7
Additional paid-in capital	470.0	466.5
Foreign currency translation adjustments	(148.8)	(153.6)
Retained earnings	706.3	925.5
Treasury stock, at cost—6,346,797 and 5,457,332 shares	(143.9)	(124.0)
Total shareholders' equity	926.4	1,157.1
	$2,289.0	$2,287.5

EXHIBIT 4

Consolidated Statement of Earnings and Retained Earnings for Avon Products, Inc., and Subsidiaries (in millions, except per share amounts)

	Year Ended December 31		
	1985	1984	1983
Net sales:			
United States	$1,582.2	$1,638.8	$1,639.7
International	887.9	966.5	967.9
	2,470.1	2,605.3	2,607.6
Cost of goods sold	959.5	1,010.5	1,052.0
Gross profit	1,510.6	1,594.8	1,555.6
Marketing, distribution and administrative expenses	1,256.3	1,297.7	1,277.5
Operating profit	254.3	297.1	278.1
Interest income	46.5	34.4	38.6
Interest expense	(63.4)	(49.9)	(43.6)
Other income (deductions)—net	(13.1)	(7.5)	(29.9)
Earnings from continuing operations before taxes	224.3	274.1	243.2
Taxes on earnings	96.1	122.2	108.3
Net earnings from continuing operations	128.2	151.9	134.9
Discontinued operations:			
Earnings, net of taxes	34.9	29.8	38.0
Loss on disposal, including taxes	(223.0)	—	—
Net (loss) earnings	(59.9)	181.7	172.9
Retained earnings, January 1	925.5	901.6	878.4
Cash dividends	159.3	157.8	149.7
Retained earnings, December 31	$ 706.3	$ 925.5	$ 901.6
Per share of common stock:			
Continuing operations	$1.61	$1.80	$1.61
Discontinued operations:			
Earnings	.44	.36	.45
Loss on disposal	(2.81)	—	—
Net (loss) earnings	$ (.76)	$2.16	$2.06
Cash dividends	$2.00	$2.00	$2.00
Average shares outstanding	79.35	83.84	83.58

EXHIBIT 5

Consolidated Statement of Changes in Financial Position for Avon Products, Inc., and Subsidiaries (in millions)

	Year Ended December 31		
	1985	1984	1983
Sources of working capital			
Net earnings from continuing operations	**$128.2**	$151.9	$134.9
Add			
Depreciation	**55.3**	52.2	41.2
Amortization of intangibles	**2.3**	1.3	.4
Deferred income taxes	**19.7**	20.3	7.3
Working capital provided from operations	**205.5**	225.7	183.8
Working capital provided from discontinued operations	**74.4**	65.2	73.8
Increase in long-term debt	**205.0**	114.1	14.2
Decrease in net asset position of discontinued operations	**166.6**	(67.3)	.8
Disposals of property	**7.8**	10.8	8.7
Treasury stock contributed to employee benefit plan	**5.4**	—	—
Common stock issued	**3.6**	5.7	40.1
	668.3	354.2	321.4
Uses of working capital			
Loss on disposal of discontinued operations	**223.0**	—	—
Cash dividends	**159.3**	157.8	149.7
Additions to property	**91.2**	104.2	110.3
Businesses acquired and sold	**75.8**	23.0	—
Purchase of treasury stock	**25.3**	124.0	—
Additions to deferred charges	**4.1**	17.2	(8.0)
Decrease in other liabilities	**7.8**	4.0	5.7
Effect of foreign currency translation adjustments on working capital	**14.4**	5.0	2.3
	600.9	435.2	260.0
Increase (decrease) in working capital	**$ 67.4**	$(81.0)	$ 61.4
Changes in components of working capital			
Cash and short-term investments	**$ (32.4)**	$(76.2)	$ 66.5
Accounts receivable	**62.1**	(24.9)	(2.2)
Inventories	**18.4**	6.6	(19.0)
Prepaid expenses	**25.3**	26.4	1.5
Notes payable	**9.0**	(3.0)	16.8
Accounts payable and accrued expenses	**(17.4)**	7.8	(80.3)
Accrued taxes	**2.4**	(17.7)	78.1
Increase (decrease) in working capital	**$ 67.4**	$(81.0)	$ 61.4

EXHIBIT 6
Industry Segments (in millions)

Industry Segments

(in millions)

	Net Sales	Operating Profit	Year Ended December 31 Identifiable Assets	Depreciation Expense	Additions To Property
1985					
Cosmetics, fragrances and toiletries	$1,609.6	$192.3	$ 963.2	$29.2	$ 35.1
Fashion jewelry and accessories	394.2	42.3	244.2	6.2	7.9
Health care	260.3	51.2	315.6	16.4	40.4
Direct response	205.2	8.8	128.8	1.2	3.3
Net assets of discontinued operations	—	—	524.9	—	—
Corporate and eliminations	.8	(40.3)	112.3	2.3	4.5
Consolidated	$2,470.1	$254.3	$2,289.0	$55.3	$ 91.2
1984					
Cosmetics, fragrances and toiletries	$1,832.3	$237.2	$ 945.2	$31.3	$ 51.8
Fashion jewelry and accessories	350.9	55.0	204.4	7.2	7.5
Health care	159.0	22.3	194.1	10.7	26.1
Direct response	186.0	2.9	100.2	.6	4.5
Other	77.6	(.5)	—	1.1	8.2
Net assets of discontinued operations	—	—	731.0	—	—
Corporate and eliminations	(.5)	(19.8)	112.6	1.3	6.1
Consolidated	$2,605.3	$297.1	$2,287.5	$52.2	$104.2
1983					
Cosmetics, fragrances and toiletries	$1,881.6	$233.6	$ 945.7	$30.9	$ 70.6
Fashion jewelry and accessories	330.2	47.3	166.7	4.8	10.2
Health care	126.6	12.9	82.5	3.6	11.9
Direct response	144.0	11.7	55.7	.6	5.4
Other	124.6	8.0	127.8	1.3	8.4
Net assets of discontinued operations	—	—	699.1	—	—
Corporate and eliminations	.6	(35.4)	179.3	—	3.8
Consolidated	$2,607.6	$278.1	$2,256.8	$41.2	$110.3

EXHIBIT 7
Geographic Areas (in millions)

Geographic Areas

(in millions)

	Net Sales	Operating Profit	Year Ended December 31 Identifiable Assets	Depreciation Expense	Additions To Property
1985					
United States	$1,581.4	$155.6	$1,126.6	$35.9	$ 68.3
Europe	290.7	32.8	182.5	5.9	7.5
Latin America	324.2	58.4	178.6	6.4	5.8
Pacific and Canada	273.0	47.8	164.1	4.8	5.1
Total international.	887.9	139.0	525.2	17.1	18.4
Net assets of discontinued operations	—	—	524.9	—	—
Corporate and eliminations	.8	(40.3)	112.3	2.3	4.5
Consolidated	$2,470.1	$254.3	$2,289.0	$55.3	$ 91.2
1984					
United States	$1,639.3	$172.4	$ 943.7	$32.9	$ 68.0
Europe	332.6	27.9	161.4	6.1	9.1
Latin America	346.0	64.7	193.5	7.3	15.1
Pacific and Canada	287.9	51.9	145.3	4.6	5.9
Total international.	966.5	144.5	500.2	18.0	30.1
Net assets of discontinued operations	—	—	731.0	—	—
Corporate and eliminations	(.5)	(19.8)	112.6	1.3	6.1
Consolidated	$2,605.3	$297.1	$2,287.5	$52.2	$104.2
1983					
United States	$1,639.1	$197.5	$ 849.7	$23.6	$ 68.1
Europe	373.9	31.1	188.0	7.3	9.1
Latin America	310.4	39.6	199.3	6.4	17.1
Pacific and Canada	283.6	45.3	141.4	3.9	12.2
Total international.	967.9	116.0	528.7	17.6	38.4
Net assets of discontinued operations	—	—	699.1	—	—
Corporate and eliminations	.6	(35.4)	179.3	—	3.8
Consolidated	$2,607.6	$278.1	$2,256.8	$41.2	$110.3

EXHIBIT 8

Ten-Year Review of Avon Prodcuts, Inc., and Subsidiaries (in millions of dollars, except per share amounts)

	1985	1984
Net Sales:		
United States	$1,582.2	$1,638.8
International	887.9	966.5
	2,470.1	2,605.3
Cost of goods sold	959.5	1,010.5
Gross profit	1,510.6	1,594.8
Marketing, distribution and administrative expenses	1,256.3	1,297.7
Operating profit	254.3	297.1
Interest income	46.5	34.4
Interest expense	(63.4)	(49.9)
Other income (deductions)—net	(13.1)	(7.5)
Earnings from continuing operations before taxes	224.3	274.1
Taxes on earnings	96.1	122.2
Net earnings from continuing operations	128.2	151.9
Discontinued operations:		
Earnings, net of taxes	34.9	29.8
Loss on disposal, including taxes	(223.0)	—
Net (loss) earnings	$ (59.9)	$ 181.7
Per share of stock:		
Continuing operations	$ 1.61	$ 1.80
Discontinued operations	(2.37)	.36
Net (loss) earnings	$ (.76)	$ 2.16
Cash dividends	$ 2.00	$ 2.00
Average shares outstanding (in millions)	79.35	83.84
% to net sales:		
Earnings from continuing operations before taxes	9.1%	10.5%
Net earnings from continuing operations	5.2	5.8
Working capital	$ 352.3	$ 284.9
Current ratio	1.65	1.53
Property—net	666.4	584.2
Capital expenditures	91.2	104.2
Total assets	2,289.0	2,287.5
Long-term debt	617.8	412.8
Shareholders' equity	926.4	1,157.1
Per share	11.69	14.47
Return on continuing operations	13.8%	13.1%
Number of employees:		
United States	18,900	18,800
International	19,500	19,500
	38,400	38,300

EXHIBIT 9

| Management's Responsibility for Financial Reporting | Report of Independent Certified Public Accountants |

Management's Responsibility for Financial Reporting

Management is responsible for all the information and representations contained in the annual report, including the financial statements, which are prepared in accordance with generally accepted accounting principles. Some elements in the statements are based on management's estimates and informed judgments.

The Company maintains systems of internal control to provide reasonable assurance that its financial records are reliable for the purpose of preparing the financial statements, that its assets are adequately protected, and that there is proper authorization and accounting for all transactions. The internal control system is supported by written policies and procedures, by the careful selection and training of qualified personnel, and by an extensive internal auditing program.

The Company's financial statements have been examined by KMG Main Hurdman, independent certified public accountants, as stated in their report. Their examination was made in accordance with generally accepted auditing standards, and included a review and evaluation of internal controls.

The Audit Committee of the Board of Directors, composed solely of outside Directors, is responsible for reviewing and monitoring the quality of the Company's accounting and auditing practices. The Committee meets several times each year with management, the internal auditors and the independent certified public accountants. The independent certified public accountants and internal auditors have complete access to management and to the Audit Committee, and meet with both to discuss their audit activities, the internal controls and financial reporting matters.

Report of Independent Certified Public Accountants

The Shareholders and Board of Directors of Avon Products, Inc.

We have examined the consolidated statement of financial condition of Avon Products, Inc. and subsidiaries as of December 31, 1985 and 1984 and the related consolidated statements of earnings and retained earnings and of changes in financial position for each of the three years in the period ended December 31, 1985. Our examinations were made in accordance with generally accepted auditing standards and, accordingly, included such tests of the accounting records and such other auditing procedures as we considered necessary in the circumstances.

In our opinion, the financial statements identified above present fairly the consolidated financial position of Avon Products, Inc. and subsidiaries at December 31, 1985 and 1984 and the consolidated results of their operations and the changes in their financial position for each of the three years in the period ended December 31, 1985, in conformity with generally accepted accounting principles applied on a consistent basis.

KMG Main Hurdman

New York, New York
January 29, 1986 (except
as to the Common
Stock Purchase note
which is dated
February 20, 1986)

EXHIBIT 10

1983	1982	1981	1980	1979	1978	1977	1976
$1,639.7	$1,598.9	$1,524.4	$1,332.1	$1,326.5	$1,233.0	$1,019.4	$ 865.1
967.9	1,111.2	1,200.8	1,237.0	1,051.0	853.3	689.3	617.1
2,607.6	2,710.1	2,725.2	2,569.1	2,377.5	2,086.3	1,708.7	1,482.2
1,052.0	1,109.8	1,108.0	960.6	903.7	759.1	619.7	544.4
1,555.6	1,600.3	1,617.2	1,608.5	1,473.8	1,327.2	1,089.0	937.8
1,277.5	1,241.6	1,220.4	1,171.1	1,036.7	880.4	718.8	617.1
278.1	358.7	396.8	437.4	437.1	446.8	370.2	320.7
38.6	39.9	49.3	39.8	34.3	29.9	22.0	20.3
(43.6)	(37.6)	(7.7)	(1.3)	(.9)	(5.8)	(4.9)	(3.6)
(29.9)	(32.0)	3.9	(3.5)	2.6	(2.7)	2.4	8.6
243.2	329.0	442.3	472.4	473.1	468.2	389.7	346.0
108.3	169.1	225.8	230.3	229.1	234.6	194.2	174.6
134.9	159.9	216.5	242.1	244.0	233.6	195.5	171.4
38.0	26.7	—	—	—	—	—	—
—	—	—	—	—	—	—	—
$ 172.9	$ 186.6	$ 216.5	$ 242.1	$ 244.0	$ 233.6	$ 195.5	$ 171.4
$ 1.61	$ 2.08	$ 3.42	$ 4.02	$ 4.06	$ 3.89	$ 3.26	$ 2.86
.45	.35	—	—	—	—	—	—
$ 2.06	$ 2.43	$ 3.42	$ 4.02	$ 4.06	$ 3.89	$ 3.26	$ 2.86
$ 2.00	$ 2.50	$ 3.00	$ 2.95	$ 2.75	$ 2.55	$ 2.20	$ 1.80
83.58	76.75	63.29	60.15	60.14	60.11	60.02	59.99
9.3%	12.1%	16.2%	18.4%	19.9%	22.4%	22.8%	23.3%
5.2	5.9	7.9	9.4	10.3	11.2	11.4	11.6
$ 365.9	$ 304.5	$ 465.3	$ 495.4	$ 505.7	$ 507.9	$ 475.3	$ 418.9
1.70	1.57	1.82	1.89	2.07	2.13	2.37	2.38
576.3	548.9	519.3	479.3	392.6	292.0	242.4	231.8
110.3	94.7	115.3	117.7	116.3	75.6	35.2	27.6
2,256.8	2,227.6	1,611.9	1,583.1	1,417.0	1,282.4	1,082.0	966.7
301.2	286.9	13.1	2.6	4.1	5.4	7.5	9.4
1,273.1	1,245.1	930.5	928.3	866.3	770.7	682.4	614.7
15.00	15.88	15.27	15.43	14.40	12.82	11.37	10.25
10.6%	12.8%	23.3%	26.1%	28.2%	30.3%	28.6%	27.9%
20,000	20,100	16,300	15,300	16,200	15,200	13,000	12,400
19,700	19,400	18,400	19,000	18,100	17,300	15,200	15,200
39,700	39,500	34,700	34,300	34,300	32,500	28,200	27,600

EXHIBIT 11
Net Sales of Principal Products (in millions)

Net Sales of Principal Products

(in millions)

	Year Ended December 31		
	1985	1984	1983
Cosmetics, fragrances and toiletries:			
Fragrance and bath products for women	$ 610.2	$ 700.9.	$ 732.0
Makeup, skin care and other products for women	659.6	727.5	709.6
Men's toiletry products	154.7	176.1	162.5
Personal care, children's and teen products	185.1	227.8	277.5
Subtotal	1,609.6	1,832.3	1,881.6
Fashion jewelry and accessories	394.2	350.9	330.2
Health care	260.3	159.0	126.6
Direct response	205.2	186.0	144.0
Other	—	77.6	124.6
Eliminations	.8	(.5)	.6
Consolidated	$2,470.1	$2,605.3	$2,607.6

Quarterly Financial Data

Quarterly data are summarized below (in millions, except per share amounts):

	Year Ended December 31, 1985*					Year Ended December 31, 1984*				
	First	Second	Third	Fourth	Year	First	Second	Third	Fourth	Year
Net sales	$529.2	$585.7	$567.8	$787.4	$2,470.1	$595.3	$676.4	$616.8	$716.8	$2,605.3
Gross profit	325.4	361.1	349.3	474.8	1,510.6	358.6	404.0	377.3	454.9	1,594.8
Net earnings from continuing operations	13.6	31.9	19.8	62.9	128.2	22.4	39.5	25.8	64.2	151.9
Discontinued operations:										
Earnings, net of taxes	9.5	8.6	5.7	11.1	34.9	7.7	8.1	4.5	9.5	29.8
Loss on disposal, including taxes	—	—	—	(223.0)	(223.0)	—	—	—	—	—
Net (loss) earnings	23.1	40.5	25.5	(149.0)	(59.9)	30.1	47.6	30.3	73.7	181.7
Per share of common stock:										
Continuing operations	$ .17	$ .40	$ .25	$ .79	$ 1.61	$ .26	$ .46	$ .30	$ .78	$ 1.80
Discontinued operations:										
Earnings	.12	.11	.07	.14	.44	.09	.10	.06	.11	.36
Loss on disposal	—	—	—	(2.81)	(2.81)	—	—	—	—	—
Net (loss) earnings	$ .29	$ .51	$ .32	$ (1.88)	$ (.76)	$ .35	$ .56	$ .36	$ .89	$ 2.16

* Previously published quarterly financial data have been restated to reflect the results of Mallinckrodt, Inc. as a discontinued operation.

Stock Market and Dividend Data

Avon common stock is listed on the New York Stock Exchange (symbol:AVP). At December 31, 1985, there were approximately 41,800 shareholders of record.

	1985		1984			Cash Dividends Per Share	
Quarter	High	Low	High	Low	Quarter	1985	1984
First	$ 23⅜	$ 19⅝	$ 25¾	$ 21	First	$ .50	$ .50
Second	21¼	17⅞	22⅜	19½	Second	.50	.50
Third	25⅝	21	25¼	21⅛	Third	.50	.50
Fourth	29	23⅜	24½	20¼	Fourth..........................	.50	.50
						$2.00	$2.00

EXHIBIT 12
Avon, Inc., Organizational Chart, 1986 (unofficial)

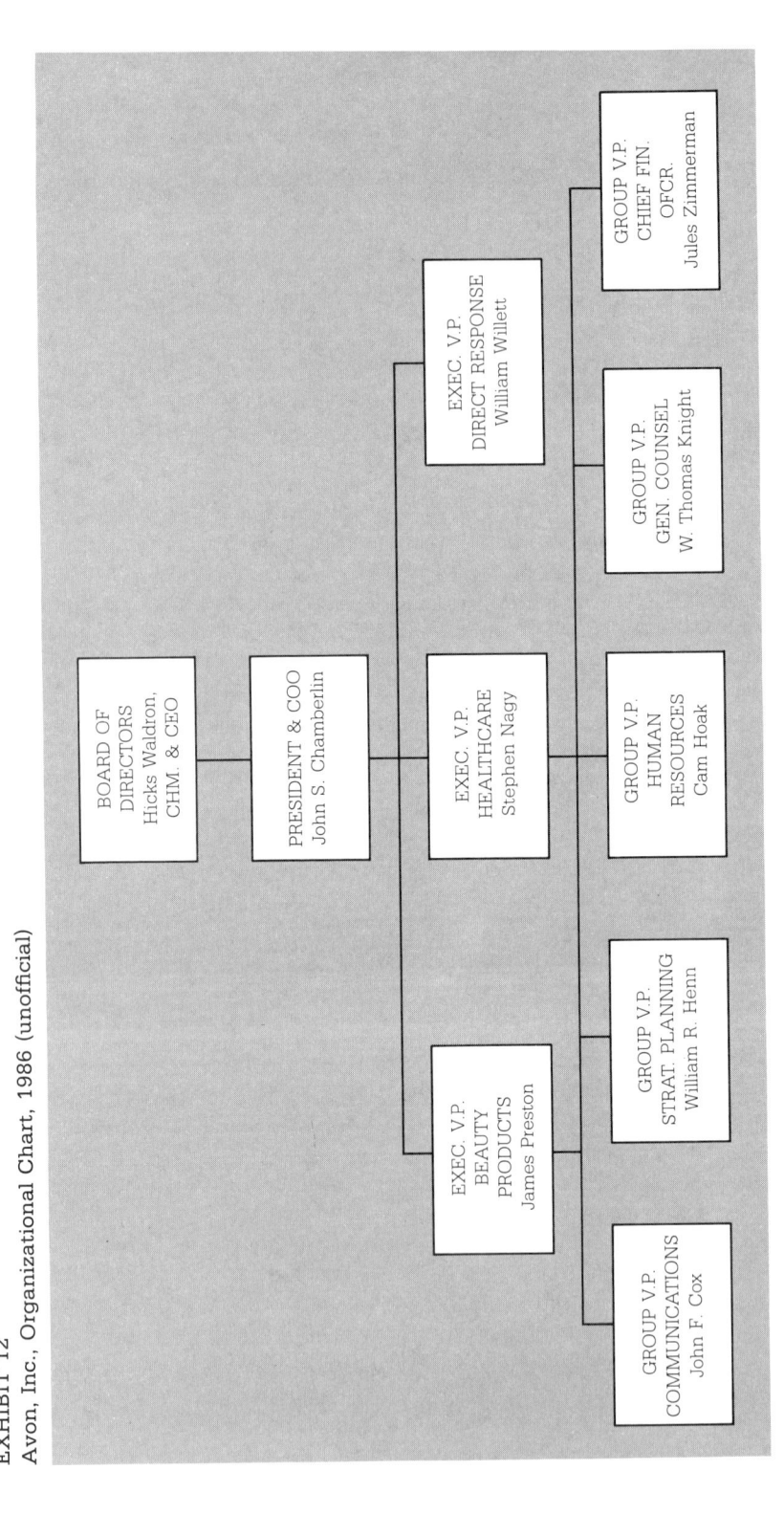

EXHIBIT 13
Management of Avon, Inc.

Board of Directors

Ruth Block*
Executive Vice President
The Equitable Life Assurance
Society of the United States

John S. Chamberlin
President and
Chief Operating Officer

Hays Clark
Retired; Former
Executive Vice President

Donald S. Fredrickson, M.D.
President and
Chief Executive Officer
Howard Hughes Medical
Institute

Stanley C. Gault
Chairman of the Board and
Chief Executive Officer
Rubbermaid Inc.

David W. Mitchell
Retired; Former
Chairman of the Board

Emil Mosbacher, Jr.*
Real Estate Investor and
Independent Oil and Gas
Producer

Merlin E. Nelson
Investment Consultant
Former Vice Chairman
AMF Inc.
(Leisure-time and
industrial products)

James E. Preston
Corporate Executive Vice
President and President, Avon
Division

Ernesta G. Procope*
President
E. G. Bowman Co., Inc.
(Insurance brokerage)

Joseph A. Rice*
Chairman of the Board
and Chief Executive Officer
Irving Trust Co. and
Irving Bank Corp.

Cecily Cannan Selby, Ph.D.
Adjunct Professor
Mathematics and Science
Education
New York University;
Lecturer and Educational
Consultant

Hicks B. Waldron
Chairman and
Chief Executive Officer

**Audit Committee Member*

Corporate Officers

Hicks B. Waldron
Chairman and
Chief Executive Officer

John S. Chamberlin
President and
Chief Operating Officer

Stephen F. Nagy
Executive Vice President

James E. Preston
Executive Vice President

William H. Willett
Executive Vice President

John F. Cox
Group Vice President,
Communications

William R. Henn
Group Vice President,
Strategic Planning and
Development

Cam Hoak
Group Vice President,
Human Resources

W. Thomas Knight
Group Vice Presicent, General
Counsel and Secretary

Jules Zimmerman
Group Vice President and
Chief Financial Officer

Vice Presidents

Philip J. Davis
Helmuth R. Fandl
Robert H. Hansen

Margro R. Long
Paul B. Markovits
Siri S. Marshall
Rainier F. Paul

Robert W. Pratt, Jr.
Virginia L. Trump

John E. Donaldson, Jr.
Vice President and Treasurer

Norman H. Werthwein
Vice President and Controller

Management Changes

Avon Products strengthened management during 1985.
   John S. Chamberlin was recruited to be the company's president and chief operating officer. He is providing the support needed by the chairman and chief executive officer. His appointment also

provides for succession and continuity of top management in the longer term.
   Stephen F. Nagy was promoted to executive vice president of Foster Medical. He has directed Foster Medical's growth to a

position of national leadership in home health care.
   The company recruited Cam Hoak to be group vice president of human resources, and William R. Henn was named group vice president of strategic planning and development.

   All four officers are members of the corporate management committee.
   General management, marketing, planning and operations talent was added in all three divisions.

Independent Accountants

KMG Main Hurdman
Park Avenue Plaza
55 East 52nd Street
New York, N.Y. 10055

Transfer Agent and Registrar

Morgan Guaranty Trust Co.
30 West Broadway
New York, N.Y. 10015

CASE 29
Hewlett-Packard, 1986

Donald F. Harvey
Research Associate: Gail Nottingham

INTRODUCTION

As John Young, chairman and chief executive officer, worked in his large well-appointed office with paneled walls and color coordinated furnishings, he reflected on his strategy for the Palo Alto-based firm. His strategic decisions had replaced the old system with a new marketing oriented strategy. Young has been reorganizing the company for survival in the computer business. Change involves risks, just as not changing does. The risk Young faces is that HP may lose the informality, the camaraderie, and the risk-taking spirit that has made it a successful company.[1]

Hewlett-Packard Company (HP), together with its consolidated subsidiaries, is engaged worldwide in the design, manufacture, marketing, and servicing of a broad array of precision electronic instruments and systems for measurement, analysis, and computation. HP operates in a single industry segment that reflects the market's demand for integrated systems solutions to specific customer problems. HP offers over 10,000 products and systems.[2]

Organizationally, it has been a loosely knit federation of highly autonomous divisions, each responsible for its own marketing. There are over fifty divisions, located in California (9), Colorado (4), Massachusetts (2), Oregon (2), Washington (3), Pennsylvania, New Jersey, Idaho, Puerto Rico, and in eleven foreign countries.[3] In the past, each division did its own manufacturing and marketing around the world, while HP headquarters oversaw strategic planning.

When John Young took over as chief executive officer (CEO) in 1978, he realized that HP had a serious problem. HP was the world's largest maker of electronic instruments, with computers about to become its main source of revenue. Yet its strategy for computers was fragmented and inconsistent.

Young realized the computer world was changing. The big corporate customers had stopped buying equipment on a piecemeal basis. They wanted compatible hardware and software. Young decided that a market-oriented structure that would offer total computer solutions to meet customer needs was necessary.

This case was prepared using published accounts and public documents for the purpose of class discussion rather than to illustrate either effective or ineffective handling of an administrative situation.

HP faces three key problems: marketing fragmentation, inability to be technically outstanding on software development, and a continued inability to meet the customer's needs.

THE ENVIRONMENT

The purpose of business is to create and keep a customer. A company must be wedded to the ideal of innovation—offering better or more preferred products in such combinations of ways, means, places, and at such prices that prospects *prefer* doing business with the company rather than with others.[4]

Electronic products are now so commonplace that many of them have taken on the characteristics of consumer products, where price is the overriding factor in buying decisions. Increasingly, industrial customers are buying computers linked with instruments for testing and process control. System capabilities and integration criteria are now important parts of the strategic directions of the customer.

Instruments were HP's primary business for the greater part of its history. Presently, computer sales account for about 55 percent of annual revenues. (See exhibits 1 and 2 for 1980 and 1984 comparison.)

Test and Measurement Equipment (T&M)

Several factors, including stagnation in industrial construction, combined to limit sales opportunities for industrial and commercial test and measurement devices in 1985. Product shipments, totaling less than $10.2 billion in 1985, grew by slightly under 3 percent, after adjustment for inflation. This rate was a significant drop from the growth rate of more than 12 percent in 1984.[5]

Despite better economic conditions in many foreign nations, the U.S. trade surplus in process control instruments declined by 5 percent in 1985. Exports increased by only 7 percent, to a total of $760 million, while imports, valued at $380 million, grew by almost 22 percent. Europe was the largest market, ordering $312 million in 1985.[6] Other purchasers were Japan, Canada, and Mexico.

Increasing competition from abroad will limit sales of many of the process industries and thus hold down investment in new plant and equipment. This factor, combined with competition in terms of both price and technology from foreign suppliers, will dampen U.S. sales. Nearly the only cause of market expansion will be increased outlays for plant modernization.

Two positive trends exist for the long term: the constant need for users to update obsolete test facilities and the increased need for testing as the electronic content of products increases. Product changes occur as chip (semiconductor) makers improve current offerings. Evolving electronics technology requires new generations of testing equipment. Test and measurement equipment is needed in all areas of the development process—design, testing, and service. Rising defense spending has boosted military use of test equipment. This increase drives the test and measurement industry to develop more sophisticated computer-controlled equipment. Thus, the long-term outlook for the T&M equipment industry is considered to be favorable.

Computers and Office Equipment

Continued improvement in price/performance levels of available equipment spurs the growth in the computer industry. The boundaries separating product classes have become blurred as performance gaps beween product categories have been filled and new technologies overtake the old. The computer industry has seen continuous technological changes as well as increased focus on service to the customer. Price cuts and/or performance increases have enlarged the market.

In the past, the rule of thumb was that for twice the price one could buy four times the performance.[7] Today, a dollar will buy more processing power at the low end of the performance range than at the high end because of the increased use of the microprocessor in the smaller systems.

Price/performance is the basis of competition in the computer industry. The price side of the equation puts pressure on margins and underscores the need to invest in automated facilities to reduce manufacturing costs. The performance side leads to shortened life cycles, resulting in uncertainty in planning, heavy commitments to R&D, and a heavy investment in advertising and marketing.

A *product* consists of both physical goods and the services associated with them. Customers select a particular product because it offers some value not found in the competing products. The product's price and performance make it more desirable than competing products.

During the early stages of development in technology-based industries, frontrunning companies often experience phenomenal growth rates. Substantial year-to-year increases in revenues and profits are typically unsustainable, as more competitors enter the market and the fight for share intensifies.[8]

International Business Machines (IBM) is expanding its dominance in almost every major market in which it competes. In 1984 IBM had revenues of $46 billion and net income of $6.6 billion. According to a user survey conducted by *Datamation*, most IBM customers said they would continue to buy most of their equipment from IBM over the next five years, not only for the safety of buying from the market leader, but also because of IBM's superior record for service and support.[9]

IBM forecasted sales of $60 billion for 1987 and has stated its corporate objective to be two-fold: achieving the highest quality products at the cheapest price.[10] Although it is difficult to realize these goals simultaneously, if accomplished the firm would position itself to the right of the computer industry's price/performance curve and have advantage in both key areas of competition.

The computer equipment industry's estimated 1985 product shipments showed an 8 percent increase over 1984, rising $53 billion.[11] The relatively low growth figure was partially due to a slowdown in purchases by business firms. Many, having purchased large amounts of equipment in previous years, concentrated on assimilating this equipment into their operations during 1985. Announcements of new products caused some users to defer purchases until the new models were available.

Business Week's "Corporate Scoreboard" listed 900 corporations and their second quarter 1986 earnings. The second-quarter performance—off 2 percent on a gain of 3 percent in sales—was better than the 13 percent drop in the second quarter of 1985. There appears to have been a steady erosion in earnings since mid-1984.[12]

Over the last two years, the stocks of technology companies have generally underperformed the market, despite their superior growth potential. The cause has likely been the declining net margins (exhibit 3) and returns on equity (exhibit 4) due to increased competition.

U.S. computer firms continue to face significant competition in both traditional and new markets. Although the extent of government involvement in the computer industry varies from country to country, typical policies to protect domestic producers include import licensing, tariffs on imports, domestic procurement preferences, and rules reserving part of the domestic market for local producers. The growing strength of the U.S. dollar was an additional factor behind the erosion of the U.S. computer trade surplus between 1981 and 1984.[13] Since 1965 seven out of ten U.S. high-technology industries have lost world market share.[14]

Although the U.S. dollar has dropped against most European currencies, it has changed little against the currencies of many developing nations such as Korea and Hong Kong, or against that of Canada.[15] The cheaper dollar needs to be accompanied by more robust economic activity abroad if U.S. exporters are to regain lost market share on the global market.

The United States accounted for 50 percent of the computer shipments in 1984 and is expected to continue to be the largest market through 1987. Japan is expected to maintain second place, followed by West Germany, the United Kingdom, and France. Demand in China and Brazil is expected to show dynamic growth.[16]

Although U.S. exports increased from 1979 to 1984 at a 20 percent compound annual rate, imports increased at a much faster 51 percent.[17] Foreign computer manufacturers, particularly the Japanese, became major suppliers to the U.S. market. Their emphasis on sales of low-priced, high-volume products, such as printers and disk storage devices, was successful.

A significant number of U.S. manufacturers moved their production facilities out of the country to Hong Kong, Singapore, Malaysia, Taiwan, and South Korea to obtain lower labor costs and stay price-competitive. By the end of 1985, U.S. companies were reportedly producing approximately half of the value of their worldwide shipments of personal computer systems, including peripherals, out of the country.[18] HP's foreign operations provided 29 percent of earnings in 1983, 32 percent in 1984, and 43 percent in 1985.[19]

Computer industry shipments through 1990 are expected to grow slightly less than the historical average of 19 percent per year.[20] Business and industrial markets will continue to aid this growth, particularly as new software becomes available.

A full-fledged recovery for the industry still seems some time away. Industry observers blame sluggish capital spending by big customers who are nervous about tax-revision legislation that could eliminate some investment tax credits.[21] Repeal of the investment tax credit—the single biggest tax break eliminated by the proposed law—will be negative for capital goods users and suppliers.

THE COMPANY

HP once relied on the inventions of its engineers to create new markets. It must now determine the needs of the market and design products to meet those needs. The business has become so complex that it is no longer possible for a designer to ask the guy at the next bench what he likes and use that as a reason to design a new product.

HP currently has three computer product lines: the HP3000 series of business and office computer systems, the HP1000 series of realtime scientific, process-control and personal computers, and the HP9000 series of engineering and technical work stations.[22] The hardware and software systems, design and development, and maintenance and enhancement requirements are different for all three series. There is little compatibility among them and interconnecting units from different series is difficult at best.

In July of 1984, HP announced a sweeping structural reorganization designed to accelerate its transition from a company run by engineers for engineers to one with the marketing clout needed to reach a wider audience and be more competitive. It was an effort to unify the previously fragmented marketing efforts of its two biggest businesses—computers and instruments.

The organizational structure shown in exhibit 5 outlines four product sectors:

- Components, measurement, and design systems
- Information systems and networks
- Manufacturing, medical, and analytical systems
- Marketing and international

These sectors are chartered to create common strategies needed to manage product lines which are increasingly interactive and for developing solutions to meet the complex needs of customers.[23]

In an August 1986 news release, John Young announced an 11 percent increase in net revenue and a 6 percent increase in net earnings for the third quarter of HP's 1986 fiscal year, which ended July 31. Orders for the period were up 25 percent over the same quarter in 1985.[24]

Young said that international orders continued to show improvement, especially when compared to the third quarter of 1985. International orders were up 19 percent to $2.493 billion. Total orders for the nine month period were up 10 percent from a year ago, totaling $5.289 billion. U.S. orders were $2.796 billion of this amount, an increase of 4 percent over 1985.[25]

Current Marketing Strategy

The personal computer business has been an uphill battle for HP ever since it first entered the market in late 1983. In 1984, HP's Personal Computer Group lost an estimated $14 million (before taxes) and was the single biggest contributor to the decline in earnings in HP's computer business.[26] In that year, HP held only 3.9 percent of the PC market share (see exhibit 6).

Sales growth for the recent HP110 as well as its first consumer personal computer, the HP150, seems to be from HP's traditional customers. The products do not sell as well in retail channels where HP has had little experience.[27]

HP is trying a new approach, conceding the race for market share of PCs to IBM. Concentration is focused on the HP3000 business market, where it is one of the larger competitors. Reliance is placed on its own sales force and also on the value-added retailer, who adds value via software, systems integration, or service and maintenance. HP is finding the use of original equipment manufacturers (OEMs) and third-party software suppliers is crucial in devising solutions for applications in which the company lacks expertise. HP is avoiding markets which require expensive distribution systems.

Seventy percent of HP's product revenue is derived through the marketing efforts of its own sales organization. The remaining 30 percent is derived through value-added resale channels, including dealers and OEMs. Sales operations are supported by approximately 27,000 individuals, including field service engineers, service personnel, and administrative support staff.[28]

HP needed a well-orchestrated line of machines for the 1980s. Instead, it had three separate computer groups, all pumping out incompatible products. The proposed solution was the Spectrum family of computers.

Spectrum is based on reduced instruction set computer (RISC) architecture. RISC computers use fewer operating instructions to process information. They are faster than other current minicomputers and can deliver equivalent power for as little as one-sixth the cost.[29]

RISC is more software than hardware intensive. RISC integrated circuits (ICs) can be easily altered in relatively short design and fabrication cycles.[30] This feature allows HP to take advantage of its in-house semiconductor processing capabilities and custom design systems for specific customer applications. Further, HP can change the chip at any time in response to changing trends in the industry.

Over time, HP plans to replace its existing lines of minicomputers—the HP3000, HP1000, and the computer-aided work station HP9000—with the Spectrum family of machines. John Young believes that the Spectrum group of products will show the ability of HP's engineers to make fundamental product contributions.[31] This product line should give HP the capability to reach new markets or be more effective in current ones.

HP is moving slowly to make sure the machine's software works. Such thoroughness has been largely responsible for HP's success in the past, but the delay could push away customers who want more computer power now. In September of 1986, a further delay of six months was announced due to software problems.

Market Share

HP is often criticized for its advertising, promotion, and dealer support programs. Technical innovation and quality are what has held HP's market share, not marketing skill.

HP's overall share of the worldwide minicomputer market slipped to 5 percent in 1985 from 5.5 percent in 1983. In the $37 billion market for commercial minis, it dropped from a 4.2 percent share in 1983 to 3.9 percent in 1985. In the $15 billion market for technical minis, HP sank to 7.8 percent, from more than 12 percent five years ago.[32] Most of this reduction in share was caused by competition from Digital Equipment Corporation (DEC), IBM, Apple, and Tandy.

In a dynamic, competitive environment, an organization must either move forward with purpose and direction or be ready for failure. Strategic management's goal is to relate the resources of the organization to long-range opportunities in the environment. To successfully complete a strategic plan, managers must understand the issue of product and market segmentation. The strategist is then able to focus the internal capabilities of the organization toward the main market segments from which it obtains its major revenues and in which it dominates the competition.

In a news release issued August of 1986, Young pointed out that HP operates in a single industry segment: the design and manufacture of measurement and computation products and systems.[33] Within this segment are four strategic business units (SBUs)—analytical instrumentation, medical electronic equipment, electronic test and measurement, and computer products.

The overall market share is revenue expressed as a percentage of the revenue of the total industry. Exhibit 6 depicts the share HP holds in relation to its major competitors; it is presented in common size and in dollar figures. Some experts believe it is more important to gain market share through a competitive advantage and aggressive strategy than it is to push for increased profits.[34]

Capital Structure

The optimal capital structure is the one which maximizes the price of the firm's stock. It almost always calls for a debt ratio which is lower than the one which maximizes earnings per share (EPS). Using leverage involves risk-return trade-off; higher leverage increases EPS (at least for a while), but risk rises continuously and at an increasing rate as debt is substituted for equity.

Risk is associated with debt; a firm's beta is a measurement of the perceived riskiness of the company to potential stockholders and increases with its degree of financial leverage. The betas of HP and its competitors are shown in exhibit 7.

Stock values are found as present values of future stream of income (dividends) and the final stock price the investor expects to receive plus an expected return on the investment. The higher the risk, the lower the price and the higher the expected return. To maximize stock price, a manager should consider actions to lower the discount rate and increase the expected growth rate, increasing the value of the firm's stock.

As a business philosophy, one of the HP corporate objectives means financing growth out of its own profits. Well-managed computer manufacturers rely more on equity and cash flow from operations to finance growth than on debt.

The environment is very volatile and the computer industry should not engage in excessive long-term debt. This research concludes that HP's objective is currently sound.

HP is strongly affected by fluctuations in currency values, as it is the thirteenth largest exporter in the United States.[35] The rise in the dollar's strength raised HP's prices in Europe about 50 percent from 1980 to 1986.[36] To maintain its market share it has shifted more of the value-added operations (manufacturing, R&D, procurement) to international markets.

Understanding the past is necessary in order to contemplate the future. The financial area determines the availability of cash resources to implement strategic actions. Financial ratios are a convenient way to summarize large quantities of financial data. They fall into five categories: liquidity, asset utilization, debt management, profitability, and common stock.[37] The 1985 income statement (see exhibit 9) and the balance sheet (see exhibit 10) will provide a set of ratios for this evaluation.

Ratio Analysis

The following ratio analysis uses the 1983, 1984, 1985, and projected 1986 data.

Liquidity

Liquidity is a measure of a firm's ability to generate sufficient cash to meet its current obligations. The most common ratio is the current ratio.

Current ratio = current assets/current liabilities

Company	1985	1984	
Hewlett-Packard	2.43	2.42	
IBM	2.28	2.11	Industry Median = 1.9
DEC	4.91	3.78	
Wang	2.31	2.08	

The higher the ratio, the greater the presumed ability of the firm to pay its current debt.

Asset Management

Average collection period = receivables/average daily sales

	1985	1984	1983
Hewlett-Packard	70.1	71.3	73.7

The high numbers signify a liberal credit policy on the part of HP.

Inventory turnover = sales/inventories

	1985	1984	1983
Hewlett-Packard	6.55	5.91	6.30

This ratio measures the average number of times per year inventory is turned over—purchased, processed, and sold. The higher the number, the greater the efficiency. The trend at HP is to have fewer lower-level parts in inventory and a higher finished goods inventory (FGI).

Fixed asset turnover = sales/fixed assets

	1985	1984	1983
Hewlett-Packard	1.98	2.17	2.18

This ratio is a measure of utilization of plant and equipment. HP's fixed assets were not as productive in 1985 as they were in 1983. This difference could be caused by investment in new equipment which is not yet fully utilized.

Total asset turnover = sales/total assets

	1985	1984	1983
Hewlett-Packard	1.15	1.17	1.13

HP is not generating a sufficient volume of business for the size of its asset investment. Sales should be increased, some assets disposed of, or both. A low turnover can mean an excess of either current or fixed assets.

Debt Management

Debt to total assets = current + long-term debt/total assets

	1985	1984	1983
Hewlett-Packard	.30	.31	.31

In 1984 and 1985, only 30 percent of HP's total financing activities were supplied by creditors.

Long-Term Debt/Total Capital (in %)

Company	1980	1981	1982	1983	1984	1985	1986
HP	1.8	1.3	1.6	2.4	2.2	2.5	2.0
IBM	11.3	12.8	12.5	10.3	11.0	11.0	12.0
DEC	22.9	3.2	2.8	2.6	10.0	15.5	8.0
Wang	52.7	34.4	36.3	27.9	22.3	34.8	34.0

Source: *Value Line*

Times interest earned = EBIT/interest charges

Because of HP's very low debt, interest charges are minimal and are not reflected as a separate item on the income statement.

Profitability Ratios

Profit margin = net profit/sales

This ratio gives the profit per dollar of sales. A low ratio can mean that the firm's sales are relatively low, that its costs are relatively high, or both (see exhibit 3).

Return on investment = net profit/total assets

	1985	1984	1983
Hewlett-Packard	.086	.129	.104

This ratio is a measure of basic earning power because assets represent the total of the resources committed to the firm.

Return on equity = net profit/common equity

This ratio measures the rate of return on the stockholders' investment, ROE. This ratio will be most affected by positive or negative leveraging (see exhibit 4).

Common Stock

Dividend payout ratio = dividends/new profit

	1985	1984	1983
Hewlett-Packard	.117	.074	.093

A low payout from a generally healthy firm indicates that earnings are being reinvested for growth. HP paid out more earnings as dividends in 1985, possibly because the firm required fewer funds for capital and equipment.

Average dividend yield = dividends per share/stock price

Company	1980	1981	1982	1983	1984	1985
HP	.6	.5	.5	.4	.5	.6
IBM	5.4	5.9	5.0	3.2	3.5	3.4
DEC	—	—	—	—	—	—
Wang	.6	.4	.4	.3	.4	.7
UNISYS	4.0	6.4	7.2	5.2	5.0	4.3

Source: *Value Line* figure

Price earnings ratio = stock price/earnings per share

Company	1980	1981	1982	1983	1984	1985
HP	16.6	18.1	19.4	24.4	14.8	17.7
IBM	10.1	10.7	10.4	12.5	10.6	12.9
DEC	14.3	14.4	11.7	19.6	15.8	14.9
Wang	29.9	25.5	35.2	30.4	19.9	NA

The P/E ratio is a measure of the degree of acceptance of the firm's stock in the market. A high ratio denotes great acceptance.

Earnings per Share

Exhibit 11 presents a time series representation of EPS for HP, IBM, Wang, and DEC. EPS represents a value measure of the stockholder.

PRODUCTION

Recently, managers within the manufacturing function at HP have recognized that the marketplace was changing so that a higher level of competition increased the emphasis on cost, timely delivery, quality, and total solutions to customer problems. A vision began that would provide HP with significant, long-term competitive advantage in the manufacturing area.

High manufacturing overhead has a dramatic effect on profit and competitiveness. Overhead costs as a percentage of value added in American industry and as a percentage of overall manufacturing costs have been rising steadily while the ratio of direct labor costs to value added has declined. Production managers have more direct leverage on improving productivity through cutting overhead than through pruning direct labor.

As America's factories step up the pace of automation, overhead costs grow in real terms because of increased support costs of maintaining and running automated equipment. Direct labor accounts for only 8 to 12 percent of total cost of American durable goods production.

Due to a decreasing labor base, HP realigned its overhead allocation system in 1986 to burden the material used in a given product with a portion of the overhead.

One concept being considered has one set of manufacturing systems, methods, and organization for existing and new products. On-line storage of unique materials, KANBAN, and real-time capacity planning are crucial aspects of the concept. Other key aspects include:

1 Support local control and decision making. The supervisor and/or people in the work group should determine what to do next.
2 Emphasize simplicity, least effort, and minimum number of transactions.
3 Remain open to new ideas. Don't be bound by tradition or what has worked in the past.
4 Design the new system so that it can be easily changed in the future.

Slower growth in the computer market affected industry employment in 1985. The employment figure for this industry remained essentially flat, after growing more than 9.5 percent in 1984.[38] Even though forecasts for 1986 were somewhat optimistic, production worker employment was expected to show little growth in that year because of large inventories. HP has also made a tremendous effort to reduce manufacturing capacity and hopes to support profit by bringing production capacity more in line with the incoming order rate.

In June 1986 HP offered two programs to help reduce its work force: a voluntary severance plan for employees in a number of select job categories and an early retirement incentive for employees who were sixty-two years of age with fifteen or more years with the company. HP offered the programs to 1,500 workers, and 1,015 employees accepted.

Materials Management

The materials management concept is used at HP. This idea is an integrated management approach to planning acquisition, conversion, flow, and distribution of production materials from raw materials to the finished product.

HP aggressively analyzes new products to determine if it is more profitable to make an item itself or to buy from outside suppliers. Internal overhead rates are still inflated due to the size of the corporation, making the use of outside suppliers attractive in many cases. An international procurement (IPO) strategy has improved the manufacturing costs, particularly when parts of high volume and low complexity are involved. IPO contacts are found in Taiwan, Korea, Japan, the United Kingdom, West Germany, and France; their services include all procurement activities. The divisions are encouraged to use IPO whenever possible for new and existing material needs.

Production control and procurement (buying, receiving, inspecting, distributing) use a common database structure to plan and control the material needs of each production site. Documentation and contracts for common component parts are handled at the corporate level, while parts (component and fabricated) unique to a division are handled autonomously.

Research and Development

Hewlett Packard spent on the average 9.98 percent of its sales on R&D during the 1981 through 1984 period.[39] Exhibit 12 shows how this expenditure compares to other companies in the industry.

HP understands that there are a number of advantages to accelerating new product introduction. The firm should enter the market early enough to profit substantially; this strategy is increasingly important as the market changes. Development costs will be less. The detailed knowledge—good and bad—about earlier product developments tends to be forgotten in a long product cycle. If the schedule is compressed, the information feedback comes quicker and is easier to use.

The approach at HP has been to accelerate the development process by teaming up R&D, marketing, manufacturing, and purchasing. The theory behind this strategy allows each area's concerns and suggestions to be on the table beginning at the early stages. The outcome of the consensus reached by this team allows the right product for the right market to be produced at a reasonable cost in a timely manner.

MANAGEMENT OF HUMAN RESOURCES

Power and achievement goals of the CEO affect the strategy of the firm. The CEO must make decisions and get others within the organization to perform efficiently. The performance of the firm is a reflection of which management style the CEO uses to define and implement the firm's strategy. HP's CEO John Young falls into the team manager category because of his emphasis on synergy among the autonomous units of the corporation.

HP's philosophy of management flows directly from the view that people are its most valuable asset. "Management by objective" (MBO) is advocated at HP; it offers freedom for individual initiative and contribution. It promotes creativity and enthusiasm and helps develop people who can step up and take on additional responsibility as the company grows.[40] HP gives the employee the tools and then expects results.

HP always has had strong traditions and policies with the goal of promoting communications: an open-door policy, coffee break discussions, and open-office floor plans. Communication has become a significant challenge, however, with an employee population of 84,000.

CONCLUSION

John Young is excited about HP's redirection and believes in the capabilities, commitment, creativity, and loyalty of the employees who will make it work. Most observers of HP, as well as insiders, credit Young with a well-conceived and bold repositioning of his company in attractive high-technology markets. Many of them, however, contend that he faces a huge challenge in making this highly praised strategy work. As John Young commented, "The fact that we have to do so many things and do them all at once is a real difference from the past. We are going outside the company more for a wider variety of expertise."[41]

If John Young can keep HP's spirit intact while reshaping the company, then the future looks good.

Notes

1 Kathleen K. Wiegner, "John Young's New Jogging Shoes," *Forbes,* November 4, 1985, 42.
2 Hewlett-Packard Company, Form 10-K, 1985, 1.
3 Standard & Poors Corporation, *Standard & Poors,* August 1986, 15.
4 Theodore Levitt, "The Globalization of Markets," *Harvard Business Review,* May–June 1983, 101.
5 U.S. Department of Commerce, "Measuring and Controlling Instruments," *U.S. Industrial Outlook,* 33–34.
6 Ibid.
7 Standard & Poors Corporation, *Standard & Poors Industry Survey* 1, April 1986, C74.
8 Ibid.
9 Ibid.
10 Interview with Roger Tracy, Hewlett-Packard Company, Spokane, Washington, September 26, 1986.
11 U.S. Department of Commerce, "Computer Equipment and Software," *U.S. Industrial Outlook,* January 1986, 28–31.
12 "Computer Scoreboard," *Business Week,* January 1986.
13 U.S. Department of Commerce, 28–32.
14 John A. Young, "Meeting Global Competition," *High Technology,* July 1985, 12.
15 Standard & Poors Corporation, *The Outlook,* August 27, 1986, 606.
16 U.S. Department of Commerce, *Industrial Outlook,* 28–36.
17 Ibid., 28–32.
18 Ibid., 28–35.
19 Hewlett-Packard, 10-K, 3.
20 U.S. Department of Commerce, *Industrial Outlook,* 28–36.
21 "Sliding Earnings, Corporate Profits Fell 5% in Second Quarter," *Wall Street Journal,* August 4, 1986, 1.
22 "A Simple Design May Pay Off Big for Hewlett-Packard," *Electronics,* March 3, 1986, 40.
23 Hewlett-Packard, Corporation Organization, December 1985.

24   *The Wall Street Journal,* August 19, 1986.

25   Ibid.

26   "Hewlett-Packard Focuses on the Office Spectrum," *Electronic Business,* August 1, 1985, 55.

27   "Why Hewlett-Packard Overhauled Its Management," *Business Week,* July 30, 1984, 112.

28   Hewlett-Packard, 10-K, 3.

29   Wiegner, "John Young's Shoes," 44.

30   Frank J. Catalano, "Hewlett-Packard Focuses on the Office Spectrum," *Electronic Business,* August 1, 1986, 46.

31   Frank J. Catalano, "John A. Young: Running a Full-Spectrum Company," *Electronic Business,* April 15, 1986, 82.

32   John W. Wilson and Gordon Bock, "Can Hewlett-Packard Put the Pieces Back Together?" *Business Week,* March 10, 1986, 114.

33   *Wall Street Journal,* August 19, 1986.

34   Donald F. Harvey, *Business Policy and Strategic Management* (Columbus, OH: Merrill Publishing Company, 1982), 343.

35   Catalano, "Hewlett-Packard Spectrum," 53.

36   "Changes," *Measure,* July–August 1986, 5.

37   Harvey, 343.

38   U.S. Department of Commerce, "Software," 28-32.

39   U.S. Department of Commerce, "Office Equipment," C75.

40   Hewlett-Packard Company, *1985 Annual Report,* 21.

41   Wiegner, "John Young's Shoes," 44.

EXHIBIT 1
Revenues by Segment, 1980

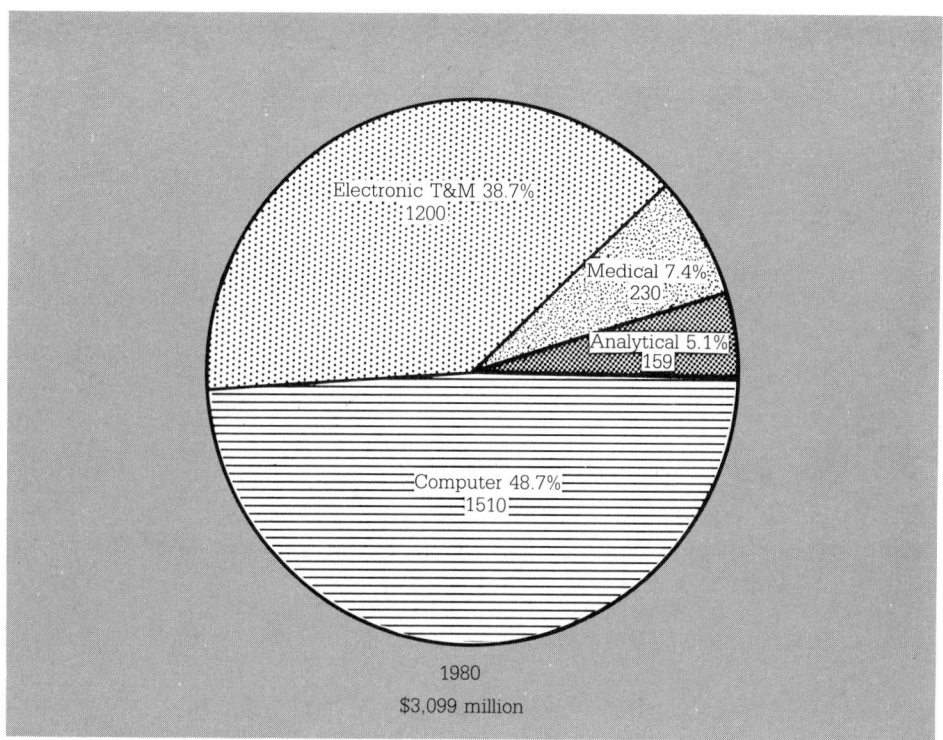

Source: August 1, 1985, issue of *Electronic Business*

EXHIBIT 2
Revenues by Segment, 1984

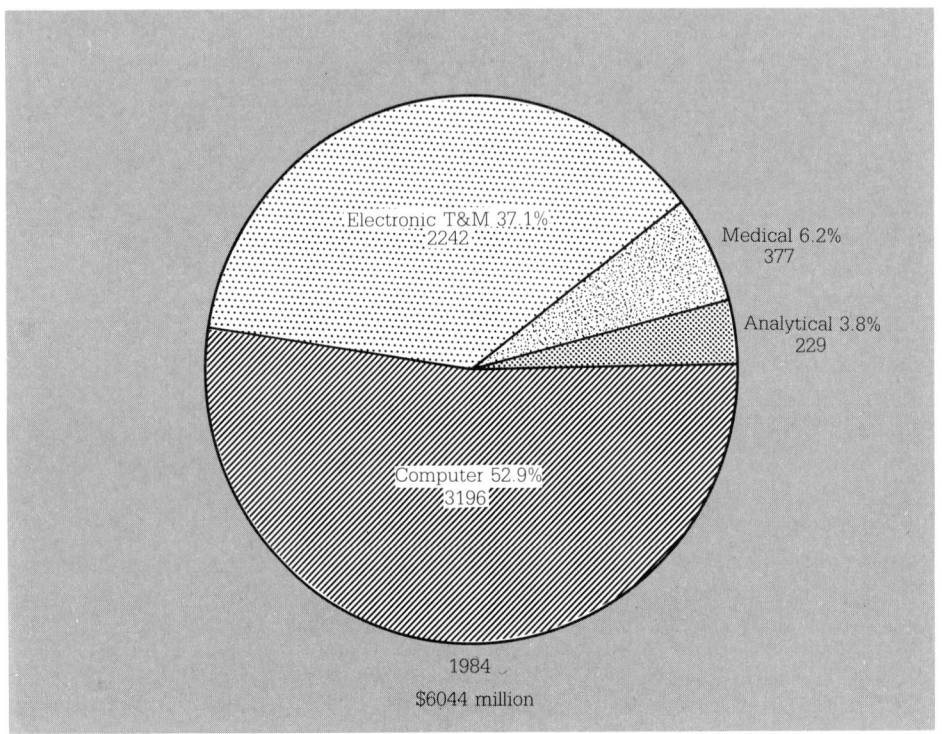

Source: August 1, 1985 issue of *Electronic Business*

EXHIBIT 3
Profit Margin (Net profit/Sales in %)

Company	1982	1983	1984	1985	1986	1987
Hewlett-Packard	9.0	9.2	9.1	7.5	7.4	7.8
IBM	12.8	13.7	14.3	13.1	11.8	12.7
DEC	10.8	6.6	5.9	5.7	8.1	9.7
Wang	9.2	9.9	9.6	.7	1.9	3.1
UNISYS	2.2	4.6	5.1	4.9	3.1	5.0

Source: *Value Line*

EXHIBIT 4
Return on Equity (in %)

Company	1980	1981	1982	1983	1984	1985
Hewlett-Packard	17.4	16.3	16.3	15.0	18.0	12.3
IBM	21.6	18.2	22.1	23.6	24.8	20.5
DEC	15.1	12.8	13.2	8.0	8.3	9.8
Wang	24.2	27.2	18.6	16.2	16.8	12.4

Source: *Value Line*

EXHIBIT 5
Organization Chart

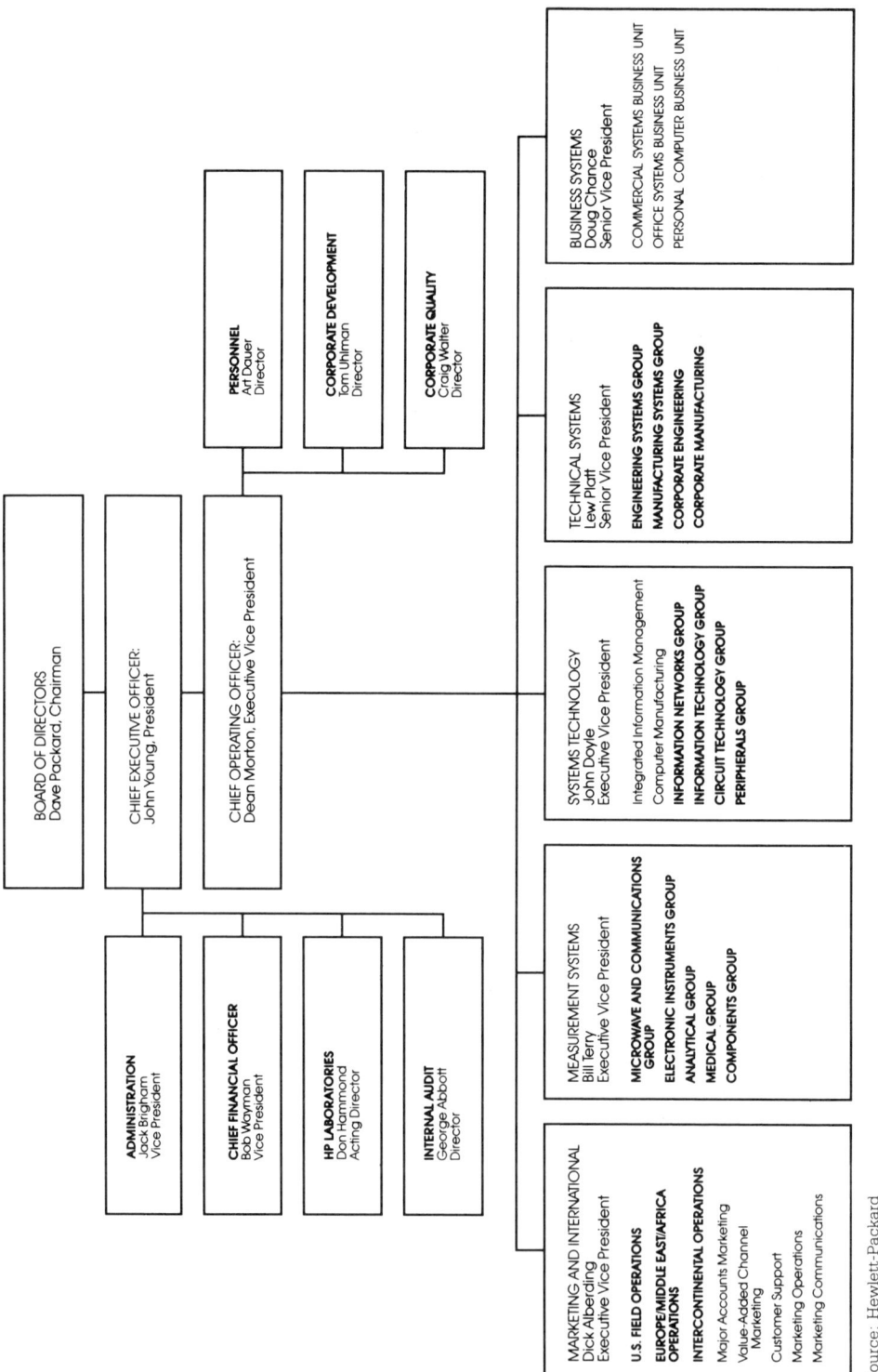

BOARD OF DIRECTORS
Dave Packard, Chairman

CHIEF EXECUTIVE OFFICER:
John Young, President

CHIEF OPERATING OFFICER:
Dean Morton, Executive Vice President

ADMINISTRATION
Jack Brigham
Vice President

CHIEF FINANCIAL OFFICER
Bob Wayman
Vice President

HP LABORATORIES
Don Hammond
Acting Director

INTERNAL AUDIT
George Abbott
Director

PERSONNEL
Art Dauer
Director

CORPORATE DEVELOPMENT
Tom Uhlman
Director

CORPORATE QUALITY
Craig Walter
Director

MARKETING AND INTERNATIONAL
Dick Alberding
Executive Vice President

U.S. FIELD OPERATIONS
EUROPE/MIDDLE EAST/AFRICA
OPERATIONS
INTERCONTINENTAL OPERATIONS
Major Accounts Marketing
Value-Added Channel
Marketing
Customer Support
Marketing Operations
Marketing Communications

MEASUREMENT SYSTEMS
Bill Terry
Executive Vice President

MICROWAVE AND COMMUNICATIONS
GROUP
ELECTRONIC INSTRUMENTS GROUP
ANALYTICAL GROUP
MEDICAL GROUP
COMPONENTS GROUP

SYSTEMS TECHNOLOGY
John Doyle
Executive Vice President

Integrated Information Management
Computer Manufacturing
INFORMATION NETWORKS GROUP
INFORMATION TECHNOLOGY GROUP
CIRCUIT TECHNOLOGY GROUP
PERIPHERALS GROUP

TECHNICAL SYSTEMS
Lew Platt
Senior Vice President

ENGINEERING SYSTEMS GROUP
MANUFACTURING SYSTEMS GROUP
CORPORATE ENGINEERING
CORPORATE MANUFACTURING

BUSINESS SYSTEMS
Doug Chance
Senior Vice President

COMMERCIAL SYSTEMS BUSINESS UNIT
OFFICE SYSTEMS BUSINESS UNIT
PERSONAL COMPUTER BUSINESS UNIT

Source: Hewlett-Packard

EXHIBIT 6
Personal Computer Market Share

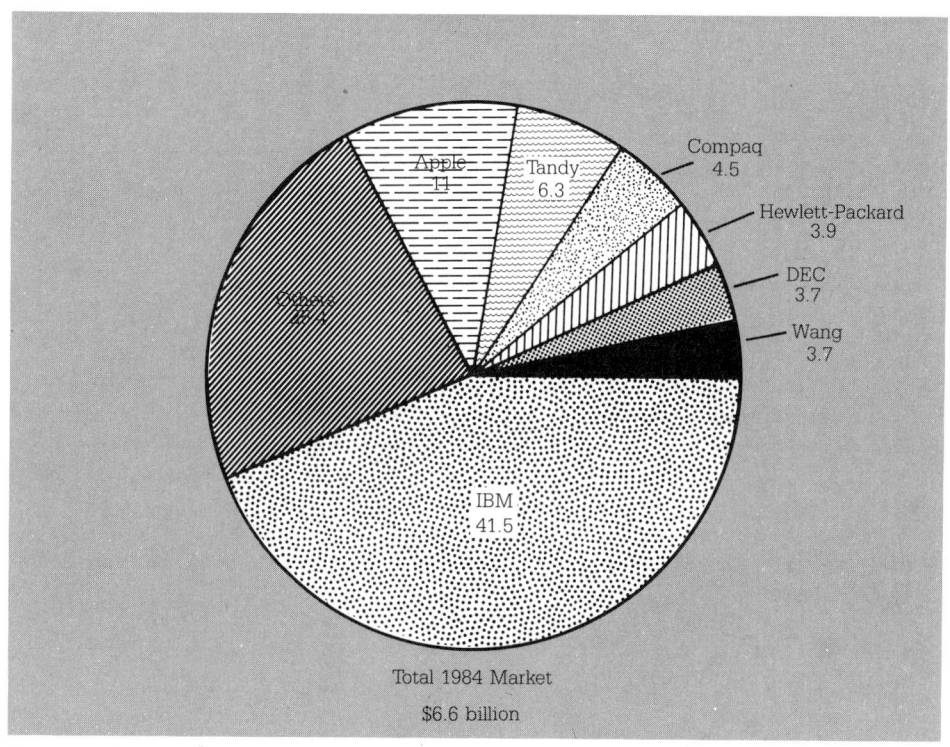

Total 1984 Market
$6.6 billion

Source: August 1, 1985 issue of *Electronic Business*

EXHIBIT 7

Company	Beta (Industry = 1.0)
Hewlett-Packard	1.30
IBM	1.05
DEC	1.25
Wang	1.50
UNISYS	1.10

Source: *Value Line*, 1103.

EXHIBIT 8
Capital structure

Company	Debt as a Percentage of Capital (1986)
Hewlett-Packard	2.0
IBM	12.0
Digital Equipment (DEC)	8.0
Wang	34.0
UNISYS	37.0

Source: *Value Line*, 1103.

EXHIBIT 9
Consolidated Statement of Earnings for the Years Ended October 31 (millions except per share amounts)

	1986*	1985	1984	1983
Net Revenue:				
Equipment	$5451	$5204	$4934	$3862
Services	1441	1301	1110	848
	6892	6505	6044	4710
Costs and Expenses:				
Cost of Goods Sold	3235	3166	2865	2195
Research and Development	805	685	592	493
Marketing	1356	1181	1066	771
Admin. & General	748	715	661	523
	6144	5747	5184	3982
Earnings before Taxes	748	758	860	728
Provisions for Taxes	269	269	313	296
Reversal of DISC Taxes**			(118)	
Net Taxes	269	269	195	296
Net Earnings	479	489	665	432
Net Earnings per Share		$ 1.91	$ 2.59	$ 1.69

*Based on first three quarters of 1986

**Reversal of DISC taxes accrued prior to 1984 due to a change in U.S. tax law.

Source: *Value Line*.

EXHIBIT 10
Consolidated Balance Sheet for the Years Ended October 31 (millions)

	1985	1984	1983
Assets			
Current assets:			
Cash and temporary cash investments	$1,020	$ 938	$ 880
Accounts and notes receivable	1,249	1,180	951
Inventories:			
Finished goods	401	373	279
Purchased parts and fabricated assemblies	592	650	469
Other current assets	80	60	53
Total current assets	3,342	3,201	2,632
Property, plant and equipment:			
Land	230	202	167
Buildings and leasehold improvements	1,653	1,416	1,102
Machinery and equipment	1,400	1,173	888
	3,283	2,791	2,157
Accumulated depreciation and amortization	1,134	923	726
	2,149	1,868	1,431
Other assets	189	84	98
Total assets	$5,680	$5,153	$4,161
Liability and shareholders' equity			
Current liabilities:			
Notes payable	$ 260	$ 217	$ 148
Accounts payable	243	281	203
Employee compensation and benefits	397	398	300
Other accrued liabilities	302	162	103
Accrued taxes on earnings	111	203	112
Other accrued taxes	63	61	54
Total current liabilities	1,376	1,322	920
Long-term debt	102	81	71
Other liabilities	92	93	46
Deferred taxes on earnings	128	112	237
Shareholders' equity:			
Common Stock and capital in excess of $1 par value (authorized: 320,000,000; issued and outstandiing: 256,916,000 in 1985, 256,478,000 in 1984, and 254,914,000 in 1983)	780	775	733
Retained earnings	3,202	2,770	2,154
Total shareholders' equity	3,982	3,545	2,887
	$5,680	$5,153	$4,161

Source: *Value Line.*

EXHIBIT 11
Time Analysis of Earnings per Share

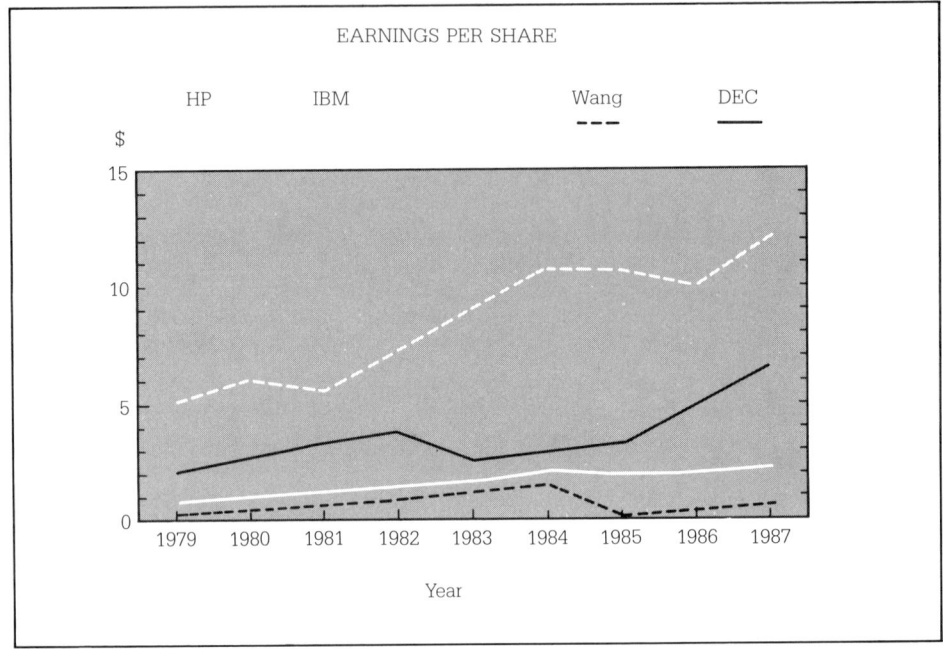

Source: Data taken from 1986 *Value Line*

EXHIBIT 12
R&D Expenditures as a Percentage of Sales

Company	1981	1982	1983	1984	1985
HP	9.7	9.97	10.47	9.79	10.5
IBM	5.55	5.97	6.26	9.14	6.9
DEC	7.85	9.01	11.06	11.29	10.7
Wang	8.05	7.50	7.64	7.35	7.7
UNISYS	5.30	5.39	5.78	5.63	5.6

Source: "Industry Surveys," *Value Line*, 1103

EXHIBIT 13
Directors and Executive Officers of Hewlett-Packard

DIRECTORS AND EXECUTIVE OFFICERS OF THE REGISTRANT

Information regarding directors is set forth under "Election of Directors" on pages 2 to 6 of the company's Notice of Annual Meeting of Shareholders and Proxy Statement, dated January 7, 1986, which pages are incorporated herein by reference.

The executive officers of the company are set forth below. All officers are elected for a one-year term.

Executive Officers

Richard C. Alberding; age 54; Executive Vice President, Marketing and International
Mr. Alberding was appointed head of the Marketing and International Sector in July 1984. He was Senior Vice President, International, from March 1983 to July 1984. He served as Vice President, Medical Products Group, from July 1981 until March 1983, and General Manager of the Medical Products Group from 1977 to 1981.

Richard W. Anderson; age 48; Vice President and General Manager, Microwave and Communications Instrument Group
Mr. Anderson served as general manager of the Computer Systems Division from 1980 until 1983 at which time he became general manager of the Microwave and Communications Instrument Group. He was elected to his present position in September 1985.

James Arthur; age 51; Vice President, U.S. Field Operations.
Mr. Arthur was elected Vice President, U.S. Field Operations in July 1984. He became a Vice President of the Company in September 1982 and was General Manager of the Computer Marketing Group from 1979 to July 1984.

Alan D. Bickell; age 49; Vice President, Intercontinental Operations
Mr. Bickell was elected Vice President in July 1984. He has been Managing Director of Intercontinental Operations since 1974.

Joel S. Birnbaum; age 47; Vice President, HP Laboratories
Mr. Birnbaum was elected to his current position in July 1984. He had been director of the Computer Research Center of HP Laboratories since joining the company in 1980. Prior to joining the company, Mr. Birnbaum was director of Computer Sciences at the Yorktown Heights facility of International Business Machines Corporation.

S. T. Jack Brigham III; age 46; Vice President Administration and General Counsel
Mr. Brigham was elected Vice President of the company in September 1982 and became Vice President Administration in January 1985. He served as Secretary of the company from May 1976 until September 1985 and has served as General Counsel since May 1976.

Douglas C. Chance; age 43; Senior Vice President and General Manager, Information Systems Group
Mr. Chance became a Vice President of the company in September 1982 and a Senior Vice President in September 1985. He became General Manager of the Information

Systems Group in July 1984. He was General Manager of the Technical Computer Group from 1979 to 1981 and General Manager of the Computer Products Group from 1981 to July 1984.

William F. Craven; age 47; Vice President and General Manager, Components Group
Mr. Craven became General Manager of the Components Group in March 1985 and was named a Vice President in September 1985. From 1981 until March 1985 he served as Corporate Director of Personnel. For the prior six years he was General Manager of the McMinnville Division of the company's Medical Products Group.

John L. Doyle; age 54; Executive Vice President, Information Systems and Networks
Prior to assuming his present position as head of the Information Systems and Networks Sector in July 1984, Mr. Doyle had been Vice President, Research and Development, since 1981. He served as Vice President, Personnel, from 1976 until 1981.

Harold E. Edmondson; age 55; Vice President, Corporate Manufacturing
Mr. Edmondson was named Vice President of Corporate Manufacturing in May 1983. He was General Manager of the Microwave and Communications Instrument Group from its formation in 1980 until May 1983 and was General Manager of the Santa Rosa Division from 1977 to 1980.

Richard A. Hackborn; age 48; Vice President and General Manager, Peripherals Group
Mr. Hackborn became a Vice President of the company in March 1983 and assumed his present position in July 1984. He served as General Manager of the Company's Information Products Group from its formation in February 1983 until July 1984. Previously, he was General Manager of the Computer Peripherals Group from August 1979 until February 1983.

William R. Hewlett; age 72; Vice Chairman of the Board
Mr. Hewlett is a co-founder of the company and has served on its Board of Directors since the company's incorporation in 1947. He has served in several executive positions, including President from 1964 to 1977, Chief Executive Officer from 1969 to 1977, and Chairman of the Executive Committee from 1977 to March 1983, when he assumed his current position.

Benjamin L. Holmes; age 51; Vice President and General Manager, Medical Products Group
Mr. Holmes became General Manager of the Medical Products Group in 1983 and was named a Vice President in September 1985. Mr. Holmes served as General Manager of the Waltham Division of the Medical Products Group from 1980 to 1983.

Franco Mariotti; age 50; Vice President, European Operations
Mr. Mariotti was appointed to his present position in July 1981 and has served as managing director of the company's European operations since 1977.

Dean O. Morton; age 53; Executive Vice President and Chief Operating Officer
Mr. Morton was elected a director of the company in September 1977. He was elected Chief Operating Officer in July 1984. Prior to assuming his current position, he had been Executive Vice President responsible for the company's Medical Products and Analytical

Instrumentation Groups since 1977. Mr. Morton is also a Director of State Street
Investment Corporation, Saga Corporation, and Xidex, Inc.

George F. Newman, Jr.; age 49; Treasurer
Mr. Newman was elected Treasurer in September 1984. He had served as the Company's
Assistant Treasurer since 1976. Mr. Newman is a director and chairman of
Hewlett-Packard Finance Company, a wholly-owned subsidiary of Hewlett-Packard
Company. He is also a director of Summit Information Systems, Inc.

Dr. Craig Nordlund; age 36; Secretary and Corporate Counsel
Mr. Nordlund joined the company as an attorney in 1977 and was named Senior Attorney
in 1980. He was appointed Assistant Secretary and Corporate Counsel in 1981 and became
Secretary in September 1985.

Alfred P. Oliverio; age 58; Senior Vice President, Major Accounts Marketing
Mr. Oliverio assumed his current position in July 1984. Prior to that time, he was Senior
Vice President, Marketing, from 1981 to July 1984 and Vice President, Marketing, from
1974 to 1981.

David Packard; age 73; Chairman of the Board
Mr. Packard is a co-founder of the company and has been a director since the company's
incorporation in 1947.[1] He has served as Chairman of the Board of Directors since 1972
and has served in several executive capacities as well, including President from 1947 to
1964. He also served as U.S. Deputy Secretary of Defense from January 1969 to December
1971. Mr. Packard is a Director of The Boeing Company and Genentech, Inc.

William G. Parzybok, Jr.; age 43; Vice President, Design Systems Group
Mr. Parzybok was elected a Vice President in September 1984 and has served in his
current position since July 1984. He was General Manager of the Company's Electronic
Measurement Group from 1981 to 1984 and Division Manager of the Loveland Instrument
Division from 1976 to 1981.

*Lewis E. Platt; age 44; Senior Vice President and General Manager, Manufacturing,
Medical and Analytical Systems*
Mr. Platt became a Vice President of the Company in March 1983 and a Senior Vice
President in September 1985. He was General Manager of the Manufacturing Systems
Group from July 1984 to January 1985. He was General Manager of the Analytical Products
Group from January 1980 to 1984 and General Manager of the Company's Waltham
Division from 1974 to 1980. Mr. Platt is also a Director of Molex, Inc., and HP Genenchem.

Charles W. Richion; age 49; Vice President and U.S. Sales Manager, U.S. Field Operations
Mr. Richion became a Vice President in September 1985. For the six years prior to that, he
served as North American General Manager for the former Computer Marketing Group.

*William E. Terry; age 52; Executive Vice President, Components, Measurement and Design
Systems*
Mr. Terry has been an Executive Vice President and Director of the company since 1980.
He is responsible for the company's Components, Measurement and Design Systems
Sector. He became a Vice President in 1974 and was General Manager of the company's

Instrument Group from 1974 to July 1984, when he became head of the Measurement, Design and Manufacturing Systems Sector. He was appointed to his present position in January 1985. He is a Director of Applied Magnetics Corporation, Kevex Corporation, and Baker Drilling Equipment Company. He also serves on the Board of Regents of Santa Clara University.

Robert P. Wayman; age 40; Vice President, Chief Financial Officer and Controller
Mr. Wayman was named Controller in January 1984 and was elected Vice President and Chief Financial Officer in September 1984. He was Deputy Corporate Controller from 1981 to 1984, and Group Controller for the company's Instrument Group from 1976 to 1981. Mr. Wayman is a Director of Hewlett-Packard Finance Company.

Cyril J. Yansouni; age 43; Vice President and General Manager, Personal Computer Group
Mr. Yansouni was elected Vice President in July 1984 and has served as General Manager of the Personal Computer Group since its formation in January 1983. He was General Manager of the Computer Terminals Group from July 1981 to 1983 and General Manager of the Grenoble Division from 1976 to 1981.

John A. Young; age 53; President, Chief Executive Officer, and Chairman of the Executive Committee
Mr. Young has served as President and Chief Executive Officer since May 1978 and has held a number of other management positions since joining the company in 1958. He is a Director of Wells Fargo & Company; Wells Fargo Bank, N.A.; and SRI International. Mr. Young is a member of the Business Council and the Business Roundtable and served as Chairman of the President's Commission on Industrial Competitiveness from 1984 to 1985. He also serves on the Board of Trustees of Stanford University.

[1]Mr. Packard did not serve as a Director during his service as United States Deputy Secretary of Defense from January 1969 to December 1971.

EXHIBIT 14
Financial Highlights

EXHIBIT 15
Consolidated Balance Sheet

October 31 (Millions)	1985	1984	1983
Assets			
Current assets:			
Cash and temporary cash investments	$1,020	$ 938	$ 880
Accounts and notes receivable	1,249	1,180	951
Inventories:			
Finished goods	401	373	279
Purchased parts and fabricated assemblies	592	650	469
Other current assets	80	60	53
Total current assets	3,342	3,201	2,632
Property, plant and equipment:			
Land	230	202	167
Buildings and leasehold improvements	1,653	1,416	1,102
Machinery and equipment	1,400	1,173	888
	3,283	2,791	2,157
Accumulated depreciation and amortization	1,134	923	726
	2,149	1,868	1,431
Other assets	189	84	98
	$5,680	$5,153	$4,161
Liabilities and shareholders' equity			
Current liabilities:			
Notes payable	$ 260	$ 217	$ 148
Accounts payable	243	281	203
Employee compensation and benefits	397	398	300
Other accrued liabilities	302	162	103
Accrued taxes on earnings	111	203	112
Other accrued taxes	63	61	54
Total current liabilities	1,376	1,322	920
Long-term debt	102	81	71
Other liabilities	92	93	46
Deferred taxes on earnings	128	112	237
Shareholders' equity:			
Common stock and capital in excess of $1 par value	780	775	733
Retained earnings	3,202	2,770	2,154
Total shareholders' equity	3,982	3,545	2,887
	$5,680	$5,153	$4,161

The accompanying notes are an integral part of these financial statements.

EXHIBIT 16
Consolidated Statement of Earnings

For the years ended October 31 (Millions except per share amounts)	1985	1984	1983
Net revenue:			
Equipment	$5,204	$4,934	$3,862
Services	1,301	1,110	848
	6,505	6,044	4,710
Costs and expenses:			
Cost of goods sold	3,166	2,865	2,195
Research and development	685	592	493
Marketing	1,181	1,066	771
Administrative and general	715	661	523
	5,747	5,184	3,982
Earnings before taxes	758	860	728
Provision for taxes	269	313	296
Reversal of DISC taxes*	—	(118)	—
	269	195	296
Net earnings	$ 489	$ 665	$ 432
Net earnings per share	$ 1.91	$ 2.59	$ 1.69

* Reversal of DISC taxes accrued prior to 1984 due to a change in U.S. tax law.
Certain amounts have been reclassified to conform to the 1985 format.
The accompanying notes are an integral part of these financial statements.

Supplementary Earnings Information, assuming the reversal of DISC taxes is applied retroactively. See Financial Review, page 27.			
Net earnings	$ 489	$ 547	$ 457
Net earnings per share	$ 1.91	$ 2.13	$ 1.79

AUTHOR INDEX

TOPIC INDEX